The European Court of Justice
Practice and Procedure

The European Court of Justice
Practice and Procedure

Second edition

K.P.E. Lasok, MA (Cantab), LLM (Exeter), PhD

Barrister, formerly Legal Secretary, Court of Justice
of the European Communities

Butterworths
London, Dublin, Edinburgh
1994

United Kingdom	Butterworth & Co (Publishers) Ltd, 88 Kingsway, LONDON WC2B 6AB and 4 Hill Street, EDINBURGH EH2 3JZ
Australia	Butterworths, SYDNEY, MELBOURNE, BRISBANE, ADELAIDE, PERTH, CANBERRA and HOBART
Canada	Butterworths Canada Ltd, TORONTO and VANCOUVER
Ireland	Butterworth (Ireland) Ltd, DUBLIN
Malaysia	Malayan Law Journal Sdn Bhd, KUALA LUMPUR
New Zealand	Butterworths of New Zealand Ltd, WELLINGTON and AUCKLAND
Puerto Rico	Butterworth of Puerto Rico, Inc, SAN JUAN
Singapore	Butterworths Asia, SINGAPORE
South Africa	Butterworth Publishers [Pty] Ltd, Durban
USA	Butterworth Legal Publishers, CARSLBAD, California; and SALEM, New Hampshire

A CIP Catalogue record for this book is available from the British Library.

ISBN 0 406 00621 0

Typeset by Phoenix Photosetting, Chatham, Kent
Printed and bound in Great Britain by Mackays of Chatham PLC, Chatham, Kent

Foreword

In a real sense the first edition of this book broke new ground. It provided a meticulously careful and most comprehensive explanation of the procedures of the European Court of Justice. It was very important for common lawyers to have it, since by and large they were not familiar either with the Statutes of the Court or the Rules of Procedure or, even less, with the numerous decisions of the Court itself, and it is in many ways the latter which indicate to the practitioner how he should conduct his case before the Court. At that time the author was able to indicate his views as to the likely outcome of procedural problems which had not been decided by the Court. He explained aspects of that procedure which were unfamiliar to the United Kingdom lawyer—questions as to admissibility, as to interim measures, as to the nature of the evidence which would be looked at.

But eleven years have passed since that first edition and things have not stood still in Luxembourg. There have been many decisions of the Court which are relevant to the chapters of this book. The author has included them either in the text or in the footnotes. The development of the Court's jurisprudence in some areas has meant that some parts of the book have had to be substantially re-written. A particular example is to be found in the chapter on interim relief. There have been many cases where interim measures have been sought. In the foreword to the first edition, it was said that 'applications for interim measures seem to me to be becoming of greater importance'. The new chapter in this book shows that that was right. It is not, however, simply a question of the volume of cases in particular situations, it is also a question of observing whether and how far the Court's approach has changed. The book shows how in more recent cases the Court has laid emphasis on the balancing of the interests of the parties in all the circumstances, thereby getting very near to the balance of convenience test which is followed by the English Courts.

This, however, is only part of the change which was needed to the first edition. At that time there was no Court of First Instance and nobody had any clear idea as to what, if any, tribunal would be established in order to relieve the heavy workload of the Court itself. Since then, we have had the Court of First Instance. It began with a limited jurisdiction but its role in dealing with competition cases has obviously been important and highly appreciated. Its procedures in some important respects differ from those of the Court and the form of its judgments is different. It was very necessary that this book should include a new section on the Court of First Instance to deal with its establishment and procedures. Now there has been another change in the jurisdiction of the Court. That jurisdiction has been widened to include all cases brought by individuals and companies. This change may not have gone far enough but at least it does something to redress the balance. The Court previously retained far too high a percentage of the cases going to Luxembourg; there is now at any rate a modest change in the balance. No doubt other changes will come.

No less important is the fact that appeals lie from the Court of First Instance to the Court of Justice. It is important that practitioners should know when they can appeal, on what grounds and within what limits. The Court of Justice has begun to consider the width of its own jurisdiction to hear appeals in respect of points of law. What is fact and what is law has always been a tease in the English Courts. Lord Denning is reputed to have said, when somebody objected that the appellants were raising what was really a question of fact, 'Mr X, if we want to hear it, we say it is a point of law, if we don't, we say it is a question of fact'. Maybe the European Court will adopt a similarly pragmatic approach.

There have been many other changes which the revised text explains. Some of them may be highly debatable. As is well known the Court of Justice has limited the length of oral speeches unless an extension is granted. There are some who think that hearings should be dispensed with in a wide range of cases. Others, like myself, think that the oral hearing is a crucial part of the Court's procedure, even if it has to be controlled to avoid prolixity and irrelevance. New rules allow for an oral hearing to be dispensed with if the parties agree and it is important that lawyers acting for parties before the Court should understand what are their rights and their options.

In the winning of cases a confident knowledge of procedure can be as valuable as a knowledge of the substantive law. The table of cases in this edition shows the range of areas covered; how many new decisions since 1983 have been included. At the time of the first edition, the author had considerable experience of Court procedures as a Legal Secretary in Luxembourg. He had also much experience as a speaker and as a writer. Now his experience has broadened in a way which is very relevant for the purposes of this book. He writes with the authority of a practitioner having considerable experience of the Court, and of the conduct of cases in this country in which European Law and access to the European Court are relevant. The text remains lucid and coherent even though necessarily very detailed. In my view it is a splendid book which every practitioner likely to be involved in European Law cases needs to have.

SLYNN OF HADLEY

Preface

Practice and procedure in the Court of Justice of the European Communities has changed significantly since the publication of the first edition of this book, due in large part to the creation of the Court of First Instance and the institution of a system of appeals from that court to the Court of Justice. The interval between the first and this edition of the book, although greater than originally intended, has fortuitously made it possible to include further changes, in particular those wrought by the extension of the jurisdiction of the Court of First Instance in 1993, the Treaty on European Union and the Agreement on the European Economic Area. It has also been possible to include more illustrations of the application of the Rules of Procedure of both courts, and of the manner in which the appellate jurisdiction of the Court of Justice is exercised, than would otherwise have been the case.

I would like to thank the President of the Court of Justice, Judge Due, and the President of the Court of First Instance, Judge Cruz Vilaça, for allowing me to pursue research at the Court when preparing this edition. I would like to express my particular thanks to Mr H von Holstein, Mr H Jung and Mrs D Louterman-Hubeau for their kindness in commenting on, and correcting various errors in, chapter 1 (needless to say, any remaining errors are my own responsibility). The publishers have proved unusually tolerant in waiting for this edition to be completed as deadline after deadline passed without it materialising. It seemed in keeping with the times that the second edition should be prepared entirely by electronic means and without the intervention of hand and pen. In the event, it was at one point unclear which of the author or his word processor was to be the first to have its existence terminated prematurely. I was fortunate, at moments of utter desperation, to receive assistance from Mrs Yvonne Cocklin. Although I believe that, initially, she entertained the unworthy thought that my difficulties were entirely due to incompetence on my part and, at one point, was toying with the idea that there emanated from my person an electro-magnetic aura that spelt doom for any electronic apparatus, she finally came to the correct conclusion that there was something wrong with the machine and not its operator.

The preparation of this edition was interrupted by the sudden and untimely death of my brother, Marc, while engaged on the restoration of a church in Istanbul, and, some three weeks later, by the birth of my daughter, Frances. To the one, the appearance of this edition comes too late; to the other, it is too soon to be appreciated. To neither could it ever be or have been of more than passing interest. Nonetheless, it seems appropriate to dedicate it to them.

This edition states the law as at 31 December 1993.

4 Raymond Buildings,
Gray's Inn, London
February 1994   KPEL

Stop Press

By Council Decision 94/149 of 7 March 1994 (OJ No L66/29 of 10 March 1994), the second part of the first sentence of Council Decision 93/350 was amended so as to effect, as from 15 March 1994, the transfer to the Court of First Instance of jurisdiction over actions brought by natural or legal persons (i) pursuant to arts 33, 35 and 40 (first and second paras) of the ECSC Treaty where such actions concern acts relating to the application of art 74 of the ECSC Treaty and (ii) pursuant to arts 173 (fourth para), 175 (third para) and 178 of the EC Treaty where such actions relate to trade protection measures within the meaning of art 113 of the EC Treaty in the case of dumping and subsidies. Decision 94/149 thus completes the transfer of jurisdiction to the Court of First Instance envisaged in Decision 93/350. The description given in this edition of the jurisdiction of the Court of First Instance should be read accordingly.

Contents

Index   725

Table of European Legislation

Page numbers printed in **bold** type indicate where the article or rule is set out.

Table of Cases

PAGE

PAGE

PAGE

PAGE

Decisions of the European Court of Justice are listed below numerically. These decisions are also included in the preceding alphabetical table.

Bibliography

Alexander, W	'The temporal effects of preliminary rulings', Yearbook of European Law, vol 8 (1988) p 11.
Alexander, W and Grabandt, E	Common Market Law Review, vol 19 (1982) p 413.
Andre, A	'Evidence before the European Court of Justice, with special reference to the *Grundig/Consten* decision', Common Market Law Review, vol 5 (1967–1968) p 35.
Arnull, A	'Article 177 and the retreat from *Van Duyn*', European Law Review, vol 8 (1983) p 365; 'The use and abuse of Article 177 EEC', Modern Law Review (1989) p 622; 'References to the European Court', European Law Review, vol 15 (1990) p 375.
Asso, B	'Le contrôle de l'opportunité de la décision économique devant la Cour Européenne de Justice', Rev Trim de Droit Européen (1976) pp 21 and 177.
Barav, A	'The exception of illegality in Community Law: a critical analysis', Common Market Law Review (1974) p 366; 'Preliminary censorship? The judgment of the European Court in *Foglia v Novello*', European Law Review, vol 5 (1980) p 433; Rev Trim de Droit Européen (1982) p 437; 'La plénitude de competence du juge national en sa qualité de juge communautaire', in L'Europe et le Droit – Mélanges en Hommage à Jean Boulouis (1991) p 1.
Bebr, G	*Judicial Control of the European Communities* (Stevens, 1962); *Development of Judicial Control of the European Communities* (Martinus Nijhoff, 1981); In *Zehn Jahre Rechsprechung des Gerichtshofs des EG* (Carl Heymanns Verlag, 1965) p 78; Common Market Law Review, vol 17 (1980) pp 371 and 525 and vol 19 (1982) p 421; 'Arbitration tribunals and Article 177 of the EEC Treaty', Common Market Law Review (1985) p 489; 'Direct and indirect judicial control of Community acts in practice: the relation between Articles 173 and 177 of the EEC Treaty', in *The Art of Governance–Festschrift zu Ehren von Eric Stein* (1987).
Bergéres, M	'La reformulation des questions préjudicielles en intérpretation par la Cour de Justice des Communautés Européennes', Recueil Dalloz Sirey (1985) p 155; *Contentieux Communautaire* (Presse Universitaire de France, 1989).
Bernhardt, R et al	*Thirty Years of Community Law* (Office for Official Publications of the European Communities, 1982).
Berri, M	'The special procedures before the Court of Justice of the European Communities', Common Market Law Review, vol 8 (1971) p 5.

Biancarelli, J   'La création du Tribunal de Premiére Instance des Communautés Européennes: un luxe ou une nécessité?', Rev Trim de Droit Européen (1990) p 1;
'Le réglement de procédure du Tribunal de Première Instance des Communautées Européennes: le perfectionnement dans la continuité', Rev Trim de Droit Européen (1991) p 543.

Biavati, P   'Limiti di applaicazione della revocazione comunitaria', Rivista Trimestríale di Diritto e Procedura Civile (1987) p 550;
'La richiesta di informazioni nel processo comunitario', Rivista Trimestriale di Diritto e Procedura Civile (1989) p 181.

Bieber, R   'On the mutual completion of overlapping legal systems: the case of the European Communities and the national legal orders', European Law Review, vol 13 (1988) p 147.

Bierry, M and Dal   'The practice followed by the Court of Justice with regard to
Ferro, A   costs', Common Market Law Review, vol 24 (1987) p 509.

di Blase, A   'Sull' efficacia interna delle sentenze emanate nei confronti degli stati membri dalla Corte di Giustizia delle Communitá Europee', Rivista di Diritto Internazionale (1973) p 486.

Borchard, G   'The award of interim measures by the European Court of Justice', Common Market Law Review, vol 22 (1985) p 203.

Borgsmidt, K   'The Advocate General at the European Court of Justice', European Law Review, vol 13 (1988) p 106.

Boulouis, J   'Nouvelles reflexions à propos du caractère "préjudiciel" de la competence de la Cour de Justice des Communautés Européennes statuant sur renvoi des juridictions nationales', Études de Droit des Communautés Européennes Mélanges offerts à Pierre Teitgen (1984).

Brealey, M   'The burden of proof before the European Court', European Law Review, vol 10 (1985) p 250.

Bridge, J   'Procedural aspects of the enforcement of European Community Law through the legal systems of the Member States', European Law Review, vol 9 (1984) p 28.

Brown, N and   *The Court of Justice of the European Communities* (Sweet & Maxwell,
Jacobs, F   1989).

Brown, N and   'Some problems of procedural law for common lawyers within
Uff, K   the community legal order', in Mélanges Dehousse, vol 2, p 269.

Capotorti, F   'Le sentenze della Corte di Giustizia delle Comunità Europee', in *La Sentenza in Europa*, p 230, Padua, CEDAM, 1988.

Cappalletti, M   'Is the European Court of Justice running wild?', European Law Review, vol 12 (1987) p 1.

Catalano, N   'Lo stile delle sentenze della Corte di Giustizia delle Comunità Europee', Il Foro Italiano (1969) p 142;
'Le procès devant la Cour de Justice des Communautés Européennes', Gazette du Palais (1970) p 161.

Chevalier, RM   'La procédure devant la Cour de Justice', in *Les Novelles: Droit des Communautés Européennes* (1969) p 391.

Chevalier, RM   '*Guide Pratique Article 177 CEE*' (Office for Official Publicaand Maidani, D   tions of the European Communities, 1982).

Cortese, E   'Sulla competenza della Corte di Giustizia delle Comunità Europee in materia di opposizione all'esecuzione', Rivisto di Diritto Europeo (1977) p 405.

Court of Justice of   *Reports of the Judicial and Academic Conference, 27–28 September 1976*
the European   (Office for Official Publications of the European Communities,
Communities   1976);
XXXV Anni, 1952–1987 (Office for Official Publications of the European Communities, 1987).

Crisham, C and   In *Essays in European Law and Integration* (ed D O'Keeffe and H G
Mortlemans, K   Schermers, Kluwer, 1982) p 43.

Cross, R	*Evidence* (Butterworths, 7th edn, 1990).
Cruz Vilaça, J	'The Court of First Instance of the European Communities', Yearbook of European Law, vol 10 (1990) p 1.
Damato, A	'L'articolo 177 del Trattato CEE ed il difetto di giurisdizione del giudice statale', Rivista di Diritto Internazionale (1986) p 315.
Dashwood, A	Legal Studies, vol 2 (1982) p 202.
Dashwood, A and Arnull, A	'English Courts and Article 177 of the EEC Treaty', Yearbook of European Law, vol 4 (1984).
Dashwood, A and White, R	'Enforcement actions under Articles 169 and 170 EEC', European Law Review, vol 14 (1989) p 388.
Dauses, M	Practical considerations regarding the preliminary ruling procedure under Article 177 of the EEC Treaty, Fordman International Law Journal, vol 10 p 538.
Dine, J, Douglas-Scott, S and Persand, I	*Procedure and the European Court* (Chancery, 1991).
Due, O	'The Court of First Instance', Yearbook of European Law, vol 8 (1988) p 1.
Evans, AC	'National courts of law resort and the European Court', Journal of the Law Society of Scotland (1983) p 201.
Everling, U	82 Michigan Law Review (1984) p 1294.
Falconetti, H	'Moyens juridiques donnés par le Traité de Rome aux avocats', Gazette du Palais (1972) p 345.
Fromont, M	'La protection provisoire des particuliers contre les décisions administratives dans les états membres des Communautés Européennes', Revue Internationale des Sciences Administratives (1984) p 309.
Funck, C	In *Zehn Jahre Rechtsprechung des Gerichtshofs des EG* (Carl Heymanns Verlag, 1965) p 60.
Galmot, Y	'Le Tribunal des Première Instance des Communautés Européennes', Revue Française de Droit Administratif (1989) p 567.
Gand, J	*Les Novelles* (Larcier, 1969) ch 1 p 295.
van Gelder	'Applications to the European Court of Justice: from reference to judgment', Journal of the Law Society of Scotland (1978) p 383.
van Ginderachter, E	'Le Tribunal de Première Instance des Communautés Européennes: un nouveau-né prodige?', Cahiers de Droit Européen (1989) p 63.
Gori, P	'L'avocat général à la Cour de Justice des Communautés Européennes', Cahiers du Droit Européen (1976) p 375.
Grass, R	L'Article 177 du Traité CEE', in *Le Droit Communautaire et International devant le Juge du Commerce* (1989) p 79.
Gray, C	'Interim measures of protection in the European Court', European Law Review, vol 4 (1979) p 80; 'Advisory opinions and the European Court of Justice', European Law Review, vol 8 (1983) p 24.
Greaves, R	'*Locus Standi* under Article 173 EEC when seeking annulment of a regulation', European Law Review, vol 11 (1986) p 119.
Grementieri, V	*Il Processo Communitario* (Dott A Giuffré, 1973); 'Profili processuali della tutela degli interessi diffusi nel diritto europeo,' Rivisto di Diritto Internazionale Privato e Processuale (1976) p 310; 'Le misure cautelari nel processo comunitario', Rivista di Scienze Giuridiche, 1988, p 87.
Harding, C	'The private interest in challenging Community action', European Law Review, vol 5 (1980) p 354.
Hartley, T	*The Foundations of European Community Law* (Clarendon Press, 1988).
von Heyderbrand, HC	'Confidential information in anti-dumping proceedings before United States courts and the European Court', European Law Review, vol 11 (1986) p 331.

van Houtte, A   'La Cour de Justice des Communautés Européenes—organisation
                     et procédure', Cahiers de Droit Européen (1983) p 3.

Hubeau, F   'Changements des règles de procedure devant les juridictions
                     communautaires de Luxembourg', in Cahiers de Droit
                     Européen (1991) p 499.

Isaac, G   'La modulation par la Cour de Justice des Communautés
                     Européennes des effets dans le temps de ses arrêts d'invalidité',
                     in Cahiers de Droit Européen (1987) p 444;
                     'Observations sur la pratique de l'intervention devant la Cour
                     de Justice des Communautés Européennes dans les affaires de
                     manquement d'états', in *Études de Droit des Communautés
                     Européennes—Mélanges Offerts à Pierre Teitgen* (1984) p 171.

Jacobs, FG   'Amendments to the Rules of Procedure', European Law
                     Review, vol 5 (1980) p 52;
                     'Proposals for reform in the organisation and procedure of the
                     Court of Justice of the European Communities with special
                     reference to the proposed Court of First Instance', in *Du Droit
                     International au Droit de l'Integration—Liber Amicorum Pierre
                     Pescatore*, p 287.

Jacobs, FG and   *References to the European Court: Practice and Procedure*
Durand A   (Butterworths, 1975).

Joliet, R   *Le Droit Institutionnel des Communautées Européennes: Le Contentieux*
                     Liège, 1981);
                     'L'Article 177 du Traité CEE et le renvoi préjudiciel', in Rivisto
                     di Diritto Europeo (1991) p 591.

Joliet, R and   'Le Tribunal de Première Instance des Communautés
Vogel, W   Européennes', Revue du Marché Commun (1989) p 423.

Joshua, J   'Proof in contested EEC competition cases: a comparison with
                     the rules of evidence in the common law', European Law
                     Review, vol 12 (1987) p 315.

Kapteyn, P and   *Introduction to the Law of the European Communities* (2d edn, L W
VerLoren van   Gormley, Kluwer/Graham & Trotman, 1989).
Themaat, P

Kennedy, T   'Paying, the piper: legal aid in proceedings before the Court of
                     Justice', Common Market Law Review, vol 25 (1988) p 559;
                     'The essential minimum: the establishment of the Court of First
                     Instance', European Law Review, vol 14 (1989) p 7.

Knaub, G   'La procédure devant la Cour de Justice des Communautées
                     Européennes', Rev Trim de Droit Européen (1967) p 269.

Koopmans, T   'Retrospectively reconsidered', Cambridge Law Journal (1980)
                     p 287;
                     'Stare decisis in European law', *Essays in European Law and Inte-
                     gration* (Ed D O'Keeffe and H G Schermers, Kluwer, 1982) p 11;
                     'La procédure préjudicielle—victime de son succès?', in *Du Droit
                     International au Droit de l'Intégration—Liber Amicorum Pierre Pescatore*
                     (1987) p 347.

Korsch, H   in *Zehn Jahre Rechtsprechung des Gerichtshofs des EG* (Carl Hey-
                     manns Verlag, 1965) p 122.

Krsjak, P   'Un jour de plaidoire à la Cour de Justice', Gazette du Palais
                     (1976) p 577.

Lagrange, M   'La Cour de Justice des Communautés Européennes: du Plan
                     Schuman à l'Union Européenne', Rev Trim de Droit Europeen
                     (1978) p 2.

La Marca, L   'La sospensione cautelare degli appalti pubblici nel proce-
                     dimento ex art 169 del Trattato di Roma', Rivista di Diritto
                     Europeo (1989) p 383.

Lang, J Temple   'The powers of the Commission to order interim measures in
                     competition cases', Common Market Law Review, vol 18 (1981)
                     p 49.

Lasok, D and Bridge, JW	*Introduction to the Law and Institutions of the European Communities* (Butterworths, 5th edn, 1991).
Lasok, KPE	'Practice and procedure before the European Court', European Competition Law Review (1981) pp 79 and 219; 'AM&S—the Court decides', European Competition Law Review (1982) p 99; 'Judicial review of issues of fact in competition cases', European Competition Law Review (1983) p 85.
Lecourt, R	'La Cour de Justice des Communautés Européennes vue de l'intérieur', in *Europaische Gerichtsbarkeit und Nationale Verfassungsgerichtsbarkeit* (ed W G Grewe, H Rupp and H Schneider, Nomos) p 261.
Lenaerts, K	'Le Tribunal de Première Instance des Communautés Européennes: genése et premiers pas', Journal des Tribunaux (1990) p 409.
Lenz, CO	'The Court of Justice of the European Communities', European Law Review, vol 14 (1989) p 127.
Lewis, C	'Retrospective and prospective rulings in administrative law', in Public Law (1988) p 78.
Lipstein, K	'*Fogia v Novello*—some unexplored aspects', in *Du Droit International au Droit de l'Intègration—Liber Amicorum Pierre Pescatore* (1987) p 373.
Louis, JV	'Le rôle de la Commission dans la procédure en manquement selon la jurisprudence récente de la Cour de Justice', in *Du Droit International au Droit de l'Intégration—Liber Amicorum Pierre Pescatore* (1987) p 387.
Louterman, D and Febvre, M	'Les incidents de procédure au sens de l'article 91 du réglement de procédure de la Cour de Justice des Communautés Européennes,' Gazette du Palais (1989) p 8.
Mackenzie Stuart, Lord	'La Cour de Justice des Communautés Europécnnes et le contròle du pouvoir discrétionnaire', Rev Int de Droit Comparé (1974) p 61; 'The Court of Justice: a personal view', in *European Governmental Studies. In Memoriam J D B Mitchell* (Sweet and Maxwell, 1983) p 118.
Mackenzie Stuart, Lord and Warner, JP	'Judicial decision as a source of Community law', in *Europaische Gerichtsbarkeit und Nationale Verfassungsgerichtsbarkeit* (eds W G Grewe, H Rupp and H Schneider, Nomos) p 273.
Mancini, F	L'articolo 177 del Trattato CEE e la cooperazione tra le giuridizioni nazionali e la Corte', Diritto Comunitario e Diritto Interno (1988) p 35.
Matthies, H	in *Zehn Jahre Rechstsprechung des Gerichtshof des EG* (Carl Heymanns Verlag, 1965) p 136.
Mêgret, C	'La portée juridique et les effets de droit de la declaration d'invalidité d'un acte communautaire prononcée par la Cour de Justice des Communautés Européennes dans la cadre de la procedure instituée par l'article 177 du Traité CEE', in *Études de Droit des Communautés Européennes—Mélanges offerts à Pierre Teitgen* (1984).
Mertens de Wilmars	'The case-law of the Court of Justice in relation to the review of the legality of economic policy in mixed-economy systems', *Legal Issues of European Integration* (1982) p 1; 'Arguments de raison et arguments d'autorité dans la jurisprudence de la Cour de Justice des Communautés Européennes', in *Arguments d'Autorité et Arguments de Raison en Droit* (Brussels, Nemesis, 1988) p 71.
Millett, T	'The new European Court of First Instance', ICLQ, vol 38 (1989) p 811; *The Court of First Instance of the European Communities* (Butterworths, 1990).

Monaco, R	'Le parti nel processo comunitario', Studi in Onore di G Morelli, *Il Processo Internazionale* (1975) vol XIV, p 563;
	'Sulla competenza delle sezioni della Corte di Giustizia delle Comunità Europee', Rivisto di Diritto Europeo (1977) p 401.
Mortlemans, K	Common Market Law Review, vol 16 (1979) p 557.
Neri, S	in *Zehn Jahre Rechtsprechung des Gerichtshofs des EG* (Carl Heymanns Verlag, 1965) p 68.
Nocerino-Grisotti	'Effetti ex nunc dell'annullamento di atti comunitari e principi dell'ordinamento italiano', in Diritto Comunitario e Degli Scambi Internationali (1988) p 421.
O'Keeffe, D	'Appeals against an order to refer under Article 177 of the EEC Treaty', European Law Review, vol 9 (1984) p 87.
Oliver, P	'Limitation of actions before the European Court', European Law Review, vol 3 (1978) p 3;
	'Interim measures, some recent developments', Common Market Law Review, vol 29 (1992) p 7.
Pastor, B and van Ginderachter, E	'La procédure en référé', Rev Trim de Droit Européen (1989) p 562.
Paulis, E	'Les effets des arrêts d'annulation de la Cour de Justice des Communautés Européennes', in Cahiers de Droit Européen (1987) p 243.
Perelman, C and Foriers, P (ed)	*Les Presomptions et les Fictions en Droit* (Bruylant, 1974); *La Preuve en Droit* (Bruylant, 1981).
Pescatore, P	*Introduction à la Science de Droit* (1978);
	'Court of Justice of the European Communities', in *Encyclopaedia of Public International Law* (North-Holland), Instalment 6 (1983) p 92;
	'Cour de Justice des Communautés Européennes—Le recours préjudiciel de l'article 177 du Traité CEE et la coopération de la Cour avec les juridictions nationales' (Office for Official Publications of the European Communities 1986).
Plouvier, L	'Le recours en revision devant la Cour de Justice des Communautés Européennes', Cahiers de Droit Européen (1971) p 428.
Rasmussen, H	'Why is Article 173 interpreted against private plaintiffs?', European Law Review, vol 5 (1980) p 112;
	'The European Court's acte clair strategy in *CILFIT*', European Law Review, vol 9 (1984) p 242;
	'Between self-restraint and activism: a judicial policy for the European Court', European Law Review, vol 13 (1988) p 28.
van Reepinghen, C and Orianne, P	*La Procédure devant la Cour de Justice des Communautés Européennes* (Larcier, 1961); Journal des Tribunaux (1961) pp 89, 111 and 125.
Rideau, J and Charrier, JL	*Code de Procedures Européennes* (Editions Litec, 1990).
Rigaux, F	'Le pouvoir d'appréciation de la Cour de Justice des Communautées Européennes a l'égard des faits', in *Miscellanea*, W J Ganshof van der Meersch, vol II, p 365.
Rosenne, S	*The World Court* (Nijhoff, 1989).
Saggio, A	'Aspetti problematici della copmetenza pregiudiziale della Corte di Giustizia delle Communità Europee messi in luce dalla giurisprudenza', Diritto Comunitario e Diritto Interno (1988) p 69;
	'Il tribunale comunitario di primo grado', Diritto Comunitario e degli Scambi Internazionali (1988) p 611.
Schermers, HG	'Factual mergers of the European Court and Commission of Human Rights', European Law Review, vol 11 (1986) p 350;
	'The European Court of First Instance', Common Market Law Review, vol 25 (1988) p 541.

Schermers, HG, Timmermans, CWA and Kellermann, AE	*Article 177 EEC: Experiences and Problems* (Amsterdam, North-Holland, 1987).
Schermers, HG and Waelbroeck, D	*Judicial Protection in the European Communities* (Kluwer, 1992).
Schneider, HG	'Towards a European lawyer', Common Market Law Review, vol 8 (1971) p 44.
Schockweiler, F	'L'execution des arrèts de la Cour', in *Du Droit International au Droit de l'Integration—Liber Amicorum Piere Pescatore* (Baden-Baden, Nomos Verlag, 1987) p 613.
Simon, D	'L'effet dans le temps des arrèts préjudiciels de la Cour de Justice des Communautés Européennes: enjeu ou pretexte d'une nouvelle guerre des juges?', in *Du Droit International au Droit de l'Integration-Liber Amicorum Pierre Pescatore* (1987) p 651.
Slusny, M	'Les mesures provisoires dans la jurisprudence de la Cour de Justice des Communautés Européennes', Rev Belge de Droit International (1967) p 127.
Slynn, G, Lasok, KPE and Millett, T	*Halsbury's Laws of England*, vol 51 (Butterworths) part 2; *Law of the European Communities* (ed D Vaughan, Butterworths) part 2.
de Soto, J	in *Zehn Jahre Rechtsprechung des Gerichtshofes des EG* (Carl Heymanns Verlag, 1965) p 48.
Tizzano, A	*La Corte di Giustizia delle Communità Europee* (Jovene, 1967); 'I provvedimenti urgenti nel processo comunitario', in *I Processi Speciali* (Jovene, 1979) p 361; Il Foro Italiano (1980) p 256; 'La Cour de Justice et l'acte unique européen', in *Du Droit International au Droit de l'Integration, Liber Amicorum Pierre Pescatore*, p 691.
Tizzano, A, and Capponi, B	Il Tribunale di Primo Grado e la Corte di Giustizia delle Communità Europee: le nuove regole di procedura Il Foro Italiano (1990) p 438.
Tommasi di Vignano, A	'Alcuni rilievi in tema di opposizione di terzo nei procedimenti dinanzi alla Corte di Giustizia delle Comunità Europee', Rivisto di Diritto Europeo (1967) p 141.
Toth, A	*Legal Protection of Individuals in the European Communities* (North Holland, 1978); 'The authority of judgments of the European Court of Justice: binding force and legal effects', Yearbook of European Law, vol 4 (1984); 'The Court of First Instance of the European Communities', *Current Issues in European and International Law* (Sweet and Maxwell, 1990) p 19; *The Oxford Encyclopaedia of European Community Law* (Clarendon Press, 1990).
Trabucchi, A	'L'efficacia erga omnes delle decisioni pregiudiziali della Corte di giustizia delle Comunità Europee', in *Cinquant' Anni nell'Esperienza Giuridica* (1988) p 104.
Tyrell, A and Yaqub, Z	*The Legal Professions in the New Europe* (Blackwell, 1993).
Ubertazzi, G	'La prova per presunzioni e il processo davanti alla Corte di Giustizia delle Comunità Europee', Rivisto di Diritto Civile (1976) p 241; 'Gli effetti ratione temporis delle sentenze preguidiziali in materia di validità degli atti comunitari', in Diritto Comunitario e degli Scambi Internazionali (1985) p 75.
Ubertazzi, LC	'Legittimazione ad agire delle associazioni di consumatori e procedimenti comunitari antitrust', Monitori dei Tribunali (1977) p 186.

Usher, J *European Court Practice* (Sweet & Maxwell, 1983);
'Exercise by the European Court of its jurisdiction to annul competition decisions', European Law Review, vol 5 (1980) p 287.

Valentine, DG *The Court of Justice of the European Communities* (Stevens & Sons, 1965).

Vandersanden, G *Contentieux Communautaire* (Bruylant, 1977).
and Barav, A

Vaughan, D and *Butterworth European Court Practice* (Butterworth, 1993).
Lasok, KPE (ed)

del Vecchio, A 'Aspetti problematici in tema di revocazione delle sentenze della Corte di Giustizia delle Comunità Europee', *Studi di Diritto Europeo in Onore di R Monaco* (Giuffré, 1977) p 227.

Vesterdorf, B 'The Court of First Instance of the European Communities after two full years in operation', Common Market Law Review, vol 29 (1992) p 897.

Waelbroeck, M, *Le Droit de la CEE*, vol 10 (Editions de l'Univeristé de Bruxelles,
Louis, JV, and 1983).
Vandersanden, G

Wall, E *The Court of Justice of the European Communities* (Butterworths, 1966).

Warner, JP Journal of the Law Society of Scotland (1975) p 47;
Journal of the Society of Public Teachers of Law, vol 14 (1976) p 15.

Wyatt, D *Foglia (No 2)*, European Law Review, vol 7 (1982) p 186.

CHAPTER 1

The Court as an institution

I Introduction

The European Court of Justice (or, to give it its full title, the Court of Justice of the European Communities) is the judicial body created by the Treaties establishing the European Coal and Steel Community, the European Economic Community and the European Atomic Energy Community.[1] Although generally styled 'the European Court', it is not to be confused with the European Court of Human Rights (which sits at Strasbourg), created under the Convention for the Protection of Human Rights and Fundamental Freedoms, of 4 November 1950. Since its inception as the Court of Justice of the European Coal and Steel Community, the Court of Justice of the European Communities has sat in Luxembourg.[2] The Treaties provide that the 'seat' of the Community institutions shall be determined by the common accord of the governments of the member states[3] but no single seat for all the institutions has ever been decided on. In 1965 the representatives of the governments of the six member states resolved, inter alia, that the provisional seat of the Court should continue to be Luxembourg[4] and it has remained there ever since. Even so it

---

1 Referred to hereafter, respectively, as 'the ECSC Treaty', 'the EC or EEC Treaty' and 'the Euratom Treaty'. The ECSC Treaty was signed at Paris on 18 April 1951; the EEC and Euratom Treaties were signed at Rome on 25 March 1957. All three have since been amended and supplemented, most recently by the Single European Act, signed on 17 and 28 February 1986 (OJ No L169 of 29 June 1987, p 1), and by the Treaty on European Union (hereafter 'the EU Treaty'), signed at Maastricht on 7 February 1992 (OJ No C191 of 29 July 1992, p 1). The last amends the EC Treaty (more familiarly known as 'the EEC Treaty'), inter alia so as to replace the term 'European Economic Community' by the term 'European Community' (see art G(A)). However, no similar amendment has been made to the other Treaties and there is no formal fusion of the Treaties. Hence, the European Court of Justice seems to remain the Court of 'the European Communities' rather than of 'the European Community'. The EU Treaty entered into force on 1 November 1993: see art R(2) and OJ No L293 of 27 November 1993, p 61. The text states the position as at the time of writing, with specific mention of the changes wrought by the EU Treaty (where applicable). Since the entry into force of the EU Treaty, it would seem that the EEC Treaty should henceforth be referred to as the EC Treaty: see EU Treaty, art G(A).
2 For an anecdotal history of the first 35 years of the Court's existence, see 'XXXV Anni, 1952–1987' (Luxembourg, Court of Justice and Office for Official Publications of the European Communities).
3 ECSC Treaty, art 77; EC Treaty, art 216; Euratom Treaty, art 189. Cf Case 230/81 *Luxembourg v European Parliament* [1983] ECR 255.
4 Decision of the representatives of the governments of the member states on the provisional location of certain institutions and departments of the Communities, art 3 (OJ No 152/18 of 13 July 1967). Article 3 also covered judicial bodies to be set up under the ECSC, EEC and Euratom Treaties and therefore applies to the Court of First Instance (see below). The decision taken by common agreement between the representatives of the governments of the member states on the location of the seats of the institutions and of certain bodies and departments of the European Communities of 12 December 1992 (OJ No C341 of 23 December 1992, p 1) confirmed Luxembourg as the seat of the Court of Justice and the Court of First Instance.

has power under the Rules of Procedure to sit in a place other than its seat in a particular instance.[5] Under art 1 of the Protocol on the Privileges and Immunities of the European Communities,[6] the premises of the Court are inviolable and exempt from search, requisition, confiscation or expropriation. Its property and assets, being those of the Communities themselves, cannot be the subject of 'any administrative or legal measure of constraint' without the Court's own authorisation. The buildings in which the Court resides are in fact owned by the government of Luxembourg and rented by the Communities.

The ECSC, EEC and Euratom Treaties were amended by the Single European Act so as to provide for the creation of a Court of First Instance to be 'attached' to the Court of Justice.[7] In 1988 the Council of Ministers acted on those amendments pursuant to a request made by the Court of Justice and adopted a decision establishing what is known as 'the Court of First Instance of the European Communities'.[8] The Court of First Instance was entrusted with exercising at first instance the jurisdiction of the Court of Justice in respect of certain matters and its seat is at the Court of Justice.[9] The members of the Court of First Instance were sworn in on 25 September 1989. By a decision dated 11 October 1989, made following the swearing-in of the Registrar of the Court of First Instance, the President of the Court of Justice declared that the Court of First Instance was duly constituted.[10] On the date of the publication of that decision in the Official Journal, the Court of First Instance was seised with the jurisdiction conferred on it by the Council of Ministers.[11]

As a result of the creation of the Court of First Instance, the organisational and institutional structure of the Court of Justice of the European Communities is somewhat complex. As an institution, the Court can be divided into two parts: the Court itself (referred to hereafter as 'the ECJ') and the Court of First Instance (referred to hereafter as 'the CFI').[12] The latter seems properly speaking to be a part of the Court although the ECSC, EEC and Euratom Treaties, as amended by the Single European Act, refer to the CFI as being 'attached' to the ECJ:[13] the Treaties do not endow the CFI with independent status as a Community institution; the Protocols on the Statute of the Court of Justice attached to the ECSC, EC and Euratom Treaties have been amended[14] so as to incorporate certain basic provisions regarding the CFI, the proceedings before it and appeals from its decisions to the ECJ, but without altering the titles of the Protocols, which still refer only to the Court of Justice. The CFI can therefore be regarded as part of the Court in an institutional sense; but that does not mean that the CFI is to be regarded in every respect as synonymous with the ECJ. For one thing, the Court still 'consists' of the ECJ

5 Rules of Procedure (Court of Justice) art 25(3) and (Court of First Instance) art 31(2).
6 Signed at Brussels on 8 April 1965.
7 Single European Act, arts 4, 11 and 26.
8 Decision 88/591 (OJ No L319 of 25 November 1988, p 1). The text of the decision was the subject of a corrigendum published in OJ No L241 of 17 August 1989, p 4. In order to avoid confusion, a corrected text of the complete decision was then published in OJ No C215 of 21 August 1989, p 1, and it is to that corrected version that reference is made. Decision 88/591 was amended by Council Decision 93/350 of 8 June 1993 (OJ No L144, p 21) of 16 June 1993.
9 Decision 88/591, arts 1 and 3, as amended.
10 OJ No L317 of 31 October 1989, p 48.
11 Decision 88/591, art 13.
12 Save where the context indicates otherwise, the term 'Court' will hereafter be used to describe the Court of Justice of the European Communities in its institutional sense, that is, as comprising both the ECJ and the CFI.
13 ECSC Treaty, art 32d; EEC Treaty, art 168a; Euratom Treaty, art 140a.
14 By Decision 88/591, as amended.

judges, 'assisted' by the ECJ advocates general;[15] it does not 'consist' of the CFI judges. Secondly, the role of the CFI is only to exercise at first instance the jurisdiction of the ECJ in regard to those matters that the Council of Ministers has specified.[16] In consequence, the CFI is to be regarded as an integral, but subordinate, part of the Court.[17] In an organisational sense, the ECJ and the CFI are separate parts of the same institution. Each of them can be further divided into two parts: on the one hand, the members of the Court[18] and their personal staffs;[19] on the other, the Registrar and the different departments (of the ECJ and the CFI, respectively) which fall within his sphere of responsibility. The Registrar of the ECJ is responsible directly for the ECJ's Registry and indirectly, through their heads of department, for the Library, Research and Documentation Directorate, the Legal Data-processing Department, the Translation Directorate, the Interpretation Division, the Information Service and the Administration. The Registrar of the CFI is responsible for the CFI's Registry and its Administration. The services of the ECJ's departments are available to the CFI, thus avoiding needless duplication.[20] In addition, there also exist the Secretariat of the Administrative Heads of the Staff Regulations Committee and the Staff Committee.

This chapter deals with the internal aspects of the Court, in particular its composition, structure and functioning, and with the division of jurisdiction between the ECJ and the CFI. Much of it, save the last aspect, is not pertinent to the conduct of proceedings before the Court but it shows how the Court works as an institution. The functioning of the Registries of the ECJ and the CFI and the internal organisation of the Court as a judicial body are clearly of importance in the administration of justice by the Court but they are of only secondary interest so far as the conduct of a particular case is concerned. For that reason, this chapter is intended only to fill in the institutional background to procedure before the Court.

II The instruments regulating the Court

The Court is a creature of the ECSC, EC and Euratom Treaties, as amended, and the basic rules governing its constitution and jurisdiction are to be found there.[21] The powers conferred on the Court by the Treaties can, of course, be modified by amending the Treaties,[22] as was done pursuant to the Single European Act, in order to create the CFI, and in other respects by the EU Treaty; other instruments, including international agreements concluded by

---

15 ECSC Treaty, arts 32 and 32a; EC Treaty, arts 165 and 166; Euratom Treaty, arts 137 and 138.
16 Decision 88/591, art 3, as amended.
17 In the same way, the advocates general of the ECJ are an integral part of the Court even though the Court does not 'consist' of them and they only 'assist' the ECJ judges: see JL da Cruz Vilaça (1990) 10 YEL 1 at p 19.
18 The judges and the advocates general, in the case of the ECJ; the judges in the case of the CFI.
19 Each member of the ECJ has a personal staff consisting of three legal secretaries, who are primarily responsible for research and drafting, a personal assistant, two assistants and chauffeur; the members of the CFI have one legal secretary, a personal assistant and an assistant. The establishments of the President of the ECJ and the President of the CFI are larger in order to take account of their additional responsibilities.
20 According to the annual report of the Court of Auditors for the financial year 1990, vol II (OJ No C324, p 1 of 13 December 1991, at p 5), the total staff employed by each Community institution at 31 December 1990 came to: Parliament, 3,387; Council, 2,066; Economic and Social Committee, 526; Commission, 17,587; Court of Justice, 738; Court of Auditors, 374.
21 Articles 31–45, 164–188 and 136–160, respectively.
22 *Opinion 1/92* [1992] ECR I-2821, para 32.

the Community, may confer additional powers on the Court provided that, in so doing, they do not change the nature of the functions of the Court as envisaged in the Treaties.[23] It is open to the Community to conclude an international agreement that has the effect of making decisions of another court binding on the Court:[24] it is not part of the essential nature of the Court, as envisaged in the Treaties, that it is supreme in all respects.[25] On the other hand, the Treaties do conceive of the Court as an institution whose decisions are binding in law and not merely advisory.[26] The Court's jurisdiction is not defined exclusively by the Treaties. At the present, the most important instruments that define its jurisdiction, apart from the Treaties, are the Convention on Jurisdiction and the Enforcement of Judgments in Civil and Commercial Matters[27] and the Convention on the Law applicable to Contractual Obligations,[28] which confer on the ECJ jurisdiction to give rulings on the interpretation of those Conventions and the acts relating to them. The Agreement on a European Economic Area[29] also extends the jurisdiction of the ECJ by providing for the possibility of the ECJ giving interpretative rulings in response to requests made by courts in EFTA countries[30] and requests made by contracting parties to the Agreement who are involved in a dispute concerning the case law regarding provisions of the Agreement that are identical in substance to corresponding rules in the EEC and ECSC Treaties and the acts adopted in implementation of them.[31]

As stated above, the Single European Act amended the ECSC, EEC and Euratom Treaties so as to provide for the creation by the Council of Ministers, at the request of the ECJ and after consulting the Commission and the Parliament, of 'a court with jurisdiction to hear and determine at first instance, subject to a right of appeal to the Court of Justice on points of law only and in

23 Ibid. If the nature of the Court's functions is to be changed, that must, and can only, be effected by amending the Treaties.
24 *Opinion 1/91* [1991] ECR I-6079, paras 39–40.
25 Save that, by virtue of the supremacy of Community law over national law, judgments of the Court bind all courts in the member states.
26 *Opinion 1/92*, above (note 22), para 33.
27 Signed in Brussels on 27 September 1968 and usually known as 'the Brussels Convention': see art 37 and the Protocol on the Interpretation of the Convention by the ECJ. The Convention has since been amended on several occasions. The present version is that as amended by the Convention on the accession of Spain and Portugal, signed in San Sebastian on 26 May 1989. A consolidated version of the Brussels Convention (and the Protocol), as amended, was published in OJ No C189 of 28 July 1990, p 1. A parallel Convention, known as 'the Lugano Convention', signed at Lugano on 16 September 1988 (see OJ No L319 of 25 November 1988, p 9), in effect extends the Brussels Convention, as amended, to the countries of the European Free Trade Association (EFTA).
28 Opened for signature in Rome on 19 June 1980 and hence known as 'the Rome Convention': see the Protocol on the Interpretation of the Convention by the ECJ (OJ No L48 of 20 February 1989, p 1).
29 Signed on 2 May 1992. The Agreement was to come into force on 1 January 1993 provided that all the Contracting Parties had deposited their instruments of ratification or approval before that date. After that date, it would enter into force on the first day of the second month following the last notification, which had to be made by 30 June 1993. After that date, the contracting parties would (if necessary) convene a diplomatic conference to appreciate the situation: see art 129(3) of the Agreement. It came into force on 1 January 1994: see OJ No L1 of 3 January 1994, p 606. The text of the Agreement is reported in [1992] 1 CMLR 921.
30 Article 107 and Protocol 34.
31 Article 111(3). The Agreement also provides for a system of exchanging information about judgments delivered by the ECJ, CFI, the EFTA court to be established pursuant to the Agreement, and the courts of last instance of the EFTA counties: art 106. Article 110 of the Agreement, which concerns the enforcement of judgments and of decisions of the EFTA Surveillance Authority or the Commission, and the suspension of enforcement, is similar to the parallel provisions in art 192 of the EC Treaty.

accordance with the conditions laid down by the Statute, certain classes of action or proceedings brought by natural or legal persons'.[32] The CFI was duly established and, within the parameters defined by the ECSC, EC and Euratom Treaties, it was entrusted with exercising 'at first instance the jurisdiction conferred on' the ECJ by the ECSC, EC and Euratom Treaties 'and by the acts adopted in implementation thereof' in respect of certain matters specified by the Council.[33]

Although each Treaty sets up its own court, and there are, as will be seen, considerable variations between the Treaties (in particular, between the ECSC Treaty on the one hand, and the EC and Euratom Treaties on the other), the member states signed a Convention on Certain Institutions Common to the European Communities on the same day the EEC and Euratom Treaties were signed, which provides, in art 3, that the jurisdiction conferred on the Court by the EEC and Euratom Treaties 'shall be exercised . . . by a single Court of Justice'. In addition, art 4 provides that, upon taking up its duties, this 'single Court of Justice . . . shall take the place of the Court provided for in Article 32' of the ECSC Treaty. The Convention included several amendments to the ECSC Treaty intended to bring it into line with the other two Treaties but the jurisdiction of the Court, as defined by each of the Treaties, has not been harmonised in this fashion so that, for example, an action for annulment under the ECSC Treaty is subject to different conditions from those applying to similar actions brought under the other two Treaties.[34]

Annexed to each Treaty is a 'Protocol on the Statute of the Court of Justice' of the Community in question. For the sake of brevity, these will be referred to as the ECSC, EC or Euratom Statute, as the case may be. The Statutes contain detailed rules covering the members of the Court and the general form of its organisation and procedure. They were amended in 1988 to take account of the creation of the CFI.[35] The only difference between the EC and Euratom Statutes appears to be the inclusion in the latter of an additional article, art 20, concerning appeals to the Court from a decision of the Arbitration Committee set up under art 18 of the Euratom Treaty. In consequence, the subsequent articles of the Statute are numbered differently from those in the EC Statute, although they have the same wording. The discrepancies between these Statutes and the ECSC Statute are more significant.

The EC and Euratom Treaties provide[36] that the Court (in the present context, the ECJ) shall adopt its own rules of procedure, which require the unanimous approval of the Council. No similar provision appears in the ECSC Treaty but art 55 of the ECSC Statute (as amended) is, in this respect, to the same effect as the EC and Euratom Treaties, save that it adds: 'The rules of procedure shall contain all the provisions necessary for applying and, where required, supplementing this Statute.' The EC and Euratom Statutes contain a similar provision.[37] Both also provide[38] that they may be amended by the Council, acting unanimously, 'as may be required by reason of measures taken by the Council' pursuant to the last paragraph of arts 165 of the EC Treaty and

---

32 ECSC Treaty, as amended, art 32d(1); EC Treaty, as amended, art 168a(1); Euratom Treaty, as amended, art 140a(1).

33 Decision 88/591, arts 1 and 3, as amended by Decision 93/350. The jurisdiction of the CFI is discussed in greater detail below.

34 Eg *Luxembourg v European Parliament* above (note 3).

35 See Decision 88/591.

36 Articles 188 and 160 respectively.

37 Articles 55 and 56 respectively, as amended.

38 EC Statute, art 56; Euratom Statute, art 57 (both as amended).

137 of the Euratom Treaty. This relates to changes in the number of members of the Court and is of limited application. In the case of the CFI, the Treaties provide that it shall establish its rules of procedure in agreement with the ECJ and that those rules shall require the unanimous approval of the Council.[39]

Although it is left to the ECJ and the CFI to draw up their rules of procedure, they must, in addition to being approved by the Council (and also, in the case of the CFI, agreed with the ECJ) follow the overall pattern set out in the Statutes. It would seem that a provision in the rules of procedure (whether of the ECJ or the CFI) may be inapplicable if it is not compatible with the Statutes.[40] The Rules of Procedure of the ECJ were first drawn up and published in 1953,[41] the Court basing them on the Rules of the International Court of Justice at The Hague,[42] as a comparison of the two sets of rules makes evident. The current Rules of the ECJ were originally published in the Official Journal in 1974 and amended on several occasions,[43] most recently to bring them up to date, take account of the creation of the CFI and remove certain deficiencies in the different language versions of the Rules.[44] References to them will be to 'RP-ECJ', followed by the number of the article in question. The Rules of Procedure deal in detail with the organisation and procedure of the ECJ and are supplemented by the 'Supplementary Rules',[45] which set out the rules relating to letters rogatory, legal aid and reports of perjury by a witness or expert. These will be referred to as 'SR'.

The procedure of the CFI is governed by Title III of the ECSC, EC and Euratom Statutes, with the exception of those provisions in that Title that are peculiar to the ECJ, any further and more detailed provisions being laid down in the Rules of Procedure to be adopted by the CFI in agreement with the ECJ and with the approval of the Council.[46] The CFI was to adopt its rules of procedure immediately upon its constitution and, until those rules entered into force, was to apply the ECJ's Rules of Procedure mutatis mutandis.[47] In the event, the Rules of Procedure of the CFI were first adopted in 1990[48] and did not come into effect until the first day of the second month following their publication in the Official Journal on 5 June 1990.[49] They were in force for less than a year. The current Rules of Procedure were adopted on 2 May 1991 and came into force on the first day of the second month of their publication in the

---

39 ECSC Treaty, art 32d(4); EC Treaty, art 168a(4); Euratom Treaty, art 140a(4).
40 See Cases 42 and 49/59 *Breedband NV v Société des Aciéries du Temple* [1962] ECR 145 at 157.
41 OJ of 7 March 1953, p 37; these Rules were replaced in 1959 (see OJ 1970, p 17).
42 Court of Justice of the European Communities, Judicial and Academic Conference 1976, Fifth Report, p 3; Van Houtte *Cahiers du Droit Européen* (1983) p 3 at 5.
43 The original version of the Rules was published in OJ No L350 of 28 December 1974, p 1; minor corrections are to be found in OJ No L102 of 22 April 1975, p 24. The amendments were published in: OJ No L238 of 21 September 1979, p 1, OJ No L199 of 20 July 1981, p 1, OJ No L165 of 24 June 1987, p 1, OJ No L241 of 17 August 1989, p 1 and OJ No L176 of 4 July 1991, p 1. The consolidated version of the Rules published in OJ No C39 of 15 February 1982, p 1 is now of historical interest.
44 At the time of writing, a complete version of the Rules of the ECJ is to be found in OJ No L176 of 4 July 1991 at p 7, which is to be read subject to the corrigenda published in OJ No L383 of 29 December 1992 at p 117.
45 OJ No L350 of 28 December 1974, p 29, as amended (see OJ No L282 of 5 October 1981, p 1 and OJ No L165 of 24 June 1987, p 4). The version published in OJ No C39 of 15 February 1982, p 1 must be read subject to the amendment made in 1987.
46 ECSC Statute, art 46; EC Statute, art 46; Euratom Statute, art 47 (all as amended by Decision 88/591). As a general rule, the provisions of the Treaties relating to the Court and, in particular, the Statutes apply to the CFI unless the Council decides otherwise: ECSC Treaty, art 32d(2); EC Treaty, art 168a(2); Euratom Treaty, art 140a(2).
47 Decision 88/591, art 11.
48 OJ No C136 of 5 June 1990, p 1.
49 See art 130 of those Rules.

Official Journal on 30 May 1991, that is, as from 1 July 1991.[50] They follow very closely the Rules of Procedure of the ECJ.[51] References to the CFI's Rules of Procedure will be to 'RP-CFI', followed by the number of the article in question. The CFI has not adopted Supplementary Rules: the matters covered by the ECJ's Supplementary Rules are dealt with directly by the CFI's Rules of Procedure.

The general principle is that procedural rules must be provided for expressly; and a rule or procedure that would have the effect of rendering an action inadmissible cannot be inferred in the absence of express provision, particularly where other rules and procedures exist which provide adequate judicial protection for a particular procedural situation.[52] In principle, procedural rules apply to all proceedings pending at the time when the rules enter into force and a fortiori to all proceedings commenced afterwards;[53] but, where there is a change in the procedural rules while a case is pending, the change does not affect a stage in the procedure that has already passed by the time of the change.[54]

RP-ECJ 15 provides that the ECJ, acting on a proposal from its President, shall adopt instructions to the Registrar. These[55] cover the duties of the ECJ's Registry, the register of cases before the ECJ, the scale of ECJ and ECJ Registry charges and the ECJ's publications. They will be referred to as 'IR'. This does not end the litany of provisions governing the Court's workings. There are, in addition, a number of sets of rules which are not published and which deal with the internal organisation of the ECJ: the 'Rules on the Internal Organisation of the Court',[56] the 'Instructions from the President of the Court to the Registrar'[57] and the 'Instructions from the Registrar to the Departments'.[58] All are collected in a looseleaf volume entitled 'General Instructions', which is intended for the ECJ's internal use and is not a legal instrument; all are concerned with rules of practice only and, in a number of respects no longer reflect current practice. At the time of writing, the CFI had not drawn up instructions to its Registrar or any internal rules similar to those described above.[59] The importance of such rules is in practice limited. In addition, there are the resolutions and decisions made from time to time by the members of the ECJ and the CFI at the administrative meetings.

50 Those rules are published in OJ No L136 of 30 May 1991, p 1 (see art 130 for the date of their coming into force).
51 The last recital to the preamble to the CFI's Rules of Procedure states that it is 'desirable that the rules applicable to the procedure before the Court of First Instance should not differ more than is necessary from the rules applicable to the procedure before the Court of Justice'.
52 Case T-1/90 *Pérez-Mínguez Casariego v Commission* [1991] ECR II-143, paras 41–43. The need for express wording applies in essence to procedural rules that bar the continuation of proceedings and not to rules or to practices that assist the conduct of a case, such as the practice applied when dealing with confidential material which, as Case 236/81 *Celanese Chemical Co Inc v Council and Commission* [1982] ECR 1183 shows, may be the subject of impromptu rules.
53 Cases 212-217/80 *Amministrazione delle Finanze dello Stato v Salumi* [1981] ECR 2735, para 9 and per Advocate General Rozes at 2755; Case 154/84 *Fleischwaren und Konserven Fabrik Schulz und Berndt GmbH v Hauptzollamt Berlin-Sud* [1985] ECR 3165, per Advocate General VerLoren van Themaat at 3169; Cases C-121 and C-122/91 *CT Control (Rotterdam) BV v Commission*, 6 July 1993, para 22.
54 Cf Case T-23/90 *Automobiles Peugeot SA & Peugeot SA v Commission* [1991] ECR II-653, paras 80–81.
55 OJ No L350 of 28 December 1974, p 33 (see also OJ No C39 of 15 February 1982, p 35), last amended in 1986 (see OJ No C286 of 13 November 1986, p 4).
56 Or 'Internal Rules', cited in the footnotes as 'GI'.
57 Or 'the President's Instructions', cited in the footnotes as 'PI'.
58 Or 'the Registrar's Instructions', cited as 'RI'.
59 Even though RP-CFI 23 provides that instructions to the Registrar shall be adopted by the CFI on a proposal from its President.

Apart from the ECSC Treaty and Statute, whose French text is the only authentic one, all the official language versions of the Treaties, Statutes and the published Rules have equal status. This occasionally leads to problems in reconciling one text with another. All the texts must, however, be interpreted to the same effect and so the meaning of a term in one language version may provide a clue to its proper meaning in another. For this reason it is unwise to place too great a reliance on the precise meaning of a word used in, for example, the English version of an article in the Rules of Procedure or on a semantic analysis of an entire passage.[60] There were certain notorious misleading translations in the Treaties, the Statutes and the Rules of Procedure. They have now been largely eliminated from the ECJ's Rules of Procedure[61] but they remain in the Treaties and the Statutes and in the reports of cases decided by the Court before the position was remedied. The word 'submissions' is one example. It has been used to translate the French word '*conclusions*' in the Treaties, the Statutes and the Rules of Procedure. Unfortunately, in French, '*conclusions*' bears a number of meanings, not all of which may happily be rendered as 'submissions'. For example, the advocate general's opinion is described as his 'submissions' in art 166 of the EC Treaty; the form of order is so described in arts 19 and 37 of the EC Statute. Where there are divergences between the different authentic language versions of a text, it can be interpreted only by a comparative linguistic analysis of all the language versions, in the light of the context and objectives of the provision in question.[62]

III   The division of jurisdiction between the ECJ and the CFI

The jurisdiction of the ECJ is, as stated above, defined for the most part in the ECSC, EC and Euratom Treaties, to which must be added any relevant conventions and other instruments. Probably the most important aspect of the ECJ's jurisdiction is its power to lay down binding and definitive interpretations of the provisions defining its jurisdiction. That gives the ECJ scope for the development of its jurisdiction where there is need in order to ensure adequate legal protection for persons subject to the law. Thus, in Case 294/83 *Parti écologiste 'Les Verts' v European Parliament*,[63] the ECJ held that, although the European Parliament is not specifically mentioned in art 173 of the EC Treaty as one of the Community institutions against which an action for annulment can be brought, an interpretation of art 173 that excluded the possibility of bringing such an action would be inconsistent with art 164 of the EC Treaty and with the general intention of the Treaty to create a complete system of legal remedies and procedures and to make a direct action available against all measures adopted by the Community institutions that are intended to have legal effect; and, in Case C-2/88 Imm. *Zwartveld*,[64] the ECJ asserted for similar reasons jurisdiction to entertain applications made by a national

---

60 This approach can lead to misunderstandings, as can be seen, in another context, from Case 157/79 *R v Pieck* [1981] QB 571, [1980] ECR 2171, where the United Kingdom government based its case on a mistranslation in the English version of a pre-Accession directive.

61 The same errors do not occur in the CFI's Rules of Procedure because of their more recent date.

62 See, generally, KPE Lasok in *Law of the European Communities*, ed. D Vaughan (Butterworths), paras 2.280 et seq.

63 [1986] ECR 1339, paras 23–25.

64 [1990] ECR I-3365.

judicial authority for the review of the discharge by the Community institutions of their duty of sincere co-operation with such authorities. The general principle remains, however, that the ECJ has no inherent jurisdiction and no power to depart from the system of remedies provided for.[65] The ECJ's implied jurisdiction, which goes beyond the jurisdiction expressly conferred on it by specific Treaty provisions, is derived from the necessity to ensure a proper and adequate system of judicial protection in the Community and underpins rather than detracts from the system of remedies expressly provided for.[66] That implied jurisdiction does not come into play merely because the Treaties do not provide expressly for a particular right of action;[67] there must be some prevailing need for the ECJ to invoke its implied jurisdiction in order to fill a lacuna in the system of remedies expressly provided for, such as where the complete absence of any other form of legal redress (including redress before the courts of the member states) creates a serious injustice and is inconsistent with the rule of law in the Community. The ECJ's extensive powers over the definition of its own jurisdiction nonetheless remain subject to the overriding power of the member states to redefine that jurisdiction by amendment of the Treaties.

The nature of the jurisdiction of the CFI is somewhat different. It has been attributed a defined part of the jurisdiction of the ECJ. Quite apart from the fact that judgments of the CFI are subject to appeal to the ECJ on points of law,[68] thus endowing the ECJ with the last word on the true scope of the jurisdiction of the CFI, it is apparent from the mechanism of the attribution of jurisdiction to the CFI that the broad approach to the definition of the ECJ's jurisdiction has no place when considering the jurisdiction of the CFI. The ECJ's jurisdiction is conferred on it by the Treaties within the context of the ECJ's overriding duty to ensure that the law is observed;[69] the CFI's jurisdiction is conferred on it by Council decision, the scope for the Council's power to attribute jurisdiction being limited by the Treaties to 'certain classes of action or proceeding' and being subject to certain express exclusions.[70] In the result, the CFI has, and can only have, attributed to it a defined part of the jurisdiction of the ECJ; and there appears to be no attribution of any implied jurisdiction.[71] That is not to say that the instruments conferring jurisdiction on the CFI must be given a narrow construction: it may be argued that, as the conferring of jurisdiction on the CFI is an exception to the general principle that the ECJ is alone among the Community institutions responsible for the administration of justice, a narrow construction is appropriate; but that seems an excessively technical and formalistic view; the purpose of conferring jurisdiction on the CFI is identified in the relevant Council decision and the provisions defining the jurisdiction so conferred are to be construed accordingly.

---

65 Cf Case 12/63 *Schlieker v High Authority* [1963] ECR 85, and Case 66/76 *CFDT v Council* [1977] ECR 305, para 8.
66 Cf Advocate General Reischl in Case 74/81 *Rudolf Flender KG v Commission* [1982] ECR 395 at 409: 'It is . . . possible to infer . . . a general principle governing the system of the ECSC Treaty . . . to the effect that, whenever measures adopted on the basis of the Treaty produce effects on undertakings which are not subject to its provisions and to which certain measures are expressly addressed, such undertakings too, may obtain judicial review of those measures, even where, as in the present case, no such right is granted *expressis verbis* in the allegedly *ultra vires* measure'.
67 Cf Case 44/81 *Germany v Commission* [1982] ECR 1855, para 7.
68 ECSC Treaty, art 32d(1); EC Treaty, art 168a(1); Euratom Treaty, art 140a(1).
69 ECSC Treaty, art 31; EC Treaty, art 164; Euratom Treaty, art 136.
70 ECSC Treaty, art 32d(1); EC Treaty, art 168a(1); Euratom Treaty, art 140a(1).
71 It may be significant that arts 3 and 4 of Decision 88/591, which identify the Treaty provisions that apply to the CFI, do not mention ECSC Treaty, art 31, EC Treaty, art 164 or Euratom Treaty, art 136.

Before turning to consider in some detail the jurisdiction of the CFI, it should be noted that the Treaty provisions enabling the creation of the CFI are expressed in general terms and, apart from defining the limits of the jurisdiction that may be conferred on it and certain other matters such as the qualifications required of its members, do not state the purpose to be served by the CFI. There are, in consequence, no preconditions for the exercise by the Community institutions of the power to propose and to decide on the establishment of a court of first instance. Although that suggests that the institutions have an unfettered discretion, it may be inferred (from the general duty imposed on the ECJ of ensuring that, in the interpretation and application of the Treaties, the law is observed) that the ECJ may request the creation of a court of first instance only where such a court is necessary in order to improve the quality of judicial protection in the Community. Further, although the Treaties place limits on the jurisdiction that may be conferred on the CFI, within those limits the choice of what jurisdiction should actually be conferred on the CFI and how that jurisdiction should be extended or reduced from time to time (within the parameters laid down in the Treaties) appears to be a matter for the Council acting at the request of the ECJ (and after consulting the Commission and the European Parliament).[72] Hence, any modification of the jurisdiction of the CFI effected after its creation must be initiated by a request from the ECJ that must similarly be necessary for improving the quality of judicial protection in the Community.

In the event, the decision to establish the CFI and the definition of the jurisdiction to be conferred on it (within the limits laid down in the Treaties) were motivated by the perceived necessity to enable the ECJ to concentrate its activities on the task of ensuring the uniform interpretation of Community law (thus maintaining the quality and effectiveness of judicial review in the Community's legal order) and by the desire to improve the judicial protection of individual interests in respect of actions requiring a close examination of complex facts.[73] The second motivation reflected in part the fact that, at the time, the Treaties limited the potential jurisdiction of the CFI to 'certain classes of action or proceedings brought by natural or legal persons' and excluded the attribution of jurisdiction in relation to actions brought by member states and Community institutions as well as references for a preliminary ruling.[74] The EU Treaty removes the limitation to cases brought by natural or legal persons and the exclusion of jurisdiction over actions brought by member states or Community institutions.

Before the EU Treaty entered into force, the jurisdiction that could be conferred on the CFI was limited as follows:

(1)   the CFI could only have jurisdiction to hear and determine cases at first instance, subject to a right of appeal on points of law to the ECJ (such a right of appeal could not therefore be excluded);

---

72 The fact that any modification to the jurisdiction of the CFI must stem from a request made by the ECJ was implicit and not expressed in clear terms in the ECSC Treaty, art 32d, the EEC Treaty, art 168a and the Euratom Treaty, art 140a, as amended by the Single European Act: see, for example Decision 88/591, art 3(3). It is, however, clear from those provisions, as amended by the EU Treaty, that the determination of the CFI's jurisdiction, as well as the proposal to create it, must be the subject of a request from the ECJ. Thus, the first amendment of Decision 88/591 affecting the jurisdiction of the CFI was made in response to a request from the ECJ: see the preamble to Decision 93/350.
73 Decision 88/591, last three recitals of the preamble. From the copious literature on the subject of the CFI and its creation, particular reference may be made to T Kennedy in [1989] 14 ELR 7; T Millett in [1989] 38 ICLQ 811; JL da Cruz Vilaça in (1990) 10 YEL 1.
74 ECSC Treaty, art 32d(1); EC Treaty, art 168a(1); Euratom Treaty, art 140a(1).

(2) the CFI's jurisdiction could relate only to certain classes of action or proceeding defined by the Council;
(3) those classes of action or proceeding were limited to those brought by natural or legal persons (the intention being to exclude actions brought by member states and Community institutions but not, it would seem, those brought by associations of natural or legal persons where such associations have capacity to bring proceedings);
(4) the CFI could not have jurisdiction to hear and determine actions brought by member states or Community institutions or references for a preliminary ruling.[75]

As stated above, the effect of the EU Treaty is to extend the CFI's potential jurisdiction by removing the limitation referred to in (3) above and the exclusion of actions brought by member states or Community institutions.

The jurisdiction actually conferred on the CFI by Decision 88/591[76] covers the following:

(1) disputes between the Communities and their servants falling within arts 179 of the EEC Treaty and 152 of the Euratom Treaty;[77]
(2) actions brought by natural or legal persons pursuant to the second paragraph of art 33 and art 35 of the ECSC Treaty, the second paragraph of art 173 and the third paragraph of art 175 of the EC Treaty or the second paragraph of art 146 and the third paragraph of art 148 of the Euratom Treaty (that is, actions for annulment or in respect of a failure to act);[78]
(3) actions under the first and second paragraphs of art 40 of the ECSC Treaty, art 178 of the EC Treaty or art 151 of the Euratom Treaty (that is, actions for damages);[79]

75 The Treaties, ibid.
76 Article 3, as amended by Decision 93/350.
77 Such actions, generally known as 'staff cases', concern in general terms disputes arising from an actual or potential employment relationship between the parties or between a person from whom the applicant derives rights and the defendant institution. They do not include actions brought by an official or other servant of the Communities that do not concern the disputed legality of an act or default of the appropriate appointing authority but concern more general questions about the exercise by a Community institution of its powers: see, for example, Case T-134/89 *Hettrich v Commission* [1990] ECR II-565, paras 21–22. Nor do they include actions brought by staff associations against a Community institution, which concern the general conditions of employment of officials and other servants of the Communities and not a particular employment relationship: see, for example, Case T-78/91 *Moat and Association of Independent Officials for the Defence of the European Civil Service v Commission* [1991] ECR II-1387.
78 Although art 3(1) of Decision 88/591, as amended, refers under subpara (b) to 'actions brought by natural or legal persons pursuant to the second paragraph of Article 3 [and] Article 35' of the ECSC Treaty, the forms of action in question are open only to undertakings or associations of undertakings referred to in art 48 of that Treaty. The terms in which jurisdiction under those provisions has been attributed to the CFI do not, and could not, alter the scope of the forms of action in question. The reference in art 3(1)(b) to 'natural or legal persons' must therefore be read subject to the more precise terminology of arts 33 and 35 of the ECSC Treaty. In relation to the EC Treaty, the CFI's jurisdiction over actions for annulment or in respect of a failure to act originally related to the implementation of the competition rules applicable to undertakings (that is, EC Treaty, arts 85 to 90 and the secondary legislation made thereunder: the secondary legislation included Council Regulation No 4064/89 – see the corrected version in OJ No L257 of 21 September 1990, p 13 – which is based in part on art 87 of the EC Treaty): see, for example, Case C-66/90 *Koninklijke PTT Nederland NV and PTT Post BV v Commission* [1991] ECR I-2723. That limitation on the CFI's jurisdiction was removed by Decision 93/350.
79 Originally, the CFI had jurisdiction only if such actions were brought by a natural or legal person in company with a staff case or an action for annulment or in respect of a failure to act over which the CFI had jurisdiction at first instance and if the object of the damages action was to obtain compensation for the damage caused by the defendant Community institution through the act or failure to act that was the subject matter of the first action. Thus, the CFI's

(4)   actions under art 42 of the ECSC Treaty, art 181 of the EC Treaty or art 153 of the Euratom Treaty (that is, actions over which the Court has jurisdiction pursuant to an arbitration clause in a contract concluded by or on behalf of the Community).

As originally worded, Decision 88/591 envisaged that, two years after the CFI had commenced operation, the Council would re-examine the ECJ's proposal that the CFI should also have jurisdiction over actions for annulment and in respect of a failure to act concerning (a) acts relating to the application of art 74 of the ECSC Treaty and (b) measures to protect trade within the meaning of art 113 of the EC Treaty in the case of dumping and subsidies.[80] The re-examination of the ECJ's proposal produced an amendment of Decision 88/591 in 1993 (see Decision 93/350) which extended the jurisdiction of the CFI.[81] That extension of the CFI's jurisdiction took effect from the first day of the second month following publication of Decision 93/350 in the Official Journal (that is, from 1 August 1993) save that (i) the extension of jurisdiction was deferred to a date to be fixed by unanimous decison of the Council in respect of annulment actions, actions brought in respect of a failure to act and damages actions brought by natural or legal persons concerning acts relating to the application of art 74 of the ECSC Treaty or measures to protect trade within the meaning of Article 113 of the EC Treaty in the case of dumping and subsidies;[82] and (ii) the extension applies to actions under an arbitration agreement where the contract in question (not the arbitration agreement) was concluded after 1 August 1993.[83] For the purpose of enabling the CFI to exercise the jurisdiction conferred on it, art 4 of Decision 88/591 (as amended) provides that the Treaty provisions dealing with the ECJ's unlimited jurisdiction in certain matters, the consequences of a declaration that an act is void or that a failure to act is contrary to the Treaty, the exception or plea of illegality, the grant of interim relief and the enforcement of judgments of the ECJ shall apply equally to the CFI.[84]

It should be observed that the attribution of jurisdiction to the CFI does not appear to involve any divestment of the jurisdiction of the ECJ. Article 3(1) of Decision 88/591 provides only that the CFI 'shall exercise at first instance the jurisdiction conferred on' the ECJ; it does not state that that jurisdiction is transferred from the ECJ to the CFI (whether or not a transferral of jurisdiction falls within the competence of the Council is doubtful). Further, the

---

jurisdiction over damages actions was contingent on it having jurisdiction over and being seised with an action for annulment or in respect of a failure to act concerning the act or default giving rise to the loss. In that situation, it does not seem that both actions had to be joined in the same application, although that would be the normal way of proceeding; separate actions could be commenced. On the other hand, it does not seem that the CFI had jurisdiction over such a damages action unless a related action for annulment or in respect of a failure to act had been commenced at the same time as, or was pending before it when, the damages action was commenced. The limitation on jurisdiction over actions for damages was removed by Decision 93/350.

80 Article 3(3) of Decision 88/591, as originally worded.
81 The CFI produced a discussion paper for consideration in the context of the 1991 inter-governmental conference on political union that set out the reasons for a more substantial extension of its jurisdiction: see (1991) 16 ELR 175.
82 At the time of writing, no such decision had been adopted.
83 Decision 93/350, art 3. Under art 4 of Decision 93/350, cases pending before the ECJ which fell within the jurisdiction of the CFI on that date and in which the preliminary report provided for in RP-ECJ 44(1) had not yet been presented were to be referred to the CFI.
84 Article 4 of Decision 88/591, as amended, also provides that certain other provisions of the Euratom Treaty (arts 49, 83 and 114b) apply to the CFI. That change was consequential upon the extension of the CFI's jurisdiction effected by Decision 93/350.

Statutes provide[85] that, where both the ECJ and the CFI have jurisdiction over actions for the annulment of the same act, the CFI may decline jurisdiction in order that the ECJ rule on both actions.[86] That method of dealing with parallel proceedings before the ECJ and the CFI presupposes that the ECJ retains jurisdiction over the matters attributed to the CFI because, otherwise, if the CFI declined jurisdiction, there would be no court with jurisdiction over the case. It seems to follow that the effect of attributing to the CFI the ECJ's jurisdiction to hear and determine certain classes of action or proceeding (at first instance) does no more than suspend, as it were, the exercise of that aspect of the ECJ's jurisdiction by the ECJ unless and until the CFI declines jurisdiction.[87] It follows, nonetheless, that when the CFI has exercised the jurisdiction attributed to it in a particular case, its judgment has the force of res judicata both as regards itself and as regards the ECJ since it is exercising (at first instance) the jurisdiction of the ECJ: the only jurisdiction that the ECJ then retains over the case is the jurisdiction to review the CFI's judgment in relation to questions of law.

IV   Composition of the ECJ and the CFI

A   The members

The judges and advocates general are members of the ECJ; the Registrar of the ECJ is usually included among their number as a matter of courtesy.[88] Articles 32 and 32a of the ECSC Treaty, arts 165 and 166 of the EC Treaty, and arts 137 and 138 of the Euratom Treaty provide that the Court shall 'consist' of what is now thirteen judges and shall be 'assisted' by what is now six advocates general. The judges and advocates general are appointed by the common accord of the governments of the member states for a renewable term of six years: every three years there is a partial replacement of the members but retiring judges and advocates general are eligible for reappointment.[89] No

---

85 ECSC and EC Statutes, art 47 (third para); Euratom Statute, art 48 (third para).

86 Thus, where a member state and two undertakings brought separate actions for the annulment of the same Commission decision, the former's action falling within the jurisdiction of the ECJ and the latter two's within the jurisdiction of the CFI, the CFI disseised itself of the proceedings brought before it and referred them to the ECJ so that it could deal with both actions at the same time: Case T-42/91 *Koninklijke PTT Nederland NV and PTT Post BV v Commission* [1991] ECR II-273.

87 The suspension of its jurisdiction over a particular case as a result of the attribution of jurisdiction to the CFI is, however, binding on the ECJ (unless and until the CFI declines jurisdiction), as can be seen from the ECSC and EC Statutes, art 47 (second para), and the Euratom Statute, art 48 (second para), which provide that, where the ECJ finds that an action falls within the jurisdiction of the CFI, it 'shall' refer the action to the CFI: for an example of such a case, see Case C-72/90 *Asia Motor France v Commission* [1990] ECR I-2181. As can be seen from the *Koninklijke PTT Nederland* case (above, ibid note 86), the CFI is obliged to accept jurisdiction in such circumstances because it is bound by the ECJ's ruling on the question of jurisdiction; but that does not prevent the CFI from declining jurisdiction on the ground that the case ought to be heard by the ECJ because of the existence of parallel proceedings pending before the ECJ.

88 The reason for the inclusion of the Registrar may be that, although the ECJ appoints its Registrar (ECSC Treaty, art 32c; EC Treaty, art 168; Euratom Treaty, art 140) but not the advocates general, the ECSC Statute (but not the later EC and Euratom Statutes) provided in art 10 that the ECJ would be 'assisted' by the advocates general and the Registrar, thus placing both on the same plane.

89 ECSC Treaty, art 32b; EC Treaty, art 167; Euratom Treaty, art 139. The mandates run from 7 October, a six-year mandate ending at the expiry of 6 October six years later and a three-year mandate ending on the same date three years after commencement. The number of judges whose mandate ends at each partial replacement of the members of the Court alternates between seven and six; the corresponding number for advocates general is three.

rules are laid down regarding the method of nominating and appointing a member of the Court. It seems to be the practice among the member states that each state is entitled to nominate one judge and the four larger member states (Germany, France, Italy and the United Kingdom) one advocate general each. It appears that the larger member states (including Spain) nominate in turn the thirteenth judge and the smaller member states the remaining advocates general.[90] The same provisions of the Treaties also provide that the number of judges and advocates general may be increased by the Council, acting unanimously, after being so requested by the Court. The CFI consists of twelve members,[91] the number being determined by the Council and not laid down in the Treaties.[92] As in the case of the members of the ECJ, the members of the CFI (all of whom are judges, there being no separate office of advocate general)[93] are appointed by the common accord of the governments of the member states for a renewable term of six years; every three years there is a partial replacement of the members but retiring members are eligible for reappointment.[94] There are no rules governing the method of nominating and appointing judges of the CFI. The practice seems to be that each member state is entitled to nominate one. As in the case of the ECJ's Registrar, the CFI's Registrar is entitled as a matter of courtesy to the same status as a member of the CFI.

The members of the ECJ are 'chosen from persons whose independence is beyond doubt and who possess the qualifications required for appointment to the highest judicial offices in their respective countries or who are jurisconsults of recognised competence'.[95] It will be observed that the second and third conditions are alternatives. The members of the CFI are 'chosen from persons whose independence is beyond doubt and who possess the ability required for appointment to judicial office'.[96] Thus, the differences between the qualifications for appointment to the ECJ and the CFI are that: a nominee to the ECJ, but not one to the CFI, can be a jurisconsult of recognised competence; a nominee to the CFI must have the ability required for appointment to judicial office, whereas a nominee to the ECJ (if not a jurisconsult of recognised

90 Cf Bulletin of the European Communities 1981, No 3, p 63 and 1986, No 1, para 1.1.2.
91 Decision 88/591, art 2(1).
92 The Council determines the composition of the CFI: ECSC Treaty, art 32d(2); EC Treaty, art 168a(2); Euratom Treaty, art 140a(2).
93 RP-CFI 2(1). The members of the CFI (with the exception of the President) may, however, be called on to perform the task of an advocate general in proceedings before the CFI: Decision 88/591, art 2(3); RP-CFI 2(2). Thus, although the task of advocate general is known both to the ECJ and to the CFI, in the case of the latter it is one that is performed on an ad hoc basis by a judge.
94 ECSC Treaty, art 32d(3); EC Treaty, art 168a(3); Euratom Treaty, art 140a(3). The members whose terms of office were to expire at the end of the first three years of the CFI's existence, at which point the first partial renewal of members would occur, were to be selected by lot immediately after the first members of the CFI had taken the oath: Decision 88/591, art 12. The number of members whose mandate ends at each partial renewal of members is not defined in the Treaties or the Statutes. In theory, it seems that it may be freely determined by the Council because the Council is entrusted with power to determine the composition of the CFI and the number of members to be the subject of partial renewal is a matter that goes to the composition of the CFI and not to the selection of its members. When the first members of the CFI were appointed, it was specified that the term of office of six of the members would be six years and that of the remaining six would be three years: Decision of the representatives of the governments of the member states of the European Communities, OJ No L220 of 29 July 1989, p 76. It is not clear whether that reflected a decision previously taken by the Council or was a decision of the governments of the member states (the distinction is an institutional one). At all events, the current practice is that the mandate of six members of the CFI comes up for renewal every three years.
95 ECSC Treaty, art 32b; EC Treaty, art 167; Euratom Treaty, art 139.
96 ECSC Treaty, art 32d(3); EC Treaty, art 168a(3); Euratom Treaty, art 140a(3).

competence) must have the qualifications for appointment to the *highest* judicial office; and, further, his or her qualifications as such must relate to the highest judicial office in the nominee's own country (a limitation that, whatever it means, does not apply in the case of an appointment to the CFI). In neither case is there any condition of nationality and it is theoretically possible, but hardly likely, that a member could be appointed who is not a national of one of the member states. In such an event, he or she would not, however, benefit in his own country from the immunity granted him by the member states.

It seems to be assumed that the conditions for appointment to the ECJ must be construed by reference to the member state proposing the nomination. Thus, the nominee of the British government must be eligible for appointment to the highest judicial office or be a jurist of recognised competence in the United Kingdom. This does not, however, appear to be so. The wording of the Treaties does not reveal whether 'in their respective countries', which relates only to the second condition for appointment to the ECJ, means the country of residence or nationality or the state making the nomination. Since the question of nomination is a practice of the member states which is not consecrated in any authoritative text, far less the Treaties themselves, the third possibility must be discarded. On balance it would appear that it is the country of nationality rather than residence which is meant but there is no certain authority for this assumption. The third condition for appointment to the ECJ, to be a jurist of recognised competence, is not linked to any country at all so that, it would seem, an expert in comparative law, international law (even Community law, perhaps) or the law of a country other than his or her place of residence or nationality may comply with this condition. So, one may conclude, would an expert in Roman or Canon law.[97] The second condition for appointment to the CFI (the ability required for appointment to judicial office) is not tied to the qualifications required for judicial appointment in any particular country, whether a member state or third country. Hence, someone who is not qualified to take up a judicial appointment in any member state is eligible for appointment to the CFI as long as he has the ability required to discharge the judicial function as perceived in general terms and not by reference to any particular judicial post.

Despite the fact that the current practice of nomination to the ECJ and the CFI may be criticised for not being based on any legal principle, it does possess certain advantages. A member of the Court is not a delegate or representative of the state nominating him: the first condition for appointment, independence, makes this clear. It is, however, advantageous that the legal systems of the member states should be fully represented on the bench, not merely in order to cope with the problem of understanding points of national law that may arise in a case, but also to give a balanced view of the legal traditions of the member states, particularly when dealing with questions concerning the principles of law on which the Treaties are based. As the ECJ pointed out in Case 155/79 *AM & S Europe Ltd v Commission*,[98] the Community is based as much on the legal interpenetration of the national legal orders as on the economic interpenetration of the member states.

The term of office of a member of the ECJ or CFI begins on the day specified in the instrument appointing him or on the date of the instrument if no day is mentioned.[99] At the first public sitting of the Court which he attends after his

---

97 On the basis of the French and Italian texts of the Treaties it is possible to argue that 'jurisconsult' means a professional legal adviser and not simply a person learned in the law.
98 [1982] ECR 1575, para 18.
99 RP-ECJ 2; RP-CFI 3.

appointment, he swears the following oath before taking up his duties: 'I swear that I will perform my duties impartially and conscientiously; I swear that I will preserve the secrecy of the deliberations of the Court.'[1] This is the same oath sworn by the Registrars of the ECJ and CFI when appointed.[2] The member then signs a solemn declaration that, both during and after his term of office, he will respect the obligations arising from his office, in particular the duty to behave with integrity and discretion regarding the acceptance of 'certain appointments or benefits' after he has ceased to hold office.[3] While holding office, members may not occupy any political or administrative office or engage in any other occupation, whether gainful or not, unless with the permission of the Council.[4] Under the ECSC Statute[5] the members also 'may not acquire or retain directly or indirectly, any interest in any business related to coal and steel during their term of office and for three years after ceasing to hold office'. The members must also reside at the place where the Court has its seat (Luxembourg)[6] but the ECJ (and, in respect of its members, the CFI) may in proper circumstances grant leave of absence to any member.[7] The ECJ settles any question concerning a member's compliance with the obligations arising from his office and his holding during office of any prohibited office or occupation.[8]

Although the parties to a case cannot apply for the composition of the ECJ or the CFI or a Chamber of either to be altered on the ground that a judge of a particular nationality is either present or absent[9], it seems that an application may be made if a member of the Court is otherwise disqualified from sitting. The Statutes[10] expressly provide that no judge or advocate general may take part in a case in which he has previously taken part as an agent or adviser or has acted for one of the parties, or has been 'called upon to pronounce' as a member of a court, tribunal or commission of enquiry or in any other capacity.[11] 'Having acted for one of the parties' refers to the case in question. If the member has acted for one of the parties in another case (for example, when in private practice before his appointment), this may be a special reason which may lead him or the President of the ECJ (or, as the case may be, the CFI) to feel that he should not sit in order to avoid a conflict of interest, whether real or suspected. It does not seem to fall within the express wording of the Statutes. If it did, those members who, before their appointment, were employed by one of

1 RP-ECJ 3(1); RP-CFI 4(1). New members of the CFI take the oath before the ECJ, the current members of the CFI being present.
2 RP-ECJ 12(5); RP-CFI 20(5). The Registrar of the CFI takes the oath before the CFI, not the ECJ.
3 RP-ECJ 3(2); RP-CFI 4(2). See ECSC Statute, arts 2 and 44; EC Statute, arts 2, 4 and 44; Euratom Statute, arts 2, 4 and 45.
4 ECSC Statute, arts 4, 13 and 44; EC Statute, arts 4, 8 and 44; Euratom Statute, arts 4, 8 and 45. In the case of the ECSC Statute, permission can be granted only by a two-thirds majority in the Council.
5 Ibid.
6 ECSC Statute, arts 9 and 44; EC Statute, arts 13 and 44; Euratom Statute, arts 3 and 45.
7 RP-ECJ 28(4); RP-CFI 34(4).
8 EC Statute, arts 4 and 44; Euratom Statute, arts 4 and 45. In the case of members of the CFI, the decision is made by the ECJ after it has heard the CFI.
9 ECSC Statute, arts 19 and 44; EC Statute, arts 16 and 44; Euratom Statute, arts 16 and 45; Case T-47/92 *Lenz v Commission* [1992] ECR II-2523, para 33 (where objection was unsuccessfully taken to the presence of the Belgian judge on the ground that the case was connected with litigation before the Belgian courts).
10 Ibid.
11 The last situation may arise, for example, where a member of the ECJ, before his appointment to it, formed part of a national court which made a reference for a preliminary ruling to the ECJ or was a member of the CFI and participated in deciding a case which was then appealed to the ECJ.

the member states would be unable to sit in a case involving that state. So far this does not appear to have happened or the point been raised; one may with some confidence conclude that, in this respect, the Statutes are to be construed narrowly. They also provide, as indicated, that if a member considers he should not sit 'for some special reason', he shall inform the President of the ECJ (or, as the case may be, the CFI). Where the same occurs to the President, he is to inform the member concerned accordingly. Any difficulties are to be resolved by a decision of the Court.[12] The Statutes, perhaps wisely, do not attempt to define what may constitute a 'special reason'. It would seem that it is for the Court to decide whether the reason given justifies the member not taking part. It does not seem that the member's own doubts about the appropriateness of him sitting bind the President or the Court although, no doubt, both would accede to the delicacy of feeling of a member. On the other hand, it would seem that, unless the Court were to decide otherwise, the President may prevent a member from sitting 'for some special reason' even if the member in question feels that the reason alleged is specious.

No procedure is laid down for an application by a party to have the composition of the ECJ, the CFI or a chamber of either changed in a particular case although, as has been remarked, the Statutes expressly exclude this only where the objection is based on nationality. The possibility must therefore remain although one would expect cogent arguments to be put forward before the ECJ (or as the case may be, the CFI) would be prepared to accede to such a request. It would appear from the Statutes that the decision is that of the Court (either the ECJ or the CFI, depending on which of them is hearing the case) and the question would arise whether a member impugned in such an application could or should sit to decide the matter. One would expect that he would not, in order to avoid the conflict of interest that would inevitably arise in appearance if not in fact.[13]

Members are totally immune from legal proceedings while they hold office but thereafter they benefit only from a partial immunity covering acts (including words spoken or written) performed by them in an official capacity.[14] Subject to any limitation period, it would seem that actions may be brought against a member after he has ceased to hold office in respect of acts performed during his term of office but otherwise than in his official capacity. The ECJ can waive a member's immunity, the decision being made by it in plenary session; as far as criminal proceedings are concerned, the member may then be tried in any of the member states but only by a court 'competent to judge the members of the highest national judiciary'.[15] It does not seem that this applies once the member has left office, unless partial immunity has been waived, nor does it apply to civil proceedings. The members also benefit from arts 12 to 15 and 18 of the Protocol on the Privileges and Immunities of the European Communities.[16] These include exemption, together with their spouses and dependants, from immigration restrictions and formalities for the registration of

12 That is, the Court (whether the ECJ or the CFI) to which the member in question belongs.
13 Although this view is disputed it would appear that, in the absence of express provision, an application to change the composition of the ECJ, the CFI or a chamber of either may be made as a procedural issue under RP-ECJ 91 or, as the case may be RP-CFI 114 (but note the *Lenz* case, above, note 9). Any factor affecting the capacity of a member in question to act judiciously may be relied on (cf van Reepinghen and Orianne *Journal des Tribunaux* (1961) at p 91).
14 ECSC Statute, arts 3 and 44; EC Statute, arts 3 and 44; Euratom Statute, arts 4 and 45.
15 Ibid. The decision whether or not to waive immunity is made by the ECJ even when it concerns a member of the CFI; but in that event the ECJ must make its decision after hearing the CFI.
16 Protocol, art 21; Decision 88/591, art 2(5).

aliens; the right to the same facilities accorded to officials of international organisations in respect of currency or exchange regulations; the right to import free of duty their furniture and effects at the time of first taking up office and the right to re-export free of duty their furniture and effects on termination of office; the right to import and re-export free of duty a motor car for their personal use; exemption from national taxation on salaries, wages and emoluments paid by the Communities. These privileges and immunities are granted solely in the interests of the Communities and it seems that the Court would be obliged to waive them if it considered waiver not to be contrary to the interests of the Community[17] unless the question arose in the context of legal proceedings against a member, in which case the Court would have discretion whether or not to waive the immunity from those proceedings. The members' salaries, allowances and pensions, together with those of the Registrars of the ECJ and CFI, are fixed by the Council, acting by a qualified majority.[18]

A member may cease to hold office through death, normal replacement, voluntary resignation or by decision of the Court;[19] there is no age for retirement. With the exception of the first and last cases, the member continues to hold office until his successor takes up his duties.[20] Normal replacement occurs when the member's term is not renewed. In other cases the vacancy can arise before the termination of his or her term of office. In that event, his or her successor is appointed for the remainder of the term[21] and may, of course, be reappointed when it expires. A member may resign voluntarily by sending a letter of resignation to the President of the Court of which he or she is a member who, in turn, passes it on to the President of the Council. The vacancy arises when the letter is received by the latter.[22]

A member may be deprived of office, pension or other benefits, by a unanimous decision of the Court,[23] if he or she 'no longer fulfils the requisite conditions or meets the obligations arising from his office'.[24] Under the ECSC Statute,[25] however, he or she may be deprived only of office and then only if he or she 'no longer fulfils the requisite conditions [of office]'; in the case of a judge (whether of the ECJ or the CFI) the decision depriving him or her of office is made (unanimously) by the (other) judges of the ECJ; in the case of an advocate general it is made (unanimously) by the Council, after the ECJ has delivered its opinion. It is doubtful if two separate procedures would have to be commenced in order to remove a judge or advocate general, one under the EEC and Euratom Treaties, another under the ECSC Treaty. The unanimous decision of the judges and advocates general of the ECJ required by the former could be taken to constitute the unanimous opinion of the judges alone (and

17 Protocol, art 18. In the case of members of the CFI, the decision seems to be one made by the ECJ.
18 Treaty Establishing a Single Council and a Single Commission of the European Communities, signed at Brussels on 8 April 1965, art 6; Decision 88/591, art 2(5). Where there is a dispute between an institution and one of its former members about the applicability of any regulations, such as those governing pensions or other benefits, a formal complaint to the institution should be made by the former member concerned before the matter is litigated before the Court: Case C-163/88 *Kontogeorgis v Commission* [1989] ECR 4189, per Advocate General Jacobs, at 4197.
19 That is, the ECJ in respect of members of the CFI as well as its own members.
20 ECSC Statute, arts 6 and 44; EC Statute, arts 5 and 44; Euratom Statute, arts 5 and 45.
21 ECSC Statute, arts 8 and 44; EC Statute, arts 7 and 44; Euratom Statute, arts 7 and 45.
22 ECSC Statute, arts 6 and 44; EC Statute, arts 5 and 44; Euratom Statute, arts 5 and 45.
23 That is, the ECJ which, in the case of a member of the CFI, decides after hearing the CFI.
24 EC Statute, arts 6 and 44; Euratom Statute, arts 6 and 45. That situation may arise, for example, where the member is so incapacitated by illness that he or she is unable to indicate his or her intention to resign voluntarily.
25 Articles 7, 13 and 44.

the opinion of the ECJ in the case of an advocate general) required by the ECSC Statute. In substance, if not in form, they would be no different. It should, however, be noted that, in the case of the ECSC Statute, all that is required is an opinion of the ECJ: it need not be in favour of removal from office, let alone unanimous. It is hardly likely, however, that the Council would act in defiance of an opinion of the ECJ because the advocate general in question would remain in office under the other two Treaties at least until the end of his term.[26]

The member in question does not take part in the deliberations over his fate[27] but he is asked by the President of the ECJ to submit his observations on the matter to the other members of the ECJ in closed session.[28] In the case of a member of the CFI, the first stage of the procedure is that the President of the CFI invites the member concerned to make representations to the other members of the CFI in closed session and in the absence of the CFI's Registrar The members of the CFI then deliberate on the question (in the absence of the member concerned) and come to a conclusion. Voting is by secret ballot and an opinion to the effect that the member concerned no longer fulfils the requisite conditions or no longer meets the obligations arising from office must be supported by the votes of at least seven judges. Where the CFI adopts such an opinion, it communicates it to the ECJ, setting out the reasons for it and particulars of the voting.[29] The procedure before the ECJ follows as in the case of a member of the ECJ. A decision of the ECJ, finding that a member (whether of the ECJ or the CFI) no longer fulfils the requisite conditions or meets the obligations arising from office, is communicated by the Registrar of the ECJ to the Presidents of the Parliament and Commission. It is also 'notified' to the President of the Council, upon which the vacancy arises.[30] Once again, the ECSC Statute is slightly different in that it requires 'notification' to all three Presidents, not just the President of the Council.[31] The difference between a 'communication' and a 'notification' seems to be this: the former simply conveys the information it contains while the latter is formal service of the document.

In the ECJ judges and advocates general and, in the CFI, judges (other than the President of the CFI and the Presidents of its chambers) rank equally in order of precedence, precedence between the members of each of the ECJ and the CFI being determined according to seniority of office and members retaining their former precedence on being reappointed; where two or more members are equally senior in terms of office, precedence is determined by age.[32] It is usual to list the members of each of the ECJ and the CFI in order of precedence starting with the President of the relevant Court and continuing

26 A sensible construction of the ECSC Statute is that it requires a decision of the ECJ recommending removal of the advocate general in question from office; in the absence of express provision requiring unanimity, a simple majority seems alone to be required. Valentine, in *The Court of Justice of the European Communities*, at p 35, takes the view that the Council's role under the ECSC Statute has been repealed. This is very doubtful.
27 ECSC Statute, arts 7 and 44; EC Statute, arts 6 and 44; Euratom Statute, arts 6 and 45; neither does the Registrar of the ECJ, see RP-ECJ 4.
28 RP-ECJ 4.
29 RP-CFI 5. The opinion and the reasons for it (but not details of the voting) should also be communicated to the member of the CFI concerned, as respect for the rights of the defence requires.
30 EC Statute, arts 6 and 44; Euratom Statute, arts 6 and 45.
31 Articles 7 and 44.
32 RP-ECJ 6; RP-CFI 6. For example, when Advocate General Sir Gordon Slynn became a judge of the ECJ, he retained the seniority that he had acquired as advocate general and was ranked above members of the ECJ who had been judges (but not members) of the ECJ for longer than he.

with the Presidents of the chambers and (in the case of the ECJ) the First Advocate General, ranked in order of seniority. Then come the rest of the members in order of seniority, the Registrar being included by courtesy at the end of the list. The members of the ECJ and the CFI are not ranked together in order of precedence. Since the CFI is a judicial body subordinate to the ECJ, its members are usually regarded as ranking below members of the ECJ.

The President of the ECJ (or, as the case may be, the CFI) is elected by the judges (of the ECJ or, as the case may be, the CFI) for a renewable term of three years after the triennial partial replacement of the members,[33] unless the current President vacates office before his term is over, in which case his successor as President is appointed only for the remainder of his term (the appointment still being renewable).[34] The election is by secret ballot, the judge who obtains an absolute majority being elected; if no one obtains an absolute majority, a second ballot is held and the judge who obtains most votes is elected. Where two or more judges obtain an equal number of votes, the oldest is elected.[35] The President's functions are described in the Rules of Procedure[36] as follows: he 'shall direct the judicial business and the administration of the Court; he shall preside at hearings and at deliberations'.[37] His precise duties will appear in due course. Apart from presiding at hearings and meetings the Presidents of the ECJ and CFI have various miscellaneous powers[38] of which the most important is to grant interim relief.[39] The President of the ECJ is also responsible for selecting the judge-rapporteurs in cases which are not automatically assigned to a chamber;[40] the President of the CFI designates the judge-rapporteurs in all cases, on the basis of a proposal from the President of the chamber to which the case has been assigned, and also designates the judge called on to perform the function of advocate general in cases where the CFI decides that an advocate general should be designated.[41] Since so much of his time is taken up with these matters, the President of the ECJ is rarely the judge-rapporteur in a case.

At present the ECJ and the CFI sit either in plenary session or in chambers. The role of the chambers will be discussed below. Each chamber has a President who is appointed by the ECJ (or as the case may be, the CFI) for a period of one year, the method of election being the same as that for the office of President of the ECJ (or, as the case may be, the CFI).[42] In cases assigned to or devolving on a chamber, the President of the chamber exercises the powers of the President of the ECJ (or, as the case may be, the CFI).[43] When the President of the ECJ (or CFI) is absent or prevented from attending or the office is vacant, the functions of President are exercised by one of the Presidents of the chambers in order of seniority; and, where at the same time all the Presidents are prevented from attending or their posts are vacant, the func-

---

33 ECSC Treaty, art 32b; EC Treaty, art 167; Euratom Treaty, art 139; RP-ECJ 7(1); Decision 88/591, art 2(1); RP-CFI 7(1).
34 RP-ECJ 7(2); RP-CFI 7(2).
35 RP-ECJ 7(3); RP-CFI 7(3).
36 RP-ECJ 8; RP-CFI 8.
37 RP-CFI 8 actually states that the President presides at 'plenary sittings', not 'hearings', which reflects the fact that cases before the CFI are ordinarily heard by chambers and exceptionally in plenary session whereas, in principle, the reverse is true of cases before the ECJ.
38 Under, for example, art 81(3) and (4) of the Euratom Treaty and art 7 of Annex II of the Staff Regulations, so far as the President of the ECJ is concerned.
39 ECSC Statute, art 33; EC Statute, art 36; Euratom Statute, art 37; RP-CFI 106.
40 RP-ECJ 9(2).
41 RP-CFI 13(2) and 19.
42 RP-ECJ 10(1); RP-CFI 15.
43 RP-ECJ 9(4); RP-CFI 16.

tions of President are exercised by one of the other judges in order of seniority.[44] The same rules apply, mutatis mutandis, where the President of a chamber is absent.[45] In the case of the ECJ, the First Advocate General is appointed by the Court in the same way and for the same period of time as the Presidents of the chambers.[46] Formerly the advocates general of the ECJ were attached to the chambers and cases were assigned to them by the President of the ECJ. At present they float and the function of distributing the cases among the advocates general is exercised by the First Advocate General, who is responsible for taking the necessary steps if an advocate general is absent or prevented from acting.[47]

In both the ECJ and the CFI, the advocate general assigned to a case assists the Court by making a reasoned submission on the case in open court, acting with complete impartiality and independence[48] but he does not participate in the deliberations between the judges that lead up to the making of the judgment.[49] As will be seen, the advocate general must also be heard before the Court makes various procedural decisions.[50] In regard to the ECJ, an advocate general acts in every case before the Court and is selected, by the First Advocate General, from among the advocates general appointed to the ECJ.[51] In regard to the CFI, an advocate general is designated from among the judges of the CFI to act only in certain cases brought before the CFI, the criteria for selecting such cases being laid down in the CFI's Rules of Procedure.[52] The designation of a judge of the CFI to perform the function of advocate general in a case is made by the President of the CFI; when a case is heard by the CFI in plenary session, it must always be assisted by a judge performing the function of advocate general; when a case is heard by a chamber of the CFI, that chamber is assisted by a judge acting as advocate general only if the CFI in plenary session has decided that there should be an advocate general.[53]

B The Registrar

The Registrars of the ECJ and the CFI are not members of their respective Courts. Each is appointed by his or her own Court[54] for a renewable term of six years.[55] The method of appointment is laid down in the Rules of Procedure. Two weeks before the date fixed for making the appointment, the President of the ECJ (or, as the case may be, the CFI) informs the members of the applications which have been made for the post.[56] The appointment is made by secret ballot, following the same procedure, mutatis mutandis, for the appointment of the

---

44 RP-ECJ 11; RP-CFI 9.
45 RP-ECJ 9(4). In the case of the CFI there is no such express provision but the same seems in any event to follow from RP-CFI 11(2).
46 RP-ECJ 10(1).
47 RP-ECJ 10(2).
48 ECSC Treaty, art 32a; EC Treaty, art 166; Euratom Treaty, art 138; Decision 88/591, art 2(3).
49 See, in the case of the CFI, Decision 88/591, art 2(3) (last sentence).
50 The role of the advocate general is discussed at length by Warner *Journal of the Law Society of Scotland* (1975) p 47; Gori *Cahiers de Droit Européen* (1976) p 375; Dashwood [1982] 2 LS 202.
51 RP-ECJ 10(2).
52 Decision 88/591, art 2(3).
53 RP-CFI 17–19. The procedure to be followed when a judge is designated to act as advocate general is discussed below.
54 ECSC Treaty, art 32c; EC Treaty, art 168; Euratom Treaty, art 140; ECSC and EEC Statutes, art 45; Euratom Statute, art 46.
55 RP-ECJ 12(4); RP-CFI 20(4).
56 RP-ECJ 12(1); RP-CFI 20(1). An application must be accompanied by full details of the candidate's age, nationality, university degrees, knowledge of languages, present and past occupations and experience, if any, in judicial and international fields: RP-ECJ 12(2); RP-CFI 20(2).

President of the Court.[57] The Registrar may be deprived of office only if he no longer fulfils the conditions required by, or no longer meets the obligations arising from, it.[58] No conditions for holding the office of Registrar appear to be specified in the Treaties, the Statutes or the Rules of Procedure. They would no doubt be considered as falling within the 'rules governing his service' which the ECJ and the CFI, respectively, are responsible for drawing up.[59] So far as is known no such rules relating to the conditions of service have been formulated by the ECJ or the CFI. Any decision on whether or not to deprive the Registrar of office is made by the Court appointing him or her after the Registrar has been given an opportunity to be heard.[60] If the office falls vacant before the Registrar's term was due to end, the ECJ (or, as the case may be, the CFI) appoints a successor for a full term of six years.[61]

The Registrar takes the same oath as that required of a judge on taking up his duties;[62] and is obliged to reside at the place where the Court has its seat.[63] He or she benefits from the same privileges and immunities under the Protocol on the Privileges and Immunities of the European Communities[64] but not those granted by the Statutes. The Statutes provide that the Court (whether the ECJ or the CFI) shall, where necessary, arrange for the replacement of the Registrar on occasions when he is prevented from attending the Court.[65] By following the same procedure for the appointment of the Registrar, the ECJ (or as the case may be, the CFI) may appoint one or more Assistant Registrars.[66] Where the Registrar is absent or prevented from attending or the post is vacant, he or she will normally be replaced by an Assistant Registrar (if any); and, where the latter is also absent or prevented from attending or the post is vacant, the President (of the ECJ or, as the case may be, the CFI) designates an official or servant to carry out the duties of Registrar.[67]

The Registrar's functions are many and varied but they may be summarised as falling into three separate categories:

(1)   RP-ECJ 23 provides that the Registrar 'shall be responsible, under the authority of the President, for the administration of the Court, its financial management and its accounts' (RP-CFI 30 is to the same effect, so far as the Registrar of the CFI is concerned)[68];

(2)   the Registrar is directly responsible for the Registry and hence is indirectly involved in the progress of cases before the ECJ (or, as the case may be, the CFI): RP-ECJ 17(1) and RP-CFI 25(1) provide that the Registrar is 'responsible, under the authority of the President, for the

---

57 RP-ECJ 12(3) and 7(3); RP-CFI 20(3) and 7(3).
58 RP-ECJ 12(6); RP-CFI 20(6).
59 In the case of the ECJ: ECSC Treaty, art 32c; EC Treaty, art 168; Euratom Treaty, art 140. In the case of the CFI: ECSC and EC Statutes, art 45; Euratom Statute, art 46.
60 RP-ECJ 12(6); RP-CFI 20(6).
61 RP-ECJ 12(7); RP-CFI 20(7).
62 RP-ECJ 12(5) and 3(1); RP-CFI 20(5) and 4(1). See also the ECSC Statute, arts 14 and 45; the EC Statute, arts 9 and 45; the Euratom Statute, arts 6 and 46.
63 ECSC Statute, arts 9 and 45; EC Statute, arts 13 and 45; Euratom Statute, arts 13 and 46.
64 Article 21; Decision 88/591, art 2(5).
65 EC Statute, arts 10 and 45; Euratom Statute, arts 10 and 46.
66 RP-ECJ 13; RP-CFI 21. They are usually titled 'Deputy Registrar'. At the time of writing, the ECJ had two and none had been appointed by the CFI.
67 RP-ECJ 14; RP-CFI 22.
68 RP-ECJ 18 and RP-CFI 26 provide that the Registrar (of the ECJ and the CFI, respectively) has custody of the seals of the Court appointing him and is responsible for its records and publications. The ECJ's Internal Rules are perhaps more succinct: art 23 provides that the Registrar (of the ECJ) is responsible for the functioning of the departments of the ECJ.

acceptance, transmission and custody of documents and for effecting service as provided for by' the Rules;
(3)   according to RP-ECJ 17(2) (RP-CFI 25(2) is to the same effect), the Registrar 'shall assist the Court, the Chambers, the President and the Judges in all their official functions' and so must attend all meetings and sittings of the ECJ (or as the case may be, the CFI) and the chambers[69] with the exception of those held to consider whether a member is to be deprived of office[70] and the deliberations of the ECJ (or CFI) on matters which do not concern its own administration (in general where the Court is considering its judgment in a case).[71]

The Registrar of the ECJ is responsible to the ECJ for all its departments but the departmental heads may submit proposals relating to their own departments to the President of the ECJ through the Registrar.[72] In the case of the Registry of the ECJ such proposals are made directly to the ECJ by the Registrar of the ECJ or his deputy.

Naturally, with all these responsibilities the Registrar is often unable to meet all his or her commitments, particularly (so far as the Registrar of the ECJ is concerned) with regard to attendance at every meeting and sitting of the Court. RP-ECJ 23 provides that, as far as the administrative functions of the ECJ's Registrar are concerned, he or she is to be assisted by an administrator; since the administration of the CFI is much smaller, there is no such provision in the CFI's Rules.[73] In matters relating to the Registry, the Registrar of the ECJ is assisted by a Deputy Registrar who acts in his place when he is absent;[74] the Registrar of the CFI does not, at present, have a deputy. Judgments are signed by the President and the Registrar[75] but it will be observed that, from time to time, judgments of the ECJ have been signed by the Deputy Registrar, a Principal Administrator or other official and even, on occasions, a legal secretary who has stood in for the Registrar at the hearing.

C Assistant rapporteurs

Acting on a proposal from the ECJ, the Council may by unanimous vote provide for the appointment of assistant rapporteurs to the ECJ and lay down the rules governing their service.[76] So far, no such proposal has been made by the ECJ. Should assistant rapporteurs be appointed, the Statutes[77] provide that they must be 'persons whose independence is beyond doubt and who possess the necessary legal qualifications'. What are the 'necessary legal qualifications' would no doubt be defined in the instrument providing for their appointment. They would be appointed by the Council, swear the same oath as that sworn by members of the Court[78] and benefit from the same immunities as the Registrar of the ECJ.[79]

The role played by the assistant rapporteurs is a little obscure. The Statutes

---

69 RP-ECJ 19; RP-CFI 27.
70 RP-ECJ 4; RP-CFI 5.
71 RP-ECJ 27; RP-CFI 33.
72 GI 55 and 56.
73 RP-CFI 30 simply provides that the CFI's Registrar will be assisted by the departments of the ECJ.
74 RP-ECJ 13. A second Deputy Registrar is in charge of the ECJ's administration.
75 ECSC Statute, arts 31 and 46; EC Statute, arts 34 and 46; Euratom Statute, arts 35 and 47; see also RP-ECJ 64(2) and RP-CFI 82(2).
76 ECSC Statute, art 16(2); EC and Euratom Statutes, art 12.
77 Ibid.
78 Ibid and RP-ECJ 24(4).
79 Protocol on the Privileges and Immunities of the European Communities, art 21.

provide that they 'may be required under conditions laid down in the Rules of Procedure to participate in preparatory enquiries in cases pending before the Court and to co-operate with the Judge who acts as Rapporteur'.[80] The Rules of Procedure of the ECJ[81] are hardly more precise, although they do say that assistant rapporteurs shall assist the President in connection with applications for interim relief and the judge-rapporteurs with their work. In so doing, the assistant rapporteurs would be responsible to the President of the Court or a chamber or a judge-rapporteur, as the case may be.[82] It is also provided that the assistant rapporteur may take part in the Court's deliberations.[83] The concept of assistant rapporteurs seems to remain very much tabula rasa and could no doubt be so defined as to provide the Court with the equivalent of the English Supreme Court masters. Their potential use as a tribunal of first instance to settle questions of fact in particular types of cases, such as staff or competition cases, has now been overtaken by the creation of the CFI.

D   Other personnel

The Statutes provide that 'officials and other servants' are to be attached to the ECJ to enable it to function and they shall be responsible to the Registrar 'under the authority of the President'.[84] The Rules of Procedure of the ECJ provide that its officials and other servants shall be appointed in accordance with the Staff Regulations and set out the oath to be taken by an official before taking up his or her duties.[85] The Staff Regulations[86] apply to all the institutions and set out a comprehensive code dealing with the employment of persons by them. 'Officials', that is to say, persons appointed to an established post in one of the institutions, are covered by the Staff Regulations for Officials; 'other servants', that is to say, temporary agents, auxiliary agents, local staff and special advisers, fall under the Conditions of Employment of Other Servants of the European Communities. Each institution possesses an 'appointing authority', which is the person or body empowered to make decisions under the Staff Regulations. In the case of the Court, the various appointing authorities are defined in a Decision dated (at the time of writing) 1 July 1992.

The Statutes provide that the President of the ECJ and the President of the CFI are to determine, by common accord, the conditions under which officials and other servants of the ECJ are to render their services to the CFI so as to enable it to function; and certain officials and servants are to be responsible to the CFI's Registrar under the authority of the CFI's President.[87] The Statutes do not provide for officials and other servants to be 'attached' to the CFI, as is the case with regard to the ECJ. The Statutes therefore seem to envisage two means of providing the CFI with the infrastructure that it requires in order to function. The first is by the ECJ making available to the CFI the services provided by the ECJ's own departments.[88] The second is by a form of assignment[89] to the CFI of

80 Ibid.
81 RP-ECJ 24(1) and (2).
82 RP-ECJ 24(3).
83 RP-ECJ 27(2).
84 ECSC Statute, art 16; EC and Euratom Statutes, art 11.
85 RP-ECJ 20.
86 See Council Regulation No 259/68 of 29 February 1968 (OJ No L56/1 of 4 March 1968) as amended.
87 ECSC and EC Statutes, art 45; Euratom Statute, art 46.
88 Thus, RP-CFI 30 provides that the CFI's Registrar shall be 'assisted' by the departments of the ECJ. The CFI's Rules of Procedure do not, of course, bind the ECJ and, in so providing, they merely state the duty of co-operation between the departments of the ECJ and the CFI that flows from the attachment of the CFI to the ECJ and from the Statutes.
89 It is not 'secondment' as that term is understood in the Staff Regulations.

officials and other servants attached to the ECJ. Strictly speaking, officials and other servants working directly for the CFI are still 'attached to' the ECJ.[90] However, since they work for the CFI, they fall within the responsibility of the CFI's Registrar, under the authority of the CFI's President. The function of appointing authority can, thus, be devolved to the CFI even though the official or other servant is in formal terms attached to the ECJ. That state of affairs is reflected in RP-CFI 28 and 29, which provide that officials and other servants whose task is to assist the President, judges and Registrar of the CFI shall be appointed in accordance with the Staff Regulations and shall take the oath taken by officials and other servants of the ECJ (the oath being taken before the CFI's President in the presence of its Registrar).

V   The structure of the Court

A   The Court and chambers

The ECJ and the CFI remain permanently in session and each fixes the time of its vacations.[91] This means nothing more than that the ECJ and CFI cease to hold hearings and give judgments during the vacation but that in other respects they continue their work. At present the vacations run from 18 December to 10 January; the Sunday before Easter to the second Sunday after Easter; and 15 July to 15 September,[92] but the dates may be changed by decision of the ECJ (or, for its own part, the CFI) in order to take account of its workload. During the vacations the functions of the President of the ECJ (or CFI) continue to be exercised in Luxembourg by the President himself, a President of one of the chambers or a judge selected by the President.[93] In cases of urgency the President may convene the judges (and, in the case of the ECJ, the advocates general) during the vacation.[94] The ECJ's Registry is closed only on the official holidays listed in Annex I of the ECJ's Rules of Procedure[95] but the Court as an institution (that is, both the ECJ and the CFI) observes the official holidays in Luxembourg.[96] Each year a list of holidays is drawn up but they apply only to the Court's officials: it is the official holidays in Annex I of the ECJ's Rules of Procedure that are important for procedural purposes; during holidays for the Court's officials that are not mentioned in Annex I, the Court is manned by a skeleton staff. The dates and times of the sittings of the ECJ, the CFI and the chambers of both are fixed by the President of those Courts and the Presidents of the chambers concerned, respectively.[97] Usually they are held on Tuesdays, Wednesdays and Thursdays each week in term time (the CFI is more flexible and does have hearings on Mondays and Fridays), with the exceptions of the weeks following Carnival Monday, Whit Monday and the week of All Saints. According to art 1 of Annex I of the ECJ's Rules of Procedure, the official holidays of the Court are New Year's Day, Easter Monday, 1 May, Ascension Day, Whit Monday, 23 June,[98] 15 August,

---

90 Since the CFI is not a Community institution in its own right but is an organ 'attached' to an institution, officials and other servants cannot be attached to it.
91 ECSC Statute, arts 17 and 44; EC Statute, arts 14 and 44; Euratom Statute, arts 14 and 45.
92 RP-ECJ 28(1); RP-CFI 34(1). It is understood that the ECJ has reduced the period of its Easter vacation to two weeks.
93 Ibid.
94 RP-ECJ 28(2); RP-CFI 34(2).
95 IR 1.
96 RP-ECJ 28(3); RP-CFI 34(3).
97 RP-ECJ 25(1) and (2); RP-CFI 31(1) and 16.
98 24 June when 23 falls on a Sunday.

1 November, 25 December and 26 December.[99] It does not seem that these comprise all the official holidays in Luxembourg.

The ECJ sits either in plenary session, for which the quorum is seven, or in chambers, for which the quorum is three.[1] If it is inquorate, a sitting in plenary session must be adjourned until there is a quorum; but, in the case of a chamber, the President of the Court is informed that the chamber is inquorate so that he can designate another judge to complete the chamber.[2] The Treaties provide[3] that it may form chambers of three or five judges 'either to undertake certain preparatory enquiries or to adjudicate on particular categories of cases'. The intention of the ECJ has been to reserve the most important cases for plenary session, cases of minor importance for chambers of three judges, and cases of middling importance for chambers of five. Each year, generally in October, the ECJ issues a decision determining the composition of the chambers. This decision is published in the Official Journal.[4] At the present time there are six chambers: the first to fourth chambers comprise three judges; the fifth and sixth chambers comprise six judges.[5]

The Treaties provide[6] that the chambers' jurisdiction to hear cases is to be defined in accordance with rules to be laid down. The rules are to be found in the ECJ's Rules of Procedure, but the principal limitation on the powers of the chambers is to be found in the Treaties themselves, which go on to provide that the ECJ must sit in plenary session when a member state or a Community institution that is a party to the proceedings so requests.[7] Since the quorum for a plenary session is seven, the ECJ has a certain area of discretion in deciding exactly how many judges must sit; in simple cases requiring the full court[8] only seven or nine judges do so.[9] RP-ECJ 9(3) provides that the ECJ shall lay down the criteria by which, as a rule, cases are to be assigned to chambers. These principles are to be found in RP-ECJ 95.

---

99 Those dates are also followed by the CFI: RP-CFI 101(2).
 1 ECSC Treaty, art 32; EC Treaty, art 165; Euratom Treaty, art 137; ECSC Statute, art 18; EC and Euratom Statutes, art 15.
 2 RP-ECJ 26(2) and (3).
 3 ECSC Treaty, art 32, EC Treaty, art 165; Euratom Treaty, art 137.
 4 RP-ECJ 9(1).
 5 See, at the time of writing, OJ No C278 of 16 October 1993, p 11. In the fifth and sixth chambers, which effectively comprise two three-judge chambers each, the sixth judge cannot sit in a case because the Treaty does not provide for the formation of chambers having more than five active members and because decisions of the Court are valid only when an uneven number of judges is sitting in the deliberations. The extra judge, who does not in consequence participate in the deliberations, is usually the President of one of the three-judge chambers forming the fifth (or sixth) chamber, the President of the other three-judge chamber being the President of the fifth (or sixth) chamber, as the case may be.
 6 Ibid.
 7 The Treaties, ibid, as amended by the EU Treaty, arts G(E)(49), H(11) and I(10). Previously, the ECJ had to sit in plenary session when it heard (i) cases brought before it by a member state or a Community institution and (ii) references for a preliminary ruling, if and in so far as the chambers did not have jurisdiction under the Rules of Procedure to give a ruling on the question referred by the national court.
 8 The classic example is an action brought by the Commission under art 169 of the EEC Treaty against a member state for failing to implement a directive within the time fixed for doing so; in many of these cases the defendant raises no defence worth considering.
 9 Usually the chamber of six judges to which the judge-rapporteur in the case belongs and one of the three-judge chambers (comprising judges other than those forming the six-judge chamber) as completed, if necessary, by the President of the Court. If at least nine judges sit the Court would not become inquorate should one of them be unable to participate in the deliberations on the judgment.

This provision covers three categories of case:

(1) appeals brought against a decision of the CFI under arts 49 of the ECSC and EC Statutes and art 50 of the Euratom Statute;[10]
(2) references for a preliminary ruling 'of a kind mentioned in Article 103' of the Rules, *semble*, all such references and similar proceedings envisaged in RP-ECJ 103;[11]
(3) any other case, with the exception of those brought by (as opposed to, so it seems, against) a member state or a Community institution.

It is unclear if the qualification applicable to the last category also applies to the first: logic suggests that, if a case brought by a member state or a Community institution should not be assigned to a chamber, the same should apply to appeals brought by a member state or a Community institution; and the structure of RP-ECJ 95(1) leaves it uncertain, in some language versions, as to whether or not the qualifying words 'with the exception of those brought by a Member State or an institution' are intended to have general application. On the other hand, cases falling within the first category can be distinguished from the typical case brought by a member state or Community institution because they originate in proceedings in respect of which the ECJ's jurisdiction is exercised by the CFI; they are not cases which are regarded as being so important that the ECJ's jurisdiction over them must be retained in its entirety by the ECJ itself. Hence, there is sound reason for construing any ambiguity in RP-ECJ 95(1) in favour of the view that all cases within the first category can be assigned to a chamber whether or not the appeal is brought by a member state or Community institution.

Cases within all three categories can be assigned to a chamber 'in so far as the difficulty or the importance of the case or particular circumstances are not such as to require that the Court decide it in plenary session'.[12] Assignment by reference to those criteria is not automatic but requires an assessment to be made of the case. In principle, the question to be considered is whether there is some reason satisfying one of the criteria of difficulty, importance or particularity that justifies retention of the case for determination by the ECJ in plenary session. The decision whether or not to assign a case to a chamber is taken by the ECJ at the end of the written procedure upon consideration of the preliminary report on the case presented by the judge-rapporteur and after hearing the advocate general assigned to the case.[13] Cases are ordinarily assigned to chambers on an ad hoc basis. A case may not be assigned to a chamber if a member state or a Community institution which is a party to, or an intervener

---

10 That is, appeals against the following decisions of the CFI: final decisions; decisions disposing of the substantive issues in part only; decisions disposing of a procedural issue concerning a plea of lack of competence or inadmissibility.
11 It would seem that the reference to RP-ECJ 103 must be understood broadly. A narrow interpretation of the word 'mentioned' would suggest that only an express mention of the provision under which the reference is made would be sufficient, which would render meaningless the use of the words 'of a kind' in RP-ECJ 95(1). Further, RP-ECJ 103(2) refers to 'references for interpretation provided for by other existing or future agreements' which, from the title to the chapter in which RP-ECJ 103 appears, seems to allude to something other than a reference for a preliminary ruling in the strict sense. It is arguable that RP-ECJ 95(1) must be construed as referring only to those proceedings described in RP-ECJ 103 as references for a preliminary ruling. However, that seems to be an excessively technical limitation to place on the scope of the power to assign a case to a chamber when it is considered that references for a preliminary ruling concerning the validity of an act of a Community institution often pose more difficulties than references concerning a question of interpretation. On that basis it is reasonable to interpret RP-ECJ 95(1) as applying generally to the proceedings envisaged in RP-ECJ 103.
12 RP-ECJ 95(1).
13 RP-ECJ 95(2).

in the proceedings, or which has submitted written observations (if the case is a reference for a preliminary ruling), requests that it be decided in plenary session.[14] The Rules of Procedure suggest that such a request should be made before the ECJ meets to decide the question of assignment to a chamber. This is not, however, stated expressly in RP-ECJ 95 and it is arguable that the ECJ could entertain a request made at any time before the date of the hearing. In practice, the ECJ has rejected requests made at a late stage in the proceedings. A request should therefore be made no later than the end of the written procedure.

As soon as proceedings in a case have begun, whether it is by application originating proceedings or lodgment of the order for reference (in a reference for a preliminary ruling), the President of the ECJ assigns the case to one of the chambers (ordinarily one with three judges) for any preparatory enquiries[15] and it will generally remain with that chamber unless it is a case which ought to be heard by the full Court or a chamber of six judges. A chamber may at any stage refer a case back to the full Court.[16] Apart from these matters, the Rules of Procedure make the chambers responsible for a number of decisions, such as those relating to legal aid[17] and the taxation of costs.[18] Although the member states and the Community institutions may, as indicated above, request a case to be decided in plenary session, no party has, with this exception, power to apply for a case to be assigned to a particular chamber or to the full Court. Representations may be made tending to show that the case deserves to be heard by the full Court but the decision rests with the ECJ itself. In consequence, when a chamber of the ECJ raises of its own motion the question whether or not a case before it should be heard by the full Court (that question may be raised by the advocate general in his opinion), it generally decides the matter for itself without giving the parties an opportunity to be heard: the question relates essentially to the organisation by the ECJ of its own procedures and the judges of the ECJ are best able to decide what is the appropriate manner of dealing with a case. In cases assigned to a chamber, the Rules of Procedure apply in the same way as to proceedings before the full Court and the President of the chamber exercises the powers of the President of the ECJ.[19] The hearing is before the chamber and judgment given by it after hearing the opinion of the advocate general.

Whereas the ECJ 'shall sit in plenary session' but 'may, however, form Chambers',[20] the CFI 'shall sit in chambers of three or five judges' (for which the

---

14 Ibid. Such a request may not be made in proceedings between the Communities and their servants which, in practical terms, means staff cases appealed from the CFI to the ECJ. In practice, all such appeals are heard by a chamber.

15 RP-ECJ 9(2).

16 RP-ECJ 95(3). In Case C-370/89 *Société générale d'entreprises électro-mécaniques v European Investment Bank* [1992] ECR I-6211, for example, the decision to refer the matter to the full Court was made following the hearing; in Cases 271/83, 15, 36, 113, 158 and 203/84 and 13/85 *Ainsworth v Commission and Council* [1987] ECR 167 (see pp 170–171), Case 192/85 *Newstead v Department of Transport and HM Treasury* [1987] ECR 4753 (see p 4763) and Case 20/85 *Roviello v Landesversicherungsanstalt Schwaben* [1988] ECR 2805 (see pp 2833–2834), the decision was made after the hearing and after the advocate general had delivered his opinion. As those cases indicate, a case may be referred back to the full Court for a variety of reasons, such as the desirability of avoiding (or resolving) a divergence in the case law of the Court in a particular area as between the decisions of different chambers; or the realisation that a case gives rise to the need to rule on the validity of a provision of secondary legislation; or the desirability of the full Court ruling on an unresolved question concerning its jurisdiction.

17 RP-ECJ 76.

18 RP-ECJ 74.

19 RP-ECJ 9(4).

20 ECSC Treaty, art 32; EC Treaty, art 165; Euratom Treaty, art 137. The use of chambers was regarded as exceptional at the time when the Treaties were signed but has since become more a matter of course. The principle (however theoretical it may in practice be) remains that the ECJ should ordinarily sit in plenary session.

quorum is three judges) but, in certain cases, 'may sit in plenary session' (for which the quorum is seven judges).[21] The constitution and composition of the chambers are determined by the CFI at the start of the legal year; the decision applies for that year only and is published in the Official Journal.[22] At present, the CFI has five chambers: the first and second of six judges, the third of three judges, and the fourth and fifth of four judges.[23] As cases come automatically before a chamber, provision must be made for their allocation as between the chambers. The Rules of Procedure provide that staff cases shall be assigned to chambers of three judges and that all other cases shall be assigned to chambers of five judges.[24] Within those parameters, the allocation of cases as between the three- and five-judge chambers, respectively, is made pursuant to criteria laid down by the CFI,[25] usually yearly, at the same time as the constitution and composition of its chambers are determined. Thus, at the time of writing, the system of allocation for the legal year running from September 1992 to August 1993 was a continuation of that first adopted by the CFI in 1989, namely, allocation to each chamber in turn in the order in which cases are registered at the Registry of the CFI, subject to any decision otherwise, made by the President of the CFI, because cases are related, or in order to ensure an even spread of the workload between the various chambers.[26] The system of allocating cases more or less automatically as between the chambers to which they have been assigned by reference to their subject matter operates without prejudice to the power of the CFI to hear a case in plenary session.[27] Cases may be heard in plenary session whenever the legal difficulty or the importance of the case or special circumstances so justify (on the same grounds a case may be referred to a chamber with a different number of judges).[28] The decision whether

---

21 Decision 88/591, art 2(4); RP-CFI 11. In relation to the quorum for plenary sessions, the Statutes incorporate the quorum rules applicable to the ECJ: ECSC and EC Statutes, art 44; Euratom Statute, art 45. Where a sitting in plenary session is inquorate, it is adjourned until there is a quorum; in the case of a chamber, the President of the chamber informs the President of the CFI who then designates a judge to complete the chamber: RP-CFI 32(2) and (3).

22 RP-CFI 10. The legal year commences in September.

23 See, at the time of writing, OJ No C206 of 30 July 1993, p 7. It will be appreciated that, as the CFI can sit only in plenary session or in chambers of three or five judges, the additional judge in the first, second, fourth and fifth chambers cannot sit in cases before those chambers. As a result, the first decision of the CFI setting up its chambers specified that they were to sit as benches of five and three judges, respectively: see OJ No C281 of 7 November 1989, p 12. The reason for the additional judge is organisational. Since the CFI has twelve judges, it is natural to divide it into two chambers of six judges, the additional judge being necessary in order to prevent the chamber from being inquorate should one of the judges fall ill or be otherwise unable to sit. The President of the CFI has various administrative and other tasks (such as the hearing of applications for interim relief) that prevent him from sitting in the three-judge chambers. That leaves only eleven judges to be allocated to those chambers, resulting in the uneven distribution between the third to fifth chambers. See further JL da Cruz Vilaça in (1990) 10 YEL 1 at pp 36–38.

24 RP-CFI 12(1).

25 RP-CFI 12(2).

26 See OJ No C281 of 7 November 1989, p 13. Thus, for example, where four applications commencing staff cases are lodged at the Registry one after the other, the first in time will be assigned to the third chamber, the second to the fourth chamber, the third to the fifth chamber and the fourth to the third chamber again (and so on for all successive staff cases). On the other hand, if all four cases were related, they might all be allocated to the same chamber and that might, in turn, require some adjustment of the system of allocation in order to ensure that that chamber was not overburdened.

27 Cf RP-CFI 12(1).

28 RP-CFI 14(1). Where a case is referred to another chamber, it can be referred only by a three-judge chamber to a five-judge chamber or vice versa; one chamber cannot refer a case to a different chamber having the same number of judges even if it wished to do so, because, for example, one or more of the judges in that other chamber have particular expertise in the subject matter of the litigation.

or not to decide a case in plenary session (or refer it to another chamber) is made by the CFI sitting in plenary session, on a proposal from the chamber currently seised with the case, and after hearing the parties and the advocate general; that chamber may make that proposal either on its own initiative or at the request of one of the parties.[29] The decision can be made at any stage in the proceedings[30] and, therefore, a request from one of the parties may in principle be made at any stage in the proceedings before the delivery of judgment. Where the initiative for the assignment of the case to the CFI in plenary session or to a larger, or smaller, chamber emanates from one of the parties, it seems that the burden lies on that party to persuade the chamber currently seised with the case that the conditions for assigning the case to the full Court (or another chamber) have been satisfied. If the chamber is not so persuaded, matters end there. It is only if the chamber is so persuaded that matters go further and the chamber puts the proposal to the CFI in plenary session.[31] Where the CFI sits in plenary session, it is assisted by an advocate general designated by the President of the CFI from among the judges of the CFI.[32] That does not mean that, even where it is only a matter of deciding whether or not a case should be heard by the full Court or a different chamber, an advocate general must be designated and express an opinion on the question.[33] In the normal course, the chamber will have given the parties an opportunity to be heard on the question, at least if the matter has been raised by one of them;[34] but the parties also have the right to be heard by the CFI in plenary session in the event that a proposal is made to it by the chamber. The right to be heard would ordinarily be exercised by the submission of written comments on the proposal and not by way of oral hearing unless the question arose only at the hearing of the case by the chamber. As soon as the application commencing proceedings before the CFI has been lodged at the Registry of the CFI, the President of the CFI assigns the case to one of the chambers[35] in accordance with the system adopted by the CFI for allocating cases. The Rules of Procedure apply in the same way to cases heard by a chamber as to cases heard by the full Court and, in cases heard by the former, the powers of the President of the CFI are exercised by the President of the chamber in question.[36]

The only material difference between cases heard by a chamber and cases heard by the full Court is that an advocate general must be designated by the President of the CFI to assist the Court when it sits in plenary session.[37] In

29 RP-CFI 51.
30 Ibid. As the practice of the ECJ indicates, the decision may be made even after the hearing and when the chamber has begun deliberating on the case.
31 Cf Case T-47/92 *Lenz v Commission* [1992] ECR II-2523, paras 30–32.
32 RP-CFI 17.
33 RP-CFI 51 states expressly and consistently with RP-CFI 17 that the advocate general shall be heard; but, although it does not even use the qualifying words 'where one has been designated', those words are implied because it would not make sense to go to the lengths of designating an advocate general for such a minor matter.
34 The position may be different where the chamber has raised the question of its own motion. In that event, the right of the parties to be heard before a decision is made is satisfied by their right to be heard by the CFI in plenary session. The hearing of the parties before the chamber makes its proposal to the full Court seems superfluous. On the other hand, where the matter is raised by one of the parties, the chamber should give the other parties an opportunity to comment (even though they will have an opportunity to be heard by the full Court if a proposal is made) because it would be wrong for the chamber to set in motion the procedure laid down in RP-CFI 51 at the behest of one party without consulting the others.
35 RP-CFI 13(1).
36 RP-CFI 16.
37 RP-CFI 17.

cases heard by a chamber, there is in principle no advocate general but an advocate general may be designated to assist a chamber in a particular case if it is considered that the legal difficulty or the factual complexity of the case so requires.[38] Whereas the designation of an advocate general is mandatory in cases heard by the full Court, in cases heard by chambers the decision to designate an advocate general is made by the CFI sitting in plenary session, at the request of the chamber seised with the case.[39] There is no provision for the matter to be raised by the parties and no deadline by which the decision must be taken. It would seem that it is open to one of the parties to request the designation of an advocate general; but it is for the chamber to decide either of its own motion or in response to such a request whether or not to put the suggestion to the full Court.[40] In contrast to the situation that applies where a case is referred to the full Court by a chamber, it does not seem that the chamber makes a proposal to the full Court that an advocate general be designated. Instead, the chamber simply makes a request to the full Court that it decide whether or not an advocate general should be designated.[41] There is no provision for the hearing of the advocate general even though the CFI must be assisted by an advocate general when it sits in plenary session.[42] At first sight, the absence of the advocate general can be explained by the fact that a decision whether or not to designate one must be made ex hypothesi before the advocate general has been designated. However, it would seem that, as a matter of principle, the requirement that an advocate general be designated to assist the CFI when sitting in plenary session applies only to decisions of substance and not to matters that relate only to the CFI's organisation or administration.[43] It does not seem to be necessary to hear the parties before the decision is taken although, if the idea originates in a representation made by one of the parties, the other parties should be given an opportunity to comment on it. The decision on the question whether or not an advocate general should be designated must be made by the time that the judge-rapporteur in the case has presented his preliminary report because the first important function of the advocate general in a case is to assist the chamber in deciding what action to take on the recommendations made the judge-rapporteur.[44] However, it

---

38 RP-CFI 18.

39 RP-CFI 19. Hitherto, an advocate general has been designated only in cases where there was no or no unambiguous case law on the point at issue: see B Vesterdorf, (1992) CMLRev 897 at 906 and 912.

40 Cf. the *Lenz* case (above, note 31).

41 The construction of RP-CFI 19 given in the text is based on the disparity in wording between that provision and RP-CFI 51.

42 RP-CFI 17.

43 It has to be said that RP-CFI 2(2) states in general terms that a judge 'may' perform the function of advocate general in a particular case 'in the circumstances specified in' RP-CFI 17 to 19, thus incorporating by reference the requirement in RP-CFI 17 that the CFI in plenary session 'shall' be so assisted, as well as the reference in RP-CFI 18 that a chamber 'may' be so assisted. RP-CFI 17 to 19 also contain no limit on the role of the advocate general. Hence, while the use of the word 'may' in RP-CFI 2(2) cannot be said to negate or override the word 'shall' in RP-CFI 17 (because the former applies also to the situation in RP-CFI 18 and not just to the situation envisaged in RP-CFI 17), there is no express exception to the rule apparently stated in RP-CFI 17. However, it seems unduly burdensome for an advocate general to be designated solely for assisting the CFI in plenary session when it is making minor decisions, such as deciding whether or not an advocate general should be designated to assist a chamber or whether or not a case should be referred to the full Court or to another chamber. The sensible interpretation of RP-CFI 17 is that it does not apply to such minor matters. Clearly, if an advocate general has already been designated by the time when some such decision must be made, he must be consulted.

44 RP-CFI 52(2). The reference to the CFI made in that provision (as in all other provisions of the Rules of Procedure) is to be understood as referring to the chamber in question: RP-CFI 11(2).

cannot be excluded that the designation of the advocate general may be made at a later stage, albeit no later than the hearing, because the essential function of the advocate general is to deliver an opinion on the case after the hearing and before the closure of the oral procedure.[45] While it is for the CFI in plenary session to decide whether or not an advocate general should be designated to assist a chamber, it is for the President of the CFI to designate the judge who will act as advocate general if the CFI so decides; it is also the President of the CFI who designates the judge who will perform the functions of advocate general in cases heard by the full Court.[46] Any one of the judges is eligible to be designated advocate general. It is not possible for the President of the CFI or the President of the relevant chamber to be designated advocate general.[47] It is understood that, where an advocate general is required in a case heard before a chamber, the practice is to designate as advocate general a judge from another chamber; in such a situation, the advocate general could then be the President of that other chamber because the function of presiding judge would be performed by the President of the chamber hearing the case.

B The Registry

The Registry, whether of the ECJ or the CFI, is the direct responsibility of the Registrar (of the ECJ or, as the case may be, the CFI). In the case of the ECJ, the Registrar is assisted by one of the Deputy Registrars who acts in his place when he is absent or prevented from attending.[48] The Registries are open to the public Mondays to Fridays from 10 a m to 12 noon and from 3 p m to 6 p m, except on Fridays (when they close at 5 p m)[49] and on the official holidays listed in Annex I of the ECJ's Rules of Procedure.[50] In addition, they are also open to the public half an hour before the commencement of every public hearing held by the Court or a chamber.[51] Outside opening hours, procedural documents may be lodged with the Court's janitor who must record the date and time of lodgment.[52] The Registries are divided into sections dealing with cases according to their procedural language. The responsibilities of the Registries relate to three broad areas of activity: (i) the keeping of the register;[53] (ii) the acceptance, transmission, custody and service of documents;[54] and (iii) assisting the Court in the discharge of its functions such as by drawing up

---

45 RP-CFI 61. It would be an infringement of an essential procedural requirement for the advocate general to deliver an opinion without having been present at the hearing of the parties.

46 RP-CFI 19 and 17, respectively.

47 RP-CFI 2(2). Decision 88/591, art 2(3) (last sentence) provides that the judge called on to perform the task of advocate general may not take part in the judgment of the case. As a result, it would seem to be inappropriate, as a matter of principle (and quite without regard to RP-CFI 2(2)), for the judge who is the presiding judge in the case to perform the functions of advocate general.

48 GI 27. The CFI may also appoint one or more Assistant Registrars to assist its Registrar: RP-CFI 21. The wording of that provision suggests that, in the absence of Instructions to the Registrar adopted by the CFI under RP-CFI 23, any such appointment would be largely inoperative because an Assistant Registrar may assist the Registrar and take his place only in so far as such Instructions to the Registrar allow. But such an interpretation seems excessively literal.

49 The Court itself is normally closed on Friday afternoons during the judicial vacations; but the Registries remain open with a skeleton staff.

50 IR 1(1); cf RP-CFI 34(3).

51 IR 1(2).

52 IR 1(1).

53 RP-ECJ 16(1); RP-CFI 24(1).

54 RP-ECJ 17(1); RP-CFI 25(1).

minutes and orders and the cause list.[55] It is often difficult to draw rigid distinctions between those activities, in particular the first and second: for example, the decisions whether or not to accept a document and whether or not to enter it on the register are often coterminous. Registry procedure is the same mutatis mutandis for both Registries. In what follows reference is often made to the rules applicable to the ECJ, in particular the Instructions to the Registrar which, pursuant to RP-ECJ 16(4), are to prescribe the rules for keeping the register of the ECJ. The practice of the Registry of the CFI is to the same effect even though it is not based on formal rules adopted by the CFI (as provided for, inter alia, in RP-CFI 24(4)). References to 'the Registrar' must be understood as referring to him and to any other person properly authorised to take his place.

1   *The register*

Each Registrar is responsible for keeping up to date the register of cases brought before the Court to which he has been appointed.[56] The register for each Court is kept in the Registry of that Court and initialled by the President of that Court; in it are entered all pleadings and supporting documents.[57] RP-ECJ 16(5) and RP-CFI 24(5) provide that 'interested persons' may consult the register and obtain copies or extracts on payment of a fee. There is no definition of what is meant by an 'interested person'. The term seems to cover the parties to a case (where they wish to consult the register in respect of some procedural document relating to the case that is entered on the register) and any other person who is able to show some legitimate interest.[58]

All procedural documents in cases before the ECJ (or, as the case may be, the CFI), including those lodged by the parties and those served on the parties by the Registrar, are entered on the register,[59] chronologically in the order in which they are lodged at the Registry, and are numbered consecutively.[60] Annexes which have not been lodged at the same time as the procedural documents to which they relate are registered separately.[61] Procedural documents should be registered as soon as they are lodged at the Registry and documents drawn up by the Court are registered on the day of issue.[62] The entry in the register is made in the language of the case and contains the information necessary for identifying the document in question, including its date and nature, a reference to the case and the date of registration.[63] When the register is corrected, a note to that effect, initialled by the Registrar, is made in the margin of the register.[64] The page numbers of the register are numbered in advance and at regular intervals the President and the Registrar are to check the register and initial it in the margin against the last entry.[65]

When a document lodged by one of the parties is registered, a note to this effect is stamped on the original (and, if the party so requests, on any copy) showing the date of registry and the registration number. The note is signed by

---

55 RP-ECJ 17(2); RP-CFI 25(2).
56 IR 11.
57 RP-ECJ 16(1); RP-CFI 24(1).
58 It should be noted that the right to consult the register does not carry with it the right to see any procedural document mentioned in that part of the register that is consulted.
59 IR 14.
60 IR 15(1).
61 IR 14.
62 IR 15(2).
63 IR 15(3).
64 IR 15(4).
65 IR 13.

the Registrar.[66] Documents drawn up by the Court bear their registration number on the first page.[67] The registration number refers to the entry on the register and has no other significance. The date is important because, in reckoning time limits, the only relevant date is that of lodgment at the Registry.[68] Where a procedural document is lodged other than on the date of its entry on the register, a note to this effect should be made on the document.[69] As has been remarked, the crucial date is that of lodgment at the Court, not entry on the register; the date marked on the document will be the latter unless the document was lodged on a different date, in which case the date of lodgment will be indicated separately. Entry on the register occurs in principle on the same day the document is lodged; but in, for example, Case 37/71 Rev *Jamet v Commission*,[70] the document was lodged on 28 December 1972 and registered only on 2 January 1973, the delay being due to the Christmas–New Year Holiday. Entries in the register and the note of registration marked on documents are 'authentic',[71] indicating compliance with the proper formalities for entry on the register.

2   *Reception and custody of documents*

Documents are lodged at the Court by handing them over to an official in the Registry of the appropriate Court or, at times when the Registry is shut, handing them to the Court's janitor.[72] The party lodging a document is entitled to ask for a receipt evidencing lodgment.[73] Where an application or other procedural document addressed to the CFI is lodged by mistake with the Registrar of the ECJ, or vice versa, it is to be transmitted immediately by the Registrar receiving it to the Registrar of the Court to which it was addressed.[74] There is no express provision equating lodgment at the wrong Registry with lodgment at the correct Registry; and the requirement that, in such a situation, the document must be transmitted 'immediately' to the correct Registry implies that lodgment at the wrong Registry has no procedural consequences (in other words, it is not a valid lodgment). In principle, the time taken to transmit the document from the Registry where it was lodged by mistake to the Registry where it should have been lodged ought not to give rise to any difficulty over the application of any relevant time limit. On the other hand, the possibility that such a mistake might give rise to such a difficulty in a particular case cannot be excluded.[75] In principle, the mistake should be noticed as soon as the document is handed over at the wrong Registry: it should appear on the face of the document that it has been lodged at the

---

66 RP-ECJ 16(2) and IR 16; RP-CFI 24(2).
67 IR 16.
68 RP-ECJ 37(3); RP-CFI 43(3). See Cases 36-38, 40, 41/58 *Simet v High Authority* [1959] ECR 157.
69 IR 4(3).
70 [1973] ECR 295.
71 RP-ECJ 16(3); RP-CFI 24(3).
72 IR 1(1).
73 IR 4(1).
74 ECSC and EC Statutes, art 47 (first para); Euratom Statute, art 48 (first para).
75 The difficulty arises only where the document is lodged at the wrong Registry, not where it is lodged by delivery to the Court's janitor because he acts for both the ECJ and the CFI. At present, the ECJ and the CFI notionally occupy different buildings. Those buildings are interconnected but have separate main entrances. Access to either Court is possible by any of the entrances. The janitors are employed by the Court in its institutional sense; the ECJ and the CFI do not employ different janitors. Were the ECJ and the CFI to occupy different buildings with different janitors for each Court, the position would appear to be the same as where a document is lodged at the wrong Registry.

Registry of a Court other than the one to which it is addressed. At that point, any difficulty can be avoided by handing the document back to the person lodging it with instructions as to where the correct Registry may be found.[76] If the document was entered on the register before the mistake was noticed, the register would have to be corrected in order to record the transmission of the document to the correct Registry. That, of course, is no bar to its immediate transmission to the correct Registry. At that point, however, it is arguable that transmission could be effected only by the Registrar. Where the mistake is noticed only after the person lodging the document has left the Court building, or where the Registry has undertaken (or, as may be the case once the document has been entered on the register, is obliged) itself to transmit the document to the correct Registry, it would be unjust if any subsequent delay in the lodgment of the document at the correct Registry were to have adverse consequences for the party concerned. The sensible solution seems to be that, so far as any relevant time limit is concerned, the document is to be regarded as having been lodged at the correct Registry on the day and at the time that it was initially lodged (at the wrong Registry); and it is understood that that is the current practice of the CFI Registry.

Where an application or other procedural document is lodged at the Registry of the Court to which it is addressed but that Court does not have jurisdiction over the proceedings to which the application or other document relates, the position is more complex. It would seem that, in the case of a procedural document subsequent to the application commencing proceedings, the error should be evident because there will be no proceedings pending in the Registry at which the document is lodged to which the document can relate. In principle, the document should be treated in the same way as a document lodged at the Registry of the Court other than that to which it is addressed. If the error is not evident, that will be due to some failure on the part of the party lodging the document to identify properly the proceedings to which it relates or, exceptionally, to the existence of different proceedings before the ECJ and the CFI having the same name and case number. In any event, the responsibility for making the error lies entirely with the party lodging the document and he must bear the consequences. Where an application commencing proceedings is addressed to and lodged at the wrong Court, the proceedings are barred from continuing before that Court and must be referred to the correct Court.[77] When the problem is fairly obvious, the practice of the ECJ's Registry is to telephone the representative of the party lodging the application and ask him (or her) to rectify the position. If the position is not rectified by the party concerned, the matter can be determined only by the Court at which the application has been lodged, not the Registrar of that Court. A decision finding such an application to be inadmissible or barred from proceeding further and referring the case to the correct Court could easily be made after such an interval of time that it would lead inevitably to the inadmissibility of the proceedings before the correct Court, thus rendering the referral of the case to that Court futile, unless the time limit for commencing the proceedings before the correct Court were observed by lodgment of the application at the wrong Court. It therefore seems to be implicit that, in those circumstances, an action has not been brought out of time merely because the application commencing proceedings was addressed to and lodged at the wrong Court and the case was not referred to the correct

---

76 It does not seem that the lodging of a document is an irrevocable act.
77 ECSC and EC Statutes, art 47 (second para); Euratom Statute, art 48 (second para). The position is considered in greater detail below: see chapter 2, section III.

Court within time. That appears to strengthen the case for saying that an application or other procedural document that has been lodged at the Court other than the one to which it is addressed is to be regarded as having been lodged at the correct Court when it is handed over, by mistake, at the Registry of the wrong Court.

Documents originating proceedings[78] are given on registration a serial number followed by a mention of the year and either the name of the applicant or the subject matter of the application in order to identify the case.[79] Since a single numerical list of all cases lodged at both Courts could not work in the absence of some system for co-ordinating the allocation of case numbers by the two Registries involved, each Registry has its own numerical list; and, in order to avoid confusion as between cases before the ECJ and cases before the CFI, the practice is for the case number allocated to ECJ cases to be preceded by the letter 'C' and that for CFI cases by 'T'.[80] Thus, the first case entered on the register of the ECJ in 1993 is Case C-1/93; while the first case entered on the register of the CFI in 1993 is Case T-1/93. Applications for interim relief, which are made separately from the document commencing the action, bear the same number as the action, followed by the letter 'R' (for example, Case C-1/93R or, as the case may be, Case T-1/93R).[81] In the same way, where subsequent proceedings are brought which must bear the same case number as the original proceedings (as happens, for example, in proceedings for the review of a judgment), one or more letters will be added after the case number in order to identify separately those subsequent proceedings; and, where there are more than one such subsequent proceedings, a figure in Roman or Arabic numerals may be added.[82] Where an appeal is brought before the ECJ from a judgment of the CFI, the proceedings before the ECJ do not use the case number given to the proceedings at first instance; a new case number is used followed by the letter 'P'.[83] If a case has been given an incorrect case number, it must be removed from the register and reentered in the register under the correct number.[84]

78 Sc as the case may be, the application in a direct action, the order for reference made by the national court in the case of references for a preliminary ruling or the application bringing an appeal from a judgment of the CFI.

79 IR 12. Strictly speaking, the case number identifies the case while the names of the parties provide a convenient method of referring to it. A brief description of what the case is about is given for the Court's internal use. In some cases, generally for reasons of confidentiality, a party may be referred to by an initial, eg Case 152/77 *B v Commission* [1979] ECR 2819. The decision to that effect may be made by the Court of its own motion or upon request. In Case 184/80 *Van Zaanan v Court of Auditors* [1981] ECR 1951, on the other hand, an unrepresented third party asked that he not be named in the judgment or the advocate general's opinion. This request was granted. In such cases a reasoned request should, it seems, be addressed to the Registrar of the Court with jurisdiction over the case. Normally the decision would be made by the Court and would apply to all stages of the proceedings. If the request is made after the advocate general has delivered his opinion, the advocate general's express consent is required because his opinion would have to be amended.

80 'T' stands for '*Tribunal*', the French term used in the title of the CFI.

81 IR 12.

82 Eg Case C-147/86 T01, Case C-147/86 T02 and Case C-147/86 T03 *POIFXG, PALSO and PSIITENSM v Greece and Commission* [1989] ECR 4103, 4111 and 4119 (third party proceedings) and Case 285/81 Rev I and II *Geist v Commission* [1984] ECR 1789 (revision).

83 Thus Case C-348/90P *European Parliament v Virgili-Schettini* [1991] ECR I-5211 was the full title of the appeal from Case T-139/89 *Virgili-Schettini v European Parliament* [1990] ECR II-535. The letter 'P' stands for '*pourvoi*', the French term for the application commencing appeal proceedings.

84 Thus, Case 235/82 Rev *Ferriere San Carlo SpA v Commission* [1986] ECR 1799 (proceedings for revision of a judgment) was, contrary to IR 12, originally registered under its own case number instead of the number of the case to which it related. By order dated 4 December 1985 it was removed from the register under the wrong number and reregistered under the correct one.

After registration, documents lodged at the Court are filed with the other documents relating to the same case. For this purpose they are numbered consecutively as they are lodged at the Registry and placed in the case file. Thus, throughout the course of the action, documents will be lodged at the Registry and given a date and registration number indicating entry on the Register; they will then be filed in accordance with the case number and given yet another number representing their position in the case file,[85] which is determined by the date of lodgment. The Registrar is responsible for maintaining the files of pending cases and for keeping them up to date.[86] The completed case file contains the originals of all the documents relating to the case that have been entered on the register;[87] and communications relating to the case between the parties and the Registry or between the Registry and the Court which are not entered on the register are kept in a separate file of correspondence relating to the case.[88]

The ECJ's internal rules also provide that the files of pending cases may be consulted in the Registry by the parties or their representatives (but not by third parties); files of completed cases are stored in the Registry and third parties have no access to them.[89] If they contain documents which the Court regards as confidential, such documents are placed in a sealed envelope and are accessible only at the written request of the party concerned and with the formal assent of the Registrar.[90] Since the internal rules were drafted, the Court has had more experience of dealing with confidential pleadings and documents. The current practice is that, where confidential treatment is accorded to a pleading or document, two versions are lodged at the Court, one confidential and the other non-confidential. The parties to a case may obtain copies of pleadings and authenticated copies of judgments and orders on payment of the appropriate charge.[91] In the case of references for a preliminary ruling, the Court's Statutes[92] provide that the decision of the national court making the reference shall be notified to the Court. Some national courts also submit their own file of the case.[93] When this happens the file may be consulted at the Registry by the parties but only the documents in it which are relevant to the substance of the dispute are translated and distributed to the members of the Court.[94] In principle, if the order for reference is properly drafted, there should be no need to refer to the national court's file of the case, if available.

The original of every pleading, accompanied by all annexes referred to

---

85 For example, the registration number may be 76102, the case number (for a case before the ECJ) C-1/93. The application in this case (assuming it to be a direct action) will, apart from the registration number, bear the number C-1/93-1, indicating that it is the first document in the case file. The next document in the case file, C-1/93-2, which will probably be the Registrar's letter to the applicant acknowledging receipt of the application, may have as its registration number 76214 because, in the meantime, more documents in other cases have been entered on the register. The case file number, like the registration number, is really for the Court's internal use. The only number of general importance is the case number (in this example, C-1/93).

86 IR 2.

87 Save that, where the Court has occasion to send a letter to a party, the signed original of the letter is sent and an initialled copy is placed in the case file.

88 The ECJ's Registry also keeps a copy of the case file which contains certified copies of all the original documents. The CFI Registry does not keep a duplicate file.

89 GI 30.

90 GI 30 and 52(3).

91 RP-ECJ 16(5); RP-CFI 24(5).

92 EC Statute, art 20; Euratom Statute, art 21.

93 If it is not submitted the Registry writes to the national court asking for it to send on the file of the case.

94 GI 36.

therein must be lodged at the Court with jurisdiction over the case, together with five copies for that Court and one for every other party to the proceedings, all copies being certified by the party lodging them.[95] The Community institutions must also provide translations, into the other official languages of the Community, of all their pleadings in the case together with the correct number of certified copies.[96] When a statement is sent to the Court in the name of a member state, the Registry must satisfy itself that the document is authentic; member states often apply to intervene in a case or make other communications by telex or facsimile and the Registry may require the authenticity of the telex or facsimile message to be confirmed or ask for the name and capacity of the signatory.[97] The fact that a communication is made by telex or facsimile or by electronic mail rather than by letter does not affect its validity, although there may be some question whether or not the formal requirements for submitting a procedural document in time have been satisfied. It is understood that communications other than procedural documents are registered even if lodged in the form of a facsimile or similar message; in references for a preliminary ruling, written observations submitted within the time limit for doing so by facsimile (and not in the form of an original plus the correct number of copies) are not registered. When the original is received, the original is registered with a note to the effect that a copy sent by facsimile was received in time. If the original is received a long time after the expiry of the time limit, the practice is to return the document and not enter it on the register despite the fact that a copy was received by facsimile within time. So far as the ECJ is concerned, the status of facsimile communications containing applications purporting to commence proceedings appears to be undecided; the practice of the CFI Registry is to regard such communications as insufficient compliance with the requirements of RP-CFI 43 (because they do not bear the original signature of the party's agent or lawyer) so that, if an original is not lodged within the relevant time limit, the proceedings have been commenced out of time and are inadmissible. On the other hand, if the relevant time limit is one that can be extended, the CFI Registry regards a facsimile communication as an implied application for an extension of time and an extension for a reasonable period is implicitly granted as long as the original arrives within that period.[98] Applications for an extension of time and communications of minor importance can be made by facsimile. Any communication made by facsimile should be sent to the facsimile machine of the relevant Registry and not to any other facsimile machine at the Court.

Defective pleadings are dealt with in a number of ways. The Registrar must decline to accept or else return without delay by registered post any pleading or other document not provided for in the Rules of Procedure or not worded in the language of the case unless otherwise expressly authorised by the President or the Court.[99] Thus, a pleading so defective as to be unrecognisable as a procedural document must ordinarily be rejected. In principle the same applies where a document is lodged after the close of the written procedure in a case (otherwise than pursuant to a request or order of the Court that it be lodged) because the Rules of Procedure envisage that in the ordinary course no further document will be lodged after that stage in the proceedings. Where the document is obviously one that should not be received, the Registrar will

95 RP-ECJ 37(1); RP-CFI 43(1).
96 RP-ECJ 37(2); RP-CFI 43(2).
97 GI 37(1).
98 See further chapter 9, p 303.
99 IR 4(2).

return it to the party concerned without consulting the President and without sending copies to the judge-rapporteur and advocate general. However, since it is possible for a new plea in law to be introduced even after the close of the written procedure where it is based on matters of fact or of law which have come to light in the course of the proceedings,[1] a document raising such a plea cannot be rejected automatically: the admissibility of the plea is to be decided in the final judgment and not before. When such a document is lodged after the close of the written procedure, the practice of the ECJ's Registry is to refer the question of its acceptance to the President (copies being sent to the judge-rapporteur and, where applicable, the advocate general).[2] If the document is accepted the other parties are given an opportunity to submit their observations. Otherwise the document is returned to the party lodging it.

If an application or other pleading does not give an address for service and the name of a person authorised and willing to accept service in Luxembourg, where it is required to do so, the consequence is that, for as long as the defect remains, service on the party concerned is effected by registered letter addressed to that party's agent or lawyer and service is deemed to be duly effected by lodging the registered letter at the post office of the place where the Court has its seat.[3] Thus, such a defect in a pleading does not require rectification (although the usual practice is for the party to be requested to rectify it); but it will be in a party's interest to remedy the defect because it is more convenient to have an address for service in Luxembourg. If an application[4] does not comply with the requirements of RP-ECJ 38(3)–(6) or, as the case may be, RP-CFI 44(3)–(5), where it is required to do so, the Registrar prescribes a reasonable period within which the application must comply with those requirements[5] and so informs the applicant by registered letter, enclosing a form for acknowledgment of receipt; if the applicant does not comply with the Registrar's directions, the latter refers the matter to the President of the Court[6] and the Court decides whether or not the failure to comply renders the application formally inadmissible (in the case of the ECJ, after hearing the advocate general).[7] No similar provision appears to deal, expressly at least, with subsequent pleadings, although IR 5(1), which is concerned with the ECJ Registrar's part in RP-ECJ 38(7), refers to 'the person . . . concerned' while RP-ECJ 38(7) speaks of 'the applicant'.[8] It is nonetheless considered that any pleading that must comply with RP-ECJ 38(3)–(6) or RP-CFI 44(3)–(5) but fails to do so is to be treated in the way indicated by RP-ECJ 38(7) or, as the case may be, RP-CFI 44(6). RP-ECJ 38(7) does not

1 RP-ECJ 42(2); RP-CFI 48(2).
2 In proceedings brought in the ECJ against a member state in respect of an alleged failure to perform an obligation imposed by the Treaties, documents evidencing compliance by that member state with its obligations are accepted, if lodged after the end of the written procedure, and served on the other party for its written observations (usually the applicant – the Commission – is asked to inform the Court within a certain period of time whether or not it intends to go on with the case).
3 RP-ECJ 38(2); RP-CFI 44(2).
4 That is, an application commencing proceedings or a particular procedure envisaged in the Rules of Procedure (such as an application to intervene, an application commencing third party proceedings or an application for revision of a judgment).
5 RP-ECJ 38(7); RP-CFI 44(6).
6 IR 5(1).
7 RP-ECJ 38(7); RP-CFI 44(6). The Registrar is not competent to rule on the inadmissibility of a pleading: see Case 131/83 *Vaupel v European Court of Justice* (15 March 1984, unreported), para 10.
8 RP-ECJ 40(1) and RP-CFI 46(1) provide that a defence must also comply inter alia with RP-ECJ 38(3)–(6) (or, as the case may be, RP-CFI 44(3)–(5)) but do not expressly incorporate RP-ECJ 38(7) and RP-CFI 44(7).

apply to proceedings commenced otherwise than by application, such as references for a preliminary ruling.

The ECJ's internal rules go into somewhat greater detail as far as defective pleadings are concerned but do not necessarily reflect accurately current practice. RP-ECJ 37(1) provides (as does RP-CFI 43(1)) that every pleading must be signed by the party's agent or lawyer. A breach of this rule is not covered by RP-ECJ 38(7) and IR 5(1) (or by RP-CFI 44(6)). The internal rules provide, however, that an application shall be registered but returned to the applicant for correction if the applicant is not represented by a lawyer (or, implicitly, an agent) or if it has been lodged with particulars of the lawyer but not signed by him.[9] It is understood that the current practice of the Registries is not to enter a pleading with such a defect on the register but to return it to the party concerned; it would be entered on the register and then returned to the party lodging it for correction only if it appeared on the face of the pleading that the party was represented by a lawyer but (through an oversight) had not been signed by him. If, by chance, it were entered on the register, that does not constitute acceptance of the admissibility of the application (or other pleading).[10] Where the application fails to name the defendant expressly (a breach of RP-ECJ 38(1) or RP-CFI 44(1) which is also not covered by RP-ECJ 38(7) or RP-CFI 44(6)) but states that it is directed against a measure of a particular Community institution, the application is registered and the applicant is then to be asked to confirm that it is made against the institution in question. The application is notified to the defendant only after the applicant's reply has been received.[11] In the case of defects referred to in RP-ECJ 38(7)[12] or RP-CFI 44(6), the application is no longer registered and notified to the defendant with a copy of the Registrar's letter to the applicant but is instead registered and retained at the Registry until the defect is remedied or the Court has declared that it is admissible notwithstanding the failure to observe the formal requirements referred to in RP-ECJ 38(7) or, as the case may be, RP-CFI 44(6).[13] When either of those events occurs, the pleading is served on the other party.[14] Although the application and defence must include a certificate that the lawyer acting for the party concerned is entitled to practise before a court of a member state,[15] the practice of the ECJ and the CFI in relation to that requirement varies. The ECJ's internal rules provide that such a certificate will not again be requested until two years after the previous one;[16] but it is understood that the current practice is to request the production of the certificate in each case. The professional identity card issued under the aegis of the CCBE is acceptable if produced within three years of its date of issue; otherwise, the card must be authenticated. The CFI Registry requires the certificate to be provided only once, the lawyer thereafter being assumed to be entitled to practise whenever he brings proceedings before the CFI. A failure to produce the certificate when requested to do so by the Court is, nonetheless,

---

9 GI 31 and 32.
10 See the *Vaupel* case, above (note 7), and also Cases 220 and 221/78 *ALA SpA and ALFER SpA v Commission* [1979] ECR 1693 and Case 73/83 *Stavridis v European Parliament* [1983] ECR 3803.
11 GI 33.
12 GI 34 must now be read subject to the amendments made to RP-ECJ 38.
13 At that stage in the proceedings, the Court is concerned only with the formal admissibility of the pleading and not with its substantial admissibility. See, for example, the procedure followed in Case T-101/92 *Stagakis v European Parliament* [1993] ECR II-63.
14 RP-ECJ 39; RP-CFI 45.
15 RP-ECJ 38(3) and 40(1); RP-CFI 44(3) and 46(1).
16 GI 35.

a formal defect which is sufficient to lead to the rejection of the application (or, as the case may be, the defence) as being inadmissible.[17]

3 Transmission and service of documents

Where the Rules of Procedure require that a document be served on a person, the task of ensuring service falls on the Registrar of the appropriate Court, not on the parties; the Registrar ensures that service is effected at the address for service of the person concerned in one of two ways: by the dispatch of a copy of the document by registered post with a form for acknowledgment of receipt; or by personal delivery of the copy against a receipt.[18] Where the first method of service is used, the document is accompanied by a note signed by the Registrar giving the number of the case and the registration number of the document, together with a brief indication of its nature.[19] In cases where a party is required to provide an address for service in Luxembourg, and has done so, service is usually effected by the second method (the Court uses its own staff for that purpose). The address for service in Luxembourg is therefore in the vicinity of the Court and preferably within the Commune de Luxembourg. Where a party is required by the Rules of Procedure to state an address for service in Luxembourg and fails to do so, service is effected by registered letter addressed to the party's agent or lawyer and is deemed to be duly effected by lodging the letter at the post office in Luxembourg.[20] The Registrar prepares and certifies the copies of the documents to be served unless the parties are obliged by the Rules of Procedure to provide certified copies for the purposes of service and have in fact provided them.[21] Where an application commencing proceedings is manifestly inadmissible, for whatever reason, it may be dismissed immediately by Court order and, in such an event, the application will be served on the other party together with a copy of the order dismissing it as inadmissible.[22]

In the case of references for a preliminary ruling, the national court's order is served by the ECJ's Registrar on the parties to the case, the member states and the Commission and the Council, if the validity or interpretation of one of its acts is in dispute.[23] It seems that, under the ECJ's internal rules, all references for a preliminary ruling are notified to the Council 'for information'.[24] When the national court's order is sent to the member states, it is accompanied by a translation made into the official language of the state in question by the Court's translation service.[25] Since, in these proceedings, the parties are not obliged to have an address for service in Luxembourg, service is made at the address for service used in the proceedings before the national court or, in its absence, at the address of the party's lawyer (or, if the party has

---

17 The *Stagakis* case (above, note 13), para 8. Where the party is represented by an agent, a failure to produce the certificate of a lawyer assisting the agent is not fatal because in that situation the agent, not the lawyer, is the party's representative: see Case T-47/92 *Lenz v Commission* [1992] ECR II-2523, para 35.

18 RP-ECJ 79; RP-CFI 100.

19 IR 3(2). For the Court's records a copy of this note is appended to the original document.

20 RP-ECJ 38(2); RP-CFI 44(2). Thus, where any time limit commences upon service of the document in question, time starts to run on the posting of the document, not upon its receipt by the person concerned.

21 RP-ECJ 79; RP-CFI 100.

22 See, for example, Case C-371/89 *Emrich v Commission* [1990] ECR I-1555, Case C-247/90 *Emrich v Commission* [1990] ECR I-3913 and Case T-78/91 *Moat and Association of Independent Officials for the Defence of the European Civil Service v Commission* [1991] ECR II-1387.

23 EC Statute, art 20; Euratom Statute, art 21; see also RP-ECJ 103(3).

24 GI 39.

25 RP-ECJ 104(1).

no lawyer, at the party's own address).[26] As far as the member states are concerned, service is made on the Minister for Foreign Affairs or the Embassy with a copy being sent to the Permanent Representative at Brussels.[27] Any written observations submitted in a reference for a preliminary ruling are served by the Registrar on all the parties (including the member states, the Council and the Commission), even if they have not themselves lodged written observations.[28] Normally the written observations will be expressed in the language of the case but a member state may submit observations in its own official language.[29] When this happens, the Registrar has the observations translated into the language of the case and served on the other parties, together with the original.[30] Translation into a further language may be required for the Court's own use and such a translation is available to the parties on request, free of charge.[31]

In direct actions, of course, the parties must give an address for service in the place where the Court has its seat, Luxembourg,[32] and the Registrar serves any documents on the parties at that address. Copies of the application and defence (less any annexes) are sent as a matter of course to the Council and the Commission so that they may decide whether the inapplicability of one of their acts is being pleaded pursuant to arts 36 of the ECSC Treaty, 184 of the EC Treaty or 156 of the Euratom Treaty.[33] Final decisions of the CFI, decisions of the CFI disposing of the substantive issues in part only and decisions of the CFI disposing of a procedural issue concerning a plea of lack of competence or inadmissibility are notified by the Registrar of the CFI not only to all the parties to the proceedings but also to all the member states and Community institutions even if they did not intervene in the case[34] so that they may consider whether or not to exercise their right of appeal. Apart from this, all persons including the member states and the Community institutions must rely on the notice of the case printed in the Official Journal[35] to determine whether they may take advantage of the procedure for intervening in a case. If they do decide to intervene, member states are entitled to use their official language, instead of the language of the case, as when taking part in a reference for a preliminary ruling; the Registrar has the application to intervene and subsequent pleadings translated into the language of the case.[36]

Apart from pleadings, the Registry also sees to the service of documents emanating from the Court itself, such as the report for the hearing, the advocate general's opinion and the judgment, etc. In the case of references for a preliminary ruling, the judgment is sent to the court making the reference

26 GI 37(4).
27 Cf GI 37(2).
28 GI 37(2).
29 RP-ECJ 29(3).
30 RP-ECJ 29(3), GI 37(2) and (3).
31 GI 37(3).
32 RP-ECJ 38(2); RP-CFI 44(2); ie the Grand Duchy. For the reasons given above, it is preferable for the address for service to be within the Commune of Luxembourg. The reason for saying that the Court's seat is to be regarded as within the Grand Duchy rather than the city (properly speaking, the Commune) of Luxembourg is that, under the Statutes, the members of the Court must reside at the place where the Court has its seat; yet many of them have resided outside the city but within the Grand Duchy. Further, on a number of occasions the Court has accepted an address for service outside the limits of the city of Luxembourg.
33 RP-ECJ 16(7); RP-CFI 24(7).
34 ECSC and EC Statute, art 48; Euratom Statute, art 49.
35 As required by RP-ECJ 16(6) and RP-CFI 24(6).
36 RP-ECJ 29(3); RP-CFI 35(3).

and certified copies to all the parties.[37] The Instructions to the Registrar state that the parties 'shall be served with the pleadings and other documents relating to the proceedings' but, where a document is very bulky and only one copy is lodged with the Registry, the Registrar, after consulting the judge-rapporteur, will inform the parties by registered letter that they may inspect it at the Registry.[38] The Registrar is, in general, responsible for the dispatch of the Court's official correspondence.[39]

4 Assistance given to the Court

The Registry sees to the distribution of procedural documents to the members of the Court. These include the pleadings, orders and decisions of the Court, letters served on the parties, transcripts, and so on.[40] If an annex to a document 'appears too bulky', the President of the Court or the chamber concerned with the case may, after consulting the judge-rapporteur, dispense with its copying and distribution, the members of the Court being simply informed that it has been lodged.[41] Every document registered is to be read by the Registry official in charge of the case as soon as it has been received in order to determine whether it needs translating[42] and whether it raises an interlocutory application such as a new claim, application for interim relief and so forth. In the latter event, a memorandum is sent to the President, judge-rapporteur and (where applicable) advocate general drawing their attention to the document.[43] The President is informed of a case as soon as the document commencing the proceedings has arrived at the Registry, by a memorandum summarising its nature and contents.[44] All documents, whether original or in translation, are distributed to the members of the Court.[45] In addition, when asked to do so by the judge-rapporteur, the Registry compiles and distributes a file of the legislation cited by the parties.[46] Reports for the hearing, judgments, interim orders and the opinions of the advocates general are supplied free of charge to third parties in a limited number and so long as stocks last.[47]

The Statutes of the Court provide that a cause list 'shall be established' by the President.[48] The Instructions to the Registrar provide that the Registrar shall draw up a cause list in the language of the cases featuring in it before every public hearing of the Court or chamber.[49] The cause list is displayed at the entrance to the courtroom in which the proceedings take place and contains the date, hour and place of the hearing, the references to the cases to be heard, the names of the parties and the names and descriptions of their agents, advisers or lawyers.[50] The Luxembourg Minister for Foreign Affairs is

---

37 Here, it is apprehended, all those who have submitted observations, whether written or oral, and the parties to the action before the national court who have not.
38 IR 3(3).
39 GI 26.
40 GI 40.
41 GI 41.
42 PI 4. All correspondence is, of course, read. So far as pleadings are concerned, in practice, in direct actions, the application commencing proceedings is read as a matter of course; other pleadings are not usually read. In references for a preliminary ruling, the order for reference, but not the written observations, is read.
43 PI 12.
44 PI 1.
45 PI 4 and 5.
46 PI 4.
47 GI 45.
48 ECSC Statute, art 28; EC Statute, art 31; Euratom Statute, art 32.
49 IP 7(1).
50 Ibid.

informed in advance of the contents of the cause list in order to ensure that the parties' representatives' rights of immunity from search and seizure etc under RP-ECJ 32 are observed.[51] The drawing up of the cause list is, of course, dependent on the fixing of the times for the hearings. This is the responsibility of the President of the Court or of the appropriate chamber.[52] It should be noted that the cause list covers not merely the oral procedure in a case (including the delivery of the advocate general's opinion) but also the handing down of the Court's judgment.

Minutes of each hearing are drawn up by the Registrar and signed by him and the President.[53] They may be inspected and copied by the parties.[54] Apart from hearings, minutes are also drawn up recording the hearing of witnesses[55] and the holding of preparatory enquiries in general.[56] Again, the parties may inspect them and take copies.[57] The minutes ordinarily record the fact that a hearing has taken place and give details of the persons involved; they are not transcripts of the hearings but, where a party makes an important statement in the course of a hearing (such as a concession, the withdrawal of a claim or an argument or an important statement of fact), that statement may well be recorded in the minutes.[58] The minutes drawn up when a witness is examined are different: they reproduce the evidence given by the witness and are checked and signed by the witness before being signed by the President or the judge-rapporteur responsible for conducting the examination and by the Registrar.[59] The minutes constitute an official record[60] and thus evidence the testimony given by the witness or, as the case may be, the events recorded in them, such as any important statement made by a party that is recorded in them.

The Registrar also draws up minutes of judgments, orders and other decisions, submitting them to the judges responsible for their signature.[61] Procedural decisions concerning a case made by the Court in administrative meetings (such as decisions concerning the allocation of the case to a chamber, the ordering of a preparatory enquiry, requests for information or documents, or the hearing) are drawn up by the Registry on the instructions of the Registrar but may take the form either of a decision or of an order, depending upon the circumstances. Ordinarily, a decision takes the form of an order where the Rules of Procedure require it to adopt that form or where the established practice of the Court is that it takes that form. Otherwise, a procedural decision will take the form of a decision. It is difficult to discern any principle behind the use of those different forms but, broadly speaking, a decision usually takes the form of a decision when it relates only to the Court's internal arrangements.[62] When in such a form it is signed by the Registrar,

---

51 IR 10. It is understood that, in practice, this rule is now obsolete. It is not known when it was last applied.
52 RP-ECJ 25(1)–(2); RP-CFI 31(1), 11(2) and 16.
53 ECSC Statute, art 27; EC Statute, art 30; Euratom Statute, art 31; RP-ECJ 62(1) and IR 7(2); RP-CFI 63(1).
54 RP-ECJ 62(2); RP-CFI 63(2).
55 RP-ECJ 47(6); RP-CFI 68(6).
56 RP-ECJ 53(2); RP-CFI 76(2).
57 RP-ECJ 53(2); RP-CFI 76(2).
58 That is certainly the practice of the CFI.
59 RP-ECJ 47(6); RP-CFI 68(6).
60 Ibid. and: RP-ECJ 53(1); RP-CFI 76(1); RP-ECJ 62(1); RP-CFI 63(1).
61 IR 3(1). For the distinction between judgments, orders and decisions, see further chapter 16, pp 493 et seq.
62 Such as decisions assigning a case to a chamber or, as the case may be, the full Court or joining a preliminary objection or other procedural issue with the substance of the case. Decisions allowing the use of another procedural language also take the form of a decision although they do, of course, affect the parties as well as the Court's internal arrangements.

entered on the register, placed in the case file and a copy is served on the parties, if need be. Otherwise the decision takes the form of an order and, after being drawn up by the Registry,[63] is approved by the President, chamber or judge-rapporteur as the case may be (and, where applicable, the advocate general), entered on the register, placed in the case file and a copy is sent to each of the parties.

Decisions fixing or extending the time limit for a step in the procedure are made by the President unless the time limit is defined in the Rules of Procedure, the Statutes or the Treaties.[64] The President of the Court (and, in the case of the ECJ, a chamber) may delegate to the Registrar power of signature for the purpose of fixing or extending those time limits which it falls to the President to prescribe or extend under the Rules of Procedure.[65] The Registrar of the ECJ has been delegated the power to fix procedural time limits in the name of the President (within certain maximum periods laid down) in respect of the lodgment of: the defence, reply, rejoinder or statement in intervention; written observations on a procedural issue raised by separate document; written observations on applications to intervene, change the language of procedure, join cases or discontinue a case, rectify, revise or interpret a judgment; written observations on applications commencing third party proceedings and applications for legal aid, stay of proceedings and for a decision on costs; statements of position from the parties regarding orders and decisions dispensing with the oral part of the procedure (where the Rules of Procedure so permit), ordering repeating or expanding a measure of enquiry, deferring the hearing of a case or staying proceedings; and replies to questions put by the Court. The ECJ's Registrar has also been delegated the power of extending (in the name of the President) those time limits. In the case of the main written pleadings, the Registrar's power to extend the time limit applies only to the first request for an extension and only if that request is for no more than one month. Otherwise the request for extension of time must be dealt with by the President (of the Court or of the relevant chamber). In the case of the CFI, it is understood that the Registrar of the CFI has been delegated authority to fix the date for the lodgment of pleadings and written observations and grant a first application for an extension of time for lodging the same if the extension requested is no more than one month; when the President is absent during Court vacations, the Registrar has more general authority (including the power to refuse an application for an extension of time) where necessary in order to ensure that the proceedings take their proper course.[66]

The Registrar must attend sittings of the Court and the chambers with two exceptions:[67] (i) meetings where the Court hears the observations of a judge who, it is alleged, 'no longer fulfils the requisite conditions or no longer meets the obligations arising from his office';[68] (ii) deliberations of the Court on questions other than those concerning its own administration.[69] The Registrar draws up the agenda of the administrative meetings of the Court and the

---

63 If the order must set out the reasons on which it is based, the judge-rapporteur undertakes that task and the order is completed by the Registry.

64 See, for example: RP-ECJ 40(2), 41(2), 42(2), 66(2) and 82; RP-CFI 46(3), 47(2), 48(2), 84(2) and 103.

65 RP-ECJ 82; RP-CFI 103(2).

66 It is understood that, when exercising that more general authority, the Registrar of the CFI would not grant extensions of time for periods longer than necessary in order to cover the period of the President's absence.

67 RP-ECJ 19; RP-CFI 27. The latter does not refer to sittings of the chambers of the CFI. Such a reference is implied: see RP-CFI 11(2).

68 RP-ECJ 4; RP-CFI 5.

69 RP-ECJ 27; RP-CFI 33.

chambers and these are submitted for the approval of the President of the Court or chamber, as the case may be.[70] He also draws up the minutes of the administrative meetings and these are approved by the Court or the President of the chamber concerned and signed by the President of the Court or chamber, as the case may be, and the Registrar himself.[71] The Registrar ensures that the decisions of the Court are executed.[72]

C   Other departments

The CFI has no departments other than its Registry. The organisation of the departments of the ECJ is determined and may be modified by the ECJ acting on a proposal from its Registrar.[73] In addition to the Registry, the ECJ comprises four services: the Library Research and Documentation Directorate, the Information Office, the Translation Directorate and the Administration. Under the Administration come a number of departments: Internal Services, Personnel, Finance and Budget, and Data Processing, none of which is of interest here. The Interpretation Division is attached to the Registry. For the sake of completeness, mention should also be made of the publications for which the Court is responsible.

1   The Library Research and Documentation Directorate

This service comprises three separate divisions. The main purpose of the library is to aid the members of the Court and its officials in their work.[74] As a result, its contents are restricted to those specialised areas relevant to the work of the Court: Community law, the laws of the member states, comparative law and international law (including the law of international institutions). The library is reserved for use by members of the Court, its officials, and authorities and officials of other Community institutions but the lawyers and agents of the parties to a case before the Court are also free to make use of it and other persons may make use of it with the permission of the library's director.[75] The library is open during the Court's working hours.[76] One of its functions is to produce for distribution and sale two bibliographies, one entitled *Legal Publications on the Subject of European Integration* and another entitled *Bibliography of European Case-law*.[77] The former consists of bibliographical references to European law other than case law, the latter to Community case law and commentaries on it.

The principal function of the Research and Documentation Division is to provide notes during the course of proceedings, as requested by a member of the Court (generally the judge-rapporteur or advocate general).[78] These notes are usually comparative studies of national law or studies of Community law relating to a particular aspect of a case before the Court and are distributed to the members of the Court and their legal secretaries. For example, in Case 155/79 *AM & S Europe Ltd v Commission*[79] the Division produced two lengthy and detailed studies of the laws of the member states concerning the confidentiality of legal communications. It also produces studies unconnected with

70 GI 29(1).
71 GI 29(4) and (5).
72 GI 29(6).
73 RP-ECJ 21.
74 GI 57.
75 GI 61.
76 Ibid.
77 GI 68.
78 GI 72 and 73.
79 [1982] ECR 1575.

a particular case but which have some bearing on the work of the Court. Among its other functions are the preparation of the headnotes to the reported cases[80] and the annual index of cases before the Court.[81] It is assisted by the Legal Data Processing Department, which is responsible for the Court's computerised information service covering for the most part decisions of the Court and Community legislation.

2 The Information Office

The Information Office falls administratively within the responsibilities of the Registrar but the President of the Court may issue directives to it.[82] It is responsible for disseminating information about the Court and making its activities widely known. It organises visits to the Court and provides information in the form of communications, lectures and conferences and the publication of documents such as the annual summary of the Court's activities.[83]

3 The Translation Directorate

The Translation Directorate is divided into sections representing all the official Community languages. There is no Irish section because, while Irish is a language that may be used in proceedings before the Court,[84] it is still not an official Community language and there is no need to translate documents into it as a matter of course. So far there has been no case in which the language of procedure was Irish. Should this arise, the Court would deal with the problem on an ad hoc basis.

The Directorate translates procedural documents, that is to say, the pleadings in a case, their annexes, the Court's communications to the parties, the report for the hearing, opinions and judgments. All such documents are translated into the language of the case (where, of course, this is necessary) and, as a matter of practice, into French, which is the common language of the Court. It is not usual for a document to be translated into any other language in the absence of a specific request.[85] Requests for translations are transmitted to the Head of the Directorate through the Registrar.[86] First priority is given to the translation of reports for the hearing, opinions and judgments, which must be ready by fixed dates. Subject to these, references for a preliminary ruling have absolute priority over other translations and must be translated and copied into all the Community languages within eight days.[87] Statements and observations relating to preliminary rulings must be translated into the language of the case and any other languages requested within 15 days of being lodged at the Registry.[88] The parties may also request translations, subject to payment of a charge, the request being made to the Registrar.[89]

4 The Interpretation Division

This Division is composed partly of officials of the Court and partly of freelance interpreters, with additional help, where needed, from staff seconded

---

80 GI 71.
81 GI 74.
82 GI 77.
83 GI 78.
84 See RP-ECJ 29(1); RP-CFI 35(1).
85 See GI 80.
86 GI 79.
87 Ibid.
88 Ibid.
89 RP-ECJ 72(b); RP-CFI 90(b).

to the Court from other Community institutions. Formerly the Court made use of interpreters seconded from the European Parliament but, as the number of hearings grew and the demands of the Parliament increased, this arrangement became less and less convenient; so, in 1980, budgetary approval was given for the creation of the Court's own interpretation service.

Interpretation into the language of the case must be ensured during hearings and shall be ensured into other Community languages at the request of a member of the Court 'having regard to their actual needs'.[90] If there are special circumstances (such as those provided for in RP-ECJ 29 and RP-CFI 35), interpretation into a language other than that of the case may be provided;[91] one example is the presence of important persons or groups at a hearing.[92] The Interpretation Division is also employed at meetings or conferences organised by the Court.[93] After the hearing in a case a transcript of the proceedings is usually distributed to the members of the Court in the language of the case and any other into which it has been interpreted.[94] The latter is not a translation but a transcript of the interpretation given at the hearing. In the case of the advocate general's opinion, which is read out in public to the Court by the advocate general in his own mother tongue, interpretation into the language of the case is always provided and a written translation into any languages requested is also normally available but, where it is not, direct interpretation may be provided.[95]

5   Official publications of the Court

The Court publishes a volume of select instruments on the organisation, jurisdiction and procedure of the Court in all the official Community languages,[96] and a series of digests of case law; but the most important of the Court's publications are those of the cases before it. RP-ECJ 68 and RP-CFI 86 provide that the Registrar (of the ECJ and, as the case may be, the CFI) shall arrange for the publication of the reports of cases. The ECJ's internal rules add that the reports shall be published in the official languages of the Community.[97] The reports cover:

(1)   judgments of the Court or a chamber (unless otherwise ordered);
(2)   interim orders;
(3)   other orders where their publication is considered desirable;
(4)   opinions given by the Court;
(5)   opinions of the advocates general.[98]

The judge-rapporteur is authorised to give the necessary instructions regarding the omission of the names of one of the parties or of third parties mentioned in the judgments, orders or opinions.[99]

Judgments and orders are published in chronological order,[1] the reports coming out in parts over the year. Since 1979 the pagination is the same for every language edition but before then only the first page of the report of each

90 GI 84.
91 See GI 86.
92 See GI 87.
93 GI 88.
94 GI 91.
95 GI 89.
96 GI 98.
97 GI 92.
98 GI 93.
99 Ibid.
 1 GI 94.

case was the same; as far as the English reports are concerned, this applies only as from 1969. As from the beginning of 1990, the reports have been retitled 'The reports of cases before the Court of Justice and the Court of First Instance' and have been divided into two sections with separate pagination.[2] The first contains the reports of cases before the ECJ and the citation of pages in that section should be preceded by 'I'; the second contains reports of cases before the CFI and the citation of pages is preceded by 'II'. Initially, each published part of the reports contained both sections but, where the volume of cases reported necessitated it, the sections were published in separate parts. Starting with the reports for 1993, cases before the ECJ and the CFI are reported in separate volumes, each issue covering one or more calendar months.

The report of a case commences with a headnote which is divided into two parts:[3] the first mentions the articles of the Treaty or any legislation involved together with various key words explaining the subject matter of the judgment; the second repeats the passages in the judgment of particular interest. As the note printed in the report states, the headnote has no binding force and is not an authentic interpretation of the judgment to which it refers.[4] The draft summary is prepared by the Research and Documentation Division and is approved by the judge-rapporteur and the other judges.[5] A brief statement of the subject matter of the case is occasionally added under the title of the judgment[6] but does not form part of the formal title of the proceedings; the judge-rapporteur is responsible for this.[7] The layout of the remaining part of the report has changed over the years.

Until the 1980s the report of the judgment consisted of two parts: the first, drawn from the report for the hearing and printed in double columns, set out the facts, the history of the proceedings and the arguments of the parties; the second was printed in one column and set out the reasoning of the judgment. It terminated in the operative part of the judgment, which was (and is) printed in heavy type and contains the Court's order. This is the passage that is read out, usually by the President, in open court when judgment is handed down. The advocate general's opinion then followed,[8] printed, as it still is, in double columns. His recommendation (the 'opinion' strictu sensu) was (and is) printed in one column.[9] In the course of the 1980s, the layout was altered because it was felt that there was some duplication between the first part of the judgment (setting out the facts, an account of the procedure followed and the arguments of the parties) and the advocate general's opinion, which often contained a summary of the same matters. The result was that the first part of the judgment was omitted from the report in all cases save those where it was considered to be necessary or desirable to include it; and the advocate-general's opinion was substituted for it in the report. After a few years there was a partial reversion to the old layout of the report in the sense that the first part of the judgment, drawn from the report for the hearing, reappeared; but the advocate general's opinion continues to precede that part of the report

---

2 The first cases decided by the CFI therefore appear in the report for 1990 even though they were decided towards the end of 1989.
3 GI 95.
4 See GI 97.
5 GI 95.
6 For example, Cases 241, 242 and 245–250/78 *DGV v Council and Commission* [1979] ECR 3017 bear the soubriquet 'Maize gritz liability'.
7 GI 96.
8 GI 94.
9 GI 96.

(now entitled 'judgment') setting out the Court's reasons and the operative part of the judgment.[10] The reports of cases before the CFI follow a slightly different format. The judgment is set out as a single document, comprising paragraphs numbered consecutively and divided by headings into sections and sub-sections, and terminating with the operative part; there is no division of the body of the report of the judgment into two parts (one essentially factual and the other setting out the CFI's reasons and its order). The advocate general's opinion (where there is one) precedes the judgment and is printed in double columns, like the opinions of the advocates general of the ECJ. Since 1989 the Court has adopted the practice of publishing certain cases in summary form only, in particular where a number of cases give rise to the same point and those following the lead case contain no additional ruling. The complete version of the judgment and, where applicable, the advocate general's opinion in such cases is available only in the language of the case (and, as regards the opinion, the language used by the advocate general) and may be obtained from the Court as long as it still has copies.

6   Publications in the Official Journal

IR 25 provides that the Registrar of the ECJ shall cause to be published in the Official Journal of the European Communities:

(1)   notices of applications originating proceedings pursuant to RP-ECJ 16(6);
(2)   notices of the removal of cases from the Register;
(3)   subject to a decision of the ECJ to the contrary, the operative part of every judgment and interim order;
(4)   the composition of the chambers;
(5)   the appointment of the President of the ECJ;
(6)   the appointment of the Registrar;
(7)   the appointment of the Assistant Registrar and the Administrator.

In addition, the ECJ's internal rules[11] provide that notices relating to requests for preliminary rulings and the assignment of jurisdiction to the chambers shall also be published. RP-CFI 24(6) provides for the publication in the Official Journal of notices of applications commencing proceedings before the CFI;[12] and the same information about the CFI is published in the Official Journal as that required by IR 25 in respect of the ECJ mutatis mutandis. Information for publication in the Official Journal is written in the language of the case and translated as soon as possible into the other official languages.[13]

RP-ECJ 16(6) provides that notices relating to applications originating proceedings shall contain the date of registration of the application, the name and permanent residence of the parties, the subject matter of the dispute and the submissions made in the application. The ECJ's internal rules[14] specify that they shall also set out the number of the case, the representatives, agents or lawyers of the applicant, the address for service, the defendants and the claim, which may be summarised. The same practice is followed in relation to applications originating proceedings before the CFI. In the case of references

10   If a case is withdrawn before judgment but after the delivery of the advocate general's opinion the opinion is normally published alone.
11   GI 99.
12   The information to be provided is the same as that required by RP-ECJ 16(6) in respect of actions before the ECJ.
13   GI 101.
14   GI 100.

for a preliminary ruling, the notice sets out the name of the national court making the reference, the parties to the action before it and the number of the case, together with the date on which the order for reference was made and when it was lodged at the ECJ, and the text of the question referred. Apart from the obvious elements, such as the number of the case and the names of the parties etc, notices of judgments or orders contain the composition of the Court (or chamber) and the operative part of the judgment.

CHAPTER 2
General outline of procedure

I Introduction

The cases that come before the Court tend to fall into one of five groups: (i) direct actions, (ii) references for a preliminary ruling, (iii) applications for interim relief, (iv) staff cases and, since 1990, (v) appeals from the CFI to the ECJ. The main procedural differences lie between the first, second and fifth. Direct actions, jurisdiction over which is divided between the ECJ and the CFI,[1] are contentious proceedings; references for a preliminary ruling, jurisdiction over which is at the time of writing reserved to the ECJ, are non-contentious proceedings; appeals from the CFI to the ECJ have procedural characteristics that set them apart from other cases because they provide the only instance of the exercise of judicial review by the ECJ over decisions of another judicial body. Applications for interim relief may be made in all direct actions, whatever their nature and whichever of the ECJ or the CFI has jurisdiction. They are one of a number of interlocutory and other proceedings that may be commenced in a direct action but, in practical terms, they are the only type which is encountered frequently. Such proceedings and the various points of procedure and practice arising in a case are dealt with in detail in subsequent chapters. Staff cases, jurisdiction (at first instance) over which is attributed to the CFI, comprise direct actions brought by present, potential or past employees of the Community institutions, or persons claiming under them, against the employing authority. Their only distinguishing feature is their subject matter and, in procedural terms, the conduct of the action before the Court is no different from that in any other direct action. This chapter considers first the procedural rules relating to the language to be used in proceedings, and then the procedure to be followed where proceedings are commenced erroneously before the ECJ or, as the case may be, the CFI, before summarising the procedure followed in direct actions, references for a preliminary ruling and appeals. Particular aspects of procedure are dealt with in greater detail in later chapters.

II The language of the case

The languages which may be used in proceedings before the Court are the official Community languages[2] together with Irish.[3] In references for a preliminary ruling the language of the case is always 'the language of the national

---

1 See chapter 1, section III.
2 Danish, Dutch, English, French, German, Greek, Italian, Portuguese and Spanish.
3 RP-ECJ 29(1); RP-CFI 35(1); see also art 7 of Council Regulation No 1 of 15 April 1958 (OJ English Special Edition, 1952–1958, p 59), as amended.

court or tribunal which refers the matter to the Court'.[4] Nonetheless, this does no more than provide a rule for selecting which of the languages used in proceedings before the Court is the language of the case; the Rules of Procedure do not appear to envisage the situation where the language of the referring court is not one of the recognised procedural languages and it is considered that, were that situation to arise, it would be necessary for the national court making the reference to the Court to express the reference in the official Community language of its own member state.[5] In the case of appeals from the CFI to the ECJ the language of the case is that of the decision of the CFI against which the appeal has been brought, without prejudice to the ECJ's power to authorise use of another language and the right of a member state participating in the appeal proceedings to use its own official language.[6] Where the appeal is brought by a member state, the exercise by that member state of its right to use its own official language in the course of the appeal does not, it would seem, result in the language of the appeal being that of the member state: even though the application commencing the appeal may be expressed in the member state's official language the language of the case remains that in which the judgment appealed against was expressed and all the other parties to the appeal are entitled and obliged to use that language unless the ECJ authorises use of another language.[7] In other proceedings, the language of the case is selected from among the recognised procedural languages by the applicant[8] save that in proceedings before the ECJ, where the defendant is a member state or a natural or legal person having the nationality of a member state, the applicant has no choice in the matter and the language of the case must be the official language of the member state in question: where

---

4 RP-ECJ 29(2), last sentence.
5 Thus, if Welsh were a procedural language of the courts in Wales (as opposed to a language that could be used for some purposes of proceedings, such as statements made by the parties in person or by witnesses), the reference would have to be made in English and not, for example, German.
6 RP-ECJ 110. It should be noted that, so far as the position of member states is concerned, RP-ECJ 110 allows a derogation, from the usual rule that the language of the appeal is that in which the judgment appealed against was expressed, only where the member state participates in the appeal as an intervener: see the fourth subpara of RP-ECJ 29(3), to which RP-ECJ 110 refers. A member state can of course participate in an appeal as the appellant (even though it was not previously a party to the proceedings before the CFI) or as a direct party to the appeal (where it was an intervener in the proceedings before the CFI). Taken literally, the derogation in RP-ECJ 110 does not apply in either of those circumstances. However the ECSC and EC Statutes, art 49, and the Euratom Statute, art 50, last sentence, provide that appellant member states are in the same position as member states which intervened at first instance; and under RP-CFI 35(3) a member state intervening in a case before the CFI is entitled to use its own official language. It therefore seems that, whether a member state participates in the appeal as an appellant or as an intervener, it is entitled to use its own official language. In those circumstances, it would be anomalous to deprive a member state of that right where it participates in the appeal as a direct party (but not an appellant) by virtue of its status as intervener in the proceedings before the CFI. Therefore, it seems that in whatever capacity it participates in an appeal a member state is entitled to use its own official language.
7 That conclusion follows from the fact that RP-ECJ 110 states that the general rule identifying the language of the appeal is 'without prejudice' (in this instance) only to the member state's entitlement itself to use its official language: the fourth subpara of RP-ECJ 29(3) does not result in all other parties to the case being obliged to use the official language of the member state concerned. Further, it would be unfair to the other parties to the appeal proceedings if they had to use the official language of the member state commencing the appeal proceedings (which might have been the only party to the proceedings before the CFI using a language other than the language of the case).
8 RP-ECJ 29(2); RP-CFI 35(2), first sentence.

it has more than one official language, the applicant can chose between them.[9] The language of the case does not change when one case is joined with another case having a different procedural language.

Save in the case of references for a preliminary ruling, the ECJ and the CFI may in cases brought before them authorise a change in the language of the case to another of the recognised procedural languages for all or part of the proceedings (and even if the language of the case has already been the subject of change).[10] This change may be made: (i) at the joint request of the parties: all the parties must concur in the application; (ii) at the request of one party: such a request may not be made by a Community institution and it can be granted only after the Court has heard the other parties and the advocate general (where there is one).[11] The Rules of Procedure do not specify whether either request should be made by application under RP-ECJ 91 or, as the case may be, RP-CFI 114. The inference from the express requirement that the Court must hear the views of both the other parties and the advocate general (where there is one) before deciding on an application made by one party (but is not obliged to hear the advocate general before considering the request made by all the parties) is that a procedure separate from RP-ECJ 91 (or RP-CFI 114) is envisaged. It is equally plausible that the divergence from the procedure set out in RP-ECJ 91 (or RP-CFI 114) simply reflects the fact that, in the first case, all the parties must apply and it is not necessary to regard the proceedings as contentious. On balance the better view is that the request should be made under RP-ECJ 91 (or, as the case may be, RP-CFI 114), simply because that provision is supposed to apply to procedural issues in general. However, it should be noted that, in Case 260/81 *Regul-Eberhardt v Commission*,[12] such a request was made simply by letter and granted after the Commission had indicated its agreement, also by letter. Such requests are rarely made and it is virtually impossible to discern what are the principles which may guide the Court in allowing or refusing a change in the language of the case.[13] In Case T-74/92 *Ladbroke Racing (Deutschland) GmbH v Commission*[13A] it was held that a request for such a change must show that the applicant's rights would otherwise be affected.

On a strict interpretation of the Rules of Procedure it could be said that a change in the language used 'for all or part of the proceedings' means that, for example, the language used for the hearing may be different from that used for the written procedure; but the language used for the hearing must be used for all purposes during the hearing. Other texts of the Rules of Procedure are not

9 RP-ECJ 29(2)(a): this provision led the ECJ to state in Case 1/60 *FERAM SpA v High Authority* [1960] ECR 165 at 170 that, unless the defendant is a Community institution, 'the language of the case is the language of the defendant'.
10 RP-ECJ 29(2)(b) and (c) (referred to, in the case of appeals, in RP-ECJ 110); RP-CFI 35(2)(a) and (b).   **11** Ibid.
12 Order of 21 October 1981: the case was subsequently withdrawn.
13 For example, in Cases 43 and 63/82 *Vereniging ter Bevordering van het Vlaamse Boekwezen (VBVB) and Vereniging ter Bevordering van de Belangen des Boekhandels (VBBB) v Commission* [1984] ECR 19 at 27, an application by three interveners to use a different language from the language of the case for their written and oral pleadings was refused even though the reason for the application was that the interveners wished to be represented by a well-known specialist in the subject matter of the litigation who could not understand or express himself in the language of the case; in Case T-1/90 *Pérez-Mínguez Casariego v Commission* [1991] ECR II-143, paras 20–22, the CFI allowed the parties to use French as the language of the case at the request of the applicant even though the applicant had commenced proceedings using Spanish: the reason for the change seems to have been that the applicant had in the meantime instructed another lawyer to represent him – the application to use another language was made under RP-ECJ 29(2)(c) (which was then applicable to CFI proceedings) but was not opposed.
13A [1993] ECR II-535, paras 14–15.

as tightly worded as the English and refer to 'use in whole or in part' of another language,[14] suggesting that, in any one part of the proceedings, the language of the case may be changed completely or only for certain purposes. This is, in fact, the interpretation adopted by the Court, as can be seen from cases such as Case 45/81 *Alexander Moksel Import-Export GmbH & Co Handels KG v Commission*[15] where the procedural language was German but an intervener was allowed to present its submissions at the hearing in English. The result was that, for the purposes of the oral procedure in that case, there were two procedural languages, German and English, but the latter was used only for the presentation of the intervener's case.

The Rules of Procedure do not provide expressly for an alteration in the language of the case so far as references for a preliminary ruling are concerned: the language of the case is that of the referring court and only the member states are entitled to use another language when taking part in the proceedings.[16] The existence of a power to change the procedural language is, therefore, a matter of debate. Nonetheless, it seems to be the Court's practice that it may entertain an application made by one of the parties to the proceedings before the referring court (other than, presumably, a member state or Community institution) to use at the hearing a language other than that of the case. The application should be made in writing and in good time before the hearing; the Court will not accede to it if the other parties to the proceedings before the referring court object. In all cases, the matter lies within the Court's discretion.

All written and oral submissions, including the documents annexed thereto,[17] must be expressed in the language of the case, which is also used when drawing up the minutes and decisions of the Court.[18] Documents which are expressed in any other language must be accompanied by a translation into the language of the case but, in the case of long documents, the translation may be confined to extracts, the Court or chamber retaining power to call at any time for a complete or fuller translation on its own motion or at the request of one of the parties.[19] This applies only to submissions made and documents lodged in the case. The result of this is that an application to intervene may be made in any of the recognised procedural languages because the applicant to intervene is not a party to the proceedings unless and until his intervention is allowed.[20] The Registrar may either decline to accept or return by registered post any pleading or document which is not worded in the language of the case.[21] Normally annexes are not returned but the party submitting them is asked to produce a translation. There seems to be no authority which settles the status of a pleading which is not expressed in the language of the case. It seems implicit in the Registrar's power to decline to accept such a pleading that it is inadmissible. The President or the Court may, however, authorise the Registrar to accept the pleading.[22] Hence, if it is served on the opposing party, an application under RP-ECJ 91 (or RP-CFI 114) to have it declared inadmissible would appear to be misconceived and the only remedy is an application for service of a translation into the language of the case; but any

---

14 Eg '*Emploi total ou partiel*'; '*uso parziale or totale*'.
15 [1982] ECR 1129.
16 RP-ECJ 29(3).
17 See, for example, Case 105/75 *Giuffrida v Council* [1976] ECR 1395 at 1405 (Advocate General Warner).
18 RP-ECJ 29(3); RP-CFI 35(3).
19 Ibid.
20 Case 30/59 *De Gezamenlijke Steenkolenmijnen in Limburg v High Authority* [1961] ECR 1 at 48.
21 IR 4(2).
22 Ibid.

relevant time limit for responding to such a document would seem to run only from service of the translation into the language of the case, not from service of the version in the language originally used. Where it is an annex which has not been lodged in the language of the case, it is certainly excessive to apply under RP-ECJ 91 (or RP-CFI 114) for the position to be regularised,[23] a simple letter to the Registrar pointing the defect out should be sufficient.

Apart from changing the language of the case the Court may also authorise the use of another language in proceedings. Automatic authorisation is given to member states by the Rules of Procedure in relation to their written and oral submissions when intervening in a case or taking part in an appeal or a reference for a preliminary ruling.[24] In the same way, the Court or chamber hearing the case may authorise a witness or expert to give his evidence in another language where he 'states that he is unable adequately to express himself in one of' the official procedural languages.[25] Curiously, the Rules of Procedure do not specify, in this context, an inability on the part of the witness or expert to express himself in the language of the case. This suggests that there is no obligation on a witness or expert to use that language; it is only when he cannot adequately express himself in any of the recognised procedural languages that authorisation is given for the use of another language. In the case both of member states and witnesses or experts, the language of the case is not changed but they are allowed to express themselves in another language; the Registrar makes arrangements for what is said to be translated into the language of the case. So far as witnesses and experts are concerned, the declaration of inability should, for practical reasons, be made in advance, even where it is simply a question of the witness or expert being better able to express himself in one recognised procedural language rather than another.

The President of the Court or chamber, when conducting the oral procedure, the judge-rapporteur, in his preliminary report (which is not, in any event, circulated to the parties) and the report for the hearing, judges and advocates general when putting questions and advocates general when delivering their opinions, may use any of the recognised procedural languages. The Registrar arranges for translation into the language of the case.[26] The advocates general normally deliver their opinions in their own maternal tongue. A judge, advocate general or one of the parties may request that things said or written in the course of proceedings be translated into one of the recognised procedural languages. The Registrar arranges for this to be done[27] and, where the request is made by one of the parties, may require the translation work to be paid for if he considers its cost to be excessive.[28] It would seem that a request submitted by a party must give reasons that the translation is required. It must be shown that the translation is necessary in order to safeguard the right to a fair trial and the Registrar must decide in each case whether sufficient reason has been shown to justify acceding to the request.[28A] Should the Registrar refuse to entertain it, application may be made to the Court under RP-ECJ 91 (or, as the case may be, RP-CFI 114). Texts drawn up either in the language of the case or in any other language authorised pursuant to RP-ECJ 29 or RP-CFI 35 are authentic.[29]

---

23 Case 14/64 *Gualco (née Barge) v High Authority* [1965] ECR 51 at 56–57 and 67 (Advocate General Roemer): the applicant was ordered to pay the costs of the application.
24 RP-ECJ 29(3) and 110; RP-CFI 35(3).   **25** RP-ECJ 29(4); RP-CFI 35(4).
26 RP-ECJ 29(5); RP-CFI 35(5).
27 RP-ECJ 30(1); RP-CFI 36(1).
28 RP-ECJ 72(b); RP-CFI 90(b): the scale of charges is to be found in IR 20.
28A *The Ladbroke* case (above, note 13A), paras 16–18.
29 RP-ECJ 31; RP-CFI 37.

There is an irrebuttable presumption of law that the Court, and all the Community institutions, are cognisant of all the official Community languages.[30] It is uncertain whether this presumption, in the case of the Court, also covers Irish. The better view is that it does not because, although Irish is a language which can be used in proceedings before the Court, it is not an official Community language for general purposes and the Court's Translation Directorate does not, therefore, include an Irish section. The consequence of this presumption is that the rules relating to the language of the case are intended primarily to benefit the parties and reduce the necessity for translations; the Court has knowledge of the existence and contents of every document submitted to it which is drawn up in an official Community language, whether or not the parties to the case understand it.[31] As a result, while a party may complain that his right to a fair trial has been infringed because a document or statement has been submitted to the Court in a language other than that of the case, he cannot rely on this fact to show that the Court was unaware of the contents of the document or statement.[32] The language rules are not peremptory requirements of the Court's procedure[33] and, if infringed, do not themselves cause the proceedings to be vitiated.

III   Conflicts of jurisdiction

The creation of the CFI and the attribution to it of part of the jurisdiction of the ECJ at first instance has created in turn the possibility of conflicts of jurisdiction between the CFI and the ECJ: in some instances one or other of the ECJ or the CFI may have jurisdiction over a particular case while the other does not; in other cases both the ECJ and the CFI may have jurisdiction.

As has been explained,[34] where an application or other procedural document addressed to the ECJ or the CFI is lodged at the wrong Registry it must be transmitted immediately by that Registry to the correct Registry[35] and proceedings will then carry on before the correct Court without there being any positive or negative conflict of jurisdiction. On the other hand, once an action has begun before either the ECJ or the CFI, it may emerge sooner or later that the Court before which it has been brought does not have jurisdiction to hear and determine it; or it may emerge that the Court in question does have jurisdiction but the same issue is also before the other Court, in which case the question arises whether the proceedings before one or other of the ECJ or the CFI should be stayed or some other step taken.

Where the CFI finds that it does not have jurisdiction to hear and determine an action in respect of which the ECJ has jurisdiction,[36] it is obliged to refer the action to the ECJ.[37] The question of the CFI's lack of jurisdiction is one that can be raised by the CFI of its own motion as soon as proceedings have been commenced before it; and, where its lack of competence is manifest, the case is simply referred to the ECJ by reasoned order without taking any further step in the proceedings, including serving the application on the defendant before

---

30   *FERAM SpA v High Authority*, above (note 9).
31   Ibid.
32   Ibid, p 170.
33   Ibid.
34   See chapter 1, section V.B(2) p 34.
35   ECSC and EC Statutes, art 47 (first para); Euratom Statute, art 48 (first para).
36   As to the jurisdiction of the ECJ and the CFI, see chapter 1, section III.
37   ECSC and EC Statutes, art 47 (second para); Euratom Statute, art 48 (second para).

the decision to refer is made.[38] The matter may also be raised by one of the parties by application under RP-CFI 114(1), in which case the President prescribes a period within which the opposite party may lodge its written response to the application.[39] Unless the Court otherwise decides, the remainder of the proceedings is oral.[40] In principle, the Court may decide, whether with or without hearing the parties (but in either event after hearing the advocate general, if there is one), to uphold or reject the application or reserve its decision until final judgment in the case.[41] In the situation under consideration, the CFI would either reject the application as unfounded or else uphold it and refer the case to the ECJ. The decision of the CFI may be the subject of an appeal to the ECJ.[42]

Where the ECJ finds that an action brought before it falls within the jurisdiction of the CFI, it likewise refers the action to the CFI, which cannot then decline jurisdiction.[43] In such a situation, it does not seem that the action before the ECJ is inadmissible in the strict sense because the ECJ has not, in principle, been deprived of jurisdiction over cases by reason of the creation of the CFI; it retains jurisdiction, in principle, but the exercise of that jurisdiction is, as it were, suspended in relation to matters falling within the jurisdiction of the CFI unless and until the CFI refers the matter to the ECJ.[44] Nonetheless, since a reference of the case by the ECJ to the CFI is mandatory, the question whether or not a case before the ECJ falls within the jurisdiction of the CFI may be raised and decided by the ECJ of its own motion.[45] By analogy with the situation where the ECJ has manifestly no jurisdiction over an action, the case may be referred to the CFI by reasoned order without taking any further step in the proceedings where it is manifest that the CFI has jurisdiction.[46] Where it is not manifest, the matter can still be raised by the ECJ at any time but its decision must be given in accordance with RP-ECJ 91(3) and (4).[47] The matter may also be raised by one of the parties by application under RP-ECJ 91(1), in which case the President prescribes a period within which the opposite party may lodge its written response to the application.[48] Unless the Court otherwise decides, the remainder of the proceedings is oral.[49] In principle the Court may decide, whether with or without hearing the parties (but in either event after hearing the advocate general), to uphold or reject the

---

38 RP-CFI 112: see, for example, Case T-78/91 *Moat and Association of Independent Officials for the Defence of the European Civil Service v Commission* [1991] ECR II-1387, para 8.

39 RP-CFI 114(2). See further below and chapter 6, p 188.

40 RP-CFI 114(3).

41 RP-CFI 114(4).

42 ECSC and EC Statutes, art 49 (first para); Euratom Statute, art 50 (first para).

43 ECSC and EC Statute, art 47 (second para); Euratom Statute, art 48 (second para).

44 Thus, the Statutes (ibid) state that the duty of the CFI to refer a case to the ECJ arises where the CFI 'finds that it does not have jurisdiction'; whereas they state that the duty of the ECJ to refer a case to the CFI arises where the ECJ 'finds that an action falls within the jurisdiction of' the CFI, not where the ECJ finds that it does not have jurisdiction. Similarly, in Case C-72/90 *Asia Motor France v Commission* [1990] ECR I-2181, the ECJ held that part of the action was manifestly inadmissible; but the part falling within the jurisdiction of the CFI was not held to be inadmissible, it was simply referred to the CFI.

45 It is an absolute bar to proceeding with a case, within the meaning of RP-ECJ 92(2), rather than a case of no jurisdiction to take cognisance of an action or manifest inadmissibility, within the meaning of RP-ECJ 92(1).

46 RP-ECJ 92(1) does not apply expressis verbis but that approach was followed in the *Asia Motor France* case (above, note 44).

47 RP-ECJ 92(2). See further below and chapter 7, p 223.

48 RP-ECJ 91(2).

49 RP-ECJ 91(3).

application or reserve its decision until final judgment in the case.[50] In the situation under consideration, the ECJ would either reject the application as unfounded or uphold it and refer the case to the CFI. The decision of the ECJ to refer the case to the CFI is binding on the CFI, with the consequence that it cannot decline jurisdiction on the ground decided by the ECJ in its decision to refer.[51]

Whether it is the CFI or the ECJ that is required to refer a case brought before it to the other Court, the Statutes do not explain what are the consequences so far as the running of time is concerned, For example, if proceedings are commenced erroneously before the CFI, in a case over which it has no jurisdiction but the ECJ does, the mistake may be discovered and the reference of the case to the ECJ made long after the expiry of the time limit for bringing proceedings before the ECJ. Must the ECJ then dismiss the proceedings as inadmissible for that reason? At first sight, the inference to be drawn from the Statutes is that an action is not to be dismissed as inadmissible due to a failure to observe a time limit when the action was initially brought in time but before the wrong Court and has been referred to the correct Court after the expiry of the relevant time limit: if it were otherwise it would be simpler for the Court before which the action was originally brought to find that it was brought before the wrong Court and then declare it to be time-barred and inadmissible without any reference to the correct Court. However, that inference does not flow inevitably from the Statutes. In many instances the reference of the case by the wrong Court to the correct Court can be effected before the expiry of the time limit for bringing proceedings; and the silence of the Statutes on the question of time may be interpreted as indicating that any such reference is without prejudice to the question of time, which must be considered by the correct Court since it is not a question that can properly be considered by the wrong Court. The approach of the CFI and the ECJ so far seems to be to regard a case referred by one of them to the other as having been commenced within time even if the reference is made, and the correct Court is seised with the case, long after the expiry of the time limit for bringing proceedings.[52] In consequence, the commencement of proceedings before the wrong Court appears to have no adverse effect on the running of time.

It is unclear whether or not an action that falls partly within the jurisdiction of the CFI and partly within the areas of jurisdiction of the ECJ that have not been assigned to the CFI can be dealt with in the same way so that the proceedings can be split and replaced by two parallel actions before both Courts.[53] In the *Asia Motor France* case,[54] part of the action was dismissed entirely as being manifestly inadmissible (as regards both the ECJ and the CFI) so that, when the remaining part was referred by the ECJ to the CFI, there was no other part of the proceedings that could have been retained by the

---

50 RP-ECJ 91(4).
51 ECSC and EC Statutes, art 47 (last sentence of second para); Euratom Statute, art 48 (last sentence of second para). Quite apart from the Statutes, the CFI appears to be bound by the decision of the ECJ either because that decision constitutes res judicata so far as the CFI is concerned (it exercises the jurisdiction of the ECJ at first instance but without depriving the ECJ of that jurisdiction to the extent that the Statutes and Rules of Procedure permit the ECJ to continue to exercise it) or because the CFI is in any event bound by decisions of the CFI on points of law.
52 See, for example, the *Asia Motor France* case (above, note 44), where the reference to the CFI was made some two months after the expiry of the time limit.
53 It is not entirely clear whether or not the splitting of an action (effectively the disjoinder of disparate claims made in the same proceedings) is possible but there seems to be no objection in principle to such a course, particularly where the parties do not object.
54 Above, note 44.

ECJ. The same occurred, so far as the CFI was concerned, in *Moat and Association of Independent Officials for the Defence of the European Civil Service v Commission.*[55] In Case C-322/91 and Case C-44/92 *Association of Independent Officials for the Defence of the European Civil Service v Commission,*[56] the original actions had been brought jointly by several persons and it was possible to split them by reference to the identity of the joint applicants and the resulting difference in their causes of action. Where part of the action could be retained by one Court and the remaining part should be referred to the other Court, the splitting of the action would, of course double the legal costs and the burden placed on the ECJ and the CFI, unless there were scope for the proceedings before one of the Courts (whether the ECJ or the CFI) to be stayed pending the outcome of the proceedings before the other Court, as envisaged by the ECSC and EC Statutes (art 47, third para) and the Euratom Statute (art 48, third para) in cases of concurrent jurisdiction. At first sight, that outcome does not appear to be satisfactory for reasons of procedural economy save in cases where there is a 'natural' split in the action, such as where the problem arises because several persons have commenced proceedings jointly rather than severally. On the other hand, it is likely that the problem would arise only in cases where dissimilar claims that would justify being pleaded in separate actions have been joined in a single application. In consequence, there are arguments for and against the solution of splitting the claims into separate actions. However, if the action were not to be split, it would seem that, if the proceedings had been commenced before the CFI, that Court would have to decline jurisdiction over the entire case and refer it to the ECJ because, otherwise, the CFI would be dealing with a case that fell in part outside its jurisdiction. If the proceedings had been commenced before the ECJ, or were referred to it in their entirety by the CFI, the ECJ could entertain the entire action because, as the power of the CFI to refer a case within its jurisdiction to the ECJ demonstrates, the jurisdictions of the ECJ and the CFI are essentially concurrent. Nonetheless, it would remain within the discretion of the ECJ to split the action and remit to the CFI the part falling within the latter's jurisdiction. In the result, it seems to be theoretically possible for the ECJ and the CFI either to take the course of splitting the action between them or to have the matter heard and determined solely before the ECJ. It is difficult to see at this juncture which solution would in the event be adopted; it may be that each case would be considered on its merits or that the splitting of the action would in the final analysis be considered the better course.

Where the subject matter of cases before the ECJ and the CFI overlap the position is as follows. Where the ECJ and the CFI are seised of cases in which the same relief is sought,[57] the same issue of interpretation is raised or the validity of the same act is called in question,[58] the CFI may in its discretion

---

55 Above, (note 38).

56 [1992] ECR I-6373 and 6387, respectively.

57 That includes the situation where actions for the annulment of the same act are brought before both the ECJ and the CFI (by different persons).

58 The cases need not be of the same procedural nature or involve the same parties. Thus, the same issue of interpretation or of validity may be raised in a reference for a preliminary ruling before the ECJ and in a direct action before the CFI. The 'validity' of an act of a Community institution is in this context to be understood as encompassing both 'validity', as that term is used in connection with references for a preliminary ruling and the plea of illegality, and 'lawfulness', as that term is used in connection with actions for annulment: it would not make sense to apply the formal distinction between those terms in the present context. Hence, it is of no consequence that the issue in the cases before the ECJ and the CFI takes the form, before the ECJ, of an enquiry into the 'validity' of an act of a Community institution in the context of a reference for a preliminary ruling and, before the CFI, of a challenge to the 'lawfulness' of the

stay the proceedings before it until such time as the ECJ delivers judgment. For its part, the ECJ may also in its discretion decide to stay the proceedings before it, in which event the proceedings before the CFI are to continue.[59] It would seem that the discretion of the Court (whether the ECJ or the CFI) should be exercised in accordance with the interests of justice in both cases and having regard, in particular, to: the stage that the proceedings have reached when the question of stay arises;[60] to the fact that, in principle, where the issue requires a close examination of complex facts, the matter is best considered by the ECJ in the light of the findings made by the CFI; and to the fact that any ruling on a point of law made by the ECJ is binding on the CFI in pari materia. It seems to follow from the fact that proceedings before the CFI shall continue to run when the ECJ decides to stay proceedings before it that, if the ECJ is the first to exercise its discretion and does so by staying the proceedings before it, that decision deprives the CFI of power to stay the proceedings before it. On the other hand, if the CFI is the first to exercise its discretion, that has no effect on the powers of the ECJ; and, further, if the ECJ were then to stay the proceedings before it, the effect would be to remove the stay of proceedings ordered by the CFI. In the normal course it does not seem likely that, if the CFI had stayed proceedings before it, the ECJ would also order a stay; it is more likely that the ECJ would take account of the CFI's decision and the reasons for it; and the proceedings before the ECJ would be continued. Where both the ECJ and the CFI are seised with applications for the annulment of the same act: in addition to its power to stay the procedings before it, the CFI can also decline jurisdiction so that the ECJ may rule on the application; and the ECJ may stay the proceedings before it, in which case the proceedings before the CFI shall continue (unless the CFI has declined jurisdiction).[61] A decision of the CFI to decline jurisdiction does not cause the proceedings to halt or to remain in limbo but results in the matter reverting to the ECJ, the exercise of whose jurisdiction over the case revives when the CFI declines jurisdiction. A decision to decline juridiction and not simply to stay the proceedings is a matter of discretion to be exercised in the interests of justice taking into account, in particular, any need for the CFI to examine the facts on which the challenge to the lawfulness of the contested act is based and the desirability of the ECJ ruling finally on the lawfulness of the contested act in the light of all relevant facts and arguments.

By way of illustration of the application of the rules just described, in Case C-66/90 and Case T-42/91, both being *Koninklijke PTT Nederland NV and PTT Post BV v Commission*,[62] the applicants (who were undertakings) had applied to the ECJ at the same time as the Netherlands for the annulment of a Commission decision made under art 90(3) of the EEC Treaty. The case brought by

---

same act in an action for annulment; or that, before the ECJ, it arises in the context of an action for annulment while, before the CFI, it arises in the form of the plea of illegality. In Case T-22/90 *Brambillo v Commission*, order of 29 November 1990, the same issue of interpretation arose in proceedings commenced before the CFI against the Commission which caused the latter to commence proceedings before the ECJ against the Council (the CFI therefore stayed the proceedings before it until the judgment of the ECJ in the action against the Council).

59 ECSC and EC Statutes, art 47 (third para); Euratom Statute, art 48 (third para).
60 For example, if proceedings before one Court have almost reached judgment whereas the proceedings before the other have only just commenced, there would seem to be no point in staying the former whereas there may be reason to stay the latter so that the defence (if it is a direct action) or the written observations (if it is a reference for a preliminary ruling) are lodged after (and can therefore take account of) the judgment in the other case.
61 Statutes, above, note 59.
62 [1991] ECR I-2723 and [1991] ECR II-273, respectively.

the Netherlands had to be dealt with by the ECJ but the other case had to be referred to the CFI. That was done; but the ECJ declined to stay the proceedings before it and, in consequence, the applicants in what was by then Case T-42/91 requested the CFI to decline jurisdiction so that both cases could be heard by the ECJ. Under the rules relating to the reference of cases to the CFI by the ECJ,[63] the CFI may not in such circumstances decline jurisdiction. As stated above, that requirement prevents the CFI from disputing the ECJ's decision on the issue of jurisdiction determined in the ECJ's decision to refer the matter to the CFI; it is without prejudice to the CFI's power to decline jurisdiction for some other reason. In the event the CFI declined jurisdiction because staying the proceedings before the CFI would not have been in the interests of justice; the applicants in the proceedings before the CFI could not intervene in the proceedings before the ECJ and, in consequence, the only way that they could be heard was by bringing their own action; it was clearly in the interests of procedural economy for the ECJ to deal with all the issues of fact and law at the same time instead of (possibly) in two stages if it rejected the action brought by the Netherlands but the other action raised different issues.

A decision whether or not to stay proceedings or, as the case may be, to decline jurisdiction may be made by the relevant Court either on its own motion or on application by one of the parties under RP-ECJ 91 or (as the case may be) RP-CFI 114.[64] A decision whether or not to stay proceedings is made by the Court or chamber seised with the case; where the case is before the ECJ the advocate general must first be heard[65] but where the case is before the CFI the parties and the advocate general (if there is one) must first be heard.[66] The proceedings may be resumed by order after following the same procedure followed when proceedings were stayed.[67] The stay takes effect on the date indicated in the order imposing the stay (or, in the absence of such indication, on the date of the order) and ends on the expiry of the period of the stay (if defined in the order imposing the stay) or on the date specified in the order lifting the stay (or, in the absence of such a date, on the date of that order); throughout the period of the stay time ceases to run for the purposes of any prescribed time limits for all parties and time begins to run afresh only from the date on which proceedings are resumed.[68] During the period of the stay time continues to run so far as persons who are not parties to the proceedings are concerned; thus, stay does not relieve any third party who wishes to intervene in the proceedings from the obligation to apply to intervene within the relevant time limit.[69] Decisions of the CFI declining jurisdiction in the circumstances discussed above are made by order which is served on the parties.[70] As in the case of decisions of the ECJ concerning the stay of proceedings there is no express requirement that such decisions be made after hearing the parties. Since such orders are the result of an exercise of the Court's discretion and may have significant consequences for the parties they should ordinarily be made only after the parties have been given an opportunity to be heard.

63 ECSC and EC Statutes, art 47 (second para); Euratom Statute, art 48 (second para).
64 As has been seen, in Case T-42/91 *Koninklijke PTT Nederland NV v Commission* (above, note 62) the decision was made on application.
65 RP-ECJ 82a(1)(a).
66 RP-CFI 78.
67 RP-ECJ 82a(1) (penultimate sentence); RP-CFI 78. The orders staying the proceedings or lifting the stay are served on the parties.
68 RP-ECJ 82a(2) and (3); RP-CFI 79(1) and (2).
69 This is provided for expressly in RP-CFI 79(1) and applies by necessary implication to cases pending before the ECJ.
70 RP-CFI 80.

IV   Direct actions

Proceedings in a direct action whether conducted before the ECJ or before the CFI develop in four phases:

(1)   the written procedure, in which the parties submit their arguments in writing;

(2)   directions and enquiries: here the Court decides after the close of pleadings what further steps are to be taken in the proceedings and, in particular, carries out enquiries into the issues of fact;

(3)   the oral procedure: this consists of the hearing and the delivery of the advocate general's opinion (where applicable); and

(4)   the judgment.

A   Written procedure

The procedure in a direct action commences with the lodgment at the appropriate Court of the application commencing proceedings. The rules relating to the form and content of the application are dealt with in chapter 9. In brief, the application must be made in writing and the original signed by the applicant's agent (in the case of a member state or Community institution) or lawyer (in the case of all other persons).[71] It must be dated and set out the applicant's name and address, the description of the signatory (ie whether he is an agent or lawyer), the name of the party against whom the application is made, the subject matter of the proceedings, the pleas in law on which the application is based, the relief sought, the nature of the evidence relied on and an address for service in the place where the Court has its seat (Luxembourg), together with the name of a person who is authorised and has expressed willingness to accept service.[72] Various other documents must be lodged at the same time which do not need to be specified here.

If the application does not comply with the requirements set out in RP-ECJ 38(3)–(6) (or, as the case may be, RP-CFI 44(3)–(5)), which concern, in essence, the various documents that must accompany the application, the Registrar requests the applicant to make good the deficiency within a reasonable period of time fixed by him. If the application has been lodged within the time limit for commencing proceedings, the fact that it is put in good order in this way only after the expiry of the time limit does not affect matters.[73] However, if the applicant fails to put his application in order or produce the required documents within the time prescribed by the Registrar, the Court must decide, after hearing the views of the advocate general (where there is one), whether or not the failure to comply with the Rules of Procedure renders the application inadmissible in point of form.[74] This procedure does not, in principle, apply to other defects in a pleading.[75] The Rules do not provide that the application must be rejected; the decision seems to lie within the discretion of the Court. It is unclear on what grounds the Court would hold the application to be admissible or reject it. Since the practice is first to write to the applicant asking him to put the application in order, the question should normally arise only if

---

71   ECSC Statute, art 22; EC and Euratom Statutes, art 19; RP-ECJ 37; RP-CFI 43.
72   Ibid; see also RP-ECJ 38 and RP-CFI 44.
73   ECSC Statute, art 22; EC and Euratom Statutes, art 19.
74   RP-ECJ 38(7); RP-CFI 44(6).
75   Case 131/83 *Vaupel v European Court of Justice* (unreported, 15 March 1984), para 9. But see p 39, above and Cases 220–221/78 *ALA SpA and ALFER SpA v Commission* [1979] ECR 1693 and Case 10/81 *Farrall v Commission* [1981] ECR 717.

he declines to do so. In that event, it is the refusal to comply with the Rules of Procedure and the Court's request that may bring about the inadmissibility of the application as much as the defect itself. Considering the nature of possible defects, some of the requirements set out in RP-ECJ 38(3)–(6) and RP-CFI 44(3)–(5) would not seem to warrant rejection of the application if they are not complied with. For example, if, in an action for annulment, the measure in question has already been published in the Official Journal, it seems excessive to regard the failure to lodge a copy of it to be sufficient to justify the rejection of the application. On the other hand, if the applicant fails to lodge a copy of the instrument constituting it, an unpublished measure whose annulment is sought, or (as the case may be) the contract or agreement giving the Court jurisdiction, such a defect may justify rejecting the application because the applicant has not given the proof required by the Rules of Procedure that it has capacity to act, that the subject matter of the proceedings exists in truth or that the Court has jurisdiction. All three factors are fundamental to the admissibility of the action.

In addition to the application commencing proceedings, the applicant may also, should need arise, apply to the President of the Court by separate document[76] for the grant of interim relief pending judgment in the action.[77]

In the case of proceedings before the ECJ, when the application has been lodged, the President of the ECJ is informed and he assigns the case to one of the chambers, for the purpose of carrying out any preparatory enquiries that may later be ordered, and designates one judge from that chamber to act as judge-rapporteur.[78] The First Advocate General is also informed of the commencement of proceedings and assigns the case to one of his colleagues as soon as the judge-rapporteur has been designated by the President.[79] In the case of proceedings before the CFI, when the application is lodged, the President of the CFI is informed and he assigns the case to one of the chambers, not for any eventual preparatory enquiries (as in the case of the ECJ) but for all the purposes of the proceedings.[80] The President of the relevant chamber then proposes (to the President of the CFI) the judge assigned to that chamber who should be designated to act as rapporteur; and the President of the CFI decides on that proposal.[81] Whether the proceedings are before the ECJ or the CFI, in assigning a case to a chamber and designating the judge-rapporteur and (where applicable) the advocate general, account is often taken of other cases concerning the same subject matter.

At this stage, and before the application has been served on the other parties, the Court may declare it to be inadmissible 'where it is clear that the Court has no jurisdiction to take cognisance' of it or where the action is 'manifestly inadmissible'.[82] The Court's decision is set out in a reasoned order. There is no provision for hearing the views of the parties and the Court exercises its power sparingly, when its lack of jurisdiction is patent.[83] In

---

76 RP-ECJ 83(3); RP-CFI 104(3).
77 See chapter 8, p 230.
78 RP-ECJ 9(2).
79 RP-ECJ 10(2).
80 RP-CFI 13(1).
81 RP-CFI 13(2). It is not clear to what extent and, if so, on what grounds the President of the CFI may refuse to designate the judge proposed by the President of the chamber. In practice the President of the CFI always acts on the proposal put to him.
82 RP-ECJ 92(1); RP-CFI 111.
83 See, for example, Case 59/79 *Fédération Nationale des Producteurs de Vins de Table et Vins de Pays v Commission* [1979] ECR 2425; Case 51/79 *Buttner v Commission* [1980] ECR 1201; Case 123/80 *B v European Parliament* [1980] ECR 1789; Case 138/80 *Borker* [1980] ECR 1975.

addition, where it appears to the Court that it has jurisdiction to hear the application but there is, or may be, an 'absolute bar' to proceeding with the case (for example, that the application may be out of time), it may at any time raise the matter of its own motion and give its decision in accordance with RP-ECJ 91(3) and (4) or, as the case may be, RP-CFI 114(3) and (4).[84] Absolute bars cannot be waived either by the parties or by the Court itself. The Court must therefore consider them, even if they have not been raised (or have been waived) by one of the parties, and may do so at any stage of the proceedings. In practice this is normally done after the close of pleadings, so that the rest of the proceedings would be devoted to the question of the admissibility of the action. However, the Court can take the point immediately after lodgment of the application. In this event, it seems that, unless it decides to allow the parties to submit written observations, it must fix the date for a hearing, pursuant to RP-ECJ 91(3) or, as the case may be, RP-CFI 114(3).

A decision of the Court to admit the application without hearing the views of the defendant might prejudice a subsequent claim by the defendant that the application was inadmissible. To avoid a possible duplication of objections, it seems logical that, when the Court raises the question of an absolute bar after lodgment of the application, it serves the application on the defendant in the usual way, informs all the parties that it intends to consider the question of the bar and fixes a date for the making of their written or oral observations. After hearing the views of the parties and those of the advocate general (if there is one), the Court either declares the application to be inadmissible or holds that it is admissible or reserves its decision until the final judgment. In either of the two latter cases, the President then fixes the time limit for the further steps in the proceedings (in the case of consideration of the bar before lodgment of the defence, the next step would be its lodgment).

In the normal course of events, the application is served on the defendant by the Registrar after it has been lodged at the appropriate Court. Where the application contains a formal defect referred to in RP-ECJ 38(7) or (as the case may be) RP-CFI 44(6), it is served after it has been corrected; but the Court may also declare the application admissible despite a failure to comply with RP-ECJ 38(7) or RP-CFI 44(6), in which case it is served despite the defect.[85] It would seem that, if the Court declares the application to be admissible despite the defect, the defendant cannot later raise the point in order to challenge the admissibility of the application. The Court's power to declare the application admissible is restricted by RP-ECJ 39 or (as the case may be) RP-CFI 45 to formal defects deriving from a failure to comply with RP-ECJ 38(7) or (as the case may be) RP-CFI 44(6) but seems to be applied, generally, to all similar defects.

Once the application has been served on him, the defendant has a choice between lodging a defence or raising a preliminary objection under RP-ECJ 91 or (as the case may be) RP-CFI 114. The defence may challenge both the admissibility and the merits of the application; a preliminary objection challenges its admissibility alone. There seems to be no reason why the defendant cannot lodge both, so long as they are in separate documents, but, if the latter is successful, the former is redundant. The defence must be lodged within one month of service of the application.[86] This time limit may be extended on

---

84 RP-ECJ 92(2); RP-CFI 113.
85 RP-ECJ 39; RP-CFI 45.
86 RP-ECJ 40(1); RP-CFI 46(1).

application to the President,[87] and, in general, one extension of time is readily granted. The application for extension may be made informally but it must give some reason why the extension sought should be granted, in particular where one has already been granted and a further extension is sought. The normal practice is to write to the President, addressing the letter to the Registrar. As a rule the Court discourages requests for the extension of time made by telephone.[88] No time limit is set for lodgment of a preliminary objection but, if it is to be lodged instead of a defence, it must clearly be lodged within the time set for lodgment of the defence. The reason is that, pursuant to RP-ECJ 94 and RP-CFI 122, the applicant may apply for judgment in default if the defendant has failed to lodge a defence within the time fixed for doing so.[89] If the defendant has not lodged a defence but has raised a preliminary objection, the applicant cannot then apply for judgment in default because the admissibility of his claim has been challenged.

The defence must set out (a) the name and permanent address of the defendant, (b) the points of law and fact relied on, (c) the form of order sought, (d) the nature of any evidence relied on, (e) an address for service in Luxembourg, and (f) the name of the person authorised and willing to accept service. It must also be accompanied by various documents which do not need to be specified here.[90] As has been said, if the defence is not lodged at the Court within the time prescribed for doing so, the applicant may apply for judgment by default. The 'time prescribed' is either one month from the service of the application on the defendant, pursuant to RP-ECJ 40(1) or (as the case may be) RP-CFI 46(1), or such other time as may be prescribed by the President upon application by the defendant under RP-ECJ 40(2) or (as the case may be) RP-CFI 46(3).

A preliminary objection to admissibility is broadly equivalent to an application to have a writ set aside for disclosing no reasonable cause of action. It is made in the form of an application that the case be dismissed and must be made by separate document.[91] The application does not put in question the substance of the claim made by the other party but alleges that it cannot be heard because the Court lacks jurisdiction or there is some other bar to proceeding with the action. It should be made only where the bar is a complete bar to the action. If it is only partial, for example if it relates to one only of a number of claims made, it is more appropriate to raise it as part of the defence to the whole action. The object of making a preliminary objection is to shorten proceedings by requesting the Court to consider the admissibility of the action alone and not delve into its merits.

The application must set out the pleas of fact and law relied on, the form of order sought and include any supporting documents.[92] When it has been lodged at the Court it is served on the applicant in the action who is given time

---

87 RP-ECJ 40(2); RP-CFI 46(3). Power to extend time in response to a first request for an extension has been delegated to the Registrar.

88 Under the ECJ's internal rules, when made in writing and lodged during the absence of the President of the Court, applications for an extension of time are to be submitted to the President of the first chamber or, in his absence, the President of the second chamber, and so on in order of seniority (PI 9); all requests for an extension of time must be submitted to the President on the day they are received at the Registry and no document agreeing to an extension may be submitted for signature without prior instructions (PI 10). Those rules must now be read subject to the delegation of power to extend time given to the Registrar.

89 See, for example, Case T-42/89 *Yorck von Wartenburg v European Parliament* [1990] ECR II-31.

90 RP-ECJ 40(1); RP-CFI 46(1).

91 RP-ECJ 91(1); RP-CFI 114(1).

92 Ibid.

by the President to submit in writing a form of order in reply to the defendant's application and the pleas of law relied on in support.[93] Thereafter the oral proceedings commence and there are no preparatory enquiries unless the Court so decides.[94] The Court comes to a decision after hearing the parties and the advocate general (if there is one). It may either decide on the application or reserve its decision until the final judgment on the case. In both the latter case and in the event that the preliminary objection is rejected, the President prescribes further time limits for further steps in the proceedings.[95] It sometimes happens that a preliminary objection is upheld only in part, in which case the action continues save in respect of the part found to be inadmissible. There is no appeal from a decision of the ECJ upholding or dismissing a preliminary objection to admissibility; where the decision is made by the CFI in proceedings pending before it an appeal lies to the ECJ.[96]

After the defence has been lodged at the Court, it is served on the applicant who is given by the President a period in which to lodge a reply; if the applicant declines to do so, pleadings are closed. If, on the other hand, a reply is lodged, it is served on the defendant, who is given a period in which to lodge his rejoinder; the pleadings then close after the lodgment of the rejoinder.[97] There is no provision for any application for summary judgment or any other abbreviation of the procedure where the defence as pleaded fails to disclose any or any reasonable defence to the claims made in the application. A notice is published in the Official Journal giving details of the application commencing proceedings[98] and third parties have three months from the date of publication in which to apply to the Court to intervene in the proceedings.[99] Where an application to intervene is allowed, the intervener is given an opportunity to submit in writing a statement in intervention setting out the form of order sought by the intervener and the pleas of law and arguments relied on in support; and each of the other parties to the proceedings is given an opportunity to submit in writing a reply to the statement in intervention.[1]

The application and the defence are the principal pleadings and should be completed by a reply and a rejoinder only where necessary. The rules relating to pleadings are considered in detail below. It suffices at this stage to make the rather obvious point that the purpose of the written pleadings is to identify the issues of fact and law that divide the parties. It should be noted that, as far as matters of fact are concerned, the pleadings also serve to identify the sources of any evidence relevant to the case. It is the Court's function, not that of the parties, to call for evidence, but it remains the duty of the parties to provide the Court with sufficient information so that it can assess how it is to exercise its powers. This information is not restricted to isolating the issues of fact but it extends to sources of evidence. The written procedure is closed by one of the following events as the case may be: failure to lodge a defence within time; waiver by the applicant of the right to lodge a reply; failure by the applicant to lodge a reply within time; waiver by the defendant of the right to lodge a

---

93 RP-ECJ 91(2); RP-CFI 114(2).
94 RP-ECJ 91(3); RP-CFI 114(3).
95 RP-ECJ 91(4); RP-CFI 114(4).
96 ECSC and EC Statutes, art 49; Euratom Statute, art 50.
97 RP-ECJ 41; RP-CFI 47.
98 RP-ECJ 16(6); RP-CFI 24(6).
99 RP-ECJ 93(1); RP-CFI 115(1). In fact time starts to run from the day after publication: see RP-ECJ 80(1)(a); RP-CFI 101(1)(a). It does not seem that RP-ECJ 81(1) (or, as the case may be, RP-CFI 102(1)), which provides that, in the case of proceedings against measures adopted by an institution, time runs from the fifteenth day after publication, applies.
 1 RP-ECJ 93(5) and (6); RP-CFI 116(4) and (5).

rejoinder; failure by the defendant to lodge a rejoinder within time; lodgment of the rejoinder. Where a third party has intervened in the proceedings the written procedure may well end after the events described above because the intervention is very often allowed at a relatively advanced stage in the written procedure involving the applicant and the defendant. In such circumstances the written procedure ends, as the case may be: on a failure by the intervener to lodge within time a written statement in intervention; on the lodgment by the other parties of their replies to the statement in intervention; or on the failure of the other parties to lodge their replies within time.

B   Directions and enquiries

After the close of pleadings, the President fixes a date on which the judge-rapporteur is to present his preliminary report on the case to the Court.[2] This report is not circulated to the parties and contains the judge-rapporteur's recommendations on how proceedings in the case should be conducted. It is discussed by the Court in an administrative meeting at which it is decided what further steps must be taken in the proceedings and the date for the hearing is fixed after hearing the views of the advocate general (where there is one).[3] In proceedings before the ECJ one decision which is usually made at this time concerns the question whether the case is to be heard by a chamber of three judges, a chamber of five, a full Court consisting only of a quorum of seven judges or the full Court comprising all the judges. This is a decision which lies almost entirely within the discretion of the Court. The rules governing the exercise of its discretion are discussed above.[4] At this point it is sufficient to recall that only a member state or a Community institution which is a party to the proceedings can by request require the Court to refer a particular case to hearing by the full Court[5] whereas other parties may simply make suggestions. A number of procedural decisions may be made by the Court at any time in the course of proceedings. Although often made before the administrative meeting it seems convenient to discuss them here.

The President of the ECJ may at any time after an advocate general has been assigned to the cases in question order that a number of cases 'concerning the same subject matter' be dealt with jointly.[6] In the same way cases before the CFI which concern the same subject matter may be joined by order of the President of the CFI.[7] Joinder does not affect the position of the parties to the actions concerned nor does it result in the actions themselves losing their separate identity; it is basically an administrative device for dealing efficiently with a number of cases giving rise to the same issues and hence to the same procedural problems. The essential criterion for joinder is therefore convenience. In the case of references for a preliminary ruling, joinder is proper if the questions referred are identical and have essentially the same object.[8] The same seems to apply, mutatis mutandis, to direct actions: if the issues are the

---

2 RP-ECJ 44(1); RP-CFI 52(1).
3 Ibid.
4 See chapter 1, section V.A.
5 RP-ECJ 95(2).
6 RP-ECJ 43.
7 RP-CFI 50.
8 Cases 117/76 and 16/77 *Albert Ruckdeschel & Co v Hauptzollamt Hamburg-St Annen* [1977] ECR 1753, Cases 124/76 and 20/77 *Moulins et Huileries de Pont à Mousson SA v Office Nationale Interprofessionnel des Céréales* [1977] ECR 1795, and Cases 187 and 190/83 *Nordbutter GmbH & Co KG and Bayerische Milchversorgungs GmbH v Germany* [1984] ECR 2553, at para 2 of the judgments.

same or there is a sufficient degree of connexity between the cases, joinder is proper unless it would not facilitate the future conduct of the proceedings.[9] However, although two or more references for a preliminary ruling may be joined, whether they come from the same[10] or different[11] national courts, the joinder of a reference for a preliminary ruling to a direct action happens rarely, if at all, and appears to be wrong in principle due to the difference in nature of the proceedings. In addition, other factors such as the language of the cases and the various procedural stages that they may have reached must be taken into account. However the fact that the cases have different procedural languages does not appear to be a bar to joinder.[12] On the other hand, joinder of future proceedings with a case nearing judgment is inconceivable.[13] Cases may be disjoined where the circumstances justifying their joinder no longer apply or new circumstances have arisen which render their continued joinder inappropriate or inconvenient for the future conduct of the proceedings. For example, in Cases 241, 242, 246–249/78 *DGV v Council and Commission*,[14] the Court disjoined one of the cases because, while agreement had been reached between the parties in all the others, which could then proceed to an adjudication on costs, no agreement had been reached in the remaining case and the Court would have to rule on the substance of the claim; in Cases 122 and 141/85 *Totaro and Dufrane v Commission*,[15] the cases were disjoined when one of them was withdrawn; Case 141/85 *Dufrane v Commission* was subsequently joined with another case[16] because of the similarity between the cases but, when Mrs Dufrane died, the cases were disjoined at the request of her personal representatives and the proceedings in Case 141/85 were stayed pending judgment in the other case.

The fact that the parties in the cases to be joined are competitors or that for some other reason the pleadings and evidence in one or all of the cases to be joined reveal secret or confidential matters that should not be disclosed to persons other than the parties to each case is not in itself an objection to the joinder of the cases: the possibility that joinder may result in the disclosure of secret or confidential material can be avoided by the parties requesting confidential treatment.[17] When examining such requests in the context of the joinder of cases, the Court's function is to resolve the conflict between the principle that business or other secrets should be respected and the principle that all parties having a potential conflict of interest must be in a position to reply to any points raised in the joined cases that adversely affect them.[18]

The decision to join several cases is made after hearing the parties and the advocate general (where there is one) and it may subsequently be rescinded.[19] Both the decision to join and that to disjoin may be made either on a request by

---

9 Case T-16/89 *Herkenrath v Commission* [1992] ECR II-275, order of 13 November 1990.
10 The *Ruckdeschel* case, above (note 8).
11 The *Pont-à-Mousson* case, above (note 8).
12 Eg Cases 40–48, 50, 54–56, 111, 113 and 114/73 *Cooperatieve Vereniging Suiker Unie UA v Commission* [1975] ECR 1663 (Re European Sugar Cartel).
13 Cases 42 and 49/59 *SNUPAT v High Authority* [1961] ECR 53 at 73.
14 [1981] ECR 1727 at 1729.
15 Order of 2 July 1987, unreported (both cases were withdrawn before judgment).
16 Case 206/85 *Beiten v Commission* [1987] ECR 5301.
17 Cases T-1 to T-4 and T-6 to T-15/89 *Rhône-Poulenc v Commission* [1990] ECR II-637 (where the CFI invited requests for confidential treatment because the cases were to be joined).
18 Ibid, para 22.
19 RP-ECJ 43; RP-CFI 50. There have also been occasions on which the Court has, with the consent of the parties, treated so-called supplementary applications as separate actions, see Case 567/79A *Flamm v Commission and Council* and Case 618/79A *Knoeppel v Commission and Council* [1981] ECR 2383 and 2387 respectively.

one or all of the parties or by the President of the ECJ (or, as the case may be, the President of the CFI) of his or her own motion (where the matter is raised by the President of his or her own motion the suggestion usually emanates from the Registry or the judge-rapporteur). A request from one of the parties need not be made by separate document as a procedural issue within the meaning of RP-ECJ 91 or RP-CFI 114 and is frequently made in the pleadings.[20] The President is not bound to accede to such requests since the matter lies within his (or her) discretion but, if all the parties are in agreement and the cases are similar in object,[21] it is apprehended that the order will be made. Where the Court raises the matter of its own motion and the parties fail to make their views on the joinder known by the date fixed for so doing, the President will simply make up his (or her) own mind.[22] The same applies where the matter is raised by one party and the other parties decline to submit observations.

The order may join direct actions for the purposes of the written procedure, the oral procedure, final judgment or all stages of the procedure.[23] Once the cases have been joined for the oral procedure, the Court might extend the joinder to the judgment stage, if it felt this to be appropriate, without hearing the parties, simply by delivering one judgment.[24] That was at a time when the Rules of Procedure specified that the decision to join cases was made by the Court itself. The Rules now provide that the decision is made by the President (whether of the ECJ or the CFI). In consequence, it would seem that an order would have to be made by the President. Similarly, the Court could join two applications and decide to rule on their admissibility in one and the same decision at the hearing concerned with their admissibility;[25] but it would appear that now the President would first have to join the cases before the Court ruled on their admissibility (although both decisions could in principle be made on the same occasion). An order joining cases for the purpose of the judgment does not preclude separate consideration of them in the same judgment.[26] So far as the earlier stages in proceedings are concerned, joinder

20 Eg in Cases 275/80 and 24/81 *Krupp Stahl A G v Commission* [1981] ECR 2489 it was made by the Commission in the defence.
21 '*Connexes par leur objet*'.
22 Eg Cases 256, 257, 265, 267/80, 5/81 *Birra Wührer SpA v Council and Commission* [1984] ECR 3693: the Court joined the cases for all purposes.
23 RP-ECJ 43; RP-CFI 50. In references for a preliminary ruling the version of RP-ECJ 103(1) in force before 1991 provided that RP-ECJ 43 applied only after the written observations had been lodged, thus leading to the inference that references for a preliminary ruling could be joined only for the purposes of the procedural stages after the end of the written procedure. The current version of RP-ECJ 103(1) provides that the Rules of Procedure apply to references for a preliminary ruling 'subject to adaptations necessitated by the nature of' such proceedings. No adaptations have been made in relation to the application of RP-ECJ 43. It may therefore be inferred that references for a preliminary ruling may in principle be joined for the purposes of the written procedure; but it seems that this is unlikely to occur in practice. However, the practice regarding the joinder of references for a preliminary ruling differs from that followed in relation to direct actions in that the parties to the preliminary ruling proceedings are not usually given an opportunity to be heard before a decision to join such cases is made.
24 See, for example, Cases 241, 242 and 245–250/78 *DGV v Council and Commission*; Cases 261 and 262/78 *Interquell Stärke-Chemie GmbH & Co v Council and Commission*; and Cases 64 and 113/76, 167 and 239/78, 27, 28 and 45/79 *Dumortier Frères SA v Council and Commission* [1979] ECR 3017, 3045 and 3091, respectively, at para 2 of the judgments.
25 Cases 31 and 33/62 *Milchwerke Heinz Wöhrmann & Sohn KG v Commission* [1962] ECR 501 at 503–504.
26 Cases 7 and 9/54 *Groupement des Industries Sidérurgiques Luxembourgeoises v High Authority* [1954–56] ECR 175 at 188 and Cases 24 and 34/58 *Chambre Syndicale de la Sidérurgie v High Authority* [1960] ECR 281 at 292.

does not prevent each party to the joined cases lodging his own pleadings and making his own submissions at the hearing. Where one of the parties appears in all the cases, however, it is usually convenient to present only one pleading covering all of the cases. One hearing would be held and one advocate general's opinion (where there is one) delivered for all the cases. Where the hearing in two or more cases is fixed for the same time, without there being a formal order joining the proceedings, the advocate general may, however, deal with all the cases in the same opinion.[27] Where cases are disjoined the remaining stages of the proceedings are conducted separately.

Proceedings may at any time be stayed by one or other of the ECJ and the CFI where both are seised of cases in which the same relief is sought, the same issue of interpretation is raised or the validity of the same act is called in question.[28] In addition: the President of the ECJ has a general power (exercisable in the form of a decision) to stay proceedings before the ECJ after hearing the advocate general and, save in references for a preliminary ruling, the parties;[29] in proceedings before the CFI a stay may be ordered in more defined circumstances. Those additional cases where proceedings before the CFI may be stayed are the following:

(1) where an appeal is brought before the ECJ against a decision of the CFI that disposes of the substantive issues in the case in part only, that disposes of a procedural issue concerning a plea of lack of competence (that is, jurisdiction) or inadmissibility or that dismisses an application to intervene;[30]
(2) where the parties jointly request a stay;[31]
(3) where third party proceedings have been brought before the CFI in respect of a judgment that is the subject of an appeal to the ECJ;[32]
(4) where proceedings for the revision of a judgment of the CFI have been commenced before the CFI and that judgment is the subject of an appeal to the ECJ;[33]
(5) where proceedings for the interpretation of a judgment of the CFI have been commenced before the CFI and that judgment is the subject of an appeal to the ECJ.[34]

In all those cases, the decision whether or not to stay the proceedings is made by the CFI in the form of an order after hearing the parties and, where applicable, the advocate general.[35] The decision whether or not to stay proceedings may be made either on the Court's own motion or on application by one of the parties under RP-ECJ 91 or (as the case may be) RP-CFI 114.[36] The

---

27 Case 28/65 *Fonzi v EAEC Commission* [1966] ECR 477 at 495 (Advocate General Roemer). The same appears to have happened in Case 238/78 *Ireks-Arkady GmbH v Council and Commission* [1979] ECR 2955 and the *DGV, Interquell* and *Dumortier* cases (above, note 24), where all the hearings were fixed for the same day and Advocate General Capotorti delivered only one opinion, despite the fact that there does not seem to have been any formal order joining them. The only order made appears to have been to join some of the cases into three separate groups for the purposes of the oral procedure.
28 See further section III above.
29 RP-ECJ 82a(1)(b). The position in references for a preliminary ruling is considered below.
30 RP-CFI 77(b).
31 RP-CFI 77(c). Eg Case T-23/92 *Cremoni v Commission*, order of 9 July 1992.
32 RP-CFI 123(4).
33 RP-CFI 128.
34 RP-CFI 129(4).
35 RP-CFI 78, 123(4), 128 and 129(4).
36 RP-CFI 77(c), which applies generally but does not limit the scope of the CFI's power to order a stay where the Rules of Procedure expressly so provide, envisages a joint request by the parties but, in practice, the CFI has discretion to raise the matter of its own motion and may do so even in response to a request made by only one party, as long as there is no objection from the other party.

proceedings may be resumed by decision of the President of the ECJ or, as the case may be, by order of the CFI after following the same procedure followed when proceedings were stayed.[37] The stay takes effect on the date indicated in the order or decision imposing the stay (or, in the absence of such indication, on the date of the order or decision) and ends on the expiry of the period of the stay (if defined in the order or decision imposing the stay) or on the date specified in the order or decision lifting the stay (or, in the absence of such a date, on the date of that order or decision); throughout the period of the stay time ceases to run for the purposes of any prescribed time limits for all parties and time begins to run afresh only from the date on which proceedings are resumed.[38] During the period of the stay time continues to run so far as persons who are not parties to the proceedings are concerned; thus, stay does not relieve any third party who wishes to intervene in the proceedings from the obligation to apply to intervene within the relevant time limit.[39]

Proceedings may be stayed where it is in the interests of justice or procedural convenience so to order: inter alia, where there are prospects that the parties may settle the dispute or that the adoption of some legislative or other measure may resolve the matters at issue;[40] where the outcome in the case will follow that in another case which can be treated as a test case or is likely to be decided first;[41] where subsequent events seemed likely to lead to further litigation rendering it unnecessary to proceed with the case;[42] or where stay was desirable in order to allow one of the parties to obtain evidence and consider its position in the light of that evidence.[43] When proceedings are resumed, they continue from where they were left at the time when the stay was imposed but the Court may require the parties to take account of any intervening events.[44]

Proceedings in staff cases are stayed automatically where the applicant has submitted to the appointing authority a complaint against an act adversely affecting him or her and has then commenced proceedings before the Court (that is, the CFI) without waiting for a response to the complaint. Ordinarily, an action commenced in such circumstances would be dismissed as inadmissible because the compulsory pre-litigation procedure in staff cases would not have been completed. A necessary condition of the admissibility of the action is that it is accompanied by an application for the suspension of the operation of the act

---

37 RP-ECJ 82a(1) (penultimate sentence); RP-CFI 78. The orders or decisions staying the proceedings or lifting the stay are served on the parties.
38 RP-ECJ 82a(2) and (3); RP-CFI 79(1) and (2).
39 This is provided for expressly in RP-CFI 79(1) and applies by necessary implication to cases pending before the ECJ.
40 Cf Case 216/84 *Commission v France* [1988] ECR 793 (in casu the hope that the infringement of the Treaty alleged against the defendant would be terminated); Case T-20/90 *Eiselt v Commission*, order of 7 February 1991 (proceedings were stayed for ten months at the joint request of the parties).
41 The situation in Case 141/85 *Dufrane v Commission* (above, notes 15 and 16). See also Cases 129 and 274/82 *Lux v Court of Auditors* [1984] ECR 4129.
42 Case T-17/90 *Camara Alloisio v Commission*, order of 15 January 1991 (proceedings were stayed sine die but were recommenced when the further litigation that was envisaged was commenced).
43 Case T-46/90 *Devillez v European Parliament*, order of 7 March 1991 (proceedings were first stayed for seven and a half weeks to allow the defendant to obtain an expert's report and then a further extension was granted when the report was obtained so that the defendant could consider what next to do).
44 For example, in Case 216/84 *Commission v France* (above, note 40), the proceedings had been stayed after the delivery of the advocate general's opinion but, when the proceedings were resumed, the Court reopened the oral procedure and asked the parties to restrict their pleadings to any points arising from national legislation that had been enacted in the meantime (see p. 801).

adversely affecting the applicant or interim measures. If the action is accompanied by such an application, it is admissible and the immediate consequence is that proceedings in the action are stayed pending the making of an express or implied decision rejecting the complaint.[45] The stay does not extend to the proceedings for interim relief since the purpose of the procedure is to enable a person adversely affected by an act to seise the Court with jurisdiction in order to obtain some form of interim relief preserving him or her from the occurrence of serious and irreparable damage while the pre-litigation procedure is still in progress. When the Court is informed that a decision rejecting the complaint has been made, the stay of the proceedings in the action is removed by a decision of the Court.[46]

Proceedings may be expedited as well as stayed. At the stage of the written procedure, proceedings are normally expedited at the initiative of the parties themselves: they may shorten the written procedure and thus speed up the disposal of the case by forgoing their right to lodge a reply or, as the case may be, rejoinder. The only provision in the Rules of Procedure dealing with expediting a case therefore concerns the position as from the oral procedure, when the progress of the case lies entirely in the hands of the Court.[47] However, the power to give a case priority over other cases is in practice exercised before the commencement of the oral procedure and may, indeed, be exercised as soon as proceedings have begun;[48] it is therefore convenient to consider it here. The Rules of Procedure provide that 'in special circumstances' the President (of the ECJ or, as the case may be, the CFI) may order that a case be given priority over others.[49] In the normal course such an order is made only on application by a party since, in the absence of such an application, setting out the reasons for it, the Court has no means of deciding whether or not one case should be given priority over another. The application should usually be incorporated in the party's first written pleading lodged at the Court: the application commencing proceedings or, as the case may be, defence;[50] a separate application seems unnecessary. If made in a subsequent written pleading or at the hearing, there would have to be particularly strong reasons to support it because, in the normal course, the failure to make an application promptly would tend to suggest that there are no particular reasons why priority should be given to the case. It is difficult to discern what may constitute the 'special circumstances' justifying the making of an order expediting the case because the reported instances of such an order being made are very few and far between. In general terms, all cases should be heard and determined as soon as possible; and an application for interim relief may be made where the normal delays in deciding a case would threaten the effectiveness of the judgment to be given by the Court.[51] The special circumstances justifying expediting a case must therefore be such as to place the case outside the normal category of cases which must suffer the delays inherent in the proper administration of justice and outside the category of cases for which some form of interim relief would be appropriate in order to cope with those

---

45 Staff Regulations, art 91(4).
46 Eg Case 90/87R *CW v Court of Auditors* [1987] ECR 1801 at 1803.
47 RP-ECJ 55(2); RP-CFI 55(2).
48 In Case 34/86 *Council v European Parliament* [1986] ECR 2155, it seems to have been exercised the day after the application commencing proceedings was registered: see pp 2157 and 2194.
49 RP-ECJ 55(2); RP-CFI 55(2).
50 In Case 34/86 *Council v European Parliament* (above, note 48) it was made in the application commencing proceedings.
51 See further chapter 8, p 230.

delays.[52] Since giving a case priority over others involves imposing on those other cases delays in their determination that would exceed what would otherwise be the case, the 'special circumstances' justifying expedition imply some public interest in the swift determination of the case that overrides the normal interest in the disposal of cases at the Court's anticipated rate of progress.[53] In weighing up the circumstances account must also be taken of the consequences of expedition for the cases affected by it and the availability of alternative possibilities, such as interim relief. Where priority is given to a case the parties will be expected to act diligently; but in practical terms that means that (if priority is ordered) the parties may not be granted any extensions of time for the lodgment of their written pleadings (save where there is very good reason) and a hearing date will be fixed at the earliest opportunity; it does not seem to be open to the Court to preclude the exercise by the parties of their right to lodge a reply or (as the case may be) a rejoinder.

Two further procedural measures generally taken at the administrative meeting remain to be considered: measures of organisation of procedure and preparatory enquiries. The distinction between those two types of measures is set out most clearly in the CFI's Rules of Procedure.[54] The ECJ's Rules of Procedure do not refer expressly to measures of organisation of procedure although such measures do feature in the practice of the ECJ and, to a considerable extent, the CFI's Rules of Procedure do nothing more than formalise a long-standing practice of the ECJ. In principle, measures of organisation of procedure and preparatory enquiries may be adopted at any time in the course of proceedings[55] but they are more usually adopted at the administrative meeting.

As defined in the CFI's Rules of Procedure, the purpose of measures of organisation of procedure is 'to ensure that cases are prepared for hearing, procedures carried out and disputes resolved under the best possible conditions'[56] and, more particularly: (i) to ensure efficient conduct of the written and oral procedure and to facilitate the taking of evidence; (ii) to determine the points on which the parties must present further argument or which call for measures of enquiry; (iii) to clarify the forms of order sought by the parties, their pleas in law and arguments and the points at issue between them; and (iv) to facilitate the amicable settlement of proceedings.[57] Measures of organisation of procedure may be prescribed, and any such measure that has already been prescribed may be modified, at any stage of the proceedings by the CFI either of its own motion[58] or on application by one of the parties.[59] The decision

---

52 Subject to the point made in the text that giving a case priority involves causing further delays to other cases before the Court, it cannot be excluded that expedition may be a more proportionate remedy than the grant of some more usual form of interim relief.
53 The facts of Case 34/86 *Council v European Parliament* (above, note 48) provide a good example.
54 See RP-CFI 64(2) and 65.
55 RP-ECJ 60 (in the case of preparatory enquiries); RP-CFI 49 (both measures of organisation of procedure and measures of enquiry). See, for example, Case T-44/90 *La Cinq SA v Commission* [1992] ECR II-1 at para 16 (an informal meeting with the parties' representatives was held while the written procedure was in course, as a result of which the applicant waived the right to lodge a reply and thus caused the written procedure to close earlier than usual).
56 RP-CFI 64(1).
57 RP-CFI 64(2).
58 As RP-CFI 49 implies. In Cases T-79, 84–86, 89, 91–92, 94, 96, 98, 102 and 104/89 *BASF AG v Commission* [1992] ECR II-315 (Re PVC Cartel) a preparatory meeting was held with the parties' representatives as a result of which certain measures of organisation of procedure were ordered (see para 6), apparently on the initiative of the CFI and as a result of certain allegations made in the written pleadings by some of the applicants.
59 RP-CFI 64(4).

to prescribe or modify a measure of organisation of procedure is made by the CFI after hearing the advocate general (if there is one) and, where the initiative has come from one of the parties, after hearing the other parties.[60] Where the procedural circumstances so require, the CFI's Registrar informs the parties of the measures envisaged by the CFI and gives them an opportunity to submit comments orally or in writing.[61] In principle, where the matter is raised by the CFI of its own motion, there is no requirement that the parties be heard before a measure of organisation of procedure is adopted: the adoption of such a measure falls within the powers of the CFI to direct its own proceedings as it thinks fit in order to dispose of cases justly and expeditiously. However, in the nature of things, the parties may have to be consulted in order to identify the most appropriate measure to adopt and select the most appropriate means of carrying it out. Where measures of organisation of procedure are prescribed by the CFI sitting in plenary session, the carrying out of the measure prescribed may be undertaken by the full Court or entrusted either to the chamber to which the case was originally assigned or to the judge-rapporteur; in the same way, where such measures are prescribed by a chamber of the CFI, they may be carried out by the chamber itself or the judge-rapporteur.[62]

The ECJ's Rules of Procedure contain no equivalent to the detailed rules laid down for the CFI concerning the adoption of measures of organisation of procedure. However, the ECJ frequently does not go to the lengths of making a formal order initiating a measure of enquiry but requests one or all of the parties (and occasionally a member state or Community institution not party to the proceedings) to supply information or produce documents. This request is made in the form of a letter from the Registrar and may ask the addressee to comply before or at the hearing. The Court may also ask the parties to argue certain points at the hearing.[63] Such requests could be regarded as informal preparatory enquiries but are in substance the same as the measures of organisation of procedure referred to in the CFI's Rules of Procedure. The continued absence from the ECJ's Rules of Procedure of any rules applying to such requests reflects in large part the fact that the simplest (and the commonest) forms of such measures do not require detailed provision in the Rules of Procedure and the fact that the more elaborate forms of such measures are unnecessary in most cases now heard by the ECJ. In contrast, the cases over which the CFI has jurisdiction at first instance tend to give rise to the kind of complex issues of fact which are best handled by means of some formal measure of organisation of procedure.[64]

Measures of organisation of procedure may take various forms. Those mentioned specifically in the CFI's Rules of Procedure[65] are the following:

---

60 RP-CFI 49, 64(1) and 64(4) (second sentence).
61 RP-CFI 64(4) (third sentence).
62 RP-CFI 64(5). In any event the advocate general (where there is one) takes part in carrying out the measures prescribed.
63 Cf Cases 83 and 94/76, 4, 15 and 40/77 *Bayerische HNL Vermehrungsbetriebe GmbH & Co KG v Council and Commission* [1978] ECR 1209 at 1212 and [1977] ECR 1222 at 1245 (Advocate-General Capotorti).
64 The simplest form of a measure of organisation of procedure is the putting of a question to the parties. Examples are legion in the case law of the ECJ. The more elaborate measures of organisation of procedure were adopted by the ECJ in actions for the annulment of Commission decisions made in application of the competition rules of the EEC Treaty. It was therefore no coincidence that, when jurisdiction at first instance over that type of case was assigned to the CFI, express provision was made in the CFI's Rules of Procedure for the adoption of measures of organisation of procedure.
65 RP-CFI 64(3). For a brief description of such measures, see B Vesterdorf, (1992) 29 CMLRev 897 at 912–915.

(1)   putting questions to the parties;[66]
(2)   inviting the parties to make written or oral submissions on certain aspects of the proceedings;
(3)   asking the parties or third parties for information or particulars;
(4)   asking for documents or any papers relating to the case to be produced;
(5)   summoning the parties' agents[67] or the parties in person to meetings.

As can be seen, some measures of organisation of procedure are virtually indistinguishable from preparatory enquiries.[68] The following provide illustrations of the type of measure encountered in practice: a meeting between the judge-rapporteur and the parties with a view to seeking a solution to the dispute (at the meeting the parties expressed their views in the light of information provided by the judge-rapporteur and in response to questions put by him; and there was a further exchange of views in writing);[69] a request that the parties indicate which annexes to their pleadings were the most important;[70] an informal meeting between the parties' representatives and the judge-rapporteur in order to determine the organisation of the oral procedure;[71] requests for information and the production of documents;[72] a request that a third party attend the hearing and be represented in order to provide the Court with any necessary information;[73] a request that the parties try to reach agreement on certain facts in issue[74] or a meeting to the same end;[75] a meeting between the parties' representatives, the judge-rapporteur and the advocate general to see if the issues can be clarified or agreed.[76] In Cases T-68, 77 and 78/89 *Società Italiano Vetro SpA v Commission*[77] the judge-rapporteur held a meeting with the parties' representatives at which he indicated to them that he wanted the reports for the hearing in the cases to be agreed and a common file of documents compiled containing everything that the parties considered to be important; he therefore asked the parties for their comments on the draft reports for the hearing and a draft list of documents. He also invited the defendant to produce the originals of the documentary evidence on which it wished to rely. The parties were able to agree the statistical evidence and the lack of any need for experts' reports; agreement was also reached on the need for witnesses and on the transcription of handwritten documentary evidence. The defendant admitted that a particular point at issue was essential to its

---

66 The parties may be asked to respond in writing before (or after) the hearing or orally at the hearing.
67 Since the member states and the Community institutions are alone represented by agents, it is implicit that the lawyer or lawyers representing the parties may also be summoned.
68 For example, requests for information and the production of documents: compare RP-CFI 64(3)(c) and (d) with RP-CFI 65(b). The difference seems to be purely formal.
69 Case 17/83 *Angelidis v Commission* [1984] ECR 2907 at 2910.
70 Case 75/84 *Metro – SB-Grossmärkte GmbH & Co KG v Commission* [1986] ECR 3021 at 3031.
71 Eg Case T-7/89 *SA Hercules Chemicals NV v Commission* [1991] ECR II-1711, para 21.
72 Eg Case T-41/90 *Barassi v Commission* [1992] ECR II-159, para 10; Case T-42/90 *Bertelli v Commission* [1992] ECR II-181, para 10; Case T-8/90 *Colmant v Commission* [1992] ECR II-469, para 13.
73 Case 23/86R *United Kingdom v European Parliament* [1986] ECR 1085, para 3 (the third party was the Commission and the formal basis for the request was EC Statute, art 21, second para).
74 Case 85/76 *Hoffmann-La Roche & Co AG v Commission* [1979] ECR 461 at 502 to 508.
75 Case 258/78 *LC Nungesser KG and Eisele v Commission* [1982] ECR 2015 at 2024.
76 Cases 100–103/80 *SA Musique Diffusion Française v Commission* [1983] ECR 1825 at 1837 (following the meeting the parties were able to define the issues of fact and law). See also Case 323/82 *SA Intermills v Commission* [1984] ECR 3809 at 3814 (the meeting appears to have been inaccurately described in the report of the case as a preparatory enquiry).
77 [1992] ECR II-1403 (Re Italian Flat Glass), paras 41–52 and 89–94.

case. Following the meeting (at which the parties also agreed that the cases should be joined) a list of documents and the report for the hearing were agreed. The defendant duly produced the originals of the documents on which it wished to rely, which revealed that the defendant had tampered with some of them.

The Court orders a preparatory enquiry when it appears from the written pleadings or any measures of organisation of procedure that have been carried out that further evidence must be sought for the purpose of resolving some or all of the issues of fact in the case.[78] The decision is made after hearing the advocate general (where there is one) but the parties are not heard unless the preparatory enquiry envisaged is the examination of a witness, the commissioning of an expert's report or the inspection of a place or thing.[79] The onus lies on the parties during the written procedure to indicate in their pleadings the facts on which they rely and, for the purposes of proof, this necessitates that they specify the means of verifying those facts (often referred to as 'offers of proof'). Where the evidence is in documentary form it must, of course, be annexed to the pleadings unless it is not in the possession or control of the party relying on it. In this event, the party should, if possible, indicate to the Court where the document may be found. The Court bases its decisions to a large extent on the recommendations of the judge-rapporteur which are usually contained in his preliminary report to the Court on the case.

A preparatory enquiry may take one of the following forms: (a) the personal appearance of the parties; (b) a request for information and production of documents; (c) oral testimony; (d) experts' reports; or (e) an inspection of the place or thing in question.[80] The decision prescribing one of these measures of enquiry is set out in a Court order which also specifies the issue or issues of fact to be determined. This order is served on the parties and they are invited to attend the enquiry.[81] Although in cases before the ECJ the order is made by the Court, the preparatory enquiry is almost invariably carried out by the chamber to which the case was originally assigned. The full Court may, however, decide to undertake the enquiry itself[82] or the enquiry may be undertaken by the judge-rapporteur.[83] In cases before the CFI, which are normally heard by a chamber and only exceptionally by the full Court, a preparatory enquiry is normally ordered by a chamber and undertaken either by the chamber itself or by the judge-rapporteur; where the case is heard by the full Court, the preparatory enquiry may be undertaken by the full Court, a chamber or the judge-rapporteur.[84] In both the ECJ and the CFI, whether it is carried out by

---

78 For example, in *BASF AG v Commission* (above, note 58) at paras 11 to 29, several applicants had alleged in the written pleadings facts suggesting that the contested decision might be vitiated by certain procedural defects. That led to a meeting with the parties' representatives, ordered by way of a measure of organisation of procedure. At that meeting there was a difference of views between the parties and, as a result of an offer of proof made by the defendant, the Court asked it to produce certain documents by way of preparatory enquiry. There was a further exchange of written pleadings between the parties concerning the documents so produced and, at the hearing, the Court ordered the defendant to produce additional evidence.

79 RP-ECJ 45(1); RP-CFI 66(1).

80 RP-ECJ 45(2); RP-CFI 65. According to the report of *SA Intermills v Commission* (above, note 76) at 3814, the ECJ in the course of its preparatory enquiries requested the judge-rapporteur and the advocate general to meet the parties before the opening of the oral procedure. Such a 'preparatory enquiry' is not expressly envisaged in the Rules of Procedure and would seem to be better classified as a measure of organisation of procedure.

81 RP-ECJ 45(1) and 46(3); RP-CFI 66(1) and 67(2).

82 RP-ECJ 44(2).

83 RP-ECJ 45(3).

84 RP-CFI 67(1).

the Court, a chamber or the judge-rapporteur, the procedure remains the same[85] and the advocate general (where there is one) takes part.[86] The manner in which the measures of enquiry are conducted is considered below.[87] The object of the preparatory enquiry is to put the Court in a position to make a finding of fact. It does not usually itself result in such a finding. When all the evidence required by the Court has been discovered, the Court may invite the parties to submit written observations by a certain date, after which the oral procedure commences.[88]

C   The oral procedure

The Statutes provide that the procedure before the Court 'shall consist of two parts: written and oral'.[89] The oral part of the procedure is therefore mandatory, not optional, so far as both the ECJ and the CFI are concerned. In addition, the oral part of the proceedings must be conducted in public unless the Court decides otherwise for serious reasons.[90] The inclusion of a public hearing in the course of judicial proceedings is generally regarded as part of the fundamental procedural guarantees accorded to the parties in legal proceedings;[91] but it is misleading to regard the requirement of an oral and, hence, public hearing as being solely in the interests of the parties to proceedings before the Court. The obligation to hear the oral submissions of the parties satisfies a public, as much as a private, concern that the parties be brought together before the Court so that each can provide a completed answer to the other's case and so that the concerns of the Court can be put to the parties and answered by them without delay. The obligation not only to hear the oral submissions of the parties but also to do so in a hearing open to the public reflects a public concern that so far as is possible justice should be administered openly. The general rule is therefore that the procedure in direct actions always contains an oral part held in public. In the Statutes and the Rules of Procedure, that general rule is dispensed with only in exceptional cases.

The Court may decide to dispense with the public nature of the hearing and exclude the public from the oral procedure only where there are 'serious reasons'; and it may so decide either of its own motion or on application by the parties.[92] An application may be made orally at the commencement of the hearing.[93] The submissions of the parties at hearings held in camera are not

---

85 RP-ECJ 46(1) and (2); RP-CFI 67(1).
86 RP-ECJ 45(3); RP-CFI 67(1).
87 See ch 11, pp 364 et seq.
88 See RP-ECJ 54.
89 ECSC Statute, art 21; EC and Euratom Statutes, art 18.
90 ECSC Statute, art 26; EC Statute, art 28; Euratom Statute, art 29.
91 Article 6(1) of the European Convention for the Protection of Human Rights and Fundamental Freedoms provides that 'in the determination of his civil rights and obligations . . ., everyone is entitled to a fair and public hearing'. It has been said that a public hearing means an oral hearing because only an oral trial can truly be said to be open to the public: *Fundamental Guarantees of the Parties in Civil Litigation*, ed M Cappelletti and D Tallon (Giuffré, 1973) at 757. Although the position of courts deciding points of law only on appeal in '*cassation*' proceedings is somewhat different (see, for example, *Axen v Germany* European Court of Human Rights, Series A No 72, (1984) 6 EHRR 195, and *Sutter v Switzerland*, ibid, Series A No 74, (1984) 6 EHRR 272), orality is an essential element in the public hearing of the parties, at least where courts of first and last instance are concerned. In this context, there appears to be no material difference between purely civil matters and the determination of rights and obligations under public law.
92 ECSC Statute, art 26; EC Statute, art 28; Euratom Statute, art 29.
93 As happened in Case 120/83R *Raznoimport v Commission* [1983] ECR 2573 and Case C-106/90R *Emerald Meats Ltd v Commission* [1990] ECR I-3377 (not referred to in the report).

published.[94] It is very rare for the Court to hold a hearing in camera. The serious reasons that may justify such a course are therefore hard to define. It would seem that a case may be heard in camera only where a party appearing in the case would be obliged to mention in the course of its address to the Court facts or matters that it, another party to the proceedings or a third party has a legitimate interest in maintaining confidential.[95] It follows from the exceptional nature of the power to hold a hearing in camera that it should be exercised only where strictly necessary. In consequence, where the revelation of the facts and matters justifying the exclusion of the public can be limited to a discrete part of the addresses of the parties to the Court, the hearing should be held in camera as to that part only and the remainder of the hearing should be held in public. It would also seem that, where an intervener has been refused access to secret or confidential documents during the written procedure in accordance with the Rules of Procedure, he (in addition to the public) may be excluded from that part of the hearing (if any) at which the secret or confidential aspects of such documents are discussed before the Court. However, there is no circumstance in which an applicant (or, as the case may be, a defendant) can be excluded from any part of the defendant's (or, as the case may be, applicant's) address to the Court.[96]

In the Rules of Procedure the hearing of the parties is dispensed with altogether only in exceptional cases, such as cases of manifest inadmissibility.[97] The existence of those exceptions does not detract from the basic principle that the substance of a person's rights and obligations cannot be determined in a direct action without a hearing. The only true exception to that principle applies in the case of proceedings before the ECJ: the ECJ's Rules of Procedure provide that, in specific cases, the ECJ may (acting on a report from the judge-rapporteur and after hearing the advocate general) decide to dispense with the oral procedure after the close of the written procedure.[98] It is implicit that the power to dispense with the oral part of the procedure can be exercised only in cases where it is apparent at the end of the written procedure that there is no need for any preparatory enquiry or measure of organisation of procedure and that the case can be decided solely on the basis of the written pleadings as they stand. As in the case of preliminary issues, it would seem that, in principle, the exercise of the power to dispense with the oral part of the procedure means that, in addition to there being no oral hearing of the parties, there is no delivery by the advocate general of an opinion on the case; but, since

---

94 RP-ECJ 56(2); RP-CFI 57. A summary of the arguments addressed to the Court at the hearing occasionally appears in the report of cases decided by the ECJ and in the body of the judgments of the CFI. It would be omitted if the hearing were held in camera. The English versions of RP-ECJ 56(2) and RP-CFI 57 suggest that the entire oral proceedings are not to be published but this is somewhat misleading: the rule does not apply to the opinion of the advocate general (where there is one).

95 Cf the *Raznoimport* case (above, note 93) (business secrets of the applicant); the *Emerald Meat* case, ibid (matters relating to a third party whose public disclosure might prejudice the interests of that third party); Case C-206/89R *S v Commission* [1989] ECR 2841, para 4, and Cases T-121/89 and T-13/90 *X v Commission* [1992] ECR II-2195, para 30 (matters relating to the applicant's medical condition).

96 See, by analogy, the position regarding the confidential treatment of documents: chapter 12.

97 RP-ECJ 92(1); RP-CFI 111.

98 RP-ECJ 44a. That provision states that the ECJ may so decide in specific cases 'after the pleadings referred to in Article 40(1) and, as the case may be, in Article 41(1) have been lodged'. Taken literally, that means that the decision can be made once the defence has been lodged and before the reply has been lodged, or between the lodgment of the reply and the rejoinder, or after lodgment of the rejoinder (that is, in the course of or at the end of the written procedure). However the intention seems to have been to refer to the last event in the course of the written procedure, whichever it might be.

the power has so far been exercised very rarely, it is difficult to discern what is the practice regarding the delivery of the advocate general's opinion.[99] As a matter of principle, a power to dispense altogether with the public hearing of the parties must be approached with the greatest of caution in case it leads to an erosion of the fundamental procedural rights of the parties and of public confidence in the proper administration of justice. The ECJ's Rules of Procedure make it clear that the ECJ may dispense with the oral part of the procedure only with the express consent of the parties.[1] That safeguard seems to satisfy any concerns that there might be about the compatibility of such a power with the fundamental procedural rights of the parties. However, it does not deal with the public interest in the open administration of justice or with the public interest in the ECJ being assisted in its task by the advocate general. It would therefore seem that the power to dispense with the oral part of the procedure is to be exercised (with the express consent of the parties) only in cases which do not give rise to issues of factual or legal complexity, which are not of general public interest and the resolution of which would not be advanced by holding a hearing. That is not to say that the parties should be required to address the Court when they do not wish to do so or see no point in doing so because they feel that they have nothing further to say. The point to be emphasised is that the decision to dispense with the oral part of the procedure is one for the ECJ to make having regard to all the relevant circumstances, not just the wishes of the parties. There may well be cases (such as disputes between Community institutions, or between a Community institution and a member state, or between member states) where the parties may well wish to avoid the embarrassment of ventilating their differences in public; but such considerations cannot override the public interest in having the dispute aired in public or in ensuring that the Court is in full possession of the material that it needs to decide the case (including an advocate general's opinion). Where the oral part of the procedure in a case is dispensed with, the ECJ can proceed to consider its decision in the case immediately after having decided to dispense with the oral part. It is unclear whether the Court's decision in the case would be made in the form of a judgment or a reasoned order. In principle, a reasoned order would not be the appropriate form but at the time of writing no practice of the ECJ had emerged.

The opening date of the oral procedure is the date of the hearing of the parties; the oral procedure terminates with the end of the hearing of the parties or, if there is an advocate general in the case, with the delivery of the advocate general's opinion. The President (of the ECJ or, as the case may be, the CFI) fixes straight away the opening date of the oral procedure where the Court decides to open the oral procedure without a preparatory enquiry or, as the case may be, a measure of organisation of procedure.[2] Where a preparatory enquiry is ordered, the President fixes the date for the opening of the oral procedure when the measures ordered have been completed.[3] The same

---

99 In Case C-377/90 *Commission v Belgium* [1992] ECR I-1229 and Case C-378/92 *Commission v Spain*, 13 October 1993, the advocate general did deliver an opinion. Since there was no hearing, the report for the hearing was replaced by a 'Judge-Rapporteur's Report' (a change of title and nothing else). For the position in the case of preliminary issues, see RP-ECJ 91(3), which similarly provides for the oral part of the proceedings to be dispensed with, in which case there is no advocate general's opinion.

1 RP-ECJ 44a. In this context 'parties' includes interveners: there is no rational basis for construing RP-ECJ 44a in a restrictive way and thus limiting the reference to 'parties' to applicants and defendants.

2 RP-ECJ 44(2); RP-CFI 53.

3 RP-ECJ 54; RP-CFI 54.

applies in proceedings before the CFI where a measure of organisation of procedure is prescribed;[4] but the practice of the ECJ is different in that, when it prescribes the equivalent of a measure of organisation of procedure, the letter informing the parties usually accompanies the notification of the date of the hearing. The opening of the oral procedure does not limit the power of the Court to order further measures of enquiry or of organisation of procedure during or after the oral procedure.[5]

In theory the Court hears cases in the order in which they are ready to be heard (ie in the order in which the preparatory enquiries are completed or, where there are no preparatory enquiries, in the order in which they are dealt with at the administrative meeting), subject to applications for interim relief, which have priority; where the preparatory enquiries in several cases are completed simultaneously, the order is determined by the date on which the proceedings in each case were commenced (ie the date on which they were first entered on the register).[6] In addition, the President may order a case to be given priority over others where there are 'special circumstances'.[7] The Court's practice is to try to give references for a preliminary ruling priority over direct actions. In fact, matters are not quite so simple because the hearings have to be fitted in where the calendar permits and by reference to the days allocated to hearings by the full Court and the chambers, respectively. In consequence, a case assigned to a particular chamber (or the Court) may be heard before another case assigned to a different chamber or the full Court, as the case may be, contrary to the proper order in which they should be heard, simply because of the availability of a hearing date. A case for which the hearing date has been fixed may be deferred where there are special circumstances.[8] The question whether or not a case should be deferred may be raised by the President on his own initiative or by the parties. Where application for deferment is made jointly by the parties, the President has discretion whether or not to make the order sought but is not required to hear any other person; where the application is made by one party[9] or the matter has been raised by the President of his own motion, the President must hear the parties and the advocate general (if there is one) before deciding whether or not to make the order.[10] An application for deferment should be made in writing, comply with RP-ECJ 37 to 38 or (as the case may be) RP-CFI 43 to 44 and set out the

---

4 RP-CFI 54. Where the parties are given an opportunity to submit written observations after the measures (of enquiry or of organisation of procedure) have been undertaken, those measures are to be taken to have been completed when the written observations have been lodged.

5 Cf RP-CFI 54. For example, in Case T-169/89 *Frederiksen v European Parliament* [1991] ECR II-1403 (paras 34 to 44), the parties were told by the Court at the end of the hearing that complementary measures of enquiry would be ordered. Those took the form of an order requiring the defendant to provide further information and produce documents relating to a particular point of fact. The information and documents produced in accordance with the order led the Court to commission an expert's report.

6 RP-ECJ 55(1); RP-CFI 55(1).

7 RP-ECJ 55(2); RP-CFI 55(2). The possibility of expediting a case is discussed above.

8 RP-ECJ 55(2) (second subpara); RP-CFI 55(2) (second subpara).

9 That is, it is opposed or the other party or parties have taken up no, or a neutral, position on the application.

10 RP-ECJ 55(2); RP-CFI 55(2). In principle, the President's power to defer a case relates only to the fixing of the date of the hearing. It is simply a question of postponing that date. There is no provision in the Rules of Procedure of either the ECJ or the CFI giving the President of either a general power to defer a case so that it may be dealt with at a later date. In practice, however, as in the case of the expediting of cases, there are instances where cases have been deferred generally. The decision to defer a case is, nonetheless, usually made after the written procedure has terminated, not beforehand.

reasons justifying putting the case back. Where it is made by one party, it should be served on the others so that they may submit their written observations.

The ECSC Statute provides that the oral procedure 'shall consist of the reading of the report presented by a Judge acting as Rapporteur, the hearing by the Court of witnesses, experts, agents and lawyers entitled to practise before a court of a Member State and of the submissions of the Advocate General'.[11] That applies to the procedure before the CFI as well as the ECJ save that in proceedings before the former the advocate general may make his submissions (that is, deliver his opinion) in writing.[12] The EC and Euratom Statutes are differently worded in that they speak of 'the hearing by the Court of agents, advisers and lawyers . . . and of the submissions of the Advocate-General, as well as the hearing, if any, of witnesses and experts';[13] but they also provide for the delivery of the advocate general's submissions in writing in proceedings before the CFI.[14] The Rules of Procedure, on the other hand, envisage that witnesses and experts are heard at the stage of preparatory enquiries and that the oral procedure commences afterwards.[15] It sometimes happens that a witness is heard immediately before the commencement of the oral procedure so that the parties and their representatives have to journey to the Court only once but, in general, witnesses do not seem to be examined during the oral procedure although the power to hear them at that stage in the proceedings is evident from the Statutes. Experts, on the other hand, are from time to time heard during the oral procedure, as will be seen.

As a rule, the oral procedure is divided into two parts: the hearing of the parties and the hearing of the advocate general's opinion[16] (where there is one). Both hearings are before the Court or chamber and the parties are invited (but are not obliged) to attend.[17] There is usually a gap of several weeks between the two so that the advocate general can prepare his opinion. The parties are informed by the Registrar of the date fixed for the hearing of their submissions and are asked to indicate for how long they are likely to address the Court so that the cause list can be drawn up. In cases heard by the full Court or by a larger chamber the parties are normally asked to keep their submissions to 30 minutes; in cases heard by a smaller chamber they are asked to speak for no more than 15 minutes. If a party does not indicate for how long he or she is likely to address the Court, the Court (or chamber) will allocate a shorter period.[18] If a party wishes to address the Court for more than the usual maximum period an application should be made to the President in good time before the date of the hearing, setting out the reasons why more time is required. Where several parties appear in the same interest they may be asked to co-ordinate their addresses to the Court in order to avoid repetition and to save time. The parties may also be asked to confine their oral submissions to particular points of concern to the Court.[19] The parties are also given a copy of a short guide to conduct at the hearing produced by the Court itself. In the event that one of the parties is unable to attend on the day fixed by the President, a request may be made for the date to be changed. Neither the

11 Article 21.
12 ECSC Statute, art 46.
13 Article 18.
14 EC Statute, art 46; Euratom Statute, art 47.
15 Cf RP-ECJ 45, 47, 54, 55 and 57; RP-CFI 54, 55, 58, 65 and 68.
16 'Submissions'.
17 From the reports of Case 224/83 *Ferriera Vittoria Srl v Commission* [1984] ECR 2349 and Case T-91/92 *Daemer v Commission*, 16 December 1993 (para 7), it would seem that the applicant did not attend the hearing of the parties.
18 Usually five minutes.
19 See, for example, Case 10/83 *Metalgoi SpA v Commission* [1983] ECR 1271 at 1274.

Statutes nor the Rules of Procedure provide a procedure for doing so but in practice it may be done by writing or telex (or even telephone if there is urgency, but there should be confirmation in writing) to the Registrar. Before the start of the hearing, the parties are served with the report for the hearing prepared by the judge-rapporteur.[20] In proceedings before the ECJ this used to form an integral part of the Court's judgment. It now comprises a self-contained section usually attached to the judgment, referred to in it and reported with it. In proceedings before the CFI the report for the hearing is drawn up solely for the purposes of the hearing. In both Courts the report consists of a summary of the facts of the case, the procedure and the arguments of the parties. It is purely descriptive and contains no findings of fact or law, although it may indicate the approach of the judge-rapporteur to the case. The parties should, however, check that it represents their side of the case accurately and if necessary write to the Registrar pointing out where it does not do so and suggesting any appropriate amendments.

The ECJ usually sits on Tuesdays, Wednesdays and Thursdays; the CFI is more flexible and may also sit on Mondays and Fridays. At the time fixed for the hearing of the case, the parties attend with their counsel in one of the courtrooms.[21] The parties' representatives wear their national robes and agents of the Community institutions wear special gowns. In the event that a party appears in person or a lawyer representing a party does not wear a gown in proceedings before the national courts before whom he or she is qualified to appear, it would seem to follow that there is no obligation to wear a gown in the proceedings before the Court. However, the President of the Court or chamber hearing the case may decide for reasons of decorum that a gown should be worn, in which case it is permissible to use one of the gowns used by the agents of the Community institutions.[22] In front of the Court bench are two tables for the parties' representatives. There is no rule laying down which is to be occupied by the applicant and which by the defendant. Generally the applicant, and those intervening in his support, and the defendant, and those supporting him, sit in separate groups. The representatives of the Commission generally sit at the table on the President's right hand but do not appear to have any prescriptive, traditional or other right to do so. Where senior counsel is accompanied by junior counsel there may not be enough room for both to sit side by side or even one behind the other. In addition, counsel addressing the Court must speak through a microphone so that what he says may be interpreted and understood by the Court. There is only one microphone for each

---

20 According to GI 17 it is supposed to be sent to them at least one week before the date of the hearing but the current practice is to aim to serve it three weeks before that date. The deadline is occasionally not met. In Case 11/63 *Lepape v High Authority* [1964] ECR 61, the applicant submitted, in an application for the reopening of the oral procedure made after the date of the hearing, that he had not received a copy of the report for the hearing and so could not challenge any inaccuracies in it. The Court held (order of 28 November 1963) that, as a copy had been duly served on him in good time, at his address for service, he was deemed to have been able to present his observations on it at the hearing, and rejected the application. Should the report for the hearing not be received at all, the party concerned should write to the Registrar for a copy. Failure to receive the report by the time the hearing has commenced does not, however, vitiate the oral procedure.

21 The ECJ uses the courtrooms on the first floor in the main court building while the CFI uses the courtrooms in the extensions to that building.

22 Thus, in Case C-168/91 *Christos Konstantinidis* [1993] ECR I-1191 (a reference for a preliminary ruling), the President required a litigant in person to wear a gown when addressing the Court. No gowns are usually worn at the hearing in an application for interim relief or in a measure of enquiry, eg where the Court or a chamber hears the testimony of a witness, but this is a matter for the President of the Court or chamber to decide.

side and there is in consequence much toing and froing in the course of a hearing in which one side or the other has more than one counsel to speak for it.

Before the case is called, counsel are invited by the Registrar, his deputy or the usher to go to the room behind the Court in order to be introduced to the members of the Court. At this point there is often an informal discussion concerning proceedings at the hearing such as the order and length of the speeches. The members of the Court, in particular the judge-rapporteur and the advocate general (where there is one), may put questions to counsel and ask them to give particular attention to certain points or issues in the case. The Court enters to the cry by the usher of 'the Court', uttered in the language of the case. The President of the Court or chamber sits in the centre with the other judges on his right and left in order of seniority. In cases heard by the full Court, he sits with the presidents of the chambers to his immediate right and left followed by the other judges (in order of seniority). The Registrar or his deputy sits to the far left of the President. In cases before the ECJ the advocate general assigned to the case sits to the President's far right. The President invites the Registrar to call the case and, after this has been done, the President opens the proceedings. As can be seen from the Statutes,[23] the hearing should commence with the reading by the judge-rapporteur of the report for the hearing. This is invariably dispensed with, the President simply saying that it can be taken as read. He then calls on counsel for the applicant to open (where a preliminary objection to the admissibility of the application has been made, it is the defendant who opens because it is he who has applied to have the action declared inadmissible). The usual order of speeches is applicant, those who have intervened in his support (in the order: member states, Community institutions, other persons), defendant, and, lastly, those who have intervened in his support. Each speaker is given an opportunity to reply. The object of the reply is to deal with the points raised by the representatives of the other parties and not to repeat the opening speech. The President may allow the parties to respond to a reply but this is, naturally, dependent on the circumstances. The President and other members of the Court may put questions to the parties.[24] Questions and interjections may be made by the members of the Court during or at the end of the speeches. The usual practice followed at the time of writing was that the members of the Court would put their questions to the parties after all the parties had made their opening speeches to the Court and before any replies. Interventions from the members of the Court are considerably less frequent than they are in, for example, British courts. At the end of the hearing, the President either declares the oral procedure to be closed or, where there is an advocate general, adjourns proceedings to a later date for the presentation of the advocate general's opinion.[25] It is not usual for the advocate general to deliver his opinion immediately after the parties have been heard although this does happen from time to time. It is sometimes said that to give the opinion straight away does not show due respect for the arguments put to the Court by the parties at the hearing. In many cases, however, there is no reason that the opinion should not be given immediately. Usually the date for the opinion is fixed after the hearing but sometimes the

---

23 ECSC Statute, art 21; EC and Euratom Statutes, art 18.
24 RP-ECJ 57; RP-CFI 58.
25 Cf RP-ECJ 59; RP-CFI 60 and 61. In Case T-5/92 *Tallarico v European Parliament*, 21 April 1993 (paras 20–23), the oral procedure was suspended at the end of the hearing to allow the parties an opportunity to settle the dispute. They were unable to do so and, when the CFI had been so informed, the oral procedure was formally closed, enabling the case to be taken to the next procedural stage (judgment).

President announces it when he adjourns the proceedings or the advocate general himself indicates when he intends to deliver it.

The conduct of the hearing is to some extent dependent on the President, who is responsible for directing it,[26] but some rules do exist in the Statutes and Rules of Procedure and in the practice of the Court. To begin with, a party may address the Court only through his agent, adviser or lawyer.[27] The Statutes provide, on the other hand, that the Court may examine experts, witnesses and the parties themselves at the hearing.[28] It is very rare for any of these persons to be formally examined at the hearing because this is usually done, if at all, at the preparatory enquiry stage of proceedings. However, it sometimes happens that the Court will hear an expert at the hearing on some technical matter which is best explained directly rather than through the medium of the party's representative.[29] The Court has tended to refuse to hear a party himself on the ground that he has his lawyer to speak for him. This occasionally causes difficulties where the 'party' also says he is an expert. In such a case, the President exercises his discretion in the light of the matter on which the party wishes to be heard. Where the party is represented by an agent[30] who is assisted by an adviser or a lawyer, both may address the Court. The parties may be requested to attend the hearing in person, in particular where the Court wishes to encourage[31] or confirm[32] an amicable settlement of the dispute. The Court may also hear a member state or Community institution which is not a party to the proceedings if it considers that it would be useful to do so.[33]

At the hearing, the President will normally refuse to admit a document unless it has already been served on the other parties to the case and they have consented to its production.[34] Where the other parties object to its production or their position is neutral, the matter remains within the discretion of the President and, in making his decision, he will take account of the importance of the document, the nature of the objections to its admission (if any), the ability of the other parties to respond to the points arising from the document at such a late stage in the proceedings and the reasons for the failure to produce the document at an earlier stage.[35] The hearing is not the proper place to adduce evidence (unless, of course, the Court has so ordered). All evidence should have been obtained in the course of the written procedure, in so far as documentary evidence is concerned, or during the preparatory enquiries. If, however, a new fact or new evidence has come to the attention of one of the

---

26 RP-ECJ 56(1); RP-CFI 56.
27 RP-ECJ 58; RP-CFI 59.
28 ECSC Statute, art 28; EC Statute, art 29; Euratom Statute, art 30.
29 For example, in Case T-30/89 *Hilti AG v Commission* [1991] ECR II-1439, the CFI heard expert economists who addressed the Court with the assistance of visual aids.
30 As is the case with member states and Community institutions only, see arts 20 of the ECSC Statute and 17 of the EC and Euratom Statutes.
31 Eg Case T-59/89 *Yorck von Wartenburg v European Parliament* [1990] ECR II-25; Cases T-33 and T-74/89 *Blackman v European Parliament*, 16 March 1993 (order of 12 July 1990).
32 Case T-140/89 *Della Pietra v Commission* [1990] ECR II-717.
33 Eg Case 23/86R *United Kingdom v European Parliament* [1986] ECR 1085 at para 3.
34 Eg Case 9/83 *Eisen und Metall AG v Commission* [1984] ECR 2071 at 2092. In Case 109/83 *Eurico Srl v Commission* [1984] ECR 3581 documents were also produced at the hearing but it is unclear whether or not the other party consented to their admission (see p 3597).
35 In Case C-156/87 *Gestetner Holdings plc v Council and Commission* [1990] ECR I-781 the President refused to admit documents at the hearing because of an inordinate delay between the end of the written procedure (at which point their importance became evident) and the point at which they were produced, for which no reason was given (the decision is not referred to in the report of the case).

parties, the proper course to adopt is either to request the Court to exercise its power under RP-ECJ 60 or (as the case may be) RP-CFI 49 to order a measure of enquiry or repeat or expand a previous enquiry; or else (if the new material is in documentary form) to make an application under RP-ECJ 91 or, as the case may be, RP-CFI 114 for leave to introduce the relevant documents.[36]

The content of a party's oral submissions should take into account the fact that the issues in the case should have been fully argued during the written procedure. The hearing is an opportunity to synthesise the issues and answer any points left outstanding in the opposing party's pleadings. Counsel may cite the pleadings, extracts from the evidence, the Court's case law etc, but extensive quotation is frowned on as being unnecessary and largely repetitive: the Court is capable of reading what is to be found in the pleadings and elsewhere. Counsel need only direct his attention to the significant extracts. As a result, the hearing is, by English standards at least, abbreviated.

Probably the most important factor to bear in mind during the hearing is the problem of language. Where necessary, counsel's submissions are interpreted simultaneously; in a French language case there will not normally be interpretation because that is the Court's working language and all its members are familiar with it.[37] However good the quality of the simultaneous interpretation, it is rarely possible to convey the full flavour and nuances of the original. It is generally better for counsel to speak freely from notes rather than read a prepared text because the latter encourages a swifter and more cursive delivery which is not always easy to interpret as the speaker is declaiming. If a written text has been prepared it is useful if the interpreters can be given a copy of it a few days before the hearing but this does not prevent counsel from diverging from his prepared text as he thinks fit. However, if he does so, he should bear in mind that the interpreters have to follow him. In any event, the delivery should be clear and at a pace that allows accurate interpretation. Presentation should for this reason be simple (for example, using a series of short sentences rather than one, long, involved sentence). Counsel are usually advised to limit their submissions to the minimum essential and not to take up all the time set aside for the hearing so that the Court can ask questions. A transcript of the hearing is made available

---

36 The latter course was adopted in Case C-213/87 *Gemeente Amsterdam and Stichting Vrouwenvaks-chool voor Informatica Amsterdam (VIA) v Commission* [1990] ECR I-221 (order of 18 April 1989) and Case C-110/89 *Commission v Greece* [1991] ECR I-2659 (order of 21 November 1990). In the first case cited the application was made two weeks before the date of the hearing. In both cases the documents in question had come to light after the party submitting them had lodged its last written pleading and therefore could not have been taken into account during the written procedure. In the first case cited the Court heard argument on the application to admit the documents at the hearing, admitted the documents because of their relevance and allowed the other party to make written submissions on them. The hearing was in consequence adjourned. In the second case cited the Court held that, after the close of the written procedure, it may authorise a party to produce those documents that appear to the Court to be useful in order to decide the case pursuant to RP-ECJ 45(2) (the equivalent provision for the CFI is RP-CFI 65). The applicant was therefore allowed to introduce documents having a direct relationship to the object of the litigation. The production of documents that provide evidence to support a party's case is not the same as the introduction of a new plea in the course of the proceedings.

37 If a member state were intervening in a case and making use of its right under RP-ECJ 29(3) or RP-CFI 35(3) to address the Court in its own official language, rather than the language of the case, interpretation would be provided even if all the members of the Court were acquainted with both. Interpretation is not merely for the benefit of the members of the Court but also for anyone else participating in the hearing.

to the Court[38] so that it has the full benefit of the parties' submissions but this is produced some time after the hearing is over and it is not then possible for points arising at the hearing which were missed at the time to be dealt with unless the Court takes the unusual step of setting a date for another hearing. Since the Court has its own transcript of the hearing it does not accept notes of the hearing made by the parties.

The advocate general delivers his opinion orally in open court in his own native language, not the language of the case (unless it happens to be his mother tongue), but the judge acting as advocate general in proceedings before the CFI may deliver his opinion in writing if he so wishes.[39] Where the opinion is delivered orally it is delivered in open court and in the presence of the judges who attended the hearing of the parties.[40] The text of the opinion is circulated to the members of the Court before its delivery and it has been questioned whether it is really necessary for the advocate general to deliver it in open court. The only justification for this seems to be that otherwise it would be uncertain whether or not the judges had read or taken the opinion into account when agreeing the judgment in the case. However that may be, the current practice is for the advocate general to read out only the concluding part of the opinion. Where in proceedings before the CFI the advocate general delivers his or her opinion in writing it is lodged at the Registry which then communicates it to the parties.[41] After the delivery of the opinion (whether orally or in writing) the President declares the oral procedure closed.[42] Where it is delivered orally a copy of the opinion is sent to the parties, if they so request,[43] and there is no purpose in them being represented when it is delivered. In his opinion the advocate general analyses the facts and points of law raised in the case and recommends to the Court a particular conclusion on them: he may also recommend that further measures of enquiry be taken,[44] that the case should be referred to the full Court or a larger chamber, or that the oral procedure should be reopened.[45]

The Court does not sit on appeal from the advocate general and in consequence the parties are not invited to comment on what he has said. The opinion is intended for the Court, not the parties, which is why it is not

---

38 Minutes of the hearing are drawn up by the Registrar and signed by him and the President; they constitute an official record of the proceedings and may be inspected by the parties at the Registry (the parties may obtain copies at their own expense): RP-ECJ 62; RP-CFI 63. The minutes are not a transcript of the hearing but they may record important statements made by the parties during the hearing: see, for example, the *Yorck von Wartenburg* case (above, note 31) at para 8. However, there is no provision in the Treaties or the Rules of Procedure allowing the Court to take formal note of a party's intention to bring an action against a Community institution: Case 141/84 *De Compte v European Parliament* [1985] ECR 1951 (para 23).

39 RP-ECJ 59(1); RP-CFI 61.

40 In Case 155/79 *AM & S Europe Ltd v Commission* [1982] ECR 1575 Advocate General Warner's opinion was delivered twice. On the first occasion it was discovered, after he had finished reading it, that one of the judges was missing. On the second occasion, with all the judges present, he simply gave his conclusions, referring to the written text of his opinion for the reasoning he followed, but not re-reading the entire opinion.

41 RP-CFI 61(1). On the first occasion on which an advocate general's opinion was delivered in proceedings before the CFI it was delivered orally: Case T-51/89 *Tetra Pak Rausing SA v Commission* [1990] ECR II-309 at 312-313.

42 RP-ECJ 59(2); RP-CFI 61(2).

43 The request may be made to the Registry. In the absence of a request the opinion is not served. Where the opinion is delivered in writing a copy is sent automatically to the parties: RP-CFI 61(1).

44 Eg Case 12/74 *Commission v Germany* [1975] ECR 181.

45 Eg Case 20/85 *Roviello v Landesversicherungsanstalt Schwaben* [1988] ECR 2805 at 2833-2834.

formally served on them (where the opinion is delivered in writing it is simply 'communicated' to them for their information). It is not proper for a party to write to the Court after the delivery of the advocate general's opinion, giving his views on it. The Court's judgment will be based on the written and oral submissions of the parties and on the advocate general's opinion. If the advocate general has misinterpreted what the parties have said, the Court may determine this by its own study of the case. It is not bound to follow the advocate general.[46]

The Court has power even at this stage in the proceedings to order that a measure of enquiry or of organisation of procedure be taken or that a previous such measure be repeated or expanded[47] and may also re-open the oral procedure[48] or order the advocate general to deliver a further opinion.[49] In the first and second cases it must hear the advocate general (where there is one). It may act either on its own motion or on application by one of the parties.[50] The power to order a measure of enquiry can be exercised at any time if the Court considers it appropriate.[51] The same criterion of appropriateness applies to the reopening of the oral procedure. The Court is sometimes led to take either step after considering the matters raised by the advocate general in his opinion.[52] Where it is a question of ordering a measure of enquiry, the determining factor is whether or not some matter of fact requires clarification. Where it is a question of reopening the oral procedure, broader considerations apply. For example, where the advocate general assigned to the case is changed after the date of the hearing but before giving his opinion[53] or a judge is unable to attend the deliberations of the Court and must be replaced by another judge who was not present at the hearing,[54] the oral procedure has to be recommenced. In such circumstances, at the second hearing the parties generally content themselves with declaring that they stand by their previous submissions and do not repeat them, the members of the Court having the benefit of the transcript of the first hearing.[55] On the other hand, the oral procedure may also be reopened because the advocate general has raised in his opinion a point of law that has not been considered by the parties;[56] where there has been an intervening change in the law;[57] or where it is considered that the Court should hear persons who were not represented at the previous hearing.[58] In such circumstances the purpose of reopening the oral

---

46 Cf Cases 36 and 71/80 *Irish Creamery Milk Suppliers Association v Ireland* [1981] ECR 735; *Delcourt v Belgium* (1979–80) 1 EHRR 35 at para 41 (European Court of Human Rights).

47 RP-ECJ 60; RP-CFI 49.

48 RP-ECJ 61; RP-CFI 62.

49 Cf Case 127/73 *BRT v SABAM* [1974] ECR 51.

50 Strictly speaking the application should be made under RP-ECJ 91 or RP-CFI 114 but it is more common for it to be made by letter and for the Court to decide the question without hearing the views of the other party. The reason for this is probably that most applications are manifestly lacking in any merit; where the matter is more debatable, the other parties are given an opportunity to submit their observations (eg Case 195/80 *Michel v European Parliament* [1981] ECR 2861).

51 Case 12/68 *X v EC Audit Board* [1969] ECR 109 at 121 (Advocate General Roemer).

52 Cf Case 140/79 *Chemial Farmaceutici SpA v DAF SpA* [1981] ECR 1 at 10.

53 Cf Cases 41, 43 and 44/73 *Générale Sucrière SA v Commission* [1977] ECR 445 at 460.

54 Cf Case 286/81 *Oosthoek's Uitgeversmaatschappij* [1982] ECR 4575 at 4584 and Case 263/81 *List v Commission* [1983] ECR 103 at 110 (where the problem arose from the death of Judge Chloros); Case 66/86 *Ahmed Saeed Flugreisen and Silver Line Reisebüro GmbH v Zentrale zür Bekämpfung Unlauteren Wettbewerbs eV* [1989] ECR 803 and Case 246/86 *Belasco v Commission* [1989] ECR 2117 (where the problem arose from the periodic partial renewal of members of the Court).

55 See, for example, the *Générale Sucrière* and *List* cases (above, notes 53 and 54).

56 Case 130/87 *Retter v Caisse de Pension des Employés Privés* [1989] ECR 865 (at 870–871).

57 The *Ahmed Saeed* case (above, note 54).

58 The *Roviello* case (above, note 45).

procedure is to consider any additional submissions that the parties may have to make.

Where application is made by a party for a measure of enquiry to be ordered or for the oral procedure to be reopened, the practice (at least of the ECJ) is to adopt a restrictive attitude. An application for a measure of enquiry may be admitted only if two conditions are satisfied: (i) it must relate to facts which are capable of having a decisive influence on the outcome of the case; and (ii) the party applying must not have been able to put them forward beforehand.[59] So far as an application to reopen the oral procedure is concerned, the Court appears to require the same conditions to be fulfilled: in Cases 2 and 3/62 *Commission v Luxembourg and Belgium*,[60] the Court rejected the application because it could not find 'anything of relevance' to justify acceding to the request and because the matters which the party applying wished to raise had been known to it before the date of the hearing and could have been argued then. In subsequent cases the Court has rejected the request because the matters sought to be raised were not decisive to resolving the dispute or simply irrelevant.[61] This does not show that it no longer applies the second condition because, the parties applying having fallen at the first hurdle, it was not necessary to consider the second.[62]

One case in which the Court does not appear to have applied the second condition is Case 195/80 *Michel v European Parliament*.[63] There the defendant had alleged a fact and the applicant conceded that it existed. On that basis the advocate general concluded that the case was inadmissible. After the delivery of his opinion, the applicant's lawyer decided to verify whether or not the fact did indeed exist. He discovered that it did not and made an application for a measure of enquiry and/or the reopening of the oral procedure. The Court ordered the latter after the defendant admitted that its assertion had been mistaken. Strictly speaking, although the matter was decisive to the case, it could have been raised beforehand had the applicant's lawyer been diligent. The Court seems to have regarded the circumstances as exceptional but, as the issue to which the fact related was the question whether or not the time limits for bringing proceedings had been observed, it is arguable that the decision is authority that the second condition does not apply where the matter in question is mandatory and should be raised by the Court of its own motion. Another exceptional case is *Irish Creamery Milk Suppliers Association v Ireland*,[64] where application was made for a measure of enquiry and/or reopening of the oral procedure so that the parties could pass comment on the advocate general's opinion and suggest how the report for the hearing might be supplemented in the light of the hearing. The Court rejected this apparently on the ground that 'all the information necessary' to enable it to decide the case was already available. It is quite clear from this that neither a measure of enquiry nor the reopening of the oral procedure will be ordered simply as a device to allow the parties to criticise the advocate general, no provision for which is

---

59 Case 77/70 *Prelle v Commission* [1971] ECR 561 (para 7).

60 [1962] ECR 425 at 445–447.

61 See Case 45/75 *Rewe-Zentrale des Lebensmittel-Grosshandels GmbH v Hauptzollamt Landau Pfalz* [1976] ECR 181 (paras 28 and 29); Case 51/75 *EMI Records Ltd v CBS United Kingdom Ltd* [1976] ECR 811 at 843; Case 26/77 *Balkan-Import-Export GmbH v Hauptzollamt Berlin-Packhof* [1977] ECR 2031 (paras 19–21).

62 Only in the *Balkan-Import-Export* case, ibid, does it seem that the second condition had been fulfilled but the matters in question were in any event irrelevant.

63 Above, note 50.

64 Above (note 46), at 745–746.

made in the Rules of Procedure.[65] On the other hand, the Court may well feel, in the light of his opinion, that it should reopen the oral procedure of its own motion.[66]

So far as the CFI is concerned, in Case T-9/89 *Hüls AG v Commission*,[67] the CFI was faced with a request for the reopening of the oral procedure for the purpose of ordering measures of enquiry directed to establishing whether or not the contested act was inexistent. The request was made some 15 months after the date of the hearing and some eight months after the delivery of the advocate general's opinion in the case. It was provoked by the fact that, in a similar case decided shortly before the request was made, the CFI had found that the contested act was inexistent because of various defects in its purported adoption. The reasons given for refusing the request were these: the mere fact that judgment had been given in the other case did not justify reopening the oral procedure;[68] the point at issue was one that it had been open to the applicant to take but it had not, even though the facts in question must have arisen before the commencement of proceedings; the Court is not obliged to initiate an investigation into the alleged inexistence of the contested act unless the parties bring forward matters sufficient to put in question the existence of the contested act (which was not the case). The CFI terminated by holding that, since the applicant's arguments could not have grounded an application for the revision of a judgment, there was similarly no ground for acceding to the request for the reopening of the oral procedure. That case was a particularly strong one for the reopening of the oral procedure having regard to the events that had happened.[69] The stance taken by the CFI indicates that it, like the ECJ, has a very reserved attitude towards applications to reopen the oral procedure (or order measures of enquiry) after the formal closure of that part of the procedure. The parallel drawn by the CFI with the conditions for entertaining an application for the revision of a judgment[70] emphasises that reserved attitude; but that approach to the criteria for deciding whether or not to reopen the oral procedure (or order a measure of enquiry at that late stage in the proceedings) does not differ in substance from the approach of the ECJ outlined above.

---

65 Case 206/81 *Alvarez v European Parliament* [1982] ECR 3369, paras 8–10.

66 Eg Cases 253/78 and 1-3/79 *Procureur de la République v Giry and Guerlain* [1980] ECR 2327, at 2359–2360, and Case 155/79 *AM & S Europe Ltd v Commission*, above (note 40), at 1616–1619.

67 [1992] ECR II-499 (paras 382–385). See also Case T-10/89 *Hoechst AG v Commission* [1992] ECR II-629 (paras 372–375); Case T-11/89 *Shell International Chemical Co Ltd v Commission* [1992] ECR II-757 (paras 372–374); Case T-12/89 *Solvay et Cie SA v Commission* [1992] ECR II-907 (paras 345–347); Case T-13/89 *ICI plc v Commission* [1992] ECR II-1021 (paras 399–401); Case T-14/89 *Montedipe SpA v Commission* [1992] ECR II-1155 (paras 389–391); Case T-15/89 *Chemie Linz AG v Commission* [1992] ECR II-1275 (paras 393–395).

68 In other words, the fact that a similar act had been held to be inexistent in another case did not deprive the contested act of the presumption of validity attaching to acts of the Community institutions; there would have to be evidence of some defect in the contested act itself rather than evidence in the nature of similar fact evidence: see the *Shell* case, ibid, para 374.

69 In the previous judgment relied on by the applicant (delivered in Cases T-79, 84 to 86, 89, 91, 92, 94, 96, 98, 102 and 104/89 *BASF AG v Commission* [1992] ECR II-315 (Re PVC Cartel)), it had been revealed that the Commission had made various significant infringements of procedure when adopting decisions in competition cases. At the hearing in those other cases, the Commission had suggested that those infringements were common. That had been repeated by representatives of the Commission to the press. Nonetheless, those statements were not considered sufficient to give cause for concern in the *Hüls* case (above, note 67) and in those related to it.

70 As to which, see chapter 16 below, pp 514 et seq.

D The judgment

In the normal course of events the Court proceeds to judgment after the delivery of the advocate general's opinion; depending upon the complexity of the case and the workload of the Court, the judgment may be delivered about a month or two after the delivery of the opinion. Not all cases proceed to judgment. The parties may, where necessary, apply to the Court for it to order the suspension of the proceedings.[71]

Further, the applicant may at any time inform the Court in writing that he wishes to discontinue proceedings, in which case the President orders the case to be removed from the Register[72] and awards costs against the applicant unless the other party has not asked for costs or the applicant establishes that discontinuance is justified by the conduct of the opposing party.[73] If the parties reach a settlement of the dispute and inform the Court that they abandon their claims before the Court rules on them, the President also orders the case to be removed from the Register,[74] the criteria for dealing with the costs being the same.[75] The case is not removed from the Register when the parties purport to settle an action for annulment or one in respect of a failure to act.[76] The reason for that seems to lie in the public interest in ensuring that the lawfulness of acts (or the failure to act) of the Community institutions be settled. It would seem that such proceedings can be terminated before judgment only if the applicant formally discontinues them;[77] but it has also been stated that once doubts as to the validity of an act (or default) of a Community institution have been aired in public they cannot be expunged by the withdrawal of proceedings and that it is inconceivable that the Court should be prevented from annulling an illegal act merely because the applicant has withdrawn.[78] It does not seem that, in a case concerning an act (or default) of interest only to the applicant, the public interest in settling the lawfulness of acts (or defaults) of the institutions would ordinarily prevail over the interest of the applicant in making an autonomous decision regarding the conduct of proceedings. At all events, the settlement of an action for annulment or in respect of a failure to act does not lead automatically to the removal of the case from the Register: before any such decision is made the parties are to be given an opportunity to explain any interest that they might have in continuing the proceedings and to answer any concern that the Court may have in allowing the proceedings to be terminated without judgment.[79] In the case of an action brought by several applicants jointly the discontinuance of the proceedings by one or more of them (whether by death, abandonment of the proceedings or, semble, as a result of a settlement with the opposing party) does not affect the position of the remaining applicants.[80]

Proceedings may also terminate without a judgment where their subject matter ceases to exist after their commencement but before the delivery of

---

71 See above. In a few exceptional cases proceedings have been suspended for very long periods (in one instance some twenty years before proceedings were eventually terminated).
72 RP-ECJ 78; RP-CFI 99. See Vandersanden and Barav *Contentieux Communautaire* (Bruylant, 1977) pp 68-69.
73 RP-ECJ 69(5); RP-CFI 87(5). Eg Case 276/83 *Commission v Greece* [1985] ECR 2751.
74 RP-ECJ 77; RP-CFI 98.
75 RP-ECJ 69(5); RP-CFI 87(5).
76 RP-ECJ 77; RP-CFI 98.
77 See, for example, Cases 109 and 114/75 *National Carbonising Co Ltd v Commission* [1977] ECR 381.
78 Case 51/87 *Commission v Council* [1988] ECR 5459 at 5469 (Advocate General Lenz).
79 Cf Cases 67, 68 and 70/85R *Kwekerij Gebroeders van der Kooy BV v Commission* [1985] ECR 1315 (para 47).
80 Case 50/84 *Bensider v Commission* [1984] ECR 3991 at 4000 (Advocate General Mancini).

judgment, or for some other reason there is no need for the Court to give judgment. In such circumstances proceedings are terminated by a decision (usually in the form of an order unless the oral procedure has by this time been opened) declaring that there is no need for the Court to give a decision.[81] The most common example of a situation where the subject matter of the action disappears in the course of proceedings, thus rendering the delivery of judgment unnecessary, is that where an act whose annulment is sought is withdrawn[82] or superseded[83] after proceedings have begun. Where the act is withdrawn and immediately replaced by another to the same effect the proceedings commenced originally against the first act can be continued against its replacement as long as the two acts are in substance identical because the subject matter of the action has not in truth disappeared.[84] The Court cannot require the defendant to maintain the contested act in force until judgment in order to preserve the subject matter of the action;[85] and any such order is unnecessary since the proceedings can be continued to judgment even if the contested act is withdrawn and not replaced as long as the applicant still has an interest in the continuation of the proceedings.[86]

The Court (or chamber) deliberates on its judgment in private and in the absence of the advocate general.[87] The draft judgment is prepared (usually in French) by the judge-rapporteur.[88] Its final form is decided by the Court (or chamber) as a body and there is no dissenting opinion. The authentic text is that in the language of the case. As the agreed version will, in most cases, be in French, the authentic version is thus a translation of the text agreed by the judges in cases where the language of the case is not French. It is vetted by a judge whose native tongue is the language of the case in order to ensure that it

---

81 Eg Case 74/81 *Rudolf Flender KG v Commission* [1982] ECR 395. In Cases 736 and 738–780/79 *Aranovitch v Commission* [1987] ECR 2425 the actions were part of a series of similar cases and the action taken as the test case was lost by the defendant. It then took the appropriate remedial action so far as all the litigants were concerned and asked the Court to declare that in the remaining cases there was no need for it to give judgment. Counsel for the remaining applicants did not have authority to discontinue the proceedings so the Court made the declaration sought by the defendant (see also Case 321/81 *Battaglia v Commission* [1987] ECR 2429.

82 Eg Cases 80–83/81 and 182–185/82 *Adam v Commission* [1984] ECR 3411 (paras 8–9).

83 Eg the situation where a regulation imposing a provisional anti-dumping duty is replaced by a regulation imposing a definitive anti-dumping duty: see, for example, Case 56/85 *Brother Industries Ltd v Commission* [1988] ECR 5655 and Cases 294/86 and 77/87 *Technointorg v Commission and Council* [1988] ECR 6077 (paras 11–14).

84 Eg Case 14/81 *Alpha Steel Ltd v Commission* [1982] ECR 749 (see also Advocate General Reischl at 775); Case 48/86R *J Cauet and B Joliet v Commission* [1986] ECR 1237 (para 4).

85 Cf the *Kwekerij Gebroeders* case (above, note 79).

86 In such circumstances that interest will ordinarily be an interest in obtaining a declaration that the contested act was unlawful for the purpose of then claiming damages. There is no such interest where a regulation imposing a provisional anti-dumping duty is replaced by one imposing a definitive duty because the unlawfulness of the former can in any event be relied on in proceedings concerning the latter: eg the *Technointorg* case (above, note 83).

87 ECSC Statute, art 29; EC Statute, art 32; Euratom Statute, art 33; RP-ECJ 27; Decision 88/591, art 2(3) (last sentence); RP-CFI 33.

88 The draft is sent to the 'reader of judgments', an official of the Court who acts under the authority of the President of the Court or, in cases allocated to a chamber, the President of the chamber concerned, and whose function is to revise the draft in order to ensure consistency in terminology and check style and presentation. The reader sends his suggestions to the judge-rapporteur and the President of the Court or the chamber, as the case may be, and his assistance may also be requested in the preparation of the draft (GI 9(a)). The necessity for the reader derives from the fact that, whereas all members of the Court know French, they cannot all draft in it easily.

corresponds to the agreed text. Occasionally there are slips.[89] The Statutes provide that the judgment must (i) state the reasons on which it is based, (ii) contain the names of the judges who took part in the deliberations, (iii) be signed by the President and the Registrar,[90] and (iv) be read in open court.[91] They add that the Court 'shall adjudicate upon costs'.[92] The Rules of Procedure are slightly more expansive and provide that the judgment shall contain:

(a) a statement that it is the judgment of the Court,
(b) the date of its delivery,
(c) the names of the President and of the judges taking part in it,
(d) the name of the advocate general (where there is one),
(e) the name of the Registrar,
(f) the description of the parties,
(g) the names of their agents, advisers and lawyers,
(h) a statement of the forms of order sought by the parties,
(i) a statement that the advocate general has been heard (where applicable),
(j) a summary of the facts,
(k) the grounds for the decision, and
(l) the operative part of the judgment, including the decision as to costs.[93]

The judgment is, in accordance with the Statutes, delivered in open court, with all the judges who took part in the deliberations present. The parties are given notice to attend to hear it[94] but only the operative part is read out and the parties are served with certified copies of the entire judgment.[95] As a result, counsel do not in practice always attend to take the judgment. The original of the judgment is signed by the President, the judges who took part in the deliberations and the Registrar, sealed and deposited at the Registry; the Registrar notes on the original the date on which it was delivered.[96] On occasion the Court delivers a so-called 'interim' or 'interlocutory' judgment, which gives a ruling on the principal issues between the parties or a direction on the law, leaving them to settle the remaining issues without prejudice to their being decided by the Court in the event that there is no agreement.[97]

---

89 Cf the variations between, on the one hand, the Danish, German and English texts and, on the other, the Dutch, French and Italian texts of para 16 of the judgment in Case 77/76 *Fratelli Cucchi v Avez SpA* [1977] ECR 987 and para 10 of the judgment in Case 105/76 *Interzuccheri SpA v Ditta Rezzano e Cavassa* [1977] ECR 1029.
90 The ECSC Statute provides that the judge-rapporteur must also sign.
91 ECSC Statute, arts 30 and 31; EC Statute, arts 33 and 34; Euratom Statute, arts 34 and 35.
92 ECSC Statute, art 32; EC Statute, art 35; Euratom Statute, art 36.
93 RP-ECJ 63; RP-CFI 81. Where a point raised in a direct action has been decided in another direct action at about the same time, the judgment in the former may simply refer to the judgment in the latter in order to explain the reasoning of the Court on that point, a copy of the judgment in the latter case being annexed to the judgment in the former: eg Case 281/84 *Zuckerfabrik Bedburg v Council and Commission* [1987] ECR 49 (para 20).
94 RP-ECJ 64(1); RP-CFI 82(1).
95 RP-ECJ 64(2); RP-CFI 82(2).
96 RP-ECJ 64(2) and (3); RP-CFI 82(2) and (3). The judgment is normally signed just before it is delivered.
97 Eg Case 238/78 *Ireks-Arkady GmbH v Council and Commission* [1979] ECR 2955; Case 170/78 *Commission v United Kingdom* [1980] ECR 417; Case 149/79 *Commission v Belgium* [1980] ECR 3881; and Cases 156/79 and 51/80 *Gratreau v Commission* [1980] ECR 3943. The recommencement of proceedings after the first judgment may be effected by letter to the Court explaining that no agreement has been reached or else that the conditions set by the Court for continuing the proceedings have been met. Although the Court generally reopens the oral procedure, it may not consider this to be necessary (see the *Gratreau* case).

Judgments of the ECJ are binding from the date of their delivery[98] and there is no appeal from them. Judgments of the CFI are also binding from the date of their delivery save that a decision of the CFI declaring a general decision (within the meaning of the ECSC Treaty) or a regulation (within the meaning of the EC and Euratom Treaties) to be void takes effect as from the date of expiry of the period for bringing an appeal against the decision before the ECJ or, where an appeal is brought within time, the date of the dismissal of the appeal by the ECJ.[99] As is clear from that provision, an appeal lies from judgments of the CFI to the ECJ; and, in the context of such an appeal, application may be made to the ECJ for the suspension of the effects of the judgment appealed against or for some other form of interim relief pending the outcome of the appeal.[1] The effects of a judgment are discussed more fully in chapter 16.

The Court may, of its own motion or on application by one of the parties, made within two weeks of delivery of the judgment, rectify clerical mistakes, errors in calculation and obvious slips.[2] This is only a slip rule and no correction of a legal error may be made by using this procedure.[3] If the Court omits to give a decision on a particular point at issue or on costs, any party may, within one month of service of the judgment, apply to the Court for it to 'supplement' its judgment. Such an application is served on the other parties in the usual manner and the President prescribes a period within which they may lodge written observations.[4] A 'point at issue', in this context, is not an argument put forward by one of the parties and refuted by the other but one of the points in the form of order, ie one of the claims put forward by one of the parties.[5]

Although there is no appeal from a judgment of the ECJ, there are two methods of seeking a review of a judgment by the ECJ itself. The first is 'third party proceedings', whereby a person not a party to the original proceedings may challenge the judgment if it is prejudicial to his rights.[6] The second method is 'revision', by which a party may seek to have the judgment revised if a new fact has since come to light which is a 'decisive factor' and which was unknown both to the Court and to the party applying for revision at the time of the judgment.[7] Lastly, there is the procedure for the interpretation of the judgment, by which any party or Community institution showing an 'interest' in a judgment of the Court may apply for it to be construed by the Court if its meaning or scope is in doubt.[8] All three procedures are considered in detail below and all three may also be relied on in relation to judgments of the CFI.[9]

V   Appeals from the CFI

An appeal may be brought before the ECJ from the following decisions of the CFI by an unsuccessful party (including an intervener) or, save in staff cases

---

98 RP-ECJ 65.

99 ECSC and EC Statutes, art 53 (second para); Euratom Statute, art 54 (second para); RP-CFI 83.

1 The Statutes, ibid. In relation to such appeals see further section V of this chapter and chapter 15, p 472.

2 RP-ECJ 66(1); RP-CFI 84(1).

3 Case 27/76 *United Brands Co v Commission* [1978] ECR 345 at 349.

4 RP-ECJ 67; RP-CFI 85. So far as the CFI is concerned, the judgment may be supplemented only if the question of costs remains undecided.

5 Both procedures are considered in more detail in chapter 16.

6 RP-ECJ 97.

7 RP-ECJ 98–100.

8 RP-ECJ 102.

9 See RP-CFI 123–124 (third party proceedings), 125–128 (revision) and 129 (interpretation).

and as the case may be, by a member state or Community institution which was not a party to the proceedings before the CFI:

(1)   final decisions;
(2)   decisions disposing of the substantive issues in a case in part only;
(3)   decisions disposing of a procedural issue concerning a plea of lack of competence or inadmissibility;
(4)   decisions dismissing an application to intervene;
(5)   decisions granting or refusing interim relief;
(6)   decisions granting or refusing a stay of enforcement of a decision of the Council or Commission.[10]

With the exception of the decisions referred to in (4) above, an appeal must be brought within two months of notification of the decisions appealed against; in the case of the decisions referred to in (4) above, the period is two weeks.[11] No appeal lies in respect of a decision of the CFI concerning only the amount of the costs to be paid or the identity of the party ordered to pay them.[12]

    An appeal is made by application to the ECJ; the application may be lodged at the Registry of either the ECJ or the CFI.[13] The application (referred to in the Rules of Procedure and hereafter as 'the appeal') must contain:

(1)   the name and address of the appellant;
(2)   the names of the other parties to the proceedings before the CFI;
(3)   the pleas in law and legal arguments relied on;
(4)   the form of order sought by the appellant;
(5)   the date on which the decision appealed against was notified to the appellant;
(6)   the appellant's address for service in Luxembourg and the name of the person who is authorised and has expressed willingness to accept service.[14]

Various documents must be attached to the appeal, including a copy of the decision appealed against, which need not be mentioned here; and the appeal must comply with the general rules governing applications made to the ECJ.[15] The scope of the appeal is limited to points of law: (a) lack of competence of the CFI; (b) breach of procedure before the CFI which adversely affects the interests of the appellant; or (c) infringement of Community law by the CFI.[16] The appeal may seek to set aside the decision of the CFI, in whole or in part, and in the same form of order as that sought at first instance, in whole or in part; a different form of order cannot be claimed and the subject matter of the proceedings before the CFI cannot be changed in the appeal.[17] The language of the appeal is that of the decision appealed against save that the ECJ may authorise use of another language in the same way as it does in direct actions, and member states are entitled to use their own official language.[18]

    Notice of the appeal is served on all the parties to the proceedings before the CFI, if necessary after the appeal has been put in order or declared admissible

---

10 ECSC and EC Statutes, arts 49 and 50; Euratom Statute, arts 50 and 51.
11 Ibid.
12 ECSC and EC Statutes, art 51 (last sentence); Euratom Statute, art 52 (last sentence).
13 RP-ECJ 111(1). Where the application is lodged at the Registry of the CFI, that Registry transmits it immediately to the Registry of the ECJ: RP-ECJ 111(2).
14 RP-ECJ 112(1) and (2).
15 RP-ECJ 112. For a fuller description of the pleading rules relating to appeals see chapter 9, pp 333 et seq.
16 ECSC and EC Statutes, art 51; Euratom Statute, art 52.
17 RP-ECJ 113.
18 RP-ECJ 110. See further section II of this chapter.

despite the existence of a formal defect.[19] Any party to the proceedings before the CFI may lodge a response to the appeal within two months of service of the notice of appeal.[20] The response must contain:

(1)   the name and address of the party lodging it;
(2)   the date on which notice of the appeal was served on him;
(3)   the pleas in law and legal arguments relied on;
(4)   the form of order sought;
(5)   the party's address for service in Luxembourg and the name of the person authorised and willing to accept service.[21]

The response must also be accompanied by certain documents which need not be mentioned here. The response may seek to dismiss the appeal, in whole or in part, or to set aside the decision of the CFI, in whole or in part; and the same form of order as that sought by the party before the CFI may be sought, in whole or in part. A different form of order cannot be sought and the subject matter of the proceedings before the CFI cannot be changed in the response.[22] The appeal and the response may be supplemented by a reply and a rejoinder or any other pleading, on application to the President made within seven days of the service of the response or the reply, as the case may be.[23] There is a right to submit a reply to a response only where the response seeks to set aside, in whole or in part, the decision appealed against on a plea of law not raised in the appeal.[24]

The proceedings follow as in a direct action and the rules relating to the introduction of new pleas in law, joinder, the presentation by the judge-rapporteur of the preliminary report on the case, the oral procedure, judgments, costs, legal aid, discontinuance, service, time limits, stay of proceedings, interim relief, intervention, assignment of cases to chambers, third party proceedings, revision and the interpretation of judgments apply mutatis mutandis.[25] The rules relating to preparatory enquiries do not apply as a matter of principle because the appeal can relate only to matters of law, not matters of fact. Appeals from a decision of the CFI dismissing an application to intervene or granting or refusing interim relief or a stay of enforcement of a decision of the Council or Commission are heard and determined by way of summary proceedings before the President.[26] An appeal does not have suspensory effect but, where appropriate, application may be made to the President of the ECJ for interim relief pending the outcome of the appeal.[27]

The procedure on appeals consists of an oral as well as a written part but the former may be dispensed with by the ECJ, acting on a report from the judge-rapporteur and after hearing the advocate general, unless one of the parties objects on the ground that the written procedure did not enable him fully to defend his point of view.[28] Where the appeal is clearly inadmissible or clearly unfounded, whether in whole or in part, the ECJ may at any time dismiss it pro tanto by reasoned order, acting on a report from the judge-

19 RP-ECJ 114.
20 RP-ECJ 115(1).
21 RP-ECJ 115(2).
22 RP-ECJ 116.
23 RP-ECJ 117(1).
24 RP-ECJ 117(3).
25 RP-ECJ 118.
26 ECSC and EC Statutes, art 50 (last para); Euratom Statute, art 51 (last para).
27 ECSC and EC Statutes, art 53; Euratom Statute, art 54.
28 ECSC and EC Statutes, art 52; Euratom Statute, art 53; RP-ECJ 120.

rapporteur and after hearing the advocate general.[29] If the appeal is well founded the ECJ quashes the decision of the CFI and either gives final judgment itself or else refers the case back to the CFI for judgment; if the case is referred back to the CFI, the CFI is bound by the decision of the ECJ on the point of law decided in the appeal.[30] Where the appeal was brought by a member state or Community institution which was not a party to the proceedings before the CFI (even as an intervener) and is upheld, the ECJ may, if necessary, state which of the effects of the decision appealed against is to be considered as definitive as between the parties to the litigation.[31]

VI References for a preliminary ruling

References for a preliminary ruling[32] are an instrument of co-operation between national courts and the ECJ which takes the form of an interlocutory step in the proceedings before a national court or tribunal designed to obtain a ruling from the ECJ on a point of Community law which has arisen in the course of the litigation between the parties.[33] The questions of Community law on which the ECJ can rule at the request of a national court concern the interpretation of the Treaties, acts of the Community institutions and certain conventions and, as the case may be, the validity of acts of the Community institutions.[34] The ECJ is alone competent to pronounce authoritatively on a question of Community law and so the procedure not only enables it to ensure the uniform interpretation and application of Community law in all the member states but it also allows a national court to seek and obtain authoritative guidance on such a point before deciding the dispute between the parties. The division of competence between the ECJ and the referring court or tribunal is not based, it has been said, 'on any hierarchical superiority of the Court but rather on a mutual exclusivity of their respective jurisdictions'.[35] The ECJ is competent to rule only on the question of Community law referred to it; the national court remains competent to decide the dispute between the parties and any other issue of fact or law. This does not, of course, mean that the referring court is free to ignore the Court's ruling on the question of the

29 RP-ECJ 119.
30 ECSC and EC Statutes, art 54; Euratom Statute, art 55.
31 Ibid.
32 See, in particular, Bebr *Development of Judicial Control of the European Communities* (Martinus Nijhoff, 1981) pp 336 et seq; Chevallier and Maidani *Guide Pratique Article 177 CEE* (1982); Hartley *The Foundations of European Community Law* (Clarendon Press, 2nd ed 1988) chaps 9 and 14; Jacobs and Durand *References to the European Court: Practice and Procedure* (Butterworths, 1975); Mortlemans (1979) 16 CMLR 557; *Article 177 EEC: Experience and Problems*, ed Schermers et al (1987); Slynn in *Law of the European Communities*, ed. D. Vaughan (Butterworths, 1990), paras 2.181 et seq.; Vandersanden and Barav *Contentieux Communautaire* (Bruylant, 1977) pp 268 et seq.
33 Cf Case 62/72 *Bollmann v Hauptzollamt Hamburg-Waltershof* [1973] ECR 269 (para 4); Case C-286/88 *Falciola Angelo v Comune di Pavia* [1990] ECR I-191 (para 7).
34 ECSC Treaty, art 41; EC Treaty, art 177; Euratom Treaty, art 150; Protocol concerning the interpretation by the Court of Justice of the Convention of 29 February 1968 on the mutual recognition of companies and legal persons (not used in practice); Protocol annexed to the Convention on Jurisdiction and the Enforcement of Judgments in Civil and Commercial Matters (referred to hereafter as 'the Brussels Convention Protocol'); First Protocol annexed to the Convention on the Law applicable to Contractual Obligations (referred to hereafter as 'the Rome Convention Protocol').
35 Bebr, p 366.

interpretation or validity of Community law with which it has been seised.[36]
The nature of the preliminary ruling procedure is such that a fully rounded
picture of the procedure requires a description of the procedure to be followed
before the national court as well as before the ECJ, an approach that strictly
speaking falls outside the scope of this work. At this point it is sufficient to
describe in general terms the proceedings before the ECJ.[37] The proceedings
before the ECJ commence with the lodgment at the ECJ's Registry of the order
for reference made by the national court. They then develop in the following
phases: written procedure; oral procedure; judgment. The procedure is
governed by the ECJ's Rules of Procedure, subject to adaptations necessitated
by the nature of references for a preliminary ruling.[38] After the delivery of
judgment by the ECJ, the proceedings before the national court continue.[39]

A   The order for reference

No express or implied requirements are laid down concerning the form and
content of the order for reference[40] and, for this reason, the Court adopts a
liberal attitude to the construction of orders for reference, interpreting them,
where necessary, so as to find the question of Community law referred when it
is not expressed clearly.[41] Where the questions referred are not framed appropriately or go beyond the jurisdiction of the ECJ, it will nonetheless do its best
to extract from all the information available to it (including the documents
before it, such as the judgment of the national court ordering the reference) the
points of Community law requiring interpretation or whose validity appears to
be at issue.[42] Nonetheless, the order for reference should contain either an
express or an implied question capable of being referred to the ECJ. The
jurisdiction of the ECJ depends upon and is defined by the question posed
(expressly or by implication): it is for the referring court alone, not the parties
or the ECJ, to determine the subject matter of the questions referred; in
consequence, the ECJ does not have jurisdiction to go outside the terms of the
reference and answer questions or problems that have not been put to it
(unless it appears that the questions put have been formulated incorrectly).[43]

---

36 See Case 29/68 *Milch- Fett- und Eierkontor GmbH v Hauptzollamt Saarbrücken (No 2)* [1969] ECR
165 (para 3): 'an interpretation given by the Court of Justice binds the national court in
question but it is for the latter to decide whether it is sufficiently enlightened by the preliminary ruling given or whether it is necessary to make a further reference to the Court'. The
effect of judgments in preliminary ruling proceedings is considered more fully in chapter 16.
37 A more detailed account of the procedure as a whole is to be found in chapter 17.
38 RP-ECJ 103(1) and (2).
39 The effect of the ruling delivered by the ECJ may be to decide the case so that the national
court has nothing further to do other than to make an order giving effect to the ruling: eg *Henn
and Darby v DPP* [1981] AC 850.
40 Case 13/61 *Kledingverkoopbedrijf De Geus en Uitdenbogerd v Robert Bosch GmbH* [1962] ECR 45 at
p 50. See also Case 101/63 *Wagner v Fohrmann and Krier* [1964] ECR 195.
41 Eg Case 228/87 *Pretura Unificata di Torino v X* [1988] ECR 5099 (paras 6–7).
42 See Case 249/84 *Ministère Public and Ministry of Finance v Profant* [1985] ECR 3237 (para 12);
Case 35/85 *Procureur de la République v Tissier* [1986] ECR 1207 (paras 9–10).
43 Eg Case 295/82 *Groupement d'Intérêt Economique Rhône Alpes Huiles v Syndicat National des Fabricants
Raffineurs d'Huile de Graissage* [1984] ECR 575 (para 12); Case 311/84 *Centre Belge d'Études de
Marché – Télémarketing SA v Compagnie Luxembourgeoise de Télédiffusion SA and Information Publicité
Benelux SA* [1985] ECR 3261 (paras 9–10); Case 247/86 *Société Alsacienne et Lorraine de Télécom-
munications et d'Electronique (Alsatel) v SA Novasam* [1988] ECR 5987 at paras 7–8 and at 6001
(Advocate General Darmon), where the national court had been asked to make a reference on
a particular point but declined to do so; Case C-337/88 *Società Agricola Fattoria Alimentare v
Amministrazione delle Finanze dello Stato* [1990] ECR I-1 (para 20); Cases C-78/90 to 83/90
Sociétés Compagnie Commerciale de l'Ouest v Receveur Principal des Douanes de la Pallice-Port [1992]
ECR I-1847 (para 15); Case C-381/89 *Syndesmos Melon tis Eleftheras Evangelikos Ekklisias v Greece*
[1992] ECR I-2111 (paras 18–19); Cases C-134 and C-135/91 *Kerafina Keramische und
Finanz-Holding AG v Elliniko Dimosio* [1992] ECR I-5699 (para 16).

However, where the question referred relates to the interpretation of a provision of Community law whose validity is fundamental to the issue in the national proceedings it seems that the ECJ should rule on the question of the validity of the provision.[44] The lack of formality concerning the order for reference can be illustrated by reference to Case 75/63 *Hoekstra (née Unger) v Bestuur der Bedrijfsvereniging voor Detailhandel en Ambachten*[45] where the referring court decided that a question of Community law had been raised but simply instructed its President to send the file of the case to the Court and it was the President, in a letter to the Registrar, who formulated the question which he said the referring court felt obliged to refer. The Court accepted this manner of proceeding but it is clearly unsatisfactory, as a matter of practice, because it may leave doubts as to whether the referring court's intentions have been properly represented. The national court may follow up the order for reference with a supplementary order for reference should it consider it to be appropriate;[46] or replace the order for reference with another one which better expresses its concerns.[47]

The Court's liberal approach to the form and content of the order for reference has, however, become less permissive over the years; more reliable guidance of a practical nature concerning the contents of the order for reference can be gleaned from the later, rather than the earlier, cases. To begin with, although the question referred can only be an abstract question of Community law, the answer depends on the context in which the question is asked. Therefore, it is helpful to the Court if the national court or tribunal sets out its findings, both of fact and national law.[48] The importance of defining properly the factual and legal matrix of the questions referred (or at least explaining the factual hypotheses on which the questions are based) is all the greater in relation to areas of Community law (such as the competition rules) where knowledge of the facts is necessary in order to provide a useful interpretation of the relevant legal provisions.[49] In addition, the referring court should explain the reasoning which led it to make the reference and the grounds on

---

44 Cf Case 20/85 *Roviello v Landesversicherungsanstalt Schwaben* [1988] ECR 2805 (para 10). Per Advocate General Mancini (at 2825–2826) the point can be taken if the national court has indicated in some way that it is concerned about the validity of the provision even if it has not requested a ruling on that point (the ECJ can consider any ground of invalidity); but it is unclear if a party to the proceedings before the referring court can raise the issue if the referring court has not considered it. See also Case 313/86 *Lenoir v Caisse d'Allocations Familiales des Alpes-Maritimes* [1988] ECR 5391 at 5410 (Advocate General Slynn): in a clear case the point can be raised by the ECJ; in case of doubt or where further argument is required the ECJ can indicate to the referring court that the question of validity is a matter to be considered. In the second alternative the ECJ would be inviting a further reference from the national court on the question of validity.

45 [1964] ECR 177 at 188–189 (Advocate General Lagrange).

46 Cf *Alsatel v Novasam* (above, note 43) at 5990.

47 Cf Case 251/83 *Haug-Adrion v Frankfurter Versicherungs-AG* [1984] ECR 4277 (para 7).

48 See Case 244/78 *Union Laitière Normande v French Dairy Farmers Ltd* [1979] ECR 2663 (paras 5–6); Cases 36 and 71/80 *Irish Creamery Milk Suppliers Association v Ireland* [1981] ECR 735 (paras 6–7); and Case 227/81 *Aubin v UNEDIC* [1982] ECR 1991 at 2008 (Advocate General Sir Gordon Slynn). Delaying the reference until the facts have been found is a matter of convenience; it is not a consideration that should be allowed to restrict the exercise of the discretion to make a reference: Case 14/86 *Pretore di Salò v X* [1987] ECR 2545 at paras 10–11.

49 Eg Cases C-320 to C-322/90 *Telemarsicabruzzo SpA v Circostel* [1993] ECR I-393 (paras 6–9); Case C-157/92 *Pretore di Genova v Banchero* [1993] ECR I-1085 (para 4); Case C-386/92 *Monin Automobiles* [1993] ECR I-2049. See also Case C-83/91 *Meilicke v ADV/ORGA AG* [1992] ECR I-4871. For that reason it is helpful if the national court sends to the ECJ its file of the case, including the pleadings of the parties and all other relevant documents. It is the practice of the Registry to ask for the file to be sent to the ECJ if the national court has not sent it with the order for reference.

which it considered an answer to the questions referred to be necessary in order to give judgment[50]; (but it would not be in the interests of procedural economy for the ECJ to refuse to answer a question referred to it merely because of a failure on the part of the referring court to explain why an answer to the question referred is necessary.[51] The national court should state reasonably clearly the question of Community law raised and the provisions of Community law in question;[52] but a failure to indicate precisely the relevant provisions of Community law is not important if they can be discerned from reading the judgment ordering the reference to be made.[53] The ECJ may decline to reply to the reference in whole or in part if it appears that there is no element of Community law which the referring court could usefully apply to the dispute before it;[54] if the question referred is expressed too generally and without reference to any specific matters making it possible to identify the concerns of the national court;[55] or if the referring court is in reality asking the ECJ to do something that properly falls within the jurisdiction of the referring court, such as applying the provision of Community law in question to the facts of the case.[56]

The admissibility of the order for reference may be raised by the ECJ of its own motion and the order for reference may be dismissed as inadmissible without any further step being taken in the proceedings.[57] Whether the question of the admissibility of the order for reference is raised by the ECJ of its own motion or by one of the parties, the order for reference cannot, it seems, be held inadmissible from the point of view of form and content, save where it is manifest that no question of Community law has arisen in the proceedings before the national court;[58] where it appears on the face of the order that the Court has no jurisdiction;[59] where it is manifest that the reference bears no relation to the real nature or object of the proceedings before the referring court;[60] or where the subject matter of the reference is not sufficiently identifiable.[61] If any of those objections to the order for reference are not manifest but

50 Case 244/80 *Foglia v Novello (No 2)* [1981] ECR 3045 (para 17); Cases 98, 162 and 258/85 *Bertini and Basignani v Regione Lazio and Unità Sanitarie locali* [1986] ECR 1885 (para 6); Case C-343/90 *Dias v Director da Alfandega do Porto* [1992] ECR I-4673 (para 19).
51 *Bertini v Regione Lazio*, above, note 50 (para 7).
52 Cf the Court's remarks in Cases 141–143/81 *Holdijk* [1982] ECR 1299 (paras 4–7) and the *Haug-Adrion* case, above, note 47 (para 9 and at 4292 per Advocate General Lenz).
53 Cases 209–213/84 *Ministère Public v Asjés* [1986] ECR 1425 (paras 14–15). See also Case C-280/91 *Finanzamt Kassel-Goethestrasse v Kommanditgesellschaft Viessmann* [1993] ECR I-971 (para 17).
54 Eg Case 132/81 *Rijksdienst voor Werknemerspensioenen v Vlaeminck* [1982] ECR 2953. See also Case C-18/92 *Chaussures Bally SA v Belgium* [1993] ECR I-2871 (paras 19–21) where the Court refused to answer a question because it was based on a hypothesis that was contradicted by the referring court's findings: in that sense, the ruling sought could not usefully be applied to the dispute before the referring court.
55 *Pretore di Salò v X* (above, note 48) at para 16.
56 Case C-320/88 *Staatssecretaris van Financiën v Shipping and Forwarding Enterprise Safe BV* [1990] ECR I-285 (para 11).
57 RP-ECJ 92(1) read with RP-ECJ 103(1). Eg Case 80/83 *Habourdin v Italocremona* [1983] ECR 3639 and Case 56/84 *Von Gallera v Maître* [1984] ECR 1769.
58 See Cases 105/79 and 68/80 *References for a Preliminary Ruling by the Acting Judge at the Tribunal d'Instance, Hayange* [1979] ECR 2257 and [1980] ECR 771 respectively.
59 Cases 104/79 *Foglia v Novello* [1980] ECR 745 and Case 244/80 *Foglia v Novello (No 2)* (above, note 50).
60 *Falciola Angelo v Comune di Pavia*, above, note 33 (para 9); Case C-368/89 *Crispoltoni v Fattoria autonoma tabacchi di Città de Castello* [1991] ECR I-3695 (para 11); Case C-186/90 *Durighello v Istituto Nazionale della previdenza sociale* [1991] ECR I-5773 (para 9); Case C-67/91 *Direccion General de Defensa de la Competencia v Asociación Española de Banca Privada* [1992] ECR I-4785 (para 26).
61 Cf the *Haug-Adrion* case (above, note 47), para 11.

may be established after more detailed scrutiny of the case, they go to the answer to be given by the ECJ to the questions referred rather than to the admissibility of the order for reference.[62] In any event, a manifest error on the part of the referring court concerning the purpose and scope of the provisions of Community law referred to in the order for reference is relevant (if at all) only to the answer to be given to the referring court and not to the question whether or not the ECJ has jursidiction to entertain the reference.[63] In principle the ECJ does not examine the circumstances in which the national court came to make the reference but it will consider those circumstances if it is manifest in the light of them that the preliminary ruling procedure has been diverted from its true purpose and is being used in the context of a contrived, spurious or non-existent dispute or if it is manifest that the provision of Community law whose interpretation is sought (or whose validity is in question) is incapable of applying to the litigation before the referring court.[64]

B The written procedure

The order for reference is notified to the Court by the referring court (not by the parties).[65] Upon receipt of the order for reference by the ECJ's Registry, it is entered on the Register in the usual way and dealt with, so far as the Court's internal procedure is concerned, like an application commencing proceedings in a direct action: the judge-rapporteur and advocate general are assigned to the case and so on. After acknowledging receipt of the order for reference the Registrar of the Court notifies it to the parties to the proceedings before the referring court, the member states, the Commission and the Council (the last if the question referred concerns the validity or interpretation of one of its acts),[66] in principle on the same day. As far as the member states are concerned, the order for reference is served in both the original language version and in a translation into the official language of the recipient member state.[67] A member state is entitled to submit observations in respect of a reference to the ECJ for the interpretation of a provision of a convention even if it is not yet a party to the convention[68] and is therefore entitled to be served with a copy of the order for reference. Service on the parties may be effected at their address

---

62 Cf Case C-159/90 *Society for the Protection of Unborn Children Ireland Ltd v Grogan* [1991] ECR I-4685 (paras 14–15).

63 Case 180/83 *Moser v Land Baden-Württemberg* [1984] ECR 2539 (paras 9–10).

64 Case 267/86 *Van Eycke v ASPA NV* [1988] ECR 4769 (para 12 and per Advocate General Mancini at 4783); Case C-150/88 *Kommanditgesellschaft in Firma Eau de Cologne and Parfumerie-Fabrik Glockengasse No 4711 v Provide Srl* [1989] ECR 3891 (para 12); Cases C-297/88 and C-197/89 *Dzodzi v Belgium* [1990] ECR I-3763 (paras 39-40); Case C-231/89 *Gmurzynska-Bscher v Oberfinanzdirektion Koln* [1990] ECR I-4003 (paras 22–23). Criminal proceedings cannot be described as a spurious or artificial dispute for these purposes: the *Asjés* case (above, note 53) at 1440 (Advocate General Lenz).

65 EC Statute, art 20; Euratom Statute, art 21. Article 5 of the Brussels Convention Protocol and Article 4 of the Rome Convention Protocol provide that the EC Treaty and Statute and the ECJ's Rules of Procedure apply to preliminary rulings made under those Protocols. For obvious reasons, the order for reference should be sent off as soon as possible, preferably by registered post.

66 The EC and Euratom Statutes, ibid; RP-ECJ 103(3). In practice all references are notified to the Council for information.

67 RP-ECJ 104(1). The ECJ allows eight to ten days for the translation of the order for reference and usually waits until all are available before notifying the order for reference to the parties, and member states, the Commission and the Council.

68 In Case 12/76 *Industrie Tessili Italiana Como v Dunlop AG* [1976] ECR 1473 (paras 5–8), a case referred under the Brussels Convention Protocol, the Court held that, by virtue of art 20 of the EC Statute, even the member states who were not yet parties to the Convention were entitled to submit observations.

for service for the purpose of the proceedings before the referring court, the address of their lawyers or, where a party is not represented, at the party's own address.[69] For this reason, it is helpful if the referring court sets out an appropriate address for service for each party in the order for reference. In this context 'parties' means all persons appearing in the proceedings before the referring court.[70] Member states are served at the Ministry for Foreign Affairs or the Embassy at Luxembourg with a copy being sent to the Permanent Representative at Brussels.[71] In the case of the Community institutions the order for reference is notified to the president and members of the institution concerned.

The persons to whom the order for reference is notified have two months from the day after notification[72] within which to submit their statements of case or written observations to the Court.[73] This period is fixed and cannot be extended on request.[74] No other person may be added to the preliminary ruling proceedings[75] unless he is first made a party to the proceedings before the national court.[76] The preliminary ruling procedure is often described as a dialogue between the referring court and the ECJ. In that sense it is not a proceeding that is inter partes; the parties are not parties in any substantive sense but only in a formal sense and, in consequence, their ability to submit observations in the course of the procedure is not part of any right to a fair hearing.[77]

The submission of written observations is not obligatory and the parties to the preliminary ruling proceedings (ie all the persons served with the order for reference) may content themselves with the submission of oral observations at the hearing.[78] In the alternative, they may decide to submit written but not oral observations. No specific requirements are laid down concerning the

---

69 GI 37(4).
70 Cf Case 2/74 *Reyners v Belgium* [1974] ECR 631 (an intervener in the national proceedings) and Case 136/78 *Ministère Public v Auer* [1979] ECR 437 ('*parties civiles*').
71 Cf GI 37(2).
72 As extended pursuant to RP-ECJ 80(2) and 81(2).
73 The EC and Euratom Statutes, ibid; RP-ECJ 103(3). There is no difference between 'statements of case' and 'written observations': for reasons of brevity the latter expression will be used here.
74 It is unclear if arts 39 of the ECSC Statute, 42 of the EC Statute and 43 of the Euratom Statute, which provide that no right shall be prejudiced by reason of the expiry of a time limit if the party concerned proves the existence of unforeseeable circumstances or of force majeure apply because no rights, stricto sensu, are at stake in the preliminary ruling procedure and the inability to submit written observations can be made up at the hearing. At all events, it seems to be the Court's practice to apply the Statutes (Mortelmans, p 564).
75 See p 154, footnote 5. The Court cannot join a third party at the request of one of the parties appearing before it: Case 19/68 *De Cicco v Landesversicherungsanstalt Schwaben* [1968] ECR 473 at 479.
76 For example, in Case 76/81 *Transporoute et Travaux SA v Minister of Public Works* [1982] ECR 417, the plaintiff before the referring court was declared insolvent after the reference had been made and its liquidators were able to submit observations in the preliminary ruling procedure only because they were given leave to continue the action by the referring court (see p 420). In Case C-262/88 *Barber v Guardian Royal Exchange Assurance Group* [1990] ECR I-1889 (at 1897–1898) the plaintiff died after the reference had been made but the referring court made an order permitting his widow to continue the proceedings in his name for and on behalf of the plaintiff's estate. That order was communicated to the ECJ.
77 *Pretore di Salò v X* (above, note 48) at 2559 (Advocate General Mancini).
78 In Case 234/83 *Gesamthochschule Duisburg v Hauptzollamt München-Mitte* [1985] ECR 327 the parties to the proceedings before the referring court did not submit any observations (para 10). Due to the short period of time allocated to parties when addressing the Court during the oral hearing it is generally unwise for a party to refrain from submitting written observations (unless it has little or nothing to say).

contents of the written observations but, as in the case of all pleadings, they should comply with RP-ECJ 37 and therefore be signed by the party's agent or lawyer;[79] be lodged together with all annexes and the correct number of certified copies; bear a date; and contain as annexes all documents relied on in support. With the exception of the member states, who may submit observations in their own official languages,[80] the parties must frame their observations in the language of the case, which is the official language of the referring court.[81] Since the object of the preliminary ruling proceedings is a decision on one or more points of Community law, the written observations should be primarily concerned with those issues and not matters of fact or of national law unless it is necessary for the purpose of deciding the issue of Community law. When the written observations are lodged at the Court it sees that any necessary translations into the language of the case are carried out and then serves on each party copies of the written observations of the other parties. The written procedure closes automatically on the expiry of the two-month period for submitting written observations (as extended on account of distance).

C The other procedural stages

After the lodgment of the written observations or the expiry of the period for doing so, the rest of the procedure follows as in a direct action from the close of pleadings (subject to certain differences explained below).[82] It need only be noted that the parties submit only one set of written observations: there is no exchange of pleadings as there is in a direct action, and the hearing is the only time at which a party in proceedings for a preliminary ruling has the opportunity to reply to what has been said by the other parties. Written observations submitted after the hearing are inadmissible.[83]

After the close of the written procedure the case is considered by the Court at an administrative meeting in the usual way. It is at this point that the decision is made about the attribution of the case to the full Court or a chamber. Since a member state or Community institution which has submitted written observations may require that the case be decided in plenary session,[84] it should request this in writing before the date of the administrative meeting.[85] It is unclear what happens if such a request is made after the Court has decided to assign the matter to a chamber. It is arguable that, in this situation, the Court no longer has power to accede to the member state's or Community institution's request unless the chamber voluntarily refers the case back to it.[86] It is, however, apprehended that neither the Court nor the chamber concerned would stand in the way of a genuine request that the matter be decided in plenary session, even if made late in time.[87] If the question referred is manifestly identical to a question on which the ECJ has already ruled, it may give its decision by reasoned order. Before doing so the ECJ must first inform the referring court, hear any observations submitted by the parties to the reference (including the member states, the Commission and the Council) and, lastly,

---

79 Save where the party concerned is entitled to appear in person: see RP-ECJ 104(2).
80 RP-ECJ 29(3).
81 RP-ECJ 29(2).
82 RP-ECJ 103(1)–(3).
83 Case 6/71 *Rheinmuhlen Düsseldorf v Einfuhr- und Vorratsstelle für Getreide und Futtermittel* [1971] ECR 719.
84 RP-ECJ 95(2).
85 The request should ordinarily be made in the written observations.
86 Cf RP-ECJ 95(3).
87 Unless, perhaps, it is made at the hearing.

hear the advocate general.[88] The obligation to inform the referring court before deciding the case by reasoned order enables the referring court to make clear to the ECJ any differences that it may perceive between the case before it and that previously decided by the ECJ. The obligation to hear the observations of the parties is adequately discharged where the earlier ruling was delivered in good time before the written observations in the case were lodged; otherwise the parties must be given an opportunity to comment specifically on the proposal to dispose of the case by reasoned order. Where the case is disposed of in that manner there is no hearing or advocate general's opinion; the judgment simply sets out in the operative part the ruling given in the previous judgment and the body of the judgment contains a reference to that previous judgment. It does not appear that a preparatory enquiry is ever ordered in the course of a reference for a preliminary ruling: the reason for that is that, in principle, the parties have their opportunity to bring forward evidence in the proceedings before the referring court[89] and the ECJ deals only with matters of law.[90] On the other hand, the ECJ may and often does adopt a measure of organisation of procedure, such as a request for the production of documents[91] or for further information.[92] The scope for such measures is limited by the fact that the ECJ may not go behind the findings of fact or of national law made by the referring court[93] or question the evidence accepted by the referring court.[94]

In a procedural sense the ECJ's only interlocutor is the referring court itself. Hence decisions taken by the ECJ in the course of proceedings relating to the expedition, stay or termination of the proceedings before judgment must ordinarily be taken at the instance of the referring court and not at the instance of the parties to the reference or another national court. Thus, once a reference has been made to the ECJ it remains seised of the reference even if the proceedings before the referring court have come to an end for some reason unless and until the referring court indicates expressly to the ECJ that it is withdrawing the reference.[95] A reference may also be withdrawn in part, as where the referring court considers that some of the questions referred have since been answered by another judgment of the ECJ; in that event the ECJ deals only with those questions referred that have not been withdrawn.[96]

---

88 RP-ECJ 104(3).

89 Case 72/83 *Campus Oil Ltd v Minister for Industry and Energy* [1984] ECR 2727 (para 11).

90 The position is considered in greater detail in chapter 10, pp 346 et seq.

91 Eg Case 5/84 *Direct Cosmetics Ltd v Customs and Excise Comrs* [1985] ECR 617 at 623, where the ECJ informed itself from a report of a UK House of Commons Committee that the judge-rapporteur had asked the United Kingdom to produce at the hearing.

92 Where a party is asked to reply to a question at the hearing but does not intend to attend the hearing, it may submit its reply in writing: see Case 158/86 *Warner Bros Inc and Metronome Video ApS v Christiansen* [1988] ECR 2605 at 2608.

93 Eg Case C-347/89 *Freistaat Bayern v Eurim-Pharm GmbH* [1991] ECR I-1747 (paras 14-17).

94 Eg Case C-332/88 *Alimenta SA v Doux SA* [1990] ECR I-2077 (para 9).

95 Cf Case C-38/89 *Ministère Public v Blanguernon* [1990] ECR I-83 at 87 (Advocate General Lenz). Thus, in Case 387/87 *Butter- und Eier Zentralgenossenschaft Oldenburg* (unreported, order of 27 October 1988), the case was removed from the register at the request of the referring court as a result of a settlement between the parties reached after the reference was made. In Case 139/88 *SA Monopole SpA v SA Compagnie des Eaux de Harre* (unreported, order of 27 October 1988), an appeal had been made against the decision to refer but the referring court had indicated that it did not want the proceedings before the ECJ to be stayed pending the outcome of the appeal. The plaintiff in the national proceedings subsequently withdrew, resulting in the termination of the action and the appeal without judgment. Both the referring court and the appeal court informed the ECJ of the termination of the proceedings and asked it to remove the case from the register. It would seem that in strictly formal terms the request need have come only from the referring court.

96 See Case C-3/90 *Bernini v Minister van Onderwijs en Wetenschappen* [1992] ECR I-1071 (para 11).

Where the decision of the referring court has been impugned directly or indirectly or, indeed, overturned in proceedings before the courts of the member state in question the reference is not for that reason alone rendered inadmissible because it must be presumed to be valid and effective unless and until formally withdrawn.[97] Where an appeal is brought before the competent national court against the referring court's decision to make the reference and the effect of the making of the appeal is to suspend the operation of the decision appealed against, the practice of the ECJ is to stay the proceedings in the reference until the outcome of the appeal is known. For the proceedings before the ECJ to be stayed in that way, the ECJ must be informed of the fact and consequences of the appeal by either the referring court itself or the court hearing the appeal.[98] If the making of the appeal does not have the effect of suspending the operation of the decision appealed against the proceedings before the ECJ will not ordinarily be stayed unless the referring court indicates that it wishes them to be stayed.[99] Where the proceedings before the ECJ are stayed pending the outcome of an appeal the referring court's file of the case is returned to it (if it is in the ECJ's possession) and a copy of the notice of appeal and the ECJ's order staying the proceedings is sent to the parties to the reference. Where the referring court's decision is upheld on appeal, the proceedings before the ECJ resume when the ECJ is so informed. The parties to the reference are then given a full period of two months (as extended, where need be, in accordance with the Rules of Procedure) in which to submit their written observations unless they had already done so before the proceedings were stayed. The President of the ECJ may give a reference for a preliminary ruling priority at the request of the referring court where there are special circumstances.[1] It does not seem that the President should accede to a request for the case to be deferred pursuant to RP-ECJ 55(2), even if made by all the parties submitting observations, without first consulting the referring court: the stay of proceedings at the request of the parties is specifically excluded in the case of references for a preliminary ruling,[2] which would suggest that the hearing of a reference for a preliminary ruling cannot be deferred at the request of the parties.

As in direct actions, a party may apply to the Court for legal aid[3] but, unlike direct actions, a party may also appear in person, without being represented by a lawyer, if he has right of audience before the referring court. The reason for this is that, as regards representation and attendance in the preliminary ruling procedure of the parties to the action before the national court, the Court 'takes account' of the referring court's rules of procedure.[4] Member

---

97 See Cases 133-136/85 *Walter Rau Lebensmittelwerke v Bundesanstalt für Landwirtschaftliche Mark-tordnung* [1987] ECR 2289 at 2304–2305 (Advocate General Lenz).

98 Thus, in Case 69/88 *Krantz GmbH & Co v Ontvanger der Directie Belastingen* [1990] ECR I-583 (see 585), where the Court was informed of the appeal and its effect by the referring court, proceedings were stayed and resumed when the appeal court upheld the referring court's decision.

99 As in Case 373/87 *Société des Auteurs, Compositeurs et Editeurs de Musique (SACEM) v Sarl La Croisette* (unreported, order of 3 February 1988), where proceedings were stayed because the referring court said that there was little point in continuing them until the outcome of the appeal was known (the decision making the reference was eventually reversed and the case removed from the register); and Cases C-100/89 and C-101/89 *Kaefer and Procacci v France* [1990] ECR I-4647 at 4651, where the referring court did not consider that the circumstances justified the staying of the proceedings when its decision had been appealed.

1 RP-ECJ 55(2): eg Case C-213/89 *R v Secretary of State for Transport, ex p Factortame* (No 2) [1990] ECR I-2433 at 2439. The request should be made in the order for reference.

2 RP-ECJ 82a(1)(b).

3 RP-ECJ 104(5): see below.

4 RP-ECJ 104(2).

states and Community institutions which are not parties to the proceedings before the national court must be represented, as is usual, by an agent. Without prejudice to the ECJ's power to give its decision in the form of an order where the questions referred are manifestly identical to questions on which the ECJ has already ruled, the procedure includes an oral part comprising, as in the case of a direct action, the hearing of the parties and the hearing of the advocate general's opinion. Acting on a report from the judge-rapporteur, after informing the parties and after hearing the advocate general the ECJ may, however, dispense with the oral part; the ECJ's power to do so is excluded if one of the parties asks to present oral argument.[5] Given the fact that, in the preliminary ruling procedure, the hearing is the only point at which a party has the opportunity to answer the case made out by an opposing party, it is clear that the exercise of the power to dispense with the oral part must be subject to the wishes of the parties. Subject to that factor, the same considerations seem to apply to the exercise of that power as in connection with the power to dispense with the hearing in a direct action.[6] At the hearing the order of speeches is normally the plaintiff or appellant before the referring court, defendant or respondent, member states, the Council and the Commission (if represented). Attendance at the hearing is not obligatory.

The Court's judgment is served on the referring court and all the persons to whom the order for reference was notified. The judgment delivered in response to a request for a preliminary ruling sets out the reasons for the ruling given but, where the issues are identical to those decided in another case (whether a preliminary ruling or a direct action), reference may simply be made to the judgment in that other case and a copy of that judgment annexed to the judgment in the former case.[7] Like all judgments, a judgment giving a preliminary ruling may be rectified where it contains clerical mistakes, errors in calculation and obvious slips.[8] However, since the judgment closes a non-contentious procedure in which the parties take no active part, other than to submit observations when so invited, none of the other procedures for supplementing,[9] interpreting[10] and reviewing[11] a judgment are applicable. If it

5   RP-ECJ 104(4). At first sight, a decision to dispense with the oral part appears to preclude the delivery of an advocate general's opinion (as in the case of direct actions). The practice is unclear: in Case C-79/91 *Knüfer v Buchmann* [1992] ECR I-6895 and Case C-331/92 *Gestion Hotelera Internacional SA v Comunidad Autonome de Canarias* (as yet unreported) the oral phase of the procedure was dispensed with but there was, nonetheless, an advocate general's opinion. It should be noted that the result of omitting the hearing was to make it impossible for the parties to comment on the implications of a judgment delivered in the course of proceedings. It would seem that, as a result of that judgment, there was no doubt about the outcome of the case and the omission of the hearing was, in consequence, justifiable (see per Advocate General Jacobs at 6908).

6   See above p 79.

7   Eg Case 195/84 *Denkavit Futtermittel GmbH v Land Nordrhein-Westfalen* [1985] ECR 3181 (where the parallel case was a direct action); Case 299/83 *SA Saint-Herblain Distribution, Centre Distributor Leclerc v Syndicat des Libraires de Loire-Océan* [1985] ECR 2515 (where the parallel case was a reference for a preliminary ruling). The past practice of the Court is now incorporated in RP-ECJ 104(3) which provides that, where a question referred to the Court is manifestly identical to a question on which it has already ruled, the Court may give the preliminary ruling sought in the form of a reasoned order referring to the previous judgment. That is done after the referring court, the parties and the advocate general have been given an opportunity to be heard.

8   RP-ECJ 66: one example is Case 244/80 *Foglia v Novello (No 2)* [1981] ECR 3045.

9   RP-ECJ 67: see Case 13/67 *Firma Kurt A Becher v Hauptzollamt München-Landsbergerstrasse* [1968] ECR 187.

10   RP-ECJ 102: see the *Becher* case (above, note 9) at 187, and Case 40/70 *Sirena Srl v Eda Srl* [1979] ECR 3169.

11   RP-ECJ 97-100.

is in some way defective or obscure, the only remedy is for the referring court to make another order for reference.[12] The judgment given by the ECJ determines conclusively the question of Community law on which it has ruled; and the judgment is therefore binding on the referring court for the purposes of the decision to be given by it in the action before it. The authority of the preliminary ruling does not prevent the referring court from making another reference (in the course of the same action before it) if the referring court encounters difficulties in understanding or applying the judgment of the ECJ or if there are new considerations which might cause the ECJ to give a different answer or if a fresh question of law has arisen; but another reference cannot be made in order to question the validity of a preliminary ruling.[13] A preliminary ruling made at the request of a court of first instance binds national courts with appellate jurisdiction[14] and is sufficient reason for any other national court faced with the same issue of Community law to decide it in the same way,[15] again without prejudice to the right of the higher court or other national court to make a further reference if it thinks it appropriate. The referring court decides the costs of the reference,[16] which means that the ECJ makes no order for costs in the final judgment so far as the parties to the proceedings before the referring court are concerned; the costs incurred by member states and Community institutions lie where they fall unless they are parties to the proceedings before the referring court, in which case the matter lies within its jurisdiction.[17]

12 The *Becher* and *Sirena* cases (above, notes 9 and 10); see also Case 135/77 *Robert Bosch GmbH v Hauptzollamt Hildesheim* [1978] ECR 855.
13 Case 29/68 *Milch- Fett- und Eierkontor GmbH v Hauptzollamt Saarbrücken* [1969] ECR 165 (para 3); Case 69/85 *Wünsche Handelsgesellschaff GmbH & Co v Germany* [1986] ECR 947 (paras 13–16). The effect of judgments in preliminary ruling proceedings is considered in chapter 16, p 497.
14 Case 338/85 *Fratelli Pardini SpA v Ministero del Commercio con l'Estero* [1988] ECR 2041 at 2058 (Advocate General Darmon).
15 Case 66/80 *International Chemical Corpn SpA v Amministrazione delle Finanze dello Stato* [1981] ECR 1191 (paras 11–14); Case 112/83 *Société des Produits de Maïs v Administration des Douanes* [1985] ECR 719 (para 16).
16 RP-ECJ 104(5).
17 Cf Cases 178–180/73 *Belgium and Luxembourg v Mertens* [1974] ECR 383 and Case 53/75 *Belgium v Vandertaelen and Maes* [1975] ECR 1647.

CHAPTER 3

Parties

The notion of a 'party' to legal proceedings can be defined in a substantive sense, as an entity benefiting from or burdened with the rights and obligations at issue in the proceedings, or in a strictly procedural sense, as an entity entitled to participate in the proceedings but not necessarily one subject to the rights and obligations which are at stake in them. In references for a preliminary ruling there are no parties in the first sense:[1] those persons who are parties to the proceedings before the referring court are entitled to submit observations in the preliminary ruling proceedings (as also are the member states, the Commission and, where appropriate, the Council)[2] in order to assist the ECJ in the discharge of its part of the dialogue between it and the referring court initiated by the making of the reference rather than for the purpose of determining any rights or obligations of the parties. This chapter is concerned primarily with the position in direct actions, where there are parties in both senses.[3] The Treaties define, in relation to each proceeding before the Court, the class of persons who may be applicant or defendant in them. For example, only the Commission can be an applicant in proceedings under art 169 of the EEC Treaty and only a member state can be a defendant.[4] In direct actions, the only other party is the intervener, who acts in defence of an interest in the proceedings and not in order to vindicate a right.[5] All these parties, applicant, defendant and intervener, can be said to possess a right to participate in proceedings but there is an additional requirement before a party can act in proceedings: he must have the capacity to exercise the right to participate in them.[6]

In broad terms, under the Treaties, the persons or entities who may be parties in proceedings can be said to fall into four categories: member states; the Communities; Community institutions; other persons or bodies.

No difficulties arise over the right to be a party or the capacity to exercise that right so far as the member states are concerned. Member states are readily

---

1 Case 14/86 *Pretore di Salò v X* [1987] ECR 2545 at 2559 (Advocate General Mancini).

2 EC Statute, art 20; Euratom Statute, art 21; RP-ECJ 103(3).

3 On the subject of parties in proceedings before the Court, see Monaco in *Il Processo Internazionale, Studi in onore di G Morrelli* p 563.

4 In proceedings under art 173 of the same Treaty, as originally worded, only the Council and the Commission were envisaged by the Treaty as capable of being a defendant while the applicant might be either a member state, the Council, the Commission or 'any natural or legal person'. The ECJ extended the class of defendants to the European Parliament (see Case 294/83 *Parti Ecologiste 'Les Verts' v European Parliament* [1986] ECR 1339, paras 23–25) and to the Court of Auditors (see Cases 193 and 194/87 *Maurissen v Court of Auditors* [1989] ECR 1045, para 42). The EU Treaty amends art 173 so as to formalise the extension of art 173 to the Parliament and so as to include the European Central Bank as a potential defendant: see art G(E)(53).

5 The position of interveners is discussed in detail below.

6 The difference can be seen in, for example, Case 135/81 *Groupement des Agences de Voyage Asbl v Commission* [1982] ECR 3799.

identifiable and, where not specifically mentioned in the Treaties, they are also comprised in the expression 'natural or legal person' or 'person'.[7] However, there may be a question about who should represent a member state in proceedings. In Community law a member state is to be understood as comprising not only the organs of central government but also the organs of local government and all branches of the legislature, executive, judiciary and administration. Entities that under national law may have legal personality distinct from that of the state in question may nonetheless be regarded as part of the state for the purposes of Community law and, in particular, the procedure before the Court. Thus, in Case 282/85 *Comité de Développement et de Protection du Textile et de l'Habillement (DEFI) v Commission*[8] the Court held that a body whose tasks were entrusted to it by a member state and whose management and policies and the interests to be protected by it were defined by the state did not represent an interest distinct from the state and so did not have a separate right of action. That principle seems to apply only where in a particular case the member state itself is implicated, as where the Commission adopts a decision addressed to a member state that concerns the activities of an entity that is regarded by Community law as forming part of the state. On the other hand, where the contested act is addressed to an entity regarded as forming part of the state, an action against that act can be brought either by that entity or by the member state itself (but not by both). Subject to those remarks, the identification of the person or body competent to represent a member state in proceedings before the Court is a matter of the internal organisation of the state concerned.

Like the member states, the Communities are easy to identify. There are three Communities, each endowed with legal personality,[9] and, in procedural terms, each is separate and distinct simply by virtue of the fact that proceedings may be brought only under or pursuant to one of the three Treaties and, hence, can involve only the Community created by that Treaty.[10] A Community is a party in rare cases, the most important of which is an action for damages, where it is the defendant. However, the Communities are not parties in a procedural sense. They do not have the capacity to exercise the right to be a party and are instead represented in legal proceedings by the Community institutions. The EC and Euratom Treaties[11] provide that the Commission represents the EC and Euratom but this relates to dealings between the Communities and third parties and to the representation of the Community before national courts; it does not mean that the Commission has a monopoly of legal representation before the Court where these Communities are concerned.[12] Hence, in staff cases, where the Court is given jurisdiction under art 179 of the EC Treaty in disputes 'between the Community and its servants', the institution or organ of the Community employing the applicant official

---

7 See, for example, Cases 7 and 9/54 *Groupement des Industries Sidérurgiques Luxembourgeoises v High Authority* [1954–56] ECR 222, where the Grand Duchy of Luxembourg was allowed to intervene under art 34 of the ECSC Statute, which provides that 'natural or legal persons' may intervene.
8 [1986] ECR 2469 (paras 17–19).
9 ECSC Treaty, art 6(1); EC Treaty, art 210; Euratom Treaty, art 184.
10 Eg Case 153/73 *Holtz and Willemsen GmbH v Council and Commission* [1974] ECR 675 at 698 (Advocate General Reischl), Case 44/76 *Milch- Fett- und Eier-Kontor GmbH v Council and Commission* [1977] ECR 393 at 412–413 (Advocate-General Reischl).
11 Articles 211 and 185 respectively.
12 Case 25/60 *De Bruyn v European Parliamentary Assembly* [1962] ECR 21 at 35 (Advocate General Lagrange); Cases 63–69/72 *Wilhelm Werhahn Hansamühle v Council* [1973] ECR 1229 at 1257 (Advocate General Roemer).

should be named as defendant, rather than the Community itself.[13] In the same way, in actions for damages brought against one of the Communities, it is the institution or institutions whose act or omission is alleged to have caused the Community to be liable which represents the Community and which, for that reason, may be named as defendant, although it is also permissible to name the Community, represented by the institution responsible.[14] This situation led Advocate General Roemer to remark in one case[15] that, in the general scheme of legal protection under the Treaties, the parties to proceedings are in principle the institutions and not the Community.

The Community institutions are those organs of the Community named as such in the Treaties.[16] Other organs created by or under the Treaties may be treated as Community institutions for procedural purposes. Thus, the European Investment Bank is not an institution but a separate body with its own legal personality.[17] As an 'organ' of the Community it is regarded as a Community institution for the purposes of actions for damages brought against the Community.[18] The European Central Bank, to be created under the EU Treaty, is also a separate body with its own legal personality[19] and is subject to a separate legal regime.[20] Nonetheless, like the European Investment Bank, it is to be regarded as a Community institution for procedural purposes. Each institution acts autonomously within the limits of its powers as defined by the Treaties.[21] However, the Treaties do not expressly state that the institutions have legal personality. It seems that, when they act within their powers, the institutions benefit from legal personality by reason of the fact that, as they represent the Communities, their acts are those of the Communities.[22] This personality is one of public law and the acts of the institutions are therefore governed by public law.[23] Originally, due to the separate legal personality of the Communities and the fact that each Treaty set up its own

13 See Case 18/63 *Wollast (née Schmitz) v Commission* [1964] ECR 85 at 96; Case 27/63 *Raponi v Commission* [1964] ECR 129 at 136; Cases 79 and 82/63 *Reynier v Commission* [1964] ECR 259 at 265; Cases 94 and 96/63 *Bernusset v Commission* [1964] ECR 297 at 306; Case 26/63 *Pistoj v Commission* [1964] ECR 341 at 351; Case 78/63 *Huber v Commission* [1964] ECR 367 at 375; Case 80/63 *Degreef v Commission* [1964] ECR 391 at 402; Case 110/75 *Mills v European Investment Bank* [1976] ECR 955 (paras 5 et seq).

14 See *Werhahn v Council*, above, note 12 (paras 7-8); *Eie-Kontor GmbH v Council and Commission*, above, note 10 (para 1 and per Advocate General Reischl, at pp 412–413).

15 *Raponi v Commission*, above, note 13 (at 142).

16 Ie the Parliament, Council of Ministers, Commission and Court of Justice. Under the EU Treaty (see arts G(B)(6), H(1) and I(1)), the Court of Auditors is included as one of the Community institutions. The Economic and Social Committee merely 'assists' the Council and the Commission (as does the Committee of the Regions created under the EU Treaty): see art 4(2) of the EC Treaty and art 3(2) of the Euratom Treaty, as amended by the EU Treaty. Neither body is formally classified as a Community institution. The Economic and Social Committee is treated as an institution under the Staff Regulations and therefore has capacity to appear before the Court in proceedings between it and one of its officials: Case 79/70 *Müllers v Economic and Social Committee of the Commission and Euratom* [1971] ECR 689 (paras 2–5). It is to be assumed that the same would apply to the Committee of the Regions.

17 EC Treaty, art 129.

18 Case C-370/89 *Société Générale des Entreprises Electromécaniques v European Investment Bank* [1992] ECR I-6211.

19 EEC Treaty, art 106(2), as amended by the EU Treaty.

20 Protocol on the Statute of the European System of Central Banks and of the European Central Bank, arts 34–35.

21 ECSC Treaty, art 6(4); EC Treaty, art 4(1); Euratom Treaty, art 3(1); Cases 7/56 and 3–7/57 *Algera v Common Assembly* [1957–58] ECR 39 at 57.

22 Cf Cases 43, 45 and 48/59 *von Lachmüller v Commission* [1960] ECR 463 at 472; Case 44/59 *Fiddelaar v Commission* [1960] ECR 535 at 543.

23 Ibid.

institutions, there were, for legal purposes, three sets of institutions, each one representing a different Community. Hence, in Case 28/64 *Müller v Commission and Euratom Councils*,[24] the action could be brought, not against the 'Council of the European Communities' but against each of the three Councils created by the Treaties, even though they shared a common secretariat. The legal unity of the institutions (but not the Communities, which remain separate legal personalities) was established by the Convention on Certain Institutions Common to the European Communities,[25] which set up a single Assembly[26] and Court of Justice for the three Communities and a single Economic and Social Committee for the EEC and Euratom, and by the Treaty establishing a Single Council and a Single Commission of the European Communities.[27] This does not, however, detract from the fact that each of the single institutions acts autonomously within its own powers: an act of the single Commission is still not an act of the Council or any other institution. Despite their autonomy among themselves, the institutions together represent each Community and, for this reason, a judgment of the Court which has the force of res judicata so far as one institution is concerned, binds the Community and, therefore, every other institution.[28]

In principle, the scheme of the Treaties is that the representation of the Communities by the institutions in legal proceedings reflects the separation of the powers of the institutions as defined in the Treaties. In most cases this is stated expressly: actions for annulment, for example, can be directed only against particular measures adopted by a specified institution;[29] the fact that another institution may have participated in the procedure leading up to the adoption of the contested act does not make that institution a proper defendant in an annulment action.[30] In other cases, such as staff disputes and, more important, actions for damages, the Treaties give no guidance. So far as the former are concerned, the matter is regulated by the Staff Regulations.[31] The rule in actions for damages is that the institution cited as defendant should be the one whose act or omission is alleged to ground the liability of the Community. This does not necessarily mean that only one institution can represent the Community in an action for damages. In Cases 63–69/72 *Werhahn v Council*[32] the applicant cited the Council for adopting the measure alleged to constitute the wrongful act and the Commission for proposing it.[33] An institution which has neither proposed nor adopted the wrongful act alleged should

---

24 [1965] ECR 237 at 247–248; see also Case 43/64 *Müller v Commission, Euratom and ECSC Council* [1965] ECR 385 at 395.

25 Signed at Rome on 25 March 1957.

26 Known as 'The Parliament'.

27 Signed at Brussels on 8 April 1965.

28 *Reynier v Commission* (above, note 13), at 265–266.

29 Cf *Reynier v Commission* (above, note 13) at 271 (Advocate General Roemer); Case 100/74 *CAM SA v Commission* [1975] ECR 1393 at 1417; Case 23/76 *Pellegrini & C Sas v Commission* [1976] ECR 1807 (para 32).

30 Eg Case 256/84 R *Koyo Seiko Co Ltd v Council and Commission* [1985] ECR 1351; Case 121/86 *Epichirisseon Metalleftikon Viomichanikon kai Naftiliakon AE v Council and Commission* [1987] ECR 1183; Case 129/86 *Greece v Council and Commission* [1987] ECR 1189; Case 150/87 *Nashua Corpn v Council and Commission* [1987] ECR 4421.

31 Proceedings must be brought against the appointing authority, ie the employing institution: see for example, Case 114/77 *Jacquemart v Commission* [1978] ECR 1697 at 1711 (order of 18 January 1978); Case 48/79 *Ooms v Commission* [1979] ECR 3121; Cases 219–228, 230–235, 237–238, 240–242/80 *André v Council and Commission* [1981] ECR 1879.

32 Above, note 12 (at para 8).

33 But see Case 253/84 *Groupement Agricole d'Exploitation en Commun (GAEC) de la Ségaude v Council and Commission* [1987] ECR 123 at 145 (Advocate General Slynn).

not be cited as defendant;[34] and, in Case 90/77 *Hellmut Stimming KG v Commission*,[35] Advocate General Mayras suggested that it is not possible to order the Community to make good damage caused by one institution when another has been cited to appear.

The last category of entities which may take part in proceedings (which includes countries other than member states) causes the most difficulty. The basic requirement is the existence of the characteristics which lie at the foundation of personality in law.[36] Initially the view taken was that it was not essential that an entity be either a legal or a natural person in the eyes of the national law governing it; bodies which did not possess legal personality in formal terms under national law might be parties to proceedings if they were endowed with the characteristics of personality which enabled them to be the subject of rights or obligations.[37] The Court identified, as the characteristics necessary for taking part in proceedings for procedural purposes, the ability, however circumscribed, to (i) undertake autonomous action and (ii) assume liability.[38] In the case of entities representing collective interests, such as trade unions, there appears to be an additional requirement: they must be truly representative of the interests which they protect or defend.[39] More recently greater emphasis has been placed on the need to satisfy the requirements of the applicable national law regarding the acquisition of legal personality. Thus, in Case 50/84 *Bensider v Commission*[40] it was held that a company in the course of formation could bring proceedings if legal personality in accordance with the relevant national law was acquired before the expiry of the period within which proceedings must be brought; if legal personality has not been acquired within that period the action is inadmissible even though there may be a practice in the member state concerned of ratifying with retrospective effect steps taken by a director of a company before its incorporation. In Case 294/83 and Case 190/84 *Parti Ecologiste 'Les Verts' v European Parliament*[41] the Court was faced with cases where, in the course of proceedings, the applicant had dissolved itself and merged with another body to form a new person to which was transferred the benefit of the original applicant's rights of action. The Court seems to have regarded the capacity to bring proceedings and the continuation of the personality of the bodies concerned as being essentially matters of national law.[42] In the result it would seem that national law ordinarily determines whether or not an entity is a legal or natural person; but that the Court will not refuse to recognise the possession of those characteristics of personality that are sufficient for participating in proceedings before the

34 Cases 56–60/74 *Kurt Kampffmeyer Muhlenvereinigung KG v Commission and Council* [1976] ECR 711 at 756 (Advocate General Reischl).
35 [1978] ECR 995 at 1013.
36 The meaning of 'legal person' in the context of Community procedural law is not necessarily the same as that in national law: see, for example, Cases 10 and 18/68 *Eridania Zuccherifici Nazionali v Commission* [1969] ECR 459 at 493 (Advocate General Roemer); Case 135/81 *Groupement des Agences de Voyage v Commission* (above, note 6) at para 10.
37 So, in *Groupement des Agences de Voyage v Commission* (above, note 6) at paras 9–12, the Court accepted that a company still in the course of formation could bring an action even though, under national law, it lacked legal personality.
38 Case 15/63 *Lassalle v European Parliament* [1964] ECR 31 at 51; Cases 41, 43–48, 50, 111, 113, 114/73 *Générale Sucrière SA v Commission* [1973] ECR 1465 at para 3.
39 See *Lassalle v European Parliament* (above, note 38) at 57 (Advocate General Lagrange); Case 175/73 *Union Syndicale v Council* [1974] ECR 917 at paras 9–13; Case 18/74 *Syndicat Général du Personnel des Organismes Européens v Commission* [1974] ECR 933 at paras 5–10.
40 [1984] ECR 3991 (paras 4–9 and see also at 4001–4005 per Advocate General Mancini).
41 [1986] ECR 1339 and [1988] ECR 1017, respectively.
42 [1986] ECR 1339 at paras 15–18 (and at 1346–1347 per Advocate General Mancini); [1988] ECR 1017 at 1026–1028 (Advocate General Mancini).

Court merely because of some technical problem under the applicable national law.[43]

Possession of the essential elements of legal personality, while sufficient to enable an entity to be a party for procedural purposes, is not necessarily sufficient to allow it a right of action: this depends on the system of remedies provided for in Community law. In the absence of express provision to the contrary, the Treaties do not enable entities representing collective interests which possess either legal personality or its essential elements to exercise a right of action held by some or all of their members or the persons or interests they represent.[44] Nor can they challenge a regulation on the basis that they group together all the persons affected by it.[45] This does not prevent such entities from defending the general interests they represent as interveners in the proceedings.[46] In general, however, they can exercise only rights of action which accrue to them personally.[47] The parent or holding company in a group of companies is in a different position. In Case 113/77 *NTN Toyo Bearing Co Ltd v Council*,[48] the applicant applied on its own behalf 'and on behalf of its subsidiaries and affiliates in the Common Market'. Apart from clarifying which were the subsidiaries and affiliates in question, no objection was taken concerning the admissibility or effectiveness of this way of proceeding.[49]

One particular restriction on the availability of rights of action concerns the ECSC Treaty which, by and large, provides that only undertakings and associations of undertakings may avail themselves of the remedies under the Treaty.[50] Undertakings are defined in art 80 of the Treaty as 'any undertaking engaged in production in the coal or the steel industry within the territories' covered by the Community[51] and, for limited purposes, 'any undertaking or agency regularly engaged in distribution other than sale to domestic consumers or small craft industries'.[52] The Court has identified the concept of an

---

43 For example, the applicant in Case 191/82 *Fédération de l'Industrie de l'Huilerie de la CEE (FEDIOL) v Commission* [1983] ECR 2913 lacked legal personality under the relevant national law but had the essential characteristics of personality and, more important, was an entity specifically envisaged by Community law as entitled to bring the proceedings in question (see at 2939–2940 per Advocate General Rozès).

44 See Cases 16 and 17/62 *Confédération Nationale des Producteurs de Fruits et Legumes v Council* [1962] ECR 471 at 479; Cases 19–22/62 *Fédération Nationale de la Boucherie en Gros et du Commerce en gros des Viandes v Council* [1962] ECR 491 at 499; *Eridania v Commission* (above, note 36) at 493 (Advocate General Roemer); *Union Syndicale v Council* (above, note 39) at 931 (Advocate General Reischl); *Syndicat Général du Personnel v Commission* (above, note 39) at 948 (Advocate General Trabucchi); Case 72/74 *Union Syndicale-Service Public Européen v Council (No 2)* [1975] ECR 401 (para 17 and, per Advocate General Reischl, at 417).

45 *Confédération Nationale des Producteurs de Fruits v Council* (above, note 44) at 480; *Fédération Nationale de la Boucherie v Council* (ibid); *DEFI v Commission* (above, note 8), para 16; Case 117/86 *Union de Federaciones Agrarias de España (UFADE) v Council and Commission* [1986] ECR 3255 (para 12).

46 *Confédération Nationale des Producteurs de Fruits v Council* (above, note 44) at 486 (Advocate General Lagrange); *Union Syndicale v Council* (above, note 39).

47 Eg Case 66/76 *CFDT v Council* [1977] ECR 305; *Groupement des Agences de Voyage v Commission* (above, note 6) at para 7; Case 43/85 *Associazione Nazionale Commerciali Internazionali Dentali e Sanitari (ANCIDES) v Commission* [1987] ECR 3131 at 3144 (Advocate General Slynn).

48 [1979] ECR 1185 at 1241 (Advocate General Warner).

49 The same approach was followed by the applicant in Case C-156/87 *Gestetner Holdings plc v Council and Commission* [1990] ECR I-781 (see 813).

50 There are some exceptions, most notably art 66(5) and actions for damages (see Cases 9 and 12/60 *Société Commerciale Antoine Vloeberghs SA v High Authority* [1961] ECR 197 at 214). Under art 34 of the ECSC Statute, only natural or legal persons may intervene.

51 The Court considered the nature of production activities in *Société Commerciale Antoine Vloeberghs SA v High Authority* (above, note 50) at 212.

52 Eg Case 1/58 *Friedrich Stork & Co v High Authority* [1959] ECR 17.

undertaking with that of a natural or legal person.[53] In consequence, two or more separate companies do not constitute an undertaking even if they are part of the same group.[54] A natural person with an interest in an undertaking is not an undertaking within the meaning of art 80,[55] but may represent an undertaking in proceedings before the Court.[56] Associations must comprise undertakings within the meaning of art 80.[57] If they do, they have a right of action, where the Treaty provides, even though the interests they represent may diverge[58] or the interests of some only of the association's members have been affected.[59] On the other hand, an association whose object is to defend and represent the interests of its members as consumers is not an 'association of undertakings' within the meaning of the Treaty, even if one at least of its members is an 'undertaking' within the meaning of art 80.[60]

The Euratom Treaty also contains a restrictive definition of some of the terms it uses to describe entities covered by it: 'person' means 'any natural person who pursues all or any of his activities in the territories of Member States within the field specified in the relevant chapter of this Treaty'; 'undertaking' means 'any undertaking or institution which pursues all or any of its activities in the territories of Member States within the field specified in the relevant chapter of this Treaty, whatever its public or private legal status'.[61] While relevant to some proceedings,[62] these limitations do not apply to the principal actions, which are open to 'any natural or legal person'.[63]

So far as other specific forms of action are concerned, reference should be made to the following. Under the Treaties,[64] staff cases may be brought by servants of the Communities, but this covers not merely persons having the status of officials or employees, other than local staff, but also their dependants and persons claiming the status of officials etc.[65] In actions brought under an arbitration clause, only parties to the clause can be party to the proceedings (other than as interveners).[66] Applications under art 1 of the Protocol on the Privileges and Immunities of the European Communities may be made by the

---

53 Cases 42 and 49/59 *SNUPAT v High Authority* [1961] ECR 53 at 80.
54 Ibid.
55 Case 12/63 *Schlieker v High Authority* [1963] ECR 85.
56 Cf Case 18/62 *Barge v High Authority* [1963] ECR 259.
57 Cases 7 and 9/54 *Groupement des Industries Sidérurgiques Luxembourgeoises v High Authority* [1954–56] ECR 175 at 189–190.
58 Case 8/57 *Groupement des Hauts Fourneaux et Aciéries Belges v High Authority* [1957–58] ECR 245 at 252; Case 13/57 *Wirtschaftsvereinigung Eisen- und Stahlindustrie v High Authority* [1957–58] ECR 265 at 276; Case 9/57 *Chambre Syndicale de la Sidérurgie Française v High Authority* [1957–58] ECR 319 at 326; Case 12/57 *Syndicat de la Sidérurgie du Centre-Midi v High Authority* [1957–58] ECR 375 at 382.
59 Case 3/54 *ASSIDER v High Authority* [1954–56] ECR 63 at 69; Case 4/54 *ISA v High Authority* [1954–56] ECR 91 at 98; Cases 140, 146, 221 and 226/82 *Walzstahl-Vereinigung and Thyssen AG v Commission* [1984] ECR 951 (paras 17–18).
60 Cases 8 and 10/54 *Association des Utilisateurs de Charbon du Grand-Duché de Luxembourg v High Authority* [1954–56] ECR 227 at 240.
61 Article 196.
62 Eg those under arts 144 and 145 of the Treaty.
63 Ie actions for annulment (art 146), a failure to act (art 148) and damages (arts 151 and 188).
64 EC Treaty, art 179; Euratom Treaty, art 152.
65 Case 116/78 *Bellintani v Commission* [1979] ECR 1585 (para 6); Case C-100/88 *Oyowe and Traore v Commission* [1989] ECR 4285 (para 7); Case 34/80 *Authié v Commission* [1981] ECR 665; Case 23/64 *Vandevyvere v European Parliament* [1965] ECR 157. For an action brought by the dependants of an official, see Cases 63 and 64/79 *Boizard v Commission* [1980] ECR 2975. It should be pointed out that the position of dependants depends on whether or not they have a right of action under the provision of the Staff Regulations relied on.
66 *Pellegrini & C Sas v Commission* (above, note 29) at para 31.

authority which is competent under national law to carry out the administrative or legal measures of constraint.[67] For the purpose of proceedings for the interpretation of a judgment, all persons are considered to be parties to the action who were parties to separate proceedings which were identical in subject matter and in the ground on which judgment was given.[68]

There are occasions when an entity possessing personality in law is held to be incapable of exercising the rights attaching to personality, eg the case of a natural person who is insane or a minor. So far as Community procedural law is concerned, such questions are governed by the personal law of the entity concerned.[69]

In the procedure before the Court there are limited possibilities of adding, removing or substituting parties.

When a party dies or becomes incapable of continuing proceedings (a phenomenon that in practice affects parties other than the Community or its institutions or the member states), no order is necessary in order to authorise the party's successors or representatives to take over the proceedings.[70] For example, in Case 92/82 *Gutmann v Commission*[71] the applicant died after the commencement of proceedings and the action was continued by his daughters as his legal successors. In Cases 239 and 275/82 *Allied Corpn v Commission*[72] one of the applicant companies was declared bankrupt after proceedings had commenced and the proceedings were continued by the receiver. In neither case does it appear that an order allowing proceedings to be continued in that way was asked from or made by the Court. In the *Gutmann* case the title of the proceedings remained unchanged but in *Allied Corpn* the title was amended and the name of the receiver substituted for that of the company, it being mentioned that the receiver was suing as such rather than in his own name. It would appear, therefore, that there is as yet no established practice concerning the title of proceedings. The applicable national law identifies the person entitled to take over the proceedings in such cases but the procedural devices by which that may be done are a matter of Community law. So far as can be seen, it is necessary to prove to the Court only that there is capacity under national law to continue the proceedings.[73] In the case of an applicant the cause of action may be extinguished upon death or supervening lack of capacity; but that is a matter of substantive Community law.[74] Where an entity is dissolved and merged with or replaced by another, the procedural consequences are in principle the same as where a party dies or becomes incapable of continuing proceedings and proceedings are continued by a successor or representative: the essential question is whether or not, in the light of the applicable national law and the intention of the persons concerned,

---

67 Case 2/68 *Ufficio Imposte di Consumo di Ispra v Commission* [1968] ECR 435 at 439.
68 Case 5/55 *ASSIDER v High Authority* [1954–56] ECR 135 at 141–142.
69 This is discussed below; see pp 195–196.
70 Case 294/83 *Parti Ecologiste 'Les Verts' v European Parliament* (above, note 41) at 1348 (Advocate General Mancini).
71 [1983] ECR 3127.
72 [1984] ECR 1005 (at 1010).
73 Application to continue may no doubt be made under RP-ECJ 91 or, as the case may be, RP-CFI 114 but the *Allied Corpn* and *Les Verts* cases are authority that it is sufficient to write to the Registrar explaining the circumstances, no order to continue being required.
74 For example, in Case 141/85 *Dufrane v Commission* (unreported, order of 23 March 1988), the applicant died and proceedings were stayed until a parallel case had been decided. The defendant lost and the question then arose as to how the *Dufrane* case should be dealt with. It was a staff case in which the applicant had sued only in order to vindicate her personal rights as an official. She made no pecuniary claim. In consequence, her successors had no interest in pursuing the action and, by reason of her death, the proceedings had lost their object.

the merged or substitute body has validly taken over the identity and the rights of the original applicant.[75] However a complete change in the person (although not the name) of the applicant during the course of proceedings appears to be impossible,[76] at least after delivery of an interlocutory judgment and possibly before: if the original applicant did not in reality have a right of action at the time of the commencement of proceedings and the true applicant did not bring proceedings in time, the position cannot be saved by substituting the one for the other in the course of the proceedings (the situation is otherwise if the original applicant validy assigns the right of action to another during the course of the proceedings). Where proceedings have been brought jointly by several applicants and one wishes to withdraw (or maintains that proceedings were brought in his name without authority) the Court will make an order removing the name of the person concerned, thus excluding him from the proceedings.[77]

Under the scheme of Community law, an action lies between an applicant and a defendant. The former must specify the person against whom the application is made[78] but the defendant is determined by reference to the nature of the action and the relief sought. An application is, therefore, inadmissible in so far as it is made against a person who lacks the capacity to be a defendant.[79] In addition, the applicant cannot extend the scope of the action by purporting, in a pleading subsequent to the application commencing proceedings, to add, as a new defendant, a third party, even if the third party has the capacity to be a defendant.[80] The joinder of other parties at the order of the Court or the request of the applicant or defendant is not expressly envisaged in either the Statutes or the Rules of Procedure although third parties may, of their own volition, apply to intervene. An intervener does not, however, have the status of an additional applicant or defendant. There are limited exceptions to this. For example, where the Commission brings an action before the Court under art 20 of the Euratom Treaty, the defendant to the proceedings is, strictly speaking, a member state or the national authority competent to grant or cause to be granted the licence in question; nevertheless, it is expressly provided that the proprietor must be heard by the Court.

The power of the Court to order, or allow, a third party to be joined (otherwise than as an intervener), in the absence of an express provision entitling it to do so, has been considered in several cases. The idea was rejected by Advocate General Roemer in his opinions in Cases 42 and 49/59 *Breedband v Société des Aciéries du Temple* and Cases 9 and 12/60 *Belgium v Société Commerciale Antoine Vloeberghs and High Authority*.[81] In his view, the structure of proceedings before the Court allowed only 'voluntary intervention' and excluded compulsory joinder of third parties.[82] Both cases were third party proceedings brought under art 36 of the ECSC Statute, which, in the authentic French version, gives persons the right to commence such proceedings against judgments '*rendus sans qu'elles aient été appelées*'. The English version says 'rendered without

---

75 Case 294/83 and Case 190/84 *Parti Ecologiste 'Les Verts' v European Parliament* [1986] ECR 1339 (paras 15–18 and per Advocate General Mancini at 1346–1348) and [1988] ECR 1017 (at 1026–1028 per Advocate General Mancini), respectively.
76 Case 250/78 *Contifex v EEC*, order of 22 September 1982 and Case 250/78 *DEKA Getreideprodukte GmbH & Co KG v EEC* [1983] ECR 421 (at 434–436, Advocate General Mancini).
77 Eg Case 167/86 *Rousseau v Court of Auditors* [1988] ECR 2705 at 2707.
78 RP-ECJ 38(1)(b); RP-CFI 44(1)(b).
79 Eg *Pellegrini & C Sas v Commission* and *André v Council and Commission* (above, notes 29 and 31).
80 Case 90/77 *Hellmut Stimming KG v Commission* [1977] ECR 2113.
81 [1962] ECR 145 and 171 at 161 and 187 respectively.
82 Other than defendants: ibid p 188.

their being heard', which does not give the full flavour of the original or that of other texts such as the German and Italian versions. The same phrase appears in arts 39 of the EC Statute and 40 of the Euratom Statute. It really means 'without being called on to appear'. The Court did not go so far as Advocate General Roemer. In *Belgium v Société Commerciale Antoine Vloeberghs and High Authority* it contented itself with holding that third party proceedings 'provide a method of recourse, on the one hand, for a third party who, having been called upon ("*appelé*") to take part in the original case, was unable to participate for justifiable reasons and, on the other hand, for any person who was not in a position to intervene'.[83] The inference is that it regarded being called on 'to take part' in the case as being equivalent to intervention: it had previously remarked that the (voluntary) intervention procedure existed in order to allow persons with an interest in the result of the proceedings to raise that matter before judgment in the case. It said nothing about the existence of a compulsory intervention procedure; neither, however, did it exclude it expressly.

The next occasion on which the problem arose was in Case 27/62 and Case 25/62 *Plaumann & Co v Commission*.[84] In both cases the applicant applied to the Court, apparently under RP-ECJ 91, for an order joining one of the member states to the proceedings. The Court decided to hear argument on the point and fixed the date for the hearing but, so far as can be seen, the matter did not go further: Case 27/62 appears to have been discontinued because it never came to judgment and, as far as Case 25/62 is concerned, it is certain that the applicant withdrew the request. In *Reynier v Commission*[85] the application was made against the EEC with the object of having the Council joined as defendant in order to obtain sight of documents and other information in its possession. The real defendant was the Commission. Advocate General Roemer remarked[86] that thought might be given to the necessity in such cases for some means of joining parties compulsorily but said that this 'has hitherto been foreign to the procedural law of the Court'.

In Case 12/69 *Wonnerth v Commission*,[87] the applicant applied for the compulsory joinder of a third party but the Court rejected this because 'compulsory intervention' was not provided for in the Rules of Procedure. Advocate General Roemer said that 'whatever one's opinion on the system of compulsory intervention and, in particular, on the question whether it could exist in our procedural law, the decisive factor is that it does not appear in the provisions at present in force governing the procedure of the Court'.[88] In Case 184/80 *Van Zaanen v Court of Auditors*[89] and Case T-1/90 *Pérez Mínguez Casariego v Commission*,[90] it was argued that the application was inadmissible because a third party affected by the issue was not joined as a party. In both cases the Court rejected this on the ground that the applicant nevertheless had an interest in obtaining judgment; the fact that a third party who could have intervened has chosen not to do so cannot be an objection to the admissibility of an action.

In the result, it is clear that, although the Court has been aware of the advantage, in some cases, of compulsory joinder of third parties, the possibility

83 Above, note 81 (at 181–182).
84 [1963] ECR 95 at 106.
85 Above, note 13: a similar situation arose in several of the staff cases decided in 1964.
86 Ibid at 271.
87 [1969] ECR 577 (para 8).
88 Ibid at 590.
89 [1981] ECR 1951, see para 13 of the judgment and also, per Advocate General Sir Gordon Slynn, p 1971.
90 [1991] ECR II-143 (paras 41–43).

has been excluded because it would require an express power in the Rules of Procedure.

A right of action may validly be assigned. In Cases 4–13/59 *Mannesmann v High Authority*,[91] the High Authority had adopted two decisions addressed to two German companies which ceased to exist, pursuant to a reconstruction of the group of which they were a part, before the decisions were communicated to them. As a result of the reconstruction, all their assets and liabilities were transferred to a third company, the applicant in the action. The Court held that the applicant could bring proceedings against the High Authority as assignee of the addressees. A similar situation arose in Case 238/78 *Ireks-Arkady GmbH v Council and Commission*[92] where an action for damages was brought by the assignee of the injured party. The assignment had been made in the context of the reorganisation of the group to which both the assignor and the assignee belonged. The Court held that there was no reason to prevent a right to compensation from being both claimed and enforced in legal proceedings by an assignee 'in circumstances such as those of the present case which do not give cause to believe that the assignment may have led to an abuse'. If a claim is validly assigned the assignor thereby ceases to be entitled to bring proceedings in respect of the claim.[93] The assignee of a right is subrogated to the right of action arising where the right is infringed and therefore an assignment of a right (for example) to payment of a refund carries with it a right to damages in respect of any unlawful refusal to pay the refund.[94]

The kind of abuse that may nullify the effect of an assignment is exemplified by Case 250/78 *DEKA Getreideprodukte GmbH & Co KG v EEC*.[95] There, a damages claim had been assigned by an insolvent company in order to avoid the extinguishment of the claim by set-off. The Court held that the assignment could not be relied on as against the Community because (i) it was abusive and (ii) the assignee had not acted in good faith since, at all material times, it knew of the abusive purpose of the assignment. The Court based its judgment on the general principles common to the laws of the member states which govern the Community's non-contractual liability under art 215 of the EC Treaty. It does not, however, seem that this approach is restricted to actions for damages: the better view is that, in any proceedings, an assignment of the cause of action may be excluded if it is found to constitute an abuse of procedure. On the other hand, it must be doubted whether the scope of the possibility of assignment is as broad in most proceedings as it is in actions for damages: it may well be accepted that a claim for damages may be assigned for a consideration to a third party unconnected with the injured party but it would appear that a claim for annulment may pass by assignment or other means only if the interest in obtaining annulment also passes, ie if the assignee is the successor to the assignor as the subject of the act sought to be annulled.

The possibility and conditions of assignment are governed by Community law but, in *Ireks-Arkady v Council and Commission*,[96] Advocate General Capotorti was of the opinion that national law governs the assignment itself.[97] In other words, both the form (e g whether notification of the assignment to the debtor

91 [1960] ECR 113 at 129, see also per Advocate General Roemer at 137.
92 [1979] ECR 2955 (para 5).
93 Cases 256, 257, 265, 267/80, 5 and 51/81 and 282/82 *Birra Wührer SpA v Council and Commission* [1984] ECR 3693 (para 7).
94 Ibid, para 12.
95 Above, note 76.
96 Above, note 92, at 2986–2987.
97 See also the *DEKA* case (above, note 76) per Advocate General Mancini.

is necessary to effect it) and the legal effect of the transaction whereby the obligation passes from one person to another, are determined by the proper law of the transaction. Hence, if the effect of the assignment under national law is to pass the benefit of the obligation but not the right of action to it, proceedings must be brought by the assignor, albeit that the benefit of the action accrues to the assignee. However, a failure to comply with an irrelevant administrative rule applicable to an assignee does not invalidate an assignment so far as Community law is concerned.[98] Further, the defendant cannot rely on its own unlawful acts in order to dispute the effectiveness of an assignment.[99] One problem that remains unresolved is the question whether the proper law of the assignment is determined by the independent election of the parties or by reference to the country with the closest connection to the subject matter of the assignment. For example, if a claim for damages, which is, ex hypothesi, a claim under Community law not national law, arises from the alleged wrongful abolition of production refunds from which an undertaking incorporated and trading in one member state would have benefited, and if, under the national law of that member state, an assignment is effective to pass the benefit of the obligation but not the right of action, may the parties to the assignment choose the national law of any member state (or a third country) most favourable for their purposes, and so avoid the limitations of the law of the country in which the assignor is established, or are they bound to comply with that law, to the exclusion of others, or some other law, even if the assignee is established in another member state or even a third country? To this question there is no clear answer. There is no doubt but that identification of the proper law of the assignment is a question of Community law. On this basis the question may well be decided on a comparative study of the laws of the member states but the better view seems to be that the parties to the assignment may select the proper law that they prefer; in the event of a failure to specify the proper law, it would appear to be that of the country with the closest connection to the transfer.

98 *Birra Wührer v Council and Commission* (above, note 93) at paras 8–10.
99 Ibid, paras 13–14.

CHAPTER 4

Representation and legal aid

I Representation and assistance

The Statutes and Rules of Procedure differentiate between 'representation' by an agent, in the case of member states and Community institutions, or by a lawyer, in the case of other persons, and 'assistance' by an adviser or lawyer. The precise significance of the terms representation and assistance is not apparent. In proceedings before the International Court of Justice, the representation of states is regarded as comprising two elements which may both be combined in the same person: political representation by an 'agent' and professional representation by an advocate or counsel. The difference between the two is that the agent is vested with full power to bind his government and take all decisions necessary in the course of the proceedings while the advocate's or counsel's authority does not go so far and statements of a binding character made through an advocate or counsel must be authorised by the agent.[1] It is arguable that this distinction was the source of the provision in the Statutes that member states and Community institutions are represented by an agent who may be assisted by an adviser or lawyer.[2] On the other hand, in, for example, French civil procedure, representation signifies not only the power to bind the party represented but also the authority to submit written pleadings. Assistance is restricted to giving legal advice to the party and submitting oral argument on his behalf but not binding him in any way. Representation may comprise assistance but the reverse is not the case.[3] Since, unlike the International Court of Justice, persons other than States (and Community institutions) may be parties before the Court, it is equally arguable that the draftsman of the Statutes had something like the French approach in mind.

The principles relating to representation and assistance are as follows.

The general rule is that member states and Community institutions are represented before the Court by an agent appointed for each case and that all other persons are represented by a 'lawyer entitled to practise before a court of a member state'.[4] The meaning of this phrase is considered below. There are two exceptions to this rule:

(1) under the ECSC Statute there is no provision relating to the representation of persons other than the member states and Community institutions; it is, therefore, to be supposed that, in all proceedings under the ECSC Treaty, the question of the representation of such persons is a matter of national law;[5]

---

1 See Rosenne *The World Court* (1989) p 117.
2 ECSC Statute, art 20; EC and Euratom Statutes, art 17.
3 See Vincent *Procédure Civile* (18th edn, 1976) paras 371 et seq.
4 Statutes, ibid.
5 See Case 18/57 *Nold KG v High Authority* [1959] ECR 41 at 48–49 of the judgment and 60 (Advocate General Roemer). In Case 75/69 *Firma Ernst Hake & Co v Commission* [1970] ECR 535, the applicant was 'represented' by the person entitled to do so under national law (see the title of the Order reported at [1970] ECR 901) and he was 'assisted' by a lawyer.

(2)   in references for a preliminary ruling, the Court 'shall take account of the rules of procedure of the national court or tribunal which made the reference' in so far as the representation and attendance of the parties to the proceedings before the national court or tribunal are concerned;[6] the meaning of this is considered below.

Where a member state or Community institution is represented by an agent, he or she may be assisted by a lawyer entitled to practise before a court of a member state in proceedings brought under the ECSC Treaty;[7] in proceedings brought under the EC or Euratom Treaties, he or she may be assisted either by an adviser or by a lawyer so entitled.[8] As far as other persons are concerned, neither the EC nor the Euratom Statute provides that their representatives may be assisted by anyone, but the ECSC Statute,[9] which of course contains no provision relating to their representation, does state that 'undertakings and all other natural or legal persons must be assisted by a lawyer entitled to practise before a court of a Member State'. Again, parties to the proceedings before a national court or tribunal making a reference for a preliminary ruling appear to be in a different position because, as has been seen, the national rules are taken into account regarding both representation and appearance. Hence it is possible for a litigant in person to submit written and oral arguments to the Court in a reference for a preliminary ruling, without being either represented or assisted by a lawyer, if he has right of audience before the national court or tribunal making the reference.[10] As will be seen, this is not possible in a direct action.

The original of every pleading must be signed by the party's agent or lawyer.[11] A 'pleading' here means any procedural document. The only exceptions to this rule are applications for legal aid[12] and, in certain circumstances, written observations in references for a preliminary ruling. Since the ECSC Statute does not require persons other than member states and Community institutions to be 'represented' by a lawyer, but only 'assisted' by one, the inference is that 'assistance' comprises the conduct of the written procedure in any action. In the *Nold* case Advocate General Roemer noted that, even under the ECSC Statute, there was a general necessity for a lawyer.[13] In Case 108/63 *Officine Elettromeccaniche Ing A Merlini v High Authority*,[14] another case under the ECSC Treaty, the party's lawyer signed and apparently submitted under a covering letter a memorandum drawn up by the party himself, lodging it as the reply. The point was taken that it was inadmissible as such. Advocate General

---

6 RP-ECJ 104(2).
7 ECSC Statute, art 20.
8 EC and Euratom Statutes, art 17.
9 Ibid art 20.
10 See, for example, Case 39/75 *Coenen v Sociaal-Economische Road* [1975] ECR 1547; Case 238/83 *Caisse d'Allocations Familiales v Meade* [1984] ECR 2631 at 2635.
11 RP-ECJ 37(1); RP-CFI 43(1). The fact that the party is himself a lawyer does not obviate the need to have the pleading signed by the party's agent or lawyer: Case 131/83 *Vaupel v European Court of Justice* (unreported, 15 March 1984) paras 8–9; Case C-126/90P *Viciano v Commission* [1991] ECR I-781 (paras 4–8). The reason is that the requirement in the Rules of Procedure is concerned not with the professional qualification of the signatory of the pleading but with his or her status as the party's representative and, therefore, as the person who has the authority to bind the party and who is subject to the obligations owed by a representative of a party to the Court.
12 RP-ECJ 76(2); RP-CFI 94(2). In Case 10/81 *Farrall v Commission* [1981] ECR 717 an application for legal aid was rejected as inadmissible but the reason for doing so is not apparent from the judgment.
13 Above (note 5), at 59.
14 [1965] ECR 1.

Roemer said[15] that it complied in formal terms with the Rules of Procedure because it had been signed by the lawyer but he doubted whether it complied with the spirit of the Rules: 'It might in fact be maintained that the obligation imposed on individuals by the [ECSC Statute] to be assisted by a lawyer has as its aim that there shall be submitted to the Court only legal opinions and explanations of fact which, having been examined by a lawyer are considered by him as fit to be put forward.' The Court was more positive and rejected the pleading as inadmissible.[16] In Cases 220 and 221/78 *ALA SpA and ALFER SpA v Commission*[17] Advocate General Capotorti held that applications purporting to commence proceedings, which were signed by the parties' legal 'representatives' but not by a 'lawyer', were inadmissible and the defect could not be cured with retrospective effect by subsequently putting them in order because the lack of representation by a lawyer is not a formal defect in a pleading.[18]

The Rules of Procedure provide that an application or defence made by a legal person governed by private law must be accompanied by proof that the authority to act granted to that person's lawyer was properly conferred on him by 'someone authorised for the purpose'.[19] This usage follows the German text of the Rules of Procedure; other versions refer to a 'representative' who is authorised to confer authority on the lawyer. In view of the discrepancy which exists between the ECSC Statute, on the one hand, and the EC and Euratom Statutes on the other, it is to be inferred that, in proceedings under the ECSC Treaty, an application[20] must be accompanied by proof that the lawyer has been validly appointed to assist the party's representative whereas, in other proceedings, the proof must relate to the lawyer's appointment as the party's representative in those proceedings. The person so appointing the lawyer may in other respects properly be described as the party's 'representative' but, for the purpose of the proceedings before the Court only, it is the lawyer appointed by him who is the representative. There appear to be no special provisions of Community law governing the appointment by a party of its representative and by him of a lawyer to assist or represent the party in proceedings before the Court so both questions are determined by national law.[21] Failure to submit proof of authority to act does not render the application a nullity but is a formal defect which can be rectified with retrospective effect;[22] and authorisation of a party's lawyer ex post facto is acceptable.[23]

Except in the case of legal persons governed by private law, proof of the lawyer's authority to act need not accompany the application or defence, although it is in the interests of the smooth running of the proceedings if this is done.[24] Nevertheless, if the lawyer's authority is challenged, the proof must be

---

15 [1965] ECR 1 at 16.
16 Ibid at 9.
17 [1979] ECR 1693.
18 The Court decided the case on another ground. See also *Farrall v Commission* (above, note 12) and *Vaupel v European Court of Justice* (above, note 11) at paras 8–9.
19 RP-ECJ 38(5)(b) and 40(1); RP-CFI 44(5)(b) and 46(1).
20 As well as all other pleadings to which RP-ECJ 38(5) and 40(1) and RP-CFI 44(5) and 46(1) apply.
21 The *Nold* case (above, note 5) at 48–49 and 60.
22 *ALA SpA and ALFER SpA v Commission* (above, note 17) at 1702 (Advocate General Capotorti); RP-ECJ 38(7); RP-CFI 44(6); see also Case 14/64 *Gualco (née Barge) v High Authority* [1965] ECR 51.
23 Cases 193 and 194/87 *Maurissen v Court of Auditors* [1989] ECR 1045 (para 33 and at 1062 per Advocate General Darmon).
24 The *Gualco* case (above, note 22) at 62-63 (Advocate General Roemer).

produced.[25] If, by mistake, the authority given is invalid, the pleading may still be admissible as long as a valid authority can be produced[26] but where the lawyer has no authority to act at all, the pleading is inadmissible. During the oral procedure a party may address the Court only through his agent, adviser or lawyer.[27]

It can be seen that both representation and assistance include the right to submit written and oral argument to the Court. The restrictions on the right to be heard, in its broad sense, relate to the quality of the person representing or assisting the party, not to his capacity as a representative or assistant. Thus a person who is an agent has an unfettered right to be heard and the same applies to one who is a lawyer, irrespective of the fact that he is representing or assisting the party; on the other hand an adviser, who can only assist, may not submit written pleadings and the party himself cannot be heard directly at all. It should, however, be borne in mind that, as has been noted above, the position in references for a preliminary ruling is different because there the Court 'takes account' of the Rules of Procedure of the national court or tribunal making the reference in so far as the parties before that court or tribunal are concerned. In consequence both written and oral observations can be lodged in such proceedings by, for example, a litigant in person, even though in a direct action he would have to be represented or assisted by a lawyer, as long as the rules of the referring court or tribunal would allow him to do so.[28] In this respect the Rules of Procedure refer only to the 'representation and attendance' of the parties before the referring court or tribunal but, as has been seen, 'representation' covers the submission of both written and oral pleadings. It will be observed, however, that the Court takes account of the rules of the referring court or tribunal, not the national rules of procedure in general or those of any higher or lower court. Hence, a party may not necessarily be represented by someone who has a right of audience before the higher or lower national court if that person has no right of audience before the referring court (and no independent right of audience before the ECJ).

In the light of the foregoing, it would seem that the precise meaning of 'representation' and 'assistance' is of little practical importance. It seems to be clear that the distinction is not the same as that in French civil procedure but that it is closer in spirit to the approach of the International Court of Justice. Put into a formula, it would appear that an adviser or lawyer who 'assists' a party may speak for him and give him legal advice, but nothing more, while an agent or a lawyer who is a party's representative can do both, and has authority to bind the party as well. Statements made by a representative of a party (whether an agent, in the case of a member state or Community institution, or a lawyer, in the case of other parties) are to be attributed in their entirety to the party in question because it is to be presumed that the representative is properly and fully authorised to represent the party in question.[29]

---

25 Ibid at 57; Case T-139/89 *Virgili-Schettini v European Parliament* [1990] ECR II-535. It should be noted that the Rules of Procedure have been amended slightly since the *Gualco* case and that both the Court's judgment and Advocate General Roemer's opinion must be read in the light of the Rules as presently framed.
26 The *Gualco* case (above, note 22) at 62–63.
27 ECSC Statute, arts 21 and 28; EC Statute, arts 18 and 29; Euratom Statute, arts 18 and 30; RP-ECJ 57 and 58; RP-CFI 58 and 59.
28 See, for example, the *Coenen* case (above, note 10).
29 Case C-290/89 *Commission v Belgium* [1991] ECR I-2851 at 2859 (Advocate General Lenz).

II   Agents, advisers and lawyers

The member states and the Community institutions are free to choose whom they like to act as agent, whether one of their officials or a person not employed by them as such, and to decide if they wish to be assisted by an adviser or lawyer.[30] The Statutes refer only to representation or assistance by an agent, lawyer or adviser, as the case may be, in the singular. On a strict interpretation, then, there can be only one representative of the party before the Court and assistance from only one adviser or lawyer. In practice it happens fairly frequently that several persons appear before the Court on behalf of a party and, in the case of persons other than a member state or Community institution, are described as 'representing' the party.[31] In principle, however, this seems to be wrong because a party should have only one representative.[32] Where there are several there is a risk of confusion because the representatives may say different things. It would seem that the reason that a party, other than a member state or Community institution, is occasionally described as having more than one representative is because the EC and Euratom Statutes do not provide for them being 'assisted' by anyone, whereas the ECSC Statute does. As far as assistance goes it is the practice to accept that an agent may be assisted by more than one adviser or lawyer and there is no theoretical objection to this, as there is in the case of a multiplicity of representatives. But if the rule that a party has only one representative before the Court were combined with the omission from the EC and Euratom Statutes of provision for assistance, except in the case of member states and Community institutions, the result would be that other persons would be limited to only one lawyer. This would not, of course, prevent the party from seeking advice from another lawyer but it would mean that the latter could not address the Court orally or in writing and it might also affect the question of costs.[33] It is to be inferred from the Court's practice that there is no restriction on the number of persons who may assist a party's representative nor any on the number who may represent a party, at least in the case of persons other than member states

---

30 Eg see Case 126/76 Costs *Firma Gebrüder Dietz v Commission* [1979] ECR 2131 (para 5). The Council and the Commission are usually represented by a member of their legal services, as agent, who is from time to time assisted by an outside lawyer (eg Case 138/79 *Roquette Frères SA v Council* [1980] ECR 3333) but, in Case 101/74 *Kurrer v Council* [1976] ECR 259, the Council's agent was a Belgian advocate. The Parliament has been represented by its Director-General for Administration, Personnel and Finance, acting as agent, assisted by an outside lawyer (see the *Roquette* case). The Court itself has been represented by its Registrar (Case 147/79 *Hochstrass v European Court of Justice* [1980] ECR 3005) or Director of Administration (Case 2/80 *Dautzenberg v European Court of Justice* [1980] ECR 3107), as agent, usually, but not always, assisted by an outside lawyer. The Court of Auditors has been represented by its Secretary (Case 184/80 *Van Zaanen v Court of Auditors* [1981] ECR 1951) and the European Investment Bank by the Director of its Directorate for Legal Affairs (Case 110/75 *Mills v European Investment Bank* [1976] ECR 955), both as agents and both assisted by outside lawyers. The practice of the member states varies. Most seem to use government legal advisers who may occasionally be assisted by an outside lawyer. The agents for Ireland and the United Kingdom tend to be the chief State and Treasury Solicitors respectively, or their assistants, assisted by outside lawyers (but not invariably: in Case 99/80 *Galinsky v Insurance Officer* [1981] ECR 941, for example, a legal adviser from the Department of Health and Social Security represented the British government and addressed the Court without the assistance of Counsel).
31 See, for example, Cases 209, 215 and 218/78 *Heintz van Landewyck Sàrl (FEDETAB) Asbl v Commission* [1980] ECR 3125.
32 This seems to have been the view of the Court in Cases 20 and 21/63 *Maudet v Commission* [1964] ECR 621.
33 See RP-ECJ 73 and RP-CFI 91 and *Maudet v Commission*, ibid.

or Community institutions in proceedings under the EC and Euratom Statutes.[34]

The member states and Community institutions have an unfettered discretion in whom to select as agent or adviser. No special qualifications are laid down for either in the Statutes or the Rules of Procedure and there is no reference to the position under national law. Hence neither the agent nor the adviser need be a qualified lawyer. It is unclear whether the latter, at least, need have any legal training. The words used in the different texts give no indication whether the adviser is to be regarded as a legal adviser or, perhaps, a technical adviser. It is a plausible argument that what is envisaged is a person who is a trained lawyer but who is not entitled to practise because, for example, he is employed by the government. On the other hand, there are certain practical advantages for a member state or Community institution to be assisted by an adviser who, while having no legal training, is an expert in any technical matters relevant to the case. In the absence of any authority on the meaning of the word 'adviser' the position is obscure. The writer, for what it is worth, inclines to the view that 'adviser' means 'legal adviser', technical advisers being covered by the term 'expert'.[35]

The Statutes[36] provide that university teachers who are nationals of a member state which entitles them to plead before a court have the same rights before the Court as lawyers. This means that, even if the university teacher is entitled under national law to appear only before certain courts or in certain proceedings, he is nevertheless on an equal footing with any lawyer from the same member state in so far as proceedings before the Court are concerned. An agent, adviser, lawyer or university teacher need not be of the same nationality or be qualified, if necessary, in the same member state as the party for whom he appears. For example, in Case 30/78 *Distillers Co Ltd v Commission*[37] the applicant, a company registered in Scotland, was represented by a Belgian lawyer, while the Commission was assisted by two Scottish advocates and the intervener, another Scottish company, by an Italian advocate. In references for a preliminary ruling, of course, someone with right of audience before the referring court can appear on behalf of a party to the proceedings before it.[38]

Although the English text of the Statutes uses the expression 'lawyer entitled to practise before a court of a Member State', the other language versions are worded differently. The French and Italian texts, for example, refer to an advocate who is a 'Member of the Bar' or 'inscribed in the professional rolls of one of the Member States'; the German version to one who is 'authorised [to practise] in one of the Member States'. In the case of proceedings under the ECSC Treaty, to which the ECSC Statute applies, the French version is to be preferred because it is the authentic text. All the texts save the English indicate that a 'lawyer' is nothing other than a practising advocate and there seems to be a clear intention to exclude other types of

---

34 In fact, in some cases to which the EC Statute applies (Case 30/78 *Distillers Co Ltd v Commission* [1980] ECR 2229 is one) both a lawyer-representative and a lawyer-assistant have been recorded as appearing on behalf of a person other than a member state or Community institution. In *Maudet v Commission* (above, note 32) the Court appeared to accept that a party other than a member state or Community institution was free to employ an adviser in addition to a lawyer representing him.

35 See also Wall *The Court of Justice of the European Communities* at p 213.

36 ECSC Statute, art 20; EC and Euratom Statutes, art 17.

37 Above, note 34.

38 Eg Case 93/83 *Zentralgenossenschaft des Fleischergewerbes v Hauptzollamt Bochum* [1984] ECR 1095 (at 1102), where one party was represented at the hearing by a tax consultant and another by a civil servant.

lawyer qualified to practise. The position, therefore, is that, under the ECSC Statute, which refers to 'lawyers' as assisting a party or an agent, the function of assistance can be discharged only by an advocate. No rule is laid down as to representation of the party save in the case of member states and Community institutions. In consequence, national law applies and a party may be represented by an English solicitor or an Italian or Dutch procurator, as the case may be. If national law does not require the party to be represented, he may appear before the Court in person but in all cases he (or his representative) must be assisted by an 'advocate'. Under the EC and Euratom Statutes, on the other hand, the function of representation may be discharged only by an agent or an 'advocate'. This does not mean that an advocate who could not represent a party under national law cannot appear on his behalf at all in proceedings before the Court: the Statutes make the advocate the party's representative. As a result, by way of example, an Italian advocate does not also have to be a procurator in order to represent a party before the Court.

The principal difficulty is to know what exactly is meant by 'advocate'. There seems no doubt but that an English barrister is, and an English solicitor may now be, an advocate within the meaning of the Statute and are therefore capable of representing a party in proceedings to which the EC and Euratom Statutes apply. On the other hand a French avoué seems to be excluded, even though he is a qualified lawyer and may represent a party in the sense understood by French law.[39] The same seems to apply to all lawyers whose function is only to 'represent' a party, within the meaning of national law, but who do not exercise the profession of an advocate.[40]

On the other hand, in Case 175/80 *Tither v Commission*,[41] which was a staff case, the applicant in a direct action was represented only by an English solicitor at a time when, in principle, the function of a solicitor was to represent a party but not to plead orally or in writing on his behalf, that being the preserve of the barrister or (in Scotland) the advocate. Like the French avoué before the fusion of that profession with that of avocat in 1971, the solicitor also had a limited right to plead on behalf of a party before certain minor courts. If all the texts of the Statutes are to be construed in the same way, there was at that time much to be said for the view that a solicitor was not an advocate within the meaning of the Statutes although it seems to have been assumed that he was.[42] No objection was taken to the appearance of the solicitor in that case. It may therefore be inferred that the Court's practice is to give a broad interpretation to the Statutes. The problem is to know whether the Court's

---

39 See Tyrrell and Yaqub, *The Legal Professions in the New Europe*, pp 116 et seq. Until 1971 the relationship between a French avocat and an avoué was analogous to, but in many respects considerably different from, that between an English barrister and a solicitor. The avoué had a right of audience before some courts but a virtual monopoly of it was held by avocats. The two professions, together with that of agrée, were merged at the end of 1971. The specific reference in the Statutes to an 'avocat' has had the effect of preventing an avoué from appearing before the Court despite the fact that he did have a right of audience before certain French courts. At the present time, it seems that the avoué represents parties before the Courts of Appeal but it is the avocat who has a monopoly of pleading.

40 For example, a Dutch or Italian procurator. In both countries most advocates are also qualified procurators (similarly, in Luxembourg it is usual for an advocate to be an avoué) but the distinction remains and appears to have been incorporated in the Statutes. Neither in Denmark nor in the Federal Republic of Germany is the legal profession divided, even formally. There is no reason to assume that 'lawyer', for the purposes of the Statutes and the Rules of Procedure, means the same as it does in Council Directive No 77/249 of 22 March 1977 (OJ No L78 of 26 March 1977, p 17).

41 [1981] ECR 2345.

42 See, for example, Schneider [1971] CMLR 49–51.

usage is to be taken as indicating that all the language versions of the Statutes are to be construed broadly and more in accordance with the English text or that they are to be construed in the light of the legal system in which the lawyer in question is entitled to practise. In the *Nold* case[43] it was accepted both by the Court and by Advocate General Roemer that the procedural law of the Community refers to national law for the purpose of determining whether a person has the capacity to appear before the Court, but this was said in the context of the requirement that the lawyer be 'entitled to practise before a court of a Member State', not in relation to the question what is the kind of lawyer so entitled envisaged by the Statute. This problem does not occur very often and it is for this reason hard to discern a particular policy of the Court in the matter. At the present it may be supposed that any practising lawyer is entitled to appear on behalf of a party if he has a right of audience before any national court, however minor, in his professional capacity and even if he is not regarded, in the jurisdicion in which he is entitled to practise, as an advocate in the strict sense. The theoretical basis for this may be that the intention of the Statutes is to give capacity to represent or assist a party to any 'lawyer' who has a right of audience before a court of a member state.[44] The use of the word 'advocate' and its equivalents is intended to indicate the function of the lawyer rather than any particular branch of the legal profession in a member state.

There is no requirement that the lawyer be entitled to practise in the member state in which he resides or works as long as he is so entitled in one, at least, of the member states. For example, an English barrister may represent a party even if his chambers are in Brussels. It does not matter that he may not be entitled to practise there as a Belgian avocat; the only test is whether he is still entitled to practise in England. Whether a lawyer is entitled to practise before a national court is a matter of national law. In the *Nold* case[45] an application was drafted by a German Rechtsanwalt (barrister) who had been suspended from practice by his local Bar Council. The question arose whether the application was invalid. It appeared that under the law governing the profession, suspension was a disciplinary measure which, if disregarded, could result in further disciplinary sanctions but it did not affect the validity of the lawyer's acts. Hence the Court concluded that, as the lawyer had not been disbarred and his suspension did not affect the validity of his acts, the application was formally valid. Advocate General Roemer suggested that the Court might still refuse to hear a lawyer against whom disciplinary proceedings had been taken[46] but the Court did not comment on this. It will be observed that the reference in the judgment to disbarment reflects the French version of the ECSC Statute, the action being one under the ECSC Treaty.

At the time of the *Nold* case the Rules of Procedure stated that a lawyer could not lodge a valid procedural document before submitting to the Registry a practising certificate. More or less the same wording was used to describe this document as is used in the current version of the Rules.[47] In the *Gualco* case[48] the Court said that, under the Rules of Procedure, a party's lawyer need only establish his professional status as a lawyer.[49] That case did not concern

---

43 Above, note 5.
44 As opposed, for example, to practising lawyers whose only function is to represent a party but who have no right of audience.
45 Above (note 5), at 49 and 89 (Advocate General Roemer).
46 Ibid.
47 Cf OJ No 6/303 of 7 April 1954, RP-ECJ 38(3) and RP-CFI 44(3).
48 Above (note 22), at 57.
49 'Avocat' in the French version of the judgment.

expressly the problem of any professional impediment barring the lawyer from acting but the question whether he had been properly appointed to act for the party. Nevertheless, when taken with the judgment in the *Nold* case, it suggests that production of a valid practising certificate does not avoid difficulties relating to the lawyer's capacity to act of the type raised in *Nold*. This is confirmed by other language versions of the Rules of Procedure because, while the English text of RP-ECJ 38(3) and RP-CFI 44(3), somewhat misleadingly, describes it as a 'certificate that he [the lawyer] is entitled to practise before a Court of a Member State', it is elsewhere identified as a document certifying that the lawyer is enrolled as a member of the bar in one of the member states.[50] The German text is a little ambiguous because it refers to it as a certificate showing that the lawyer is authorised to practise as an advocate but the Court's interpretation seems to be that it only establishes the lawyer's professional status as such,[51] in other words that he has not been disbarred or struck off. It cannot be regarded as constituting irrefutable proof of capacity to appear on behalf of a party. If there is other evidence of an impediment to his acting, the certificate cannot defeat it.

It seems clear from the *Nold* case that the effect of such evidence on the lawyer's capacity to act depends on whether or not it shows that he is prevented from acting as a matter of national procedural law or by virtue of the disciplinary or ethical rules that bind him as a member of the professional body to which he belongs. If the former prevent the lawyer wholly or partly from acting on behalf of his client, the same impediment applies in the context of proceedings before the Court.[52] Thus, in Case 142/85 *Schwiering v Court of Auditors*,[53] where the defendant contested the right of the applicant's lawyer to act for him on the ground that the lawyer was a Commission official who was on leave from the Commission in order to carry out his functions as an elected member of the European Parliament, the lawyer produced certificates showing that he was inscribed on the roll of certain German courts. On that basis, the ECJ concluded that the requirements of the Rules of Procedure had been satisfied: had the lawyer's status as a Commission official (or, indeed, as an elected member of the European Parliament) prevented him from acting under national procedural law, he could not have remained inscribed on the roll. On the other hand, if the lawyer has breached a disciplinary or ethical rule, the Court seems to have discretion whether or not to hear him. Written pleadings presented by him must be accepted as being admissible and cannot be excluded from consideration but the Court may refuse to hear oral argument depending on the gravity of the infraction. Theoretically a breach of a professional rule is a matter for the profession to decide on, not the Court, but it may be so grave a breach as to reflect upon the dignity of the Court, in which case the Court may exercise its powers under RP-ECJ 35(1) or, as the case may be, RP-CFI 41(1).[54] Where the breach of a professional rule of conduct is a ground under national procedural law for withdrawing or reducing the lawyer's capacity to act for the party, the matter is no longer a disciplinary or ethical problem which is the concern only of the appropriate professional body.

50 See, for example, the French and Italian versions.
51 Sc as barrister or advocate.
52 For example, if the lawyer can submit written pleadings but not oral argument, the same applies in proceedings before the Court; if he is totally barred from acting, he is totally barred before the Court.
53 [1986] ECR 3177 (order of 26 September 1985, unreported).
54 Those Rules allow the Court to exclude an adviser or lawyer from the proceedings where his conduct is incompatible with the dignity of the Court. Its application in this context is a deduction from the *Nold* case and there is, so far as is known, no precise authority on the point.

The question whether an English barrister may appear on behalf of a client without being instructed by a solicitor would be answered by applying these principles. Any arrangement made between the Bar Council and the Law Society of England and Wales and any rule of etiquette of the Bar does not affect right of audience before the Court under the Statutes and the Rules of Procedure. But if the barrister's right of audience before an English court is conditional on there being an instructing solicitor, he has no right of audience before the Court if that condition is not fulfilled. As it happens, the necessity to be instructed by a solicitor appears to be a rule of etiquette which is now of limited application and which does not affect a barrister's capacity to plead on behalf of his client. As a result, the Court must accept written pleadings submitted by the barrister and does not appear to retain any discretion whether or not to hear oral argument from him. Any disciplinary proceedings which might be brought concern the Bar Council. The Court is not in a position to take a view on matters of professional etiquette in a member state nor would such a breach of etiquette (if any) appear to be incompatible with the dignity of the Court. The fact that, in a particular case, an English judge might exercise his discretion not to hear a barrister who appeared without an instructing solicitor is irrelevant. The only question is whether it is a rule of English procedural law that the absence of an instructing solicitor deprives the barrister of the capacity to appear on behalf of a party (which appears not to be the case).

The rule that, in references for a preliminary ruling, the Court 'shall take account' of the rules of procedure of the referring court so far as concerns the representation and attendance of the parties to the proceedings before that court[55] appears to have two possible interpretations: (i) the Court is bound to apply the referring court's rules of procedure, even if they are more restrictive than the Court's own Rules; or (ii) the Court only applies the referring court's rules in the event that a party is represented by a person who has right of audience before the referring court but not before the Court itself. The effect of the first interpretation is that, on the one hand, member states and Community institutions which are parties to the proceedings before the referring court cannot be represented by an agent before the Court unless they could have been so represented before the referring court or they elect to appear before the Court pursuant to their right under the Statutes and not their right as parties to the proceedings before the referring court; on the other hand, other persons may plead in person, if they could have done so before the referring court, but may find themselves unable to use a lawyer entitled to practise before the Court, if he could not appear before the referring court. The effect of the second interpretation is that the usual rules concerning representation and assistance in proceedings before the Court continue to apply but the Court has power to extend the right of audience to persons (eg a litigant in person or unqualified legal adviser) competent to appear before the referring court. The Court does not appear to have revealed how RP-ECJ 104(2) is to be construed. It is to be inferred from a few cases[56] that the second interpretation suggested is the correct one.

---

55 RP-ECJ 104(2). The national court's rules of procedure are in any event to be construed subject to the provisions of Directive No 77/249, above (note 40).

56 Eg Case 234/81 *E I Du Pont de Nemours Inc v Customs and Excise Comrs* [1982] ECR 3515, where one of the parties before the referring court was represented by a Scots advocate who did not, ordinarily, have right of audience before the referring court.

III   Rights and immunities

The Statutes[57] provide that agents, advisers and lawyers 'shall, when they appear before the Court, enjoy the rights and immunities necessary to the independent exercise of their duties, under conditions laid down in rules drawn up by the Court.'[58] The Rules of Procedure provide that the privileges, immunities and facilities made available by them 'are granted exclusively in the interests of the proper conduct of proceedings'.[59] The form of words used in the Statutes to justify the grant of rights and immunities to agents, advisers and lawyers is not repeated in the Rules of Procedure. The explanation for this seems to be not so much the desire to avoid needless repetition as that the Statutes set out the purpose for which the rights and immunities are granted and all the immunities, privileges and facilities specified in the Rules of Procedure are to be interpreted in the light of this purpose; the Rules of Procedure set out the conditions under which the immunities, privileges and facilities are granted. As a result, the immunities and so forth mentioned in the Rules of Procedure cannot be applied or defined as being other than for the purpose of safeguarding the independent exercise of the functions of an agent, adviser or lawyer, even if it would be in the interests of the proper conduct of proceedings to do so. On the other hand, even if they do secure the independent exercise of those functions, the immunities etc may not be relied on if this would be contrary to the interests of the proper conduct of proceedings.

The conclusion to be drawn from this approach is that there is no special right or privilege for the benefit of the parties themselves to be found in the Statutes or the Rules of Procedure other than those which may form part of the rules of natural justice, or the right to a fair trial (more usually referred to as 'the rights of the defence'). The rights given to agents, advisers and lawyers are intended to aid the discharge of their functions as such and are not a protection, albeit indirect, of the party on whose behalf they appear.[60] They do, however, apply to university teachers with a right of audience.[61]

The phrase in the Statutes, 'when they appear before the Court', suggests that the rights and immunities apply only during the physical appearance of the agent, adviser or lawyer before the Court. Other language versions do not say 'when' but 'who appear before the Court', or some similar phrase. A less elliptical way of putting what the Statutes seem to mean is 'who appear on behalf of a party in proceedings before the Court'. This indicates that the rights and immunities attach by reason of a person's quality as an agent, adviser or lawyer and not by reference to a period of time. Secondly, it is not physical appearance before the Court that matters but appearance on behalf of a party. This seems evident from the facts that some agents, advisers and lawyers may not 'appear' in person[62] and that immunity from suit covers what the agent, adviser or lawyer has written.[63] 'Appearance' seems to comprise the

---

57 ECSC Statute, art 20; EC and Euratom Statutes, art 17.
58 Although 'duties' is the word used in the English version of the Statutes, other texts refer to 'functions' and it is this term that will be used henceforth.
59 RP-ECJ 34; RP-CFI 40. The English version of RP-ECJ 34 seems to have been taken from the German text. The French and the Italian versions, for example, refer to the 'interests of proceedings', not to the 'proper conduct of proceedings'. It does not seem, however, that there is any difference in substance between these two formulations. The German and English versions just give more precise expression to what is meant in the French and Italian versions.
60 But see Usher *European Court Practice* at p 223.
61 RP-ECJ 36; RP-CFI 42.
62 Eg in a reference for a preliminary ruling when only written observations are lodged.
63 See RP-ECJ 32(1); RP-CFI 38(1).

functions of 'representing' a party and 'assisting' his representative. In the context of a procedure which places as much emphasis on written pleadings as does procedure before the Court, a narrow construction of 'appearance' is difficult, if not impossible, to justify.

The privileges, immunities and facilities made available in the Rules of Procedure are of little importance in practice and do not appear ever to have been invoked.

A Immunity from suit

Immunity in respect of words spoken or written concerning the case or the parties is enjoyed by 'agents representing a State or an institution' and by 'advisers and lawyers'.[64] Both categories must be 'appearing before the Court or before any judicial authority to whom the Court has addressed letters rogatory'.[65] Agents thus benefit not from any general immunity but from an immunity restricted to 'appearance' before the Court or 'any judicial authority' etc; an agent would for these purposes be representing a member state or Community institution only in proceedings before the Court[66] and immunity is in any event granted only in the interests of the proper conduct of such proceedings.[67] The immunity is that of the agent, adviser or lawyer, not the party.

The immunity covers both the written and oral pleadings in a case in so far as they relate to the matter before the Court. For example, a libel of a third party inserted in a pleading would not be covered by immunity unless its subject matter related to the dispute between the parties.[68] It is a question of fact whether the words do relate to the case or the parties. Apart from the pleadings themselves, all other remarks, whether oral or written, which are addressed to the Court would appear to fall within the category of material which may be covered by immunity but it is unclear whether immunity may extend to communications passing between persons entitled to immunity concerning, for example, the conduct of proceedings and their possible settlement, but not made to or before the Court and perhaps not in the Court building. In the absence of any authority, no firm answer can be given. The writer inclines to the view that immunity should be narrowly construed. The most that can be said is that words addressed to the Court are prima facie covered by immunity; with regard to those addressed to other persons, whether or not they are themselves entitled to immunity, evidence would have to be adduced to show that lack of immunity would be detrimental to the proper conduct of proceedings and the independent exercise of the functions of their author before it could be said that they might be covered by immunity. It seems better to adopt a pragmatic approach. Depending on the circumstances, a ruling on the question whether immunity applies might be obtained either by way of a reference for a preliminary ruling or in an application under RP-ECJ 91 or, as the case may be, RP-CFI 114 during the course of proceedings.

64 Including university teachers.
65 RP-ECJ 32(1); RP-CFI 38(1).
66 In the case of letters rogatory, the examination of the witness or expert before the competent judicial authority in a member state is made in the context of an action before the Court and the national authority is deputed by the Court to carry out the examination. It can therefore properly be described as proceedings before the Court.
67 RP-ECJ 34; RP-CFI 40.
68 A libel of the opposing party would, of course, be covered by immunity even if its subject matter was not connected with the dispute because the Rules of Procedure state expressly that immunity attaches to words spoken or written which concern the parties.

Since the words may be written, it follows that immunity does not apply only to persons physically present before the Court at the time when they are expressed. Nevertheless the implication from the Rules of Procedure is that the speaker or writer has capacity to address the Court. In consequence, no immunity would cover words addressed to the Court by a lawyer who is not entitled to practise before a court of a member state. The same appears to apply even if it is right that words directed at a person other than the Court may be covered by immunity because the privilege is only that of someone who is representing a party or assisting a representative. Unless the lawyer in question is an agent or adviser he can do neither if he is not qualified to practise before the court of a member state. The immunity applies whatever the nature of proceedings in which the words were spoken or written. The Statutes make clear that proceedings before a national judicial authority pursuant to letters rogatory, which are a step in proceedings before the Court, are covered. By parity of reasoning, the same would apply should the Court entrust a preparatory enquiry to an Assistant Rapporteur.[69]

It is unclear whether immunity attaches only from the point at which proceedings commence and ends with the final judgment or whether it must be given a wider field of application. The commencement of a direct action, for example, is marked by the lodgment of the application at the Court. It is obvious that the application must have been written before being lodged. If it contains a libel of the opposing party and he or another obtains a copy before the date of lodgment, is it covered by immunity? Common sense suggests that it is. As with defining the matter covered by immunity, the touchstone is the purpose of the privilege. It would be tempting to say that all preparatory acts which lead directly to the commencement of proceedings are covered by immunity (for example, a draft of the application which contains the libel) but the better view is probably to consider each case as it arises. By way of principle it seems right to say that words spoken or written between the commencement of proceedings and final judgment are prima facie covered by immunity but, with regard to words spoken or written at other times, there must be evidence to show that the inapplicability of immunity would be detrimental to the proper conduct of proceedings and the independent exercise of the functions of the agent, adviser or lawyer concerned. It should be noted that the final judgment may not in fact terminate the proceedings: there might be a further application for the Court to supplement its judgment[70] or a dispute as to costs.[71] Nevertheless, it seems right to take the date of final judgement as marking the prima facie end of proceedings.

Immunity may be relied on whatever the type of proceedings brought against the agent, adviser or lawyer, whether criminal or civil. Nor is there any time limit to its effectiveness. Clearly, if immunity lasted only for the length of time of the proceedings before the Court, it would not fulfil its function effectively because the person aggrieved by the words in question would simply delay commencing proceedings against their author until after the Court had delivered judgment. Once the conditions for benefiting from immunity have been fulfilled, therefore, it lasts unless and until the Court decides to waive it. The question of waiver is considered below.

---

69 Although the Statutes provide for this possibility (see art 16(2) of the ECSC Statute and art 12 of the EC and Euratom Statutes), no Assistant Rapporteurs have ever been appointed and the Rules of Procedure are silent on the matter.
70 RP-ECJ 67; RP-CFI 85.
71 RP-ECJ 74; RP-CFI 92.

B Exemption from search and seizure

Papers and documents relating to the proceedings are exempt from search and seizure.[72] This privilege is enjoyed only by agents, advisers and lawyers, not by the parties or anyone else. The Rules of Procedure leave many questions unanswered concerning its scope but it seems reasonable to put the position as follows.

'Papers and documents relating to the proceedings' covers all written pleadings, notes of evidence, documentary evidence, drafts, memoranda and so forth relevant to the case before the Court. It is not restricted to material that is brought into existence for the purpose of being presented to the Court but extends to all material which forms part of the brief or file of the party's representative or his adviser. It is uncertain to what extent protection may be extended, in the light of modern conditions, to material which is not in the form of a paper or document. The teleological method of interpretation would, it is submitted, suggest that it is content rather than physical form which attracts protection: the exemption from search and seizure is not granted just because certain papers and documents are papers and documents; it is the fact that they relate to the proceedings that is the determining criterion. Ascertaining whether or not that criterion is satisfied can be done only by assessing the contents.[73] The conclusion is that material relating to proceedings is not deprived of protection merely because it lacks the physical form of a 'paper' or 'document'. Computerised records cannot therefore be searched for records of material relating to proceedings and it must be doubted whether telephone conversations conducted by an agent, adviser or lawyer relating to proceedings may be tapped.

Protection is not restricted to material found in the possession of the agent, adviser or lawyer, for example in his pocket or briefcase or in his office; it also extends to papers sent by him to the Court. It is doubtful if it covers communications moving from the agent, adviser or lawyer to the party he represents or assists, or to material such as copies of any advice given found in the possession of the party because these, ex hypothesi, no longer form part of the file or brief of the agent, adviser or lawyer. On the other hand, a communication relating to the proceedings and sent to him by the party (or third party) is protected from search and seizure because it is destined to form part of the brief. Although not, strictly speaking, in the power or control of the agent, adviser or lawyer if consigned to the post or found in the possession of the party or his servant while being taken to the agent, adviser or lawyer, such material may properly be regarded as protected on the ground that the intended recipient has putative possession of it by reason of the intention of the true possessor that it should form part of the brief. By analogy a telephone conversation between the agent, adviser or lawyer and another person which relates to the proceedings would also be protected, whether or not the former initiated the communication.

Exemption from search and seizure applies in particular to the passage of papers and documents from one part of the Community to the Court at Luxembourg and vice versa but its object is to prevent access to the Court from being blocked, hindered or prejudiced by acts of public authority and so it may apply generally, not just at the moment when the material passes across the frontier of a member state. Assuming that all the other conditions for benefiting from exemption are fulfilled, it prevents any search or seizure by any

---

72 RP-ECJ 32(2)(a); RP-CFI 38(2)(a).
73 See the second part of RP-ECJ 32(2)(a) and RP-CFI 38(2)(a).

public authority in the Community. Thus, for example, the powers of the police or the Inland Revenue under English law cannot be used to obtain sight or the seizure of material relating to proceedings before the Court. In the same way, the protection applies where a private person seeks to enlist the aid of a public authority to enforce a right to search or seize documents: the English procedure of discovery and similar rights cannot be used, where the protection applies, even at the suit of a private person. The crucial question is whether it is sought to rely on an exercise of public authority in order to search or seize. The Community institutions are also bound by this rule and their powers are to be construed subject to the Court's Rules of Procedure in the absence of a specific provision modifying or overriding them.

Protection attaches when the physical form embodying the material relating to the proceedings comes into existence. It is arguable that, like immunity from suit, it continues indefinitely after the close of the proceedings on the ground that the agent, adviser or lawyer might be deterred from assembling the material, whether for the purpose of preparing the case or for presentation to the Court, by the risk of a search or seizure immediately after the close of proceedings. In fact, on a strict construction of the Rules of Procedure, it is possible to say that a search or seizure may be effected at any time after the hearing because the proper conduct of the proceedings by the agent, adviser or lawyer can no longer be jeopardised: the opinion of the advocate general (where there is one) and the decision of the Court will be based on the submissions and disclosures of the parties that have previously been made and would not be influenced by the search or seizure. It is doubtful if this is correct because, at the very least, there is the possibility of the reopening of the oral procedure after the delivery of the advocate general's opinion,[74] quite apart from any proceedings subsequent to the final judgment. For example, an application for revision of a judgment may be made up to ten years after the date of the final judgment.[75] It can be said with some confidence that material which comes into existence after the date of the final judgment is not protected unless it relates to other proceedings but there is good reason to believe that, once material is protected, it remains protected indefinitely. It must be admitted, however, that the justification for maintaining protection after the end of the proceedings is considerably less than in the case of immunity from suit and hence a heavier burden lies on a person relying on the protection to prove that it is justified. The most that can be said is that protection is not in principle ruled out after final judgment but that it depends on the facts of the case if its maintenance remains in the interests of the proper conduct of proceedings and the independent exercise of the functions of agent, adviser or lawyer. The justification of the protection is not, directly at least, that a party may be deterred from making a disclosure to the Court by the fear of a search or seizure but that the agent, adviser or lawyer may be prevented from putting the party's case fully to the Court and properly carrying out his functions, which comprise a duty to be frank to the Court.

In the event of any dispute concerning the right to protection, the papers or documents must be sent immediately to the Court for inspection in the presence of the Registrar and the person concerned.[76] The Rules of Procedure envisage that the customs officials or police may seal the papers or documents before sending them to the Court. It is, no doubt, arguable that the specific

---

74 RP-ECJ 61; RP-CFI 62.
75 ECSC Statute, art 38; EC Statute, art 41; Euratom Statute, art 42.
76 RP-ECJ 32(2)(a); RP-CFI 38(2)(a).

mention of these two branches of public authority indicates that they alone are prevented from searching or seizing papers and documents and they alone have power to refer the matter to the Court in the event of a dispute. Such a narrow construction seems artificial in the light of the purpose of the protection. The Rules of Procedure appear to contemplate that it is when a dispute arises that the police or the customs may be involved, for example where an investigating authority has recourse to either in order to enforce its power to search and seize in the event that there is a refusal to comply with it. There is nothing which suggests that the Rules do anything more than set out a procedure for transmitting the material to the Court. In consequence, once the power to search and seize is challenged, the material must be sent to the Court forthwith. If the police or the customs are involved, they are responsible for doing so and have discretion whether or not to seal the material. If another authority with power to search or seize is concerned, it ought by analogy to do the same, but, if it can enforce its powers only by calling in aid the police or customs, the matter can be referred to the Court only when this has been done. Before then there is, ex hypothesi, no risk of enforcement of the search or seizure: it can happen only if the person concerned consents to it. Where the power cannot be exercised without the person concerned's consent, there is no need to rely on the exemption from search and seizure given by the Rules.

The Rules do not specify who is to inspect the material. It is implied that verification is undertaken by the Court in the presence of the Registrar and the person concerned.[77] It is not clear whether the Court can delegate this function to a chamber or a judge or whether the advocate general (where there is one) must be involved. Since disputes may be either trivial or important, it seems that the better view is that the Court is primarily responsible for deciding, after inspecting the material, whether it is protected or not. However, it may, in the first instance, delegate this function to a chamber or a single judge. The chamber or judge, after seeing the material, may either decide the question or refer it to the full Court for decision. In either event, the decision is made in the form of an order. Where the Court or a chamber is involved, the advocate general assigned to the case (where there is one) must be heard before the decision is made. He does not deliver an opinion in public but gives his views orally.[78] The Registrar must be present when the material is opened and inspected; the agent, adviser or lawyer concerned is also there and may be asked questions. The investigating authority involved cannot, ex hypothesi, attend, nor do the parties to the proceedings. Whether there is a hearing of the two sides to the dispute[79] is a matter for the discretion of the Court or chamber.

C The right to foreign currency

Agents, advisers and lawyers are entitled to 'such allocation of foreign currency as may be necessary for the performance of their duties'.[80]

This does not, of course, mean that they are entitled to be financed by the State or anyone else. It is intended to remove exchange control restrictions which would jeopardise the proper performance of these duties. While the English text specifies 'foreign currency', the French version speaks of '*devises*', which is wide enough to cover means of effecting a payment abroad other than

---

77 Ie the agent, adviser or lawyer.
78 See the analogies offered by preparatory enquiries and applications for interim relief.
79 The agent, adviser or lawyer and the investigating authority.
80 RP-ECJ 32(2)(b); RP-CFI 38(2)(b). This presupposes the inapplicability of the general Treaty provisions.

currency. It seems logical to construe the Rules broadly, not restricting them to any particular means of payment. In this sense the right can be defined as the facility to make without hindrance such payments abroad as are necessitated by the performance by the agent, adviser or lawyer of his or her duties. Strictly speaking, the right is simply to the allocation of 'foreign currency' and so it would be compatible with the rules to allow the allocation but fix the exchange rate at a prejudicially high level. If there were evidence that this was done with the intention of preventing the allocation it could, it seems, quite properly be characterised as a breach of the Rules.[81] On the other hand it does not seem that the right entitles the agent, adviser or lawyer to a preferential exchange rate. Since the right is that of the party's agent, adviser or lawyer, not the party himself, it follows that it applies only to the former's disbursements. In consequence, a party could not claim that he must have the facility to pay a foreign-based lawyer or, in particular, the person willing to accept service on his behalf in Luxembourg. The problem lies in the extent to which the agent, adviser or lawyer can rely on the right. Can he claim the allocation of foreign currency so that he may be paid by the client or does the right extend only to the sums disbursed by him? If the party instructs a person based abroad, he has no entitlement to an allocation to pay the latter by a direct transfer of funds. He must pay his agent, adviser or lawyer[82] in the member state in question and the payee may use the right to an allocation of foreign currency to take the money out of the country. It is unclear whether an allocation could be obtained in respect of the whole sum. It is certainly the case to the extent that it covers the payee's own disbursements. The price for his services, where it excludes his own costs, does not, perhaps, 'enable' the performance of his duties but it can be regarded as a condition of performance in that, if there is no prospect or possibility of payment, the agent, adviser or lawyer may refuse to act. It is not easy to see where the line should be drawn. It can be argued that it is in the interests of the proper conduct of proceedings that a party should be entitled to be represented or assisted by the agent, adviser or lawyer he wishes and should neither be influenced in the making of his choice by the fear that a foreign lawyer will not be paid in foreign currency nor be threatened with having to choose another representative during the course of proceedings because of an inability to overcome exchange control restrictions. It can also be said that the power to prevent or hinder the payment of an agent, adviser or lawyer is detrimental to the independent performance of his functions. On the other hand, where the agent, adviser or lawyer is not based abroad the allocation of foreign currency is justified only in order to cover the disbursements made abroad. These can be divided into two parts: disbursements made for the purpose of preparing the case; and those made for the purpose of appearing before the Court. On any view of the Rules, both are covered. Should the agent, adviser or lawyer be entrusted with the function and, at least in the first instance, with the financial burden and responsibility for the retaining of another adviser or lawyer based abroad, it would seem that he would have a right to a foreign currency allocation for this purpose too, although this would not, as has been said, apply if the party were to retain the additional adviser or lawyer directly.

81 The only sanction would seem to be an action for damages or the commencement of proceedings against the member state concerned by the Commission (or another member state) in order to obtain a declaration that it had failed to fulfil its obligations under the Treaty. There might, however, be some more practical relief available under national law and the Court could in such circumstances grant legal aid from Community funds.
82 In practice it would only be the last.

In brief, then, the privilege appears to cover all disbursements made by the agent, adviser or lawyer in another member state for the purpose of preparing the case and appearing before the Court, whether or not he is based abroad, and also the price of the services of a foreign-based agent, adviser or lawyer. It should be noted that the person who accepts service on behalf of the party in Luxembourg is rarely his agent, adviser or lawyer. There is no requirement that that person be a lawyer or have legal training but it is often the case that this is so and that he is called on by the party to perform other services. In so far as his expenses are borne in the first instance by the party's agent, adviser or lawyer, they would seem to be covered by the privilege. On the other hand, if borne directly by the party, it would have to be decided whether they could be described as payments made necessary in the performance of the duties of an agent, adviser or lawyer. Ordinarily the answer would be in the negative because the person who accepts service is no more than a letterbox but, if he does happen to be a lawyer and the sum due is to be paid as fees, the payment is seemingly regarded as made necessary in the performance of the duties of an adviser or lawyer.[83] As far as costs are concerned, additional services performed by the person who accepts service are not recoverable[84] but it is doubtful how far the Rules relating to costs can be taken as a suitable analogy: the standard of what is a necessary or indispensable expense for the purpose of the proceedings[85] is not necessarily the same as that for determining what is necessary for the performance of the duties of the agent, adviser or lawyer. If the person who accepts service does also act as an adviser or lawyer, he should be treated as such for the purposes of the right to a foreign currency allocation.

D Free movement

Agents, advisers and lawyers also enjoy the right to 'travel in the course of duty without hindrance'.[86] Again, this does not benefit the party on whose behalf they appear: he may be prevented from attending the hearing but not they. Other texts use a slightly different phrasing from the English: 'free movement to the extent necessary for the performance of their duties'.

What is 'necessary' should not be too narrowly construed. For example, it is not strictly 'necessary' for someone to appear on behalf of a party at the hearing, whether in a direct action or in a reference for a preliminary ruling: the absence of someone to speak for him will not result in the party losing the case by default, least of all in the latter proceedings, which are non-contentious and in which it frequently happens that a party is not represented at the hearing. Nevertheless, it is part of the duties of a representative to appear in person on behalf of the party before the Court and it is certainly in the interests of the proper conduct of proceedings that he should be heard. Whether other journeys around or to and from the Community are 'necessary' is largely a question of fact. It is part of the duties of an agent, adviser or lawyer to be fully apprised of the party's case and, if this should necessitate a trip abroad, he should be entitled to it.

The right of free movement does not appear to give a right to enter private premises, for example those of the opposing party. As in the case of the other privileges and facilities mentioned in RP-ECJ 32(2) and RP-CFI 38(2), it is a right as against public authority and relates to the exercise of public powers.

---

83 Cases 20 and 21/63 *Maudet v Commission* [1964] ECR 621.
84 Ibid.
85 See RP-ECJ 73(b); RP-CFI 91(b).
86 RP-ECJ 32(2)(c); RP-CFI 38(2)(c). See also the general Treaty provisions on free movement.

RP-ECJ 33 and RP-CFI 39 provide that, in order to benefit from the privileges, immunities and facilities mentioned in RP-ECJ 32 and RP-CFI 38, of which free movement is one, the agent, adviser or lawyer must furnish proof of his status. This is considered in detail below. The inference, however, is that the right of free movement can be exercised simply on presentation of the proof of status referred to by RP-ECJ 33 and RP-CFI 39 (presumably supported by proof of the identity of the person bearing the proof of status) so that there would be no need of further documentation in order to pass from one member state to another. Immigration officers being what they are, one would still be advised to keep one's passport or identity card. It is doubtful if the right of free movement could be relied on to enable the (temporary) release from prison of the agent, adviser or lawyer. This is a largely theoretical question since it is doubtful if a member state or Community institution would in practice select as its agent or adviser a convict or that a lawyer would remain entitled to practise before the court of a member state while serving time. On the other hand, restrictions may be imposed by national law on the free movement of a person which might not affect his capacity to plead, such as binding over on condition not to be found in a particular place or not to move from it, or the French rules relating to internal exile. These, it would seem, no longer apply to an agent, adviser or lawyer in so far as the performance of his duties are concerned.

E   The entitlement to rely on a right or immunity

In order to benefit from the above-mentioned 'privileges, immunities and facilities', the person entitled to them must furnish proof of his 'status'.[87] In the case of agents, the proof of status is 'an official document issued by the State or institution which they represent'; in that of advisers and lawyers it is 'a certificate signed by the Registrar'.[88] A copy of the agent's proof of status must be 'forwarded without delay' to the Registrar by the member state concerned. It seems that this should be done when the document is first issued, which ought to be when the agent is appointed, not when the document is first used to support a claim. Failure to give a copy to the Registrar does not appear to destroy the value of the document but it would seem that the object of notifying the Registrar is so that the validity of the document may be checked by approaching the Court. The certificate signed by the Registrar is also drawn up by him and given to the adviser or lawyer if he so requests and if it is 'required for the proper conduct of proceedings'.[89] An application for such a certificate should therefore be made (in writing) to the Registrar, setting out why it is required for the proper conduct of proceedings. It does not seem that the adviser's or lawyer's position as such is sufficient in itself to give him a right to official proof of his status. The certificate is limited in validity 'to a specified period, which may be extended or curtailed according to the length of the proceedings'.[90] Application for it to be extended or curtailed should be made to the Registrar. The Rules, however, imply that the Registrar may also act on his own motion. There is no provision for an appeal from a decision of the Registrar to the Court.

The fact that the proof issued by the Registrar is limited in point of time does not of itself indicate that the privileges granted by the Rules of Procedure are

87 RP-ECJ 33; RP-CFI 39.
88 Ibid.
89 IR 9.
90 RP-ECJ 33; RP-CFI 39.

equally limited: the certificate is proof of status and does not determine whether an adviser or lawyer has been validly appointed to appear on behalf of a party before the Court nor does it act as proof that the substantive requirements for benefiting from one of the privileges have been satisfied. A fortiori it cannot limit the existence of the privilege in question. On the other hand, it is a formal sine qua non for enjoyment of the privilege. If it be accepted that immunity in respect of words spoken or written concerning the case or the parties, for example, exists after the end of the proceedings, the problem of taking advantage of that immunity some time after their end arises. RP-ECJ 33 and RP-CFI 39 suggest that the Registrar's certificate should usually be issued for a period not exceeding the length of proceedings but there is nothing to say that another cannot be applied for after that time. So, in the event of proceedings being commenced in respect of words spoken or written by an adviser or lawyer, he may apply to the Registrar for a certificate evidencing that he satisfied at the relevant time the formal requirements for reliance on RP-ECJ 32(1) or, as the case may be, RP-CFI 38(1).

The French and Italian versions of RP-ECJ 33 and RP-CFI 39 indicate that proof of status must be given before claiming the privilege in question.[91] The inference is that a claim to a privilege may be refused unless it is preceded or accompanied by presentation of proof of status. The Rules do not, however, suggest that anything else is needed in order to benefit from RP-ECJ 32 or RP-CFI 39. So, for example, in the case of a lawyer who wishes to travel to Luxembourg to plead before the Court, presentation of the Registrar's certificate to an immigration officer (and, where necessary, presentation of proof that he or she is the person referred to in the certificate) should without more entitle him or her to enjoy the right to free movement, apparently without the necessity to produce evidence that the journey is necessary to perform his or her duties as the party's lawyer. This could be taken as suggesting that the immigration officer is not entitled to question him at the time of the passage across the frontier as to, for example, the date of the hearing or, at least, to require a reply to such a question. It is doubtful if this is correct. The proof of status seems intended only to be evidence that the holder benefits from the privileges in general but not that he or she benefits from the particular privilege in question under the circumstances existing at the material time. The conclusion appears to be that, unless the agent, adviser or lawyer shows, prima facie, that the substantive conditions for benefiting from the Rules of Procedure have been fulfilled, his claim to a privilege may be denied despite presentation of his proof of status. Nonetheless, the only proof that may be required of him is that which is reasonably necessary to establish the claim. Otherwise, the requirement of proof could itself be a means of thwarting the purpose lying behind the existence of the privileges. The only exception to this Rule seems to be exemption from search and seizure because RP-ECJ 32(2)(a) and RP-CFI 38(2)(a) state specifically that the matter must be referred to the Court once a dispute has arisen. This occurs when the power to search or seize is opposed, rather than when the investigating authority challenges the claim to exemption.

F Waiver and loss of entitlement to a right or immunity

The second sentence of RP-ECJ 34 and RP-CFI 40 provides that the Court may waive immunity 'where it considers that the proper conduct of proceedings will not be hindered thereby'. This refers to the condition upon which all

91 This seems to be borne out by the German version as well.

the privileges, immunities and facilities set out in RP-ECJ 32 and RP-CFI 38 are granted, which is specified in the first sentence of RP-ECJ 34 and RP CFI 40, ie that they are 'exclusively in the interests of the proper conduct of proceedings'. If the Court considers that this condition is no longer satisfied, it will waive immunity. 'Immunity' is not, here, a compendious term for the bundle of rights, privileges and facilities specified in RP-ECJ 32 and RP-CFI 38. That seems to follow clearly from the difference in wording, reproduced in all the texts, between the first and second sentences of RP-ECJ 34 and RP-CFI 40: the first sentence refers to 'privileges, immunities and facilities'[92] and the second just to 'immunity'. The Court does not, therefore, have express power to waive the privileges and facilities mentioned in RP-ECJ 32(2) and RP-CFI 38(2).[93] The existence of this express power in relation to immunity does, however, indicate that immunity is not lifted automatically but only by a decision of the Court. It seems also to exclude waiver by the person benefiting from it.

No procedure is specified in the Statutes or elsewhere for applying for waiver of immunity. In these circumstances, it seems appropriate to follow that set out in RP-ECJ 91 or, as the case may be, RP-CFI 114. Questions concerning the right to rely on RP-ECJ 32(1) or RP-CFI 38(1) may, of course, arise in the context of proceedings before a national court; but, although a reference for a preliminary ruling could be made concerning the interpretation to be given to the Rules of Procedure and the extent of any privilege, immunity or facility, it would not be possible to use this procedure in order to request the Court to waive immunity.[94] The burden lies on the party seeking waiver to show that it would not prejudice the proper conduct of proceedings. It is possible to argue on the basis of, for example, the Italian text of RP-ECJ 34 and RP-CFI 40, that it is the proper conduct of the proceedings in the action in which the words were said or spoken that matters, not the proper conduct of proceedings in general. Hence there is no objection to lifting immunity once the action is over because the proper conduct of proceedings which have terminated can no longer be prejudiced. The full phrase used in the first sentence of RP-ECJ 34 and RP-CFI 40 is, however, 'the interests of the proper conduct of proceedings'[95] and it is this that the second sentence means to refer to when it uses the abbreviated phrase 'the proper conduct of proceedings'.[96] The 'interest' in this context lies in upholding the legitimate expectation of the agent, adviser or lawyer that he may fully and freely present the case of the party on whose behalf he appears without risk of being prosecuted or sued in respect of what he has said or written.

Since there is no provision for waiver of the privileges and facilities set out in RP-ECJ 32(2) and RP-CFI 38(2), whether by the Court or by the person benefiting from them, it would seem that they end automatically once they are no longer in the interests of the proper conduct of proceedings. The right to free movement would seem to disappear as a matter of course once proceedings have terminated but that to an allocation of foreign currency appears to persist for as long as the agent, adviser or lawyer retains any outstanding pecuniary obligations necessitating its invocation which relate to the performance of his

---

92 In the German text only to 'privileges', but all the same, a different word is used in the second sentence.
93 Vandersanden and Barav, op cit take the opposite view, see p 34.
94 Unless the proceedings were regarded as analogous to the type of situation dealt with by the ECJ in Case C-2/88 Imm *Zwartveld* [1990] ECR I-3365.
95 Or, in Italian, 'the interests of the proceedings'.
96 Cf the other language versions.

functions. A problem arises in relation to exemption from search and seizure. Although falling within RP-ECJ 32(2) and RP-CFI 38(2), and so described as a 'privilege' or 'facility', its legal form is closer to that of an immunity. The structure of RP-ECJ 32 and 34 and RP-CFI 38 and 40 nevertheless seems to prevent it from being considered an immunity for the purposes of RP-ECJ 34 and RP-CFI 40. In addition, if it is right that exemption applies even after the termination of proceedings, the situation may arise that papers and documents are exempt from search and seizure despite the fact that the Court may be prepared to lift immunity from suit in respect of them. This would avail nothing because the material could not be seized in order to be made the subject of proceedings. However, if the Court is prepared to waive immunity, exemption is also likely to disappear because it could no longer be said to be 'exclusively in the interests of the proper conduct of proceedings', as required by the first sentence of RP-ECJ 34 and RP-CFI 40. The reason for this is that, where both rights apply at the same time, they pertain to the same subject matter[97] and the same test for their application applies. In consequence, if a claim to exemption is upheld, there are no grounds for waiving immunity from suit in respect of the contents of the papers or documents. On the other hand, the rejection of the claim brings in its train a finding that there are also grounds for waiving immunity. Nonetheless, a decision of the Court rejecting the claim to exemption is not equivalent to one lifting immunity.

Under RP-ECJ 35(1) and RP-CFI 41(1) an adviser or lawyer[98] (but not an agent) 'who uses his rights for purposes other than those for which they were granted, may at any time be excluded from the proceedings'. This applies to the rights of an adviser or lawyer in general and not just those rights specified in RP-ECJ 32 and RP-CFI 38. As far as the latter are concerned, the Rules of Procedure do not exclude the application of any remedies under national law should an adviser or lawyer abuse his (apparent) right to enjoy a privilege, immunity or facility, eg professional disciplinary proceedings or a prosecution. RP-ECJ 35(1) and RP-CFI 41(1) simply specify what action the Court can take in the interests of the proper conduct of its own proceedings.

IV Obligations

The Statutes[99] also provide that, as regards the advisers and lawyers who appear before it, 'the Court shall have the powers normally accorded to courts of law, under conditions laid down' in the Rules of Procedure.[1] The Rules of Procedure state that an adviser or lawyer, but not an agent, may at any time be excluded from the proceedings if (i) his conduct towards the Court, a chamber, a judge (including the President), an advocate general or the Registrar is 'incompatible with the dignity of the Court' or (ii) he 'uses his rights for purposes other than those for which they were granted'.[2]

The decision to exclude is made in the form of an order by the Court or chamber after the adviser or lawyer in question has been given 'an opportunity to defend himself'.[3] This means that the rules of natural justice must be observed before the decision is taken. There is no requirement that the adviser

---

97 Ie words spoken or written which relate to the proceedings.
98 Including a university teacher with a right of audience before the Court.
99 ECSC Statute, art 20; EC and Euratom Statutes, art 17.
1 ECSC Statute, art 20, refers only to 'lawyers'.
2 RP-ECJ 35(1); RP-CFI 41(1).
3 Ibid.

or lawyer be represented by someone. Equally there is no requirement that the decision be taken by members of the Court other than those before whom the incident had occurred. In the case of a hearing before the full Court, of course, this would in any event be impossible. The advocate general's opinion (in cases before the ECJ) is heard before the order is made and is given in private. In specifying an order made by the Court or chamber, the Rules of Procedure appear to exclude a decision made by the President of the Court (or a chamber) in proceedings for interim relief heard by him alone. In such proceedings he sits neither as 'the Court' nor as a chamber. The fact that the Statutes authorise the Court to give effect to the broad principle stated by them in its Rules of Procedure indicates that the enunciation of the principle in the latter is a full and comprehensive statement of the powers which the Court may exercise.[4] However, neither the Rules of Procedure nor the Statutes refer to the President: the lacuna is complete. In this situation it seems right to have recourse to the principle that the Court and, in this case, its members possess the implied powers necessary for the proper functioning of any judicial authority. Hence RP-ECJ 35 and RP-CFI 41 apply by analogy in proceedings before a single judge, mutatis mutandis.

The effect of the decision is to deprive a party of the adviser or lawyer appearing for him during the course of the proceedings. It follows that the decision must be made when the incident occurs or is brought to the attention of the Court so that the exclusion of the adviser or lawyer from the proceedings harms the interests of the party less than if it were to take effect at a more advanced stage. Proceedings are stayed for a period fixed by the President when the order is made so that the party concerned can appoint another adviser or lawyer[5] but the more advanced they are the less easy it is for someone else to replace the adviser or lawyer. If proceedings are allowed to continue without action being taken against the offender, once the incident has come to light, the Court, chamber or judge must be taken to have waived the breach. After the hearing is over there is no point in making an order. It is not clear from the Rules of Procedure whether the Court has power to exclude an adviser or lawyer from the proceedings by reason of an incident which took place in the context of another action. The power is certainly exercisable only in relation to current proceedings and not proceedings in general[6] but the phrasing of the Rules is wide enough to allow the Court to make such an order in every case in which a particular adviser or lawyer appears if it is of the opinion that a breach by him of his obligations to the Court in earlier proceedings merits it. Once made, the order has immediate effect[7] but can be rescinded at any time.[8]

Although the English and German texts of the ECJ's Rules of Procedure refer to behaviour 'towards the Court, a Chamber, a Judge, an Advocate General or the Registrar', the French and Italian versions simply say 'towards the Court, a Chamber or a Magistrate'.[9] In this context 'magistrate' means an official of the Court who exercises judicial functions. There is therefore no difference in substance between the texts. The CFI's Rules of Procedure do not

---

4 See the analogy provided by third party proceedings: Cases 9 and 12/60 *Belgium v Société Commerciale Antoine Vloeberghs and the High Authority* [1962] ECR 171 at 187–188 (Advocate General Roemer).
5 RP-ECJ 35(2); RP-CFI 41(2).
6 See, for example, the Italian text.
7 RP-ECJ 35(1); RP-CFI 41(1).
8 RP-ECJ 35(3); RP-CFI 41(3).
9 'Magistrat' and 'magistrato' respectively.

refer expressly to a chamber of the CFI but the reference is implied by virtue of RP-CFI 11(2). They also do not refer to the advocate general but, in the CFI, only a judge can act as advocate general in a case; separate reference to the advocate general would therefore have been superfluous. The Registrar is included in both the ECJ's and the CFI's Rules of Procedure because, although he is not a 'judge', he is in charge of the administrative aspect of judicial proceedings and acts as the Court's mouthpiece in dealing with the parties prior to and after the hearing.

The omission from the Rules of agents does not mean that they can be as abusive as they like to the Court with complete impunity. Should the situation warrant it, the Court may have recourse to its implied powers.

'Conduct . . . incompatible with the dignity of the Court' covers a wide range of activities: in Case 108/63 *Officine Elettromeccaniche Ing A Merlini v High Authority*,[10] Advocate General Roemer suggested that it might include the submission by a lawyer of a pleading drawn up by his client and not checked by him to see if it was fit to be lodged. Another example is deliberately misleading the Court; but it seems unnecessary to set out a catalogue of examples here. It should be noted that the CFI's Rules of Procedure refer to 'conduct . . . incompatible with the dignity of the Court of First Instance', which does not point to conduct that is in some respect different in nature or degree from conduct incompatible with the dignity of the ECJ; it simply means that the conduct in question must relate to the CFI or its members and Registrar, not to the ECJ and its members or Registrar. The second ground for excluding an adviser or lawyer from proceedings is abuse of the rights attaching to the functions of adviser or lawyer.[11] It is not restricted to those privileges, immunities and facilities specifically recognised by the Rules of Procedure but encompasses any misuse by the adviser or lawyer of his position as such.

V Legal aid

The Statutes contain no provision relating to legal aid but two articles in the Rules of Procedure of the ECJ (RP-ECJ 76 and 104(5)) and four in the Rules of Procedure of the CFI (RP-CFI 94 to 97) do. RP-ECJ 76 and the parallel provisions in the CFI's Rules of Procedure apply to contentious proceedings before the Court; RP-ECJ 104(5) applies to references for a preliminary ruling. The reason there are two separate provisions seems to be that, in the normal course of events, the question of legal aid in references for a preliminary ruling would have arisen and been dealt with at the stage of the proceedings before the referring court since the reference procedure constitutes a step in those proceedings. The provision in the ECJ's Rules of Procedure for legal aid in such cases therefore provides something of a safety net to be used when the primary source of funds is unavailable.

A Contentious proceedings

RP-ECJ 76(1) and RP-CFI 94(1) provide that a party who is wholly or in part unable to meet the costs of the proceedings may at any time apply for legal aid. The words 'wholly or in part' indicate that the party concerned need not be entirely indigent; it is sufficient if he or she is unable to fund all the costs of the

---

10 [1965] ECR 1 at 16.
11 Cf the different language versions of RP-ECJ 35(1) and RP-CFI 41(1).

proceedings, irrespective of the extent of the shortfall. 'Party' covers all persons and bodies capable of taking part in the proceedings, whether legal or natural or lacking in personality; and whether an applicant, defendant or intervener. The application for legal aid may also be made prior to the commencement of proceedings, at which point, of course, the applicant cannot really be described as a 'party' stricto sensu.[12] When made before the proceedings have commenced, it need not be made through a lawyer[13] and, at least where it appears justified, has the effect of suspending the running of any time limit for the commencement of proceedings (always assuming that the application for legal aid is made before the expiry of such a time limit.[14] It is unclear whether an application for legal aid made once proceedings have begun must be made through a lawyer. The application for legal aid is an exception to the general rule that all pleadings must be submitted by a lawyer.[15] The wording of the exception is broad enough to cover all applications for legal aid irrespective of the stage in proceedings at which they are submitted but it is to be found in RP-ECJ 76(2) and RP-CFI 94(2), which deal specifically with applications made before the commencement of proceedings; it does not form part of the more general provision found in RP-ECJ 76(1) and RP-CFI 94(1). The inference is that an application for legal aid made after the commencement of proceedings must be signed by a lawyer. This could have harsh results if, for some reason, the litigant's money were to run out midway through the proceedings but before he had time to apply for legal aid through his lawyer. In view of this, and despite the absence of any authority, the position can be put as follows: an application for legal aid made before the commencement of proceedings may be made without the intervention of a lawyer; one made after proceedings have begun should be made by the party's lawyer but, if not, may still be admissible if the applicant gives a good and sufficient reason. It would seem that it would have to be shown that the absence of the lawyer was due to an event beyond the applicant's control which he could not reasonably have foreseen or avoided.

The role of the lawyer aside, the application must comply with the requirements of RP-ECJ 37 or, as the case may be, RP-CFI 43 and be framed in the language of the case. It must be accompanied by evidence of the applicant's need of assistance, 'in particular', the Rules go on to say, 'by a document from the competent authority certifying his lack of means'.[16] Where the application is made prior to the commencement of proceedings, it must also 'briefly state the subject of such proceedings'.[17] These are the only requirements stated expressly in the Rules. RP-ECJ 76(3) and RP-CFI 94(2), however, imply that legal aid shall be refused 'where there is manifestly no cause of action': the implication derives from the provision in the Rules of Procedure that the chamber, which is entrusted with deciding whether or not the application for legal aid should be refused, must also consider whether or not there is

---

12 RP-ECJ 76(2); RP-CFI 94(2).
13 Ibid. In Case 10/81 *Farrall v Commission* [1981] ECR 717, however, the application was rejected as inadmissible. It is to be supposed that the reason was that the Court considered that the applicant manifestly had no cause of action (see RP-ECJ 76(3) and RP-94(2)) but no reason was given in the Court order.
14 Case T-92/92AJ *Lallemand-Zeller v Commission* [1993] ECR II-31.
15 Or an agent; see RP-ECJ 37(1) and RP-CFI 43(1) and *Merlini v High Authority* (above, note 10).
16 RP-ECJ 76(1); RP-CFI 94(1).
17 RP-ECJ 76(2); RP-CFI 94(2). This appears to be an allusion to RP-ECJ 38(1)(c) and RP-CFI 44(1)(c) which provide that an application commencing proceedings must set out the 'subject-matter of the proceedings'.

manifestly no cause of action, which would seem to have no meaning unless the manifest absence of a cause of action were a ground for refusing the application. Where the application is made after the commencement of proceedings, this can be determined by looking at the pleadings; if the application is made beforehand, it must therefore show a prima facie case.[18]

Evidence of the applicant's need of assistance comprises (i) his personal means and (ii) the calls likely to be made on him by his lawyer. As far as the latter is concerned it seems to be sufficient to state the estimated cost of the proceedings and the (estimated) amount of the legal aid sought. The applicant's personal means must be proved. The Rules suggest that it is not essential that the applicant submit a document from the 'competent authority' but, quite clearly, such a document is likely to have greater probative value than the applicant's own declaration. It seems in fact to be the Court's practice to require production of a certificate of means from the competent authority. If such a document is not submitted, the application may be rejected for lack of proof.[19] The Rules do not specify what is 'the competent authority'. Another 'competent authority' is named in SR 4 and RP-CFI 95(2) but this seems to refer to the national authority responsible for appointing a lawyer where the applicant either does not indicate his choice of a lawyer or the Court considers his choice unacceptable. It is to be supposed that the competent authority under RP-ECJ 76(1) and RP-CFI 94(1) is the national body responsible for assessing a person's financial position for the purpose of granting legal aid under national law. If there is no such body it is difficult to say what other organisation could be competent, probably the revenue or social security services. In England the competent authority, for natural persons, would appear to be the Legal Aid Board. As far as legal persons are concerned, it may be the authority with whom the audited accounts are registered.[20]

The function of the competent authority is only to produce a certificate of lack of means, not to determine the question whether the applicant is entitled to legal aid. The certificate should in consequence show a complete picture of the applicant's financial situation. It is not enough if it simply certifies that the applicant is poor enough to qualify for legal aid under national law. The Court would be in a position to deduce from this that the applicant is unable to meet the cost of proceedings but this is unsatisfactory because, on the one hand, the Court would be bound by national criteria concerning the entitlement to legal aid and, on the other, it could not determine whether the applicant is wholly or partly unable to meet the costs save by relying on further information given by the applicant himself. The Court is not bound by the view expressed by the competent authority: it must assess the proof of lack of means itself in the light of the costs likely to be incurred by the applicant. It may be that it would decide that the competent authority had not taken into account a source of

---

18 In Case T-13/91R *Harrison v Commission* [1991] ECR II-179 the applicant was unable to demonstrate that he had such a case and the request for legal aid was refused (see para 27).

19 See Case 30/80 *Fedele v Parliament* (unreported, order of 24 April 1980), where the applicant submitted copies of his employer's tax declarations showing his earnings but failed to produce a certificate from the competent authority. In the *Harrison* case, ibid the request for legal aid was not accompanied by any information establishing that the applicant was in need, not even a certificate from the competent authority (see para 27). In the *Lallemand-Zeller* case (above, note 14), a letter from the national social services was relied on successfully.

20 It is understood that in Case 96/80 *Jenkins v Kingsgate (Clothing Productions) Ltd* [1981] ECR 911, the Court asked for the applicant company's audited accounts filed at the Companies Registry. On the other hand, in Case T-131/89 *Cosimex GmbH v Commission* (case withdrawn; order of 5 July 1990), the applicant produced its accounts but no certificate attesting its lack of means and the application for legal aid was dismissed.

income which it should have taken into account or vice versa. For example, national law might prescribe that a spouse's income should be considered. The Court is not bound by national law and must decide this matter for itself. The competent authority determines what are the applicant's financial resources, nothing more.

Decisions granting legal aid give no reasons[21] and it is therefore impossible to say what criteria the Court adopts when deciding whether to grant legal aid, and if so, how much. This is a situation in which inspiration from national law is of little value since it will only indicate where policy, rather than principle, has fixed the criteria to be taken into account. For the same reason, the rules adopted by the member state in which the applicant resides can be of little relevance. They may, for example, constitute a serious attempt to assess capacity (or incapacity) to pay legal costs in the context of the prevailing charges made by lawyers in that member state. This is of little use if costs of representation or assistance before the Court are in practice higher than those for appearances before a national court or if the applicant wishes to employ foreign counsel. In this situation one can do nothing more than say that the Court must adopt a commonsense approach in its assessment of the applicant's financial capacity to bear the costs of the action. One obvious rule seems to be that it is the applicant's disposable resources that should be taken into account: his house, the tools of his trade and a portion of his income reasonably sufficient to ensure his subsistence, and so forth, should be left out of account. In the case of legal persons it is a little more difficult to suggest criteria. The test here would seem to be not whether the accounts show a profit but whether the payment of costs would be so onerous as to endanger the company's capacity to pay its debts as they arise and risk its bankruptcy or winding up. In companies with a modest profit margin the payment of costs could cause severe cash flow problems and lead to its liquidation even though, after all the debts were paid, there might still be something left for the shareholders. The commonsense approach would indicate that a company is entitled to legal aid if the burden of costs would threaten its commercial existence.

In brief, the test for the grant of legal aid is whether or not the applicant is 'unable' to meet the costs of the proceedings and this means inability to incur the expense on top of all normal and reasonable outgoings.

The Rules appear to envisage aid not only to pay the costs of the applicant's lawyer but also those he must pay if he loses the case, because RP-ECJ 76(1) and RP-CFI 94(1) refer compendiously to the 'costs of the proceedings'.[22] This does not seem to be contradicted by RP-ECJ 76(5) and RP-CFI 97(3), which provide that, in its decision as to costs, the Court may order the payment to the cashier of the Court of the whole or part of any sums advanced as legal aid. Against this it could well be said that, as a matter of principle, the Court should assist impecunious parties only in shouldering the financial burden of presenting their side of the case rather than act as an insurer for them against the risk of losing. SR 5 certainly implies that 'costs' in the context of legal aid means the expense of bringing the action rather than the overall expenses incurred, such as costs awarded against the legally aided party, and it seems that, in general, the Court tends to grant legal aid only for bringing the

---

21 RP-ECJ 76(3); RP-CFI 94(2).

22 This seems to be borne out by other texts of the Rules but the French, for example, differentiates between the costs of the proceedings in RP-ECJ 76 ('frais de l'instance') and costs simpliciter ('dépens').

action.[23] There does not seem to have been a case in which a party has claimed legal aid in order to help him bear the costs of losing. The point therefore appears to remain open. The most that can be said is that the power to grant legal aid to cover the costs awarded against the applicant exists but it is not the Court's practice, so far, to exercise it. In consequence a successful party who is awarded costs must have recourse to the normal procedures under national law in order to recover them from the assisted party. If the legally aided party wins and is awarded costs, the Court may order that the sums advanced as legal aid be paid to the Court by the losing party[24] or, as suggested by Advocate General Sir Gordon Slynn in the *Tither* case,[25] by ordering that any sum obtained by way of damages should be used first to satisfy the debt to the Court. Where costs should ordinarily be awarded against the party granted legal aid, the Court may order the repayment of all or part of the sums advanced by it.[26] It is the Registrar's function to obtain the recovery of the legal aid ordered to be repaid.[27] This will be done by bringing proceedings for execution of the Court's order in the member state in which the legally-aided party is resident.

When the application for legal aid is lodged at the Court, the President designates a judge to act as rapporteur and the chamber to which he belongs decides whether it should be granted after considering the written observations of the other party and after hearing the advocate general (where there is one).[28] Quite apart from the question whether the applicant's financial position justifies the grant of legal aid, the chamber must also consider whether or not there is 'manifestly no cause of action'; if there is manifestly no cause of action, it seems that legal aid must be refused.[29] As worded, the Rules of Procedure appear to envisage an application made by the party initiating the action, not the defendant. Almost invariably, the defendant in contentious proceedings before the Court is either a Community institution or a member state, neither of which would normally be expected to be in need of legal aid. However, it is possible for a person other than a Community institution or a member state to be a defendant to proceedings, as was, for example, the case in the third party proceedings brought by one steel company against the High Authority and three other steel companies.[30] Further, an intervening party may also be able to apply for legal aid, where appropriate. The words 'manifestly no cause of action' should therefore be interpreted, in such cases, as also meaning 'manifestly no defence to the action' and 'manifestly no case in the intervention'.

The Rules of Procedure indicate that the Court considers this question only after the other parties have been given an opportunity to submit written observations. This would mean that, where the Court decided to dismiss the action itself as inadmissible of its own motion under RP-ECJ 92 or RP-CFI 111, and without hearing the parties, it could not reject the accompanying application for the grant of legal aid until it had served the application on the

---

23 Most orders granting legal aid set out the figure awarded, which is intended to cover the fees and incidental expenses of the applicant's lawyer, but nothing more (the sum is expressed in the currency in which the lawyer is to be paid).
24 See Case 175/80 *Tither v Commission* [1981] ECR 2345 (para 21).
25 Ibid.
26 RP-ECJ 76(5); RP-CFI 97(3). See Case 25/68 *Schertzer v European Parliament* [1977] ECR 1729.
27 RP-ECJ 76(5); RP-CFI 97(3).
28 RP-ECJ 76(3); RP-CFI 94(2). Usually the chamber and the judge-rapporteur to whom the case has been assigned deal with the application for legal aid.
29 RP-ECJ 76(3); RP-CFI 94(2).
30 Cases 42 and 49/59 *Breedband NV v Société des Aciéries du Temple* [1962] ECR 145.

other parties and awaited their observations. In Case 233/82 *K v Germany and European Parliament*[31] the Court avoided this by applying RP-ECJ 92 instead of RP-ECJ 76(3) on the ground, so it seems, that the latter refers to the absence of a cause of action whereas the former speaks of a manifest lack of jurisdiction and the Court had previously dismissed the action on this ground. From this it is to be inferred that RP-ECJ 76(3) (and RP-CFI 94(2)) refer only to the substance of the case; where it is inadmissible there is no need to hear the parties before refusing to grant legal aid. This appears to be an application by analogy of RP-ECJ 92(1) (see also RP-CFI 111). In one sense, one would expect RP-ECJ 92(2) and RP-CFI 113 to apply to the request for legal aid because the previous dismissal of the action on the ground that it was inadmissible is an absolute bar to the continuation of the ancillary proceedings for the grant of legal aid. In principle, that is correct; but the dismissal of the action also means that there is no need to rule on the request for legal aid because the action to which it relates no longer exists.[32]

The decision of the chamber gives no reasons and there is no appeal from it[33] but the chamber may at any time of its own motion or on application withdraw legal aid if the circumstances upon which it was granted change.[34] In the order granting legal aid the Court also orders that a lawyer be appointed to act for the applicant.[35] Usually it accepts the applicant's own choice but, if he does not name his lawyer himself or the Court considers his choice unacceptable, the Registrar sends a copy of the order granting legal aid and the application to the authority named in Annex II of the Supplementary Rules. This Annex sets out the authority competent in each member state to suggest to the Court a lawyer who may represent the applicant. The competent authorities in the United Kingdom are the Law Societies of England and Wales, Scotland and Northern Ireland. The function of the competent authority is only to make suggestions; the power to make a decision appointing a lawyer to act for the applicant remains the Court's. It seems that the competent authority is determined by the member state in which the applicant resides. This is not expressly stated in SR 4 and RP-CFI 95(2) but it emerges from Annex II, where it is so provided for the purpose of determining the authority competent in respect of persons living in different parts of the United Kingdom. So, for an English person resident in Belgium, the competent authority would be the Belgian Minister of Justice rather than the Law Society of England and Wales.[36] Legal aid is granted out of the Court's budget; the Court has power to

31 [1982] ECR 3637.

32 Eg Case C-130/91 *Instituto Social de Apoio ao Emprego e à Valorização Profissional and Interdata (Centro de Processamento de Dados Lda) v Commission* [1992] ECR I-69.

33 RP-ECJ 76(3); RP-CFI 94(2).

34 RP-ECJ 76(4); RP-CFI 96.

35 SR 4; RP-CFI 95(1). In practice this is not always done, see, for example, Case 66/81 *Pommerehnke v Bundesanstalt für Landwirtschaftliche Marktordnung* [1982] ECR 1363 (order of 16 March 1982); Case 240/81 *Einberger v Hauptzollamt Freiburg* [1982] ECR 3699 (order of 1 April 1981). In Case 145/83 *Adams v Commission* [1985] ECR 3539, the applicant was granted legal aid with no maximum amount fixed coupled with an order that a lawyer be appointed for him. The applicant applied for certain named lawyers to be appointed and the Court so ordered, specifying that the amount of fees and disbursements due by way of legal aid would be fixed at the end of the case. In the course of the proceedings the applicant's lawyers were changed at his request, thus indicating that, when legal aid has been granted, any change in the applicant's lawyers must be approved by the Court.

36 However, it should be noted that, in the *Lallemand-Zeller* case (above, note 14), the CFI appointed a Luxembourg lawyer for the applicant after giving the latter an opportunity to name the lawyer of his choice but without, it would seem from the report of the case, making enquiry of the competent authority in the member state where the applicant resided (France) or, indeed, of any other competent authority.

adjudicate on the lawyer's disbursements and fees and the President may, on application, order that he receive an advance of the legal aid granted.[37] Such an application is usually to be made in the application for legal aid. Where legal aid is granted in response to an application made before the commencement of proceedings, the Court must specify the date from which the running of time for the commencement of proceedings (suspended as a result of the making of the application for legal aid) recommences. That date will ordinarily be the date on which the order granting legal aid is notified to the applicant.[38] Thus, in an action for annulment under art 173 of the EEC Treaty brought by an individual resident in the United Kingdom, for which the time limit for bringing proceedings is two months and ten days, if the application for legal aid was lodged at the Court one month after time had started to run, the application for annulment would have to be lodged within one month and ten days of the notification of the decision granting legal aid. Clearly, in such a situation, the later the application for legal aid is made, the less time is left for the drafting of the application commencing proceedings once legal aid has been granted.

B References for a preliminary ruling

RP-ECJ 104(5) provides that 'in special circumstances the Court may grant, by way of legal aid, assistance for the purpose of facilitating the representation or attendance of a party'. As has been seen, 'representation', in the scheme of the Rules, covers the submission of both written and oral observations.[39] Legal aid is not normally granted for the attendance of a party (as distinct from the party's lawyer) at the hearing. It would seem that the only justification for doing so would be if the party were a litigant in person before the referring court.

The 'special circumstances' which may justify the grant of legal aid are difficult to define because the Court has given no public guidance on the matter but they may be taken to include all circumstances in which, if assistance is not given by the Court, the party in question will simply be unable to present his side of the case. That might be where, as in *Lee v Minister for Agriculture*[40] there is no provision for legal aid in the member state from which the reference comes, either generally or specifically, in relation to references to the Court. Another reason might be a refusal by the national authority competent to grant legal aid to extend it to cover the reference to the Court.[41] In such a case the question would, of course, arise whether or not the party's financial position is such as to justify financial assistance. Whether the Court would step in if the national authority, in breach of the applicable national rules, declined to grant legal aid for the reference is a moot point. It is arguable that, in such a case, there is no justification for the Court granting legal aid because the party has a right to it under national law and should therefore make use of the remedies open to him under that law, in order to force the

---

37 SR 5 and RP-CFI 97(2). The English text specifies an application made by the lawyer. Other language versions do not support this and, in the *Tither* case (above, note 24), an advance was ordered on application by the party, not his lawyer. As a result, it must be concluded that the English text is misleading and that the application can be made by the party. Indeed this is likely to be more usual.

38 The *Lallemand-Zeller* case (above, note 14).

39 See Case 152/79 *Lee v Minister for Agriculture* [1980] ECR 1495.

40 Ibid.

41 This appears to have been the situation in Case 320/82 *D'Amario v LVA Schwaben* [1983] ECR 3811 (order of 7 July 1983).

national authority to release the money, before turning to the Court: by parity of reasoning, the Court would not be justified in granting legal aid if the party had made no attempt at all to obtain it under national law. On the other hand, it would clearly be unfair if the party were to lose his chance of presenting his case to the Court because of delays in obtaining legal aid under national law. In consequence, the Court might well take the view that, where it is impossible or unlikely that legal aid will be granted in time for the hearing, it shall exercise its powers under RP-ECJ 104(5). In that situation it could no doubt subject the grant to the condition that the sum awarded would be repaid if and when the national authority's responsibility for legal aid were established. As in the case of RP-ECJ 76, RP-ECJ 104(5) describes the beneficiary of legal aid as a 'party', thus clearly indicating that he may be either a legal or a natural person. However, in the only case in which an application for legal aid was made by a legal person, it was turned down by the Court.[42] As is usual, no reason for doing so was given and it is possible that the view was taken that 'party' must be restricted to natural persons. It is also possible that the Court found that there were no special circumstances justifying the grant of legal aid so the point remains open.

Although RP-ECJ 104(5) makes no express reference to RP-ECJ 76, it is to be supposed that the Court would adopt the same criteria for granting assistance and that the same formal requirements apply, mutatis mutandis, to the application for assistance. This being so, it would be possible to make the application before the order for reference has been sent to the Court although probably not before the date of the order for reference. It is doubtful if legal aid can be refused on the ground that the applicant has shown no prima facie case[43] because proceedings for obtaining a preliminary ruling are non-contentious and there is no cause of action in dispute before the Court. This requirement does not therefore seem to be applicable.[44] It is unclear whether or not the Court would impose an analogous test; for example, whether or not the point of Community law raised in the reference is 'manifestly clear' so that representation of the parties is not necessary in order that justice be done. Since the grant of assistance lies within the Court's discretion, one cannot exclude the possibility that this might be a reason for refusing an application for legal aid in an exceptional case. As a matter of principle, however, if the order for reference is admissible, the Court should grant assistance to an impecunious party, all other conditions for doing so having been fulfilled.

The application for legal aid should state the circumstances relied on in support of the application and, in particular, indicate what the position regarding legal aid is so far as the national proceedings are concerned. If legal aid has been granted (or refused) by the competent national authority, a copy of its decision should be attached to the application because, even if it relates only to the proceedings before the referring court, it will be of some assistance to the ECJ. The (estimated) amount of the legal aid sought should be stated. The means used to establish the party's indigence have included: a statement from the party's employer and a declaration made under oath by the employee

---

42 *Jenkins v Kingsgate (Clothing Productions) Ltd* (above, note 20).
43 See the reference in RP-ECJ 76(3) to 'manifestly no cause of action'.
44 The Court does have jurisdiction to scrutinise the proceedings before the referring court for the purpose of determining the admissibility of the order for reference (see pp 100–101, above) but it does not seem that, if the reference were admissible, the Court would remain competent to assess the arguments of the parties before the national court for the purpose of deciding whether or not they had a case that was sufficiently arguable to justify the grant of legal aid.

herself as to her income;[45] a statement of personal circumstances;[46] a certificate of property and income;[47] a declaration concerning the party's personal and economic situation and a statement from her lawyer indicating his fees and disbursements.[48] Legal aid in references for a preliminary ruling has been granted for the purposes of the hearing alone, because that was what was requested.[49] The other parties to the reference proceedings are not given an opportunity to submit observations on the application for legal aid.

C Payment and recovery of sums advanced

The order granting legal aid usually sets a limit to the amount which the Court is prepared to cover. This is only, however, a limit; it is not a definitive statement of the party's entitlement come what may. Should the situation arise that it is insufficient to cover the expenses actually incurred, an application may, it seems, be made for a supplementary grant but evidence would have to be produced to show that circumstances had changed since the date of the original application because, otherwise, the second application could be construed as a disguised attempt to get round the rule that there is no appeal from the Court's order[50] and it might, therefore, be regarded as vexatious.

An application for the payment of the legal aid awarded by the Court is made to the Registrar but he is obliged to require particulars of the costs incurred.[51] It is not sufficient, therefore, for the application for payment simply to mention the amount found in the order granting legal aid. It must go further and show what costs justifying the payment have been incurred. It does not seem that a party is entitled to the whole sum awarded merely if he shows that some costs have been incurred, unless, under the terms of the order, legal aid were paid out as a lump sum compensation for them.[52] Rather, he is entitled to be reimbursed for the expenses he has in fact disbursed up to the amount set by the order granting legal aid. The particulars given should, as a matter of practice, be supported by some evidence justifying the costs, if any.

The payment of the legal aid due is ordered by the Registrar against a receipt or other proof of payment and, if he thinks that the amount claimed is excessive, he may of his own motion reduce it or order payment by instalments.[53] There is no provision for an appeal to the Court against any decision made by him. In the case of an advance payment of legal aid ordered by the President under SR 5(2) or, as the case may be, RP-CFI 97(2), the Registrar has no power to require production of particulars of costs but (at least in the

---

45 Case 379/87 *Groener v Minister for Education and City of Dublin Vocational Educational Committee* [1989] ECR 3967 (order of 8 November 1988). In Case C-251/89 *Athanasopoulos v Bundesanstalt für Arbeit* [1991] ECR I-2797 (order of 3 May 1990) there was simply a declaration under oath.
46 Case 186/87 *Cowan v Trésor Public* [1989] ECR 195 (order of 10 February 1988).
47 Case 344/87 *Bettray v Staatsecretaris van Justitie* [1989] ECR 1621 at 1625.
48 Case C-33/89 *Kowalska v Freie und Hansestadt Hamburg* [1990] ECR I-2591 (order of 3 May 1990).
49 Case 125/88 *Criminal proceedings against HFM Nijman* [1988] ECR 3533 (order of 14 December 1988).
50 See RP-ECJ 76(3) and RP-CFI 94(2) (last sentence).
51 IR 21(1). The English text refers to an 'advance payment' but this is misleading. An advance payment of legal aid, which may be ordered by the President on application by the party's lawyer, is provided for in SR 5(2) and RP-CFI 97(2); but RP-ECJ 76(5) and RP-CFI 97(1) make no mention of it. IR 21(4) deals with the advance payment under SR 5(2); IR 21(1) is concerned only with 'advancing' or paying what may be due.
52 An order specifying a lump sum by way of legal aid has been made in the past, generally covering legal fees (eg the order in the *D'Amario* case, above, note 41).
53 IR 21(2).

case of the ECJ's Registrar) he may still reduce the amount if he considers it to be excessive or order payment by instalments.[54] This appears to allow the ECJ's Registrar to derogate from the President's decision but it may be no more than a slip in the drafting of the rules.

When a party granted legal aid, whether in the context of a direct action or a reference for a preliminary ruling, has incurred Registry charges, RP-ECJ 76(5) or, as the case may be, RP-CFI 97(3) applies[55] and the costs are initially borne by the Court itself but may be recovered in the order for costs at the end of the action. It is unclear whether, in a reference for a preliminary ruling, the Court can recover sums paid out as legal aid. RP-ECJ 104(5) provides that it is for the referring court to 'decide as to the costs of the reference' but this seems to apply to decisions determining who is to pay the costs and does not entirely exclude the possibility that the Court may recover legal aid from an assisted party who has been awarded costs by the referring court. Normally, in a direct action, the Court orders repayment of the amounts paid over as legal aid in the order for costs.[56] It is therefore arguable that, in the judgment giving the preliminary ruling, the Court can also order that the legal aid be reimbursed by the party ordered by the referring court to pay the costs of the reference. The alternative view seems to be that legal aid granted in proceedings for a preliminary ruling is not recoverable. The former hypothesis has the merit of tying in with the problem of the recovery of Registry charges in references for a preliminary ruling.

Where sums advanced as legal aid are recoverable under RP-ECJ 76(5) or, as the case may be, RP-CFI 97(3), the Registrar, whose responsibility it is to obtain their repayment, first sends a written demand by registered post stating the amount due, the method of payment and the date by which payment should be made.[57] If his request is not complied with within the time fixed for doing so, he asks the Court to adopt an 'enforceable decision'.[58] Under the Treaties only judgments of the Court are enforceable[59] so it would seem that the decision must, strictly speaking, be in this form. The Registrar then takes the steps necessary to execute the judgment pursuant to the Treaties.[60]

---

54 IR 21(4).
55 IR 19.
56 See above p 147.
57 IR 22(1).
58 IR 22(2).
59 ECSC Treaty, art 44; EC Treaty, art 187; Euratom Treaty, art 159. But see chapter 16, section IX.
60 ECSC Treaty, art 92; EC Treaty, art 192; Euratom Treaty, art 164. IR 22(2) suggests that it is the Court which orders the enforcement of the decision but this is an obvious tautology and it stems from a simple mistranslation. The Court, in the person of the Registrar, is the 'person concerned' for the purposes of art 192 of the EEC Treaty and 164 of the Euratom Treaty. In *Schertzer v European Parliament* (above, note 26), the applicant had received legal aid but lost the case. As it was a staff case, the Court ordered each party to bear its own costs and the applicant to repay the sums advanced as legal aid. In 1979 the Court adopted an order (unreported) requiring payment of the latter and leaving it to the Registrar to fix the method and time for repayment. The order said that it should be enforced ('l'execution forcée . . . sera requise') if the money was not paid on time.

CHAPTER 5

Intervention

I Introduction

The persons who are the main or immediate parties to proceedings before the Court are identified at the commencement of the proceedings. Other persons are unable to join or be joined as a party to the proceedings otherwise than by means of the procedure known as intervention. Different actions may be joined at different stages of the proceedings but joinder results only in consolidation of the proceedings, not consolidation of the actions or the joinder of a new party. The procedure known as third party proceedings is a method of reviewing a judgment of the Court which may be invoked by third parties to the proceedings before the Court (hence the title given to the procedure). But the only true procedure enabling someone who is not a party to proceedings at their commencement to become a party later on is intervention. In Cases 42 and 49/59 *Breedband NV v Société des Aciéries du Temple* and Cases 9 and 12/60 *Belgium v Société Commerciale Antoine Vloeberghs SA and High Authority*,[1] which both concerned third party proceedings, the Court pointed out that, since it is in the interests of justice and legal certainty that persons having an interest in the result of proceedings before the Court shall be prevented as far as possible from asserting this interest after judgment has been delivered, the procedure of intervention exists in order to allow them to do so at an earlier stage. Nevertheless, intervention does not, as will be seen, give the intervener rights in the proceedings as extensive as those of a party in the true sense, although the intervener is equally bound by the Court's judgment.

Four sets of provisions deal with the intervention of someone who is not strictly speaking a party to a case before the Court:

(1) Articles 20 and 21 respectively of the EC and Euratom Statutes make specific provision for the submission of observations by the member states, the Commission and the Council in references for a preliminary ruling; no similar provision exists in the ECSC Statute but the want is made up by RP-ECJ 103(3). This right is distinct from intervention in the true sense because references for a preliminary ruling are non-contentious proceedings.

(2) All three Statutes contain broadly comparable provisions for intervention in contentious proceedings.[2]

(3) The ECSC Statute[3] allows the member states to intervene in proceedings

---

1 [1962] ECR 145 and 171 at 158 and 181 respectively.
2 ECSC Statute, art 34; EC Statute, art 37; Euratom Statute, art 38. The English text refers to intervention in a 'case' but other texts use a word which has the more specific meaning of a dispute or litigation.
3 Article 41.

brought under art 89 of the ECSC Treaty, ie in disputes between the member states concerning the application of the ECSC Treaty.

(4) RP-ECJ 123 provides for intervention in appeals to the ECJ from the CFI. The right to intervene applies to those categories of potential interveners in contentious proceedings recognised by the Statutes (see (2) above). Interveners in an appeal can only be third parties to the proceedings in which the judgment or decision appealed against was delivered; if they had been parties to those proceedings, even as interveners, they would automatically be parties to the appeal.[4]

Only the last three types of intervention will be discussed here. It will be observed that the restriction of the second type to contentious proceedings means that it is not possible for a person other than a member state, the Commission or the Council to be heard in a reference for a preliminary ruling unless he was a party to the proceedings before the referring court.[5]

II   Who can intervene

The EC and Euratom Statutes[6] declare that member states and Community institutions may intervene in cases[7] before the Court; other persons may do so if they show that they have an interest in the outcome of the case but their right to do so is restricted to cases between Community institutions, on the one hand, and persons other than member states or Community institutions, on the other. They have no right to intervene at all in an action between member states, between Community institutions or between member states and Community institutions. In contrast, the ECSC Statute[8] gives the right to intervene to 'natural or legal persons establishing an interest in the result of any case submitted to the Court', without any restriction.

Under the EC and Euratom Statutes, then, member states and Community institutions have a general right to intervene but 'other persons' and, in the context of the ECSC Statute, all 'natural or legal persons', must show an interest in the result of the case.[9] Since no specific provision is made in the ECSC Statute for intervention by member states[10] and Community institutions, it must be supposed that they may intervene only if they can be

4 However, in the case of an appeal from a decision of the CFI dismissing an application to intervene, it would seem that only the parties to the *intervention* proceedings could be parties to the appeal: an applicant to intervene becomes a party to the action only if the application to intervene is upheld and, by the same token, the parties to the action are not parties to the intervention proceedings unless they have been asked by the CFI to submit observations on the application to intervene (and have done so).

5 Applications made by a person, other than a member state or a Community institution, to intervene in a reference for a preliminary ruling were rejected in Case 6/64 *Costa v ENEL* [1964] ECR 614 and Case 212/81 *Caisse de Pension des Employés Privés v Bodson* [1982] ECR 1019. In the former the Court took the view that the limitation of the right to submit observations in a reference for a preliminary ruling to 'the parties, the member states, the Commission and, where appropriate, the Council' (EC Statute, art 20) impliedly excluded any possibility of submitting observations, so far as a private person or undertaking was concerned, if he were not a party to the proceedings before the referring court. The only way of submitting observations in such a situation would therefore seem to be to seek to be joined to the proceedings before the referring court.

6 Articles 37 and 38 respectively.

7 Ie contentious proceedings.

8 Article 34.

9 'Other persons' and 'natural or legal persons', respectively, include third countries.

10 Other than in the context of art 41.

described as 'natural or legal persons' and can show an interest in the result of the case. There seems to be no difficulty with the first condition as far as the member states are concerned.[11] With regard to Community institutions, how-ever, the matter is a little obscure. Article 6 of the ECSC Treaty provides that the Community has legal personality and that it shall be 'represented' by its institutions, 'each within the limits of its powers'. The Community, therefore, has legal personality but its institutions do not.[12] If the Community has an interest in the result of a case brought under the ECSC Treaty, it may intervene through one of the institutions. If one of the institutions is already a party to the case, it is doubtful (though by no means clear) that another institution may intervene because it is arguable that the interests of the Community are already adequately represented. If no Community institution were involved in the case, the question of representation would no doubt be decided by reference to the subject matter of the dispute, the institution within whose competence it fell being a proper representative of the Community.[13] The question of interest is dealt with below.

It is arguable that the phrase 'natural or legal person' in the ECSC Statute is not as wide a description as the expression 'other persons' used in the EC and Euratom Statutes because it implies that, to intervene, a person must be recognised either as a natural person or as a legal person. In the context of the EC Statute, the Court has held that the right to intervene does not extend to entities lacking legal personality or its basic aspects[14] but what this appears to mean is that an applicant to intervene does not have to be recognised as a legal person in formal terms: it is sufficient if it possesses the elements of legal personality. It is to be supposed that the same approach would be taken in relation to the ECSC Statute, despite its more specific wording.[15]

At all events, the right to intervene has been accorded, inter alia, to a third country;[16] an unincorporated association;[17] the Italian National Union of Consumers, a body not possessing legal personality in Italian law;[18] the Federation of European Bearing Manufacturers Associations;[19] the Consul-tative Committee of the Bars and Law Societies of the European Communi-ties (the 'CCBE'), a body lacking in legal personality, which represents lawyers' professional associations in the member states;[20] the Bureau Européen des Unions de Consommateurs, an umbrella group covering con-sumers' organisations in the Community, which has legal personality under

---

11 See, for example, Cases 7 and 9/54 *Groupement des Industries Sidérurgiques Luxembourgeoises v High Authority* [1954–56] ECR 175 at 222 and Case 30/59 *De Gezamenlijke Steenkolenmijnen in Limburg v High Authority* [1961] ECR 1 at 48.

12 See Cases 7/56 and 3–7/57 *Algera v Common Assembly* [1957–58] ECR 39 at 58.

13 Bebr in *Judicial Control of the European Communities* (1962) p 169, takes the view that Community institutions cannot intervene under the ECSC Statute. In the case of the EC and Euratom Statutes, of course, the problem of representation does not arise because the Community institutions may intervene as of right: see Case 138/79 *Roquette Frères SA v Council* [1980] ECR 3333 (paras 17–21); Case 114/81 *Tunnel Refineries Ltd v Council* [1982] ECR 3189, order of 30 September 1981.

14 Case 15/63 *Lassalle v European Parliament* [1964] ECR 31 at 50.

15 See the *Lassalle* case (ibid) at 54 (Advocate General Lagrange).

16 Cases 91 and 200/82 *Chris International Foods Ltd v Commission* [1983] ECR 417.

17 Cases 16 and 17/62 *Confédération Nationale des Producteurs de Fruits et Légumes v Council* [1962] ECR 471 at 488–489.

18 Cases 41, 43–48, 50, 111, 113 and 114/73 *Générale Sucrière SA v Commission* [1973] ECR 1465.

19 See Case 113/77 *NTN Toyo Bearing Co Ltd v Council* [1979] ECR 1185. Here the Court took account of the fact that the Association, which had been formed in Germany, had capacity to intervene in similar proceedings under German law and costs could be recovered against it.

20 Case 155/79 *A M & S Europe Ltd v Commission* [1982] ECR 1575, order of 7 May 1980.

Belgian law;[21] and the European Council of Chemical Manufacturers' Federation.[22] A number of professional or trade organisations were allowed to intervene in Cases 197–200, 243, 245 and 247/80 *Ludwigshafener Walzmühle Erling KG v Council and Commission.*[23] A German trade union also applied but its application was rejected because it was held that it had not shown an interest in the result of the case.[24] The Court order does not discuss the question whether the union could be regarded as a 'person', although there is some authority that trade unions may intervene.[25]

As has been remarked, legal personality in formal terms is not the criterion determining capacity to intervene, at least in actions brought under the EC and Euratom Treaties; neither is the fact that a particular body can be classified in the same group, such as that of trade or professional associations, as another body which has been allowed to intervene in a previous case. The Court's approach is set out most clearly in the following two cases. In *Lassalle v European Parliament*[26] the Court appeared to identify independence and responsibility as the two qualities required by a body for the purpose of intervening, both being regarded as forming part of the basic aspects of legal personality. The case concerned an application to intervene made by the Parliament's Staff Committee. The Court seems to have held that it lacked independence and responsibility because it was only a component of the Parliament which was, of course, the defendant in the action. In *Générale Sucrière SA v Commission*[27] the Court held that 'bodies not having legal personality may be permitted to intervene if they display the characteristics which are at the foundation of such personality, in particular, the ability, however circumscribed, to undertake autonomous action and to assume liability'. In subsequent cases the question whether an applicant to intervene has fulfilled these two conditions has rarely been challenged, opposition to intervention generally being centred on the question whether the applicant to intervene has shown sufficient interest in the case to justify allowing the intervention. In consequence there has been little futher elaboration of this formula by the Court.

By analogy to the *Lassalle* case, it is arguable that even an entity possessing legal personality under national law may not be entitled to intervene unless it is independent vis-à-vis both the applicant and the defendant to the proceedings. For example, where a subsidiary which is wholly owned or controlled by one of the parties seeks to intervene, it could be said that, in real terms, it is the alter ego of the party due to its position of dependence. There appears to be no clear authority on this point. The better view seems to be that an entity which is recognised as possessing legal personality under national law is deemed to have the capacity to be an intervener (without prejudice to the question – considered below – whether or not it has an independent interest justifying its intervention); it is only if the entity in question does not possess legal personality in formal terms that the substantive test adopted by the Court is to be applied.

21 Cases 228 and 229/82 *Ford v Commission* [1984] ECR 1129, orders of 21–22 September 1982 (the proceedings for interim relief) and 1 December 1982 (the intervener had been a complainant to the Commission).
22 Case 236/81 *Celanese Chemical Co Inc v Council and Commission* [1982] ECR 1183.
23 [1981] ECR 3211 (see, for example, the orders of 18 February and 11 March 1981).
24 [1981] ECR 1041.
25 See Case 18/74 *Syndicat Générale du Personnel des Organismes Européens v Commission* [1974] ECR 933 at 953 (Advocate General Trabucchi). Staff unions were allowed to intervene in Case 3/83 *Abrias v Commission* [1985] ECR 1995 (order of 8 December 1983) and interventions by such organisations in staff cases have been frequent since then.
26 Above, note 14.
27 Above (note 18), see p 1468.

Since the purpose of the intervention is to enable a third party to protect an interest which may be affected by the result of the case, rather than to vindicate a right which he may possess, the significance of legal personality to capacity to intervene is, in theoretical terms, comparatively little: for example, a group of persons can be said to have a (collective) interest in the outcome of a case even though the group does not constitute one legal person; but the possession of a single legal right by the group, as opposed to the bundle of rights possessed individually by those comprising it, presupposes that the group has legal personality. Capacity to intervene depends largely, therefore, on whether the group can act independently, ie whether it can appoint its own representative, and assume liability for the costs incurred by it, rather than on the question whether it can be said to possess an autonomous right or interest. In the nature of things it is likely to fail the latter test.

In the same way, the question of legal personality aside, a party is not prevented from intervening in a case, assuming that all conditions for intervening are fulfilled, merely because it for some reason lacks capacity to be a party to the action. For example, in Cases 3 to 18, 25, 26/58 *Erzbergbau AG v High Authority*,[28] the interveners were six German Länder; the cases were applications for the annulment of two High Authority decisions made under art 33 of the ECSC Treaty. This gives the Court jurisdiction to hear actions brought by a member state, the Council and undertakings or associations as defined in the Treaty. In consequence the Länder, although capable of intervening, did not have capacity to bring the action themselves.[29] In Case 45/81 *Alexander Moksel Import-Export GmbH & Co Handels KG v Commission*,[30] an action for annulment of a Commission regulation pursuant to art 173 of the EEC Treaty, the intervener was barred by the two-month time limit in art 173 from itself bringing an action for annulment but that did not affect its capacity to intervene. The conclusion seems to be that a person may intervene even if he were prevented from bringing the action himself because of the expiry of a time limit or some other ground of inadmissibility. It should be borne in mind, however, that he would still have to show an interest in the result of the case.[31]

As a general rule it can be said that the absence of a right of action against a party is not, per se, a bar to intervening because the object of intervention is to protect an interest and not to enforce a right. But the absence of a right may, depending on the circumstances, reflect the inexistence of a relevant interest justifying intervention.

---

28 [1960] ECR 173. See also Case 13/60 *Geitling Ruhrkohlen–Verkaufsgesellschaft mbH v High Authority* [1962] ECR 83 at 143.

29 See also Case 25/59 *Netherlands v High Authority* [1960] ECR 355.

30 [1982] ECR 1129.

31 Bebr, *Judicial Control* pp 169–172 takes the view that the right to intervene is restricted to persons who are under the jurisdiction of the Community (ie covered by the Treaties), or a member state, and he goes so far as to say that an undertaking trading outside the Community cannot intervene unless it owns enterprises within the Community. The basis for this view is uncertain: the object of intervention is not to enable the intervener to enforce a legal relationship that may exist between him and the party *against* whom he intervenes, whence the capacity to intervene of persons who have no locus standi as parties in the true sense. In consequence the argument that, by ratifying the Treaties, the member states could only bind and confer rights on persons under their jurisdiction, is considerably weakened. The only 'right' the intervener relies on is the right to intervene and that is made subject, in particular, to the condition that he shows an interest in the result of the case. An undertaking based in a third country but trading within the Community may, depending on the facts, show such an interest. It seems artificial to exclude intervention simply because the undertaking is not based in the Community. In any event, a Swedish company was allowed to intervene in Case 792/79R *Camera Care Ltd v Commission* [1980] ECR 119, and a third country in *Chris International Foods Ltd v Commission* (above, note 16).

Intervention in an action between member states by a person other than another member state or a Community institution is specifically excluded by the EC and Euratom Statutes.[32] On the other hand, no such restriction applies under the ECSC Statute. Furthermore, art 41 of the ECSC Statute, which provides that member states have the right to intervene in proceedings brought by one member state against another under art 89 of the ECSC Treaty, only appears to derogate from the rule in art 34 of the ECSC Statute, which provides that a natural or legal person can intervene in a case only if it shows an interest in the result of it. The consequence seems to be that a natural or legal person other than a member state can intervene in an action brought under art 89, if it shows an interest in the result, but has no right to do so.

III   Interest

Under the EC and Euratom Statutes[33] member states and Community institutions need not justify their application to intervene. The same applies, as has been remarked, to applications to intervene made by a member state under art 41 of the ECSC Statute. In consequence, in cases to which the EC and Euratom Statutes and art 41 of the ECSC Statute apply, member states and Community institutions have a right to intervene (subject only to compliance with the procedural rules governing applications to intervene). In all other cases, however, the applicant's entitlement to intervene is contingent upon the intervener establishing 'an interest in the result of the case'. It does not seem that there is any formal difference in the application of this test to member states and Community institutions under the ECSC Statute and to other persons. Nevertheless, just as the interest which one individual may have in a case may differ from that of another, so the interest of a member state or a Community institution may differ in substance from that of an individual.

In principle, an interest in the result of the case means an interest in the operative part of the final judgment which the parties ask the Court to deliver.[34] The intervener will be aware of the form of order submitted by the applicant from the notice of the case published in the Official Journal. In principle, an interest in the success of the arguments put forward by one of the parties is not enough.[35] In practice, in certain cases the distinction between an interest in the result of the case and an interest in the success of the arguments put forward by one of the parties has become blurred; as will be seen, where a case establishes a principle of general application, a third party affected by the operation of that principle may be entitled to intervene.

In Cases 9 and 12/60 *Belgium v Société Commerciale Antoine Vloeberghs SA and High Authority*[36] the Court considered the question whether the notice of Case

---

32 Articles 37 and 38 respectively.
33 Ibid.
34 Case 111/63 *Lemmerz-Werke GmbH v High Authority* [1965] ECR 716 at 717 and 722 (Advocate General Roemer). The facts were that the action concerned an individual decision addressed to the applicant requiring it to pay a sum due under the scrap equalisation scheme. The intervener was another steel undertaking in the same position as the applicant. Its interest in the case was that, if the applicant were successful, the High Authority would have to change its policy, but the intervener had no direct interest in the validity of the decision challenged in the action and hence no interest in the resolution of the dispute between the parties. Its interest was purely collateral. See also the *Générale Sucrière* case (above, note 18).
35 Cases 56 and 58/64 *Etablissements Consten SARL and Grundig-Verkaufs-GmbH v Commission* [1966] ECR 382 at 385; Cases 116, 124 and 143/77 *GR Amylum NV and Tunnel Refineries Ltd v Council and Commission* [1978] ECR 893.
36 Above, note 1.

9/60 published in the Official Journal revealed an interest in the case justifying the Belgian government's intervention. The test it seems to have adopted is that the interest must be both direct and specific (or concrete).[37] An abstract interest in the observance of the Treaty would not justify the intervention of a member state in any and every action.[38] The application in Case 9/60 had claimed damages in respect of a wrongful act or omission of the High Authority and, for this reason, the Belgian government could not have been aware of any interest in the outcome of the case because the Court's judgment could only have either awarded damages to the applicant or dismissed the action. There could have been no effect on the Belgian government's position. On the other hand, had the action claimed the annulment of a High Authority decision, the Belgian government would probably have had an interest in intervening because the effects of the Court's judgment would have been felt by persons other than the applicant. The interest is therefore revealed by an effect on the intervener's position. In general terms, a person's interest to intervene is confirmed by his possession of a right of action in respect of the subject matter of the dispute, whether or not that right of action has been exercised in time or at all.[39] By way of example, a person who is the addressee of a decision challenged in the action quite clearly has sufficient interest to intervene.[40] However, it should not be inferred that an interest to intervene arises only when the person concerned could himself have brought proceedings. The advantage of the ability to intervene in an action is that it enables persons with an interest in a case but without a cause of action to make their views known. Before illustrating the nature of the interest required to ground an application to intervene in a case by reference to the case law of the Court, consideration will be given to the problems posed by interventions by bodies representing a collective interest and by the identity or near identity of the intervener's interest with that of the party in whose support the intervener is intervening.

The cases concerning interventions by representative bodies suggest that the requirement that the intervener's interest in the result of the case be direct and concrete is broadly construed. A representative or collective body would seem to have an interest if the persons it represents have one.[41] That interest may itself be clearly direct: for example, where a regulation requires the

---

37 See also the *Amylum* case (above, note 35) at para 9.

38 Ie one brought under the ECSC Treaty, where every potential intervener, even a member state, must show an interest in the result of the case.

39 Eg Case 150/86 *Union Sidérurgique du Nord et de l'Est de la France SA (USINOR) v Commission* (unreported, order of 28 January 1987); Case C-156/87 *Gestetner Holdings plc v Council and Commission* [1990] ECR I-781 (order of 16 December 1987); Case T-35/91 *Eurosport Consortium v Commission* [1991] ECR II-1359 (para 15). In the first and second cases cited, the order allowing the application to intervene states expressly that the fact that the intervener has brought its own action does not remove the right to intervene in other proceedings.

40 See for example, Cases 10 and 18/68 *Société Eridania Zuccherifici Nazionali v Commission* [1969] ECR 459 and Case 130/75 *Prais v Council* [1976] ECR 1589.

41 *Producteurs de Fruits v Council* (above, note 17); see also the intervention of the Comité française de la Semoulerie Industrielle in *Ludwigshafener Walzmühle Erling KG v Council and Commission* (above, note 24) (order of 21 January 1981) and the intervention of Intellectual Property Owners Inc (a non-profit-making association of companies, universities and independent inventors with extensive portfolios of intellectual property rights potentially affected by the proceedings) in Case C-241/91P *Radio Telefis Eireann v Commission* and Case C-242/91P *Independent Television Publications Ltd v Commission*, unreported (orders of 25 March 1992). In Case 9/82 *Øhrgaard and Delvaux v Commission* [1983] ECR 2379 and Case 10/82 *Mogensen v Commission* [1983] ECR 2397, applications to intervene made by a Danish association were rejected because, it seems, the cases concerned an internal recruitment competition in which it had no interest.

abolition of quantitative restrictions on imports, the effect of its annulment on national producers of the goods in question cannot be other than direct.[42] On the other hand, in the *Générale Sucrière* case,[43] the action was brought by a number of undertakings against a Commission decision finding that they had infringed the competition rules and requiring them to terminate the infringement. A body representing Italian consumers was allowed to intervene on the basis that the correct application of the competition rules not only ensures that the Common Market operates normally but benefits consumers; the extent of the intervention was, however, limited to the Commission's decision as it related to the effects of the restrictive practice in Italy. In *A M & S Europe Ltd v Commission*[44] the action claimed the annulment of part of the Commission decision requiring the applicant to disclose certain documents. Annulment would have affected no one but the parties, A M & S and the Commission; disclosure would have affected only A M & S's interests, and possibly those of the persons or undertakings mentioned in the documents. The CCBE intervened, however, on the basis that, since the documents were alleged to be privileged from disclosure because they were, or contained, communications passing between a lawyer and his client, the Court's decision would affect the enforcement of the rules of professional conduct binding lawyers in the member states by the CCBE and the national professional organisations represented by it; in addition, the result of the case would have a bearing on the rights and duties of individual lawyers throughout the Community. Similarly, in Case C-241/91P *Radio Telefis Eireann v Commission* and Case C-242/91P *Independent Television Publications Ltd v Commission*,[45] Intellectual Property Owners Inc (an association incorporated in a third country) intervened on the basis that the Commission and third parties might seek to interpret the judgment under appeal in such a way as to have direct and adverse consequences for the members of the association in relation to the exercise by them of their intellectual property rights. The rights of the members of the association were not in fact in dispute in the proceedings; it was the possibility that the judgment would be used as a precedent in other cases that gave rise to the intervention of the association. In contrast, in the *Ludwigshafener Walzmühle* case,[46] an action for damages based on the alleged wrongful fixing of wheat prices, the Court rejected an application to intervene made by a German trade union which relied on the favourable effect, in particular on job prospects, which the action would have on the trade union's members if it were successful. This, the Court held, was an indirect effect of the potential result of the case and far too removed to justify the intervention of the union.

More recently, applications to intervene in staff cases made by staff or trade unions have been upheld on the ground that such bodies are generally allowed to intervene (in staff cases) where the outcome of the proceedings is such as to affect a collective interest represented by the applicant to intervene and the case is therefore of general importance: in effect, the intervener is seeking to obtain for its members the rights sought by the party in whose support the intervener is intervening.[47] A

42 *Producteurs de Fruits v Council* (above, note 17).
43 Above, note 18.
44 Above, note 20.
45 Above (note 41), orders of 25 March 1992.
46 Above (note 23), see order of 8 April 1981.
47 Case T-49/89 *Mavrakos v Council* [1990] ECR II-509 (order of 8 December 1989 – the case concerned a change in practice affecting an entire category of officials, including members of the intervener); Case T-110/89 *Pincherle v Commission* [1991] ECR II-635 (order of 12 December 1989); Case C-107/90P *Hochbaum v Commission* [1992] ECR I-157 (order of 10 October 1990); Case T-84/91 *Meskens v European Parliament* [1992] ECR II-1565 (paras 10–14); Case C-242/90P *Commission v Albani* (unreported, order of 15 November 1990); Case C-244/91P *Pincherle v Commission* (opinion of Advocate General Darmon, para 47).

body representing collective interests may in such circumstances have an interest to intervene even though none of its members is directly affected by the dispute.[48] Such a body may also have an interest to intervene where an individual does not. For example, in Case T-121/89 *X v Commission*,[49] a case concerning the defendant's refusal to recruit the applicant on grounds of health, the CFI allowed a staff union to intervene because the case did not concern just the interests of one person (the applicant) but the practice of the defendant's medical services which in principle fell within the scope of the collective interests with which the union was concerned. An application to intervene made by an individual official was rejected because neither his status as such nor his obligation to have an annual medical examination gave him a direct and actual interest in the relief sought by the applicant. An application to intervene made by the Belgian League for Human Rights was rejected because its vocation (to support any person whose fundamental rights have been affected) did not have a sufficiently close connection with the case; further, the action did not concern human rights as such but the legality of certain recruitment procedures.[50] A body representing collective interests may in any event have an interest to intervene in its own right, for example where the case may lead the Court into defining the rights of such bodies;[51] or where the body's interest to intervene derives from its participation in the proceedings leading up to the adoption of the contested act.[52]

A slightly different problem is posed by the question whether or not an intervener's interest must be distinct from that of the party in whose support the intervener wishes to intervene. This problem has arisen in cases where there is some particularly close link between that party and the intervener, such as where the intervener is a member or component part of the party, with the consequence that the intervener's interest is merged with or indistinguishable from the interest of the party.[53] In *Producteurs de Fruits v*

---

48 Cases C-193 and C-194/87 *Maurissen and European Public Service Union v Court of Auditors* [1990] ECR I-95 (order of 10 February 1988 in Case C-194/87): the intervener comprised professional organisations or trade unions with the consequence that its character as a representative body could not be put in doubt merely because none of the defendant's officials was a member of the intervener; the point at issue was one that did not concern the relationship between the defendant and its officials alone. In many staff cases, the point at issue will be of general importance in that sense because the Staff Regulations apply to all the Community institutions.

49 [1992] ECR II-2195 (order of 13 February 1990).

50 The emphasis on the general nature of the issue in the case (and therefore on the general importance of the final decision) when considering, and justifying, an intervention by a trade union is more pronounced in other cases, such as Case 431/85 *Diezler v Economic and Social Committee* [1987] ECR 4283 (order of 25 June 1986 – a group of officials being candidates for election to the staff committee allowed to intervene); Case 148/88 *Albani v Commission* (unreported, orders of 13 June and 13 December 1988 – staff unions but not individuals allowed to intervene – the case was withdrawn after being transferred to the CFI); Case T-41/90 *Barassi v Commission* [1992] ECR II-159 (order of 28 January 1991).

51 *Maurissen and European Public Service Union v Court of Auditors* (above (note 48), order of 10 February 1988 in Case C-194/87).

52 The classic example is that of the associations representing Community industry in dumping investigations. Complaints to the Commission alleging dumping and requesting corrective action in the form of the imposition of an anti-dumping duty must be made by the Community industry affected by the alleged dumping and, for that reason, are made almost invariably by associations comprising the undertakings affected. Such associations participate in the ensuing administrative proceedings and have an interest to intervene (in support of the Community institutions) in actions for the annulment of the regulation imposing the duty.

53 In that sense, the situation is the converse of that where a body representing a collective interest wishes to intervene in support of a party who is a member of that representative body. Where there is no link in an institutional or personal sense but merely a commonality of interest, it does not seem that a problem arises: see, for example, Case 273/85R *Silver Seiko Ltd v Council* [1985] ECR 3475 (para 6), where the argument that the intervener's interests were adequately represented by the defendants (in whose support the intervener wished to intervene) was rejected.

Council,[54] the Court appears to have rejected the view that the intervener's interest in the case must be distinct from that of the party which he supports, which tends to suggest that even a wholly owned subsidiary cannot be barred from intervening on the ground that its interest is in substance the same as that of its parent. However, in Case 323/82 *Intermills v Commission*[55] it appears to have been argued that subsidiaries of the applicant did not have sufficient interest to intervene. The Court rejected this on the ground that the applicant had only a minority shareholding in the subsidiaries so that it could not be excluded that the latter had an interest of their own to represent in the proceedings, which could be taken to indicate that wholly owned subsidiaries would not have an interest in intervening in support of the parent company. In Case 358/85 *France v European Parliament*,[56] the applicant sought the annulment of a resolution of the European Parliament and various members of the Parliament applied to intervene under art 34 of the ECSC Statute because they had participated in the drafting of the contested resolution and were MEPs. Their applications were rejected on the grounds that it was for the defendant institution to decide how to organise its defence; that the interest of the interveners was not distinct from that of the defendant; and that it is contrary to the system of judicial protection in the Community for members of an institution to be entitled to intervene in support of the institution. By the same token, a commissioner could not intervene in support of the Commission and a minister in the government of a member state could not intervene in support of the Council (which consists of representatives of the member states). That principle has not been taken so far as to exclude intervention by a member state in support of the Council (even though that seems to be a logical conclusion), presumably because the EC and Euratom Statutes expressly confer on the member states a right to intervene.[57] On the other hand, in Case 143/84 *Vlachou v Court of Auditors*,[58] a case concerning a decision of a selection board, a member of that board was allowed to intervene, albeit only in order to refute the applicant's allegations that he had infringed the Staff Regulations. Thus, it may be that a member of a Community institution may be able to intervene in support of the institution if he (or she) is personally impugned in the action. The question whether or not the principle, that members of a Community institution cannot (ordinarily at least) intervene in support of that institution, applies also to the persons or bodies recognised by Community law as forming part of a member state is largely of academic interest: with the exception of actions under the ECSC Treaty, persons other than Community institutions and member states cannot intervene in actions in which member states are applicants or defendants; although the question might arise in other actions if both a member state and a person or body regarded as forming part of that state sought to intervene. It is certainly arguable that the same principle applies.[59] If so, such a person or body would not ordinarily have an interest to intervene in a case in which the member state in question had already intervened; but, if that person or body had been allowed to intervene

54 Above (note 17), at 488; see also the cases cited in note 96, p 167, below.
55 [1984] ECR 3809 (see order of 22 June 1983).
56 [1986] ECR 2149 and [1988] ECR 4821 (order of 3 July 1986, see [1988] ECR at 4836–4837 per Advocate General Mancini).
57 The other view is that the fact that the Council consists of 'representatives' of the member states (ECSC Treaty, art 27; EC Treaty, art 146; Euratom Treaty, art 116) is in itself sufficient to say that the members of the Council are not the member states but the natural persons representing the member states from time to time.
58 [1986] ECR 459 (para 8 and per Advocate General Lenz at 463).
59 Cf Case 282/85 *Comité de Développement et de Protection du Textile et de l'Habillement (DEFI) v Commission* [1986] ECR 2469 (paras 17–19).

before the member state applied to do so, it does not seem that the member state's application would cause the intervention of that person or body to be revoked[60] and it is doubtful if the member state's application could be refused (on the ground that its interest was already represented in the proceedings) because (in actions under the EC and Euratom Treaties) a member state has a right to intervene without any need to show an interest.

Passing now to particular examples of what constitutes an interest to intervene, in Cases 7 and 9/54 *Groupement des Industries Sidérurgiques Luxembourgeoises v High Authority* and Cases 8 and 10/54 *Association des Utilisateurs de Charbon de Grand-Duché de Luxembourg v High Authority*[61] Luxembourg had an interest in the proceedings because they concerned the question whether the system for subsidising domestic fuel introduced by the Luxembourg government was compatible with the Treaty. In Cases 24 and 34/58 *Chambre Syndicale de la Sidérurgie de l'Est de la France v High Authority*[62] the French government intervened in an action brought by eight French undertakings and associations for the annulment of a High Authority decision refusing to take action to require the German government to modify transport tariffs that were alleged to discriminate against non-German undertakings, presumably because French economic interests in general were threatened; and in Case 30/59 *De Gezamenlijke Steenkolenmijnen in Limburg v High Authority*[63] the action concerned the High Authority's acquiescence in the granting of a bonus to miners in Germany which was financed from public funds so the German government had an interest to intervene in order to defend the system it had introduced. In contrast, it was five Dutch undertakings which sought to intervene in Case 25/59 *Netherlands v High Authority*,[64] an action brought by the Dutch government under art 88 of the ECSC Treaty for the annulment of a High Authority decision recording that the member states had failed to fulfil their obligations under the Treaty in that they had not published or notified to the High Authority the scales, rates and other tariff rules applied to the carriage by road of coal and steel for hire or reward. The decision went on to set out the measures which the member states had to take in order to comply with their obligations and set a time limit for compliance. The interveners were either carriers or users of the goods in question and were directly affected by the decision. Their interest in the outcome of the case was unquestionable but the Court limited the scope of their intervention by holding that they had an interest in the annulment of part but not the whole of the decision. That part was the High Authority's finding that there had been a failure to comply with the Treaty because this necessitated an interpretation of the Treaty provisions. On the other hand, the interveners had no interest in the annulment of the obligations with which the High Authority had required the member states to comply in its decision.

A party to a (restrictive) agreement or practice has an interest in an action brought to annul a decision of the Commission requiring it to be terminated,[65] exempting it from prohibition or withholding the benefit of exemption[66] or

---

60 It is still an open question whether or not the Court can reconsider an application to intervene once it has been allowed: see *Vlachou v Court of Auditors* (above, note 58), order of 16 October 1985.

61 [1954–56] ECR 222 and 241.

62 [1960] ECR 281.

63 [1961] ECR 1.

64 Above (note 29) at 386–389.

65 The intervener supported the Commission: Case 71/74R & RR *Nederlandse Vereniging voor de Fruit-en-Groentenimporthandel (FRUBO) v Commission* [1974] ECR 1031, 1095.

66 Cases T-29 and T-30/90 *Quantel SA v Commission* (unreported, order of 23 January 1991): the intervener supported the Commission.

declaring that it is not prohibited;[67] so has a person whose contractual or property rights are affected by the agreement.[68] At a more general level, the complainant in competition cases has an interest in an action brought to annul the Commission's decision;[69] so also have any undertakings whose marketing policy is affected by the restrictive practice in question,[70] consumers in general[71] and persons whose commercial interests are directly affected by the decision.[72] If the Court's decision would have decisive effect on other proceedings between one of the parties and the intervener pending before a national court, there is sufficient interest to intervene.[73] For example, an insurance company has an interest to intervene in support of the defendant institution in an action for the annulment of a decision refusing to acknowledge that the death of an official was caused by an occupational disease where, if the action were successful, a claim would be made for which the insurance company would ultimately be liable.[74]

In *Moksel v Commission*[75] it was argued that the intervener had no interest because it could not benefit from the applicant's success. The action was for the annulment of a Commission regulation and the intervener could not itself bring an action for annulment because the time for doing so had expired. The Commission relied on Case 92/78 *Simmenthal SA v Commission*[76] for the proposition that, if the applicant won, the regulation would be annulled only as far as it was concerned so the intervener could gain nothing from the action. The Court held[77] that, even if the intervener had no direct interest in the case, it did have an interest in the outcome, at least in regard to the reasoning behind the judgment. In contrast, when a similar situation arose in Case 56/85 *Brother Industries Ltd v Commission*,[78] the application to intervene was refused. There, a purchaser of machines manufactured by one Japanese company (Silver Seiko)

---

67 Eg Case T-125/90 *Filtrona Española SA v Commission* (unreported, order of 15 February 1990).
68 Case T-157/89 *Algemene Financieringsmaatschappij Nefito BV v Commission* (unreported, order of 25 September 1990).
69 Case 73/74 *Groupement des Fabricants de Papiers Peints de Belgique v Commission* [1975] ECR 1491; Case 28/77 *Tepea BV v Commission* [1978] ECR 1391; Case 30/78 *Distillers Co Ltd v Commission* [1980] ECR 2229; Cases 209–215 and 218/78 *Heintz Van Landewyck Sàrl (FEDETAB) v Commission* [1980] ECR 3125 at 3130–3131 and 3144; Case 60/81 *IBM Corpn v Commission* [1981] ECR 2639 (order of 13 May 1981); Cases 76, 77 and 91/89R *Radio Telefis Eireann v Commission* [1989] ECR 1141 (para 3); Case T-65/89 *BPB Industries plc and British Gypsum Ltd v Commission* (unreported, order of 18 January 1990).
70 Cases 43 and 63/82 *De Vereniging ter Bevordering van het Vlaamsche Boekwezen v Commission* [1984] ECR 19 (order of 10 March 1982).
71 The *Générale Sucrière* case (above, note 18). See also the *Ford* cases (above, note 21) and Case T-29/92 *Vereniging van Samenwerkende Prijsregelende Organisaties in de Bouwnijverheid (SPO) v Commission* [1993] ECR II-1 (para 22) (in the latter case it was, however, regarded as significant that the consumers in question were distinct from the general body of consumers affected by the practices in question).
72 *Van Landewyck v Commission* (above, note 69): several Belgian trade associations (with legal personality under Belgian law) which traded in the products in question.
73 *Consten and Grundig v Commission* (above, note 35); *SPO v Commission* (above, note 71), paras 17–20, where the intervener's interest was retained after the national proceedings pending at the time of the application to intervene had been withdrawn because it was still possible for proceedings to be recommenced against the intervener (paras 21–22); in *BPB Industries plc and British Gypsum Ltd v Commission* (above, note 69) the intervener was merely contemplating claiming damages against the applicants before the national courts on the basis of the contested decision.
74 Case 189/82 *Seiler v Council* [1984] ECR 229 (at 234); Case T-122/89 *Ferrandi v Commission* [1990] ECR II-517 (order of 23 January 1990).
75 Above, note 30.
76 [1979] ECR 777.
77 Order of 15 July 1981.
78 [1988] ECR 5655 (order of 3 October 1985).

applied to intervene in support of an action brought by another Japanese manufacturer (Brother) for the annulment of a regulation imposing an anti-dumping duty on the products of both manufacturers. It was held that Brother's claim was for the annulment of the regulation in so far as it applied to Brother; the intervener's interest was in the annulment of the regulation in so far as it applied to Silver Seiko; therefore the intervener had no interest in the outcome of the action brought by Brother. It is true that the ruling in the *Moksel* case comes very close to admitting, as an interest in the result of the case, an interest in the success of a particular argument but the explanation probably is that, if the regulation were annulled, the intervener might rely on this in an action before a national court. The same criticism can be raised in regard to the CCBE's intervention in the *A M & S* case, but there again, on closer analysis, the explanation can be seen to lie in the fact that the documents in question were, for the most part, communications to or from a lawyer belonging to one of the professional bodies represented by the CCBE. The interest of the CCBE lay, therefore, not in establishing the existence of a principle of confidentiality, as a general proposition, but in protecting the right of confidentiality of the lawyers concerned, which was directly threatened by the proceedings. The situation in the *Brother* case was different because Silver Seiko had brought an action of its own[79] and the intervener's position would therefore be affected by the outcome of that action, not the outcome of the *Brother* action.

Case 246/81 *Bethell v Commission*,[80] on the other hand, was an action brought primarily under art 175 of the EEC Treaty for a declaration that the Commission had failed to act and, alternatively, under art 173, for the annulment of a letter sent by the Commission to the applicant. Ten airlines were allowed to intervene. It seems that the applications to intervene were based on the argument that it was, in their view, necessary to protect their rights, which they felt were directly or indirectly challenged in the action. Lord Bethell's essential complaint was that the Commission had not acted to combat restrictive practices in the field of air transport. It seems likely that the interventions were allowed because of the claim under art 173. There could have been no interest in the failure of the primary claim, as it was pleaded. The failure to act as alleged was said to be a failure to say that the Commission was going to act against the restrictive practices in question or, on the contrary, to say that it was not going to act. None of the interveners could properly be said to have an interest in this. They would be affected if the Commission did or did not act but they would not be affected by a simple declaration of intention from the Commission saying whether it would or would not act.[81] On the other hand, the annulment claim was based on the contention that the letter sought to be annulled constituted a decision finding that there had not been an infringement of the competition rules. The interveners undoubtedly had an interest in

---

79 Cases 273/85 and 107/86 *Silver Seiko Ltd v Council* [1988] ECR 5927. The *Brother* action was brought against the regulation imposing a provisional anti-dumping duty whereas the *Silver Seiko* action was brought against the regulation imposing a definitive anti-dumping duty. However, the first action was devoid of purpose because the adoption of a definitive anti-dumping duty supersedes any provisional duty. In consequence, so far as the intervener was concerned, the *Silver Seiko* action was alone relevant to its interests.

80 [1982] ECR 2277.

81 It is arguable that the airlines' interest could have been grounded on their interest in obtaining a finding that the Commission was under no duty to act owed to the applicant. The difficulty with this is that any such obligation is a bare duty to act, not one to act in a particular way: an obligation binding the Commission to take steps to end an alleged restrictive practice among the airlines cannot be predicated from an obligation to adopt a position one way or another on the matter; it could be based only on some other article of the Treaty or secondary legislation.

this part of the action. In Case 6/70 *Borromeo Arese v Commission*[82] a similar situation arose. This concerned an application under art 175 for a declaration that the Commission had infringed the Treaty by failing to adopt a decision laying down rules to be followed in the wording of leases of agricultural land consequent upon the enactment of a draft Italian law dealing with the method of fixing the rents for agricultural land. A lessee of land in Italy sought to intervene in support of the Commission, saying that he had a material interest in the application of the Italian law. The application to intervene was rejected on the ground that he had not shown a concrete link between his individual interest and the object of an action under art 175.

The judgment in *Belgium v Société Commerciale Antoine Vloeberghs SA and High Authority*[83] suggests that intervention in an action for damages is not, in general, possible and an application to intervene in such an action was rejected in *Amylum v Council and Commission*.[84] As has been seen, however, interventions from a number of organisations were admitted in the *Ludwigshafener Walzmühle* case,[85] though it is not clear why. Since the basis of the claim for damages in that case was the alleged wrongful fixing of wheat prices, it is possible that the interest was held to lie in obtaining a judgment that would establish that fact. One could conclude, therefore, that an interest to intervene in a damages action may be established if the liability of the Community alleged is based on an act, omission or state of affairs whose wrongfulness or illegality affects the position of the intervener.[86] Thus, in Case 253/84 *Groupement Agricole d'Exploitation en Commun (GAEC) de la Ségaude v Council and Commission*,[87] it was held that, in an action for damages resulting from a normative act, the form of order sought by the applicant (which determines whether or not the intervener has an interest to intervene) is to be understood as concerning not only the award of damages in favour of the applicant but also the incidental finding that the contested act is unlawful. Ordinarily, an intervener in a damages action who supports the applicant has no interest in the award of damages to the applicant[88] and cannot himself claim the award of damages because interveners are limited to supporting the relief claimed by the applicant or defendant and may not raise a direct claim of their own even if they have an independent right of action in respect of that claim.[89] For those reasons, the interest to intervene must be found elsewhere.

Where the object of the action is the annulment of a refusal by the Commission to grant interim relief, the person against whom relief would have been granted has sufficient interest to intervene for that reason alone.[90] The interest required to intervene in proceedings for interim relief brought before the Court is in principle no different from that required to intervene in the action to which those proceedings relate: it is certainly the case that the entitlement to

---

82 [1970] ECR 815, order of 16 June 1970, unreported.
83 Above, note 1.
84 Above, note 35. See also Case 114/83 *SICA and SIPEFEL v Commission* [1984] ECR 2589 at 2591 (order of 19 October 1983). The applicants to intervene wished to intervene as parties in their own right, that is, as something more than interveners in the strict sense. Similarly, in the *Brother* case (above, note 78), the intervener also purported to claim damages.
85 Above, note 23.
86 Eg *Chris International Foods v Commission* (above, note 16).
87 [1987] ECR 123 (order of 20 March 1985).
88 The possibility cannot be excluded that a creditor of the applicant may have an interest.
89 Cf *Eurosport Consortium v Commission* (above, note 39) (para 15), where the intervener's intervention was expressly limited to supporting the applicant's form of order. The inability of the intervener itself to claim damages seems to have been one of the objections to the applications to intervene cited in note 84 above.
90 Case T-44/90 *La Cinq SA v Commission* [1992] ECR II-1 (order of 31 January 1991).

intervene in the former is contingent upon there being an entitlement to intervene in the latter (although a decision on an application to intervene in interim relief proceedings does not need to await a decision on the application to intervene in the main action)[91] but there seems to be no additional requirement for intervention in interim relief proceedings.[92] The same applies where the application for interim relief is made in the context of an appeal to the ECJ from a judgment or decision of the CFI.[93] Proceedings for the interpretation of a judgment are ancillary to the proceedings leading up to the delivery of the judgment in question. As a general rule, therefore, proceedings for the interpretation of a judgment concern only the parties to the judgment (including interveners). In consequence, intervention in the interpretation proceedings by a person who was not a party to the judgment is not possible unless the interpretation requested relates specifically to another case between the intervener and one of the parties to the judgment (in which case the intervener must be allowed to intervene in order to protect his rights of the defence).[94]

It seems clear from the cases that, to justify intervention, the result of the case must affect the intervener's legal position,[95] his economic position[96] (this is the basic justification for intervening in competition cases)[97] or, possibly, his freedom of action.[98] The effect must flow directly from the precise subject

91 Indeed, decisions allowing interventions in interim relief proceedings are commonly made some time before the decisions allowing the intervention in the main proceedings: see p 174 below.

92 Eg *Radio Telefis Eireann et al v Commission* (above, note 69) (at para 3).

93 Case C-242/90P-R *Commission v Albani* [1990] ECR I-4329 (para 5): third parties whose appointments had been put in doubt by the judgment appealed against.

94 Case 9/81-Interpretation *Court of Auditors v Williams* [1983] ECR 2859 (para 7).

95 See, for example, *Consten and Grundig v Commission* and *Fruit-en-Groentenimporthandel FRUBO v Commission* (above, notes 35 and 65). In this context such an effect is to be distinguished from the binding effect of the Court's judgment.

96 See *Producteurs de Fruits v Council* (above, note 17) and possibly the *Ludwigshafener Walzmühle* case (above, note 23). In the *Ford* cases (above, note 21), which were applications for interim relief made by two members of the Ford group in the context of two actions against the Commission for the annulment of a decision ordering the applicants, by way of interim measures, to resume the sale of right-hand-drive cars in Germany for direct importation by purchasers into the United Kingdom, two dealers of Ford vehicles in England and Scotland applied to intervene. The President rejected their applications on the ground that, having regard to the information before him, they had not shown 'a sufficiently defined interest' to be allowed to intervene. It seems that the dealers argued that, if relief were not granted, the Commission's decision would gravely affect their commercial position. The President's orders suggest that the applications were dismissed because the dealers did not establish with sufficient certitude that they would be so affected. An alternative view is that they did not show an interest above and beyond that of any other Ford dealer. The validity of this approach is extremely doubtful. The criterion required is an interest in the result of the case, not a greater interest than any other interested person. If two persons have such an interest, it is not reasonable to reject an application to intervene made by one simply because he has no greater interest than the other, the latter having chosen not to intervene. In competition cases, it is true, the class of potential interveners can be vast due to the economic interests involved; in *Ford*, for example, every car dealer in the United Kingdom could be said to have had an interest to intervene because of the economic or commercial effects of the renewed import of cheaper right-hand-drive vehicles from Germany. This is the defect in the use of economic interests as the guiding criterion for intervention. Nevertheless, once such a criterion has been adopted, it cannot simply be discarded in some cases, but not in others, because the class of potential interveners is particularly large. The Court, however, allowed the interventions in the action (order of 2 February 1983).

97 It was expressly adopted in, for example, the *Japanese Ball-Bearing* cases (above, note 19) and Case 26/76 *Metro-SB-Grossmärkte GmbH & Co KG v Commission* [1977] ECR 1875, orders of 30 November 1977 and 30 November 1976 respectively, where trade associations were allowed to intervene because the nature of their economic interest in the actions was the same as that of the applicants.

98 *A M & S Europe Ltd v Commission* (above, note 20).

matter of the dispute, which is to be settled in the operative part of the judgment, and not be collateral to it; it must be concrete, or real, and not abstract or theoretical. A mere 'moral' interest is not sufficient to support a claim to intervene. In Case 40/79 *Mrs P v Commission*[99] an official of the Commission had divorced his wife and then died. His ex-wife claimed a widow's pension under the Staff Regulations, whereupon the deceased's mother applied to intervene in support of the Commission and in her capacity as *'subrogée-tutrice'*, or supervising guardian, of the deceased's two children, one of whom was in her custody. Her interest was alleged to be two fold: on the one hand she claimed a moral interest in ensuring that her son's ex-wife was not recognised as his widow; on the other, the orphans' pensions granted by the Commission to the children would be halved if the ex-wife received a widow's pension. The Court held that the application to intervene was inadmissible in so far as it was based on her 'moral interest' because the judgment in the case could not decide the question of the ex-wife's status. The same approach to the assessment of the interest required to intervene is followed in appeals brought before the ECJ against judgments or decisions of the CFI.

IV   Rights of the intervener

Under the EC and Euratom Statutes[1] 'submissions' made in an application to intervene are limited to supporting the 'submissions' of one of the parties. Under the ECSC Statute[2] they may also request the rejection of the 'submissions' of one of the parties. In this context, 'submissions' appears to mean 'form of order'.[3] The rule indicates the subordinate nature of intervention: unlike a party to the action in a full sense, the intervener cannot determine the scope of the proceedings by introducing a new claim which he thinks ought to have been made;[4] he can only support or request the rejection of the case already made by one of the parties with the authority of his presence in court and the ingenuity of the arguments he puts forward. He cannot in consequence make a claim of his own even if he has a separate right of action in respect of that claim[5] and cannot claim any relief in respect of himself.[6] As the Rules of Procedure[7] put it, the intervener must accept the case as he finds it. The intervener is not, however, bound to put forward positive arguments in favour of the total acceptance or rejection of the case put by one of the parties. He may remain silent in regard to, for example, the applicant's claim for damages, and

---

99 [1979] ECR 3299.
1 Articles 37 and 38 respectively.
2 Article 34.
3 See Case 111/63 *Lemmerz-Werke v High Authority* [1965] ECR 716 at 717–718 and 722 (Advocate General Roemer).
4 See Case 114/83 *SICA and SIPEFEL v Commission* [1984] ECR 2589 at 2591–2592, order of 19 October 1983.
5 Case T-35/91 *Eurosport Consortium v Commission* [1991] ECR II-1359 (para 15). In Case C-155/91 *Commission v Council* [1993] ECR I-939 (paras 22–24), that limitation on the rights of the intervener was construed particularly strictly. The Commission claimed the annulment of a Council directive. The intervener (the European Parliament) claimed the annulment of one specific provision of the directive. That claim was rejected as inadmissible because it did not have the same object as the Commission's claim. At first sight, on the basis that the greater includes the lesser, one would have thought that the intervener's claim was within the scope of the applicant's claim. It was, nonetheless, materially different from the latter.
6 As RP-ECJ 93(1)(e) and RP-CFI 115(2)(e) indicate.
7 RP-ECJ 93(4); RP-CFI 116(3).

concentrate his arguments on the claim for annulment which accompanies it. Or he may limit the scope of his intervention to the single point which he regards as being decisive for the purpose of obtaining the relief sought or the one in relation to which his intervention would be most valuable. Naturally, the points dealt with in the intervention must be relevant to the claims in the action; if not, the application to intervene would be inadmissible because the intervener has no interest justifying his intervention if he intends only to ventilate a question which is not pertinent to the dispute between the parties.

The forms of order of the parties to an action should be directly contradictory. To the extent that they are not, no issue lies between the parties. To intervene in support of the form of order of one party is therefore, in substance, to request the rejection of the other party's form of order, and vice versa. In this sense the EC and Euratom Statutes mean the same as the ECSC Statute, although they do not expressly state that the intervener may reject the 'submissions' of one of the parties. In practice an intervener always intervenes 'in support' of a party, even if the object is to 'reject' the other party's case. The phraseology of the ECSC Statute indicates that an intervener can either support or reject a party's form of order but not do both. If the intervener found himself in disagreement with part of one party's case but not the whole of it, he could in consequence only support the rest of it and remain silent with regard to the part with which he disagreed. He could not actively oppose it unless he intervened in support of the other party, in which case he would find himself in the same dilemma as far as part, at least, of that party's case was concerned. The Court has, however, interpreted the EC Statute liberally, and allowed an intervener to support different points in both parties' forms of order.[8] Due to the similarity of wording, with regard to the Euratom Statute, and of effect, with regard to the ECSC Statute, the same interpretation seems to apply to all three Statutes. In practice, that liberal construction may benefit member states and Community institutions with the right to intervene rather than other interveners who must in principle demonstrate an interest in supporting the form of order of one side or the other. Having said that, it should be observed that RP-ECJ 93(1) and RP-CFI 115(2) require the application to intervene to set out 'the form of order sought, by one or more of the parties, in support of which the intervener is applying for leave to intervene'. It may be that the reference to 'one or more of the parties' is to be understood as referring to 'one or more of the parties in the same interest', thus covering the situation where there are several applicants or several defendants, rather than opposing parties. The true construction of those Rules is unclear.

The difference in wording between the Statutes may be important where one party has conceded a claim made in the other party's form of order. When this happens there is no longer any issue between the parties, to the extent of the concession. Under the EC and Euratom Statutes, where the intervener's right is, in principle, to support one party's form of order, the concession

---

8 An intervention in support of both parties may give rise to confusion. In Case 258/78 *LC Nungesser KG and Kurt Eisele v Commission* [1982] ECR 2015 (order of 30 January 1980), the German government had originally applied to intervene in order to expound its views on certain legal aspects of the case without explaining which. In a subsequent telex it explained that it wished to support the applicant's claim for annulment in relation to part of the decision attacked and to support the defendant's case in relation to other issues. In Cases T-68, T-77 and T-78/90 *Società Italiano Vetro SA et al v Commission* [1992] ECR II-1403 (Re Italian Flat Glass) (paras 36–42), the United Kingdom intervened in part in support of the applicant and in part in support of the defendant. The defendant asked the CFI to require the United Kingdom to choose which party it supported. The United Kingdom said that it would limit its oral submissions to supporting the applicant on one point and that satisfied the defendant.

precludes intervention because, if the intervener has supported the form of order of the party making the concession, he cannot continue to support a claim in that form of order which is no longer being made. In contrast, under the ECSC Statute, the intervener may not be bound by the concession because his right is not restricted merely to supporting one party's form of order: he can seek the rejection of that of the other party. In consequence, when the concession is made, his right to support the conceding party's form of order disappears with the conceded claim but it is arguable that his right to seek the rejection of the other party's form of order is unaffected. This possibility does not exist under the other Statutes because the rejection of one form of order which is implicit in the support given to the other results as a matter of fact and not as of right. To allow an intervener to continue to oppose a claim made in an action to which the ECSC Statute applies after that claim has been conceded by the party in whose support the intervener has intervened would, however, allow the intervener to override the wishes of the principal parties in the litigation. It is therefore doubtful that the Court would so construe the ECSC Statute. The intervener is in any event bound by concessions made before the date of his intervention[9] and could not seek to oppose a claim that had been the subject of a concession before his intervention was allowed.

Although the intervener must, subject to what has already been said, accept the action as it is defined in the parties' forms of order, this does not mean that he is bound in every respect by the way in which they have conducted it. It is common to divide the submissions in a case into pleas (often referred to in the case law as 'grounds'), exceptions and arguments. The first are matters of fact or law upon which the claims made in the form of order are based. Exceptions are specific defences or objections to bringing the claim or action. Arguments are the exposition of the pleas (or grounds) and exceptions relied on. In his opinion in Case 30/59 *De Gezamenlijke Steenkolenmijnen in Limburg v High Authority*[10] Advocate General Lagrange doubted whether the intervener could rely on pleas or exceptions (translated in the English text of his opinion as 'submissions' and 'objections' respectively) which are not relied upon by the parties because they must remain in control of the proceedings. On the other hand, the intervener could, in his opinion, raise new grounds or exceptions of the sort which the Court may consider of its own motion.[11] In brief, therefore, an intervener would be restricted to the issues as defined by the parties in their pleadings and his only freedom would lie in the choice of arguments, whether of fact or of law, which he might use to support one side's view of a particular issue, and in the possibility of raising a point which the Court would otherwise be bound to consider of its own motion if the parties failed to do so. The Court made it clear that an intervener can make use of any argument, even if it conflicts with those advanced by the party in whose support the intervener has intervened. As the intervener had not sought to introduce a new ground or exception, the judgment is, in other respects, not particularly informative.

In Cases 42 and 49/59 *SNUPAT v High Authority*,[12] which was decided a month after the *Steenkolenmijnen* case, the intervener did raise several exceptions relating to the admissibility of the action which were not put forward by the defendant. The Court accepted that the intervener's right to make these

---

9 RP-ECJ 93(4); RP-CFI 116(3).

10 [1961] ECR 1.

11 Points which are '*d'ordre public*' (translated as 'public policy') and which the Court cannot ignore, even if not relied on by the parties, if it is to discharge its duty to ensure that the law is observed.

12 [1961] ECR 53.

points 'cannot be disputed in the present case, since these exceptions or arguments seek the rejection of the applicant's conclusions'.[13] Advocate General Lagrange does not seem to have considered this matter in his opinion. It is arguable that the Court's view was compatible with that expressed by him in *Steenkolenmijnen* on the basis that all admissibility points must be considered by the Court even if they are not raised by the parties; so the *SNUPAT* case would be an example of the second exception to the general rule that the intervener is confined to the dispute as defined by the parties themselves. But that was not in fact the reason given by the Court. In Cases 27 to 29/58 *Compagnie des Hauts Fourneaux et Fonderies de Givors v High Authority*[14] the Court appears to have envisaged the intervener raising a point not open to one of the parties to raise but the judgment is in this respect too obscure to rely on as an authority.

As a matter of principle, the intervener should only be able to raise matters which the party he supports could have relied on had he thought of them. Otherwise the intervener's subordinate role would disappear and he would become a true party to the action, which is not the intention of the Statutes and the Rules of Procedure. The same line of reasoning would support Advocate General Lagrange's view expressed above. On the other hand, what was formerly the second paragraph of RP-ECJ 93(5) and is now the first paragraph has been cited[15] to support the theory that new pleas can be relied on by the intervener. In its present form RP-ECJ 93(5) states, as does RP-CFI 116(4):

'The President shall prescribe a period within which the intervener may submit a statement in intervention. The statement in intervention shall contain: (a) a statement of the form of order sought . . .; (b) the pleas in law and arguments relied on by the intervener; (c) where appropriate, the nature of any evidence offered.'

RP-ECJ 93(5), as formerly worded, referred only to the intervener's 'grounds for his submissions'. 'Grounds' could, here, have been intended to cover both arguments and pleas or objections which the Court could take of its own motion. The current wording of RP-ECJ 93(5) and RP-CFI 116(4) appears to suggest even more strongly that the intervener may raise matters of fact and law that have not previously been raised by the parties, without any limit to those points that the Court is obliged to raise of its own motion. There is very little recent authority on the question and, at the time of writing, hardly anything in relation to the current wording of RP-ECJ 93(5) and RP-CFI 116(4). In Case 253/84 *GAEC v Council and Commission*[16] Advocate General Slynn suggested that an argument that is inadmissible when advanced by a main party (applicant or defendant) because it is contrary to RP-ECJ 42(2) is admissible when advanced by an intervener; in Case 233/85 *Bonino v Commission*[17] Advocate General Darmon suggested that an intervener cannot raise a fresh issue unless it is based on matters of fact or law that came to light in the course of the procedure.[18] In Cases C-305/86 and C-160/87 *Neotype Techmashexport GmbH v Commission and Council*[19] the intervener supported the defendants and raised an objection to the admissibility of the action which the defendants disputed but it was not necessary to consider the question whether or not an

13 See 75.
14 [1960] ECR 241 at 258.
15 See Vandersanden and Barav, op cit, pp 473–474.
16 [1987] ECR 123 (at 153–154).
17 [1987] ECR 739 (at 753–754).
18 Those cases must now be read subject to the current wording of RP-ECJ 42(2).
19 [1990] ECR I-2945 (at 2970–2971 and para 18).

intervener can raise a point disputed by the party in whose support it intervenes because the point could be taken by the Court of its own motion. In Case C-313/90 *Comité International de la Rayonne et des Fibres Synthétiques (CIRFS) v Commission*[20] it was held that an intervener cannot raise an objection to the admissibility of the action; but any arguments directed to the admissibility of the action may be considered by the Court of its own motion. In that case, the objection to admissibility in question had been expressly disclaimed by the party in whose support the intervener had intervened. While an intervener may well be precluded from raising a preliminary objection to admissibility (which would involve the intervener in initiating a procedural step that ex hypothesi the principal parties had decided not to initiate), to preclude an intervener from disputing the admissibility of the opposing party's claim or pleading would seem to be inconsistent with the *SNUPAT* case. The *CIRFS* and *SNUPAT* cases may be reconciled by saying that an intervener may raise an admissibility point as long as the party in whose support he has intervened has not expressly conceded the point or renounced any reliance upon it.

In the absence of a definitive ruling by the Court, the better view may be that the intervener can rely on all pleas, objections and arguments which the party he supports could have raised, even if the intervener would be prevented for some reason from relying on them in an action brought by himself,[21] save where the party supported by the intervener has already expressly conceded the point or renounced any reliance upon it. The fact that the intervener must accept the case as he finds it[22] does not mean that the intervener is precluded from raising a new point in his statement in intervention unless he can invoke RP-ECJ 42(2) or, as the case may be, RP-CFI 48(2): the intervener is not restricted in his intervention by any failure of the party whom he supports to raise a point before the intervention was allowed. It is only after the intervention has been allowed and the intervener becomes a party to the proceedings that RP-ECJ 42(2) or (as the case may be) RP-CFI 48(2) applies to him. In view of the intervener's subordinate role, he cannot initiate the various proceedings of which an applicant or defendant may avail himself, in particular, proceedings for interim relief. That does not prevent him from intervening in those proceedings.[23]

---

20 [1993] ECR I-1125 (paras 20–23 and see the opinion of Advocate General Lenz, paras 47–49). The *CIRFS* case was followed in Case C-225/91 *Matra SA v Commission* [1993] ECR I-3203 (paras 12–13).

21 Bebr, op cit, pp 175–176, on the other hand, says that new grounds cannot be added by the intervener, giving as an example the case of an application for the annulment of a general decision brought under art 33 of the ECSC Treaty by an undertaking. Such applications are admissible only if a misuse of powers is alleged. If the application was based on another ground for annulment, its admissibility could not be cured if the intervener made out a case for annulment based on a misuse of powers. This is a powerful argument against the power of an intervener to adduce new grounds because, on Bebr's hypothesis, the intervener would in substance take over the role of applicant. If it can be accepted as far as admissibility is concerned (because, if the action goes, there is nothing to support the intervention) it does not necessarily follow that the same line of reasoning must be accepted with regard to the merits of the action. (See also Berri (1971) 8 CMLR 5 at 13–14.)

22 RP-ECJ 93(4); RP-CFI 116(3).

23 Cases 71/74R & RR *Fruit-en-Groentenimporthandel Frubo v Commission* [1974] ECR 1031; Cases 6 and 7/73R *ICI SpA and Commercial Solvents Corpn v Commission* [1973] ECR 357; Case 109/75R *National Carbonising Co Ltd v Commission* [1975] ECR 1193; Cases 113/77R and 113/77R-I *NTN Toyo Bearing Co Ltd v Council* [1977] ECR 1721.

V Procedure

Interveners are represented in proceedings in the same way as other parties.[24] An application to intervene must be made[25] within three months of the publication in the Official Journal of the notice of the case[26] or, in relation to applications to intervene in an appeal made to the ECJ from a judgment or decision of the CFI, within three months of the date on which the appeal was lodged.[27] Those time limits cannot be extended.[28] Appeals made to the ECJ are the subject of a notice published in the Official Journal in the same way as any other application commencing proceedings; but the period within which the application to intervene in an appeal must be lodged starts to run from the date of lodgment of the appeal, not the date of publication of the notice in the Official Journal. That is the only difference of practical importance between the procedure in appeals and that in direct actions heard by the ECJ so far as intervention is concerned.[29]

The notice published in the Official Journal contains details of the subject matter of the dispute, the claims in the application and a summary of the contentions and the main arguments adduced in support.[30] It does not give details of the defence and may, indeed, be published before the defence has been lodged at the Court. In consequence, the decision to intervene must usually be made on the basis of the contents of the application as set out in the notice and in ignorance of the defendant's defence. The difficulties which this may cause to a person who wishes to intervene in support of the defendant's form of order are apparent rather than real: unless the defendant concedes the action, his form of order will be precisely contrary to the applicant's form of order.[31] As has been seen, an intervener is not bound by the arguments put forward by either party so the opportunity to intervene is not prejudiced if he is ignorant of either. It is the form of order that matters.[32]

If the defendant fails to lodge a defence, the applicant may apply for judgment in default under RP-ECJ 94 or RP-CFI 122. It is tenable that, under the ECSC Statute, intervention against the applicant is possible because it would take the form of a request for the rejection of the applicant's form of order. On the other hand, this is certainly not possible under the other two Statutes because, in the absence of a defence, there is no form of order, other

---

24 RP-ECJ 93(1) (last sentence); RP-CFI 115(3).
25 Ie lodged at the Court.
26 RP-ECJ 93(1); RP-CFI 115(1).
27 RP-ECJ 123.
28 Not even at the request of a member state: Case 74/82 *Commission v Ireland* [1984] ECR 317 (order of 22 September 1982).
29 RP-ECJ 118.
30 RP-ECJ 16(6); RP-CFI 24(6).
31 Thus, in the *Neotype Techmashexport* case (above, note 19), order of 8 May 1987, the objection to the application to intervene (which was based on the ground that it was inadmissible because it was made before the defendant, in whose support the intervener wished to intervene, had lodged its defence) was dismissed, the Court holding that, in such circumstances, an application to intervene in support of the defendant is to be construed as being made in opposition to the applicant's form of order and on the assumption that the defendant will oppose that form of order.
32 In Cases T-29 and T-30/90 *Quantel SA v Commission* (unreported, order of 23 January 1991), where the intervener applied to intervene in support of the defendant before it knew what position the defendant was going to adopt, the application to intervene was allowed since the intervener had shown an interest in the result of the case and had applied within time. The implication is that the fact that the intervener may be intervening in support of a point that does not form part of the defendant's defence is not relevant to the admissibility of the application to intervene.

than that of the applicant, to support. Under the ECSC Statute the failure to lodge a defence does not preclude an intervention against the applicant.[33] However, an application to intervene should not normally be granted unless and until the defence has been served because, at least under the EC and Euratom Statutes, it may be rendered otiose by the defendant's concession of the dispute, implied by his failure to serve a defence. Although intervention in support of the defendant may be nugatory if there is no defence, it is probable, but by no means settled, that it revives and there is no necessity to make a second application to intervene, if the defendant applies to set aside judgment by default. If the intervention has not been allowed before then, it would seem that the application can be made after the defendant has lodged his application to set aside, which initiates a proceeding distinct from that initiated by the applicant in the action.

In the case of applications for interim relief, it does not seem to be necessary for an application to intervene in those proceedings to be made if the intervener's application to intervene in the action has already been granted. On the other hand, if it has not already been granted or the intervener has not yet applied to intervene in the action, he must make two applications, which may be contained in the same document, one to intervene in the proceedings for interim relief and the other to intervene in the action itself. This may be illustrated by Cases 60 and 190/81R *IBM Corpn v Commission*.[34] There the application for interim relief was made after the Court had allowed the intervener's intervention in the first action, Case 60/81. A month later IBM began a second action, Case 190/81, and made a second application for interim relief. Both applications for interim relief were heard together. No order was made allowing the intervener to intervene in the first application, Case 60/81R, because its intervention in the action had already been allowed; but an order was made allowing it to intervene in the second application for interim relief, Case 190/81R, because its intervention in that action had not been allowed.[35]

An application to intervene in proceedings for interim relief is made to the judge dealing with the case.[36] His decision allowing or rejecting the application to intervene does not bind the Court (or chamber), which remains competent to decide on the question of intervention in the action.[37] It is unclear what happens where there is, or may be, a conflict between the judge and the Court. It would seem that the former is bound by a prior decision of the Court, admitting intervention in the action, on the basis that intervention in the action comprises intervention in all ancillary or interlocutory proceedings, such as those for interim relief. It would also be illogical to find that a person can intervene to protect his interest in the outcome of the action but not intervene in proceedings designed to safeguard that outcome. On the other hand, where the judge has first rejected intervention, the putative intervener might seek to use the Court's subsequent admission of his intervention in the

---

33 Berri, (1971) 8 CMLR 5 at 11.

34 [1981] ECR 1857.

35 Separate orders for intervention in the action and in the proceedings for interim relief were made, on the same day, in Cases 43 and 63/82R *VBVB and VBBB v Commission* [1982] ECR 1241 (orders of 10 March 1982).

36 Usually the President of the Court or one of the chambers.

37 Cf Cases 228 and 229/82 *Ford v Commission* [1984] ECR 1129. As in Cases 76, 77 and 91/89R *Radio Telefis Eireann v Commission* [1989] ECR 1141 (para 3), an application to intervene in interim relief proceedings is normally granted only in respect of those proceedings and not in respect of the main action.

action to reverse the judge's decision.[38] It is doubtful if this is possible, despite the fact that, as has been said, intervention in the action would appear to comprise intervention in the proceedings for interim relief, simply because the intervener would remain bound by the judge's decision; the Court does not have power to reverse decisions of the judge made in summary proceedings heard by him. The position is different where the Court has admitted the intervention in the action before the matter comes before the judge: here the decision of the Court avoids the necessity for applying to the judge; if application is made, it must be allowed on the basis of the Court's prior decision. There is, however, no authority for this and the point remains open to argument.

Several persons may apply to intervene in the same application.[39] Where the intervener applies to intervene in several, but not all, cases which have been joined, the intervention is admitted in relation to all,[40] unless it would be inadmissible in relation to some. In the *Ludwigshafener Walzmühle* case,[41] which comprised several distinct actions joined by order of the Court, a German trade union sought to intervene after the time limit set for doing so had expired in all but one of them. It was objected that to admit the intervention would allow the intervener to intervene indirectly in all the actions despite the time bar. The Court dismissed the application to intervene on other grounds, but it would seem, as a matter of principle, that if an application to intervene is made in circumstances in which it is within time or otherwise admissible only in relation to one of a number of joined cases, the application should be allowed as to that case alone. In practice this may mean that the intervener is in no worse a position than if he had intervened in all the cases but, on the one hand, the mere fact that the cases have been joined should not give rise to a right to intervene where one would not otherwise exist; on the other hand, it would be perverse to exclude intervention in the one case in which it is certainly admissible simply because it is inadmissible with regard to the other joined cases.

It has also been suggested[42] that intervention is not possible unless the action has been accepted as admissible. There seems to be no reason that this should be so, given that the intervener may himself raise arguments against the admissibility of the action.[43] In addition, since admissibility is very often decided at the same time as the merits of the case, the result of this approach would be to exclude intervention entirely. There are, of course, cases where the intervener states expressly that he seeks to challenge only the foundation of a party's claim or defence, not its admissibility. In such cases the intervener must be taken to have waived any objection to admissibility and it is right to restrict intervention to the substance of the case. On the other hand, where the intervener does not expressly waive any objection to admissibility, he has every interest to be heard if, for example, the Court decides to deal with admissibility before turning to the merits of the action. It does not seem that the intervener can himself raise an objection to admissibility under RP-ECJ

---

38 Assuming, of course, that the Court made its decision on the intervention before the hearing of the application for interim relief.
39 This happened in Case 25/59 *Netherlands v High Authority* [1960] ECR 386 and Case 246/81 *Bethell v Commission* [1982] ECR 2277.
40 Cases 152–186, 203, 204, 219/81 *Ferrario v Commission* [1983] ECR 2357 (order of 29 October 1981).
41 [1981] ECR 3211.
42 See Bebr, op cit, p 171, and Vandersanden and Barav, op cit, p 461, footnote 7.
43 See the *SNUPAT* case (above, note 12) (but see also the *CIRFS* and *Matra* cases, above, note 20).

91(1) or RP-CFI 114(1) because the role of intervention does not seem to entitle an intervener to take positive steps in the proceedings.[44] When a preliminary objection has been made there is no point in excluding the intervener from that part of the proceedings because he can still raise the admissibility point again if the Court considers the substance of the case. The object of proceedings under RP-ECJ 91 and RP-CFI 114, which is to settle the issue of admissibility before turning to the merits, would then be lost. The right of the intervener to challenge admissibility, which is now well established, seems to carry with it the right to be heard if a preliminary objection to admissibility is raised and a right to reopen the question of admissibility if the preliminary objection is rejected without the intervener being heard.[45] It seems to be the Court's practice to hear the intervener at the preliminary objection unless he evinces an intention only to intervene in regard to the merits.[46]

The application to intervene must comply with RP-ECJ 37 and 38 or, as the case may be, RP-CFI 43 and 44 and in addition contain:

(1)   a description of the case;
(2)   a description of the parties;
(3)   the name and address of the intervener;
(4)   the intervener's address for service in Luxembourg;
(5)   the form of order sought by one or more of the parties in support of which the intervener seeks to intervene; and
(6)   except in the case of applications to intervene made by member states or Community institutions,[47] a statement of the reasons establishing the intervener's interest in the result of the case.[48]

In most cases the application will be very short: the member states often apply by means of a telex or a facsimile message a few lines long.[49] Where the applicant must show an interest to intervene the bulk of the application will be taken up with this. Interveners often explain at length the substantial points of their intervention but this does not appear to be necessary.[50] The Rules of Procedure used to provide that the application to intervene should set out an indication of the evidence relied on by the intervener. At that time, there was authority that the application should mention the evidence relied on only if the

---

44 There does not, however, appear to be any authority on this point save the *CIRFS* case (above, note 20) per Advocate General Lenz. If the *CIRFS* and *Matra* cases (above, note 20) are to be understood as precluding the raising of an admissibility point by an intervener even where the party supported by the intervener has unintentionally failed to do so, it seems to follow necessarily that an intervener cannot raise a preliminary objection to admissibility.

45 Sed quaere if admissibility is settled before the date of intervention: see RP-ECJ 93(4); RP-CFI 116(3).

46 See, for example, Case 60/81 *IBM Corpn v Commission* [1981] ECR 2639; Case 45/81 *Moksel v Commission* [1982] ECR 1129.

47 Strictly speaking, of course, member states and Community institutions intervening in actions to which the ECSC Statute applies should state the reasons justifying an interest in the result of the case.

48 RP-ECJ 93(1); RP-CFI 115(2).

49 In Case 792/79R *Camera Care v Commission* [1980] ECR 119, the Registrar asked the intervener to submit a written application to intervene, but the reason for this was that the intervener had previously sent a telex saying that it wished to apply for leave to intervene: the telex did not therefore constitute an application to intervene and the Court wanted to know for certain whether or not such an application was going to be made. In *Moksel v Commission* (above, note 46) a company did apply by telex to intervene.

50 In *SNUPAT v High Authority* (above, note 12) order of 20 January 1960, unreported, the Court held that the intervener had to set up the grounds for his submissions in the pleading lodged after the intervention was admitted but not in the application to intervene.

intervener's interest was doubtful, not if it was manifest.[51] This suggested that evidence relating to the intervener's arguments of substance did not have to be set out in the application to intervene.[52] The Rules of Procedure no longer require the intervener's evidence to be indicated in the application to intervene. Nonetheless, it would seem that, where the intervener's interest to intervene turns on matters of fact, any evidence supporting the existence of that interest should be indicated in the application and, where in documentary form, annexed to it. It is essential that the application to intervene should set out clearly those parts of the parties' forms of order that the intervener supports or opposes.[53] If this is not done, the application is certainly inadmissible but the Court may, through the Registrar, ask for it to be clarified.[54] As long as the defect is remedied within the time limit for intervening, the application is admissible: in the *Ludwigshafener Walzmühle* case[55] a defective application was cured by telex.

The provision in RP-ECJ 38(7) and RP-CFI 44(6) allowing the Registrar to prescribe a reasonable period for an applicant to put his application in order does not apply to the contents of the application to intervene as specified by RP-ECJ 93(1) and RP-CFI 115(2): these mirror the requirements of RP-ECJ 38(1) and (2) and RP-CFI 44(1) and (2); but RP-ECJ 38(7) and RP-CFI 44(6) apply only to the requirements set in RP-ECJ 38(3)–(6) and RP-CFI 44(3)–(5), respectively, so it may be deduced that RP-ECJ 38(7) does not apply to RP-ECJ 93(1) and that RP-CFI 44(6) does not apply to RP-CFI 115(2).[56] On the other hand, compliance with the requirements set out in

---

51 The *SNUPAT* case (above, note 12), order of 20 January 1960. However, in Case C-179/87 *Sharp Corpn v Council* [1992] ECR I-1635 (order of 3 February 1988) the applicant objected to an application to intervene in support of the defendant on the ground that the application did not indicate the evidence relied on. The Court dismissed the objection because the Rules of Procedure, as they then stood, did not require the intervener to submit offers of proof and documents complementing those already submitted by the parties (thus implying that the obligation to indicate in the application to intervene the evidence relied on did relate to the intervener's substantive submissions in the case – at least where they raised matters of fact going beyond those raised by the applicant and defendant).

52 This was logical given that the arguments themselves would be contained in the pleading lodged after the intervention had been allowed.

53 RP-ECJ 93(1)(e) and RP-CFI 115(2)(e) refer only to the forms of order that the intervener supports but, as explained above, if the intervener intervenes in support of the defendant but before the defence is lodged, it is easier to oppose the applicant's form of order rather than support the defendant's form of order (which is ex hypothesi non-existent or unknown). The statement in intervention may in any event set out a form of order supporting or opposing a party's form of order (see RP-ECJ 93(5)(a); RP-CFI 116(4)(a)) so it seems illogical to limit the form of order mentioned in the application to intervene to that which the intervener supports.

54 This was done in the *Nungesser* case (above, note 8) in relation to the German government's application to intervene. The order allowing the intervention was made only after the German government's clarification had been lodged at the Court. This was done within time so the question did not arise whether a clarification out of time would render the application inadmissible.

55 Above (note 41), see order of 21 January 1981.

56 If the applicant fails to lodge an application to intervene which does comply with the Rules of Procedure, within time, it will be rejected on the ground of inadmissibility. In *IBM Corpn v Commission* (above, note 46), the British government applied to intervene without specifying which party's form of order it supported or rejected and to what extent, on the basis that member states have a right to intervene under the EEC Statute. The precise reasoning behind this assumption is not altogether clear. The furthest that the EEC and the Euratom Statutes go is to give member states and Community institutions a right to intervene without showing an interest in the result of the case. There is nothing to suggest that, unlike 'other persons', they are not restricted to supporting the submissions (ie form of order) of one of the parties. From the *Nungesser* case (above, note 8) it seems to be the Court's view that they are so restricted: it follows that member states must set out in their applications to intervene the precise object of their intervention. The Court did not rule on the British government's application in the *IBM* case because it was limited to the substance of the action, which was dismissed as being inadmissible after a preliminary objection had been raised by the defendant.

RP-ECJ 38(3)–(6) and RP-CFI 44(3)–(5), which must also be satisfied, is dealt with under RP-ECJ 38(7) or, as the case may be, RP-CFI 44(6), where need be.[57] The application to intervene may be drawn up in any of the languages accepted by the Court because, until the Court allows the intervention, the intervener is not a party to the proceedings and therefore is not obliged to use the language of the case.[58]

Lodgment of the application does not automatically entitle the applicant to join in the proceedings.[59] A decision has to be made on the application. The application to intervene is therefore served on the parties, who are given an opportunity to submit written or oral observations on it.[60] Usually the parties are asked to submit written observations but that requirement has been dispensed with where the intervener applies to intervene in an application for interim relief and there is not sufficient time to wait for the submission of observations in writing. In such a situation the Court (that is, the President or the judge hearing the application) decides whether or not to admit the intervention at the hearing in the proceedings for interim relief. After the parties have been heard on the application to intervene, the President (or judge) makes his decision and then continues with the hearing on the application for interim relief.[61] It has been the practice of the ECJ in recent years also to dispense with written and oral observations on applications to intervene made by member states on the ground that they have a right to intervene (as long as the application is made within time) and that therefore giving the other parties to the case an opportunity to submit observations on such an application is pointless. That practice was very unfair to the parties because they often heard of the intervention of a member state at a late stage and at a point in the proceedings at which they were barred from replying in writing to an intervener's written submissions. The Rules as currently worded provide a solution to that problem because the parties may now be allowed to reply to the intervener's written statement in intervention.[62] Even so, the practice of not informing the parties of a member state's application to intervene is not to be encouraged because it fails to take account of the fact that the opportunity of submitting observations on such an application enables a party to claim confidential treatment for any secret or confidential documents before the Court.[63]

---

57 In Cases C-193 and C-194/87 *Maurissen and European Public Service Union v Court of Auditors* [1990] ECR I-95 (order of 10 February 1988), for example, the intervener produced the mandate given to its lawyer but only parts of its statutes (see RP-ECJ 38(5)). Those parts were, however, sufficient to establish its objects, functions and general characteristics for the purpose of determining whether or not it had capacity to be an intervener. There was therefore no need to submit the complete text of the statutes. In Case C-156/87 *Gestetner Holdings plc v Council and Commission* [1990] ECR I-781 (order of 26 November 1987), the Court seems to have relied solely on the statement in one provision of the intervening association's statutes, that its object was to represent the Community industry concerned and undertake defensive action against unfair and illegal practices, for the purpose of concluding that it possessed the characteristics of personality required in order to intervene.

58 *De Gezamenlijke Steenkolenmijnen v High Authority* (above, note 10): the intervener was the Federal Republic of Germany and the Rules of Procedure in force at the time did not incorporate a provision such as the fourth sub-paragraph of RP-ECJ 29(3). See also Case 150/86 *Union Sidérurgique du Nord et de l'Est de la France (USINOR) v Commission* (case withdrawn, order of 28 January 1987). It is in any event doubtful if this provision applies to applications to intervene.

59 *De Gezamenlijke Steenkolenmijnen v High Authority* (above, note 10).

60 RP-ECJ 93(2); RP-CFI 116(1).

61 See the *Commercial Solvents* case; *Fruit-en-Groentenimporthandel Frubo v Commission*; *National Carbonising Co Ltd v Commission*; *NTN Toyo Bearing Co v Council*; above, note 23.

62 RP-ECJ 93(6); RP-CFI 116(5).

63 See RP-ECJ 93(3); RP-CFI 116(2).

No formal requirements are laid down for the written observations on the application to intervene but they should in principle comply with RP-ECJ 37 or, as the case may be, RP-CFI 43. Very often observations are submitted in the form of a telex or facsimile message.[64] It is very rare for there to be oral argument on an application to intervene.[65] The intervener has no right of reply to the observations of the parties on his intervention[66] but the President or, as the case may be, the Court may allow a reply if the circumstances justify it. A decision on the application to intervene is not necessary if the action is withdrawn or discontinued.[67] Otherwise the decision whether or not to allow the intervention is made in all cases, other than in appeals to the ECJ, by the President in the form of an order; but, instead of making the decision himself, he may refer the application to the Court.[68] In the case of applications to intervene in appeals to the ECJ, the decision is made by the ECJ in the form of an order and after the advocate general has been heard.[69] In the case of applications to intervene in cases before the CFI, the order made by the President or, as the case may be, the Court must be reasoned if it dismisses the application[70] because an appeal lies from such an order to the ECJ.[71] The appeal can be brought only by the applicant to intervene and it must be lodged within two weeks of notification to that applicant of the decision dismissing the application.[72] The appeal is heard and determined in summary proceedings before the President of the ECJ.[73] No appeal lies against a decision of the CFI (or its President) allowing an application to intervene.

If the intervention is allowed, the intervener receives a copy of every document served on the parties but the President may withhold documents which are secret or confidential if one of the parties so requests.[74] A request for confidential treatment of documents already before the Court cannot be made as against an intervener after his application to intervene has been allowed.[75] In consequence, a party (whether applicant or defendant) who wishes to keep

64 Eg Case 60/81 *IBM Corpn v Commission* (above, note 46).
65 Eg the *Lemmerz-Werke* case (above, note 3), at 719 (Advocate General Roemer).
66 Case 25/59 *Netherlands v High Authority* [1960] ECR 355.
67 Eg Case T-9/90 *Van der Stijl and Cullington v Commission* (unreported, order of 5 November 1990).
68 RP-ECJ 93(2); RP-CFI 116(1). It is apprehended that an application would be referred to the Court by the President if it gave rise to some point of principle requiring clarification. For an example of such a reference see Case T-84/91 *Meskens v European Parliament* [1992] ECR II-1565.
69 RP-ECJ 123.
70 RP-CFI 116(1) (last sentence). Orders allowing an application to intervene, whether in proceedings before the ECJ or in proceedings before the CFI, need not give any reasons but often do.
71 ECSC and EC Statutes, art 50 (first sentence); Euratom Statute, art 51 (first sentence).
72 Ibid.
73 ECSC and EC Statutes, art 50 (last sentence); Euratom Statute, art 51 (last sentence). See further chapter 15.
74 RP-ECJ 93(3); RP-CFI 116(2). See *VBVB and VBBB v Commission* (above, note 35), order of 10 March 1982: in the order allowing the intervention, the Court asked one of the applicants (which had claimed confidential treatment) to inform the Court which documents should be given confidential treatment and to provide the reasons therefor (in the event, at that stage there were no documents on the file which had to be kept secret from the intervener). In Case C-136/89 *Hyundai Merchant Marine Co Ltd v Commission* (unreported, order of 4 July 1990) and Case C-66/90 *Koninklijke PTT Nederland NV and PTT Post BV v Commission* (reported sub nom Cases C-48 and C-66/90 *Netherlands v Commission* [1992] ECR I-565) (unreported order of 5 December 1990), the applicants were ordered to prepare a non-confidential version of their pleadings for service on the intervener, only documents not capable of such treatment being withheld in their entirety from the intervener.
75 Cases C-133 and C-150/87 *Nashua Corpn v Commission and Council* [1990] ECR I-719 (order of 16 March 1988 in Case C-150/87).

certain secret or confidential material from an intervener must claim confidential treatment either by application when the secret or confidential document is lodged at the Court or in the written observations submitted to the Court in response to the application to intervene. Any restrictions on the disclosure of secret or confidential documents to the intervener may then be set out in the order allowing the intervention or the order may suspend the transmission of the documents served on the parties to the intervener until the question of confidential treatment has been resolved.[76] In principle, interveners are entitled to see every document served on the main parties and it is only by derogation from that principle that certain documents or parts of documents may be withheld on account of their secret or confidential nature. In consequence, the Court must be satisfied that confidential treatment is justified before it will withhold a document or a part of a document from an intervener. When deciding whether or not a claim to confidential treatment is justified, the Court must try to reconcile the legitimate concern of the party in question to prevent substantial damage to its interests and the intervener's legitimate concern to have the information necessary in order to enable it to assert its rights fully and put its case to the Court; account must also be taken of certain principles of law, such as the protection of lawyer–client confidences.[77] The party claiming confidential treatment must therefore explain precisely which documents or parts of documents are said to be secret or confidential.[78] A waiver of confidentiality vis-à-vis a main party to the action (whether applicant or defendant) does not constitute a waiver of the right to claim confidential treatment vis-à-vis an intervener.[79] Confidential treatment may be given to parts of the pleadings as well as to documentary evidence.[80] Where confidential treatment is accorded to a document, it is not disclosed to any intervener, including a member state.[81] Although a principal party (whether applicant or defendant) can claim confidential treatment as against an intervener, an intervener cannot claim confidential treatment as against a principal party[82] and, it may be, cannot claim confidential treatment as against another intervener.[83]

---

76   The latter course was adopted in the *VBVB and VBBB* case (above, note 35) and in Case T-30/89 *Hilti AG v Commission* [1990] ECR II-163.

77   The *Hilti* case (ibid) at para 11. For an account of the CFI's assessment of the claim to confidential treatment, see paras 12–23 of the judgment.

78   Ibid.

79   Ibid, paras 12–14.

80   Eg Case 273/85R *Silver Seiko Ltd v Council* [1985] ECR 3475 (para 6).

81   *Gestetner Holdings Plc v Council and Commission* (above, note 57), order of 16 December 1987.

82   See chapter 12.

83   In Case C-172/87 *Mita Industrial Co Ltd v Council* [1992] ECR I-1301, one intervener claimed confidential treatment not as against the main parties but as against an association comprising its commercial rivals which had intervened in support of a party opposing the first intervener. The ECJ refused to give confidential treatment to the documents in question even though there was no dispute about their confidential nature and even though confidential treatment had been given to the information in question vis-à-vis the association concerned both in the administrative proceedings prior to the commencement of the action and in parallel proceedings before the ECJ. No reasons were given and it is not clear whether or not an order was drawn up. The decision nonetheless seems to be wrong in principle because an intervener is a party once its application to intervene is allowed and, on that basis, is entitled to claim confidential treatment as against another intervener (but not as against a principal party) on the basis of RP-ECJ 93(3) or RP-CFI 116(2). Further, there is no reason in principle that an intervener should not be allowed confidential treatment of secret or confidential material vis-à-vis another intervener where the circumstances justify it. If, in such circumstances, confidential treatment is refused, the intervener should apply to withdraw the pleadings and documentary evidence lodged at the Court and replace them with an edited version that omits the secret or confidential material (which was what was done in the *Mita* case).

When the intervention is allowed, the President prescribes a period within which the intervener may submit a written statement in intervention.[84] This period can be extended on application.[85] The statement in intervention must be expressed in the language of the case save that member states, when they intervene, are entitled to use their official languages, as opposed to the language of the case, in both their written and oral submissions.[86] The Court may, however, exercise its power under RP-ECJ 29(2)(c) or, as the case may be, RP-CFI 35(2)(b) to allow an intervener to use a language other than that of the case, if it so requests.[87] The Rules of Procedure do not specify any formal requirements for the statement in intervention but RP-ECJ 37 or, as the case may be, RP-CFI 43 applies, as they do to all pleadings. So far as its content is concerned, the statement in intervention must set out:

(1)   a statement of the form of order sought by the intervener in support of or opposing, in whole or in part, the form of order sought by one of the parties;
(2)   the pleas in law and arguments relied on by the intervener; and
(3)   where appropriate, the nature of any evidence offered.[88]

Those matters do not have to be set out in that order; and it is common for the first to be last. The fact that the intervener should indicate the nature of the evidence relied on shows that the reference to 'pleas in law and arguments relied on by the intervener' is not intended to preclude reliance upon arguments based on matters of fact. The nature of the evidence relied on (if any) is pleaded in the statement in intervention in the same way as in an application commencing proceedings or defence.[89]

Initially the parties were allowed to answer the case made out by the intervener in writing. Then the Rules of Procedure were amended so as to exclude that possibility. The parties were in consequence able to deal with the intervener's written case only in their written pleadings[90] or at the hearing. That was very unsatisfactory, particularly when the Court began to control the time taken by the parties in their oral submissions to the Court. The Rules currently provide that, after the statement in intervention has been lodged, the President will, where necessary, prescribe a time limit within which the parties (including other interveners) may reply to that statement.[91] Therefore, if the statement in intervention is lodged at a time when the other parties still have at

---

84 RP-ECJ 93(5); RP-CFI 116(4). The intervener is not obliged to submit its case in writing: in Case 34/86 *Council v European Parliament* [1986] ECR 2155 (at 2157 per Advocate General Mancini) one intervener contented itself with submitting oral argument alone.
85 RP-ECJ 82; RP-CFI 103.
86 RP-ECJ 29(3); RP-CFI 35(3). All other interveners, including Community institutions, must use the language of the case once their application to intervene has been allowed unless the Court rules otherwise.
87 See *De Gezamenlijke Steenkolenmijnen v High Authority* (above, note 10) at 50; in *Moksel v Commission* (above, note 46) the Court required the intervener's written observations to be in the language of the case (German) but the oral observations could be in English. However, in *VBVB and VBBB v Commission* (above, note 35), order of 22 September 1982, several interveners were not allowed to submit either written or oral observations in a language other than that of the case. No reason was given for this decision. In Case 53/85 *AKZO Chemie BV and AKZO Chemie UK Ltd v Commission* [1986] ECR 1965 (order of 10 July 1985), the intervener was allowed to use a language other than the languge of the case for the written and oral procedure. It is doubtful if the Court has adopted any particular practice in the matter.
88 RP-ECJ 93(5); RP-CFI 116(4).
89 See chapter 9.
90 Unless the written procedure had already ended or their last written pleading had been lodged.
91 RP-ECJ 93(6); RP-CFI 116(5).

least one written pleading to lodge, the simplest solution is for them to deal with the statement in intervention in that pleading. If necessary, the President may extend the time limit for lodging any outstanding written pleadings so that the parties can take account of the intervener's written submissions. On the other hand, if the statement in intervention is lodged after a party has lodged its last written pleading, the President should give that party an opportunity to reply in writing to the statement in intervention in the form of an additional pleading. The 'necessity' for a written reply to the statement of intervention is a matter for the parties to consider (they may believe that it is sufficient to make oral submissions in reply at the hearing); it does not seem that the President can decide the 'necessity' for a written reply without prejudging the case to some extent. No requirements of form or content are laid down in the Rules of Procedure for any written reply to the statement in intervention. RP-ECJ 37 or, as the case may be, RP-CFI 43 must be complied with. Otherwise, the reply need only answer the case made out by the intervener. It does not seem that the reply need contain a form of order because the form of order of the party submitting the reply will be contained in its principal pleadings.[92] At the hearing, the intervener addresses the Court in the same way as a principal party. Given the fact that secret or confidential documents may be withheld from an intervener, such material should not be mentioned by another party at the hearing. If it is necessary to mention it, application would have to be made for that part of the hearing to be held in camera, with the intervener excluded. Since such a step runs contrary to the general principle that the hearing is held in public, strong reasons would have to be given for it.

It is unclear whether or not the President or the Court can reconsider an application to intervene once it has been allowed or revoke leave to intervene. The question was raised in Case 143/84 *Vlachou v Court of Auditors*,[93] a staff case where the applicant ('V') sought the annulment of a decision appointing another official ('K') to a particular post. K intervened in support of the defendant. K was married to another official ('S'), who had brought an action against the defendant for the annulment of the decision appointing V to a different post. Both K and S were represented by the same lawyer. The defendant believed that the object of K's intervention in V's action was to obtain sight of certain documents and pass knowledge of them to S so that she could use that knowledge in her action against the defendant. The defendant therefore applied to the Court for it to reconsider its decision to allow K's intervention.[94] The Court made its decision expressly without deciding whether or not it could reconsider an application to intervene. It dismissed the defendant's request solely on the ground that K had a valid interest in supporting the defendant. It would therefore seem that, even if the grant of leave to intervene could be reconsidered or revoked, that could be so only upon discovery of a new fact affecting the intervener's entitlement to intervene.[95] Where it is feared that an intervener wishes to use information acquired as a

---

92 The application, defence or statement in intervention, as the case may be.
93 [1986] ECR 459 (order of 16 October 1985).
94 At that time, decisions on applications to intervene were made by the Court. If the same situation arose under the Rules of Procedure as they are currently worded, the application would be made to the President.
95 Such as, presumably, evidence that the intervener had ceased to exist or to possess the characteristics or personality required for intervention in proceedings before the Court or, where relevant, evidence that the intervener did not have or no longer had an interest to intervene.

result of its participation in the proceedings for purposes unconnected with the proceedings, application may be made for secret or confidential documents to be withheld from the intervener;[96] but the Rules of Procedure contain no provision empowering the Court to direct an intervener to use the documents to which he is entitled to have access for the purposes only of the proceedings.[97]

96 See above pp 179–180.
97 The *Hilti* case (above, note 76) at para 23.

CHAPTER 6

Procedural issues

RP-ECJ 91 and RP-CFI 114 set out the procedure for applying to the ECJ and the CFI, respectively, for a decision on 'a preliminary objection or other preliminary plea not going to the substance of the case'.[1] They are used principally to raise a preliminary objection to the admissibility of the action or, in the case of the CFI, a preliminary objection to its competence (that is to say, its jurisdiction). That type of procedural issue, together with the related provisions contained in RP-ECJ 92 and RP-CFI 111–113, is discussed in the following chapter, as is the raising by the Court of its own motion under RP-ECJ 92(2) or RP-CFI 113 of the question whether or not there is an absolute bar to proceeding with a case even though it is admissible. Those questions aside, there is no apparent limit to the types of 'preliminary plea not going to the substance of the case' which may be the subject of an application under RP-ECJ 91 or RP-CFI 114 other than that they must not impinge on the dispute concerning the merits of the case (whence their 'preliminary' nature). That limit can be illustrated by reference to Case 22/59 *Macchiorlatti Dalmas e Figli SaS v High Authority*.[2] There the defendant produced a document which appeared to have emanated from the applicant. The latter applied, under the predecessor to RP-ECJ 91, for the Court to rule on the legal value of the document. No evidence was produced tending to invalidate it and the Court took the view that, in substance, the applicant wanted it to rule on the issue of fact to which the document related. Since this impinged on the merits of the case, the application was rejected as inadmissible. The case also illustrates the essentially procedural nature of the applications that may be made.[3] As the word 'plea' is mainly used in the Rules of Procedure to describe the grounds on which a party bases its case, the term 'issue' or 'procedural issue' will be used to describe preliminary pleas in order to avoid confusion.

In brief, RP-ECJ 91 and RP-CFI 114 set out the procedure to be followed for raising all procedural matters which may require a formal decision of the Court, before the substance of the case is settled in the final judgment, other than those specifically provided for elsewhere in the Rules of Procedure. A matter should not be raised if it does not require a formal decision. For example, in Case 30/78 *Distillers Co Ltd v Commission*,[4] Advocate General Warner pointed out that the point in question could have been dealt with at

---

1 RP-ECJ 91(1). RP-CFI 114(1) is worded slightly differently: 'a decision on admissibility, on lack of competence or other preliminary plea not going to the substance of the case'. The difference is essentially cosmetic. Vandersanden and Barav, op cit, p 46, adopt an analytical approach to the types of decision that can be made which is based on the French text of RP-ECJ 91 but, in view of the relative poverty of authority, it seems appropriate to be more pragmatic.
2 Order of 17 November 1959 (unreported).
3 See also Cases 46/87 and 227/88 *Hoechst AG v Commission* [1989] ECR 2859 at 2907–2908 (Advocate General Mischo).
4 [1980] ECR 2229.

the hearing and, for this reason, although the application under RP-ECJ 91 should, in his view, have been allowed, the applicant should have borne the costs of it.[5] In addition, the object of the procedure is to deal only with the matter raised and not with anything connected with the substance of the case. The Court will not, therefore, allow the submission of further written pleadings concerning the substance of the case;[6] and the procedure cannot be used in order to obtain an early ruling on a point of law that may well decide the case one way or the other (other than one relating to the admissibility of the proceedings). Typical examples of the type of plea that may be raised under RP-ECJ 91 and RP-CFI 114 are applications for: confidential treatment of pleadings or evidence; withdrawal of a document from the file; a measure of enquiry; the production of documents; reopening of the written or oral procedure; stay of proceedings. Other examples are set out in their procedural context in various places in this book or can be drawn directly from the case law. RP-ECJ 91 can be invoked in references for a preliminary ruling.[7]

The unusual feature of the *Macchiorlatti Dalmas* case[8] was that it seemed to the Court that the application was made only in order to decide an issue of fact relating to the merits of the case and not the procedural issue whether the document was admissible as evidence. In other cases, applications have been accepted as admissible because they raised issues concerning the evidence that had to be decided before the Court considered the merits of the case. For example, in *Mirossevich v High Authority*[9] the applicant contested the authenticity of two documents submitted by the defendant. At that time the Rules of Procedure contained a specific provision empowering the Court to verify disputed documents, the procedure following that set out in the predecessor to RP-ECJ 91. Since the defendant conceded that it would not use one of the documents, the application was, to that extent, pointless but, in relation to the second document, the Court held that the matter would be dealt with as a measure of enquiry. A similar situation arose in Cases 9 and 58/65 *Acciaierie San Michele SpA v High Authority*,[10] where the applicant applied under RP-ECJ 91 for an order that the defendant produce the original of a document on the ground that the copy given to the applicant appeared to be incomplete. By this time the specific provision for the verification of the authenticity of a document had disappeared. The defendant eventually produced the original to the Registrar who compared it with the applicant's photocopy and ascertained that the two corresponded. The Court took official notice of this fact. In Cases C-89, C-104, C-114, C-116, C-117 and C-125 to 129/85 *A Ahlström Osakeyhtio v Commission*[11] several applicants applied for an order that certain documents could not be relied on by the defendant because they had been produced too late in the administrative procedure leading up to the making of the contested decision. That application was joined to the substance of the case: the arguments relied on in its support were identical to those relied on in support of the

---

5 See also Case 14/64 *Gualco (née Barge) v High Authority of the ECSC* [1965] ECR 51 at 67–68 (Advocate General Roemer).
6 Cf Case 34/65 *Mosthaf v Euratom Commission* [1966] ECR 521; Case 10/55 *Mirossevich v High Authority* [1954–56] ECR 333 at 336, order of 20 January 1956 (unreported).
7 Eg Case C-16/90 *Detlef Nolle v Hauptzollamt Bremen-Freihafen* [1991] ECR I-5163 (order of 16 May 1991): an application for the production of documents.
8 Above, note 2.
9 Above, note 6.
10 [1967] ECR 1 at 3.
11 [1993] ECR I-1307 (para 29 and see the opinion of Advocate General Darmon at paras 55–57). The admissibility of the evidence did not require a decision because the issue to which it related was decided on other grounds: see para 54 of the judgment.

claim for the annulment of the contested act. The application was thus an inappropriate use of RP-ECJ 91 because, on the assumption that the argument was that the documents were inadmissible as evidence against the applicant, that argument (and the consequences if it were correct)[12] were matters going to the substance of the case which were not suited to a preliminary determination. In Case C-213/87 *Gemeente Amsterdam and Stichting Vrouwenvakschool voor Informatica Amsterdam (VIA) v Commission*[13] and Case C-110/89 *Commission v Greece*[14] the applicants applied under RP-ECJ 91 for leave, and were allowed, to lodge further documents that had come to light after the end of the written procedure.

In Case 28/65 *Fonzi v Euratom Commission*[15] and the *Distillers* case,[16] a party applied under RP-ECJ 91 for certain documents to be removed from the file on the grounds of confidentiality. In both cases the application was allowed in part.[17] In the same way, in Cases T-1 to T-4 and T-6 to T-15/89 *Rhône-Poulenc v Commission*,[18] the CFI invited the parties to request confidential treatment for their pleadings and annexes as a result of the joinder of the cases, treating the matter as a procedural issue under RP-ECJ 91 (which was applicable to proceedings before the CFI at that time). Confidential treatment will not be given to matters that are not genuinely secret or confidential or deserving of protection from disclosure in the interests of justice.[19] In Case C-327/86 *Herkenrath v Commission*[20] the defendant applied under RP-ECJ 91 for the withdrawal from the Court file of a document introduced by the applicant on the ground that it was an internal note that had come into the applicant's possession by irregular means. The applicant was asked, but failed, to submit observations in reply. The Court therefore concluded that the defendant's application was justified and ordered the document to be withdrawn.[21] In Cases C-116 and C-149/88 *Hecq v Commission*[22] the applicant applied under RP-ECJ 91 for the production by the defendant of a document. The defendant produced the document to the Court but claimed that it should be excluded from consideration because of its confidential nature. The Court order was therefore limited to that point: the Court considered that the document added nothing useful and therefore ordered it to be excluded from consideration without ruling on whether or not it was confidential.

12 Namely, that it would have to be considered whether or not the defendant had sufficient other evidence to establish its case against the applicant.

13 [1990] ECR I-221.

14 [1991] ECR I-2659 (order of 21 November 1990).

15 [1966] ECR 477 at 506.

16 Above (note 4), see p 2237, order of 28 March 1979 (unreported).

17 It is unclear whether the application for confidential treatment of certain documents, made in Case 236/81 *Celanese Chemical Co Inc v Council and Commission* [1982] ECR 1183, was based on RP-ECJ 91, although, no doubt, it could have been.

18 [1990] ECR II-637 (paras 22–25).

19 Eg Case C-54/90 *Weddel & Co BV v Commission* [1992] ECR I-871 (order of 15 May 1991), where an application for the exclusion from the file of the record of the examination of certain witnesses by a national court was dismissed because a summary of the meeting to which that evidence related was being relied on in other proceedings.

20 Order of 15 June 1989 (the case is reported sub nom Case T-16/89 *Herkenrath v Commission* [1992] ECR II-275).

21 A similar situation arose in Case C-352/88 *Commission v Ireland* (unreported, order of 6 July 1989), where the defendant relied on an internal document emanating from the applicant. The latter applied under RP-ECJ 91 for the withdrawal of the document. That was not a case in which the document had come into the defendant's hands by irregular means. Nonetheless, it conceded the application for the withdrawal of the document and the Court made the order without needing to consider the confidential nature of the document.

22 [1990] ECR I-599 (order of 28 June 1989).

When application is made for the production of evidence, the Court has tended to deal with the matter in the context of preparatory enquiries rather than specifically as a separate procedural issue.[23] This means that, although the application is, in formal terms, admissible, the Court will consider whether or not to accede to it only when deciding what measures of enquiry are necessary in order to resolve the issues of fact in the case.

Other problems concerning the conduct of proceedings which have been brought before the Court under RP-ECJ 91 or RP-CFI 114 include applications for a third party to be joined to the proceedings[24] or to be substituted for one of the parties;[25] applications for the reopening of the written[26] or oral procedure[27] or for the suspension of proceedings.[28] In several cases an application has been made to 'strike out' or have rejected as inadmissible part of the opposing party's pleadings. In *Mosthaf v Euratom Commission*[29] reliance was placed on RP-ECJ 42(2) but the application was rejected on the ground that the opposing party had simply denied the applicant's argument on one point and not added a fresh issue. In Case 44/76 *Milch-, Fett- und Eier-Kontor GmbH v Council and Commission*,[30] on the other hand, the applicant applied for an order that the defendant delete from the defence a sentence that was alleged to be irrelevant, incorrect and defamatory. The latter conceded the point by redrafting the offending sentence but Advocate General Reischl took the view that the applicant was nevertheless entitled to the costs of the issue. A similar situation arose in Case 119/77 *Nippon Seiko KK v Council and Commission*.[31] Lastly, Case 76/63, an action commenced by the applicant in Cases 19 and

23 See, for example, Cases 24 and 34/58 *Chambre Syndicale de la Sidérurgie de l'Est de la France v High Authority* [1960] ECR 281, order of 3 March 1959 (unreported); Case 18/63 *Wollast née Schmitz v Commission* [1964] ECR 85, order of 13 November 1963 (unreported); Cases 19, 65 and 76/63 *Prakash v Euratom Commission* [1965] ECR 533 at 545 and Case 68/63 *Luhleich v Euratom Commission* [1965] ECR 581 at 591, orders of 28 October 1963 (unreported). In Case 118/83 *CMC Cooperativa Muratori e Cementisti v Commission* [1985] ECR 2325, however, the decision on the application was reserved to the final judgment (see order of 29 February 1984, unreported). In the *Detlef Nolle* case (above, note 7), a reference for a preliminary ruling, the application for the production of documents was dismissed on the ground that the document in question was not relevant to the question referred.
24 Case 25/62 *Plaumann & Co v Commission* [1963] ECR 95 at 106 (see also Case 27/62, order of 6 December 1962, unreported): the applicant applied for the Federal Republic of Germany to be joined and the Court decided to hear argument but the application was eventually withdrawn.
25 Case 250/78 *Deka (formerly Contiflex) v EEC* [1983] ECR 421, order of 22 September 1982 (unreported): the applicant had purportedly assigned its right to damages to a third party and applied for an order requiring the defendant to pay the money to it; the Court reserved its decision for the final judgment.
26 In Case T-5/90 *Marcato v Commission* [1991] ECR II-731 (order of 24 January 1991), where the applicant had failed to lodge a reply in time, thus causing the written procedure to close, the parties and the Court were in agreement that, due to the complexity of the case, it was desirable for there to be a complete written procedure.
27 Eg Case 11/63 *Lepape v High Authority* [1964] ECR 61, order of 28 November 1963 (unreported): a week after the hearing the applicant applied under RP-ECJ 91 for the Court to take account of certain declarations made and reopen the oral procedure because he, allegedly, had not received a copy of the report for the hearing before the date of the hearing and so could not challenge any inaccuracies in it; the Court dismissed the application on the ground that, as the report had been duly served in good time at the address for service, the applicant was deemed to have been able to present any observations on it at the hearing.
28 Case 9/65 *Acciaierie San Michele SpA v High Authority* [1967] ECR 27 (see also Case 6/65 *Merisider v High Authority*, order of 22 June 1965, unreported): the applicant applied for suspension pending judgment of the Italian Constitutional Court on the lawfulness of the Italian statute giving effect to the ECSC Treaty; the Court dismissed the application on its merits.
29 Above, note 6.
30 [1977] ECR 393, see pp 405 and 421.
31 [1979] ECR 1303, see p 1273 (Advocate General Warner).

65/63 *Prakash v Commission*,[32] was 'an interpretative application and in so far as necessary an application originating proceedings' whose object seems to have been to clarify the scope of the form of order in Case 65/63. It was eventually discontinued but, in an order removing the case from the Register, the Court suggested (but without deciding the point) that, at most, such a proceeding could be brought only under RP-ECJ 91.

An application under RP-ECJ 91 or RP-CFI 114 is made by separate document.[33] As a result, to raise, for example, an objection to the admissibility of the action in the defence does not constitute a preliminary objection within the meaning of RP-ECJ 91 or RP-CFI 114 and the matter would be dealt with separately only if the Court decided to raise it of its own motion under RP-ECJ 92 or, as the case may be, RP-CFI 111 or 113.[34] The same applies where a procedural issue is raised in an application commencing proceedings, a defence, reply or rejoinder, and not in a separate application. The application should comply with RP-ECJ 37 or, as the case may be, RP-CFI 43. RP-ECJ 91(1) and RP-CFI 114(1) state that it must set out 'the pleas of fact and law relied on and the form of order sought by the applicant' and that 'any supporting documents must be annexed to it'. If the pleas of fact and law relied on are not set out,[35] or there is no form of order,[36] the application may be rejected as inadmissible. It should also state the names of the parties to the proceedings, and, where necessary, comply with RP-ECJ 38(2)–(5) or, as the case may be, RP-CFI 44(2)–(5).[37]

After the application has been lodged, it is served on the other parties and the President fixes a period within which they are to present their written replies to the application.[38] The period may be extended on application.[39] The answer is not given a particular name, such as a defence, reply or even observations, in the Rules of Procedure, nor is anything laid down concerning its form or contents save that it must contain a form of order and the pleas in law relied on in support.[40] Usually the form of order will seek the dismissal of the application and costs. In other respects the answer should comply with RP-ECJ 37 (or RP-CFI 43) and, by analogy, RP-ECJ 40 (or RP-CFI 46), mutatis mutandis.

The written part of the procedure ends with the lodgment of the reply[41] and the Court then decides whether to make its decision on the application immediately or not. There are no preparatory enquiries; RP-ECJ 91(3) and RP-CFI 114(3) provide that the remainder of the proceedings shall be oral 'unless the Court decides otherwise'. More often than not, there is no hearing.

---

32 [1965] ECR 574.

33 RP-ECJ 91(1); RP-CFI 114(1).

34 Cf Case 47/65 *Kalkuhl v European Parliament* [1965] ECR 1011 and Case 543/79 *Birke v Commission and Council* [1981] ECR 2669 at para 30 of the judgment.

35 *Nippon Seiko KK v Council and Commission* (above, note 31) at 1273–1274 (Advocate General Warner).

36 Case 55/64 *Lens v European Court of Justice* [1965] ECR 837 at 840.

37 It is equally essential that an indication is given of the case to which the application relates. On the other hand, matters already mentioned in an earlier pleading, such as the address for service, do not have to be repeated. Where the application raises a preliminary objection as to admissibility, it often replaces the defence and should therefore comply with the requirements of RP-ECJ 40 or, as the case may be, RP-CFI 46, mutatis mutandis.

38 RP-ECJ 91(2); RP-CFI 114(2).

39 RP-ECJ 82; RP-CFI 103.

40 RP-ECJ 91(2); RP-CFI 114(2).

41 However, in Cases 532, 534, 567, 600, 618 and 660/79 *Amesz v Commission and Council* [1981] ECR 2569 the Council, which had made the application under RP-ECJ 91, wrote to the Court, maintaining its position, after the lodging of the reply.

In that event, although it occasionally happens that the Court makes a formal order stating that there will be none,[42] it is more usual for this to be omitted; after hearing the views of the advocate general (which are not, in this event, published), where there is one, the Court issues an order upholding or rejecting the application or reserving its decision on the matter for final judgment.[43] In the case of preliminary objections as to admissibility, an order upholding the application, which very often starts by explaining that the Court does not think that there are grounds for opening the oral procedure, terminates the proceedings and includes an order for costs.[44] In all other cases the action continues and the President prescribes new time limits for the further steps in the proceedings.[45]

The criterion adopted by the Court for deciding whether or not to open the oral procedure has been expressed in various ways: for example, where there is 'need'[46] or there are 'grounds'[47] for doing so or where it is 'necessary'.[48] The different terms used express the same idea: if it is possible to come to a decision on the basis of the written submissions, the oral procedure will not be opened.[49] It should be observed that the notion of 'need', 'necessity' or 'grounds' is not immutable and varies according to the nature of the decision which the Court feels it must take. By way of illustration, in the case of a preliminary objection as to admissibility, the Court must be convinced by the written submissions that the action is inadmissible before it can dismiss it without hearing the parties. If there is some doubt, the oral procedure should be opened. On the other hand, it does not have to be convinced beyond doubt if it takes the view that it is better to reserve a decision on admissibility until the final judgment. If the Court has serious doubts on the merits of the objection to admissibility, it should, in general, decide to reserve its decision until the final judgment in order to avoid prolonging the proceedings: if there is a hearing on the application made under RP-ECJ 91 or RP-CFI 114, and the Court decides at the end of the day to reject it, the action continues, there will be a second hearing, advocate general's opinion (where applicable) and judgment, adding several months to the total length of the proceedings.

If the Court decides to open the oral procedure, the date is fixed for the hearing and the proceedings follow as in an ordinary direct action: after the hearing the advocate general (where there is one) delivers his opinion in open court and the Court then makes its decision. Once again, the Court may decide

---

42 Eg Case 19/72 *Thomik v Commission* [1972] ECR 1155, order of 4 October 1972 (unreported).

43 RP-ECJ 91(4); RP-CFI 114(4). Eg Case 175/83 *Culmsee v Economic and Social Committee and Council* [1984] ECR 3321 and Case T-3/90 *Prodifarma v Commission* [1991] ECR II-1 (para 16).

44 See, for example, Cases 59 and 60/79 *Fédération Nationale des Producteurs de Vins de Table et Vins de Pays v Commission* [1979] ECR 2425 and 2429 respectively.

45 RP-ECJ 91(4); RP-CFI 114(4). In Case T-11/90 *HS v Council* ([1992] ECR II-1869, order of 15 January 1991), the defendant's preliminary objection to admissibility was joined to the substance, the order stating that the rest of the written procedure would in particular enable the parties to clarify their position regarding the issues in the case.

46 Case 192/80 *Geist v Commission* [1981] ECR 1387; Case 141/80 *Hebrant (née Macevicius) v European Parliament* [1980] ECR 3509; Case 48/79 *Ooms v Commission* [1979] ECR 3121; Cases 219–228, 230–235, 237–238, 240–242/80 *André v Council and Commission* [1981] ECR 1879.

47 *Fédération Nationale v Commission* (above, note 44).

48 Case 618/79A *Knoeppel v Commission and Council* [1981] ECR 2387; Case 567/79A *Flamm v Commission and Council* [1981] ECR 2383; Case 295/83 *Parti Ecologiste 'Les Verts' v European Parliament* [1984] ECR 3331; Case 296/83 *Parti Ecologiste 'Les Verts' v European Parliament* [1984] ECR 3335.

49 Eg Case 82/84 *Metalgoi SpA v Commission* [1984] ECR 2585; Cases 83 and 84/84 *NM v Commission and Council* [1984] ECR 3571 (para 8); Case 135/84 *FB v Commission* [1984] ECR 3577 (para 5).

between upholding the application under RP-ECJ 91 or RP-CFI 114, dismissing it or reserving its decision until the final judgment. Save where it upholds a preliminary objection as to admissibility, the action continues and the President prescribes new time limits for the further steps in the proceedings.[50] The Court may decide to reserve a decision on admissibility if the question cannot be disentangled from the substance of the case[51] but it is more usual for the issue to be resolved immediately.

50 RP-ECJ 91(4); RP-CFI 114(4).
51 Cf Cases 106, 107/63 *Alfred Toepfer KG and Getreide-Import Gesellschaft v Commission* [1965] ECR 429.

CHAPTER 7

Admissibility

I Introduction

An objection to the admissibility of a proceeding before the Court is not a true defence to the claim made or answer to the issues of substance raised, but a plea that the Court is barred for some reason from entertaining the proceeding with the result that it must dismiss it without considering the merits of the case.[1] It is usual to distinguish between the admissibility of the cause of action and the admissibility of the application commencing proceedings. If the action is inadmissible, it follows that the application is also barred; on the other hand, if the former is admissible, the inadmissibility of the application does not, in itself, prevent the proceedings from being recommenced. Another division lies between objections to admissibility which are mandatory and must be raised by the Court of its own motion, irrespective of the wishes of the parties, and objections which can be raised only by the parties so that a failure to plead them means that they are waived. A third possible division is between the general conditions of admissibility applicable in most proceedings and the particular conditions applicable in specific types of proceedings. The latter are adequately dealt with in most of the leading books on the principal actions which can be brought before the Court[2] and are only briefly touched upon here. The object of this chapter is simply to give a general description of the different objections to admissibility and the procedures by which they may be raised and decided.

By way of general remark, the admissibility of an action is determined by reference to the situation prevailing when the proceedings are commenced; if at that time the conditions for bringing proceedings are not satisfied, the action is inadmissible unless the defect is rectified subsequently but within the period for bringing the proceedings.[3] Further, an objection to the admissibility of proceedings commenced by a person cannot be avoided by that person joining in an application made by other persons against whom the objection cannot be raised: an application brought jointly by several persons is not admissible in respect of them all if, in relation to some of them, it is inadmissible; equally, it is not inadmissible in relation to them all but is admissible in respect of those applicants who are able to satisfy the conditions required for its admissibility.[4]

---

1 See generally De Soto in *Zehn Jahre Rechtsprechung des Gerichtshofs der E.G.* pp 48 et seq.
2 Eg Bebr, op cit; Hartley, *The Foundations of European Community Law* (2d edn, Clarendon Press); Schermers and Waelbroeck, op cit.
3 Case 50/84 *Bensider v Commission* [1984] ECR 3991 (para 8).
4 Ibid at 4000 (Advocate General Mancini).

II   Objections to admissibility

A   Lack of jurisdiction

The Court's competence (that is to say, its jurisdiction) to hear a matter is defined in the Treaties and the other instruments giving it jurisdiction. All proceedings must therefore be founded on a specific provision or provisions; the Court has no inherent jurisdiction[5] and cannot be given jurisdiction simply by the consent of the parties.[6] Where the contested act is based on more than one of the Treaties or relates simultaneously and indivisibly to the spheres of more than one Treaty, an action is admissible if and to the extent that the jurisdiction of the Court and the remedies provided for by the relevant provisions of any one of the Treaties are applicable.[7] The Court's lack of jurisdiction is something which the Court must raise of its own motion.[8] RP-ECJ 92(1) and RP-CFI 111-112 provide that, 'where it is clear that the Court has no jurisdiction to take cognisance of an action' and, specifically in the case of the CFI, where there is 'manifest lack of competence', the Court may 'give a decision on the action', which means that it is either dismissed as inadmissible or, as the case may be, referred to whichever of the ECJ or the CFI does have jurisdiction over it. The division of jurisdiction between the ECJ and the CFI has already been described.[9] Lack of jurisdiction is also an 'absolute bar to proceeding with a case' within the meaning of RP-ECJ 92(2) and RP-CFI 113.[10]

Lack of jurisdiction can be considered under two headings: ratione materiae and ratione personae. In the first the Court has no jurisdiction by reason of the subject matter of the proceedings. In the second the Court lacks jurisdiction over one or both of the parties. Without attempting a comprehensive statement of the situations in which the Court lacks jurisdiction, the position can broadly speaking be illustrated by the following examples.

In general, the Court lacks jurisdiction ratione materiae when the relief sought in the proceedings falls outside the scope of the relief that it is empowered to grant.[11] In references for a preliminary ruling the Court lacks

---

5 See chapter 1, section III.
6 Its jurisdiction to arbitrate and to settle disputes between the member states referred to it by special agreement is conferred on it by the Treaties (arts 42, 181 and 153, on the one hand, and 89, 182 and 154, on the other, of the ECSC, EC and Euratom Treaties respectively). Jurisdiction may also be conferred on it by national law but this is again by virtue of a Treaty provision (art 43 of the ECSC Treaty). For the Court's reluctance to entertain references for a preliminary ruling submitted to it by consent of the parties to the proceedings before the referring court, see Case 104/79 *Foglia v Novello* [1980] ECR 745 and Case 244/80 *Foglia v Novello (No 2)* [1981] ECR 3045 (and the abundant literature which has grown up concerning both cases).
7 Case 230/81 *Luxembourg v European Parliament* [1983] ECR 255; Case 222/83 *Municipality of Differdange v Commission* [1984] ECR 2889 (para 6).
8 Eg Case T-19/90 *von Hoessle v Court of Auditors* [1991] ECR II-615 (para 28).
9 See chapter 1, section III. For the referral of a case from the Court lacking jurisdiction to the Court with jurisdiction, see chapter 2, section III.
10 Eg Cases 31 and 33/62 *Milchwerke Heinz Wöhrmann & Sohn KG and Alfons Lüttick GmbH v Commission* [1962] ECR 501 and Cases 105/79 and 68/80 *References for a Preliminary Ruling by the Acting Judge at the Tribunal d'Instance, Hayange* [1979] ECR 2257 and [1980] ECR 771.
11 Eg Case 81/83 *Acciaiere e Ferriere Busseni SpA v Commission* [1984] ECR 2951 (para 25); Case 53/84 *Adams v Commission* [1985] ECR 3595 (claim for a declaration made in an action for damages); Case 162/84 *Vlachou v Court of Auditors* [1986] ECR 481 at 487 per Advocate General Lenz (claim for mandatory order in a staff case); Case 53/85 *Akzo Chemie BV and Akzo Chemie UK Ltd v Commission* [1986] ECR 1965 at para 3 (claim for the return of documents); Case 15/85 *Consorzio Cooperativo d'Abruzzo v Commission* [1987] ECR 1005 (para 18); Cases 142 and 156/84 *British American Tobacco Co Ltd and R J Reynolds Industries Inc v Commission* [1987] ECR

jurisdiction ratione materiae where the questions which it has been called on to answer do not concern the interpretation or, as the case may be, the validity of the acts specified in the provision conferring jurisdiction on the Court;[12] where it is manifest that the dispute before the referring court is contrived or fictitious in character;[13] or where it is manifest that the subject matter of the reference is irrelevant to the litigation before the referring court.[14] In an action for annulment, the Court lacks jurisdiction ratione materiae where the contested act does not exist;[15] where it does not have the required legal effect;[16] where the contested act is not one adopted by a Community institution;[17] where the defendant does not have jurisdiction over the matter in dispute;[18] or where, in order to decide the case, the Court would have to rule on the compatibility of a provision of national law with Community law.[19] An action for damages may be inadmissible by reason of its subsidiary character having regard to the

4487 at para 13 (claim for a mandatory order in an action for annulment); Case 207/86 *Asociación Professional de Empresarios de Pesca Comunitarios (Apesco) v Commission* [1988] ECR 2151 at para 31 (idem); Case 108/88 *Cendoya v Commission* [1989] ECR 2711 at paras 8–9 (claim for declarations); Case T-1/90 *Pérez-Mínguez Casariego v Commission* [1991] ECR II-143 at para 91 (claim for a mandatory order in relation to execution of a judgment); Case C-63/89 *Les Assurances du Crédit et Compagnie Belge d'Assurances Crédit SA v Council and Commission* [1991] ECR I-1799 at para 30 (claim for injunction in a damages action); Case C-199/91 *Foyer Culturel du Sart-Tilman v Commission* [1993] ECR I-2667 at paras 17–18 (claim for payment of a sum of money in an action for annulment).

12 For example, the Court does not have jurisdiction to apply a provision of Community law to the facts of a particular case or to rule on the validity of a provision of national law: eg Case 237/82 *Jongeneel Kaas v Netherlands* [1984] ECR 483 (para 6); Case 97/83 *CMC Melkunie BV* [1984] ECR 2367 (para 7); Cases 91 and 127/83 *Heineken Brouwerijen v Inspecteur der Vennoot-schapsbelasting* [1984] ECR 3435 (para 10); Case 137/84 *Ministère Public v Mutsch* [1985] ECR 2681 (para 6); Case 298/84 *Iorio v Azienda Autonoma delle Ferrovie dello Stato* [1986] ECR 247 (para 8); Case 54/85 *Ministère Public v Mirepoix* [1986] ECR 1067 (para 6). The Court also cannot answer a question relating to the interpretation of an act that has not been adopted: Case 93/78 *Mattheus v Doego* [1978] ECR 2203. But it has also been held that the objection that the reference raises no question of Community law goes to the answer to be given to the referring court and not to the jurisdiction of the Court: Case C-159/90 *Society for the Protection of Unborn Children Ireland Ltd v Grogan* [1991] ECR I-4685 (paras 14–15).

13 Eg Case 104/79 *Foglia v Novello* and Case 244/80 *Foglia v Novello (No 2)* (above, note 6); Case 267/86 *Van Eycke v ASPA NV* [1988] ECR 4769 (para 12 and at 4783 per Advocate General Mancini); Cases C-297/88 and C-197/89 *Dzodzi v Belgium* [1990] ECR I-3763 (para 40); Case C-231/89 *Gmurzynska-Bscher v Oberfinanzdirektion Köln* [1990] ECR I-4003 (para 23).

14 Eg *Dzodzi v Belgium* (ibid) para 40; *Gmurzynska-Bscher v Oberfinanzdirektion Köln* (ibid) para 23; Case C-368/89 *Crispoltoni v Fattoria Autonoma Tabacchi di Città di Castello* [1991] ECR I-3695 (para 11); Case C-186/90 *Durighello v Istituto Nazionale della Previdenza Sociale* [1991] ECR I-5773 (para 9).

15 Eg Case T-64/89 *Automec Srl v Commission* [1990] ECR II-367 (para 41); Cases T-79, T-84 to T-86, T-89, T-91, T-92, T-94, T-96, T-98, T-102 and T-104/89 *BASF AG v Commission* [1992] ECR II-315 (Re PVC Cartel); Case T-16/91 *Rendo NV v Commission* [1992] ECR II-2417 (para 39); Case T-46/90 *Devillez v European Parliament*, 30 June 1993 (para 12).

16 Eg Case T-135/89 *Pfloeschner v Commission* [1990] ECR II-153 (paras 11–14); Case C-64/93 *Donatab Srl v Commission* [1993] ECR I-3595.

17 Eg Case 46/81 *Benvenuto* [1981] ECR 809 (the act was adopted by a member state); Case C-97/91 *Oleificio Borelli SpA v Commission* [1992] ECR I-6313 (paras 9–10); Cases C-181 and C-248/91 *European Parliament v Council and Commission* [1993] ECR I-3685 para 12 (acts of representatives of the member states acting otherwise than in their capacity as members of the EC Council are not subject to judicial review by the Court).

18 Eg Cases 75, 146 and 147/88 *Bonazzi-Bertottilli v Commission* [1989] ECR 3599 (paras 21–22).

19 Eg Case C-347/87 *Triveneta Zuccheri SpA v Commission* [1990] ECR I-1083 (the Court can rule on the compatibility of national law with Community law in the context of an action brought under arts 169 or 170 of the EEC Treaty and the similar provisions in the ECSC and Euratom Treaties; but it would prejudge the outcome in such proceedings to deal with such an issue in the context of an action for annulment).

available national remedies;[20] and, where it is based on the alleged illegality of an act of a Community institution, it is inadmissible if the act in question has no legal effects.[21] Another example of lack of jurisdiction ratione materiae is the use of an inappropriate procedure. In Cases 114–117/79 *Fournier née Mazière v Commission*[22] the wife and children of an official brought actions for damages under art 215 of the EEC Treaty based on the unlawfulness of the official's conditions of employment. Article 179 of the Treaty gives the Court exclusive jurisdiction over disputes between the Community and its officials. The Court therefore declined jurisdiction, holding: 'It would be contrary to the system of legal remedies adopted by Community law for rectifying irregularities in conditions of employment to concede that by a misuse of procedure an action for damages based on the same facts may be brought by the members of the family of an official or other servant acting on their own behalf, even if they allege that they have personally suffered damage in this connection. These actions do not therefore fall within the second paragraph of Article 215 of the Treaty'.[23]

In relation to lack of jurisdiction ratione personae, the Court has no jurisdiction over a reference for a preliminary ruling made by a court or body that is not competent to make such a reference[24] or by a court that would otherwise be entitled to make a reference save that there is no dispute pending before it.[25] Similarly, the Court has no jurisdiction ratione personae over proceedings brought by individuals against a member state.[26] Actions for the annulment of a regulation imposing an anti-dumping duty are admissible only in so far as particular persons (generally exporters or producers) are concerned.[27] Pursuant to art 91(2) of the Staff Regulations, staff cases must be directed against the official's appointing authority; the Court does not, therefore, have jurisdiction over an action brought against an institution other than the appointing authority.[28] Lack of jurisdiction ratione personae is often barely distinguishable from the next ground of admissibility to be considered.

B   No locus standi

Locus standi, in this context, means that a person falls within the category of persons who may bring or appear before the Court in a specified type of

---

20 Eg Case 175/84 *Krohn & Co Import-Export GmbH & Co KG v Commission* [1986] ECR 753 (paras 27–29); *Les Assurances du Crédit v Council and Commission* (above, note 11) at 1817 (Advocate General Tesauro).

21 Case C-50/90 *Sunzest (Europe) and Sunzest (Netherlands) v Commission* [1991] ECR I-2917; Case C-117/91 *Bosman v Commission* [1991] ECR I-4837.

22 [1980] ECR 1529.

23 For a similar case see Case 46/75 *IBC Srl v Commission* [1976] ECR 65.

24 Eg Case 56/84 *Von Gallera v Maître* [1984] ECR 1769.

25 Eg Case 338/85 *Fratelli Pardini SpA v Ministero del Commercio con l'Estero* [1988] ECR 2041 (paras 10–14 and at 2056–2060 per Advocate General Darmon).

26 Eg Case 276/86 *Belkacem v Germany* [1986] ECR 3975; Case C-285/90 *Tsitouras v Greece* [1991] ECR I-787.

27 Eg Case 240/84 *NTN Toyo Bearing Co Ltd v Council* [1987] ECR 1809 (paras 5–7); Case 255/84 *Nachi Fujikoshi Corpn v Council* [1987] ECR 1861 (paras 6–8); Case 256/84 *Koyo Seiko Co Ltd v Council* [1987] ECR 1899 (paras 5–7); Case 258/84 *Nippon Seiko KK v Council* [1987] ECR 1923 (paras 6–8).

28 Eg Cases 219–228, 230–235, 237–238, 240–242/80 *André v Council and Commission* [1981] ECR 1879; Case 567/79A *Flamm v Commission and Council* [1981] ECR 2383; Case 618/79A *Knoeppel v Commission and Council* [1981] ECR 2387; Case 307/85 *Gavanas v Economic and Social Committee and Council* [1987] ECR 2435 (paras 7–9). For an ordinary action for annulment under art 173 of the EEC Treaty, see Case 100/74 *CAM SA v Commission* [1975] ECR 1393 at 1396: the action had originally been begun against both the Commission and the Council but the Court ruled that it was inadmissible in so far as it was directed against the latter because the measure challenged was an act of the Commission.

proceeding. The absence of locus standi may be raised by the Court of its own motion.[29] The rules defining locus standi differ from action to action. For example, an undertaking cannot bring proceedings under art 33 of the ECSC Treaty unless it is regularly engaged in production or distribution within the meaning of art 80 of the ECSC Treaty. That indicates an activity that is normal, ordinary or effective (but not merely occasional); and that requirement is not satisfied where the undertaking in question has only just been formed.[30] No such requirement applies to actions for annulment brought under the EC Treaty. In some cases one of the conditions of locus standi is that the person has sufficient interest. The classic example is the action for annulment. All three Treaties provide, in varying terms, that a natural or legal person[31] may apply for the annulment of a measure which 'concerns' them. In the context of the ECSC Treaty this has been held to refer to the 'interest' which the applicant has in the annulment of the measure.[32] In actions for annulment under the EC and Euratom Treaties, on the other hand, where a natural or legal person may challenge a decision, other than one addressed to that person, only if it is of direct and individual concern to him,[33] the 'concern' which must be shown is a formal requirement which distinguishes a particular category of natural or legal persons from the general class of those persons who may be affected by or wish to complain of the measure in question. All other conditions having been fulfilled, the applicant has established his locus standi to bring proceedings when he shows this 'direct and individual concern'. However, as will be seen, this does not necessarily mean that the applicant has sufficient interest to obtain the annulment of the measure.[34]

C Lack of capacity

Lack of capacity to act in proceedings is a matter which primarily concerns legal and natural persons other than the member states and the Community institutions. This ground of inadmissibility applies where, although the party in question may have locus standi, his capacity to act is challenged by reason of, for example, the fact that he is a minor or, in the case of legal persons, no proper authority is given for participating in the proceedings. There are very few cases concerning lack of capacity and, it seems, no clear authority determining whether this is an objection which can be waived by the other parties or must be taken by the Court of its own motion.[35]

---

29 De Soto, *Zehn Jahre Rechtsprechung*, p 56.
30 *Bensider v Commission* (above, note 3) at 4002–4003 (Advocate General Mancini).
31 So far as the ECSC Treaty is concerned, undertakings or associations: see art 33. The government of a self-governing territory dependent upon a member state is to be regarded as a 'natural or legal person' and not as a member state for these purposes: Case C-298/89 *Gibraltar v Council* [1993] ECR I-3605 (para 14).
32 Case 30/59 *De Gezamenlijke Steenkolenmijnen in Limburg v High Authority* [1961] ECR 1 at 16 and 37 (Advocate General Lagrange). This probably means sufficient interest to bring proceedings (ie locus standi) and does not refer to the interest necessary to allow the claim for annulment to proceed to judgment: the two matters were considered separately by the Court in Cases 7 and 9/54 *Groupement des Industries Sidérurgiques Luxembourgeoises v High Authority* [1954–56] ECR 175 at 190–193.
33 See arts 173 and 146 respectively.
34 In Case 70/87 *Fédération de l'Industrie de l'Huilerie de la CEE (Fediol) v Commission* [1989] ECR 1781 (at 1801), however, Advocate General van Gerven suggested that, if the contested act was addressed to the applicant and of direct and individual concern to him, the action is admissible and no further requirements need be satisfied.
35 In Case 18/62 *Barge v High Authority* [1963] ECR 259, the applicant seems to have been the legal representative of the undertaking in question: see per Advocate General Lagrange at 284.

The law governing capacity is the applicable national law in the sense that that law determines whether or not and, if so, to what extent, the acts of a person or body can have legal effect. The applicable national law does not itself determine the question of capacity so far as proceedings before the Court are concerned: that is a matter governed by Community law which is to be decided by reference to the capacity of the person or body concerned, as defined by the applicable national law.[36]

In the case of legal persons the applicable national law is the law of the country in which the legal person in question was incorporated;[37] where an unincorporated association or body lacking legal personality is involved, it is the national law governing its activities.[38] So far as natural persons are concerned, it is their personal law but the position regarding what that law may be is a little unclear. For other purposes[39] the Rules of Procedure tend to refer to the country of residence. There seems no better solution to the problem of determining the personal law but there appears to be no authority on the point so far as capacity to act is concerned.[40] Other alternatives appear to be the law of the country of which the person in question is a national or the law which has the closest connection to the subject matter of the dispute. One solution which must, however, be rejected, for obvious reasons, is that the Court may pick and choose between different possible national laws, selecting, presumably, the one most favourable to the person in question. Although this approach has a certain air of plausibility,[41] it would create uncertainty. When a party dies or becomes incapable of continuing proceedings, the applicable national law identifies the person competent to take over the proceedings but the procedural devices whereby this is done are a matter of Community law. So far as can be seen, it is necessary only to prove to the Court that there is capacity under national law to continue the proceedings.

D   Lack of interest

It has earlier been observed that the locus standi required to bring some proceedings incorporates a condition that the applicant show sufficient interest. In addition, the applicant must invariably show that he has sufficient interest in obtaining the relief sought.[42] To take a simple example, art 173 of the EC Treaty defines the category of persons (other than member states, the

---

36 Hence lack of capacity to be a party to proceedings under national law is not necessarily an objection to capacity to be a party to proceedings before the Court: the essential question is whether or not the capacity recognised by the applicable national law possesses the char-acterisics required by Community procedural law (see the *Bensider* case (above, note 3) at 4005 per Advocate General Mancini).

37 Case 18/57 *I Nold KG v High Authority* [1959] ECR 41.

38 Cf Case 2/68 *Ufficio Imposte di Consumo di Ispra v Commission* [1968] ECR 435 at 439 and per Advocate General Roemer at 447; Case 294/83 *Parti Ecologiste 'Les Verts' v European Parliament* [1986] ECR 1339 (paras 15–18 and 1346–1348 per Advocate General Mancini).

39 See, in particular, Annex II of the Supplementary Rules, which identifies the competent authority for the purpose of appointing a lawyer to act for a party in receipt of legal aid.

40 In Case 18/70 *Duraffour v Council* [1971] ECR 515 an action was brought by the widow of a deceased official 'acting on her own behalf and as a legal guardian of her infant children'. They appear to have been of French nationality but resided in Brussels. It is unclear what was the national law applicable to determine the widow's capacity to act on behalf of the children.

41 Why, for example, should a person be held incapable of undertaking legal proceedings before the Court, because in one member state he would lack capacity, if in another member state he would not?

42 Cf Case 13/86 *von Bonkewitz-Lindner v European Parliament* [1987] ECR 1417 (para 6); Case 134/87 *Vlachou v Court of Auditors* [1987] ECR 3633 (para 8). See also the comments of Advocate General Mancini in *British American Tobacco Co Ltd and R J Reynolds Industries Inc v Commission* (above, note 11) at 4546–4549.

Council or the Commission) capable of seeking review of the legality of an act of the Council or the Commission, as legal or natural persons to whom a decision has been addressed or to whom a decision addressed to another person is of direct and individual concern. There is no express requirement that an applicant should show an interest in having the legality of the act in question reviewed in addition to showing that he falls within the category of potential applications as so defined. Nonetheless, it is well established that the admissibility of the action is contingent on there being an 'interest', sometimes called a 'legal' interest, in the result of the case: the Court does not entertain proceedings brought just for the sake of litigating or to establish a point that is purely abstract or academic. In consequence, in Case 88/76 *Société pour l'Exportation des Sucres SA v Commission*,[43] the Court held the application to be inadmissible due to the lack of any legal interest, even though the applicant in principle had locus standi to bring it: because of its lack of retrospective effect the measure challenged did not in fact apply to the applicant. There was therefore no point in annulling the measure.[44] Lack of interest in bringing proceedings is an absolute bar to the proceedings and may be considered by the Court of its own motion.[45]

Whether or not an applicant has sufficient interest is assessed by reference to the circumstances existing at the moment the application commencing proceedings is lodged at the Court.[46] If, due to a change of circumstances after that date, the applicant ceases to have any interest in continuing with the proceedings, the action is not inadmissible but there is no reason for the Court to proceed to judgment and the continuation of proceedings may well be an abuse of process entitling the Court to order the applicant to pay the costs arising after the date on which the proceedings should have been discontinued.[47] The interest required to support an application has been described as 'legitimate, present, vested and sufficiently clear';[48] and it has been held that a person must have a vested and actual interest or, if the interest concerns a future situation, the impact on that situation must be immediate and certain.[49] In many respects the interest required is similar, mutatis mutandis, to that required in order to intervene in a direct action.[50] The basic requirement is that the action, if successful, will lead to a change in the applicant's position; it

---

43 [1977] ECR 709.
44 See also Cases 81 and 119/85 *Union Sidèrurgique du Nord et de l'Est de la France (USINOR) v Commission* [1986] ECR 1777 (para 18), where the Court considered of its own motion whether or not the contested decision actually affected the applicant.
45 Case 245/85 *Geist v Commission* [1987] ECR 2181 at 2190 (Advocate General Darmon).
46 Cases 5–11, 13–15/62 *Société Industriale Acciaierie San Michele v High Authority* [1962] ECR 449 at 460; Case 14/63 *Forges de Clabecq SA v High Authority* [1963] ECR 357 at 371; Case T-58/92 *Moat v Commission*, 16 December 1993 (para 32).
47 Cf Cases 5, 7 and 8/60 *Meroni & Co, FERAM and SIMET v High Authority* [1961] ECR 107 at 111-112; *Forges de Clabecq SA v High Authority* (ibid) at 376 (Advocate General Lagrange); Case 15/67 *Bauer v Commission* [1967] ECR 397 at 402; Case 43/74 *Guillot v Commission* [1977] ECR 1309 at 1340 (Advocate General Capotorti) (see also paras 13–14 of the judgment); Case 243/78 *Simmenthal SpA v Commission* [1980] ECR 593 (paras 9 and 11). The remarks in the *Bauer* case (at 402) and Case 33/68 *Rittweger v Commission* [1969] ECR 393 (para 9), which tend to suggest that an application may become inadmissible, after it has been lodged, if the defendant concedes the action by voluntarily granting the relief sought, are not compatible with the other authorities, of which the *Simmenthal* case is a good example. There the Court held that the applicant had no interest in the proceedings after judgment had been handed down in an earlier case. This event took place after the proceedings had been commenced. The application was in consequence dismissed, but not because it was inadmissible.
48 Case 17/78 *Deshormes (née La Valle) v Commission* [1979] ECR 189 (paras 10–12).
49 Case T-138/89 *Nederlandse Bankiersvereniging and Nederlandse Vereniging van Banken v Commission* [1992] ECR II-2181 (para 33).
50 See pp 158 et seq.

is not essential for the applicant to show that a right will be vindicated.[51] It is enough if the result of the action would be to bring about a change for the better in the applicant's material position[52] or a return to his original position.[53] Hence the fact that, in an action for annulment, the applicant has complied with the contested act pending judgment does not deprive the applicant of an interest in obtaining a decision finding it to be void.[54] If the result of the action would be actually inconsistent with the applicant's legitimate interests, the applicant has no interest in proceeding with the action.[55] The same applies where the action is brought against a measure that the applicant has requested (unless it met his request in part only and, if he were successful, he might be able to better his position).[56] The prospect of a change for the better need not be certain.[57] The fact that the change may prove contrary to the applicant's immediate material position is irrelevant[58] if the result is to remedy an unlawful situation[59] (but a private individual does not usually have sufficient interest to make a point of general importance which does not affect his position).[60]

A person has an interest in the annulment of a decision addressed to him which indicates a course of conduct which he must pursue.[61] But an applicant has no interest in obtaining a judgment which will establish that he was in the right, once the defendant has satisfied the claims made.[62] On the other hand, even if the action cannot improve the applicant's immediate material position, sufficient interest may exist if the circumstances are likely to recur, and the judgment will therefore cause the defendant to avoid re-creating or repeating an unlawful situation,[63] or if the judgment will affect other proceedings.[64]

---

51 Cf Case 26/68 *Fux v Commission* [1969] ECR 145; Cases 10 and 18/68 *Eridania Zuccherifici Nazionali v Commission* [1969] ECR 459 at 491 (Advocate General Roemer); Case 236/82 *Brautigam v Council* [1985] ECR 2401 (para 21); *Geist v Commission* (above, note 45) para 15; *von Bonkewitz-Lindner v European Parliament* (above, note 42) para 8. In Case 148/79 *Korter v Council* [1981] ECR 615, Advocate General Capotorti said (at 634): 'An interest to sue exists where the decision which is requested of the Court is a means of making good the damage allegedly done to the applicant's material interest by the conduct of the defendant.'

52 Eg Case 58/75 *Sergy v Commission* [1976] ECR 1139 (para 5). 'Material' here can mean financial (see Case T-46/90 *Devillez v European Parliament*, 30 June 1993, para 16) but is not limited to that type of interest: an official, for example, may have an interest in preferring some duties to others (Case 7/77 *Ritter Von Wüllerstorff und Urbair v Commission* [1978] ECR 769 at para 11). In a case where the interest is financial, the argument that the action is inadmissible for lack of interest because of absence of sufficient proof of any obligation to pay the sum claimed goes to the substance of the case and not to its admissibility: Case T-86/91 *Wery v European Parliament* [1993] ECR II-45 (para 26).

53 Eg Case 92/78 *Simmenthal SpA v Commission* [1979] ECR 777 (para 32).

54 Cases 172 and 226/83 *Hoogovens Groep BV v Commission* [1985] ECR 2831 (paras 18–19).

55 Case 134/87 *Vlachou v Court of Auditors* (above, note 42) paras 9–10.

56 Case 55/88 *Katsoufros v Court of Justice* [1989] ECR 3579 at 3586 (Advocate General Tesauro).

57 *Fux v Commission* (above, note 51); Case 4/73 *J Nold KG v Commission* [1974] ECR 491 (para 3).

58 *Forges de Clabecq SA v High Authority* (above, note 46) at 376 (Advocate General Lagrange).

59 Case 20/68 *Passetti-Bombardello v Commission* [1969] ECR 235 (para 6); Cases 55–76, 86, 87, 95/71 *Besnard v Commission* [1972] ECR 543 (paras 24–26).

60 Case 85/82 *Schloh v Council* [1983] ECR 2105 (para 14); Case 204/85 *Stroghili v Court of Auditors* [1987] ECR 389 (paras 8–12); Case 111/86 *Delauche v Commission* [1987] ECR 5345 (para 32).

61 Cases 193 and 194/87 *Maurissen v Court of Auditors* [1989] ECR 1045 (para 19).

62 *Bauer v Commission* (above, note 47); Case 108/86 *GdM v Council and Economic and Social Committee* [1987] ECR 3933.

63 Case 92/78 *Simmenthal SpA v Commission* (above, note 53); Case 45/86 *Commission v Council* [1987] ECR 1493 at 1506–1507 (Advocate General Lenz); *Apesco v Commission* (above, note 11) para 16.

64 Case 77/77 *Benzine en Petroleum Handelsmaatschappij BV v Commission* [1978] ECR 1513: potential liability of the applicant; Case 76/79 *Karl Könecke Fleischwarenfabrik GmbH & Co KG v Commission* [1980] ECR 665 (para 9): potential liability of the defendant; Case 223/85 *Rijn-Schelde-Verolme Maschinenfabrieken en Scheepswerven NV v Commission* [1987] ECR 4617 (paras 9–11): potential liability of the applicant.

Present uncertainty as to a future, contingent right may give rise to a 'legitimate, present, vested and sufficiently clear interest'.[65] Injury to reputation may also constitute sufficient interest[66] as may the loss of a chance.[67] An applicant lacks sufficient interest if he has, by his own actions, made the grant of the relief sought pointless.[68] The same is true where the ground relied on for annulling a measure is a procedural defect in its adoption but the measure could certainly be confirmed in substance, in the absence of a mistake of law or of fact.[69] The addressees of a judgment have an interest in the way in which it is executed.[70]

The position in certain types of case (which may provide useful analogies in other cases) can be illustrated by the following examples. In staff cases, voters and candidates in an election have an interest in challenging the lawfulness of the electoral procedure.[71] Candidates admitted to take part in a recruiting competition have an interest in the subsequent conduct of the competition.[72] An official who is not eligible for a particular post or for promotion has no interest in disputing the legality of steps taken to fill the post or those taken in the promotion procedure;[73] but the fact that an official who is eligible for, but has been refused, appointment to a particular post has taken up another post in another Community institution does not mean that he no longer has an interest in the annulment of the decision refusing to appoint him because he may always be transferred back to the first institution and a post in another institution is not necessarily equivalent to what he might otherwise have been entitled to.[74] Similarly, a retired official has no interest in the annulment of a decision appointing another person to a post to which he can no longer lay claim but he may still have an interest in claiming damages;[75] and, for the same reason, he has an interest in the annulment of a decision excluding him, before his retirement, from a list of candidates for promotion.[76] An interest in not having one's prospects of promotion reduced and not being subject to 'unlawful' competition from another official is, however, a future and hypothetical interest that cannot found an action.[77] Any official who is a member of a staff or

---

65 *Deshormes née La Valle v Commission* (above, note 48) (paras 10–12); Case 167/86 *Rousseau v Court of Auditors* [1988] ECR 2705 (para 7).
66 Case 155/78 *Miss M v Commission* [1980] ECR 1797 (para 6); *Benzine en Petroleum v Commission* (above, note 64); *Katsoufros v Court of Justice* (above, note 56) para 11 and at 3586–3587 (Advocate General Tesauro).
67 Cases 81–88/74 *Marenco v Commission* [1975] ECR 1247 (para 10).
68 Eg *Marenco v Commission* (ibid) para 6.
69 See Case 90/74 *Deboeck v Commission* [1975] ECR 1123 (paras 12–15 and the authorities cited by Advocate General Warner at 1140–1142); Case 9/76 *Morello v Commission* [1976] ECR 1415 (para 11); Case 30/78 *Distillers Co Ltd v Commission* [1980] ECR 2229 (para 26 and, per Advocate General Warner, at 2290); Case 117/81 *Geist v Commission* [1983] ECR 2191 (para 7); Case 432/85 *Souna v Commission* [1987] ECR 2229 (para 20); Case T-27/92 *Camera-Lampitelli v Commission*, 15 July 1993 (para 53).
70 Case T-38/89 *Hochbaum v Commission* [1990] ECR II-43 (para 8).
71 Case 54/75 *De Dapper v European Parliament* [1976] ECR 1381 (para 27); Cases 146 and 431/85 *Diezler v Economic and Social Committee* [1987] ECR 4283 (para 9).
72 *Hochbaum v Commission* (above, note 70) para 8.
73 Case 126/87 *Del Plato v Commission* [1989] ECR 643 (para 20); Case T-30/90 *Zoder v European Parliament* [1991] ECR II-207; Case T-51/90 *Moretti v Commission* [1992] ECR II-487 (para 22). By the same token, if the official's complaint about being excluded from a competition is unfounded, he does not have a legitimate interest in contesting any steps taken in the course of the competition after his exclusion from it: Case 108/88 *Cendoya v Commission* [1989] ECR 2711 (para 27).
74 Case T-156/89 *Mordt v Court of Justice* [1991] ECR II-407 (paras 34–36).
75 Case T-20/89 *Moritz v Commission* [1990] ECR II-769 (paras 16 and 18).
76 Case T-82/89 *Marcato v Commission* [1990] ECR II-735 (paras 53–54); *Moat v Commission* (above, note 46) paras 31–33.
77 *Stroghili v Court of Auditors* (above, note 60) paras 8–12.

trade union has an interest in challenging a decision affecting the activities of that organisation;[78] and a decision addressed to a staff or trade union which mentions one of its members is of interest to that member.[79] Certain acts may be challengeable in a staff case if they affect the moral interests or future perspectives of an official and even if they do not affect his material interests.[80] In actions for annulment, an applicant has no interest in the annulment of the contested act unless the operative part of the act affects him adversely; recitals in the preamble to the contested act or findings made in the reasoning given for it cannot be challenged at all unless they form part of the reasoning supporting a provision in the operative part of the act that adversely affects the applicant.[81] In general, only measures capable of directly affecting a specific legal situation may be regarded as adversely affecting the applicant.[82] In actions for the annulment of regulations imposing an anti-dumping duty, there is no interest in challenging the regulation imposing a provisional duty (otherwise than in support of a claim for damages) because such a duty is payable definitively only pursuant to the regulation imposing a definitive duty (an interest does lie in challenging the latter regulation).[83] It has been suggested that a person has no interest in seeking the annulment of an individual act before it has been notified because, until then, the act has no effect;[84] but if the premature commencement of proceedings is defective for that reason, which is doubtful,[85] that defect will disappear as soon as the act is notified and can no longer be a bar to the continuation of the proceedings since ex hypothesi the limitation period will not yet have expired.

It is usually said that the member states do not need to show interest or locus standi.[86] The reason for this is that, in general, the member states are given an unfettered right to participate in proceedings before the Court; and the justification for this is that, as contracting parties to the Treaties, the member states have both the capacity and an undeniable interest in ensuring that the Treaties are properly interpreted and applied. If that proposition were to be accepted without qualification, futile or purposeless actions initiated by member states would be admissible even if they were not well founded. At all events, the theory that member states are presumed to have sufficient interest to commence proceedings does not receive unqualified support from the Statutes of the Court: witness, for example, art 34 of the ECSC Statute and arts 39 and 40 of the EC Statute. Member states do not have to show an interest in the result of the case when intervening in actions brought under the EC and Euratom Treaties, but that is because it is expressly provided in the EC and Euratom Statutes (arts 37 and 38 respectively) that they may intervene, only persons other than a member state or a Community institution having to show such an interest. In view of the absence of a presumption or rule drawn from

78 *Maurissen v Court of Auditors* (above, note 61) para 18.
79 Ibid para 20.
80 Case T-47/90 *Bade (née Herremans) v Commission* [1991] ECR II-467 (para 26).
81 *Nederlandse Bankiersvereniging* (above, note 49) para 31.
82 Cf Cases 269 and 292/84 *Fabbro v Commission* [1986] ECR 2983 (para 9 – a staff case).
83 Cases C-305/86 and C-160/87 *Neotype Techmashexport GmbH v Commission and Council* [1990] ECR I-2945 (paras 13–16).
84 Cases 358/85 and 51/86 *France v European Parliament* [1988] ECR 4821 at 4838 (Advocate General Mancini).
85 Cases 172 and 226/83 *Hoogovens Groep BV v Commission* [1985] ECR 2831 (para 8).
86 Eg Case 45/86 *Commission v Council* (above, note 63) para 3 and at 1504 (Advocate General Lenz); Case 68/86 *United Kingdom v Council* [1988] ECR 855 (Re Agricultural Hormones) (at 875 per Advocate General Lenz); Case 131/86 *United Kingdom v Council* [1988] ECR 905 (Re Protection of Battery Hens) (para 6).

the instruments defining the Court's jurisdiction, that the member states are held to have sufficient interest, it is a reasonable inference, from the cases establishing that other persons must show such an interest even when this requirement is not stated expressly in the Treaty or other provision giving the Court jurisdiction in the matter, that the same requirement applies to the member states. However, in the nature of things, their interest is different from and more broadly defined than that of other persons. Hence, while it cannot be said that, as a matter of principle, member states invariably have an interest in proceedings, it can be affirmed that, as a matter of fact, they will do so in all but the most exceptional cases.[87] It is therefore accurate to state that member states do not need to show an interest of the same kind as that required of ordinary litigants.

The position of Community institutions is, in principle, no different from that of member states, in particular in relation to actions for annulment, although there may be a difference in the nature of the interest which a Community institution may have in proceedings.[88] In relation to the Commission's interest in commencing and continuing proceedings against a member state under art 169 of the EEC Treaty, the Court held in Case 167/73 *Commission v France*[89] that the Commission 'does not have to show the existence of a legal interest, since, in the general interest of the Community, its function is to ensure that the provisions of the Treaty are applied by the Member States and to note the existence of any failure to fulfil the obligations deriving therefrom, with a view to bringing it to an end'. What this really means is that the Commission does not have to show an individual interest in the result of each case brought under art 169 because, by reason of its functions, it has a general interest in the result of such proceedings. This interest is present when the member state concerned has failed to comply with the Commission's reasoned opinion by the date for doing so fixed by the Commission.[90] If, between that date and the commencement of proceedings before the Court, the member state does so comply, the Commission still has an interest in continuing the action[91] in order to ensure that Community law is properly administered and applied[92] or to establish the member state's liability towards other member states, the Community or private persons.[93] On the other hand, proceedings brought under art 169 in respect of the future conduct of a member state are inadmissible: in such proceedings, the risk of future unlawful conduct only provides the interest in bringing proceedings against past conduct.[94]

---

87 See, by way of analogy, the position with regard to intervention in direct actions brought under the ECSC Treaty. But note Case 230/81 *Luxembourg v European Parliament* [1983] ECR 255 (para 24).
88 Cf Case 22/70 *Commission v Council* [1971] ECR 263 (paras 56–61). But see Case 45/86 *Commission v Council* (above, note 63) para 3 and at 1504–1507 per Advocate General Lenz (an action for annulment); Case 302/87 *European Parliament v Council* [1988] ECR 5615 at 5628 (Advocate General Darmon), an action in respect of a failure to act.
89 [1974] ECR 359 (para 15).
90 Case 7/61 *Commission v Italian Government* [1961] ECR 317 at 326; Case 240/86 *Commission v Greece* [1988] ECR 1835 (para 16). In Case 51/83 *Commission v Italy* [1984] ECR 2793 (at 2809) Advocate General Lenz suggested the date of the commencement of the action.
91 Case 95/77 *Commission v Netherlands* [1978] ECR 863 at 874 (Advocate General Reischl).
92 Case 26/69 *Commission v France* [1970] ECR 565 (paras 11–13).
93 Case 39/72 *Commission v Italy* [1973] ECR 101 (paras 9–11); Case 240/86 *Commission v Greece* (above, note 90) para 14. If damage has been caused by a member state to an individual through an infringement of Community law, there may be liability in damages under national law: Case 60/75 *Russo v AIMA* [1976] ECR 45 (para 9); Cases C-6 and C-9/90 *Francovich v Italy* [1991] ECR I-5357.
94 Case C-217/88 *Commission v Germany* [1990] ECR I-2879 at 2890 (Advocate General Jacobs).

E Prescription[95]

1 General remarks

The laying down of reasonable time limits is an application of the fundamental principle of legal certainty[96] which also requires that clear and precise wording should be used.[97] It is not precluded by the Human Rights Convention.[98] Failure to observe a reasonable time limit may result in the loss of the right to bring proceedings, that is, loss of 'the opportunity to bring the facts forming the subject of the action before the Court for examination of the substance of the case',[99] and is the classic example of an objection to the admissibility of an action.[1] In general, delay is a ground of inadmissibility only if there is express provision to this effect. Such a provision may take the form of a specific time limit or a power granted to a specified person or body to fix a time limit. For example, art 173 of the EEC Treaty imposes a fixed time limit of two months within which application must be made for the review of the legality of an act of the Council or the Commission other than a recommendation or opinion. If this time limit is not respected, an application made under art 173 will be rejected as inadmissible because the cause of action is barred. On the other hand, RP-ECJ 40(2) and RP-CFI 46(3) provide that the time limit for serving the defence in an action, which is one month, can be extended, on application, by the President of the Court. If the time limit fixed by him is not respected, the applicant may apply for judgment by default, in which case the defendant has lost the opportunity to serve a defence and can oppose the application only at the hearing.[2] Limitation periods must be fixed in advance[3] but there are no general principles of law concerning the length of the period.[4] Time limits are governed exclusively by Community law and are not subject to rules of national law.[5] In the case of an application made by several persons, the question whether or not it has been made in time is to be decided by reference to each of the applicants considered separately.[6]

If there is no provision for a time limit, the Court cannot impose one of its own motion.[7] For example, the possibility of bringing an action for damages

---

95 See Oliver (1978) 3 ELRev 3.
96 Case 33/76 *Rewe-Zentralfinanz eG and Rewe- Zentral A-G v Landwirtschaftskammer für das Saarland* [1976] ECR 1989 (para 5); Case 34/65 *Mosthaf v Euratom Commission* [1966] ECR 521 at 531.
97 Case 44/81 *Germany v Commission* [1982] ECR 1855 (para 16).
98 Case 257/85 *Dufay v European Parliament* [1987] ECR 1561 (para 10).
99 Case 20/65 *Collotti v European Court of Justice* [1965] ECR 847 at 850; see also Cases 220 and 221/78 *ALA SpA and ALFER v Commission* [1979] ECR 1693 at 1700 (Advocate General Capotorti). But not all time limits define mandatory limitation periods: see, for example, Case 13/69 *Van Eick v Commission* [1970] ECR 3; Case 20/88 *Roquette Frères SA v Commission* [1989] ECR 1553, paras 11–13 (an action for damages).
 1 *Collotti v European Court of Justice*, ibid at 853 (Advocate General Roemer). It should be noted, however, that in some member states the expiry of a time limit for bringing proceedings is regarded as determining the right of action and thus as going to the substance of a claim rather than to its admissibility. The same approach can occasionally be seen in decisions of the Court.
 2 RP-ECJ 94(1); RP-CFI 122(1).
 3 Case 41/69 *ACF Chemiefarma NV v Commission* [1970] ECR 661 (paras 17–20).
 4 Case 155/79 *A M & S Europe Ltd v Commission* [1982] ECR 1575 at 1631 (Advocate General Warner).
 5 Case 209/83 *Ferriera Valsabbia v Commission* [1984] ECR 3089 (para 12).
 6 Case 264/83 *Delhez v Commission* [1985] ECR 2179 (para 15).
 7 Cf *ACF Chemiefarma NV v Commission* (above, note 3), paras 17–20. The remark in Case 120/73 *Gebrüder Lorenz GmbH v Germany and Land Rheinland Pfalz* [1973] ECR 1471 (para 4) that, in proceedings under art 93 of the EC Treaty, the Commission must act within a reasonable period, is not the imposition of a period of prescription, as has been suggested (Oliver, p 6). On the other hand, the judgment in Case 59/70 *Netherlands v Commission* [1971] ECR 639 does

based on the Community's non-contractual liability under arts 178 and 215 of the EC Treaty is, with certain exceptions, prescribed five years after the occurrence of the event giving rise to liability.[8] In consequence, when an official of the Commission brought an action for damages, it was pleaded that he was out of time because proceedings were commenced after the expiry of the five-year period. The applicant, however, relied not only on arts 178 and 215 but also on art 179, which gives the Court exclusive jurisdiction over disputes between the Community and its officials 'within the limits and under the conditions laid down in the Staff Regulations'. This means, the Court held, that a dispute between an official and an institution concerning compensation for damage, where it originates in the employment relationship between the parties, falls exclusively under art 179 and the time limit on bringing actions for damages under arts 178 and 215 does not apply. The only time limits applicable are those contained in the Staff Regulations. The Court dismissed the application as inadmissible not because the five-year limitation period had not been complied with but because the three-month time limit specified in the Staff Regulations for applying to the Court after the end of the pre-litigation administrative procedure had not been observed.[9] The result of this is that there is no time limit on actions for damages falling under art 179 (other than those set out in the Staff Regulations) and so, in Case 106/80 *Fournier v Commission*,[10] the claim for damages was admissible even though it was in part based on events which had taken place and damage which had occurred more than five years before the commencement of proceedings.[11] In the same way, there is no time limit for bringing proceedings under art 169 of the EC Treaty;[12] and a measure can be impeached out of time if it contains such serious and manifest defects as to render it non-existent.[13] Nonetheless, in cases where there is no time limit for bringing proceedings, it would seem that an excessive delay in bringing them may effectively bar the proceedings if the defendant can show that the delay has prejudiced its ability to defend itself.[14] There is no limitation period in the Treaties regarding actions for damages in respect of breach of contract and delay is relevant only if there is a contractual limitation period or the delay is such as to constitute waiver of the right of action.[15] Thus, delay in commencing proceedings is not ordinarily an objection to their admissibility unless a relevant limitation period has expired. Further the lawfulness of an act may be challenged, either because the contested act implements a normative measure which is invalid[16] or because acts preliminary to the contested act are unlawful[17], without the failure to contest the normative measure or the preliminary acts in question being

appear to go against *Chemiefarma*. It can, however, be interpreted as holding that an applicant may be regarded as being estopped from commencing proceedings or as having waived the right to do so or as having no interest in proceeding with an action against a failure to act, once an 'unreasonable' period has elapsed after the defendant has made its position clear.
8 EC Statute, art 43.
9 Case 9/75 *Meyer-Burckhardt v Commission* [1975] ECR 1171.
10 [1981] ECR 2759.
11 Parts of the claim were rejected as inadmissible for other reasons. See also Case 317/85 *Pomar v Commission* [1987] ECR 2467.
12 Case C-96/89 *Commission v Netherlands* [1991] ECR I-2461 (paras 14–16); Case C-317/92 *Commission v Germany* (as yet unreported) per Advocate General Darmon, paras 5–9.
13 Case 15/85 *Consorzio Cooperativo d'Abruzzo v Commission* [1987] ECR 1005 (para 10); Case 226/87 *Commission v Greece* [1988] ECR 3611 (para 16).
14 *Commission v Greece* (ibid).
15 See Case 25/60 *De Bruyn v European Parliamentary Assembly* [1962] ECR 21 at 27–28.
16 EC Treaty, art 184. Eg Case 181/85 *France v Commission* [1987] ECR 689 at 703 (Re Countervailing Charge on French Ethyl Alcohol) (Advocate General Slynn).
17 Eg Case 307/85 *Gavanas v Economic and Social Committee and Council* [1987] ECR 2435 (para 16).

regarded as acquiescence in their unlawfulness or otherwise as precluding reliance upon their unlawfulness.

2 Prorogation of and derogation from time limits

RP-ECJ 82 and RP-CFI 103 provide that any time limit prescribed pursuant to the Rules of Procedure may be extended by whoever prescribed it. This applies only to the 'procedural' time limits such as those for the lodging of pleadings.[18] In contrast, the 'substantive' time limits, such as those whose expiry bars the commencement of proceedings, cannot be extended under RP-ECJ 82 or RP-CFI 103 or, indeed, RP-ECJ 38(7) or RP-CFI 44(6), which allow defective applications to be put in order.[19] It may be inferred from RP-ECJ 82 and RP-CFI 103 that the procedural time limits are not peremptory so that a failure to comply with them cannot be raised by the Court of its own motion and may be cured, even retroactively, by the application of RP-ECJ 82 or, as the case may be, RP-CFI 103.[20] On the other hand, the normal practice is that a time limit cannot be extended in response to an application for an extension of time submitted after the expiry of the relevant period. The substantive time limits are mandatory[21] and, with the apparent exception of the time limit for commencing a damages action,[22] a failure to comply with them must be raised by the Court of its own motion.[23] In the absence of an express provision allowing derogation from their application, neither proof that a party was justified in delaying nor the fact that the delay was not due to his fault are sufficient to justify overriding them.[24] Such a provision is to be found in each of the Statutes,[25] which provide: 'No right shall be prejudiced in consequence of the expiry of a time limit if the party concerned proves the existence of unforeseeable circumstances or of force majeure.' However, it seems that, in addition to unforeseeable circumstances or force majeure, a time limit may not be a bar if the delay in commencing proceedings is attributable to 'excusable error' on the part of the applicant, that is to say, exceptional circumstances or where the defendant has behaved in such a way as to induce confusion in the mind of a party acting in good faith and with due diligence.[26]

18 Cf Cases 220 and 221/78 *ALA and ALFER v Commission* [1979] ECR 1693 at 1700 (Advocate General Capotorti).
19 Ibid.
20 Cf the reasoning of the Court in Case 1/60 *FERAM v High Authority* [1960] ECR 165 at 170, an analogous situation.
21 Cases 25 and 26/65 *SIMET and FERAM v High Authority* [1967] ECR 33 at 49 (Advocate General Gand); Case 33/72 *Gunnella v Commission* [1973] ECR 475 (para 4 and see the authorities cited by Advocate General Mayras at 484); Cases 122 and 123/79 *Schiavo v Council* [1981] ECR 473 (para 22); Case 227/83 *Moussis v Commission* [1984] ECR 3133 (para 12); Case 302/85 *Pressler-Hoeft v Court of Auditors* [1987] ECR 513 (para 5); Case T-119/89 *Teissonnière v Commission* [1990] ECR II-7 (para 26); Case T-58/92 *Moat v Commission*, 16 December 1993, para 39. But note Cases 14, 16, 17, 20, 24, 26, 27/60 and 1/61 *Meroni & Co v High Authority* [1961] ECR 161 at 173.
22 Case 20/88 *Roquette Frères SA v Commission* [1989] ECR 1553 (para 12 and at 1562–1564 per Advocate General Darmon); Case C-55/90 *Cato v Commission* [1992] ECR I-2533 (Per Advocate General Darmon at para 10 of his opinion). The fact that the applicant asserts that an action for damages has been brought within time (in order to forestall any such objection that the defendant might raise) does not justify the conclusion that such an objection has been raised or entitle the Court to take the point: the *Roquette* case at 1564.
23 Eg Case T-19/90 *von Hoessle v Court of Auditors* [1991] ECR II-615 (paras 23–24).
24 Case 32/72 *Wasaknäcke Knäckebrotfabrik GmbH v Einfuhr- und Vorratsstelle für Getreide und Futtermittel* [1972] ECR 1181; Case 209/83 *Valsabbia SpA v Commission* [1984] ECR 3089.
25 ECSC Statute, art 39; EC Statute, art 42; Euratom Statute, art 43.
26 Case 25/68 *Schertzer v European Parliament* [1977] ECR 1729 (para 19); Case T-12/90 *Bayer AG v Commission* [1991] ECR II-219 (paras 28–29); Cases T-33 and T-74/89 *Blackman v European Parliament*, 16 March 1993 (paras 32–34).

There seems little doubt but that a party is entitled to have RP-ECJ 82 or, as the case may be, RP-CFI 103 applied in his favour where he proves such circumstances to exist but the Statutes and the principle of excusable error are primarily intended to apply to substantive time limits.

The concept of excusable error is to be narrowly construed because the application of substantive time limits is mandatory. It applies where, for example, the delay in bringing proceedings arises because the behaviour of the defendant has obscured the identity of the body competent to deal with any essential pre-litigation steps and rendered the date of the commencement of the relevant time limit uncertain.[27] On the other hand, the fact that the defendant notified the contested act to the applicant's head office whereas previously all communications were sent to the applicant's legal service is not an exceptional circumstance liable to create an excusable error, nor is the fact that the defendant failed to dispute an acknowledgment of receipt wrongly dated by the applicant.[28] Similarly, the fact that the defendant, for reasons of its own, deals with a request made out of time does not re-establish a right which is definitely time-barred.[29]

In *SIMET and FERAM v High Authority*[30] Advocate General Gand took the view that 'unforeseeable circumstances' and 'force majeure' are 'external events beyond the control of the person under the obligation, of a kind which that person could not foresee and the consequences of which he could not imagine'. In Case 284/82 *Acciaierie e Ferriere Busseni v Commission*[31] the Court held that, in general terms, 'force majeure' envisages, in its essentials, external circumstances which make it impossible for the required action to be taken before the expiry of the limitation period; even if it does not presuppose absolute impossibility, there must still be abnormal difficulties which (i) are independent of the will of the person concerned and (ii) appear inevitable even if every useful precaution is taken.[32]

The *SIMET and FERAM* case concerned two applications which were sent by post and arrived at the Court out of time. The advocate general did not accept that the Statutes applied to postal delays because these are always foreseeable and should be catered for. The Court did not comment on this so the point seems still to remain open.[33] The fact relied on by both the Court and the advocate general was that the delay in lodging the applications arose after they had arrived in Luxembourg. The Court held that the four days required to transmit the applications from Luxembourg railway station to the Court

---

27 The *Schertzer* case (ibid).
28 *Bayer AG v Commission* (above, note 26) paras 31 and 35–40.
29 The *Moussis* case (above, note 21), para 13.
30 Above, note 21 at 50.
31 [1984] ECR 557 (para 11 and at 570–572 per Advocate General Reischl). See also Case 224/83 *Ferriera Vittoria v Commission* [1984] ECR 2349 (para 13); the *Valsabbia* case (above, note 24) paras 21–22, where the applicant could have got over the difficulty by invoking RP-ECJ 38(7) (para 25); Cases 98 and 230/83 *Van Gend en Loos v Commission* [1984] ECR 3763 (para 16).
32 The concept of force majeure has been explored by the Court in a number of cases, albeit in a context different from that under consideration here: see, for example, Case C-334/87 *Greece v Commission* [1990] ECR I-2849; Case C-335/87 *Greece v Commission* [1990] ECR I-2875.
33 See also *ALA SpA and ALFER v Commission* (above, note 18) at 1700 (Advocate General Capotorti). On the other hand, in Case 264/82 *Timex Corpn v Council and Commission* [1985] ECR 849 (order of 28 April 1983), the Court applied art 42 of the EC Statute in a case where an application to intervene had been sent by registered post and, in the normal course, would have arrived at the Court before the expiry of the period for applying. At the time of the Court's order, over three months after the application had been sent off, it still had not arrived. It is arguable that, while postal *delays* do not fall within art 42, the complete disappearance of a missive does.

constituted 'unforeseeable circumstances' and enabled it to treat the day the applications arrived in Luxembourg as the day of their lodgment at the Registry. This suggests that the Statutes operate, not to extend the time limit, but to create a fictitious date within the time period applicable, at which the event in question (there, lodgment of the application) would have occurred had it not been for the unforeseen circumstances or force majeure.[34] In the *Busseni* case[35] the application commencing proceedings was lodged out of time because the decision challenged in the application had been notified to the applicant, a steel company, at a time when the business had been closed down and the company was in a form of receivership under Italian law. In consequence, it was said, the management was prevented from knowing of the communication of the decision. The Court rejected this on the ground that, on the facts, the company had not been put in liquidation and its management had not ceased to be responsible for the conduct of its affairs. The company had remained active and there were in consequence no abnormal and inevitable difficulties or external events independent of the will of the management which might have justified a failure to open correspondence. In contrast, in Case 349/85 *Denmark v Commission*[36] an application to intervene was made out of time as a result of confusion induced in the intervener by the Court's Registry as to the date of the start of the limitation period.[37] The Court considered that, as the failure to observe the time limit was the result of reliance upon an erroneous statement made by the Registry, it was the consequence of unforeseen circumstances.

The following do not constitute unforeseen circumstances or force majeure: the unavailability of any lawyer and the fact that the local law libraries are shut for the holidays, at least where there is a period of ten days outside the holiday period and while time is still running;[38] the fact that, at the material time, the applicant was closed for business, its staff in receipt of state benefits and its sole director absent for personal reasons (because he could have made any necessary administrative arrangements to cover his absence);[39] the fact that the defendant did not reply to the applicant's request that any decision be addressed to the applicant's central administration;[40] internal problems within the applicant concerning the communication of information;[41] the fact that the provision setting out the time limit had not been translated into the applicant's mother tongue (at least where he must have had a satisfactory knowledge of at least one other Community language);[42] strikes (at least where they have been announced in the Press);[43] an exceptional malfunctioning of the postal system (at least where the time actually allowed for posting was less than the extension of time granted under the Rules of Procedure to take

---

34 Cf the *Timex* case (ibid).
35 Above (note 31) paras 12–14.
36 [1988] ECR 169 (order of 15 October 1986).
37 The period is three months running from publication of the notice of the case in the Official Journal: RP-ECJ 93(1); RP-CFI 115(1). The issue of the Official Journal containing the notice was dated 31 December 1985 but it did not appear until 22 April 1986. The Registry told the intervener that it considered the date of publication to be 28 April 1986 because that was the day when the Court received the issue in question. The intervener relied on that statement. As a result, its application to intervene was made out of time.
38 The *Valsabbia* case (above, note 24), paras 23–24.
39 *Ferriera Vittoria v Commission* (above, note 31) para 14.
40 Case 42/85 *Cockerill–Sambre SA v Commission* [1985] ECR 3749 (para 12).
41 Ibid.
42 Case 276/85 *Cladakis v Commission* [1987] ECR 495 (paras 10–12).
43 Case 70/86 *Commission v Greece* [1987] ECR 3545 (Re Late Budget Payments) (para 9).

account of distance);[44] events taking place after the expiry of the limitation period.[45]

In staff cases the three-month period for applying to the Court, under art 91(1) of the Staff Regulations, against a decision of the appointing authority rejecting the official's complaint starts to run again when an express decision is made after the complaint has been rejected by implied decision but before the three-month period has expired.[46] Although this applies only where the express decision is adopted within that period, time starts to run again only when it is notified to the official (and so may begin running after the original period has expired) unless any delay in notification is attributable to him and not to the institution.[47]

The Statutes[48] also provide for 'periods of grace based on considerations of distance' to be laid down in the Rules of Procedure. These are set out in Annex II of the ECJ's Rules of Procedure[49] and are not new periods but extensions of the period in question[50] which are intended to compensate for the delays inherent in communicating from the seats of the institutions to the different parts of the Community.[51] They apply only to the period for applying to the Court and not generally to all time periods, such as those within which an institution is to act.[52] The periods of grace are calculated by reference to the place where the party concerned (not his lawyer) is habitually resident.[53] A party's 'habitual residence' is a question of fact and it seems that it is sufficient if he has lived in a particular place for a 'considerable' length of time, irrespective of his motives for doing so.[54] In addition, RP-ECJ 80(2) and RP-CFI 101(2) provide that, if a period 'would otherwise end on a Saturday, Sunday or an official holiday, it shall be extended until the end of the first following working day'. The official holidays envisaged are listed in Annex I of the ECJ's Rules of Procedure.[55] Time does, nevertheless, continue to run *during* official holidays, Saturdays, Sundays and vacations,[56] including holidays in the member states.[57]

44 Case C-59/91 *France v Commission* [1992] ECR I-525 (para 10): the extensions of time on account of distance are granted automatically specifically for the purpose of catering for postal delays.
45 Ibid (para 11).
46 Article 91(3) of the Staff Regulations.
47 Case 5/76 *Jänsch v Commission* [1976] ECR 1027.
48 ECSC Statute, art 39; EC Statute, art 42; Euratom Statute, art 43. See also RP-ECJ 81(2); RP-CFI 102(2).
49 For all parties, save those habitually resident in the Grand Duchy of Luxembourg, the periods of grace are as follows: Belgium, two days; Federal Republic of Germany, the European territory of France and the Netherlands, six days; the European territory of Denmark, Greece, Ireland, Italy, Spain, Portugal (with the exception of the Azores and Madeira) and the United Kingdom, ten days; other European countries and territories, two weeks; the Azores and Madeira, three weeks; other countries, departments and territories, one month.
50 *SIMET and FERAM v High Authority* (above, note 21) at 49 (Advocate General Gand).
51 Cf Cases 36–38, 40 and 41/58 *SIMET v High Authority* [1959] ECR 157.
52 Cases 5, 7, 13–24/66 *Firma E Kampffmeyer v Commission* [1967] ECR 245 at 272 (Advocate General Gand); Case 195/80 *Michel v European Parliament* [1981] ECR 2861 at 2882 (Advocate General Sir Gordon Slynn).
53 Case 28/65 *Fonzi v Euratom Commission* [1966] ECR 477 at 491; see also Case 31/65 *Fonzi v Euratom Commission* [1966] ECR 513.
54 Case 28/65 *Fonzi v Euratom Commission* [1966] ECR 477 at 498 (Advocate General Roemer). The length of time in that case was less than a year. The habitual residence of a Community institution is where its decision-making functions (nor particular services) are located, subject to any formal decision determining its location: Case C-137/928 *Commission v BASF AG* (as yet unreported) per Advocate General van Gerven (paras 4–7).
55 They are: New Year's Day, Easter Monday, 1 May, Ascension Day, Whit Monday, 23 June (or 24, where 23 is a Sunday), 15 August, 1 November, 25 and 26 December.
56 RP-ECJ 80(1)(d)–(e); RP-CFI 101(1)(d)–(e).
57 The *Valsabbia* case (above, note 24) para 12.

3   The running of time

Two problems generally arise in relation to the running of time: the identification of the event or act that causes time to start running; and the calculation of the limitation period.

The Treaties usually provide that time starts to run on or from the occurrence of a particular event. The Rules of Procedure derogate from this by providing, first, that the day during which the event or action from which the period is to run occurs shall be excluded when reckoning any period of time prescribed by the Treaties, the Statutes or the Rules of Procedure themselves;[58] and, secondly, that time for commencing proceedings against a measure adopted by an institution runs from the day following receipt of notification of it or, 'where the measure is published, from the 15th day after publication' in the Official Journal.[59] Those derogations also affect the calculation of the limitation period. The provision that, in the case of measures published in the Official Journal, time runs from the 15th day after publication has been described as 'nothing more than a closer definition of the concept of "notification" that is to say clarification as to the beginning of the period, which is lacking in the Treaty itself'.[60] As that remark indicates, it is not so much the occurrence of the event in question as knowledge of its occurrence on the part of the person concerned that is the important factor when identifying the point at which time starts to run.

In actions for annulment, the event causing time to start to run under all three Treaties is the notification or publication of the contested act[61] save that, under the EC and Euratom Treaties[62] and, so far as actions under the ECSC Treaty are concerned, under the Court's case law,[63] time starts to run as from the day on which the contested act 'came to the knowledge of' the applicant where it is not notified or published. As has been seen, where the contested act is published in the Official Journal, time in fact starts to run from the 15th day after publication. It seems reasonably clear that that applies where proceedings are brought against a measure which must be published in the Official Journal; and there is no provision in the Rules of Procedure that excludes its application in the case of a measure that need not be, but is, published in the Official Journal. The questions nonetheless arise whether or not publication is in all circumstances sufficient to cause time to start running; and whether or not an earlier event may cause it to do so.

It would seem that, strictly speaking, notification is service of a measure on the person to whom it is addressed. A measure is notified not when it is sent but when it is received in such a state as to enable the addressee to take full cognisance of it.[64] A formal error in the name or title given to the addressee

---

58 RP-ECJ 80(1)(a); RP-CFI 101(1)(a).

59 RP-ECJ 81(1); RP-CFI 102(1). 'Publication' means that the measure is made available to the public in all the official Community languages at the Office for Official Publications of the European Communities, Luxembourg, and the date of publication is that on which this is first done, whatever the date appearing on the issue of the Official Journal in question: Case 99/78 *Weingut Gustav Decker KG v Hauptzollamt Landau* [1979] ECR 101 (para 3); Case C-337/88 *Società Agricola Fattoria Alimentare (SAFA) v Amministrazione delle Finanze dello Stato* [1990] ECR I-1 (para 12).

60 Case 88/76 *Société pour l'Exportation des Sucres SA v Commission* [1977] ECR 709 at 731 (Advocate General Reischl).

61 ECSC Treaty, art 33; EC Treaty, art 173; Euratom Treaty, art 146.

62 Ibid.

63 Case 236/86 *Dillinger Hüttenwerke AG v Commission* [1988] ECR 3761 (para 14); Case C-180/88 *Wirtschaftsvereinigung Eisen- und Stahlindustrie v Commission* [1990] ECR I-4413 (para 22).

64 Case 58/88 *Olbrechts v Commission* [1989] ECR 2643 (para 10); Case 374/87 *Orkem v Commission* [1989] ECR 3283 (para 6); Case T-54/90 *Lacroix v Commission* [1991] ECR II-749 (para 29).

does not invalidate the notification, at least where the addressee realised at the material time that an error had been made.[65] If the form of the notification is such that the person concerned is not put in a position in which he can exercise his rights, the notification is ineffective.[66] It is not necessary that the addressee or any particular person (such as the managing director or legal adviser of the addressee) has actual knowledge of the contents of the notification as long as it has actually been received.[67] Hence notification to the head office of a company is sufficient; companies have no right to require a Community institution to send the notification to any other place or to a particular person.[68] In the case of an unpublished measure, receipt of a letter that expresses precisely and unequivocally a reasoned decision will be regarded as a notification sufficient to cause time to start running in preference to a subsequent communication.[69] In the case of measures challenged by a person other than the addressee, time starts to run when the applicant receives knowledge of the measure, notification not applying ex hypothesi.[70] Knowledge means that the applicant is sufficiently apprised of the measure that he can identify it and ascertain both its precise content and the reasons for it in such a way as to be able to decide whether or not he can institute proceedings.[71] Where the person concerned has knowledge of the existence of an act that may affect his position but insufficient knowledge to identify it or ascertain its precise content and the reasons for it, he lies under a duty to make a request, within a reasonable time after first receiving knowledge of the possible existence of the act, for the whole text of the act; time will ordinarily start running from receipt of the complete text of the act but, if no such request is made, time will start running from the point at which the request should have been made (that is, from the expiry of a reasonable period of time after the person concerned first had knowledge of the possible existence of the act in question).[72] If such a request is made within a reasonable period of time but the institution concerned fails to provide a complete text of the act, the inference is that time does not start to run[73] at least unless and until the act is either published in the Official Journal or notified to the applicant; the alternative view is that time does start to run, the applicant being entitled to have the act annulled for lack of reasons. Whether or not the person concerned has sufficient knowledge of the possible existence of an act affecting him to put him on enquiry is a question of fact. Possession of such knowledge may be inferred from the fact that the relevant information was in his possession or in the public domain or in the possession of a committee on which that person was represented[74] or, presumably, known to an employee of the person concerned or, possibly, a company within the same group.[75]

---

65 Case 82/84 *Metalgoi SpA v Commission* [1984] ECR 2585.

66 Case 76/79 *Karl Könecke Fleischwarenfabrik GmbH & Co KG v Commission* [1980] ECR 665 (para 7 and at 683 per Advocate General Reischl).

67 *Ferriera Vittoria v Commission* (above, note 31) para 11; the *Cockerill-Sambre* case (above, note 40) para 10.

68 The *Cockerill-Sambre* case (ibid) para 1.

69 Case C-12/90 *Infortec-Projectos e Consultadoria Lda v Commission* [1990] ECR I-4625.

70 See, for example, Case 135/81 *Groupement des Agences de Voyages asbl v Commission* [1982] ECR 3799 (paras 15–18).

71 Hearsay evidence is insufficient to constitute knowledge of a measure for the purposes of art 173 of the EEC Treaty: Case 118/83R *CMC Cooperativa Muratori e Cementisti v Commission* [1983] ECR 2583 at para 48 (Judge Pescatore).

72 *Dillinger Hüttenwerke AG v Commission* (above, note 63) para 14; *Wirtschaftsvereinigung Eisen- und Stahlindustrie v Commission* (above, note 63) para 22; Case C-102/92 *Ferriere Acciaierie Sarde SpA v Commission* [1993] ECR I-801 paras 18–19.

73 Cf the *Dillinger Hüttenwerke* case (ibid) at 3775 (Advocate General Darmon).

74 The *Wirtschaftsvereinigung Eisen- und Stahlindustrie* case (above, note 63) paras 25–27.

75 Cf *Orkem v Commission* (above, note 64) para 6.

Statements from a national authority that fail to show clearly and unequivocally that the Community institution concerned has made a definitive ruling are insufficient to establish that the applicant has knowledge.[76]

In the case of measures which have not been notified (or not notified effectively) to the person concerned and are published in the Official Journal (whether or not they must be published), publication starts time running only if it gives sufficient information to amount to complete knowledge of the measure.[77] If it does not, time starts to run a reasonable time after publication if the published information is sufficient to put the applicant on notice of the existence of a measure which may affect his legal position and thus oblige him to make enquiries as to its exact content.[78] Publication in the Official Journal is notice to all the world and an applicant cannot claim that he did not have knowledge of the measure or was not put on enquiry simply because he did not read the relevant part of the Official Journal. Publication is, however, notice only of what is published so that the mere mention of a measure in the Official Journal does not cause even a reader of the Official Journal to have knowledge of the precise contents of the measure. In *Karl Könecke Fleischwarenfabrik GmbH & Co KG v Commission*[79] Advocate General Reischl took the view that, where a contested measure is published, even though publication is not required, and also notified to the persons concerned, the time for bringing proceedings under art 173 starts to run from whichever of the dates is later in time. The Court held that time ran from the 15th day of publication of the measure (a Commission decision) on the basis that the earlier communication of the decision to the applicant did not contain any details 'which would have permitted the applicant to identify the decision taken and to ascertain its precise content in such a way as to enable it to exercise its right to institute proceedings'.[80] The inference is that it is the first event in time which starts time running, not the last. Similarly, in Cases 358/85 and 51/86 *France v European Parliament*[81] Advocate General Mancini took the view that, where the applicant has full knowledge of the contested act before it is published in the Official Journal, time runs from the acquisition of knowledge and not from publication.

Where the event causing time to start running is notification, it is for the party claiming that the action is out of time to prove the date on which the contested act was notified; in the absence of proof of the date of receipt, the Court has no basis on which to conclude that the proceedings have been brought out of time unless there is other convincing evidence to that effect.[82] Where the same act has been notified more than once and at different times or in different countries so that the date of the expiry of the limitation period varies depending upon which notification is relied on, it is an open question

76 Case 378/87 *Top Hit Holzvertrieb GmbH v Commission* [1989] ECR 1359 (paras 14–15).
77 Cases 89 and 91/86 *L'Etoile Commerciale and Comptoir National Technique Agricole v Commission* [1987] ECR 3005 at 3014 (Advocate General Cruz Vilaça).
78 Cases 10 and 18/68 *Società Eridania Zuccherifici Nazionali v Commission* [1969] ECR 459 at 488–489 (Advocate General Roemer); Case 69/69 *Alcan Aluminium Raeren SA v Commission* [1970] ECR 385 at 396–397 (Advocate General Gand). But see Cases 31 and 33/62 *Milchwerke Heinz Wöhrmann & Sohn KG and Alfons Lütticke GmbH v Commission* [1962] ECR 501 at 511 (Advocate General Roemer).
79 Above (note 66) at 682 but see 683.
80 Ibid, para 7; see also at 683 (Advocate General Reischl).
81 [1988] ECR 4821 (at 4838–4839).
82 *Olbrechts v Commission* (above, note 64) para 10; Case T-1/90 *Pérez-Mínguez Casariego v Commission* [1991] ECR II-143 (para 37). Notification should therefore be effected by registered letter with an acknowledgment of service: eg the *Ferriera Vittoria* case (above, note 31) para 9; the *Cockerill-Sambre* case (above, note 40) para 8; *Bayer AG v Commission* (above, note 26) paras 18–20.

whether or not the applicant should be given the benefit of the longest limitation period.[83] It is sufficient protection of the procedural rights of the applicant to take the limitation period that terminates earlier rather than later; but it cannot be excluded that there may be cases where it is more appropriate to take the period terminating later.[84]

In the case of actions for damages, time starts to run as from the date on which liability accrues. The non-contractual liability of the Community depends on the following factors: (i) a wrongful act; (ii) damage; and (iii) a causal connection between them. It follows that time starts to run only when all three factors are in existence. In Cases 256, 257, 265, 267/80 and 5/81 *Birra Wührer SpA v Council and Commission*[85] the Court therefore held that the limitation period cannot begin 'before the date on which the injurious effects of the unlawful measures adopted by the Community were produced', rejecting as the date on which time began to run the dates on which those measures entered into force and were published. The Statutes[86] provide that proceedings in matters arising from non-contractual liability 'shall be barred after a period of five years from the occurrence of the event giving rise thereto'. That event is normally, as has just been seen, the occurrence of the damage flowing from a wrongful act. In the case of damage occurring over a period of time, damage caused outside the limitation period is not recoverable but that does not prevent compensation from being awarded in respect of damage arising during the limitation period.[87] However, the expiry of the limitation period is not a valid defence to an action for damages where the applicant became aware of the event giving rise to liability belatedly and without any fault or lack of diligence on his part.[88] The inference is that, as in the case of actions for annulment, the crucial question is whether or not the applicant has, or should by exercising reasonable diligence have had, knowledge of all the factors necessary for him to decide whether or not to commence proceedings (and, in the context of an action for damages, submit an application for compensation to the responsible Community institution within a reasonable time).

Passing now to the calculation of the limitation period, periods expressed in days, weeks, months or years are to be calculated as follows:

(1)   the period is to be calculated from the moment at which the relevant event occurs or the relevant action takes place, the day during which that event occurs or that act takes place being excluded;

(2)   a period expressed as a number of days ends with the last of the relevant number of days;

(3)   a period expressed as a number of weeks, months or years ends with the expiry of whichever day in the last week, month or year is the same day of

---

83 The point was left open in Case T-106/89 *Norsk Hydro A/S v Commission* (unreported, order of 19 June 1990), where the contested act was notified to the applicant in the United Kingdom (in respect of which the extension of time on account of distance is ten days) and Norway (in respect of which it is four weeks).

84 For example, where notification is effected first at a branch office or subsidiary and then at the head office in another country and it would in the circumstances be unfair to calculate the limitation period by reference to the first notification.

85 [1982] ECR 85 and [1984] ECR 3693 (para 15); see also Case 51/81 *De Franceschi SpA Monfalcone v Council and EC Commission* [1982] ECR 117.

86 ECSC Statute, art 40; EC Statute, art 43; Euratom Statute, art 44.

87 The *Birra Wührer* case (above, note 85) at [1984] ECR 3693 (paras 19–23).

88 Case 145/83 *Adams v Commission* [1985] ECR 3539 (paras 50–51): the event giving rise to liability could not have been known to the applicant before the preparatory enquiries undertaken by the Court in the proceedings.

the week, or falls on the same date, as the day during which the event or action from which the period is to be calculated occurred or took place;

(4)   in a period expressed in months or years, if the day on which it should expire does not occur in the last month, the period ends with the expiry of the last day of that month;

(5)   a period expressed in months and days is reckoned first in whole months and then in days;

(6)   periods are not suspended if they include official holidays, Saturdays, Sundays or the judicial vacations;[89]

(7)   the period is extended on account of distance by adding to the end of the period the relevant extension of time;[90]

(8)   if the period would otherwise end on a Saturday, Sunday or official holiday, it is extended to the end of the next following working day.[91] It should be noted that a period can start or run through but not end on a Saturday, Sunday or official holiday.

Thus, if one supposes two actions under art 173 of the EC Treaty for the annulment of a Commission decision notified to one applicant in the United Kingdom at 15.30 hours on 20 December and notified to the other at 15.30 hours on 30 December, the calculation of the periods for commencing proceedings is as follows: the period laid down by art 173 is two months, as extended on account of distance by ten days; in the first action the period begins at 00.00 hours on 21 December and in the second it begins at 00.00 hours on 31 December because the day on which the event causing time to start running (notification of the decision) is excluded from consideration; the calculation of the number of months is done by reference to calendar months and not periods of 30 or 31 days; in the first action the first month ends on 21 January and in the second action it ends on 31 January (that is, at 00.00 hours on those days); in the first action the second month ends on 21 February, at 00.00 hours (or, to put it another way, at 24.00 hours on 20 February) and in the second action the second month ends on the last day of February (28 or 29, depending upon whether or not that year is a leap year),[92] at 24.00 hours; the ten days on account of distance are then added, which brings the period to 2 March in the first action (assuming that February has 28 days) and to 10 March in the second action; ordinarily, the limitation period will end at 24.00 hours on those dates; if 2 or 10 March is a Saturday, the period is extended to 24.00 hours on the next following working day (Monday 4 or 12 March); the same applies if 2 or 10 March is a Sunday; if, on this example, the Monday following Saturday (or Sunday) 2 or 10 March were Easter Monday (an official holiday of the Court), the period would end at 24.00 hours on the Tuesday as being the next following working day after Saturday/Sunday 2 or 10 March.

The position in an action brought under art 175 of the EEC Treaty in respect of a failure to act is as follows. The defendant institution must first be called upon to act and must then define its position within two months.

---

89   RP-ECJ 80(1); RP-CFI 101(1). The Rules of Procedure now codify the case law as set out in *SIMET and FERAM v High Authority* (above, note 21) at 48 (Advocate General Gand); Case 152/85 *Misset v Council* [1987] ECR 223 (paras 7–11 and at 228–232 per Advocate General Mancini); *Cladakis v Commission* (above, note 42) para 8; *France v Commission* (above, note 44), para 6.

90   RP-ECJ 81(2); RP-CFI 102(2).

91   RP-ECJ 80(2); RP-CFI 101(2).

92   The fact that the event causing time to start running in the second action occurred on the penultimate day in December does not mean that the limitation period should end on the penultimate day in February.

Supposing the letter calling on the institution to act to have been delivered to the institution at 15.30 hours on 20 December, the period of two months starts to run at 00.00 hours on 21 December; it expires at 24.00 hours on 20 February (or, to put it another way, at 00.00 hours on 21 February). If the institution has not defined its position by then, the person concerned has a further two months in which to bring proceedings before the Court. To that further period of two months is to be added the extension of time on account of distance.[93] Supposing the person concerned to be resident in the United Kingdom, the period for applying to the Court starts at 00.00 hours on 21 February and expires at 24.00 hours on 30 April (subject to any further extension to the end of the next following working day if 30 April is a Saturday, Sunday or an official holiday of the Court).

The running of time may be interrupted or suspended where, before the expiry of the time limit for commencing proceedings and before the application commencing proceedings has been lodged, an application is made for legal aid. It would seem that the running of time is interrupted or suspended only if the application for legal aid is granted; and time starts running again as from the date of notification to the applicant of the order granting legal aid.[94] Further, in the case of actions for damages, the Statutes provide for the interruption of the limitation period 'if proceedings are instituted before the Court or if prior to such proceedings an application is made by the aggrieved party to the relevant institution of the Community'. In the former event, the date of the lodgment at the Registry of the application marks the institution of proceedings and the suspension of the time period. It would seem that the proceedings envisaged are those claiming damages in respect of the wrongful act and not other proceedings, for example an action for the annulment of the wrongful act. In the event that application is made to the 'relevant' Community institution, which would be the institution representing the Community in any action for damages, the proceedings must be instituted within the period provided for in the Treaty applicable for the bringing of an action for annulment or an action in respect of a failure to act. In other words, the Statutes give an injured person an option between commencing an action for damages before the Court or seeking a settlement of the matter. The running of the limitation period is suspended in the latter event while negotiations last but, when they terminate in a decision with which the injured person is unsatisfied or a failure to make a decision, the injured person must commence an action for damages within the period fixed, respectively, for bringing an action for annulment or one in respect of a failure to act if he wishes to take advantage of the suspension of the limitation period. This does not, however, mean that the action is barred if either period is not observed, merely that the suspension of the running of the limitation period does not operate during the negotiation period if the action is not commenced timeously after the end of the negotiations. Hence, if negotiations begin one year after time has started to run and end after two years with no result satisfactory to the injured person, he still has two years in which to commence proceedings and does not have to rely on the suspension of the limitation period. On the other hand, if the negotiations had lasted five years, the action would be barred unless the running of time were suspended and, in order to avail himself of this, the injured person must

---

93 The periods set out in Annex II of the ECJ's Rules of Procedure are calculated by reference to the distance of a party from the place where the Court has its seat, Luxembourg. In consequence, they have no application to the time limits applicable to proceedings involving other institutions, a fortiori those whose seat is not at Luxembourg.
94 Case T-92/92AJ *Lallemand-Zeller v Commission* [1993] ECR II-31.

commence proceedings within the additional time period specified in the Statutes.[95]

A party cannot avoid the effects of the expiry of a time limit for bringing proceedings against a measure by attacking a subsequent measure confirming the first[96] unless there is a 'new fact of such a character as to alter the essential circumstances and conditions which governed the adoption of the first measure'.[97] The existence of a new fact shows that the later measure is not a purely confirming measure but alters the legal situation which existed beforehand.[98] A judgment of the Court annulling a measure can be a new factor only so far as the parties to the proceedings closed by the judgment or persons directly affected by the measure annulled are concerned.[99] On the other hand, the discovery of a new fact revealing that the contested act was made on an erroneous basis and which the applicant did not know and could not have known beforehand may also be sufficient to reopen the time limit for challenging the act.[1]

F Connexity

The Treaties create a system of remedies which are, in general and in principle, separate and independent. It sometimes happens, however, that an applicant seeks to avoid the consequences of his actual or envisaged lack of success in obtaining a particular form of relief by dressing up the action as something other than what it really is, intending, by this means, to obtain the same relief by a different form of action. A typical example is an action for damages which is nothing more than an action for annulment in masquerade.[2]

---

95 ECSC Statute, art 40; EC Statute, art 43; Euratom Statute, art 44. See Cases 42 and 49/59 *SNUPAT v High Authority* [1961] ECR 53 at 92 (Advocate General Lagrange); *Kampffmeyer v Commission* (above, note 52) at 260; and Case 11/72 *Giordano v Commission* [1973] ECR 417 (paras 5–7).

96 Case 17/71 *Tontodonati v Commission* [1971] ECR 1059 (para 3).

97 *SNUPAT v High Authority* (above, note 95) at 76; *Pressler-Hoeft v Court of Auditors* (above, note 21), para 6.

98 Cf Case 34/65 *Mosthaf v Euratom Commission* [1966] ECR 521 at 530; Case 58/69 *Elz v Commission* [1970] ECR 507 at 513 (Advocate General Gand); Case 22/70 *Commission v Council* [1971] ECR 263 at 279.

99 Case 43/64 *Müller v Euratom and ECSC Councils* [1965] ECR 385 at 397; Case 46/64 *Schoffer v Commission* [1965] ECR 811 at 816; Cases 50, 51, 53, 54, 57/64 *Loebisch v Commission, Euratom and ECSC Councils* [1965] ECR 825 at 831; Case 55/64 *Lens v European Court of Justice* [1965] ECR 837 at 841; Case 52/64 *Pfloeschner v Commission* [1965] ECR 981 at 987; Case 5/65 *Saudray v Commission* [1965] ECR 993 at 997; Case 12/65 *Bauer v Commission* [1965] ECR 1003 at 1009; Case 47/65 *Kalkuhl v European Parliament* [1965] ECR 1011 at 1014; *Mosthaf v Euratom Commission* (ibid) at 530.

1 Eg Case 219/84 *Powell v Commission* [1985] ECR 3629.

2 In Case 59/65 *Schreckenberg v Euratom Commission* [1966] ECR 543 the applicant requested that he be promoted with retrospective effect and, when the Commission refused, brought an action for the annulment of the refusal and, in the alternative, for damages. The damages claimed were not in fact assessed in the light of the loss actually suffered but by reference to what would have been the case had the Commission's decision been annulled. The Court held (at 550): 'Although a party may take action by means of a claim for compensation without being obliged by any provision of law to seek the annulment of the illegal measure which causes him damage, he may not by this means circumvent the inadmissibility of an application which concerns the same illegality and has the same financial end in view.' See also Case 28/65 *Fonzi v Euratom Commission* [1966] ECR 477; Case 4/67 *Muller (née Collignon) v Commission* [1967] ECR 365; Case 53/70 *Vinck v Commission* [1971] ECR 601; Case 11/72 *Giordano v Commission* [1973] ECR 417; Cases 15–33, 52, 53, 57–109, 116, 117, 123, 132, 135–137/73 *Schots (née Kortner) v Council, Commission and European Parliament* [1974] ECR 177; Cases 4 and 30/74 *Scuppa v Commission* [1975] ECR 919 at 940–941 (Advocate General Trabucchi); Case 9/75 *Meyer-Burckhardt v Commission* [1975] ECR 1171; Cases 56–60/74 *Kurt Kampffmeyer Mühlenvereinigung KG v Commission and Council* [1976] ECR 711 at 750–755 (Advocate General Reischl); Case

In this situation the rejection of the action for annulment will bring in its train the automatic rejection of the action for damages whether or not the two claims are made separately or in the same proceedings. It is not necessary that the disguised action follows after proceedings which have turned out unsuccessfully for the applicant: if, for example, an action for annulment was not brought at all and the time limit for doing so has expired, a subsequent claim which is in substance no more than an action for annulment will still be inadmissible.[3] The crucial question is whether there is so close a connection between the claim made and a different, inadmissible claim that the former must be rejected. This depends on an analysis of the nature in law of both claims: where the subject matter of and the relief sought in both claims are found to be materially identical, the connection is sufficient to entrain the inadmissibility of the claim made.[4]

In the case of parallel claims for annulment and damages, the connection between them does not invariably mean that the inadmissibility of the one leads to the inadmissibility of the other.[5] If that were so, a legal or natural person, who could not bring an action for the annulment of a regulation, would also not be able to bring a claim for damages based on an allegation that the regulation was unlawful. Instead, the rule is that, where the applicant has no locus standi to bring a connected claim, its inadmissibility does not result in the inadmissibility of the claim for damages.[6] The reason for this is that the objection to admissibility based on connexity is intended to prevent abuse of process. There is no abuse if the applicant could not, in any event, have brought the connected claim. Per contra, if the object is to evade a peremptory rule barring a connected claim which could have been raised. Hence most of the connexity cases concern attempts to get round a time bar.

G   Failure to comply with a preliminary procedure

Some proceedings before the Court may be commenced only after the completion of a pre-litigation procedure: the most frequent examples are (i)

129/75 *Hirschberg v Commission* [1976] ECR 1259; Case 167/80 *Curtis v Commission and European Parliament* [1981] ECR 1499 at 1532–1533 (Advocate General Capotorti); Case 33/80 *Albini v Council and Commission* [1981] ECR 2141; Case 543/79 *Birke v EC Commission* [1981] ECR 2669; Case 106/80 *Fournier v Commission* [1981] ECR 2759 at 2777–2780 (Advocate General Sir Gordon Slynn); Case 401/85 *Schina v Commission* [1987] ECR 3911; Case 346/87 *Bossi v Commission* [1989] ECR 303 (paras 31–35); Case T-27/90 *Latham v Commission* [1991] ECR II-35 (paras 36–39); Case T-20/92 *Moat v Commission*, 13 July 1993 (para 46).

3 The problem of a time-barred action for annulment dressed up as a claim for damages has also, in some cases, been resolved by holding (i) that the applicant is precluded from relying on the illegality of an act in order to obtain the relief sought (eg the *Giordano* case, ibid para 4) or (ii) that the damage really flows from the applicant's own failure to bring an action for annulment in time (eg the *Schreckenberg* case, ibid at 555 (Advocate General Roemer)).

4 For cases in which the connection was not sufficiently close, see Case 79/71 *Heinemann v Commission* [1972] ECR 579; Case 106/80 *Fournier v Commission* (above, note 2).

5 *Scuppa v Commission* (above, note 2) (Advocate General Trabucchi); Case 155/85 *Strack v European Parliament* [1986] ECR 3561 at 3569–3570 (Advocate General Mischo); Case 253/86 *Sociedade Agro-Pecuaria Vicente Nobre Lda v Council* [1988] ECR 2725 at 2736 (Advocate General Mischo); Case T-5/90 *Marcato v Commission* [1991] ECR II-731 (para 49).

6 Eg Cases 9 and 12/60 *Société Commerciale Antoine Vloeberghs SA v High Authority* [1961] ECR 197 (the connected claim was one in respect of a failure to act); Case 25/62 *Plaumann & Co v Commission* [1963] ECR 95 (the damages action was instead rejected as 'unfounded': see the explanation given by Advocate General Dutheillet de Lamothe in Case 4/69 *Alfons Lütticke GmbH v Commission* [1971] ECR 325 at 343); Case 4/69 *Alfons Lütticke GmbH v Commission*, itself; Case 5/71 *Aktien-Zuckerfabrik Schöppenstedt v Council* [1971] ECR 975; Cases 9 and 11/71 *Compagnie d'Approvisionnement de Transport et de Crédit SA and Grands Moulins de Paris SA v Commission (No 2)* [1972] ECR 391; Case 43/72 *Merkur – Aussenhandels GmbH v Commission* [1973] ECR 1055.

actions brought against a member state alleging a failure to fulfil an obligation under the Treaty;[7] (ii) actions in respect of a failure to act;[8] and (iii) staff cases.[9]

In the first, the preliminary procedure is intended, on the one hand, to compel the Commission to clarify the Treaty obligations of the member state and the respects in which it is alleged to be in default and, on the other hand, to allow the member state to comply of its own accord with the requirement of the Treaty or else comment on the allegations made or justify its conduct so that an accommodation on the matter may be reached without the need for recourse to the Court.[10] Rigid respect of the procedure is unnecessary[11] as long as its objectives are satisfied. Naturally, if the preliminary procedure is omitted altogether or is carried out in such a defective manner as to affect adversely the member state's rights of the defence, the ensuing action is inadmissible.[12] In some respects, the most important stage is the delivery of the Commission's reasoned opinion because this defines the scope of any subsequent proceedings. This opinion must contain a coherent statement of the reasons which have led the Commission to believe that the member state has failed to fulfil its obligations.[13] The subject matter of the proceedings before the Court cannot diverge from that defined in the reasoned opinion[14] save in so far as its scope is lessened by a concession or settlement of part of the case. This does not mean that the Commission is bound by the strict terms of the reasoned opinion; for example, as long as the nature of the alleged infringement has been identified, it does not matter if the national measure specified in the reasoned opinion has been repealed and replaced by another measure to the same effect;[15] and, where the Commission complains of a single act whose effects extend over a long period of time (or, possibly, a series of recurring acts that are identical in nature), as opposed to a number of distinct infringements of the Treaty, it may include in the proceedings before the Court events taking place after the date of the reasoned opinion.[16]

7   EC Treaty, arts 169 to 170; Euratom Treaty, arts 141 to 142. The position under art 88 of the ECSC Treaty is somewhat different in this respect because the applicant is the allegedly defaulting member state and so a defect in the pre-litigation procedure would be relied on as a ground for annulling the Commission's decision.
8   ECSC Treaty, art 35; EC Treaty, art 175; Euratom Treaty, art 148.
9   Staff Regulations, arts 90 to 91.
10 Cf Case 20/59 *Italy v High Authority* [1960] ECR 325 at 346–347 (Advocate General Roemer); Case 74/82 *Commission v Ireland* [1984] ECR 317 (paras 12–13); Case 85/85 *Commission v Belgium* [1986] ECR 1149 (para 11); Case 199/85 *Commission v Italy* [1987] ECR 1039 (para 7).
11 Case 45/64 *Commission v Italy* [1965] ECR 857 at 871 (Advocate General Gand).
12 Eg Case 51/83 *Commission v Italy* [1984] ECR 2793 (paras 4–8); Case 293/85 *Commission v Belgium* [1988] ECR 305 (the pre-litigation procedure was not carried out validly because the Commission did not give the defendant adequate time limits).
13 Case 7/61 *Commission v Italy* [1961] ECR 317 at 327; Case 325/82 *Commission v Germany* [1984] ECR 777 (paras 8–9).
14 Case 7/69 *Commission v Italy* [1970] ECR 111; Case 193/80 *Commission v Italy* [1981] ECR 3019; *Commission v Ireland* (above, note 10), para 20; Case 166/82 *Commission v Italy* [1984] ECR 459 (paras 16–20); Case 23/84 *Commission v United Kingdom* [1986] ECR 3581 (para 49); Case C-217/88 *Commission v Germany* [1990] ECR I-2879 (paras 11–12); Case C-152/89 *Commission v Luxembourg* [1991] ECR I-3141 (para 9); Case C-198/90 *Commission v Netherlands* [1991] ECR I-5799 (paras 14–16); Case C-279/89 *Commission v United Kingdom* [1992] ECR I-5785 (para 17); Case C-105/91 *Commission v Greece* [1992] ECR I-5871 (para 12); Case C-157/91 *Commission v Netherlands* [1992] ECR I-5899 (para 17); Case C-237/90 *Commission v Germany* [1992] ECR I-5973 (paras 20–22); Case C-210/91 *Commission v Greece* [1992] ECR I-6735 (paras 9–12); Case C-296/92 *Commission v Italy*, 12 January 1994, paras 11–12.
15 Case 45/64 *Commission v Italy* (above, note 11); Case C-105/91 *Commission v Greece* (above, note 14) para 13. But see Case 124/81 *Commission v United Kingdom* [1983] ECR 203.
16 Case 309/84 *Commission v Italy* [1986] ECR 599 (Re Vineyard Reductions) (para 15 and at 601–602 per Advocate General VerLoren van Themaat).

In the second, the object of the preliminary procedure is to put the defendant institution on notice by calling on it to act. The aim of this is to require the institution to define its position expressly or by implication from its silence. If the institution is not put on notice, a subsequent action alleging a failure to act is inadmissible.[17] The same ensues if the subject matter of the action is different from that of the notice calling on the institution to act.[18]

So far as staff cases are concerned, the preliminary procedure is intended 'to enable and encourage an amicable settlement of [the] difference which has arisen between officials or servants and the administration'.[19] A failure to comply with the procedure leads to the inadmissibility of the action before the Court and, although the scope of the action is not bound to the strict terms of the complaint submitted at the pre-litigation stage to the administration, the subject matter must remain the same.[20] Nonetheless, the Court construes the complaint liberally because it is, in theory at least, submitted by the applicant himself without the aid of (professional) legal advice;[21] and where, in the proceedings before the Court, the applicant invokes a plea not raised beforehand solely because of a change in position made by the defendant in the course of the pre-litigation procedure, the defendant is not entitled to object to the new plea.[22] The preliminary procedure is, however, purposeless in cases where the administration has no power to alter the decision of which the applicant complains. The most notable example of this is the decision of a selection board. In consequence the action can, and should, be begun within three months (as extended by any periods of grace, etc) of notification of the selection board's decision. If the applicant should, instead, go through the preliminary procedure, his eventual action before the Court is out of time and, therefore, inadmissible. The Court has, nevertheless, accepted the admissibility of such actions on the ground that the Staff Regulations are in this respect obscure and misleading so that it would be inequitable to deprive the applicant of his rights.[23] The position is otherwise where the prior lodging of a complaint might have served some useful purpose, such as where it is essential

17 Case 17/57 *Gezamenlijke Steenkolenmijnen in Limburg v High Authority* [1959] ECR 1 at 8.
18 Cases 41 and 50/59 *Hamborner Bergbau AG v High Authority* [1960] ECR 493 at 505.
19 Case 58/75 *Sergy v Commission* [1976] ECR 1139 (para 32); Case 173/84 *Rasmussen v Commission* [1986] ECR 197 (para 12); Case T/58/92 *Moat v Commission*, 16 December 1993 (para 39).
20 The *Sergy* case (ibid) para 33; Cases 75 and 117/82 *Razzouk and Beydoun v Commission* [1984] ECR 1509 (para 9); Cases 259/84 and 259/84R *Strack v European Parliament* [1985] ECR 453; Case 174/83 *Amman v Council* [1985] ECR 2133; Case 175/83 *Culmsee v Economic and Social Committee* [1985] ECR 2149; Case 176/83 *Allo v Commission* [1985] ECR 2155 (para 19); Case 233/83 *Agostini v Commission* [1985] ECR 2163 (para 19); Case 247/83 *Ambrosetti v Commission* [1985] ECR 2171 (para 19); Case 264/83 *Delhez v Commission* [1985] ECR 2179 (para 25); Case 52/85 *Rihoux v Commission* [1986] ECR 1555 (para 15); Case 130/86 *Du Besset v Council* [1986] ECR 2619; Case 242/85 *Geist v Commission* [1987] ECR 2181 (para 9); Case 16/86 *GP v Economic and Social Committee* [1987] ECR 2409; Case 224/87 *Koutchoumoff v Commission* [1989] ECR 99 (para 10 and at 111 per Advocate General Tesauro); Case 346/87 *Bossi v Commission* [1989] ECR 303 (paras 27–28 and at 313–316 per Advocate General Darmon); Case 126/87 *Del Plato v Commission* [1989] ECR 643 (para 14); Case T-57/89 *Alexandrakis v Commission* [1990] ECR II-143 (paras 9–11); Case T-19/90 *von Hoessle v Court of Auditors* [1991] ECR II-615 (para 33); Case T-146/89 *Williams v Court of Auditors* [1991] ECR II-1293 (paras 56–57 and 63–64); Case T-60/91 *C v Commission* [1991] ECR II-1395 (para 16); Case T-29/91 *Castelletti v Commission* [1992] ECR II-77; Case T-4/92 *Vardakis v Commission*, 30 March 1993 (paras 16–17).
21 See, for example, the *Sergy* case (above, note 19); Case 23/74 *Küster v European Parliament* [1975] ECR 353; Case 54/77 *Herpels v Commission* [1978] ECR 585; *Rasmussen v Commission* (above, note 19), para 13.
22 Case T-86/91 *Wery v European Parliament* [1993] ECR II-45 (paras 24–25).
23 See Case 34/80 *Authié v Commission* [1981] ECR 665 at paras 6–8 and the authorities cited by Advocate General Warner at 686–687.

for the defendant to know the complaints made by the applicant in order to see whether or not the dispute can be settled.[24]

A failure to comply with a preliminary procedure appears to be an objection which the Court can raise of its own motion.[25] The requirement to go through a preliminary procedure in certain cases is not to be confused with some general requirement that the scope of proceedings before the Court must not go beyond the confines of the dispute between the parties as it has developed in the course of the events leading up to the commencement of the action. No such general requirement exists. Apart from those cases where a preliminary procedure must be followed before the commencement of legal proceedings, there is no requirement that the scope of an action be limited to the matters expressly in dispute in the course of the events prior to the commencement of proceedings. Hence, in an ordinary action for annulment, the applicant's case against the contested act is not limited to the matters of dispute raised with the author of the contested act before its adoption; the Court is seised of all the elements of fact and of law taken into account by the author of the act when it adopted the act.[26] In the same way, when the defendant in Cases 314 and 315/86 *de Szy-Tarisse v Commission*[27] objected that, in an action concerning the defendant's failure to comply with an earlier judgment of the Court, the applicant's claim for compensation must be inadmissible because it had not been included in the application that was the subject of the earlier judgment, that objection to admissibility was dismissed: the claim for compensation arose in the normal way out of the preliminary procedure followed immediately prior to the commencement of proceedings and could not be excluded merely because, at some stage in the history of the dispute, before that preliminary procedure had been commenced, the dispute was different in scope.

H   Lis pendens

The objection of lis pendens may be raised where an action before the Court (whether the ECJ or the CFI) duplicates other proceedings pending before the same Court (including a different chamber of the same Court); the objection of lis alibi pendens may be raised where an action before the ECJ duplicates other proceedings pending before the CFI or vice versa. Both objections may be taken by the Court of its own motion.

Lis pendens may be raised against an action challenging an act which merely confirms an earlier measure contested in other proceedings where the same submissions are made.[28] The actions in question must be between the

---

24 Eg Case 168/83 *Pasquali-Gherardi v European Parliament* [1985] ECR 83 (para 11) and, in general, claims for damages (see, for example, Case T-46/90 *Devillez v European Parliament*, 30 June 1993 (para 43), and Cases T-17/90, T-28/91, T-17/92 and T-27/92 *Camara Alloisio v Commission*, 15 July 1993 (paras 46–49).

25 Case 7/69 *Commission v Italy* (above, note 14); *Alexandrakis v Commission* (above, note 20), para 8; *C v Commission* (above, note 20), paras 11–16. The remark in para 3 of the judgment in Case 255/78 *Anselme (née Heirwegh) v Commission* [1979] ECR 2323 is to be explained by the Court's practice in staff cases.

26 Eg Case 298/83 *CICCE v Commission* [1985] ECR 1105 (paras 19–20).

27 [1988] ECR 6013 (paras 10–13).

28 Cases 45 and 49/70 *Bode v Commission* [1971] ECR 465 (para 11); Cases 58 and 75/72 *Perinciolo v Council* [1973] ECR 511 (para 5); a similar situation arose in *Compagnie d'Approvisionnement de Transport et de Crédit SA v Commission* (above, note 6), paras 9–11; but see also Cases 26 and 86/79 *Forges de Thy-Marcinelle et Monceau SA v Commission* [1980] ECR 1083, especially at 1077 (Advocate General Capotorti).

same parties, have the same purpose and be based on the same submissions.[29] Minor differences in the formulation of the relief sought in the actions in question do not prevent the objection from applying as long as the effect of the judgments to be delivered in them (if the applicant were successful) would be the same.[30] The objection does not apply where the first action was inadmissible for a particular reason and the second action, albeit the same, is not affected by that particular ground of inadmissibility;[31] nor does it apply to an action for annulment brought in respect of an act adopted after the commencement of proceedings in respect of a failure to act and in response to the request to act initiating those proceedings.[32]

In the case of a parallel action before another court (that is, one other than the ECJ or, as the case may be, the CFI), the inadmissibility of proceedings before the Court may ensue if the latter has no jurisdiction to hear the matter but not on the basis of mere concurrency.[33] In consequence, the objection of lis alibi pendens does not normally apply to the situation where other proceedings are pending before a national court, an international tribunal or a court in a third country because the Court's jurisdiction does not overlap with theirs. Since the jurisdictions of the ECJ and the CFI do overlap, the objection of lis alibi pendens may in principle be raised where similar actions are pending before both Courts. In that event, however, one or other of the ECJ and the CFI stays the proceedings before it and there is then no need or justification for raising the objection.[34]

I Res judicata

As the Court put it in Cases 79 and 82/63 *Reynier v Commission*[35] 'the force of res judicata prevents rights confirmed by a judgment of the Court from being disputed anew'. Hence, when the Court has delivered a final judgment on the substance of an action, a subsequent application having the same purpose and relating to the same cause of action is inadmissible.[36] Similarly, where the Court has upheld the lawfulness of part of a measure by rejecting the applicant's claims that it should, to that extent, be annulled, the matter cannot be raised again, in subsequent proceedings brought by the same person, even if the subject matter of the later action is a different measure which reproduces the lawful parts of the earlier measure.[37] Res judicata is also capable of applying to certain decisions of a procedural nature.[38]

29 Cases 358/85 and 51/86 *France v European Parliament* [1988] ECR 4821 (para 12); Case T-28/89 *Maindiaux v Economic and Social Committee* [1990] ECR II-59 (para 23). Note Case 53/84 *Adams v Commission* [1985] ECR 3539 at 3554 (Advocate General Mancini).
30 Cases 146 and 431/85 *Diezler v Economic and Social Committee* [1987] ECR 4283 (paras 13–16).
31 Ibid (para 12).
32 Cases C-15/91 and C-108/91 *Buckl & Söhne OHG v Commission* [1992] ECR I-6061 (paras 19–20).
33 Cases 64 and 113/76, 167 and 239/78, 27, 28 and 45/79 *Dumortier Frères SA v Council* [1979] ECR 3091 (para 7).
34 ECSC and EC Statutes, art 47 (last paragraph); Euratom Statute, art 48 (last paragraph). See further chapter 2, section III, p 57.
35 [1964] ECR 259 at 266.
36 Eg Case 57/70 *Van Eick v Commission* [1971] ECR 613 at 618; Case 192/80 *Geist v Commission* [1981] ECR 1387; Cases 159 and 267/84, 12 and 264/85 *Ainsworth v Commission* [1987] ECR 1579 (paras 3–4).
37 Case 14/64 *Gualco (née Barge) v High Authority* [1965] ECR 51.
38 Eg Case T-16/89 *Herkenrath v Commission* [1992] ECR II-275, where the case had originally been brought before the ECJ and, at that stage, the defendant had successfully applied under RP-ECJ 91 for an order excluding an internal document annexed to the applicant's pleadings. The case was subsequently transferred to the CFI, at which point the applicant applied to have the document reintroduced on the ground that he had not been heard before the ECJ

The extent of the effect of res judicata is defined by reference to the operative part of the judgment and to the reasoning in the judgment which supports it.[39] The effect covers only those questions of fact and law actually or necessarily decided in the judgment.[40] In consequence, res judicata is no obstacle to the admissibility of a subsequent action which, although it has the same parties and subject matter as earlier proceedings, raises issues different from those already considered by the Court.[41] A fortiori, where only the parties are the same and, although the proceedings concern the same Treaty provision, the subject matter is different.[42] However, res judicata is not restricted to cases where the proceedings are exact duplicates of earlier proceedings which have already been concluded: it may also, in certain cases, be raised where the parties are different, as long as the subject matter and the issues remain the same. For example, the effect of the annulment of a measure by the Court is erga omnes.[43] As a result, if a person not a party to proceedings in which the Court has found a measure affecting him to be void, brings an action in order to achieve the same objective, he will be met by the plea of res judicata and the action rejected as inadmissible.[44] On the other hand, when the judgment rejects an application for annulment, its effect is only inter partes.[45] The effect of res judicata may be avoided only by commencing one of the exceptional procedures for reviewing judgments of the Court.[46]

Res judicata is not a ground for rejecting a reference for a preliminary ruling as inadmissible because, although a preliminary ruling is binding on the

made its previous order. The CFI rejected the application on the ground that the applicant had not demonstrated that force majeure or unforeseen circumstances had prevented him from being heard at the material time. Nonetheless, the inference is that the decision in question determined the matter and prevented the CFI from considering the question de novo. It may also be inferred that procedural decisions made without a party being heard in accordance with the Rules of Procedure do not have the force of res judicata. Certain procedural decisions do not have the finality of a decision having the force of res judicata: see, for example, decisions granting or refusing interim relief, which may be reconsidered at any time – RP-ECJ 84(2) and 87–88; RP-CFI 105(2) and 108–109.

39 The *Gualco* case (above, note 37) at 64 (Advocate General Roemer); Case 30/76 *Küster v European Parliament* [1976] ECR 1719 at 1731 (Advocate General Reischl).

40 Case C-281/89 *Italy v Commission* [1992] ECR I-347 (para 14).

41 See, for example, the *Gualco* case (above, note 37); Cases 29, 31, 36, 39–47, 50 and 51/63 *Des Laminoirs, Hauts Fourneaux, Forges, Fonderies et Usines de la Providence SA v High Authority* [1965] ECR 911 at 951–952 (Advocate General Roemer).

42 Eg Cases 2-10/63 *Società Industriale Acciaiarie San Michele v High Authority* [1963] ECR 327 at 339–340.

43 *Küster v European Parliament* (above, note 39) at 1731–1732 (Advocate General Reischl). In contrast, the interpretation of the law on which the annulment decision is based has the effect of res judicata only as regards the parties to the original proceedings: Case 292/84TP *Bolognese v Scharf and Commission* [1987] ECR 3563 (para 9).

44 Case 5/55 *ASSIDER v High Authority* [1954–56] ECR 135 at 146 (Advocate General Lagrange). In fact, in the case to which he refers, the earlier judgment was delivered after the commencement of proceedings, which is why the Court held that there was no need for it to give judgment on annulment and yet did not reject the applications as inadmissible (the previous judgment was that in Case 1/54 *France v High Authority* [1954–56] ECR 1; the Court also did not refrain from giving judgment in or declare admissible the second action in the series, Case 2/54 *Italy v High Authority* [1954–56] ECR 37, because the judgment in both cases was delivered on the same date). It should be observed that, if an earlier judgment annuls an individual decision, res judicata binds only the parties to those proceedings: eg *Schots (née Kortner) v Council, Commission and European Parliament* (above, note 2) para 36.

45 The *ASSIDER* case (ibid), Advocate General Lagrange; see also Bebr, op cit, at p 149.

46 See further chapter 16, pp 507 et seq. For example, in Case 219/87 *Hoogovens Groep BV v Commission* [1989] ECR 1717, Advocate General Lenz considered that the applicant was precluded from calling into question the legal position resulting from a previous judgment which annulled part only of the contested act because the applicant had taken no step to have the judgment supplemented under RP-ECJ 67 (see 1727–1728).

referring court, it may always make a second order for reference, if it thinks it necessary or desirable.[47] As far as other courts are concerned, a preliminary ruling does not constitute res judicata but they remain bound by the authority of the ruling[48] with the result that a national court or tribunal against whose decisions there is no judicial remedy under national law is no longer bound to refer to the Court a question of Community law which is materially identical to the one answered in the Court's ruling.[49] Where a question referred to the Court for a preliminary ruling is manifestly identical to a question on which the Court has already ruled, the Court does not dismiss the reference as inadmissible by virtue of res judicata but gives its decision in the form of a reasoned order which refers to the previous judgment (usually a copy of the latter is attached to the order.[50]

J Defective pleadings

An objection to the admissibility of the application, or any other pleading, does not, as such, challenge the foundation of the action and is commonly based on a procedural irregularity in the pleading, such as a failure to have it signed by the party's agent or lawyer. The Court must consider whether a pleading is inadmissible by reason of a procedural irregularity, if necessary of its own motion, because the provisions governing the form of a pleading relate to the Court's right to exercise its powers as well as to the interests of the opposing parties.[51] Even so, not every defect may lead to the inadmissibility of a pleading: in the case of a failure to comply with the requirements of RP-ECJ 38(3) to (6) or, as the case may be, RP-CFI 44(3) to (5), the Court has discretion whether or not to admit the pleading as admissible if it has not been put in order within the time limit set by the Registrar for doing so.[52] It is apprehended that the Court would only accept a pleading suffering from such a defect, after the party lodging it had been given an opportunity to remedy it but had failed or refused to do so, if the circumstances were very exceptional. If, on the other hand, the defect is cured, but after the expiry of the period laid down for doing so, the pleading is admissible.[53]

47 Case 29/68 *Milch-, Fett- und Eierkontor GmbH v Hauptzollamt Saarbrücken (No 2)* [1969] ECR 165 (paras 2–3); Case 69/85 *Wünsche Handelgesellschaft GmbH & Co v Germany* [1986] ECR 947 (paras 13–16).
48 Case 112/76 *Manzoni v Fonds National de Retraite des Ouvriers Mineurs* [1977] ECR 1647 at 1661–1663 (Advocate General Warner).
49 Cases 28–30/62 *Da Costa en Schaake NV v Nederlandse Belastingadministratie* [1963] ECR 31 at 38.
50 RP-ECJ 104(3).
51 Cases 19 and 21/60, 2 and 3/61 *Société Fives Lille Cail v High Authority* [1961] ECR 281 at 294; Case 219/78 *Michaelis v Commission* [1979] ECR 3349 at 3361–3362 (Advocate General Capotorti). The Court acted of its own motion, inter alia, in Case 83/63 *Krawczynski v Euratom Commission* [1965] ECR 623 (the reply); Case 55/64 *Lens v European Court of Justice* [1965] ECR 837 (an application made under RP-ECJ 91); Case T-64/89 *Automec Srl v Commission* [1990] ECR II-367 (para 74).
52 RP-ECJ 38(7) and 39; RP-CFI 44(6) and 45; Cases 193 and 194/87 *Maurissen v Court of Auditors* [1989] ECR 1045 at 1062 (Advocate General Darmon). Thus, a failure to lodge a lawyer's certificate of entitlement to practise is not a procedural irregularity where the party is represented by an agent whom the lawyer is merely assisting; but it is a procedural irregularity of some consequence if the lawyer is the party's representative: compare Case T-47/92 *Lenz v Commission* [1992] ECR II-2523 (para 35) and Case T-101/92 *Stagakis v European Parliament* [1993] ECR II-63 (para 8). An application may be regularised ex post facto: *Maurissen*, and cf para 33 of the judgment.
53 At least where it has not caused the proceedings to be delayed: Case 2/68 *Ufficio Imposte di Consumo di Ispra v Commission* [1968] ECR 435 at 443 (Advocate General Roemer).

It is arguable that a defective pleading is one 'not provided for in the Rules of Procedure' within the meaning of IR 4(2) with the result that the Registrar of the ECJ must decline to accept it unless expressly authorised by the President of the ECJ or the ECJ itself. Such authorisation is to be found in the ECJ's internal rules but it does not prejudice a subsequent finding by the Court that the pleading is inadmissible: IR 4(2) concerns only its entry on the Register.[54] In the case of defects other than those under RP-ECJ 38(3)–(6) and RP-CFI 44(3)–(5), it is unclear whether they may be remedied after the pleading has been lodged. In Case 10/81 *Farrall v Commission*,[55] where the applicant made several applications without being represented by a lawyer (contrary to RP-ECJ 37(1)), the Registrar requested him to put them in order by causing them to be lodged by a lawyer. According to the report of the case, this request was made under RP-ECJ 38(7), which at the time applied only to a failure to comply with RP-ECJ 38(2)–(6) and which currently applies only to a failure to comply with RP-ECJ 38(3)–(6). The same practice was considered in Cases 220 and 221/78 *ALA SpA and ALFER v Commission*,[56] where Advocate General Capotorti indicated that other defects do not fall within the scope of RP-ECJ 38(7) with the result that, for example, a failure to submit a pleading signed by a lawyer cannot be made good, the pleading being inadmissible. The scope of RP-CFI 44(6) (the equivalent of RP-ECJ 38(7) so far as proceedings before the CFI are concerned) is to be construed accordingly. Since the pleadings in question in that case had, in any event, been lodged out of time the Court did not have to consider this point. There is provision in the ECJ's internal rules[57] that, where an applicant is not represented by a lawyer, the application should be registered and then returned to him for correction. But a new application signed by a lawyer would have to be lodged in time in order to save the action.[58]

At all events, not every defect falling outside the scope of RP-ECJ 38(7) or RP-CFI 44(6) leads to the inadmissibility of a pleading.[59] Some certainly do, such as the failure to set out a form of order when required;[60] a failure to comply with art 19 of the EEC Statute and RP-ECJ 38(1)(c) or RP-CFI 44(1)(c) (in casu a claim for an unspecified form of damages).[61] Others, such as a failure to date the pleadings, probably do not. The Court appears to adopt a flexible approach, the basic criterion for deciding whether or not a procedural defect leads to the inadmissibility of the pleading being its effect on the Court's ability properly to exercise its powers in the case and on the right of the other parties to a fair trial.[62]

The inadmissibility of a pleading is not irredeemable: as long as any relevant time limits are observed, the position can be remedied by submitting

---

54 Eg Case 229/81 *CODEMI SpA v Euratom Commission* [1982] ECR 377: the Registrar could have declined to accept the document in question but the Court authorised its entry on the Register, subsequently rejecting it as inadmissible after hearing argument.
55 [1981] ECR 717. See also Case 73/83 *Stavridis v European Parliament* [1983] ECR 3803.
56 [1979] ECR 1693, see 1700–1702. See also Case 131/83 *Vaupel v European Court of Justice* (15 March 1984, unreported).
57 GI 31.
58 The *Vaupel* case (above, note 56), para 9.
59 The *Gualco* case (above, note 37) at 63 (Advocate General Roemer).
60 Eg *Lens v European Court of Justice* (above, note 51); Case 48/70 *Bernardi v European Parliament* [1971] ECR 175 (at 189 per Advocate General Roemer).
61 The *Automec* case (above, note 51), paras 72–77.
62 See, in particular, Cases 46 and 47/59 *Meroni & Co v High Authority* [1962] ECR 411. For example, in *Lenz v Commission* (above, note 52) para 36, the fact that annexes to a pleading had not been communicated to the other party in the language of the case was regarded as sufficient to justify a request by the other party for an extension of time for the lodging of the next pleading but it was not regarded as being in other respects a procedural defect.

a document in the proper form. This does not cure the defect in the previous pleading but is admissible in its own right.[63] In addition, where a second application is lodged commencing proceedings having the same subject matter as those begun by an earlier, defective application, and the two cases are joined, the admissibility of the second application may cover the inadmissibility of the first and allow the arguments made in it to be considered by the Court.[64]

III Raising an objection

A General remarks

An objection to admissibility may be raised either by the parties or, in certain cases, by the Court of its own motion. In references for a preliminary ruling, an objection to the admissibility of the order for reference may be raised by the Court or the parties at any time. In a direct action the matter is usually raised by the defendant in the defence or by way of a preliminary objection to admissibility under RP-ECJ 91 or, as the case may be, RP-CFI 114;[65] if raised in the rejoinder or at the hearing, it constitutes a fresh issue within the meaning of RP-ECJ 42(2) or, as the case may be, RP-CFI 48(2) and may itself be inadmissible unless it is a point that the Court is obliged to take of its own motion.[66] Where admissibility is challenged only in the defence, the matter is resolved in the final judgment unless the Court decides of its own motion to raise it as a separate issue under RP-ECJ 92 or, as the case may be, RP-CFI 111 or 113; or the parties agree at the close of pleadings that it would be more convenient to have the issue of admissibility decided first.[67] A preliminary objection to admissibility should be raised under RP-ECJ 91 or RP-CFI 114 only if the ground relied on is a complete bar to the whole action and is distinct from the issues raised in relation to the substance of the case.[68] If it relates to some only but not all of the claims made, it should be raised in the defence and the matter left to the final judgment. Otherwise, the preliminary objection

---

63 Cf *ALA SpA and ALFER v Commission* (above, note 56) at 1702 (Advocate General Capotorti).
64 *Forges de Thy-Marcinelle et Monceau SA v Commission* (above, note 28), para 4.
65 The fact that RP-ECJ 91 and RP-CFI 114 make special provision for raising an objection to admissibility does not preclude the defendant from challenging admissibility in the defence. Eg Case 10/55 *Mirossevich v High Authority* [1954–56] ECR 333, order of 17 March 1956, unreported (see p 336 of the Report): the applicant applied for an objection to admissibility raised in the rejoinder to be struck out because it was in breach of RP-ECJ 69 which, as then worded, provided for the raising of preliminary objections, as under the current RP-ECJ 91. The Court rejected the application, holding that neither RP-ECJ 69 nor any other provisions required an objection to admissibility to be raised by separate document; the defendant had only elaborated in the rejoinder an objection made in the defence. Normally an objection to admissibility is raised by the defendant but, in *Lens v European Court of Justice* (above, note 51) at 843–844, Advocate General Roemer appears to have accepted in principle that the applicant may also raise the matter as a preliminary issue under RP-ECJ 91.
66 Eg Cases 54-60/76 *Compagnie Industrielle et Agricole du Comté de Loheac v Council and Commission* [1977] ECR 645 (paras 2–4). It is generally considered that a point that can be raised at any time by the Court of its own motion – which includes all admissibility points – may also be raised at any stage in the proceedings by the parties: eg the *Del Plato* case (above, note 20) at 651 (Advocate General Darmon).
67 Eg Case 106/80 *Fournier v Commission* [1981] ECR 2759 (see at 2774); Cases 91 and 200/82 *Chris International Foods Ltd v Commission* [1983] ECR 417.
68 Where there is a close relationship between the question of admissibility and the substance of the action, it is usually appropriate to proceed directly to consider the latter: eg Case 64/82 *Tradax Graanhandel BV v Commission* [1984] ECR 1359, para 12.

would serve only to lengthen proceedings rather than shorten them. Moreover, where an application is manifestly unfounded, the Court may decline to consider a doubtful admissibility point and content itself with dismissing the case on its merits.[69] For similar reasons the Court may refuse to consider an objection to the admissibility of a part only of the applicant's claims where the issues raised by that part would have to be decided by it in any event or involve consideration of disputed facts.[70] The question of admissibility may also be indistinguishable from the substance of the case in that, if the action is founded, it is also admissible (because the question of admissibility turns on the existence or otherwise of the right or interest that entitles the applicant to judgment).[71]

The power of the Court to raise the question of admissibility of its own motion is defined in RP-ECJ 92 and RP-CFI 111 and 113. Under the first paragraph of RP-ECJ 92 and under RP-CFI 111 the Court may dismiss an action on the ground that it clearly has no jurisdiction to take cognisance of it or on the ground that the action is manifestly inadmissible. The Court may so order even before the application commencing proceedings has been served on the other parties to the proceedings. Under the second paragraph of RP-ECJ 92 and under RP-CFI 113, the Court 'may at any time of its own motion consider whether there exists any absolute bar to proceeding with a case'. Those provisions may be invoked where the objection to proceeding with the case is not clearly established and the matter may require investigation or where the action is admissible but there is some other reason it should not proceed further. The procedure followed is similar to that followed where an objection is raised by a party under RP-ECJ 91(1) or, as the case may be, RP-CFI 114(1). Neither RP-ECJ 91 nor RP-ECJ 92 applies to appeals from the CFI.[72] It therefore seems that a preliminary objection to the admissibility of an appeal cannot be made by a party, although its admissibility can be challenged in the written response to the notice of appeal or at the hearing. The ECJ may of its own motion dismiss the appeal in whole or in part where it is clearly inadmissible or clearly unfounded.[73]

B Dismissal for manifest lack of jurisdiction or inadmissibility

RP-ECJ 92(1) and RP-CFI 111 apply in the case of 'actions'. The previous wording of the former referred to 'an application lodged . . . in pursuance of' RP-ECJ 38(1), which gave rise to various problems: did RP-ECJ 92(1) apply to defective applications, applications lodged otherwise than under RP-ECJ 38(1) and to proceedings commenced otherwise than by application? The current wording of RP-ECJ 92(1) (and the wording of RP-CFI 111) resolves some but not all of those difficulties. To begin with, the elimination of the qualifying words 'lodged . . . in pursuance of' RP-ECJ 38(1) or, as the case may be, RP-CFI 44(1) undoubtedly broadens the scope of RP-ECJ 92(1) and RP-CFI 111. On the other hand, the term now used in the English version of

---

69 Case 218/80 *Kruse v Commission* [1981] ECR 2417 (para 5); Cases 193–198/82 *Rosani v Council* [1983] ECR 2841 (paras 9 and 17); Case T-91/92 *Daemen v Commission*, 16 December 1993.
70 Case C-119/88 *Aerpo v Commission* [1990] ECR I-2189 (paras 13–14) (the action was there dismissed as unfounded; if the applicant had been right on the substance, it would then have been necessary to consider the admissibility of the relevant part of the claim and, if appropriate, to reject it as inadmissible); Cases T-6 and T-52/92 *Reinarz v Commission*, 26 October 1993 (para 50).
71 Eg Case T-108/89 *Scheuer v Commission* [1990] ECR II-411 (paras 24–31); Case C-170/89 *Bureau Européen des Unions de Consommateurs v Commission* [1991] ECR I-5709.
72 RP-ECJ 118.
73 RP-ECJ 119. See further chapter 15, Section VI, p 479.

the Rules of Procedure conveys the impression that the scope of those provisions is broader than may be the case: the word 'action' is very general and may be construed narrowly, so as to encompass all direct actions, or broadly, so as to encompass all proceedings before the Court. Other language versions do not convey the same impression. The French text, for example, uses the word *'requête'* which is the equivalent of the word 'application' in the former English version of RP-ECJ 92(1). The implication is that RP-ECJ 92(1) and RP-CFI 111 apply at the least to actions commenced by an application within the meaning of art 22 of the ECSC Statute and art 19 of the EC and Euratom Statutes. That they apply generally to all proceedings begun by application, even if not envisaged by arts 22 of the ECSC Statute and 19 of the EC and Euratom Statutes, appears from Case T-4/89 Rev *BASF AG v Commission*.[74] Thus, appeals from decisions of the Euratom Arbitration Committee, which are dealt with in art 20 of the Euratom Statute (the application commencing proceedings before the Court being made under RP-ECJ 101), and other procedures, such as those for interim relief, third party proceedings, legal aid, intervention and so forth, are covered.[75] The fact that the application is defective in some respect other than that the Court has no jurisdiction to entertain it or that it is manifestly inadmissible does not prevent the application of RP-ECJ 92(1) or RP-CFI 111.[76] The apparent limitation of the scope of RP-ECJ 92(1) and RP-CFI 111 to applications means that they do not cover references for a preliminary ruling, which are dealt with in arts 20 and 21 of the EC and Euratom Statutes, respectively, and are not commenced by an 'application'. However, RP-ECJ 92(1) has been applied to such cases, no doubt on the basis that RP-ECJ 103(1) provides generally for the application of the Rules of Procedure to references for a preliminary ruling.[77]

Once the application has been lodged, the Court may at any time thereafter dismiss it by reasoned order after hearing the advocate general (where there is one) either on the ground of a clear absence of jurisdiction or on the ground of manifest inadmissibility. RP-ECJ 92(1) and RP-CFI 111 specifically provide that the order may be made 'without taking further steps in the proceedings'. The Court is not obliged to hear the views of the parties before making its decision: indeed, the object of RP-ECJ 92(1) and RP-CFI 111 is to enable the Court to act of its own motion and reject an application immediately. This necessarily means that the ground of rejection must be manifest on the face of the application so that any argument on the point is futile. As illustrations of the use made of RP-ECJ 92(1) and RP-CFI 111, reference may be made to the following cases.

In Case 51/79 *Buttner v Commission*,[78] a staff case, the Court declared that it had no jurisdiction because, under the Staff Regulations, actions may be brought challenging the legality of an 'act adversely affecting' the applicant adopted by or on behalf of the appointing authority and the case itself concerned the contents of a report drawn up by a private company, which

---

74 [1992] ECR II-1591 (para 17). RP-ECJ 92(1) does not, however, apply to applications commencing an appeal to the ECJ from a judgment or decision of the CFI: RP-ECJ 118.
75 In Case 233/82 *K v Germany and European Parliament* [1982] ECR 3637, the ECJ appears to have applied RP-ECJ 92(1) to an application for legal aid.
76 The Court does not have to wait for a defect in the application to be corrected by the applicant before rejecting it as inadmissible because of lack of jurisdiction: this appears to have happened in *K v Germany and European Parliament* (ibid) where the application was made by the applicant in person and did not, therefore, comply with RP-ECJ 37(1).
77 References for a preliminary ruling have been dismissed on the basis of RP-ECJ 92(1) as being manifestly inadmissible in Case 80/83 *Habourdin v Italocremona* [1983] ECR 3639; Case 56/84 *Von Gallera v Maitre* [1984] ECR 1769; Case 318/85 *Unterweger* [1986] ECR 955.
78 [1980] ECR 1201.

could not constitute such an act. A similar situation arose in Case 123/80 *B v European Parliament*,[79] another staff case, in which the applicant claimed the annulment of a letter informing him of a draft decision which would be adopted by the defendant: this was clearly a preparatory act and not one adversely affecting the applicant. Cases 114 to 117/79 *Fournier (née Mazière) v Commission*[80] were brought under arts 175 and 215 of the EEC Treaty by the wife and children of an official alleging that damage had been caused to them by the defendant's failure to address an unspecified act to the official. The Court held that this method of proceeding fell outside the scope of art 215 because a legal remedy already existed for rectifying irregularities in the employment of an official. Case 46/81 *Benvenuto*[81] was an application for a declaration that certain Italian regulations governing the premium rate and general conditions of motor insurance were contrary to art 85 of the EC Treaty and therefore void: the Court, of course, has no jurisdiction under the EC Treaty to annul acts of a member state and therefore dismissed the application, before it had been served on the named defendants, on the ground that it 'clearly had no jurisdiction' to hear it. Similar situations arose in Case 276/86 *Belkacem v Germany*[82] and Case C-285/90 *Tsitouras v Greece*.[83] Lastly, the application in Case 229/81 *CODEMI SpA v Euratom Commission*[84] took the form of a letter written by the president of an Italian court asking for the enforcement of an order made by him against the Commission. Whereas, in all the other cases cited, the Court appears to have acted under RP-ECJ 92(1) or RP-CFI 111 without hearing argument, in this case the letter was served on the parties to the proceedings before the Italian court and they were invited to lodge written observations. The Court rejected the application because it fell outside the scope of any known procedure. The *CODEMI* case indicates that the Court has discretion whether or not to reject the application out of hand and may instead ask the parties to submit written (or oral) observations. This is exceptional. Normally the Court makes the order in an administrative meeting after hearing the views of the advocate general (where there is one) and, were it considered necessary to hear argument from the parties, the procedure envisaged in RP-ECJ 92(2) or, as the case may be, RP-CFI 113 could be followed.

C Summary dismissal

RP-ECJ 92(2) and RP-CFI 113 retain the same wording as the former version of RP-ECJ 92, before it was amended in 1979. They provide that the Court 'may at any time of its own motion consider whether there exists any absolute bar to proceeding with a case'. This power can be exercised in all proceedings[85] with the exception only of appeals to the ECJ from a judgment or decision of the CFI.[86] The expression 'absolute bar' is rendered in French as '*les fins de*

79 [1980] ECR 1789.
80 [1980] ECR 1529.
81 [1981] ECR 809.
82 [1986] ECR 3975.
83 [1991] ECR I-787.
84 Above, note 54.
85 Other language versions do not in fact refer to a bar to proceeding 'with a case' so no special meaning attaches to the use of the word 'case'. RP-ECJ 92(2) and RP-CFI 113 do not allow a party to sidestep RP-ECJ 42(2) or, as the case may be, RP-CFI 48(2) and raise a fresh issue out of time (see Case 110/81 *Roquette Frères SA v Council* [1982] ECR 3159 at para 33 of the judgment) but, obviously, RP-ECJ 42(2) and RP-CFI 48(2) are no bar to raising a claim which the Court can take of its own motion (eg Case 31/69 *Commission v Italy* [1970] ECR 25 at para 8).
86 RP-ECJ 118.

non-recevoir d'ordre public' and a similar phrase is used in the Italian version of RP-ECJ 92(2)[87] but the German text is different again.[88] There is some uncertainty concerning the precise meaning of the phrases used. The expression used in the French text points to an objection to the admissibility of the cause of action (not just the application commencing proceedings) which is '*d'ordre public*' and must therefore be raised by the Court of its own motion. This has led one writer to suggest that RP-ECJ 91 applies to objections to the admissibility of the application[89] and RP-ECJ 92 to objections to the admissibility of the cause of action.[90]

Although it seems to be accepted that any ground of admissibility may be raised by a party under RP-ECJ 91 or, as the case may be, RP-CFI 114, it is nevertheless true that the wording of the different language versions of RP-ECJ 92(2) and RP-CFI 113 indicates, as the English text has it, absolute bars to the continuation of proceedings. That seems to include, in addition to the inadmissibility of the action, any other reason that the proceedings should not proceed to judgment.[91] The problem, however, lies in the question whether or not RP-ECJ 92(2) and RP-CFI 113 allow the Court to reject a case where there exists any such bar or only where the bar is itself mandatory and cannot be waived by the parties. The different texts of RP-ECJ 92(2) and RP-CFI 113, of which some, as has been mentioned, contain no express reference to mandatory bars, may be reconciled by saying that all absolute bars are mandatory and must be raised by the Court of its own motion or else by saying that, where a particular language version refers only to mandatory bars, any ambiguity in the other language versions should lead to them being given a narrow construction in order to ensure consistency as between the different texts of the Rules of Procedure. Since any point going to the admissibility of the proceedings can be raised by the Court of its own motion,[92] the difficulty seems to arise only in relation to those absolute bars that do not concern admissibility, such as the question whether or not the action has lost its purpose. In any event, given the fact that the Court may hear the parties before dismissing an action under RP-ECJ 92(2) or RP-CFI 113, the Court can raise of its own motion any absolute bar to proceeding with a case and, if there is doubt as to whether or not it is a bar that may be, and is intended to be, waived by a party, the matter can be resolved by hearing the parties. It would certainly be

---

87 '*L'improcedibilità per motivi di ordine pubblico*'.
88 '*unverzichtbare Prozessvoraussetzungen fehlen*': absence of an indispensable requirement for bringing an action.
89 '*Exceptions*' in the French text.
90 See De Soto, *Zehn Jahre Rechtsprechung* p 50.
91 Eg Case 19/85 *Grégoire-Foulon v European Parliament* [1985] ECR 3771, where the action lost its purpose after the commencement of proceedings because the defendant withdrew the contested act (an additional claim raised in the reply was inadmissible). In Case 248/86 *Bruggemann v Economic and Social Committee* [1987] ECR 3963, the action was dismissed under RP-ECJ 92(2) as being inadmissible for lack of interest, that finding approximating to a finding that there was no case on the substance.
92 *Lens v European Court of Justice* (above, note 51) at 844 (Advocate General Roemer); Cases 67 to 85/75 *Lesieur Cotelle et Associés SA v Commission* [1976] ECR 391 (para 12 and at 419 per Advocate General Warner); Case 219/78 *Michaelis v Commission* [1979] ECR 3349 at 3361–3362 (Advocate General Capotorti); Case 155/78 *Miss M v Commission* [1980] ECR 1797 at 1813 (Advocate General Capotorti); Case 135/81 *Groupement des Agences de Voyages v Commission* [1982] ECR 3799 (Advocate General Rozes); Case T-60/91 *C v Commission* [1991] ECR II-1395 (para 11); Case T-16/91 *Rendo NV v Commission* [1992] ECR II-2417 (para 39). *Compagnie Industrielle et Agricole du Comté de Loheac v Council and Commission* (above, note 66) may be distinguished because no reasoning or arguments were addressed to the Court in support of the objection.

illogical for the Court to be able to dismiss a case because of some bar which the party concerned could and might waive.

RP-ECJ 92(2) and RP-CFI 113 have been invoked, with increasing frequency in recent years,[93] in respect of: lack of jurisdiction;[94] prescription;[95] lis pendens;[96] lack of interest;[97] failure to comply with a preliminary procedure;[98] res judicata;[99] and where the action, although not inadmissible, had become devoid of purpose after the commencement of proceedings.[1]

The Court may act under RP-ECJ 92(2) or RP-CFI 113 at any stage in the proceedings. In Case 200/87 *Giordani v Commission*,[2] for example, it acted after the hearing because the defendant had not made clear whether or not it was disputing the admissibility of the action. When the Court raises an objection to admissibility under RP-ECJ 92(2) or RP-CFI 113, it gives its decision in accordance with RP-ECJ 91(3) and (4) or, as the case may be, RP-CFI 114(3) and (4). In other words, a date is fixed for a hearing at which the parties will be invited to deliver their oral submissions on the point unless the Court considers either that the parties should first make their submissions in writing or that there is no need to hear the parties (in which case the Court proceeds to make its decision).[3] There are no preparatory enquiries. The Court will not hear oral argument if the documents before it contain all the information that it requires in order to make a decision.[4] After hearing the advocate general (where there is one), the Court decides either to uphold the objection to proceeding with the case, in which event the action is dismissed, or to reject it, in which event the proceedings continue, the President prescribing new time limits for the further steps that follow. The Court may also decide to reserve its decision until final judgment, in which event the President prescribes new time limits for the next stages in the proceedings.

D   Dismissal on application

Any party may raise a preliminary objection to admissibility under RP-ECJ 91 or, as the case may be, RP-CFI 114(1). The procedure under those provisions

---

93 See generally the *Del Plato* case (above, note 20) at 650–651 (Advocate General Darmon).
94 Eg Cases 31 and 33/62 *Milchwerke H Wöhrmann & Sohn KG and Alfons Lütticke GmbH v Commission* [1962] ECR 501; Case 43/76 *Reference for a Preliminary Ruling from the Tribunal de Grand Instance, Melun*, order of 30 June 1976 (unreported); Cases 105/79 and 68/80 *References for a Preliminary Ruling by the Acting Judge at the Tribunal d'Instance, Hayange* [1979] ECR 2257 and [1980] ECR 771; Case 138/80 *Borker* [1980] ECR 1975.
95 Eg Case 55/64 *Lens v European Court of Justice* (above, note 51); Case 47/65 *Kalkuhl v European Parliament* [1965] ECR 1011 (at least 15 other unreported cases were dismissed, apparently for the same reason, in 1965 and one in 1968); *Vaupel v European Court of Justice* (above, note 56); Case 317/85 *Pomar v Commission* [1987] ECR 2467.
96 Eg Cases 45 and 49/70 *Bode v Commission* [1971] ECR 465; *Perinciolo v Council* (above, note 28).
97 Eg Case 108/86 *GdM v Council and Economic and Social Committee* [1987] ECR 3933.
98 Eg Case 13/86 *von Bonkewitz-Lindner v European Parliament* [1987] ECR 1417 (paras 5–7).
99 Cases 159 and 267/84, 12 and 264/85 *Ainsworth v Commission* [1987] ECR 1579 (paras 3–4).
1 *Grégoire-Foulon v European Parliament* (above, note 91) para 7.
2 [1989] ECR 1877 (para 10).
3 RP-ECJ 91(3) and RP-CFI 114(3) provide that 'unless the Court decides otherwise, the remainder of the proceedings shall be oral'. That gives the Court discretion as to how the proceedings shall be conducted. The inference from the exclusion of RP-ECJ 91(2) and RP-CFI 114(2) is that the proceedings do not normally include a written part; but it would have been inappropriate to incorporate those provisions in the procedure under RP-ECJ 92(2) and RP-CFI 113 because they concern proceedings begun by application and not by the Court of its own motion. In consequence, the reference to the discretion under RP-ECJ 91(3) and RP-CFI 114(3) does not appear to exclude as a matter of principle the lodging of written submissions should the Court consider it to be desirable.
4 Eg Case 216/83 *Parti Ecologiste 'Les Verts' v Commission and Council* [1984] ECR 3325; Case 297/83 *Parti Ecologiste 'Les Verts' v Council* [1984] ECR 3339.

'plainly aims at allowing the admissibility of applications to be argued at an early stage of the procedure, in order to save the parties, where appropriate, from having to engage in unnecessary argument on the substance of the case. The sole condition required for the employment of that procedure is that consideration of the substance of the case should not be broached.'[5] In most cases it is the defendant who raises the objection, for obvious reasons. It is unclear whether an intervener can do so. It is established that an intervener may raise an objection to admissibility not considered by the party in whose support he has intervened[6] and may, of course, argue in favour of an objection which has been made. On the other hand, to allow an intervener to raise such an objection as a preliminary issue under RP-ECJ 91 or RP-CFI 114 would enable him to take the direction of the case out of the hands of the parties stricto sensu. This seems to be contrary to the essentially subordinate role of interveners in the proceedings. It would seem, instead, that an intervener is restricted to raising the objection in his observations.[7] This does not, of course, preclude the Court from taking the point under RP-ECJ 92 or, as the case may be, RP-CFI 111 or 113.

The procedure under RP-ECJ 91 and RP-CFI 114 has already been considered.[8] At this point it suffices to say that, when a preliminary objection to admissibility is raised, the facts of the case are, strictly speaking, irrelevant. The reason for this is that, on the one hand, the purpose of raising the objection at a preliminary stage is to dispose of the case without more ado (hence there are no preparatory enquiries in order to ascertain whether or not the facts alleged are true) and, on the other hand, the substance of the case does not fall for consideration. In the nature of things, some grounds of inadmissibility, in particular lack of locus standi or of interest, cannot be assessed without looking at the facts. In some cases, the contention of the party raising the objection is that, even if the allegations of fact made by the opposing party are true, the action is still inadmissible. This puts the Court in a dilemma: if it hears the objection and then decides to reject it, it may subsequently find that the facts alleged are not true and the action is, after all, inadmissible; on the other hand, if the decision on admissibility is reserved until final judgment, the Court may find that the time spent on the further pleadings, any preparatory enquiries and the oral procedure, was wasted because the objection must be upheld. Its decision whether or not to hear the objection as a preliminary issue is therefore reached after assessing the importance of the facts of the case to the question of admissibility and the persuasiveness of the objection raised. When admissibility is clearly dependent on facts which the parties do not agree or are not prepared to admit for the purpose of deciding this question, the decision on admissibility can only be reserved until the final judgment. This suggests that, in such a case, a preliminary objection should not be raised at all, the admissibility of the action simply being challenged in the defence. The same seems to apply where only part of the action is inadmissible and the raising of a preliminary objection to that part will not reduce the scope of the case significantly.[9]

---

5 Case 20/65 *Collotti v European Court of Justice* [1965] ECR 847 at 853 (Advocate General Roemer).
6 See Cases 42 and 49/59 *SNUPAT v High Authority* [1961] ECR 53 at 75.
7 Case C-313/90 *CIRFS v Commission* [1993] ECR I-1125 opinion of Advocate General Lenz at paras 47–49. See p 172 above.
8 See chapter 6, pp 188 et seq.
9 Cf *Aerpo v Commission* above, note 70 (paras 13–14), where the Court declined to consider the defendant's arguments on admissibility because it would have to rule on the substance of the case in any event.

CHAPTER 8

Interim relief

I Introduction

As set out in the Treaties, the powers of the Court to grant interim relief comprise four distinct remedies:

(1)   suspension of the application of an act challenged in an action before the Court;[1]
(2)   interim measures pending the final decision in a case before the Court;[2]
(3)   suspension of the enforcement of a decision of the Court itself;[3] and
(4)   suspension of the enforcement of a measure adopted by another institution.[4]

To these the chapter of the ECJ's Rules of Procedure which deals with interim relief adds a fifth: compulsory inspections under art 81 of the Euratom Treaty. This is not really a species of interim relief and seems to have been included in the chapter only because of certain procedural similarities to proceedings for interim relief. It is considered elsewhere.[5] Interim relief is also available in the context of appeals to the ECJ from judgments or decisions of the CFI.[6] In substance, the relief available comprises the remedies referred to in (1) to (4) above; and the conditions that must be satisfied before relief can be granted are the same as in the case of the grant of interim relief in the context of proceedings brought directly before the ECJ or the CFI and otherwise than by way of appeal.[7] The chief characteristics of proceedings for interim relief, whether brought before the ECJ or the CFI, are that they are summary and heard by a single judge, the President of the Court or a chamber. It is very rare for an application to be dealt with by the full Court. In addition, most applications are made in the context of litigation which is already before the Court. For reasons of clarity the proceedings to which the application for interim relief relates will be referred to as the 'action'.

The nature of interim measures was discussed at length by Advocate General Capotorti in his opinion in Cases 24 and 97/80R *Commission v France*[8] but his remarks seem to be broadly applicable to the various categories of

---

1 ECSC Treaty, art 39; EC Treaty, art 185; Euratom Treaty, art 157.
2 ECSC Treaty, ibid; EC Treaty, art 180; Euratom Treaty, art 158. As can be seen from the wording of art 39 of the ECSC Treaty, suspension of the application of an act challenged in an action before the Court is nothing more than a particular type of interim measure but the EC and Euratom Treaties deal with them separately and the same approach will be followed here.
3 ECSC Treaty, arts 44 and 92; EC Treaty, arts 187 and 192; Euratom Treaty, arts 159 and 164.
4 ECSC Treaty, art 92; EC Treaty, art 192; Euratom Treaty, art 164.
5 See chapter 17, pp 600–601.
6 ECSC and EC Statutes, art 53; Euratom Statute, art 54.
7 Cf Case C-345/90P-R *European Parliament v Hanning* [1991] ECR I-231 (para 26). The procedural aspects of applications for interim relief made in the context of appeals to the ECJ from the CFI are discussed in chapter 15, section VII, pp 479 et seq.
8 [1980] ECR 1319.

relief, of which interim measures are one, available to a litigant in a direct action in order to preserve his rights pending judgment, and which are here referred to as 'interim relief'. The topic was also the subject of extensive analysis by Advocate General Tesauro in Case C-213/89 *R v Secretary of State for Transport, ex p Factortame Ltd.*[9] The opinions of Advocates General Capotorti and Tesauro can be summarised as follows.

The need for interim relief arises from the hiatus between the point in time at which a right comes into existence and the point in time at which its existence is established definitively by a judicial decision having the force of res judicata which is enforceable against the parties to the dispute. The fact that a right must wait for a judicial decision before its existence is established definitively does not mean that, in the meantime, it is not an accrued right or is something less than a right or is less worthy of protection; it is simply that, until the Court is in a position to give final judgment in the dispute between the parties, it is not able to give one party or the other the specific and definitive judicial protection of the right in issue that flows from a judgment binding the parties to the dispute. Given such a situation, the purpose of interim relief is to ensure that the passage of the time needed by the Court to deliver a final judgment does not have the effect of depriving the right irredeemably of its substance.[10]

The three characteristics of interim relief, then, are its connexity with the substance of the action, its temporary nature and the requirement that it does not prejudice the Court's final decision in the action. The first indicates that the procedure for interim relief is an integral part of the proceedings in the action and is 'intended to prevent the effectiveness of the decision from being jeopardised by a situation which is incompatible with the realisation of the rights of one party'.[11] It necessarily follows that the interim relief sought must be capable of preventing the effectiveness of the final decision from being jeopardised;[12] and that the risk of jeopardy relates to the rights claimed in the action and not other rights.[13] The temporary nature of the relief granted, which ensures that it does not prejudice the final decision by producing a situation which is irreversible, is another indication of the ancillary nature of the role played by the procedure in the context of the action: 'It is the [final] judgment which definitively determines the rights and obligations of the parties with an authority and effectiveness which are logically greater than that of the interim measure'.[14] The requirement that the relief granted does not prejudice the Court's final decision in the action 'is justified . . . on at least three grounds: first of all the relationship between the interim measure and the judgment, characterised . . . by the ancillary nature of the first, would be reversed if the judgment were influenced or anticipated by the interim measure; secondly, the summary nature of the proceedings in an application for interim measures would not make it possible to reach a decision capable of

9 [1990] ECR I-2433 at 2451 et seq.
10 Ibid at 2455–2457.
11 [1980] ECR 1319 at 1337.
12 Eg Case 25/85R *Nuovo Campsider v Commission* [1985] ECR 751 (para 23); Case 206/89R *S v Commission* [1989] ECR 2841 (paras 15–17); Case 246/89R *Commission v United Kingdom* [1989] ECR 3125 (para 38); Case C-257/90R *Italsolar SpA v Commission* [1990] ECR I-3841 (paras 17–21).
13 Eg Case C-313/90R *Comité International de la Rayonne et des Fibres Synthétiques v Commission* [1991] ECR I-2557 (paras 19–26), where the applicant's success in the action would not have prevented the occurrence of the harm from which it sought to be protected by the grant of interim relief; the relief claimed therefore went beyond the scope of the action and was not necessary in order to preserve the effectiveness of a judgment upholding the rights claimed by the applicant.
14 [1980] ECR 1319 at 1337.

affecting the substance of the case without seriously affecting the rights of the parties; thirdly, resumption of the normal course of the proceedings in the . . . action after their interruption by the interim measure would lose all purpose if the main problem for decision had already been decided by way of the order for interim measures.'[15] In the nature of things, however, an application for interim relief may be dependent on a point of law that, when decided, resolves the entire dispute between the parties.[16] The requirement that the grant of relief should not prejudice the outcome in the action applies as much to the effects of the final judgment on the legal position of the parties before the date of judgment as to its future effects.[17] It is worth emphasising that, at the stage at which the decision whether or not to grant interim relief is made, the Court is ex hypothesi in no position to come to a decided view on the rights at issue. All such rights are therefore to be regarded, for the purposes of granting or refusing interim relief, as claimed or putative rights. In particular, the presumption of validity from which acts adopted by the Community institutions benefit unless and until a competent court rules that the act is invalid[18] does not in principle place a Community institution in a better position than any other party at the interim relief stage where the validity of the act is in dispute; and it certainly does not operate so as to bar a claim for such relief as against such an act.[19] Lastly, the relief granted must not impose on the party against whom it is granted and on any third parties affected by the grant of relief any burden that is greater than necessary in the circumstances of the case.[20]

Each type of interim relief is here treated separately before consideration of the conditions for the grant of relief.

II   The four types of interim relief

A   Suspension of an act challenged before the Court

Actions brought before the Court[21] and appeals to the ECJ from judgments or decisions of the CFI[22] do not have suspensory effect, save as otherwise provided in the Euratom Treaty,[23] but the Court (whether the ECJ or the CFI) has power to suspend the application of an act challenged before it and the ECJ has power to suspend the application of an act in issue in an appeal from

---

15 Ibid at 1338.
16 Case 792/79R *Camera Care Ltd v Commission* [1980] ECR 119, is a rare example. Ordinarily, the outcome in proceedings for interim relief does not produce definitive statements of the law (other than those relating to the grant of relief) because the order made is of its nature without prejudice to the eventual decision on the substance of the case: Case 352/88R *Commission v Italy* [1989] ECR 267, para 22. In Case 120/83R *Raznoimport v Commission* [1983] ECR 2573, however, the doubts expressed by Judge Mertens de Wilmars about the defendant's case in the course of the interim relief proceedings seem to have proved so persuasive that the action proceeded no further. Similarly, in Case 214/86R *Greece v Commission* [1986] ECR 2631, Judge Mackenzie Stuart found that only a certain amount could have been deducted by the defendant from the applicant's entitlement, thus defining the scope of the action and also resulting in an order that the defendant refrain from all measures of enforcement in relation to the excess (see paras 16–17 and the operative part of the order).
17 Case C-40/92R *Commission v United Kingdom* [1992] ECR I-3389 (para 29).
18 See Case 101/78 *Granaria BV v Hoofproduktschap voor Akkerbouwprodukten* [1979] ECR 623 (para 4).
19 The *Factortame* case (above, note 9) at 2458–2459 (Advocate General Tesauro).
20 Cf Cases 76, 77 and 91/89R *Radio Telefis Eireann v Commission* [1989] ECR 1141 (para 19); Case T-45/90R *Speybrouck v European Parliament* [1990] ECR II-705 (para 36).
21 ECSC Treaty, art 39; EC Treaty, art 185.
22 ECSC and EC Statutes, art 53 (first para); Euratom Statute, art 54 (first para).
23 Euratom Treaty, art 157.

the CFI.[24] In regard to acts whose lawfulness or validity is in issue in proceedings before the CFI, it should be observed that, whereas a judgment or decision of the CFI normally takes effect when it is delivered, a judgment declaring a general decision within the meaning of the ECSC Treaty or a regulation within the meaning of the EC and Euratom Treaties to be void takes effect only as from the date of expiry of the period for appealing from the judgment or, where an appeal is brought within time, as from the date of the dismissal of the appeal (if it is dismissed). Such general decisions or regulations thus remain in force even after the CFI has delivered a judgment finding them to be void, without prejudice to any application made to the ECJ for their suspension or any other interim measure.[25] Thus, in the context of appeals from the CFI to the ECJ, the occasion for an application for suspension to be made to the ECJ may arise where the CFI has upheld the lawfulness of a measure other than a general decision or regulation or where it has either upheld the lawfulness of, or declared void, a general decision or regulation. Under the Statutes,[26] time for bringing an action against the Community in respect of its non-contractual liability ceases to run if proceedings are begun before the Court or if, prior to such proceedings, the aggrieved party makes an application to the appropriate Community institution; but that does not result in the suspension of any act of the Community institutions, such as the act causing the loss.

In references for a preliminary ruling the referring court suspends the proceedings before it upon making the order for reference[27] but this is the automatic effect of making the reference and requires no intervention by the Court. The stay of the proceedings before the referring court in such circumstances is not an interim measure and does not satisfy any requirements of interim protection of the disputed rights.[28] If any such protection is necessary, that is a matter for the referring court, not the Court. The referring court decides whether or not to grant such interim relief as may be available under national law in accordance with the requirements of national law subject to two qualifications: where interim relief is sought in order to protect a right under Community law, any rule of national law which constitutes the sole obstacle to the grant of relief must be set aside (that is, where the substantive conditions for the grant of relief are satisfied, a provision of national law may not be relied on in order to refuse the relief sought);[29] and, where an act of a member state or emanation of the state is impugned in domestic proceedings on the ground that it implements an act of a Community institution that is unlawful under Community law, the national court may grant interim relief in the form of suspension of the operation of the domestic measure in question where, first, it entertains serious doubts about the validity of the act of the Community institution concerned, secondly, it refers the question of the validity of the Community act to the Court (unless the Court is already seised of that question), and thirdly, the criteria employed by the Court in deciding whether or not to grant interim relief in similar cases are satisfied.[30]

24 Treaties, ibid; Statutes, ibid; RP-ECJ 83(1); RP-CFI 104(1).
25 ECSC and EC Statutes, art 53 (second para); Euratom Statute, art 54 (second para).
26 ECSC Statute, art 40; EC Statute, art 43; Euratom Statute, art 44.
27 EC Statute, art 20; Euratom Statute, art 21.
28 *R v Secretary of State for Transport, ex p Factortame Ltd* (above, note 9) at 2451–2452 (Advocate General Tesauro).
29 Ibid. The question whether or not Community law may confer a right to interim relief in proceedings before national courts even where no such right or no appropriate form of relief is available under national law alone is an a matter of some debate.
30 Cases C-143/88 and C-92/89 *Zuckerfabrik Süderdithmarschen AG and Zuckerfabrik Soest GmbH v Hauptzollamt Itzehoe and Hauptzollamt Paderborn* [1991] ECR I-415. See further chapter 17, section G.7, p 565.

Passing now to consideration of the power of the Court to suspend the application of an act challenged before it, the English version of the EC and Euratom Treaties refers to 'the contested act' while the ECSC Treaty specifies 'the contested decision or recommendation';[31] and, to complete the picture, the first paragraph of RP-ECJ 83(1) and RP-CFI 104(1) refers to 'any measure adopted by an institution . . . only if the applicant is challenging that measure in proceedings before the Court'. Those words indicate that the power to grant relief is restricted to cases where the lawfulness of a particular act, decision or recommendation is at stake. This does not mean that an application for relief can be made only in actions for annulment: the lawfulness of an act (of a Community institution) may also be in issue in actions against a member state for failing to fulfil its obligations under the Treaty, in actions for damages where the source of the Community's liability is alleged to lie in an unlawful (as opposed to wrongful) act[32] and in cases where its legal effect is dependent on another act which is challenged in the action.[33] In the same way, suspension in the context of appeals to the ECJ is not necessarily to be limited to appeals from judgments of the CFI delivered in actions for annulment. However, in the nature of things, most applications for suspension are made in the context of actions for annulment. Suspension of an act of a Community institution is not likely to arise in actions against a member state for failing to fulfil its obligations under the Treaty. It is arguable that that form of relief is in principle inappropriate in an action for damages because the only relief that may be sought in such an action is compensation for the loss suffered, not an order prohibiting the defendant from continuing with the conduct causing the loss; but the alternative view is that suspension is an appropriate form of interim (albeit not final) relief because it may limit the eventual liability of the defendant or preserve the applicant from future loss that might not be compensatable by an award of damages. It would seem that, if interim relief were to be granted, the applicant would have to be faced with a threat of loss that was either not such as could be compensated by an award of damages or disproportionately great by comparison to the inconvenience to the defendant of granting relief.

It would seem that relief cannot be granted in a reference for a preliminary ruling which raises the question of the validity of an act of one of the institutions because of the non-contentious nature of such proceedings: there is no lis between the parties in the proceedings before the Court and its jurisdiction is limited to the questions contained in the national court's order for reference. This is made clear by the wording of the Treaties: the power to suspend application of an act follows from the fact that 'actions brought before' the Court do not have suspensory effect. References for a preliminary ruling are not 'actions brought before' it. As pointed out above, the solution is for the party concerned to apply to the referring court for interim relief against any steps taken at the national level to implement the impugned Community act.[34]

If the order can be made only in proceedings in which the lawfulness of an act is at stake, it seems to follow that relief can be granted only in relation to acts whose lawfulness can be challenged. There is no difficulty in defining

---

31 Articles 185, 157 and 39, respectively.

32 In Cases C-51 and C-59/90R *Comos-Tank BV v Commission* [1990] ECR I-2167 (at para 33), Judge Due left open the question whether or not an application for suspension is admissible in an action for damages.

33 See, for example, Case 23/74R *Küster v European Parliament* [1974] ECR 331. Relief can relate only to that part of a general decision which is implemented by the act challenged in the action: see Case 258/80R *Metallurgica Rumi SpA v Commission* [1980] ECR 3867 at para 16.

34 See Oliver in (1992) 29 CMLRev 7 at 9–10.

those acts under the ECSC Treaty which, as has been noted, restricts the power to suspend to decisions or recommendations. These comprise most, but not all, the legally binding acts of the institutions under that Treaty. In Cases 35/62 and 16/63R *Leroy v High Authority*,[35] for example, it appears to have been held that relief could not be granted in relation to a provision of the Staff Regulations on the ground that it did not constitute a 'measure' within the meaning of RP-ECJ 83(1). At that time the ECSC Staff Regulations were contained in a 'Regulation' adopted pursuant to the original version of art 78 of the ECSC Treaty.

Under the EC and Euratom Treaties, the term used, 'act', is far less clear than 'decision or recommendation'. To begin with, it could conceivably be taken to cover acts of a member state or even a private person. The Rules of Procedure, however, specify that relief can be granted only in relation to a 'measure adopted by an institution'. Since there does not appear to be a direct authority on the point, it seems to be arguable that the Rules of Procedure are more restrictive in this respect than the EC and Euratom Treaties would indicate. But it would be hazardous in the extreme to frame an application for the suspension of the application of an act under art 185 of the EC Treaty or art 157 of the Euratom Treaty when the author of the act is not a Community institution; all the more so given that the same relief is available under art 186 of the EC Treaty or art 158 of the Euratom Treaty in the form of interim measures.

In Case 21/59R *Italy v High Authority*[36] Judge Donner suggested that the power to suspend application related to acts of the High Authority or, where appropriate, those of third parties which affected the applicant. This statement was made in the context of art 39 of the ECSC Treaty, which covers both suspension and interim measures. Since the former is indisputably limited to acts of a Community institution, the reference to measures taken by third parties seems to be restricted to interim measures and, in Cases 31 and 53/77R *Commission v United Kingdom* and Case 61/77R *Commission v Ireland*[37] the Commission applied for suspension of the measures adopted by the two defendant member states in the form of an application for interim measures.

Article 173 of the EC Treaty and art 146 of the Euratom Treaty provide that the Court may review the legality of 'acts' of the Council and the Commission 'other than recommendations and opinions'. This indicates that recommendations and opinions are acts within the meaning of the Treaties. For the purposes of defining the 'acts' which may be suspended under art 185 of the EC Treaty or art 157 of the Euratom Treaty, the term must be given a narrower meaning consonant with the context in which it is to be applied. As a result, the act in question must be susceptible to attack before the Court and must have effects which can be suspended. For example, in *Italy v High Authority*[38] the Italian government sought the suspension of a decision of the High Authority made under art 88 of the ECSC Treaty, which provides that the High Authority may record in a reasoned decision its finding that a member state has failed to fulfil its obligations under the Treaty and require the member state concerned to remedy this situation within a specified period of time. Sanctions can be imposed only after that period has expired. Judge Donner held that suspension could not be ordered because the decision was not a measure of 'application': it was declaratory and imposed no extra

---

35 [1963] ECR 213.
36 [1960] ECR 351.
37 [1977] ECR at 921, 937 and 1411.
38 Above, note 36.

obligation on the member state concerned; the setting of a time limit for compliance with the Treaty is a prerequisite for the application of sanctions and a decision to apply them could no doubt have been suspended. Similarly, in Case T-19/91 *Société d'Hygiène Dermatologique de Vichy v Commission*[39] Judge Cruz Vilaça dismissed an application for the suspension of the operation of a Commission decision withdrawing the protection from fines afforded to agreements notified to the Commission under Regulation No 17 on the ground that such a decision makes no order against the person to whom it is addressed requiring it to alter its behaviour and thus does not require enforcement; it merely informs the undertaking concerned of the Commission's provisional opinion and, as such, is incapable of causing serious and irreparable damage and thus of being suspended. An act is something positive and, for this reason alone, an applicant cannot force an institution to act by alleging a failure to act contrary to the Treaty and then applying to the Court for this failure to be suspended.

There seems to be no significance in the use of the word 'measure' rather than 'act' in the Rules of Procedure. It probably reflects the difference in wording between the EC and Euratom Treaties, on the one hand, and the ECSC Treaty on the other. In any event the same term is used, for example, in the Italian and French texts of the EC and Euratom Treaties and the Rules of Procedure.[40]

The extent to which a regulation or other provision of general effect may be considered an act or measure for the purpose of granting relief has given rise to particular problems which seem to relate more to the interest of the applicant in obtaining the suspension of a measure of general effect than to the question of principle, whether or not such a measure is capable of being suspended by an order of the Court. In *Leroy v High Authority*[41] suspension of a provision of general effect was refused, although the reason may have been that it was not part of a 'decision or recommendation' within the meaning of the ECSC Treaty. 'Decisions' in that context may be of general effect and so one would be entitled to conclude that, under the ECSC Treaty, such measures may be suspended. In Case 44/75R *Firma Karl Könecke v Commission*,[42] however, an application made under arts 185 and 186 of the EC Treaty but requesting the suspension of a regulation, Judge Lecourt held that, 'save in exceptional circumstances making it possible to single out the applicant from other persons subject to the law', the effect of a general provision cannot be regarded as being that of a 'measure' within the meaning of RP-ECJ 83(1). In Case 92/78R *Simmenthal SpA v Commission*,[43] Judge Kutscher seemed to admit the theoretical possibility of suspending a regulation but dismissed the application on the ground that the drastic consequences of doing so were out of proportion to the individual interest which the applicant wished to safeguard.[44] On the other hand, in the *Japanese Ball Bearing* cases[45] he found no difficulty in ordering

39 [1991] ECR II-265 (para 20).
40 The German version, like the English, uses different words: '*Handlung*' in the EC and Euratom Treaties and '*Massnahmen*' in the Rules of Procedure.
41 Above, note 35.
42 [1975] ECR 637.
43 [1978] ECR 1129.
44 See also Case 243/78R *Simmenthal SpA v Commission* [1978] ECR 2391; in Case 166/78R *Italy v Council* [1978] ECR 1745, the application was dismissed on other grounds, as were those in Cases 48/79R *Ooms v Commission* [1979] ECR 1703 and 33/80R *Albini v Council and Commission* [1980] ECR 1671.
45 Cases 113/77R and 113/77R-I *NTN Toyo Bearing Co Ltd v Council* [1977] ECR 1721; Case 119/77R *Nippon Seiko KK v Council and Commission* [1977] ECR 1867; Case 121/77R *Nachi Fujikoshi Corpn v Council* [1977] ECR 2107.

the suspension of the regulation in question. These cases are, however, distinct from other cases concerning regulations because the measure in dispute was expressly aimed at the applicants and later found by the Court to constitute, in part at least, a decision which was of direct and individual concern to them.[46] A clearer authority that measures of general effect may, in theory at least, be suspended is Case 258/80R *Metallurgica Rumi SpA v Commission*.[47] In Case 119/86R *Spain v Council and Commission*[48] and Case 128/86R *Spain v Commission*,[49] a member state applied for the suspension of various regulations without raising any apparent objection to its entitlement to do so. Further, in art 53 of the ECSC and EC Statutes and art 54 of the Euratom Statute, it is provided that, in the case of an appeal from a decision of the CFI declaring a regulation to be void, the regulation in question remains in effect until the appeal has been disposed of (at which point its lawfulness will finally be settled) 'without prejudice, however, to the right of a party to apply to the Court of Justice, pursuant to' art 39 of the ECSC Treaty, arts 185 and 186 of the EC Treaty or, as the case may be, arts 157 and 158 of the Euratom Treaty 'for the suspension of the effects of the regulation which has been declared void or for the prescription of any other interim measures'. The reference to arts 185 of the EC Treaty and 157 of the Euratom Treaty would be otiose unless the suspension of 'the contested act', within the meaning of those provisions, also meant the suspension of a regulation.

It may therefore be concluded that a regulation or other provision of general effect is an act or measure which may be suspended by application under the first paragraph of RP-ECJ 83(1) or RP-CFI 104(1). In the ordinary course, the applicant for relief would be able to obtain only partial suspension of a measure having general effect: as will appear from the discussion of the conditions that must be satisfied in order to justify the grant of relief, an applicant for relief must generally demonstrate the necessity for relief in order to ward off a threat to the applicant's own interests, not those of a third party; hence, in the case of a measure having general effect, relief can be granted only to the extent that the measure affects the applicant and not to the extent that it affects other persons.[50]

Although the English text of the Treaties refers to the 'suspension' of the 'application' of the act in question, the Rules of Procedure[51] speak of the suspension of the 'operation' of the measure. There is no such variation in some of the other texts[52] and, like the use of 'measure' and 'act', it seems to be of no consequence. Other texts of the Treaties tend to use a word closer to 'execution' than 'application' or 'operation' but, as can be seen from the cases, the latter expressions appear to be more accurate because they avoid the connotations of a word like 'execution'. When the application or operation of the act is suspended, it ceases to have legal effect and no steps can therefore be taken to execute or enforce it. On the other hand, an application to suspend execution or enforcement, which is properly made under RP-ECJ 89 or RP-CFI 110, aims at the measures taken to secure compliance with the act but not at its other legal effects. A failure to appreciate this distinction led the

---

46 A similar situation arose in Case 232/81R *Agricola Commerciale Olio Srl v Commission* [1981] ECR 2193.
47 Above (note 33) para 9.
48 [1986] ECR 2241 (Re Export Deposits).
49 [1986] ECR 2495.
50 As will be seen, the Commission and the member states may apply for interim relief in order to protect a more general interest represented by them.
51 RP-ECJ 83(1); RP-CFI 104(1).
52 Eg the French and Italian; the German version is, however, different.

applicant in Case 107/82R *AEG Telefunken AG v Commission*[53] to apply for suspension of enforcement before the Commission had taken any such steps. The President nevertheless interpreted the application for relief as implying that what was really sought was suspension of the operation of the act.

The effect of the relief which may be granted is negative only, in the sense that the act (or measure) in dispute ceases to have any effect until the order granting suspension lapses. It is not, of course, necessary to apply to suspend the application of the entirety of the act. It is often the case, particularly in competition matters, that only a part of the measure needs to be suspended and so the applicant can, and should, select that part of it which justifies suspension. The order that can be made suspends only the direct results of the measure[54] and has no positive effects other than those flowing immediately from suspension. In consequence, it has been held that suspension of a negative administrative act is inconceivable because the grant of such relief in respect of such an act cannot possibly alter the applicant's position.[55] For example, in several cases application has been made for the suspension of a decision refusing to grant an authorisation. The object of the application was, in substance, to obtain grant of the authorisation but this was not a result flowing from the suspension of the refusal and the applications were in consequence rejected.[56] In such a situation the only possible remedy is to apply for an order that authorisation be granted by way of an interim measure.[57] Whether such an application would be successful will be considered below. Similarly, suspension of the application of a Commission decision finding that there has been an infringement of art 85(1) of the EEC Treaty and ordering the infringement to be terminated does not amount to making the restrictive practice in question provisionally valid: the Court does not have this power.[58] Another example is provided by Case 91/76R *De Lacroix v European Court of Justice*,[59] where the applicant had requested the suspension of the operation of a decision rejecting her candidature for a post and a declaration that she be allowed, in consequence, to take part in the competition. This was rejected because suspension of the decision would not result in her admission to the competition. The most that the Court could do was order the suspension of the whole recruitment procedure. To admit the applicant to the competition would reverse the decision, not suspend it.[60]

Application may be made for the suspension of the application of an act that is itself a form of interim relief and whose annulment is sought in the action, such as a Commission decision adopting interim measures in a competition case[61] or a regulation imposing a provisional anti-dumping duty.[62] In such

53 [1982] ECR 1549.

54 *Leroy v High Authority* (above, note 35).

55 *S v Commission* (above, note 12) para 14.

56 See Case 19/59R *Geitling Ruhrkohlen-Verkaufsgesellschaft mbH v High Authority* [1960] ECR 34 and Case 50/69R *Germany v Commission* [1969] ECR 449.

57 As was done, unsuccessfully, in Case 25/62R I *Plaumann & Co v Commission* [1963] ECR 123 (see also Case 25/62R II, ibid, at 126).

58 Case 71/74R and RR *Nederlandse Vereniging voor de Fruit- en Groentenimporthandel v Commission* [1974] ECR 1031; Cases 209–215 and 218/78R *Heintz van Landewyck Sarl v Commission* [1978] ECR 2111.

59 [1976] ECR 1563.

60 See also Case 4/78R *Salerno v Commission* [1978] ECR 1; *S v Commission* (above, note 12) para 16.

61 Eg Case T-23/90R *Automobiles Peugeot SA and Peugeot SA v Commission* [1990] ECR II-195; Cases T-24 and T-28/92R *Langnese-Iglo GmbH and Schöller Lebensmittel GmbH & Co KG v Commission* [1992] ECR II-1713 and 1839.

62 Eg the *Raznoimport* case (above, note 16). The admissibility of an action for the annulment of such a regulation, upon which the admissibility of the application for interim relief depends, should now be considered in the light of later cases, in particular Cases C-305/86 and C-160/87 *Neotype Techmashexport GmbH v Commission and Council* [1990] ECR I-2945 (paras 13–16).

cases, if the criteria that must be satisfied in order to justify the grant of relief have been satisfied, it may not be possible to preserve the position pending judgment by merely suspending the operation of the contested act: suspension would risk causing the occurrence of the events that the contested act sought to avoid and thus might bring about serious and irreparable damage to the person whose interests were protected by the contested act. Therefore, interim measures rather than suspension may be the more appropriate form of relief.[63]

If the measure in question is not going to be applied or has no practical effect, such as where the defendant has already taken steps to suspend its operation or has given an undertaking not to apply it, the order will not be made.[64] If made, the Court's order will not necessarily suspend the act pending judgment in the action if an earlier date for the lapse of the order is justified.[65] For example, if the contested act is due to expire before the date of judgment and may then be replaced by another measure, suspension can in principle be granted only for the period while the contested act remains in force; if it is replaced by another measure, the applicant must bring an action, and any necessary application for interim relief, against that measure; the Court cannot make an order that would in effect prevent the Community institution concerned from exercising its powers after the expiry of the contested act.[66] The application for suspension cannot be made before the measure has come into existence, even if there is a possibility that it may be adopted,[67] and it must be made before the measure is applied or has taken effect.[68]

B Interim measures

The EC and Euratom Treaties[69] state that the Court may prescribe 'any necessary interim measures' in 'any cases before it'. Article 39 of the ECSC Treaty simply says that the Court may prescribe 'any other necessary interim measures' in the context of actions brought before it. The second paragraphs of RP-ECJ 83(1) and of RP-CFI 104(1) are a little more specific. They provide that an application for interim measures is admissible 'only if it is made by a party to a case before the Court and relates to that case'. This seems to make it impossible for an intervener to apply for the adoption of interim measures: his status in the proceedings is not that of a party stricto sensu because he has no right, other than to support or oppose the case made by the applicant or defendant. It seems that an application for interim measures can be made in the context of an application for interim measures, in order to preserve the situation until the judge decides whether or not to grant relief pending judgment in the action.[70]

An example of an application made by a party which did not relate to the case is to be found in Case 186/80R *Suss v Commission*.[71] There, an official of the Commission claimed by way of interim measure the communication to him of

---

63 Eg the *Langnese-Iglo* case (above, note 61) paras 29–35. See further below.
64 See further below in connection with the requirement of urgency (pp 261 et seq.)
65 Cases 6 and 7/73R *Istituto Chemioterapico Italiano SpA and Commercial Solvents Corpn v Commission* [1973] ECR 357; Case 20/74R *Kali-Chemie AG v Commission* [1974] ECR 337 and 787.
66 Case 294/86R *Technointorg v Commission* [1986] ECR 3979 (paras 20–27).
67 See Case 51/79R II *Buttner v Commission* [1979] ECR 2387.
68 Case 67/63R *SOREMA v High Authority* [1964] ECR 174; Case 68/63R *Luhleich v Euratom Commission* [1965] ECR 618; Cases 19 and 65/63 *Prakash v Euratom Commission* [1965] ECR 576; Case 61/76R II *Geist v Commission* [1976] ECR 2075; Case 121/77R *Nachi Fujikoshi Corpn v Council* (above, note 45); Case 92/78R *Simmenthal SpA v Commission* (above, note 43).
69 Articles 186 and 158 respectively.
70 See the *Commercial Solvents* case (above, note 65).
71 [1980] ECR 3501 (para 16).

the report of an Invalidity Committee. No such claim formed part of the application commencing the action nor was it pertinent to any issue between the parties. The claim was therefore rejected. Similarly, in *Leroy v High Authority*[72] the applicant claimed that no official should be appointed to fill the post that he had occupied until the High Authority refused to integrate him as an established official. He sought the annulment of this refusal but annulment would not have resulted in his integration, merely in the necessity for the High Authority to reconsider whether or not to integrate him. In consequence, the claim that the post should be kept open for him, pending judgment in the action, was rejected. The relevance of the claim for interim measures to the action is not a matter of whether or not the relief sought is identical to that claimed in the action but whether it will preserve the efficacy of a judgment in the applicant's favour. In neither the *Suss* nor the *Leroy* case did the relief sought in the claim for interim measures relate in this sense to the relief sought in the action. In *Leroy*'s case in particular, even had annulment resulted in his establishment as an official, he had no right to be appointed to a specific post and therefore no right to require the High Authority to keep any particular post vacant for him.

Applications for interim measures have been made in proceedings under arts 93(2) and 169 of the EEC Treaty, as well as in actions for annulment.[73] Where the object is to suspend the operation of a measure whose author is not a Community institution or which is not covered by art 185 of the EC Treaty, art 175 of the Euratom Treaty or the first part of art 39 of the ECSC Treaty, the relief sought should be suspension by way of an interim measure.[74]

In principle, interim measures are of a conservatory nature and apply in particular, but not invariably, to cases where positive action is required in order to prevent the Court's final judgment from being rendered nugatory by the passage of time or the occurrence of some event. Nevertheless, the President's power to take positive steps to preserve the position of the parties does not extend to the taking of administrative decisions which are the responsibility of another institution or to the substitution of his own discretion for that of another institution.[75] In Case 25/62 *Plaumann & Co v Commission* the applicant made two applications for interim measures,[76] each claiming that the Court should declare that the defendant was obliged to authorise the German government to suspend partly the imposition of customs duties on imported clementines. The case arose from a Commission decision refusing to authorise the German government to do so which was challenged by a German importer. Judge Donner held that, while such an order was not clearly excluded by art 186 of the EC Treaty, it could be justified only 'by wholly exceptional circumstances and if there were very good reasons for thinking that the party concerned would otherwise suffer serious and irreparable damage'. This is, of course, significantly different from an application that the

---

72 Above, note 35.
73 At one time it was thought that, in actions against a member state for a declaration that the state concerned has failed to fulfil a Treaty obligation, the only form of interim relief that could be granted was an interim declaration. The Court has never taken that view and has been prepared to grant whatever form of relief seems appropriate in order to prevent the damage alleged from occurring.
74 See, for example, Case 61/77R *Commission v Ireland* (above, note 37) and at 953–956 (Advocate General Reischl).
75 The *Geitling* case and *Germany v Commission* (above, note 56); the *Küster* case (above, note 33); *Nederlandse Vereniging voor de Fruit- en Groentenimporthandel v Commission* (above, note 58); Case 109/75R *National Carbonising Co Ltd v Commission and National Coal Board* [1975] ECR 1193.
76 Above, note 57.

Court should itself take the measures requested. In a later case Judge Mackenzie Stuart held that, where the defendant institution enjoys a wide discretion, the Court cannot interfere in interim proceedings at least in the absence of solid evidence of a misuse of powers.[77]

The reluctance on the part of the judges to interfere is generally attributable to the fact that the grant of relief would in such circumstances amount to giving the applicant the benefits of a final judgment before the soundness of the applicant's case in the action had been properly assessed, thus rendering the continuation of the action otiose.[78] The situation is all the more delicate where the applicant is challenging a decision of a Community institution (in practice, the Commission) to grant or refuse interim relief and is claiming interim relief in respect of that decision. For example, in Case 109/75R *National Carbonising Co Ltd v Commission*[79] Judge Lecourt regarded the application as requesting the suspension of the effect of a decision refusing to take emergency measures, which would amount to a decision of the Judge ordering such measures and impinging on the powers of the Commission. He therefore ordered that the Commission take the measures it thought 'strictly necessary' for the preservation of the position until final judgment. The control of the Court, was, in his view, restricted to reviewing the measures taken by the Commission, not dictating to it the precise measures it should adopt. The same approach was taken by the Court as a whole in Case 792/79R *Camera Care Ltd v Commission*.[80] That concerned an application for an order that the Commission require two companies to continue to supply goods to the applicant and take the measures necessary to ensure adequate supplies during an investigation under Regulation No 17 or pending the final hearing of the action. The action was itself for a declaration that the Commission had acted unlawfully in failing to take such steps and therefore brought into question the Commission's powers to adopt measures of interim relief in the context of competition investigations. The Court's decision on the application for interim relief largely concerned this question. After deciding that the Commission did have power to adopt interim measures, the Court referred the matter back to the Commission so that it might take a decision on the request.

So far as the grant of interim relief is concerned, there appears to be no difference in principle between cases where the applicant seeks relief in respect of a failure by the Commission to exercise its power to grant relief, cases where the relief granted by the Commission is inadequate (both being situations where the applicant is the person who sought relief from the Commission) and cases where the applicant is the person against whom the Commission has granted relief, the application to the Court then being for the suspension of the Commission's order or its modification in order to reduce the burden imposed on the applicant. The application to the Court for interim relief in all those cases takes very much the form of an appeal from the Commission's decision, the applicant having, in effect, to show why it was wrong in the circumstances. In consequence, to plead a specific form of relief has certain advantages over a general claim that the Court order the Commission to do what is necessary or a claim that the Commission should reconsider the request for interim measures.[81] From the

---

77 *Nuovo Campsider v Commission* (above, note 12) para 30.
78 Eg the *Nuovo Campsider* case ibid para 24; Case 321/88R *Sparr v Commission* [1988] ECR 6405 (para 9).
79 Above, note 75.
80 Above, note 16.
81 The latter claim is in any event inadmissible, at least in an action for the annulment of the decision not to grant relief, because it encroaches on the substance of the action against the Commission and is inconsistent with the division of functions between the Commission and the Court: Case T-131/89R *Cosimex GmbH v Commission* [1990] ECR II-1 (Judge Cruz Vilaça).

Commission's point of view, it has done what is necessary (even if that is nothing at all) and there is no reason for it to reconsider the situation (in the absence of a new fact). The applicant must show that the Commission should have acted (if the case concerns a failure on its part to adopt interim relief) or should have adopted a more apposite form of relief (if the case concerns a decision granting interim relief). In the first situation, the President may avoid any risk of prejudicing the final judgment by giving a general instruction to the Commission, unless he takes the view that the application should be rejected. In the second situation (where the applicant may be the person in whose favour the Commission acted but is more likely to be the person against whom the Commission's decision was directed), the function of the judge hearing the application for interim relief is in principle to cut down the effects of the contested act (where necessary) so as to ensure that it operates solely as an interim measure[82]. In some instances, the appropriate remedy may therefore be the suspension of the offending part of the decision but, in others, the judge may have to take positive steps by way of interim measures in order to ensure that the interests of all the persons affected are properly respected.[83]

It is probably sufficient to plead that the Court should order the Commission to take the necessary steps, where the Commission has not acted at all, for then the basic question is whether the Commission was right to hold that there was no necessity to act. If the Commission has acted, but inadequately to protect the applicant's position or wrongly so as to damage the applicant's position, it is probably better to plead a specific form of relief because it is necessary to show that the Commission had not adopted a measure that it should and could have adopted. It should be observed, however, that the reluctance to order a specific form of interim measure applies only where the defendant is an institution, invariably the Commission, which may exercise a discretion to preserve the applicant's position. In other cases it is in practice indispensable to apply for, and order, relief which is sufficiently precise so that all concerned know what is required and further disputes will be avoided.[84]

In Case 50/69R *Germany v Commission*[85] Advocate General Gand took the view that art 186 of the EEC Treaty refers, in essence, to protective measures in financial disputes and is not applicable, for example, to actions for the annulment of a decision under art 226 of the EC Treaty. It seems to have been argued that the Court might authorise protective measures to be taken by a member state by way of an interim measure although art 226(2) gives this power to the Commission. The Court's refusal to take this step was based on its lack of competence to substitute itself for the Commission. Thus *Germany v Commission* really highlights the difference between asking the Court to exercise a discretion granted to an institution and asking it to order that institution to exercise its discretion. It is not an authority that interim measures can only, or must usually, be granted in financial disputes. Very often a financial dispute will concern the exercise of a power by a Community institution. That does not prevent the Court or the President from ordering a payment to be made, where the circumstances justify it.

The possibility of obtaining money payments by way of interim measures seems to have been accepted in principle by Judge Donner in Case 68/63R

---

82 Cases 228 and 229/82R *Ford Werke AG and Ford of Europe Inc v Commission* [1982] ECR 3091, para 14 (Judge Mertens de Wilmars); the *Automobiles Peugeot* case (above, note 61) para 24 (Judge Cruz Vilaça).
83 Eg the *Langnese-Iglo* case (above, note 61).
84 See, for example, Case 42/82R *Commission v France* [1982] ECR 841 at 866 (Advocate General Sir Gordon Slynn).
85 Above, note 56.

Luhleich v Euratom Commission,[86] a staff case in which the applicant claimed an allowance for his needs pending judgment. Although the application was dismissed, he held that such an allowance could be granted as an interim measure if the action was manifestly well founded. In both this and Cases 19 and 65/63 *Prakash v Euratom Commission*[87] a separate claim was also made for a salary advance. This appears to have been rejected because it was in reality dependent on the success of a further claim for suspension of the decision terminating the applicant's appointment. It would clearly have been inconsistent to reject the claim that the applicant's employment with the defendant institution should continue and then uphold the claim for payment of the salary. The rejection of the first necessarily entailed rejection of the second. In Case 44/59 *Fiddelaar v Commission*[88] the applicant claimed a specific sum as an advance on salary arrears or such other sum as equity might determine. It was not established that the applicant's financial position required payment of the whole sum claimed so a lesser amount was ordered to be paid which was sufficient to cover his immediate needs. The defendant had in fact conceded that this amount was due. In Case T-45/90R *Speybrouck v European Parliament*[89] the defendant was ordered to pay the applicant the equivalent of the allowances due to her as a result of the termination of her contract of employment (the lawfulness of which was at issue in the proceedings) until the allowances were actually paid by the institution responsible for doing so (a third party), in order to preserve the applicant from the consequences of any administrative delays in their payment.

Claims for the payment of money run up against the objection that, if the action is successful, the money will be paid in any event so the only damage caused to the applicant is that arising from being kept without his money in the period before judgment. In so far as that damage is pecuniary or financial in nature, it is doubtful if it can in the normal course of events be described as serious and irreparable damage justifying the grant of some form of interim relief. Usually the situation can be remedied at judgment by an award of interest. On the other hand, if the action is lost, it is the other party who will have been deprived of his money and the applicant will have to pay it back,[90] if he is able to do so. Therefore, it is usually necessary to demonstrate that damage of a non-pecuniary nature will ensue. Where, however, the applicant seeks to retain money which he is required to pay by the decision attacked in the action, it is more likely that relief will be granted (although here the relief would normally be suspension of the operation of the decision rather than an interim measure stricto sensu).

In the *Luhleich* and *Prakash* cases one of the interim measures claimed was an order for the production of documents. Abandoned in *Luhleich*, the claim was rejected by Judge Donner in *Prakash* on the ground that it was for the Court or chamber dealing with the case to decide such a question, not the judge on an application for interim relief. In subsequent cases, similar requests have been made for the defendant to hold an enquiry[91] and for

---

86 Above, note 68.
87 Above, note 68.
88 [1960] ECR 555.
89 Above, note 20 (paras 28–37).
90 See *Albini v Council and Commission* (above, note 44). In Cases T-278/93R, T-555/93R, T-280/93R and T-541/93R. *Jones v Council and Commission*, 1 February 1994 (para 54), a claim for an advance payment of damages was rejected because it would prejudge the outcome of the case and there was no direct link between the damage with which the applicant was supposedly threatened pending judgment and the damage for which compensation was sought.
91 Case 114/83R *SICA and SIPEFEL v Commission* [1983] ECR 2315 (paras 6–9).

the Court to appoint an expert to look into certain factual aspects of the case.[92] An order to produce documents, appoint an expert to make a report or, generally, to enquire into the facts of the case is usually made as part of the preparatory enquiries undertaken after the close of the written procedure; and there is an appropriate procedure for obtaining such an order.[93] There is therefore no question of the applicant's position being prejudiced by the passage of time unless, for example, the documents in question are in imminent danger of destruction (or a potential witness is on the point of death). Even in that event it is doubtful if interim relief is the proper remedy because its object is in principle to preserve the applicant's position pending judgment so that the Court's decision is not rendered nugatory, not assist the making of that decision. The correct procedure seems to be to write to the Registrar requesting the Court to order a preparatory enquiry immediately so that the evidence is taken before it is destroyed or otherwise ceases to exist; and an application, for what is in effect a measure of enquiry, dressed up as an application for interim measures will usually be dismissed because an incorrect procedure has been followed. On the other hand, if there is reliable evidence that evidence relevant to the issues in the case is going to be destroyed and will have ceased to exist before a preparatory enquiry can be undertaken, it may be appropriate to seek an order restraining the person in possession of the evidence from destroying it before any necessary preparatory enquiries have been made: although the destruction of evidence does not in itself deprive a judgment in the applicant's favour of its full effects, it may have just as serious an effect on the applicant's rights by depriving him of the opportunity to obtain a judgment in his favour. The risk that the opposing party in a case will destroy relevant evidence is an exceptional circumstance which must ordinarily be proved to the satisfaction of the Court; it cannot be inferred from the mere fact that the opposing party is or may be in possession of evidence that favours or may favour the applicant's case.[94] In any event an application for interim measures cannot be used, as a substitute for discovery proceedings, in order to obtain sight of relevant documents in the hands of the other party before lodging the defence, reply or rejoinder or in order to define what constitutes the evidence relevant to the case.[95]

In an application for the suspension of a measure under the first paragraph of RP-ECJ 83(1) or of RP-CFI 104(1), the measure must be contested in the action. Under the second paragraph of RP-ECJ 83(1) and of RP-CFI 104(1), an application for an interim measure is admissible if it 'relates' to the case before the Court. The test is therefore less stringent than that for suspension. However, as Cases 18/65R *Gutmann v Euratom Commission*[96] shows, suspension may be applied for as an interim measure. Gutmann was suspended from his duties and then transferred to another post. He submitted a complaint to the Commission and, when it was rejected, appealed to the Court. In the

---

92 Case C-358/89R *Extramet Industrie SA v Council* [1990] ECR I-431 (para 26); Case C-106/90R *Emerald Meats Ltd v Commission* [1990] ECR I-3377 (paras 28–30). In the latter case the defendant applied for an expert to be appointed to determine the applicant's claim but, since the defendant maintained that it had no power to adopt a measure that would satisfy the applicant (a submission that the judge seemed to consider well founded), an expert's opinion could not be of 'decisive influence' and the request was dismissed.

93 See chapter 11, p 364.

94 Case 121/86R *Anonimos Eteria Epichiriseon Metalleftikon Viomichanikon kai Naftiliakon AE v Council and Commission* [1986] ECR 2063 (para 17); Case 129/86R *Greece v Council and Commission* [1986] ECR 2071 (para 17).

95 Cases 121 and 122/86R *Anonimos Eteria Epichiriseon Metalleftikon Viomichanikon kai Naftiliakon AE v Council and Commission* [1987] ECR 833 (paras 15–16).

96 [1966] ECR 135.

meantime the Commission issued a vacancy notice concerning his original post, inviting candidates to apply for it. If Gutmann won his action, what would happen if the Commission had appointed someone to the post before the date of the judgment? The decision to issue the vacancy notice was not directly in issue and in fact, in order to challenge it, Gutmann would have had to have brought a separate action. Before doing so, he applied for the notice to be suspended as an interim measure under art 158 of the Euratom Treaty. The Commission naturally objected that the vacancy notice could not be suspended because it was not challenged in the action but Judge Lecourt brushed that aside as being too formalistic: the action related to the removal of Gutmann from his post and so put in question the fact that it was vacant; the application to suspend the operation of the vacancy notice was therefore an inevitable consequence of the action challenging the decision holding the post to be vacant.[97] In principle, the Court's power to suspend, by way of interim measures, the operation of an act other than the contested act may be exercised only if the acts in question were adopted by the same institution and that institution is a party to the proceedings (in practice, therefore, the defendant).[98]

As can be seen, the relief sought by way of interim measure can be wide-ranging in nature; but it may not be contrary to Community law,[99] beyond the Court's jurisdiction[1] or be such as to deprive the action of its purpose or render it nugatory.[2] The nature of the interim relief sought does not have to be the same as that of the relief sought in the action.[3] The relief granted in decided cases or considered as within the Court's jurisdiction to grant includes: the ordering of an expert's report;[4] an order preventing the defendant institution from concluding a contract or from allocating funds for its performance, if concluded;[5] an order that the defendant propose to a particular committee that a product be included on a list of authorised products and inform the member states of that fact;[6] an order extending the time for paying import duties.[7] In Cases 160 and 161/73R *Miles Druce & Co Ltd v Commission*[8] the origins of the dispute lay in a proposed take-over of the applicant by Guest, Keen and Nettlefolds Ltd ('GKN'). The applicant requested the Commission

---

97 To like effect see also *Küster v European Parliament* (above, note 33). See also *SICA and SIPEFEL v Commission* (above, note 91).
98 Case 133/87R *Nashua Corpn v Commission* [1987] ECR 2883, paras 7–8.
99 See *Commission v France* (above, note 84) para 19.
1 Case 191/88R *Co-Frutta Sarl v Commission* [1988] ECR 4551 (para 24).
2 Case 74/85R *Remy v Commission* [1985] ECR 1185 (paras 9–10); Case 231/86R *Breda-Geominera-ria v Commission* [1986] ECR 2639 (para 18).
3 The classic example is provided by actions brought under art 169 of the EC Treaty: the only relief that can be sought in the action is a declaration but the interim relief that may be sought may be, and invariably is, entirely different in nature (commonly an order that the defendant state suspend any measures that it has implemented or is about to implement that would alter the status quo). Where the nature of the relief sought in the application is the same as that sought in the action (in casu suspension of the operation of a measure whose annulment is claimed), it has been held that the relief sought cannot be ordered in an application for interim measures because it would amount to a provisional annulment of the contested measure: Case 292/84R *Scharf v Commission* [1984] ECR 4349 (para 10). It is not clear why relief should be refused for that reason alone.
4 Case 318/81R *Commission v CODEMI* [1982] ECR 1325. As can be seen from the later cases discussed above, such an order is unusual.
5 Case 118/83R *CMC v Commission* [1983] ECR 2583 (para 53).
6 Case 65/87R *Pfizer International Inc v Commission* [1987] ECR 1691: the object was to restore the status quo.
7 Case 160/84R *Oryzomyli Kavallas OEE v Commission* [1984] ECR 3217 (para 9).
8 [1973] ECR 1049.

to exercise its powers under art 66(5) of the ECSC Treaty to prevent the take-over and, on the Commission refusing to act, brought an action to have the refusal annulled. The application for interim measures claimed a broad selection of types of relief: in brief, an order that GKN (i) acquire no shares in the applicant, (ii) not exercise the voting rights attached to its shares, (iii) not exercise its right to call a general meeting and (iv) not propose a resolution in the event of a general meeting being held. The application was not granted for various reasons but it was never suggested that such relief might fall outside the Court's power. In such a case, however, the Court would not, as explained above, be likely to order the Commission to adopt a specific form of relief unless it was clear that no other was adequate to preserve the position of the applicant. Indeed in a subsequent application[9] Judge Lecourt ordered the Commission to take 'all necessary measures' to preserve the status quo. By this time the Commission's decision on the merger was imminent but it had said that it would include in a decision allowing the merger a provision deferring its entry into force until three weeks after notification to the interested parties, thus allowing the applicant time to commence proceedings against it and, if necessary, apply to the Court for interim relief. In fact, however, this does not seem to have given any protection to the applicant until then: GKN could complete the take-over and then cause the applicant to discontinue its action. In consequence the Commission was ordered to ensure that the entry into force of its decision should not be before a certain date and to take all the necessary measures to ensure that no action was taken until then.[10] It is an open question whether or not, by way of interim measure, the Court can order national authorities not involved in the proceedings to apply a measure contested in the action in a particular way.[11] Where the issue is the interpretation of a provision of Community law, proceedings for interim relief are not an appropriate method for providing the Community institutions with an interpretation that may be relied on as providing a solid basis for future legislative developments: any ruling on the correct interpretation of a provision of Community law made at the interim relief stage is necessarily without prejudice to the final judgment.[12] As in the case of the suspension of an act challenged before the Court, the justification for granting relief may disappear if the party concerned gives an undertaking to the Court that satisfies it that there is no need to grant relief.[13]

C   Suspension of the enforcement of a decision of the Court

RP-ECJ 89 and RP-CFI 110 provide that the same rules as those relating to the suspension of the operation of a measure adopted by an institution and to the adoption of any other interim measure apply to applications to suspend the enforcement of a decision of the Court. Where the decision whose enforcement is to be suspended is a decision of the ECJ, the application is made to the ECJ; where the decision in question is that of the CFI, the application is made to the CFI save that, if the decision is the subject of an appeal to the ECJ, application

9   Cases 160, 161, 170/73R II *Drule & Co v Commission* [1974] ECR 281.
10   What would happen when the Commission approves a take-over can be seen from Case 3/75R *Johnson and Firth Brown Ltd v Commission* [1975] ECR 1 and, in relation to take-overs and mergers authorised by the Commission under Council Regulation No 4064/89 (OJ 1989 No L395/1), from Case T-96/92R *Comité Central d'Entreprise de la Société Générale des Grandes Sources v Commission* [1992] ECR II-2579.
11   Cases C-51 and C-59/90R *Comos-Tank BV v Commission* [1990] ECR I-2167 (para 33).
12   Case 352/88R *Commission v Italy* [1989] ECR 267 (para 22).
13   See further below in connection with the requirement of urgency (pp 261 et seq.)

may be made to the ECJ for an interim measure in the form of the suspension of the operation of the decision appealed against.[14]

The object of suspension is to halt the proceedings, initiated in a member state under arts 44 and 92 of the ECSC Treaty, arts 187 and 192 of the EC Treaty or arts 159 and 164 of the Euratom Treaty, for the enforcement of the decision by the competent authority under national law. Enforcement, in this sense, is to be contrasted with 'execution' of the judgment, which may be stayed pursuant to: RP-ECJ 94(3) or, as the case may be, RP-CFI 122(3), where the judgment has been delivered in default of defence; or RP-ECJ 97(2) or, as the case may be, RP-CFI 123(2) in the context of third party proceedings. As in the case of applications to suspend the operation of a measure adopted by any other institution, the object of 'stay of execution' is to suspend the legal effects of the decision rather than the proceedings taken under national law to enforce it.[15] Where appropriate, the order suspending enforcement of the decision must set a date on which it will expire.[16] A decision rejecting an application for confidential treatment of a party's pleadings is not susceptible of 'enforcement' in the sense used in this context and cannot therefore be suspended.[17]

D Suspension of the enforcement of a measure adopted by another institution

As in the case of the previous type of interim relief, this remedy applies where a measure adopted by an institution is to be enforced by the authorities of a member state pursuant to art 92 of the ECSC Treaty, art 192 of the EC Treaty or art 164 of the Euratom Treaty. Only the Court has jurisdiction to suspend enforcement by the national authorities: national courts have jurisdiction only over complaints that enforcement is not being carried out correctly.[18] Where the operation of a measure has been suspended, of course, the question of suspending its enforcement never arises.

Although RP-ECJ 89 and RP-CFI 110, which also apply here, refer to 'any measure adopted by another institution', it is only those measures specifically envisaged by the articles of the Treaties just cited that are in question. The Euratom Treaty contains no express limitation on the type of measure that is enforceable but the ECSC and EC Treaties both refer to decisions (of the High Authority, Council or Commission respectively) 'which impose a pecuniary obligation'. These alone are said to be enforceable. The EEC Treaty goes even further and specifies decisions which impose the obligation 'on persons other than States'. The same rules govern the grant of this form of relief as the other types[19] and it is in general analogous to the suspension of the enforcement of a decision of the Court.

---

14 Case T-77/91R *Hochbaum v Commission* [1991] ECR II-1285 (paras 19–23); Cases C-372/90P, C-372/90P-R and C-22/91P *Samenwerkende Elektriciteits-produktiebedrijven NV v Commission* [1991] ECR I-2043, para 11 (the ECJ can entertain an application for the suspension of a decision of the CFI only in the context of an appeal to the ECJ against that decision).

15 In third party proceedings the rules to apply are those set out in RP-ECJ 83 to 88 or RP-CFI 104 to 109; and the conditions for obtaining 'stay of execution' under RP-ECJ 97(2) and RP-CFI 123(2) are the same as those for obtaining the suspension of the operation of a measure of an institution: see Cases 42 and 49/59 *Breedband NV v Société des Aciéries du Temple* [1962] ECR 167.

16 RP-ECJ 89; RP-CFI 110.

17 Cases C-133 and C-150/87 *Nashua Corpn v Council* [1990] ECR I-719, order of 19 May 1988 in Case C-150/87 (unreported).

18 EC Treaty, art 192; Euratom Treaty, art 164.

19 RP-ECJ 89; RP-CFI 110.

E   Effect of the grant of relief on unrepresented third parties

Interim relief is sought almost invariably by the applicant in an action against the defendant in the proceedings or a measure adopted by the defendant. In a few cases, however, the question has arisen of the Court's powers in relation to persons other than the defendant (such as an intervener or a third party). The problem has three aspects: Can the Court take into account the position of persons who are not parties to the proceedings? If it can, can the Court make an order directed at a party other than the defendant in the action? And can the Court make an order directed to a party to the proceedings which will have an adverse effect on other persons?[20]

In relation to the first aspect, as will be explained in greater detail below,[21] hitherto only member states and Community institutions (or at least the Commission) have been held to be entitled to rely on a threat to third parties in order to establish the existence of a threat of serious and irreparable damage.[22] In virtually all applications for interim relief, the party opposing the grant of relief is either a member state or a Community institution. In consequence, the ability of the Court to take the interests of unrepresented third parties into account appears at first sight to depend upon the identity of the party invoking them. However, the better view seems to be that, whereas the applicant for relief may rely only upon a threat of serious and irreparable damage to it or (in the case of a member state or the Commission) to the interests that it represents, the defendant may properly rely upon a threat either to itself (including the interests that it represents) or to third parties: the threat relied on by the applicant goes to its personal entitlement to relief; the threat to the defendant and to others goes to the propriety of the exercise by the Court of its powers in the circumstances of the case.

In relation to the second and third aspects, in Cases 160 and 161/73R *Miles Druce & Co Ltd v Commission*[23] the first application made for interim relief sought orders binding GKN, a person appearing in the proceedings as an intervener. The application was not granted for various reasons; but there was no suggestion that an order could not have been made against a person represented before the Court as an intervener. The problem whether or not the Court can impose an obligation on a person not party to the proceedings or present only as an intervener was avoided in the second application made in the *Miles Druce* case[24] because the party bound by the order (the Commission) did have power to control the activities of the third party (GKN). There is no doubt that, where this solution is possible, it will be preferred to an order directed at the third party; but it does not remove the problem entirely. In Case 133/87R *Nashua Corpn v Commission*[25] Judge Mackenzie Stuart refused to

---

20 It may of course be that an order granting interim relief has a beneficial effect on unrepresented third parties, such as where the Commission or a member state seeks relief in order to protect some legitimate interest from serious and irreparable damage pending judgment. The problem of the effect of an order on unrepresented third parties arises only where the effect in question is adverse to their interests.
21 See section III.C – *Serious and irreparable damage*, pp 268 et seq.
22 Eg Case 61/77R *Commission v Ireland* [1977] ECR 937. In Case 260/82R *NSO v Commission* [1982] ECR 4371, a threat to the members of the applicant organisation was relied on but, since a threat to them was, in effect, a threat to the applicant, such a threat is not in the same category as a threat to a third party stricto sensu. See also Cases 228 and 229/82R *Ford Werke AG and Ford of Europe Inc v Commission* [1982] ECR 3091 and Case 1/84R *Ilford SpA v Commission* [1984] ECR 423.
23 Above, note 8.
24 Above, note 9.
25 [1987] ECR 2883 (paras 7–8).

order, by way of interim measures, the suspension of a measure adopted by a Community institution that was not a party to the proceedings. In Cases T-24 and T-28/92R *Langnese-Iglo GmbH and Schöller Lebensmittel GmbH & Co KG v Commission*,[26] on the other hand, the relief granted limited the rights conferred on the interveners by the contested act without any question being raised about the appropriateness of ordering relief that would have an adverse effect on intervening parties.

When suspension of a measure is ordered, the application is usually made in the context of an action challenging the measure in question and the defendant is in consequence the author of it. It may be that, as a result of the suspension of the measure, third parties (eg member states) in the process of applying or taking steps to implement it must cease to do so[27] or may have to take other steps (which may need to be specified in the order granting relief).[28] In such circumstances, the third party has an interest in the case only in the sense that it is the person charged with applying or implementing the measure. In other respects, its position is unaffected by suspension and it does not have any interest that should be taken into account when deciding whether or not to grant relief. In consequence, even if the order granting suspension were to contain an order directed at a third party requiring the third party to implement the suspended provision (or the measure containing the suspended provision) in a particular way,[29] that would not be an invasion of the rights or interests of the third party which would constitute an objection in principle to the grant of relief. On the other hand, in Case 26/76R *Metro-SB-Grossmärkte GmbH & Co KG v Commission*[30] the applicant requested the suspension of the operation of a Commission decision that, inter alia, exempted under art 85(3) of the EEC Treaty a series of agreements which set up a distribution system and which would otherwise have been prohibited under art 85(1). Judge Mertens de Wilmars rejected the request on the ground that it fell outside the scope of an urgent interim measure intended to safeguard the applicant's interests because of its effect on third parties (that is, the parties to the series of agreements): suspension would have brought into question the lawfulness and enforceability of the arrangements made by them. The application also included a request that measures be taken to ensure that the applicant could obtain supplies from one of the third parties. This was rejected on other grounds but it seems to be implicit that, if the applicant can obtain relief elsewhere, whether from the Commission or national courts, the Court will not act. In the two *Simmenthal* cases, the *Grandes Sources* case and the *Vittel* case[31] the question again arose of the effect on third parties unrepresented before the Court but, like the first claim in the *Metro* case, the effect was indirect in the sense that the Court was asked to make an order directed to the other party which would have repercussions on the position of third parties. Nevertheless Judge Kutscher and, following him, Judge Cruz Vilaça said that, even if it

26 [1992] ECR II-1713 and 1839.
27 This was envisaged by Judge Donner in Case 21/59R *Italy v High Authority* [1960] ECR 351 and happened in the *Japanese Ball Bearing* cases (Cases 113/77R and 113/77R-I *NTN Toyo Bearing Co Ltd v Council*, Case 119/77R *Nippon Seiko KK v Council and Commission*, Case 121/77R *Nachi Fujikoshi Corpn v Council* [1977] ECR 1721, 1867 and 2107).
28 Case 23/86R *United Kingdom v European Parliament* [1986] ECR 1085, in particular para 23.
29 See *United Kingdom v European Parliament*, ibid.
30 [1976] ECR 1353.
31 Case 92/78R *Simmenthal SpA v Commission* [1978] ECR 1129; Case 243/78R *Simmenthal SpA v Commission* [1978] ECR 2391; *CCE de la SG des Grandes Sources v Commission* (above, note 10) paras 36-41; Case T-12/93R *Comité Central d'Entreprise de la Société Anonyme Vittel v Commission*, [1993] ECR II-449 (Order of 2 April 1993) and order of 6 July 1993.

were possible to grant as interim relief a remedy which would deprive unrepresented third parties of their rights, it would be justified only if the applicant were exposed to a situation threatening his very existence.

The position therefore seems to be that, in principle, the Court cannot grant relief where to do so would affect adversely the rights of unrepresented third parties unless, perhaps, the applicant for relief were faced with a threat to its very existence (and the adverse effect on the third parties concerned of granting relief is not as serious). A fortiori, the Court cannot make an order that is actually directed at an unrepresented third party. On the other hand, where the third party concerned is before the Court as an intervener, relief affecting the rights of the intervener may be granted and an order directed at the intervener may be made (without the applicant for relief needing to show a threat to its very existence). Where it is appropriate to grant relief affecting or potentially affecting the position of unrepresented third parties, an order may be made where the party to the proceedings to whom the order is addressed (whether a Community institution or a member state) has the power to control the activities of the unrepresented third parties. If no party to the proceedings has such a power over the unrepresented third parties, it is at present unclear whether or not an order can be made at all. On the other hand, an order may be directed at a third party whose rights or interests have not been adversely affected by the grant of relief where necessary in order to ensure that the consequences of the relief granted are properly understood.[32]

III   Conditions for the grant of relief

The orders granting or refusing interim relief are not always unanimous in their presentation of the conditions on which relief is to be granted. The principal reasons for this are that the Court's case law has been built up piecemeal on the basis of decisions which are usually made by a single judge (the President of the Court or a chamber); in addition, time is of the essence and it is rarely possible to do more than make a quick appreciation of the facts as they appear at the time. As a result, there are considerable variations in the terminology used and in the importance given in different cases to particular situations of fact. It is unwise to place too much reliance on the precise manner in which the judge has formulated the conditions for granting relief, above all in cases where relief was refused, because he is likely to have concentrated on one particular point which will decide the question rather than to have canvassed all the points. Even where the order is granted, it is to be expected that there will be variations as the case law has evolved over the years.

The only guidance given by the Treaties, the Statutes or the Rules of Procedure as to what are the conditions for making an order is to be found in RP-ECJ 83(2) and RP-CFI 104(2) which state that an application for relief must 'state the subject matter of the proceedings, the circumstances giving rise to urgency and the pleas of fact and law establishing a prima facie case for the interim measures applied for'. The essential characteristic of a measure of interim relief is that it preserves the position of the parties pending the final decision in the action in order to prevent the final decision from being rendered nugatory by the passage of time or a supervening event. Hence its temporary nature, which has a formal aspect (in that an order granting relief cannot in any event survive the delivery of final judgment) and a real aspect (in that an order granting relief cannot create a state of affairs that may outlast the order

---

32 Case 23/86R *United Kingdom v European Parliament* (above, note 28).

itself).[33] The present state of the case law was summed up by the the then President of the ECJ, Judge Mertens de Wilmars, in Cases 60 and 190/81R *International Business Machines Corpn v Commission*[34] as follows:

'It is clear from the consistent case law of the Court that measures of this nature cannot be considered unless the factual and legal grounds relied on to obtain them establish a prima facie case for granting them. In addition there must be urgency in the sense that it is necessary for the measures to be issued and to take effect before the decision of the Court on the substance of the case in order to avoid serious and irreversible damage to the party seeking them; finally they must be provisional in the sense that they do not prejudge the decision on the substance of the case'.

'Prejudge', in this context, means that they do not 'decide disputed points of law or of fact or neutralise in advance the consequences of the decision to be given subsequently on the substance of the action'.[35]

It is important to note that the mere fact that an action has been commenced before the Court does not mean that the applicant is entitled to anticipate the outcome of the proceedings and obtain all or part of the benefit of a final judgment in his favour, by means of an application for interim relief, as soon as proceedings have been commenced. That restraint applies just as much to the Court: it is obliged to allow the opposing party the opportunity to present written and oral argument as provided for in the Rules of Procedure and must properly consider the arguments presented by the parties and the evidence relating to the facts in issue before making its decision. The Rules of Procedure contain no provision for obtaining judgment by a summary or expedited procedure where the defendant has no defence;[36] and the possibility of applying for interim relief does not provide a substitute for such a procedure. In consequence, subject perhaps to the point about to be considered, the strength of the applicant's case against the defendant is not a factor that would in itself justify the grant of relief; nor is the fact that the applicant for relief is prepared to offer a security.[37] The possible exception to that general proposition emerges from *International Business Machines Corpn v Commission* where it was argued that, where relief is sought against an act which is manifestly unlawful, it is unnecessary to show that any other damage may be caused if relief is not granted: the gravity of the breach of the law is sufficient justification for making an order. This point was not decided by the President because he took the view that the acts in question did not 'appear to be measures lacking even an appearance of legality, and as such to require their operation to be suspended forthwith'.[38] The same claim was made in Case 46/87R *Hoechst AG v Commission*[39] where, again, it was not dismissed as a matter of principle but was

---

33 See RP-ECJ 86(4); RP-CFI 107(4).
34 [1981] ECR 1857 (para 4).
35 Case 206/81R *Alvarez v European Parliament* [1981] ECR 2187 at para 6 (Judge Mackenzie Stuart); Case 269/84R *Fabbro v Commission* [1984] ECR 4333 (para 3).
36 Judgment can be obtained where the defendant fails to lodge a defence within time: see RP-ECJ 94 and RP-CFI 122. That does not apply where a defence is lodged within time but it fails to disclose any or any seriously arguable defence. In that event, the applicant can only waive the right to lodge a reply and thus foreshorten the written procedure.
37 Case 240/84R *NTN Toyo Bearing Co Ltd v Council* [1984] ECR 4093 (para 6).
38 Above, note 34 (para 7). Note Case 293/82R *De Compte v European Parliament* [1982] ECR 4331 at para 12 (Judge Mackenzie Stuart): a Community institution cannot be prevented by an application for interim measures from carrying on with a procedure that will later be annulled because of a procedural defect.
39 [1987] ECR 1549 (paras 28–32).

rejected because the applicant did not succeed in showing that the contested act was manifestly unlawful. The point therefore remains open; but it seems clear from the *IBM* case that, for this argument to succeed, it must be shown beyond any shadow of doubt that the act in dispute is unlawful. If the opposing party can raise a doubt as to that fact, the argument fails and the applicant can succeed only if he shows that the usual criteria required for the grant of relief are satisfied. It should be observed that, in this context, the argument that the contested act is manifestly unlawful is not so much an argument that the defendant clearly has no defence to the action as an argument that the illegality is so serious that it constitutes in itself damage justifying the grant of relief and is such that there is no interest in maintaining the effectiveness of the contested act pending judgment.

The requirement that there be a threat of serious and irreparable damage provides the Court with the justification for departing from the general principle that the commencement of proceedings does not itself have suspensory effect or entitle the applicant to some immediate form of relief and with the justification for making an order before it is in a position to deliver final judgment.[40] In principle, once the party seeking relief has shown a prima facie case and the necessity for immediate action to avoid serious and irreversible damage, he is entitled to an order unless the opposing party can show that he, too, would suffer serious and irreversible damage, if relief were ordered. In order to oppose the grant of relief, it is not sufficient to prove that the opposing party would be adversely affected or inconvenienced by the grant of relief; it must be shown that the relief granted would itself render the Court's final judgment nugatory so far as the opposing party is concerned. The criteria determining the grant or refusal of relief appear to be the same for all cases and no criteria in addition to those outlined above appear to apply. However, the cases in which relief may be granted differ significantly from one another. Broadly speaking, they can be divided into the following categories:

(1)   cases where a legal or natural person (including a member state or Community institution) seeks relief in respect of an individual act threatening serious and irreparable damage;

(2)   cases where a member state or Community institution seeks relief against a general normative act threatening serious and irreparable damage;

(3)   cases where the Commission (or, theoretically, a member state) seeks relief against an act (or omission) of a member state threatening serious and irreparable damage.

In the first two categories, the contested act, being an act of a Community institution, benefits from a presumption as to its validity.[41] That presumption is not in itself a bar to the grant of interim relief.[42] The question is whether or not that presumption (which can also be taken to express an interest, on the part of the Community or the Community institution that adopted the contested act, in its continued application unless and until it is found to be invalid by a competent court) raises an additional obstacle to the grant of relief that may not apply in the third category of cases, even where a member state may be

---

40   As noted above, the fact that the applicant for relief is prepared and able to compensate the defendant for the consequences of obtaining the relief sought by providing a security is insufficient justification: *NTN Toyo Bearing Co Ltd v Council* (above, note 37).

41   Eg Case 101/78 *Granaria BV v Hoofdproduktschap voor Akkerbouwprodukten* [1979] ECR 623 (para 4).

42   Cf Case C-213/89 *R v Secretary of State for Transport, ex p Factortame Ltd (No 2)* [1990] ECR I-2433 at 2458 (Advocate General Tesauro).

said to have a comparable interest in the application of its legislative or other acts pending a finding by a competent court that those acts are invalid by reason of a conflict with a provision of Community law. As between the first and second categories of cases, the question is whether or not the particular or, as the case may be, the general nature of the contested act makes any (and, if so, what) difference to the assessment of the interest in its continued application.

At first sight, the facts that the criteria applied by the Court when deciding whether or not to grant interim relief are applied in all cases without exception and that they are particularly difficult for an applicant for relief to satisfy lead to the conclusion that those criteria, when satisfied, override any interest of whatever nature opposing the grant of relief: in short, however great the interest of the Community or a Community institution or a member state in the continued application of the contested act, it cannot be more important than the interest of the Community in ensuring that judgments of the Court are effective, which is an essential guarantee of respect for the rule of law in the Community.[43] However, in some cases reference has been made to a 'balance of interests' or 'balance of convenience' and in other cases the usual criteria applied by the Court have been construed in a more strict or more lax way. Although the case law does not as yet demonstrate a consistent and formalised division of cases into different categories so far as the application of the criteria for the grant of relief is concerned, there are traces of the emergence of such a division which it is as well to bear in mind when examining the cases.

The question of manifest illegality aside, the conditions for granting interim relief can be considered to fall under the following headings:

(1) prima facie case;
(2) urgency;
(3) serious and irreparable or irreversible damage; and
(4) the role of the balance of convenience or balance of interests.

A   Prima facie case

The requirement of a prima facie case can be understood in various ways. At one level it refers to the degree of examination that the Court can give to an application: the proceedings are summary and subject to the pressure of time; they are not suitable for painstaking analysis. Thus, in Case T-29/92R *Vereniging van Samenwerkende Prijsregelende Organisaties in de Bouwnijverheid v Commission*,[44] Judge Cruz Vilaça stated that a detailed analysis of the issues in the case was impossible all the more so because an applicant is limited to referring to the pleas of fact and law relied on by him in the action and to asserting that it cannot reasonably be asserted that the action is without foundation; the judge hearing the application for relief must consider the applicant's arguments to see if they put in doubt the opposing party's case. Therefore, a prima facie case for the grant of relief does not mean that the applicant's case must be clear and obvious;[45] it means that the application for relief must not be manifestly

---

43 The only exception appears to be the case where, although the applicant for relief has satisfied the criteria for the grant of relief, the making of the order would inflict serious and irreparable damage on the other party to the proceedings (or an unrepresented third party); but in such circumstances the relief sought could not be *interim* relief in the true sense of that term because it would have permanent effects. That being so, the Court would not in any event have jurisdiction to make the order.
44 [1992] ECR II-2161, at para 34.
45 Cf Case T-44/90 *La Cinq SA v Commission* [1992] ECR II-1 (paras 60–62).

unfounded.[46] It is occasionally said that there must at least be 'fumus boni iuris', on the ground, no doubt, that there is no smoke without fire. The degree of certainty required when a final decision is made in the case is not required at the interim relief stage.[47] It does not follow that there is some limit to the matters which the judge hearing the application can properly look at before deciding whether or not a prima facie case has been shown: for example, the judge is not prevented from examining in detail the application commencing proceedings and the evidence adduced in support of it, if he has the time to do so.

At another level, the requirement of a prima facie case refers to the case that the applicant must present. That falls into two parts: the case to which the application for relief relates (that is, the action); and the case for the grant of relief. In principle, the applicant must have a prima facie case both as to admissibility and as to substance in relation both to the action and to the application for relief: the 'fumus boni iuris' presupposes that the applicant for relief has a good case so far as the action is concerned just as much as a good case for the grant of relief before judgment. In consequence, the applicant must show that he has a prima facie case in the action, not just the proceedings for interim relief taken by themselves.[48] In most cases, the consideration expressed to be given to the requirement of a prima facie case in fact focuses on the action; the prima facie case for the grant of relief is usually examined by reference to the requirements of urgency, serious and irreversible (or irreparable) damage and, where appropriate, the balance of convenience or balance of interests (save in those cases where the admissibility of the application for relief is also an issue). In this section, therefore, the requirement of a prima facie case will be considered first in relation to the admissibility of the application for relief and then in relation to the admissibility and substance of the action. The remaining aspects of the prima facie case will be dealt with separately in relation to the requirements of urgency, serious and irreparable damage and the balance of convenience or of interests.

The applicant will naturally be unable to show a prima facie case if the application for interim relief is itself inadmissible. There are various reasons why that may be so. For example: an application may in general be inadmissible if it fails to state the circumstances giving rise to urgency or the factual or legal grounds capable of justifying the grant of the relief sought;[49] an application for the suspension of the operation of a measure adopted by an institution may be inadmissible if the measure is not contested in the action[50] or if the measure has already taken effect;[51] the application may also be inadmissible if its subject

46 Cases 31 and 53/77R *Commission v United Kingdom* [1977] ECR 921 (Advocate General Mayras).

47 Cf Case T-23/90 *Automobiles Peugeot SA v Commission* [1991] ECR II-653 (para 61), a case concerning the analogous situation of interim relief granted by the Commission.

48 Case 809/79R *Pardini SpA v Commission* [1980] ECR 139; Case 173/82R *Castille v Commission* [1982] ECR 4047.

49 Case 2/65R *Ferriera Ernesto Preo e Figli v High Authority* [1966] ECR 231; *NTN Toyo Bearing Co Ltd v Council* (above, note 37) para 7; Case 90/87R *CW v Court of Auditors* [1987] ECR 1801 (para 8); Case 378/87R *Top Hit Holzvertrieb GmbH v Commission* [1988] ECR 161 (paras 19–20).

50 Case 2/59R *Niederrheinische Hütte AG v High Authority* [1960] ECR 162 (the order refers to an 'earlier concomitant action', the phraseology used in RP-ECJ 63, as then worded, which alludes to the action in the context of which the application for relief is made); *Scharf v Commission* (above, note 3) para 5; Cases C-66/91 and C-66/91R *Emerald Meats Ltd v Commission* [1991] ECR I-1143 (para 33).

51 Case 67/63R *SOREMA v High Authority* [1964] ECR 174; Cases 3–18, 25, 26/58 *Erzbergbau v High Authority* [1960] ECR 220.

matter does not relate to an (admissible) claim made in the action[52] or if the action has been or is to be dismissed as inadmissible[53] (an aspect to be considered in more detail below); an application may be rejected as inadmissible because it is a misuse of procedure, such as where the matter should first have been taken up with the other party because there was a separate, and more appropriate, procedure for dealing with the situation;[54] it may be dismissed as inadmissible for lack of interest, such as where the relief sought cannot assist the applicant;[55] or where the relief sought falls outside the jurisdiction of the Court to grant before final judgment or at all.[56] The application may also become devoid of purpose where the circumstances that might otherwise have justified the grant of relief cease to apply before the decision on the application is made;[57] but in that event no decision would be made on the application and it would not be held to be inadmissible.

Passing now to consideration of the action, although it is well established that, in considering whether or not to grant interim relief,[58] the chances of success of the action cannot be ignored,[59] some cases show a certain disinclination to consider the foundation of the action, particularly where it is alleged to be inadmissible.[60] The reason for this seems to be the desire to keep separate and distinct the functions of the judge and the Court: it is for the Court to decide on the action and for the judge to decide on the application for interim relief. Nevertheless, the judge may have to adopt a view as to the merits or admissibility of the action. In the nature of things that view cannot prejudice the Court's decision in the action,[61] even when the application for interim relief is heard by the Court itself and not a judge,[62] because the decision on the application is generally made before the close of the written procedure and in

---

52 Case 186/80R *Suss v Commission* [1980] ECR 3501; Case 18/65R *Gutmann v Euratom Commission* [1966] ECR 135; Case 88/76R *Société pour l'Exportation des Sucres v Commission* [1976] ECR 1585; Case T-10/91R *Bodson v European Parliament* [1991] ECR II-133 (in particular paras 17–18); Case C-257/93R *van Parijs v Council and Commission*, 6 July 1993; Case C-282/93R *Comafrica SpA v Council and Commission*, 6 July 1993.

53 Case C-68/90R *Blot and Front National v European Parliament* [1990] ECR I-2177; *Emerald Meats Ltd v Commission* (above, note 50) para 33; Case C-295/92R *Landbouwschap v Commission* [1992] ECR I-5069; Case C-276/93R *Chiquita Banana Co BV v Council*, 6 July 1993; Case C-287/93R *Simba SpA v Council*, 6 July 1993; Case C-288/93R *Comaco Srl v Council*, 6 July 1993; Case C-64/93R *Donatab Srl v Commission*, 9 July 1993. For an example of the close connection between the admissibility of the action and the admissibility of the application for relief, see *Ilford v Commission* (above, note 22) paras 5–7.

54 *Bodson v European Parliament* (above, note 52) paras 18–19.

55 Eg Case 107/89R *Calurla-Boch v European Parliament* [1989] ECR 1357 (the object of the relief sought was to allow the selection board to take account of the applicant's certificates but it was common ground that the applicant had succeeded at that stage of the competition and failed only at the later, oral, stage); Case C-206/89R *S v Commission* [1989] ECR 2841 (the relief sought was suspension of the operation of a negative administrative decision which could not have the positive consequences that the applicant sought to achieve); Case C-106/90R *Emerald Meats Ltd v Commission* [1990] ECR I-3377 (paras 22–27).

56 Eg Case 321/88R *Sparr v Commission* [1988] ECR 6405 (Judge Grevisse); Case T-131/89R *Cosimex GmbH v Commission* [1990] ECR II-1 at paras 12–14 (Judge Cruz Vilaça); *Hochbaum v Commission* (above, note 14) paras 19–23.

57 Cases T-10/92R to T-12/92R and T-14/92R to T-15/92R *SA Cimenteries CBR v Commission* [1992] ECR II-1571 (para 28).

58 Sc suspension of the operation of a measure adopted by an institution.

59 Case 50/69R *Germany v Commission* [1969] ECR 449 (Advocate General Gand); *CMC v Commission* (above, note 5) para 63.

60 See, for example, Case 18/57 *Nold KG v High Authority* [1957–1958] ECR 121; Case 28/65R *Fonzi v Euratom Commission* [1966] ECR 508; Case 109/75R *National Carbonising Co v Commission* [1975] ECR 1193.

61 Case 19/78R *Authié v Commission* [1978] ECR 679.

62 Case 42/82R *Commission v France* [1982] ECR 841 at 864 (Advocate General Sir Gordon Slynn).

the absence of a comprehensive examination of the facts. The summary nature of the proceedings precludes a decision based on a profound and painstaking analysis of the facts and of the relevant law. There is no contradiction, therefore, if the Court should make an order on the basis of a particular finding of fact or law, but subsequently reject that finding in the final judgment in the light of further argument and after a more prolonged period of reflection.[63] Although the preliminary view of the action taken by the judge at the interim relief stage does not and cannot prejudge the final decision to be made in the action, some judges have nonetheless demonstrated extreme reluctance to be drawn into expressing an opinion on the merits of the action.[64] That approach is understandable where the judge's view of the action is unfavourable to the applicant since, if the relief sought were refused for that reason and the Court took another view in the judgment, the applicant might then have been mistakenly deprived of all or part of the benefit of the judgment. Probably for that reason Judge Donner once took the view that the foundation of the action comes into question only when it has been established that the circumstances justify grant of relief.[65] Subsequent practice has been to the contrary.[66] Nonetheless, even though the assessment of the action is not supposed to involve a detailed examination of the contentions raised by the applicant in the action, those contentions should be developed sufficiently clearly; otherwise, they may be left out of account when deciding whether or not there is a prima facie case.[67] As long as the applicant has demonstrated that he has a prima facie case in respect of the admissibility and the merits even of only a part of the action, the requirement of a prima facie case has been satisfied pro tanto and the applicant's failure to establish a prima facie case in respect of another part of the action is irrelevant[68] unless the claim for interim relief is dependent upon there being a prima facie case for that other part.

As far as the admissibility of the action is concerned, it has been said that it is not for the judge to consider it[69] and that he cannot in any event decide it;[70] the alleged inadmissibility of the action, it has been said, is not, per se, a ground for the inadmissibility of the application for interim relief[71] and, when considering the latter, the judge must not, in any event, prejudice questions relating to the former.[72] There are indications to the contrary: for example, in *Firma Karl Könecke v Commission*[73] Judge Lecourt held that, where the grant of interim measures may hinder the application of a series of regulations, the applicant may lie under a particularly heavy duty to show that his action is admissible. In *Camera Care v Commission*[74] Advocate General Warner said that an application for interim relief may be rejected if the action is clearly inadmissible. In Case 231/86R *Breda-Geomineraria v Commission*[75] an application for relief was

---

63 Cf Case 23/86R *United Kingdom v European Parliament* (above, note 28) para 37.
64 Eg Case 25/85R *Nuovo Campsider v Commission* [1985] ECR 751 (para 24); Cases 67, 68 and 70/85R *Kwekerij Gebroeders van der Kooy BV v Commission* [1985] ECR 1315 (para 43); Case 62/86R *AKZO Chemie BV v Commission* [1986] ECR 1503 (paras 14–18).
65 Case 31/59 *Acciaieria e Tubificio di Brescia v High Authority* [1960] ECR 98.
66 See, for example, Case 61/77R *Commission v Ireland* (above, note 22); Case 42/82R *Commission v France* (above, note 62); Case T-13/91R *Harrison v Commission* [1991] ECR II-179.
67 Case 152/88R *Sofrimport Sarl v Commission* [1988] ECR 2931 (para 12).
68 Case 146/85R *Diezler v Economic and Social Committee* [1985] ECR 1805 (paras 4 and 12).
69 *Fonzi v Euratom Commission* (above, note 60).
70 *Suss v Commission* (above, note 52).
71 Ibid.
72 Case 75/72R *Perinciolo v Council* [1972] ECR 1201.
73 [1975] ECR 637.
74 [1980] ECR 119 at 133.
75 Above, note 2 (para 17).

dismissed because the action was premature and inadmissible; in Case 50/84R *Bensider v Commission*[76] it was held that an application for relief should be rejected if the action has been brought out of time.

It is apparent from the nature of the proceedings, however, that, while the judge may have to decide on the admissibility of the application for interim relief, he has no power to make a decision on the admissibility of the action because that is not in issue before him; on the other hand, the admissibility of the action may, nevertheless, be an element to be taken into account when considering the question whether the applicant has shown a prima facie case for the grant of interim relief.[77] The view which the judge may form of the admissibility of the action does not, and cannot, amount to a decision on that issue which binds the parties because the only issue with which he is seised is the question whether or not to grant interim relief.[78] Even so, the tendency in the cases is for the judges to entertain serious reservations about any consideration of the admissibility of the action.[79] The general rule is that the admissibility of the action should not be considered at all at the interim relief stage. The only exception to that rule appears to be the situation where the action is said to be manifestly inadmissible or, to put it another way, where there is nothing to support any claim that it is admissible.[80] Even if the admissibility of the action is in doubt, the requirement of a prima facie case has been satisfied (at least to that extent) where the question of the inadmissibility of the action requires further consideration and cannot be said to be manifest[81] or where 'it cannot be stated categorically' that the action will not be held admissible.[82] The prima facie admissibility of the action may be established by reference to an assertion of fact made by the defendant even if it is unsupported by evidence.[83]

In relation to the substance of the case, if the action is manifestly without foundation[84] or there is no substantial basis for the claims made in it[85] or the

76 [1984] ECR 2247 (para 24).

77 Eg *CMC v Commission* (above, note 5) para 37.

78 The judge cannot even rule on the lawfulness of a regulation challenged in the proceedings: see Case 92/78R *Simmenthal SpA v Commission* (above, note 31).

79 Eg Case 23/86R *United Kingdom v European Parliament* (above, note 28) para 12; Case 351/85R *Fabrique de Fer de Charleroi v Commission* [1986] ECR 1307 (para 13); Case 360/85R *Dillinger Hüttenwerke AG v Commission* [1986] ECR 1319 (para 13); *Pfizer International Inc v Commission* (above, note 6) para 15.

80 Eg *Diezler v Economic and Social Committee* (above, note 68) para 3; Case 221/86R *Group of the European Right and National Front Party v European Parliament* [1986] ECR 2969 (para 19); Case 82/87R *Autexpo SpA v Commission* [1987] ECR 2131 (para 15); Case 376/87R *Distrivet SA v Council* [1988] ECR 209 (para 21); Case 160/88R *Fédération Européenne de la Santé Animale v Council* [1988] ECR 4121 (paras 22–30); Case C-117/91R *Bosman v Commission* [1991] ECR I-3353 (paras 7–9); *SA Cimenteries CBR v Commission* (above, note 57) paras 44–48; the *Grandes Sources* case (above, note 31) para 31. In Case 23/87R *Aldinger v European Parliament* [1987] ECR 2841 (para 8) and Case 209/87R *Association des Aciéries Européennes Indépendants (EISA) v Commission* [1987] ECR 3453 (para 10), Judge Schockweiler considered that the raising of a 'serious ground of inadmissibility' was sufficient to put the admissibility of the action in issue: see also Case 214/87R *Cockerill Sambre v Commission* [1987] ECR 3463 and Case 223/87R *Associazione Industrie Siderurgiche Italiane (ASSIDER) v Commission* [1987] ECR 3473.

81 Eg the *Group of the European Right* case, ibid; *EISA v Commission*, ibid paras 10–11; *Distrivet SA v Commission*, ibid paras 21–26; *SA Cimenteries CBR v Commission*, ibid paras 52–54; the *Grandes Sources* case ibid paras 31–35; the *Vittel* case (above, note 31, order of 2 April 1993) paras 20–26. Thus, even the 'serious doubts' entertained by Judge Mackenzie Stuart about the admissibility of the action in Case 117/86R *Union de Federaciones Agrarias de España (UFADE) v Council and Commission* [1986] ECR 2483 (para 31) and in *Co-Frutta SARL v Commission* (above, note 1) para 23 did not in themselves justify the rejection of the application.

82 *Aldinger v European Parliament* (above, note 80) para 9 (Judge Schockweiler).

83 *Autexpo SpA v Commission* (above, note 80) paras 18–19.

84 *Johnson and Firth Brown v Commission* (above, note 10); Case 260/85R *Tokyo Electric Co Ltd v Council* [1985] ECR 3467 (para 15).

85 Case 731/79R *B v European Parliament* [1979] ECR 3629.

applicant has failed to produce sufficient evidence or argument to establish a prima facie case,[86] the application for interim relief can and should be dismissed. Judge Donner used to take the view that there had to be 'a strong presumption' that the action was well founded or at least that it should be prima facie clearly well founded;[87] and, after considering the case law in a subsequent case, Advocate General Gand came to the similar conclusion that relief would be granted if the applicant's case 'clearly appears well founded or if there is at least a strong presumption that it is well founded'.[88] In one case, Judge Sørensen said that it had to be possible to anticipate the Court's decision;[89] in another, Judge Mackenzie Stuart said that the applicant's arguments 'cannot be regarded as so clear that they can be accepted by the Court without serious risk of prejudging the arguments which must be presented on the substance of the case'.[90] Such cases appear to be the exceptions. In other cases it has been said that the applicant's case against the defendant does not need to be 'clear and flagrant'.[91] It is sufficient if there is a 'certain degree of probability' that the action is well founded;[92] if it is 'arguable';[93] 'prima facie valid';[94] 'prima facie sound';[95] 'based on serious considerations such as to make the legality of [the measures whose annulment was sought] seem doubtful to say the least';[96] gives rise to 'serious dispute', 'cannot be rejected without further consideration';[97] is based on 'cogent arguments',[98] 'pertinent arguments'[99] or 'relevant arguments'[1] which it will be necessary to examine in greater detail or more thoroughly in the main action; if 'it cannot be ruled out' that the contested act may be declared void[2] or it is 'impossible to

---

86 Case 57/86R *Greece v Commission* [1986] ECR 1497 (para 11); Case 108/88R *Jaenicke Cendoya v Commission* [1988] ECR 2585 (para 21).

87 See Cases 43, 44 and 48/59 *von Lachmüller v Commission* [1960] ECR 489; Case 68/63R *Luhleich v Euratom Commission* [1965] ECR 618 and Cases 19 and 65/63A *Prakash v Euratom Commission* [1965] ECR 576 (allowances for needs pending judgment). He seemed, however, to have taken a less strict view in Case 25/62R II *Plaumann & Co v Commission* [1963] ECR 126. See also Case 346/82R *Favre v Commission* [1983] ECR 199.

88 Case 50/69R *Germany v Commission* (above, note 59) at 455.

89 Case 4/78R *Salerno v Commission* [1978] ECR 1.

90 *Kwekerij Gebroeders van der Kooy BV v Commission* (above, note 64) para 43.

91 *La Cinq SA v Commission* (above, note 45) paras 60–62 (dealing with the analogous requirement applied by the Commission when deciding whether or not to exercise its powers to grant interim relief in competition cases).

92 Case 61/77R *Commission v Ireland* (above, note 22) (Advocate General Reischl); *CMC v Commission* (above, note 5) at para 37.

93 *Camera Care Ltd v Commission* (above, note 74) at 134 (Advocate General Warner).

94 Cases 24 and 97/80R *Commission v France* [1980] ECR 1319 at 1341 (Advocate General Capotorti).

95 Case 42/82R *Commission v France* (above, note 62) at 864 (Advocate General Sir Gordon Slynn).

96 Case 232/81R *Agricola Commerciale Olio Srl v Commission* [1981] ECR 2193 (Judge Mertens de Wilmars); *Fabbro v Commission* (above, note 35) para 6; *Scharf v Commission* (above, note 3) para 8 (Judge Kakouris). Cf Case 92/88R *Associazione Industrie Siderurgiche Italiane (ASSIDER) v Commission* [1988] ECR 2425 (para 14).

97 *Ford Werke AG and Ford of Europe Inc v Commission* (above, note 22) para 8 (Judge Mertens de Wilmars); Case 120/83R *Raznoimport v Commission* [1983] ECR 2573.

98 Case 23/86R *United Kingdom v European Parliament* (above, note 28) para 37.

99 Judge Mackenzie Stuart in: Case 250/85R *Brother Industries Ltd v Council* [1985] ECR 3459 (para 14); Case 273/85R *Silver Seiko Ltd v Council* [1985] ECR 3475 (para 15); Case 297/85R *Towa Sankiden Corpn v Council* [1985] ECR 3483 (para 13); Cases 277 and 300/85R *Canon Inc v Council* [1985] ECR 3491 (para 14); *Fabrique de Fer de Charleroi v Commission* (above, note 79) para 25; *Dillinger Hüttenwerke AG v Commission* (above, note 79) para 26.

1 Case 221/86R *Group of the European Right v European Parliament* [1986] ECR 2969, para 28 (Judge Mackenzie Stuart).

2 Case 160/84R *Oryzomyli Kavallas OEE v Commission* [1984] ECR 3217, para 6 (Judge Mackenzie Stuart).

predict the outcome' and the possibility that the Court may uphold the applicant cannot be excluded;[3] if there is a 'real dispute' supported by 'sound arguments';[4] if the action raises 'delicate and complex problems'[5] or 'serious problems';[6] is 'not without foundation' or 'not prima facie without foundation';[7] 'does not appear to be devoid of all foundation',[8] is 'not manifestly unfounded' or 'without foundation'[9] or is 'not, at first sight, altogether without foundation';[10] is supported by 'weighty factors';[11] reveals 'factors which are prima facie capable of calling into question the lawfulness' of the contested act';[12] raises questions of principle on which the Court has not yet had occasion to rule;[13] or turns on disputed questions of fact that cannot be determined at the interim relief stage without prejudging the action.[14] It is also relevant if the defendant's case is prima facie erroneous[15] or gives rise to serious doubts;[16] the mere fact that the issues are hotly disputed may make it impossible to say that the applicant's case lacks any foundation.[17]

In Case 278/84R *Germany v Commission*[18] the test apparently adopted by Judge Mackenzie Stuart was that the applicant's most important submission gave rise to an interpretation of the relevant Community legislation that 'cannot be regarded as so obvious that the Court can accept it without a serious risk of prejudging the arguments to be presented on the substance of the case'. In the context of the decision, that does not seem to mean that the applicant is obliged to produce a case that is 'obvious' in that sense: the order seems to mean that the applicant's case fell short of being so strong that it could be treated as evident without any risk of the Court coming to a different view in its final judgment; but it is implicit that, even so, the applicant's case

---

3 Case 90/87R *CW v Court of Auditors* [1987] ECR 1801, para 11 (Judge Kakouris).
4 Case 141/84R *De Compte v European Parliament* [1984] ECR 2575, para 11 (Judge Galmot).
5 Case 78/83R *Usinor v Commission* [1983] ECR 2183 at para 8 (Judge Mertens de Wilmars); Cases 76, 77 and 91/89R *Radio Telefis Eireann v Commission* [1989] ECR 1141, para 14 (Judge Koopmans); Case C-280/93R *Germany v Council* [1993] ECR I-3667, para 21 (the ECJ); Case C-296/93R *France v Commission*, 16 July 1993; Case C-307/93R *Ireland v Commission*, 16 July 1993.
6 Case T-23/90R *Automobiles Peugeot SA and Peugeot SA v Commission* [1990] ECR II-195, para 22 (Judge Cruz Vilaça).
7 Case 246/89R *Commission v United Kingdom* [1989] ECR 3125, para 33 (Judge Due); Case C-195/90R *Commission v Germany* [1990] ECR I-2715, para 19 (Judge Due); Case C-272/91R *Commission v Italy* [1992] ECR I-457, para 24 (Judge Due).
8 Case 56/89R *Publishers' Association v Commission* [1989] ECR 1693, para 31 (Judge Due).
9 Case 270/84R *Licata v Economic and Social Committee* [1984] ECR 4119 (para 8); Case 146/85R *Diezler v Economic and Social Committee* [1985] ECR 1805, para 12 (Judge Kakouris); Case T-39/90R *Samenwerkende Elektriciteits-produktiebedrijven NV v Commission* [1990] ECR II-629, para 23, Case T-45/90R *Speybrouck v European Parliament* [1990] ECR II-705, para 21 and Cases T-7/93R and T-9/93R *Langnese-Iglo GmbH v Commission* [1993] ECR II-131, para 39 (all Judge Cruz Vilaça).
10 Case 23/87R *Aldinger v European Parliament* [1987] ECR 2841, para 14 and Case 24/87R *Virgili v European Parliament* [1987] ECR 2847, para 14 (both Judge Schockweiler).
11 Case C-195/90R *Commission v Germany* (above, note 7) paras 27 and 30 (per curiam).
12 *Speybrouck v European Parliament* (above, note 9) para 20 (Judge Cruz Vilaça).
13 Case C-345/90P-R *European Parliament v Hanning* [1991] ECR I-231 (paras 29–30).
14 Case 154/85R *Commission v Italy* [1985] ECR 1753 (para 18); Case 293/85R *Commission v Belgium* [1985] ECR 3521 (para 18); Case 62/86R *AKZO Chemie BV v Commission* [1986] ECR 1503 (para 18).
15 Case 351/85R *Fabrique de Fer de Charleroi v Commission* [1986] ECR 1307 (para 22); Case 360/85R *Dillinger Hüttenwerke AG v Commission* [1986] ECR 1319 (para 23).
16 Case 1/84R *Ilford v Commission* [1984] ECR 423, paras 11, 14–18 and 20 (Judge Mertens de Wilmars); Case T-21/93R *Peixoto v Commission* [1993] ECR II-463, para 24 (Judge Cruz Vilaça).
17 Cases T-24 and T-28/92R *Langnese-Iglo GmbH and Schöller Lebensmittel GmbH & Co KG v Commission* [1992] ECR II-1839 (para 27).
18 [1984] ECR 4341 (para 17).

was sufficiently strong for the purposes of the interim relief proceedings. In some instances, the requirement of a prima facie case has been regarded as such a low threshold test that, in effect, the burden lies on the defendant to demonstrate that the applicant has no case. For example, in Case 76/88R *La Terza v Court of Justice*,[19] an action for the annulment of a decision refusing to allow the applicant to work on a part-time basis after she had been allowed to do so for several years, Judge Due considered that it was necessary for the defendant to show the existence of new circumstances necessitating immediate termination of part-time working and said that the reasons set out in the contested act were so scant and stereotyped as to justify in themselves the commencement of proceedings. A different situation arises where the defendant fails to reply to the applicant's contentions regarding the action when responding to the application for interim relief. It has been said that such behaviour makes it impossible for the judge hearing the application to come to a conclusion on the relevance, accuracy and nature of the contested facts; but that means neither that the defendant must be taken to admit the applicant's assertions nor that the applicant's claim cannot be dealt with; it simply means that the judge must limit himself to taking note of those factors showing that there is a real dispute between the parties and that the applicant's case is supported by sound arguments.[20]

Despite the variation in mode of expression, the meaning of the requirement of a prima facie case seems clear; the judge does not have to be convinced that the applicant will win the action but he must be convinced that it is possible that the applicant may do so.[21] Since the material available to him when coming to a conclusion on this point is incomplete, the judge does not have to be so scrupulous when searching for evidence as he would have to be when arriving at a final view of the question: the fact that the evidence is incomplete or that the opposing party shows that there is a doubt as to the inferences that are to be drawn from it does not justify a finding that the applicant has no case.[22] On the other hand, if the applicant's case imposes on him a particularly heavy burden of proof or persuasion, such as where the applicant maintains that the contested act is non-existent, it may be easier to say that a prima facie case has not been shown; and, in such circumstances, the applicant may have to advance 'serious and concrete indications' supporting his contentions in order to meet the requirement of a prima facie case.[23] The relative weakness of

---

19 [1988] ECR 1741 (paras 19–21).

20 *De Compte v European Parliament* (above, note 4) paras 9–11 (Judge Galmot).

21 Cf the phraseology used to justify the opposite conclusion: 'manifestly without foundation' in Case 3/75R *Johnson and Firth Brown Ltd v Commission* [1975] ECR 1; 'clearly inadmissible' in Case 792/79R *Camera Care Ltd v Commission* [1980] ECR 119 (Advocate General Warner); 'prima facie serious problems' in Case 114/83R *SICA and SIPEFEL v Commission* [1983] ECR 2315, para 5 (Judge Mertens de Wilmars); 'prima facie unfounded' in Case 175/86R *RM v Council* [1986] ECR 2511, para 27 (Judge Bahlmann); 'devoid of all relevance' in Case 304/86R *Enital SpA v Council and Commission* [1987] ECR 267, para 15 (Judge Mackenzie Stuart). In contrast, in Case 293/84R *Sorani v Commission* [1985] ECR 251 (para 6), Judge Bosco considered that the applicant's submissions 'do not, at first sight, seem particularly solid' and, in Case 48/86R *Cauet and Joliet v Commission* [1986] ECR 1237 (paras 27–30), Judge Mackenzie Stuart concluded that the applicant had not shown a prima facie case because 'on a first reading' of the relevant legislation 'it appears reasonable to conclude' that the defendant was right.

22 Cf Case 18/57 *Nold KG v High Authority* [1957–58] ECR 121 at 127 (Advocate General Roemer) (in German law full proof is not required in similar proceedings). But see Case 20/81R *Arbed SA v Commission* [1981] ECR 721 at paras 18 and 21. Initially the burden lies on the applicant to show that he has an arguable case.

23 Case T-29/92R *Vereniging van Samenwerkende Prijsregelende Organisaties in de Bouwnijverheid v Commission* [1992] ECR II-2161 (para 33).

the applicant's case may have to be weighed against the seriousness of the consequences of withholding relief before concluding that there is or is not a prima facie case.[24]

Apart from the admissibility of the application for relief and the chances of success for the action, an assessment of the case for relief made out by the applicant must also take account of the nature of the relief sought. If it is inappropriate in the light of the claims made in the action or is excessive, relief may be refused.[25] Some judges have suggested that a balance of convenience or balance of interests test is to be applied[26] and this is considered below.

B Urgency

Urgency is not determined by reference to the speed with which the applicant applies for relief but by the extent to which the applicant needs to obtain relief before judgment in order to avoid certain damage.[27] The applicant must show that, if the judge does not make the order, serious and irreparable damage will be caused before the Court can give judgment in the action (or, as it is sometimes more colourfully put, that the applicant cannot await the outcome of the proceedings without having personally to sustain damage that would result in serious and irreversible consequences for him).[28] If no urgency in this sense is proved, the application will be rejected.[29] More specifically, if the Court can give judgment in the action before the damage is likely to occur,[30] there is no necessity for an order to be made.[31] The time factor apart, the nature of the relief sought may also be relevant to the question of urgency: the relief sought should be of such a nature as to prevent the occurrence of the alleged damage before judgment is delivered.[32] There is no urgency justifying an order suspending the operation of a measure adopted by an institution if there is no reason to fear that it will be implemented or enforced or if it will have no practical effect.[33] It is sufficient to disprove urgency that the defendant

---

24 Ibid paras 37–38 (those paragraphs in the order are ambiguous in that they may in the alternative be construed as suggesting the application of a balancing test after the applicant has been found to have a prima facie case; but the explanation given in the text is believed to be the correct construction).

25 See Case 91/76R *De Lacroix v European Court of Justice* [1976] ECR 1563; Case 121/77R *Nachi Fujikoshi Corpn v Council* [1977] ECR 2107; Case 4/78R *Salerno v Commission* [1978] ECR 1; Case 19/78R *Authié v Commission* [1978] ECR 679; Case 92/78R *Simmenthal SpA v Commission* [1978] ECR 1129; Case 243/78R *Simmenthal SpA v Commission* [1978] ECR 2391; Case 74/85R *Remy v Commission* [1985] ECR 1185 (paras 9–10).

26 See, for example, Judge Sørensen in the *Salerno* and *Authié* cases and Judge Kutscher in the *Simmenthal* cases, ibid.

27 *Aldinger v European Parliament* (above, note 10) para 13; *Virgili v European Parliament* (above, note 10) para 13.

28 Case 809/79R *Pardini SpA v Commission* [1980] ECR 139; Cases 24 and 97/80R *Commission v France* [1980] ECR 1319 (Advocate General Capotorti); Case 20/81R *Arbed SA v Commission* (above, note 22); Case 142/87R *Belgium v Commission* [1987] ECR 2589 (para 23); Case 111/88R *Greece v Commission* [1988] ECR 2591 (para 15); Case C-225/91R *Matra SA v Commission* [1991] ECR I-5823 (para 19).

29 Case 2/65R *Ferriera Ernesto Preo e Figli v High Authority* [1966] ECR 231.

30 Sc before the decision, the suspension of whose operation has been claimed, takes effect or before the state aid causing the alleged distortion of competition would be paid.

31 Case 6/72R *Europemballage Corpn and Continental Can Corpn Inc v Commission* [1972] ECR 157; *Matra SA v Commission* (above, note 28) paras 24–25.

32 Case 246/89R *Commission v United Kingdom* (above, note 7) para 38; Case C-40/92R *Commission v United Kingdom* [1992] ECR I-3389 (para 31).

33 Case 2/59R *Niederrheinische Hütte A G v High Authority* [1960] ECR 162; Case 21/59R *Italy v High Authority* [1960] ECR 351; Case 60/63R *Acciaierie Ferriere Pietra Oddino v High Authority* [1965] ECR 27; Case 322/87R *Frank v Court of Auditors* [1987] ECR 4375 (para 19).

institution satisfies the applicant's concerns;[34] or gives an undertaking that it will not apply the measure or will apply it only in such a way as to remove the threat to the applicant;[35] or, where the threat to the applicant's position comes from a third party, if the third party gives an undertaking not to act.[36] In the same way, there is no urgency if the occurrence of the threat is contingent upon events or the behaviour of third parties and it is insufficiently certain that those events will occur or that the third parties in question will behave in the way feared.

In applications for the suspension of an act challenged before the Court, the Court will usually accept an undertaking (if made) from the author of the measure that it will not be applied and will then dismiss the application.[37] Whereas, in the case of suspension, the undertaking must ordinarily be given by the author of the act in question (that is, the defendant), in the case of an application for interim measures an appropriate undertaking may be given by any party to the proceedings (including an intervener) who is in a position to ensure that the applicant for relief will not be threatened with serious and irreparable damage pending judgment.[38] Undertakings made by or on behalf of a Community institution should be made (and, if made, relied on) only if given by the agent of the institution concerned (otherwise, the undertaking will have been given by a person who may not have authority to give it, in which case it might quite properly be repudiated by the institution concerned). When made by the institution's agent, formal note is to be taken of the undertaking.[39] It would appear that, when an undertaking is given in that way, it cannot be repudiated by the hierarchical superior of the institution's agent but can properly be withdrawn only by the institution itself or an official duly authorised to do so by that institution; until properly withdrawn, the undertaking must therefore be complied with by the officials of the institution concerned, at whatever level, as if it were (as in principle it is) a direct instruction emanating from the persons comprising the institution (such as the College of Commissioners, in the case of the Commission). Even when given by the institution's agent, however, such undertakings appear to have no legal

---

34 Eg Cases 82 and 83/85R *Eurasian Corpn Ltd v Commission* [1985] ECR 1191 (para 25).

35 *Acciaierie Ferriere Pietra Oddino v High Authority* (above, note 33); Case 31/79R *Société des Aciéries de Montereau v Commission* [1979] ECR 1077; Case 45/84R *EISA v Commission* [1984] ECR 1759 (paras 12–14).

36 Cases 160 and 161/73R *Miles Druce & Co Ltd v Commission* [1973] ECR 1049.

37 Eg Case 68/63R *Luhleich v Euratom Commission* [1965] ECR 618; *Acciaierie Ferriere Pietro Oddino v High Authority* (above, note 33); *Société des Aciéries de Montereau v Commission* (above, note 35); Cases 161 and 162/80R *Carbognani and Zabetta v Commission* [1980] ECR 2655; *EISA v Commission* (above, note 35) paras 12–14; Case 78/86R *Costacurta v Commission* [1986] ECR 1231; Case C-385/89R *Greece v Commission* [1990] ECR I-561 (para 10). The Court is not always fortunate in its dealings with the institutions. In the fourth case mentioned, the application requested the suspension of what was alleged to be a decision transferring the applicants, who were officials of the Commission, from Rome to Brussels. At the hearing the Commission said that it did not intend to implement the 'decision' until a formal decision had been adopted so the purpose of the application was in substance already achieved and the claim for suspension was otiose. Judge Pescatore agreed and held that there was no need to give judgment on the application. On the same day he also heard the application in Case 163/80R *Jacobucci v Commission* [1980] ECR 2661, which concerned the same situation. In view of the Commission's declaration, Jacobucci withdrew her application for suspension and it was removed from the Court's register. That very evening, it seems, the Commission adopted a decision transferring the applicants.

38 Eg Case 260/85R *Tokyo Electric Co Ltd v Council* [1985] ECR 3467 (paras 16–17), undertakings given by an intervener. In Case 45/87R *Commission v Ireland* [1987] ECR 1369, the defendant was able to give an undertaking which was effective up to a particular date but stated that it could not maintain the status quo thereafter in the absence of an order (para 3).

39 Eg *Tokyo Electric Co Ltd v Council*, ibid paras 16–17.

force as between the institution and the applicant for relief save that they may create a legitimate expectation, on the part of the latter, that they will be performed unless and until properly withdrawn. Undertakings given by or on behalf of a member state must similarly be made by the agent of the member state; those given by or on behalf of any other party must be made by that party's representative. In all cases, formal note should be taken of the giving of an undertaking. The effectiveness of such an undertaking is dependent upon the good faith of the party giving it. If the party giving the undertaking fails to perform it, the opposing party may renew its application for suspension or, as the case may be, interim measures and may well have an independent cause of action for damages in respect of any loss suffered between the breach of the undertaking and the grant of interim relief in consequence of the failure to perform the undertaking;[40] but it would seem that the Court could award damages in such circumstances only where a Community institution has failed to perform an undertaking, the liability of other parties in respect of breach of an undertaking ordinarily being a matter for the competent national court. When a party withdraws an undertaking, it should inform the Court and the opposing party or parties so that any appropriate action may be taken in order to maintain the status quo; otherwise, the party giving the undertaking may be acting in breach of the other party's legitimate expectations.

Urgency may also be disproved where the opposing party gives not so much an undertaking concerning the position pending judgment but a concession regarding the situation after the date of judgment which ensures that the judgment will be fully effective despite any change in circumstances in the meantime. Thus, if the defendant gives an assurance that a recruitment procedure will not affect the applicant's rights, if he wins the action, the applicant will then have no interest in pursuing the application for relief because the continuation of the recruitment procedure will not be prejudicial to the effectiveness of the final judgment.[41] In one case an application was made for the suspension of a sale of olive oil by tender on the basis that, if the applicants made unconditional offers, this would be taken as a waiver of their property rights in the oil, whereas, if they made conditional offers, these would be rejected. Relief on this ground was refused because the defendant institution conceded that an unconditional offer would not be a waiver of the applicant's rights and the judge incorporated this concession in his decision.[42]

Where the application for interim relief seeks the same relief as that claimed in the action, no order may be made for fear of prejudging the action since the relief will by its nature be permanent rather than temporary.[43] But an order may be made if the applicant shows that he is presented with an imminent

---

40 It should be made clear that the failure to perform the undertaking does not provide the applicant for relief with a right to claim suspension or interim measures. However unattractive the behaviour of the party concerned might be thought to be as a result of its failure to perform the undertaking, interim relief could be ordered only if the requirements for granting it were satisfied. Clearly, if those requirements were not satisfied and the applicant's renewed application were unsuccessful, the failure to perform the undertaking would not, in the event, have caused the applicant recoverable loss unless the applicant was successful in the action.

41 Cases 98 and 99/63R *Reynier v Commission* [1964] ECR 276; *Carbognani and Zabetta v Commission* (above, note 37); Case 89/82R *Wölker v Commission* [1982] ECR 1323; Case 241/84R *Pizzinato v Commission* [1984] ECR 3619 (paras 9–10); Case 64/86R *Sergio v Commission* [1986] ECR 1081 (para 9).

42 Case 232/81R *Agricola Commerciale Olio Srl v Commission* [1981] ECR 2193.

43 Case 731/79R *B v European Parliament* [1979] ECR 3629; Case 794/79R *B v European Parliament* [1979] ECR 3635; Cases 24 and 97/80R *Commission v France* (above, note 28); Case C-40/92R *Commission v United Kingdom* (above, note 32) para 29.

threat or that the status quo is threatened.[44] Where necessary, the interim relief sought should therefore be distinguished from the relief sought in the action either by a difference in their nature or, where they are the same in nature, by their temporal scope.

Where it is the defendant who has the power to alter or maintain the status quo, urgency (in the sense of a change in the status quo) cannot be inferred merely from the fact that proceedings have commenced and may be disproved by the stance taken by the defendant before the making of the application for relief.[45] In particular, there is ordinarily no urgency where there already exists a mechanism for preserving the position, even if the operation of that mechanism is dependent upon some action on the part of the defendant or a third party.[46] There is in consequence no need for the judge to act unless there is evidence that the defendant (or the third party) will or may by his act or omission cause the status quo to be ended; in that event the judge may order the defendant to take the steps necessary to preserve the status quo or impose some other appropriate form of relief.[47] The status quo is ordinarily the situation prevailing at the time when the application for relief is made. In most cases, the application is made at the commencement of the action, in which case the status quo ante is taken to be the situation prevailing before then. In actions for annulment, the status quo can be taken to be the situation prevailing immediately before the adoption of the contested act[48] at least where the applicant for relief has commenced proceedings promptly and without undue delay.[49] In proceedings that are commenced only after a compulsory pre-litigation procedure, it is unclear whether the status quo ante is to be taken to be the situation prevailing at the commencement of litigation or that prevailing at some earlier time, such as at the commencement of the pre-litigation procedure or some point during it.[50] In principle, for the purpose of the grant of interim relief, the status quo should ordinarily be taken to be the situation prevailing at the time when the application for relief is made; but it cannot be excluded that, in some cases, it may be more just to take the situation prevailing at an earlier point in time. In Case 154/85R *Commission v Italy*,[51] for example, the status quo was taken to be the situation prevailing immediately before the first of the events causing the Commission to commence the pre-litigation procedure, thus resulting in the defendant being required to revert to the position as it had been nearly a year before relief was granted. The fact that the applicant for relief is obliged to go through a pre-litigation procedure before proceedings can be commenced before the Court and an

---

44 *Miles Druce & Co Ltd v Commission* (above, note 36); Case 318/81R *Commission v CODEMI SpA* [1982] ECR 1325; Case 171/83R *Commission v France* [1983] ECR 2621; but see also *Authié v Commission* (above, note 25).

45 Case C-40/92R *Commission v United Kingdom* (above, note 32) paras 27 and 31.

46 Case C-280/93R *Germany v Council*; Case C-296/93R *France v Commission*; Case C-307/93R *Ireland v Commission* (all above, note 5).

47 Cases 160, 161, 170/73R II *Miles Druce & Co Ltd v Commission and GKN* [1974] ECR 281; Case C-40/92R *Commission v United Kingdom* (above, note 32).

48 Eg Case 65/87R *Pfizer International Inc v Commission* [1987] ECR 1691 (paras 25–26).

49 The mere fact that proceedings have been commenced within the limitation period may not be sufficient to take the status quo back to the situation prevailing before the adoption of the contested measure if the threat to the applicant is such that a prudent litigant would and could have commenced proceedings at an earlier point during the running of the limitation period.

50 In practical terms, this difficulty concerns proceedings brought in respect of a failure by a member state to fulfil a Treaty obligation: see ECSC Treaty, art 88; EC Treaty, art 169; Euratom Treaty, art 141.

51 Above, note 14 (para 21).

application for interim relief can be made gives the opposing party an opportunity to alter the prevailing state of affairs to its advantage, or allow that state of affairs to alter, while the pre-litigation procedure is taking its course; and in particular cases it may be regarded as unjust to allow the opposing party to take advantage of the delays caused by the pre-litigation procedure, at least where the opposing party has been made fully aware of the point at issue and cannot rely upon some countervailing interest.[52] On the other hand, where the commencement and conduct of the pre-litigation procedure lie entirely within the discretion of the applicant for relief, delay on the part of the applicant in commencing the pre-litigation procedure or a failure on its part to pursue with dispatch the conduct of that procedure may militate against the selection of an early point in time as identifying the status quo. Cases where a date before the making of the application for relief is taken for the purpose of establishing the status quo are not, strictly speaking, exceptions to the general rule that interim relief is concerned with maintaining the status quo and not with the reversal of a state of affairs existing at the time application is made because one of the functions of interim relief is to *restore* the status quo.[53]

Although, as has been said, urgency is a function of the need to grant relief before judgment and not of the speed with which the applicant has applied for relief, delay in making an application may negative urgency[54] either by suggesting that there is no real need to act before judgment[55] or by allowing the situation to change to the detriment of the applicant for relief: urgency is always to be assessed by reference to future events and not by reference to a change in circumstances which has already occurred by the time when application is made[56] save in cases where the applicant applies promptly in order to restore the status quo after the occurrence of an unforeseen event.[57] It should be noted that this does not mean that an applicant for relief can be criticised for not making the application at the outset of the proceedings: an applicant for relief should apply for interim relief only when it appears that damage is likely to be caused before judgment can be delivered. In the nature of things, the circumstances of a particular case may be such that that risk is apparent at the outset or apparent only when the action is well advanced. Where, at the commencement of proceedings, a future event likely to cause serious and irreparable damage to the applicant is perceived as occurring relatively far off in point of time, an application for relief made at that stage of the action risks being dismissed as premature; there is in consequence sound reason for delaying the application for relief until the occurrence of the future event is imminent.[58] In such circumstances, delay does not create an artifical degree of

---

52 Case 293/85R *Commission v Belgium* (above, note 14), where the relief granted in effect restored the status quo at the beginning of the academic year even though it had already started when proceedings before the Court were commenced, appears to be an example of such a case.
53 Cf Case 352/88R *Commission v Italy* [1989] ECR 267 (para 23). Other things being equal, maintenance of the status quo (particularly if it is long-standing) is preferable to any alteration of it: cf *Radio Telefis Eireann v Commission* (above, note 5) para 15; *Publishers' Association v Commission* (above, note 8) para 35.
54 Case 28/65R *Fonzi v Euratom Commission* [1966] ECR 508; Cases 31 and 53/77R *Commission v United Kingdom* [1977] ECR 921 (Advocate General Mayras).
55 Cf Case 194/88R *Commission v Italy* [1988] ECR 5647 (para 16), where the defendant's reliance on a threat to public health and the environment if relief were granted was rejected because the competent national body had itself acted in a dilatory fashion.
56 Cf Case 57/89R *Commission v Germany* [1989] ECR 2849 (para 18).
57 If the event is foreseeable, it may form part of the status quo: cf *Ilford v Commission* (above, note 16) paras 22–23.
58 Eg *Aldinger v European Parliament* (above, note 10) paras 11–13; *Virgili v European Parliament* (above, note 10) paras 11–13.

urgency but simply reflects a previous absence of urgency. There is authority that, if a measure is already in force when an application to suspend its operation is made, it is impossible to say that suspension is urgent.[59] That is not necessarily so in all cases; it depends upon the nature of the measure whose suspension is sought and on whether it takes effect at a given moment or over a given period of time (which passed before the application for relief was made) or has future effects in that, although already in force, it will apply to a future situation or will continue to regulate the situation. For example, the urgency to suspend a decision to transfer the applicant for relief from one post to another, which is expressed to take effect only several months after it was made and came into force, increases with the passage of time; and whereas, at the time the decision was adopted, there might not then have been any urgency at all to justify an application for suspension, the closer one gets to the date on which the decision has its effect, the greater the degree of urgency if no judgment is yet in sight.[60] In an application for interim measures, as opposed to suspension, however, it does not seem that the current application of the measure in question is a bar to relief.[61] The basic rule seems to be that, if the measure has already taken effect, no relief can be given[62] unless it may continue to have effect and thus may give rise to serious and irreparable loss in the future.[63] The judge can order relief only in respect of the future loss.[64] In the case of measures which have already taken effect, there is urgency if there is no evidence of a real possibility of avoiding future loss from their continued application.[65]

In general, there is no urgency if there is no discernible causal connection between the events giving rise to the application for relief and the threat of serious and irreparable damage relied on;[66] or if any change in circumstances pending judgment would be reversed automatically or deprived automatically of any prejudicial effect on the applicant for relief by a judgment in his (or her) favour[67] (in consequence, the judge must first decide whether or not the applicant's success in the action would make it possible to reverse the

---

59 Case 61/76R II *Geist v Commission* [1976] ECR 2075. But see *Ilford v Commission* (above, note 16).

60 The *Aldinger* and *Virgili* cases (above, note 10).

61 Case 61/77R *Commission v Ireland* [1977] ECR 1411.

62 Case 10/82R *Morgensen v Commission* [1982] ECR 325; Case 39/83R *Fabius v Commission* [1983] ECR 2147.

63 Cf Case 67/63R *SOREMA v High Authority* [1964] ECR 174; Cases 19 and 65/63A *Prakash v Euratom Commission* [1965] ECR 576; *Luhleich v Euratom Commission* (above, note 37); *Geist v Commission* (above, note 59); Case 61/77R *Commission v Ireland* (above, note 61); *Nachi Fujikoshi Corpn v Council* (above, note 25); Case 92/78R *Simmenthal v Commission* (above, note 25); Case 42/82R *Commission v France* [1982] ECR 841.

64 *Nachi Fujikoshi Corpn v Council* (above, note 25); *SICA and SIPEFEL v Commission* (above, note 21); Case 57/89R *Commission v Germany* (above, note 56) para 18.

65 Case 42/82R *Commission v France* (above, note 63) at 865 (Advocate General Sir Gordon Slynn.)

66 Case 82/87R *Autexpo SpA v Commission* [1987] ECR 2131 (para 24); Case 191/88R *Co-Frutta Sarl v Commission* [1988] ECR 4551 (paras 20–21); Case C-242/90P-R *Commission v Albani* [1990] ECR I-4329 (paras 22–25), the judgment of the CFI which the applicant sought to have suspended was not capable of giving rise to the damage feared.

67 Eg Case 341/85R *van der Stijl v Commission* [1985] ECR 3795 (para 12); Case 46/87R *Hoechst AG v Commission* [1987] ECR 1549 (para 34); Case 209/87R *Association des Aciéries Européennes Indépendantes (EISA) v Commission* [1987] ECR 3453 (para 22); Case 214/87R *Cockerill Sambre v Commission* [1987] ECR 3463 (para 22); Case 223/87R *Associazione Industrie Siderurgiche v Commission* [1987] ECR 3473 (para 22); Case 85/87R *Dow Chemical Nederland BV v Commission* [1987] ECR 4367 (para 17); Case 229/88R *Cargill BV v Commission* [1988] ECR 5183 (para 19); Case 171/89R *Gonzalez Holguera v European Parliament* [1989] ECR 1705 (paras 13–14); Case T-155/89R *Buccarello v European Parliament* [1990] ECR II-19 (para 12); Cases T-10 to T-12, T-14 and T-15/92R *SA Cimenteries CBR v Commission* [1992] ECR II-1571 (para 56).

situation);[68] or if the applicant's position could be adequately protected in other proceedings (in casu, proceedings brought before national courts).[69] Urgency also will not be demonstrated where the purpose of the relief sought is to maintain a state of affairs that is itself a disruption of the status quo and appears to be unlawful.[70] In an action to suspend the operation of a recruiting competition, urgency is not established if the applicant is young enough to take part in a forthcoming competition.[71] There is no urgency if the applicant can protect his rights adequately by bringing another action.[72] Dissemination of a report whose contents and conclusions are only under discussion, so that no decision is yet contemplated, does not give rise to urgency:[73] there must be more than just a possibility that an act adversely affecting the applicant may be adopted.[74] In the same way, the continuation of an administrative investigation[75] does not justify relief.[76] In a case where the applicant for relief seeks an order enabling it to fill a post, the facts that the post was vacant for several months before the dispute between the parties arose and that the person appointed to it was authorised to occupy it on a part-time basis for over a year indicate that there is no urgency; it is therefore for the applicant to demonstrate some objective need to fill the post before judgment by showing, for example, that there has been a significant increase in the volume of work to be done.[77] There is no urgency to suspend a measure that does no more than require an undertaking to produce documents which make it possible for the defendant institution to monitor the development of trade: such a measure is not likely to influence the behaviour of the undertaking and, in consequence, is not likely to cause harm justifying suspension.[78] On the other hand, the requirement of urgency is satisfied in the case of a measure that has an immediate influence on the action of an undertaking, such as by deterring it from a lawful development of its business;[79] or where the national authorities are about to take action on the basis of the contested act.[80]

In all cases, however, it is not sufficient to demonstrate that a measure contested in the action is about to be put into effect or that the status quo is about to be altered in some other way. In addition to those matters, it is necessary to show that serious and irreparable damage will result before judgment can be given.[81]

---

68 *Radio Telefis Eireann v Commission* (above, note 5) para 15.
69 Case 310/85R *Deufil GmbH & Co KG v Commission* [1986] ECR 537 (paras 21–22); Case 303/88R *Italy v Commission* [1989] ECR 801 (para 25); Case C-40/92R *Commission v United Kingdom* (above, note 32) para 30; Case T-12/93R *Comité Central d'Entreprise de la Société Anonyme Vittel v Commission*, 6 July 1993.
70 Cases 67, 68 and 70/85R *Kwekerij Gebroeders van der Kooy BV v Commission* [1985] ECR 1315 (paras 41–44).
71 *Salerno v Commission* (above, note 25).
72 Case 186/80R *Suss v Commission* [1980] ECR 3501.
73 Case 51/79R *Buttner v Commission* [1979] ECR 1727.
74 Case 51/79R II *Buttner v Commission* [1979] ECR 2387.
75 Sc into an alleged infringement of the competition rules.
76 Cases 60 and 190/81R *International Business Machines Corpn v Commission* [1981] ECR 1857; Case 173/82R *Castille v Commission* [1982] ECR 4047; *De Compte v European Parliament* (above, note 4).
77 Case C-35/92P-R *European Parliament v Frederiksen* [1992] ECR I-2399 (paras 20–22).
78 Case 37/84R *EISA v Commission* [1984] ECR 1749 (para 11).
79 Case 45/84R *EISA v Commission* (above, note 35) para 11.
80 *Oryzomyli Kavallas OEE v Commission* (above, note 2) para 7; *Italy v Commission* (above, note 69) para 25.
81 Eg Case 378/87R *Top Hit Holzvertrieb GmbH v Commission* [1988] ECR 161 (para 18). Urgency is an aspect of serious and irreparable harm: Case T-44/90 *La Cinq SA v Commission* [1992] ECR II-1 (para 29).

C Serious and irreparable damage

In principle, damage that may be caused to a third party is irrelevant to a claim for interim relief: only that affecting the applicant can be relied on in order to ground a claim for relief.[82] It would appear from Case T-96/92R *Comité Central d'Entreprise de la Société des Grandes Sources v Commission*[83] that employees' organisations may in principle rely on a threat to the jobs of their members (at least where they exist in order to represent the interests of the employees of a particular undertaking).

In the case of member states, the position is more complex. Some cases suggest that the damage relied on may be any damage caused to any person within their frontiers or any damage to their national interest.[84] In other cases, member states have been precluded from relying on damage other than damage with which they have been 'personally' threatened, thus excluding reliance on damage to persons within their frontiers.[85] The cases can be reconciled by saying that member states can rely upon damage to persons or interests which they represent save where those persons or interests could be adequately and more conveniently protected otherwise than by the member state in question, such as by an action brought by the persons concerned themselves. Thus, where the person threatened with damage is the recipient of a (proposed) state aid whose grant has been prohibited by the contested act, that person, as well as the member state proposing to grant the aid, has a right of action against the contested act; since that person is able to protect its interests by itself bringing proceedings and, in those proceedings, seeking interim relief, it (rather than the member state concerned) should bear the responsibility of protecting its own position; if it does not consider it necessary to commence proceedings and seek interim relief, it is not for the member state to do so in its stead (although the member state is clearly entitled to seek the annulment of the contested act in order to establish the lawfulness of the grant of the state aid).[86] Although that

82 Case 12/64R *Ley v Commission* [1965] ECR 132; Case 22/75R *Küster v European Parliament* [1975] ECR 277; Case 269/84R *Fabbro v Commission* [1984] ECR 4333 (para 9); Case 292/84R *Scharf v Commission* [1984] ECR 4349 (paras 12–14); *Fabrique de Fer de Charleroi v Commission* (above, note 15), para 27; *Dillinger Hüttenwerke AG v Commission* (above, note 15) para 28; Case 55/86R *Asociacion Provincial de Armadores de Bugues de Pesca de Gran Sol de Pontevedra (Arposol) v Council* [1986] ECR 1331 (para 6); *Belgium v Commission* (above, note 28) paras 23–24; *Top Hit Holzvertrieb GmbH v Commission*, ibid, para 18; Case 111/88R *Greece v Commission* (above, note 28) para 15; Case 112/88R *Crete Citron Producers' Association v Commission* [1988] ECR 2597 (para 20); Case C-313/90R *Comité International de la Rayonne et des Fibres Synthétiques v Commission* [1991] ECR I-2557 (para 24). But see Cases 228 and 229/82R *Ford Werke AG and Ford of Europe Inc v Commission* [1982] ECR 3091 (para 10); *Ilford v Commission* (above, note 16) para 21; Case 92/88R *Associazione Industrie Siderurgiche Italiane (ASSIDER) v Commission* [1988] ECR 2425 (para 24); *Publishers' Association v Commission* (above, note 8) para 35.
83 [1992] ECR II-2579 (paras 43–47).
84 Case 166/78R *Italy v Council* [1978] ECR 1745 (the action was brought to annul several Council regulations, the damage relied on to justify relief being suffered by the Italian cereal starch industry; the application was rejected on the ground that there was no evidence of serious and irreparable damage, not on the ground that the type of damage relied on did not justify relief); Case 171/83R *Commission v France* (above, note 44); Case 278/84R *Germany v Commission* (above, note 18) para 19; Case 57/86R *Greece v Commission* [1986] ECR 1497 (para 12); Case 303/88R *Italy v Commission* (above, note 69) para 24, damage to the Italian economy resulting from the risk that the recipients of certain state aids might go out of business (the argument was rejected on the facts).
85 Case 142/87R *Belgium v Commission* (above, note 28) paras 23–24; Case 111/88R *Greece v Commission* (above, note 28) paras 14–16; Case 303/88R *Italy v Commission* (above, note 69) para 23; Case 32/89R *Greece v Commission* [1989] ECR 985 (para 16); Case C-356/90R *Belgium v Commission* [1991] ECR I-2423 (para 24).
86 See also the situation that gave rise to the applications in Case 111/88R *Greece v Commission* (above, note 28) and *Crete Citron Producers' Association v Commission* (above, note 82).

approach appears to reconcile most cases, it does not fit every one of them.[87] For example, in Case 119/86R *Spain v Council and Commission*[88] Spain sought the suspension of various regulations on the ground that they were seriously damaging Spanish exports because exporters had to lodge a security and that, together with the formalities and additional expense involved, had caused a significant fall in exports and a consequent loss of market share and outlets. The application was dismissed essentially for evidential reasons but not because Spain had invoked a type of damage that could not be relied on in such an application. At about the same time, the Spanish exporters made a similar application which was dismissed on essentially the same grounds.[89] In Case C-280/93R *Germany v Council*[90] the ECJ expressed the principle to be applied in more general terms as being that, as the member states may act in defence of general interests at the national level (in particular, economic and social interests), they may rely on any threat to an entire sector of the national economy, in particular threats to employment and to the cost of living.

In the case of the Community institutions, the damage may be that which would be suffered by them qua institution[91] and, at least in the case of the Commission,[92] any damage to the interests of the Community,[93] including a threat to the rule of law in the Community or to persons whose rights under Community law are threatened.[94] The same applies where the Commission (at least) opposes an application for relief: for example, when an undertaking which has been involved in a restrictive practice applies for the suspension of the operation of a Commission decision finding the practice to be contrary to the competition rules, the Commission may, it would seem, rely on the effect suspension would have on the victims of the practice in order to oppose the application, even though the effect on the Commission qua institution would be neither serious nor irreparable; the Commission represents the Community public interest in the proper application of the competition rules. It is not clear to what extent there are limits to the interests that a Community institution

---

87 In fact, the inability of a member state to rely upon a threat to a person or interest within its borders seems to arise almost only in state aid cases where the person or interest in question is the recipient or beneficiary of the state aid. In consequence, it may be that that inability is a peculiar featue of state aid cases which does not apply in most other areas.

88 [1986] ECR 2241 (Re Export Deposits). See also Case 128/86R *Spain v Commission* [1986] ECR 2495.

89 Case 117/86R *Union de Federaciones Agrarias de España (UFADE) v Council and Commission* [1986] ECR 2483. Judge Mackenzie Stuart expressed some doubt about the admissibility of the exporters' action but nonetheless decided their application for interim relief on the ground that they had failed to show the urgency of the situation.

90 Above (note 5) para 27.

91 Eg Case C-345/90P-R *European Parliament v Hanning* [1991] ECR I-231 (paras 32–33).

92 The position regarding the other Community institutions is unclear. It is tenable that each institution may rely only on a threat to the interests represented by it. The Commission represents broader interests than do the other institutions because of its more wide-ranging powers to ensure the observance of Community law: ECSC Treaty, art 8; EC Treaty, art 155; Euratom Treaty, art 124.

93 See, for example, *Commission v Ireland* (above, note 61); Case 42/82R *Commission v France* (above, note 63); Case 171/83R *Commission v France* (above, note 44); *Ley v Commission* (above, note 82) at 134; Case 154/85R *Commission v Italy* [1985] ECR 1753 (para 19); Case 45/87R *Commission v Ireland* [1987] ECR 783, para 32 (damage to the Commission 'as guardian of the interests of the Community').

94 Eg Case 293/85R *Commission v Belgium* [1985] ECR 3521 (para 23; in casu, the interests of students in a member state); Case 194/88R *Commission v Italy* [1988] ECR 5647 (paras 6 and 16); Case 246/89R *Commission v United Kingdom* [1989] ECR 3125 (in casu, the rights of owners and operators of certain fishing vessels; it should be noted that the Commission commenced proceedings for interim relief after the persons concerned had failed to obtain interim relief from the competent national courts).

may rely on. In Case 3/75R *Johnson and Firth Brown v Commission*[95] the Commission had adopted a decision authorising the take-over of the applicants. They applied for the operation of the decision to be suspended. There was no doubt that its operation would cause serious and irreparable damage to the applicants. Judge Lecourt found that suspension of its operation would cause equally serious and irreparable damage to the creditors of the company whose shares in the applicants were to be sold in order to effect the take-over. The creditors had an interest in having the shares sold as soon as possible and had intervened in the proceedings. In consequence suspension was not granted but other relief was. It is doubtful if the threat to the creditors could properly be said to be subsumed in the Community public interest represented by the Commission: the Commission's powers were to be exercised for the purpose of maintaining a healthy steel industry whereas the interveners' interest was purely pecuniary. It was not necessary to decide that question because the judge could take account of the interest of the creditors since they had intervened in the proceedings.[96]

The serious and irreparable nature of the loss alleged must be assessed 'in concreto'.[97] The applicant cannot rely on a risk of damage which does not arise from the act of another but has been brought on by himself[98] or on a risk that the applicant has knowingly assumed.[99] The risk must be sufficiently certain and arise directly from the act whose annulment is sought in the action.[1]

The two adjectives most commonly used to describe the damage with which the applicant must be threatened are 'serious' and 'irreversible', although 'irreparable' is sometimes used instead of the latter. There appears to be no significant difference between 'irreversible' and 'irreparable'. Both words, 'serious' and 'irreversible' or 'irreparable', tend to be used together.[2] Some early cases, however, suggest that there must be a risk of irreparable or at least serious damage,[3] rather than the risk of damage that is both serious and irreparable. In Cases 24 and 97/80R *Commission v France*[4] Advocate General Capotorti treated both terms as being synonymous: 'the applicant should be exposed to serious, in the sense of "irreparable" damage'. This appears to be

95 [1975] ECR 1.
96 Compare Cases 6 and 7/73R *Istituto Chemioterapico Italiano SpA and Commercial Solvents Corpn v Commission* [1973] ECR 357. There the applicants sought to have annulled a Commission decision requiring them to terminate forthwith a restrictive practice which comprised a refusal to supply a company called Zoja. Zoja intervened in the proceedings and Judge Lecourt held that the potential damage to it, if interim relief were granted, had to be taken into account. It would seem, however, that Zoja's intervention was not strictly necessary in order to bring its interest before the Court because it was an interest that the Commission could properly represent.
97 *Agricola Commerciale Olio Srl v Commission* (above, note 42).
98 Case 220/82R *Moselstahlwerk GmbH & Co Kg v Commission* [1982] ECR 2971; Case 338/82R *Albertini and Montagnani v Commission* [1982] ECR 4667; Case 347/82R *Alvarez v European Parliament* [1983] ECR 65.
99 *Ilford v Commission* (above, note 16) paras 22–23. The acceptance by the applicant of a known risk may be inferred from an objective assessment of what a reasonable person in the position of the applicant could reasonably be expected to have known. It is not necessary to establish what the applicant actually knew or believed at the material time.
1 Case T-96/92R *Comité Central d'Entreprise de la Société Générale des Grandes Sources v Commission* [1992] ECR II-2579 (para 46); Case C-280/93R *Germany v Council* [1993] ECR I-3667 (para 41); Case T-12/93R *Comité Central d'Entreprise de la Société Anonyme Vittel v Commission*, 6 July 1993; Case C-296/93R *France v Commission*, 16 July 1993; Case C-307/93R *Ireland v Commission*, 16 July 1993.
2 See, for example, Case 42/82R *Commission v France* [1982] ECR 841, a decision of the full Court.
3 See, for example, Case 31/59 *Acciaieria e Tubificio di Brescia v High Authority* [1960] ECR 98; Case 17/64R *Suss v High Authority* [1964] ECR 617.
4 [1980] ECR 1319 at 1341.

the currently accepted approach in the sense that the phrase 'serious and irreparable damage' is regularly repeated in the orders and is clearly used as a formula to describe the damage that must be proved, whose separate elements are not subject to semantic analysis.[5] This must be borne in mind when referring to old cases which do appear to draw a distinction between 'serious' and 'irreparable' or 'irreversible' damage.[6]

Whatever the way of expressing the formula to be used, the test seems to have remained the same over the years: as Advocate General Capotorti put it,[7] the damage must be 'such as to make the ultimate judgment pointless, so that in the absence of interim measures there would be no purpose in the ultimate judgment'. The effect of the damage is therefore to be measured by reference both to the position of the applicant for relief and to the purpose of the action. For that reason, proof of moral damage, even if 'serious and irreparable' as far as the applicant's feelings are concerned, is insufficient: moral damage does not prejudice the effect of the final judgment. Put another way, the test for irreparable damage is that it is impossible to safeguard the applicant's position retroactively if he wins the action,[8] the object of interim relief being to prevent the final judgment from being rendered worthless by the passage of time and the infliction of damage that is irreversible.[9] If the result of a failure to grant interim relief is simply disadvantageous to the applicant, but not irreversibly so, the order will not be made.[10] Nevertheless, it would seem that, if the disadvantage suffered by the applicant is serious, and an obstacle to carrying out its commercial activities[11] or, possibly, disproprortionate having regard to the interest of the defendant in leaving matters as they are in the absence of interim relief,[12] relief may be granted. In cases where relief is sought in respect of a measure granting some form of interim relief that has been challenged in the action, the relevant question is whether or not the contested measure, if put into operation immediately, risks causing damage considerably in excess of the inevitable but temporary disadvantages arising from a true conservatory measure.[13] In one case it was suggested that, if dismissal of the application for relief would lead to an 'almost hopelessly involved situation', relief might be granted.[14] The fact that the applicant succeeded in obtaining relief in a

---

5 An example is Case 20/81R *Arbed v Commission* 1981] ECR 721 (para 14), where the damage in question comprised the quarterly fixing of steel quotas at a level which the applicants alleged was too low. They applied for an increase of the quotas by way of interim relief. The damage was, on the facts, certainly irreversible or irreparable because, even if they won the action, the judgment could not, other than by an award of damages, which were not claimed, compensate for the production lost in the time leading up to the date of the judgment. On the other hand, the increases sought were relatively small and this led the President to hold that the fixing of the quotas at a level that was too low 'cannot be regarded as being such as to cause serious and irreparable damage to undertakings of the size of the applicants'. If 'serious' were truly a distinct attribute of the damage that must be proved, the order would have referred to it alone and not to 'serious and irreparable damage'.

6 It should also be noted that, in a few more recent cases, the distinction between 'serious' and 'irreparable' can be observed, possibly reflecting a more relativist approach on the part of some judges to the justification for granting relief.

7 Cases 24 and 97/80R *Commission v France* (above, note 4) at 1342. Cf Cases 67, 68 and 70/85R *Kwekerij Gebroeders van der Kooy BV v Commission* [1985] ECR 1315 (para 47).

8 Case 29/66R *Gutmann v Euratom Commission* [1967] ECR 241.

9 Case 50/69R *Germany v Commission* [1969] ECR 449 (Advocate General Gand).

10 Cases 3–18, 25, 26/58A *Erzbergbau v High Authority* [1960] ECR 220; Case 120/83R *Raznoimport v Commission* [1983] ECR 2573.

11 Case 18/57 *Nold KG v High Authority* [1957–58] ECR 121 at 124 (a decision of the ECJ).

12 Case 44/88R *De Compte v European Parliament* [1988] ECR 1669 (para 31).

13 Case T-23/90R *Automobiles Peugeot SA and Peugeot SA v EC Commission* [1990] ECR II-195 (para 24).

14 Cases 42 and 49/59 *Breedband NV v Société des Aciéries du Temple* [1962] ECR 145.

previous case does not relieve him of the obligation to demonstrate that the conditions required for the grant of relief have been satisfied in the case pending before the Court.[15]

Ex hypothesi the damage has not occurred at the time of the application. If it has, relief is not granted save in respect of any future damage that may arise before judgment can be delivered.[16] It is sufficient to show that damage[17] is a possibility[18] but the possibility must be real or concrete and the potential damage actual and specific; a risk of indefinite or hypothetical future damage is not sufficient to ground a claim for relief.[19] The fact that the situation giving rise to the threat of damage is temporary and is likely to or will inevitably end before the delivery of judgment is not a reason for refusing to grant relief where the damage likely to be caused during the relevant period (if relief were refused) is serious and irreparable.[20] In Case 112/88R *Crete Citron Producers' Association v Commission*[21] it was suggested that the damage must be the 'direct' result of the act challenged in the action. That appears to mean that relief may be sought only in order to restore the position to what it was intended to be before the acts prompting the application for relief but not in order to provide the applicant with some collateral advantage: in casu, where the intended consequence of a measure is to restore a member state's balance of payments, the suspension of the operation of an act repealing that measure can be based only on the resultant damage to the balance of payments and not on the collateral advantage obtained by exporters from the measure in the form of a reduction in their production costs and a consequent increase in their incomes. In many cases, however, distinctions between so-called 'direct' and 'indirect' or 'collateral' consequences lack substance. In the *Crete Citron Producers* case itself, the measure adopted to safeguard Greece's balance of payments took the form of an authorisation to grant export aid. The contested act withdrew that authorisation. In the circumstances, it seems somewhat artificial to say that the direct result of the authorisation was not that the exporters concerned continued to benefit from export aid but that Greece's balance of payments continued to be assisted by the exports facilitated by the export aid. In contrast, there is a justifiable distinction between damage that is the 'direct' or 'immediate' consequence of the situation with which the Court is confronted and damage that is merely an indirect consequence, in the sense that there is no direct or immediate causal connection between the damage relied on and the situation as it currently stands. Thus, suspension of a measure is not justified if the damage relied on could not result directly from the continued operation of the act in question but would result only if further steps were taken.[22]

The following situations have been held to constitute neither serious nor

15 Case 44/88R *De Compte v European Parliament* (above, note 12) para 32.
16 Eg Cases C-143/88 and C-92/89 *Zuckerfabrik Süderdithmarschen AG v Hauptzollamt Itzehoe* [1991] ECR I-415 (para 29). See footnote 63, p 266, above.
17 Described in the decision as 'immediate and irreversible'.
18 Cases 209–215 and 218/78R *Heintz Van Landewyck Sarl v Commission* [1978] ECR 2111.
19 Case 142/87R *Belgium v Commission* [1987] ECR 2589 (para 25); Case 209/87R *Association des Aciéries Européennes Indépendantes (EISA) v Commission* [1987] ECR 3453 (paras 17–19); Case 214/87R *Cockerill Sambre v Commission* [1987] ECR 3463 (paras 17–19); Case 223/87R *Associazione Industrie Siderurgiche Italiane (ASSIDER) v Commission* [1987] ECR 3473 (paras 17–19); Case T-24/93R *Compagnie Maritime Belge Transport NV v Commission* [1993] ECR II-543 (para 34).
20 Case 270/84R *Licata v Economic and Social Committee* [1984] ECR 4119 (para 16); Case 209/87R *EISA v Commission* and the *Cockerill Sambre* and *ASSIDER* cases (ibid) para 22; Cases T-24 and T-28/92R *Langnese-Iglo GmbH & Schöller Lebensmittel GmbH & Co KG v Commission* [1992] ECR II-1839 (see in particular para 26).
21 [1988] ECR 2597 (paras 19–20).
22 Eg Case 269/84R *Fabbro v Commission* [1984] ECR 4333 (paras 12–13).

irreparable damage: financial loss, where it can be passed on to the applicant's customers,[23] does not threaten the applicant's continued existence,[24] can be quantified (for the purpose of compensation)[25] or can be compensated[26] – in general, being kept out of one's money is not *necessarily* serious or irreparable damage[27] unless the damage (of a non-pecuniary nature) that would ensue constitutes serious and irreparable damage;[28] damage, such as the loss of the opportunity to tender for the purchase of goods or exclusion from a market, which can be assimilated to financial loss (and which is therefore assessed in the same way as financial loss);[29] an inability to use certain budgetary appropriations in a particular year for specified purposes where, if the final judgment was favourable, the appropriations could be used in the next financial year;[30] in staff cases, assignment to another department[31] or the continuance of a recruiting competition, even if a third party is, in consequence, appointed to the post in dispute, because the applicant can always challenge the decision appointing the third party to the post[32] or apply for another vacant post;[33] dissemination of a report whose contents and conclusions are still under discussion, when there is no more than just a possibility of it being acted upon;[34] dissemination of business secrets where their continued confidentiality is protected by other legal provisions and there is no evidence that such provisions risk being ignored;[35] being kept out of one's money or being forced to buy goods on the market at higher prices,[36] at least in an action for damages (sed quaere in an action for annulment) because the loss can be made good in the judgment;[37] the continuance of the Commission's investigations into an

23 Case 25/62R I *Plaumann & Co v Commission* [1963] ECR 123.
24 Case 160/84R *Oryzomyli Kavallas OEE v Commission* [1984] ECR 3217 (para 8); Case 160/84R II *Oryzomyli Kavallas OEE v Commission* [1984] ECR 3615; Case 310/85R *Deufil GmbH & Co KG v Commission* [1986] ECR 537 (paras 23–24); Case 304/86R *Enital SpA v Council and Commission* [1987] ECR 267 (para 16); Cases C-51/90R and C-59/90R *Comos-Tank BV v Commission* [1990] ECR I-2167 (para 24).
25 The *Comos-Tank* case (ibid) para 24.
26 Cases 82 and 83/85R *Eurasian Corpn Ltd v Commission* [1985] ECR 1191 (paras 26–27); Case 229/88R *Cargill BV v Commission* [1988] ECR 5183 (paras 16–18); Case 32/89R *Greece v Commission* [1989] ECR 985 (para 19); Case C-195/90R *Commission v Germany* [1990] ECR I-3351 (para 38); Case C-257/90R *Italsolar SpA v Commission* [1990] ECR I-3841 (para 15); Case C-358/90R *Compagnia Italiana Alcool Sas di Mario Mariano & Co v Commission* [1990] ECR I-4887 (para 26); Case T-21/93R *Peixoto v Commission* [1993] ECR II-463 (para 28).
27 Case 62/74R *Vellozzi v Commission* [1974] ECR 895; Case 141/84R *De Compte v Parliament* [1984] ECR 2575 (para 4); Case 221/86R *Group of the European Right and National Front Party v European Parliament* [1986] ECR 2969 (paras 38–41).
28 Eg Case 90/87R *CW v Court of Auditors* [1987] ECR 1801 (paras 12–14); Case T-45/90R *Speybrouck v European Parliament* [1990] ECR II-705 (paras 23–30).
29 Case C-358/90R *Compagnia Italiana Alcool Sas di Mario Mariano & Co v Commission* (above, note 26) paras 27–28.
30 Case 23/86R *United Kingdom v European Parliament* [1986] ECR 1085 (paras 42–46), where it was the defendant who had asserted that serious and irreparable damage would so result, if the relief sought were granted.
31 Case 69/83R *Lux v Court of Auditors* [1983] ECR 1785: the reason was that the applicant had retained his post.
32 Case 17/64R *Suss v High Authority* (above, note 3); Case 176/88R *Hanning v European Parliament* [1988] ECR 3915 (para 13): this is contradicted by several other cases, see below.
33 Case 206/89R *S v Commission* [1989] ECR 2841 (para 18).
34 Case 51/79R *Buttner v Commission* [1979] ECR 1727; Case 51/79R II *Buttner v Commission* [1979] ECR 2387.
35 Case T-39/90R *Samenwerkende Elektriciteits-produktiebedrijven NV v Commission* [1990] ECR II-649 (paras 31–33).
36 Case 809/79R *Pardini SpA v Commission* [1980] ECR 139; Case 25/85R *Nuovo Campsider v Commission* [1985] ECR 751 (para 22).
37 Case 33/80R *Albini v Council and Commission* [1980] ECR 1671; Case 294/86R *Technointorg v Commission* [1986] ECR 3979 (para 28).

alleged infringement of the competition rules;[38] breach of the rules of natural justice, if the party's position is safeguarded by another procedure;[39] a refusal to allow an institution's internal messenger service to be used for the distribution of trade union information (because the trade union was still free to distribute the material itself);[40] a refusal to give the applicant time off work to attend trade union meetings (because the applicant was not actually prevented from attending meetings; and, if he was successful in the action, the periods deducted from his holiday entitlement in order to take account of the time taken up by the meetings could be restored by way of compensation);[41] use of a particular voting system in elections to a staff committee;[42] being obliged to maintain prices at a certain level, where there is no evidence of any loss of customers to competitors as a result;[43] damage related more to difficulties inherent in a member state's legal system than to the contested act;[44] a threat to less than 0.4% of the market[45] or only 0.24% of the applicant's business;[46] a loss of revenue equivalent to 0.26% of turnover or a loss of market share equivalent to 3% of turnover (in the case of the latter, at least where there is no indication that such a loss threatens the applicant's existence or is irrecoverable);[47] a loss of relative position and reductions in deliveries that are substantially less than 1%;[48] in state aids cases, the prohibition of the grant of such aid does not cause serious and irreparable damage if there are other (lawful) ways of achieving the object of the aid,[49] if the aid in question does not have a decisive effect on the investment decisions of the intended beneficiaries, there is time to adjust to the contested act and if no important investment plans would be prevented as a result of its continued application,[50] or if the recipient would otherwise still be able to meet its obligations;[51] the grant of such aid does not cause serious and irreparable damage to a competitor if, without it, the undertakings concerned would have gone ahead with their plans, albeit on a lower scale;[52] the cost of providing a guarantee;[53] a risk of a creditor's action should the applicant (a member state) cause the recipient of state aid to be declared bankrupt in implementation of the contested act;[54] damage that can be avoided by taking advantage of the procedures available under domestic law;[55] a hypothetical and indeterminate threat of damage to the economy of a

38 Cases 60 and 190/81R *International Business Machines Corpn v Commission* [1981] ECR 1857.
39 Case 122/83R *De Compte v Parliament* [1983] ECR 2151.
40 Case 193/87R *Maurissen v Court of Auditors* [1987] ECR 3445 (paras 15–16).
41 Ibid (para 17).
42 Case 63/88R *Maindiaux v Economic and Social Committee* [1988] ECR 1659 (para 28).
43 Case 62/86R *AKZO Chemie BV v Commission* [1986] ECR 1503 (para 26).
44 Case 82/87R *Autexpo SpA v Commission* [1987] ECR 2131 (paras 24–25).
45 Case 97/85R *Union Deutsche Lebensmittelwerke GmbH v Commission* [1985] ECR 1331 (para 20): the applicants' primary concern was the possible extension of the acts complained of to the rest of the Community and their application was in that sense premature.
46 Case T-23/90R *Automobiles Peugeot SA and Peugeot SA v Commission* (above, note 13) paras 25–28; Case T-23/90 *Automobiles Peugeot SA and Peugeot SA v Commission* [1991] ECR II-653 (para 76).
47 *Comos-Tank BV v Commission* (above, note 24) paras 25–26 and 30–31.
48 Case 92/88R *Associazione Industrie Siderurgiche Italiane (ASSIDER) v Commission* [1988] ECR 2425 (paras 26–27).
49 Case 57/86R *Greece v Commission* [1986] ECR 1497 (para 12).
50 Case 248/84R *Germany v Commission* [1985] ECR 1813 (para 11).
51 Case C-356/90R *Belgium v Commission* [1991] ECR I-2423 (para 25).
52 Case C-225/91R *Matra SA v Commission* [1991] ECR I-5823 (paras 21–25).
53 Case 213/86R *Montedipe SpA v Commission* [1986] ECR 2623 (para 23); *Technointorg v Commission* (above, note 37) para 28.
54 Case 142/87R *Belgium v Commission* (above, note 19) para 25.
55 *Deufil GmbH & Co KG v Commission* (above, note 24) paras 21–22; Case 142/87R *Belgium v Commission* (above, note 19) para 26.

member state;[56] temporary deprivation of a sum representing, in one instance, less than 1% of a member state's external deficit and, in another, just over 4% of a member state's annual expenditure (even where the amount in question increases an already considerable budgetary deficit);[57] the loss of almost all sales in the Community, where the applicant nonetheless remains profitable because demand for its products on markets outside the Community is still buoyant and there is no imminent threat to the applicant's survival;[58] in the case of a member state, a threat to the stability of its balance of payments where the exports concerned represented less than 1% of the member state's total exports;[59] imposition of a penalty where the fine (or other sanction) is small in relative terms[60] or its imposition may be avoided by conduct in compliance with the law[61] that does not itself cause serious and irreparable damage and where there is adequate protection against the unlawful imposition of the penalty;[62] the withdrawal of protection from fines afforded by Regulation No 17;[63] a requirement to provide information;[64] administrative inconvenience;[65] a loss of potential profits (at least where the loss is small by comparison with the applicant's existing business);[66] a loss of competitiveness due to late entry into the market (too uncertain to justify relief);[67] a threat to plans for future marketing efforts[68] or a very short period in which it would be impossible for the applicant to plan its business (in casu, three weeks);[69] a loss of income, where the loss is made up in sufficient part to avoid serious and irreparable damage by the grant of various benefits and allowances;[70] withdrawal of a claim in return for compensation when the other party accepts that the claim can be reintroduced if the basis for calculating the compensation is found to be unlawful in other proceedings;[70A] a prohibition on performing an agreement.[70B]

It should be noted that, where the applicant for relief has knowingly placed itself voluntarily in a particular situation in which it is at risk, the damage arising therefrom is liable to be regarded as having been accepted by the applicant and, for that reason, as not constituting serious and irreparable damage.[71] The failure to obtain an advantage (such as a financial benefit) from

---

56 Case 303/88R *Italy v Commission* [1989] ECR 801 (para 24): the damage was said to result from the risk that the recipients of certain state aids might go out of business if the Commission's decision requiring the recovery of the aids were implemented; but the undertakings in question accounted for only 2.5% of production in the sector concerned and there was no evidence that would make it possible to evaluate the alleged risk.

57 Case 214/86R *Greece v Commission* [1986] ECR 2631 (para 20); Case 32/89R *Greece v Commission* (above, note 26) paras 17–18.

58 Case C-358/89R *Extramet Industrie SA v Council* [1990] ECR I-431 (paras 18 and 23).

59 Case 111/88R *Greece v Commission* [1988] ECR 2591 (paras 17–18).

60 Case 46/87R *Hoechst AG v Commission* [1987] ECR 1549 (paras 33 and 35).

61 Case 55/86R *Arposol v Commission* [1986] ECR 1331 (para 18); Case T-23/90R *Automobiles Peugeot SA and Peugeot SA v Commission* (above, note 13) para 32.

62 The *Arposol* case (ibid) para 19.

63 Case T-19/91 *Société d'Hygiène Dermatologique de Vichy v Commission* [1991] ECR II-265 (para 20).

64 Case C-213/91R *Abertal SAT Lda v Commission* [1991] ECR I-5109 (paras 19–20).

65 Ibid (paras 21–22).

66 Case 352/88R *Commission v Italy* [1989] ECR 267 (para 25).

67 Ibid (para 26).

68 Case C-40/92R *Commission v United Kingdom* [1992] ECR I-3389 (para 30).

69 The *Autexpo* case (above, note 44) paras 24–25.

70 *Speybrouck v European Parliament* (above, note 28) para 28; Case T-51/91R *Hoyer v Commission* [1991] ECR II-679 (para 22).

70A Cases T-278/93R, T-555/93R, T-280/93R and T-541/93R *Jones v Council and Commission*, 1 February 1994, para 53.

70B *CMBT v Commission* (above, note 19) para 33.

71 Case 1/84R *Ilford SpA v Commission* [1984] ECR 423 (paras 21–23), where relief was granted only in respect of the period during which the applicant was not on notice that its supplies might be the subject of interruption.

which a person has not previously benefited under the status quo is not serious and irreparable damage, at least where a change in the status quo is necessary in order to enable the person concerned to obtain it.[72] In contrast, where a person has a chance of obtaining a future benefit, the loss of that chance by an alteration in the status quo may be serious and irreparable damage. It is unclear if damage to reputation constitutes serious and irreparable damage.[73] In the ordinary way, damage to reputation would be cured by a final judgment in the applicant's favour which would have the effect of restoring the applicant's name and reputation. Such damage could not therefore be regarded as irreparable, even if it were serious. If damage to reputation were, as is sometimes claimed, to manifest itself in the form of loss of business or income in the period pending the delivery of final judgment, it would fall to be assessed as loss of business or loss of income, rather than damage to reputation, when deciding whether or not it constituted serious and irreparable damage.

The following situations have been held not to constitute irreparable or irreversible damage: the disclosure of confidential information to Commission inspectors, at least if the inspectors are bound by an oath of secrecy;[74] the absence of a right to claim reimbursement of money (wrongly or mistakenly) paid out, if the competent authority has at least a discretion to reimburse and if it is not certain that it will not exercise its discretion to do so;[75] a request that the applicant submit proposals for terminating an infringement of the competition rules (as opposed to being required to terminate it forthwith or by a date likely to be before the judgment in the action);[76] an inability to import or sell perishable goods which are in cold storage, unless it is shown that it is impossible to prevent damage to the goods;[77] in staff cases, exclusion from a recruiting competition, if there is sufficient likelihood of another competition being held before the applicant reaches the age limit for candidates[78] or, where the object of the competition is to create a reserve list of candidates, if the candidate can be admitted to the list before it closes (assuming that he wins the case and passes the competition);[79] delay in paying money due;[80] inability to practise as a doctor, at least if the applicant had previously acted only in an administrative capacity (a staff case);[81] inconvenience and extra expense in moving from one country to another (because it can be compensated for in damages);[82] the termination of an official's employment (for the same reason);[83] financial loss if it is otherwise recoverable under Community law or national law;[84] a refusal to extend an invitation to a visiting expert and a

---

72 Case 352/88R *Commission v Italy* (above, note 66) paras 23–25; Case C-195/90R *Commission v Germany* [1990] ECR I-3351 (paras 42–43).

73 Such a claim was made in Case 118/83R *CMC v Commission* [1983] ECR 2583 (para 51) and in Case T-23/90R *Automobiles Peugeot v Commission* (above, note 13) para 30, but rejected on the facts. In *Hoechst AG v Commission* (above, note 60) para 33, the applicant relied unsuccessfully on non-material damage in the form of a bare infringement of its constitutional rights.

74 *Acciaieria e Tubificio di Brescia v High Authority* (above, note 3): the application was for the suspension of the operation of a decision ordering an inspection; Case 37/84R *EISA v Commission* [1984] ECR 1749 (para 1).

75 Case 25/62R I *Plaumann & Co v Commission* (above, note 23) but see below.

76 Case 6/72R *Europemballage Corpn and Continental Can Co Inc v Commission* [1972] ECR 157.

77 Case 44/75R *Firma Karl Könecke v Commission* [1975] ECR 637.

78 Case 4/78R *Salerno v Commission* [1978] ECR 1; *S v Commission* (above, note 33) para 18.

79 Case 142/82R *Copine v Commission* [1982] ECR 1911; Case 293/84R *Sorani v Commission* [1985] ECR 251 (para 8).

80 Case 48/79R *Ooms v Commission* [1979] ECR 1703; Case 214/86R *Greece v Commission* (above, note 57) para 21.

81 Case 129/80R *Turner (née Krecke) v Commission* [1980] ECR 2135.

82 Case 174/80R *Reichardt v Commission* [1980] ECR 2665.

83 Case 347/82R *Alvarez v European Parliament* [1983] ECR 65.

84 Case 42/82R *Commission v France* (above, note 2) at 865 (Advocate General Sir Gordon Slynn); Cases 24 and 97/80R *Commission v France* (above, note 4) at 1342 (Advocate General Capotorti);

change in an official's responsibilities (the latter if the defendant accepts that the official would be reinstated if he wins the action);[85] in the case of an application to suspend the operation of a Commission decision granting an exemption under art 85(3) of the EEC Treaty, it was held that no order would be made because there was no proof that it was impossible for the applicant to comply with the exempted agreement or that compliance would cause irreparable loss;[86] a significant fall in exports (unless there is evidence of a loss of certain markets);[87] a loss of market share (or of relative position in the market) where it is potentially recoverable in the event of a change in the law[88] or where it is easily recoverable or the loss can be quantified;[89] generally, any form of damage that may be prevented or reversed by bringing other proceedings, including proceedings before national courts.[90]

The following have been found to constitute serious and irreparable damage: loss of income by an official who has been dismissed and cannot find work, aliter if he is in a position to get another job;[91] where rights and benefits may be conferred on third parties which would be difficult to withdraw if the action succeeded,[92] the filling of a post, in an action challenging the decision leaving it vacant;[93] the vacancy of a post for a lengthy period;[94] a risk of having to change an appointment;[95] a serious disturbance in the business and interests managed by the applicant[96] or a serious effect on established distribution systems that may create changes in the market that might be very difficult or impossible to reverse;[97] the exclusion of the applicant's product from the market, resulting in a significant drop in orders, where the lost market share is being taken over by competing products and it would be difficult, if not impossible for the applicant's product to regain its previous position;[98] a 93% decline in an undertaking's imports;[99] the risk of closure of part of a business

Case 278/84R *Germany v Commission* [1984] ECR 4341 (para 22); *Hoechst AG v Commission* (above, note 60) para 35; Case 44/88R *De Compte v European Parliament* (above, note 12) para 31; *Hoyer v Commission* (above, note 70) para 19; Case T-52/91R *Smets v Commission* [1991] ECR II-689 (para 20).

85 Case 338/82R *Albertini and Montagnani v Commission* [1983] ECR 145.
86 Case 26/76R *Metro-SB-Grossmärkte GmbH & Co KG v Commission* [1976] ECR 1353.
87 Case 119/86R *Spain v Council and Commission* [1986] ECR 2241 (Re Export Deposits) (para 30); Case 117/86R *Union de Federaciones Agrarias de España (UFADE) v Council and Commission* [1986] ECR 2483 (para 30); Case 128/86R *Spain v Commission* [1986] ECR 2495 (para 30).
88 Case 92/88R *ASSIDER v Commission* (above, note 48) para 28.
89 The *Comos-Tank* case (above, note 24) paras 30–31.
90 Eg Case 85/87R *Dow Chemical Nederland BV v Commission* [1987] ECR 4367 (paras 17–18); Case 32/89R *Greece v Commission* (above, note 26) para 16; Cases T-10 to T-12, T-14 and T-15/92R *SA Cimenteries CBR v Commission* [1992] ECR II-1571 (para 56). The statement to the contrary in Case T-44/90 *La Cinq SA v Commission* [1992] ECR II-1 (paras 79–81), which was made in the context of the analogous powers of the Commission to grant interim relief in competition cases, is unsupported by the case law on the grant of interim relief by the Court.
91 Cases 43, 45 and 48/59 *Eva von Lachmüller v Commission* [1966] ECR 489.
92 Case 15/63R *Lassalle v European Parliament* [1964] ECR 57; Case C-272/91R *Commission v Italy* [1992] ECR I-457 (para 27).
93 Case 18, 35/65R *Gutmann v Euratom Commission* [1966] ECR 135.
94 Case 176/88R *Hanning v European Parliament* [1988] ECR 3915 (para 14); Case C-345/90P-R *European Parliament v Hanning* [1991] ECR I-231 (para 32).
95 Ibid [1991] (para 33).
96 Case 45/71R *GEMA v Commission* [1971] ECR 791 (para 3 – but see also para 4); Cases 228 and 229/82R *Ford Werke AG and Ford of Europe Inc v Commission* [1982] ECR 3091.
97 Cases 76, 77 and 91/89R *Radio Telefis Eireann v Commission* [1989] ECR 1141 (para 18); Case 56/89R *Publishers' Association v Commission* [1989] ECR 1693 (paras 33–34); Cases T-24 and T-28/92R *Langnese-Iglo GmbH & Schöller Lebensmittel GmbH & Co KG v Commission* [1992] ECR 1839 (para 29); Cases T-7/93R and 9/93R *Langnese-Iglo GmbH v Commission* [1993] ECR II-131 (paras 40–42).
98 Case 65/87R *Pfizer International Inc v Commission* [1987] ECR 1691 (paras 18–19).
99 Case T-23/90 *Automobiles Peugeot v Commission* (above, note 46) para 72.

and the tying up of substantial investments (consequent upon a Commission decision ordering an infringement of the competition rules to be terminated forthwith);[1] the threat of a take-over which may result in the applicant withdrawing the action;[2] loss of interest on a deposit, at least in an action for annulment;[3] the payment of a considerable sum of money forthwith (where it was doubtful if it could be recovered[4]) and the loss of interest resulting therefrom, having regard to the possible duration of the action and the rates of interest applicable at the time;[5] 'serious difficulties' to an industry (the applicant was a member state);[6] the making of payments or binding commitments to make payments, before the date of judgment, where it would be very difficult or impossible to recover the sums in question if the applicant were successful in the action;[7] the possibility that students will not be enrolled if they are unable or unwilling to pay a disputed fee;[8] being driven out of business;[9] the imposition of import controls creating a considerable backlog of goods waiting to be imported into a member state and preventing their disposal on the importing country's market;[10] the inability to reconstruct a restrictive practice or marketing arrangements if the decision banning them were annulled;[11] the conclusion of a contract awarded to a competing tenderer;[12] cutting off an undertaking's sources of supply, at least where its stocks are insufficient to enable it to trade until the date of judgment in the action;[13] depriving a person of money and thus compelling him to sell property on unfavourable terms, permanently depriving him of a part of his assets, where a judgment in his favour would not allow him to recover his property on the same terms;[14] damage to family relationships or the educational prospects of a member of the family and damage to health;[15] the holding of elections to a staff committee;[16] in the case of a person elected member of a staff committee for a limited period of time, preventing that person from participating in meetings of the staff committee;[17] in the case of a fishing vessel, the loss of the right to fly

---

1 Case 20/74R *Kali-Chemie AG v Commission* [1974] ECR 337 and 787.
2 Case 3/75R *Johnson and Firth Brown Ltd v Commission* [1975] ECR 1.
3 Case 88/76R *Société pour l'Exportation des Sucres v Commission* [1976] ECR 1585. But see Case 221/86R *Group of the European Right and National Front Party v European Parliament* [1986] ECR 2969 (paras 38–41): the obligation to take out a loan and pay interest on it does not constitute serious damage where the applicant can afford to pay the interest.
4 Cases 113/77R and 113/77R-I *NTN Toyo Bearing Co Ltd v Council* [1977] ECR 1721 (an action for annulment); Case 119/77R *Nippon Seiko KK v Council and Commission* [1977] ECR 1867; Case 121/77R *Nachi Fujikoshi Corpn v Council* [1977] ECR 2107. In the last case some money had already been paid but the President refused to order that the applicant should be reimbursed. Cf Case 25/62R I *Plaumann & Co v Commission* [1963] ECR 123.
5 Case 258/84R *Nippon Seiko KK v Council* [1984] ECR 4357 (paras 16–17): the application was rejected on other grounds.
6 Case 166/78R *Italy v Council* [1978] ECR 1745; Case 171/83R *Commission v France* [1983] ECR 2621.
7 Case 23/86R *United Kingdom v European Parliament* [1986] ECR 1085 (paras 41–46).
8 Case 293/85R *Commission v Germany* [1985] ECR 3521 (paras 20–23).
9 Cases 209–215 and 218/78R *Heintz Van Landewyck Sarl v Commission* [1978] ECR 2111; Case 154/85R *Commission v Italy* [1985] ECR 1753 (para 19); Case 152/88R *Sofrimport Sarl v Commission* [1988] ECR 2931 (para 32); Case C-195/90R *Commission v Germany* [1990] ECR I-3351 (para 39).
10 Case 42/82R *Commission v France* [1982] ECR 841.
11 Cases 43 and 63/82R *VBVB and VBBB v Commission* [1982] ECR 1241; Case 260/82R *NSO v Commission* [1982] ECR 4371; Case T-29/92R *Vereniging van Samenwerkende Prijsregelende Organisaties in de Bouwnijverheid v Commission* [1992] ECR II-2161 (para 31).
12 Case 118/83R *CMC v Commission* [1983] ECR 2583 (para 52).
13 Case 1/84R *Ilford SpA v Commission* [1984] ECR 423 (para 21).
14 Case 141/84R *De Compte v European Parliament* [1985] ECR 2575 (paras 5–6).
15 Case 90/87R *CW v Court of Auditors* [1987] ECR 1801 (paras 12–14); Case 24/87R *Virgili v European Parliament* [1987] ECR 2847 (para 17); Case 76/88R *La Terza v Court of Justice* [1988] ECR 1741 (para 18); Case T-21/93R *Peixote v Commission* [1993] ECR II-463 (para 37).
16 Case 146/85R *Diezler v Economic and Social Committee* [1985] ECR 1805.
17 Case 270/84R *Licata v Economic and Social Committee* [1984] ECR 4119 (para 14).

the flag of a member state and the consequent cessation of fishing activities;[18] irremediable changes in market shares which would make the development and completion of the common transport policy more difficult;[19] a loss of professional expertise.[20]

Applications for the suspension of the operation of regulations imposing definitive anti-dumping duties have given rise to an assessment of serious and irreparable harm that is different from that in other cases.[21] Originally, relief was granted (inter alia) on the ground that the financial consequences of the imposition of definitive duties were serious and, because it was uncertain whether or not the sums in question would be recovered in full if the applicant were successful in the action, irreparable.[22] Such damage is, of course, a direct, necessary and intended consequence of the adoption of an anti-dumping duty. Although the duty is imposed by regulation, it is well established that exporters to the Community of the goods subject to the duty who are identified in the relevant regulation are entitled to seek the annulment of the regulation in proceedings under article 173 of the EEC Treaty: so far as such persons are concerned, the regulation is regarded as a decision of direct and individual concern to each of them. The threat of damage that can be relied on in support of an application for suspension is the threat to the exporter making the application of financial loss caused to a subsidiary, branch or agency in the Community which is liable to pay the anti-dumping duty when the goods are imported into the Community.[23] A different tack was taken in Case 258/84R *Nippon Seiko KK v Council*,[24] where Judge Mackenzie Stuart suggested that an applicant had to show some special damage in addition to the consequences likely to arise in every case where an anti-dumping duty is imposed.[25] That approach was followed by him in Case 77/87R *Technointorg v Council*[26] and by Judge Due in Case 69/89R *Nakajima All Precision Co v Council*[27] and Case C-358/89R *Extramet Industrie SA v Council*.[28] The result of that approach is that an applicant cannot rely upon a threat of serious and irreparable damage to

---

18 Case 246/89R *Commission v United Kingdom* [1989] ECR 3125 (para 37).

19 Case C-195/90R *Commission v Germany* (above, note 9), paras 39-40.

20 Case T-51/91R *Hoyer v Commission* [1991] ECR II-679 (para 24); Case T-52/91R *Smets v Commission* [1991] ECR II-689 (para 25).

21 Applications for the suspension of regulations imposing provisional, as opposed to definitive, anti-dumping duties are in principle inadmissible on the ground that there is ordinarily no interest in challenging such a regulation: Cases C-305/86 and C-160/87 *Neotype Techmashexport GmbH v Commission and Council* [1990] ECR I-2945 (paras 13–16). Such regulations are in any event a form of interim relief pending the decision whether or not to adopt a definitive duty; and, were an application for interim relief to be admissible, it would in principle have to be dealt with in the same way as any other application made in respect of an administrative measure adopting interim relief: see Case 120/83R *Raznoimport v Commission* [1983] ECR 2573; Case 294/86R *Technointorg v Commission* [1986] ECR 3979.

22 Eg *NTN Toyo Bearing Co Ltd v Council* (Judge Kutscher), *Nippon Seiko KK v Council and Commission* and *Nachi Fujikoshi Corp v Council* (all above, note 4).

23 In principle, therefore, the fact that the duty is imposed by a legislative measure (a regulation) is not relevant to the application for suspension save that the case law indicates that the consequences of granting relief must be considered (an aspect of the exercise of the discretion to grant relief that is dealt with in the next section of this chapter and that is not relevant to the question whether or not a threat of serious and irreparable damage to the applicant has been established).

24 Above, note 5 (para 20).

25 Applications for the suspension of a regulation imposing a definitive anti-dumping duty made in the following year were dismissed by Judge Mackenzie Stuart on other grounds: see, for example, Case 250/85R *Brother Industries Ltd v Council* [1985] ECR 3459.

26 [1987] ECR 1793 (paras 16–17 and 19).

27 [1989] ECR 1689 (para 10).

28 [1990] ECR I-431 (paras 20–21).

him which is 'inherent' in the measure whose suspension is sought. Further, the applicant cannot rely upon such a threat even if it is likely to have a particularly devastating effect upon him by reason of some factor peculiar to him (such as the fact that the applicant has only one customer in each member state and, if deprived of that customer, will lose all its existing markets),[29] save (perhaps) where the threat is so devastating as to give rise to an imminent risk to the survival of the applicant.[30] In consequence, it is not at all clear what damage short of the destruction of the applicant can possibly constitute serious and irreparable damage sufficient to ground a claim for relief. What is clear is that, so far as the definition of serious and irreparable damage is concerned, the approach taken in relation to anti-dumping duties is atypical, not to say anomalous.

Where the damage relied on is pecuniary, the attitude of the Court has hardened in recent years.[31] Formerly, the determining factor for characterising such damage as serious and irreparable damage was whether or not it was recoverable as a direct consequence of the applicant winning the action (if he did do so). As a result, pecuniary loss might not be serious and irreparable in the context of an action for damages or in proceedings where the Court had unlimited jurisdiction and could award damages even though the claim was only for annulment. On the other hand, in an action for annulment where the Court did not have unlimited jurisdiction, the loss might well be serious and irreparable unless it would be fully compensated by the annulment of the measure in question. For example, if the effect of annulment were the repayment to the applicant of money wrongfully withheld, plus interest thereon, in order to show that there was risk of serious and irreparable damage there would have to be evidence that the delay in payment of the sum in question (resulting from the need to wait until final judgment) would cause damage which could not be compensated by payment of interest. The more recent case law indicates that pecuniary damage is not in principle serious and irreparable unless there are exceptional circumstances.[32] The assumption is that pecuniary loss is always recoverable in some way or form; whether it is recoverable as a direct consequence of the final judgment or as a result of bringing further proceedings does not matter. If pecuniary loss is or may be recoverable only in part, the question then arises whether or not the inability to achieve compensation in total would result in serious damage or at least damage to the applicant that is out of proportion to the interest of the defendant in avoiding the grant of relief.[33] Even if pecuniary loss is eventually recoverable, serious and irreparable damage may still be caused in the meantime; but, in relation to that issue, the case law exhibits a very reserved attitude towards claims made by legal persons. It is often stated that there must be proof that, in the meantime, the applicant's very existence is under

---

29 The *Nakajima* case (above, note 27) paras 11–12.

30 The *Extramet* case (above, note 28) para 23.

31 See, for example, Case 351/85R *Fabrique de Fer de Charleroi v Commission* [1986] ECR 1307 (paras 28–34); Case 360/85R *Dillinger Hüttenwerke AG v Commission* [1986] ECR 1319 (paras 27–33).

32 Eg Case 44/88R *De Compte v European Parliament* [1988] ECR 1669 (para 31); Case T-45/90R *Speybrouck v European Parliament* [1990] ECR II-705 (paras 23–24); Cases C-51 and C-59/90R *Comos-Tank BV v Commission* [1990] ECR I-2167 (para 24); Case C-195/90R *Commission v Germany* (above, note 9) para 38; Cases C-143/88 and C-92/89 *Zuckerfabrik Süderdithmarschen AG v Hauptzollamt Itzehoe* [1991] ECR I-415 (para 29); Case C-213/91R *Abertal SAT Lda v Commission* [1991] ECR I-5109 (para 24).

33 Cf Case 44/88R *De Compte v European Parliament* (ibid) para 31.

threat[34] whereas a more realistic test would be whether or not the conduct of the applicant's business would be materially affected for the worse.

Where the damage consists not simply of pecuniary loss but of an injury to property rights, not even an award of damages may prevent such damage from being considered serious and irreparable. In Case 232/81R *Agricola Commerciale Olio Srl v Commission*,[35] the applicants were designated as the purchasers of a quantity of olive oil sold by lot at a fixed price pursuant to a Commission regulation. In two subsequent regulations the Commission purported to repeal the first regulation and offered the same amount of oil for sale by tender. The applicants claimed that they had acquired property rights in the oil under the first regulation and applied for the annulment of the other two and an order suspending their operation. Apart from the threatened loss of their property rights, the applicants also argued that, if they participated in the sale by tender, they would suffer a heavy financial burden and could not be sure of obtaining precisely the same lots sold to them under the first regulation. On top of that they had difficulty in obtaining oil from other sources. The Commission argued that this did not constitute serious and irreparable loss because an action for damages could be brought. The President rejected this on the ground that the loss 'cannot be offset by the prospect of an unspecified amount of compensation in the future when all the evidence suggests that [the applicants] are being deprived of their property'. It is at this stage unclear whether the same approach will be followed in future or be superseded by a greater tendency to transmute certain forms of damage into pecuniary loss. In Case C-358/90R *Compagnia Italiana Alcool Sas de Mario Mariano & Co v Commission*,[36] for example, a situation similar to that in the *Agricola Commerciale Olio* case arose and the applicant complained that it would be excluded from the market for alcohol for use in the fuel sector as a result of the defendant's decision not to take action on the tenders received but to open new tender procedures under different conditions. The damage was characterised as financial in nature and, since there was no evidence that it could not be made good in its entirety, the application for relief was dismissed.[37] In many instances, damage of a commercial nature can be remedied by an award of financial compensation and, in such cases, as long as the loss is quantifiable there seems no particular reason that interim relief need be granted unless the disruption caused to the applicant or the difficulty in obtaining financial compensation is disproportionately great having regard to the interest of the opposing party in avoiding the grant of interim relief.

D The balance of interests

In most cases the decision whether or not to order relief is made solely on the basis of the evidence put forward by the applicant to show that he is threatened with serious and irreparable damage. In some cases, however, the Court has also considered the damage that may be caused to others if the relief sought is granted and has sought to balance the interests in the case. The frequency of such cases has grown in recent years and they now seem to represent an established development in the case law on interim relief.[38] However, the

34 Eg the *Comos-Tank* case (above, note 32) para 24.
35 [1981] ECR 2193.
36 [1990] ECR I-4887 (para 28).
37 The action was one for annulment and damages.
38 For relatively early suggestions that the Court or judge balances the respective interests of the parties when deciding whether to order interim relief see Slusny (1967) Rev Belge Droit Int, 127 and 146; Gray (1979) ELR 80 et seq. (citing the practice of the International Court of Justice and of English courts); Temple Lang (1981) CMLR 49 at 51, footnote 5 (citing the practice of English courts); Bebr *Development of Judicial Control of the European Communities* pp 145–146.

expression 'balance of interests' (occasionally also 'balance of convenience') has been used to express a variety of different operations and it is as well to be clear about the sense in which the interests at stake can be balanced in the context of the grant or refusal of interim relief.

As a matter of principle, the decision whether or not to grant relief cannot and does not depend upon nothing more than the finding that one party or the other lies under the greater risk of damage if relief is refused or, as the case may be, granted: the authorities indicate without any ambiguity that the starting point is for the applicant to show that he is under the threat of serious and irreparable damage. Anything less than that is not good enough. The applicant must therefore satisfy an irrelative test (in the sense that it requires no examination of the relative positions of the applicant and the opposing party or parties). When the risk threshold is set so high for the applicant, it necessarily follows that mere inconvenience to the defendant or the possibility that, in relative terms, the damage to the defendant resulting from the grant of relief may be greater than the damage with which the applicant is threatened (if relief is not granted) cannot bar the claim for relief.

In order to counter the case for the grant of relief, the defendant (or, as explained above, unrepresented third parties) would have to be threatened with serious and irreparable damage (as that expression is understood in the context of interim relief), if relief were ordered. There is no doubt that this is in principle a good answer to a claim for relief because: ex hypothesi, serious and irreparable damage to the defendant would render the final decision in the action otiose and this would be contrary to the principle that interim relief is only temporary and does not prejudice the effect of the final judgment;[39] and, secondly, in the case of a threat to third parties, it is well established that a threat of serious and irreparable (or at least serious) damage to the rights or interests of third parties bars a claim for interim relief unless the applicant's very existence is under threat. It is in that sense that occasional statements in the case law, to the effect that the judge must weigh up all the interests involved, are to be understood.[40] In the ordinary case, the plea that serious and irreversible damage may be caused to the defendant (or to third parties) does not, however, cause the judge to balance that risk with the risk to the applicant: if the effect of granting relief is to cause such damage, it falls in principle outside the judge's powers to order it. In consequence, if it is not probable that such damage will be caused to the defendant (or to third parties), the judge rejects the defendant's plea. If it is probable, he either rejects the applicant's claim entirely or awards a different kind of relief which will safeguard the applicant's position but either will not render final judgment in the action nugatory as far as the defendant is concerned or will not inflict serious or serious and irreparable damage on third parties.

It is really only in cases where, although the extent of the threats to the applicant and the defendant is the same (that is, the damage is serious and irreparable), the degree of probability of the threats to the opposing parties differs that

---

39 If the damage with which the defendant is threatened would arise in any event and even if relief were not granted, it cannot be relied on as an objection to the grant of relief: Case 194/88R *Commission v Italy* [1988] ECR 5647 (para 17).

40 Eg Case 278/84R *Germany v Commission* [1984] ECR 4341 (para 20), where the grant of relief would have prejudiced the Court's final judgment by creating a serious disturbance of the market (see para 21); Case T-96/92R *Comité Central d'Entreprise de la Société Générale des Grandes Sources v Commission* [1992] ECR II-2579 (paras 36–41) and Case T-12/93R *Comité Central d'Entreprise de la Société Anonyme Vittel v Commission* [1993] ECR II-449 (para 30) and order of 6 July 1993, where the grant of relief would have affected the exercise of a third party's voting rights, thus seriously affecting the operations of a group of companies, or prolonged a situation of dominance on a market in such a way as to risk having irreversible effects on competition.

the judge is called on to perform a balancing exercise: he must then weigh, on the one hand, the nature of the threat to one party and the likelihood that it will materialise before judgment against, on the other hand, the nature of the threat to the other party and the likelihood that that threat will materialise before judgment. Theoretically, the balancing exercise should be limited to the degree of probability of the threat to either party because the nature (or rather extent) of the threat is identical: serious and irreparable damage.[41] Depending upon the circumstances of the case, however, the balancing exercise may relate to either or both of the nature of the threat and the degree of probability that it will materialise: in the present state of the case law, it cannot be excluded that, even where the damage with which both parties are threatened (depending upon whether relief is granted or refused) is serious and irreparable and the degree of probability of the damage being caused before judgment is the same, the judge may be entitled to examine more specifically the nature and extent of the threat to each party in order to identify which is intrinsically the more serious.[42] Such an approach appears to have more merit than the alternative solution, which is that the judge refuses to grant relief, even though the applicant is faced with serious and irreparable damage, simply because, if relief were granted, the defendant would then be faced with serious and irreparable damage (the probability of the threats materialising being the same). At first sight, that alternative appears to be a sensible solution because there is ordinarily no good reason that, before final judgment is given and the respective rights and duties of the parties have been determined, the judge should transfer a risk of serious and irreparable damage from one party to the other. The mechanistic application of that approach could, however, create injustice in particular cases, such as where the threats to both parties, while being threats of damage that is serious and irreparable in the technical sense in which that expression is used, are nonetheless different in nature (such as where the damage to the applicant is to its commercial interests whereas the damage to the defendant is to the interests of the Community in disposing of intervention stocks)[43] or extent (such as where the imposition of an anti-dumping duty would cause serious and irreparable damage to the business of an exporter to the Community but the suspension of the measure imposing the duty pending final judgment would cause serious and irreparable damage to the business of many undertakings in the Community).[44] In such cases, if no solution is available which would ward off the threats to both parties, the just solution may be to lessen the threat to one party or the other, which may lead to a sharing of the risk as between the opposing parties.[45] Such cases may also be resolved by balancing the opposing interests of the parties in obtaining relief or, as the case may be, ensuring the continued effectiveness of the disputed measure: in a balancing exercise of that sort, the status quo and the past attitudes of the parties may play an important part.[46] It should be

---

41 For an example of the balancing of probabilities, see Cases 76, 77 and 91/89R *Radio Telefis Eireann v Commission* [1989] ECR 1141 (paras 15–18); Case C-280/93R *Germany v Council* [1993] ECR I-3667 (paras 49–54); *Peixoto v Commission* (above, note 15) paras 36–39.

42 That appears to have been done in Case C-345/90P-R *European Parliament v Hanning* [1991] ECR I-231 (para 33).

43 The *Compagnia Italiana Alcool* case (above, note 36) para 29.

44 Cf the test suggested in Case 77/87R *Technointorg* (above, note 26) para 17.

45 Eg Cases T-24 and 28/92R *Langnese-Iglo v Commission* [1992] ECR II-1839 (paras 26–35); Cases T-7 and T-9/93R *Langnese-Iglo v Commission* [1993] ECR II-131 (paras 3–45).

46 Eg *Radio Telefis Eireann v Commission* (above, note 41) para 15; Case 56/89R *Publishers' Association v Commission* [1989] ECR 1693 (para 35). In Case 45/87R *Commission v Ireland* [1987] ECR 1369 (paras 32–33) the comparison was between the applicant's interest in ensuring observance of Community law and the defendant's interest in putting an early end to a health

emphasised that the balance of interests referred to here applies where one or other of the parties is threatened with serious and irreparable damage whether the judge grants the relief sought or refuses it; such an approach is not necessary where one or other of the parties is faced with a threat falling short of serious and irreparable damage.

A different kind of balancing of interests applies where the judge is considering the form of the relief to be granted. In that situation, the applicant has ex hypothesi satisfied all the conditions for the grant of relief. The judge is then concerned only to ensure that the relief ordered is proportionate in the sense that it is effective and imposes on the opposing party and on third parties burdens that go no further than is absolutely necessary in order to provide the degree of protection to which the applicant is entitled.[47]

It remains to be considered whether or not there is authority for the application of a balance of interests, or balance of convenience, test that is different from the test discussed above, in particular, whether or not relief may be granted or refused on the basis that the damage with which one party is threatened is more important in nature or extent than the damage with which the other party is threatened and even if the damage in question is not 'serious and irreparable' in the technical sense. The cases requiring comment in this connection fall broadly speaking into three categories:

(1)   cases in which a threat to third parties was considered;
(2)   those in which it was a threat to the defendant (or to an interest represented by the defendant) that was taken into account;
(3)   applications for the suspension of the operation of a regulation or measure of general effect.

The cases falling within the last category give rise to particular problems and will be examined separately.

The first[48] and second[49] categories[50] for the most part comprise cases where

hazard; in Case C-272/91R *Commission v Italy* [1992] ECR I-457 (para 28) the comparison was between the defendant's interest in rapid automation of a public lottery and the applicant's interest in preventing infringements of fundamental rules of Community law in circumstances where there had already been one judgment against the defendant.

47 Eg Case 293/85R *Commission v Belgium* [1985] ECR 3521 (para 24); *Speybrouck v European Parliament* (above, note 32) para 36. The principle of proportionality also requires that the means used be proportionate to the aim sought in the sense that, even if the means used are both effective and the minimum necessary to achieve the desired aim, their adverse consequences must be outweighed by the benefits derived from achieving the desired aim. That aspect of the principle of proportionality does not need to be considered at the stage of selecting the relief to be granted because the application of the criteria for the grant of relief (in particular the requirement that the applicant be threatened with serious and irreparable damage) will have rendered it otiose.

48 Cases 6 & 7/73R *Istituto Chemioterapico Italiano SpA and Commercial Solvents Corpn v Commission* [1973] ECR 357; *Johnson and Firth Brown Ltd v Commission* (above, note 2); Case 91/76R *De Lacroix v European Court of Justice* [1976] ECR 1563; Case 4/78R *Salerno v Commission* [1978] ECR 1; Case 19/78R *Authié v Commission* [1978] ECR 679; Case 142/82R *Copine v Commission* [1982] ECR 1911; Cases 228 and 229/82R *Ford Werke AG and Ford of Europe Inc v Commission* [1982] ECR 3091; Case 173/82R *Castille v Commission* [1982] ECR 4047; Case 114/83R *SICA and SIPEFEL v Commission* [1983] ECR 2315; Cases 67, 68 and 70/85R *Kwekerij Gebroeders van der Kooy BV v Commission* [1985] ECR 1315 (para 45); Case 57/86R *Greece v Commission* [1986] ECR 1497 (para 12); Case 221/86R *Group of the European Right and National Front Party v European Parliament* [1986] ECR 2969 (paras 38–41); Case 161/87R *Muysers and Tulp v Court of Auditors* [1987] ECR 2381 (para 13); Case 63/88R *Maindiaux v Economic and Social Committee* [1988] ECR 1659 (para 28); *European Parliament v Hanning* (above, note 42) para 33; the *Grandes Sources* case (above, note 40) paras 36–41.

49 Cases 42 & 49/59 *Breedband NV v Société des Aciéries du Temple* [1962] ECR 145; Case 15/63R *Lassalle v European Parliament* [1964] ECR 57; Cases 18, 35/65R *Gutmann v Euratom Commission* [1966] ECR 135; Case 29/66R *Gutmann v Euratom Commission* [1967] ECR 241; Case 22/75R

the test adopted was whether or not the defendant or third parties would suffer serious and irreparable damage if relief were ordered; or where the application was either upheld or rejected on other grounds and the judge went on to pass some observations on the alleged threat to the defendant or to third parties. There are serious difficulties in the way of construing such cases as showing the existence of a balance of interests or balance of convenience test[51] because remarks to the effect that there is no threat or risk of detriment to the defendant can be interpreted simply as emphasising the fact that the defendant had not come anywhere near establishing a risk of serious and irreparable damage which would justify refusing relief. They do not indicate that the judge would have dismissed the application had a threat of a lower degree been proved.

The cases falling within the first and second categories which do lend some apparent support for a balance of interests or balance of convenience test in a sense different from that discussed above are the following. *De Lacroix v European Court of Justice*[52] was a confused case: Judge Donner treated the application as one for the suspension of a competition held by the Court to fill three vacant posts. He said that to grant relief would cause serious difficulties for the Court, because there was a need to fill the posts as soon as possible, and serious inconvenience for the other candidates. In *Salerno v Commission, Authié v Commission* (both decisions of Judge Sørensen), *Copine v Commission* and *Castille v Commission* (both decisions of Judge Bosco),[53] which also concerned recruitment or promotion procedures, the applications were rejected on other grounds but the judges, following *De Lacroix*, added that the balance of convenience did not favour the granting of relief. In *Reichardt v Commission*,[54] an application for the suspension of the operation of a decision transferring the applicant, Judge Mertens de Wilmars held that, apart from urgency, the only issue in the case was whether the application of the decision would cause irreversible damage which could not be remedied if it were annulled or damage which would be out of proportion to the interest of the defendant. Similar remarks appear in some of his other decisions: for example, in *Arbed v Commission*[55] he assessed the extent of the damage with which the applicants were threatened by reference only to their capacity to bear it, which suggests a balancing approach. In his opinion in Case 42/82R *Commission v France* Advocate General Sir Gordon Slynn referred to the balance of convenience[56]

Küster v European Parliament [1975] ECR 277; *De Lacroix v European Court of Justice* (ibid); Cases 31 and 53/77R *Commission v United Kingdom* [1977] ECR 921 at 931 (Advocate General Mayras); *Salerno v Commission* (ibid); *Authié v Commission* (ibid); Case 174/80R *Reichardt v Commission* [1980] ECR 2665; Case 20/81R *Arbed v Commission* [1981] ECR 721; Case 78/83R *USINOR v Commission* [1983] ECR 2183; Case 42/82R *Commission v France* [1982] ECR 841 (Advocate General Slynn); Case 347/82R *Alvarez v European Parliament* [1983] ECR 65; Case 270/84R *Licata v Economic and Social Committee* [1984] ECR 4119 (para 14); Case 97/85R *Union Deutsche Lebensmittelwerke GmbH v Commission* [1985] ECR 1331 (para 21); Case 45/87R *Commission v Ireland* (above, note 46) para 33; *Muysers and Tulp v Court of Auditors* (ibid) para 13; Case 23/87R *Aldinger v European Parliament* [1987] ECR 2841 (para 17); *Virgili v European Parliament* (above, note 15) para 17; *Maindiaux v Economic and Social Committee* (ibid) para 28; Case 176/88R *Hanning v European Parliament* [1988] ECR 3915 (para 9); Case 246/89R *Commission v United Kingdom* (above, note 18) para 39; *Speybrouck v European Parliament* (above, note 32) para 36; *European Parliament v Hanning* (above, note 42) para 33.

50 As can be seen, some cases fall into both categories.

51 Other than as described above.
52 Above, note 48.
53 Above, note 48.
54 Above, note 49.
55 Above, note 49. See also the *Ford* case (above, note 48) para 14, and *Usinor v Commission* (above, note 49) para 8. Note Case 141/84R *De Compte v Parliament* (above, note 14) (Judge Galmot).
56 Above (note 10) at 867.

but, since he had earlier accepted that the applicant had shown that there was a threat of serious and irreparable damage, it is possible that he considered that the defendant would also have to show the existence of such a threat in order to justify the rejection of the application. In Case 176/88R *Hanning v European Parliament*,[57] Judge Moitinho de Almeida said that the applicant had to be threatened with irreversible damage but that the relief granted must not be out of proportion to the defendant's interest in having the contested act applied. That suggests that the applicant could in principle obtain relief if he or she were threatened with irreversible damage of a minor nature unless the defendant could demonstrate a risk of more serious (but equally irreparable) damage if relief were granted. In *Speybrouck v European Parliament*,[58] a case concerning the termination of the applicant's contract of employment, Judge Cruz Vilaça said that it was necessary to balance the interests of the parties to avoid serious and irreparable damage to the applicant and also avoid obliging the defendant to maintain the employment relationship in a situation in which mutual confidence was lacking. In that context, however, he seems to have been envisaging the balancing exercise undertaken when selecting the appropriate form of relief to grant and not any exercise to be undertaken when deciding whether or not relief ought to be granted as a matter of principle.

Thus, a review of the cases falling within the first and second categories, taken within the general context of the case law, reveals no certain authority for the propositions that relief may be granted, in the absence of proof of serious and irreparable damage, merely on the ground that the threat to the applicant outweighs that to the defendant; or that relief may be refused, if the applicant does show that there is risk of irreparable damage, merely on proof of some threat to the defendant which is less than serious and irreparable. There are, clearly, a few cases which are not easy to explain and which are best regarded as anomalies since the case law, when taken as a whole and subjected to proper analysis, simply does not support the view that relief is, as a matter of practice, granted or refused on the basis of an assessment or balance of the respective interests of the parties alone. There is no doubt but that such a balance can be drawn when the judge is deciding what is the most appropriate form of relief to order: he must, in accordance with the principle of proportionality,[59] ensure that the relief granted is adequate to achieve its objective of preserving the status quo and that it does not impose an excessive burden on the defendant to the application in comparison with some other, equally appropriate, form of relief.[60] Nonetheless, it is not a condition of entitlement to relief in general (as opposed to a specific form of relief) that the balance of the interests of the parties weighs in favour of the applicant.

On the other hand, several decisions made by Judge Mertens de Wilmars and the decision of Judge Moitinho de Almeida in Case 176/88R *Hanning v European Parliament*[61] indicate that they did employ the balance of interests or balance of convenience approach. The explanation for this probably lies in the fact that they did not require proof of serious and irreparable damage in order to ground a claim for relief, particularly (in the case of Judge Mertens de Wilmars) where the applicant was prepared to lodge a security under RP-ECJ

---

57 Above (note 49) para 9.
58 Above (note 32) para 36.
59 It will be noted that arts 39 of the ECSC Treaty, 186 of the EC Treaty and 158 of the Euratom Treaty refer to the adoption of the 'necessary' interim measures.
60 This seems to be the true explanation of Case 26/76R *Metro-SB-Grossmärkte GmbH & Co KG v Commission* [1976] ECR 1353, which has been cited as authority for the balance of convenience approach.
61 Above, note 49.

86(2). There is insufficient evidence in the case law to infer that their decisions can be taken to herald a shift in approach.[62]

One important category of cases in which special problems have arisen comprises cases involving measures of general effect. They are too few in number to have produced a settled and consistent line of authority.

In Case 44/75R *Firma Karl Könecke v Commission*[63] Judge Lecourt held that, save in exceptional cases making it possible to single out the applicant from other persons, the judge cannot consider the effect of a general provision as amounting to that of a 'measure' within the meaning of RP-ECJ 83(1); on the other hand, where the application is for relief by way of an interim measure (as opposed to suspension of the operation of the provision in question), the applicant must prove in a particularly clear fashion that he is concerned directly and individually by the provision. The action was for the annulment of several Commission regulations and, in adopting those two tests, Judge Lecourt seems to have been influenced by the conditions for the admissibility of an action for annulment brought by a natural or legal person under art 173 of the EC Treaty. Neither test was expressly mentioned by Judge Kutscher in the *Japanese Ball Bearing* cases[64] nor by Judge Mertens de Wilmars in Case 232/81R *Agricola Commerciale Olio Srl v Commission*.[65] The probability is that, in all these cases, the regulations in question plainly singled out the applicants and were therefore, prima facie at least, of direct and individual concern to them.

In the two *Simmenthal* cases,[66] in contrast, the applicants sought the suspension of the operation of a Commission decision fixing the Community selling prices and import quotas for beef and veal and of several regulations. As far as the first was concerned, Judge Kutscher refused to grant relief on the ground that it would deprive unrepresented third parties of their rights. Even if it were possible, he held, it would be justified only if the applicant were exposed to a threat to its very existence. Suspension of the operation of the regulations was simply held to be out of all proportion to the interests which the applicants wished to safeguard. It should be noted that the decision was addressed to the member states so the action for annulment would have been admissible only if the decision was of direct and individual concern to the applicants. In addition, the decision was in substance a measure of general effect, as was amply demonstrated by the fact that it impinged on the rights of third parties, because it was an administrative measure intended to achieve a particular regulatory effect on an entire sector of the common agricultural policy.

In a number of cases in which the suspension of regulations imposing anti-dumping duties was sought, Judge Mackenzie Stuart emphasised the need to balance all the interests concerned by the case and compare the effect on the applicant, if relief were not granted, with the effect on Community industry (generally represented by an intervener in the proceedings), if it were granted.[67] In parallel, he also developed the principle, followed in later anti-

---

62 In particular, such an inference seems to be contradicted by decisions such as the Court's judgment in Case 42/82R *Commission v France* (above, note 10).
63 [1975] ECR 637.
64 Cases 113/77R and 113/77R-I *NTN Toyo Bearing Co Ltd v Council*, Case 119/77R *Nippon Seiko KK v Council and Commission*, Case 121/77R *Nachi Fujikoshi Corpn v Council* (above, note 4).
65 Above, note 35.
66 Case 92/78R *Simmenthal SpA v Commission* [1978] ECR 1129 and Case 243/78R *Simmenthal SpA v Commission* [1978] ECR 2391.
67 Case 250/85R *Brother Industries Ltd v Council* (above, note 25) para 17; Case 273/85R *Silver Seiko Ltd v Council* [1985] ECR 3475 (para 18); Case 297/85R *Towa Sankiden Corpn v Council* [1985] ECR 3483 (para 16); Cases 277 and 300/85R *Canon Inc v Council* [1985] ECR 3491 (para 17).

dumping cases, that the applicant must demonstrate both a threat to it of special damage over and above that arising in the normal course from the imposition of an anti-dumping duty and the absence of any appreciable injury to Community industry if relief were granted.[68] The reasoning behind that approach seems to be that, otherwise, the usual conditions required for the grant of interim relief would be easily satisfied and, if relief were then granted, the effect would be to frustrate the purpose of the regulation imposing the duties. On the other hand, in the *Sofrimport* case,[69] a case concerning regulations limiting imports of apples into the Community (that is, trade protection measures similar in objective to anti-dumping duties), Judge Mackenzie Stuart did not, at least expressly, adopt the same approach followed by him in anti-dumping cases. The *Sofrimport* case was, however, one where there was evidence that, if relief were not granted, the applicant would be forced to cease trading and there was no indication that, if relief were granted, it would cause a serious disturbance of the market.

In all these cases, save *Agricola Commerciale Olio Srl v Commission*,[70] the judges have stressed that account must be taken of the effect of granting relief in the public interest. This has been expressed in different ways: Judge Lecourt spoke both of the public interest and the impact on administrative action; Judge Kutscher of an appreciable detriment to the Community, the effect on the public budget and the rights of third parties; Judge Mackenzie Stuart of the effect on Community industry, which the contested regulations sought to protect. In consequence it seems possible to summarise the cases as follows. Where an application for interim relief is made in respect of a measure of general effect, the applicant must, in addition to the other conditions required for the grant of relief, show that:

(1)   the measure is of direct and individual concern to him or singles him out for special treatment, in the technical sense used in the context of the admissibility of the action;[71]

(2)   it threatens him with damage over and above that normally arising from a measure of that type;[72] and

(3)   the applicant's private interest in obtaining relief outweighs the public interest in refusing it. In assessing the public interest weighing against the grant of relief, broader considerations may have to be taken into account than the question whether or not serious and irreparable damage may be caused.

IV   Procedure

An application for suspension of the operation of an act contested in the action may be made only by the person challenging the act.[73] An application for

---

68 Case 258/84R *Nippon Seiko KK v Council* (above, note 5) paras 19–20; Case 77/87R *Technointorg v Council* (above, note 26) paras 16–20.

69 Above, note 9 (paras 32–33).

70 Above, note 35.

71 It is not enough to show that, because of some idiosyncrasy, the applicant just happens to be affected to a greater extent than others: it must be possible to determine that this is within the intendment of the measure. But see Case 258/80R *Metallurgica Rumi SpA v Commission* [1980] ECR 3867.

72 The fact that such special damage arises by reason of some particular weakness or peculiarity of the applicant and is not within the intendment of the contested measure appears to be irrelevant.

73 RP-ECJ 83(1), first sentence; RP-CFI 104(1), first sentence.

interim measures may be made by any party to the action.[74] In practice, applicants for interim measures are almost invariably applicants in the action.[75] Interveners are not thought to be 'parties' for the purpose of making an application for interim measures. In the case of the suspension of the enforcement of a decision of the Court or of any measure adopted by another institution, there is no definition of the persons who may apply.[76] It is thought that an application may be made by anyone with sufficient interest, typically the person against whom the decision or other measure is being enforced. An application for interim relief may also be made (to the President of the ECJ) in the context of an appeal (to the ECJ) from a judgment of the CFI.[77] In that context, the applicant may be 'a party' to the appeal where the relief sought is the suspension of the effects of a regulation which has been declared void by the CFI or any other interim measure,[78] that is (it would seem), the appellant (even if an intervener before the CFI) or any other party. There seems to be no reason to confine that broad right to seek relief to the case of a judgment of the CFI declaring a regulation to be void: the limits to the right to seek relief in the context of an appeal seem to be limited only by the ability of the applicant to demonstrate that the conditions for granting relief have been satisfied. The procedure followed when seeking interim relief in the context of an appeal is the same as when application is made in the context of a direct action brought before the ECJ.[79]

An application for interim relief may be made at any stage as long as it is not made so late in the day as to have lost any usefulness.[80] An application for suspension of the operation of a measure or for interim measures must be made by separate document[81] and may be held to be inadmissible if made in the application commencing the action, rather than separately.[82] An application for the suspension of the enforcement of a decision of the Court or of any measure adopted by another institution must also be made by separate document but need not be made in the context of an action pending before the Court.[83] Whatever the nature of the relief sought, the general form of the application is the same as that for an application commencing proceedings in a direct action but it must comply with RP-ECJ 83(2) or, as the case may be, RP-CFI 104(2) as well as RP-ECJ 37 and 38 or, as the case may be, RP-CFI 43 and 44.[84] As a result, it must state the applicant's name and address, the name of the defendant, the name and address of the person authorised to accept

74 RP-ECJ 83(1), last sentence; RP-CFI 104(1), last sentence.

75 Case C-106/90R *Emerald Meats Ltd v Commission* [1990] ECR I-3377 (paras 28–30) provides a rare example of the defendant applying for a form of interim relief (appointment of an expert).

76 See RP-ECJ 89; RP-CFI 110.

77 ECSC and EC Statutes, art 53; Euratom Statute, art 54.

78 Ibid, second para.

79 RP-ECJ 118.

80 *Aldinger v European Parliament* (above, note 49) para 11; *Virgili v European Parliament* (above, note 15) para 11.

81 RP-ECJ 83(3); RP-CFI 104(3).

82 See Case 108/63 *Officine Elettromeccaniche Ing A Merlini v High Authority* [1965] ECR 1; Case 32/64 *Italy v Commission* [1965] ECR 365 at 372; Case 81/83 *Acciaierie e Ferriere Busseni v Commission* [1984] ECR 2951 at 2966 (Advocate General Lenz).

83 For example, where the validity of the contested act is disputed in proceedings before a national court and has been the subject of a reference for a preliminary ruling, an application to suspend the enforcement of the measure may be made to the Court (where necessary) without the need to commence proceedings directly before the Court.

84 RP-ECJ 83(3); RP-CFI 104(3).

service in Luxembourg;[85] it must bear a date, be signed by the party's agent or lawyer, as the case may be, be lodged with the required number of copies and also be drawn up in the language of the case. Most of the documents which are required to accompany an application will in any event be annexed to the application commencing the action and it is apprehended that, where this is so, a simple reference to them in the application for interim relief is sufficient to comply with RP-ECJ 38 and RP-CFI 44. Different applications may be dealt with together, like similar actions, if they have the same purpose and are closely connected.[86]

The matters of substance which are required to be set out in the application for interim relief are defined partly in RP-ECJ 38 and RP-CFI 44 and partly in RP-ECJ 83(2) and RP-CFI 104(2). They comprise:

(1)   the subject matter of the dispute;
(2)   the circumstances giving rise to urgency;
(3)   the pleas of fact and law establishing a prima facie case for the interim relief applied for;
(4)   the form of order sought; and
(5)   the evidence relied on.

It is not essential to set them out in this order or to set them out in this way. Basically the application falls into three parts.

The first part consists of a description of the dispute between the parties and the arguments advanced by the applicant. This need not be as detailed as the application commencing the action, in order to avoid repetition.[87] Its purpose is to set out the context of the application for relief and show that the applicant has an arguable case in the action.[88]

The second part deals with the need for urgency and the risk of serious and irreparable damage. The summary nature of proceedings for interim relief means that a full scale investigation into the facts is not to be expected, nor is it required; but the judge must be given reasonable cause to believe that the conditions for obtaining relief have been fulfilled. The degree to which the nature of the proceedings entitles the judge hearing the application to rely upon assertions made by one or other of the parties that are not supported by evidence is controversial; and different judges have taken different views.[89] In consequence, even if only as a matter of precaution, the applicant must produce any relevant documents in his possession or control and indicate with precision any other source of evidence such as testimony.

The third part consists of the form of order, in which the prayer for relief is set out. The relief sought should be set out in precise terms and be clearly

---

85 If an address for service in Luxembourg is not specified, service will be effected in accordance with RP-ECJ 38(2) or RP-CFI 44(2). If the application commencing the action gives an address for service in Luxembourg but the application for interim relief does not, it may be assumed that the omission is an oversight and, in the interim relief proceedings, service should be effected in the normal way at the address for service in Luxembourg.
86 Eg Cases 82 and 83/85R *Eurasian Corpn Ltd v Commission* [1985] ECR 1191 (para 4).
87 Some pleaders annex a copy of the application commencing the action to the application for interim relief.
88 The suggestion in *Vereniging van Samenwerkende Prijsregelende Organisaties in de Bouwnijverheid v Commission* (above, note 11) para 34, is that the applicant need only list the grounds relied on in the application commencing the action and assert that that application cannot reasonably be said to be without foundation (but the judge must still verify whether or not that is so).
89 See pp 295–298.

justified by reference to the matters set out in the body of the application.[90] It is nevertheless admissible to add a plea for 'further or other relief' because the judge may decide that, while the relief sought is not appropriate, some other form of relief should be ordered. In contrast to other proceedings, the judge is not faced with a choice between granting the order sought by the applicant or refusing it altogether. He may, and often does, make his decision on the basis of what is appropriate in order to preserve the position pending judgment in the action.[91] For the same reasons, the application may be amended in the course of the proceedings in response to any change in circumstances which may affect the nature of the relief to be granted;[92] but otherwise any change in the nature or extent of the relief sought must remain within the scope of the claim as originally formulated.[93] As is usual, the applicant should ask for costs, although the normal order is for the question of costs to be decided in the final judgment. In other respects, the relief that can be claimed is limited to that proper to interim relief proceedings and may not include, for example, a claim for symbolic damages.[94] An application not made in the proper form may, of course, be rejected as inadmissible.[95]

The application may be rejected as inadmissible without being served on the opposing party if the action to which it relates is also rejected as being outside the Court's jurisdiction, manifestly inadmissible or the subject of an absolute bar.[96] Otherwise, the application is served on the other party in the usual way and the President prescribes 'a short period' for the submission of any written or oral observations.[97] The reference to 'written or oral observations' suggests that the President may fix a date for the hearing of the application without giving the other party the opportunity to answer the application in writing. The usual practice is for the President to invite, and receive, written observations from the opposing party and then to decide whether or not further oral observations are necessary, unless the matter is so urgent that there is no time for written observations. The omission of an opportunity to submit written or, as the case may be, oral observations does not, of course, deprive the opposing party altogether of his right to be heard since he will invariably be given the opportunity to be heard either orally or in writing, if not in both forms, unless the application is so obviously inadmissible or unfounded that it can be dismissed immediately. It is to be noted that no 'defence' is lodged in response to the application. Instead, proceedings are analogous to those for intervening in a case and the emphasis is less on their contentious nature. The opposing party's observations should answer the

---

90 In Case 107/82R *AEG Telefunken AG v Commission* [1982] ECR 1179 and 1549, the application sought suspension of the enforcement (ie execution) of a Commission decision imposing a fine on the applicants. The Commission naturally argued that relief was neither urgent nor necessary because no proceedings had begun before a national court for the recovery of the sums due. The President, however, construed the application as impliedly seeking the suspension of the operation of the decision. This would cause its enforcement to be suspended by freezing its legal effects. It should be observed that it is not always possible to save an application in this way.

91 Cf *Ilford v Commission* (above, note 13).

92 *Eurasian Corpn Ltd v Commission* (above, note 86) paras 14–16; Case 48/86R *J Cauet and B Joliet v Commission* [1986] ECR 1237 (para 4), where the parties agreed that the proceedings should continue as against a decision which replaced the decision that had originally been contested.

93 Case 293/85R *Commission v Belgium* (above, note 47) para 4, where at the hearing the applicant narrowed the scope of the relief sought; Case C-280/93R *Germany v Council* (above, note 41) paras 15–16.

94 Case C-35/92P-R *European Parliament v Frederiksen* [1992] ECR I-2399 (paras 25–26).

95 See Case 731/79R II *B v European Parliament* [1980] ECR 829.

96 Eg Cases 264/88 and 264/88R *Valle Fernandez v Commission* [1988] ECR 6341.

97 RP-ECJ 84(1); RP-CFI 105(1).

assertions made in the application for relief and may, where appropriate, request an alternative order to that proposed by the applicant.[98]

The President has power to grant the application even before the defendant's observations have been submitted.[99] This situation may arise in cases of extreme urgency where it is necessary to preserve the position pending the receipt of the defendant's observations on the application for relief and the eventual decision on the application.[1] For example, in Case 107/82R *AEG Telefunken AG v Commission*[2] the Commission had, in brief, adopted a decision requiring the payment of a fine within three months. AEG lodged an application commencing proceedings for the annulment of the decision some four weeks before the fine was to be paid and also applied for the operation of the decision to be suspended. The President granted relief without hearing the Commission, five days after the lodgment of the application for interim relief, suspending the operation of the relevant part of the decision pending a final decision on the application. Similarly, in Cases 228 and 229/82R *Ford Werke AG and Ford of Europe Inc v Commission*[3] the Commission had exercised its powers to order interim measures pending the termination of an investigation under art 85 of the EEC Treaty, and the applicant had commenced an action for the annulment of the order so made. An application for the suspension of the operation of the Commission's order was also made, only a few days before the order was to come into effect. The President promptly suspended its operation pending a decision on the application for interim relief made by Ford on the ground that 'it is desirable in the interests of the proper administration of justice not to put this measure into effect before the parties have had the opportunity of stating their views during these proceedings relating to an application for interim measures'. In Cases 6 and 7/73R *Istituto Chemioterapico Italiano SpA and Commercial Solvents Corpn v Commission*[4] the applicant specifically asked for relief pending a decision on the application for interim relief. It is good practice for such a request to be made where the applicant believes that the occurrence of serious and irreparable damage is imminent. In such cases, the lack of time to consider the matter makes it impossible for the judge dealing with the application to make a proper assessment of the cases for and against the grant of relief; the decision to grant relief may therefore be based more on the seriousness and degree of imminence of the threat and less on a profound analysis of the applicant's case in the action.[5] Where necessary, the order may go further than the relief sought by the applicant.[6] Such an order

---

98 The opposing party generally requests the rejection of the form of order proposed by the applicant for relief. It is almost unheard of for the opposing party itself to claim some form of interim relief; but such a claim was made in the *Emerald Meats* case (above, note 75) paras 28–30, where it was dismissed as unnecessary, not inadmissible.
99 RP-ECJ 84(2); RP-CFI 105(2).
 1 See, for example, Case 293/82R *De Compte v European Parliament* [1982] ECR 4001; Case 338/82R *Albertini and Montagnani v Commission* [1982] ECR 4667; Case 214/86R *Greece v Commission* [1986] ECR 2505; Case 45/87R *Commission v Ireland* [1987] ECR 783; Cases T-24 and T-28/92R *Langnese-Iglo GmbH & Schöller Lebensmittel GmbH & Co KG v Commission* [1992] ECR II-1713; Case T-29/92R *Vereniging van Samenwerkende Prijsregelende Organisaties in de Bouwnijverheid v Commission* [1992] ECR II-2161 (para 8); Case 12/93R *CCE Vittel and CE Pierval v Commission* [1993] ECR II-449.
 2 [1982] ECR 1179 and 1549.
 3 [1982] ECR 2849.
 4 [1973] ECR 357. A holding order may also be made pending the decision in another case: Case T-554/94R *Abbott Trust v Council and Commission*, 12 January 1994.
 5 Eg Case 194/88R *Commission v Italy* [1988] ECR 4547; Case C-195/90R *Commission v Germany* [1990] ECR I-2715 (paras 18–20).
 6 Case 221/86R *Group of the European Right and National Front Party v European Parliament* [1986] ECR 2579.

may be made by the President immediately even though the final decision on the application for interim relief is to be made by the Court itself.[7] Where the order is made without hearing the views of the defendant to the application, it may subsequently be varied or cancelled, either on application or by the President of his own motion.[8] It is arguable that this also applies where the defendant to the application has failed to submit his observations within time but this is uncertain: since the proceedings are not wholly contentious, because of the judge's interest in ensuring that the Court's final judgment is not rendered nugatory, the order cannot be made merely on the ground that the defendant to the application had impliedly consented to it by failing to submit any observations in time, as is the case where judgment in contentious proceedings is obtained in default of a defence; in consequence, it is arguable that, where the judge has granted relief, in the absence of submissions from the defendant, his order can be varied or cancelled only where there is a change in circumstances.[9]

Before making his decision, the President may order a preparatory enquiry[10] but it has not so far been the practice to do so.[11] The usual practice is for there to be a hearing. The rules do not specify that there must be a hearing: this is a matter for the President to decide in the light of the facts of the case, the arguments of the parties and the degree of urgency. He may be satisfied that a decision can be made on the basis of the written submissions only.[12] The hearing is held before the President alone[13] although, if he wishes, he may invite the advocate general, the judge-rapporteur or anyone else, if he has a mind to, to attend. The decision on the application must be reasoned and is served on the parties 'forthwith'.[14] There is no appeal from an order of the President of the ECJ;[15] an order of the President of the CFI, or of the CFI itself (or one of its chambers) may be appealed to the ECJ, the appeal being heard by the President of the ECJ by way of summary procedure (that is, the same procedure followed in an application made directly to the President of the ECJ for interim relief).[16] The order (whether made by the President of the ECJ or of the CFI) may at any time be varied or cancelled on application on account of a

---

7 Case C-195/90R *Commission v Germany* [1990] ECR I-3351 (para 4).
8 RP-ECJ 84(2); RP-CFI 105(2). Eg Case 194/88R *Commission v Italy* [1988] ECR 4559 (original order extended until the date of the final order on the application for interim relief in order to preserve the position until the hearing of the application).
9 RP-ECJ 87; RP-CFI 108.
10 RP-ECJ 84(2); RP-CFI 105(2).
11 A rare instance of the ordering of a preparatory enquiry is Case 285/81R *Geist v Commission* (unreported), where the applicant was asked to produce evidence of his financial circumstances (verified, where possible, by a public authority or accountant) but declined to do so. As a result, the Court was unable to rule on the application. No further step was taken in the interim relief proceedings until 29 September 1983, when the application was dismissed on the ground that, as final judgment had been given in the action, there was no need to rule on the application for interim relief.
12 See, for example, Case 60/63R *Acciaierie Ferriere Pietro Oddino v High Authority* [1965] ECR 27; 338/82R *Albertini and Montagnani v Commission* [1983] ECR 145; Case 69/83R *Lux v Court of Auditors* [1983] ECR 1785; Case 241/84R *Pizzinato v Commission* [1984] ECR 3619 (para 3).
13 Robes are not usually worn unless the President decides otherwise. The hearing is generally conducted in an informal manner. Although the case is usually heard by the President alone, the hearing is not, in formal terms, in camera. A party may, however, apply in writing or orally at the hearing itself for the proceedings to be heard in camera (see Case 120/83R *Raznoimport v Commission* [1983] ECR 2573).
14 RP-ECJ 86(1); RP-CFI 107(1).
15 RP-ECJ 86(1). See Cases 12 and 29/64 *Ley v Commission* [1965] ECR 107 at 121.
16 ECSC and EC Statutes, art 50 (second and third paras); Euratom Statute, art 51 (second and third paras).

'change of circumstances'.[17] Similarly, where the application has been dismissed, the applicant is not barred from making a further application where there are 'new facts'.[18] Both applications should be made in the usual form and it is to be supposed that proceedings are the same as for an application for interim relief under RP-ECJ 83 et seq or, as the case may be, RP-CFI 104 et seq, mutatis mutandis. Even where an application for interim relief must in principle be dismissed, it may be appropriate to grant some form of relief covering the period after the dismissal of the application in order to prevent the time taken to decide the matter from causing the applicant difficulties.[19]

The order granting relief is normally limited to preserving the position of the applicant and not third parties;[20] and it will go only so far as is necessary in order to preserve the position.[21] Where appropriate, provision may be made for monitoring compliance with the order.[22] An order granting interim relief in the form of suspension of the enforcement of a decision of the Court or of any measure adopted by another Community institution must, where appropriate, specify the date on which the interim measure is to lapse.[23] That date may be indicated either as a calendar date or by reference to the occurrence of some relevant event, such as the date of any judgment ruling on the validity or interpretation of the decision or measure in question (which cannot normally be predicted with accuracy). An order granting suspension of the operation of a measure challenged in an action before the Court or any other interim measure must have only an interim or temporary effect and must be without prejudice to the decision of the Court on the substance of the case;[24] unless the order fixes the date on which the relief granted is to lapse,[25] the order lapses automatically when final judgment in the action is delivered.[26] Since the suspension of the operation of a contested act and other forms of interim measures (with the exception of the suspension of the enforcement of a decision of the Court or other measure) are granted solely in the context of proceedings before the Court and must not prejudice the Court's final judgment in the action, it follows that, in principle, such relief cannot survive the delivery of final judgment. It would therefore seem that the order granting such relief cannot specify, as the date on which the order is to lapse, a date after the delivery of judgment. The discretion to limit the temporal effect of the order operates within the period before the ending of the action by the delivery of

17 RP-ECJ 87; RP-CFI 108. See, for example, Case C-272/91R *Commission v Italy* [1992] ECR I-457 and 3929.
18 RP-ECJ 88; RP-CFI 109.
19 Eg Cases T-10 to 12 and T-14 to 15/92R *SA Cimenteries CBR v Commission* [1992] ECR II-1571 (para 58).
20 Eg the order made in Case 23/86R *United Kingdom v European Parliament* [1986] ECR 1085.
21 Eg Cases 76, 77 and 91/89R *Radio Telefis Eireann v Commission* [1989] ECR 1141 (paras 19–20); Case 56/89R *Publishers' Association v Commission* [1989] ECR 1693 (paras 38–40); Case T-45/90R *Speybrouck v European Parliament* [1990] ECR II-705 (paras 31–37), where the defendant was ordered to pay certain sums due from a third party in case, and for so long as, the third party was in delay in paying them; *Vereniging van Samenwerkende Prijsregelende v Commission* (above, note 1) paras 39–42.
22 Eg Case 154/85R *Commission v Italy* [1985] ECR 1753 (para 21); Case 293/85R *Commission v Belgium* [1985] ECR 3521.
23 RP-ECJ 89; RP-CFI 110.
24 RP-ECJ 86(4); RP-CFI 107(4).
25 Where necessary, the application for relief may be renewed if the duration of the original order is limited: see, for example, Case 160/84R *Oryzomyli Kavallas OEE v Commission* [1984] ECR 3217 (para 9), where the original order was in principle a holding order designed to preserve the position so that the applicant could, if need be, obtain further evidence to support the claim for relief (the subsequent proceedings are reported in [1984] ECR 3615).
26 RP-ECJ 86(3); RP-CFI 107(3). Eg Case 78/83R *USINOR v Commission* [1983] ECR 2183.

final judgment. Since the date of the final judgment is not usually predict-
able, it would appear that, if the order does specify a date which happens to
fall after the delivery of the final judgment, the order lapses automatically
when final judgment is delivered and is not prolonged until the date specified
in it. It is for the Court, in the final judgment, and not for the President (or,
as the case may be, the Court or a chamber) in an earlier interim relief order,
to deal in an appropriate manner with the situation in the event that there is
some compelling reason why the final judgment should not take effect when
it is delivered. By the same token, where interim relief is granted in the
context of proceedings before the CFI and the CFI's final judgment is the
subject of an appeal to the ECJ, the interim relief order expires in principle
on the delivery of the CFI's judgment and the continuation of the relief
granted until then is a matter for the President of the ECJ to decide in the
context of the appeal proceedings.

The Statutes[27] provide only that the President of the Court may hear
applications for interim relief. Should he be prevented from sitting, his place is
taken by one of the presidents of the chambers, in order of seniority, and,
should there be no president of a chamber available, one of the judges, in order
of seniority.[28] Cases may be assigned to a chamber and never be heard by the
full Court but the application for interim relief in such cases is ordinarily heard
by the President of the Court. The President (of the ECJ or, as the case may be,
the CFI) may decide that, although there is no reason preventing him from
sitting, the application is one best considered by the Court (or, as the case may
be, by the chamber to which the action has been assigned). This usually occurs
only in cases of real difficulty or importance and, when it happens, the Court
(or chamber) will decide the issue, setting aside for the time being all the other
cases before it in order to deal with the application expeditiously. The procedure is the same as that where the President alone decides the question: the
Court (or chamber) may grant the application before hearing the other side
but a decision so made may be reviewed; the other party is asked to submit
written or oral observations and a preparatory enquiry may be ordered.[29] The
decision of the Court (or chamber) is given only after hearing the advocate
general, where there is one.[30] When the Court is seized of the application it has
the same powers as those entrusted to the President and its order has no effect
on its final judgment in the action.

Passing now to consideration of the evidential requirements in interim relief
proceedings,[31] in Cases 53/65R *Arturo Mondini SpA v High Authority* and 1/66R
SpA Acciaierie e Ferriere Stefana Fratelli v High Authority[32] Judge Hammes rejected
an application because it was based on mere assertions and did not adduce any
evidence or refer to any material of probative value which would support those

27 ECSC Statute, art 33; EC Statute, art 36; Euratom Statute, art 37.
28 RP-ECJ 85, 11 and 6; RP-CFI 106 and 6.
29 RP-ECJ 85; RP-CFI 106. However, the hearing is before the full Court (or chamber) and
    gowns are worn.
30 Ibid. In cases before the CFI, an advocate general would be heard only in the event that the
    matter were dealt with by the CFI in plenary session: RP-CFI 17.
31 Where, due to the urgency of the situation, the judge grants relief before hearing the other
    party, the evidential requirements are much less even than when the judge is considering the
    matter in the light of the other party's observations. Thus, in Case 194/88R *Commission v Italy*
    (above, note 5), Judge Mackenzie Stuart remarked that the applicant's assertions 'may, at this
    stage of the proceedings, be regarded as true'. At a later stage in the interim relief proceedings,
    the judge must inevitably be more sceptical.
32 [1966] ECR 17 and [1967] ECR 283 respectively.

assertions.[33] At least in the case of matters that can easily and most appropriately be proved by documentary evidence, such as the capacity of the applicant to bear financial loss or damage, a failure to produce such evidence cannot be remedied by mere unsupported assertion.[34] In relation to other matters, not all judges have adopted as strict an approach as Judge Hammes. In *Ford v Commission*[35] Judge Mertens de Wilmars felt able to make a preliminary assessment of one issue of fact on the basis of statements made at the hearing; in Cases 82 and 83/85R *Eurasian Corpn Ltd v Commission*[36] Judge Koopmans was able to accept the assertions of the parties as reliable evidence; in Case 148/88R *Albani v Commission*[37] Judge Due rejected one of the applicant's submissions on the basis of certain assertions of fact made by the defendant at the hearing. Where the assertions made by the applicant are unsupported by any evidence but are expressly conceded by the opposing party, no difficulty seems to arise.[38] On one view, if the opposing party fails to contest the applicant's assertions, the opposing party should be taken to concede them, at least for the purposes of the interim relief proceedings. However, in Case 141/84R *De Compte v European Parliament*,[39] Judge Galmot took the view that, if the opposing party fails to reply to the applicant's assertions, that does not betoken acceptance of them; the judge hearing the application must still ascertain whether or not there is a real dispute between the parties and whether or not the applicant's claims are supported by sound arguments. Where the applicant's assertions are disputed by the opposing party and there is conflicting evidence before the judge, the judge is inevitably drawn into considering the sufficiency of the evidence relied on by the parties,[40] save where one party does not 'seriously' contest an assertion made by the other party.[41] Where there is a dispute between the parties, there seems to be nothing to prevent the judge from coming to a provisional conclusion. However, in Case 250/85R *Brother Industries Ltd v Council*,[42] where the question of the threat of damage was hotly contested between the parties, Judge Mackenzie Stuart considered that, in such a situation, it was impossible to accept the figures submitted by one party in preference to those submitted by another party

33 See also Judge Mackenzie Stuart in Case 310/85R *Deufil GmbH & Co KG v Commission* [1986] ECR 537 (para 23), a requirement of 'convincing evidence'; the same in Case 92/88R *Associazione Industrie Siderurgiche Italiane (ASSIDER) v Commission* [1988] ECR 2425 (para 24), a requirement of 'cogent evidence'; Judge Due in Case 148/88R *Albani v Commission* [1988] ECR 3361 (para 18), a requirement of 'firm evidence'; Judge Mackenzie Stuart in Case 191/88R *Co-Frutta Sarl v Commission* [1988] ECR 4551 (para 21), a requirement of 'objective evidence'; Judge Joliet in Case C-35/92P-R *European Parliament v Frederiksen* [1992] ECR I-2399 (para 21).

34 Case 44/88R *De Compte v European Parliament* [1988] ECR 1669 (paras 33–36). Compare Case 234/82R *Ferriere di Roe Volciano v Commission* [1983] ECR 725 with Case 348/82R *IRO v Commission* [1983] ECR 1237.

35 Above, note 3.

36 [1985] ECR 1191 (paras 17–21).

37 Above, note 33 (para 24). There seems to have been nothing to controvert the assertions made by the defendant.

38 Cf Case 82/87R *Autexpo SpA v Commission* [1987] ECR 2131 (paras 18–19), where Judge Mackenzie Stuart felt able to accept the prima facie admissibility of the action on the basis of an assertion of fact (made by the defendant) that was unsupported by evidence.

39 [1984] ECR 2575 (paras 9–11).

40 Eg Case 119/86R *Spain v Council and Commission* [1986] ECR 2241 (Re Export Deposits) (paras 25–30); Case 128/86R *Spain v Commission* [1986] ECR 2495 (paras 25–30); Case 57/89R *Commission v Germany* [1989] ECR 2849 (paras 19–22); Case C-280/93R *Germany v Commission*, [1993] ECR I-3667.

41 Eg Case 154/85R *Commission v Italy* (above, note 22) para 20.

42 [1985] ECR 3459 (para 16). See also Case 273/85R *Silver Seiko Ltd v Council* [1985] ECR 3475 (para 17); Case 297/85R *Towa Sankiden Corpn v Council* [1985] ECR 3483 (para 15); Cases 277 and 300/85R *Canon Inc v Council* [1985] ECR 3491 (para 16).

without prejudicing the substance of the case unless there were other factors weighing in favour of the view of one or other of the parties. In such a situation, the evidence adduced by the party opposing the application seems to cancel the effect of the evidence adduced by the applicant; the case is then to be decided on the basis of the burden of proof, which lies on the applicant, resulting in the dismissal of the application.[43]

The standard of proof in interim relief proceedings is not as high as in direct actions. In Case 18/57 *Nold KG v High Authority*,[44] Advocate General Roemer pointed out that 'full proof' is not necessary and only a prima facie case need be shown. In *Ford v Commission*[45] Judge Mertens de Wilmars referred to 'a degree of probability sufficient for the purposes of this order'. On the other hand, in Case 250/85R *Brother Industries Ltd v Council*[46] (a dumping case), Judge Mackenzie Stuart required from the applicant 'reliable and uncontested evidence' to the effect that the grant of relief would not cause damage to Community industry. In contrast, in Case 152/88R *Sofrimport Sarl v Commission*[47] (also a trade protection, albeit not a dumping, case) he was prepared to accept that, at first sight, grant of the relief sought would not lead to a serious disturbance of the market in the Community. The difference in approach between those cases is really a reflection of their different factual circumstances and not a matter of legal principle. In Case 160/84R *Oryzomyli Kavallas OEE v Commission*[48] Judge Mackenzie Stuart referred to a lack of 'convincing' evidence but was nonetheless prepared to grant relief because of the scale of the alleged threat to the applicant, which suggests that a weakness in the evidence relied on need not be a barrier to the grant of relief but may be a factor to be taken into account when deciding whether or not to grant relief or to grant it only for a short period in order to preserve the position until the applicant has obtained better evidence. In Case 246/89R *Commission v United Kingdom*,[49] when considering the effectiveness of the relief sought by the applicant, Judge Due considered that 'the possibility could not be excluded' that that relief would be effective in certain cases.

The position can therefore be summarised as follows. It is for the applicant to demonstrate a prima facie case for relief and for the opposing party to negate the material relied on by the applicant or else to demonstrate a prima facie case for the existence of some bar to the grant of relief (such as that it would cause serious and irreparable damage). Each party's assertions ought to be supported by evidence, where available. The evidence and assertions of each party must be sufficiently persuasive but need not be 'convincing' in the sense that, at the interim relief stage, the judge hearing the application is required to come to a provisional and not a definitive view of the position. Whether or not evidence or an assertion is sufficiently persuasive depends in large part on the extent to which it is contested by the other party and on the gravity and degree

---

43 The *Brother* case para 18; *Silver Seiko* para 19; *Towa Sankiden* para 17; *Canon* para 18 (all above, note 42).
44 [1957–58] ECR 121 at 127.
45 Above, note 3 (para 7). See also Cases C-51 and C-59/90R *Comos-Tank BV v Commission* [1990] ECR I-2167 (para 29) and Case C-213/91 *Abertal SAT Lda v Commission* [1991] ECR I-5109 (para 24), where Judge Due referred to 'the required degree of probability' without explaining what that degree was.
46 Above, note 42 (para 17). See also *Silver Seiko* para 18, *Towa Sankiden* para 16 and *Canon* para 17 (all above, note 42).
47 [1988] ECR 2931 (para 33).
48 Above, note 25 (paras 8–9). See also Case 160/84 R II *Oryzomyli Kavallas OEE v Commission* [1984] ECR 3615.
49 [1989] ECR 3125 (para 38).

of imminence of the threat of damage to either party depending upon whether or not relief is granted.

The operation of an order granting relief may be made subject to the lodging by the applicant of a security[50] or any other condition fixed by the President. The purpose of requiring a security is to cover the situation where the party ordered to provide it (the applicant for relief) is liable for the sum covered by the security and there is a risk that it may become insolvent and therefore unable to pay the sum due.[51] In consequence, the lodging of a security will not be required if the applicant would be able to pay the sum due[52] or if the security relates to an amount that the applicant is not otherwise liable to pay. Thus, the requirement to provide a security is not intended to ensure that the opposing party is compensated by the applicant for any loss caused to the opposing party as a result of the grant of relief should the applicant lose the action or should it eventually turn out that relief should not have been granted, unless the applicant would otherwise be liable in respect of that loss.[53] In the result, the cases where a security has been required are those where relief has been sought in respect of the payment of a sum of money (usually a fine).[54] In such cases, the judge's willingness to make the order, or to put it another way, his willingness to accept that the conditions for granting relief are fulfilled, may be affected by the applicant's willingness to lodge a security. For example, in *AEG Telefunken AG v Commission*[55] and Case 86/82R *Hasselblad (GB) Ltd v Commission*[56] the President suspended the operation of two Commission decisions imposing fines on the applicants subject to the condition that the latter should provide bank guarantees covering the amounts of the fines. In the first case the guarantee had already been given. In the second case the President found that the applicant had not shown that there existed 'exceptional circumstances . . . such as to justify the granting of a suspension without the provision

---

50 RP-ECJ 86(2); RP-CFI 107(2); Cases C-143/88 and C-92/89 *Zuckerfabrik Süderdithmarschen AG v Hauptzollamt Itzehoe et al* [1991] ECR I-415 (para 32). The word actually used is 'enforcement' but 'operation', as it is used in RP-ECJ 83(1) and RP-CFI 104(1), is perhaps more accurate because it is the legal effect of the order which is made conditional on the lodging of a security, not the possibility of 'enforcing' or 'executing' it within the meaning of, for example, RP-ECJ 89, RP-CFI 110 or art 192 of the EEC Treaty.

51 Case C-195/90R *Commission v Germany* (above, note 7) para 48. In that case, the Commission relied on a comparative study of national law indicating that, where a state acts to enforce the law rather than to protect its own proprietary or contractual interests, it is required to lodge a guarantee only in highly exceptional circumstances: see Oliver, (1992) 29 CMLRev 7 at 8.

52 Case C-195/90R *Commission v Germany* (ibid) para 49.

53 *Commission v Germany* suggests that, at least in proceedings under EEC Treaty, art 169, the applicant for relief (the Commission) may be liable in damages to the opposing party in respect of any loss resulting from the grant of relief (presumably in the event that the applicant loses the action); but that is an inference from para 49 of the judgment and it cannot be relied on in support of some general proposition that, in all proceedings, the applicant for relief may be so liable. The other view is that the applicant for relief is not ordinarily liable for the loss arising directly from the grant of relief (if any) because the proximate cause of that loss is not the applicant's decision to apply for relief but the decision of the Court to grant it. Further, it would be contrary to public policy to make the Court liable for any loss arising from the exercise of a judicial discretion (save in very exceptional cases). Having said that, it is not to be excluded that the Community may be liable to compensate a member state for loss arising from the grant of interim relief in the course of unsuccessful infringement proceedings brought against that member state. The basis for liability would be a general obligation to compensate rather than liability based on fault lying in the commencement of infringement proceedings or the exercise of the power to grant interim relief.

54 In Case 160/84R *Oryzmoyli Kavallas* (above, notes 25 and 48) relief was granted subject to provision of a bank guarantee covering the payment of customs duties.

55 Above, note 2.

56 [1982] ECR 1555.

of a guarantee', but suspended the operation of the decision subject to the provision of a guarantee within eight weeks. If one were not obtained within that time, the order granting suspension would lapse. A similar order was made in Case 263/82R *Klöckner Werke A G v Commission*[57] but the applicant was unable to obtain the security required and made a second application for relief without this condition. The President rejected it on the ground that it had neither been shown nor affirmed that the applicant had tried to negotiate the grant of a bank guarantee.[58] When the operation of a decision imposing a fine is suspended on condition that the applicant provide a bank guarantee, the applicant cannot claim the costs of providing the guarantee, if it is successful in the action, because, in the absence of the order, the applicant would have had to pay the fine forthwith.[59] As a result of the availability of interim relief in such cases where a bank guarantee was provided by the applicant, the Commission adopted the policy of refraining from seeking payment of fines imposed by it on undertakings if they commenced proceedings for the annulment of the decision imposing the fine and also provided a security for the eventual payment of the fine in the event that they were unsuccessful. That policy made it no longer necessary for the Court to grant interim relief in such cases, although the Court will do so should the need arise[60] and, in particular, where there are exceptional circumstances (namely, that the applicant is a small undertaking which either cannot provide the security required or would suffer serious and irreparable damage if it did so).[61]

Those cases concern the giving of security by the applicant for relief. In Case 293/85R *Commission v Belgium*,[62] Belgium was ordered to suspend the exaction of discriminative fees for vocational training but the order provided that students (that is, third parties to the proceedings) benefiting from the order had to give a personal undertaking in writing to pay the fees in question if the action against Belgium were dismissed. An example of another sort of condition to which the order may be made subject is Cases 43 and 63/82R *VBVB and VBBB v Commission*,[63] which concerned a Commission decision finding that a restrictive agreement infringed art 85 of the EEC Treaty and requiring the infringement to be terminated. Relief was granted on condition that the sanctions against breach of the agreement set out in it were not applied if persons bound by the agreement did not comply with its terms.

57 [1982] ECR 3995 and 4225. See also *Ferriere di Roe Volciano v Commission* and *IRO v Commission* (both above, note 34); Case 78/83R *USINOR v Commission* (above, note 26).
58 The same approach was originally followed in cases where applicants sought the suspension of the operation of regulations imposing anti-dumping duties: see, for example, Cases 113/77R and 113/77R-Int *NTN Toyo Bearing Co Ltd v Council* [1977] ECR 1721. It was abandoned when a more restrictive view was taken of the conditions for the grant of interim relief in such cases: see Case 258/84R *Nippon Seiko KK v Council* [1984] ECR 4357; Case 77/87R *Technointorg v Council* [1987] ECR 1793.
59 Case 78/83 *USINOR v Commission* [1984] ECR 4177 at 4206–4207 (Advocate General Slynn).
60 As it did in Case 62/84R *USINOR v Commission* [1984] ECR 2643.
61 Eg Case 392/85R *Finsider v Commission* [1986] ECR 959; Case 213/86R *Montedipe SpA v Commission* [1986] ECR 2623.
62 Above, note 22 (para 24).
63 [1982] ECR 1241.

CHAPTER 9

Pleading

I Introduction

For procedural purposes, a distinction is often drawn between 'procedural documents' and 'communications'. The former comprise the pleadings (application, defence, reply, rejoinder and so forth) and other documents, generally requiring action on the part of the Court (applications for an extension of time and the like), lodged by the parties at the Registry and procedural acts of the Court (such as notifications of procedural documents and procedural decisions). The latter comprise a heterogeneous collection of documents (such as the written consent given by a party to a proposal to dispense with the oral part of the procedure before the ECJ)[1] which are difficult to list or define. Broadly speaking, procedural documents are those documents that mark the passage of proceedings from one stage to another; communications are any other document. Procedural documents are subject to certain formal requirements; communications are not. With the exception of the most obvious examples, the classification of a particular document as a procedural document or as a communication is often unclear; and the treatment of some documents is on occasion inconsistent with their classification. The distinction between procedural documents and communications and the consequences of that disinction are therefore best regarded as matters of practice rather than logic. In case of doubt about the correct classification of a document, it is better to draw it up and lodge it as if it were a procedural document.

The pleadings in a case (by which is meant the statement of a party's case, whether or not accompanied by a statement of the order sought from the Court and whether relating to the Court's final judgment or to some preliminary or procedural point) are written and, where there is a hearing, oral. The former are more important, the role of oral pleadings in the Court's procedure being very limited and, in most cases, little more than an adjunct to the written pleadings. This chapter is concerned only with the latter.[2] All pleadings are addressed to the Court and are intended to inform it, as well as the other parties, of a party's case. In consequence, certainly in contentious proceedings, a pleading must satisfy two duties: one owed to the Court of explaining how the party wishes it to exercise its powers and the reasons why; and a second, owed to the opposing party, of setting out clearly the case which he must answer.[3] The Rules of Procedure do not lay down any standard form of

---

1 See RP-ECJ 44a.
2 Oral pleadings are discussed above: see pp 78 et seq.
3 Eg Cases 46 and 47/59 *Meroni & Co v High Authority* [1962] ECR 411 at 419; Cases 19 and 21/60, 2 and 3/61 *Société Fives Lille Cail v High Authority* [1961] ECR 281 at 294; Case T-21/90 *Generlich v Commission* [1991] ECR II-1323 (para 31).

pleading, nor has any emerged in practice, although there are certain basic requirements relating to the form and content of written pleadings. As a result, practice and the influence of national legal traditions play a large part in the drafting and presentation of pleadings. The object of this chapter is to set out the basic rules and these may be subject to specific exceptions.

II General rules

Procedural documents and communications must comply with the rules relating to the language to be used in proceedings. In addition, RP-ECJ 37 and RP-CFI 43 set out several requirements which must be fulfilled by 'every pleading', that is, every procedural document.[4] In fact, however, the Rules of Procedure sometimes provide expressly that RP-ECJ 37 or, as the case may be, RP-CFI 43 apply mutatis mutandis to specific pleadings,[5] sometimes that they apply only in part[6] and sometimes remain silent.[7] It is, therefore, open to argument that RP-ECJ 37 and RP-CFI 43 are not applicable to every written submission to the Court.[8] Nonetheless, it would seem that, at least as a matter of practice, RP-ECJ 37 or, as the case may be, RP-CFI 43 should be complied with unless there is express provision otherwise in the Rules of Procedure. The requirements set out in RP-ECJ 37 and RP-CFI 43 are the following.

(1) The original of every pleading must be signed by the party's agent or lawyer.[9] The only exceptions to this appear to be applications for legal aid[10] and written observations submitted in references for a preliminary ruling.[11] In other cases a pleading may be rejected as inadmissible if it does not comply with this requirement.[12] It is not sufficient if the (agent or) lawyer has simply signed or adopted something drafted by the party himself;[13] he must at least have examined the pleading.[14] The fact that the party concerned is himself a lawyer does not obviate the need for the pleading to be signed by the lawyer representing the party:[15] the purpose

---

4 See, for example, the French version of the Rules of Procedure. The terms 'pleading' and 'procedural document' are in this context interchangeable.
5 Eg RP-ECJ 83(3), 93(1), 94(4), 97(1) and 102(1); RP-CFI 104(3), 115(2), 122(4), 123(1) and 129(1).
6 Eg RP-ECJ 101(2).
7 Eg RP-ECJ 76, 91, 94(1), 103–104, 107 and 109; RP-CFI 94, 114 and 122(1).
8 In Case 2/68 *Ufficio Imposte di Consumo di Ispra v Commission* [1968] ECR 435 at 442, Advocate General Roemer suggested that RP-ECJ 37 and 38 might apply *by analogy* to an application for an order allowing an applicant to enter the premises of the Joint Research Centre establishment at Ispra and did not, it must be supposed, think that RP-ECJ 37 applied directly to such a pleading.
9 RP-ECJ 37(1); RP-CFI 43(1).
10 RP-ECJ 76(2); RP-CFI 94(2).
11 This follows from RP-ECJ 104(2) which requires the Court to 'take account' of the rules of procedure of the referring court regarding the representation and attendance of the parties to the proceedings before it. In consequence, if a party to the proceedings before the referring court is entitled to plead his case in person or with the assistance of someone other than a lawyer, that party may in the preliminary ruling proceedings before the ECJ submit written observations signed otherwise than by a lawyer.
12 Case 108/63 *Officine Elettromeccaniche Ing A Merlini v High Authority* [1965] ECR 1 (the applicant's reply); Case 10/81 *Farrall v Commission* [1981] ECR 717 (the application commencing proceedings); Case 131/83 *Vaupel v European Court of Justice*, 15 March 1984, unreported.
13 *Officine Elettromeccaniche Ing A Merlini v High Authority* (ibid).
14 Ibid, per Advocate General Roemer at 16.
15 The *Vaupel* case (above, note 12); Case C-126/90P *Viciano v Commission* [1991] ECR I-781 (paras 4 and 8).

of the rule is to ensure that the pleading has been adopted and lodged by the person who bears the responsibility for the conduct of the proceedings on behalf of the party.

(2)   Every pleading must bear a date.[16]

(3)   The original of every pleading must be lodged, accompanied by all annexes referred to therein and the requisite number of certified copies.[17] The party lodging the pleading certifies that the copies are true copies by marking this on each one. The required number of copies is five for the Court and one each for every other party to the proceedings (including interveners). There seems to be an agreement between the Community institutions that, in addition, they lodge all the copies needed by the Court (the Court's needs are greater than the rules suggest). The institutions are also required to produce translations of all their pleadings into the other official Community languages within a time limit set by the Court[18] and the same applies to documents annexed to the pleadings. In fact, however, it appears to be the practice to lodge French translations of the pleadings and annexes alone unless the Court requests otherwise. The rules relating to the number of copies to be lodged apply equally to translations.

(4)   To every pleading must be annexed a file containing all the documents relied on in support of the pleading, together with a schedule listing them.[19] The annexes should be expressed in the language of the case.[20] Hence, a document written in another language should be accompanied by a translation into the language of the case. If that is not done, the opposing party may be entitled to ask for an extension of time in order properly to consider the document; but a failure to provide a translation of the document into the language of the case is not otherwise a defect of procedure.[21] It is good practice to ensure that the annexes are readily identifiable and legible. As a result, documents which are entirely or partly in manuscript should be accompanied by a typewritten transcription. In the case of lengthy documents, the relevant extracts may be annexed but the whole document or a copy of it must be lodged at the Registry.[22] All the documents *mentioned* in the pleading do not need to be annexed; it is only those *relied on* in support of the claims made in the pleading that must be.[23] A failure to annex relevant documents may embarrass the other party in the preparation of his case, but is not necessarily a ground for holding the pleading to be inadmissible.[24] The requirement to annex relevant documents is in principle a formal requirement regarding the presentation of evidence in proceedings; it is not a condition of the proof of facts in issue[25] and does not amount to a requirement that the party lodging the pleading demonstrate at least a prima facie case for his claims on the (documentary) evidence.

---

16 RP-ECJ 37(3); RP-CFI 43(3).
17 RP-ECJ 37(1); RP-CFI 43(1).
18 RP-ECJ 37(2); RP-CFI 43(2).
19 RP-ECJ 37(4); RP-CFI 43(4).
20 Case 105/75 *Giuffrida v Council* [1976] ECR 1395 at 1405 (Advocate General Warner).
21 Case T-47/92 *Lenz v Commission* [1992] ECR II-2523 (para 36).
22 RP-ECJ 37(5); RP-CFI 43(5).
23 See, in the case of an application, Case 171/86 *Union Sidérurgique du Nord et de l'Est de la France SA (USINOR) v Commission*, unreported (order of 28 January 1987, para 19); and, in the case of a defence, Case 201/86 *Spie-Batignolles v Commission* [1990] ECR I-197 (unreported order of 16 December 1987, para 13).
24 Cf Cases 95-98/74, 15 and 100/75 *Union Nationale des Coopératives Agricoles de Céréales v Commission and Council* [1975] ECR 1615 (para 4).
25 Case 171/86 *Usinor* (above, note 23).

Although RP-ECJ 37 and RP-CFI 43 require that a pleading be signed, the Rules of Procedure do not specify that the body of the pleading must be presented in any particular form (typed, manuscript). On occasion a manuscript pleading has been received and no objection seems ever to have been taken as to its admissibility on this ground alone. Nonetheless, there are obvious practical difficulties in reading a manuscript and it is better to have pleadings typed.

Sometimes pleadings are submitted in the form of a telex or facsimile message.[26] Since a telex clearly cannot be 'signed', even if the name of the agent or lawyer appears on the message, and a facsimile message can only reproduce a signature affixed to another document (the original of the facsimile message), it is arguable that a telex or facsimile message can be regarded only as a warning to the Court that a pleading is about to be lodged and does not itself constitute lodgment. The better view seems to be that a telex or facsimile message is to be regarded as a copy of the pleading and that its lodgment at the Court in that manner is not effective lodgment.[27] It should, therefore, as a rule, be followed by lodgment of the original and the remaining copies within the relevant time limit. On the other hand, documents that can safely be classified as 'communications' may be lodged by telex or facsimile machine. Where the original of a procedural document is lodged after the expiry of a time limit, the question may arise whether the position is saved if a preceding telex or facsimile message was lodged in time. The Rules of Procedure do not envisage this situation because they suppose that copies are presented at the same time as the original.[28] In addition, it seems to be the lodgment of the original of the pleading that is important from the point of view of the reckoning of time limits. In consequence, on a strict construction of the Rules, the lodgment of a copy, such as a telex or facsimile message, amounts to communication of the contents of a pleading but does not constitute its lodgment and, therefore, has no effect on the running of time.[29] It would seem an exceptionally harsh result if the lodgment of the original out of time due to, for example, postal delays, were to result in its inadmissibility even though an accurate copy had been lodged within time. It is possible that, in such circumstances, the Court would not be too inflexible and would regard the pleading as having been made in time as long as the position were regularised by the lodgment of the original.[30] At all events, the lodgment of a copy (in the form of a telex or facsimile message) does not appear to be adequate compliance with the Rules and must, in the ordinary course, be completed by lodgment of the original pleading. If the lodgment of a copy in the form of a telex or facsimile message is to be regarded as lodgment within any relevant time limit, it would seem that the entire message must have been received at the Court before the expiry of the time limit. If, for example, the final page or pages (in particular, the page containing the agent's or lawyer's signature) of a pleading or communication sent by facsimile are not received until after the expiry of the time limit

26 For example, in Case 276/83 *Commission v Greece* [1985] ECR 2751, the defendant consented to the withdrawal of the action by facsimile message. If a pleading or communication is sent to the Court by facsimile machine, it should be sent to the number of the machine in the appropriate Registry and not to any other facsimile number held by the Court.
27 See Case C-122/90 *Emsland-Stärke v Commission*, unreported (order of 15 May 1991).
28 RP-ECJ 37(1); RP-CFI 43(1).
29 See the *Emsland-Stärke* case (above, note 27). The problem was not discussed in Cases 281, 283–285 and 287/85 *Germany, France, Netherlands, Denmark and United Kingdom v Commission* [1987] ECR 3203 because the pleading in question was in any event lodged out of time (see para 5 and per Advocate General Mancini at 3229–3230).
30 See the practice of the Court, as described in chapter 1, section VB p 38.

(whether because the message is particularly long or because the Court's facsimile machine runs out of paper[31] or because of an interruption in transmission), it would seem that the pleading as a whole must be regarded as having been lodged out of time. It is appreciated that that may seem to be a harsh result, particularly where the main parts of the pleading have been received before the expiry of the time limit. On the other hand, a line must be drawn somewhere; and, since the time limits for lodging pleadings are extended by ample periods to take account of the distance of a party from the place where the Court has its seat, there seems to be sufficient justification for adopting a strict view regarding the lodging of pleadings at the very end of that extended time limit. The application of a time limit may not be circumvented by lodging a pleading in instalments.[32]

In all cases where a pleading is to be served by the Court on other persons, it must be lodged at the Court in such a state that service is possible: a party cannot impose on the Court any condition seeking to restrict service where service is required by an instrument governing the Court's procedure or by considerations of natural justice or the rights of the defence. A pleading which is lodged purportedly subject to any such condition may be rejected by the Court.[33]

If a party wishes to obtain confidential treatment for its pleadings as against another party (ordinarily an intervener), it must first apply to the Court under RP-ECJ 91 or, as the case may be, RP-CFI 114 for such confidential treatment.[34] In the case of pleadings, confidential treatment is normally limited to the assertions of fact in the pleading that relate to or reveal the contents of documentary or other evidence that is entitled to confidential treatment. The confidential treatment of pleadings is therefore ancillary to that of evidence.[35] Confidential treatment will not be granted unless the material in question is genuinely secret or confidential[36] and it is in the interests of justice to protect such material.[37]

---

31 It does not seem that, in the latter event, the party lodging the pleading could invoke exceptional circumstances or force majeure (see ECSC Statute, art 39; EC Statute, art 42; Euratom Statute, art 43) because the risk that the machine might run out of paper is foreseeable as a possibility. Any prudent person would inform the Court in advance that the pleading was being sent by facsimile machine so that the Court's machine could be checked to see that it had sufficient paper and so that someone would be in attendance in case the message was incomplete for some reason.

32 Case 321/85 *Schwiering v Court of Auditors* [1986] ECR 3199 (order of 15 June 1988, para 2, in taxation proceedings after the judgment), where a party was given a date by which written observations on the application for taxation were to be submitted and lodged its observations within time, indicating that it would submit further written observations shortly. Those further observations were lodged out of time and were therefore excluded from consideration because there had been no request to extend the time limit.

33 Cf Case 236/81 *Celanese Chemical Co Inc v Council and Commission* [1982] ECR 1183 at para 2 (a direct action); Case 6/81 *Industrie Diensten Groep BV v J A Beele Handelmaatschappij BV* [1982] ECR 707 (a reference for a preliminary ruling).

34 Application may be made at or after the commencement of proceedings. If not already applied for by the time when a person has applied to intervene, the application should be made in the party's written observations on the application to intervene: see pp 179–180.

35 For the confidential treatment of evidence, see chapter 12, pp 405–406.

36 Eg information about a party's prices that was not public knowledge: Case C-66/90 *Koninklijke PTT Nederland NV and PTT Post BV v Commission* (reported sub nom Cases C-48 and C-66/90 *Netherlands v Commission* [1992] ECR I-565), order of 5 December 1990.

37 Cf Case C-54/90 *Weddel & Co BV v Commission* [1992] ECR I-871 (order of 15 May 1991), where the Court refused to exclude from the file a record of the examination of certain witnesses by a national court because a summary of the meeting to which the testimony of the witnesses related was being relied on in other proceedings.

III Pleadings in direct actions

A Applications commencing proceedings

RP-ECJ 38 and RP-CFI 44 set out minimum requirements concerning the contents of the application and the documents which must be annexed to it.

1 Contents

The application must set out the following.

(1) The name and address of the applicant.[38] The applicant should be clearly identifiable, either by express reference or, at the least, indirectly from the contents of the application.[39] One application may be brought by several applicants,[40] in which case the name and address of each of them must be given. The criteria determining whether or not a joint application should be made are the same as those applied by the Court when deciding whether to join different proceedings.[41]

(2) The designation of the party against whom the application is made,[42] that is, an indication or description of the defendant.[43] A slip in the naming of the defendant does not make the application inadmissible as long as it does not affect the right to a fair trial[44] or the applicant's intention is clear;[45] formal defects in the description of the defendant may be rectified even after lodgment of the application and, as a last resort, at the delivery of judgment.[46] Where not stated expressly, it is sufficient if the defendant can be identified from the contents of the pleading.[47] It does not appear to be necessary to give the defendant's address. Normally one person is named as defendant but, in actions against the Community, it often happens that several Community institutions, usually the Council and the Commission, are cited.

---

38 RP-ECJ 38(1)(a); RP-CFI 44(1)(a).

39 Eg *Ufficio Imposte di Consumo di Ispra v Commission* (above, note 8), at 439 and 443 (Advocate General Roemer).

40 Eg Case 50/74 *Asmussen v Commission and Council* [1975] ECR 1003, an action brought by 59 persons.

41 Case 13/57 *Wirtschaftsvereinigung Eisen- und Stahlindustrie v High Authority* [1957–58] ECR 265 at 277, see also at 317 (Advocate General Lagrange). In Cases 18 and 19/64 *Alvino and Benoit v Commission* [1965] ECR 789 some of the original forms of order were mutually incompatible as between different applicants and so their interests in the case might conflict but the inconsistencies were withdrawn in the reply (see 796).

42 RP-ECJ 38(1)(b); RP-CFI 44(1)(b).

43 This reflects art 19 of the EC and Euratom Statutes, the English version of which refers to the name of the party against whom the application is made. Article 22 of the ECSC Statute, on the other hand, does not make identification of the defendant a requirement at all.

44 Cases 63-69/72 *Wilhelm Werhahn Hansamühle v Council* [1973] ECR 1229 (para 8). Thus, where an action for damages is directed against a Community institution and not the relevant Community, the action is not inadmissible because the defect is purely formal: Case 353/88 *Briantex SAS and Di Domenico v EEC and Commission* [1989] ECR 3623 (para 7 and at 3631 per Advocate General Jacobs).

45 Case 44/76 *Milch-, Fett- und Eier-Kontor GmbH v Council and Commission* [1977] ECR 393 at 413 (Advocate General Reischl); Case 85/86 *Commission v Board of Governors of the European Investment Bank* [1986] ECR 2215.

46 Case 85/86 *Commission v Board of Governors of the European Investment Bank* [1988] ECR 1281 at 1297 (Advocate General Mancini).

47 *Ufficio Imposte di Consumo di Ispra v Commission* (above, note 8) at 443–444 (Advocate General Roemer); *Commission v Board of Governors of the European Investment Bank* (ibid) para 6.

(3)   The subject matter of the dispute and a summary of the pleas in law on which the application is based.[48]

(4)   The form of order sought by the applicant.[49] The expression 'form of order' is often rendered in the English texts as 'conclusions' or 'submissions', which can cause confusion. It refers to the claim for relief.

(5)   The nature of any evidence founded upon by the applicant (often referred to as the 'offer of proof').[50] The applicant should annex to the application all documents relied on by him[51] but, in the nature of things, some relevant documents may not be in his possession or control and some facts in issue may be provable only by other forms of evidence such as testimony. Such evidence can be produced only pursuant to a court order and the applicant should, therefore, indicate with precision the evidence whose production he wishes the Court to order by way of a preparatory enquiry for the purpose of proving each and every fact in issue. Where the case raises points of law alone and no facts are in issue, this requirement is otiose.[52]

(6)   The applicant's address for service in Luxembourg and the name of a person who is authorised and has expressed willingness to accept service.[53] What is required is the name of a *person* (no objection has so far been raised to the use of a legal, as opposed to a natural, person) and a declaration of his willingness to accept service on behalf of the applicant. If the application does not contain this information, service on the applicant is effected by registered letter addressed to the applicant's agent or lawyer unless and until the position is rectified.[54] The address of a person in Luxembourg who is willing to accept service is necessary so that the Court can contact the applicant with ease. There are no qualifications for accepting service, other than an address in Luxembourg, but it is advisable for a party to choose someone with the technical means to transmit documents without delay to the party or its agent or lawyer.[55]

The Rules of Procedure do not prescribe a particular order or form in which these requirements must be expressed and the Court has not sought to impose a particular formal style of pleading. Nonetheless, applications can, in general, be said to fall into three parts: title; submissions; and form of order.

The body of the application sets out the submissions of fact and law which entitle the applicant to the relief sought, which is defined in the form of order. These are the most important parts of the application: for the purposes of

---

48 RP-ECJ 38(1)(c); RP-CFI 44(1)(c); ECSC Statute, art 22; EC and Euratom Statutes, art 19. According to Advocate General Roemer (Case 18/69 *Fournier v Commission* [1970] ECR 249 at 285) a clear exposition of the claims made must be given in the application itself 'or at least in a written pleading submitted to the Court within the time limit for making an application'.

49 RP-ECJ 38(1)(d); RP-CFI 44(1)(d).

50 RP-ECJ 38(1)(e); RP-CFI 44(1)(e).

51 RP-ECJ 37(4); RP-CFI 43(4).

52 Cases C-213/88 and C-39/89 *Luxembourg v European Parliament* [1991] ECR I-5643 at 5673 (Advocate General Lenz).

53 RP-ECJ 38(2); RP-CFI 44(2).

54 Ibid. The application is admissible even if no address for service in Luxembourg is given. Under the Rules of Procedure as previously worded, the applicant was obliged to provide an address for service in Luxembourg, otherwise the application would be dismissed as inadmissible (see Case 297/84 *Sahinler v Commission* [1986] ECR 443); but the application would be admissible if that defect was remedied unless, perhaps, it was remedied after the time fixed for doing so by the Registrar and had caused the proceedings to be delayed (*Ufficio Imposte di Consumo di Ispra v Commission*, above, note 8, at 442–443 per Advocate General Roemer).

55 The address for service should be somewhere in the vicinity of the Court and preferably within the Commune of Luxembourg because the Court effects service in Luxembourg by hand.

admissibility, it is essential that the application has a form of order and sets out the facts and pleas in law invoked in support of it; as long as the application states the minimum necessary in order to identify the relief sought and the factual and legal grounds relied on, the requirements of admissibility have been satisfied and any deficiencies in the presentation of the case made out in the application go to the substance of the case.[56] It is comparatively rare for either of those parts of the application to be omitted entirely; most of the decided cases concern statements of the grounds relied on and forms of order which are said to be deficient in some respect. It may be observed in passing that the subject matter of the dispute should be evident from the statement of the grounds relied on and the form of order but, for the purposes of exposition, those two parts of the application will be commented on separately.[57]

2 Title

The title identifies the nature of the pleading and the action which it commences. Of the requirements in RP-ECJ 38 and RP-CFI 44 set out above, it comprises (1), (6) and (2) in that order.[58] The Statutes,[59] but not the Rules of Procedure, also require the 'description of the signatory' of the pleading[60] to be mentioned. This is usually set out after either (1) or (6) depending on the taste of the draftsman. After (2) there generally follows the designation of the pleading (in this case 'application'). This is not the only conceivable method of entitling the application; sometimes the pleading is headed by the word 'application' and the names, etc of the parties follow. Since the word 'application' is often qualified by a brief description of the nature of the proceedings, the full title may be somewhat as follows:

In the Court of Justice of the European Communities
(*or, as the case may be*:
In the Court of First Instance of the European Communities)

A B of [*address*], represented by C D, barrister, with an address for service in Luxembourg at the office of E F of [*address in Luxembourg*],

Applicant

against

Commission of the European Communities,[61]

Defendant

---

56 Cases C-213/88 and C-39/89 *Luxembourg v European Parliament* (above, note 52) paras 20–21 and pp 5670 and 5672–5673 per Advocate General Lenz.

57 Although the admissibility of an action is determined by reference to the situation prevailing when the application is lodged, it would seem that a technical ground of inadmissibility applicable at that stage may not render the application (and the action) inadmissible if it is cured within the period for commencing proceedings: Case 50/84 *Bensider v Commission* [1984] ECR 3991 (para 8).

58 The usual way of identifying the action to which a pleading relates is to quote the number of the case and the names of the parties. The number of the case cannot, of course, be used in the application which commences the proceedings because it is added by the Court when the application is lodged at the Registry.

59 ECSC Statute, art 22; EC and Euratom Statutes, art 19.

60 Ie the applicant's agent or lawyer: see RP-ECJ 37(1); RP-CFI 43(1).

61 For obvious reasons, the address of most defendants (ie Community institutions and member states) is usually known.

Application made under Articles 173 and 174 of the EEC
Treaty for a declaration that Commission Decision No 83/
1004 of 12 December 1983 is void.[62]

As can be seen, when set out in this way, the title also states the subject matter
of the dispute.[63] For this it is essential to give sufficient details to establish the
subject matter with certainty.[64] In actions for annulment it is, in particular,
necessary to identify clearly the measures sought to be annulled; if this is not
done, the application may be inadmissible.[65] In Case T-50/89 *Sparr v Commission*[66] the application did not provide sufficient information to enable it to be
classified so the Court classified it from the procedural point of view and did
not dismiss it as inadmissible because it was defective.

3   Submissions

An application which does not contain any statement of the submissions relied
on is inadmissible;[67] but if the failure to adduce any argument in the application relates only to one claim out of several, the Court may simply refuse to
consider that claim.[68] That part of the application setting out the applicant's
submissions must be drafted 'in such a way that the essential features of the
grounds on which it is based can be clearly discerned and it is possible to
distinguish the provisions on which the action is founded'.[69] The term
'grounds' is used in the Statutes[70] and was used in the English version of the
Rules of Procedure and in the case law to describe what, since the amendment
of the ECJ's Rules of Procedure in 1991, are now called 'pleas in law' (the latter
is the term that will be used henceforth save in quotations from the case law).
The grounds or pleas in law are the matters of law raised by the applicant to
justify grant of the relief sought. In support of each plea the applicant may
adduce any number of arguments and may add to them at will in the course of
the proceedings[71] but the application is intended to state the pleas relied on
exhaustively and, as a general rule, the scope of the action cannot subsequently be broadened by the addition of new pleas not mentioned in it.[72] There are,

---

62 Some pleadings say 'to the President and Members of the Court of Justice of the European
Communities' (or 'to the President and Members of the Court of First Instance of the
European Communities') or simply 'In the case of . . .'.
63 As far as admissibility is concerned, it is not necessary to mention expressly the Treaty
provision under which the action is brought (Cases 2–10/63 *Société Industriale Acciaierie San
Michele v High Authority* [1963] ECR 327 at 341) but to make such an omission is an
unsatisfactory way of pleading.
64 See Case 4/69 *Alfons Lütticke GmbH v Commission* [1971] ECR 325 (para 2).
65 See Case 30/68 *Lacroix v Commission* [1970] ECR 301 (paras 21–26).
66 [1990] ECR II-539 (para 5).
67 Case 2/54 *Italy v High Authority* [1954–56] ECR 37 at 59 (Advocate General Lagrange); Case
9/55 *Société des Charbonnages de Beeringen v High Authority* [1954–56] ECR 311 (see also Advocate
General Lagrange, at 266).
68 Case C-132/88 *Commission v Greece* [1990] ECR I-1567 (para 15).
69 Case 219/78 *Michaelis v Commission* [1979] ECR 3349 at 3360 (Advocate General Capotorti);
Generlich v Commission (above, note 3) paras 31–32. In Case C-61/90 *Commission v Greece* [1992]
ECR I-2407 (para 15), a point made by one party was rejected because it was insufficiently
precise and detailed. The fact that the defendant chooses to respond to a particular point only
in the rejoinder does not indicate that the application is defective in that respect: the *Generlich*
case (para 33).
70 ECSC Statute, art 22; EC and Euratom Statutes, art 19.
71 Eg Case 2/54 *Italy v High Authority* (above, note 67) at 51; Case 2/56 *Geitling Selling Agency for
Ruhr Coal v High Authority* [1957–58] ECR 3 at 17; Case 2/57 *Compagnie des Hauts Fourneaux de
Chasse v High Authority* [1957–58] ECR 199 at 206; Cases 9 and 12/60 *Société Commerciale Antoine
Vloeberghs SA v High Authority* [1961] ECR 197 at 215; the *Generlich* case (above, note 3) para 32.
72 Case 18/57 *Nold KG v High Authority* [1959] ECR 41 at 51.

in principle, two exceptions to this: pleas which are mandatory and must be raised by the Court of its own motion even though they have not been pleaded;[73] and pleas based on matters of law or of fact which come to light in the course of the procedure.[74] Both are considered below. Unless one of those exceptions applies, the only way that a new plea not mentioned in the application can be brought before the Court is by commencing a second action (always assuming that the time for doing so has not yet expired); but if the second action repeats any plea made in the first action, it will to that extent be inadmissible by virtue of the principle of lis pendens.[75]

When the Statutes[76] provide that there need only be a 'brief' statement of the pleas relied on and the Rules of Procedure refer to a 'summary' of those pleas, what is meant is that, although all the pleas must be set out and none may be left out, each one can be stated shortly and without a lengthy, comprehensive exegesis of the arguments used in support.[77] The statement in the application may be completed in the course of the proceedings.[78] Nonetheless, the pleas must be specified with sufficient particularity as to (i) their nature and content, (ii) the facts on which they are based and (iii) the rules of law invoked: it must be possible to identify the complaints made and the essence of the arguments invoked in support of them.[79] It should be emphasised that the test used to decide whether or not a pleading is insufficiently clear is whether or not the opposing party was able to adopt a position on the case in the light of it and whether or not the Court is able to exercise its powers of review.[80] For the purposes of satisfying the requirements of the Rules of Procedure, it is not necessary for the application to set out a good case: the strength of the case shown in the application goes to the foundation

73 Eg Case 2/54 *Italy v High Authority* (above, note 67) at 52.
74 RP-ECJ 42(2); RP-CFI 48(2). Before 1991, the Rules of Procedure were more restrictive in that a new plea (other than one that the Court could take of its own motion) could be introduced only if based on matters of law or fact which had come to light during the *written* procedure; the current version of the Rules allows the introduction of new pleas based on matters that have come to light after the close of the written procedure.
75 Cases 175 and 209/86 *M v Council* [1988] ECR 1891 at 1905 (Advocate General Mancini); Cases 358/85 and 51/86 *France v European Parliament* [1988] ECR 4821 (paras 7–12); Case C-157/89 *Commission v Italy* [1991] ECR I-57 (paras 5–7 and at 73 per Advocate General van Gerven).
76 Ibid note 70.
77 Case 25/62 *Plaumann & Co v Commission* [1963] ECR 95 at 120 (Advocate General Roemer).
78 Eg Case 18/60 *Worms v High Authority* [1962] ECR 195 at 203; Case 281/82 *Unifrex v Commission and Council* [1984] ECR 1969 (para 15); Case 118/83 *CMC Cooperativa Muratori e Cementisti v Commission* [1985] ECR 2325 (para 33), where the Court asked the applicant to present more detailed arguments at the hearing; Case T-82/89 *Marcato v Commission* [1990] ECR II-735 (para 74); Case C-243/89 *Commission v Denmark* [1993] ECR I-3353 (para 17). But contrast Cases T-33 and T-74/89 *Blackman v European Parliament*, 16 March 1993 (paras 64–65).
79 Case 111/63 *Lemmerz-Werke GmbH v High Authority* [1965] ECR 677 at 696; the *Blackman* case (ibid) para 64. Examples of failure to plead sufficiently precisely are: Case T-1/90 *Pérez-Mínguez Casariego v Commission* [1991] ECR II-143 (paras 57 and 62); Case C-330/88 *Grifoni v Euratom* [1991] ECR I-1045 (paras 17–18); Case C-63/89 *Les Assurances du Crédit et Compagnie Belge d'Assurance Crédit SA v Council and Commission* [1991] ECR I-1799 (para 25); Cases T-68, T-77 and T-78/89 *Società Italiano Vetro SA v Commission* [1992] ECR II-1403 (Re Italian Flat Glass) (paras 83–84); Case C-157/91 *Commission v Netherlands* [1992] ECR I-5899 (para 12); Case C-306/91 *Commission v Italy* [1993] ECR I-2133 paras 23–28 (see also paras 12–17 of the opinion of Advocate General Gulmann). For examples of applications held to be sufficiently clear despite the protestations of the defendant, see *CMC Cooperativi Muratori e Cementisti v Commission* (ibid) at 2331 (Advocate General VerLoren van Themaat); *Weddel & Co BV v Commission* (above, note 37) para 16 and at 883–884 (Advocate General van Gerven).
80 *Unifrex v Commission and Council* (above, note 78) paras 14–15 and at 1991 (Advocate General Mancini). Case T-85/92 *De Hoe v Commission* [1993] ECR II-523, para 20.

of the action.[81] The application should be brief and avoid unnecessary repetition but it should not be too concise.[82] The Court may be prepared to interpret the application freely if the defendant is not prejudiced thereby.[83] If the application does nothing more than set out various legal provisions and judicial authorities but fails to indicate the facts and circumstances relied on to support the claims made against the defendant, it will be held to be inadmissible because such a manner of pleading makes it impossible for the Court to rule on the case.[84] If an application is defective in this respect, the defect may be cured if the proceedings are joined to other proceedings having the same subject matter;[85] otherwise, the application will be inadmissible or excluded from consideration to the extent of the defect.[86] However, even a confused application is admissible if it has not misled the defendant.[87]

The applicant is not obliged to identify the pleas relied on properly or at all by reference to their legal classification as set out in the Treaties or elsewhere:[88] it is enough if they are designated 'in terms of their substance' as long as they are sufficiently clear.[89] On the other hand, an abstract statement is insufficient[90] and so is a formal reference to all the grounds mentioned in the Treaty:[91] the applicant must give particulars of the constituent elements of the plea.[92] This means that he must set out the precise facts relied on: the defendant is 'obliged to reply only to facts explicitly defined and to refute only clear and precise allegations'; he must be allowed to submit his defence with full knowledge of the facts at issue.[93] The applicant is not, however, bound to plead precisely facts which it is not possible for him to identify accurately and which are within the knowledge of the defendant.[94] So, for example, in an action for

---

81 Cf Case 126/83 *STS Consorzio per Sistemi di Telecomunicazione via Satellite SpA v Commission* [1984] ECR 2769 at 2782 (Advocate General VerLoren van Themaat). In consequence, where an argument advanced in support of a plea is itself unsupported, the argument is defective and should be rejected as such (as in Cases T-17/90, T-28/91 and T-17/92 *Camara Alloisio v Commission*, 15 July 1993, paras 86–91) and not because it is inadmissible.

82 Case 46/69 *Reinarz v Commission* [1970] ECR 275 at 286 (Advocate General Roemer); Case 76/86 *Commission v Germany* [1989] ECR 1021 at 1035 (Advocate General Jacobs).

83 Eg Cases 25 and 26/65 *SIMET and FERAM v High Authority* [1967] ECR 33 at 43; Case C-188/88 *NMB (Deutschland) GmbH v Commission* [1992] ECR 1689 (para 20), where the application claimed the annulment of the defendant's 'policy' but was construed as aiming at the decisions applying that policy.

84 Case C-347/88 *Commission v Greece* [1990] ECR I-4747 at 4770 (Advocate General Tesauro); Case C-52/90 *Commission v Denmark* [1992] ECR I-2187 (paras 17–19).

85 Eg Cases 26 and 86/79 *Forges de Thy-Marcinelle et Monceau SA v Commission* [1980] ECR 1083 (para 4).

86 Cf Case 277/82 *Papageorgopoulos v Economic and Social Committee* [1983] ECR 2897 (para 14).

87 *Pérez-Mínguez Casariego v Commission* (above, note 79) paras 45–49.

88 *Nold KG v High Authority* (above, note 72) at 66 (Advocate General Roemer); *Société Fives Lille Cail v High Authority* (above, note 3) at 295; *San Michele v High Authority* (above, note 63) at 348 (Advocate General Roemer).

89 The *Société Fives Lille Cail* case (ibid) at 295; the *San Michele* case (ibid) (see also per Advocate General Roemer at 348); Case 338/82 *Albertini and Montagnani v Commission* [1984] ECR 2123 (para 5); Cases C-363/88 and C-364/88 *Finanziaria Siderurgica Finsider SpA v Commission* [1992] ECR I-359 at 394 (Advocate General van Gerven), where the applicant's written and oral pleadings made it clear that the action was based on a further Treaty provision in addition to the one mentioned expressly in the application.

90 The *Société Fives Lille Cail* case (above, note 3); Case T-33/91 *Williams v Court of Auditors* [1992] ECR II-2499 (para 32).

91 *Lemmerz-Werke GmbH v High Authority* (above, note 79) at 705 (Advocate General Roemer).

92 'An indication of the essence of the arguments which will be of decisive importance in the evaluation of the submissions put forward': ibid at 705 (Advocate General Roemer). Cf Case 235/82 *Ferriere San Carlo v Commission* [1983] ECR 3949 (para 22); *De Hoe v Commission* (above, note 80) paras 21–26.

93 *Meroni & Co v High Authority* (above, note 3) at 419; see also the *Société Fives Lille Cail* case (above, note 3) and the *Blackman* case (above, note 78).

94 See *Alvino and Benoit v Commission* (above, note 41) at 797.

annulment, a failure to state in the application the date and contents of the contested act is not a defect, at least where the applicant is not in possession of sufficient information to be more precise than he has been.[95] Also in an action for annulment, it is not enough simply to allege one of the grounds for annulment mentioned in the Treaties: particulars must be given of the respects in which it is relied on.[96] In an action for damages, the applicant must give particulars of the wrongful acts alleged, the damage caused and the causal connection between them.[97]

The rules of law relied on by the applicant should be identifiable[98] although a specific reference to them is not necessary if they can be determined with sufficient clarity from a reading of the application.[99] The wrong citation of a provision of Community law does not cause the application or the ground to which it relates to be inadmissible[1] although it undoubtedly goes to the substance of the claim.

In several damages actions the defendant has objected that the applicant has not produced the figures on which the claim is based. The rule is that 'a claim for any unspecified form of damages is not sufficiently concrete and must therefore be regarded as inadmissible'.[2] In the nature of things, however, it may not be possible to assess the extent of the damage caused at the outset of proceedings, particularly where the damage is imminent or still continuing. In such circumstances, it is permissible for more detailed information concerning the claim to be produced at a later stage in proceedings, even if the result is to alter the amount claimed in the light of new or better information, at least as long as the defendant has an opportunity to reply;[3] but the applicant must plead the existence of special circumstances making it impossible for him to

---

95 Case C-157/90 *Infortec-Projectos e Consultadoria Lda v Commission* [1992] ECR I-3525 (paras 11-15).

96 The *Société Fives Lille Cail* case (above, note 3); a complaint stated in vague terms and not based on any specific argument must be rejected at once (see Case 19/58 *Germany v High Authority* [1960] ECR 225 at 239). See also Case 14/59 *Société des Fonderies de Pont à Mousson v High Authority* [1959] ECR 215 at 233.

97 *Meroni & Co v High Authority* (above, note 3); *Plaumann & Co v Commission* (above, note 77) at 120 (Advocate General Roemer); Case T-64/89 *Automec Srl v Commission* [1990] ECR II-367 (para 73); Case C-44/92 *Association of Independent Officials for the Defence of the European Civil Service v Commission* [1992] ECR I-6387 (paras 10–12). In Case 90/78 *Granaria BV v Council and Commission* [1979] ECR 1081 Advocate General Capotorti took the view that a lack of proof regarding the causal connection between the wrongful act alleged and the damage caused goes to the substance of the case rather than the admissibility of the application (see 1097–1098). In Case 346/87 *Bossi v Commission* [1989] ECR 303 at 316, Advocate General Darmon said that a failure to plead a causal connection is not fatal if one can easily be inferred from the facts.

98 *Michaelis v Commission* (above, note 69) at 3360 (Advocate General Capotorti); see also *Ufficio Imposte de Consumo di Ispra v Commission* (above, note 8) at 444 (Advocate General Roemer).

99 Case 62/65 *Serio v Euratom Commission* [1966] ECR 561 at 568 and at 575 (Advocate General Roemer); Case T-18/90 *Jongen v Commission* [1991] ECR II-187 (para 13).

1 Case 12/68 *X v Audit Board* [1969] ECR 109 (para 7).

2 Case 5/71 *Aktien Zuckerfabrik Schöppenstedt v Council* [1971] ECR 975 (para 9); Case 3/66 *Alfieri v European Parliament* [1966] ECR 437 at 447; Case 68/63 *Luhleich v Euratom Commission* [1965] ECR 581 at 605. See also Case 40/75 *Société des Produits Bertrand SA v Commission* [1976] ECR 1; Case T-64/89 *Automec Srl v Commission* [1990] ECR II-367 (para 73); Case T-28/90 *Asia Motor France SA v Commission* [1992] ECR II-2285 (paras 48–51), where the particulars given related to the period before the defendant could have been held liable. In Case T-63/89 *Latham v Commission* [1991] ECR II-19 (para 43) an unparticularised claim for damages was simply dismissed.

3 See, for example, Cases 29, 31, 36, 39–47, 50, 51/63 *Fonderies et Usines de la Providence v High Authority* [1965] ECR 911 at 934–935; Case 59/83 *Biovilac NV v Commission* [1984] ECR 4057 (para 9 and at 4085, Advocate General Slynn); Cases 279, 280, 285 and 286/84 *Walter Rau Lebensmittelwerke v Commission* [1987] ECR 1069 at 1095 (Advocate General Lenz); Case C-330/88 *Grifoni v Euratom* [1991] ECR I-1045 at 1057–1058 (Advocate General Tesauro).

indicate the precise extent of the damage suffered or the amount claimed[4] or, at the least, must plead the precise nature of the loss so that the defendant can plead to the application even if it does not know the exact sum claimed.[5] In the case of damage that is imminent, the claim in the application can be framed as a claim for a declaration that the Community will be liable but, in such circumstances, the threat of damage must be foreseeable with a sufficient degree of certainty;[6] if the damage alleged is a mere possibility or is contingent on some event which has not taken place or may not take place, the claim must be dismissed.[7] The claim may also be rejected if the applicant fails to provide particulars of the loss when asked by the Court to do so.[8] It has been suggested that the applicant cannot increase the amount claimed beyond the amount specified in the application[9] but it would seem that that may be so only in cases where there is no excuse for the failure to indicate the correct amount in the application and not in cases where the applicant is going no further than being more precise than he could have been at an earlier stage in the proceedings.[10] In other cases the Court has been asked to give an interlocutory judgment deciding the question of the defendant's liability, the question of the amount recoverable being settled in the light of this decision.[11] When this happens, the applicant must still give sufficient particulars to enable the opposing party to defend itself and the Court to rule on the dispute but they need not be as detailed concerning the damage alleged to have been suffered as they would otherwise have to be:[12] the scope of the claim may not, however, be extended after interim judgment on liability has been delivered.[13] An action for a declaratory judgment on the issue of liability in which the loss is not adequately particularised or in which the claim is for a nominal sum by way of damages is therefore inadmissible.[14] Where a claim is made for damages to be fixed ex aequo et bono, generally in cases of non-material loss such as damage to reputation, the Court fixes the amount due at its own discretion[15] but the exact nature of the non-material loss must still be identified.[16] A claim for compensatory interest must be pleaded specifically and proved by evidence of loss caused by the delay in payment but a claim for default interest is implicit

4 *Automec Srl v Commission* (above, note 2) paras 75–76; Case T-37/89 *Hanning v European Parliament* [1990] ECR II-463 (para 82).
5 Case 253/86 *Sociedade Agro-Pecuaria Vicente Nobra Lda v Council* [1988] ECR 2725 (para 18 and page 2736 per Advocate General Mischo).
6 *Biovilac v Commission* (above, note 3) para 9; Case 147/83 *Binderer v Commission* [1985] ECR 257 (para 19).
7 Case 257/83 *Williams v Court of Auditors* [1984] ECR 3547 (para 28); the *Binderer* case (ibid) paras 20–21.
8 Case 253/84 *Groupement Agricole d'Exploitation en Commun (GAEC) de la Ségaude v Council and Commission* [1987] ECR 123 (paras 12–13).
9 *Grifoni* (above, note 3) at 1057–1058 (Advocate General Tesauro).
10 Case 224/87 *Koutchoumoff v Commission* [1989] ECR 99 (para 11 and at 112 per Advocate General Tesauro).
11 See, for example, Case 74/74 *CNTA v Commission* [1975] ECR 533; Cases 56–60/74 *Kurt Kampffmeyer Mühlenvereinigung KG v Commission and Council* [1976] ECR 711; Case 44/76 *Milch-Fett- und Eier-Kontor GmbH v Council and Commission* [1977] ECR 393; Case 90/78 *Granaria BV v Council and Commission* [1979] ECR 1081.
12 Ibid; Case C-87/89 *Société Nationale Interprofessionelle de la Tomate v Commission* [1990] ECR I-1981 at 2002 (Advocate General Lenz).
13 Cases 532, 534, 567, 600, 618, 660/79 and 543/79 *Amesz v Commission* [1985] ECR 55 (para 9); Case 131/81 *Berti v Commission* [1985] ECR 645 (paras 16–18).
14 Case C-119/88 *Aerpo v Commission* [1990] ECR I-2189 at 2205 (Advocate General Jacobs).
15 Eg Case 18/78 *Mrs V v Commission* [1979] ECR 2093 (para 19), where the Court held that symbolic damages would be enough and ordered payment of a sum corresponding to one 'European Monetary Unit'.
16 Case 346/87 *Bossi v Commission* [1989] ECR 303 (para 37).

in any claim for damages and does not require any prior request for payment or proof of damage.[17] Where the defendant is or is alleged to be liable to several persons jointly, a failure to specify in the application how the damages are to be apportioned between the applicants does not affect the admissibility of the application.[18]

In the particular cases of actions brought by the Commission against a member state alleging a failure by the latter to comply with its obligations under the EC or Euratom Treaties and staff cases, the scope of the action is determined by the application but the claims made in the application must have been raised against the defendant in the pre-litigation stage of the procedure.[19] The application need not be a perfect copy of the claims raised beforehand[20] and it is sufficient if a claim was raised implicitly in the course of the pre-litigation procedure.[21] On the other hand, a failure to include in sufficient detail in the application a point elaborated in the pre-litigation procedure may be fatal.[22] In actions brought by the Commission against a member state, a change in the law that takes place after the commencement of proceedings (other than one that makes no material difference to the original matters of complaint) cannot be relied on against the defendant.[23]

References to what has been said in other proceedings or in other documents are not sufficient to comply with the requirement to state the pleas relied on[24] and, when both parties adopt this practice, it has been regarded by the Court as unacceptable because it makes it impossible to check the exact content and significance of the submissions and arguments put forward.[25] Such references are, therefore, regarded as inadmissible[26] save where:

(1)   the two cases are so closely connected that they are or will be joined;[27]
(2)   the proceedings have been commenced after the completion of a mandatory pre-litigation procedure, in which case limited reference may be

---

17 Case 158/79 *Roumengous (née Carpentier) v Commission* [1985] ECR 39 (para 14 and at 41–42, Advocate General Mancini).
18 Case 267/82 *Développement SA and Clemessy v Commission* [1986] ECR 1907 (para 19).
19 Case T-134/89 *Hettrich v Commission* [1990] ECR II-565 (paras 11–19); Case C-157/91 *Commission v Netherlands* [1992] ECR I-5899 (para 17).
20 Case C-347/88 *Commission v Greece* [1990] ECR I-4747 at 4768–4769 (Advocate General Tesauro); Case C-105/91 *Commission v Greece* [1992] ECR I-5871 (para 13), where the national legislation had changed in the meantime but the system complained of had remained the same.
21 Case T-18/90 *Jongen v Commission* [1991] ECR II-187 para 22. The Court is more likely to be indulgent to the applicant in a staff case than to the Commission in an action against a member state.
22 *Hettrich v Commission* (above, note 19) para 16; Case C-347/88 *Commission v Greece* (above, note 20), paras 28–30 and at 4766 (Advocate General Tesauro); Case C-110/89 *Commission v Greece* [1991] ECR I-2659 (para 6 and at 2676 per Advocate General Lenz), a point raised only at the hearing.
23 Cases 194 and 241/85 *Commission v Greece* [1988] ECR 1037 at 1045 (Advocate General Cruz Vilaça).
24 Case 9/55 *Société des Charbonnages de Beeringen v High Authority* [1954–56] ECR 311 at 325; Case C-43/90 *Commission v Germany* [1992] ECR I-1909 (paras 7–8 and at 1924 per Advocate General Darmon).
25 Cases 19 and 65/63 *Prakash v Euratom Commission* [1965] ECR 533 at 546.
26 Ibid; but they do not bring about the inadmissibility of the entire application if it otherwise conforms to the Rules of Procedure (Case 4/69 *Alfons Lütticke GmbH v Commission* [1971] ECR 325, para 2).
27 *Société des Charbonnages de Beeringen v High Authority* (above, note 24); see also Case 8/55 *Fédération Charbonnière de Belgique v High Authority* [1954–56] ECR 245 at 266 (Advocate General Lagrange). In Case 61/77 *Commission v Ireland* [1978] ECR 417, a direct action, the Court took account of certain arguments raised in parallel preliminary ruling proceedings 'in order that all aspects of the dispute may be fully examined' (para 21), even though the two cases were not joined. This is exceptional and is probably to be explained by the fact that direct actions are not joined to references for a preliminary ruling even where the proceedings are heard and decided at the same time.

made to the pre-litigation exchanges in order to clarify the scope of the action and the arguments relied on in the application;[28] and
(3)   the Court permits such references to be made.[29]

Statements contained in the application which are disclaimed by the applicant are not regarded as forming part of the case made out by him.[30] There is no provision for the amendment of the pleas and arguments set out in the application[31] although corrections of typing errors and other slips are permitted. The only possibility of changing what has been said is by addition or concession in the reply or at the hearing.

The Court may take some pleas of its own motion and, when these are raised by the applicant, they must be considered even though they do not appear in the application.[32] Such issues are those which 'bring into question matters of such importance that the Court "would disregard the rule of law which it has the duty of seeing observed, if the decision which it gives does not take account thereof"'.[33] For the most part they appear in actions for annulment and include the following: infringement of an essential procedural requirement;[34] lack of reasoning in a decision;[35] lack of competence.[36]

Although RP-ECJ 38(1) and RP-44(1) mention the nature of any evidence founded upon by the applicant after the form of order, there is no requirement that the application should end with a list of the evidence relied on. It seems to be better practice to set out the nature of any relevant evidence after each assertion of fact made in the body of the application; although some pleaders place immediately before the form of order a distinct section of the application devoted to evidence which indicates the nature and source of the evidence relied on in support of the assertions of fact made earlier in the application.[37]

---

28 Case C-347/88 *Commission v Greece* (above, note 20) at 4767 (Advocate General Tesauro).
29 Case T-82/89 *Marcato v Commission* [1990] ECR II-735 (paras 22–24).
30 Case 111/63 *Lemmerz-Werke GmbH v High Authority* [1965] ECR 677 at 696.
31 But see *Milch- Fett- und Eier-Kontor GmbH v Council and Commission* (above, note 11) at 421 (Advocate General Reischl).
32 Case C-70/88 *European Parliament v Council* [1991] ECR I-4529 at 4544–4545 (Advocate General van Gerven).
33 Case 36/72 *Meganck v Commission* [1973] ECR 527 at 539 (Advocate General Mayras, quoting from Odent, *Cours de Contentieux Administratif*, a textbook on French administrative law). In Cases 209–215 and 218/78 *Heintz van Landewyck Sarl v Commission* [1980] ECR 3125 at 3302, Advocate General Reischl said that the Court could raise of its own motion 'particularly important issues'.
34 Case 2/54 *Italy v High Authority* [1954–56] ECR 37 at 52; Case 6/54 *Netherlands v High Authority* [1954–56] ECR 103 at 112; Case 20/59 *Italy v High Authority* [1960] ECR 325 at 347 (Advocate General Roemer); Case C-291/89 *Interhotel v Commission* [1991] ECR I-2257: but not all procedural defects (see Case 101/79 *Vecchioli v Commission* [1980] ECR 3069, para 19 and at 3099 (Advocate General Warner).
35 Case 18/57 *Nold KG v High Authority* [1959] ECR 41 at 52; Case 4/73 *Nold KG v Commission* [1974] ECR 491 at 512 (Advocate General Trabucchi); *Hanning v European Parliament* (above, note 4), para 38; Case T-115/89 *Gonzalez Holguera v European Parliament* [1990] ECR I-831 (para 37); Case T-45/90 *Speybrouck v European Parliament* [1992] ECR II-33 (para 89); Case T-11/91 *Schloh v Council* [1990] ECR II-203 (para 83); Case T-61/89 *Dansk Pels-dryavlerforening v Commission* [1992] ECR II-1931; Case T-65/89 *BPB Industries plc and British Gypsum Limited v Commission* [1993] ECR II-389 (para 98).
36 Case 19/58 *Germany v High Authority* [1960] ECR 225 at 233; *Meganck v Commission* (above, note 33) at 540 (Advocate General Mayras); and Case 110/81 *Roquette Frères SA v Council*, [1982] ECR 3159 (para 34).
37 For example, where one of the grounds relied on in a claim for annulment is misuse of powers, the allegation should be particularised by reference to specific facts. In respect of each fact alleged, the means of proving it should be set out, eg 'The applicant relies on the documents annexed hereto and on the testimony of A B of [address and occupation]'. In the case of witnesses, it should be explained why a particular person is competent to give evidence. There is no reason that the content of the evidence should not be annexed to the pleading in the form of a statement or declaration under oath (this has been done in some cases) but there may be tactical reasons why a party would not wish to do so.

The case law shows what are the minimum requirements for complying with the Statutes and the Rules of Procedure. It is obviously better practice to seek to do more than just the minimum.

4 Form of order

The inclusion of a form of order in the application is an essential condition of its admissibility[38] and omission of the form of order cannot be cured by subsequent amendment.[39] The form of order defines the relief sought by the applicant (not the pleas relied on)[40] and is usually expressed as setting out the order which the applicant wishes the Court to make. The relief sought should be set out unequivocally and precisely for two reasons: (i) if it is ambiguous or obscure the Court may be led to give judgment ultra petita or to fail to give judgment on one of the heads of claim; and (ii) the defendant must be in a position to know exactly the case which he must answer.[41] The fact that the form of order is unclear does not lead inevitably to the inadmissibility of the application: the form of order should be construed in the light of the application as a whole, and the statements of the pleas relied on in particular;[42] in general terms, how the claims made are expressed does not affect their admissibility as long as what is claimed is discernible.[43] Where necessary, the Court may ask the applicant to clarify the order sought.[44] A mistake made by the applicant when formulating the form of order goes to the substance of the case, not the admissibility of the action (although it cannot be excluded that the discordance between the form of order and the pleas invoked in its support may be so great as to render it pointless to rule on the substance of the case).[45]

The applicant is entitled only to the relief claimed expressly or by implication

---

38 Cf Case 55/64 *Lens v European Court of Justice* [1965] ECR 837 at 840; Case 110/63A *Willame v Euratom Commission* [1966] ECR 287 at 291; Case 17/68 *Reinarz v Commission* [1969] ECR 61 at para 47; Case 48/70 *Bernardi v European Parliament* [1971] ECR 175 at 189 (Advocate General Roemer).

39 *Bernardi v European Parliament* (ibid).

40 Invoking the invalidity of a regulation in support of a claim for the annulment of a decision is a plea and therefore does not need to figure in the form of order: Case C-188/88 *NMB (Deutschland) GmbH v Commission* [1992] ECR 1689 (para 25).

41 See Cases 46 and 47/59 *Meroni & Co v High Authority* [1962] ECR 411 at 419.

42 Case 33/59 *Compagnie des Hauts Fourneaux de Chasse v High Authority* [1962] ECR 381 at 393 (Advocate General Lagrange); *Meroni & Co v High Authority* (ibid) at 419–420. See also Cases 25 and 26/65 *SIMET and FERAM v High Authority* [1967] ECR 33; Case 2/68 *Ufficio Imposte di Consumo di Ispra v Commission* [1968] ECR 435 at 437–438 and at 449 (Advocate General Roemer); Case 419/85 *Commission v Italy* [1987] ECR 2115 (Re Community Driving Licence) (para 8); Case 307/85 *Gavanas v Economic and Social Committee and Council* [1987] ECR 2435 (para 12); Case 190/84 *Parti Ecologiste 'Les Verts' v European Parliament* [1988] ECR 1017 at 1029 (Advocate General Mancini), where the application identified the acts whose annulment was sought by reference to their subject matter for want of more precise information concerning them, without interfering with the defendant's ability to marshal its defence; *Bossi v Commission* (above, note 16) paras 15–18, where the act whose annulment was sought was identified by drawing inferences from the body of the application; Case T-119/89 *Teissonière v Commission* [1990] ECR II-7 (para 20); *BPB Industries v Commission* (above, note 35) para 162.

43 Case 135/87 *Vlachou v Court of Auditors* [1988] ECR 2901 at 2908 (Advocate General Lenz). If the contested act is unclear, that may excuse a lack of clarity in the applicant's form of order: Case 214/83 *Germany v Commission* [1985] ECR 3053 at 3069 (Advocate General VerLoren van Themaat).

44 Eg *Meroni & Co v High Authority* (above, note 41); Case 804/79 *Commission v United Kingdom* [1981] ECR 1045 at 1053.

45 Case C-217/91 *Spain v Commission*, 7 July 1993 (opinion of Advocate General Gulmann, para 7). The Court took a different view: see paras 12–17.

in the form of order contained in the application.[46] There is no provision for amendment of the form of order and while, in some cases,[47] the Court has not excluded entirely the possibility of amendment, the furthest it has gone is to allow a change in the wording, but not the subject matter, of the order sought.[48] For example, in Case 25/62 *Plaumann & Co v Commission*[49] the applicant originally claimed a declaration that the defendant was liable to compensate him for future damage arising from a wrongful act. In the reply this was converted into a claim for a specified sum by way of damages. The Court held this to be a 'permissible amplification' of the claim made in the application: as Advocate General Roemer pointed out,[50] the amendment simply quantified the damage claimed. In the same way, in Case C-243/89 *Commission v Denmark*,[51] the Court stated that the form of order may be expressed in more precise terms in a later pleading in order to take account of information coming to light in the course of the proceedings. In such cases the amplification or particularisation of the form of order is not an extension of its true scope. The only exceptions to the rule that the Court cannot grant relief other than that claimed in the application are:

(1) where a mandatory ground has been raised which would entrain the annulment of a contested measure in its entirety but the applicant has sought only its partial annulment;[52]

(2) where the Court has unlimited jurisdiction;[53]

(3) where, after the commencement of proceedings for annulment, the act challenged is amended or replaced by another measure which is identical in nature and subject matter to the act first challenged, in which case the applicant may amend the form of order in a subsequent pleading or (if the second act was adopted after the close of the written procedure) at the hearing but must do so expressly;[54]

---

46 See Case 8/56 *ALMA v High Authority* [1957–58] ECR 95 at 100 (the Court there had unlimited jurisdiction); Case 44/59 *Fiddelaar v Commission* [1960] ECR 535 at 542; *Compagnie des Hauts Fourneaux de Chasse v High Authority* (above, note 42) at 388; *Reinarz v Commission* (above, note 38) para 47; Cases 173/82, 157/83 and 186/84 *Castille v Commission* [1986] ECR 497 at 502 (Advocate General Lenz); Case 191/84 *Barcella v Commission* [1986] ECR 1541 (paras 5–6 and at 1543 per Advocate General Darmon); Case 7/86 *Vincent v European Parliament* [1987] ECR 2473 (at 2486 per Advocate General Cruz Vilaça); Case 278/85 *Commission v Denmark* [1987] ECR 4069 (para 37); *Spain v Commission* (above, note 45) paras 12–17; Case T-6 and T-52/92 *Reinarz v Commission*, 26 October 1993, para 38; Case T-65/91 *White v Commission*, 12 January 1994, para 83.

47 Eg *Compagnie des Hauts Fourneaux de Chasse v High Authority* (ibid); *Meroni & Co v High Authority* (above, note 41) at 420.

48 See, for example, Case 232/78 *Commission v France* [1979] ECR 2729 (para 3); Case 124/81 *Commission v United Kingdom* [1983] ECR 203 (para 6); Case T-41/89 *Schwedler v European Parliament* [1990] ECR II-79 (para 34). A new claim raised subsequently to the application cannot be saved by severing it and treating it as a separate action: Case T-22/92 *Weissenfels v European Parliament*, 26 October 1993, paras 27–29.

49 [1963] ECR 95 at 108.   **50** At 118.

51 [1993] ECR I-3353 (para 20).   **52** Case 37/71 *Jamet v Commission* [1972] ECR 483 (para 12).

53 *Fiddelaar v Commission* (above, note 46) at 542–543; Case 23/69 *Fiehn v Commission* [1970] ECR 547 (para 17); Case 24/79 *Oberthür v Commission* [1980] ECR 1743 (para 14). See also *ALMA v High Authority* (above, note 46) at 100 and Cases 27 and 39/59 *Campolongo v High Authority* [1960] ECR 391 at 415 (Advocate General Roemer). Contra, see Case 267/85 *Luttgens v Commission* [1986] ECR 3417 (para 6), inadmissibility of a claim for compensation introduced during the oral procedure. Even where the Court has unlimited jurisdiction, it cannot order the defendant to take measures to comply with the judgment: Case T-156/89 *Mordt v Court of Justice* [1991] ECR II-407 (para 150).

54 Case 14/81 *Alpha Steel Ltd v Commission* [1982] ECR 749 (para 8); Case 48/86R *J Cauet and B Joliet v Commission* [1986] ECR 1237 (para 4); *Automec Srl v Commission* (above, note 2), paras 67–68. Where an act that cannot be challenged is replaced by one that can, such an amendment is not possible because the subject matter of the action would then be changed: *Automec* (para 69).

(4) where the applicant brought an action in respect of the defendant's
failure to act and, in the course of the proceedings, the defendant adopted
a challengeable act;[55]
(5) in interim relief cases, where there is a change of circumstances requiring
a corresponding change in the relief sought and the ability of the opposing party to defend itself is not affected;[56] and
(6) where the applicant concedes a head of claim in whole or in part.[57]

Subject to the exceptions referred to above, the Court is precluded only from
awarding relief that goes outside the scope of that claimed in the application; it
is not precluded from granting less than the relief claimed in circumstances
where the Court concludes that the applicant's claim is founded, but not to the
extent claimed in the form of order in the application.

A number of claims may be joined in the form of order, whether made cumu-
latively or alternatively, even if they are different in nature, such as a claim for
annulment and one for damages.[58] There is no requirement that different claims
be expressed in some order of priority but an ordering of the claims made into
primary, secondary and, where appropriate, other claims is consistent with the
Rules of Procedure.[59] Where the claims made are inconsistent, they should be
expressed as alternative claims. If that is not done expressly in the application,
the Court will construe them as being alternative claims, in which case the
applicant will be precluded from seeking as a subsidiary form of relief a claim
that is wider than the claim regarded by the Court as being the primary claim
made.[60] A claim for default interest is usually implicit in any claim for damages
but a claim for compensatory interest is a distinct claim which must be pleaded
specifically.[61] A claim for costs should always be made unless the applicant does
not wish to recover costs if he should be successful.[62] A claim for 'further or other

---

55 Case 103/85 *Stahlwerke Peine-Salzgitter AG v Commission* [1988] ECR 4131 (paras 11–12). The
CFI seems to have taken a different view in *Asia Motor France SA v Commission* (above, note 2),
para 43.
56 Cases 82 and 83/85R *Eurasian Corpn Ltd v Commission* [1985] ECR 1191 (paras 15–16). In Case
C-280/93R *Germany v Council* [1993] ECR I-3667 (paras 15–16), the changes in the relief
sought do not seem to have reflected a change in circumstances but were simply alternative
claims whose admissibility was to be assessed by reference to the scope of the relief originally
sought.
57 Case 11/63 *Lepape v High Authority* [1964] ECR 61 at 69; Cases 18 and 19/64 *Alvino and Benoit v
Commission* [1965] ECR 789; Case 214/83 *Germany v Commission* (above, note 43) para 19; Case
293/85R *Commission v Belgium* [1985] ECR 3521 (para 4). A concession can only be deduced
from an express statement or unambiguous conduct: Case 1/74 *Giry v Commission* [1974] ECR
1269 at 1282 (Advocate General Trabucchi, citing the maxim 'nemo res suas iactare
praesumitur').
58 Cases 7 and 9/54 *Groupement des Industries Sidérurgiques Luxembourgeoises v High Authority* [1954–
56] ECR 175 at 189 and at 206 (Advocate General Roemer) (a claim for annulment and a
claim for a declaration); Cases 7/56 and 3–7/57 *Algera v Common Assembly* [1957–58] ECR 39 at
64; *Plaumann & Co v Commission* (above, note 49) at 118–119 (Advocate General Roemer)
(claims for annulment and for damages).
59 Case 214/83 *Germany v Commission* (above, note 43), para 20 and at 3069–3070 (Advocate
General VerLoren van Themaat): the Court is not obliged to consider alternative or subsidiary claims unless it dismisses the principal claims made.
60 *Vlachou v Court of Auditors* (above, note 43) paras 2–3 and at 2908 (Advocate General Lenz).
61 *Roumengous v Commission* (above, note 17) at 41–42 (Advocate General Mancini). Claims for
compensatory interest were dismissed because they were not made in the application in that
case (para 14 of the judgment) and in a number of other cases, including *Amesz v Commission*
(above, note 13) para 17; Case 737/79 *Battaglia v Commission* [1985] ECR 71 (para 13); *Berti v
Commission* (above, note 13) paras 16–18; Case C-320/81 *Acerbis v Commission* [1990] ECR I-563
(para 23).
62 Cases 92 and 93/87 *Commission v France* [1989] ECR 405 at 436 (Advocate General van
Gerven). By failing to claim costs in the application (or, so far as the defendant is concerned, in
the defence), a party risks losing the right to claim them entirely: Case 298/83 *CICCE v
Commission* [1985] ECR 1105 (para 32).

relief' should normally be made only in cases where the Court has unlimited jurisdiction. Where claims are joined improperly, the application is not inadmissible for that reason alone: the proper course is to disjoin the claims.[63] Claims may be improperly joined where there is no (factual) connection between them[64] or where they comprise distinct actions which are governed by different procedural rules.[65] A claim made in the form of order which is outside the Court's powers to order is inadmissible[66] but may be construed as an argument in support of any admissible claims.[67]

5   Attachments

To the application should be annexed the following:

(1)   A certificate showing that the lawyer acting for the applicant is entitled to practise before a court of a member state.[68] RP-ECJ 38 and RP-CFI 44 say that it is the lawyer himself who must lodge the certificate (not the applicant) and do not expressly provide that it must accompany the application. It is to be inferred from RP-ECJ 38(7) and RP-CFI 44(6), however, that the certificate must be annexed to the application because, if it is not, the Registrar must prescribe a reasonable period within which the *applicant* is to produce it. If he fails to do so, the Court may reject the application on the ground of want of form.[69] The certificate is essential for determining whether the requirements that a party be represented by, and that the pleadings lodged on his behalf have been signed by, a lawyer entitled to practise before the courts of a member state have been properly complied with.[70] There are no rules defining what may constitute a certificate. It is, nonetheless, quite clear that it must be a document which shows that the lawyer fulfils the requirement in the Rules of Procedure for acting on behalf of a party in proceedings before the Court and that it must be issued by a national authority competent to do so.

(2)   In actions for annulment or against a failure to act, the measure whose annulment is sought or documentary evidence of the date on which the defendant institution was requested to act.[71] The object of this is to identify clearly the subject matter of the action and a failure to comply

63   Cf *Groupement des Industries Sidérurgiques Luxembourgeoises v High Authority* (above, note 58) at 206 (Advocate General Roemer); for examples of disjoinder, see Case 567/79A *Flamm v Commission and Council* [1981] ECR 2383 and Case 618/79A *Knoeppel v Commission and Council* [1981] ECR 2387.

64   *Groupement des Industries Sidérurgiques Luxembourgeoises v High Authority* (ibid).

65   Case 40/71 *Richez-Parise v Commission* [1972] ECR 73 (paras 2–3). The applicant sought annulment of an act and the revision of a judgment. The Court found it possible to adjudicate on both claims in one judgment because the latter was made in the alternative and, in substance, sought a similar result to the former.

66   *Fiddelaar v Commission* (above, note 46) at 542; *Mordt v Court of Justice* (above, note 53) para 140.

67   Case 150/84 *Bernardi v European Parliament* [1986] ECR 1375 (para 24).

68   RP-ECJ 38(3); RP-CFI 44(3). The meaning of entitlement to practise before a court of a member state is discussed at pp 125–129. It is understood that the Court will accept a professional identity card issued in the form agreed by the CCBE, at least if it has been issued or validated within the previous year.

69   Eg Case T-101/92 *Stagakis v European Parliament* [1993] ECR II-63.

70   In consequence, where a party is entitled to be, and is, represented by an agent who has signed the pleadings, a failure to produce a certificate for the lawyer assisting the agent is not a procedural irregularity: Case T-47/92 *Lenz v Commission* [1992] ECR II-2523 (para 35).

71   RP-ECJ 38(4); RP-CFI 44(4). See also the ECSC Statute, art 22, and the EC and Euratom Statutes, art 19. The ECSC Statute specifies, in the case of proceedings against an implied decision, 'documentary evidence of the date on which the request was lodged'. This does not appear to differ in substance from the requirement in the EC and Euratom Statutes.

with this requirement may lead to the inadmissibility of the application.[72] In the nature of things, this requirement can be satisfied only if the applicant is in possession of a true copy of the measure whose annulment is sought or of the evidence required. In actions in respect of a failure to act, the applicant can be expected to have evidence of the request to act but, in actions for annulment, it often happens that the applicant knows or believes that a challengeable act has been made, or purportedly made, but does not possess a true copy of it.[73] In such circumstances, the applicant may ask the author of the act (that is, the intended defendant in the proceedings) to supply a true copy so that it may be attached to the application. However, it is not unknown for the author of the act to refuse to comply with such a request. In cases where the applicant is not in possession of a true copy of the contested act, the applicant's failure to attach a true copy to the application cannot be a procedural defect and cannot be relied on by the defendant (being the author of that act) in order to challenge the admissibility of the application. Where the application is put in order after the expiry of the time limit for bringing proceedings, the applicant is not barred from continuing the action,[74] at least if he has complied with the time limit set by the Registrar for producing the missing evidence. Where this time limit has not been respected, the application may be inadmissible on the ground of want of form[75] but the action is not necessarily time-barred. If the measure whose annulment is sought has been published in the Official Journal by the time the application is lodged it does not seem that a failure to annex a copy of it would lead to the inadmissibility of the application as long as the measure is clearly identifiable by a citation of the appropriate part and page number of the Official Journal. There is, however, no authority for this so it would be wise to annex a copy of the measure to the application in all cases.

(3) In the case of applications made by a legal person governed by private law, (a) 'the instrument or instruments constituting or regulating that legal person or a recent extract from the register of companies, firms or associations or any other proof of its existence in law' and (b) 'proof that the authority granted to the applicant's lawyer has been properly conferred on him by someone authorised for the purpose'.[76] The object of this requirement is to establish the existence of the applicant, its capacity to initiate legal proceedings and the fact that it is properly represented.

---

72 Cf Case 30/68 *Lacroix v Commission* [1970] ECR 301.
73 For example, the applicant may have been informed orally of the existence of a decision of direct and individual concern to him or may have nothing more than a letter which suggests that such a decision has been made but does not constitute a copy of the decision.
74 ECSC Statute, art 22; EC and Euratom Statutes, art 19.
75 RP-ECJ 38(7); RP-CFI 44(6).
76 RP-ECJ 38(5); RP-CFI 44(5). A failure to attach to the application a copy of the instrument constituting or regulating the applicant can lead to the inadmissibility of the application: Case 289/83 *GAARM Groupement des Associations Agricoles pour l'Organisation de la Production et de la Commercialisation des Pommes de Terre et Légumes de la Région Malouine v Commission* [1984] ECR 2789. It is not fatal as long as a copy is produced in the course of the proceedings: Cases 193–194/87 *Maurissen v Court of Auditors* [1989] ECR 1045 (paras 31–32). In principle, a complete copy of the instrument should be attached but, in Case C-194/87 *Union Syndicale v Court of Auditors*, order of 10 February 1988 (judgment reported as Cases C-193 and C-194/87 *Maurissen v Court of Auditors* [1990] ECR I-95), an association which had applied to intervene (and which therefore had to produce the instrument constituting or regulating it) annexed to its application part only of its statutes; that was held to be sufficient compliance with the Rules of Procedure because the parts disclosed to the Court were enough to establish the objects, functions and general characteristics of the association.

Proof that the applicant is properly represented may be by production of 'a company's documents of constitution, an extract from the commercial register and an authority ad litem'.[77] In the case of a company governed by English law, it would be necessary to produce the memorandum and articles of association or an extract from the Companies Register and, for example, a copy of any resolution of the board of directors authorising the commencement of proceedings and the appointment of the lawyer, although it is more frequent to produce only the memorandum and articles of association and a declaration before a notary. Where the commencement of proceedings or the appointment of the applicant's lawyer has been effected or authorised by a director, officer or organ of the applicant whose power so to do does not appear on the face of the instrument constituting or regulating the applicant which has been attached to the application, it is necessary to provide further evidence to establish that proceedings have been properly commenced and the lawyer properly appointed. It will be observed that, in the case of a legal person governed by public law, there is no similar requirement. This does not mean that such persons are presumed to have capacity to bring proceedings and to be properly represented. The silence of the Rules of Procedure suggests nothing more than that they are not obliged to annex evidence of either fact to the application. Should the defendant challenge capacity or the lawyer's authority to act, the applicant would be bound to produce the evidence. In order to avoid difficulties and delays in the proceedings[78] it is better to annex such evidence to the application even though there is no express requirement to do so. The same applies in the case of applicants whom the Court recognises as having capacity to bring proceedings but who are not legal persons under national law.[79] When the Rules of Procedure were drafted, it was probably not envisaged that persons lacking legal personality in the formal sense could bring proceedings. As far as such persons are concerned, the question of their existence and capacity to bring proceedings and be represented before the Court is all the more delicate and liable to be challenged by the opposing parties.

(4)   In actions brought before the Court pursuant to an arbitration clause contained in a contract concluded by or on behalf of the Community[80] or pursuant to a special agreement concluded between member states,[81] a copy of the arbitration clause in the contract or the special agreement in question.[82] Where the provision under which the Court has jurisdiction is contained in or made applicable by several documents, all should be produced.[83]

(5)   The authority to act of the applicant's lawyer. This is not expressly required by the Rules of Procedure[84] and, hence, a failure to annex the

---

77   *Ufficio Imposte di Consumo v Commission* (above, note 42) at 443 (Advocate General Roemer). GI 34 refers to 'an extract from a trade register or a declaration before a notary'.

78   Cf *Ufficio Imposte di Consumo v Commission* (ibid). It is understood that the Court requires compliance even from a member state.

79   Eg an unincorporated association.

80   ECSC Treaty, art 42; EC Treaty, art 181; Euratom Treaty, art 153.

81   ECSC Treaty, art 89; EC Treaty, art 182; Euratom Treaty, art 154.

82   RP-ECJ 38(6).

83   Cf Case 23/76 *Luigi Pellegrini and CSAS v Commission* [1976] ECR 1807: an arbitration clause was contained in a draft agreement which was incorporated into the contract between the parties orally, later confirmed in writing; the applicant showed that the arbitration clause applied by producing the correspondence passing between the parties.

84   Although RP-ECJ 38(5)(b) and RP-CFI 44(5)(b) require it by implication.

authority to the application does not entitle the Court to reject it on the ground of want of form.[85] Nonetheless, proof of authority to act should be produced at some time and a failure to do so when challenged may lead to the inadmissibility of the application.[86] It is, of course, arguable that the grant of authority (without retrospective effect) after the expiry of a time limit for the bringing of proceedings does lead to the inadmissibility of the action: the first application is inadmissible because the lawyer lodging it had no authority to do so and a subsequent application is inadmissible because it is out of time. In the interests of the smooth running of the proceedings, the Court has always, as a matter of practice, required an authority to be produced with the application.[87] Adequate proof is a signed statement by the applicant or, in the case of a legal person, a natural person properly authorised to do so, indicating that the lawyer has been given authority to act. The Community institutions and some member states also produce proof that the agent representing them has authority to act but this is not necessary unless requested by the Court.

(6) A file containing all the documents relied on in support of the claims made and a schedule listing those documents.[88]

B The defence

The minimum requirements concerning the defence are to be found in RP-ECJ 40(1) and RP-CFI 46(1) and (2) which, in addition, apply to the defence the provisions of RP-ECJ 38(2) to (5) and RP-CFI 44(2) to (5), respectively.

1 Contents

The defence must state:

(1) The name and address of the defendant.
(2) The arguments of fact and law relied on. The defendant does not have to set out any 'pleas', only the arguments of fact and law on which he relies in order to rebut the case made out by the applicant.
(3) The form of order sought. Usually this requests the rejection of the application and costs.
(4) The nature of any evidence offered by the defendant.
(5) An address for service in Luxembourg and the name of a person authorised and willing to accept service.[89]

Like the application, the defence usually falls into three parts: title; submissions; and form of order.

2 Title

The title is the same as that in the application with the addition of the case number (which the Court will have indicated to the defendant when serving

---

85 Case 14/64 *Gualco (née Barge) v High Authority* [1965] ECR 51 at 57.
86 It does not seem that, if the authority to act is conferred on the lawyer after the lodgment of the application, the application is inadmissible, at least where the authority is retrospective: Cases 193 and 194/87 *Maurissen v Court of Auditors* [1989] ECR 1045 (para 33 and at 1062, Advocate General Darmon).
87 GI 34. Cf the *Gualco* case (above, note 85) at 62–63 (Advocate General Roemer).
88 See p 302.
89 The consequences of failing to provide an address for service in Luxembourg are the same as in the case of an application.

the application), the name of the person representing the defendant and, where necessary, the defendant's address and address for service in Luxembourg.[90] For example:

In the Court of Justice of the European Communities:

Case C-400/93

(*or, as the case may be*:

In the Court of First Instance of the European Communities:

Case T-400/93)

A B of [address], represented by C D, barrister, with an address for service in Luxembourg at the office of E F of [address in Luxembourg],

Applicant

against

Commission of the European Communities, 200 rue de la Loi, B-1049 Brussels, represented by G H, a member of its Legal Service acting as Agent, with an address for service in Luxembourg at the offices of I J, a member of its Legal Service, Jean Monnet Building, Kirchberg,

Defendant

Defence

3   Submissions

The submissions are often divided into two parts: those relating to the admissibility of the application or the action and those going to the merits of the claim. There appear to be no technical rules concerning admissions so that a failure to deny expressly or by implication an assertion of fact or of law in the application is not inevitably treated as an admission of the assertion.[91] On the other hand, a failure to contest an assertion made in the application may be taken to indicate that, although the assertion is not formally admitted by the defendant, no issue arises in the proceedings in respect of it; and the defendant may then be precluded from subsequently seeking to contest the assertion (should it wish to do so).[92] Since the main written pleadings in a direct action are the application and defence, the reply and rejoinder being optional supplementary pleadings, it is incumbent on the defendant to plead specifically in the defence to those allegations in the application that it wishes to contest. If the defendant fails to reply to a particular point made in the application, the applicant (and the Court) may reasonably conclude that the defendant is not raising a defence to that point. Further, in relation to that point, the applicant has nothing to reply to; and, in principle, the written procedure must therefore

---

90 It is not necessary to set out the subject matter of the action. There is no obligation on the defendant to use the same style as the applicant when setting out the title.

91 Cf Case 166/82 *Commission v Italy* [1984] ECR 459 (para 21); Case 141/84R *De Compte v European Parliament* [1984] ECR 2575 (paras 10–12). In the *De Compte* case the problem arose in the context of interim relief proceedings and before the defendant had lodged its defence. It may well be that, at such an early stage in an action, a defendant may have a legitimate reason for not wishing to commit itself in relation to the facts of the case. No such justification can be relied on by the time the defendant must lodge its defence.

92 Cf Case 21/84 *Commission v France* [1985] ECR 1355 (para 10).

be taken to be closed pro tanto in regard to that aspect of the case.[93] Technicalities apart, it is obviously better practice to deal clearly with each and every allegation in the application. If not, there is risk of confusion and the possibility that adverse inferences may be drawn from the state of the pleadings.

The defence should not canvass matters which do not fall within the scope of the proceedings; to the extent that it does so, it may be inadmissible.[94] As in the application, each assertion of fact should be supported by a reference either to a document which has been produced to the Court in the application or is annexed to the defence, or to the other types of evidence relied on. The obligation (applicable to all pleadings) to annex to the defence a file of all the documents relied on does not oblige the defendant to annex documents in the possession of third parties (at least where those third parties fall outside the control of the defendant).[95]

4 Form of order

In most cases the form of order in the defence requests the Court to dismiss the application and award costs in favour of the defendant[96] but it is occasionally necessary to plead in more detail.[97] If the defence contains no form of order at all, it seems to be open to the applicant to apply for judgment by default on the ground that no defence in proper form has been lodged within time.[98] If the applicant should fail to apply for judgment by default, proceedings continue in the normal way and the absence of the form of order is relevant only to any claim for costs that the defendant may later make.[99] It is arguable that, where the submissions made in the defence make it clear that the defendant does not concede the applicant's claims, the absence of a form of order in the defence is just a formal defect (because neither the applicant nor the Court can have been misled about the defendant's position) and the defendant cannot be precluded from rectifying the situation by including a proper form of order in the rejoinder.[1] The same possibilities of amending, supplementing or extending the defence are available as in the case of the application, mutatis mutandis.

There is no express provision enabling a defendant to raise in the defence a separate claim against the applicant: the scope of the defence is limited to answering the claim made by the applicant and so any claims which the

---

93 If a rigorous attitude were not taken with regard to the duty of the defendant to answer in the defence all the assertions made in the application that the defendant wished to contest, there would be a risk that the defendant would seek to steal a march on the applicant by reserving its main points of argument for the rejoinder, thus depriving the applicant of a fair opportunity to answer the defendant's case in writing.
94 Cf Case 48/69 *ICI Ltd v Commission* [1972] ECR 619 (order of 11 December 1969, unreported). The defendant lodged a defence containing several references to documents concerning other proceedings. The Court took the view that this was capable of embarrassing the applicant when answering the case made out by the defendant and held that the defence should be purged of the references to matters falling outside the scope of the proceedings. It therefore sent the defence back to the defendant and set a new date for the lodgment of an acceptable pleading.
95 Case 201/86 *Spie-Batignolles v Commission* [1990] ECR I-197 (unreported order of 16 December 1987, para 16).
96 If the defendant fails to include a claim for costs and introduces it only in the rejoinder, it may be dismissed as inadmissible: the *CICCE* case (above, note 62) para 32.
97 Where, for example, part of the applicant's claim is conceded.
98 RP-ECJ 94(1); RP-CFI 122(1). See further, chapter 16, section V, pp 500 et seq.
99 Case C-290/89 *Commission v Belgium* [1991] ECR I-2851 at 2859–2860 (Advocate General Lenz, citing Case 28/69 *Commission v Italy* [1970] ECR 187 at 190).
 1 Cf Case 28/69 *Commission v Italy* (ibid). That does not mean that the defendant can claim costs if no such claim was made in the defence: cf Case 298/83 *CICCE v Commission* [1985] ECR 1105 (para 32).

defendant may wish to raise can normally be made only by commencing a separate action. There is no possibility, as there is, for example, in English civil procedure, of adding a counterclaim to the defence. The nature of the system of remedies in Community law is such that the possibility of cross-claims rarely arises and circuity of action is not the problem that it is in a national legal system. Nothing, however, prevents the defendant from raising a separate claim if it can be pleaded as a defence.[2] Hitherto this situation has arisen only in actions for damages.

In Case 250/78 *DEKA Getreideprodukte GmbH & Co KG v Council and Commission*[3] the Court upheld the applicant's claim for damages and ordered the parties to agree the amount due to be paid. The following year, while negotiations were still in progress between the applicant and the Council and Commission, the German government claimed from the applicant a sum, twice as great as the damages claimed, which was due to it by way of export refunds paid over by a mistake induced by the fraud of a director of the applicant. This debt was assigned to the Commission, which asserted that the applicant's damages claim was thereby extinguished. The Court accepted this. It is to be observed that both the claim for damages (for non-payment of production refunds) and that for the repayment of the export refunds arose from the operation of the Common Agricultural Policy; the debt owed by the applicant to the German government, like the claim for damages, concerned sums chargeable to the Community budget and did not constitute a wholly independent obligation. In substance, the two claims were closely connected in their subject matter despite the fact that, due to the administrative structure of the Common Agricultural Policy, two separate persons – the Community and a member state – were responsible in respect of each claim. The case is not, therefore, authority that a claim for damages can be extinguished by the assignment of an unconnected claim, eg one in respect of unpaid income tax. It is at this stage unclear how close the connection between the claims must be in order to allow one to be set off against the other. The Court is likely to proceed case by case on the basis of comparative studies of national law. Nonetheless, it is reasonable to assume that one claim may extinguish another in whole or in part if, having regard to the nature and basis in law of the two claims, it would be inequitable to uphold the one without taking into account the other. The *DEKA* case suggests that set-off is not restricted to claims which are true defences[4] and may apply whenever it is the only practicable method of vindicating the defendant's rights.[5]

5   Attachments

The defence must be accompanied by:

(1)   A certificate showing that the lawyer acting for the defendant is entitled to practise before a court of a member state.[6]

(2)   In actions for annulment or against a failure to act, the measure whose

---

2   In Cases 4–13/59 *Mannesmann v High Authority* [1960] ECR 113 the applicants claimed to set-off their claims for damages against the obligation, imposed on them by the High Authority in a number of decisions contested in the action, to repay equalisation payments made out of the Scrap Equalisation Fund. The Court did not find it necessary to consider these claims. It is doubtful if an applicant can properly claim a set-off in an action for annulment.

3   [1983] ECR 421, see also [1979] ECR 3017.

4   Ie those based on a vice in the applicant's own claim.

5   Cf para 14 of the judgment.

6   Cf RP-ECJ 38(3); RP-CFI 44(3).

annulment is sought or documentary evidence of the date on which the defendant was requested to act.[7]

(3)   Where the defendant is a legal person governed by private law, the instrument or instruments constituting or regulating it (or a recent extract from the register of companies, firms or associations or any other proof of the defendant's existence in law) and proof that the authority granted to the defendant's lawyer has been properly conferred on him by someone authorised for the purpose.[8]

(4)   In a staff case brought before the CFI, the complaint made under art 90(2) of the Staff Regulations and the decision rejecting the complaint, together with a statement of the dates on which the complaint was submitted and on which the decision was notified.[9]

(5)   The authority to act of the defendant's agent or lawyer.

(6)   A file of the documents relied on in support of the defence and a schedule listing those documents.[10]

Save where indicated otherwise below, the rules applicable to the attachments to the application commencing proceedings apply also in the case of the defence. Where (2) and (4) have already been complied with by the applicant, as should be the case, it does not appear to be necessary for the defendant to repeat the exercise. The Rules of Procedure do not provide that a defective defence may be put in order in the same way that, pursuant to RP-ECJ 38(7) and RP-CFI 44(6), an application may be. The reason for this may be that, as the time limit for lodging the defence can be extended by the President,[11] there is no need for a provision like RP-ECJ 38(7) and RP-CFI 44(6): if a defence is rejected on the ground of want of form, the defendant can be given an extension of time in which to cure the defect (if it is curable) and there is no risk that rights will in the meantime be barred by the expiry of a substantive time limit, as may happen in the case of a defective application.[12]

C Reply and rejoinder

The application and the defence are the principal pleadings in a direct action. They may be supplemented, if need be, by a reply from the applicant and a rejoinder from the defendant.[13] The written procedure closes if the applicant waives the right to lodge a reply or fails to lodge the reply within the period fixed for doing; the same happens where the defendant waives the right to lodge a rejoinder in response to the reply or fails to lodge the rejoinder within the time for doing so. In such circumstances, if the applicant or, as the case may be, the defendant wishes to lodge a reply (or rejoinder) out of time,

---

7 Cf RP-ECJ 38(4); RP-CFI 44(4).
8 Cf RP-ECJ 38(5); RP-CFI 44(5).
9 RP-CFI 46(2).
10 See p 302.
11 RP-ECJ 40(2); RP-CFI 46(3).
12 On the other hand, the period for lodging the defence cannot be extended if no application for an extension of time has been made within the period; and an extension cannot be obtained on the basis of the ECSC Statute, art 39, the EC Statute, art 42, or the Euratom Statute, art 43 (in the absence of proof of unforeseeable circumstances or force majeure): Case T-42/89 *Yorck von Wartenburg v European Parliament* [1990] ECR II-31 (para 4). It is therefore arguable that, if a defective defence is lodged within time, an extension of time designed to allow the defect to be cured cannot be granted once the original period for lodging the defence has expired. The better view seems to be that a purely formal defect in the defence does not invalidate the lodgment of the defence within the period for doing so and therefore does not prevent such a defect from being remedied subsequently.
13 RP-ECJ 41(1); RP-CFI 47(1).

application must be made under RP-ECJ 91 or RP-CFI 114 for the written procedure to be reopened[14] unless the purpose of the pleading is to raise a new plea in law under RP-ECJ 42(2) or RP-CFI 48(2).[15] The reply or, as the case may be, rejoinder is almost invariably drafted in order to answer the points made in the pleading immediately preceding it (that is, the defence or reply and any statement in intervention of an intervener)[16] – although that does not prevent a party from adducing new arguments in respect of the issues as they are defined in the application and defence[17] – and without the benefit of any evidence other than that previously disclosed in the proceedings or in the possession of the party in question (that is, the applicant, in the case of the reply, or the defendant, in the case of the rejoinder). However, a party is not precluded from applying to the Court for the production of documents or some measure of enquiry to be carried out in order to prepare the reply or, as the case may be, the rejoinder. The possibility of making such an application was not excluded in Case 171/86 *USINOR v Commission*[18] but the Court indicated that convincing arguments would have to be adduced in support of it.

Apart from the general rules applicable to all pleadings, no requirements are laid down concerning the form and content of the reply and rejoinder. In practice, they usually follow the format of the application and defence. The title, of course, remains the same unless proceedings have been discontinued so far as one of the parties is concerned or a third party has been joined as an intervener.[19] Since the function of the reply and rejoinder is to complete and clarify, in the light of the opposing parties' pleadings, what has been said in the application or defence, it is not, in principle, possible to amend the forms of order in the application or defence and no new issues can be raised, although those already canvassed can be expanded by the addition of new arguments. Further evidence may be adduced, in the form of documents, or indicated in the reply or rejoinder but reasons should be given for the delay in production.[20] The evidence may relate either to a fact already in issue between the parties or to one that has come to light in the course of the written procedure and which gives rise to a new issue admissible pursuant to RP-ECJ 42(2) or, as the case may be, RP-CFI 48(2). Evidence which was not produced or referred to in the application or defence through an oversight may be indicated in the reply or rejoinder.[21] It is not necessary to repeat in the reply or rejoinder points made in

---

14 See Case T-5/90 *Marcato v Commission* [1991] ECR II-731 (order of 24 January 1991), where the applicant failed to lodge a reply in time, apparently because the applicant's lawyer had asked a colleague to prepare the reply and it had not been lodged in time due to illness and secretarial errors. The written procedure was reopened because the opposing party accepted, and the Court agreed, that, due to the complexity of the case, it was in the interests of justice that there be a complete written procedure.

15 In Cases C-116/88 and C-149/88 *Hecq v Commission* [1990] ECR I-599 (at 602) the defendant failed to lodge a rejoinder in time. Its application for an extension of time to do so was rejected by the President on the ground that the circumstances did not fall within RP-ECJ 42, thus indicating that, as the written procedure had closed, the application could be upheld only if its purpose was to raise a new plea in law.

16 See Case C-70/88 *European Parliament v Council* [1991] ECR I-4529 at 4544 (Advocate General van Gerven).   17 Ibid.

18 Unreported order of 28 January 1987 (para 24). The application was made in connection with the preparation of the reply. The Court remarked that knowledge of the content of the contested act should normally be sufficient.

19 The applicant cannot add a new defendant in the reply: Case 90/77 *Hellmut Stimming KG v Commission* [1977] ECR 2113; Case 62/83 *Eximo v Commission* [1984] ECR 2295 at 2318 (Advocate General Lenz). Where a third party has been joined as an intervener, the words 'supported by', followed by his name, address, the name of his representative and the address for service, are added after that of the party in whose support he has intervened.

20 RP-ECJ 42(1); RP-CFI 48(1).

21 Case 19/77 *Miller International Schallplatten GmbH v Commission* [1978] ECR 131 at 162 (Advocate General Warner): papers forgotten in an old file.

an earlier pleading. Thus, where the defendant denies an assertion of fact made in the application, it is not necessary to set out in the reply a denial of that denial. On the other hand, it is necessary for a party to take up a position in the reply or, as the case may be, the rejoinder in respect of every point made in the opposing party's earlier pleading (that is, the defence or reply) that is not covered by an assertion made in the application or, as the case may be, the defence.[22] A general denial of all the opposing party's assertions will normally make it clear that a party does not accept those points made by the opposing party that he does not choose to answer specifically. In that context, it should be noted that, where the applicant waives the right to lodge a reply, or the defendant waives the right to lodge a rejoinder, neither answers (in writing) the assertions made by the opposing party in the defence or, as the case may be, the reply. However, it has never been considered that, in giving up the right to answer in writing, the party concerned must be taken to have conceded the assertions made by the opposing party in the last pleading lodged by him. On the contrary, the assumption is that the party waiving the right to submit a further pleading takes issue with the assertions made in the latest pleading to be lodged. In effect, therefore, there is an implied joinder of issue on the pleadings as they stand when the written procedure ends.

RP-ECJ 42(2) and RP-CFI 48(2) provide: 'No new plea in law may be introduced in the course of proceedings unless it is based on matters of law or of fact which come to light in the course of the procedure.' Before 1991 the Rules of Procedure provided that no new plea in law (then described as a 'fresh issue') could be raised unless it was based on matters of law or of fact coming to light in the course of the *written* procedure. As Advocate General Mischo pointed out in Cases 46/87 and 227/88 *Hoechst AG v Commission*,[23] that produced a lacuna in the Court's procedure: a fresh issue could not be raised in respect of matters of fact or of law coming to light between the close of the written procedure and the date of judgment.[24] In consequence, he suggested that RP-ECJ 42(2) should also apply to fresh issues based on facts coming to light after the end of the written procedure; and that suggestion was incorporated into the Rules of Procedure when they were amended in 1991. The previous case law still provides reliable guidance regarding what constitutes a new plea in law (or 'fresh issue') based on matters of law or of fact which have come to light in the course of the procedure, always bearing in mind that the right to introduce a new plea in law is now more extensive.

RP-ECJ 42(2) and RP-CFI 48(2) indicate that, in principle, the scope of an action is restricted to the issues between the parties as they are defined in the application and the defence; it is by way of exception to that principle that one or other of the parties may introduce a new plea in law based on matters of law or of fact coming to light in the course of the procedure. That exception apart, neither the applicant nor the defendant can broaden the areas of dispute,

---

22 Eg Case C-375/90 *Commission v Greece* [1993] ECR I-2055 (paras 29 and 34–35), where the applicant failed to contest assertions made by the defendant, leading the Court to conclude that the applicant failed on the issues in question. Some assertions made by the opposing party do not need a specific reply: for example, as pointed out in Case 166/82 *Commission v Italy* [1984] ECR 459 (paras 19–22), the mere fact that the applicant has failed to reply to suggestions made by the defendant that the applicant has narrowed the scope of the action does not establish that the scope of the action has in fact been narrowed; for that to be so, there would have to be some express concession by the applicant.
23 [1989] ECR 2859 at 2908–2909.
24 In fact, there was some authority that such an issue could be raised: see p 332. It was perhaps more accurate to state that the then wording of RP-ECJ 42(2) suggested the existence of a lacuna that was in the process of being filled by a practice adopted from time to time by the Court. The amendment of RP-ECJ 42(2) removed any risk that the Court's practice might be regarded as being at variance with its Rules of Procedure.

whether of fact or of law, in a pleading subsequent to the application or, as the case may be, the defence or at the hearing. Any attempt to do so is inadmissible.[25] That general prohibition on the extension of the scope of proceedings applies just as much where the proceedings are the subject of an appeal to the ECJ[26] and where, at the close of the appeal proceedings, the ECJ remits the case to the CFI for judgment[27] but it does not, of course, prevent a party from elaborating the submissions made in connection with an existing issue.[28] Further, the Rules of

25 See, for example, Case 9/55 *Société des Charbonnages des Beeringen v High Authority* [1954–56] ECR 311 at 326; Case 18/57 *Nold v High Authority* [1959] ECR 41 at 51; Cases 27–29/58 *Compagnie des Hauts Fourneaux de Givors v High Authority* [1960] ECR 241 at 256; Cases 19 and 21/60, 2 and 3/61 *Société Fives Lille Cail v High Authority* [1961] ECR 281 at 295; Cases 17 and 20/61 *Kloeckner and Hoesch v High Authority* [1962] ECR 325 at 347; Cases 56 and 58/64 *Consten SA and Grundig Verkaufs GmbH v Commission* [1966] ECR 299 at 335–356 (Advocate General Roemer); Case 16/67 *Labeyrie v Commission* [1968] ECR 293 at 311 (Advocate General Roemer); Cases 54–60/76 *Compagnie Industrielle et Agricole du Comté de Loheac v Council and Commission* [1977] ECR 645 (paras 2–4); Case 68/77 *IFG v Commission* [1978] ECR 353 at 378 (Advocate General Capoporti); Case 12/79 *Hans-Otto Wagner GmbH Agrarhandel KG v Commission* [1979] ECR 3657 (para 8 and at 3678 per Advocate General Warner); Case 43/79 *Mencarelli v Commission* [1980] ECR 201 at 216 (Advocate General Mayras); Case 11/81 *Firma Anton Dürbeck v Commission* [1982] ECR 1251; Case 119/81 *Kloeckner v Commission* [1982] ECR 2627 at 2678–2679 (Advocate General VerLoren van Themaat); Case 110/81 *Roquette Frères SA v Council* [1982] ECR 3159 (para 31); Case 59/83 *Biovilac v Commission* [1984] ECR 4057 (para 24); Case 150/84 *Bernardi v European Parliament* [1986] ECR 1375 (para 22); Case 25/86 *Suss v Commission* [1986] ECR 3929 (para 9); Cases 279, 280, 285 and 286/84 *Walter Rau Lebensmittelwerke v Commission* [1987] ECR 1069 (paras 38–39 and at 1096 per Advocate General Lenz); Case 95/86 *Ferriere San Carlo SpA v Commission* [1987] ECR 1413 (para 5); Case 7/86 *Vincent v European Parliament* [1987] ECR 2473 at 2486 (Advocate General Cruz Vilaça); Case 262/83 *Commission v Italy* [1987] ECR 3073 (para 24 and at 3084–3085 per Advocate General Cruz Vilaça); Case 208/85 *Commission v Germany* [1987] ECR 4045 (para 9); Case 298/86 *Commission v Belgium* [1988] ECR 4343 (para 8 and at 4355 per Advocate General Cruz Vilaça); Cases 260/85 and 106/86 *Tokyo Electric Co Ltd v Council* [1988] ECR 5855 at 5909 (Advocate General Slynn); Case 305/87 *Commission v Greece* [1989] ECR 1461 at 1469 (Advocate General Jacobs; the Court refused to consider the point on the ground that it was not supported by any new evidence: see para 11); Case C-121/86 *Anonimos Etaireia Epicheiriseon Metalleftikon Viomichanikon kai Naftiliakon AE v Council* [1989] ECR 3919 at 3937 (Advocate General Tesauro); Case T-33/90 *Von Bonkewitz-Lindner v European Parliament* [1991] ECR II-1251 (para 55); Case C-230/89 *Commission v Greece* [1991] ECR I-1909 (para 14); Case T-45/90 *Speybrouck v European Parliament* [1992] ECR II-33 (para 88); Case T-16/90 *Panagiotopoulou v European Parliament* [1992] ECR II-89 (paras 69–74); Cases T-68, T-77 and T-78/89 *Società Italiano Vetro SA v Commission* [1992] ECR II-1403 (para 82); Case C-282/90 *Industrie-en Handelsonderneming Vreugdenkil BV v Commission* [1992] ECR I-1937 (para 10 and at 1949 per Advocate General Darmon); Case C-385/89 *Greece v Commission* [1992] ECR I-3225 (para 21); Case C-97/91 *Oleificio Borelli SpA v Commission* [1992] ECR I-6313 (para 18); Case T-84/92 *Nielsen and Möller v Economic and Social Committee*, 28 September 1993, para 38 (the CFI refused to consider the offer of proof made in connexion with the new plea because it did not establish why the new plea could not have been made earlier – para 39); Case C-55/91 *Italy v Commission*, 6 October 1993, para 40.

26 See RP-ECJ 113(1) (second indent), 113(2), 116(1) (second indent), 116(2) and 118 (which applies RP-ECJ 42(2) to appeal proceedings).

27 RP-CFI 120 (which applies RP-CFI 48(2)); Case T-43/89RV *Gill v Commission*, 23 March 1993 (para 47).

28 Eg Case 2/54 *Italy v High Authority* [1954–56] ECR 37 at 51; Case 2/57 *Compagnie des Hauts Fourneaux de Chasse v High Authority* [1957–58] ECR 199 at 206; Case 19/58 *Germany v High Authority* [1960] ECR 225 at 239; Cases 9 and 12/60 *Société Commerciale Antoine Vloeberghs SA v High Authority* [1961] ECR 197 at 215; Cases 29, 31, 36, 39–47, 50 and 51/63 *Fonderies et Usines de la Providence v High Authority* [1965] ECR 911 at 935; Cases 209–215 and 218/78 *Heintz van Landewyck Sarl v Commission* [1980] ECR 3125 at 3302 (Advocate General Reischl); Case 306/81 *Verros v European Parliament* [1983] ECR 1755 (para 9); the *Walter Rau* case (above, note 25) at 1095 (Advocate General Lenz); Case 257/86 *Commission v Italy* [1988] ECR 3249 (para 15 and at 3259–3260 per Advocate General Darmon); Case C-163/88 *Kontogeorgis v Commission* [1989] ECR 4189 at 4197 (Advocate General Jacobs); Case T-37/89 *Hanning v European Parliament* [1990] ECR II-463 (para 38); Case T-16/91 *Rendo NV v Commission* [1992] ECR II-2417 (para 96); Case C-338/92 *Compagnie d'Entreprise CFE v European Parliament*, 20 October 1993, paras 7–9; Case T-59/92 *Caronna v Commission*, 26 October 1993, para 34.

Procedure do not prevent the Court from taking a point of its own motion.[29] On occasion, the Court has preferred to consider the merits of a new plea rather than dismiss it as inadmissible; but those seem to be cases where the plea could be rejected with little difficulty and with less trouble than by applying RP-ECJ 42(2) or RP-CFI 48(2).[30] The inability to raise a new plea in law (other than as permitted by RP-ECJ 42(2) and RP-CFI 48(2)) applies just as much to interveners as it does to the applicant and defendant.[31] That does not mean that, if the applicant or defendant is precluded from raising a plea in law which has been omitted from the application or defence, an intervener is similarly barred from raising the issue in its statement in intervention; it simply means that an intervener is barred from raising a new plea *after* lodging the statement in intervention (unless RP-ECJ 42(2) or, as the case may be, RP-CFI 48(2) may be relied on).[32]

A matter of law, such as the (alleged) unlawfulness of a regulation, cannot be relied on to justify adding a new plea in law if it was capable of being known and pleaded at an earlier stage[33] unless, so far as the applicant is concerned, it arises from a proposition of law adopted in the defence;[34] for a new fact to be able to justify raising a new plea in law, it must not have existed or must not have been known to the applicant when the action was commenced or to the defendant when the defence was lodged[35] or, if known beforehand, its relevance to the case must not have been known.[36] In Case C-279/89 *Commission v United Kingdom*,[37] Advocate General Gulmann doubted whether a judgment delivered after the commencement of proceedings could justify raising a new plea (the reason being, in essence, that the principle of law decided in the judgment is ordinarily capable of being raised at the proper time, the judgment merely strengthening the force of the argument). When a new plea in law is raised during the procedure, the President may, acting on a report of the judge-rapporteur and after hearing the advocate general (where there is one), allow the other party time to answer it even after the expiry of the normal procedural time limits.[38] This is without prejudice to the admissibility of the plea, which is decided in the final judgment.[39] Where a new plea in law is

29 Eg Case 131/83 *Vaupel v European Court of Justice*, unreported (para 5); Cases C-133 and C-150/87 *Nashua Corpn v Commission and Council* [1990] ECR I-719 at 743 (Advocate General Mischo), where the defendant had originally accepted that the application was admissible but reversed its position at the hearing.

30 Eg Case 401/85 *Schina v Commission* [1987] ECR 3911 (para 15).

31 Case 233/85 *Bonino v Commission* [1987] ECR 739 at 753–754 (Advocate General Darmon).

32 Cf Case 253/84 *Groupement Agricole d'Exploitation en Commun (GAEC) de la Ségaude v Council and Commission* [1987] ECR 123 at 153–154 (Advocate General Slynn).

33 *Roquette v Council* (above, note 25) para 31; see for example, Case 114/76 *Bela-Mühle Josef Bergmann KG v Grows Farm GmbH & Co KG* [1977] ECR 1211 at 1243 (Advocate General Capotorti); Case C-135/92 *Fiskano AB v Commission* (unreported, per Advocate General Darmon, paras 49–56).

34 Cases 12 and 29/64 *Ley v Commission* [1965] ECR 107 at 119; Cases 63–69/72 *Wilhelm Werhahn Hansamuhle v Council* [1973] ECR 1229 at 1273–1274 (Advocate General Roemer).

35 *Firma Anton Dürbeck v Commission* (above, note 25) para 17; *Miller International Schallplatten GmbH v Commission* (above, note 21); Case 145/83 *Adams v Commission* [1985] ECR 3539 at 3552 (Advocate General Mancini), where the relevant fact on which the defendant's liability was based was not discovered until a preparatory enquiry held in the course of the proceedings; Case 5/85 *AKZO Chemie BV and Akzo Chemie UK Ltd v Commission* [1986] ECR 2585 (paras 14–17), points based on facts known to the party before the action was brought; Case 246/84 *Kotsonis v Council* [1986] ECR 3989 (para 18), a point based on documents not produced until after the close of the written procedure; Case T-22/92 *Weissenfels v European Parliament*, 26 October 1993, paras 33–35.

36 Case T-12/89 *Solvay & Cie SA v Commission* [1992] ECR II-907 (para 47).

37 [1992] ECR I-5785 at 5809–5810 (Re Fishing Licences).

38 RP-ECJ 42(2); RP-CFI 48(2). Eg Case 131/87 *Commission v Council* [1989] ECR 3743 at 3746 (Re Trade in Animal Glands).

39 Ibid. Thus, the application made in Case 129/85 *British Columbia Forest Products Ltd v Commission*, order of 27 September 1988, [1989] 4 CMLR 22, for the striking out of certain passages in the rejoinder seems to have been misconceived as well as unfounded.

raised during the written procedure, it is normally incorporated in the plead-ing (reply or rejoinder) and it is only where it appears in the rejoinder that it may be necessary for the President to allow the other party (the applicant) time to answer it in writing.

The object of the restriction on the raising of new pleas in law is twofold:[40] to pre-vent a time limit from being evaded[41] and to safeguard the opposing party's right to be heard.[42] In a number of cases, therefore, when a new plea in law has been rejected as inadmissible, the Court or Advocate General has noted that the opposing party had not had an adequate opportunity to answer it.[43] It has in consequence been suggested that RP-ECJ 42(2) (and therefore RP-CFI 48(2)) should not be rigidly applied where no time limit is involved[44] or where the other party has had an adequate opportunity to reply to the point.[45] Advocate General Reischl has ex-pressed the opinion that RP-ECJ 42(2) (and therefore RP-CFI 48(2)) is not applied if it is felt to be expedient not to apply it,[46] but there is no clear authority for this unless it is taken to be an allusion to the suggestions just mentioned.

RP-ECJ 42(2) and RP-CFI 48(2) do not in terms apply to an amendment of the form of order in the application or defence or to a change in the subject matter of the action; and the addition of a new claim cannot, in consequence, be based on them.[47] While a concession may be made[48] or the form of order clarified[49] in the reply or rejoinder, a substantial change in the nature of the

---

40 Case 219/78 *Michaelis v Commission* [1979] ECR 3349 at 3361–3362 (Advocate General Capotorti).
41 *Société Fives Lille Cail v High Authority* (above, note 25) at 295; Case 36/72 *Meganck v Commission* [1973] ECR 527 at 539 (Advocate General Mayras); *Wilhelm Werhahn Hansamuhle v Council* (above, note 34) at 1273–1274 (Advocate General Roemer); Case 19/85 *Grégoire-Foulon v European Parliament* [1985] ECR 3771 (para 8); *Walter Rau Lebensmittelwerke v Commission* (above, note 25) at 1096 (Advocate General Lenz); Case 374/87 *Orkem v Commission* [1989] ECR 3283 at 3335 (Advocate General Darmon). This usually applies to issues raised in the reply.
42 See Case 46/75 *IBC v Commission* [1976] ECR 65 at 89 (Advocate General Warner); Case 112/78 *Kobor v Commission* [1979] ECR 1573 at 1581 (Advocate General Capotorti); Case 30/78 *Distillers Co Ltd v Commission* [1980] ECR 2229 at 2291–2292 (Advocate General Warner); Case 24/79 *Oberthür v Commission* [1980] ECR 1743 at 1764–1765 (Advocate General Mayras); Cases 118–123/82 *Celant v Commission* [1983] ECR 2995 (para 20).
43 Eg Cases 244 and 245/85 *Cerealmangimi SpA and Italgrani SpA v Commission* [1987] ECR 1303 (para 23 and at 1320 per Advocate General Mischo); Case 323/87 *Commission v Italy* [1989] ECR 2275 at 2296 (Advocate General Jacobs); Case C-282/90 *Industrie-en Handelsonderneming Vreugdenkil BV v Commission* [1992] ECR I-1937 at 1949 (Advocate General Darmon).
44 *Fonderies et Usines de la Providence v High Authority*, (above, note 28) at 951 (Advocate General Roemer); *Wilhelm Werhahn v Council*, (above, note 34) at 1273–1274 (Advocate General Roemer).
45 *Kobor v Commission* (above, note 42) (Advocate General Capotorti); *Distillers Co Ltd v Commis-sion* (above, note 42) (Advocate General Warner); *Oberthür v Commission* (above, note 42) (Advocate General Mayras); Case C-279/89 *Commission v United Kingdom* [1992] ECR I-5785 at 5809–5810 (Re Fishing Licences) (Advocate General Gulmann). Cf Case 78/83 *USINOR v Commission* [1984] ECR 4177 at 4207 (Advocate General Slynn).
46 Cases 56–60/74 *Kurt Kampffmeyer Mühlenvereinigung KG v Commission and Council* [1976] ECR 711 at 754; see also the *Dürbeck* case (above, note 25) at 1275.
47 Case 267/85 *Luttgens v Commission* [1986] ECR 3417 (para 6 and at 3429 per Advocate General Cruz Vilaça); Case T-41/89 *Schwedler v European Parliament* [1990] ECR II-79 (para 34); Case T-20/92 *Moat v Commission*, 13 July 1993 (para 45). There have been cases where the Court has dismissed a new claim as unfounded rather than as inadmissible, possibly because it was less troublesome to deal with the claim on that basis: eg Case 7/86 *Vincent v European Parliament* [1987] ECR 2473 (contrast paras 24–27 with 2486 per Advocate General Cruz Vilaça: one explanation of the case is that, as the Court had unlimited jurisdiction, the new claims were not inadmissible).
48 Cases 18 and 19/64 *Alvino and Benoit v Commission* [1965] ECR 789.
49 Case 28/64 *Müller v Council and Euratom Council* [1965] ECR 237 at 249; Cases 18 and 35/65 *Gutmann v Euratom Commission* [1966] ECR 103 at 125 (Advocate General Roemer); Case 2/68 *Ufficio Imposte di Consumo di Ispra v Commission* [1968] ECR 435 at 449 (Advocate General Roemer); Case 74/74 *CNTA v Commission* [1975] ECR 533 para 5; Case 17/78 *Deshormes v Commission* [1979] ECR 189 at 212 (Advocate General Reischl); see also Cases 19 and 65/63 *Prakash v Euratom Commission* [1965] ECR 533 at 576 but compare *Bernardi v European Parliament* (above, note 25) paras 2–4.

action or the relief sought (even in the alternative) is inadmissible.[50] There is in consequence a tendency to take a variation in a party's claims into account only as argument on the interpretation to be given to the relief originally sought.[51] The only exception to this appears to be where a new factor intervenes during the course of the proceedings and it would not be in the interests of the administration of justice and due process or it would be inequitable in all the circumstances to disallow an amendment and require proceedings to be started again. This occurred in *Alpha Steel v Commission*[52] where the applicant sought the annulment of a decision which was replaced by another decision after the commencement of proceedings. The defendant claimed that the applicant should therefore have commenced a new action against the latter. The Court rejected this and allowed an amendment of the form of order, extending it to cover the second decision.[53] As a result, it does not seem that the reply or rejoinder need contain a form of order unless it is intended to concede or clarify a claim or rely on a new factor justifying a substantial change in the relief sought.

D Subsequent pleadings

In theory there are no further written pleadings after the rejoinder. Where the applicant waives his right to lodge a reply or the defendant waives his right to lodge a rejoinder, the pleadings end with the defence and the reply, respectively.[54] A subsequent pleading which purports to 'complete' the written procedure is in principle inadmissible[55] unless lodged in connection with a new plea in law admissible pursuant to RP-ECJ 42(2) or RP-CFI 48(2) or in response to a request made by the Court. Thus, where a new plea in law based on a matter of law or of fact coming to light in the course of the written procedure is introduced in the rejoinder, the other parties may be given by the President, either on application or of his own motion, time to submit a further pleading dealing with the admissibility and substance of the new plea.

There is considerable authority against the admission of new pleas after the

---

50 Case 17/57 *Gezamenlijke Steenkolenmijnen in Limberg v High Authority* [1959] ECR 1 at 8; Case 83/63 *Krawczynski v Euratom Commission* [1965] ECR 623 at 633 and 640; Case 17/68 *Reinarz v Commission* [1969] ECR 61 para 47; Case 232/78 *Commission v France* [1979] ECR 2729 para 3; Case 125/78 *GEMA v Commission* [1979] ECR 3173 para 26 and 3201–3202 per Advocate General Capotorti); Case 124/81 *Commission v United Kingdom* [1983] ECR 203 (para 6); Case C-180/88 *Wirtschaftsvereinigung Eisen-und Stahlindustrie v Commission* [1990] ECR I-4413 at 4433–4434 (Advocate General Darmon); Case T-14/89 *Montedipe SpA v Commission* [1992] ECR II-1155 (para 38); Case T-48/90 *Giordani v Commission*, 1 July 1993, para 94 (claim for moral damage rejected because raised only at the hearing). See also Case 24/71 *Meinhardt (née Forderung) v Commission* [1972] ECR 269 at 280 (Advocate General Roemer), where the applicant amended the form of order in the reply and then reverted to the original claim for relief at the hearing. The Court did not rule on the admissibility of the amendments made by the parties to the forms of order in *Deka Getreideprodukte GmbH & Co KG v Council and Commission* (above, note 3).
51 Eg Case C-87/89 *Société Nationale Interprofessionnelle de la Tomate v Commission* [1990] ECR I-1981 at 1993 (Advocate General Lenz).
52 Case 14/81 [1982] ECR 749 at para 8.
53 The same approach was followed in Case 103/85 *Stahlwerke Peine-Salzgitter AG v Commission* [1988] ECR 4131 (paras 11–12), where the ECJ allowed an action in respect of a failure to act to be transformed into an action for annulment.
54 See RP-ECJ 44(1); RP-CFI 52(2).
55 Eg Case 10/55 *Mirossevich v High Authority* [1954–56] ECR 333 (order of 20 January 1956), unreported: the Court rejected a pleading lodged by the applicant after the lodgment of the rejoinder. In Case 62/83 *Eximo v Commission* [1984] ECR 2295 (see 2299) the applicant appears to have lodged a 'supplementary pleading'. Its admissibility was reserved to the final judgment but, since the applicant's case was dismissed, it was not necessary for the Court to rule on admissibility.

close of the written procedure and, in particular, at the hearing,[56] based on the grounds that (i) RP-ECJ 42(2) (before it was amended in 1991) envisaged the raising of such pleas during the written procedure only and must be taken implicitly to have excluded their raising during the oral procedure, and (ii) the opposing party does not have an adequate opportunity to answer a new plea (as opposed to an argument) raised for the first time after the close of the written procedure or at the hearing.[57] In fact, however, RP-ECJ 42(2) only excluded the raising of new pleas which were not based on matters of fact and law that had come to light during the written procedure; it did not expressly exclude the raising of a new plea which was based on such a matter but which could not have been raised beforehand, eg a new plea raised by the applicant and based on a matter which emerged for the first time after the lodgment of the reply. In that situation, even before the amendment of RP-ECJ 42(2) to allow a new plea to be raised in relation to a matter of fact or law coming to light at any time in the course of the procedure, it seems that the new plea was admissible at the hearing[58] or might be raised (by the applicant) in a supplementary pleading.[59] The current wording of RP-ECJ 42(2) and RP-CFI 48(2) makes the position plain by allowing the Court to admit a new plea whether it is based on a matter of fact or law that has come to light during or after the written procedure. Where a party wishes to raise a new plea after the close of the written procedure, application may be made in writing or orally at the hearing.[60] A written application must comply with the general rules applicable to pleadings. No other requirements are laid down in the Rules of Procedure. It would seem that the application would set out the matter of fact or law which has come to light, aver that it was not known and could not have been pleaded beforehand and state the new plea to be raised and the arguments relied on in support of it. The form of order in the application would comprise a prayer that the Court admit the issue.[61] At that stage in the proceedings, the Court is not concerned with the question whether or not the new plea is admissible in accordance with RP-ECJ 42(2) or RP-CFI 48(2); the only

---

56 The Court may also reject as inadmissible a clarification of the relief sought which is made at the hearing: Case 30/68 *Lacroix v Commission* [1970] ECR 301, para 26.

57 See Case 12/68 *X v Audit Board* [1969] ECR 109 at 121 (Advocate General Gand); *Meganck v Commission* (above, note 41) at 539 (Advocate General Mayras); Case 46/75 *IBC v Commission* [1976] ECR 65 at 89 (Advocate General Warner); *GEMA v EC Commission* (above, note 50) at 3201–3202 (Advocate General Capotorti); Cases 103–109/78 *Société des Usines de Beauport v Council* [1979] ECR 17 at 31 (Advocate General Warner); Case 730/79 *Philip Morris Holland BV v Commission* [1980] ECR 2671 at 2704 (Advocate General Capotorti); Case 323/87 *Commission v Italy* [1989] ECR 2275 at 2296 (Advocate General Jacobs).

58 Case 21/65 *Morina v European Parliament* [1965] ECR 1033 at 1040.

59 *Distillers Co Ltd v Commission* (above, note 42): the Court found it unnecessary to give a ruling on the admissibility of the pleading because it considered the matters raised to be irrelevant (see para 29) but Advocate General Warner did think it was admissible because the other parties had had an opportunity to answer the points raised (see 2292).

60 The basis in the Rules of Procedure is uncertain: in the *Distillers* case reliance appears to have been placed on RP-ECJ 42(2) but it only sets out a procedure for dealing with fresh issues raised in the course of the written procedure. The better view seems to be that the application may be made under RP-ECJ 91 or, as the case may be, RP-CFI 114. If the application is made orally at the hearing, there must be some very good reason why it was not made beforehand: the Court has been known to refuse to take at the hearing even points going to the admissibility of the action (which it is usually regarded as obliged to consider whether or not the point is raised by the parties) where they turn on matters of fact that have not been the subject of debate between the parties at an earlier stage in the proceedings.

61 It is unclear if the application need include a prayer for the costs of the application to be awarded to the applicant. Such a prayer would in principle be encompassed in the general prayer for costs normally included in the principal pleading of the party concerned (the application or defence).

relevant question is whether or not the other parties should be given an opportunity to answer the application in writing. If the nature and content of the application suggest that the other parties should be given that opportunity, the President will then fix a date by which they must submit an answer in writing. The answer must be limited to the points raised in the application and may contain a form of order requesting the rejection of the application as inadmissible or the dismissal of the new plea as unfounded.

In the course of the proceedings the Court may ask the parties to submit observations on a point, answer questions or supply evidence or information, etc. The pleadings containing the answers to such requests should comply with the basic rules governing all pleadings and should avoid unnecessary formalism. The titles should be sufficient to identify the case to which the pleading relates but it does not appear to be necessary to comply to the letter with the requirements that apply to the application commencing proceedings and the defence. The opposing party may reply to the answer given at the hearing; a written pleading in reply is in principle inadmissible and so can be lodged only at the invitation or with the consent of the Court. Where evidence has been produced pursuant to a request or order of the Court, the opposing party may be given an opportunity to submit evidence in rebuttal[62] but his only opportunity to submit observations on the evidence produced is at the hearing unless the Court decides to invite the parties to submit written observations.[63]

E Pleadings in ancillary proceedings

As a general rule, applications in ancillary proceedings (interim relief, intervention, third party proceedings and so forth) follow the same pattern as the application commencing the action. If a form of order is not included, the pleading may be inadmissible, at least where it is required expressly.[64] It is arguable that all applications must contain a form of order even in the absence of an express requirement in the Rules of Procedure because, otherwise, they are to be construed as articulating a wish on the part of the applicant, not a request for the Court to make an order. There is no clear authority for this but it seems the better course to ensure that there always is a form of order. The form of order should request in precise terms the relief which is sought. In applications for interim relief it may also include a claim for 'further or other relief' because the President may find that, while the application should not be dismissed, an order in the form set out in the application is not appropriate. When the Rules of Procedure specify that a party is to submit 'observations', the pleading is framed in the same way as an application or defence and is entitled 'observations'. It is debatable whether it is necessary to include a form of order but this is usually done, even if the relief sought is only an award of costs.

IV Pleadings in appeals

A Application commencing appeal

An appeal from the CFI is commenced by application whether it is made against a final judgment of the CFI, a judgment or order disposing of the

---

62 RP-ECJ 45(4); RP-CFI 66(2).
63 RP-ECJ 54; RP-CFI 64. Eg Case 318/86 *Commission v France* [1988] ECR 3559 at 3563, where the applicant submitted certain information to the Court with the leave of the Court and the defendant was allowed to make submissions on the information.
64 Case 110/63A *Willame v Euratom Commission* [1966] ECR 287 at 291; Case 55/64 *Lens v European Court of Justice* [1965] ECR 837 at 840.

substantive issues in part only of the case or disposing of a procedural issue concerning a plea of lack of competence or inadmissibility, an order dismissing an application to intervene or an order granting or refusing some form of interim relief.[65] In all cases, the rules relating to the form and content of the application are the same. Like any pleading, the application must comply with the general rules set out in RP-ECJ 37[66] and must be in the language of the case.[67] The Rules of Procedure refer to the application both as such and as 'the appeal'.[68] The appeal can therefore be taken to have the general form of an application (and thus comprises the title, submissions and form of order) while being entitled 'Appeal'.

1   Contents

The appeal must contain the following:

(1)   the name and address of the appellant;
(2)   the names of the other parties to the proceedings before the CFI;
(3)   the pleas in law and legal arguments relied on;
(4)   the form of order sought by the appellant;[69]
(5)   the appellant's address for service in Luxembourg;[70]
(6)   the date on which the decision appealed against was notified to the appellant.[71]

Since the appeal is limited to points of law, there is no express provision for the inclusion of an indication of any evidence relied on by the appellant: in principle, all the relevant facts have been found by, or are contained in the judgment or order of, the CFI; and, if that is not so, it may be a ground for setting aside the judgment or order appealed against, with or without a remission of the matter to the CFI, but is not in other respects relevant. A failure to set out the address for service in Luxembourg does not render the appeal inadmissible; it simply results in the use by the Court of the alternative form of service provided for in RP-ECJ 38(2).

2   Title

The title may satisfy the requirements set out in (1), (2), (5) and (6) above. It should identify both the nature of the pleading (as an appeal) and also the subject of the appeal because, where the appeal concerns a decision dismissing an application to intervene or granting or refusing interim relief, the appeal is heard by summary procedure.[72] In consequence it is desirable for the Registry officials to be able to see at a glance the type of appeal in question. As in the case of all other pleadings, there is no specific form for the title of a pleading but the following seems to be an appropriate form to follow in the case of appeals:

In the Court of Justice of the European Communities

AB of [address], represented by CD, barrister, with an address for service in Luxembourg at the office of EF of [address in Luxembourg],

---

65   RP-ECJ 111(1).
66   RP-ECJ 112(1), last sentence; for those general rules, see page pp 301 et seq.
67   RP-ECJ 110. A member state may use its own language but any other appellant must use the language of the case unless the Court authorises use of another language at the joint request of the parties to the appeal.
68   See, for example, RP-ECJ 112.
69   RP-ECJ 112(1).
70   RP-ECJ 38(2), applied by RP-ECJ 112(1), last sentence.
71   RP-ECJ 112(2).
72   ECSC and EC Statutes, art 50; Euratom Statute, art 51.

Appellant

against

(1)   Commission of the European Communities
(2)   GH,

Respondents

Appeal against a [judgment/order] of the Court of First Instance of the European Communities [state chamber, where applicable] of [date] in Case T-1001/93 *AB v EC Commission, supported by GH*, notified to the Appellant on [date].

An alternative approach, which reflects more closely the title used in some of the reported cases is:

In the Court of Justice of the European Communities

AB of [address], represented by CD, barrister, with an address for service in Luxembourg at the office of EF of [address in Luxembourg],

Appellant

Appeal against the [judgment/order] of the Court of First Instance of the European Communities [state chamber, where applicable] of [date] in Case T-1001/93 *AB v EC Commission, supported by GH*, notified to the Appellant on [date],

the other parties to the proceedings being:

(1)   Commission of the European Communities
(2)   GH

It will be observed that the title does not set out the case number of the appeal: the appeal does not inherit the case number used for the original action before the CFI but is given a new case number when it comes before the ECJ. All the parties (including interveners) must be mentioned, listed preferably in the order in which they appeared in the original proceedings, that is, applicant, followed by any interveners in its support, and then the defendant, followed by any interveners in its support. Thus, where the appellant is the defendant in the original proceedings, the applicant in the original proceedings will be the first respondent, followed by any interveners; and, if the appellant is an intervener, the first respondent will be the original applicant, followed by any interveners in its support, and then the defendant, followed by any interveners in its support. The Rules of Procedure do not require the appellant to set out the address, address for service and name of representative of the other parties, which will in any event be found in the papers of the case at first instance.[73] In the examples given above, no particular qualification has been given to the judgment or order appealed against (other than its date and the case in which it was delivered). If the appeal concerns an order dismissing an application to intervene or granting or refusing interim relief, it should be described in more detail: for example 'the order dismissing the Appellant's application to intervene' or 'the order refusing to grant the interim relief sought by the Appellant' or 'the order granting interim relief'.

---

73 It would no doubt be helpful to set out each party's address, address for service and name of representative but it could be misleading to do so since a party might have changed one or other or might decide to use a different address for service or representative for the purposes of the appeal.

3   Submissions

The submissions are limited to one or more of the following grounds of appeal: lack of competence of the CFI; a breach of procedure before the CFI which adversely affects the interests of the appellant; infringement of Community law by the CFI.[74] A ground of appeal which contests a finding of fact made at first instance is inadmissible;[75] but a ground of appeal which disputes the legal characterisation of a factual situation is not inadmissible.[76] Further, the appellant cannot rely on a ground or plea that he did not rely on, or failed to pursue, at first instance[77] or a ground that is based on evidence that was not before the CFI[78] save perhaps where the new ground or plea is one that can be taken by the Court of its own motion.[79] The ground of appeal relied on must be identified and, in principle, all the arguments relied on to develop the submission must be set out in the appeal because there may be no further exchange of written pleadings after the lodgment of the response(s) to the appeal. It would seem that the same approach followed in relation to applications generally is to be followed in relation to appeals: the pleading must be sufficiently clear to enable the Court to exercise its powers and to enable the other parties to the proceedings to understand the issues and respond to them. It must therefore indicate precisely those parts of the judgment of the CFI which are contested in the appeal and the legal arguments relied on in support of the objection taken to each of those parts.[80] An appeal is inadmissible if it merely repeats, refers to or reproduces word for word the pleas and arguments put to the CFI.[81] Therefore, even if it is necessary to place reliance in the appeal on substantially the same pleas and arguments as those used before the CFI, they must be reformulated as objections to the relevant parts of the judgment appealed against.

4   Form of order

The appeal must contain a form of order. In principle, the relief that can be sought is limited to: an order setting aside the decision appealed against in

---

74 ECSC and EC Statutes, art 51; Euratom Statute, art 52; Case C-132/90P *Schwedler v European Parliament* [1991] ECR I-5745 at 5757 (Advocate General Tesauro); Case C-346/90P *F v Commission* [1992] ECR I-2691 (paras 6–7). By way of illustration, the following are not grounds of appeal: that the CFI dealt with an objection to admissibility separately without joining it to the substance and that the appellant was required to have his application signed by a lawyer even though he himself was a lawyer (Case C-126/90P *Viciano v Commission* [1991] ECR I-781 (paras 4–8)); that the CFI failed to assess properly the pre-litigation correspondence for the purpose of calculating a time limit and that the CFI erred in finding that an assessment of a medical committee was medical in nature (Case C-346/90P *F v Commission* [1992] ECR I-2691 (paras 8–11 and 17–18)).

75 Case C-115/90P *Turner v Commission* [1991] ECR I-1423 (para 13); Case C-283/90P *Vidranyi v Commission* [1991] ECR I-4339 (paras 12–13); Case C-132/90P *Schwedler v European Parliament* (ibid) para 11; Case C-107/90P *Hochbaum v Commission* [1992] ECR I-157 (para 9); Case C-378/90P *Pitrone v Commission* [1992] ECR I-2375 (para 12); Case C-18/91P *V v European Parliament* [1992] ECR I-3997 (paras 15–17 and 42–44); Case C-35/92P *European Parliament v Frederiksen* [1993] ECR I-991 (opinion of Advocate General van Gerven, para 2); Case C-354/92P *Eppe v Commission*, 22 December 1993, paras 29 and 33.

76 Case C-145/90P *Costacurta v Commission* [1991] ECR I-5449 at 5459 (Advocate General van Gerven); *Schwedler v European Parliament* (ibid) at 5758 et seq (Advocate General Tesauro).

77 *V v European Parliament* (above, note 75) para 21; *Eppe* (above, note 75), para 13; Case C-36/92P *NV Samenwerkende Electriciteits-produktiebedrijven v Commission* (unreported, per Advocate General Jacobs, paras 66–67, where the point in question was considered to be an amplification of a point put to the CFI). Contra Case C-283/90P *Vidranyi v Commission* (above, note 75) at 4358 (Advocate General Lenz).

78 Case C-126/90P *Viciano v Commission* (above, note 74) para 10.

79 Per contra Case C-348/90P *European Parliament v Virgili-Schettini* [1991] ECR I-5211 at 5222 (Advocate General Lenz).

80 Case C-244/92P *Kupka-Floridi v Economic and Social Committee* [1993] ECR I-2041 (para 9).

81 Ibid (paras 10–11); *Eppe* (above, note 75), paras 7–8.

whole or in part; an order granting the relief sought before the CFI in whole or in part; and costs.[82] In the ordinary course, the form of order will comprise all three heads: a prerequisite of an order granting the relief sought at first instance is the making of an order setting aside the decision appealed against; and it would be unusual for an appellant to forgo the opportunity to claim costs. If it considers that an appeal is well founded, the ECJ has power to quash the decision appealed against and then either give final judgment itself or remit the matter to the CFI for judgment. The Rules of Procedure do not state so expressly, but it seems to be permissible to include, where appropriate, a claim that the ECJ remit the matter to the CFI after setting aside the decision appealed against. In most cases, no doubt, the appellant will prefer the ECJ to set that decision aside and then grant the relief sought by him; but it cannot be excluded that in a particular case it will be more appropriate for the matter to be remitted. In that event, there seems to be no objection to the appellant claiming that the decision appealed against be set aside and the matter remitted to the CFI.[83] The subject matter of the proceedings at first instance may not be changed in the appeal and, to the extent that the appeal goes beyond the scope of the form of order in the proceedings at first instance, it is inadmissible.[84] In consequence, where the appellant claims that the ECJ should itself decide the matter at issue (after setting aside the judgment appealed against), the appellant is limited to claiming before the ECJ the relief he claimed in his application, defence or, as the case may be, statement in intervention in the proceedings before the CFI (subject to any subsequent concession made by the appellant).

5 Attachments

The following must be attached to the appeal:

(1) the decision appealed against;[85]
(2) a certificate showing that the lawyer acting for the applicant is entitled to practise before a court of a member state.[86]

If either is not attached to the appeal, the Registrar is to prescribe a period within which the defect is to be rectified; and, if the appellant fails to rectify the defect within that period, the Court must decide (after hearing the advocate general) whether or not that failure renders the application formally inadmissible.[87]

B Response

Notice of the appeal is served on all the parties to the proceedings before the CFI (save, of course, the appellant)[88] and each is entitled to lodge a response in

---

82 RP-ECJ 113(1). An appeal cannot be made solely on the question of costs: ECSC and EC Statutes, art 51 (last sentence); Euratom Statute, art 52 (last sentence).
83 The fact that an order remitting the matter to the CFI is not one of the forms of relief listed in RP-ECJ 113(1) does not seem to preclude the inclusion of such a claim in the form of order: on one view, the possibility of making such an order is implicit in the first form of relief listed in RP-ECJ 113(1) (setting aside the decision appealed against) where the second (granting the relief sought at first instance) is not granted when the appeal is upheld.
84 RP-ECJ 113(2); Case C-283/90P *Vidranyi v Commission* (above, note 75) paras 9–10 and at 4359, per Advocate General Lenz.
85 RP-ECJ 112(2).
86 RP-ECJ 112(1), last sentence, which refers to RP-ECJ 38(3).
87 RP-ECJ 112(3), applying RP-ECJ 38(7).
88 RP-ECJ 114.

writing within two months of service of the notice.[89] It follows that the respondents may include parties who supported the appellant's case at first instance (such as intervener) as well as parties who opposed that case. In consequence, the response is not necessarily a hostile pleading.

1　Contents

The response must contain:

(1)　the name and address of the party lodging it;
(2)　the date on which notice of the appeal was served on him;
(3)　the pleas in law and legal arguments relied on;
(4)　the form of order sought by the respondent;[90]
(5)　the respondent's address for service in Luxembourg.[91]

The response may therefore be divided into three parts: title (which may comprise (1), (2) and (5) above); submissions; and form of order.

2　Title

The title may follow that used in the appeal, with the addition of the case number (supplied by the Court), the respondent's address, the date on which the notice of the appeal was served and the description of the pleading, as follows:

In the Court of Justice of the European Communities

Case C-2002/93P

AB of [address] represented by CD, barrister, with an address for service in Luxembourg at the office of EF of [address in Luxembourg],

Appellant

against

(1)　Commission of the European Communities
(2)　GH,

Respondents

Response of GH of [address], represented by IJ, barrister, with an address for service in Luxembourg at the office of KL of [address in Luxembourg], made in consequence of the notice of the appeal of AB served on [date].

3　Submissions

The submissions must be set out in full because a further exchange of written pleadings may not take place. Since the relief sought may include not only the dismissal of the appeal but also the setting aside of the decision appealed against or the relief sought by the respondent in the proceedings before the CFI,[92] the scope of the submissions need not be limited to answering the points made in the appeal. Indeed, it would seem that a respondent may make out an entirely different case (from that set out in the appeal) for the setting aside or variation of the decision appealed against, as long as he does not change the

---

89 RP-ECJ 115(1). The time limit for lodging the response cannot be extended.
90 RP-ECJ 115(2).
91 RP-ECJ 38(2), applied by virtue of RP-ECJ 115(2), last sentence.
92 Eg Case C-346/90P *F v Commission* (above, note 74) at 2698.

subject matter of the proceedings[93] or seek some form of relief other than that sought at first instance.[94] As in the case of the appeal, the response is limited to matters of law, not fact, and, where the response seeks the setting aside of the CFI's decision or the award of the relief claimed at first instance, it would seem that the respondent may rely only upon pleas advanced at first instance,[95] although he is not limited to those pleas advanced at first instance that were actually considered in the CFI's decision.[96]

4 Form of order

The relief that may be sought in a response comprises:[97]

(1) an order dismissing the appeal, in whole or in part;
(2) an order setting aside the decision appealed against, in whole or in part;
(3) the same relief, in whole or in part, sought in the proceedings before the CFI;
(4) costs.

As in the case of the appeal, a different form of order from that sought at first instance cannot be included in the response; and the subject matter of the proceedings before the CFI cannot be changed in the reponse.[98] A claim for nominal damages representing the moral damage resulting from a dilatory and vexatious appeal is inadmissible; the appropriate way of dealing with an abusive appeal is to reject it as manifestly inadmissible or unfounded.[99]

5 Attachments

The only attachment to the reponse is a certificate showing that the lawyer acting for the respondent is entitled to practise before a court of a member state.[1]

C Subsequent pleadings

There is no right to lodge a reply and rejoinder after the response has been lodged save where a response seeks to set aside, in whole or in part, the decision appealed against on the basis of a plea in law not raised in the appeal. In that event, the appellant and any other party to the appeal proceedings (save, of course, the respondent who raised the issue in his response) may submit a reply on that plea alone within two months of the service of the response in question.[2] Otherwise, a further written pleading may be submitted only with the leave of the President. Thus, save where a response seeks to set aside the decision appealed against on the basis of a plea different from one raised in the appeal, the written procedure ends with the lodgment of the response (or,

---

93 RP-ECJ 116(2).
94 RP-ECJ 116(1), second indent.
95 As is the case with regard to the appellant: see *V v European Parliament*, (above, note 75) para 21.
96 Case C-185/90P *Commission v Gill* [1991] ECR I-4779 at 4803 (Advocate General Jacobs).
97 RP-ECJ 116(1). A claim for an order setting aside the decision appealed against is admissible notwithstanding the expiry of the period for appealing before the response was lodged; Case C-136/92P *Commission v Lualdi* (unreported, per Advocate General Lenz, paras 113–117).
98 RP-ECJ 116(1) and (2).
99 Case C-35/92P *European Parliament v Frederiksen* [1993] ECR I-991 (opinion of Advocate General van Gerven, para 12). Hence, a respondent in the appeal has no greater right to seek a specific form of relief than at first instance: if Case C-53/92P *Hilti AG v Commission* (unreported, per Advocate General Jacobs, para 59).
 1 RP-ECJ 38(3), applied by RP-ECJ 115(2), last sentence. In contrast to the position regarding the appeal, the Rules of Procedure do not apply RP-ECJ 38(7). It is arguable that that is an oversight and that RP-ECJ 38(7) applies, by analogy at least, in the event that the certificate is not produced.
 2 RP-ECJ 117(2).

more accurately, the last response where there are several) unless the President allows a reply to be lodged.

Leave to lodge a further pleading is sought by application made in writing within seven days of the service of the response or, as the case may be, the reply. The President may give leave if he 'considers such further pleading necessary and expressly allows it in order to enable the party concerned to put forward its point of view or in order to provide a basis for the decision on the appeal'.[3] Where the President gives leave to a party to lodge a reply, any other party who wishes to lodge a rejoinder in response to the reply must apply to the President for leave; the leave given to lodge a reply does not open up automatically a right to respond in writing to the reply. The basis on which leave may be given to respond to a reply is the same as that on which leave may be given to lodge the reply. The Rules of Procedure also refer to the lodging of 'any other pleading',[4] which seems to be an allusion to a further pleading that does not reply to a previous pleading but supports it.

It is to be observed that the President cannot give leave of his own motion. He can act only in response to an application from a party. However, that does not appear to preclude the Court from requesting the parties to make additional submissions in writing on a particular point should it think it desirable. Only two grounds may justify the grant of leave by the President. The first relates specifically to the position of the party seeking leave: where a further pleading is 'necessary . . . in order to enable the party concerned to put forward its point of view'. The second relates to the position of the Court: where a further pleading is 'necessary . . . in order to provide a basis for the decision on the appeal'. In relation to both grounds, the decision of the President is based on his assessment of the position. He is not obliged to grant leave merely because a request has been made. In consequence, a request must set out the reasons justifying the exercise of the President's discretion in favour of allowing a further pleading. It does not appear to be necessary for the President to allow any of the other parties to make submissions in response to the application. If they are concerned by the grant of leave, where it is sought in relation to the lodgment of a reply, they have the opportunity to respond by applying to lodge a rejoinder; they do not appear to have a legitimate interest to object to the lodgment of a rejoinder because, ex hypothesi, the party applying is simply responding to the leave given to another party to lodge a reply.

A subsequent pleading (whether reply, rejoinder or other) should set out the title of the appeal followed by the submissions that the party lodging the pleading wishes to make. RP-ECJ 42(2) applies, as in an ordinary direct action.[5] In consequence, a subsequent pleading may not raise a new plea in law unless it is based on matters of fact or law which have come to light in the course of the procedure. In view of the fact that the form of order in the appeal or, as the case may be, the reponse cannot, in principle, be amended, it does not seem that a subsequent pleading need contain a form of order.

D Pleadings in ancillary proceedings

Pleadings in ancillary proceedings (interim relief, intervention and so forth) are in principle no different (save as to title) from similar pleadings in a direct action.[6]

---

3 RP-ECJ 117(1).
4 RP-ECJ 117(1) and (3).
5 RP-ECJ 118.
6 See section III.E, p 333 above.

E Pleadings after referral back to the CFI

Where the ECJ sets aside a judgment or order of the CFI, it may decide the matter itself or refer it back to the CFI for decision.[7] Where the written procedure had not been completed before the CFI when the judgment referring the case back to the CFI was delivered (such as where the CFI gave judgment on a preliminary objection to the admissibility of the action and the ECJ annulled its decision), the written procedure is resumed, at the stage which it had reached previously, by means of measures of organisation of procedure adopted by the CFI.[8] On the other hand, where the written procedure had been completed by the time when the judgment referring the case back to the CFI was delivered (such as where the judgment appealed to the ECJ was a final judgment of the CFI), further written pleadings may be lodged.

Those further written pleadings are referred to in the Rules of Procedure as 'statements of written observations'.[9] The parties are not obliged to lodge such statements. The applicant in the proceedings is entitled to do so within two months of the service on him or her of the ECJ's judgment. If lodged within time, the applicant's statement is served on the defendant(s). The defendant is then entitled to lodge a statement within the month following the communication to him or her of the applicant's statement. If the applicant's statement was lodged well within the period of two months fixed for doing so, the defendant is entitled to more time in which to lodge a statement because the time allowed to the defendant for lodging a statement may in no case be less than two months from service on him or her of the ECJ's judgment. When the defendant's statement (if any) is lodged, the statements of both the applicant and the defendant are communicated at the same time to the intervener(s). The intervener, like the defendant, is then entitled to lodge a statement within the month following the communication of the other parties' statements, save that the time for doing so may not be less than two months from the service on the intervener of the ECJ's judgment.[10] A further round of statements of written observations supplementing the first may be allowed by the CFI if the circumstances justify it; a party has no right to reply in writing to the statements made by any of the other parties.[11]

Statements of written observations retain the number and title of the proceedings before the CFI,[12] to which should be added 'Statement of written observations submitted by . . .'. The statement must comply with the general rules applicable to all pleadings.[13] The body of the statement sets out the party's observations, that is, submissions on the issues of fact and law remaining to be decided by the CFI in the light of the ECJ's judgment. It is clearly unnecessary and undesirable to repeat matters covered adequately in the pleadings already lodged at the Court. The starting point for a party's submissions is therefore the state of the case as it has been left by the judgment of the ECJ. RP-CFI 48 applies[14] to the first statement of written observations lodged by a party at the CFI just as much as to any supplementary statement

---

7 ECSC and EC Statutes, art 54; Euratom Statute, art 55.
8 RP-CFI 119(2). See further chapter 15, pp 486 et seq.
9 RP-CFI 119(1) and (3).
10 RP-CFI 119(1).
11 RP-CFI 119(3).
12 See Case T-43/89RV *Gill v Commission*, 23 March 1993. As can be seen, the only change is the addition of the letters 'RV' to the case number.
13 RP-CFI 43, which applies by virtue of RP-CFI 120.
14 By virtue of RP-CFI 120: see the *Gill* case (above, note 12) para 47.

with the consequence that no further evidence may be offered and no new plea in law may be introduced unless an exception to the general prohibition on the introduction of new evidence and new pleas in law can be relied on. A new plea may be raised if it is based on the findings made by the CFI in the judgment appealed against or on any statement made by the ECJ in its judgment.[15] It is doubtful if statements of written observations need to contain a form of order: in principle, the relief that the parties may seek can be no different from that sought at the outset of the proceedings so the inclusion of a form of order would be repetitive. Until the CFI has made a ruling on the point, however, it would be advisable to include a form of order.[16] Ordinarily, a statement of written observations will not require any attachments.

V   Pleadings in references for a preliminary ruling[17]

The only written pleadings in a reference for a preliminary ruling are the parties' written observations.[18] The Rules of Procedure do not impose any requirements regarding the form and contents of the written observations. They usually fall into four parts: title; an explanation of the facts and circumstances giving rise to the reference; submissions on the questions referred; and recommendations on the form of the answer to be given to the referring court.[19] In the case of parties to the proceedings before the referring court who are represented before the Court by the same person representing them before the referring court, it would not appear to be necessary to adduce evidence of the representative's capacity to represent them in the preliminary ruling proceedings or his authority to do so, as is required in the case of direct actions, because both may be presumed from the fact that the representative has represented the party in question in the proceedings before the referring court. On the other hand, if the representative is different in the preliminary ruling proceedings, it would seem that evidence of capacity and authority to act should be produced.

For the title of the observations it is enough to indicate with sufficient clarity the case to which the pleading relates. This is normally done by setting out the case number and the title of or the names of the parties to the proceedings before the referring court. The name of the person on whose behalf the pleading is lodged should also be set out, together with an address for service, which need not be in Luxembourg. The title may, therefore, take the following form:

In the Court of Justice of the European Communities

Case C-401/93

A B Ltd

against

C D Ltd

15 The *Gill* case (above, note 12) paras 48–49.
16 The statements lodged in the *Gill* case included forms of order.
17 See Atkin's Court Forms, Vol 17.
18 In arts 20 and 21 of the EC and Euratom Statutes, respectively, and RP-ECJ 103(3) reference is made to 'statements of case or written observations'. No practical significance appears to attach to either expression.
19 In cases where the admissibility of the order for reference may be in doubt, it is usual to set out any submissions on this point before turning to the questions referred.

> Observations submitted on behalf of A B Ltd of [address] represented by E F, Barrister, with an address for service at [address].

Since the object of the reference is to obtain a preliminary ruling on a question of Community law, a recitation of the facts of the case is usually necessary only in order to clarify or supplement the order for reference in a material particular. The role of fact-finding in proceedings for a preliminary ruling is discussed below[20] and the pleading of fact should be considered in the light of the principles set out there. The submissions on the questions referred are generally set out in separate headings relating to each question unless the logical connection between two or more questions is so great that it is not convenient to deal with them separately. For the same reason, it may not be convenient to examine each question in the same sequence as that adopted in the order for reference. The submissions should be limited to those relevant to the questions referred.[21] There is no form of order. By analogy, however, the observations often end with the parties' suggestions concerning the answer to be given to the referring court.[22] These may also be placed individually, at the end of the submissions devoted to each question.

The Court makes no order for costs so far as the parties to the proceedings before the referring court are concerned and the costs of any member state or Community institution which chooses to submit observations lie where they fall, so there is no need for any party submitting observations to claim costs. To the written observations should be annexed the signatory's authority to act for the party on whose behalf the observations are submitted. There is no restriction on the raising of new points at the hearing, which is normally the only time at which it is possible to comment on the matters raised by the other parties in their observations.

---

20 See chapter 10, pp 346 et seq.
21 In Cases 50-58/82 *Administrateur des Affaires Maritimes Bayonne v Dorca Marina* [1982] ECR 3949 (para 13), for example, the Court refused to consider an argument on the ground that it did not fall within the scope of the order for reference.
22 Eg 'For these reasons it is respectfully submitted that the question set out in the order for reference should be answered as follows: (1) Examination of the question has not revealed any factor which renders Regulation No . . . invalid (or: Regulation No . . . is invalid); (2) Article . . . of Regulation No . . . is to be interpreted to the effect that . . .'.

CHAPTER 10

Evidence

I Introduction

The principal subject of this and the following three chapters is the proof of the existence of facts, not law, from material (evidence) which is either primary, in the sense that it constitutes the direct perception of a fact, or secondary in the sense that the perception of the fact is not achieved directly, through the senses, but indirectly through inference. The degree of elaboration necessary in the drawing of inferences depends on the nature of the evidence used. This chapter deals with the role of evidence and fact-finding in proceedings before the Court and the anomalous topic of the proof of law. The three following chapters deal with the proof of facts by means of measures of enquiry, the exclusion of evidence and, lastly, rules of evidence.

II The role of evidence in proceedings before the Court[1]

The importance of fact-finding in a particular case depends in part on the nature of the proceedings and in part on the way the case is pleaded. If, for example, the parties are agreed on the facts, the Court does not normally seek to reopen the issues of fact. This does not, however, mean to say that the Court is invariably bound by concessions made by the parties. The nature of proceedings before it is neither wholly accusatorial nor entirely inquisitorial.[2] The inquisitorial character of proceedings stems, in essence, from the Court's function, as defined by the Treaties,[3] to ensure that the law is observed. It is also inherent in its jurisdiction, which enables it to give judgment on matters involving the public interest and not just the private interest of the parties. For example, an action for damages brought against the Community may put in question the lawfulness of an act of one of the institutions. The Court's decision on the issue can therefore have repercussions on matters other than the applicant's entitlement to damages. In some cases, such as staff cases, the interests involved can be said to be purely private but these tend to be exceptional. More often, when the Court gives judgment on the lawfulness of an act of an institution or its interpretation, the public, Community interest is also at stake and requires that the Court take a positive role in the disposal of the case. There is, nevertheless, a distinction to be drawn between the existence of a power to investigate a question of fact, even against the wishes of the parties, which reveals the inquisitorial side of the Court's procedure, and the

---

1 See, inter alia, Rigaux, *Miscellanea W. J. Ganshof van der Meersch*, Volume II, p 365; Asso (1966) Rev Trim Droit Européen 21 and 177; Bebr *Development of Judicial Control of the European Communities*, (1981) pp 125 et seq; Hartley *The Foundations of European Community Law*.
2 See, for example, André [1967] 5 CMLR 38 et seq.
3 ECSC Treaty, art 31; EC Treaty, art 164; Euratom Treaty, art 136.

exercise of that power. The Court is not bound in any and every case to carry out a detailed investigation into every conceivable question of fact. Its duty to ensure that the law is observed is tempered by the need to ensure that cases are decided expeditiously so that justice is not denied by delay. The Court is only bound to take those steps that are sufficient to ensure that justice is done. It is under no duty to undertake excessive measures. In consequence, where certain facts are not disputed by the parties or are not in doubt, there is no reason for the Court to exercise of its own motion its powers of investigation.

One of the features of the way the Court operates is its willingness to rely on *ipse dixit* rather than evidence in order to establish the existence of a fact,[4] To some extent this is a development which has been forced on the Court by its increased workload: in earlier days, as can be seen from the reports, it took pains to gather the evidence necessary to decide issues of fact. It also reveals an assumption, but not a presumption, held by the Court that the member states and the Community institutions can be relied on to give an accurate present-ation of the material facts. This supposes not only that the member states and Community institutions would not deliberately seek to mislead the Court but also that they are conscientious in setting out the true position and avoiding unintentional misrepresentations. Where the parties to proceedings are either member states or Community institutions, it is no doubt sufficient to proceed on this basis: both parties have, in general, sufficient resources and adequate access to relevant information to look after themselves; if a fact asserted by one party is not challenged, or is expressly conceded, by the other party, what need is there for the Court to interfere? On the other hand, where natural or legal persons are involved as parties,[5] the situation is somewhat different. There is no equivalence of position, or anything approaching it, even when the natural or legal person does have extensive resources, as, for example, in the case of a large multinational corporation. The reason is that the relationship between the member states and the Community institutions is at times so close that material evidence in the form, for example, of internal documents, is more likely to be known to all parties concerned. A natural or legal person, however, even if a large and wealthy multinational corporation, may easily be kept ignorant of relevant evidence held by a Community institution or a member state (generally the former). In these circumstances it is dangerous for the Court to rely on *ipse dixit*: justice cannot be done, and is certainly not seen to be done, where one party is not required to produce evidence in support of the assertions of fact made by it. Even when the parties are in an equivalent position, *ipse dixit* may not be reliable where the assertion is made at a stage in the proceedings at which the other party is unable to take up an informed position in regard to the assertion; and, in such circumstances, evidence is required.[6]

For the purpose of considering the role of evidence, it is convenient to distinguish between non-contentious proceedings, principally references for a preliminary ruling, and contentious proceedings.

4 For example, in Case 28/83 *Forcheri v Commission* [1984] ECR 1425 (para 17), the Court took 'formal notice' of statements of facts made by an intervening member state and, on the basis of those facts, found in favour of the defendant (in whose support the state had intervened); in Case 64/85 *Watgen v Caisse de Pension des Employés Privés* [1988] ECR 2435 (at 2446–2447), Advocate General Mancini remarked on the fact that, in an earlier case, the Court had made a finding about the effect of national legislation even though no proof of the relevant facts had been furnished to it.
5 In practice, in actions against a Community institution or in references for a preliminary ruling.
6 Cf Case 323/87 *Commission v Italy* [1989] ECR 2275 at 2296 (Advocate General Jacobs).

A   Non-contentious proceedings

The role of evidence in non-contentious proceedings depends upon the nature of the proceedings and the relevance to them of findings of fact. In principle, the fact that proceedings are non-contentious in nature means that fact-finding is inquisitorial rather than accusatorial and, in consequence, that there is no evidential burden of proof (although there may well be a legal burden of proof arising as a matter of substantive law).

The most important category of non-contentious proceedings is the reference for a preliminary ruling. In this proceeding the Court is seised of a question of Community law relating to the interpretation or validity of, as the case may be, a provision of the Treaty, a Convention or an act of one of the institutions or some other body. The question arises in the context of litigation before a national court or tribunal. Three categories of fact can be identified in proceedings for a preliminary ruling: (i) those relating to the admissibility of the reference; (ii) those relating to the dispute between the parties before the national court; (iii) those relating to the answer to the question of law put to the Court. Before dealing in detail with those different categories of fact, it should be noted, as a general observation, that the parties to the proceedings before the referring court have their chance to bring forward evidence in the proceedings before that court and not in the preliminary ruling proceedings before the Court.[7] The parties who can appear only in the preliminary ruling proceedings (the member states, Council and Commission) do not have the opportunity to bring forward evidence in the proceedings before the referring court. To the extent that an investigation of the facts can be undertaken by the Court, they are therefore restricted to bringing forward evidence in the course of the preliminary ruling proceedings. The facts that, as will be seen, the Court may assess the evidence, make findings in relation to certain facts in order to come to a conclusion on the question referred to it and take account of evidence not before the referring court, do not discharge the parties to the proceedings before the referring court from the duty to bring forward their evidence at that stage, before the reference is made, rather than thereafter. In cases where the facts are or may be critical to the Court's ruling, it is all the more necessary for the parties to the proceedings before the referring court, and for the referring court itself, to ensure that the relevant facts are found, so far as it lies within the power of the parties to adduce evidence in relation to them and of the referring court to find them. Where the Court finds it necessary to look at facts other than those set out in the order for reference or to assess evidence, it may inform itself from reports made by a national authority;[8] unchallenged information or statistics furnished by some of the parties before it;[9] facts found in a direct action involving one of the parties and dealing with the same situation.[10]

1   Facts relating to admissibility

By and large, the Court does not take cognisance of the facts of the case other than for the purpose of understanding the context in which the reference was

---

7 Case 72/83 *Campus Oil Ltd v Minister for Industry and Energy* [1984] ECR 2727 (para 11).
8 Case 5/84 *Direct Cosmetics Ltd v Customs and Excise Comrs* [1985] ECR 617 at 623.
9 Case 148/85 *Direction Générale des Impôts and Procureur de la République v Forest and Minoterie Forest SA* [1986] ECR 3449 (para 11); Case 433/85 *Feldain v Services Fiscaux du Département du Haut Rhin* [1987] ECR 3521 (para 16).
10 Case C-27/90 *SITPA v ONIFLHOR* [1991] ECR I-133 (para 18).

made and its ruling must be given;[11] but it does consider certain matters relating to the admissibility of the order for reference: such as whether the referring court is a body competent to make the reference,[12] whether the question referred relates to a matter on which a reference can be made[13] or whether it is 'quite obvious' that the question of law bears no relation to the actual nature of the case or to the subject matter of the proceedings before the national court.[14] The Court is not usually in a position to appreciate the relevance of the questions of law raised in the order for reference and the necessity for a preliminary ruling because it does not have direct knowledge of the facts.[15] In consequence, it is in no position to question the assessment made by the referring court; aliter if the lack of relevance or necessity is clear on the face of the order for reference.[16] In Case 93/78 *Mattheus v Doego Fruchtimport und Tiefkuhlkast eG*,[17] where there were suspicions that the reference had been made by the national court simply because a contract between the parties provided for a reference to be made, Advocate General Mayras took the view that it was not right to assess how seriously the dispute between the parties was taken by the national court, even if there were suspicions that it was in fact a fictitious dispute.

In Case 104/79 *Foglia v Novello*[18] the Court did investigate and draw conclusions from the facts leading up to the making of the order for reference, holding that it did not have jurisdiction to entertain the reference because there was, in its view, no genuine dispute between the parties. The referring court then made a second order for reference[19] asking, inter alia, what were the Court's powers of appraising the facts found by a national court in the order for reference. The Court then ruled that it should be put in such a position by the referring court that it could make any assessment necessary for the discharge of its functions in the context of preliminary rulings in particular for the purpose of determining whether it is competent to answer the reference. This seems to make it clear that the Court does have power to find facts for the purpose of determining admissibility but the judgment is not clear as to the precise extent of this power. In his opinion, Advocate General Sir Gordon Slynn suggested that the Court can look only at the order for reference or the

---

11 See, for example, Case 6/64 *Costa v ENEL* [1964] ECR 585 at 593; Case 20/64 *Albatros Sàrl v SOPECO* [1965] ECR 29 at 34; Case 2/67 *De Moor v Caisse de Pension des Employés Privés* [1967] ECR 197 at 205; Case 13/68 *Salgoil SpA v Italian Ministry for Foreign Trade* [1968] ECR 453 at 459; Case 10/69 *Portelange SA v Smith Corona Marchant International SA* [1969] ECR 309 at 315; Case 17/81 *Pabst and Richarz KG v Hauptzollamt Oldenburg* [1982] ECR 1331 at para 12; Case 167/84 *Hauptzollamt Bremen-Freihafen v J Henr Drinert, Holzimport* [1985] ECR 2235 (para 12).
12 Eg Case 61/65 *Vaassen (née Göbbels) v Beambtenfonds voor het Mijnbedrijf* [1966] ECR 261 at 272–273; Case 36/73 *Nederlandse Spoorwegen NV v Minister Verkeer en Waterstaat* [1973] ECR 1299 at 1317–1320 (Advocate General Mayras); Case 17/76 *Brack v Insurance Officer* [1976] ECR 1429 at 1456 (Advocate General Mayras); Case C-24/92 *Corbiau v Administration des Contributions* [1993] ECR I-1227. But see Case 65/81 *Reina v Landeskreditbank Baden-Württemberg* [1982] ECR 33 at paras 6–8.
13 Case 105/79 *Preliminary Ruling by the Acting Judge at the Tribunal d'Instance, Hayange* [1979] ECR 2257.
14 The *Salgoil* case (above, note 11); Case 126/80 *Salonia v Poidomani and Giglio* [1981] ECR 1563 (para 6); Case 166/84 *Thomasdünger GmbH v Oberfinanzdirektion Frankfurt-am-Main* [1985] ECR 3001 (para 11); Case C-286/88 *Falciola Angelo SpA v Comune di Pavia* [1990] ECR I-191 (paras 8–9).
15 See, for example, Case 43/71 *Politi SAS v Ministry of Finance of the Italian Republic* [1971] ECR 1039; Case 83/78 *Pigs Marketing Board (Northern Ireland) v Redmond* [1978] ECR 2347.
16 The *Salgoil* case (above, note 11) and the *Salonia* case (above, note 14).
17 [1978] ECR 2203.
18 [1980] ECR 745: see Barav, 5 ELR 443; Bebr (1980) 17 CMLR 371; Wyatt, 6 ELR 447.
19 Case 244/80 *Foglia v Novello (No 2)* [1981] ECR 3045.

file of the case: if it was apparent from either that the order for reference was not admissible, the Court could refuse to deal with the reference (but, it seems, had discretion whether or not to do so); if it was not apparent, it was to be supposed that the reference was admissible.

Assuming that this approach is right, the referring court should set out in the order for reference the basis for making it so that the Court can decide whether or not it is obliged to answer it.[20] If it appears on the face of the order (as completed, where need be, by the file accompanying it) that the reference is inadmissible, the Court is under no duty to answer it and may send the matter back to the referring court.[21] Where there is a conflict between the order for reference and the file of the case sent to the Court by the referring court, the order for reference should be preferred because that is the instrument which seises the Court with jurisdiction. The file is relevant only in so far as it explains or supplements the order for reference. It is unclear whether the Court may decide to answer the reference despite the fact that it is inadmissible. The judgment in the first *Foglia v Novello* case[22] seems to have held that the absence of a duty to answer the reference meant that the Court had no jurisdiction to do so, not that the Court had discretion whether or not to answer it. If the order for reference is not ex facie inadmissible, the Court remains under a duty to answer but it would seem that, if the order is obscure or doubt is thrown upon it in the observations of a party, the Court has discretion (but no duty) to delay giving judgment until the national court has clarified the question. The Court cannot, however, reject the order as inadmissible simply because it is obscure or some doubt as to its admissibility has been raised, unless inadmissibility is manifest on the face of the order (as explained or completed, where need be, by the file of the case).[23] A fortiori, the Court cannot order a measure of enquiry in order to find any facts relating to the issue of admissibility.

2 Facts relating to the dispute between the parties

It is well established that the referring court has exclusive jurisdiction over the facts relating to the dispute before it.[24] The facts of the dispute give rise to the issue of Community law referred to the Court and may therefore influence how the Court approaches the question of law referred to it and how the Court expresses the ruling to be given. That issue should be defined in the light of the

---

20 Eg Cases 98, 162 and 258/85 *Bertini v Regione Lazio* [1986] ECR 1885 (para 6); Case C-343/90 *Dias v Director da Alfandega do Porto* [1992] ECR I-4673 (paras 19–20).
21 Eg *Bertini v Regione Lazio*, (ibid) para 8; Case 267/86 *van Eycke v ASPA NV* [1988] ECR 4769 (paras 12–13 and at 4783, Advocate General Mancini).
22 Above, note 18.
23 Thus, in Case 6/84 *Nicolet Instrument v Hauptzollamt Frankfurt am Main-Flughafen* [1985] ECR 765 (para 7), where the Commission expressed a reservation about the admissibility of the reference in its written observations but withdrew those reservations at the hearing, the Court considered it unnecessary to examine them even though, ordinarily, the Court is obliged to consider of its own motion the admissibility of proceedings brought before it.
24 See, for example, Case 51/74 *Van der Hulst's Zonen CV v Produktschap voor Siergewassen* [1975] ECR 79 (para 12): Case 48/75 *Royer* [1976] ECR 497 (para 16); Case 51/75 *EMI Records v CBS United Kingdom Ltd* [1976] ECR 811 at 854 (Advocate General Warner); Case 104/77 *Firma Wolfgang Oehlschläger v Hauptzollamt Emmerich* [1978] ECR 791 (para 4); Case 36/79 *Denkavit Futtermittel GmbH v Finanzamt Warendorf* [1979] ECR 3439 (para 12 and at 3461, Advocate General Reischl); *Campus Oil* (above, note 7) para 10; Case 253/83 *Kupferberg v Hauptzollamt Mainz* [1985] ECR 157 (para 13); Case C-332/88 *Alimenta SA v Doux SA* [1990] ECR I-2077 (para 9).

facts in the order for reference[25] and, once it is so defined, the Court cannot go behind it because the extent of its jurisdiction is determined by the order for reference.[26] The Court may interpret the order for reference but cannot redraft it.[27] Where it does not contain any findings of fact or is deficient in this respect, the Court may in principle make enquiries or consider evidence[28] or make assumptions[29] in order to clarify the issue raised in the order for reference; but the Court cannot itself decide any issues of fact relating to the dispute between the parties and, if it were to do so, its findings would not bind the national court, since they could have been made only for the purpose of defining the issue of Community law with which the Court is seised by the order for reference. Since the preliminary ruling procedure is intended to deal with questions of law only (even though the questions of law raised may give rise to subsidiary issues of fact), it seems to follow that matters of fact relating to the context of the reference should not be the subject of investigation by the Court (in the event that they are not set out adequately in the order for reference) unless they are agreed between the parties or, if in dispute, are such that the Court may come to a (provisional) conclusion, for the purposes of the reference, without prejudicing the utility of the ruling given or the resolution of the issue by the referring court.[30]

The two most detailed analyses of the role of evidence in references for a preliminary ruling cover facts falling within this second category and come from the advocate general's opinion in *EMI v CBS* and *Denkavit Futtermittel v Finanzamt Warendorf*.[31] The former concerned the question whether trademark rights could be used to prevent the importation of trademarked goods from a third country and so the interpretation of the EC Treaty. The parties before the Court produced a considerable amount of documentary evidence relating, not to the question of interpretation *stricto sensu* but to the general context of the dispute. Advocate General Warner took the view that this evidence could be looked at for two purposes only:[32] (i) to explain and complete the facts stated in the order for reference, in so far as the conclusions to be drawn from the evidence were common ground; and (ii) for enlightenment concerning the issues between the parties in so far as they disagree on what are the conclusions to be drawn from the evidence. He went on, however, to say that, where the reference concerned the validity of an act of an institution, the Court could admit evidence on a relevant issue of fact.[33]

The *Denkavit* case also involved a question of interpretation: whether Community law forbade certain action to be taken if a given state of affairs existed. The Commission challenged the accuracy of the assumption that that state of

---

25 In consequence, if the order for reference does not set out the factual background, the Court may not be able to answer the question referred to it: see, for example, Cases C-320 to C-322/90 *Telemarsicabruzzo SpA v Circostel et al* [1993] ECR I-393.

26 In particular, the Court cannot go behind the facts found by the national court on the basis of a mere oral statement by counsel: see Case 137/78 *Henningsen Food Inc v Produktschap voor Pluimvee en Eiren* [1979] ECR 1707 at 1723 (Advocate General Warner).

27 *EMI v CBS* (above, note 24) at 854 (Advocate General Warner).

28 Eg Case 191/83 *Salzano v Bundesanstalt für Arbeit* [1984] ECR 3741 (para 8), reliance on documents before the Court in order to make a finding of background relevance to the question of interpretation raised.

29 Case 243/83 *Binon & Cie v Agence et Messageries de la Presse* [1985] ECR 2015 (para 21).

30 In general, that will be so only where the disputed facts are simple in nature or where no serious issue arises in respect of them.

31 Above, note 24.

32 *EMI v CBS* (above note 24), at 854–855.

33 See also Cases 80 and 81/77 *Société les Commissionnaires Réunis Sàrl v Receveur des Douanes* [1978] ECR 927 at 957.

affairs did exist. Once again the issue of fact did not relate to the question of Community law but to the context in which it was to be applied. Advocate General Reischl said that the Court was bound by the facts found by the referring court and that the response to the question in the order for reference had to be framed on the basis that those facts did indeed exist;[34] however, he went on to say that he had considerable misgivings over whether the Court is unconditionally bound by findings of fact which are subject to well-founded doubts concerning their accuracy and relevance to the resolution of the dispute before the referring court. He thought that the Court might be bound by an agreement between the parties, but not in regard to facts relating to the validity of a provision of Community law. In such a case the Court[35] 'is entitled to adopt a critical stance, nay perhaps even bound to investigate the questions of fact at issue. Further the same must however be assumed if . . . it is a question of the interpretation of Community law for the purpose of assessing the validity of a national provision. If this depends on a particular economic situation as a whole and if there are serious doubts regarding the assessment made by the national court, then it seems to me hardly sustainable that the Court should simply overlook it and give an interpretation of Community law in respect of facts which are probably not true.'

In that case, the national court's findings were based solely on statements made by the plaintiff before it which had been accepted by the defendant without checking them. He therefore took the view that, even in a reference concerning the interpretation of a provision of Community law, the Court can correct the facts found, but 'only if it is clearly possible from the documents, that is to say, without additional, time-consuming evidence, for which there is basically no place in proceedings for *interpretation*'.[36] It is not the Court's usual practice to correct the facts found by the national court, even if serious doubts are raised concerning their accuracy, in proceedings for interpretation. It is more likely for the Court to take the dispute on the facts into account when framing its answer to the question. The facts are not, of course, directly relevant to the problem of interpretation itself[37] but certainly affect the way the Court's answer is to be put. It is not therefore necessary to consider the accuracy or otherwise of the findings of fact.[38] The situation is, as will be seen, completely different in proceedings concerning the validity of a provision of Community law, where the facts do affect that question and are not simply general background material of no relevance to the issue before the Court.

3   *Facts relating to the reference*

Facts determining the answer to the question of law posed in the order for reference fall, as a matter of principle, within the exclusive jurisdiction of the

34 Above, note 24 at 3461.
35 Ibid at 3461–3462.
36 Ibid at 3463; his emphasis.
37 Save in cases where the teleological method of interpretation is used, in which case the relevant facts are properly to be regarded as falling within the category of facts relevant to the question of law referred to the Court, rather than the category of facts relating to the dispute between the parties.
38 Eg Case 99/83 *Fioravanti v Amministrazione delle Finanze* [1984] ECR 3939 (para 10), where the referring court assumed a fact and one of the parties produced documentary evidence that suggested that the fact was wrongly assumed, but the Court left the question to the referring court; Case C-345/88 *Bundesamt für Ernährung und Forstwirtschaft v Butterabsatz Osnabrück-Emsland* [1990] ECR I-159 (para 14), where a fact suggested in the question referred was not apparent from the documentary evidence but the Court limited itself to proceeding on the basis that that fact existed, saying that it was for the referring court to verify the assumptions on which the reference was made.

Court and it is not bound by findings made by the national court which relate to that aspect of the case, rather than to the background to the question referred. If the national court could bind the Court in so far as the factual basis to the question of law referred were concerned, the Court would no longer be in a position to ensure that the law is observed: the rulings given by the Court on a particular matter would vary from case to case, depending on the facts found by the referring court, giving rise to uncertainty in the law and reducing the preliminary ruling to a judgment on a hypothesis. However, since the preliminary ruling procedure is designed to be a step, in the proceedings before the referring court, which is in principle concerned only with a question of law, the usual practice is to rely on the findings of fact made by the referring court even where they relate to the question of law that has been referred, unless those findings are put in issue in the course of the preliminary ruling procedure.

In the nature of things, facts determining the interpretation of a provision of Community law give rise to few disputes. They comprise such things as (i) the text of the provision itself and (ii) evidence other than the text of the provision to be interpreted that is relevant to the interpretation to be given, such as preparatory documents (for example, the minutes of the Council or a Commission working paper which may be relevant to the intention behind the provision) or evidence relating to the effect in practice of the different contending interpretations of the provision (which may be useful in deciding which interpretation is to be preferred). A dispute over the text of the provision in question, as opposed to the meaning to be given to it, is almost unheard of.[39] Preparatory documents are not usually considered to be material which may be relied on for the purposes of interpretation, as opposed to ascertainment of the object or intention of the draftsman; and, even then, are usually considered to be relevant only if they have been published, in which case little difficulty arises in regard to proving them. Reference to the practice of the contracting parties to an international convention has been rejected as an aid to the construction of a provision.[40] Where evidence of the different consequences of the different contending interpretations of a provision is relevant, it is clearly better for the material facts to be found in the order for reference.[41] Where it is argued that a provision is to be interpreted by analogy to another provision, it is necessary to demonstrate that the factual substratum of both provisions is the same, which may well involve the Court in examining evidence in addition to the facts found in the order for reference.[42] Facts giving rise to the problem of interpretation, as opposed to those relating to its solution, may also fall within the jurisdiction of the Court to determine, particularly where the Court is in a better position than the referring court to establish their existence or non-existence.[43]

---

39 In Case 22/81 *R v Social Security Comr, ex p Browning* [1981] ECR 3357 the text was the English version of art 50 of Council Regulation No 1408/71 of 14 June 1971 (OJ No L149/2 of 5 July 1971), which had been subjected to various amendments and corrections over the years. Counsel for one party placed great emphasis on the meaning of the word 'fixed', which appeared in the version he was working from, and Counsel for the other party placed equally great emphasis on the meaning of the word 'determined' which was used in another version.

40 Case 236/83 *University of Hamburg v Hauptzollamt Münster-West* [1984] ECR 3849 (para 23): the reason seems to have been that reliance was placed on assumptions regarding the intentions of the other contracting parties rather than on established facts.

41 See, for example, Case C-372/88 *Milk Marketing Board of England and Wales v Cricket St Thomas Estate* [1990] ECR I-1345.

42 Case 74/87 *D Goerrig GmbH v Hauptzollamt Geldern* [1988] ECR 2771 (para 13).

43 Cf Case 327/82 *Ekvo v Produktschap voor Vee en Vlees* [1984] ECR 107 (para 10), in casu, variations in cutting and boning methods as between the member states that led to variations in the meaning given to terms used in Community legislation.

Facts which are pertinent to the validity of an act of an institution may be the subject of findings made by the national court in the order for reference or may not even be the subject of dispute between the parties to the proceedings before the national court. The first situation arose in Case 131/77 *Firma Milac, Gross- und Aussenhandel Arnold Nöll v Hauptzollamt Saarbrücken*,[44] where the validity of a regulation turned on the question whether the price of powdered whey depended on the price of skimmed milk powder. The referring court made the order for reference on the basis of certain findings on this point to which it had come after considering the facts. The existence of those findings did not prevent the Court from carrying out its own investigation, which confirmed the conclusions of the referring court.

An example of the second situation is Case 245/81 *Edeka Zentrale AG v Germany*.[45] There an action had been brought by an importer against the German authority responsible for the issue of import licences for preserved mushrooms. The latter had rejected an application for import licences on the ground that their issue had been suspended by a Commission regulation. The dispute concerned the validity of that regulation, which determined the validity of the refusal to grant the licences. The regulation had suspended the grant of import licences in respect of goods from those third countries which did not agree to limit their exports to the Community and its validity depended in part on how the Commission had conducted the negotiations on self-limitation agreements with third countries. The defendant in the proceedings before the German court had no direct knowledge of the negotiations but it did not challenge certain assertions as to the facts made by the applicant and conceded others. From a procedural point of view, it could have been said that, as far as the German court was concerned, the issues of fact had to this extent been determined in favour of the applicant by the time that the order for reference was made, even though the unchallenged or conceded facts had not in substance been incorporated in the order for reference and formally adopted by the referring court. Nevertheless the Court did review the facts.

One of the reasons why the Court should not be bound by findings made by the referring court or concessions made by the parties to proceedings before it, which relate to the answer to be given to the question of law in the order for reference, is that, as in the *Edeka* case, the facts may not be within the capacity of the referring court to determine or the parties to prove because neither has access to the evidence on which a reliable conclusion can be based. The Court's duty to ensure that the law is observed could not properly be discharged if its decision on the validity of a provision of Community law were based on findings that were probably unsafe, unreliable or untrue.[46]

In both the *Milac* and *Edeka* cases the Commission challenged the facts found by or agreed before the national court so there was, to that extent, an issue of fact before the Court when it came to consider the question of law put to it. Had the Commission conceded the facts, would the Court have been bound to accept the concession? Clearly not. Proceedings for obtaining a preliminary ruling are non-contentious and so a concession of fact does not remove an issue from the competence of the Court to decide, as may happen where its function is to decide a *lis* between the parties: the object of the

---

44 [1978] ECR 1041.
45 [1982] ECR 2745.
46 Thus, in Case 291/86 *Central-Import Münster GmbH & Co KG v Hauptzollamt Münster* [1988] ECR 3679 (paras 25–30), the facts relevant to the validity of the contested measure were proved by evidence adduced by the Commission in the course of the proceedings before the Court.

preliminary ruling procedure is not to determine the legal position of the parties inter se[47] but to consider a matter of public interest.[48] It seems, however, that the Court may, in its discretion, accept a concession where it is made by a party submitting observations who has knowledge of the facts. Such a concession can be relied on. A concession made by a party who has no knowledge of the facts is unsafe. In both cases the Court remains free to seek evidence on the point by ordering a measure of enquiry or exercising its other powers. It is not necessary to refer the matter back to the national court for further findings and this would, indeed, be fruitless in most cases because any relevant evidence is likely to be in the possession of Community institutions or other persons or bodies within the control of the Court, not the referring court.[49] Although the decision to accept a concession should, in principle, be based on whether or not its maker has knowledge of the facts conceded, it would seem that the Court may take other relevant factors into account, such as the relative importance of the fact in question and whether or not the person making the concession might have some interest other than in revealing the truth when admitting the fact.

Findings of fact made by the Court for the purpose of answering the question referred to it bind the referring court by virtue of the principle of res judicata,[50] but only in regard to the question of law decided by the Court. In consequence the national court is free to ignore them for the purpose of deciding the dispute before it.

The extent to which it is necessary to investigate material questions of fact, even in cases concerning the validity of a provision of Community law, is determined in part by the terms of the order for reference. In several early cases it was said that the Court could only consider grounds of invalidity raised by the referring court in the order for reference and could not consider additional arguments put by the parties, save in exceptional circumstances. For example, in Cases 73 and 74/63 *Internationale Crediet-en Handelsvereniging NV Rotterdam v Minister van Landbouw en Visserij*,[51] Advocate General Roemer said: 'a national court cannot pose a completely general question on the validity or invalidity of acts of the institutions in its order making the reference . . . [It] must clearly state the questions on which it requests a preliminary ruling and must indicate the grounds which are said to entail the invalidity of a particular act. That is as far as the opinion of the Court of Justice may extend. If it were otherwise, the matter in dispute, other than in annulment proceedings, would not be precisely defined and the Court would have to make an examination from all imaginable points of view, which might be contrary to the intention of the parties in the national proceedings'.[52]

47 Case 13/61 *Kledingverkoopbedrijf De Geus en Uitenbogerd v Bosch GmbH* [1962] ECR 45 at 61 (Advocate General Lagrange).

48 Case 127/73 *BRT v SABAM* [1974] ECR 51 at 69 (Advocate General Mayras).

49 The Community institutions are, of course, obliged to give active assistance to the national courts, so far as it lies within their power to do so, by producing documents or authorising their officials to give evidence: Case C-2/88 Imm *Zwartfeld* [1990] ECR I-3365 (para 22). Nonetheless, once the matter is before the Court in the form of a reference for a preliminary ruling, it would delay the final determination of the proceedings unnecessarily for the Court to refer the matter back to the referring court instead of seeking the relevant evidence and deciding the question of fact itself.

50 See, for example, Case 112/76 *Manzoni v Fonds National de Retraite des Ouvriers Mineurs* [1977] ECR 1647 at 1661–1663 (Advocate General Warner). National courts may also be obliged to adopt findings on matters of Community law made by the Court in parallel proceedings before it: cf Cases 106–120/87 *Asteris AE v Greece and EEC* [1988] ECR 5515, para 18 and at 5528 (Advocate General Slynn).

51 [1964] ECR 1 at 26 and 28.

52 To similar effect, see Case C-323/88 *SA Sermes v Directeur des Services des Douanes de Strasbourg* [1990] ECR I-3027 at 3038–3040 (Advocate General van Gerven).

Although he excluded an exhaustive examination of the question of validity, he did accept that the order for reference could be given an extensive interpretation so as to cover questions not raised expressly by it. Nevertheless, the parties could still not extend the scope of the order for reference unilaterally.[53] The Court held the measure in question to be valid 'in the absence of any other defect which can be examined by the Court of its own motion'.[54] In Case 5/67 *Beus GmbH & Co v Hauptzollamt München-Landsbergerstrasse*[55] Advocate General Gand, while basically following the same approach as that of Advocate General Roemer, also said that the Court 'cannot hold a measure to be valid if it appears to [it] to be vitiated by a defect of such gravity that it ought to be raised' by the Court of its own motion. More recently, in Case 11/74 *Union des Minotiers de la Champagne v French Government*[56] Advocate General Trabucchi said that 'the task of this Court, in proceedings for the preliminary examination of the validity of Community acts is not to test, in a thorough and definitive manner, the legality of the act in question but solely to declare whether the doubts in the matter expressed or merely referred to by the national court are well founded'.[57]

In fact, the scope of the Court's enquiry into different grounds of invalidity depends very much on the wording of the question referred to it. If the question concerns a specific ground,[58] the Court's jurisdiction is restricted to that ground. If, however, it was manifest that the measure was invalid for another reason, the Court would not be ensuring that the law is observed if it refrained from examining that ground and drawing the national court's attention to it. But the Court is clearly not bound to consider any and every conceivable argument. Nor does it do so in practice. A judgment finding that a measure is valid usually states that no cause has been shown to cast doubt on the validity of the measure; it is never said that the measure is valid. In consequence, it is always possible to challenge the validity of the measure again, in subsequent proceedings, on a ground or on facts other than those considered by the Court.

It is more usual for the question in the order for reference to be phrased in general terms[59] and for the arguments which have occurred to the national court to be set out in the order for reference. In such a case, the order for reference often, but not invariably, reflects the submissions made by the parties to the proceedings. In this situation the question to be answered by the Court is not restricted to any particular ground of invalidity and there is in consequence no reason to limit argument to the grounds that may be set out in the body of the order for reference: these are mentioned for the purpose of informing the Court of the issues between the parties and show the preoccupations of the national court but they do not limit the Court's jurisdiction in answering the question, which is defined by the question itself. If, therefore, a new ground of invalidity is put forward by one of the parties, the Court can

---

53 But see Case 17/67 *Firma Max Neumann v Hauptzollamt Hof Saale* [1967] ECR 441 at 460, where he suggested that the Court was not bound to consider only the points of law raised by the national court in the order for reference but could look at points raised by the parties.

54 [1964] ECR at 14.

55 [1968] ECR 83 at 108.

56 [1974] ECR 877 at 888.

57 Thus, in Cases 50-58/82 *Administrateur des Affaires Maritimes, Bayonne v Dorca Marina* [1982] ECR 3949 (para 13) the Court refused to consider an argument that the disputed regulation infringed general principles of law on the ground that that issue did not fall within the scope of the reference.

58 For example: 'is such and such a regulation invalid because the Council did not give adequate reasons?'

59 For example: 'is such and such a regulation valid?'

consider it. It does not extend the scope of the order for reference because the crucial part, the question referred, is quite general.[60] Nevertheless, the Court tends only to consider the arguments addressed to it and gives the same cautious reply if it finds the measure to be valid. It is undoubtedly true that it is easier to deal with a case in which the national court asks a specific question but the mere fact that the question asked is in general terms, or no findings are made which narrow down the scope of the reference, does not make it inadmissible.[61]

Although facts relating directly to the question of the validity of the contested act thus seem to fall within the jurisdiction of the Court to find, the question whether or not a finding of invalidity in relation to one case may be relied on in relation to another case may depend upon facts that lie within the jurisdiction of the referring court.[62]

The validity of a provision of Community law cannot be reviewed by reference to rules or concepts of national law.[63] In Cases 21–24/72 *International Fruit Co NV v Produktschap voor Groenten en Fruit*[64] the Court held that its jurisdiction to review validity under art 177 of the EC Treaty extends to all grounds capable of invalidating a provision of Community law including, where applicable, rules of international law. In later cases, however, the grounds of review have been stated variously to be restricted (at least in cases where the measure in question involves an assessment of complex economic facts) to patent error and misuse of power;[65] manifest error, misuse of power or a clear exceeding of the bounds of the relevant institution's discretion;[66] or manifest error and manifest failure to observe Community law.[67] This appears to mean that, when an institution has not simply applied the law to the facts but has appreciated, assessed or drawn inferences from the facts before acting, the Court's jurisdiction to review does not normally extend to the appreciation, assessment or inference made. The Court may always determine whether the institution took into account facts that were relevant in law, whether the facts were correctly found and whether the institution acted lawfully, given the correctness of its assessment. But the Court cannot review

60 See, for example, *Beus GmbH & Co v Hauptzollamt München-Landsbergerstrasse* (above, note 55) at 96.

61 See, for example, Cases 103 and 145/77 *Royal Scholten Honig (Holdings) Ltd and Tunnel Refineries Ltd v Intervention Board for Agricultural Produce* [1978] ECR 2037 at 2012 (Advocate General Reischl); the *Foglia v Novello* cases (above, notes 18 and 19); Cases 141–143/81 *Holdijk, Mulder and Alpuro* [1982] ECR 1299 (paras 4–8): the relevance of and necessity for the reference are different matters.

62 Case 112/83 *Société Produits de Mais SA v Administration des Douanes et droits indirects* [1985] ECR 719 (para 13).

63 Case 11/70 *Internationale Handelgesellschaft mbH v Einfur und Vorratsstelle für Getreide und Futtermittel* [1970] ECR 1125 (para 3).

64 [1972] ECR 1219 (paras 5–7).

65 See Case 57/72 *Westzucker GmbH v Einfuhr- und Vorratsstelle für Zucker* [1973] ECR 321 (para 14); Case 78/74 *Deuka, Deutsche Kraftfutter GmbH BJ Stolp v Einfuhr und Vorratsstelle für Getreide und Futtermittel* [1975] ECR 421 (para 9); Case 5/75 *Deuka Deutsche Kraftfutter GmbH BJ Stolp v Einfuhr und Vorratsstelle für Getreide und Futtermittel* [1975] ECR 759 (para 4).

66 Case 55/75 *Balkan Import-Export GmbH v Hauptzollamt Berlin-Packhof* [1976] ECR 19 (para 8); Case 29/77 *SA Roquette Frères v France* [1977] ECR 1835 (paras 19–20); Case 136/77 *Firma A Racke v Hauptzollamt Mainz* [1978] ECR 1245 (para 4) (see also Case 37/70 *Rewe-Zentrale des Lebensmittel-Grosshandels GmbH v Hauptzollamt Emmerich* [1971] ECR 23 at 42 (Advocate General Dutheillet de Lamothe)).

67 Case 2/77 *Hoffmann's Stärkefabriken AG v Hauptzollamt Bielefeld* [1977] ECR 1375 at 1405 (Advocate General Mayras); in Case 126/81 *Wünsche Handelsgesellschaft v Germany* [1982] ECR 1479, Advocate General Rozés referred only to manifest error but it seems that this was the only ground then in issue. See also Case 345/82 *Wünsche v Germany* [1984] ECR 1995 (para 21).

the measure by substituting its own assessment of the facts for that of the institution, except when the institution's assessment is itself tainted with illegality.[68]

B   Contentious proceedings

In direct actions, the importance of evidence depends on the provisions giving the Court jurisdiction. Broadly speaking these fall into three categories:

(1)   those which set a specific limitation to its jurisdiction over the facts;[69]
(2)   those which set no specific limitation;[70]
(3)   those which provide that the Court has 'unlimited jurisdiction'.[71]

Save in respect of the last category, which comprises, in general, certain specified types of financial dispute[72] and in which the Court can examine all matters of fact and law,[73] the Court's jurisdiction may be limited not only by an express stipulation but also by the nature and object of the proceedings. For example:

Article 18 of the Euratom Treaty is one of the rare provisions which appear expressly to exclude review by the Court of the facts of the case because the grounds of review are restricted to 'the formal validity of the decision and to the interpretation of the provisions of this Treaty'. Article 33 of the ECSC Treaty gives the Court jurisdiction to annul decisions or recommendations of the Commission 'on grounds of lack of competence, infringement of an essential procedural requirement, infringement of this Treaty or of any rule of law relating to its application, or misuse of powers'. It is not expressly stated that it has power to annul on the ground of a mistake of fact but this is implied: if the basis in fact of an exercise by the Commission of its powers is wrong, it follows necessarily that the exercise is wrong in law on one of the grounds set out in art 33. However, that provision goes on to say: 'The Court may not, however, examine the evaluation of the situation, resulting from economic facts or circumstances, in the light of which the [Commission] took its decisions or made its recommendations save where the [Commission] is alleged to have misused its powers or to have manifestly failed to observe the provisions of this Treaty or any rule of law relating to its application.' The significance of this is discussed below. For the moment, it is sufficient to point out that art 33 of the ECSC Treaty, like art 18 of the Euratom Treaty, contains an express stipulation limiting, albeit to different degrees, the Court's powers of review in

---

68 In Case 6/54 *Netherlands v High Authority* [1954–56] ECR 103, an action brought under art 33 of the ECSC Treaty, which also excludes the review of assessments or evaluations of economic facts or circumstances save where there is a misuse of powers or a manifest failure to observe the provisions of the Treaty or any rule of law relating to its application, the Court construed the latter exception as resulting, in that case, only 'from the finding by the Court of the existence of an economic situation which prima facie reveals no necessity for the contested measure in the pursuit of the objectives set out in Article 3 of the Treaty' (see p 115). The Court's approach to reviewing the validity of measures in references for a preliminary ruling, even those brought under the other Treaties, seems to be broadly the same in this respect as that required by art 33. This being the case, a manifest failure to observe Community law or a clear overstepping of the institution's discretion appears to be covered by saying that the Court can always review whether the institution was wrong in law, whatever the accuracy of its evaluation of the facts (see below).
69 Eg arts 33 of the ECSC Treaty and 18 of the Euratom Treaty.
70 Eg arts 37 of the ECSC Treaty and 173 of the EC Treaty.
71 Eg arts 36 and 88 of the ECSC Treaty and 172 of the EC Treaty.
72 Not all cases in which the Court has unlimited jurisdiction concern financial disputes: see, for example, art 88 of the ECSC Treaty.
73 See Bebr *Development of Judicial Control of the European Communities* pp 125 et seq.

regard to the facts. This limitation necessarily restricts the importance of fact-finding in proceedings under those two provisions.

In contrast, art 173 of the EC Treaty, which gives the Court jurisdiction to annul (among others) acts of the Council and the Commission other than recommendations and opinions on the same grounds to be found in art 33 of the ECSC Treaty, contains no restriction on its power to review an 'evaluation of the situation, resulting from economic facts or circumstances'. It therefore falls, for present purposes, within the second category of provisions giving the Court jurisdiction. Nevertheless the Court has proceeded to impose on itself a limitation similar to that set out in art 33. The reason for this is that the object of an action for annulment is the review by the Court of the lawfulness of an act and the review of an exercise of discretion falls outside the scope of the proceedings.

On the other hand, art 37 of the ECSC Treaty gives the Court jurisdiction to determine whether a Commission decision, (i) recognising the existence of a situation which is of such a nature as to provoke fundamental and persistent disturbances in the economy of a member state and prescribing the steps to be taken to end it or (ii) refusing expressly or impliedly to recognise the existence of such a situation, is 'well founded'. It is not stated that the Court has unlimited jurisdiction nor is there any express stipulation indicating, or limiting, the grounds of review. Like art 173 of the EC Treaty, art 37 falls in the second category mentioned above. Unlike proceedings under art 173, however, the Court has extremely wide powers of review since art 37 gives it jurisdiction to assess the economic position of the member states and examine whether, in view of this situation, the measures adopted may be considered necessary and appropriate.[74] The Court's jurisdiction is thus broader than in proceedings in which the lawfulness of a measure is at issue but, even so, the Court does not have power to remake the Commission's decision and so its jurisdiction is not, strictly speaking, unlimited. The difference between jurisdiction under art 33 of the ECSC Treaty, or art 173 of the EC Treaty, and art 37, is that, whereas the end result is a judgment upholding a measure or declaring it to be void, the Court has power under the last of those provisions to decide whether the act is 'well founded', not just 'lawful'.

The object of proceedings in which the Court has unlimited jurisdiction is not simply the review of a measure, which may be annulled if it is held to be unlawful or not well founded, but the remaking of it. Hence the Court can substitute its own judgment in the matter for that of the body whose decision is in question, even when it is necessary to overturn an evaluation of fact or some other exercise of discretion.[75] An additional consequence is that the Court is not bound merely to grant or refuse the relief sought in the applicant's form of order: it may order other relief even if it has not been pleaded.[76] In general, the Court is given unlimited jurisdiction by express provision in the Treaties or subordinate legislation. For example, art 17 of Council Regulation No 17 of 6

---

74 See Cases 2 and 3/60 *Niederrheinische Bergwerks-AG v High Authority* [1961] ECR 133 at 146 and per Advocate General Lagrange at 152–153; Case 13/63 *Italy v Commission* [1963] ECR 165 at 182–183.

75 See Bebr *Judicial Control* pp 129–131. In Case 1/56 *Bourgaux v Common Assembly* [1954–56] ECR 361 at 375, Advocate General Roemer suggested that unlimited jurisdiction does not entitle the Court to review every exercise of a discretion but he seems subsequently to have qualified this (for example, in Case 13/69 *Van Eick v Commission* [1970] ECR 3, he said that the Court could not substitute its own evaluation for that of the Commission *because* it did not have unlimited jurisdiction in the matter). The remark was made in connection with the discretion of the Community institutions to order their own internal affairs and it is doubtful if it applies outside staff cases, if at all.

76 Eg Case 24/79 *Oberthür v Commission* [1980] ECR 1743.

February 1962[77] provides that the Court has unlimited jurisdiction 'to review decisions whereby the Commission has fixed a fine or periodic penalty' in the exercise of its powers under the Regulation.[78] What this means is that the Court can review all matters of fact and law in connection with such a decision; it can therefore substitute its own assessment of the facts for that of the Commission and substitute its own assessment of the gravity of the infringement or the appropriateness of the sanction imposed by the Commission, when considering whether the fine or periodic penalty should be reduced, increased or cancelled. It should be noted, however, that the Court's unlimited jurisdiction is usually restricted to the financial aspects of the dispute (in competition cases, the imposition of a fine). Hence, while the Court may come to its own assessment in relation to such aspects, it cannot substitute its own assessment of the case for that of the body whose act is in question in respect of other aspects of the dispute.[79] Evidence plays its most influential role, therefore, in cases where the Court has unlimited jurisdiction.

As can be seen, the most important limitation on the Court's powers, so far as facts are concerned, is that, in proceedings in which the object is the annulment of an act, it cannot normally review evaluations of the facts or the exercise of a discretion. In the context of art 33 of the ECSC Treaty, the position is as follows. Although the Court can review any findings of fact made by the Commission, it cannot review the conclusions drawn from those facts by the Commission when evaluating the situation,[80] save under the conditions mentioned in art 33. While the restriction of the Court's powers of review set out in this provision does not expressly apply to an evaluation of facts or circumstances which are not 'economic', the nature of the proceedings means that the Court cannot, in general, review any evaluation.

A misuse of powers is the exercise of a power for a purpose other than that for which it was given. As far as a manifest failure to observe the provisions of the Treaty or any rule of law relating to its application is concerned, 'manifest' means that 'a certain degree is reached in the failure to observe legal provisions so that the failure to observe the Treaty appears to derive from an obvious

77 JO 204/62 of 21 February 1962, English Special Edition 1959–1962 p 87.
78 The ultimate source of this provision is art 172 of the EEC Treaty. In Case 41/69 *ACF Chemiefarma NV v Commission* [1970] ECR 661 at 704, Advocate General Gand remarked that the 'dispute as a whole is brought before the Court so that it has full power to consider the facts and, according to the view it takes as to the existence of the alleged infringements and their gravity, it may uphold, cancel or reduce the fine or, if necessary, increase it'. It is interesting to observe that, although Case 61/80 *Coöperatieve Stremsel-en Kleurselfabriek v Commission* [1981] ECR 851 did not involve a fine, so the Court would not, in theory, have unlimited jurisdiction, the judgment was based in part on the finding that the object of the restrictive practice was to prevent competition despite the fact that the decision challenged did not find this but was based on the fact, put at issue by the applicant, that the practice had this effect.
79 Thus, in Cases 176 and 177/86 *Houyoux v Commission* [1987] ECR 4333 (para 16), a staff case (in respect of which the Court has unlimited jurisdiction in relation to disputes of a financial character), the Court held that it could of its own motion award the successful applicant financial compensation for the damage caused by the defendant's maladministration. In Case T-156/89 *Mordt v Court of Justice* [1991] ECR II-407 (para 150), on the other hand, the Court held that it could not order the defendant to take specific measures to comply with the judgment, even though it had unlimited jurisdiction; and, in Case 228/83 *F v Commission* [1985] ECR 275 (para 34), it held that it could not substitute its own judgment for that of the appointing authority except in the case of a manifest error or misuse of powers. It was the non-pecuniary nature of the matters at issue in *Mordt* and *F v Commission* that precluded the Court taking the same approach as in *Houyoux*.
80 See *Netherlands v High Authority* (above, note 68) at 114; Case 2/56 *Geitling Selling Agency for Ruhr Coal v High Authority* [1957–58] ECR 3 at 18; Case 13/60 *Geitling Ruhrkohlen Verkaufsgesellschaft mbH v High Authority* [1962] ECR 83 at 116; Cases 154, 205, 206, 226–228, 263, 264/78, 31, 39, 83 and 85/79 *Ferriera Valsabbia SpA v Commission* [1980] ECR 907 (para 50).

error in the evaluation, having regard to the provisions of the Treaty, of the situation in respect of which the decision was taken'.[81]

When raising either ground in order to establish jurisdiction to review an evaluation of economic facts or circumstances, it is not necessary to adduce 'full proof' of the allegations made but it is equally insufficient to make a mere assertion: the ground relied on must be supported by 'appropriate evidence'.[82] This appears to mean that sufficient evidence must be produced to set up a prima facie or arguable case.[83] Similarly, when an undertaking or association of undertakings seeks the annulment of a general decision or recommendation under art 33, it can do so only on the ground of a misuse of powers and so need only formally allege (with reasons being given) that there has been a misuse of powers affecting it in order to establish the admissibility of the action; proof that there actually has been a misuse of powers goes to the substance of the case, not its admissibility.[84] Nonetheless, even for admissibility, it would seem that the applicant must produce sufficient evidence to set up a prima facie case.

The restriction imposed by art 33 is not limited to the 'evaluation' of facts and circumstances stricto sensu. As the Court pointed out in Cases 15 and 29/59 *Société Metallurgique de Knutange v High Authority*,[85] it extends to the expediency[86] of the measures adopted because review of expediency would necessarily entail review of the evaluation made. This does not leave discretionary powers unfettered by the possibility of review: as Advocate General Lagrange pointed out in the same case,[87] 'power of discretion does not mean arbitrary power. The High Authority must respect the Treaty and the general principles of law, particularly when it adopts regulations and in doing so makes use of legislative power. Yet it enjoys a margin of discretion within the limits which you [the Court] have already had occasion to trace in some important judgments.' The same applies to evaluations:[88] a decision based on an evaluation is only partly outside the jurisdiction of the Court to review;[89] the power of appraisal given to the institution does not affect the Court's jurisdiction to see if the decision is right in law.[90]

---

81 *Netherlands v High Authority* (above, note 68) at 115.
82 Ibid.
83 See *Valsabbia v Commission* (above, note 80) at para 12.
84 Case 3/54 *ASSIDER v High Authority* [1954–56] ECR 63 at 69; Case 8/55 *Fédération Charbonnière de Belgique v High Authority* [1954–56] ECR 245 at 257.
85 [1960] ECR 1 at 10.
86 'Opportunité'.
87 Above, note 85 at 13.
88 While it is possible to distinguish (subjective) evaluations of facts from (subjective) evaluations of what is an expedient solution to a problem, as defined by an evaluation of facts, the one rests on the other and both characterise a discretionary power. For this reason, the limitation on the Court's powers of review under art 33 of the ECSC Treaty, although expressed to apply to the evaluation of a situation of fact, reveals in substance a general restriction on the review of discretionary powers (cf Asso, above, note 1). The extent of the discretion afforded to a Community institution depends on the Treaty or legislative provision giving it power to act.
89 Cases 36–38 and 40/59 *Geitling Ruhrkohlen-Verkaufsgesellschaft mbH v High Authority* [1960] ECR 423 at 439.
90 Case 14/61 *Koninklijke Nederlandsche Hoogovens en Staalfabrieken NV v High Authority* [1962] ECR 253 at 268. See also at 284 (Advocate General Lagrange); 'legal [sic] control must be exercised in the normal conditions of an application for annulment of a decision. It is for the Court to investigate whether the different reasons stated in the contested decision are, on the one hand, correct in substance and, on the other, such as to justify the decision in law. In particular, the Court must review the administration's concept of the legal nature of the interests which it must take into consideration and it is only within these limits that the discretionary power of the High Authority can be exercised.'

In brief, under art 33 of the ECSC Treaty, the Court has power to determine whether the facts taken into account were correctly found and relevant in law and whether the institution correctly interpreted and applied the law. But it cannot, in general, review the deductions drawn from the facts, including assessments of expediency when a discretionary power is being exercised.

In annulment cases where the Court's powers of review in regard to the facts are not expressly limited by the Treaty provision on which its jurisdiction is founded, the same limitation as that found in art 33 of the ECSC Treaty applies. This can be seen from the first staff case heard by the Court, Case 1/55 *Kergall v Common Assembly*,[91] an action brought under art 42 of the ECSC Treaty. Advocate General Roemer observed: 'in so far as the regularity of an administrative decision is at issue, review by the Court is subject to the same limits as for a direct application for annulment. The Court will therefore examine whether the measure was legal and whether the limits of the discretionary power were respected. But it is not also required to assess whether the administrative measure was appropriate.'[92] In consequence, in that and succeeding cases, the Court held that the evaluation of a person's capacity to carry out his duties falls within the discretion of the appointing authority[93] as does the selection of candidates for a post.[94] At the present time, the Court has unlimited jurisdiction in staff disputes of a financial character by virtue of an express provision to this effect[95] but this was not so when the first staff cases were decided by the Court.

In Case 24/62 *Germany v Commission*,[96] an action under art 173 of the EC Treaty, the Court accepted that its powers of review could be limited, not by the Treaty provision giving it jurisdiction, but by the nature of the powers whose exercise it was reviewing. After examining the relevant articles of the EC Treaty, the Court concluded that the Commission's discretionary power under art 25 was exercised by it independently and without any fetter, subject only to limits which are laid down by the Treaty and whose respect is reviewed by the Court.[97] The same approach was taken in Case 34/62 *Germany v Commission*,[98] also an application made under art 173 of the EC Treaty. Advocate General Roemer said that the exercise of discretionary powers could be reviewed but: 'only the actual area of discretion, to which the balancing and evaluation of the various decisive criteria belong, is not subject to legal [sic] review. It can be submitted to judicial review only by means of a complaint of misuse of powers, so that the Court cannot substitute its own reasons for the reasons why the Executive considered its decisions to be appropriate. There appears to me to be no doubt that the facts upon which a discretionary decision is based are subject to judicial review. In this connection we do not only have to think of the existence of the conditions for action laid down in a provision but also of the whole background of facts which determine and characterise discretionary decisions.'

91 [1954–56] ECR 151: see para A(b) of the judgment and 165 (Advocate General Roemer).
92 'Elle n'est pas tenue d'apprécier aussi l'opportunité de la mesure administrative'.
93 Eg Case 10/55 *Mirossevich v High Authority* [1954–56] ECR 333 at 342 and 351 (Advocate General Lagrange).
94 Eg *Bourgaux v Common Assembly* (above, note 75) at 368 and 374–375 (Advocate General Roemer).
95 Article 91(1) of the Staff Regulations.
96 [1963] ECR 63 at 68.
97 The English version of the judgment is misleading because it can be taken as indicating that the discretionary power is subject to review by the Court. The French version, on the other hand, makes it clear that the Court can only determine whether or not the Commission has overstepped the limits of its discretion; it cannot review the exercise of the discretion itself.
98 [1963] ECR 131 at 146–147 and 152 (Advocate General Roemer).

Similarly, in Case 13/63 *Italy v Commission*[99] the Court declined, in proceedings under art 173, to review an assessment made by the Commission because it was not 'clearly erroneous'. Advocate General Lagrange pointed out that the Commission was free to act within the limits of its discretionary powers and, after examining the facts and matters of the case, he concluded that it had kept within the limits of its 'power of appraisal' and had not made an error of law or of fact. He did, however, hold that the decision in question could be attacked if there were misuse of powers. Review of the Commission's power under art 85(3) of the EC Treaty to grant exemption from art 85(1) is like review of decisions adopted under the corresponding provisions of the ECSC Treaty: 'the exercise of the Commission's powers necessarily implies complex evaluations on economic matters. A judicial review of these evaluations must take account of their nature by confining itself to an examination of the relevance of the facts and of the legal consequences which the Commission deduces therefrom. This review must in the first place be carried out in respect of the reasons given for the decisions which must set out the facts and considerations on which the said evaluations are based.'[1]

The question whether or not there is some limitation on the Court's power to review evaluations of facts depends, in the first place, on whether or not the provision under which the defendant acted granted it a discretionary power. If so, in actions concerning the lawfulness of the defendant's acts, the Court is restricted to determining whether the defendant took into account facts that were relevant in law, whether those facts were correctly found and whether the defendant correctly interpreted the provision authorising it to act. But the Court cannot substitute its own evaluation of the facts for that made by the defendant; its power of review extends to what is reviewable and not to the making of executive decisions.[2] In the nature of things, evaluations of facts and assessments of what is an apposite solution, particularly in complex economic matters, do not always produce answers that can be described objectively as being right or wrong; the more complex the basic facts, the more likely it is that a number of equally acceptable interpretations can be identified. In such circumstances, the Court cannot always say that a decision-making body was wrong to adopt one rather than another. To do so is not to review the decision made, a judicial function, but to remake it, which is, in principle, an executive or administrative function.[3] Apart from proceedings in which the Court has unlimited jurisdiction, the cases in which the Court will, exceptionally, review an evaluation or assessment, which have been mentioned above in connection with references for a preliminary ruling, are instances in which it is possible to

99 Above, note 74 at 178 and 183–184, 189 (Advocate General Lagrange).
1 Cases 56 and 58/64 *Etablissements Consten SARL and Grundig-GmbH v Commission* [1966] ECR 299 at 347; Case 17/74 *Sadolin & Holmblad A/S members of the Transocean Marine Paint Association v Commission* [1974] ECR 1063 (para 16); Case 71/74 *Nederlandse Vereniging voor de Fruit- en Groentenimporthandel (Frubo) v Commission* [1975] ECR 563 (para 43); Case 26/76 *Metro-SB-Grossmärkte GmbH & Co KG v Commission* [1977] ECR 1875 (paras 45 and 50); Case 30/78 *Distillers Co Ltd v Commission* [1980] ECR 2229 at 2286–2287 (Advocate General Warner). Cf Cases 36–38 and 40/59 *Geitling v High Authority* [1960] ECR 423.
2 Cf Cases 35/62 and 16/63 *Leroy v High Authority* [1963] ECR 197 at 207: 'the applicant's criticisms are not directed against the material accuracy of findings of fact which are capable of objective verification, nor against assessments which may be objectively reviewed, but against complex value-judgments the merits of which, by their very nature and subject, cannot be reviewed by the Court'. In Case 29/70 *Marcato v Commission* [1971] ECR 243 (para 7) the Court declined to review an assessment involving 'complex value judgments which, by their very nature, are not capable of objective proof'.
3 See generally Lagasse *L'Erreur Manifeste d'Appréciation en Droit Administratif* (Brussels, 1986).

say that the evaluation or assessment is, for one reason or another, objectively wrong.[4]

In relation to those matters of fact that may be in issue in the proceedings before the Court, facts alleged by one party which are not disputed by the other party are often (but not invariably) considered to be established, with the consequence that their formal proof becomes unnecessary.[5] Facts in issue must ordinarily be proved by sufficient evidence adduced by the party alleging the fact or in the course of a measure of enquiry ordered by the Court. A submission which is unsupported by evidence will be rejected.[6]

III   Proof of law

Although proof of facts is of particular concern here, it is not out of place to consider briefly at this stage the proof of law, both Community and 'foreign' law, whether it be that of a member state or a third country.

Community law may be proved by reference to the official texts of the Treaties or other instruments or by reference to the Official Journal. Not all measures having legal effect may be published in the Official Journal. The Statutes provide[7] that an application commencing proceedings for annulment must be accompanied by the measure challenged in the action. Ordinarily, production of a document which appears to embody the measure in question is sufficient proof of the measure to satisfy that procedural rule; but that does not preclude any dispute over the questions whether or not the document at issue actually embodies the measure, whether or not the measure has the required legal characteristics (for example, whether or not it constitutes in law a challengeable act) and whether or not it exists at all.[8] Certified copies of judgments of the Court are provided to the parties;[9] authenticated copies are obtainable on request.[10] For the purposes of argument (as opposed to enforcement) decisions of the Court are normally established by citation from the *European Court Reports*. Proof of the meaning of a text of Community law is to be found in the authentic text. Where there are several authentic texts in different

---

4 To these cases may be added Case 13/69 *van Eick v Commission* [1970] ECR 3 at 21 (Advocate General Roemer), Case 46/72 *De Greef v Commission* [1973] ECR 543 (para 46) and Case 228/83 *F v Commission* [1985] ECR 275 (para 34), staff cases in which the Court did not have unlimited jurisdiction, and in which it was held that an evaluation or assessment could be reviewed only if it contained an obvious error or was outrageously severe (*van Eick*) or was clearly excessive or an abuse of power (*De Greef*) or a manifest error or misuse of powers (*F v Commission*). A common lawyer would probably have said that the question was whether a reasonable person could have come to such a conclusion on the facts (cf Case 34/80 *Authié v Commission* [1981] ECR 665 at 689 (Advocate General Warner); the Court referred in para 13 of the judgment to 'exceeding the limits of authority' and 'mistake'). In view of the wide range of formulations adopted at different times, it seems clearer to say that the test is whether the evaluation or assessment is objectively wrong (cf Case 343/82 *Michael v Commission* [1983] ECR 4023 (para 24)).

5 Cf Case 21/84 *Commission v France* [1985] ECR 1355 (para 10); Case C-375/90 *Commission v Greece* [1993] ECR I-2055 (paras 29 and 34–35).

6 Case 346/82 *Favre v Commission* [1984] ECR 2269 (paras 31–32).

7 ECSC Statute, art 22; EC and Euratom Statutes, art 19.

8 See, for example, Cases T-79, T-84 to T-86, T-89, T-91, T-92, T-94, T-96, T-98, T-102 and T-104/89 *BASF AG v Commission* [1992] ECR II-315 (Re PVC Cartel), where what had every appearance of being a Commission decision was found on investigation to be non-existent as such.

9 RP-ECJ 64(2); RP-CFI 82(2).

10 Cf IR 20.

languages, they must all be taken into account as evidence of the meaning.[11] Drafts and other preparatory material may constitute proof of the intention of or the object sought to be achieved by the draftsmen[12] but are not proof of the meaning of the text itself.[13]

There are no rules relating to the proof of 'foreign' law. The only question relates to the weight which can be attached to the evidence submitted to the Court. Photocopies of official publications setting out the text of legislation or court decisions are adequate proof; so may be testimony from a witness.[14] In the case of the national laws of the member states, the Court is aided by its Research and Documentation Division and the knowledge and expertise of its members. It is not, therefore, constrained to rely on the presentations made by the parties, even by agreement between them, and may, indeed, reject views which do not accord with its own knowledge.[15] In references for a preliminary ruling, the Court does not question statements of national law made by the referring court in the order for reference[16] but, in the absence of any such statements, it may draw inferences from information provided by the parties or from the evidence.[17]

11 The sole authentic text of the ECSC Treaty is French (see art 100) but the EEC and Euratom Treaties were drawn up in four equally authentic texts: German, French, Italian and Dutch (arts 248 and 225 respectively). The Official Journal was in the beginning published in the four original official languages of the Communities. After the accession to the Community of first Denmark, Ireland and the United Kingdom, then Greece and, more recently, Spain and Portugal, the Official Journal also began to be published in Danish, English, Greek, Spanish and Portuguese. Various pre-accession acts were translated into the languages of the new members and are authentic versions as from the date of accession: see, for example, art 155 of the 1972 Act of Accession, as amended, and art 147 of the 1979 Act of Accession. The Acts of Accession also provide that the Danish, English, Greek, Portuguese and Spanish texts of the EEC and Euratom Treaties are authentic versions (see, for example, arts 160 and 152 respectively of the 1972 and 1979 Acts of Accession). The authentic version of judgments of the Court is that drawn up in the language of the case: RP-ECJ 31; RP-CFI 37.
12 See, for example, Case 6/54 *Netherlands v High Authority* [1954–56] ECR 103 at 116.
13 See, for example, Case 155/79 *AM & S Europe Ltd v Commission* [1982] ECR 1575, per Advocate General Warner. For a review of methods of interpretation used by the Court, see the reports to the Judicial and Academic Conference, held by the Court in 1976, presented by Judge Kutscher and F Dumon; and *Law of the European Communities* (ed Vaughan), paras 2.280 et seq.
14 There are no rules concerning the qualifications necessary for giving evidence of 'foreign' law.
15 See, for example, *AM & S v Commission* (above, note 13) per Advocate General Sir Gordon Slynn at 1651.
16 Eg Case 116/84 *Criminal proceedings against Henri Roelstraete* [1985] ECR 1705 (para 10).
17 Case 293/83 *Gravier v City of Liège* [1985] ECR 593 (paras 3, 13 and 14).

CHAPTER 11

Measures of enquiry

I Introduction

The parties do not have a right or power to submit evidence save in the case of documentary evidence which is in their possession. The power to submit such evidence is set out in RP-ECJ 37(4) and RP-CFI 43(4), which provide that, to every pleading, there must be annexed the documents relied on in support of it.[1] However, this power is really a duty binding the parties to submit the relevant evidence, rather than a right or privilege to do so. A similar duty binds Community institutions, in proceedings under the ECSC Treaty against decisions adopted by them, to transmit to the Court all the documents relating to the case.[2] In so far as other forms of evidence are concerned, there is no duty to present such evidence to the Court but a duty to specify its existence in the pleadings.[3] It should be noted that, save in relation to the duty binding Community institutions in proceedings under the ECSC Treaty, the duty to produce documents in the party's possession or to specify other sources of evidence is restricted to material which the party wishes to rely on. There is no duty[4] to produce evidence which contradicts one's own case.

Necessity imposes on the parties the obligation to do all in their power to ensure that the Court is in possession of everything that is needed for it to decide the issues of fact in their favour. For this, as will be seen, the parties must provide the Court with adequate material on which to judge precisely what measures of enquiry, if any, are to be ordered. Beyond that, there is authority that the parties lie under a duty owed to the Court to ensure that evidence and sources of evidence are placed before it fairly and accurately; it seems to follow from this that they are also under a duty not to mislead the Court as to the existence or non-existence of a relevant fact, whether by act or omission, by word or by silence. In one case,[5] Advocate General Lagrange said that the adversary nature of proceedings in a direct action obliged the parties 'to collaborate with a view to enabling the Court to decide, with all the facts at its disposal', an issue before it. It seems to be this duty which led him to say: 'even when the defendant is an administrative body it must, at least within certain limits, produce the documents or the information which it alone possesses in its capacity as a public authority'. Unfortunately, such a principle is incorporated expressly only in art 23 of the ECSC Statute, which has a

---

1 The Court may also allow a party to produce a thing for its inspection, see below, p 402.
2 ECSC Statute, art 23.
3 See RP-ECJ 38(1)(e) and 40(1)(d); RP-CFI 44(1)(e) and 46(1)(d).
4 Outside art 23 of the ECSC Statute. It is, of course, arguable that this provision simply reflects a general principle of judicial control of administrative action in the Community.
5 Cases 29, 31, 36, 39–47, 50 and 51/63 *Laminoirs Hauts Fourneaux, Forges Fonderies et Usines de la Providence SA v High Authority* [1965] ECR 911 at 944.

limited field of application.[6] As far as the duty lying on the Community institutions is concerned, Advocate General Lagrange is something of a voice crying in the wilderness because, in practice, the institutions are almost notorious for their reticence.[7]

The same responsibilities exist in references for a preliminary ruling as in direct actions. The only difference is that the scope of any enquiries which may be made by the Court is limited in the former by the questions set out in the order for reference and in the latter by the parties in their pleadings. The Court can exercise its powers of investigation only to the extent that they are necessary for resolving the issues with which it is seised: It is not entitled to indulge in an investigation going beyond the confines of the action as determined by the parties' pleadings or the order for reference. Nevertheless, although its jurisdiction in a case is limited to the issues of fact to which the case gives rise, the Court's powers of investigation are not restricted by the nature of the evidence or sources of evidence adduced by the parties. No party has a right to prove facts in any particular way. Hence the Court is not obliged to restrict its investigation of the facts to the documents produced in the pleadings;[8] it is not bound to accede to a party's desire to prove a fact by, for example, the testimony of a string of witnesses. The means to prove facts lie within the discretion of the Court to order.[9]

6 But it also seems to apply to staff cases. In Case 18/70 *Duraffour v Council* [1971] ECR 515 (para 31), the Court held that 'it is for the defendant institution, as the appointing authority, to cooperate with those claiming under one of its servants in order to discover the truth'. See also at 533 (Advocate General Roemer).

7 For example, in Case 52/81 *Firma Werner Faust OHG v Commission* [1982] ECR 3745, the Commission had asked certain third country producers to limit their exports to the Community and then had suspended the issue of import licences save in regard to goods from countries which had agreed to self-limitation. There was an issue concerning the negotiations between the Commission and the third countries involved prior to the suspension of the issue of import licences. The applicant produced a series of telexes, passing between third parties, which showed that the Commission had asked Taiwan to export no more than a certain amount and that Taiwan had agreed to this limitation before the suspension. There was, however, no direct evidence that the telex containing the Taiwanese agreement to limit exports was shown to the Commission. The Commission asserted that there had been no self-limitation agreement with Taiwan (but produced no documents or other evidence) and that the suspension of import licences in respect of products from Taiwan was therefore lawful. Subsequently, in Case 245/81 *Edeka Zentrale AG v Germany* [1982] ECR 2745, a reference for a preliminary ruling which gave rise to the same issue, the Court asked the Commission to give further information about the negotiation of the self-limitation agreements with third countries. The Commission, represented by the same person as in the *Faust* case, replied in writing and again asserted (without producing any documents, etc) that there had been no agreement with Taiwan. At the hearing, however, counsel for Edeka relied strongly on the telexes produced in the *Faust* case and, in the face of this, the Commission's representative finally admitted that the Commission had known of the Taiwanese reply to its request to limit exports before the issue of import licences was suspended. The Commission had, in fact, simply ignored the Taiwanese guarantee for what were said to be administrative reasons but it is extraordinary that this was never said in the *Faust* case and that no documents or other evidence were ever produced. The result of this behaviour was to leave the Court, at least until the hearing in the *Edeka* case, with the impression that the Commission had never known of the Taiwanese telex.

8 In Case T-3/90 *Prodifarma v Commission* [1991] ECR II-1 (para 3) the Court of its own motion took account of the facts set out in the file in a connected case.

9 Eg Case T-1/90 *Pérez-Mínguez Casariego v Commission* [1991] ECR II-143 (para 94); Case T-26/89 *De Compte v European Parliament* [1991] ECR II-781 (paras 224–229); Case T-53/91 *Merger v Commission* [1992] ECR II-2041 (para 26); Case T-33/91 *Williams v Court of Auditors* [1992] ECR II-2499 (para 31).

II   Ordering a measure of enquiry

At the close of pleadings, the Court considers the case in an administrative meeting and decides what further steps are necessary for its swift and efficient disposal. Among these steps is the acquisition of further evidence. RP-ECJ 45(1) and RP-CFI 66(1) state that the Court 'shall prescribe the measures of enquiry that it considers appropriate by means of an order setting out the facts to be proved', after hearing the views of the advocate general. These measures are defined in RP-ECJ 45(2) and RP-CFI 65 'without prejudice' to the powers of the Court set out in arts 24 and 25 of the ECSC Statute, 21 and 22 of the EC Statute and 22 and 23 of the Euratom Statute. Under the Statutes, the Court may require to produce all documents and to supply all information which it considers desirable (i) the parties,[10] (ii) their representatives or agents[11] or (iii) the governments of the member states.[12] It may also require to supply all information which it considers necessary for the proceedings (i) those member states or (ii) those Community institutions which are not parties to the case.[13] In addition, the Court may entrust 'any individual, body, authority, committee or other organisation it chooses' with the task of giving an expert opinion[14] or holding an enquiry.[15] The Statutes also provide for the hearing of witnesses[16] and for the examination of the parties themselves.[17] RP-ECJ 45(2) and RP-CFI 65 specify five types of measure of enquiry that the Court may order:

(1)   the personal appearance of the parties;
(2)   a request for information and production of documents;
(3)   oral testimony;
(4)   experts' reports; or
(5)   an inspection of the place or thing in question.

This is not a list of the means of proving a fact but an enumeration of the powers which the Court may exercise; it is not exhaustive because it is 'without prejudice' to the powers contained in the articles of the Statutes expressly referred to.

Despite the fact that it is for the Court to order a measure of enquiry, the burden lies, in the first instance, on the parties, in a direct action, to indicate the steps necessary for the purpose of investigating an issue of fact. The inquisitorial character of proceedings in a direct action extends only to the method of obtaining evidence; it remains the responsibility of the parties to set up their own cases.[18] To begin with, the relevant facts must be put in issue: if the facts are not disputed[19] or not disputed in any serious

---

10   ECSC Statute, art 24; EC Statute, art 21; Euratom Statute, art 22.
11   ECSC Statute, ibid.
12   Ibid.
13   EC Statute, art 21; Euratom Statute, art 22; it will be observed that the Court does not have the same power, in so far as Community institutions are concerned, under the ECSC Statute.
14   ECSC Statute, art 25; EC Statute, art 22; Euratom Statute, art 23.
15   ECSC Statute, ibid.
16   ECSC Statute, art 28; EC Statute, art 23; Euratom Statute, art 24.
17   ECSC Statute, ibid; EC Statute, art 29; Euratom Statute, art 30.
18   In the case of actions brought by the Commission against member states, it has been said that it is for the Commission, and not the Court, to ensure that all necessary evidence is before the Court: Case 169/82 *Commission v Italy* [1984] ECR 1603 at 1631 (Advocate General VerLoren van Themaat); Case 141/87 *Commission v Italy* [1989] ECR 943 (para 17 and at 972, Advocate General Jacobs).
19   See Case 21/84 *Commission v France* [1985] ECR 1355 (para 10).

way,[20] the Court may well conclude that there is sufficient evidence available to make appropriate findings of fact without the need for any measure of enquiry. Where a party alleges a fact or seeks to put in issue a fact alleged by another party, it is not enough to rely on assertion alone; there must be at least the appearance of some substance behind the assertion. By way of example, in Cases 42 and 49/59 *SNUPAT v High Authority*[21] an intervener based certain arguments on the wording of a contract which it did not produce because it was confidential. The Court held that, since it was relying on a document in its own possession, it should have adduced proof of its allegations by disclosing the contract: 'it is not acceptable to rely on the Court to take the initiative in obtaining for itself by measures of enquiry information intended to prove the cogency of the argument relied upon by the intervener, which itself possesses that information'. The Court 'taking note of the reservations and hesitations' of the intervener, did not order production and simply said that it was unnecessary to consider the arguments because of lack of proof.[22] A similar situation arose in Case 14/64 *Gualco (née Barge) v High Authority*.[23] There a series of arguments was put forward by the applicant, who did not produce any documents to 'support her assertions or render them plausible'. The Court therefore rejected them as unfounded, holding that there was no need to order the measures of enquiry (testimony) suggested by the applicant on the ground, seemingly, that, by failing to produce any evidence at all, she had failed to set up the arguments as worthwhile to investigate, even though all the evidence had in fact been in her possession or at her disposal. The offers of proof, the Court held, 'are not supported by any facts worthy of consideration'.[24] The necessity to plead specifically was again emphasised in Case 51/65 *ILFO v High Authority*,[25] where the applicant asked for measures of enquiry to be adopted, including the ordering of an expert's report, and said that it was ready to produce all necessary documents to prove its allegations. The Court rejected this because no evidence had been adduced to justify such measures and the grounds on which the application was based were also 'too imprecise'. Advocate General Gand said measures of enquiry 'could only be ordered if the applicant first put forward specific facts . . . of such a nature as to justify further study and a reconsideration of the High Authority's decision'. In Cases 19 and 65/63 *Prakash v Euratom Commission*[26] the Court said that the ordering of

---

20 See Case C-96/89 *Commission v Netherlands* [1991] ECR I-2461 (paras 21–22), where the applicant relied on inferences drawn from the documents while the defendant failed to indicate any basis on which those inferences could be said to be unfounded; Case C-110/89 *Commission v Greece* [1991] ECR I-2659 (paras 10–16 and at 2680–2682, Advocate General Lenz), where the applicant's case was based inter alia on newspaper reports but the defendant failed to adduce any evidence to counter that relied on by the applicant, despite being invited to do so, and proved unable to explain itself effectively.
21 [1961] ECR 53.
22 Ibid, at 84 and 85.
23 [1965] ECR 51.
24 Ibid at 59–60. See also Case 2/65 *Preo e Figli v High Authority* [1966] ECR 219 at 231 (Advocate General Gand). The parties had agreed that an expert should be appointed to ascertain the facts but, for a reason not mentioned in the report, he did not do so. The applicant then asked for witnesses to be heard. The advocate general said that this request should be rejected for several reasons: (i) the applicant had declined to have the matter settled by an expert; (ii) 'it limits itself to bringing before you mere allegations quite unsupported by any shred of evidence'; and (iii) it was 'hazardous' to prove facts as remote in time as those in question by means of witnesses who were mostly employees of the applicant. The second reason was, he said, sufficient to reject the request. See also Case 119/81 *Kloeckner AG v Commission* [1982] ECR 2627 (para 8).
25 [1966] ECR 87 at 96–97 and 101.
26 [1965] ECR 533 at 554.

an expert's report in order to resolve an issue of fact would be justified only if the facts already proved raised a presumption in favour of the applicant's argument because the burden of proof rested on him. In Case T-156/89 *Mordt v Court of Justice*[27] the applicant raised a point at the hearing but did not develop the factual basis for it so the CFI concluded that there was no reason to order a measure of enquiry.[28]

The conclusions to be drawn from the cases cited seem to be the following: the Court will not undertake a fishing expedition on behalf of one of the parties; for this reason, simply to raise an argument is not sufficient to cause the Court to investigate its basis in fact; some justification must be put forward to show that the matter is worth investigating further. This appears to mean that a contention must be supported by sufficient evidence or indications as to make it arguable. If a party refrains from producing, for this purpose, (documentary) evidence which is in its possession or at its disposal, the Court may infer that the contention is not supported by sufficient evidence and refuse to order a measure of enquiry.[29] For a measure of enquiry to be ordered, it must be shown, then, that:

(1)   an argument has been raised which is relevant to deciding the case;[30]
(2)   the argument cannot be accepted or rejected without finding certain facts;
(3)   a measure of enquiry is necessary in order to find those facts.[31]

So far as the first of these requirements is concerned, a relevant argument is one which is pertinent to the resolution of the dispute, ie one whose acceptance or rejection determines whether the relief sought is to be granted or not, either directly or indirectly.[32] At the close of pleadings it is usually possible to decide which arguments are relevant and which are not. At that stage, which is the point at which the decision to order a measure of enquiry is usually made, all the relevant arguments are still to be considered by the Court although, in the judgment, it may find that one issue settles the case and it is not necessary to decide the others. As a matter of principle, it is not possible to establish whether an argument is necessary, as opposed to relevant, to the decision in the action, before the parties have fully presented their cases to the court and the advocate general has delivered his opinion. Even then, some points may require further clarification, which is why the Court has power to reopen the oral procedure and to order a measure of enquiry at any time.[33] In consequence, sufficient evidence should be obtained to find the facts relating to all

---

27   [1991] ECR II-407 (para 126).
28   See also Case 323/87 *Commission v Italy* [1989] ECR 2275 (at 2296, Advocate General Jacobs).
29   Thus, in Cases 169/83 and 138/84 *Leussinck-Brummelhuis v Commission* [1986] ECR 2801 (paras 16–17), where the defendant was best able to provide evidence on a particular issue of fact, but did not do so, the uncertainty as to what was the truth led the Court to accept the applicant's contentions. This is not invariably the practice: in Case T-35/89 *Albani v Commission* [1990] ECR II-395 (paras 48–49), the Court ordered one party to produce documents in order to enable it to discharge the burden of proof under which it lay.
30   Cf Case 403/85 *F v Commission* [1987] ECR 645 (para 9), where the measure of enquiry sought did not relate to matters relevant to the legal issues in the case.
31   In some cases, those requirements are rolled up into one: thus, in Case 212/86 *Imperial Chemical Industries plc v Commission*, order of 11 December 1986 (reported sub nom Case T-13/89 *Imperial Chemical Industries plc v Commission* [1991] ECR II-1021, see per Judge Vesterdorf at [1991] ECR II-867 at 889–891), where a request was made under RP-ECJ 91 for the production of documents, the Court held that the test was whether or not production was indispensable for the judicial review of the contested act.
32   Cf Case 224/87 *Koutchoumoff v Commission* [1989] ECR 99 (para 19), where the measure of enquiry did not relate to an issue that the Court had to decide.
33   RP-ECJ 60 and 61; RP-CFI 49 and 62.

the relevant arguments, not just the most important or promising ones. In practice, however, it often happens that a measure of enquiry is not ordered or, where there has been a formal application for such a measure to be ordered, the decision to order a measure of enquiry is reserved to the judgment in the action simply because it appears to the Court at the close of the written procedure that the case may be decided on a ground other than that to which the proposed measure of enquiry relates.[34] Thus, in practice (and whatever principle may suggest), a measure of enquiry will not usually be ordered unless it is necessary in order to decide a point that is not merely relevant but essential to the disposal of the case.

In relation to the second requirement referred to above, the question whether or not a particular argument or point cannot be accepted or rejected without finding certain facts needs no further elaboration. In contrast, the third requirement (that a measure of enquiry is necessary in order to find the relevant facts) does merit further exploration. In dealing with this requirement, it should be borne in mind that the proposal to order a measure of enquiry may emanate from the Court itself, from the party seeking to establish a particular point or from the party contesting an assertion made by an opposing party. The Court will not order a measure of enquiry of its own motion unless it has concluded that the evidence before it is deficient in some material respect.[35] In that sense, the Court's assessment of the need for a measure of enquiry is objective: the Court's concern is to decide the case properly; it has no interest in any particular outcome to the case. Where the initiative comes from a party, the test to be applied by the Court is in principle the same: the party applying for a measure of enquiry must demonstrate that the evidence before the Court is deficient and that the measure of enquiry sought is both necessary and sufficient to make up for that deficiency.[36] Where the measure is sought by the party asserting the existence of the fact in

---

34 Eg Case 118/83 *CMC Cooperativa Muratori e Cementisti v Commission* [1985] ECR 2325 (paras 20–25), where the application for the production of documents was reserved to the final judgment and, in the meantime, the opposing party voluntarily produced cetain documents, thus obviating the need for a formal order (the course of events incidentally demonstrates the disadvantages of reserving the decision on the application to the final judgment: if the opposing party had not produced the documents voluntarily, what would the Court have done in the final judgment?). The complications and delays that may arise when the ordering of a measure of enquiry is left until late in the procedure can be illustrated by Case T-169/89 *Frederiksen v European Parliament* [1991] ECR II-1403 (paras 34–44).

35 Thus, in Case 246/84 *Kotsonis v Council* [1986] ECR 3989 (para 20) the Court heard evidence because there were discrepancies in the documentary evidence before it. In Case C-169/84 *Société CdF Chimie Azote et fertilisants SA and Société Chimique de la Grande Paroisse SA v Commission* [1990] ECR I-3083 (para 28) an expert's report was ordered because the parties had provided contradictory information concerning certain facts in issue. In contrast, in Case C-248/89 *Cargill BV v Commission* [1991] ECR I-2987, the advocate general advised the Court to accept the defendant's offer of proof of a fact and the Court therefore decided that there was no need to verify the fact by hearing testimony. In Case 105/87 *Morabito v European Parliament* [1988] ECR 1707 (para 7), a case where the defendant failed to lodge a defence within time, the Court held that, since the applicant's assertions were supported by documentary evidence, they could be regarded as proved for the purposes of the proceedings.

36 So, in Cases 19 and 65/63 *Prakash v Commission* and Case 83/63 *Krawczynski v Euratom Commission* [1965] ECR 533 and 623, at 561 and 641 respectively, the Court took the view that it was not necessary to admit the offers of proof made by the parties because it had all the information necessary to decide the dispute. See also Case 16/67 *Labeyrie v Commission* [1968] ECR 293 at 304; Case 110/75 *Mills v European Investment Bank* [1976] ECR 1613 at 1635, where Advocate General Warner said that a document produced to the Court need not be served on the other party because it did not, in his view, say anything new; Case T-1/90 *Pérez-Mínguez Casariego v Commission* [1991] ECR II-143 (para 94); Case T-53/91 *Merger v Commission* [1992] ECR II-2041 (para 26).

question, the nature and source of the evidence are clearly relevant: if the nature of the evidence is documentary and if the relevant documents can be expected to be in the possession of the party in question, the need for a measure of enquiry is questionable (because, in principle, all the relevant evidence should be attached to the party's pleadings) and the fact that that party has requested a measure of enquiry tends to suggest that the assertion of fact is unsupported by relevant evidence. The position is different where the nature of the evidence (such as where it takes the form of testimony) or its source (such as where it is documentary in nature but the documents are in the possession of another party or a third party) is such that the party making the assertion could not adduce the evidence in the absence of a Court order. Even in such circumstances, whether or not an order will be made depends in large part on the attitude of the opposing party. Where the existence of the asserted fact is conceded by the opposing party, there is, of course, no need for a measure of enquiry because the fact is not in issue. Where the opposing party denies the asserted fact, it is in issue and, in principle, a measure of enquiry is necessary. However, there are cases where the Court has refused to order a measure of enquiry sought by a party opposing an assertion of fact made by the other party on the ground that, in order to obtain such an order, a party must demonstrate that there are doubts about the accuracy of the other party's assertions.[37] Thus, where a party makes an assertion of fact or, at the least, a prima facie plausible assertion, it is not enough simply to deny the assertion; the opposing party must indicate that there is some reasonable doubt about the assertion. In consequence, whether the measure of enquiry is sought by the party making the assertion or the party opposing it, the factor determining whether or not a measure of enquiry is ordered is whether or not there is a reasonable doubt about the truth of the assertion. The position is different where the assertion is one of law, even though it is dependent upon the existence or otherwise of certain facts. Thus, in Case C-49/88 *Al-Jubail Fertiliser Co v Council*[38] it was held that the mere assertion that the rights of the defence have been respected is not good enough; evidence to support the assertion must be produced.

In relation to measures of enquiry sought by a party, an additional factor to be taken into account is the nature and extent of the measure of enquiry sought. The fact that there is a reasonable doubt about the truthfulness of an assertion does not justify the making of an order that is disproportionate.[39] Therefore, a measure of enquiry will not be ordered if it is unnecessary to investigate the facts for the purpose of accepting or rejecting a relevant argument. For example, in Case 3/65 *SA Métallurgique d'Espérance-Longdoz v High Authority*[40] the Court refused to accede to the applicant's request that

---

37 Eg Case 171/86 *USINOR v Commission*, order of 28 January 1987, para 21 (the case was subsequently withdrawn). In Case C-157/89 *Commission v Italy* [1991] ECR I-57 (para 15 and at 77 and 80, Advocate General van Gerven), the Court did not order any preparatory enquiries but asked the parties to specify, on the basis of scientific publications, their factual allegations; the defendant disputed the probative value of the publications relied on by the Commission but that objection was dismissed on the ground that the defendant had not produced alternative scientific studies challenging the data relied on by the other party. In Case C-96/89 *Commission v Netherlands* [1991] ECR I-2461 (paras 21–22) the defendant failed to produce the slightest evidence ('*commencement de preuve*') to contradict the applicant's assertions. In Case C-110/89 *Commission v Greece* [1991] ECR I-2659 (at 2680–2682, Advocate General Lenz) the applicant's evidence comprised newspaper reports but the defendant failed to produce anything to affect the value of that evidence.

38 [1991] ECR I-3187 (para 20 and the opinion of Advocate General Darmon, para 83).

39 Case 171/86 *USINOR v Commission*, (above, note 37) para 23.

40 [1965] ECR 1065 at 1084; see also Case T-82/89 *Marcato v Commission* [1990] ECR II-735 (para 81).

witnesses be examined because, even if the facts alleged were true, the claim would still have to be rejected; in Cases 15 and 29/59 *Société Métallurgique de Knutange v High Authority*[41] the Court declined to examine certain disputed facts because they could not influence the decision in the case; and in Case 21/64 *Macchiorlatti Dalmas and Figli v High Authority*[42] the Court did not hear testimony because its content would not have revealed a fact capable of supporting the point being made. In Case 60/82 *Cowood v Commission*[43] the Court invited the applicant to suggest the names of witnesses who might give evidence on the issues of fact. The Court decided not to hear the witnesses proposed because, even if that evidence could be accepted, it did not relate to any relevant facts.[44]

Once it is established that an enquiry is necessary in order to ascertain the existence of a relevant fact, the question arises, what measure of enquiry is to be adopted? It is up to the parties to indicate in their pleadings the precise method of proving a fact which is most appropriate. In the case of witnesses this is done by specifying the person or persons to be called to give evidence and explaining why they are competent to do so in relation to the facts in question.[45] The same approach should, it seems, be adopted, mutatis mutandis, as far as other sources of evidence are concerned. The Court will not order a measure of enquiry if the evidence that may be obtained is obviously unreliable,[46] a fortiori if the party requesting the measure of enquiry has declined to produce or assent to the production of more trustworthy evidence.[47] In Case 35/67 *Van Eick v Commission*[48] the Court laid down rules for the exercise, by a Disciplinary Board convened under the Staff Regulations, of the power to call witnesses. It held that the Board was 'bound in the exercise of its powers to observe the fundamental principles of the law of procedure', so it would appear that the same rules bind the Court. Hence: 'In accordance with these principles [the Court] could not refuse to comply with an application for the examination of witnesses, once this request clearly indicates the facts on which there is reason to hear the witness or witnesses named and the reasons which are likely to justify their examination. It is, however, for the [Court] to assess both the relevance of the application in relation to the subject matter of the dispute and the need to examine the witnesses named. The [Court] could, in principle, take the view that the examination of only some of the witnesses called by the applicant was sufficient for the purposes of the enquiry into the case.'

If the parties do not request the ordering of a measure of enquiry, the Court

---

41 [1960] ECR 1 at 8; see also Case 13/60 *Geitling Ruhrkohlen-Verkaufsgesellschaft mbH v High Authority* [1962] ECR 83 at 116, where the Court did not consider errors of fact (sc 'trifling' discrepancies of fact) which did not in fact or in law affect the decision at issue; Case 29/70 *Marcato v Commission* [1971] ECR 243 at 247; Case C-106/90R *Emerald Meats Ltd v Commission* [1990] ECR I-3377 (paras 28–30).

42 [1965] ECR 175 at 189.

43 [1982] ECR 4625.

44 See also *Williams v Court of Auditors* above, note 9 (para 31).

45 See RP-ECJ 47(1), last sentence; RP-CFI 68(1), last sentence; and see further below, pp 388 et seq.

46 See, for example, *Gualco (née Barge) v High Authority* and *Preo e figli v High Authority* (above, notes 23 and 24 at 66 and 231 respectively (Advocates General Roemer and Gand): in both cases the applicant requested witnesses to be called to give evidence in respect of events taking place several years beforehand. Both advocates general doubted the competence of the persons concerned to give reliable testimony in view of the lapse of time. In the first case there was further reason for doubt because the applicant did not indicate why the witnesses would be in a position to give relevant testimony; in the second, the advocate general drew attention to the fact that the witnesses were employees of the applicant.

47 Ibid at 59 and 231 respectively.

48 [1968] ECR 329 at 342. Cf Cases 43 and 63/82 *VBVB and VBBB v Commission* [1984] ECR 19 (para 18).

can, of course, consider the matter of its own motion. Although it is not bound to accede to a request that is made, it should do so, as the *van Eick* case shows, in so far as the issues of fact are relevant and the measure sought is necessary or appropriate for the resolution of the issues.

III   Conduct of measures of enquiry

The Court has power at any time to order a measure of enquiry to be taken or a previous enquiry to be repeated or expanded, after hearing the views of the advocate general.[49] A measure of enquiry is normally ordered after the close of pleadings and prior to the opening of the oral procedure. It would appear that the Court does not order a measure of enquiry to be taken or repeat or expand a previous enquiry unless it seems to it to be appropriate to do so in order to decide the case.[50] The parties may apply for a measure of enquiry to be ordered but, at least in the case of an application made after the close of the oral procedure, it may be admitted only 'if it relates to facts which are capable of having a decisive influence and which the party concerned was not able to put forward before the close of the oral procedure'.[51] In most cases the Court reopens the oral procedure when it orders a measure of enquiry after the advocate general has delivered his opinion but this is not necessary. The parties' right to be heard on the evidence is inherent in any measure of enquiry and it is not necessary to reopen the oral procedure in order to allow them to comment on the results of the enquiry.[52] This would be necessary, however, if the advocate general were to be allowed to make his views known formally.

A measure of enquiry is prescribed by a Court order, made after hearing the views of the advocate general, which sets out the facts to be proved and is served on the parties.[53] The procedure followed is dealt with in detail below in relation to each type of measure. In essence, the enquiry is conducted by the Court, a chamber or the judge-rapporteur.[54] It is very rare for the full Court to

49 RP-ECJ 60; RP-CFI 49. See, for example, Case 5/67 *Beus GmbH & Co v Hauptzollamt München Landsbergerstrasse* [1968] ECR 83 (note p 107) (a reference for a preliminary ruling); *Preo v High Authority*, (above, note 24 at 255) (there was no second advocate general's opinion); Case 43/74 *Guillot v Commission* [1977] ECR 1309 at 1323 (witnesses were heard after the first hearing and the Court then adjourned proceedings to allow the parties to submit written observations); Case 190/73 *Officier van Justitie v van Haaster* [1974] ECR 1123 at 1128 (reference for a preliminary ruling); Case 111/63 *Lemmerz-Werke GmbH v High Authority* [1965] ECR 677 at 688; Case 37/64 *Mannesmann AG v High Authority* [1965] ECR 725 at 738; Case 36/72 *Meganck v Commission* [1973] ECR 527 at 529 (the oral procedure was not reopened as well); *Duraffour v Council* (above, note 6); *Usines de la Providence v High Authority* (above, note 5); Case 40/79 *P v Commission* [1981] ECR 361 at 370 (the oral procedure was not reopened); Case 785/79 *Pizziolo v Commission* [1981] ECR 969; Case 170/78 *Commission v United Kingdom* [1980] ECR 417 (Re Excise Duties on Wine).
50 Case 12/68 *X v Audit Board* [1969] ECR 109 at 121 (Advocate General Gand) (cf RP-ECJ 45(1)); see chapter 2, pp 77–78 and 88–90.
51 Case 77/70 *Prelle v Commission* [1971] ECR 561 at 566, and the authorities cited above at pp 88–90.
52 See RP-ECJ 45(4) and 46(2) and (3); RP-CFI 66(2) and 67. The oral procedure was not reopened in, for example, *Preo v High Authority*, *Meganck v Commission* and *P v Commission* (above, notes 24 and 49). In some cases, however, it may be necessary to reopen the oral procedure if new evidence is admitted, in order to allow the other party to comment upon it: see *Mills v European Investment Bank* (above, note 36 at 1635) (Advocate General Warner).
53 RP-ECJ 45(1); RP-CFI 66(1). The order may be amended or supplemented with little difficulty. In Case T-35/89 *Albani v Commission* (above, note 29) at paras 26–33 the Court had ordered two witnesses to be examined on a certain day. On the day in question, one of the parties suggested that a third person be examined and the Court so ordered.
54 RP-ECJ 45(3) and 46(1); RP-CFI 67(1).

be involved.[55] Normally each case heard before the ECJ is assigned to a chamber for the purpose of carrying out any preparatory enquiries, even before these are envisaged,[56] and the chamber exercises the powers vested in the Court under the Rules of Procedure, the President of the chamber similarly exercising those of the President of the Court.[57] Cases heard before the CFI are assigned to and dealt with by a chamber unless the matter is referred to the full Court; in consequence, any preparatory enquiries are carried out by a chamber unless they are entrusted to the judge-rapporteur.[58] In cases before the ECJ it is rare for an enquiry to be entrusted to the judge-rapporteur alone.[59] The advocate general 'takes part' in the measure of enquiry, whoever is entrusted with it, but does not 'conduct' it.[60]

Not all enquiries necessitate a hearing but some, eg oral testimony, do. The Rules of Procedure are silent on how the hearing is to be conducted in the context of an enquiry managed by the full Court or the judge-rapporteur. In the case of the ECJ, RP-ECJ 46(2) says, in this connection, 'Articles 56 and 57 of these Rules shall apply to proceedings before the Chamber.' The inference is that RP-ECJ 56 and 57 also apply where the enquiry is in the hands of the Court. Presumably the same is true, mutatis mutandis, where it is the judge-rapporteur who is in charge. On the other hand, it can also be argued that the Rules of Procedure do not envisage the judge-rapporteur continuing to conduct an enquiry if it necessitates a hearing. The practice of the Court offers no guidance on this point. It may be that the better view is that, once he is entrusted with an enquiry, it is up to the judge-rapporteur to decide whether any hearing that may have to be held is to be heard by him. If he does so decide, RP-ECJ 56 and 57 apply correspondingly. In consequence, the hearing is conducted by the President (of the Court or the chamber) or by the judge-rapporteur and it may, depending on the circumstances, be heard in public or in camera.[61] The President (or judge-rapporteur) may put questions to the parties' representatives, and so may the other judges and the advocate general.[62] Although no provision similar to RP-ECJ 46(2) appears in the Rules of Procedure of the CFI, it is assumed that the position is the same.

---

55 Save, for example, in an order requesting the production of documents or information, or in an inspection of the place or thing in question: see below pp 383–388 and 402–403.
56 RP-ECJ 9(2); in *Preo v High Authority*, (above, note 24 at 224, and Case 74/74 *CNTA v Commission* [1976] ECR 797 at 799, for example, the enquiry was assigned to the Second Chamber.
57 RP-ECJ 46(1).
58 In Cases T-68, T-77 and T-78/89 *Società Italiana Vetro SpA v Commission* [1992] ECR II-1403 (Re Italian Flat Glass) (order of 7 May 1991) the judge-rapporteur was ordered inter alia to identify all relevant documents referred to by the parties, identify any others, ensure any necessary transcriptions and translations, decide whether or not it was necessary to examine witnesses and, if so, whom, proceed to any measures of organisation of procedure and, to those ends, convoke the parties and ask them any necessary questions. That order, as can be seen, related more to measures of organisation of procedure under RP-CFI 64 than to measures of enquiry under RP-CFI 65.
59 In Case 23/81 *Commission v Royale Belge* [1983] ECR 2685, the enquiry was assigned to the judge-rapporteur but, as it concerned an expert's report, this was in any event necessary in view of RP-ECJ 49(2). On the other hand, in Case 132/81 *Rijksdienst voor Werknemerspensionen v Vlaeminck* [1982] ECR 2953, the order reopening the oral procedure also assigned any necessary measures of enquiry to the judge-rapporteur. Both this and the *Royale Belge* case were heard by a chamber. It is supposed that the judge-rapporteur is more likely to be entrusted with a preparatory enquiry in this situation than when the case is heard by the full Court.
60 RP-ECJ 45(3); RP-CFI 67(1).
61 RP-ECJ 56.
62 RP-ECJ 57.

The Rules of Procedure also provide that the parties are 'entitled to attend the measures of enquiry'.[63] An enquiry which consists of an order for the production of documents does not readily lend itself to the notion that a party has a right to 'attend'. On the other hand, the rules relating to the hearing of testimony and experts' reports expressly state that the parties may attend the enquiry and ask questions.[64] That reflects a general principle of procedural law.[65] It also seems to be the ECJ's practice when carrying out an inspection under RP-ECJ 45(2)(e).[66] The Rules of Procedure do not, however, expressly provide that the parties have a right to give their views on the evidence obtained by the enquiry. Nevertheless, this seems implicit in their right to attend and is the usual practice.[67] RP-ECJ 54, which deals with the close of the preparatory enquiry, indicates only that, in cases before it, the ECJ is not bound to allow the parties to comment on the evidence in writing.

RP-ECJ 45(4) and RP-CFI 66(2) state: 'Evidence may be submitted in rebuttal and previous evidence may be amplified.' The phrasing used is slightly ambiguous in that it suggests either that it lies within the discretion of the Court to allow the submission of evidence in rebuttal etc or that this is a facility of which the parties may take advantage, if they so wish, but as of right. Both views are tenable, given that the calling of evidence is in general the responsibility of the Court but that, as a matter of principle, the Court cannot refuse to accept relevant evidence from one party which would tend to rebut evidence produced at the behest of the Court by the other party. On balance it is preferable to regard RP-ECJ 45(4) and RP-CFI 66(2) as indicating that the matter lies within the discretion of the Court because, while the submission of evidence in rebuttal could, arguably, be left to the parties, the amplification of previous evidence cannot. There is no textual reason to consider the two parts of the rule independently. The exercise of the Court's discretion under the rule would appear to be guided by the same principles that apply to the ordering of a measure of enquiry and with due regard for the rights of the defence. There are very few cases in which it is evident that evidence was submitted in rebuttal. In Case 32/62 *Alvis v Council*[68] the order prescribing the measure of enquiry invited the defendant to name its witnesses on the issues of fact before a certain date, the right of rebuttal being left to the applicant, who was given the same period of time in which to name his witnesses. An order so framed is, however, comparatively unusual. In Case 89/83 *Hauptzollamt Hamburg-Jonas v Dimex Nahrungsmittel Im-und Export GmbH*,[69] a reference for a preliminary ruling, the Court asked one of the parties to confirm or rebut a statement of fact made by the other party. The report of Cases 56 to 60/74 *Kampffmeyer Muhlenvereingung KG v Commission and Council*[70] says that, after the Court had decided to hear several witnesses, the Commission put in a written statement concerning one of the issues of fact on which they were to be examined. This statement 'submitted evidence in rebuttal', in the form of documents and a request that other persons should be heard as witnesses on the issue in question. From this it can be seen that 'evidence in rebuttal' need not be of the same type as the evidence it seeks to rebut and that it is up to the parties to

63 RP-ECJ 46(3); RP-CFI 67(2).
64 RP-ECJ 47(4) and 49(5); RP-CFI 68(4) and 70(5).
65 Case 141/84 *De Compte v European Parliament* [1985] ECR 1951 (paras 17–18).
66 Below pp 402–403.
67 Eg Case 232/81 *Agricola Commerciale Olio v Commission* [1984] ECR 3881 at 3884; Case 264/81 *Savma v Commission* [1984] ECR 3915 at 3918.
68 [1963] ECR 49, order of 1 February 1963, unreported.
69 [1984] ECR 2815 at 2821.
70 [1976] ECR 711 at 716.

adduce evidence or sources of evidence which may rebut that produced by or at the request of the opposing party. In Case T-36/89 *Nijman v Commission*,[71] a party sought to adduce witness evidence in order to rebut the conclusions of an expert's report. That offer of proof was dismissed as inadmissible. The explanation seems to be that the evidence could have been drawn to the attention of the Court at an earlier stage in the proceedings (indeed, before the expert's report was ordered), no reason was given for the delay in producing it and, further, the party concerned had never asserted previously what it was now asserting on the basis of the 'new' evidence. The case thus shows that evidence in rebuttal cannot be used in order to remedy a failure to adduce evidence at the proper time; and that evidence in rebuttal is limited to countering the impact of the evidence produced by the measure of enquiry and cannot extend to questioning the assumptions on the basis of which the measure of enquiry was ordered.

At the close of the preparatory enquiry either the Court may give the parties an opportunity to comment on the evidence obtained in writing, a period being fixed for the submission of written observations, or the President sets the date for the opening of the oral procedure and the parties may comment on the evidence at the hearing.[72] In Case T-169/89 *Frederiksen v European Parliament*,[73] the procedure followed was more complex: the defendant had been requested to produce documentary evidence in the course of the proceedings and had duly done so but, at the end of the hearing, the Court was not satisfied that it was in full possession of all the necessary evidence; it informed the parties that it was going to order a complementary measure of enquiry and subsequently ordered the defendant to provide further information and documents on a particular question of fact; the information and documents produced by the defendant caused the Court to order an expert's report. In Case 232/81 *Agricola Commerciale Olio v Commission* and Case 264/81 *Savma v Commission*,[74] the Court had originally opened the oral procedure without any preparatory enquiries but asked the defendant to reply to certain questions and provide certain information. The defendant's response caused measures of enquiry to be ordered, resulting in a further round of enquiries.

IV The personal appearance of the parties

The parties cannot be required to give evidence as witnesses[75] although, under the Statutes, they may be required to produce documents and supply information[76] and the Court has power during the hearing to question them, albeit that they can only plead through their representatives.[77] In consequence, if a question is put directly to the party at the hearing, the answer must come from the lips of his representative.[78] The parties are not normally obliged to be

71 [1991] ECR II-699 (paras 26–29).
72 RP-ECJ 54. RP-CFI 54 simply provides that the date for the opening of the oral procedure is fixed when any measure of enquiry has been completed; but it is implicit that the parties may either be allowed to comment on the evidence in writing or else submit oral argument at the hearing.
73 [1991] ECR II-1403 (paras 34–36).
74 [1984] ECR 3881 at 3884 and 3915 at 3918, respectively.
75 Case 10/55 *Mirossevich v High Authority* [1954–56] ECR 333, order of 4 June 1956, unreported.
76 ECSC Statute, art 24; EC Statute, art 21; Euratom Statute, art 22.
77 ECSC Statute, art 28; EC Statute, art 29; Euratom Statute, art 30.
78 Where this would be impracticable, the President has been known to allow the party to address the Court itself.

present in court at the hearing but the Court may order them to be present in person under RP-ECJ 45(2)(a) or, as the case may be, RP-CFI 65(a). In the case of legal persons and bodies lacking legal personality, appearance is by the natural person competent to represent them under national law. The same rule seems to apply as far as the member states are concerned, but the position is not entirely clear and it is arguable that appearance is by the agent appointed to represent a member state in proceedings before the Court. How a Community institution can appear in person other than by its agent is obscure.[79]

It is comparatively rare for a party to be ordered to appear in person by way of a measure of enquiry. In theory the order must set out the facts which are to be proved.[80] No details of the procedure which is to be followed appear in the Rules of Procedure or elsewhere. The general rules for the conduct of a measure of enquiry[81] indicate that the other parties are entitled to attend; the hearing is held in open court unless it is decided otherwise; the members of the Court may put questions to the party ordered to be present. It does not seem that the other parties can put questions directly but they may ask the Court to do so. The party ordered to be present cannot be required to swear to the veracity of what he says and it is to be inferred that there is no sanction if he conceals or falsifies any evidence because power to impose a sanction is not to be found expressly stated in the Rules of Procedure or elsewhere and, since it would affect the liberties of the individual, an express provision would be necessary to establish its existence. Moreover, the Statutes provide[82] only that the Court can take 'formal note' of a refusal to give the information requested by it. There is therefore no sanction other than this if the party refuses either to appear before the Court or to make a statement or answer questions. As is usual, an official record is made of the proceedings and signed by the President and the Registrar.[83]

In practice the decision to order a party to appear in person is taken by the Court at the administrative meeting and the formal order circulated to the parties is drawn up on the basis of the note of the decision made in the minutes of the meeting. Generally speaking, there appear to be two types of situation in which a party is ordered to attend in person: where the object is that the party may be asked to reply to questions or comment on the content of the testimony given by a witness; and where the object is to obtain information, particularly specialised or technical information. In the first situation the order usually says that a certain person is to be 'heard as a witness' in relation to some issue of fact and that the party is to be 'heard as a party' or simply ordered to attend the hearing of the witness.[84] In the second situation the measure of enquiry takes the usual form, there being an order specifying the questions to be put to

79 In Case 98/76 *Trevor v Court*, order of 4 April 1977, unreported (the case was withdrawn before judgment) both parties were ordered to be heard in order to resolve certain question of fact: the Court was represented by the Registrar. In Case T-59/89 *Yorck von Wartenburg v European Parliament* [1990] ECR II-25, the European Parliament was ordered to attend in person at the hearing by means of a representative duly empowered by the Parliament to bind it by his statements; but that was in the context of an attempt by the CFI to achieve an amicable settlement of the dispute, presumably by way of a measure of organisation of procedure under RP-CFI 64(3)(e), not the giving of evidence.
80 RP-ECJ 45(1); RP-CFI 66(1).
81 See RP-ECJ 46, 56 and 57; RP-CFI 67.
82 ECSC Statute, art 24; EC Statute, art 21; Euratom Statute, art 22.
83 RP-ECJ 53; RP-CFI 76.
84 See, for example, Case 43/74 *Guillot v Commission* [1977] ECR 1309; Case 29/78 *Delfino v Commission*, order of 23 January 1979, unreported (the case was later withdrawn and never came to judgment); Cases 59 and 129/80 *Turner (née Krecké) v Commission* [1981] ECR 1883 at 1892.

the party or parties or the issues of fact on which they are to give evidence. Occasionally the hearing is held in camera but the other parties are invited to attend.[85] This situation is to be distinguished from instances where there is an informal meeting between the parties and their representatives and the Court[86] to discuss the procedural aspects of the case, such as the need to order measures of enquiry, or to see if the issues in the case can be clarified or agreed.[87]

The weight to attach to the evidence given by a party in person depends, as in the case of any other witness, on a number of factors such as the extent to which it is supported by other evidence, such as documents or testimony, the appearance of the party when answering questions and the obvious factor that the party has an interest in putting across a story favourable to his own case.[88] A party's evidence may corroborate or confirm other evidence.[89] In Case 18/57 *Nold KG v High Authority*[90] Advocate General Roemer said that written declarations made by the partners in the applicant undertaking had no probative value because they were neither testimony nor documentary evidence, although he appears to have accepted that they had some corroborative value. The Court did not, however, take this line. It seems to have accepted the evidence of the written attestations.[91] The parties' evidence may also be of considerable value where technical matters are involved. In Case 228/83 *F v Commission*[92] Advocate General Mancini said that, when seeking to establish the facts concerning alleged punishable conduct, the most effective and clearest means of separating fact from fiction, the relevant from the irrelevant and the intentional from the unintentional, is direct confrontation between the parties.

Two rough rules can be said to lie at the heart of the Court's treatment of evidence from a party:

---

85 See, for example, Case 1/55 *Kergall v Common Assembly* [1954–56] ECR 151 at 153 (parties ordered to appear in person in camera in order to supply full information and any relevant documents concerning the questions of fact set out in the order); Case 37/64 *Mannesmann A G v High Authority* [1965] ECR 725 at 738 (parties ordered to attend in the Deliberation Room to provide certain technical information: see also Case 111/63 *Lemmerz-Werke GmbH v High Authority* [1965] ECR 677 at 688); *Trevor v Court* (above, note 79); Case 74/74 *CNTA v Commission* [1976] ECR 797 at 799 (parties ordered to appear before the Second Chamber, the applicant being invited to answer the questions specified in the order and to produce documents in support of its answers; it was also said that the applicant's representative should be accompanied by those members of the applicant's staff best placed to explain the facts); Case 54/75 *De Dapper v European Parliament* [1976] ECR 1381, order of 20 October 1976, unreported (the matter had been referred to the Second Chamber which ordered the parties and their representatives to attend at the Deliberation Room in order to give certain information and answer questions); Case 155/78 *M v Commission* [1980] ECR 1797 at 1801 (applicant ordered to appear in person at a hearing in camera); Case 142/78 *Exner (née Berghmans) v Commission* [1979] ECR 3125 at 3129 and 3136 (applicant ordered to appear at the hearing and give evidence).
86 Ie usually the judge-rapporteur and the advocate general.
87 See, for example, Case 258/78 *LC Nungesser KG and Kurt Eisele v Commission* [1982] ECR 2015; Cases 100–103/80 *Pioneer v Commission* [1983] ECR 1825; RP-CFI 64(3)(e).
88 See the treatment given by Advocate General Warner in Case 102/75 *Petersen v Commission* [1976] ECR 1777 at 1802.
89 See the *Guillot* case (above, note 84) at 1337.
90 [1959] ECR 41 at 61.
91 See Rec V at 111. In Cases 173/82, 157/83 and 186/84 *Castille v Commission* [1986] ECR 497 (see at 504, Advocate General Lenz), the position was slightly different because the 'evidence' on which a party based certain allegations made about a third party comprised letters that had been written by that party himself. The underlying principle, of course, is that a person can only give evidence of what he himself knows.
92 [1985] ECR 275 at 284.

(1)   the less important the subject matter is to the issues in the case, the more likely is the evidence to be trustworthy (so, for example, background information which helps to an understanding of the case is more likely to be worth relying on than evidence relating to a critical issue of fact); and

(2)   evidence which tends to go against the party's own case is likely to be more reliable than evidence which tends to support it.

IV   Requests for information and the production of documents

Information and documents may be produced by the parties (or, as the case may be, by third parties) either by legal compulsion or voluntarily. The instances of legal compulsion can be divided into two: automatic production by operation of law; and production pursuant to a Court order or request. The three forms of production will be considered in turn. By way of introductory remark, it should be noted that a document is of probative value if it constitutes independent evidence of the existence of a fact. Hence, a party cannot create documentary evidence of a fact by setting out his assertions in the form of a document and producing that document as evidence.[93] It is in part for that reason that internal documents (that is, documents drawn up by a party for its own use) are commonly regarded as lacking in probative value:[94] in substance, they are nothing more than assertions made by that party. However, such documents do have probative value where they are used to establish the knowledge or belief of the party concerned at the material time or, generally, where the internal procedures of the party concerned (usually a Community institution) are relevant to an issue in the case.

A   Production by operation of law

There is no general provision in Community law for the automatic production and disclosure of documentary evidence, with one exception: art 23 of the ECSC Statute. This provides that, when proceedings are begun (under the ECSC Treaty) against a decision of a Community institution, that institution 'shall transmit to the Court all the documents relating to the case'.[95] This provision has been the subject of very little judicial exegesis but certain conclusions concerning its application can be drawn from Case 2/54 *Italy v High Authority*.[96]

---

93 Cases 173/82, 157/83 and 186/84 *Castille v Commission* (above, note 91) at 504 (Advocate General Lenz); Case C-330/88 *Grifoni v Euratom* [1991] ECR I-1045 at 1060 (Advocate General Tesauro). In Cases 193 and 194/87 *Maurissen v Court of Auditors* [1989] ECR 1045 (at 1066) Advocate General Darmon went so far as to say that 'no document purporting to support a party's allegations which emanates from that party should be taken into account by the Court'.

94 Eg Case C-49/88 *Al-Jubail Fertiliser Co v Council* [1991] ECR I-3187 (Advocate General Darmon at para 82 of his opinion). In contrast, in Case 318/81 *Commission v CODEMI* [1985] ECR 3693 (para 47) certain internal documents were held to be of no probative value because they were contradicted by evidence from experts, which tends to suggest that they would otherwise have been regarded as having probative value.

95 Article 26 of the Staff Regulations provides that, in staff cases, the official's personal file is to be sent to the Court. That is not the same as art 23 of the ECSC Statute because the official's personal file does not necessarily contain any or all of the documentary evidence relating to the dispute before the Court. The obligation to disclose the personal file provides the Court with background information relating to the official concerned and with the exchanges between the official and the employing institution made during the compulsory pre-litigation procedure.

96 [1954–56] ECR 37.

There Italy had applied for the annulment of several High Authority decisions. At the hearing it applied for the High Authority to be invited to produce, in accordance with art 23, all documents relating to the case. The Court held that the High Authority had been bound to forward all documents and that Italy's application to force production was admissible because it was entitled to think that art 23 would have been complied with and could not know whether this was so before the hearing. In consequence, it is possible to say that the duty to produce to the Court all documents arises upon service on the defendant institution of the application commencing proceedings and it is not necessary for the applicant to make a special application. It is not, however, clear whether the institution should perform its obligation to disclose before lodging its defence or before the time for lodgment of the reply. As a matter of practice, it should produce the documents as soon as is possible. No doubt the applicant may apply for an extension of the time fixed for lodging the reply to allow him to take into account documents produced or to await their production. Nevertheless the limit of any extension remains within the discretion of the President and it cannot be said that the applicant (or the defendant institution) can cause proceedings to be halted indefinitely pending production. As long as the applicant is given adequate opportunity to comment on the documents produced and, if necessary, permitted to submit new arguments based on them, his interests will not be adversely affected if the written procedure is allowed to continue.

If the applicant does not challenge the defendant institution's failure to comply with art 23 before the hearing, this does not constitute waiver of any right to challenge it later on in the proceedings, in the absence of any express disclaimer. Nevertheless, if the question is raised only after the hearing it is still open to the defendant to argue that the applicant has acquiesced in the disposal of the case on the basis of the information which has been disclosed.

It should, however, be borne in mind that art 23 imposes a duty without specifying to whom that duty is owed. The behaviour of the applicant may preclude him from protesting against a failure to comply with art 23 but it does not prevent the Court from ordering the production of documents if it thinks it necessary in the public interest to do so.

Article 23 does not specify in detail the documents which are to be produced. It is only all those 'relating to the case'. This means that every document, without exception, which has a bearing on the subject matter of the dispute should be transmitted to the Court. This does not mean that all these documents will be communicated to the other parties to the proceedings. In *Italy v High Authority* the Court said that it had power to authorise parts of the documents disclosed to be omitted and, if necessary, to examine the documents in camera.[97] Its order in the case did, in fact, authorise the High Authority to erase the names of the persons taking part in the meeting of which minutes were to be produced and also any reference which could allow them to be identified.[98] The documents should, even so, be produced to the Court in toto, accompanied, where necessary, by a reasoned application that all or part of specified documents should be excluded from the file. In the absence of any such application, the Court is entitled to conclude that there is no objection to disclosure of all the documents, in their entirety, to the other parties.

In *Italy v High Authority*, where art 23 was not complied with, the Court did not in fact order production of all documents but only the minutes and

---

97 See ibid at 54–55 of the judgment.
98 See ibid at 42.

opinions of the ECSC Consultative Committee, reserving the right, if necessary, to call for production of minutes of the Council and the High Authority. It is evident from this that the duty to disclose covers all documents held by the defendant institution, not just those brought into being by it. It also suggests that the duty to disclose binds the institution as representative of the Community so that it is no reason for withholding a particular document to say that it is held by an institution or body which is not named as defendant to the proceedings: the Court did not order production of the Council minutes only because this was not considered necessary, not because the Court had no power to do so in an application made to ensure the proper observance of art 23. The point is, however, unclear and it seems to remain open to argument that the defendant institution is only bound to produce documents it has in its possession. If so, this does not, of course, prevent the Court from requesting the production of documents held by another institution, under art 24 of the ECSC Statute. The *Italy v High Authority* case does show that, if an order is made for an institution to comply with art 23, it may be restricted to those documents which the Court considers necessary.[99] This presupposes that the Court is in a position to know what is or is not necessary for it to decide the dispute but, in most cases, there is likely to be little disagreement over the documents that should be called for because the proceedings will, or should, identify the issues and narrow down the category of documents that are both relevant and necessary. Even so, the effect is that the applicant may not be able to add a new ground to his claim on the basis of a new fact which might be found in documents which are relevant to the case but are not necessary for deciding it as it has hitherto been pleaded. This is a factor which should be considered by the Court when deciding whether to limit its order to comply with art 23.

Where a large number of documents are produced, some of which are said to be confidential and should not be disclosed to the parties, no precise procedure for dealing with the problem is provided for. In theory all the documents produced should be disclosed to the other parties. It is only if an objection is raised to their disclosure that the Court may select which are to be shown to the parties and which withheld. In the absence of any objection, there does not seem to be any power entitling the Court to sift through the documents in order to sort out those which it deems to be so interesting or useful as to warrant disclosure to the other parties. Such an approach is difficult to justify.

Where an institution has doubts as to the relevance of a document, the proper course would seem to be to apply to the Court for it to rule on the question. The application could be made in two ways, either by transmitting the document to the Court, annexed to an application that the Court order that it falls outside the scope of art 23, or by simply describing the nature and contents of the document in such an application.[1] As in the case of an objection

---

99 In Case 3/54 *ASSIDER v High Authority* and Case 4/54 *ISA v High Authority* [1954–56] ECR 63 and 91 respectively, the High Authority did not, it seems, comply with art 23 and, at the hearing, the applicant asked for the production of all documents relating to the case (at 65 and 94). The Court rejected this, holding that there was already sufficient evidence available to the Court (at 71 and 100).

 1 The application would be made under RP-ECJ 91 or, as the case may be, RP-CFI 114, the first paragraph of which says that 'any supporting documents must be annexed to it'. This seems to refer to the documentary evidence relied on to base the application, not, as in the present situation, the document which is the subject matter of the application. Nevertheless, in case of doubt, the document in question should be annexed to the application. If it were regarded as being particularly sensitive, it could be placed in a sealed envelope, a description of its nature and contents being included in the application. If not annexed, the Court may still call for its production in order to settle the issue: in practice it may be difficult to decide whether the document is material to the case without looking at it (cf the procedure adopted in Case 236/81 *Celanese Chemical Co Inc v Council and Commission* [1982] ECR 1183).

to disclosure based on other grounds, such as confidentiality, it can only be speculated what procedure the Court may adopt to decide the question. In Case 155/79 *AM & S Europe Ltd v Commission*,[2] where a similar problem arose in relation to documents ordered to be produced by the Commission during a competition investigation, only the judge-rapporteur and the advocate general actually saw the documents, a report on them being prepared and circulated to the other members of the Court and the parties, but not the documents themselves. The same approach could be adopted in the present situation. Alternatively, a chamber could be entrusted with the function of ascertaining the contents of the document as a preparatory enquiry. If the Court subsequently found that the document should not be disclosed, it would not then be prejudiced because it had seen it and those of its members who had seen it could refrain from taking any further part in the proceedings without affecting the Court's capacity to decide the action. A different procedure is followed where a party wishes to retain the confidentiality of pleadings or evidence in relation to another party (ie an intervener) or where cases have been joined and a party to one of the joined cases wishes to retain confidentiality in relation to a party to the other joined case. In those circumstances, however, the Court is concerned with material that a party wishes to disclose voluntarily to the Court as part of its case (subject to protection from disclosure justified on some ground of confidentiality) whereas, in the situation under consideration, the Court is concerned with material that a party is obliged by law to disclose.

The mere fact that a particular document is described as being confidential does not, of itself, render it privileged from disclosure;[3] there must be some evidence to support the assertion.[4] A complete list of the grounds which may be relied on to justify withholding a document cannot be drawn up with any degree of certainty because of the lack of authority on the subject. Clearly a document can be withheld because it does not relate to the case but the notion of 'relating' to the case before the Court is one that can be defined only by the Court, not any other body or institution, because it depends on the correct interpretation to be given to the ECSC Statute. Of the other grounds that may be relied on, it seems reasonably certain that an institution is not bound to disclose a document if this would lead to a contravention of some provision of Community law. For example, art 47 of the ECSC Treaty provides that the Commission 'must not disclose information of the kind covered by the obligation of professional secrecy'. Any breach of professional secrecy may give rise to an action for damages. In consequence, it is arguable that the Commission cannot be bound by art 23 of the ECSC Statute to disclose a document containing such information. On the other hand, in Cases 36, 37, 38 and 40/59 *Geitling Ruhrkohlen-Verkaufsgesellschaft mbH v High Authority*[5] which, so far as can be seen, concerned a request for information made by the Court, not the production of documents under art 23, the High Authority wrote to the Court to say that it had reservations about answering one of the questions put by the Court because this might lead to a breach of art 47. The Court therefore made an order allowing it to supply the information sought but omitting the business names and addresses of the persons in question. In the case of documents, of course, the removal of all references which might indicate the person supplying the document in question, even if possible, seriously affects its

2 [1982] ECR 1575.
3 Case 110/75 *Mills v European Investment Bank* [1976] ECR 1613 at 1635 (Advocate General Warner).
4 See the *AM & S* case (above, note 2).
5 [1960] ECR 423 at 437.

probative value. However, the *Geitling* case appears to suggest that art 47 does not exempt an institution *entirely* from an obligation to produce evidence in proceedings before the Court: the request for information was made under art 24 of the ECSC Statute which, although it specifies no sanction for a breach, nevertheless imposes an obligation to produce documents and information when the Court so requests; art 23, likewise, obliges an institution to produce documents. If the Court could require production of information falling within art 47, subject to certain safeguards intended to protect the essential core of professional secrecy, it seems to follow that the same applies to automatic production of documents under art 23.

Where an obligation not to disclose information arises neither expressly nor by necessary implication from a provision of the Treaty but from a provision of secondary legislation, the question may arise whether or not it is valid. If it is not, it cannot, in any event, override art 23. A right to withhold information may also be derived from the general principles of Community law.[6] In this respect an institution cannot rely on the confidentiality of the relationship between a lawyer and his client, save in respect of communications passing between it and an independent lawyer,[7] but it is not excluded that an institution may rely on some other privilege based on the public interest.[8] It is unclear to what extent art 23 would override any such privilege: the better view is that any conflict between it and a right to withhold information is to be resolved by balancing the public interests in favour of and militating against disclosure.[9]

B   Voluntary production

It is a general rule that to every pleading (by which is meant every formal procedural document addressed to the Court) is annexed a file containing the documents relied on in the body of the pleading.[10] This rule does not require the disclosure of all documentary evidence in the possession of a party, only that on which he wishes to rely.[11] It is bad practice to produce a document for the first time at the hearing, without giving the other parties adequate notice of it. The Court's 'Notes for the Guidance of Counsel at Oral Hearings' say that a document produced after the close of the written procedure will not be admitted, save in exceptional circumstances and with the agreement of the other parties. Occasionally they may wish to consent to production only if they

---

6 See the *AM & S* case (above, note 2).
7 Ibid.
8 In Case 18/70 *X v Council* [1972] ECR 1205, some documents ordered to be produced by the Court were withheld by the defendant's medical officer on the ground that they were covered by the principle of medical secrecy (see at 1211, Advocate General Roemer). The Court did not seek to force their disclosure but instead appointed an expert to examine the question of fact to which they related. More detailed consideration was given to the question in Case 155/78 *M v Commission* [1980] ECR 1797, which is, so far, the leading case on the point (see especially the opinion of Advocate General Capotorti).
9 See *Mills v European Investment Bank* (above, note 3) (Advocate General Warner). It would appear from Case 28/65 *Fonzi v Euratom Commission* [1966] ECR 477 at 506–507 that, if disclosure is 'essential for the efficient administration of justice', the Court may require the production of relevant but confidential evidence.
10 RP-ECJ 37(4); RP-CFI 43(4).
11 In Case 52/81 *Faust v Commission* [1982] ECR 3745, the applicant set out in his pleading the gist of an exchange of telexes but did not annex copies of the telexes themselves to the pleading. The Court requested him to produce the telexes and he did so. It does not seem to be necessary to annex copies of documents which are referred to in the documents relied on although it is, within limits, good practice to do so, if the document is important. In any event, the Court may, if it thinks appropriate, ask for such a document to be produced.

are allowed the opportunity to submit further written or oral observations on the document. In consequence, the party producing the document may be penalised for its late production in the order for costs.[12] On the other hand, even if the other parties raise no formal objection to the production of a document after the close of the written procedure, the admissibility of the document is still a matter for the Court to decide and there have been cases where the Court has refused to allow the production of relevant documents.[13]

C Production by Court order

The Court has power under the Statutes[14] to require the production and supply of 'all documents and . . . all information which [it] considers desirable'. Under the ECSC Statute, the order requiring production or supply may be directed to the parties, their representatives or agents, and the governments of the member states. Hence no Community institution may be so requested unless it is a party.[15] Under the EC and Euratom Statutes the request can only be made of the parties but the Court can also require the member states and Community institutions who are not parties to the case 'to supply all information which [it] considers necessary for the proceedings'. Under the Rules of Procedure, a request for information and the production of documents is listed among the measures of enquiry that the Court may adopt 'without prejudice' to the provisions of the Statutes[16] and is also listed among the measures of organisation of procedure that may be prescribed by the CFI.[17] Such a request is made, like all measures of enquiry or of organisation of procedure, if the Court considers it 'appropriate'.[18]

It seems that the Court may exercise either its powers under the Statutes, for which there are no formal requirements, or its power under the Rules of Procedure, which requires the making of a formal order setting out the facts to be proved in the event that the request for the production of documents takes the form of a measure of enquiry.[19] By and large, the Court adopts the informal approach (which, in the case of the CFI is more properly characterised as a measure of organisation of procedure), the request being made in a letter sent through the Registrar.[20] The Court usually requests an answer before the

---

12 Eg Case 56/77 *Agence Européenne d' Intérims SA v Commission* [1978] ECR 2215 at 2230 and 2238.
13 Eg Case C-156/87 *Gestetner Holdings plc v Council and Commission* [1990] ECR I-781, where the Court refused to admit certain documents at the hearing, despite the fact that the opposing parties raised no formal objection, because no reason was given to explain why they had not been produced earlier (the relevance of the documents in question had become apparent only at the end of the written procedure but there had been sufficient time between then and the date of the hearing for the documents to have been produced).
14 ECSC Statute, art 24; EC Statute, art 21; Euratom Statute, art 22.
15 However, in Cases 32, 52 and 57/87 *Industrie Siderurgiche Associate (ISA) v Commission* [1988] ECR 3305 (at 3307) the Court requested the Council, which was not a party to the proceedings, to produce extracts of the minutes of its meetings (and the Council obliged).
16 RP-ECJ 45(2); RP-CFI 65.
17 RP-CFI 64(3).
18 RP-ECJ 45(1); RP-CFI 66(1).
19 RP-ECJ 45(1); RP-CFI 66(1).
20 For example, in Case 208/80 *Lord Bruce of Donnington v Aspden* [1981] ECR 2205 a reference for a preliminary ruling, the Registrar's letter conveyed the request of the Court that the Parliament answer certain questions and produce relevant documents by a certain date, enclosing a copy of the questions set out in the order for reference. The Court invited the Parliament to send an authorised representative to attend the hearing with a view to helping the Court with any additional information. A letter was also sent to the Council asking it 'to be good enough to supply the Court' with certain documents referred to by the parties (sc extracts from the Council minutes and a letter from the President of the Council to the President of the

hearing so that all the parties have the opportunity to consider the information or documents well beforehand. A formal order made under RP-ECJ 45 or RP-CFI 66(1) will request the production of information or documents relating to a question of fact specified in the order by a specified date. Usually any information sought is presented to the Court in written form but the Court may ask for it to be given orally by the representative of the party at the hearing or by some other person.[21] Like the informal approach under the Statutes, however, no sanction is laid down if the order is ignored. In the case of orders summoning a witness, there is specific provision for the enforcement in the member states of a measure adopted by the Court in the event that the witness fails to appear.[22] No such provision exists in the case of an order requiring the supply of information or the production of documents so it is to be inferred that the order is unenforceable.[23]

Three terms are used to describe the criterion for requesting the supply of information or the production of documents, whether formally or informally: 'desirable',[24] 'necessary'[25] and 'appropriate'.[26] Despite the difference in their semantic meaning, the first and third appear to reflect the same approach: that the Court must be guided by what steps appear to it to be in the interests of the proper disposal of the case (the same approach to be followed when deciding whether or not the CFI's power to prescribe a measure of organisation of procedure is to be exercised).[27] The second word, however, applies in the context of requests directed at member states and Community institutions who are not parties to the case and which are made under the EC and Euratom Statutes. Its use, in contrast to the word 'desirable', which appears in the same articles of the Statutes, indicates that, in proceedings under the EC and Euratom Treaties, the Court must adopt a different test when considering whether to exercise its powers in this respect. Instead of simply deciding what seems advantageous or useful for the resolution of any issues of fact, the Court must go further and consider whether the information or documents can be obtained from another source. If they can, it is not 'necessary' for the proceedings that a member state or Community institution which is not a party to them should be approached.

In Case 2/54 *Italy v High Authority*[28] the Court used the word 'necessary', in another context, to mean essential for the resolution of the dispute. Sometimes it is possible to say that a particular category of document is not 'necessary', in this sense, to deciding the case. But necessity can only be judged before the document has been disclosed and it may happen that what appears to be a necessary document is found, on examination, to be irrelevant. It is not for the member state or Community institution to decide for itself whether the Court's

Parliament annexed to the minutes) (see at 2209). A slightly different situation arose in Case T-9/92 *Automobiles Peugeot v Commission* [1993] ECR II-493 (para 12) where, for the sake of good order, the Court asked the parties for their agreement that certain documents produced in earlier proceedings between the same parties could be used in the current proceedings.

21 Eg in Cases 59 and 129/80 *Turner (née Krecké) v Commission* [1981] ECR 1883 the Court heard evidence from a doctor, just before the hearing, for the purpose of information only (see at 1903). The doctor did not take the oath.
22 RP-ECJ 48(4); RP-CFI 69(4).
23 The Treaties refer only to the enforcement of 'judgments' of the Court: see ECSC Treaty, art 44; EC Treaty, art 187; Euratom Treaty, art 159. See further below pp 534 et seq.
24 ECSC Statute, art 24; EC Statute, art 21 (first sentence); Euratom Statute, art 22 (first sentence).
25 EC Statute, art 21 (second sentence); Euratom Statute, art 22 (second sentence).
26 RP-ECJ 45(1); RP-CFI 66(1).
27 See RP-CFI 64(1) and (2).
28 [1954–56] ECR 37. See also Cases T-6 and T-52/92 *Reinarz v Commission*, 26 October 1993, para 116.

request is a proper one. Therefore a request for production should be complied with even if the member state or Community institution, having the benefit of knowledge of the contents of the document, believes that it is not necessary for deciding the case. In such a situation it would seem that the member state or Community institution could apply to the Court, by letter or under RP-ECJ 91 or, as the case may be, RP-CFI 114,[29] for the document to be excluded from the Court's file. In all cases the Court has a discretion to refuse to make a request where, even if it would aid the resolution of an issue of fact, the revelation of a document or certain information might be contrary to other interests which may outweigh those in favour of the proper disposal of the dispute between the parties. For example, it may not be in the public interest that a particular document or class of documents be disclosed even if they are material to the case.

It is for the Court itself to determine whether or not to exercise its powers; it is not bound to act in accordance with a request made by one of the parties and it can act in the absence of such a request. Nevertheless, the burden lies on the parties in the first instance to make clear what are the questions of fact and to indicate so far as possible how best they may be resolved. The parties themselves have no power to request or require the production of documents or information by another party or a third party. They may, however, set out in their pleadings the documents or categories of documents which they feel the Court should order to be produced. Alternatively, an application can be made under RP-ECJ 91 or, as the case may be, RP-CFI 114 for the production of documents.[30] A request can also be made informally, by letter.[31]

29 It should be observed that the use of RP-ECJ 91 and RP-CFI 114 in this way is not sanctified by any authority. RP-ECJ 91 and RP-CFI 114 specify that a 'party' may apply but, in this case, the applicant would not, ex hypothesi, be a 'party' within the meaning of arts 21 and 22 of the EC and Euratom Statutes respectively. It is arguable that, once the Court has made a request under the Statute, the addressee of the request is a 'party' to the case thenceforth as far as procedural matters connected with the request are concerned. This would then enable it to take advantage of RP-ECJ 91 and RP-CFI 114. A less formalistic approach is to say that reliance on RP-ECJ 91 or RP-CFI 114 is unnecessary because any difficulties concerning the request can be sorted out on an informal basis between the Court and the member state or Community institution concerned. The difficulty with this is that it leaves the parties, stricto sensu, with no role to play in regard to a matter which may turn out to be very important for the case.

30 See, for example, Case 33/59 *Compagnie des Hauts Fourneaux de Chasse v High Authority* [1962] ECR 381 at 386 and Cases 46 and 47/59 *Meroni & Co v High Authority* [1962] ECR 411 at 417 (the applicants applied for further measures of enquiry, sc permission to submit further documents and that the defendant be ordered to answer certain questions and produce documents; the application was granted in part, the defendant being ordered to produce a report, a decision on the request for questions to be asked being reserved and the applicant being allowed to submit the documents specified in the order); Cases 9 and 58/65 *Acciaierie San Michele SpA v High Authority* [1967] ECR 1 at 3 (the applicant applied, inter alia, for an order that the High Authority produce the original of an annex to a letter; it produced the original to the Registrar, who compared it with the photocopy received by the applicant, and the Court took formal note of this); Cases 24 and 34/58 *Chambre Syndicale de la Sidérurgie de l'Est v High Authority* [1960] ECR 281, order of 3 March 1959, unreported (the applicant requested that the High Authority should produce a number of documents, some mentioned generally, eg correspondence relating to the matter exchanged between the High Authority and the German government, minutes of meetings of the High Authority relating to the dispute, some specifically, eg several documents referred to in a letter; the Court dealt with the request in the general context of the measures of enquiry necessary in the case); Case 18/63 *Wollast (née Schmitz) v Commission* [1964] ECR 85 order of 13 November 1963, unreported; Cases 19 and 65/63 *Prakash v Euratom Commission* [1965] ECR 533 at 545 and Case 68/63 *Luhleich v Euratom Commission* [1965] ECR 581 at 591 (unreported orders of 28 October 1963: as in the *Schmitz* case, application was made for the production of certain documents but the Court merely reserved its decision); Case 212/86 *Imperial Chemical Industries plc v Commission* (reported as Case T-13/89 [1991] ECR II-1021), order of 11 December 1986 (see per Judge Vesterdorf [1991] ECR II-867 at 889–891).

31 Case 76/69 *Rabe v Commission* [1971] ECR 297, order of 6 May 1970, unreported.

An order for the production of documents may be very extensive in scope: in Cases T-160 and T-161/89 *Kalavros v Court of Justice*,[32] the defendant was ordered to produce all documents relating to the contested act, a form of order equivalent to the automatic disclosure of relevant documents provided for in art 23 of the ECSC Statute. An application for the production of documents, which seeks the disclosure of the internal files or documents of a party which is a Community institution, is regarded as requesting an exceptional measure of enquiry. Normally, such applications are made in the context of proceedings for the annulment of a measure adopted by the institution in question. In such cases, the measure of enquiry sought will not be ordered unless the circumstances surrounding the making of the contested act give rise to serious doubts about the real reasons of the institution concerned and to suspicions that there has been a misuse of powers. It is therefore necessary for those doubts and suspicions to be raised by the applicant as part of the case for the annulment of the contested act and it is also necessary for there to be some objective foundation for them. Mere assertion is not good enough.[33] Where internal documents are relevant, the party in possession of them may be ordered to produce the original or, depending upon the nature of the document, a certified copy.[34]

In Case C-201/86 *Spie-Batignolles v Commission*[35] it was held that the Court will not order the production by a party of documents drawn up by third parties, at least where the actions of the third party are outside the party's control. In fact, it is occasionally the case, particularly in competition cases where an undertaking seeks the annulment of a Commission decision finding the existence of an infringement of the competition rules, that a party may be in the possession of relevant evidence taking the form of documents drawn up by a third party, and the Court may well require such evidence to be produced.[36] In consequence, the ruling in the *Spie-Batignolles* case should be understood as referring to documents drawn up by a third party which are not in the possession of the party concerned (and which that party could not obtain from the third party as of right) or which have come into the possession of the party in circumstances which indicate that that party is either not free to disclose them as it wishes or is free to disclose them only for certain limited purposes (which do not include disclosure in proceedings before the Court or, generally, public disclosure). By way of illustration, the *Spie-Batignolles* case was an action for damages based on the alleged wrongful conduct of the Commission regarding the preparation and implementation of two contracts concluded between the applicant and a third country (Rwanda). The Commission could not be required to disclose official correspondence in its possession emanating from the Rwandan authorities without overriding the legitimate interest of those authorities in maintaining the confidentiality of their communications with the Commission. On the other hand, where in the course of an investigation under the EC competition rules the Commission

---

32 [1990] ECR II-871 (paras 14–15).
33 Cases 142 and 156/84 *British American Tobacco Co Ltd and R. J. Reynolds Industries Inc v Commission* [1986] ECR 1899 (paras 11–12); Case C-201/86 *Spie-Batignolles v Commission* [1990] ECR I-197, order of 16 December 1987 (para 20); *Imperial Chemical Industries plc v Commission* (above, note 30).
34 Eg Case 69/83 *Lux v Court of Auditors* [1984] ECR 2447 at 2450 (order for the production of the minutes of a meeting of the defendant or, at the very least, a certified copy of the passages in the minutes relating to the contested act).
35 Above (note 33) paras 16–17.
36 Eg Cases T-68, T-77 and T-78/89 *Società Italiano Vetro SA v Commission* [1992] ECR II-1403 (Re Italian Flat Glass) (para 41).

comes into possession of documents drawn up by third parties which are relevant to the investigation, such documents are liable to be used by the Commission for the purposes of the investigation and cannot, in consequence, be excluded from any subsequent obligation to disclose relevant evidence that attaches in the course of proceedings before the Court (subject, of course, to the question of the protection of business secrets).

If a person refuses to comply with a request of the Court, the most it can do is to take 'formal note' of the refusal.[37] It may also, however, draw inferences from the refusal. There is no obligation on it to do so nor any rules as to what inferences it may draw but, in the nature of things, its decision on the facts may be coloured by a refusal of a person to produce the information or documents requested. There are very few cases in which a party or a member state or Community institution not a party to the proceedings has declined to comply with a request of the Court. In Case T-35/89 *Albani v Commission*[38] a party was able to comply in part only with an order to produce documents because some of the documents in question had been destroyed. That caused the Court to hear evidence from the persons who had destroyed them. In Case 110/75 *Mills v European Investment Bank*[39] the Court asked the defendant to produce a document 'on the simple principle that the Court may always order production of a document that is referred to in a document that is itself in evidence'.[40] The defendant initially refused to comply on the ground that (i) the document was irrelevant and (ii) it was confidential, but later relented. In Cases 42 and 49/59 *SNUPAT v High Authority*,[41] on the other hand, the intervener refused to produce a document on which it relied because it was confidential. It said it was willing to produce the document to a person bound by professional secrecy, in the presence of the judge-rapporteur, or to the defendant but its arguments depended on an interpretation of certain parts of the document which could only be appreciated in their context. The Court took note of the intervener's reservations and hesitations and did not order production but simply rejected its arguments because of lack of proof. Similarly, in Cases 117/76 and 16/77 *Ruckdeschel & Co v Hauptzollamt Hamburg-St Annen*,[42] the Council and the Commission relied on certain facts to support the validity of a regulation. The plaintiffs in the action before the national court disputed the correctness of those facts and the Court asked the Council and the Commission to produce evidence in support of their assertions. The Council did not reply to the request. Advocate General Capotorti remarked: 'The Council and the Commission have not therefore been in a position to provide the information requested of them by the Court.' He then went on to say: 'In the circumstances the conclusion must be drawn that there is no evidence of the facts to which the two institutions attached importance.'[43]

A refusal from the adverse party to produce any evidence may lead to the inference that the assertion is well founded. It is less clear if this inference can be drawn where the refusal emanates from someone who is not a party to the

---

37 ECSC Statute, art 24; EC Statute, art 21; Euratom Statute, art 22. See Case T-25/90 *Schönherr v Economic and Social Committee* [1992] ECR II-63 (paras 30–31): the failure to comply with the order was one of the factors taken into account in the decision to annul the contested act.
38 [1990] ECR II-395 (paras 48–49).
39 Above (note 3).
40 Ibid per Advocate General Warner at 1634.
41 [1961] ECR 53 at 85.
42 [1977] ECR 1753.
43 Ibid at 1784. See also Case 19/77 *Miller International Schallplatten GmbH v Commission* [1978] ECR 131 (paras 21–22).

proceedings. If he has an interest in seeing the assertion rejected, it may be that the inference could be drawn. For this reason, if there is some ground for the refusal to comply, such as the public interest in favour of non-disclosure, it ought to be revealed to the Court. This may avoid the drawing of unnecessary inferences. On the other hand, the Court may persist in its request either by rejecting the reason given or by suggesting that the matter be resolved by a chamber or a judge unconnected with the case looking at the material in question. Only if these suggestions were rejected or the material were not disclosed after the chamber or judge had come to a view in favour of disclosure, would the Court then be entitled to draw inferences from the refusal to comply with the request.

There is no provision for the case where information or documents are concealed or misleading, inaccurate or forged material is produced in purported compliance with a request. It is to be supposed that, if such action were taken within the knowledge or with the connivance of a party's adviser or lawyer, this would constitute conduct 'incompatible with the dignity of the Court' within the meaning of RP-ECJ 35(1) or RP-CFI 41(1) and the adviser or lawyer could be excluded from the proceedings. If the matter comes to light before the judgment is given, the evidence in question may, of course, and should be, rejected, the Court drawing what inferences it may from the relevant facts, of which the incident in question would be one. If it comes to light after the date of judgment, it may give rise to proceedings for revision[44] if all the other conditions for revision of a judgment are satisfied. There is no provision analogous to those in respect of defaulting witnesses.[45]

VI   Oral testimony

The Statutes provide[46] that witnesses may be heard 'under conditions laid down in the Rules of Procedure' and that they may be heard on oath.[47] The EC and Euratom Statutes[48] further specify that the oath may be in the form laid down in the Rules of Procedure or in that laid down by the law of the country of the witness. In the alternative the Court may, instead of examining the witness itself, order him or her to be heard by the judicial authority in the place of his permanent residence.[49] Thus there are two separate methods of examining a witness: by the Court and through letters rogatory. The parties must be given an opportunity to be heard before a measure of enquiry in the form of oral testimony is ordered, whether the testimony is taken directly by the Court or through letters rogatory.[50]

The ECSC Statute[51] distinguishes between witnesses who have concealed or falsified facts in relation to which they have testified or been examined by the Court and witnesses who have 'defaulted'. With regard to the former, 'the Court is empowered to report the misconduct to the Minister of Justice of the State of which the witness or expert is a national, in order that he may be subjected to the relevant penal provisions of the national law';[52] with regard to

---

44 See pp 514 et seq.
45 Eg ECSC Statute, art 28; EC Statute, art 24; Euratom Statute, art 25.
46 ECSC Statute, art 28; EC Statute; art 23; Euratom Statute, art 24.
47 ECSC Statute, ibid; EC Statute, art 25; Euratom Statute, art 26.
48 Ibid.
49 EC Statute, art 26; Euratom Statute, art 27.
50 RP-ECJ 45(1); RP-CFI 66(1).
51 Article 28.
52 It is to be noted that it seems to be assumed that the witness is from one of the member states.

the latter, the Court has 'the powers generally granted to courts and tribunals, under conditions laid down in rules drawn up by the Court and submitted for the approval of the Council, acting unanimously'. The EC and the Euratom Statutes are framed differently. They provide that any 'violation' of an oath by a witness shall be regarded by each member state as the wrong or offence it would constitute if it had been committed before a national court with jurisdiction in civil proceedings; at the instance of the Court, the member state concerned shall prosecute the offender before the competent national court.[53] As far as 'defaulting' witnesses are concerned, the Court, as under the ECSC Statute, has the powers generally granted to courts and tribunals and may impose pecuniary penalties under conditions laid down in the Rules of Procedure.[54]

A Examination of witnesses by the Court

The Rules of Procedure state, first, that the Court may order certain facts to be proved by witnesses either of its own motion or on application by a party but in both cases after hearing the views of the advocate general, the order setting out the facts to be proved;[55] and, secondly, that the Court may by order summon a witness either of its own motion or on application by a party or at the request of the advocate general.[56] This has led to the suggestion[57] that two separate orders are made. The first comprises the order, envisaged also in RP-ECJ 45(1) and RP-CFI 66(1), which opens the measure of enquiry and specifies the issues of fact which are to be investigated and the witnesses who are to be called. The second order is the one actually summoning the witnesses. Whatever may have been the practice of the Court in former times, the present position seems to be that the decision to hear testimony is made at the Administrative Meeting and one order drawn up on the basis of the minutes of that meeting (after the parties have been given an opportunity to be heard).[58] This order sets out:

(1) the surname, forenames, description and address of the witnesses;
(2) an indication of the facts on which they are to be examined; and
(3) where appropriate, particulars of the arrangements made by the Court for reimbursement of expenses incurred by the witnesses and of the penalties which may be imposed on a defaulting witness.[59]

An example of one such order is set out in the report of Case 18/63 *Wollast (née Schmitz) v Commission*.[60] The order is then served on the parties and the witnesses cited in it.[61]

Where a party applies for the summoning of a witness, he must set out both the precise facts upon which the witness is to be heard and the reasons justifying his examination.[62] If the party does not show that the witness is in a position to give relevant evidence, the Court will not summon him.[63] The

---

53 EC Statute, art 27; Euratom Statute, art 28.
54 Ibid, arts 24 and 25 respectively.
55 RP-ECJ 47(1); RP-CFI 68(1).
56 Ibid.
57 Wall *The Court of Justice of the European Communities – Jurisdiction and Procedure* pp 240–241.
58 RP-ECJ 45(1); RP-CFI 66(1).
59 See RP-ECJ 47(2); RP-CFI 68(2).
60 [1964] ECR 85 at 95.
61 RP-ECJ 47(2); RP-CFI 68(2).
62 RP-ECJ 47(1); RP-CFI 68(1).
63 Eg Case 14/64 *Gualco (née Barge) v High Authority* [1965] ECR 51 at 66 (Advocate General Roemer); Case 60/82 *Cowood v Commission* [1982] ECR 4625 (para 13); Case 403/85 *F v Commission* [1987] ECR 645 (para 9).

Rules of Procedure do not specify whether the application must be made by separate document. It can and, as a matter of good practice, should be made in the pleadings: RP-ECJ 38(1)(e) and 40(1)(d) and RP-CFI 44(1)(e) and 46(1)(d) state that the application and defence, respectively, must set out 'the nature of any evidence offered in support'; where a fact upon which a party wishes to rely can be proved only by testimony, the party should specify this in the pleading. In addition, the witness ought to be clearly identified, by name, address, occupation and competence as a witness, so that the Court can assess his capacity to give evidence. Alternatively, the application can be made separately and, it would seem, at any time. The formal requirements of such an application are set out in RP-ECJ 37 and RP-CFI 43 and it must be made in the language of the case.

The Rules of Procedure leave it unclear whether the application is made under RP-ECJ 47(1) or RP-CFI 68(1) or, as a procedural issue, under RP-ECJ 91 or RP-CFI 114. If made as a procedural issue (that is, by separate document and not in the body of a pleading), the procedure set out in the latter articles would have to be followed. Although parties have on occasion requested witnesses to be heard,[64] it is not evident that the matter was raised under RP-ECJ 91 or RP-CFI 114. The Court may make the summoning of the witness conditional on the deposit with the Court's cashier of a sum which it considers to be sufficient to cover the taxed costs. Where the decision to summon the witness is made by the Court of its own motion, however, the cashier advances the funds necessary.[65] The Court order summoning witnesses specifies the precise question of fact upon which each witness is to be examined. In order to make the order, therefore, the Court must be in a position to know what are the important issues of fact in the case and who are the persons best qualified to give evidence on them. It is the duty of the parties, in their pleadings, and, if necessary, in a formal application for the summoning of witnesses, to place the Court in this position. In some early cases, the Court was able to determine only the issues of fact on which testimony was required. It then made an order requiring the parties to indicate in writing the persons who could give evidence on the issues specified in the order.[66] More recently, in cases before the ECJ, there has been a growing tendency to hold an informal meeting between the judge-rapporteur, the advocate general and the parties and their representatives to sort out such questions; in cases before the CFI that tendency has been formalised as measures of organisation of procedure.[67]

The parties have two weeks from the date of service of the Court's order on them to object to the summoning of a particular witness.[68] The grounds upon which the objection may be based are that the witness is (a) not competent, (b)

64 See, for example, Case 44/59 *Fiddelaar v Commission* [1960] ECR 535 at 545–546; *Gualco v High Authority* (above, note 63); Case 11/64 *Weighardt v Euratom Commission* [1965] ECR 285; Case 3/65 *SA Métallurgique d' Espérance-Longdoz v High Authority* [1965] ECR 1065; Case 2/65 *Preo e Figli v High Authority* [1966] ECR 219; Case 77/70 *Prelle v Commission* [1971] ECR 561.

65 RP-ECJ 47(3); RP-CFI 68(3). Ie where the Court decides to hear witnesses of its own motion, the costs are borne by it: see, for example, Case 10/55 *Mirossevich v High Authority* [1954–56] ECR 333. This is, however, without prejudice to the Court's power to order that one of the parties shall bear the burden of such costs at the end of the day.

66 See Case 68/63 *Luhleich v Euratom Commission* [1965] ECR 581 (the order also required the parties to give reasons why each witness proposed should be examined, to limit their proposals to the minimum necessary and to communicate the proposals to both the Court and the other parties); Case 34/65 *Mosthaf v Euratom Commission* [1966] ECR 521; *Cowood v Commission* (above, note 63).

67 See RP-CFI 64.

68 RP-ECJ 50(2); RP-CFI 73(2).

not a proper person or (c) any other reason.[69] The basic, but not only, objection to a witness would seem to be that there exists some circumstance which would render the probative value of his testimony worthless, even if it is given under oath.[70] Apart from specifying that the objection must set out the grounds on which it is based and the evidence relied on,[71] the Rules of Procedure make no further specific provision. As in the case of applications for the summoning of a witness, it is unclear whether the objection is to be dealt with in accordance with RP-ECJ 91 or RP-CFI 114 or not. At all events, it is to be supposed that the Court would not decide to uphold the objection without hearing the views of the other parties and, if need be, the witness himself. If no objection is made within the period for doing so, it is unclear whether or not any objection may be raised thereafter. In principle, the existence of an express time limit for the raising of an objection leads to the inference that the parties are precluded from raising any objection after the expiry of the time limit. However, it does not seem that a party could be precluded from raising an objection thereafter if it were based on a material fact that had come to the attention of the party concerned only after the expiry of the time limit. In that event, the objection should be raised promptly. If a party is aware of an objection or potential objection to the examination of a person as a witness and nonetheless fails to raise an objection or even agrees to the examination of the person concerned as a witness, that party will be taken to have acquiesced in the examination and will be precluded from asserting that the examination of the person concerned was a procedural defect.[72] In such circumstances, while the admissibility of the testimony given by the witness cannot be contested, it is still open to the parties, or any one of them, to rely on the objection (where appropriate) in order to undermine the weight to be attached to the testimony of the witness.

Witnesses who have been duly summoned are obliged to attend to give evidence.[73] There is no provision making any particular person or category of persons uncompellable as a witness. If a witness fails to appear before the Court, it may impose a fine of not more than ECU 5,000 and order a further summons to be served at his own expense.[74] If the witness gives a 'valid excuse' for not appearing, he may be discharged from the obligation to pay the fine;

---

69 RP-ECJ 50(1); RP-CFI 73(1).
70 In Case C-244/92P *Kupka-Floridi v Economic and Social Committee* [1993] ECR I-2041 (paras 12–19), the appellant contested a judgment of the CFI on the ground, inter alia, that a person examined as a witness by the CFI could not have given testimony as such because, by his conduct before the commencement of the action, he had made himself a party to the case (although he had not participated in the proceedings as an intervener or other party). That claim was dismissed because the appellant had in fact acquiesced in the examination of the person concerned as a witness. It was not necessary for the Court to consider the question whether or not a party is competent to give evidence as a witness. In principle, an objection that a person cannot be heard as a witness because he or she is a party to the proceedings is a technical objection to the form of the Court order: if the person concerned is a party, he or she should be ordered to be 'heard as a party' and not 'as a witness'. It is not an objection to the competence of the person concerned to give evidence; and any difference in the probative value of the evidence given which results from the fact that the person concerned is a party goes to the assessment of the evidence given and not to its admissibility. Lastly, it is doubtful if an employee of a party is to be regarded as a party to the proceedings for the purpose of giving oral evidence: employees, whether they be officials of a Community institution or employed by an undertaking which is a party to the proceedings, are invariably examined as witnesses and not as parties.
71 RP-ECJ 50(2); RP-CFI 73(2).
72 *Kupka-Floridi v Economic and Social Committee* (above, note 70).
73 RP-ECJ 48(1); RP-CFI 69(1).
74 RP-ECJ 48(2); RP-CFI 69(2).

and the amount may be reduced at the request of the witness where he establishes that it is disproportionate to his income.[75] Otherwise the fine or a decision requiring his attendance may be enforced in accordance with the usual rules for enforcing a judgment.[76] It does not seem that, when a witness defaults, the Court must first consider fining him before seeking to enforce a second order requiring him to give evidence. It lies within its discretion whether or not to fine or commence proceedings to have its order enforced. It may, indeed, decide to take no action at all. In Cases 19 and 65/63 *Prakash v Euratom Commission*[77] the Court ordered testimony to be heard from several witnesses. One lived in the United States of America and did not appear but sent a written reply to the questions on which he was to give evidence. The Court decided to dispense with his testimony and add his letter to the file. In Case 3/66 *Alfieri v European Parliament*[78] a similar approach was adopted when one of the witnesses excused himself on valid grounds (unspecified in the report) and submitted a written declaration. This was read out at the hearing with the consent of the parties. Although the Statutes declare[79] that the Court has 'the powers generally granted to courts and tribunals and may impose pecuniary penalties' in respect of defaulting witnesses, these powers are said to be exercisable under the conditions laid down in the Rules of Procedure, which refer only to a power to fine and a power to require appearance before the Court. It does not, therefore, seem that, under the Rules of Procedure as presently worded, the Court exercises any other powers.

However he may be summoned, whether by the Court of its own motion or at the request of one of the parties, the witness remains a witness of the Court and gives his evidence to it; the parties are given notice to attend at the examination of the witness but are not obliged to do so.[80] The President of the Court (or chamber)[81] first establishes the identity of the witness[82] and then informs him that he will be required to 'vouch the truth' of his testimony in the manner laid down in the Rules of Procedure.[83] He also instructs the witness to tell the truth and warns him of the criminal liability which he may incur under national law in the event of a failure to do so.[84]

Witnesses may be heard:

(1)   on oath, taken in the form laid down in the Rules of Procedure or in the manner specified by the law of the country in which the witness resides;[85]
(2)   after making an affirmation, if the law of the country in which he resides so provides and in the manner laid down by it;[86] or
(3)   without taking an oath or affirming, if the law of the country in which he resides provides for neither but after being instructed by the President that he must tell the truth and being warned of any criminal liability under national law if he fails to do so.[87]

---

75 RP-ECJ 48(3); RP-CFI 69(3).
76 RP-ECJ 48(4); RP-CFI 69(4).
77 [1965] ECR 533 at 545.
78 [1966] ECR 437 at 446.
79 ECSC Statute, art 28; EC Statute, art 24; Euratom Statute, art 25.
80 RP-ECJ 47(4); RP-CFI 68(4).
81 It will in fact be almost invariably the president of a chamber, see RP-ECJ 9(2) and RP-CFI 13(1).
82 By asking him to give his name, address and occupation.
83 RP-ECJ 47(4); RP-CFI 68(4). See also RP-ECJ 124; RP-CFI 71.
84 RP-ECJ 124(1); RP-CFI 71(1).
85 EC Statute, art 25; Euratom Statute, art 26; RP-ECJ 124(2); RP-CFI 71(2).
86 RP-ECJ 124(2); RP-CFI 71(3).
87 Ibid.

The way in which the witness gives his evidence depends very much on how the chamber entrusted with the measure of enquiry wishes to conduct the proceedings. The Rules of Procedure envisage that the witness first makes a deposition and then answers questions which may be put to him by the judges, the advocate general, or the representatives of the parties.[88] On occasion, however, the entire examination may be conducted by the judge-rapporteur or the parties may be allowed to examine the witnesses themselves. Since the witness is the Court's, there is no examination and cross-examination in the sense understood in the context of proceedings in an English court. Instead, subject to the control of the President, the parties, through their representatives, may put questions to the witness, confront him with any documents, etc. The end result, where this happens, is very similar to the examination of a witness in an English court. Questions may be asked of the witness either directly or through the President. It is a fundamental procedural rule that, at least in cases where a person is threatened with a decision adverse to his or her interests, that person or his representative is entitled to attend the examination of a witness and put or have put to the witness there and then any question that may be useful to his defence.[89] An additional witness, not included in the Court order, may be examined on the same occasion as the other witnesses if the Court should consider it appropriate.[90] Gowns are not normally worn at the examination of witnesses.

After giving his evidence, the witness swears or affirms the truth of what he has said[91] (unless relieved from doing either).[92] The Registrar then has a record of the evidence, which constitutes the official record of the proceedings, drawn up and signed by him, the President or (as the case may be) judge-rapporteur and the witness.[93] The examination of the witness is tape recorded and it is the transcript of the recording that is signed. The oath that the witness must take is as follows: 'I swear that I have spoken the truth, the whole truth and nothing but the truth';[94] but he may also take the oath laid down by his national law.[95] The Court may, after hearing the parties, exempt a witness from taking the oath.[96] Where national law allows the witness in legal proceedings to make an affirmation equivalent to an oath as well as or instead of it, he may make such an affirmation under the conditions and in the form prescribed by national law.[97] If national law does not provide for an oath or an affirmation, the President simply instructs the witness to tell the truth and reminds him of the penalties under national law for not doing so.[98] After the examination of a witness, a supplementary statement made by the witness may be accepted by the Court.[99]

If a witness refuses to give evidence, take the oath or affirm without 'good reason' he may be fined up to ECU 5,000[1] but may be discharged from the obligation to pay if he has a 'valid excuse'.[2] The fine may also be reduced at the

88 RP-ECJ 47(4); RP-CFI 68(4).
89 Case 141/84 *De Compte v European Parliament* [1985] ECR 1951 (paras 17–18).
90 Case T-35/89 *Albani v Commission* [1990] ECR II-395 (paras 26–33).
91 RP-ECJ 47(5); RP-CFI 68(5).
92 RP-ECJ 124(2), last sentence; RP-CFI 71(3), last sentence.
93 RP-ECJ 47(6); RP-CFI 68(6).
94 RP-ECJ 47(5); RP-CFI 68(5).
95 RP-ECJ 124(2); RP-CFI 71(2).
96 RP-ECJ 47(5); RP-CFI 68(5).
97 RP-ECJ 124(2); RP-CFI 71(3).
98 RP-ECJ 124(1) and (2); RP-CFI 71(1) and (3).
99 Case 246/84 *Kotsonis v Council* [1986] ECR 3989 (para 22).
 1 RP-ECJ 48(2); RP-CFI 69(2).
 2 RP-ECJ 48(3); RP-CFI 69(3).

request of the witness where he establishes that it is disproportionate having regard to his income.[3] The decision imposing a fine is enforced in the same way as a judgment of the Court.[4] It is not entirely clear what may be a good reason or valid excuse for not giving evidence, taking the oath or affirming. The existence of any privilege entitling a witness to refuse to give evidence seems to be a matter of Community law, but there is practically no authority as to its existence and the grounds on which it might be invoked. In Case 155/79 *AM & S v Commission*[5] the Court recognised the confidentiality of the lawyer–client relationship and, although the case actually concerned the Commission's powers to require the disclosure to it of documents, it is to be supposed that a lawyer, as defined in the judgment, may refuse to give evidence on confidential matters falling within the scope of the relationship with his client.[6] The fact that the Court does respect confidentiality based on other grounds is evident from Case 155/78 *M v Commission*,[7] where the Court made an order requiring several doctors to give evidence 'subject always to the limits imposed by their rules of professional conduct'.[8] In some member states it is unlawful for certain classes of person to give evidence relating to a confidential relationship; to do so can result in them being prosecuted under the code of criminal law. Hence it is uncertain whether the Court proceeds on the basis that it will not require a witness to give evidence where it would be contrary to his national law to do so or might lead to the imposition of a penalty; or whether it simply respects certain confidential relationships. In view of the various links with the law of the country in which the witness resides (concerning the method of taking an oath or affirming and the sanctions for violating the oath or concealing or falsifying evidence), it is arguable that a witness is entitled to refuse to give evidence on the ground that to do so would be contrary to national law.[9] Whether the existence of a privilege against self-incrimination should be accepted, is another question.[10] It also seems right that the Court should respect the confidentiality of certain relationships even in the absence of any rule of national, or indeed written Community, law forbidding a breach of confidence, as a matter of public policy. At this stage in the development of the Court's case law, it is, however, impossible to say whether, and if so to what extent, the Court is prepared to limit the exercise of its powers to require evidence to be given in a particular case.

The ECSC Statute provides[11] that, where a witness has concealed or falsified facts on which he has testified or been examined by the Court, it may report the matter to the Minister of Justice of the member state of which the witness is a national so that he may be subjected to the appropriate sanction under national law. The EC and Euratom Statutes[12] provide that 'a Member State shall treat any violation of an oath by a witness or expert in the same manner as if the offence had been committed before one of its courts with jurisdiction in civil proceedings. At the instance of the Court, the Member

---

3 Ibid.
4 RP-ECJ 48(4); RP-CFI 69(4).
5 [1982] ECR 1575.
6 For the same reason, one of the parties may object that he is not a competent witness regarding such matters.
7 [1980] ECR 1797 at 1801.
8 It seems that, in this case, the Court regarded the doctors' reliance on medical secrecy as excessive but it does not seem to have taken any action against them.
9 Against this see *M v Commission* (above, note 7 at 1821) (Advocate General Capotorti).
10 See, in a different context, Case 374/87 *Orkem v Commission* [1989] ECR 3283 (paras 28–35).
11 Article 28.
12 Articles 27 and 28 respectively.

State concerned shall prosecute the offender before its competent court.' It will be observed that, while the EC and Euratom Statutes simply refer to a 'violation of an oath', and do not therefore cover the situation where the witness has only affirmed but has nevertheless deliberately lied to the Court, the ECSC Statute speaks of a concealment or falsification of evidence. The EC and Euratom Statutes also specify that the violation of the oath is to be regarded as if it had occurred before a national court with jurisdiction in civil proceedings whereas the ECSC Statute does not.

The Rules of Procedure envisage that, when a witness violates his oath or conceals or falsifies evidence, the Court reports the matter to the member state concerned.[13] The procedure is that, after hearing the advocate general, the Court refers the matter to the competent authority of the member state specified in Annex III of the Supplementary Rules.[14] The criterion for selecting the competent authority is the place where the witness resides.[15] The competent authority then acts. It would seem from the Statutes that the competent authority is bound to prosecute the witness and has no discretion to refrain from doing so.[16] The Court's report appears to be made in the form of an order which is served by the Registrar on the competent authority and which sets out the facts and circumstances causing the Court to refer the matter.

It would seem that both the competent authority and the judicial authority responsible for deciding the witness's guilt are bound by the findings of fact made by the Court. The judicial authority's function is only to decide whether they constitute an offence under national law. This does not mean that it cannot supplement those findings where necessary. For example, the witness's state of mind may be an ingredient of the offence but the Court's order may only set out the facts and respects in which he did not tell the truth. In this event, the judicial authority can and must investigate the witness's state of mind. What it cannot do is call into question the Court's finding of fact.

Witnesses are entitled to have their travelling and subsistence expenses reimbursed[17] and to be paid compensation for any loss of earnings.[18] The cashier of the Court may make a payment towards travelling and subsistence expenses in advance[19] but compensation for loss of earnings is paid only after the witness has given evidence.[20] An application for payment of expenses or compensation is made by the witness to the cashier of the Court. The Rules of Procedure do not lay down any formal requirements but it seems that it should be in writing and addressed to the Registrar. Evidence must be produced to justify a claim for loss of earnings and particulars must be given of the costs for

---

13 RP-ECJ 125(c).
14 SR 6; RP-CFI 72(1).
15 This follows from the identification of the competent authority in the constituent parts of the United Kingdom, which is based on residence, and it is to be supposed that the same test applies as between the member states.
16 SR 6 contains a somewhat cryptic reference to what is now RP-ECJ 124 and it is arguable that the intention was that a prosecution could be made whenever national law allowed it, even if the witness had only affirmed. All three Statutes envisage that the Rules of Procedure may supplement them (ECSC and EC Statutes, art 55; Euratom Statute, art 56) and this may also apply to the Supplementary Rules (but see RP-ECJ 125). RP-ECJ 124(1) and RP-CFI 71(1) appear to assume that there may be criminal liability if a witness does not tell the truth even if he has neither sworn an oath nor affirmed.
17 RP-ECJ 51(1); RP-CFI 74(1).
18 RP-ECJ 51(2); RP-CFI 74(2).
19 RP-ECJ 51(1); RP-CFI 74(1).
20 RP-ECJ 51(2); RP-CFI 74(2).

which any advance payment is requested.[21] The Registrar orders the payment of the sums due and requires a receipt or acknowledgment of payment.[22] If he is of the opinion that the amount applied for is excessive, he may reduce it of his own motion or order it to be paid by instalments.[23] There is no provision for an appeal against his decision.[24]

Where the witness is summoned by the Court at the behest of one of the parties, the Court may require, as a condition of summoning the witness, that that party deposit with the Court's cashier a sum which it considers to be sufficient to cover the taxed costs of hearing the witness; on the other hand, if the witness is summoned by the Court of its own motion, the cashier shall advance any sums necessary in connection with the examination.[25] This does not preclude the Court from ordering, in the judgment closing proceedings, one of the parties to bear the costs of hearing witnesses, even where they were summoned by the Court of its own motion.[26] In such an event, the costs of the preparatory enquiry normally follow the event.[27]

B   Letters rogatory

The EC and Euratom Statutes specifically provide[28] that the Court may order a witness to be examined by a judicial authority in the place where he resides permanently. The order may be made on application by a party or by the Court of its own motion[29] and in any event after the parties have been given an opportunity to be heard.[30] No conditions are expressly laid down in the Rules of Procedure regarding the form and content of an application made by a party. RP-ECJ 37 and RP-CFI 43 apply in any event but it would also seem that the applicant, as in the case of an application for the examination of a witness by the Court, should set out the facts on which the witness should be examined, the reasons he should be examined and the justification for recourse to letters rogatory.

Letters rogatory are issued in the form of an order which sets out the name, forenames, description and address of the witness, the facts on which he is to be examined, the parties, their agents, lawyers or advisers, their address for service and a brief description of the subject matter of the dispute.[31] The order is served on the parties by the Registrar,[32] who also sends it to the competent authority in the member state in which the witness is to be examined.[33] Annex I of the Supplementary Rules identifies the competent authority for each member state.[34] The country in which the examination is to take place is that

---

21 IR 21(1).
22 IR 21(2).
23 Ibid.
24 IR 21(1) mentions only 'advance payments' but it seems that it really means 'advances' simpliciter.
25 RP-ECJ 47(3); RP-CFI 68(3).
26 Eg Cases 40–48, 50, 54–56, 111, 113 and 114/73 *Suiker Unie UA v Commission* [1975] ECR 1663 at 2025 (Re European Sugar Cartel).
27 Cf Case 43/74 *Guillot v Commission* [1977] ECR 1309 (para 110): they may also be divided between the parties, see Cases 56–60/74 *Kampffmeyer Muhlenvereinigung KG v Commission and Council* [1976] ECR 711 (para 24).
28 Articles 26 and 27 respectively.
29 RP-ECJ 52; RP-CFI 75(1).
30 RP-ECJ 45(1); RP-CFI 66(1).
31 SR 1; RP-CFI 75(2).
32 Ibid.
33 SR 2; RP-CFI 75(3).
34 The Minister of Justice in Belgium, Denmark, France, Greece, Ireland, Italy, Luxembourg, the Netherlands, Portugal and Spain, the Federal Minister of Justice in Germany and the Secretary of State in the United Kingdom.

where the witness resides permanently.[35] Where necessary, the order is accompanied by a translation into the official languages of the member state to which it is addressed.[36] The competent authority passes the order on to the judicial authority that has power under national law to carry out the examination[37] and it is this authority which must give effect to the letters rogatory, in accordance with the national law applied by it.[38] Once the order has been executed the judicial authority gives the order embodying the letters rogatory, any documents arising from its implementation and a detailed statement of the costs to the competent authority, which sends them on to the Registrar.[39] The Registrar then has all these documents translated into the language of the case.[40]

The Court bears the costs of the letters rogatory but may, where appropriate, charge them to the parties.[41] In the first instance, the Registrar instructs the cashier of the Court to refund the costs directly to the body designated by the competent authority (which need not be the judicial authority which carried out the examination) in the currency of the member state concerned and against proof of payment.[42] As can be seen, these costs are those incurred by the body responsible for implementing the letters rogatory, not the costs incurred by the parties. It is the former alone that may be borne by the Court unless it decides to charge them to the parties. So far as is known, letters rogatory have been used only once.[43]

VII   Experts' reports

Under the Statutes[44] the Court can at any time entrust the task of giving an expert opinion to 'any individual, body, authority, committee or other organisation it chooses'. The ECSC Statute provides for the compilation of a list of individuals or bodies approved by it as experts but this has never been done. It also provides, in addition to giving an expert opinion, for the holding of an enquiry. This is not, however, specifically referred to in the five types of measures of enquiry set out by the Rules of Procedure.[45] Either it is to be taken to be included in 'experts' reports' or the list is not to be regarded as exhaustive. Experts' reports have been ordered, inter alia, to assess the quality of a translator's work,[46] an official's mental state[47] and the applicant's qualifications and abilities;[48] to examine the rates for and conditions of transport of mineral fuels,[49] price rises and the market in dyestuffs[50] and the economic

---

35 EC Statute, art 26; Euratom Statute, art 27.
36 SR 2; RP-CFI 75(3).
37 Ibid.
38 Ibid.
39 Ibid.
40 Ibid.
41 EC Statute, art 26; Euratom Statute, art 27; SR 3; RP-CFI 75(4).
42 IR 21(3).
43 In Case 160/84 *Oryzomyli Kavallas OEE v Commission* [1985] ECR 675.
44 ECSC Statute, art 25; EC Statute, art 22; Euratom Statute, art 23.
45 See RP-ECJ 45(2); RP-CFI 65.
46 Case 10/55 *Mirossevich v High Authority* [1954–56] ECR 333.
47 Case 12/68 *X v Audit Board* [1969] ECR 109 and Case 18/70 *X v Council* [1972] ECR 1205.
48 Case 785/79 *Pizziolo v Commission* [1981] ECR 969.
49 Cases 24 and 34/58 *Chambre Syndicale de la Sidérurgie de l'Est v High Authority* [1960] ECR 281.
50 Case 48/69 *ICI Ltd v Commission* [1972] ECR 619: see also Case 49/69 *Badische Anilin und Soda-Fabrik AG v Commission*, Case 51/69 *Farbenfabriken Bayer AG v Commission*, Case 52/69 *Geigy AG v Commission*, Case 53/69 *Sandoz AG v Commission*, Case 54/69 *Française des Matières Colorantes SA (Francolor) (now SA Produits Chimiques Ugine Kuhlmann) v Commission*, Case 55/69 *Cassella Farbwerke Mainkur AG v Commission*, Case 56/69 *Farbwerke Hoechst AG v Commission* and Case 57/69 *ACNA v Commission* [1972] ECR 713, 745, 787, 845, 851, 887, 927 and 933, respectively.

consequences of certain gas tariffs;[51] to verify the conclusions drawn in the contested act, the evidence relied on and the characteristics of the market;[52] and to investigate the damages claimed and the issues of fact between the parties.[53] On occasion, the parties have themselves submitted an expert's report or, at the hearing, an expert has addressed the Court on behalf of one of the parties.[54] In neither case is this, strictly speaking, the hearing of expert evidence within the meaning of the Statutes and the Rules of Procedure. In the first case, the evidence tendered by the party is documentary and, in the second, it is either testimony or a parole plea as to the facts. In principle, the ordering of an expert's report is inconsistent with proceedings under art 169 of the EEC Treaty.[55]

The decision to obtain an expert's report (or, it seems, to hold an enquiry)[56] is made by the Court in the form of an order[57] after the parties have been given an opportunity to be heard.[58] In contrast to the position with regard to witnesses, the Rules of Procedure do not expressly state that the order may be made either on application by one of the parties or by the Court of its own motion. It would, nevertheless, appear that a party may apply for an expert's report to be obtained or an enquiry held, the application being in the same form as for the summoning of a witness.[59] The Court's order appoints the expert, defines his task and sets a time limit for the making of his report.[60] The Court may request the parties or one of them to lodge a security for the costs of the expert's report.[61] The order is then served on the parties, who have two weeks after service to make any objection to the appointment of the expert.[62] They cannot complain about the other contents of the order. The objection is made in the same form and must be based on the same grounds as in the case of a witness.[63] The usual order is that the parties should, by a specified date, agree between themselves the person to be appointed as the expert and that, if they fail to agree, either the Court shall appoint one or more persons[64] or there shall be two experts nominated by the parties.[65] On the other hand, in Case 785/79 *Pizziolo v Commission*[66] and, so it would seem, the *Dyestuffs* cases,[67] the order was that, failing agreement between themselves, each party should send

51 Case C-169/84 *Société CdF Chimie Azote et Fertilisants SA and Société Chimique de la Grande Paroisse SA v Commission* [1990] ECR I-3083.
52 Cases C-89, C-104, C-114, C-116, C-117, C-125 to C-129/85 *A Ahlström Osakeyhtio v Commission* [1993] ECR I-1307 (paras 31–32 and 137–138).
53 Cases 29, 31, 36–47, 50 and 51/63 *Laminoirs, Hauts Fourneaux, Forges, Fonderies et Usines de la Providence v High Authority* [1965] ECR 911.
54 In Case 204/80 *Procureur de la République v Vedel* [1982] ECR 465, a reference for a preliminary ruling, the Court asked the French government to send a representative to the hearing, accompanied by an expert.
55 Case 141/87 *Commission v Italy* [1989] ECR 943 (para 17 and at 972, Advocate General Jacobs).
56 See IR 8.
57 RP-ECJ 49(1); RP-CFI 70(1). In Case 318/81R *Commission v CODEMI SpA* [1982] ECR 1325 an expert was appointed as an interim measure, not a measure of enquiry.
58 RP-ECJ 45(1); RP-CFI 66(1).
59 In *Pizziolo v Commission* (above, note 48) the request was made in the Reply, see 973.
60 RP-ECJ 49(1); RP-CFI 70(1).
61 RP-ECJ 49(2); RP-CFI 70(2).
62 RP-ECJ 50(2); RP-CFI 73(2).
63 RP-ECJ 50; RP-CFI 73.
64 See, for example, *Chambre Syndicale de la Sidérurgie v High Authority* (above, note 49) order of 26 June 1959, unreported; *Usines de la Providence v High Authority* (above, note 53); Cases T-32 and 39/89 *Marcopoulos v Court of Justice* [1990] ECR II-281 (paras 12–16).
65 Case 23/81 *Commission v Royal Belge* [1983] ECR 2685, order of 9 December 1981, unreported.
66 Above (note 48).
67 [1972] ECR 619, 713, 745, 787, 845, 851, 887, 927 and 933.

in its nomination, giving reasons for its objections to the other party's proposal. In the event, the parties to the *Pizziolo* case proposed one expert each and agreed that they should nominate a third. The Court accepted this suggestion just as, in the *Dyestuffs* cases, it had accepted the parties' agreement that there should be two experts.[68] In Case 318/81 *Commission v CODEMI*[69] the Court ordered that the report should be drawn up by a panel of experts and nominated the chairman of the panel, ordering him to choose the other members from lists of names submitted by the parties. In Case C-169/84 *Société CdF Chimie Azote et Fertilisants and Société Chimique de la Grande Paroisse SA v Commission*[70] the order underlines the appropriateness of agreement between the parties on the identity of the expert because, in the absence of agreement, they would each have to nominate one expert who together would nominate a third. Clearly, from the point of view of the costs involved, one expert is better than three. In Case T-169/89 *Frederiksen v European Parliament*[71] the Court asked the parties to agree the expert but one of the parties contested the need for an expert's report and did not co-operate in the nomination of an expert. In consequence, the Court appointed the expert of its own motion.

The expert receives a copy of the order appointing him and is given all the documents necessary for carrying out his task.[72] He is supervised by the judge-rapporteur (even where formal control of the preparatory enquiry has been assigned to a chamber) who is entitled to be present during his investigations and who is to be kept informed of his progress.[73] The expert himself has no powers of investigation. If, for example, he requires a document which is not in his possession or that of the Court, he must ask the Court to require its production unless the possessor is willing to disclose it at the expert's own request.[74] Similarly, he has no power to enter premises. The Rules of Procedure expressly provide[75] that the Court may order witnesses to be examined by it, if the expert so requests, the examination following the usual rules. In the *CODEMI* case,[76] however, the Court's order provided expressly that the board of experts could hear witnesses and call for the production of documents.

The expert's opinion is restricted to the points expressly referred to in the order appointing him[77] and is given in the form of a report.[78] The report should

---

68 See [1972] ECR at 647; in Case 2/65 *Preo e Figli v High Authority* [1966] ECR 219 the Court assigned the conduct of preparatory enquiries to the Second Chamber, it heard the parties in camera and they agreed on the appointment of an expert (see at 224).
69 [1985] ECR 3693 (at 3696–3697).
70 [1990] ECR I-3083.
71 [1991] ECR II-1403 (paras 36–41).
72 RP-ECJ 49(2) and IR 8; RP-CFI 70(2). Eg *Mirossevich v High Authority* (above, note 46) at 353. In Case 12/68 *X v Audit Board* [1970] ECR 291, the expert was to have access to the parties and both the defendant's medical advisers and the applicant's doctors were to give him all useful information; in *Pizziolo v Commission* (above, note 48; order of 30 November 1981, unreported) the order specified that a copy of the Court's judgment, the order appointing the experts and all pleadings and annexes should be served on the experts.
73 RP-ECJ 49(2); RP-CFI 70(2).
74 So, in *Pizziolo v Commission* (above, note 48) the experts approached the Court for additional documents. The Court, through the Registrar, then asked the parties if they agreed to their production (which they did) and also requested them to draw up a list of agreed documents.
75 RP-ECJ 49(3); RP-CFI 70(3).
76 Above (note 69).
77 RP-ECJ 49(4); RP-CFI 70(4). If a party wishes to object that the report goes beyond the scope of the matters on which the expert was ordered to report, he should raise the objection immediately (usually in written observations on the report). If any such objection is not raised until the hearing in the case, it may be dismissed as inadmissible: Case T-36/89 *Nijman v Commission* [1991] ECR II-699 (paras 30–31).
78 RP-ECJ 49(5); RP-CFI 70(5).

be submitted to the Court within the time limit set in the order but it would seem that the Court may extend the time if so requested.[79] It does not seem that the President alone has power to extend time because the original time limit is contained in a Court order and the Rules of Procedure give him no express authority to override it.[80] No formal requirements as to the contents of the report are laid down. Where more than one expert has been appointed, the report is the report of them all. That does not mean that the experts must be unanimous: the practice of appointing an uneven number of experts indicates that the report may be based on the opinion of the majority. After presenting his report the expert takes the following oath in the presence of the Court: 'I swear that I have conscientiously and impartially carried out my task.'[81] However, after hearing the parties, the Court may exempt the expert from taking the oath[82] and, as in the case of witnesses, the oath may be taken in the manner laid down by the expert's own national law or he may affirm or simply be warned by the President of the criminal liability he may have incurred under national law if he has not carried out his task conscientiously and impartially.[83]

The Court may, after the presentation of the report, order that the expert be examined.[84] In this event, the parties are given notice to attend the examination, which is conducted as if the expert were a witness and may be ordered by letters rogatory.[85] The parties may also be allowed to submit written observations or questions. There is no specific provision that the report be served on the parties but it is the practice to do so;[86] service of the report on the parties appears to be implied in the right of the parties to attend the examination of an expert and ask him questions.[87] The expert is examined on his report but not on matters falling outside the definition of his task contained in the order appointing him. The procedure for examining an expert varies from case to case.[88] In *Chambre Syndicale de la Sidérurgie v High Authority*[89] the Court allowed the parties and the advocate general time to put written questions to the expert and the latter gave written replies. In *Usines de la Providence v High Authority*[90] only the defendant thought it necessary to submit observations on the expert's report. There was then an examination in open court under RP-ECJ 49(5), at

---

79 See *Usines de la Providence v High Authority* (above, note 53) at 934.
80 RP-ECJ 82 and RP-CFI 103(1) provide only that the person who has prescribed a time limit under the Rules of Procedure may extend it.
81 RP-ECJ 49(6); RP-CFI 70(6).
82 Ibid.
83 RP-ECJ 124; RP-CFI 71(1)–(3).
84 In the *Société CdF Chimie Azote* case (above, note 70) at 3085–3086, the parties were asked for their views on whether or not the experts should give oral evidence and take the oath. They did not consider that either step was necessary and did not formulate any question on the report to be put to the experts.
85 EC Statute, art 25; Euratom Statute, art 26; RP-ECJ 49(5), 52 and 124; SR 1–3; RP-CFI 70(5) and 75.
86 Where the report contains confidential matters, such as business secrets of one of the parties or a third party, a non-confidential version of the report may be prepared for disclosure to the parties: see *Société CdF Chimie Azote* (above, note 70) at 3085–3086, where the Court sent the non-confidential version prepared by it to the experts for their approval before serving it on the parties.
87 They may also inspect his report at the Registry and take copies of it at their own expense (see RP-ECJ 53(2); RP-CFI 76(2)).
88 Useful descriptions of the procedure followed may be found in Cases T-32 and T-39/89 *Marcopoulos v Court of Justice* [1990] ECR II-281 (paras 12–16); *Nijman v Commission* (above, note 77) paras 11 et seq; *Frederiksen v European Parliament* (above, note 71) paras 34 et seq.
89 Above (note 49) see at 292.
90 Above (note 53) see 933–934.

which the expert presented an oral report on the defendant's observations and took the oath. Subsequently he wrote a letter to the Court containing certain corrections he wished to be made to his report in the light of the oral examination. *X v Audit Board* and the *Dyestuffs* cases[91] followed a similar pattern but, in Case 18/70 *X v Council*,[92] due to the sensitivity of the evidence, the expert gave his presentation and was extensively examined and cross-examined by the parties at the hearing in camera. After he had made his observations and taken the oath, the hearing was resumed in public.

The function of an expert is basically to give an opinion on questions of fact but, on occasion and depending on the scope of his remit, he may be called on to examine questions of mixed fact and law. His conclusions do not constitute a decision on the matters submitted for his consideration but evidence of how they are to be resolved. It remains for the Court to decide the question, taking account of all the evidence including the expert's report and whether or not the expert has followed the right approach in law.[93] The Court is not bound by his conclusions and may review them.[94] In *Société CdF Chimie Azote*[95] the Court accepted the findings in the report because it contained 'detailed and consistent reasoning . . . based on precise information'. The Court may also decide that a further report should be ordered.[96] A party cannot rely upon evidence (such as the testimony of a witness) in order to undermine the conclusions of an expert unless that evidence was offered at an earlier stage in the proceedings (and erroneously left out of account) or could not have been offered before the expert made his report.[97]

The same sanctions apply to an expert who fails properly to discharge his duties as to a witness.[98] Where an expert is unable to produce his report, the Court may have recourse to a different measure of enquiry in order to obtain the evidence sought.[99] Like witnesses, experts are entitled to have their travel and subsistence expenses reimbursed[1] and to fees in respect of their services.[2] The former may be paid in advance but the latter are paid only after the expert has performed the task entrusted to him.[3] A request for the payment of these should be made to the Registrar but, if he considers the request to be excessive, he may reduce it of his own motion or order payment by instalments and there is no express provision for an appeal against his decision.[4]

---

91 Above, notes 72 and 50 respectively, see pp 293 and 648 respectively.

92 [1972] ECR 1205 at 1207 and 1212.

93 For example, in *Commission v CODEMI* (above, note 69) at 3701, Advocate General Slynn accepted a finding made by the experts because it 'followed the right approach' when calculating the sums due.

94 See, for example, *Chambre Syndicale de la Sidérurgie v High Authority* (above, note 49) at 310 et seq, and *Usines de la Providence v High Authority* (above, note 53) at 940. In *A Ahlström Osakeyhtio v Commission*, (above, note 52), Advocate General Darmon thought that the opinion of the experts was doubtful and that it was therefore difficult for the Court to base its judgment on it (see paras 432–433 of his opinion); but the Court concluded that the experts' report could be relied on.

95 Above, note 70 para 31.

96 This was done in the *Dyestuffs* cases (above, note 50) see 667.

97 *Nijman v Commission* (above, note 77) paras 26–29.

98 ECSC Statute, art 28; EC Statute, art 27; Euratom Statute, art 28; SR 6; RP-CFI 72.

99 Cf Cases T-33 and T-74/89 *Blackman v European Parliament* [1993] ECR II-249 (para 18) where, for some reason, the experts appointed by the Court were unable to contact each other and produce a report. The Court therefore ordered certain persons to be heard as witnesses.

1 RP-ECJ 51(1); RP-CFI 74(1).

2 RP-ECJ 51(2); RP-CFI 74(2).

3 Ibid.

4 IR 21.

VIII   Inspection of the place or thing in question

An inspection may be ordered only after the parties have been given an opportunity to be heard.[5] The object of inspection is to enable the Court to appreciate a relevant fact at first hand. No precise rules are laid down for the conduct of an inspection.

There seem to have been only two occasions on which the Court has inspected a place.[6] In Case 14/59 *Société des Fonderies de Pont-à-Mousson v High Authority*[7] the problem before the Court was whether molten pig iron was a product covered by the ECSC Treaty and whether the Treaty covered foundries. The Court decided to inspect the foundry premises and wished to see it in action. The inspection took place with the parties and their representatives present. The Court requested that technicians employed by both parties should also be present to explain the manufacturing process and answer any questions that might be put by the Court or the parties' representatives. Advocate General Lagrange regarded the visit as 'interesting and amply commentated'.[8] In Cases 42 and 49/59 *SNUPAT v High Authority*[9] the Court inspected the premises of two steel undertakings which had intervened in the case, which put in issue the criterion of 'local integration' adopted by the High Authority for the administration of the scrap equalisation scheme, ie whether group scrap was 'own arisings' or 'bought scrap'. At the time of the inspection, which seems to have followed the same format as the inspection in the *Pont-à-Mousson* case, questions were asked of the interveners and statements made. The value of the inspection was expressed by Advocate General Lagrange[10] in these terms: 'As regards the technical aspects of integration, they are well known to the Court because of the complete explanation which it received during its visit to the premises and from the memories which it has no doubt retained regarding that visit which was so interesting in every respect.'

Inspection of a thing by way of a measure of enquiry is comparatively rare;[11] more often a party volunteers to produce an article for the Court's information. This mostly happens in tariff classification cases. By way of example, the Court has been shown gramophone records,[12] a laughing sack[13] and various items made from what was alleged to be artificial stone.[14] The Court does not, in general, refuse to admit things which a party proffers as evidence to

---

5 RP-ECJ 45(1); RP-CFI 66(1).
6 Three, according to Van Houtte *Cahiers de Droit Européen 1983* p 3 at p 21.
7 [1959] ECR 215 at 224.
8 Ibid at 237.
9 [1961] ECR 53, see at 72, 84–85 and 87.
10 Ibid at 100.
11 In Case 22/76 *Import Gadgets Sàrl v LAMP SpA* [1976] ECR 1371, the Court requested one of the parties to produce for inspection a 'laughing device' which Advocate General Warner described in his opinion as 'a small battery-powered gadget, in a pink plastic casing, which, when a button on it is pressed, makes a noise like human laughter. In the case of this particular specimen the laughter was masculine and somewhat sardonic' (see 1377). Similarly, in Case 798/79 *Hauptzollamt Köln-Rheinau v Chem-tec* [1980] ECR 2639 (see 2648) the Court asked for a specimen of the disposable gas-masks in dispute and received a box of several assorted varieties, some of which were demonstrated to the Court at the hearing.
12 Case 51/75 *EMI Records v CBS United Kingdom Ltd* [1976] ECR 811.
13 The *Import Gadgets* case (above, note 11) see 1379.
14 To wit, a large slab, a triangular piece of broken slab, a basin with plastic overflow pipe attached and a statue of a tiger: Case 234/81 *Du Pont de Nemours Inc v Customs and Excise Comrs* [1982] ECR 3515.

illustrate a point in his argument but it is sparing in the exercise of its power to call for production of a thing. In consequence, if a party wishes to have something inspected by the Court, it is often better simply to lodge the item in question at the Registry, preferably before the hearing.[15] The other parties are, of course, allowed to inspect it.

---

15 In particular if the item is not known to the other parties. In tariff classification cases, however, the item is generally a sample and the other parties usually have knowledge of what it is like. It is sufficient, then, to bring the sample along to the hearing (as was done in Case 317/81 *Howe and Bainbridge BV v Ober-finanzdirektion Frankfurt am Main* [1982] ECR 3257: a bale of sailcloth in its wrappings).

CHAPTER 12

Exclusion of evidence

I Introduction

Evidence is produced to the Court and disclosed to the parties. On occasion a party objects either to producing evidence or to its disclosure to another party; it also happens that a party seeks to have excluded from the proceedings evidence which has already been produced to the Court or disclosed to the parties.[1] Both situations are dealt with here. The Court is concerned only with evidence that is relevant to an issue in the case and will not, therefore, consider irrelevant evidence when reaching a decision, even though it may have been disclosed and form part of the file of the case.[2] In consequence, objections to the production or disclosure of evidence, in theory, arise only in connection with relevant evidence, whereas an application to remove evidence from the file may also concern irrelevant evidence which the Court will not, in any event, consider but which may, for example, be confidential.

II The power to exclude evidence

The Court has power to withhold secret or confidential documents from an intervener in direct actions[3] but the general rule is that all evidence must either be disclosed to the parties or left out of account altogether. The basis for that approach is that a party's rights cannot be determined on the basis of evidence which has not been disclosed to him or her; but, as the judgment will not, in principle, determine the rights of an intervener, there is no objection in principle to the withholding of evidence from him (or her).

As the Court put it in *SNUPAT v High Authority*:[4] 'It would infringe a basic principle of law to base a judicial decision on facts and documents of which the parties themselves, or one of them, have not been able to take cognisance and in relation to which they have not therefore been able to formulate an opinion.'

---

1 It should be noted that a distinction is to be drawn between the exclusion of evidence from consideration in a case because, for example, it is irrelevant and the exclusion of evidence from the proceedings. The former requires no formal step on the part of the Court and usually follows as a matter of course from the nature of the evidence; it relates to the substance of the case. For example, in Case C-343/87 *Culin v Commission* [1990] ECR I-225 (para 15 and at 234, Advocate General Mischo) a later correction made to the statement of reasons in the contested decision was simply left out of account (because it was submitted after the commencement of proceedings and, in consequence, could not be admissible as evidence of the reasoning followed when the decision was made). The latter requires a formal Court order and relates not to the substance of the case but to the procedural admissibility of the evidence in question (that is, its inclusion in the file of the case).
2 Cf Cases 40–48, 50, 54–56, 111, 113 and 114/73 *Coöperative Vereniging Suiker Unie UA v Commission* [1975] ECR 1663 (Re European Sugar Cartel) (para 327).
3 RP-ECJ 93(3); RP-CFI 116(2).
4 Cases 42 and 49/59 [1961] ECR 53 at 84.

For this reason, the Court was not willing in that case to accept conditions which were sought to be imposed on the production of a relevant document.[5] Similarly, in Case 6/81 *Industrie Diensten Groep BV v J A Beele Handelmaatschappij BV*,[6] a reference for a preliminary ruling, the Court refused to accept a written answer to a request made by it for the disclosure of information because the party submitting the answer objected to it being served on the opposing party. The Court asked for a document to be produced which could be served on all the parties.[7] The exception to this rule, which applies against interveners, but not, as the *SNUPAT* case shows, in their favour, is justified only because of the intervener's ancillary role in a direct action. Where, on the other hand, the information which a party wishes to keep confidential is only of peripheral importance from the point of view of the evidential value of a document, the Court may agree to the information being suppressed. For example, in Case C-64/88 *Commission v France*,[8] the applicant relied on certain reports in order to establish its case against the defendant but claimed confidentiality for the reports on the ground that confidential treatment was necessary in order to guarantee the future effectiveness of its inspectors and protect the third parties referred to in the reports. The Court therefore asked the applicant to produce non-confidential versions of the reports for use in the proceedings. The defendant claimed that the non-confidential versions could not be relied on because it was unable to identify the incidents mentioned in them. That objection was dismissed on the ground that the omissions from the reports were not such as to prevent the defendant from carrying out cross-checks against its own reports. Thus, in that case, the material omitted from the reports produced for use by the Court and disclosure to the other party did not prevent the other party from defending itself.[9] Evidence which is withdrawn or excluded in this way is not considered by the Court.

A party may apply for confidential treatment for documents which it wishes to produce to the Court. The Court has discretion whether or not to accede to this request but, where the request is accepted in principle by the other parties, it is apprehended that the Court would not reject it. The effect of confidential treatment is simply that the documents in question may be disclosed only to the other parties to the proceedings, who are bound not to show or pass on the information contained in them to third parties, and not to the interveners; in addition, the information contained in them will not be made public in the report of the case published in the *European Court Reports*. In the leading case concerning confidential treatment, *Celanese v Council and Commission*,[10] the Court ordered that its President should decide upon any requests for confidential treatment after examining the documents in question and hearing the views of the other parties. If he refused to grant confidential treatment, the

5 One of the interveners wished to rely on the terms of a contract but did not want it to be shown to the applicant and another intervener, who were its competitors. It said that it was willing to reveal the document to any person bound by professional secrecy, in the presence, if need be, of the judge-rapporteur, or to the High Authority. The Court applied the same rule to proceedings before the Commission in competition investigations: see Case 85/76 *Hoffman-La Roche & Co AG v Commission* [1979] ECR 461 (para 14).
6 [1982] ECR 707. See also Case 236/81 *Celanese Chemical Co Inc v Council and Commission* [1982] ECR 1183.
7 It construed 'opposing party' to mean, in this context, all parties within the meaning of art 20 of the EC Statute. In the *Celanese* case the Court rejected a 'confidential' pleading.
8 [1991] ECR I-2727 (para 11 and at 2736, Advocate General Lenz).
9 See also Case 30/78 *Distillers Co Ltd v Commission* [1980] ECR 2229, where the applicant asked that certain figures mentioned in a written reply to a request for information be kept confidential so the Court simply deleted them from the text.
10 Above, note 6: the proceedings were later discontinued.

party applying could withdraw the documents, in which case they could not be relied on at all in the proceedings. The Court, however, reserved the right to exclude from the file those documents which, if it considered them, would have to be made public in the judgment or the advocate general's opinion. The effect of exclusion would be that the documents concerned would be ignored completely. The Court does not accept claims to confidential treatment at face value but will require a claim to be justified and, where necessary, will carry out its own assessment of the claim.[11] The fact that, for the purposes of the proceedings, a party has waived the right to claim confidential treatment for a particular adminicle as against the opposing party does not preclude him seeking confidential treatment as against an intervener and in order to prevent publication of the information in question in the judgment and report of the case.[12]

A party may also apply under RP-ECJ 91 or, as the case may be, RP-CFI 114 for an adminicle of evidence to be excluded from consideration by the Court. Article 33(7) of the old Rules of Procedure[13] provided that the authenticity of a document could be challenged under what was then the equivalent of RP-ECJ 91. This procedure was used for the purpose of excluding an adminicle on the ground that it did not constitute relevant evidence.[14] Although art 33(7) no longer forms part of the Rules of Procedure, it is still possible to bring before the Court under RP-ECJ 91 or RP-CFI 114 a dispute concerning the admissibility of evidence. In Cases 18 and 35/65 *Gutmann v Euratom Commission*,[15] for example, both parties referred to the Court, as a procedural issue, the question whether two written witness statements annexed to the rejoinder were admissible, although the matter was, in the event, settled between them. Similarly, in Case 25/68 *Schertzer v European Parliament*[16] the defendant contested the validity and authenticity of certain documents produced by the applicant. The President ordered the originals of the documents to be produced and, after the defendant had submitted written observations, there was a hearing in camera as a result of which the Court authorised the documents to be lodged and the defendant was allowed to submit further observations.[17]

---

11   Case T-30/89 *Hilti AG v Commission* [1990] ECR II-163 (paras 10–11); Cases T-1 to T-4 and T-6 to T-15/89 *Rhône-Poulenc v Commission* [1990] ECR II-637 (paras 22–25).
12   *Hilti AG v Commission* (ibid) paras 12–14.
13   OJ 7 March 1953 p 37 at 44.
14   See Case 10/55 *Mirossevich v High Authority* [1954–56] ECR 333; the applicant applied contesting the authenticity of two documents produced by the defendant. The latter subsequently waived reliance on the first document and the Court ordered an enquiry into the authenticity of the second (at 336). This was a translation which the defendant had produced in order to show that the applicant was obviously incapable to act as a translator. The applicant first claimed not to be the author of the document (she only made manuscript alterations to it: see 352) but then conceded that it was 'legally authentic', although it did not represent the true position. The authenticity of the document, ie whether it really was a translation into Italian made by the applicant from a French original, was proved by documents produced by the defendant and corroborating evidence from witnesses (at 343). The Court also obtained an expert's opinion on the quality of the translation but this did not relate to the question of 'authenticity'. In Case 22/59 *Macchiorlatti Dalmas v High Authority* (order of 17 November 1959, unreported: the case was removed from the Register before judgment) the defendant produced in the course of proceedings a document which appeared to have emanated from the applicant. The latter applied to the Court for it to rule on the legal value of the document but no evidence was produced tending to invalidate it. The Court held that, in substance, the applicant wished it to rule on the issue to which the document related and rejected the application as inadmissible because matters relating to the substance of the case could not be decided in such proceedings.
15   [1966] ECR 103 at 115.
16   [1977] ECR 1729 at 1732.
17   The proceedings were then stayed pending judgment in several actions brought before French courts, among them claims that the applicant had committed forgery and uttered a forged document. The latter were eventually dismissed.

In Case 30/78 *Distillers v Commission*[18] the applicant applied under RP-ECJ 91 to have certain documents withdrawn from the file on the case. The Commission argued that the Court had no power to accede to this request but the latter held that the power to authorise withdrawal of documents is essential for the interests of the proper administration of justice. Some of the documents in question were not of importance to the case whereas others constituted 'an essential part' of the administrative procedure before the Commission and had been relied on in the proceedings before the Court. Withdrawal was therefore authorised only in regard to the former category.[19] This was not the first case in which an application had been made to have certain documents excluded from consideration by the Court, although it was the first in which the Court's power to do so was challenged and the Court expressly held that it existed. Under the old Rules of Procedure such a power was in any event implied in art 33(7), at least in the case of documents whose 'authenticity' was not upheld. Even after the removal of art 33(7) from the Rules of Procedure in 1960,[20] the Court's power to order the removal of documents from the file was unquestioned.

For example, in Case 28/65 *Fonzi v Euratom Commission*[21] the Commission applied for an order that certain documents annexed to the reply be removed from the file. The Court ordered one of the documents in question to be excluded from consideration but reserved its decision on the rest of the application to the final judgment. The document initially removed from the file comprised draft minutes of a meeting of the Commission[22] and its retention in the file was held to be 'capable of amounting to a violation of the secrecy of the deliberations of the Commission . . . in a matter which is unconnected with the present dispute'. The reason why it was excluded was its lack of relevance rather than the fact that it was confidential. This follows from the order of the Court which required production of the Commission's minute-book so that the Court could look at the minutes of the same meeting. Production of the minutes was 'essential for the efficient administration of justice' in order that the Court could be placed in possession of the authentic text of a decision in issue in the case. The procedure adopted was that the parties should attend before the judge-rapporteur; the Commission would produce the minute-book and the judge-rapporteur would make a copy of the relevant part. The other documents sought to be excluded were a copy of a report made by a private detective agency on the activities of two colleagues of the applicant prior to their employment by the Commission and a telex passing between two officials of the Commission.[23] Advocate General Roemer took the view that neither document was relevant to a decision in the case but only the removal from the file of the report need be considered, if the Court also thought it to be irrelevant, because it was capable of prejudicing persons who were not parties to the proceedings.[24] The Court decided that the report should be excluded because it was 'capable of prejudicing third parties not involved in the present proceedings and unable to defend themselves'. On the other hand, it decided not

---

18 Above, note 9, order of 28 March 1979, unreported, see p 2237 of the report.
19 The same approach was followed in Case 246/86 *S C Belasco v Commission* [1989] ECR 2117, order of 3 February 1988 (paras 5–6), where the intervener applied for certain documents annexed to the reply to be excluded because they made adverse comments about a third party. The Court declined to exclude the documents because the matters in question were relevant to the case but it suppressed a part of one of the documents which was not important to the case.
20 See OJ 1960, pp 17 et seq.
21 [1966] ECR 477 at 490, 492–493 and 506.
22 See ibid at 480 and 496.
23 See ibid at 480, 493 and 503.
24 Ibid at 503.

to exclude the telex because it was relevant to the proceedings and 'manifestly incapable of prejudicing the rights of third parties'.[25] Exclusion of documents on the ground of their lack of relevance is relatively common.[26]

It is not, however, necessary to raise an objection to an adminicle of evidence formally under RP-ECJ 91 or RP-CFI 114. In Cases 197–200, 243, 245 and 247/80 *Ludwigshafener Walzmühle Erling KG v Council and Commission*[27] the Commission objected at the hearing and the Court decided then and there that the document in question, which had been lodged by the interveners, should be withdrawn from the file and that the extracts from it reproduced in the body of the intervener's observations should be considered 'non-existent'. The document appears to have been a draft report prepared by officials of the Commission which was not approved by it and never submitted to the Council. The interveners said that it had been distributed at a meeting of the 'Advisory Committee on Cereals', which included representatives of the various industrial and trade sectors involved, and given to them by someone attending the meeting. The Commission's view was that the document had been improperly obtained: at the meeting in question, there was an oral report but the document was not distributed because it had not been submitted to the Commission for its approval; furthermore, the front page of the copy placed before the Court, which would show its origin and date etc, was missing. The interveners were unable to say who had given them the document and why it was incomplete.

Advocate General VerLoren van Themaat thought that it was going too far to say that persons can never make use of confidential and internal Commission documents because it was well known that such documents are frequently leaked and even published. It was 'an exaggeration and a disregard of practice' to say that this made any internal proposals or discussions impossible. As a result, the burden lies on the institution to show in each case that use of such documents is inadmissible. The document in question, however, apart from being confidential and internal, was also incomplete and its nature therefore confusing; the Commission's view that the members of the Advisory Committee could not legitimately have taken cognisance of it was not rebutted by the interveners. He regarded these as the reasons for the Court's decision to exclude the document from consideration. In its judgment the Court simply said that it found that 'there exists . . . a doubt both as to the actual nature of the contested document and as to whether the interveners obtained it by proper means. In the circumstances, the document must be removed from the file, together with the quotations from it included in the intervening party's

---

25 Ibid at 493.

26 For example, in Case 352/88 *Commission v Ireland* (order of 6 July 1989) the applicant applied to exclude an internal document of its own that was relied on by the defendant; the document was ordered to be excluded essentially because it related to a matter on which there was no issue in the case. In Cases C-116 and C-149/88 *Hecq v Commission* [1990] ECR I-599 (order of 28 June 1989) the applicant had applied under RP-ECJ 91 for the production of a document; the defendant produced it but claimed that it should be excluded from consideration; the Court excluded it because it added nothing useful to the case, without needing to rule on its confidential character. In Cases T-47 and T-82/89 *Marcato v Commission* [1989] ECR II-231 (order of 6 December 1989) and Case T-5/90 *Marcato v Commission* [1991] ECR II-731 (paras 3–5), various documents adduced by the defendant were excluded from consideration on application by the applicant because they related to events after the contested act and added nothing useful to the resolution of the dispute. In Case C-308/87 *Grifoni v Euratom*, 3 February 1994 (judgment, para 7; per Advocate General Tesauro, para 4), documents proving the applicant's income were unadmissible because they contributed other information given previously. Other documents were admissible because they were produced at the Court's request. The excluded documents were not relevant to the pleaded case.

27 [1981] ECR 3211 (paras 13–16 and at 3241).

statement.' Although neither the Court nor the advocate general relied expressly on it as a ground for excluding the document, it appears from the latter's opinion that the report was 'irrelevant as far as the formation of the Commission's and Council's definitive opinion is concerned'.

The cases indicate that the Court alone has the power to derogate from the general rule that all evidence must be disclosed and the parties themselves are not entitled to withhold evidence or attach conditions to its disclosure unilaterally. Evidence may be withheld from an intervener but not from a party unless it is of no evidential significance to the issues in the case. Evidence which is excluded for some reason is excluded totally and is treated, for the purposes of the case, as being non-existent. A party (including an intervener) may apply for an adminicle of evidence to be excluded. Ordinarily the application should be made under RP-ECJ 91 or RP-CFI 114. It is unclear whether an intervener is a 'party', within the meaning of this provision, for the purpose of making such an application. While it seems that an intervener cannot raise a preliminary objection,[28] it would be excessively formalistic to say that he also cannot raise a procedural issue under RP-ECJ 91 or RP-CFI 114. The better view appears to be that an intervener is a party within the meaning of RP-ECJ 91 or RP-CFI 114 so far as matters falling within the scope of the intervention are concerned, but there is no authority on this. An intervener would therefore be advised to make an application based on RP-ECJ 91 or, as the case may be, RP-CFI 114 and the Court's implied power to make the order, in the alternative. It should be noted that, since the intervener must accept the case as he finds it at the time of his intervention,[29] an application can probably be made to exclude evidence only if it has been placed before the Court after the intervention. This again, however, is a point on which there is no authority. As can be seen from the *Ludwigshafener Walzmühle* case, an application need not necessarily be made in writing under RP-ECJ 91 or RP-CFI 114 but it would seem that there should be some justification for not raising the matter formally as a procedural issue.

There appear to be, in essence, two grounds on which evidence may be excluded: lack of probative value and impropriety in its production. The fact that evidence contains scandalous material (in the sense that it is damaging to the reputation of a person) is not sufficient to justify the exclusion of the evidence (whether or not the scandalous material is true) if the evidence, or the parts of it containing the scandalous material, are relevant to the issues in the case.[30]

III   Lack of probative value

Evidence may be excluded for lack of probative value where, for example, it lacks relevance or authenticity or is confidential. Of these, the most important (in the sense of being the ground encountered most frequently in practice) is lack of relevance: any adminicle which is irrelevant to the issues in a case is capable of being excluded whether or not it is confidential. However, lack of relevance is not of itself sufficient to exclude an adminicle of evidence, as opposed to not taking it into account in deciding the case.[31] There must be

28 See p 229.
29 RP-ECJ 93(4); RP-CFI 116(3).
30 Cf *S C Belasco v Commission* (above, note 19) paras 5–6.
31 For example, in Case C-330/88 *Grifoni v Euratom* [1991] ECR I-1045 (para 10 and at 1058–1059, Advocate General Tesauro) a legal requirement that an agreement be in writing rendered evidence of an oral agreement legally irrelevant; but the fact that such evidence could not be taken into account did not mean that it should be excluded from the Court file. Similarly, in competition cases, credible evidence which the Commission did not reveal to the

some further reason for taking further steps to exclude it, such as that it is confidential or that it may prejudice third parties. Lack of authenticity comprises cases where an adminicle is found not to be genuine. Confidentiality may be included under the heading 'lack of probative value' because the claim that an adminicle of evidence is confidential constitutes in substance an assertion that, so far as concerns the proceedings in which the claim is raised, the adminicle is deprived of any probative value in deciding the case by reason of its confidential nature. Hitherto, claims of confidentiality have fallen into one of five categories:

(1)   national security;[32]
(2)   business secrets;[33]
(3)   administrative confidences;[34]
(4)   medical secrecy;[35] and
(5)   lawyer–client confidences.[36]

It is not excluded that other categories of confidentiality may be recognised by the Court on the basis of the principles common to the member states.[37]

Confidentiality of whatever sort can be waived, in certain circumstances, by the person for whose benefit it exists.[38] It would seem that confidentiality is deemed to be waived as soon as an adminicle has been produced but it may be reasserted to exclude the adminicle if it is not relevant to a decision on the issues in the case.[39] Subject to this exception, administrative confidentiality is deemed to be waived, as a matter of law, in proceedings instituted under the ECSC Treaty against a decision of a Community institution, so far as documentary evidence relating to the case is concerned.[40] The confidentiality of business secrets and administrative confidences is not absolute and may be overridden where it is in the interests of the efficient administration of justice.[41]

undertaking concerned or on which the undertaking was not given an adequate opportunity to present its views during the course of the proceedings before the Commission, is inadmissible as proof of a fact found in the Commission's decision: eg Cases 100–103/80 *Musique Diffusion Française SA v Commission* [1983] ECR 1825 (paras 29–30 and 65). Such evidence is therefore legally irrelevant; but that is a factor that goes to the substance of the case and not to the question whether or not such evidence should be formally excluded from the proceedings.

32 See art 223(1) of the EC Treaty and Case 115/82 *Commission v Italy* (later withdrawn).
33 Eg the *SNUPAT* case (above, note 4); *BV Industrie Diensten Groep v J A Beele Handelmaatschappij BV* (above, note 6); *Distillers v Commission* (above, note 9); *Celanese v Council and Commission* (above, note 6).
34 Eg *Fonzi v Euratom Commission* (above, note 21); the *Ludwigshafener Walzmühle* case (above, note 27).
35 Eg Case 18/70 *X v Council* [1972] ECR 1205 (see 1211); Case 155/78 *M v Commission* [1980] ECR 1797.
36 Case 155/79 *A M & S v Commission* [1982] ECR 1575.
37 See ibid at para 18.
38 For information protected by professional secrecy, see Cases 41/69 *ACF Chemiefarma NV v Commission*, 44/69 *Buchler & Co v Commission* and 45/69 *Boehringer Mannheim GmbH v Commission* [1970] ECR 661, 733 and 769 respectively; for medical secrecy, where the position is more complicated than the other categories of confidentiality recognised by the Court, see *M v Commission* (above, note 35); for lawyer–client confidences, see the *A M & S* case (above, note 36) para 28.
39 This follows from the *Distillers* case (above, note 9). It does not apply where a document is produced for the purpose of deciding whether it may benefit from confidential treatment: see the *A M & S* and *Celanese* cases (above, notes 36 and 6).
40 Article 23 of the ECSC Statute. There is in fact no clear authority for this and the writer keeps his options open in the discussion of administrative confidentiality below.
41 *Fonzi v Euratom Commission* (above, note 21); Case 110/75 *Mills v European Investment Bank* [1976] ECR 1613 at 1635 (Advocate General Warner). Since business secrecy is of less public importance than administrative confidentiality, it seems to follow that, if the latter can be overridden, so can the former.

The same seems to apply to medical secrecy.[42] In *A M & S v Commission*, however, the Court defined the scope of lawyer/client confidentiality narrowly and linked it to the right to a fair trial.[43] It is therefore arguable that confidentiality, as so defined, gives an absolute privilege unless it is waived. Confidentiality on grounds of national security is also absolute and cannot be overridden where it is based on art 223 of the EC Treaty and as long as no 'improper use' has been made of the privilege within the meaning of art 225.

An adminicle is confidential by reason of the circumstances in which it came into existence, but only for so long as it is treated as being confidential: if it is published at large, confidentiality ceases even though it may originally have been confidential.[44] On the other hand, the fact that an adminicle has been circulated to several people does not mean that it is no longer confidential as against the world: in Cases 209 to 215 and 218/78 *Heintz van Landewyck Sarl (FEDETAB) v Commission*[45] the Court held that 'information in the nature of a trade secret given to a trade or professional association by its members and thus having lost its confidential nature vis-à-vis them does not lose it with regard to third parties'.

The types of confidentiality which have been considered by the Court may be briefly described as follows.

A National security

The ECSC Treaty does not contain any express provision protecting national security, presumably because of its object of creating 'the basis for a broader and deeper community among peoples long divided by bloody conflicts'[46] as much as its limited scope. Article 223(1) of the EC Treaty, however, provides: 'No Member State shall be obliged to supply information the disclosure of which it considers contrary to the essential interests of its security.' This privilege is restricted to information relating to 'the essential interests' of the security of a member state and does not, therefore, apply to all information relating to national security. Although the test of what is essential is subjective, the right to invoke art 223(1) may be reviewed by the Court under art 225 at the suit of the Commission or any member state. No proceedings have ever been brought before the Court under this provision so it is a little difficult to define with authority what is the scope of the Court's powers of review and, hence, the scope of the privilege to withhold information. It seems, nonetheless, that a member state is only entitled to refuse to supply information which falls within a class or category of matters, defined objectively by the Court in the light of the purpose and objectives of the Treaty and the principles common to the member states, relating to 'security'. Secondly, the information in question must relate to the security of the member state invoking the privilege, not any other member state or a third country. This is a question which is also subject to review by the Court. Next, the information must concern the 'essential interests' of national security. It would appear that it is left to the member state concerned to define what are its 'essential interests' in the matter of its security and to determine whether the disclosure of information of such a nature as to comply with the three preceding criteria is

---

42 *M v Commission* (above, note 35).
43 'The rights of defence', see above (note 36) para 21 of the judgment.
44 See, for example, the remarks of Advocate General VerLoren van Themaat in the *Ludwigshafener Walzmühle* case (above, note 27); Case C-281/87 *Commission v Greece* [1989] ECR 4015 (para 10).
45 [1980] ECR 3125 (para 46).
46 See the preamble.

'contrary' to those interests.[47] Nevertheless, the Court would be entitled to find that a member state was making improper use of the privilege if it were manifest that essential interests were not involved or that disclosure was not contrary to them. In the face of a judgment against it the member state could no longer withhold the information.

The parallel provisions in the Euratom Treaty are more elaborate because it is envisaged that information whose disclosure is liable to harm the defence interests of one or more member states is the subject of a security system to be elaborated in secondary legislation.[48] Nonetheless, there is no express provision preventing, as a general rule, disclosure to the Court of matters subject to a security system, should the need arise, and this would, in any event, appear to be contrary to the nature of the system envisaged in the Treaty, which allows disclosure subject to observance of the appropriate security measures. This does not exclude the possibility that, in a particular case, disclosure may be prohibited but this depends on the proper interpretation to be given to the relevant Treaty provisions and the secondary legislation applicable. So far as can be seen, no secondary legislation purports to prohibit disclosure to the Court.

A refusal to produce material on grounds of national security is rare. One of the few cases in which a party has declined to produce information or evidence on this ground is Case 115/82 *Commission v Italy*,[49] an action brought under art 169 of the EEC Treaty in which it was alleged, inter alia, that certain restrictions on the export of various types of sea-going vessel were prohibited by art 34 of the Treaty. Without expressly relying on art 223(1), the Italian government attempted to justify the restrictions on the ground that the vessels in question were of military importance but refused to give any details on the basis that this would compromise national security.

B   Business secrets

Save in the case of the withholding of evidence from an intervener[50] or where different cases have been joined,[51] there is no authority to the effect that relevant evidence may be withheld or excluded because it is a business or trade secret. The most that can be said is that, on the basis of the *Distillers* case, irrelevant or unimportant evidence may be excluded on this ground.[52] In order

---

47 Cf Case 222/84 *Johnston v Chief Constable of the Royal Ulster Constabulary* [1986] ECR 1651 (para 26).

48 Articles 24 et seq and 194; see Council Regulation (Euratom) No 3 of 31 July 1958 (OJ 1958 p 408, English Special Edition, 1952–1958, p 63).

49 Above (note 32).

50 Case T-30/89 *Hilti AG v Commission* [1990] ECR II-163 (paras 11 and 19–22).

51 *Rhône-Poulenc v Commission* (above, note 11) para 22.

52 The same would appear to be true, in general, for any adminicle which can be said to be confidential in nature. The true test of the strength of a claim to confidentiality is when it is made in order to justify the withholding or exclusion of relevant evidence. The decision in the *Celanese* case (above, note 6) which could be taken as suggesting that relevant evidence may be withheld or excluded because of business secrecy, was based in part on art 8 of Council Regulation No 3017/79 of 20 December 1979 (OJ No L339/1) and in part on the fact that the defendants conceded confidential treatment for the documents. As has been said, this took the form only of a ban on publication to interveners and third parties, it did not prevent disclosure to the Court or to the opposing parties. The case is exceptional because the Court allowed documents to be disclosed, on a conditional basis, for the purpose of deciding whether they were confidential and entitled to such treatment. Its decision not to take into account documents whose publication could not be avoided was the corollary to the confidential protection afforded to them. For these reasons, the case should be regarded as an application of RP-ECJ 93(3) and not as authority that the evidence in question could be withheld or excluded *simply* because it was a business secret.

to determine whether or not an adminicle contains material that constitutes a business secret, account must be taken not only of the nature of the information in question but also its age: some business secrets lose their character as such or the value of their remaining secret in a much shorter period of time than others.[53]

C Administrative confidences

As far as administrative confidences are concerned, both the member states and the Community institutions appear to be in the same position but the problem of the disclosure of administrative confidences has arisen only in relation to the latter. The Court's jurisdiction over acts of the institutions necessarily means that administrative confidentiality cannot be raised against it. If this were not so, the institutions could in many cases prevent effective judicial review of their acts by withholding relevant evidence on the ground that it is confidential. The principle, therefore, is that, whatever the position regarding third parties, administrative confidences are not privileged from disclosure in proceedings before the Court. Case 260/80 *Andersen v Council*[54] shows that there must be some further reason relating to the nature or content of an administrative confidence to justify excluding it from consideration or, semble, refusing to disclose it. It should be noted, however, that the Court does not have power to force disclosure.

Administrative confidentiality falls into two parts: confidences contained in internal communications; and confidences obtained from contacts with third parties. The latter are often protected by the principle of professional secrecy.[55] Therefore, unauthorised disclosure is prohibited as a matter of law. In both cases, however, the evidence is not privileged absolutely from disclosure in proceedings before the Court and the Court may require it to be produced, subject, if need be, to certain safeguards to protect the essential core of confidentiality.[56] It is worth nothing that, under art 19 of the Staff Regulations, the duty binding officials of the Community institutions not to disclose in legal proceedings information obtained in the performance of their duties without permission from the appointing authority, does not apply where the official concerned is giving evidence before the Court; but this dispensation seems to apply only in cases concerning officials or former officials.

D Medical secrecy

Medical secrecy has come up for consideration in staff cases in the context of the obligation binding the appointing authority to give reasons for any decision adversely affecting an official or servant of an institution.[57] The Court has held

53 Cf the *Hilti* case (paras 19–22), and the *Rhône-Poulenc* case (para 23) (both above, note 11).
54 [1984] ECR 177 (paras 5–6).
55 See, for example, art 47 of the ECSC Treaty (the obligation in art 47 applies whether the information is obtained lawfully or not: per Judge Donner in Case 31/59 *Acciaieria e Tubificio di Brescia v High Authority* [1960] ECR 98) and art 20 of Regulation No 17, OJ 1962, p 204.
56 See Case 2/54 *Italy v High Authority* [1954–56] ECR 37 at 42 (internal communications) and Cases 36–38 and 40/59 *Geitling v High Authority* [1960] ECR 423 at 437 (professional secrecy): in both cases the Court allowed the persons who had uttered the confidences to remain anonymous. In *Italy v High Authority* it described this as an 'exceptional measure'. The same expedient was used by the Commission in Case 85/76 *Hoffmann-La Roche & Co AG v Commission* [1979] ECR 461 (paras 16–19) but it is unclear whether this was done with the permission of the Court, although the information was revealed pursuant to a request made by it. The Court's unwillingness to exclude administrative confidences unless there is good reason can be seen from *Andersen v Council* (above, note 54).
57 Eg Case 121/76 *Moli v Commission* [1977] ECR 1971; Case 75/77 *Mollet v Commission* [1978] ECR 897; *M v Commission* (above, note 35).

that the obligation to give reasons is tempered by the confidentiality of medical secrets, which means that, save in exceptional circumstances, it is left to the individual doctor to decide whether to communicate to those whom he is treating or examining the nature of the condition from which they may be suffering.[58] The need to give reasons is satisfied if the person concerned requests the information to be imparted to another doctor of his own choice. In proceedings before the Court, however, it seems that confidential information obtained by a doctor examining or treating a person may and, where the Court requires, must be disclosed. The authority for this is *M v Commission*.[59] There the Court found that the laws of the member states recognised certain limitations to the confidentiality of the relationship between a patient seeking treatment and a doctor. It selected three sets of circumstances from which such limitations could 'in particular' result:

(1)   'where the person concerned has expressly given his consent' (to the lifting of confidentiality);
(2)   'where the doctor's involvement takes place in the context of administrative checking procedures so that the spontaneous confidential relationship which is the basis of professional secrecy does not exist';
(3)   'where reliance on such confidentiality would have the result of obstructing the normal course of justice'.

The apparent limitation of confidentiality to the relationship between a patient seeking treatment and a doctor giving it seems too narrow because the case actually concerned a medical examination made for the purpose of deciding whether a candidate for a post was physically fit for the performance of her duties. Subject to the second set of circumstances identified by the Court, it would seem that confidentiality extends to any medical information obtained during an examination even if the person concerned is not seeking treatment, as the Court's earlier decisions[60] had suggested. The Court proceeded to hold: 'In this case it must be observed that the applicant has expressly given her consent to all relevant information relating to the medical examinations which were carried out being given to the Court. The medical examinations in question were carried out pursuant to the Staff Regulations in the context of an administrative recruitment procedure the legality of which must, at every stage, be capable of review by the Court. In these circumstances the refusal to give any information whatever concerning the basis of the medical records and the reliance, by the doctors in the confidence of the Commission, on the confidentiality of medical findings as grounds for refusing to provide any useful indication has the result of making it impossible for the Court to carry out the judicial review entrusted to it by the Treaty and the Staff Regulations.'

It seems possible to attribute each part of this extract from the judgment to one of the sets of circumstances imposing a limit on confidentiality.[61] If this were so, it would seem to follow that the applicability of the third followed from the fact that the first two also applied, thus suggesting that all three are

---

58   Ibid.
59   Above, note 35, paras 18–20.
60   *Moli v Commission* and *Mollet v Commission* (above, note 57).
61   If so, however, the examinations would not have been confidential by virtue of the second set of circumstances. Although this may be supported by reference to the apparent exclusion of examinations as capable of constituting a confidential relationship between doctor and patient, it is hard to place in the context of the case: if the examinations did not give rise to a confidential relationship, the applicant's consent to the disclosure of the information would be irrelevant because it was not confidential.

cumulative and that one alone may not be sufficient to lift confidentiality. A similar approach was adopted by Advocate General Capotorti,[62] who formulated the principle that professional (here medical) secrecy cannot be relied on in judicial proceedings 'at least where . . . a dispute between a public employee and the administration is involved, where, moreover, the medical examinations have been carried out on behalf of the administration and not at the request or in the interests of the patient and where, finally, the person concerned agrees to the information in the possession of the doctor being disclosed to the Court'. Later on he reformulated it as 'a duty on the doctor, within the compass of disputes between a public employee and the administration and provided that the patient's consent has been given, to provide an administrative court with information acquired in the course of medical examinations carried out at the request of the authority'.

E Lawyer–client confidences

As defined in *A M & S v Commission*[63] the confidentiality of the lawyer–client relationship has three characteristics:

(1)   it serves the requirement 'that any person must be able, without constraint, to consult a lawyer whose profession entails the giving of independent legal advice to all those in need of it';
(2)   it applies to 'communications . . . made for the purposes and in the interests of the client's rights of defence' (ie the right to a fair trial); and
(3)   the communications 'emanate from independent lawyers, that is to say, lawyers who are not bound to the client by a relationship of employment'.

The *A M & S* case actually concerned the question whether confidentiality applied in the context of an investigation carried out by the Commission under the competition rules. The judgment establishes that confidentiality applies, not only in proceedings before the Court, but also in administrative proceedings which may result in a decision directly affecting the person seeking to take advantage of confidentiality. In consequence, protection covers communications made after the initiation of any procedure which will or may result in such a decision and earlier written communications which have a relationship to the subject matter of that procedure. The communications must concern legal advice, not, for example, business advice.

There are frequent references in the judgment to communications 'emanating' from an independent lawyer. This would tend to suggest that only documents containing legal advice and drawn up by the lawyer would be protected, but not a request for legal advice. This seems to be wrong. The Court says that the principle of confidentiality serves the requirement that persons may be able to consult a lawyer whose profession entails the giving of independent legal advice. This shows that the act of the client in requesting legal advice and the act of the lawyer in giving it were both present in the mind of the Court. In addition, there are a number of references (more in the French text of the judgment than in the authentic, English version; but the former provides the form of words on which the judges agreed) to an 'exchange' of communications. An exchange is two-way. Lastly, of the documents in respect of which the claim to protection was upheld, one (No 5), according to Advo-

---

62 [1980] ECR at 1820–1821.
63 Above (note 36); see (1982) ECLR 99.

cate General Sir Gordon Slynn's opinion,[64] comprised requests for legal advice made by executives of A M & S to a solicitor in private practice.

The judgment indicates that, in order for the communications to be protected, the lawyer involved must possess the following qualities:

(1)   he must be entitled to practise in one of the member states;
(2)   he must be bound by rules of professional ethics and discipline laid down and enforced in the general interest by institutions with power to do so;
(3)   he must not be bound to the client by any employment relationship; and
(4)   the exercise of his functions must be subject to the overriding interests of justice.

The reason for this approach seems to be that the Court regarded the lawyer's role as 'collaborating in the administration of justice by the courts' and as providing 'in full independence, and in the overriding interests of that cause [ie the administration of justice], such legal assistance as the client needs'.

The phrase 'lawyer entitled to practise' is not used in the French version of the judgment. This says '*avocat inscrit au barreau*' and indicates what would more aptly be described in English as a 'barrister'. The English phrasing of the judgment is to be preferred for the simple reason that three of the documents recognised by the Court as protected (Nos 4, 5 and 7) were sent by or to a solicitor in private practice. The judgment is not, therefore, to be understood as applying only to practising lawyers who are barristers or advocates but to all practising lawyers who possess the qualifications set out in the judgment. It is likely that the Court intended to refer to those persons defined as 'lawyers' in Council Directive No 77/249 of 22 March 1977[65] but this is not entirely clear because the judgment also refers to the Court's Statutes.

It excluded lawyers entitled to practise in third countries even though they otherwise fulfil the strict requirements of independence, etc, specified by it. The reason for this is obscure and particularly so given that, at the time some of the documents in the case were drawn up, Britain was not a member of the Community and so correspondence with British lawyers would not have been protected on the basis of the Court's own definition. It is arguable that the judgment is to be interpreted as holding that a document which is not protected at the time when it comes into being may later become protected once all the conditions for protection have been fulfilled. As far as employed lawyers are concerned, Advocate General Sir Gordon Slynn pointed out that, in some member states, they were subject to professional ethics and discipline while in others they were not. At first blush, the judgment is sufficiently unclear to suggest that, if an employed lawyer is also entitled to practise and his ethical and disciplinary obligations as a practising lawyer effectively outweigh his contractual obligations to his client so that he can in truth be said to be independent and bound by the overriding interests of justice, communications passing between him and his client are protected. The Court, however, withheld protection from every document involving an employed lawyer so the employment relationship must itself be regarded as sufficient to negative the existence of protection.

The Court appears to have rejected the view that documents summarising legal advice are protected[66] but it upheld the claim to protection made in respect of communications containing legal advice which had been sent to an

64   [1982] ECR at 1643.
65   OJ No L78/17.
66   In contrast, in Case T-30/89 *Hilti AG v Commission* [1990] ECR II-163 (paras 15–18) the CFI seems to have regarded internal notes of advice from external lawyers as protected.

executive of a company in the same group as A M & S and which had then been passed on to it. In doing so the Court seems to have accepted that the common interest of the members of a group of companies may justify the retention of confidentiality in respect of documents drawn up by or for one member of the group and found in the possession of another.[67]

It seems that, when a claim to protection from disclosure on grounds of confidentiality arises before the evidence in question has been produced to the Court, it must be supported by evidence of such a nature as to demonstrate that it fulfils the conditions for being granted legal protection: a bare claim is not enough.[68] The Court may, in its discretion, call for production of the evidence in question. In *AM & S v Commission* only the judge-rapporteur and the advocate general actually saw the documents but that was a case heard by the full Court. In the event that the matter were heard by a chamber, all the judges could look at the material without prejudicing any subsequent proceedings.

IV Improperly obtained evidence

The second ground on which evidence may be excluded, impropriety in its production, seems to have been raised in only a few cases.[69] In *Hoffmann-La Roche v Commission* the applicant claimed that the procedure initiated by the Commission, which resulted in the decision challenged in the action, was irregular because the applicant's own internal documents had come into possession of the Commission by unlawful means. This claim was later abandoned and the Court did not, therefore, rule upon it; it did, however, state that it was not an issue which should be examined by it of its own motion.[70] It is doubtful, given the circumstances in which the claim was made, that this can be regarded as authority that an impropriety in the obtaining of evidence can never be raised by the Court of its own motion, even when the impropriety directly affects the course of proceedings before the Court itself. The point remains open but it is submitted that, as a general rule, where evidence has been obtained by improper means from a party to the action (including interveners), it is for that party to object to the inclusion of the evidence; if an objection is not made, both the confidentiality of the evidence and the impropriety in its production are taken to be waived. The Court may, however, raise of its own motion the admissibility of evidence improperly obtained from a person not a party to the proceedings.

In the *Ludwigshafener Walzmühle* case[71] Advocate General VerLoren van Themaat took the view that it was for the Commission, which raised the question of inadmissibility, to prove it. The Court, on the other hand, merely intimated that the existence of a doubt as to whether the evidence was

---

67 Cf *Heintz van Landewyck Sàrl (FEDETAB) v Commission* (above, note 45) para 46.

68 Cf *A M & S v Commission* (above, note 36): there the Court dealt with the procedure to be followed when such a claim is raised as against the Commission but it seems right to apply the same rules, mutatis mutandis, when the claim is made in proceedings before the Court (eg the *Celanese* case (above, note 6).

69 *Hoffmann-La Roche v Commission* (above, note 5); the *Ludwigshafener Walzmühle* case (above, note 27); Case 232/84 *Commission v Tordeur* [1985] ECR 3223; Cases 31 and 35/86 *Levantina Agricola Industrial SA (LAISA) v Council* [1988] ECR 2285; Case 352/88 *Commission v Ireland*, order of 6 July 1989 (the point did not need to be decided); Case C-281/87 *Commission v Greece* [1989] ECR 4015; Case T-16/89 *Herkenrath v Commission* [1992] ECR II-275. No impropriety was alleged in *Andersen v Council* (above, note 54).

70 *Hoffmann-La Roche* (ibid) at para 7 of the judgment.

71 Above (note 27).

obtained by proper means could be enough to exclude it. In consequence it would seem that the burden lies on the party seeking to exclude evidence on this ground to show that there is doubt as to the propriety of its production. It is then for the party producing the document to satisfy the Court that this doubt is unfounded. Mere assertion is not enough to establish that the party producing the document has acted improperly or to cast on that party the burden of proving that the document was obtained properly.[72] On the other hand, once the issue has been raised, a failure by the party producing the document to explain the position will lead the Court to conclude that the allegation of an impropriety is founded and to exclude the document from consideration.[73] It is not sufficient for the party producing the document to assert it was given the document by a third party and has no reason to suspect any impropriety: evidence must be produced of the circumstances in which the document was obtained at every stage at which it passed from one person to another. Thus, in Case 232/84 *Commission v Tordeur*[74] Tordeur stated that he had obtained the documents from a trade union which had been given them by the Commission itself. The Commission denied that it had given them to the trade union. At the hearing the Court excluded the documents from the file on the ground that Tordeur was unable to prove that it had in fact done so. In Cases 31 and 35/86 *Levantina Agricola Industrial SA (LAISA) v Council*[75] the applicant said that the document had come into its hands without any indication of its origin or confidential nature; there was nothing to lead it to believe that the defendant's consent was necessary in order to rely on the document. Nonetheless, although the Court did not exclude the possibility that internal documents may legitimately form part of the file, it excluded the document on the ground that the applicant could not prove that it had acquired the document in a regular manner.

What constitutes an impropriety in the obtaining of evidence is not at this stage entirely clear due to the lack of authorities. It would seem, however, that impropriety is not restricted to the use of unlawful or dishonest means in obtaining the evidence: it is sufficient if there is a breach of a confidence or the abuse of a position of trust.[76] In addition, it is not necessary that the party producing the evidence is the person who has used improper means: it is sufficient that he has (innocently) received the evidence from the hands of a

---

72 Case C-281/87 *Commission v Greece* [1989] ECR 4015 (para 11 and at 4024, Advocate General Jacobs).

73 Case 327/86 *Herkenrath v Commission*, order of 15 June 1989 (reported sub nom Case T-16/89 [1992] ECR II-275). When the case was transferred to the CFI, the applicant sought to contest the decision of the ECJ to exclude the document on the ground that the letter from the ECJ asking the applicant to submit observations on the allegation that the document had been obtained improperly had been lost in the post. The opposing party claimed that the matter was now res judicata but the CFI dismissed the application on the ground that the letter had been delivered to the applicant's address for service in Luxembourg and there was no suggestion that force majeure or unforeseen circumstances had prevented the applicant from responding within time.

74 [1985] ECR 3223, order of 19 March 1985.

75 [1988] ECR 2285, order of 15 October 1988.

76 To these may be added procedural defects in obtaining the evidence, if Cases 18 and 35/65 *Gutmann v Euratom Commission* [1966] ECR 103 at 118 are to be regarded as an example of the exclusion of improperly obtained evidence. According to Advocate General Roemer (at 130) the evidence comprised statements taken by the Commission from the applicant's former subordinates; the applicant was not given an opportunity to defend himself or confront his accusers and he was not shown the texts of the statements. It is possible that the Court rejected the evidence because of these procedural irregularities but it could also be because the evidence was of doubtful credibility in view of the fact that the deponents had not been properly examined on their statements.

person guilty of the impropriety.[77] Where the party concerned has come into possession of evidence emanating from the opposing party without any impropriety, the mere fact that the opposing party would ordinarily require its consent to be given to production of the evidence in proceedings before the Court and has not been asked for, or given, its consent is insufficient to establish any impropriety or other reason justifying the exclusion of the evidence.[78] It is unclear whether the Court is obliged to exclude evidence improperly obtained or whether it has a discretion in the matter. The better view seems to be the latter because there may well be cases where the impropriety is only trivial or purely formal and it would be excessive to exclude the evidence. The burden would nevertheless lie on the party seeking to rely on the evidence to show that the public interest in favour of its disclosure outweighed that in favour of its exclusion.

77 Cf the *Ludwigshafener Walzmühle* case (above, note 27), where the intervener had received the document from a third party.
78 Case 260/80 *Andersen v Council* [1984] ECR 177 (paras 5–6).

CHAPTER 13

Rules of evidence

I Introduction

Advocate General Warner said, on one occasion, 'there are, as far as I can discern, no rules of evidence'.[1] There is a great deal of truth in this. The common law rules of evidence are largely exclusionary because the tribunal of fact was generally a jury and it was therefore important to prevent unreliable evidence from being put to it. This approach is naturally out of place when facts are to be found by a body trained to do so. In civil law countries attempts were made to reduce the intellectual process of weighing up the cogency of evidence and coming to a decision on it to technical formulae. These were gradually swept away and replaced simply by the criterion that the judge should be convinced.[2] Although there are cases where Community legislation has determined what is to be the proof of a fact,[3] these are exceptional. Where Community law lays down no requirements of proof, any appropriate means of proof may in principle be used.[4] In addition, the case law of the Court contains very few statements on questions of evidence. This is not surprising given that, in the realm of evidence, rules other than the most rudimentary tend to be artificial and difficult to reconcile with what goes on in the real world.

II The burden of proof

The 'burden of proof' can be understood in two ways: (i) the burden of proving one's case (the legal burden); (ii) the burden of adducing evidence to prove a fact (the evidential burden). The general rule, which, so far as both burdens are concerned, determines the party on whom the burden of proof lies, is expressed in the maxim ei incumbit probatio qui dicit, non qui negat: it is for the party who asserts a proposition or a fact to prove it; a party does not bear

---

1 (1976) 14 JSPTL 15.
2 'Intime conviction'.
3 See, for example, art 10 of Directive No 73/23 of 19 February 1973 (OJ No L77 of 26 March 1973 p 29) and Case 815/79 *Cremonini and Vrankovich* [1980] ECR 3583 (paras 9–10); Regulation No 3214/75 of 3 December 1975 (OJ No L323 of 15 December 1975 p 1), which provides that a valid certificate of origin must be accepted as proof of the origin of the goods; and Cases 15 and 16/76 *France v Commission* [1979] ECR 321 (aids paid in disregard of the formal requirements as to proof). See also Case C-27/92 *Möllmann-Fleisch GmbH v Hauptzollamt Hamburg-Jonas* [1993] ECR I-1701.
4 Cases 225 and 241/81 *Toledano Laredo and Garilli v Commission* [1983] ECR 347 (para 13). So far as the national authorities (and probably the Community institutions) are concerned, what constitutes an appropriate form of proof may, however, be determined by general principles of Community law: eg Case 199/82 *Amministrazione delle Finanze v San Giorgio SpA* [1983] ECR 3595.

the burden of proving purely negative facts.[5] However, the application of this principle and the very existence of a burden of proof, including the need (if any) to distinguish between the two senses of the term, depend on the nature of the proceedings. The existence of the legal burden presupposes that the proceedings are contentious; the legal burden has, in principle, no place in non-contentious proceedings. The evidential burden, on the other hand, can be said to exist wherever there are facts to be proved and whatever the nature of the proceedings; but the allocation of this burden is dependent on whether the proceedings are inquisitorial or accusatorial in character.

Even a cursory reading of the judgments and opinions in preliminary rulings does reveal the application by the Court of a burden of proof relating to the ascertainment of a fact. By way of example, in Cases 117/76 and 16/77 *Firma Albert Ruckdeschel & Co and Diamalt AG v Hauptzollamt Hamburg-St Annen*[6] the Court had asked the Council and the Commission to supply evidence to support certain assertions made by them. Adequate proof was not forthcoming and Advocate General Capotorti said: 'in the circumstances the conclusion must be drawn that there is no evidence of the facts to which the two institutions attached importance'. This tends to suggest that, in references for a preliminary ruling, each party who submits written or oral observations to the Court must discharge a burden lying on him to satisfy it that the assertions of fact he makes are true. Since the preliminary ruling procedure is in theory non-contentious, there should be no legal burden of proof. An indication to the contrary is to be found in Case 126/81 *Wünsche Handelgesellschaft v Germany*,[7] where Advocate General Rozès said that the burden of proof lay on Wünsche to show that the Commission had exceeded its discretion.[8]

In direct actions both the applicant and the defendant lie under a duty to adduce the documentary evidence and sources of evidence on which they rely to prove an assertion of fact[9] but the power to call for the production of evidence lies with the Court. Hence any allocation of the burden of adducing evidence to prove a fact, even in direct actions, must, in practice, be reduced to the pleading stage of the procedure, at which the parties put forward the documents and sources of evidence on which they rely. In this connection, Advocate General Gand once said:[10] 'I do not think that it is right to apply with undue strictness the concept of "burden of proof". . . In the final analysis, a reasonable degree of certainty must be attained on examining the documents produced by each of the parties and the reply made to them by the opposing party, subject to the Court's power, if it considers that the matter is insufficiently clear, to make an order for' a measure of enquiry. Similarly, in Cases 29, 31, 36, 39–47, 50 and 51/63 *Laminoirs, Hauts Fourneaux, Forges Fonderies et Usines de la Providence SA v High Authority*[11] Advocate General Lagrange remarked, in the context of a claim for damages: 'the onus of proof lies with the injured

---

5 Case T-117/89 *Sens v Commission* [1990] ECR II-185 (para 20). For examples of the burden of proof attaching to the party making an assertion, see Case 51/83 *Commission v Italy* [1984] ECR 2793 (para 17); Case 55/83 *Italy v Commission* [1985] ECR 683 (paras 15–16); Case 56/83 *Italy v Commission* [1985] ECR 703 (paras 15–16); Case 3/86 *Commission v Italy* [1988] ECR 3369 (para 13); Case 290/87 *Commission v Netherlands* [1989] ECR 3083 (paras 11 and 20).
6 [1977] ECR 1753 at 1784.
7 [1982] ECR 1479 at 1496.
8 In a subsequent case, Case 345/82 *Wünsche Handelgesellschaft v Germany* [1984] ECR 1995 (at 2025–2026), Advocate General Rozès said that the burden of proof is a matter for the national court, applying national rules of procedure.
9 RP-ECJ 38(1)(e) and 40(1)(d); RP-CFI 44(1)(e) and 46(1)(d).
10 In Case 8/65 *Acciaierie e Ferriere Pugliesi SpA v High Authority* [1966] ECR 1 at 12.
11 [1965] ECR 911 at 943–944.

party. However the defendant must not remain inactive. It is incumbent on him to produce to the Court all the evidence which can be used to dispute the relevance of the evidence put forward by the party opposing him. Even when the defendant is an administrative body it must, at least within certain limits, produce the documents or the information which it alone possesses in its capacity as a public authority. Briefly, therefore, although the parties oppose each other, they are required, and indeed precisely because they are opponents, to collaborate with a view to enabling the Court to decide, with all the facts at its disposal, whether the damage is sufficiently proved.'

The remarks of Advocate General Gand evince a natural unwillingness that cases should be decided on the basis of the burden of proof (that is, that where there is lingering uncertainty the decision should go against the party bearing the legal burden); and both advocates general indicate that the way of avoiding such an outcome is co-operation between the parties and the Court in the production of all relevant evidence, the parties by producing the evidence in their possession and the Court by exercising its powers to order a measure of enquiry. Thus, while one party may bear the legal burden of proof, both parties may lie under a duty to adduce evidence relevant to an issue of fact connected with it. The limit to the evidential burden lying on the parties is, however, the inability of the parties to adduce certain evidence in the absence of any exercise by the Court of its powers. Another example of this is Case 18/70 *Duraffour v Council*.[12] The facts were that the applicant, the widow of a deceased official of the Council, applied for the lump sum payable under the Staff Regulations when an official dies. The issue was whether the official had committed suicide, thus entitling the Council to withhold the money. A dispute arose over the question whether it was for the applicant to prove that the deceased had not committed suicide, to justify the claim, or whether it was for the defendant to prove that he had, to justify rejecting the claim. Advocate General Roemer came to a view on this point after a comparative study of national law, finding that 'in public law cases . . . the Court plainly has the power to order measures of enquiry of its own motion. This accords with the principle that in proceedings of this nature there is strictly speaking no individual burden of proof but rather an obligation, in fact on both parties, to co-operate effectively to discover the facts'.[13] The Court seems to have held that the burden of proving the issue lay with the applicant[14] but that the defendant also was bound 'as the appointing authority, to co-operate . . . in order to discover the truth'.[15]

The conclusion seems to be that, even in contentious proceedings, there is, strictly speaking, no allocation of the burden of adducing evidence as between the parties. Both lie under an equal duty to the Court to produce evidence or sources of evidence relating to the issues of fact in the case.[16] Nevertheless, in contentious proceedings, only one party bears the risk if an issue of fact is not proved. In consequence, where the evidence produced to the Court, considered as a whole, is inconclusive as to the existence or non-existence of a fact

12 [1971] ECR 515: see also the subsequent proceedings, reported sub nom *X v Council* [1972] ECR 1205.
13 Ibid at 533.
14 See [1972] ECR at 1212 (Advocate General Roemer).
15 [1971] ECR 515 (para 31).
16 The existence of such a duty, bearing on both parties, nonetheless presupposes that, in contentious proceedings, the applicant has demonstrated that its assertions have substance and raise questions that the defendant must answer. The defendant's duty to adduce relevant evidence does not come into play at all if the applicant fails to present a case that calls for an answer.

in issue, the Court is entitled to find that the legal burden of proof has not been discharged to that extent[17] but it does not do so on the basis that the party bearing the legal burden has failed to produce sufficient evidence to support his case. In proceedings before the Court, which are semi-inquisitorial in character, the production of sufficient evidence to decide an issue of fact is, in the final analysis, a matter for the Court to decide. The most that the parties can be held to do is to set up their own cases and give the Court sufficient documentary evidence and indications of sources of evidence[18] so that, if the matter still remains in doubt, the Court can exercise its own investigative powers. The parties cannot force the Court to act nor can they produce, of themselves, testimony or evidence that is not in their own possession or control. It follows that judgment cannot, in general, be given against a party on the basis that he has failed to produce sufficient evidence.

The one exception to this general rule appears to be the situation where the evidence in question is in the sole possession of one only of the parties. That party then bears the burden of producing the evidence. For example, in Case 45/64 *Commission v Italy*,[19] the Commission brought an action alleging that the Republic of Italy had infringed art 96 of the EEC Treaty, which requires that any tax refund paid on the exportation of goods must not exceed the internal taxation previously levied on them. So far as is relevant for present purposes, the burden of the Commission's complaint was that exports of certain products benefited from a flat-rate refund calculated by reference to their weight and not to the various taxes which had previously been imposed. The inevitable result of this, it was alleged, was that the amount of certain refunds would exceed the actual tax burden. The defendant asserted that the burden lay on the Commission to prove that the refunds were greater than those authorised by the Treaty and, certainly, if the Commission lost on this issue, it would lose the case. However, the information necessary to decide whether the refunds exceeded the tax burden was in the possession of the Italian government and the only figures it had ever produced tended to suggest that the flat-rate system did contravene art 96. The Court held that it was for the defendant, not the Commission, to prove that the system complied with the Treaty by producing the evidence. In Cases 169/83 and 136/84 *Leussinck-Brummelhuis v Commission*[20] the applicants claimed that a road accident had been caused by the defendant's negligence. The accident had occurred because the tread came away from a tyre on a car belonging to the defendant which was being driven by a chauffeur employed by the defendant at a time when the car was being used for a mission authorised by the defendant. The official report of the accident said that the detachment of the tread could be attributed to a number of possible causes (poor maintenance, inadequate inspection of the vehicle, negligent use). The defendant was best placed to provide the Court with any evidence enabling it to determine exactly what the cause was; but the defendant failed to produce any evidence. In consequence, the Court construed the uncertainty against the defendant and found that the accident had been caused by negligence for which the defendant was responsible. Those cases appear to show

17 Cf Case 23/81 *Commission v Royale Belge* [1983] ECR 2685 (paras 22–25).
18 It was the failure to comply with this duty, the evidential burden applicable at the stage of the written procedure (at which point proceedings are still accusatorial in character), that led the Court to reject an allegation made by the applicant in Case 107/82 *AEG v Commission* [1983] ECR 3151 (para 130).
19 [1965] ECR 857 at 867 and at 874–875 (Advocate General Gand). For the subsequent proceedings, see [1969] ECR 433. But see also Cases 96/81 *Commission v Netherlands* and 97/81 *Commission v Netherlands* [1982] ECR 1791 and 1819, respectively, at paras 6–8.
20 [1986] ECR 2801 (paras 15–17).

that a party cannot rely on the fact that the opposing party bears the burden of proving his case in order to avoid producing evidence.[21]

In the same way, in Case 19/77 *Miller International Schallplatten GmbH v Commission*,[22] where the applicant refused to produce its accounts in order to support the plea that a fine imposed by the Commission should be reduced because it was 'extremely burdensome', the Court dismissed the application, remarking that the applicant had prevented verification of its assertion. It is to be observed that the Court did not draw the inference from the failure to produce the accounts that the evidence to support the assertion did not exist nor did it find in favour of the Commission on the issue of fact. The applicant had failed to discharge the evidential burden imposed on it by the Court when the Court requested production of the accounts; that made it impossible to resolve the issue of fact one way or the other; judgment was therefore given against the applicant because it bore the legal burden of proof.

There are some cases which appear to suggest that there may be an allocation of the burden of adducing evidence as between the parties. In Case 10/55 *Mirossevich v High Authority*[23] the Court described a particular fact as a 'serious presumption' in support of the applicant's claim; it was for the defendant to rebut the presumption but evidence sufficient to do so had not been produced. This suggests, not only that the burden of adducing evidence may lie as between the parties, but also that it may shift in the course of proceedings. Similarly, in Cases 19 and 65/63 *Prakash v Euratom Commission*[24] the Court held that to order an expert's report would be justified only 'if the facts already proved raised a presumption in favour of the applicant's argument, since the burden of proof rests, generally speaking, on him'. Advocate General Gand said: 'in this case the burden of proving the accuracy of the facts which might be called in question does not fall on the defendant institution'. Since the Court refers to a presumption 'in favour of the applicant's argument', it may well have been thinking of the normal burden of proving one's case which would determine who has the burden of persuading the Court to order a measure of inquiry. A slightly different situation arose in Case C-65/91 *Commission v Greece*,[25] where the applicant produced photocopies of certain documents to prove its case and the defendant failed to produce any evidence or explanation to negative the inferences to be drawn from the photocopies. The totality of the evidence before the Court was sufficient to discharge the (legal) burden of proof lying on the applicant; any other evidence would have been in the possession of the defendant alone but it failed completely to produce anything that might weaken the force of the evidence produced by the applicant.

That the legal burden of proof exists in contentious proceedings is apparent from, for example, cases such as Case 6/54 *Netherlands v High Authority*,[26] Case 8/55 *Fédération Charbonnière Belgique v High Authority*,[27] Case 34/62 *Germany v Commission*,[28] Case 23/76 *Pellegrini & C SAS v Commission*,[29] Case 277/82

21 See also the explanation given by Advocate General Jacobs of Case 272/86 *Commission v Greece* [1988] ECR 4875 (see in particular paras 21 and 31) in Case 141/87 *Commission v Italy* [1989] ECR 943 at 972; Case T-58/92 *Moat v Commission*, 16 December 1993, para 65.
22 [1978] ECR 131 (para 21). See also Case 285/81R *Geist v Commission* (unreported), order of 29 September 1983 (para 4).
23 [1954–56] ECR 333: see 343–344 and 352 (Advocate General Lagrange).
24 [1965] ECR 533 at 554 and 569 (Advocate General Gand).
25 [1992] ECR I-5245 (paras 9–10).
26 [1954–56] ECR 103.
27 [1954–56] ECR 245 at 302.
28 [1963] ECR 131.
29 [1976] ECR 1807 (para 30).

Papageorgopoulos v Economic and Social Committee,[30] where the Court held that an allegation of misuse of powers had not been proved sufficiently in law. In theory this burden does not shift in the course of proceedings, whatever the burden of adducing evidence may do. On the other hand, in Case 12/74 *Commission v Germany*[31] Advocate General Warner said that, in proceedings under art 169 of the EEC Treaty, the burden might shift.[32] The explanation for this seems to lie in the distinction between propositions advanced to show that the opposing party has not discharged the burden lying on him to prove his case and pleas raised to rebut the case made out.[33] This can be illustrated by reference to actions for damages. It is well established that the applicant must prove the existence and the amount of the loss[34] and, therefore, where the claim seeks the reimbursement of sums paid out to a national authority without cause, the applicant must prove that he has exhausted all possibility of recovering the money under national law in order to establish the loss for which the Community may be made liable.[35] In the *Kampffmeyer*[36] and *Becher*[37] cases the applicants proved the existence of the loss. It had arisen from the withdrawal of a zero levy with effect from a certain time of day; normally levies remained applicable throughout the whole day. The defendant pleaded that the applicants should also have to prove that the relevant contracts were made either before the relevant time or without knowledge of the change. The Court regarded this as reversing the burden of proof. The defendant was in substance arguing that its liability should be reduced because the applicants had contributed to the loss through lack of foresight; in raising the burden of proof point the defendant was trying to force the applicants to prove that they had not contributed to the loss. Strictly speaking this was a separate issue raised by the defendant and it followed that the burden lay on it to show that the applicants had contributed to the loss, not the other way around. In the same way, in Case 238/78 *Ireks-Arkady GmbH v Council and Commission*[38] the defendants argued that the loss incurred by the applicants could have been avoided by passing on the effect of it to customers in the form of higher prices. Advocate General Capotorti regarded this as raising a separate plea so that the burden of proving that the loss could have been passed on lay with the defendants.[39]

In a few cases the Court has identified where the burden lies in relation to particular issues. For example, it has been held that, in staff cases, it is for the party alleging that the application is out of time (ie the defendant institution) to prove the date of the notification of the rejection of a complaint; if the rejection is not sent by registered post or some similar means, the institution cannot adduce conclusive evidence concerning the date of notification and the applicant is therefore entitled to the benefit of any doubt as to the start of any limitation period.[40] On the other hand, where the completion of a pre-

---

30 [1983] ECR 2897 (para 13).
31 [1975] ECR 181 at 213.
32 See also *Acciaierie e Ferriere Pugliesi SpA v High Authority* (above, note 10).
33 Cf *Commission v Royale Belge* (above, note 17) para 25.
34 See, for example, Case 49/65 *Ferriere e Acciaiere Napoletane SpA v High Authority* [1966] ECR 73 at 82; Case 74/74 *CNTA v Commission* [1976] ECR 797 at paras 13 and 17.
35 See Cases 5, 7 and 13–24/66 *Firma E Kampffmeyer v Commission* [1967] ECR 245 at 264.
36 Ibid.
37 Case 30/66 *Firma Kurt A Becher v Commission* [1967] ECR 285.
38 [1979] ECR 2955.
39 Ibid at 3006. See also Cases 256, 257, 265, 267/80, 5 and 51/81, 282/82 *Birra Wührer v Council and Commission* [1984] ECR 3693 (para 28 and at 3737–3738, per Advocate General VerLoren van Themaat).
40 Case 108/79 *Belfiore v Commission* [1980] ECR 1769 (para 7); Cases 193 and 194/87 *Maurissen v Court of Auditors* [1989] ECR 1045 (para 46). This appears to be a principle of general application: see Cases 32 and 33/58 *SNUPAT v High Authority* [1959] ECR 127 at 136.

litigation procedure is a prerequisite of the admissibility of the action, the burden lies on the applicant to prove that the pre-litigation procedure has been properly completed.[41] The burden lies on the party alleging a misuse of powers to prove the allegation by reference to objective, relevant and consistent evidence.[42] Again, in staff cases, the burden lies on the applicant to adduce evidence to show that the contested decision is contrary to the interests of the service.[43] Article 60(1) of the ECSC Treaty prohibits certain pricing practices, in particular discriminative practices involving the application by a seller of dissimilar conditions to comparable transactions. Where the Commission finds that there has been discrimination of this nature, it is for the undertaking challenging the Commission's decision to show that the conditions were not dissimilar or that the transactions were not comparable.[44] According to Advocate General Warner the burden lies on the defendant institution in staff cases to prove the reason for an official's dismissal.[45] In actions for annulment or for damages (the latter where based on the unlawfulness of an act of the defendant), the burden of proving unlawfulness lies on the applicant.[46] In actions under art 169 of the EEC Treaty, the burden (both legal and evidential) lies on the Commission to prove that there has been a failure on the part of the defendant to fulfil its obligations under the Treaty[47] but the burden lies on the defendant to prove a defence (such as that its measures are proportionate[48] or benefit from a derogation).[49] In actions relating to the clearance of accounts, it is for the defendant (the Commission) to prove that the applicant (a member state) has infringed the rules and for the applicant to prove that the defendant erred in calculating the financial consequences;[50] save where no distinction can be drawn between those aspects of the dispute, in which case the entire burden falls on the applicant.[51] In contrast, where an assignee of a right claims damages, the burden lies on him to prove an infringement of the right; it is not necessary for him to prove that he gave the assignor value to the equivalent of the amounts claimed in exchange for the assignment of the right.[52] The Court will adopt the ordinary and natural inferences to be drawn

---

41 Eg Case 152/87 *Montgomery v European Parliament* [1987] ECR 4899 (para 9).
42 Case T-108/89 *Scheuer v Commission* [1990] ECR II-411 (paras 50–53).
43 Ibid (para 48).
44 Case 29/67 *Société De Wendel v Commission* [1968] ECR 263 at 278, see also at 288 (Advocate General Roemer).
45 Case 110/75 *Mills v European Investment Bank* [1976] ECR 1613 at 1627–1628.
46 Case 204/84 *Sideradria Industria Metallurgica SpA v Commission* [1986] ECR 1415 (para 11), an action for annulment; Case 244/83 *Meggle Milchindustrie GmbH & Co KG v Council and Commission* [1986] ECR 1101 (paras 26–27), an action for damages.
47 Case 298/86 *Commission v Belgium* [1988] ECR 4343 (para 16); Case 141/87 *Commission v Italy* [1989] ECR 943 (para 17); Case 290/87 *Commission v Netherlands* [1989] ECR 3083 (para 11); Case C-62/89 *Commission v France* [1990] ECR I-925 (para 37); Case C-244/89 *Commission v France* [1991] ECR I-163 (para 35 and at 184, Advocate General Jacobs); Case C-249/88 *Commission v Belgium* [1991] ECR I-1275 (para 6); Case C-157/91 *Commission v Netherlands* [1992] ECR I-5899 (para 12); Case C-210/91 *Commission v Greece* [1992] ECR I-6735 (paras 22–23).
48 Case 324/82 *Commission v Belgium* [1984] ECR 1861 (para 31).
49 Case 199/85 *Commission v Italy* [1987] ECR 1039 (paras 14–15).
50 Case 347/85 *United Kingdom v Commission* [1988] ECR 1749 (Re Dual Pricing for Milk) (para 16); Case C-8/88 *Germany v Commission* [1990] ECR I-2321 (para 28 and at 2351–2353, Advocate General van Gerven); Case C-281/89 *Italy v Commission* [1991] ECR I-347 (para 19 and at 356, Advocate General Mischo); Case C-48/91 *Netherlands v Commission* 10 November 1993 (opinion of Advocate-General Lenz, paras 39–48).
51 *Italy v Commision*, ibid (para 20 and at 356); Case C-55/91 *Italy v Commission*, 6 October 1993, paras 14, 35 and 71.
52 *Birra Würhrer v Council and Commission* (above, note 39) paras 31–32.

from evidence unless the party wishing the Court to come to a different conclusion discharges the burden of proving that other conclusion.[53]

The relationship between the two burdens of proof can be illustrated by considering an action for the annulment of a Commission decision finding that the applicant has infringed the competition rules. The legal burden lies on the applicant to show that the decision is wrong as a matter of law.[54] The applicant may allege that the Commission erred when it found a particular fact on which it based its decision. If this assertion is not made out, the applicant risks losing the case. Both parties must produce the documents in their possession and inform the Court of the other sources of evidence on which they rely in order to support the positions they adopt on the issue of fact. The Commission, in particular, must reveal the evidence on the basis of which it found the disputed fact[55] because the essential question is whether or not, at the time when the contested decision was adopted, the Commission had sufficient evidence to support its findings.[56] Thus, whereas the legal burden lies on the applicant, the primary evidential burden lies on the defendant.[57] If the Commission successfully demonstrates that the evidence at its disposal at the time when the decision was adopted was sufficient in law to support its findings, the evidential burden shifts to the applicant to produce evidence to establish that those findings were erroneous.[58] In practice, due to the particular characteristics of the judicial review of Commission decisions in application of the competition rules, the discharge of the evidential burden is more complex.

To the extent that the undertaking does not raise an issue relating to the inferences drawn from evidence used by the Commission of which it had knowledge and an opportunity to rebut in the proceedings before the Commission, the Court is entitled to assume that the Commission's findings are not challenged. In relation to those findings which are challenged, in strict theory the Commission should, no doubt, produce all the evidence at its disposal when it adopted the decision which relates to the disputed findings of fact, not just a selection of the evidence which tends to support them. The Court can exercise its powers of review and determine whether or not the evidence at the Commission's disposal was sufficient in law to support its findings only if the Court is in a position to assess the weight of the evidence relied on by the Commission; and the weight of any particular adminicle depends not only on its intrinsic value but also on its relationship with other adminicles.[59] In

---

53 Case 338/82 *Albertini and Montagnani v Commission* [1984] ECR 2123 (para 30); Case 12/83 *Bähr v Commission* [1984] ECR 2155 (paras 15–17); Case 346/82 *Favre v Commission* [1984] ECR 2269 (para 25); Case T-7/89 *Hercules Chemicals NV SA v Commission* [1991] ECR II-1711 (paras 43–44 and 145).

54 Eg Cases 43 and 63/82 *VBVB und VBBB v Commission* [1984] ECR 19 (paras 34 and 59).

55 Cf Case 41/69 *ACF Chemiefarma NV v Commission* [1970] ECR 661 at 708 (Advocate General Gand).

56 Case T-30/89 *Hilti AG v Commission* [1991] ECR II-1439 (para 44).

57 In this type of situation, the applicant should be in possession of all the evidence relied on by the Commission in support of its findings because, in the course of the proceedings leading up to the adoption of its decision, the Commission lies under a duty to reveal to the undertakings whose conduct is being investigated all the evidence relied on against them. Any other evidence which has not been revealed to the undertakings concerned is inadmissible in support of any findings made against them. Nonetheless, the Commission bears the evidential burden of producing *to the Court* the evidence on which it relied in support of its findings.

58 *Hercules Chemicals NV SA v Commission* (above, note 53) paras 43–44 and 145; Case T-15/89 *Chemie Linz AG v Commission* [1992] ECR II-1275 (para 44).

59 For example, the weight to be given to a particular document relied on by the Commission may have to be revised considerably if it is found that the Commission was also in possession of a number of other documents of equal probative value which all suggest that the facts were otherwise than as suggested by the first document.

practice, the parties often content themselves with producing to the Court only the evidence relied on by the Commission which they believe is important enough to look at. This is not necessarily all the evidence available to the Commission. Apart from evidence referred to expressly in the decision, the Commission may have implicitly based its findings on, or been influenced by, other evidence, some of which may not have been disclosed to the undertaking concerned. Where the Commission has not disclosed evidence to the undertaking concerned and has not given the undertaking an opportunity to rebut such evidence in the course of the proceedings before the Commission, the Commission has disabled itself from relying on that evidence in the proceedings before the Court in order to support the findings made against the undertaking.[60] The evidential burden lying on the Commission cannot be discharged by reliance upon such evidence. However, such evidence may be of assistance to the undertaking because it may be exculpatory in nature or else may tend to weaken the force of the evidence expressly relied on by the Commission. Ex hypothesi, the undertaking is not in a position to draw the Court's attention to such undisclosed evidence in any specific way: the most that the undertaking can do is to make the general assertion that the Commission may be in possession of evidence that may assist the undertaking, an assertion that would ordinarily be regarded as insufficient to justify a measure of enquiry such as an order that the Commission produce all undisclosed evidence in its possession. By continuing to conceal (consciously or unconsciously) any undisclosed evidence in its possession, the Commission can give an entirely false picture of the conclusiveness of the proof on which it relied expressly to make its findings.[61] It is for this reason that the duty binding the Commission to produce to the Court all the evidence on which a disputed finding is based covers no more and no less than all the evidence relating to that finding, including material inadmissible as incriminatory evidence in the proceedings before the Court. The Commission cannot avoid the duty to reveal the evidence in its possession by, for example, pleading that it neither admits nor denies the existence of the disputed fact, thus leaving, as the only 'assertion' of fact requiring proof, the applicant's contention that the fact did not exist. For pleading purposes, the Commission is bound by the decision attacked unless it concedes that the decision was wrong in whole or in part. The Court reaches a conclusion on the issue of fact after considering all the evidence at its disposal. If the Commission does not produce any evidence at all, the Court is entitled to conclude that it had no grounds for finding the fact and the decision may be annulled, to the extent that it turns on the existence of the fact, even if the applicant has not been able to produce any evidence to show that the fact did not exist. A failure on the part of the applicant to produce any evidence does not normally affect the resolution of the dispute because, in the nature of things, the Commission could only have found the fact in its decision on the basis of evidence in its possession or at its disposal. Evidence available to the applicant and not to the Commission is relevant only in so far as it tends to contradict or weaken the evidence relied on by the Commission.

---

60 Case 322/81 *Nederlandsche Banden-Industrie Michelin v Commission* [1983] ECR 3461 (para 9) and note 87, p 431.
61 See, for example, Cases T-68, T-77 and T-78/89 *Società Italiano Vetro SA v Commission* [1992] ECR II-1403 (Re Italian Flat Glass) (paras 89–94).

The crucial role played by the evidence on which the Commission based its findings has been emphasised in several cases[62] but it should not be forgotten that the burden still lies on the applicant to prove that the Commission erred in finding a relevant fact, in the sense that it is the applicant that risks losing the case if the assertion that the Commission erred is not made out. That the Commission is required to disgorge the evidence relating to a disputed finding of fact simply reflects the fact that only it knows exactly where all that evidence is to be found, not that the 'burden of proof', in a general sense, has shifted to it.[63] The burden of proof lying on the applicant is discharged if the Court determines that the Commission was not in possession of evidence which was sufficiently conclusive to ground its findings of fact; and, for that purpose, the Court may take into account evidence produced after the date of the Commission's decision which contradicts the evidence relied on by the Commission.[64] It is not necessary for there to be enough evidence to show that a fact in issue found by the Commission did not exist although the burden of proof is also discharged where this is the case. On the other hand, where the evidence relied on by the Commission is sufficient in law to support a finding of fact in the decision but all the evidence produced to the Court leaves the matter inconclusive (as where further evidence throws doubt on some material relied on by the Commission but is not sufficient to set up a positive case that the fact was wrongly found) the question whether or not the legal burden lying on the applicant has been discharged depends upon the degree of doubt and, hence, upon the standard of proof.

III   The standard of proof

Although it can be taken to be the rule that the Court must be convinced of the existence of a fact, there is very little authority on what is necessary to convince it or, in other words, on what is the standard of proof required. In Case 6/54 *Netherlands v High Authority*[65] the Court alluded at one point to full proof ('*une preuve complète*') but its reference in the *Mirossevich* case[66] to a 'serious presumption' can also be taken as indicating what is an adequate standard in the absence of any contradictory evidence or argument.[67] In *Usines de la Providence v High Authority*[68] Advocate General Roemer referred to 'convincing proof' and 'complete proof' ('*preuve intégral*'); in Case 8/65 *Acciaierie e Ferriere*

62 See, for example, Cases 40–48, 50, 54–56, 111, 113 and 114/73 *Coöperative Vereniging Suiker Unie UA v Commission* [1975] ECR 1663 (Re European Sugar Cartel) (paras 210 and 418–420 and at 2061, Advocate General Mayras); Case 6/72 *Europemballage Corpn and Continental Can Co Inc v Commission* [1973] ECR 215 (para 37); Case 27/76 *United Brands Co v Commission* [1978] ECR 207 (paras 264–267).

63 When reading Advocate General Warner's remarks in Cases 6 and 7/73 *Istituto Chemioterapico Italiano SpA and Commercial Solvents Corpn v Commission* [1974] ECR 223 at 269 and those of Advocate General Sir Gordon Slynn in Cases 100–103/80 *Musique Diffusion Française SA v Commission* [1983] ECR 1825, it should be borne in mind that neither advocate general expressly distinguishes between the two senses in which the expression 'burden of proof' is used, although the distinction between them is apparent in what is said.

64 Eg Cases 29 and 30/83 *CRAM and Rheinzink v Commission* [1984] ECR 1679 (paras 16–20).

65 Above (note 26) at 115.

66 Above (note 23).

67 See also the *Prakash* case (above, note 24) 'a presumption in favour of the applicant's argument'.

68 Above (note 11) at 961. In the *Europemballage* case (above, note 62) at 262 he seems to have considered that the test to apply when examining the Commission's findings in competition cases was whether or not they had been proved 'beyond doubt' or had 'a certain and unassailable foundation'.

Pugliesi v High Authority,[69] on the other hand, Advocate General Gand spoke of a 'reasonable degree of certainty' (*'une certitude raisonable'*). In *Duraffour v Council*[70] the Court seemed to regard it as sufficient if there were 'sufficiently weighty, clear and uncontradictory circumstantial evidence not contradicted by contrary circumstantial evidence' (*'présomptions suffisamment graves, précises et concordantes non-contredites par des présomptions contraires'*); in the subsequent proceedings, Advocate General Roemer said that probability bordering on certainty was not necessary, it being sufficient if 'substantial indications give rise to a high degree of probability' (*'des indices graves établissent un haut degré de probabilité'*).[71] In more recent cases the Court has specified a 'body of concordant evidence';[72] 'sufficiently precise and coherent proof';[73] less helpfully, proof *'à suffisance de droit'* (sufficiently proved in law) or 'sufficiently clear evidence';[74] 'specific and concrete evidence';[75] a 'firm, precise and concordant body of evidence'.[76] At least in competition cases, where there is any reasonable doubt, the benefit of that doubt must be given to the undertaking(s) accused of unlawful conduct.[77] In actions for damages it may be difficult for the applicant to discharge the burden of proving the extent of the loss suffered. Difficulties in calculating the loss do not, however, prevent the applicant from recovering. If all the evidence available has been put forward, realistic approximations are sufficient and it is not necessary to reach an exact assessment of the damage as long as it is possible to arrive at an 'acceptable' approximation on the basis of facts that are 'sufficiently reliable'.[78] In applications for interim relief it may be sufficient if there is 'a degree of probability sufficient for the purposes' of the proceedings.[79] In the *Polypropylene* cases,[80] where the applicants applied for the oral procedure to be reopened in order to argue that certain defects of procedure had rendered the contested decision non-existent, the Court required them to demonstrate on a balance of probabilities that the contested decision was vitiated by the defects in question (a test that the applicants failed). It should be noted that that standard of proof was required in order to justify the procedural step of reopening the oral procedure, indicating that a higher standard of proof would have been required to establish the non-existence of the decision.[81]

---

69   Above, note 10 at 12.
70   Above, note 12 at para 30.
71   Case 18/70 *X v Council* (above, note 12) at 1213.
72   Cases 154, 205, 206, 226–228, 263 and 264/78 and 31, 39, 83 and 85/79 *Ferriera Valsabbia SpA v Commission* [1980] ECR 907 (para 129).
73   Cases 29 and 30/83 *Compagnie Royale Asturienne des Mines SA (CRAM) and Rheinzink GmbH v Commission* [1984] ECR 1679 (para 20).
74   Eg *AEG v Commission* (above, note 18) inter alia at para 136; Case C-35/88 *Commission v Greece* [1990] ECR I-3125 (para 31); Case C-96/89 *Commission v Netherlands* [1991] ECR I-2461 (paras 21–22); *Hilti AG v Commission* (above, note 56) para 44; *Hercules Chemicals NV SA v Commission* (above, note 53) para 75.
75   Case 290/87 *Commission v Netherlands* [1989] ECR 3083 (para 20); Case T-73/89 *Barbi v Commission* [1990] ECR II-619 (para 45).
76   Cases C-89, C-104, C-114, C-116, C-117, C-125 to C-129/85 *A Ahlström Osakeytiö v Commission* [1993] ECR I-1307 (para 127).
77   Case T-1/89 *Rhône-Poulenc SA v Commission* [1991] ECR II-867 at 954 (Judge Vesterdorf). Cf *CRAM and Rheinzink v Commission* (above, note 73) para 16.
78   *Usines de la Providence v High Authority* (above, note 11) at 938–939, see also 943–944 (Advocate General Lagrange) and 961 (Advocate General Roemer).
79   Cases 228 and 229/82R *Ford Werke AG and Ford of Europe Inc v Commission* [1982] ECR 3091 (para 7).
80   Eg Case T-9/89 *Hüls AG v Commission* [1992] ECR II-499. See B. Vesterdorf in (1992) 29 CMLRev 897 at 909 (note 16).
81   The non-existence of a contested act must usually be so evident as to leave no room for any doubt at all about the non-existence of the act. The problem in the *Polypropylene* cases arose from the fact that the decision contested in those cases appeared on its face to have been properly adopted. However, it was alleged to have been vitiated by the same defects as those

The Court does not yet seem to have settled on a specific formula to express the standard of proof required to convince it of the existence of a fact. The absence of such a formula from the case law does not, of course, necessarily mean that it does not exist: the Court may well have decided for itself what degree of proof is necessary without publishing its views to the world. At one time, the position was sufficiently uncertain as to leave it a plausible supposition that each judge applied the standard of proof adopted in the legal system in which he was trained. The resultant decision on an issue of fact therefore appeared to spring from a pot pourri of national standards which might differ in terms of formulation, if not also in degree. The position is still not entirely clear. For reasons of legal certainty it would probably be better if the Court identified one standard of proof. That adopted by Advocate General Gand in Case 8/65 seems to be one of the better candidates.

IV   The golden rule

The laws of the member states contain many rules excluding relevant evidence[82] or, which comes to much the same, defining what may constitute proof of a fact.[83] With the exception of the limited circumstances in which relevant evidence may be excluded from the proceedings (because it lacks probative value for the purposes of the proceedings or has been improperly obtained) or must be excluded from consideration (because it is legally irrelevant), the Court does not apply such artificial rules of proof: the only criterion, the golden rule, is the credibility of evidence.[84] As has been remarked, rules specifying what is proof of a fact are occasionally found in Community legislation. The validity of such rules does not appear to have been tested before the Court. It is to be supposed that the Court would apply them unless it were shown that there was no justification, whether commercial, administrative or economic, for their existence and that they tended to affect adversely the right to a fair trial or infringed some other principle of Community law.[85] Thus, in Case C-330/88 *Grifoni v Euratom*,[86] the Court held that a legal requirement that an agreement be in writing excluded evidence of an oral agreement.

In practice, the most important derogation from the golden rule is the rule in competition cases that credible evidence which the Commission did not reveal to the undertaking concerned or on which the undertaking was not given an adequate opportunity to present its views during the course of the proceedings before the Commission, is inadmissible as proof of a fact found in the Commission's decision which tends to incriminate the undertaking.[87] As a result, only

which had affected the decision contested in Cases T-79, T-84 to T-86, T-89, T-91, T-92, T-94, T-96, T-98, T-102 and T-104/89 *BASF AG v Commission* [1992] ECR II-315 (Re PVC Cartel), which also appeared on its face to be a decision that had been properly adopted but, on investigation, had been shown to be so vitiated by procedural defects that it was held to be non-existent.

82 Eg the rule against hearsay evidence.
83 Eg the necessity for written evidence in certain matters under art 1341 of the French Civil Code.
84 *Rhône-Poulenc SA v Commission* (above, note 77) at 954 (Judge Vesterdorf).
85 Cf Case 199/82 *Amministrazione delle Finanze v San Giorgio* [1983] ECR 3595 (paras 13–14).
86 [1991] ECR I-1045 (para 10 and at 1058–1059, Advocate General Tesauro).
87 *Musique Diffusion Française SA v Commission* (above, note 63) paras 29–30 and 65; *AEG v Commission* (above, note 18) paras 24–30; *Nederlandsche Banden-Industrie Michelin v Commission* (above, note 60) paras 7–8; *VBVB and VBBB v Commission* (above, note 54) para 25; Case C-62/86 *AKZO Chemie BV v Commission* [1991] ECR I-3359 (paras 21 and 24); Case T-9/89 *Hüls AG v Commission* [1992] ECR II-499 (paras 38–39 and 46).

documents mentioned in the Statement of Objections notified by the Commission to the undertaking concerned[88] (or mentioned in some similar communication sent to the undertaking by the Commission before the making of the final decision at the end of the administrative proceedings) or appended to it, and on which the undertaking has been given an adequate opportunity to defend itself can be relied on as against the undertaking in the proceedings before the Court. Documents appended to the Statement of Objections but not mentioned in it may be used as evidence only if the undertaking could reasonably infer from the Statement of Objections the conclusions that the Commission intended to draw from them; documents produced by the undertaking concerned in reply to the Statement of Objections can also be used to incriminate it because, in producing them, the undertaking must have known that they could be used against it by the Commission.[89] Documents that, for those reasons, are inadmissible for the purpose of incriminating an undertaking may, however, be admissible in the proceedings before the Court for the purpose of exculpating the undertaking,[90] in which case the document in question appears to be admissible only in respect of the exculpatory passages.[91]

In general, the credibility or probative value of evidence is assessed by reference to common sense or ordinary experience of affairs. In the same way, the inferences to be drawn from evidence are those which follow in the ordinary and natural way from the evidence.[92] Evidence must be evaluated in the same way irrespective of the identity of the person or party from whom it has been obtained.[93] Arguments against the probative value of evidence must be sufficiently precise and detailed if they are to be accepted.[94] The Court's approach to assessing evidence can be illustrated by the following cases.

In Case 18/57 *Nold KG v High Authority*[95] the partners in the applicant undertaking produced during the proceedings written declarations, tending to show that they had given an oral authority to act on behalf of the undertaking to one E Nold, in order to prove that he had such authority when he caused an application commencing proceedings to be lodged on his behalf. Advocate General Roemer held that the declarations did not constitute either testimony or documentary evidence but, when taken with the fact that, at the material time, Nold had negotiated and concluded agreements on behalf of the undertaking, they indicated that he had been empowered to act on its behalf.[96] The Court seems to have regarded the declarations as being credible enough in themselves. In the *Valsabbia* case,[97] one of the applicants said that the Commission had wrongly relied on prices entered by hand on a series of invoices;

---

88 More specifically, those mentioned in relation to the legal assessment made by the Commission in the Statement of Objections and not just in relation to the factual background to the case: *A Ahlström Osakeytiö v Commission* (above, note 76) para 138.

89 Eg the *Hüls* case (above, note 87) para 39; Case T-11/89 *Shell International Chemical Co Ltd v Commission* [1992] ECR II-757 (paras 55–59).

90 Such as where the document incriminates the undertaking in relation to one aspect of the case alleged against it by the Commission but exculpates it in relation to another aspect of that case.

91 The *Shell* case (above, note 89) para 57.

92 Case 338/82 *Albertini and Montagnani v Commission* [1984] ECR 2123 (para 30).

93 Cf Case 143/84 *Vlachou v Court of Auditors* [1986] ECR 459 (para 18).

94 Case C-61/90 *Commission v Greece* [1992] ECR I-2407 (para 15).

95 [1959] ECR 41.

96 Ibid at 61. Capacity to institute proceedings is determined by the national law governing the applicant but German law did not require a power to act to be in writing. The question was therefore one of Community procedural law: did the evidence indicate that power had been given orally?

97 Above (note 72) paras 172–174.

annotations such as these, it maintained, were of no probative value because they were 'extraneous to the real contractual relationship'. This argument was dismissed because the Commission produced corroborative evidence in the form of telexes and the written testimony of its inspector.

The *Suiker Unie* case[98] gave rise to several evidential problems. Two of the applicants contended that correspondence passing between third parties[99] could not be used against them. The Court held that it could accept as evidence of an undertaking's conduct correspondence exchanged between third parties, 'provided that the content thereof is credible to the extent to which it refers to the said conduct'.[1] It rejected both the view that one of the third parties might have invented what it said and the argument that the documents in question should not be taken literally, although they were damning, because it would be 'even more unusual' for an undertaking to 'simulate in letters and documents conduct likely to lay it open to sanctions'.[2] In addition, it was useless to deny the evidential value of the documents on the ground that a third party recorded or kept them for the sole purpose of rendering the other party to the correspondence liable to be proceeded against by the Commission.[3] The evidence contained in the documents could be used in general against all the applicants.[4] Credibility is not affected simply because there is a conflict of interest between the person making a statement and the person of or about whom it is made; all relevant factors affecting credibility should be taken into account, such as corroborative evidence.[5] If there is sufficient evidence to establish as a matter of law the existence of a fact, the Court does not have to consider the credibility of further evidence tending to the same conclusion,[6] at least if its lack of credibility would not in turn affect the credibility of the evidence relied on to establish the fact. The Court may exclude from consideration an adminicle whose probative value is not evident and cannot be demonstrated by the party relying on it.[7]

In the *Polypropylene* cases,[8] Judge Vesterdorf considered that, to be credible, testimony should be given by persons with direct knowledge of the facts; testimony from other persons or a failure to bring forward witnesses in relation to a fact that can only, or can best, be proved by testimony may weaken the credibility of the evidence actually given. In the case of a witness, his or her demeanour when under examination as well as the substance of the testimony given are clearly of importance.[9] In the case of a document, the plausibility of the information set out in it, its origin, the circumstances in which it was drawn up, the person(s) for whom it was intended and its contents are all relevant

98 Above note 62.
99 Sc between one of the applicants in another of the joined cases and a third party unconnected with the proceedings.
1 *Suiker Unie* (above, note 62) para 164 of the judgment.
2 Ibid paras 160–161 of the judgment.
3 Ibid para 163 of the judgment.
4 Ibid para 574 of the judgment.
5 See ibid paras 271–274 of the judgment. Another example of a case in which hearsay evidence was admitted is Case 52/81 *Faust v Commission* [1982] ECR 3745.
6 Cases 100–103/80 *Musique Diffusion Française SA v Commission* [1983] ECR 1825 (para 60).
7 Cases C-89, C-104, C-114, C-116, C-117 and C-125 to C-129/85 *A Ahlström Osakeytiö v Commission* [1993] ECR I-1307, paras 68–69, where the Commission was unable to specify how a particular document proved the identity of the parties to an alleged concerted practice.
8 See Case T-1/89 *Rhône-Poulenc SA v Commission* [1991] ECR II-867 at 955–957.
9 In that respect, it is a defect in the procedure followed when examining a witness that not all the judges who will decide the case are present when a witness is examined. Unless the judges who were not present at the time rely on the impression made by the witness on those judges who were present, there is a risk that those judges who were not present may give the testimony a different value from that given to it by the judges who were present.

factors when determining credibility. The facts that the document was drawn up in close connection with the events described in it and, in the case of confidential matters, without the intention of being made public, can be highly significant.[10] On the other hand, in Case C-35/88 *Commission v Greece*[11] Advocate General Mischo doubted the evidential value of purely internal documents, preferring documents which are intended to be made public.[12] The most that can be said is that the internal nature of a document may be relevant to its probative value, the degree to which it is relevant varying on the precise nature of the document and the surrounding circumstances. The incomplete nature of a document may deprive it of credibility[13] but not the fact that only a photocopy, not the original, is produced in evidence.[14] Where different adminicles corroborate one another or, on the other hand, are in conflict, the credibility of the evidence as a whole or of particular adminicles is affected, as the case may be, in a positive or negative way.[15]

In the *Polypropylene* cases[16] the Court upheld the reliance placed by the Commission on a handwritten record of a telephone conversation between the marketing director of one of the undertakings involved in the proceedings and an unknown person. The note of the conversation was believed to have been written in the first part of 1977 (some 15 years before the judgment). It was very terse but contained precise information about the terms of an agreement said to have been made by four other undertakings. The author of the note did not remember precisely the circumstances in which he had written it. Even so, the note was unambiguous. There was an explanation for the form that it took.[17] The author's imprecise recollection of the circumstances did not affect the evidential value of the note because its contents indicated that the information set out in it had been provided by one of the undertakings referred to in it; the precision of the information showed that it was not the product of gossip or invention.[18] It should also be noted that the credibility of the document was supported by the reaction to it of the undertakings named in it (at least two of them made admissions consistent with the note) and by subsequent events later in 1977. In relation to documents in general, the Court preferred the contemporaneous notes of meetings as records of their purpose to the assertions later made by the undertakings.[19] In assessing the notes of meetings,

---

10 In *Rhône-Poulenc* (above, note 8) Judge Vesterdorf pointed out that, in many instances, the people used by the undertakings to explain the documents away were in-house or independent lawyers, not the company employees concerned. He regarded that as significant (albeit not decisive) because it is surprising that it should be necessary to have recourse to explanations given by someone other than the persons directly involved. The lesson seems to be that, where documentary evidence is relied on, it is necessary for a party to provide evidence from a direct participant in the events recounted in or purportedly proved by the documents in order to dispel any misconceptions arising from the documents.
11 [1990] ECR I-3125 at 3144.
12 See also Case C-49/88 *Al-Jubail Fertiliser Co v Council* [1991] ECR I-3187 (para 82 of the opinion of Advocate General Darmon). In *Commission v Greece* (ibid) the Court relied on the document but also referred to corroborative evidence: see paras 21 and 26 of the judgment.
13 Case 152/87 *Montgomery v European Parliament* [1987] ECR 4899 (para 9).
14 Cf Case C-65/91 *Commission v Greece* [1992] ECR I-5245 (paras 9–10), where the Commission successfully relied on photocopies of documents. That was, however, a case where the authenticity of the photocopies could easily have been checked by the opposing party.
15 Eg Case T-80/91 *Campogrande v Commission* [1992] ECR II-2459 (para 18). The fact that one adminicle is corroborated by another does not guarantee the objectivity of the evidence if both are derived from the same source: Case C-48/91 *Netherlands v Commission*, 10 November 1993, para 25.
16 Above, note 8.
17 'The anti-competitive object of the note was a reason for its author to leave the least trace possible.'
18 Case T-11/89 *Shell International Chemical Co Ltd v Commission* [1992] ECR II-757 (para 86).
19 Ibid (para 116).

Judge Vesterdorf placed some weight on the consideration that it is hardly plausible that large undertakings will send to important meetings people who are not able to express in a reasonable and trustworthy manner what happened at the meetings.[20]

According to Judge Vesterdorf in the *Polypropylene* cases,[21] economic analysis may also be important but it is of limited use and cannot be a substitute for the legal assessment of primary facts. In the *Woodpulp* case[22] Advocate General Darmon expressed similar hesitations about the expert evidence commissioned by the Court in that case, but the Court does not seem to have had such reservations.[23] There is no formal bar to reliance on evidence produced in other proceedings. For example, in Case 34/80 *Authié v Commission*,[24] testimony given several years beforehand in a previous case was admitted as evidence and, in Case 245/81 *Edeka Zentrale AG v Germany*,[25] a reference for a preliminary ruling, telexes produced in a previous direct action were relied on. But it would seem that the evidence must have been properly obtained.[26]

V   Presumptions[27]

The word 'presumption' is generally used to describe either a conclusion that a fact (often termed the 'presumed fact' or 'inferred fact') exists which may, or must, be drawn if some other fact (often termed the 'primary fact' or 'basic fact') is proved or admitted; or a conclusion which must be drawn (usually without the need for any evidence to support it) unless and until the contrary is proved. Presumptions are defined, sometimes in legislation and sometimes in case law. When defined in case law they very often, but not invariably, reflect the Court's appreciation, based on general experience and knowledge of the facts in a particular case, of what constitutes proof of a fact in issue (that is, they are examples of the first sense in which the word 'presumption' is used).[28] Presumptions in the second sense identified above are rules of evidence which

---

20 Experience might suggest some reservations about that assumption. However, it is a reasonable basis on which to assess contemporaneous notes and it is the only basis on which they can properly be assessed by the Court (and the Commission) in the absence of some kind of indication (presumably in the form of the testimony of an appropriate witness) as to the true ability of the author of such notes to make an accurate record.

21 Above, note 8 at 957.

22 *Ahlström Osakeytiö* (above, note 7) in particular at paras 74–127 of the judgment and paras 432–433 of the opinion of Advocate General Darmon.

23 That was, however, a case where the expert evidence was used largely to cast sufficient doubt on the findings made by the Commission to justify dismissing those findings, as opposed to setting up a positive case contradicting the Commission's findings.

24 [1981] ECR 665 para 12.

25 [1982] ECR 2745. Where the Court wishes to use evidence produced in other proceedings, it may exercise its powers under the Statutes, as was done in Cases 80-81/77 *Les Commissionaires Réunis Sàrl v Receveur des Douanes* [1978] ECR 927 (see 930).

26 Cases 18 and 35/65 *Gutmann v Euratom Commission* [1966] ECR 103 at 118 and 130 (Advocate General Roemer). The judgment is obscure. The Court held that it could not 'assess the value of the evidence produced because the conditions under which the statements were taken by the Commission's security service while the case was in progress do not enable the Court to exercise its powers of review'. Advocate General Roemer's opinion goes into greater detail but it is unclear whether the Court's objection was to the procedural defects in the obtaining of the evidence (the opposing party was never allowed to confront the persons who made the statements or shown the statements themselves) or its general lack of credibility.

27 Ubertazzi (1976) Riv di Dir Civ 241; for presumptions in general, see *Les Présomptions et les Fictions en Droit* (ed Perelman and Foriers) (Bruylant, 1974) and *Cross on Evidence* (7th edn) pp 124 et seq.

28 Cf Pescatore *Introduction à la Science du Droit* (1978) para 143.

apply in all cases, whether or not they are founded upon experience. Since presumptions of the first sort are based on the application of the same deductive processes to proven facts, it follows that the same presumed or inferred facts are to be found even in different cases where the proven primary facts are the same. In that sense, the predictability of presumptions in the first sense used above (where the primary facts are the same) may lead to the conclusion that they also are rules of evidence; but that is an erroneous description because, in principle, the rule of evidence is the requirement that the same deductive processes be applied to evidence, the presumption being nothing more than a conclusion of fact which follows from the application of that rule. All presumptions, whatever their origin, are either rebuttable or irrebuttable.

An example of the first sense in which the word 'presumption' may be, and has been, used by the Court is to be found in *Duraffour v Council*,[29] where it held that a fact could be deduced from 'sufficiently weighty, clear and uncontradictory circumstantial evidence'. In fact, the phrase used in the French text, which has already been quoted, is as follows: '*présomptions suffisamment graves, précises et concordantes*'. It is clearly inspired by art 1353 of the French Civil Code and means simply that the existence of a fact may be inferred from the existence of other facts which are sufficiently weighty, clear and uncontradictory and are of such a nature as to indicate the existence of the unknown fact. In other words, the inference made by the Court can be based only on a proven fact which (i) in the light of experience indicates the existence of the unknown (or otherwise unproven) fact and (ii) is sufficiently persuasive or convincing as such an indication, when compared with all the other material evidence. Most of the references to presumptions which appear in the Court's judgments in fact concern inferences of this type.[30] For example, in Case 107/82 *AEG v Commission*[31] the Court held that it is not necessary to prove that a wholly owned subsidiary has been influenced by the commercial policy of the parent company since this follows necessarily from the fact that the guiding intelligence of both companies is the same. In contrast, proof of the existence of parallel conduct between undertakings does not lead to the inference (or presumption) that there is a concerted practice between them within the meaning of art 85 of the EC Treaty unless concertation is the only plausible explanation for such conduct[32] or the parallel conduct was preceded by an exchange of information between the undertakings concerned.[33] Similarly, proof that a document has been sent by post does not lead to the presumption that the document was actually received (unless it was sent by registered post).[34] A failure to deny having received a communication does not lead to any inference as to the date on which it might have been received.[35]

There is no rule requiring evidence in corroboration in order to support an inference. The necessity for corroboration depends in each case on the persuasiveness of the proved facts which are relied on as evidence of the presumed or

29 [1971] ECR 515 at 525.
30 Cf Case 10/55 *Mirossevich v High Authority*, [1954–56] ECR 333 at 343 and 352 (Advocate General Lagrange); Case 13/60 *Geitling Ruhrkohlen-Verkaufsgesellschaft mbH v High Authority* [1962] ECR 83 at 105; Case 13/63 *Italy v Commission* [1963] ECR 165 at 176.
31 [1983] ECR 3151 (para 50).
32 Cases 29 and 30/83 *CRAM and Rheinzink v Commission* [1984] ECR 1679 (para 20); see also the *Ahlström Osakeytiö* case (above, note 7) para 71.
33 Eg the *Shell* case (above, note 18) para 149.
34 Case T-117/89 *Sens v Commission* [1990] ECR II-185 (para 18); *Al-Jubail Fertiliser Co v Council* (above, note 12) para 22 of the judgment and paras 86–88 of the opinion of Advocate General Darmon.
35 Case 58/88 *Olbrechts v Commission* [1989] ECR 2643 (paras 11–12).

inferred fact. Whether or not the proved facts are capable of supporting the existence of a particular fact is normally to be decided in the light of ordinary experience[36] but this is sometimes lacking in matters of a technical and, in particular, economic nature. The Court may therefore have recourse to the special experience of experts in the relevant field.[37] As a general rule, a presumption cannot take the place of proof[38] and must therefore be based on some evidence.

Presumptions of the second type, which are generally applicable rules of evidence, have the effect, where they are rebuttable, of shifting the burden of proof, and, where they are irrebuttable, come close in nature to legal fictions. Several such presumptions can be found in the case law of the Court. For example: all the Community institutions have cognizance of every official Community language (irrebuttable);[39] omnia praesumuntur rite esse acta (rebuttable: there must be evidence raising some doubt as to its truth);[40] a formal reply made by a Community institution in formal correspondence is a decision (rebuttable).[41] Another such presumption appears to be the (rebuttable) presumption that an agreement or concerted practice within the meaning of art 85 of the EEC Treaty comes into existence by reason of the mere participation of an undertaking in a meeting between other undertakings to discuss anti-competitive arrangements, thus avoiding the need for proof of actual agreement or concertation and rendering irrelevant proof derived from the subsequent behaviour of the undertakings concerned that there was no agreement or concertation.[42] Such presumptions overlap with principles governing the construction of legislative texts. For example: in dubio pro libertate (rebuttable: the intention of the legislator must be clear).[43] It is comparatively rare, however, for the Court expressly to adopt a presumption of this sort.

It is not possible to give a complete list of the presumptions that may be found in Community legislation. The most important are probably those in arts 35 of the ECSC Treaty, 175 of the EC Treaty, 148 of the Euratom Treaty and 90 of the Staff Regulations, which all provide, in effect, that silence over a specified period constitutes an implied decision against which proceedings can be brought. This presumption is irrebuttable: the fact that an express decision was adopted outside the period in question is neither here nor there.[44] The existence of a general power to adopt presumptions in secondary legislation

---

36 Eg Case 338/82 *Albertini and Montagnani v Commission* [1984] ECR 2123 (para 30).
37 See, for example, Case 48/69 *ICI Ltd v Commission* [1972] ECR 619; Case 261/78A *Interquell Stärke-Chemie GmbH & Co KG v EEC* [1982] ECR 3271, an interesting example of proof by inference.
38 Cases 193 and 194/87 *Maurissen v Court of Auditors* [1989] ECR 1045 (para 47); Case 290/87 *Commission v Netherlands* [1989] ECR 3083 (para 11); Case C-334/89 *Commission v Italy* [1991] ECR I-93 (paras 10–11 and at 100 per Advocate General van Gerven).
39 Case 1/60 *FERAM v High Authority* [1960] ECR 165 at 170.
40 Case 113/77 *NTN Toyo Bearing Co Ltd v Council* [1979] ECR 1185 at 1247 (Advocate General Warner); Cases 43 and 63/82 *VBVB and VBBB v Commission* [1984] ECR 19 para 14; Case 244/81 *Klöckner-Werke AG v Commission* [1983] ECR 1451 (para 12); Cases T-79, T-84 to T-86, T-89, T-91, T-92, T-94, T-96, T-98, T-102, T-104/89 *BASF AG v Commission* [1992] ECR II-315 (Re PVC Cartel) (paras 97–102).
41 Case 151/83 *Société Aciéries et Laminoirs de Paris v Commission* [1984] ECR 3519 at 3540–3541 (Advocate General Slynn).
42 Eg Case T-9/89 *Hüls AG v Commission* [1992] ECR II-499 (paras 125–127, 168 and 170).
43 Case 6/72 *Europemballage and Continental Can Co Inc v Commission* [1973] ECR 215 at 255 (Advocate General Roemer); see also Case 169/80 *Administration des Douanes v Gondrand Frères SA* [1981] ECR 1931 (paras 17–18).
44 Cf Case 79/70 *Müllers v Economic and Social Committee and Euratom Councils* [1971] ECR 689 at 698.

seems to follow from the Court's acceptance of its own power to create presumptions, as rules of evidence in its case law. However, the power to incorporate a particular presumption in a particular legislative act is another matter. In Case 32/65 *Italy v Council and Commission*[45] the Court rejected the possibility that a Council Regulation adopted under art 87 of the EEC Treaty, which empowered the Commission to grant exemption from art 85(1) in respect of certain types of restrictive agreement, could create a presumption that all agreements of the specified types fell within art 85(1). The ability to establish presumptions in secondary legislation seems, therefore, to be subject to review by the Court. Community legislation benefits from a presumption of validity which can be rebutted only if the act in question is found to be invalid by a competent court.[46] This does not prevent the validity of the act from being challenged, for example, before a national court; it prevents the effectiveness of the act from being denied unless and until there is a finding of invalidity made by a competent court[47] and, in the meantime, the operation of the act may be suspended by the Court[48] or the operation of national implementing measures may be suspended by the competent national courts.[49]

45 [1966] ECR 389 at 406. See also Case 199/82 *Amministrazione delle Finanze v San Giorgio* [1983] ECR 3595.
46 Eg Case 101/78 *Granaria BV v Hoofproduktschap voor Akkerbouwproducten* [1979] ECR 623 (para 4). The competent court is the Court itself: Case 314/85 *Foto-Frost v Hauptzollamt Lübeck-Ost* [1987] ECR 4199.
47 The *Granaria* case (ibid) para 5. A finding of invalidity has retrospective effect unless the Court decides to limit the temporal effect of the judgment.
48 See chapter 8.
49 Cases C-143/88 and C-92/89 *Zuckerfabrik Süderdithmarschen AG and Zuckerfabrik Soest GmbH v Hauptzollamt Itzehoe and Hauptzollamt Paderborn* [1991] ECR I-415.

CHAPTER 14

Costs

I Introduction

The Statutes provide[1] that the Court shall 'adjudicate' on costs. The Court's power to adjudicate is exercised at two different stages in the proceedings: (i) a decision as to costs is given in the operative part of every judgment[2] that is final and in every order closing the proceedings;[3] (ii) disputes concerning the taxation of costs recoverable pursuant to the decision in the final judgment or order closing the proceedings are heard by the Court.[4] The rules relating to the award of costs affect directly the liability of the parties and, in consequence, the parties are entitled to have that liability determined at the end of the proceedings by reference only to the rules applicable when the proceedings commenced.[5]

II The award of costs

A Preliminary rulings

Every judgment must contain a decision as to costs. The position with regard to the judgment in a reference for a preliminary ruling is somewhat unusual because such proceedings are in the nature of an interlocutory step in the proceedings before the referring court. In Case 13/61 *Kledingverkoopbedriff De Geus en Uitdenbogerd v Bosch GmbH*[6] Advocate General Lagrange noted that, in proceedings under art 177 of the EEC Treaty, the Court does not hear 'parties' in the strict sense of the word because the procedure is 'entirely within the realm of public policy'. He suggested four ways for the question of costs to be resolved:

(1) costs to be borne by the Court because the procedure is a matter of public policy;
(2) costs to be borne by the party losing before the national court;
(3) costs to be borne by the party whose arguments on the reference are rejected by the Court; and
(4) each party to pay its own costs.

---

1 ECSC Statute, art 32; EC Statute, art 35; Euratom Statute, art 36.
2 RP-ECJ 63; RP-CFI 81.
3 RP-ECJ 69(1); RP-CFI 87(1).
4 RP-ECJ 74(1); RP-CFI 92(1).
5 Case T-23/90 *Automobiles Peugeot SA and Peugeot SA v Commission* [1991] ECR II-653 (paras 80–81). The difficulty had arisen as a result of an intervening change in the liability of the principal parties regarding the costs of interveners. By parity of reasoning, it is arguable that the liability of an intervener in regard to costs is to be determined by reference to the rules applicable at the time when the intervention was made and not those applicable when the action commenced.
6 [1962] ECR 45 at 71.

He preferred the last. The Court, however, has adopted a different approach, now incorporated in RP-ECJ 104(5), which provides: 'it shall be for the national court or tribunal to decide as to the costs of the reference'. This does not mean that the referring court has jurisdiction to decide all the costs of the reference. As far as the parties to the proceedings before the referring court are concerned, the order for costs in the judgment of the Court states that a decision on costs is for the referring court to decide but, in the case of costs incurred by a member state or Community institution which has submitted observations and is not a party to the proceedings before the referring court, the order states that costs are irrecoverable. Hence, the 'costs of the reference' are those incurred by the parties to the original action.[7] It has, however, been suggested[8] that the Court does have jurisdiction to rule on the recoverability of costs incurred by reason of a preparatory enquiry, even in references for a preliminary ruling. Furthermore, where a member state or Community institution, which is a party to the proceedings before the referring court, submits observations in the preliminary ruling proceedings as such, rather than as a party (as where it is represented by an agent instead of a person with right of audience before the referring court) the usual order will be made with the result that the costs of the reference are irrecoverable by the member state or Community institution in question even if it wins the proceedings before the referring court and would ordinarily be entitled to costs.[9] Where a reference for a preliminary ruling is followed by a direct action bought before the Court concerning the same issues, a party to both proceedings cannot claim in the direct action the costs incurred by it in the preliminary ruling proceedings.[10]

In the *Bollmann* case[11] the question arose whether the procedure for the recovery of costs and the recoverability of costs incurred by the parties to the proceedings before the national court, in the context of the reference, were to be decided according to national law or the Court's Rules of Procedure. It was argued that, since RP-ECJ 103(1), which refers to the procedure in references for a preliminary ruling (as then worded), incorporates RP-ECJ 43 'et seq',[12] the rules relating to costs were similarly incorporated. The Court rejected this argument on the ground that RP-ECJ 69–75 referred only to costs in contentious proceedings and did not, therefore, apply to references for a preliminary ruling. The Court concluded that 'the recovery of costs and the recoverability of expenses necessarily incurred by the parties to the main action for the purposes of an application for a preliminary ruling under art 177 of the EEC Treaty are governed by the provisions of national law applicable to the said proceedings'.[13] It continued: 'it devolves on the competent national courts to consider, in the context of their national law, the extent to which matters incidental to an application for a preliminary ruling should be taken into account'.[14]

---

7   Cf Case 62/72 *Bollmann v Hauptzollamt Hamburg-Waltershof* [1973] ECR 269 (para 6).
8   Ibid at 280 (Advocate General Roemer).
9   See Case 105/80 *Desmedt v Commission* [1981] ECR 1701 at 1712: this was a reference for a preliminary ruling made by a Belgian court in an action brought against the Commission. As a party to the proceedings before the referring court, the Commission should have been represented by a person with a right of audience before the referring court, but instead it chose to submit observations through an agent, as a Community institution.
10   Case 318/81 *Commission v CODEMI* [1985] ECR 3693 at 3705 (Advocate General Slynn).
11   Above, note 7.
12   The current version of RP-ECJ 103(1) refers more generally to 'the provisions of these Rules'. The effect is therefore the same as it was at the time of the *Bollmann* case (ibid).
13   Ibid para 6.
14   Ibid para 7.

B Interlocutory orders and judgments

In the case of interlocutory orders and judgments which are not final, such as one rejecting an objection to admissibility, in which case the action continues until judgment on the merits of the case, the decision on costs is usually reserved until the final judgment or order.[15] On the other hand, where the order or judgment is final (for example, where an application to intervene is rejected)[16] an order for costs will be made.[17] In Case C-72/90 *Asia Motor France v Commission*[18] the judgment was partly final and partly interlocutory in the sense that the action was held to be inadmissible in part and, as to the remainder, was remitted to the CFI. The unsuccessful party was therefore ordered to pay the costs only in respect of that part of the costs attributable to the part of the action held to be inadmissible; as to the rest, the decision on costs was left to the CFI.

C Intervention

Member states and Community institutions which intervene in proceedings bear their own costs; other persons may be ordered to bear their own costs.[19] In relation to persons other than member states and Community institutions, as a general rule, where the application to intervene is rejected, the intervener pays the costs, subject to the rules set out below. If the intervention is allowed, the intervener is normally entitled to the same order as to costs as the party in whose support he has intervened. Thus, if the party supported by the intervener wins, the intervener is, in the normal course of events, entitled to his costs as against the losing party, even if he does not put forward any arguments not made by the successful party,[20] unless the arguments he did put forward were all rejected by the Court,[21] in which case the intervener bears his own costs. Where the party supported by the intervener loses, the intervener pays his own costs and also all those incurred by the opposing party on account of the intervention:[22] the liability to pay the opposing party's costs is often joint and several with the liability of the party in whose support the intervener intervened and any other interveners supporting that party.[23] However, in Case 24/71 *Meinhardt (née Forderung) v Commission*[24] the intervener was ordered

15 Cf Case T-30/89 *Hilti AG v Commission* [1990] ECR II-163.
16 See Cases 197–200, 243, 245, 247/80 *Ludwigshafener Walzmühle Erling KG v EEC* [1981] ECR 1041.
17 See, for example, the orders in Case 238/78 *Ireks-Arkady GmbH v EEC* [1981] ECR 1719 and Cases 241, 242, 246–249/78 *DGV v EEC* [1981] ECR 1727, which completed two earlier interlocutory judgments (reported at [1979] ECR 2955 and 3017) by removing the cases from the Register and deciding who should bear the costs.
18 [1990] ECR I-2181 (para 21).
19 RP-ECJ 69(4); RP-CFI 87(4). Originally, all interveners were in principle treated in the same way (although there was a tendency in the case law for intervening member states to be ordered to bear their own costs) and it was not until the amendment of the Rules of Procedure in 1991 that a mandatory rule was introduced providing that member states and Community institutions should bear their own costs.
20 Case 130/75 *Prais v Council* [1976] ECR 1589 at 1600 and at 1609 (Advocate General Warner).
21 Case 792/79R *Camera Care Ltd v Commission* [1980] ECR 119, order of 17 December 1980, unreported.
22 See Case 113/77 *NTN Toyo Bearing Co v Council* [1979] ECR 1185 at 1211 (and at 1274–1275 (Advocate General Warner)); Case 118/77 *ISO v Council* [1979] ECR 1277 at 1300; Case 119/77 *Nippon Seiko KK v Commission* [1979] ECR 1303 at 1334; Case 120/77 *Koyo Seiko Co Ltd v Council and Commission* [1979] ECR 1337 at 1359–1360; Case 121/77 *Nachi Fujikoshi Corpn v Council and Commission* [1979] ECR 1363 at 1385.
23 Cases 296 and 318/82 *Netherlands and Leeuwarder Papierfabriek v Commission* [1985] ECR 809 (para 32).
24 [1972] ECR 269 at 279, see also Case 40/79 *Mrs P v Commission* [1981] ECR 361 at 375.

to pay only his own costs. If the case is withdrawn or discontinued by the party in whose support the intervener intervened, the intervener is usually ordered to bear its own costs, irrespective of the chances of success in the action or similar proceedings.[25] If the case is withdrawn or discontinued by the party against whom the intervener intervened, the intervener is normally entitled to its costs against that party at least as long as the party in whose support the intervener intervened is entitled to its costs against the withdrawing or discontinuing party.[26] If an intervener has not asked for costs, it will in any event be ordered to bear its own costs.[27]

D   Interim relief

Applications for interim relief are normally the subject of an order for costs in the final judgment closing proceedings: an order for costs in the final judgment or order includes by implication the costs of any interim proceedings.[28] But, in Case 2/59R *Niederrheinische Hütte AG v High Authority*,[29] where no action had been commenced at the time the application for interim relief was heard, costs were not reserved but awarded against the applicant, the application being dismissed; and, in Case C-295/92R *Landbouwschap v Commission*,[30] where the action had previously been dismissed as inadmissible, the applicant was ordered to pay the costs of the interim relief proceedings in the order dismissing those proceedings as inadmissible.[31] So far as can be seen, costs normally follow the event.[32] Thus, in Cases 59 and 129/80 *Turner (née Krecke) v Commission*[33] the defendant, who lost the action, was ordered to pay all the costs, including those of the application for interim relief, even though the applicant lost that part of the case. In Case T-45/90 *Speybrouck v European Parliament*[34] the same occurred, even though the interim relief granted was not exactly the relief that had been sought, but the situation was regarded as exceptional.[35] The Court may apply the other rules for awarding costs mentioned below.[36] For example, in Cases 98 and 99/63 *Reynier and Erba v Commission* the applicants discontinued as a result of a statement made by the defendant at the hearing in

25 Eg Case 150/86 *Union Sidérurgique du Nord et de l'Est de la France (USINOR) v Commission*, order of 8 March 1988.
26 Eg Case 308/85 *Nippon Seiko KK v Council*, order of 3 February 1988.
27 Case T-3/90 *Vereniging Prodifarma v Commission* [1991] ECR II-1 (para 47).
28 Case T-50/89 *Sparr v Commission* [1990] ECR II-539 (para 9).
29 [1960] ECR 162.
30 [1992] ECR I-5069. See also Case C-276/93R *Chiquita Banana Co BV v Council*, 6 July 1993 (two other orders to the same effect were made on that day).
31 As the interim relief proceedings were still pending when the action was dismissed as inadmissible, the costs of those proceedings could not have been included in the order for costs made when the action was dismissed.
32 Cases 16–18/59 *Geitling Ruhrkohlen-Verkaufsgesellschaft v High Authority* [1960] ECR 17 at 26; Case 68/63 *Luhleich v Euratom Commission* [1965] ECR 581 at 607; Case 82/84 *Metalgoi v Commission* [1984] ECR 2585; Case 100/86 *Cauët and Joliot v Commission* [1987] ECR 3379 (para 24).
33 [1981] ECR 1883 and at 1921.
34 [1992] ECR II-33 (paras 107–113).
35 The President's order in the interim relief proceedings had recognised that the defendant owed a particular duty to the applicant. The defendant nonetheless failed to comply with that order, forcing the applicant to make a second application for interim relief. At the hearing of that second application, the defendant undertook to comply with the first order. In consequence, the applicant withdrew the application for interim relief.
36 Eg Cases 64, 71–73 and 78/86 *Sergio v Commission* [1988] ECR 1399 (paras 55–57), where the applicant lost but the defendant was ordered to pay all the costs, including those incurred in the interim relief proceedings (in which the defendant had been successful). The *Speybrouck* case (above, note 34) provides an example of the application of the fourth and sixth rules set out below (pp 446 and 453).

the proceedings for interim relief. That statement also caused those proceedings to be terminated in the defendant's favour. Because the statement would have made the action unnecessary, had it been made earlier, the Court ordered the defendant to bear all the costs, including those of the summary proceedings.[37] On the other hand, in *Halyvourgiki Inc v Commission*,[38] where the applicant discontinued the action and was ordered to bear the costs, the Court also ordered each party to bear its own costs in respect of the application for interim relief. Where an application for interim relief is withdrawn or discontinued, the costs are usually dealt with on the same basis as when an action is withdrawn or discontinued.[39] If a party objects to bearing the costs of interim relief proceedings, it should say so in its pleadings in order (if possible) to avoid the normal order being made.[40]

E Appeals

The ECJ makes a decision as to the costs of an appeal where the appeal is unfounded (in which case it is dismissed and the proceedings come to an end) or where the appeal is well founded and, instead of remitting the case to the CFI, the ECJ itself gives final judgment in the case.[41] In principle, where the appeal is dismissed, the ECJ rules only on the costs of the appeal (including those of any ancillary proceedings in the appeal, such as interim relief proceedings) because the CFI's decision remains intact and therefore caters for the costs at first instance. On the other hand, where the appeal is well founded and the ECJ itself gives judgment, the ECJ decides on the costs at first instance as well as on appeal.[42] Where the appeal is well founded but the case is remitted to the CFI, the ECJ reserves the costs to be dealt with by the CFI in its final judgment in the case[43] and, under RP-CFI 121, the CFI applies the usual rules applied in any final judgment or order.[44] For its part, when awarding costs, the ECJ follows the same rules as those applied in any final judgment or order[45] save that:

(1)　in staff cases RP-ECJ 70 (the eighth rule for the award of costs in a final judgment or order described below) applies only in the case of appeals brought by a Community institution and, in appeals brought by an official or other servant, the Court may order the parties to share the costs, where equity so requires, in derogation from RP-ECJ 69(2) (which sets out the normal rule that the unsuccessful party pays the costs and provides for the apportionment of costs between several unsuccessful parties);[46]

37　See Cases 79 and 82/63 *Reynier and Erba v Commission* [1964] ECR 259 at 268 and 276.
38　Cases 39, 41, 43, 85, 88, 121/81, order of 25 November 1981.
39　See further below pp 453 et seq.
40　Case T-50/89 *Sparr v Commission* (above, note 28) para 9.
41　RP-ECJ 122 (first subpara).
42　Eg Case C-345/90P *European Parliament v Hanning* [1992] ECR I-949 (paras 39–42).
43　Case C-185/90P *Commission v Gill* [1992] ECR I-4779 at 4814 (no reasons given); Case C-68/91P *Moritz v Commission*, per Advocate General van Gerven (para 28); Case C-86/92P *Samenwerkende Electriciteits-produktiebedrijven v Commission* (unreported, opinion of Advocate General Jacobs, para 73).
44　See, for example, Case T-43/89RV *Gill v Commission* [1993] ECR II-303 (paras 66–67).
45　RP-ECJ 118, which applies (inter alia) RP-ECJ 69 to the procedure followed on appeals. RP-ECJ 69(5) is referred to expressly in RP-ECJ 122 (third subpara). For an example of the award of costs on the withdrawal of an appeal, see Cases C-372/90P, C-372/90P-R and C-22/91P *Samenwerkende Electriciteits-produktiebedrijven NV v Commission* [1991] ECR I-2043. For an example of the award of costs when both parties have appealed and both appeals are dismissed, see Case C-346/90P *F v Commission* [1992] ECR I-2691.
46　RP-ECJ 122 (second subpara). It should be noted that there is no reference to appeals brought by a person who is not an official, other servant or Community institution, such as an appeal brought by a staff union. It would seem that the second indent of RP-ECJ 122 (second subpara) may be applied by analogy to such appeals. Cf Case C-244/91P *Pincherle v Commission*, 22 December 1993, paras 37–38.

(2)   when an appeal brought by a member state or Community institution which did not intervene in the proceedings before the CFI is held to be well founded, the ECJ may order that the parties share the costs or that the successful appellant pay the costs which the appeal has caused an unsuccessful party to incur.[47]

It is unclear whether or not, in general, a person who has not previously intervened in support of a party and who does so only at the appeal stage should be entitled to costs if the interest supported by him is successful in the appeal.[48]

F   Final judgments and orders

The Court has a wide discretion with regard to awarding costs in the final judgment or order. In principle, when the Court awards costs, it states only who has to bear them and, if necessary, whether or not a party has to bear all or part of another party's costs; it is not appropriate to identify a specific sum by way of costs unless and until there is a dispute between the parties as to the amount of recoverable costs.[49] The Rules of Procedure lay down the following eight principles on which the award is made.

1   The normal order

The normal order is that costs are to be paid by the unsuccessful party but this order will be made only if costs have been asked for.[50] If this has not happened, the unsuccessful party cannot be ordered to pay the costs incurred by the successful party and so each party must bear its own costs.[51] The costs must be claimed in express terms; an elliptical or ambiguous claim (in casu, a claim for costs to be awarded in accordance with the Rules of Procedure) may not be considered to be a claim that the opposing party be ordered to bear the costs.[52] Although the English version of the Rules of Procedure specifies that costs must have been asked for 'in the successful party's pleading', this does not prevent a successful intervener from being awarded costs[53] nor does it prevent the Court from awarding costs, if they have not been asked for in the written

---

47 RP-ECJ 122 (fourth indent). The reason for that provision is that, save in staff cases, member states and Community institutions have a right to commence an appeal against judgments or orders of the CFI, even if they were not parties to the proceedings before the CFI: ECSC and EC Statutes, art 49 (third subpara); Euratom Statute, art 50 (third subpara). In consequence, they may cause the parties to the case before the CFI to incur costs as a result of the appeal even though those parties were content with the judgment of the CFI or, at least, were not prepared to contest it in an appeal to the ECJ.
48 The fact that a large number of persons intervened for the first time in the appeal proceedings in Case C-242/90P *Commission v Albani*, 6 July 1993, in support of the successful appellant may well have been the main factor leading to the Court ordering each party to bear its own costs.
49 Case 265/83 *Suss v Commission* [1984] ECR 4029 at 4054–4055 (Advocate General Lenz).
50 RP-ECJ 69(2) (first sentence); RP-CFI 87(2) (first sentence). That order was made in Cases 316/82 and 40/83 *Kohler v Court of Auditors* [1984] ECR 641 (para 36), where the applicant was successful in the first action but unsuccessful in the second, which had been brought as a result of certain erroneous arguments put forward by the defendant in response to the applicant's first complaint.
51 Cases 23, 24 and 52/63 *Usines Emile Henricot SA v High Authority* [1963] ECR 217 at 225; Case 23/76 *Luigi Pellegrini & C SAS v Commission* [1976] ECR 1807 at 1822 (joint defendant); Case 138/79 *Roquette Frères SA v Council* [1980] ECR 3333 at 3361; Case 139/79 *Maizena GmbH v Council* [1980] ECR 3393 at 3425; Case 294/83 *Parti Ecologiste 'Les Verts' v European Parliament* [1986] ECR 1339 (para 56).
52 Case C-255/90P *Burban v European Parliament* [1992] ECR I-2253 (para 26).
53 Case 130/75 *Prais v Council* (above, note 20) at 1600 and 1609–1610 (Advocate General Warner).

pleadings, as long as they have been claimed at the hearing.[54] Where the successful party has asked in its pleadings for costs to be dealt with otherwise than by applying the normal rule (in casu, by asking for a particular rule as to costs to be applied), there is no need for the Court to consider disposing of the costs in any other way.[55]

The general principle that costs follow the event appears to be based on the theory that the litigation has been brought about unnecessarily by the actions of the losing party. Thus, in Case 70/63A *High Authority v Collotti and European Court of Justice*,[56] costs were awarded against the applicant, whose application was held to be inadmissible, because it had instituted proceedings 'without due cause'.[57] The rule is without prejudice to the other principles set out in the Rules of Procedure, so that even a successful party may be ordered to pay all or part of the costs if the circumstances justify it.[58] By reference to the reason for the rule about costs following the event, costs may still be awarded against a successful defendant if it was reasonable for the applicant to institute proceedings.[59]

2 The sharing of costs between losing parties

Where there are several unsuccessful parties, the Court must decide how the costs are to be shared between them.[60] By way of example: in Cases 41, 43 and 44/73 *Générale Sucrière SA v Commission*,[61] proceedings for the interpretation of a judgment of the Court, the applicants and those of the defendants who submitted observations in support of them failed in their arguments and the Court ordered each to bear its own costs and, since there were eight of them, one-eighth of the Commission's costs; in Cases 32 and 36–82/78 *BMW Belgium SA v Commission*,[62] the unsuccessful applicants had challenged a Commission decision imposing fines of varying amounts on them and the Court ordered each one to pay a part of the Commission's costs corresponding to the percentage that the fine imposed on it bore to the total amount of the fines;[63] in Case 264/82 *Timex Corpn v Council and Commission*[64] the unsuccessful parties were ordered to pay the costs jointly and severally.[65]

---

54 *NTN Toyo Bearing Co v Council* (above, note 22) at 1210–1211 and 1274 (Advocate General Warner) (a successful applicant); Case 155/79 *AM & S Europe Ltd v Commission* [1982] ECR 1575, per Advocate General Warner (a successful intervener); Case T-64/89 *Automec Srl v Commission* [1990] ECR II-367 (para 79). But see Cases 92 and 93/87 *Commission v France and United Kingdom* [1989] ECR 405, para 31 and at 436 (Advocate General van Gerven): in that case, the successful party had asked for costs in written comments submitted in response to a document produced by the opposing party as a result of a request made by the Court at the hearing; in consequence, strictly speaking, the claim for costs was not made in the successful party's pleadings, whether written or oral. In Case 298/83 *CICCE v Commission* [1985] ECR 1105 (para 32) the successful party asked for costs only in the rejoinder and the claim was therefore held to be inadmissible. That case appears to be exceptional.
55 Case 280/85 *Mouzourakis v European Parliament* [1987] ECR 589 (para 15).
56 [1965] ECR 275 at 280.
57 'sans motif légitime'.
58 *Usines Emile Henricot SA v High Authority* (above, note 51).
59 Cases 53 and 54/63 *Lemmerz-Werke GmbH v High Authority* [1963] ECR 239 at 255 (Advocate General Roemer).
60 RP-ECJ 69(2) (last sentence); RP-CFI 87(2) (last sentence).
61 [1977] ECR 445 at 464.
62 [1979] ECR 2435 at 2483.
63 See also Cases 29, 31, 36, 39–47, 50 and 51/63 *Fonderies et Usines de Providence v High Authority* [1966] ECR 139 at 142–143.
64 [1985] ECR 849 (para 34).
65 See also Case 222/83 *Commune de Differdange v Commission* [1984] ECR 2889 (para 14); *Cauët and Joliot v Commission* (above, note 32) para 24.

3   Cases of mixed success and failure

Where each party succeeds on some and fails on other heads of claim, the Court may order that the costs be shared or that the parties shall bear their own costs.[66] There are many examples of the Court dividing the costs on the basis of the issues lost and won.[67] For example, in Case 18/76 *Germany v Commission*,[68] the Commission failed on one head and the applicant on the rest so the latter was ordered to pay its own costs and three-quarters of those of the Commission. In Cases 40–48, 54–56, 111, 113 and 114/73 *Suiker Unie UA v Commission*[69] and the *Woodpulp* case[70] the costs of preparatory enquiries (the examination of witnesses and experts' reports) were ordered to be paid by the party who lost on the issues to which the enquiries related. In Case 238/78 *Ireks-Arkady GmbH v EEC* and Cases 241, 242, 246–249/78 *DGV v EEC*[71] the Court appeared to suggest that a reduction of the sum claimed in a damages action might justify sharing the costs. In Case 86/82 *Hasselblad (GB) Ltd v Commission*,[72] each party (including the intervener) was ordered to bear its own costs. In Case 131/86 *United Kingdom v Council*[73] the applicant was successful but its main point was rejected by the Court and it won on an alternative submission so each party was ordered to bear its own costs. In Case 11/82 *Paraiki-Patraiki v Commission*,[74] the contested decision was annulled in part only and the defendant was therefore ordered to pay part of the applicants' costs as well as its own.

4   Exceptional circumstances

Where the circumstances are exceptional, the Court may order that the costs be shared or that the parties bear their own costs.[75] It is not easy to reduce to a formula the conditions under which the Court will regard the circumstances as being exceptional and thus justifying a departure from the general rule that costs follow the event. Sometimes there is no apparent reason for the Court so deciding;[76] on other occasions the cases seem contradictory;[77] many of the cases are staff cases and for this reason cannot be relied on in other contexts;[78] lastly, there seems to be an overlap with the fifth rule on costs. The question whether circumstances are exceptional for costs purposes is largely a matter of fact left to the appreciation of the judges.

---

66 RP-ECJ 69(3) (first sentence); RP-CFI 87(3) (first sentence).
67 Eg Cases 532, 534, 567, 600, 618, 660/79 and 543/79 *Amesz v Commission* [1985] ECR 55 (para 19).
68 [1979] ECR 343. See also Case 165/82 *Commission v United Kingdom* [1983] ECR 3431.
69 [1975] ECR 1663 at 2025 (Re European Sugar Cartel).
70 Cases C-89, C-104, C-114, C-116, C-117, C-125 to C-129/85 *A Ahlström Osakeytiö v Commission* [1993] ECR I-1307 (para 203, and see also para 205).
71 [1981] ECR 1719 and 1727.
72 [1984] ECR 883 (para 59 and at 932, Advocate General Slynn).
73 [1988] ECR 905 (Re Protection of Battery Hens) (para 41).
74 [1985] ECR 207 (para 45): in relation to some of the applicants, the action was held to be inadmissible and they had to pay all their own costs but there was no order that they should pay any of the Commission's costs (in so far as the Commission's costs had been increased by their participation in the action).
75 RP-ECJ 69(3) (first sentence); RP-CFI 87(3) (first sentence).
76 Eg Case 26/75 *General Motors Continental NV v Commission* [1975] ECR 1367 at 1380–1381:
77 Cf Case 153/73 *Holtz and Willemsen GmbH v Council* [1974] ECR 675, Case 74/74 *CNTA v Commission* [1976] ECR 797 and Cases 116 and 124/77 *GR Amylum NV and Tunnel Refineries Ltd v Council and Commission* [1979] ECR 3497.
78 The relationship between an official and the employing institution imposes greater responsibilities on the latter to treat the former fairly and the Court is more ready to vindicate those responsibilities by an award of costs than in disputes between other persons and a Community institution.

From the decided cases it is possible to give some idea of the type of situation that the Court has found to be exceptional. For example, in two cases, joined for the oral procedure and treated by the parties as joined for the written procedure, the applicant won the first and the defendant the second. The Court found that it was impossible to determine the costs attributable to each case and simply ordered the parties to bear their own costs.[79] The same order may be made 'in view of the complexity of the questions raised' in the action[80] or in view of the 'general interest' in the question.[81] On the other hand, where a series of frauds have been carried out on a Community scheme, persons may be induced to sue for damages for fear that their claims may later have been barred when the scheme is wound up; they cannot be 'blamed' for this and, even if they lose, each party may be ordered to bear its own costs.[82] The circumstances are exceptional where: the defendant's behaviour may have induced the applicant to bring the action[83] or undoubtedly encouraged[84] or been a factor in the decision to commence proceedings;[85] the decisive factor in starting the action was the defective drafting of a decision[86] or the silence of the legislation as to the correct legal position;[87] sloppy administrative practices have been a contributory factor to the applicant's decision to go to law in order to clarify his position[88] or there was a lack of clarity in the defendant's conduct;[89] the successful party knew in advance that any proceedings would be

79 Cases 275/80 and 24/81 *Krupp Stahl AG v Commission* [1981] ECR 2489 at 2518.
80 Cases 2 and 3/60 *Niederrheinische Bergwerks AG v High Authority* [1961] ECR 133 at 148; Case 74/81 *Rudolf Flender KG v Commission* [1982] ECR 395, per Advocate General Reischl.
81 Case 175/73 *Union Syndicale, Massa and Kortner v Council* [1974] ECR 917 at 927.
82 Cases 46 and 47/59 *Meroni & Co v High Authority* [1962] ECR 411 at 423.
83 *Usines Emile Henricot SA v High Authority* (above, note 51) (the High Authority had not in fact asked for costs) and Case 28/63 *Koninklijke Nederlandsche en Staalfabrieken NV Hoogovensen v High Authority* [1963] ECR 231 at 236 (in both cases the High Authority was ordered to bear three-quarters of the costs even though the applicants lost); Case 118/83 *CMC Cooperativa Muratori e Cementisti v Commission* [1985] ECR 2325 (para 50); Case T-40/91 *Ventura v European Parliament* [1992] ECR II-1697, paras 62–63 (the inducement took the form of leading the applicant to believe that he had a claim – the defendant was ordered to bear its own costs and three-quarters of those of the applicant); Case T-25/92 *Palacios v Economic and Social Committee* [1993] ECR II-201 (paras 54–55); Case T-46/90 *Devillez v European Parliament*, 30 June 1993 (para 48); Case T-22/92 *Weissenfels v European Parliament*, 26 October 1993, para 96.
84 Case 32/62 *Alvis v Council* [1963] ECR 49 at 57 (the Council was ordered to pay four-fifths of the costs); Case T-156/89 *Mordt v Court of Justice* [1991] ECR II-407, para 166 (the defendant, the successful party, had withheld information from the applicant which would have been important when deciding whether or not to bring proceedings).
85 Cases 783 and 786/79 *Venus and Obert v Commission and Council* [1981] ECR 2445 at 2463, where the Commission was ordered to pay costs of the proceedings; Case 150/84 *Bernardi v European Parliament* [1986] ECR 1375 (para 53), where the irregular notification of the draft of the contested decision to the applicant by an official lacking the appropriate authority 'may have played a part' in the decision to bring proceedings.
86 Case 14/63 *Forges de Clabecq SA v High Authority* [1963] ECR 357 at 374 (the parties bore their own costs); Case T-7/90 *Kobor v Commission* [1990] ECR II-721, para 43 (defective phrasing of the draft decision and inappropriate wording in the decision as adopted – defendant ordered to pay half the applicant's costs); Case T-64/89 *Automec Srl v Commission* [1990] ECR II-367, para 80 (defendant contributed to the emergence of the dispute by the ambiguous wording of a letter but the applicant persisted with the proceedings once the matter had been clarified and introduced an inadmissible claim for damages so the defendant was ordered to pay only one half of the applicant's costs).
87 Case 26/67 *Danvin v Commission* [1968] ECR 315 at 323: the defendant was ordered to pay three-quarters of the applicant's costs; Case 18/70 *X v Council* [1972] ECR 1205 (it was equitable to order the defendant to pay all the costs); Case 89/76 *Commission v Netherlands* [1977] ECR 1355 at 1366 (it was reasonable that each party bear its own costs).
88 Case 83/63 *Krawczynski v Euratom Commission* [1965] ECR 623 at 641: the Commission was ordered to bear its own costs and two-fifths of the applicant's.
89 Case 61/74 *Santopietro v Commission* [1975] ECR 483 at 491: the defendant was ordered to pay all the costs.

inadmissible but did not tell the applicant in time;[90] the behaviour of the defendant has influenced the way in which the applicant formulated his submissions and induced him to make submissions that he would not have made had he known the true facts.[91] An additional factor may be the offensive behaviour of a senior official employed by the defendant.[92] In an action for damages, the applicant may have had 'sufficient reason' to bring the action[93] or could reasonably have considered himself injured by the defendant's act[94] or the defendant's acts may be capable of rendering it liable, even though there is no proof of loss.[95] More generally, the applicant may have had 'good reason to consider itself justified in asking the (defendant) to explain' the matter before the Court.[96] The cause of the action may be a misunderstanding between the parties.[97] It may have failed because the defendant requested the applicant to wait, with the result that the action became time-barred[98] or because the defendant suggested a change in the subject matter of the application.[99] On the other hand, if the applicant could have avoided litigation,[1] or shortened the proceedings[2] by taking proper steps, he may be ordered to pay costs even if he wins. Where the action is brought solely in order that a provision of one of the Treaties is properly complied with, this may be held to be an exceptional circumstance.[3] Similarly, in Case 165/87 *Commission v Council*[4] the action for

90 Case T-54/90 *Lacroix v Commission* [1991] ECR II-749, para 41 (the defendant's behaviour had also contributed in other ways to the commencement of proceedings; the defendant was ordered to pay half the applicant's costs).
91 Case 267/85 *Luttgens v Commission* [1986] ECR 3417 (para 13).
92 *Krawczynski v Euratom Commission* (above, note 88).
93 *Holtz and Willemsen GmbH v Council* (above, note 77) at 697: each party was ordered to bear its own costs. But see the *Amylum* case (above, note 77).
94 Cases 56-60/74 *Kurt Kampffmeyer Mühlenvereinigung KG v Commission and Council* [1976] ECR 711 at 747: each party bore its own costs and half of those of the preparatory enquiries.
95 Case 74/74 *CNTA v Commission* [1976] ECR 797 at 806: each party bore its own costs. The English version of the judgment says that 'the conduct of the Commission was calculated to render the Community liable' but this is a mistranslation: the French version says it was *'de nature à engager'* the Community's liability.
96 Case 23/76 *Luigi Pellegrini & C SAS v Commission* (above, note 51) at 1822: each party was ordered to bear its own costs. See also Case 230/81 *Luxembourg v European Parliament* [1983] ECR 255 (para 65); Case T-28/90 *Asia Motor France SA v Commission* [1992] ECR II-2285 (paras 56–57), an action in respect of a failure to act.
97 Case 52/70 *Nagels v Commission* [1971] ECR 365 at 373: it was therefore 'just' that the defendant pay half the applicant's costs; see also Case 34/65 *Mosthaf v Euratom Commission* [1966] ECR 521 at 532.
98 Case 79/70 *Müllers v Economic and Social Committee* [1971] ECR 689 at 698: the defendant was ordered to pay the applicant's costs.
99 Case 7/69 *Commission v Italy* [1970] ECR 111 at 117.
 1 Case 797/79 *Tiberghien (née Peuteman) v Commission* [1980] ECR 3921 at 3936: this was a staff case, which explains why the parties were ordered to bear their own costs; had the Court considered the applicant to have behaved unreasonably or vexatiously it might have ordered her to pay all the costs, but her behaviour seems to have been considered something less than this as the decision was based on the first sentence of RP-ECJ 69(3), not the second. In Case 188/84 *Commission v France* [1986] ECR 419 (para 41) the failure of the defendant to co-operate at the pre-litigation stage compelled the applicant to bring proceedings and, although the action was dismissed, each party was ordered to bear its own costs.
 2 Case 170/78 *Commission v United Kingdom* [1983] ECR 2265 at para 30: the Commission was ordered to bear its own costs because the case was brought without adequate preparation, thus causing the proceedings to be prolonged.
 3 Case 66/76 *CFDT v Council* [1977] ECR 305 at 311: each party bore its own costs. A French trade union sued over its exclusion from the ECSC Consultative Committee. The action was dismissed as inadmissible but it was held to be an exceptional circumstance 'when a trade union institutes proceedings with the sole aim of ensuring that the Consultative Committee is representative, a requirement expressly laid down by Article 18 of the Treaty'.
 4 [1988] ECR 5545 (Re Harmonised Commodity Descriptions) (para 23).

annulment was dismissed because the illegality found to exist was regarded as a purely formal defect which did not vitiate the contested act; but each party was ordered to bear its own costs because the applicant's case had been upheld to a substantial extent. If the action enables a mistake committed by the defendant to be recognised by it and corrected,[5] or arises from a situation which the defendant recognises should be remedied,[6] the defendant may be ordered to pay part of the applicant's costs even though the latter has lost. In Cases T-10 to T-12 and T 15/92 *Cimenteries CBR SA v Commission*[7] the CFI held that it was not appropriate to order the successful party to pay the costs because it could not be said to have acted contrary to the case law of the Court (the action being dismissed as inadmissible but not as being unfounded) and its acts could not be said to have been manifestly unlawful. That suggests that, where an action is dismissed as being inadmissible but the defendant appears to have acted unlawfully or contrary to the Court's case law, the circumstances are sufficiently exceptional to justify ordering the defendant to pay all the costs.

The common factor in most of these cases is that the successful party was for some reason responsible for instigating the proceedings or causing them to fail in a manner that the Court regarded as inequitable.

5 Unreasonable or vexatious conduct

A party, even if successful, may be ordered to pay costs which the Court considers him to have unreasonably or vexatiously caused the other party to incur.[8] In some cases it is not always easy to discern whether the Court regarded the circumstances as exceptional, and so as falling under the preceding rule, or showing that costs were unreasonably or vexatiously caused. Sometimes the same situation is classified in one case as unreasonable behaviour and in another as an exceptional circumstance; and sometimes the Court has simply stated that a party has caused the other party to incur costs, without qualifying that consequence as unreasonable or vexatious.[9] In one case it was suggested that greater use should be made of this rule in view of the Court's excessive workload.[10] It is arguable that most of the cases which appear to have been decided under the previous rule should have been based on this one. Some support for this can be drawn from Advocate General Roemer's opinion in Cases 53 and 54/63 *Lemmerz-Werke GmbH v High Authority*,[11] where he suggested the single criterion of the 'reasonableness' of the legal proceedings: only if the commencement of proceedings was unreasonable should the party whose unreasonable attitude brought them about be burdened with costs. This approach would reduce the 'exceptional circumstances' relevant to the preceding rule to cases where, for example, it is impossible to make an accurate apportionment of the costs or where the public interest has been served by bringing the action. Nonetheless, the state of the case law does not suggest that this is the approach adopted by the Court,

---

5 Case 110/63A *Willame v Euratom Commission* [1966] ECR 287 at 293.

6 Case T-41/90 *Barassi v Commission* [1992] ECR II-159 (para 57); Case T-42/90 *Bertelli v Commission* [1992] ECR II-181 (para 57).

7 [1992] ECR II-2667 para 53.

8 RP-ECJ 69(3) (last sentence); RP-CFI 87(3) (last sentence). Case 146/84 *De Santis v Court of Auditors* [1985] ECR 1723 at 1729–1730 (Advocate General Slynn).

9 Eg Case 76/84 *Rienzi v Commission* [1987] ECR 315 (paras 25–26).

10 Case 147/83 *Münchener Import-Weinkellerei Herold Binderer GmbH v Commission* [1985] ECR 257 at 265 (Advocate General VerLoren van Themaat).

11 [1963] ECR 239 at 255.

however attractive it might be. Most of the decisions concern 'unreasonable costs' but, as in the case of the preceding rule, a large number are staff cases and are not necessarily relevant to situations which may occur other than in the context of the relationship between an official and his employing institution.

The following are examples of unreasonableness. Where the applicant is induced by the defendant's conduct to lodge two applications although one would have sufficed, the defendant is responsible for the costs of the unnecessary application.[12] But once the applicant should have realised that he had no grounds for proceeding with the redundant action, it is unreasonable for him to continue proceedings and he should discontinue it: if he does not, he is at risk as to the costs thereafter incurred.[13] Where the applicant was misled by the defendant[14] and induced[15] or impelled[16] by his conduct to make the application[17] or else led to delay commencing proceedings until the action was time-barred,[18] the defendant may be ordered to bear all or part of the costs. The same may happen where the action arises 'largely as a result' of conduct of the defendant in adopting a particular procedure which evinces a lack of consideration for the applicant and shows a general failure to observe good administrative practice.[19] Similarly, where the defendant fails to dispel a misunderstanding on the part of the applicant,[20] supplies him with incorrect information,[21] creates a misleading

12 Cases 15 and 29/59 *Société Métallurgique de Knutange v High Authority* [1960] ECR 1 at 10: it had in fact conceded this and said it was willing to bear the costs.
13 Cases 35/62 and 16/63 *Leroy v High Authority* [1963] ECR 197 at 208.
14 Case 200/87 *Giordani v Commission* [1989] ECR 1877, para 29 (the applicant was caused to formulate the application in a particular way); Case 25/83 *Buick v Commission* [1984] ECR 1773 (para 22).
15 Case 49/64 *Stipperger v High Authority* [1965] ECR 521 at 527 (the defendant was ordered to pay the costs); Case 282/81 *Ragusa v Commission* [1983] ECR 1245; Case 343/82 *Michael v Commission* [1983] ECR 4023, para 31 (sloppy drafting of a decision); Case 69/83 *Lux v Court of Auditors* [1984] ECR 2447, para 41 (the defendant had contributed to a large extent to the dispute by failing to provide the applicant with a proper and express statement of the reasons for the contested decision); Case 302/85 *Pressler-Hoeft v Court of Auditors* [1987] ECR 513, para 14 (the contested decision had been formulated in terms which could have caused the applicant to believe that the action was admissible).
16 Cases 109 and 114/75 *National Carbonising Co Ltd v Commission* [1977] ECR 381 at 390–391 (Advocate General Mayras): each party should bear its own costs.
17 See also Case 122/77 *Claes (née Agneessons) v Commission* [1978] ECR 2085 at 2102 (Advocate General Reischl); Case 268/86 *Clasen v European Parliament* [1988] ECR 2453 (para 22).
18 Case 40/71 *Richez-Parise v Commission* [1972] ECR 73 at 80–81: the defendant claimed that the applicant should pay the costs because the action was out of time (since it was a staff case, the normal order would be for each party to bear its own costs even if the applicant lost) but the Court rejected this and made the normal order because of the defendant's behaviour.
19 Case 125/80 *Arning v Commission* [1981] ECR 2539 at 2555; Case 147/83 *Münchener Import* (above, note 10) at 265 (Advocate General VerLoren van Themaat) (a failure by the defendant to advise interested parties clearly and promptly of a problem over possible alternative translations of legislation in a situation where the defendant had raised expectations and where proceedings could have been avoided); Case 7/86 *Vincent v European Parliament* [1987] ECR 2473, paras 28–29 (delay in producing the applicant's periodic report); Cases 64, 71–73 and 78/86 *Sergio v Commission* [1988] ECR 1399, paras 55–57 (the applicant could not be blamed for bringing proceedings for the annulment of decisions for which sufficient reasons were not given); Cases T-160 and T-161/89 *Kalavros v Court of Justice* [1990] ECR II-871, paras 79–82 (the defendant repeatedly failed to give reasons for the contested act, thus giving rise to grounds for considering that its conduct had led the applicant into bringing proceedings); Case T-27/90 *Latham v Commission* [1991] ECR II-35, paras 52–53 (proceedings provoked largely by the defendant's maladministration).
20 Case 101/77 *Ganzini v Commission* [1978] ECR 915 at 922: the defendant was ordered to pay all the costs.
21 Case 137/79 *Kohll v Commission* [1980] ECR 2601 at 2614: it was 'equitable' for the defendant to pay all the costs; Case T-44/92 *Delloye v Commission* [1993] ECR II-221 (paras 26–29) – errors in a competition notice.

impression,[22] is guilty of arbitrary conduct,[23] prolongs proceedings by making erroneous assertions[24] or shows lack of regard to an employee,[25] or itself brings about an abnormal situation which arouses in the applicant understandable but unjustified expectations.[26] But it is not unreasonable or vexatious that the defendant failed to adopt an express decision in response to the applicant's pre-litigation complaint[27] or clarified his position only two weeks or so before the action commenced.[28]

On the other hand, where the defendant concedes the applicant's claims after the action has begun by granting the relief sought, costs may be awarded against him;[29] but the applicant, although not bound to discontinue once the concession is made, has no interest in proceeding further and costs thereafter incurred must be considered as having been incurred unreasonably through his own conduct.[30] Where the litigation could have been avoided by greater diligence in producing relevant information on the part of the applicant,[31] the applicant is himself largely responsible for the situation of which he complains,[32] the applicant failed to make a proper examination of the case before commencing proceedings[33] or an interlocutory application is made unnecessarily,[34] the applicant has caused the defendant to incur costs unreasonably. Per contra, where it is the defendant who has withheld relevant information,[35] or who is responsible for the Court ordering an avoidable

22 Case 76/84 *Rienzi v Commission* (above, note 9) paras 25–26.
23 Case 148/79 *Korter v Council* [1981] ECR 615 at 629: the defendant to bear all the costs.
24 Case T-1/92 *Tallarico v European Parliament* [1993] ECR II-107 (para 76).
25 Case 60/80 *Kindermann v Commission* [1981] ECR 1329 at 1342: the applicant got to hear of a decision affecting him from his colleagues; 'the Commission might have taken care to inform the applicant first' (the defendant bore half the applicant's costs). See also Case 263/81 *List v Commission* [1983] ECR 103, at paras 30–31 of the judgment.
26 Case 218/80 *Kruse v Commission* [1981] ECR 2417 at 2424: the defendant ordered to pay all costs.
27 Case 277/84 *Jänsch v Commission* [1987] ECR 4923, paras 24–25 (the applicant was thus compelled to bring proceedings in order to avoid forfeiting any legal rights); Case 1/87 *Picciolo v Commission* [1988] ECR 711 (para 49); Case T-18/90 *Jongen v Commission* [1991] ECR II-187 (para 41).
28 Case 116/78 *Bellintani v Commission* [1979] ECR 1585 at 1611–1612 (Advocate General Reischl).
29 Case 33/68 *Rittweger v Commission* [1969] ECR 393 at 398: after the commencement of proceedings the defendant lodged a statement of the applicant's rights but clarified it only in a letter annexed to the rejoinder (the defendant was ordered to pay all the costs); Case 74/72 *Di Blasi v Commission* [1973] ECR 847 at 856–857 (defendant ordered to pay all the costs).
30 Cases 5, 7, 8/60 *Meroni & Co FERAM and SIMET v High Authority* [1961] ECR 107 at 111–112; Case 15/67 *Bauer v Commission* [1967] ECR 397.
31 Case 18/62 *Barge v High Authority* [1963] ECR 259 at 282: the applicant owed her partial success in the action to the Court's insistence on the production of certain documents; with greater diligence she could have produced similar information earlier.
32 Case 731/79 *B v European Parliament* [1981] ECR 107 at 112; applicant ordered to pay all the costs.
33 Case 51/83 *Commission v Italy* [1984] ECR 2793, paras 19–20 (both parties were partly unsuccessful and the applicant had not formally claimed costs in the application); Case C-52/91 *Commission v Netherlands* [1993] ECR I-3069 para 46 (the lack of adequate preparation caused the applicant to amend its claims several times making the defence to them difficult).
34 Case 113/77 *NTN Toyo Bearing Co Ltd v Council* [1979] ECR 1185 at 1273 (Advocate General Warner): an application was made to strike out part of the rejoinder because it contained information irrelevant to the case; even though the application should be allowed, it was held to be excessive because it would have been sufficient to point out the fact at the hearing.
35 Case 111/83 *Picciolo v European Parliament* [1984] ECR 2323, para 30 (questions put to the defendant by the Court made it possible for the applicant to assess the reasons for the contested decision so he could not be criticised for having brought the proceedings); Case T-1/90 *Pérez-Mínguez Casariego v Commission* [1991] ECR II-143, para 98 (the defendant had failed to prove that the contested decision had been communicated to the applicant and the decision had lacked reasoning).

measure of enquiry[36] or fixing a second hearing because of the late presentation of relevant information.[37] The defendant may also be ordered to pay the costs if the Court rejects the application on a ground contested by the defendant[38] or despite the existence of an error of law on the part of the defendant.[39]

In staff cases the applicant has been ordered to pay all the costs where the application was manifestly inadmissible or its inadmissibility could easily have been foreseen and the defendant's costs were therefore incurred unreasonably[40] but, in other cases, the same behaviour has been characterised as an abuse of the process of the Court.[41] To persist in an action in the manifest absence of any real interest or useful purpose in continuing with it has also been described as an abuse of process.[42] In another case it was said to be vexatious.[43] It is probable that the two terms indicate the same basic idea. Under the Staff Regulations, an institution can require an official to resign if, after he has taken leave on personal grounds and the leave has come to an end, he twice refuses a post offered to him. When this actually happened in one case, the official concerned applied for the annulment of the decision requiring him to resign. The Court held this was vexatious.[44] It is also vexatious to bring a legal action when the same result could be achieved by means of an existing administrative procedure.[45] It is likely, although the Court did not say so expressly, that to bring an action simply as a delaying tactic is vexatious.[46] Claims which lack any justification but which place a burden on the defendant and the Court in refuting them are to be discouraged and may be considered vexatious.[47] In Case 19/87 *Hecq v Commission*[48] the successful defendant argued that the action had been vexatious because the applicant was himself the author of the measures of which he had complained. The Court rejected that claim on the ground that the information at its disposal did not enable it to determine who was responsible. In an opinion providing several indicia of

36 Case 12/68 *X v Audit Board* [1970] ECR 291 at 295.
37 Case 56/77 *Agence Européenne d'Interims SA v Commission* [1978] ECR 2215 at 2238: the defendant was ordered to pay the costs of the second hearing, necessitated in order to allow the applicant to consider information produced only at the first hearing.
38 Case 88/76 *Société pour l'Exportation des Sucres v Commission* [1977] ECR 709. The point was that the applicant was seeking the annulment of part of a regulation on the ground that it had been published (as opposed to adopted) only after the material time. The defendant contended that the regulation was both valid and did apply retrospectively. The Court rejected the application because the regulation could not have effect before it was published and therefore did not affect the applicant. In substance, though not in formal terms, it granted what the applicant was seeking.
39 Case 248/86 *Brüggemann v Economic and Social Committee* [1987] ECR 3963 (para 11).
40 Case 47/70 *Kschwendt v Commission* [1971] ECR 251; Case 227/83 *Moussis v Commission* [1984] ECR 3133 (paras 15–17); Case 25/86 *Suss v Commission* [1986] ECR 3929 (para 12); Case 204/85 *Stroghili v Court of Auditors* [1987] ECR 389 (para 15).
41 Case 57/70 *Van Eick v Commission* [1971] ECR 613 at 619.
42 Case 243/78 *Simmenthal SpA v Commission* [1980] ECR 593.
43 Cases 122 and 123/79 *Schiavo v Council* [1981] ECR 473 at 492.
44 Case 108/79 *Belfiore v Commission* [1980] ECR 1769 at 1784.
45 Cases 6 and 97/79 *Grassi v Council* [1980] ECR 2141 at 2162.
46 Case 123/80 *B v European Parliament* [1980] ECR 1789 and Case 123/80R *B v European Parliament* [1980] ECR 1793.
47 Case 54/77 *Herpels v Commission* [1978] ECR 585 (para 54). This was a claim for damages for the cost of consulting a lawyer at the preliminary administrative stage of a staff action. The object of the pre-litigation procedure is to obtain a resolution of the dispute without the need to go to law. However, because the defendant failed in its claims that the action was inadmissible, the Court ordered each party to bear its own costs, even though the applicant did in fact lose. Note also Cases 36, 37 and 218/81 *Seton v Commission* [1983] ECR 1789; Cases 118–123/82 *Celant v Commission* [1983] ECR 2995 (para 33).
48 [1988] ECR 1681, para 50 and at 1695–1696 (Advocate General Mischo).

what may constitute vexatious conduct, Advocate General Mischo considered that the action was not manifestly abusive because it was not manifestly inadmissible or unfounded; the applicant had not made any excessive charges; the action was not manifestly intended to cause delays; the applicant was not otherwise able to have the contested measures reviewed; the defendant had not determined who was responsible for the events giving rise to the contested measures and had not given the applicant an opportunity to comment on the contested measures before their adoption. Proceedings concerning the implementation by the defendant of a judgment of the Court cannot be said to be abusive or vexatious where the defendant itself had experienced difficulties in implementing the judgment and had applied for an interpretation of the judgment.[49] An action cannot be regarded as unreasonable or vexatious, even if it had little prospect of success, if the applicant had an interest in bringing it[50] or the case concerned a factually complex problem.[51]

Whereas the preceding rule appears to cover cases where the Court regarded it as equitable to apportion the costs instead of making the usual order, this rule seems to apply to two different types of case: that where the costs have been unnecessarily incurred and that where there has been abuse of process or other behaviour which must be discouraged. In both cases it would seem that the conduct complained of must have caused additional costs to be incurred.[52] Conduct during the proceedings before the Court may be regarded as unreasonable or vexatious just as much as conduct beforehand.[53]

6   Costs on discontinuance or withdrawal of proceedings

A party who discontinues or withdraws from proceedings shall be ordered to pay the costs (if they have been applied for in the opposing party's pleadings). If the latter has not asked for costs, each party shall bear its own costs.[54] A different order will be made only where the party who discontinues or withdraws applies for the costs to be borne by the opposing party (and such an order appears to be justified by the conduct of that party) or where the parties have come to an agreement on costs (in which case, the decision on costs is in accordance with the agreement).[55]

Although the English text uses two terms, 'discontinue' and 'withdraw', the French and Italian versions use only one, which picks up the expression used in the title to RP-ECJ 77–78 and RP-CFI 98–99: 'discontinuance', in the English version. Those provisions deal with the situation where the parties reach a settlement or the applicant discontinues the proceedings. It is possible, therefore, to interpret this rule on costs as applying only in those situations and not where, for example, one or more claims are settled or conceded but the rest of the action still continues. The German version of this rule, however, refers both to withdrawal of the action and withdrawal of a claim. This may have led

---

49 Case 134/84 *Williams v Court of Auditors* [1985] ECR 2225 (para 21).
50 Case 135/87 *Vlachou v Court of Auditors* [1988] ECR 2901, para 32 and at 2909 (Advocate General Lenz).
51 Case T-63/91 *Benzler v Commission* [1992] ECR II-2095, paras 34–36 (the successful party had also claimed that the opposing party should bear all the costs because the amount claimed was derisory; but the Court considered that the former's estimate of the amount at stake was manifestly wrong).
52 Case 31/71 *Gigante v Commission* [1976] ECR 1471 at 1472.
53 See in particular Case 140/86 *Strack v Commission* [1987] ECR 3939 (para 18).
54 RP-ECJ 69(5); RP-CFI 87(5). See, for example, Cases 78/81 and 78/81R *Bernardi v European Parliament* [1981] ECR 1467.
55 Rules of Procedure, ibid.

Advocate General Reischl to suggest in Case 148/73 *Louwage v Commission*[56] that the costs should not be awarded in the applicant's favour because, although he had won on some issues, he had withdrawn the rest. The Court did not follow him and ordered the defendant to pay all the costs but it is not clear why. It seems an unduly restrictive interpretation to limit the application of this rule to cases where the entire action is withdrawn. The consequence of such a construction would be that there would be no provision in the Rules of Procedure dealing expressly with the withdrawal of a claim.[57] The better view is, therefore, that this rule also applies to the withdrawal of one or more claims, even if the entire action is not withdrawn or discontinued.[58] In the nature of things, an order under this rule relating to the claims that had been withdrawn or discontinued would not be made until judgment on the outstanding claims.

The previous version of RP-ECJ 69(5)[59] provided that the discontinuing or withdrawing party would be ordered to pay the costs unless the discontinuance or withdrawal was justified by the conduct of the other party. The current version of the rule allows the Court to order that other party to bear the costs 'if this appears justified by the conduct of that party', thus apparently extending the circumstances in which the Court may exercise its discretion. The principal reason a party other than the discontinuing or withdrawing party may be ordered to pay the costs remains the situation where the discontinuance or withdrawal was the consequence of the conduct of the other party. The burden lies on the discontinuing or withdrawing party to show why the other party should be ordered to bear the costs.[60]

Very often the parties come to an agreement between themselves as to the costs.[61] If one party seeks to go back on an agreement on costs after the Court has been informed that the parties have agreed to the withdrawal of the proceedings, the Court will award the costs on the basis of the agreement earlier reached between the parties and will not entertain submissions that put the agreement in question.[62] Where a case is withdrawn by agreement between

---

56 [1974] ECR 81 at 98.

57 Unless such an event were, for example, to be considered an exceptional circumstance.

58 That interpretation was followed in the following cases (the judgments often refer to RP-ECJ 69(4) which was the equivalent, at the time, of RP-ECJ 69(5)): Case 116/82 *Commission v Germany* [1986] ECR 2519 (paras 33–34); Case 306/84 *Commission v Belgium* [1987] ECR 675 (paras 9–13); Case 412/85 *Commission v Germany* [1987] ECR 3503 (paras 21–24); Case 54/87 *Commission v Italy* [1989] ECR 385 (para 20).

59 RP-ECJ 69(4).

60 Where at first sight the other party's conduct has led to the withdrawal or discontinuance of the proceedings, the burden may shift to that other party to demonstrate that the withdrawing or discontinuing party should, after all, bear the costs. Thus, in Case 196/84 *ROGESA v Commission*, order of 18 September 1985, the applicant withdrew when the defendant modified the contested act. At first sight, the withdrawal was justified by the defendant's action. The defendant claimed that it modified the contested act as a result of new information produced by the applicant after the commencement of proceedings and applied for the applicant to bear the costs. The Court ordered the defendant to bear the costs because it did not offer any proof of its assertions to contradict the applicant's claim that withdrawal had been justified by the defendant's conduct.

61 See, for example, Cases 16–18/59 *Geitling Ruhrkohlen-Verkaufsgesellschaft mbH v High Authority* [1960] ECR 17 at 26; Case 289/85 *Italy v Commission* [1987] ECR 5321. In Case 792/79R *Camera Care Ltd v Commission* (the proceedings for interim relief are reported at [1980] ECR 119) the applicant and defendant reached agreement on costs as between themselves but the intervener persisted in a claim that its costs should be borne by the other parties. The Court ordered it to bear its own costs on the ground that the arguments it had put forward in the proceedings for interim relief had been rejected by the Court: 'in these circumstances the interveners cannot demand that their costs should be charged to the principal parties' (order of 17 December 1980, unreported).

62 Case 163/86 *Papageorgiadis v European Parliament*, order of 18 March 1987.

the parties and there is also agreement on the costs, the usual practice of the ECJ is simply to remove the case from the register. The usual practice of the CFI is to remove the case from the register by an order which provides for the costs in the way agreed between the parties.[63] Where there is no agreement on costs, the Court makes its own decision.[64]

In principle, the fact that cases are joined makes no difference to the manner in which the rule is applied.[65] The same seems to apply where a number of persons appear in the same case as applicants or, as the case may be, defendants.[66] Where some of a number of joined cases are discontinued by the applicants, they may be ordered to pay only part of the defendant's costs, even if the defendant is the same in every action, not because the defendant's conduct has justified the discontinuance but because only part of the defendant's total costs is attributable to the discontinued actions.[67]

There are not very many instances where the Court has given a ruling on what conduct may be considered as justifying a party in withdrawing or discontinuing. In general, a concession by the defendant of the applicant's claims or a change in the defendant's position after the commencement of proceedings that renders the further continuation of the proceedings needless will justify the withdrawal or discontinuance of the proceedings and lead to an order that the defendant pay the costs.[68] In one case the defendant revoked the decision challenged in the action, thus rendering the action purposeless. The defendant had promised to do so before the action commenced but the Court held that this fact did not make the action abusive or vexatious because the promise was made close to the expiry of the time limit for challenging the decision. Discontinuance was therefore justified by the defendant's conduct.[69] It is to be inferred that, in other circumstances, it may be abusive or vexatious to start proceedings where the defendant has given an assurance that it will act, even though it has not yet done so. It would seem that conduct of the types illustrated above in connection with the fourth and fifth rules may justify an order for costs in favour of the discontinuing party.[70]

On the other hand, in Case T-45/89 *Association des Acieries Européennes Indépendantes v Commission*,[71] each party was ordered to bear its own costs because, although the defendant's conduct had precipitated the commencement of proceedings and the situation had been remedied (at the express

---

63 Eg Case T-59/89 *Yorck von Wartemburg v European Parliament* [1990] ECR II-25; Case T-5/89 *Rydalm v Commission*, order of 13 February 1990.

64 In Case T-153/89 *Martin and Millet v Commission*, order of 11 October 1990, the withdrawal was justified by the attitude of the defendant and it was ordered to pay the costs subject to any other division of the costs agreed between the parties.

65 Eg Cases 80–83/81 and 182–185/82 *Adam v Commission* [1984] ECR 3411 (paras 8–16).

66 Cf Case C-169/84 *Société CdF Chemie Azote et Fertilisants SA v Commission* [1990] ECR I-3083 (para 54), where one of two applicants discontinued by letter in the middle of the proceedings but the defendant eventually lost. The discontinuing applicant was ordered to pay one-third of the defendant's costs incurred before the discontinuance (there being in total three parties).

67 See Cases 39, 41, 43, 85, 88, 121/81 *Halyvourgiki Inc v Commission* order of 25 November 1981; of the six actions, two were discontinued and the applicants in them ordered to bear their own costs and one-third of those incurred by the defendant up to the date of the discontinuance.

68 Cases 46 and 47/59 *Meroni & Co v High Authority* [1962] ECR 411; Cases 123/81 and 123/81R *Krupp Stahl AG v Commission* [1981] ECR 2391; Case 4/85 *Commission v Greece* [1987] ECR 4383; Case 132/85 *Commission v Greece* [1987] ECR 5293; Case 54/87 *Commission v Italy* [1989] ECR 385 (para 20); Case C-376/90 *Commission v Belgium* [1992] ECR I-6153 (para 31).

69 Case 118/81 *Dillinger Huttenweke AG v Commission*, order of 14 October 1981, unreported.

70 See also Cases 79 and 82/63 *Reynier and Erba v Commission* [1964] ECR 259 at 274–276 (Advocate General Roemer).

71 Order of 5 March 1991; a similar situation arose in Case 202/86 *Chambre Syndicale des Eaux Minérales et de Sources v Commission*, order of 30 September 1987.

request of the Court) only very late in the proceedings, thus causing the applicant to withdraw, diligent conduct on the applicant's part could have avoided the litigation. Similarly, in Case 138/85 *Commission v Greece*,[72] where the Commission had brought proceedings under art 169 of the EEC Treaty in the mistaken belief that the provision of Greek law in question had been introduced after the accession of Greece to the Community, and withdrew the proceedings after Greece had indicated in response to a question put by the Court that the provision had been introduced long beforehand, each party was ordered to bear its own costs because a communication from Greece before the commencement of proceedings should have warned the Commission to investigate matters further.[73] In Case 299/87 *Commission v Ireland*,[74] also proceedings under art 169, each party was ordered to bear its own costs because the defendant had complied with its Treaty obligations just before the commencement of proceedings and had told the Commission by telephone and facsimile machine but did not inform the Commission formally until after their commencement: the Commission should therefore have known what the position was before it started the action but the defendant was also at fault in not informing the Commission officially. In Case 369/87 *Armada Supply Ltd v Commission*[75] the commencement and withdrawal of the proceedings were not regarded as caused by any action of the defendant (it was clear that no decision capable of being annulled had been adopted and that a related claim in respect of a failure to act was premature) so the applicant was ordered to pay the costs. In Case 272/87 *Federacciai, Federazione Imprese Siderurgiche Italiane v Commission*[76] the applicant withdrew because of a judgment delivered by the Court in another case but the Court still ordered the applicant to bear the costs because it failed to show why the judgment in question had caused its interest in continuing the proceedings to disappear.

Where proceedings are settled, it may be that neither party makes a concession which makes it possible to say that the consequent termination of the proceedings has resulted from the conduct of either of them; it may also be that the proceedings are terminated by all the parties and not any one of them. In such circumstances, if the parties cannot agree between themselves on how the costs should be borne, it would seem that the next following rule should apply because it would be unjust to impose the burden of paying the costs on the party who discontinues or withdraws where the termination of the proceedings is the result of a genuine compromise between the parties or a decision made by them all. If a party might be penalised in costs in such a situation, the parties might be discouraged from settling disputes or indicating to the Court at the earliest opportunity that the dispute has been settled.[77] In fact, the present rule has been applied where a party has withdrawn or

---

72 Order of 3 October 1986.
73 The fact that each party was ordered to bear its own costs indicates that Greece should have made a clear and unequivocal statement of the position much earlier than was the case.
74 Order of 14 June 1988.
75 Order of 19 May 1988.
76 Order of 28 September 1989.
77 A settlement usually, but not always, includes provision for the costs of the proceedings. Where it does not do so, a party may either refuse to discontinue or withdraw the proceedings or else agree to discontinue or withdraw them and have the question of costs dealt with by the Court. The fact that the parties have reached agreement on all aspects of the case save the question of costs does not mean that the present rule is to be applied: there must in addition be a clear and unconditional withdrawal or discontinuance of the proceedings (see Case T-73/91 *Gavilan v European Parliament* [1992] ECR II-1555 (para 26)).

discontinued as a result of a settlement and it has not been possible to say that the other party's conduct led to the termination of the proceedings.[78]

7 Costs where a case does not proceed to judgment

Where a case does not proceed to judgment, the costs are in the discretion of the Court.[79] The English version of the Rules of Procedure is not very happily phrased because it suggests an overlap with the previous rule. In fact what is meant is that, despite the fact that the action has been settled, conceded or no longer requires judgment to be given, it has not been discontinued or withdrawn so that it is left to the Court to terminate the proceedings.[80] This it does in a decision finding that there is no ground for proceeding to judgment. Advocates General Roemer and Reischl took the view that, when this happens, the Court's discretion in the matter of costs is to be exercised after taking into account all the circumstances and making a summary assessment of the parties' chance of success.[81] This does not prevent the Court from awarding costs against one of the parties, even though he would probably have won the action, if there are exceptional circumstances or costs have been unreasonably or vexatiously incurred.[82] The assessment of the chances of success is summary in the sense used in the context of proceedings for interim relief[83] and does not require a profound analysis of the issues: a prima facie test is sufficient.[84]

In the past, the Court did not tend to explain how it exercised its discretion. It was therefore unclear to what extent the Court accepted the theory adopted by Advocates General Roemer and Reischl. In one case, Cases 7 and 9/54 *Groupement des Industries Sidérurgiques Luxembourgeoises v High Authority*,[85] the Court did appear to have made the order on the basis of an assessment of the applicant's chances of success.[86] It was, however, clear that the Court would take into account the behaviour of the parties,[87] but it seemed that even a high degree of unreasonable and reprehensible conduct must have caused additional costs to be incurred before the Court would award costs against a

---

78 Cases C-372/90P, C-372/90P-R and C-22/91P *Samenwerkende Electriciteits-produktiebedrijven NV v Commission* [1991] ECR I-2043, paras 11–13 (the order was made after first deciding that the proceedings had not been vexatious and that the settlement had largely satisfied the applicant's concerns; each party was ordered to bear its own costs).
79 RP-ECJ 69(6); RP-CFI 87(6). Before the amendment of the ECJ's Rules of Procedure in 1991, the relevant rule was RP-ECJ 69(5) and that is the rule referred to in the previous case law.
80 Eg Case 75/83 *Ferriere San Carlo v Commission* [1983] ECR 3123; Case 256/81 *Paul's Agriculture Ltd v Council and Commission* [1983] ECR 1707.
81 Case 103/63 *Rhenania Schiffahrts- und Speditionsgesellschaft mbH v Commission* [1964] ECR 425 at 432; *Bauer v Commission* (above, note 30) at 405; *Di Blasi v Commission* (above, note 29) at 864; Case 31/71 *Gigante v Commission* [1975] ECR 337 at 350; Case 74/81 *Flender KG v Commission* [1982] ECR 395.
82 See the *Gigante* and *Flender* cases, ibid.
83 See chapter 8, pp 257–260.
84 *Di Blasi v Commission* (above, note 29).
85 [1954–56] ECR 175 at 202–203.
86 The first claim did not proceed to judgment because the High Authority eventually adopted the decision which the applicant was seeking. The Court simply said that 'it may be considered' that the claim was well founded. It is unclear whether it actually examined the question in greater or lesser detail or simply took the view that, as the applicant had got what it wanted, it could be inferred that it had the better case. See also Cases 15/64 and 60/65 *Moreau v Euratom Commission* [1966] ECR 459 at 468: the defendant conceded the application 'by implication'. In the *Rhenania* case (above, note 81) the Court merely held that there was no need for it to consider to what extent the application was admissible and well founded; the circumstances of the case and the course of the proceedings were sufficient for it to decide that each party should bear its own costs (see at 429). See also *Ferriere San Carlo v Commission* (above, note 80).
87 See *Meroni & Co v High Authority* and *Groupement des Industries Sidérurgiques Luxembourgeoises v High Authority* (above, notes 68 and 85 respectively.)

party.[88] There are not very many cases in which it was clear that the Court had applied this rule[89] so it was hard to discern any general trend.

The more recent case law can be summarised as follows. Where neither party has asked for costs, each shall be ordered to bear its own costs.[90] Where the defendant has conceded the applicant's claims or satisfied them in full after the commencement of proceedings but before the delivery of judgment, the defendant will be ordered to pay the costs save to the extent that the further continuation of the proceedings by the other party is unjustified;[91] but, if the applicant was nonetheless left in a state of uncertainty about his or her position and, for that reason, did not discontinue the proceedings, the defendant will be ordered to pay all the costs.[92] The same applies in actions in respect of a failure to act where the defendant adopts a position after the commencement of proceedings.[93] Where the defendant has acknowledged that its conduct was responsible for the commencement of proceedings and that the applicant's claims were essentially well founded, the defendant will be ordered to pay the costs.[94] Where proceedings have not been withdrawn by one party because the other has refused to dispose of the costs in accordance with the agreement between the parties settling the dispute between them, the Court will terminate the proceedings by order requiring the defaulting party to pay the costs in accordance with the settlement agreement.[95] The defendant will be ordered to pay the costs where the applicant has died after the commencement of proceedings but would otherwise have been successful in the action.[96] In Case 242/86 *Ireland v Commission*,[97] the defendant was ordered to pay the costs

88 Case 31/71 *Gigante v Commission* [1976] ECR 1471 at 1472: this was a staff case and the usual order was made, each party to bear its own costs.

89 For example, in *Bauer v Commission* (above, note 30) the Court did not proceed to judgment on the application but the decision on costs does not mention RP-ECJ 69(5), which was, at that time, the equivalent of RP-ECJ 69(6). The reason seems to be that it did give judgment on a claim in the reply (see at 403). In *Di Blasi v Commission* (above, note 29) part of the case did not proceed to judgment but again the Court did not refer to what is now RP-ECJ 69(6) in the decision on costs. The same thing happened in *Moreau v Euratom Commission* (above, note 86).

90 Case C-118/91 *France v Commission*, 18 November 1992.

91 Cf Case T-81/91 *Feltz v European Parliament* [1992] ECR II-1827 (paras 27–28); Case C-222/92 *Syndicat Français de l'Express International v Commission*, 18 November 1992 (where the defendant withdrew the contested act after the commencement of proceedings as a result of certain facts brought to its attention in the application).

92 Case 14/84 *Hansen-Meyer v Economic and Social Committee* [1984] ECR 4317, para 14 (the Court had put certain questions to the defendant in order to ascertain whether or not the applicant had any interest in continuing the proceedings but the defendant did not reply until the hearing).

93 Case 377/87 *European Parliament v Council* [1988] ECR 4017 (para 12); Case 383/87 *Commission v Council* [1988] ECR 4051 (para 12). In Case T-55/89 *Solomon & Peres Ltd v Commission*, order of 9 February 1990, however, each party was ordered to bear its own costs.

94 Case 321/81 *Battaglia v Commission* [1987] ECR 2429. The same applies where the defendant's actions provoked the litigation, whatever the merits of the case: Cases T-89/91, T-21/92 and T-89/92 *X v Commission*, 25 November 1993, para 53 (each party ordered to pay own costs: see para 54).

95 Case 43/83 *De Naeyer v Commission* [1987] ECR 3569, paras 9–11 (the defaulting party was also ordered to pay the costs incurred by the other party in obtaining a medical examination pursuant to a measure of enquiry ordered by the Court which was regarded by the parties as indispensable for the conclusion of the settlement agreement and, therefore, of the litigation.

96 Case 141/85 *Dufrane v Commission*, order of 23 March 1988 (the case had been joined with another action – in which the applicant was later successful – and disjoined upon the death of the applicant, the proceedings then being stayed; the death of the applicant deprived the action of its purpose because she had made no pecuniary claim that could have been taken over by her successors; the Court was therefore presented with a situation in which it could conclude with certainty that the applicant would have won the action and, further, no costs had been incurred unnecessarily after her death).

97 [1988] ECR 2895 (para 9).

because the applicant could not reasonably be reproached for having commenced proceedings in view of the imminent expiry of the time limit for doing so and the conditional nature of the assurances given by the defendant (and which the defendant had complied with only in the course of proceedings). In Cases 294/86 and 77/87 *Technointorg v Commission and Council,*[98] the first action did not proceed to judgment because the contested act was replaced by the act contested in the second action. The applicant lost the second action and was therefore ordered to pay the costs of the first action.[99] In Cases 167 and 168/87, 28 and 123/88 *Organizacion de Productores Asociados de Grandes Atuneros Congeladores de España v Commission*[1] the contested act was annulled in parallel proceedings and replaced by a measure which took account of the applicant's claims but, since there were serious doubts about the admissibility of the action, each party was ordered to bear its own costs. Although, as can be seen, the parties' respective chances of success are a factor to be taken into account, they are not the only factor and, even if a party might be considered to be facing a losing battle, other factors may weigh against an order that that party bear the costs. Thus, in Case T-73/91 *Gavilan v European Parliament*[2] the Court proceeded on the assumption that the action might be inadmissible but concluded that, because the defendant had placed the applicant in a position of unjustified professional uncertainty and had not remedied the position for years until even after the commencement of proceedings, the defendant should bear its own costs and half of the applicant's. In Case C-54/91 *Germany v Commission*[3] a claim was settled after the commencement of proceedings but the applicant's claim for costs was rejected on the ground that the settlement had resulted from a reconsideration of the position by the defendant in the light of new evidence produced by the applicant: had that evidence been produced earlier, a settlement could have been achieved without the need for litigation. In essence, therefore, the premature nature of the claim barred the applicant's right to costs.

There was some doubt whether or not this rule applies where part only of the action does not proceed to judgment.[4] It would seem that, for the reasons given above in connection with the previous rule, it does so apply.[5]

8 Staff cases

In proceedings between the Communities and their officials or other servants, the institution shall bear its own costs without prejudice to the power of the Court to order a party to pay costs which the Court considers that party to have unreasonably or vexatiously caused another party to incur.[6] This rule applies whether it is the employing institution or the official or other servant who is the applicant. In several cases the Court has applied this rule where proceedings were brought under the Staff Regulations by a person who was not an official or other servant.[7] It seems that it is to be interpreted broadly, so

---

98 [1988] ECR 6077 (para 52).
99 This was not a situation where the substitution of the first contested act by the second was unforeseeable: the former was a regulation imposing provisional anti-dumping duties which, in the nature of things, is replaced by a regulation imposing definitive duties or else expires. If the substitution had been unforeseeable, the defendant would have been ordered to pay the costs of the first action.
1 1989] ECR 55 (paras 7–10).   **2** [1992] ECR II-1555 (paras 28–31).
3 [1993] ECR I-3399.
4 Cf Advocate General Roemer's opinion and the Court's judgment in Case 74/72 *Di Blasi v Commission* [1973] ECR 847.
5 Case C-54/91 *Germany v Commission* (above, note 3) appears to be an example.
6 RP-ECJ 70; RP-CFI 88.
7 Eg Case 18/70 *X v Council* [1972] ECR 1205 (the widow of a deceased official); Case 23/64 *Vandevyvere v European Parliament* [1965] ECR 157 and Case 34/80 *Authié v Commission* [1981] ECR 665 (unsuccessful candidates in a competition).

as to cover all persons entitled to bring proceedings under the Staff Regulations and Conditions of Employment, including persons claiming the status of an official or other servant of the Communities.[8] By reason of this rule, the normal order in a staff case, when the defendant institution wins, is that each party shall bear its own costs. This rule does not apply if the action is not brought under a provision of the Treaties or subordinate legislation specifically governing staff disputes,[9] and the Court may depart from it where the conditions for applying the fifth rule referred to above apply, for example, where the manner of conducting proceedings is abnormal and abusive.[10]

G   Costs of execution

Costs necessarily incurred by a party in enforcing a judgment or order of the Court shall be refunded by the opposite party on the scale in force in the State where the enforcement takes place.[11] This rule does not apply to preliminary rulings, which are not enforced as such but are applied by the national court which made the reference.

III   Recoverable costs

A   General

Recoverable costs are those which may be recovered by the Court and those which may be recovered by the party in whose favour an award of costs is made.

RP-ECJ 72 and RP-CFI 90 provide that proceedings before the Court are free of charge, so that, normally, no costs are recoverable by the Court. There are four exceptions to this:

(1)   'Where a party has caused the Court to incur avoidable costs the Court may, after hearing the Advocate General, order that party to refund them';[12]

(2)   'where copying or translation work is carried out at the request of a party, the cost shall, in so far as the Registrar considers it excessive, be paid for by that party on the scale of charges referred to in' RP-ECJ 16(5) or, as the case may be, RP-CFI 24(5);[13]

(3)   sums payable to witnesses and experts under RP-ECJ 51 or RP-CFI 74;[14]

(4)   legal aid.[15] The last is considered elsewhere.[16]

There does not appear to be any case in which a party has caused the Court to incur 'avoidable' costs and it is difficult to be precise about what such costs might entail. The normal costs incurred in the running of the Court appear to

---

8 Cases 75 and 117/82 *Razzouk and Beydoun v Commission* [1984] ECR 1509 per Advocate General Sir Gordon Slynn; Case 43/84 *Maag v Commission* [1985] ECR 2581 (para 28).

9 Cf Case 64/80 *Giuffrida and Campogrande v Council* [1981] ECR 693.

10 Case 338/82 *Albertini & Montagnani v Commission* [1984] ECR 2123 (para 52); Case 227/83 *Moussis v Commission* [1984] ECR 3133 (para 16); Cases T-57 and T-75/92 *Yorck von Wartenburg v European Parliament*, 28 September 1993, para 77.

11 RP-ECJ 71; RP-CFI 89.

12 RP-ECJ 72(a); RP-CFI 90(a). Where the matter arises before the CFI, there is no express requirement that the advocate general (where there is one) be heard.

13 RP-ECJ 72(b); RP-CFI 90(b).

14 RP-ECJ 73(a); RP-CFI 91(a). Eg Case 23/81 *Commission v Royale Belge* [1983] ECR 2685 (para 28).

15 RP-ECJ 76(5); RP-CFI 97(3).

16 Chapter 4, pp 143 et seq.

be excluded. That seems to leave the costs of unnecessary copying or translation work and preparatory enquiries, other than those envisaged elsewhere. The second exception is self-explanatory. Detailed rules for the imposition of charges for copying or translation work are set out in the Instructions to the Registrar. No Registry charges may be imposed other than those referred to in Section Three of the Instructions,[17] art 20 of which defines Registry charges by reference to RP-ECJ 72(b) and sets out the scale to be applied. In RP-ECJ 72(b) and RP-CFI 90(b) the word 'excessive' appears to refer to the cost of the work rather than its volume. The inference is that copies and translations may be obtained free of charge unless the demand is such that, in the opinion of the Registrar, the Court is caused to incur 'excessive' costs. In this situation the party requesting the work is charged at the rate specified in IR 20. The sum due may be paid either in cash to the Court cashier or by bank transfer to the Court account at the bank named in the demand for payment.[18] Where the party has been granted legal aid, IR 19 provides that RP-ECJ 76(5) applies. It therefore seems that the Court bears the costs in the first instance but may recover them as amounts advanced as legal aid in the decision on costs in the final judgment.

RP-ECJ 51 and RP-CFI 74 provide that witnesses and experts are entitled to (i) reimbursement of their travel and subsistence expenses and (ii) compensation for loss of earnings, in the case of witnesses, and fees for their services in the case of experts. Where it is the Court which has paid out such sums, it is entitled to recover them from one of the parties if it so orders. The same applies where the Court has paid the expenses of letters rogatory.[19] Where a party has applied for a witness to be heard, the Court may make the summoning of the witness conditional upon the deposit with the Court's cashier of a sum which the Court considers sufficient to cover the taxed costs of hearing the witness.[20]

Costs recoverable by the party in whose favour an award of costs is made are defined by RP-ECJ 73 and RP-CFI 91 as: (a) sums payable to witnesses and experts under RP-ECJ 51 and RP-CFI 74, respectively; and (b) 'expenses necessarily incurred by the parties for the purpose of the proceedings, in particular the travel and subsistence expenses and the remuneration of agents, advisers or lawyers'.

Sums payable to witnesses and experts are usually paid by the losing party[21] but are recoverable under the first heading only where the Court has ordered the witnesses to be heard or the expert to make a report by way of a preparatory enquiry; the fees of an expert consulted by a party of his own motion are recoverable, if at all, only under the second heading.[22] Where witnesses are heard in their capacity as officials of an institution which is a party to the proceedings, the costs of their examination are borne by the institution[23] but this seems to apply only to compensation for loss of earnings: travel and subsistence expenses would still appear to be borne by the party ordered to pay the costs generally.[24] Where the Court has already advanced or paid sums due to a witness or expert, the party ordered to pay the costs reimburses the Court.

---

17 IR 17.
18 IR 18.
19 EC Statute, art 26; Euratom Statute, art 27; SR 3; RP-CFI 75(4).
20 RP-ECJ 47(3); RP-CFI 68(3).
21 Cases T-33 and T-74/89 *Blackman v European Parliament* [1993] ECR II-249 (para 101).
22 Cases 19, 20/74 *Kali-Chemie A G v Commission* [1975] ECR 499 (unreported order of 1 December 1976).
23 Cases 19 and 65/63 *Prakash v Euratom Commission* [1965] ECR 533 at 561.
24 See, by analogy, Case 126/76 *Firma Gebrüder Dietz v Commission* [1979] ECR 2131.

The only costs recoverable under the second heading are those 'necessarily incurred . . . for the purpose of the proceedings'. 'Proceedings' means 'proceedings before the Court'[25] and so no costs are recoverable which were incurred at any pre-litigation stage, for example, during the administrative procedure in a staff case or the preliminary exchanges leading up to an action against a failure to act on the part of a Community institution.[26] On the other hand, this does not mean that no costs at all can be recovered for work done prior to the commencement of proceedings: if this were so, a party would not be able to recover in respect of fees due to his lawyer for drafting the application commencing proceedings. It seems, instead, that costs may be recovered for expenses incurred in preparing for the commencement of proceedings. Such expenses must, however, be 'necessary'. This means 'necessary to resolve the dispute'[27] and it can best be illustrated by reference to each head of costs in question.

B   Witnesses and experts

In one case the Court allowed the recovery of the costs of one expert consulted by a party but not a second because the latter's report was not necessary to resolve the dispute;[28] in another, such expenses were not held to be necessary because the party had decided not to rely on the report in its pleadings and the Court had subsequently ordered an expert's report itself.[29] In Case 43/83 *De Naeyer v Commission*[30] the Court allowed the recovery of the costs of a medical examination which had been ordered by way of a measure of enquiry and which had been regarded by the parties as indispensable to the settlement of the case.

C   Remuneration of agents, advisers and lawyers

As a general rule, it is not necessary for the purpose of the proceedings to be represented or assisted by more than one lawyer or adviser and any additional expenses so incurred are not recoverable.[31] Despite the fact that some Community institutions, particularly the Council and the Commission, possess a legal service staffed by trained lawyers, it is accepted that the remuneration of an outside lawyer, acting as agent or assistant to the agent of the institution, is necessarily incurred for the purpose of the proceedings and therefore recoverable.[32] On the other hand, the remuneration of an official of the institution is not recoverable because it lies within the scope of his employment to assist, give

---

25 Cf RP-ECJ 72; RP-CFI 90.
26 Case 75/69 *Ernst Hake & Co v Commission* [1970] ECR 901 (para 1 of the order).
27 Two early orders refer to the necessity to vindicate or ensure the adequate defence of the rights of the party awarded the costs: Case 18/57 *Nold KG v High Authority* [1959] ECR 41 (unreported order of 30 June 1959); Case 35/58 *Worms v High Authority* (unreported order of 17 November 1959).
28 *Kali-Chemie AG v Commission* (above, note 22).
29 Case 49/69 *Badische Anilin- und Sodafabrik AG v Commission* [1972] ECR 713, order of 12 June 1975, unreported.
30 [1987] ECR 3569 (para 11).
31 Cases 20 and 21/63 *Maudet v Commission* [1964] ECR 621 at 622–623 (the reasoning seems to have been based on the French version of RP-ECJ 73(b) which refers to agents, advisers and lawyers in the singular; other texts, such as the English and German, do not); Case 73/74 *Groupement des Fabricants de Papiers Peints de Belgique v Commission* [1975] ECR 1491 (unreported order of 5 July 1976); Cases 106 and 107/63 *Toepfer v Commission* [1965] ECR 429 (unreported order of 16 May 1966); Case 18/57 *Nold KG v High Authority* (above, note 27).
32 *Dietz v Commission* (above, note 24), para 6. In previous cases the Court had allowed an institution to recover as costs the remuneration due to an adviser (Case 25/62 *Plaumann & Co v Commission* [1963] ECR 95, unreported order of 28 November 1963) and a lawyer (Cases 9 and 58/65 *Acciaierie San Michele SpA v High Authority* [1968] ECR 259) but without giving reasons.

advice to and defend the interests of the institution; in consequence, his remuneration is not an expense incurred for the purpose only of the proceedings in question.[33] Fees due in respect of the provision of an address for service in Luxembourg are also recoverable but are restricted to 'fees for acceptance of service in the proper sense' and do not include fees relating to the provision of other services such as legal advice or supervision of the conduct of proceedings.[34] In this connection it would seem that, when considering whether fees due to the second adviser or lawyer are recoverable costs, the Court would take into account the importance of the case and the difficulties to which it gives rise.[35] In one case the Court disallowed a claim for the costs of consulting a university professor because the consultation related to a problem of domestic law which did not present particular difficulties.[36]

D Travel and subsistence expenses

In general, the travel and subsistence expenses which are recoverable are those incurred by the agent, adviser or lawyer[37] but where the agent, adviser or lawyer is involved in several cases heard on the same day or occasion, travel and subsistence expenses are not recoverable in respect of the same journey or the same day more than once only.[38] Where an institution is represented by one of its officials, it may still recover his travelling expenses and daily subsistence allowance even though his remuneration is not recoverable.[39] A claim for travel and subsistence expenses incurred by the party's lawyer in travel outside the Community may be rejected unless there is proof of circumstances requiring travel outside the Community, such as the absence of a representative of the party in the Community or the inadequacy of modern means of communication.[40] The same would seem to apply, as a matter of principle, to travel within the Community.

The travel and subsistence expenses of witnesses and experts are normally covered by RP-ECJ 73(a) or, as the case may be, RP-CFI 91(a). When an expert falls to be dealt with under RP-ECJ 73(b) or RP-CFI 91(b), the test is whether or not expenses were necessarily incurred and so, if fees are not, on this basis, recoverable, nor are travel and subsistence expenses. The same applies in the case of supernumerary advisers and lawyers. A party's travel and subsistence expenses are recoverable only if

---

33 The *Dietz* case.
34 *Maudet v Commission* (above, note 31): fees for acceptance of service seem to be limited to office and correspondence expenses. Fees for acceptance of service were awarded, inter alia, in Case 49/65 *Ferriere e Acciaierie Napoletane SpA v High Authority* [1966] ECR 73 (unreported order of 6 October 1966); Case 8/65 *Acciaierie e Ferriere Pugliesi SpA v High Authority* [1966] ECR 1 (unreported order of 13 July 1966); *Toepfer v Commission* (above, note 31).
35 These are certainly two of the criteria adopted by the Court when taxing costs (see below) and would seem to apply when the Court decides whether it was necessary for the party to be represented or assisted by more than one person, as in the analogous situation where the party consults an expert of its own motion: see Cases 241, 242, 246–249/78 *DGV v EEC* [1981] ECR 1731 (para 5 of the order).
36 Case 102/84 *Dillinger Hüttenwerke AG v Commission* (case withdrawn) order of 22 May 1985.
37 Case 24/79 *Oberthür v Commission* [1981] ECR 2229 (para 2 of the order).
38 Case 238/78 *Ireks-Arkady GmbH v Council and Commission* [1981] ECR 1723 and *DGV v EEC* (above, note 35), para 5 of the order.
39 *Dietz v Commission* (above, note 24). In actions against member states, the Commission does not claim the legal costs awarded against the member state concerned on condition that, in such actions, a successful member state will not claim its legal costs from the Commission: answer given by Mr Delors to Written Question No 2256/91 (OJ No C102 of 22 April 1992, pp 39–40).
40 Case 65/87 *Pfizer International Inc v Commission* (unreported order of 22 September 1988, para 8).

his presence at the hearing is necessary. This may be the case if:

(1)   the Court has requested the party to be present in person;
(2)   the hearing concerns the taking of evidence relating to events experienced by the party;[41] or
(3)   the course of such events is extremely complicated and the main point at issue before the Court,[42] in which case the presence of the party may be useful to help the Court disentangle the facts.

Where the facts necessary for deciding the case are largely to be found in documents before the Court, it is not necessary for the party to be present[43] unless the documents themselves present the facts in a way which is obscure or confused.

E   Miscellaneous

Office expenses,[44] postal, telephone, telex and photocopying charges[45] and any taxes due on sums payable which themselves constitute recoverable costs[46] are recoverable. Sums claimed for care and consideration are not.[47] The costs of a bank guarantee obtained in order to avoid the immediate enforcement of the contested decision while judgment is pending are not recoverable because they are not incurred for the purpose of the proceedings.[48] In general, it would seem that miscellaneous expenses are recoverable if they are shown to have been necessarily incurred.

IV   Taxation

A   Commencement of taxation proceedings

An application to the Court for the taxation of costs is made under RP-ECJ 74(1) or, as the case may be, RP-CFI 92(1). The Rules of Procedure do not lay down any particular requirements as to the form and content of the application. As usual, RP-ECJ 37 or RP-CFI 43 governs form and presentation while RP-ECJ 38 or RP-CFI 44 applies, by analogy, to the contents. It would appear to be sufficient, for the purpose of compliance with RP-ECJ 38(5)(a) or RP-CFI 44(5)(a), to refer to the application commencing proceedings in the case, or, as the case may be, the defence; but the other requirements should probably be set out in the application for taxation, particularly where a lengthy interval has elapsed between the date of judgment and the making of the application. Taxation proceedings are normally given the same number and title as the action to which they relate (save that, in some instances, one or more letters are added after the case number in order to indicate that the

---

41 Eg Case 68/63 *Luhleich v Euratom Commission* [1965] ECR 581 (unreported order of 13 July 1966).

42 *Oberthür v Commission* (above, note 37), para 3 of the order.

43 Ibid.

44 *Ferriere e Acciaierie Napoletane SpA v High Authority* (above, note 34).

45 *Ireks-Arkady GmbH v Council and Commission* and *DGV v EEC* (above, notes 38 and 35), para 5 of the order.

46 *Ernst Hake & Co v Commission* (above, note 26), para 3 of the order (VAT: the Court reduced the amount claimed to take account of a reduction in the fees it held to be recoverable).

47 Case 10/55 *Mirossevich v High Authority* [1954–56] ECR 333 (unreported order of 12 July 1957).

48 Case 183/83 *Krupp Stahl AG v Commission* [1987] ECR 4611. The guarantee was required by the Commission as one of the conditions for it refraining from taking steps to enforce the decision. The other condition was the commencement of proceedings before the Court for the annulment of the decision.

proceedings are ancillary to the main action) but the application is not usually made against every other party to the original proceedings: the defendant in the taxation proceedings is the party with whom a dispute has arisen in regard to the costs.[49] The language of the proceedings is determined by the usual rules[50] and will normally be that of the case. It seems to be possible for the Court to tax the costs without the need for a formal application to that effect where the case is before the Court for the purpose of awarding costs and it is apparent that there is a dispute between the parties as to the amount of the costs. Thus, in Case 43/83 *De Naeyer v Commission*,[51] where the parties had agreed to withdraw the action consequent upon a settlement of the dispute, and the applicant refused to withdraw because the defendant objected to paying the applicant's costs pursuant to the settlement, the matter came before the Court for an order terminating the proceedings (on the ground that there was no need to give judgment) and disposing of the costs. The only remaining issues between the parties seem to have concerned the heads of costs which the defendant should pay and the amount of the costs to be paid. Although no formal application for taxation seems to have been made, the Court made a formal order awarding the costs to the applicant in accordance with the settlement and then immediately proceeded to tax the costs. Needless to say, the Court can deal with the matter in that way only if the dispute between the parties concerning the amount of the costs to be paid is sufficiently clear and there is enough information before the Court to enable it to tax the costs.

There is no time limit for the making of an application under RP-ECJ 74(1) or RP-CFI 92(1)[52] but the party awarded costs should send a detailed account of the costs claimed to the opposing party within a reasonable time. There is little guidance as to what may or may not constitute a reasonable time. In the *Dietz* case,[53] the party ordered to pay the costs argued that the right to recover costs had been lost because six months had elapsed before a claim for costs was made. The Court rejected this argument on the ground that a claim had been made 'within a reasonable period which can by no means be taken to imply that [the party awarded costs] had waived its right'. This leaves the matter open because the Court does not actually hold that silence over a long period of time can constitute waiver, only that it did not constitute waiver in that case. Nonetheless, a reasonable inference from the *Dietz* case is that the party awarded costs should not be inactive for so long that it may be taken to have waived its right to claim payment of the costs. In order to avoid difficulties of this nature, it should be sufficient to make a formal claim intended to preserve the position until a more detailed account can be drawn up. Such a claim is

---

49 For example, in Case 4/73 *Nold Kohlen- und Baustoffgrosshandlung v Commission* [1975] ECR 985, the application for taxation was lodged by the interveners in the original action and made against the applicant, who had been ordered to bear the costs. The defendant to the original action was not a party to the taxation proceedings because no dispute over costs had arisen between it and the applicant. The same situation arose in Case C-157/87Dep *GIMELEC v Electroimpex* (unreported order of 16 October 1991) but, in contrast to the *Nold* case, the order in the *GIMELEC* case did not bear the same title as the original proceedings (Case C-157/87 *Electroimpex v Council* [1990] ECR I-3021): the case number remained the same, with the addition of the letters 'Dep' (meaning '*dépens*', or 'costs'), but the intervener, who had applied for taxation, was named as the applicant and the applicant in the action (Electroimpex) was named as the defendant in the taxation proceedings.

50 See chapter 2, pp 52 et seq.

51 [1987] ECR 3569.

52 See *Acciaierie San Michele SpA v High Authority* (above, note 32).

53 Above (note 24), para 1 of the order.

made to the party ordered to pay the costs and does not start off any proceedings or the running of any time limit.

A condition precedent to the making of an application to the Court for the taxation of costs is the existence of 'a dispute concerning the costs to be recovered'.[54] An application to be relieved of the costs, made by the party ordered to pay them, is not such a dispute: it relates to the award of the costs and not their amount. Hence it cannot be made under RP-ECJ 74(1) or RP-CFI 92(1).[55] The earliest time at which an application can be lodged is the moment when the party ordered to pay the costs disputes the claim made by the party awarded costs. In order to narrow down the area of any potential dispute it is therefore useful if the claim is itemised. A dispute arises not only when the party ordered to pay the costs challenges the amount claimed or a particular head of costs but also where he declines or refuses to pay all or part of the sum claimed: for example, in Case 6/72 *Europemballage Corpn and Continental Can Co Inc v Commission (No 2)*[56] the defendant, who had been ordered to pay the costs, paid over a sum which the applicant considered did not match the costs recoverable under RP-ECJ 73. On the other hand, in Case 25/65 *SIMET v High Authority*,[57] the High Authority was ordered to pay the costs and, shortly after the judgment was handed down, the applicant's representative sent an account of the fees and expenses due. The High Authority replied saying that its practice was to wait until the Court had settled the fees due before paying them and suggesting that the applicant apply to the Court under RP-ECJ 74. The applicant duly did so, the High Authority not opposing the application and leaving the matter to the Court which dismissed it as inadmissible because there was no dispute 'regarding either the amount of the costs to be recovered or their payment' at the time the application was made. The same thing happened in *Acciaierie San Michele SpA v High Authority*[58] but several months later the High Authority applied alleging that the costs claimed by the applicant were excessive. This time the applicant pleaded that the application was inadmissible because it was, in effect, seeking a variation of the previous order made and the Rules of Procedure made no provision for appeals. The Court rejected this, holding that the proceedings did not amount to an appeal from the previous order because it had decided only the admissibility of the application then made by Acciaierie San Michele and not the substance of the dispute between the parties; an application for taxation is always admissible whenever one of the parties disputes the costs and, as the High Authority had, by the time of the second application, raised a dispute, it was admissible.

Once a dispute has arisen, it does not matter which party makes the application for taxation.[59] The only object of the taxation of costs to be recovered under RP-ECJ 74 and RP-CFI92 is to determine, where necessary, the amount of the costs and fees which, having regard to all the facts of the case, must be borne by the unsuccessful party by way of recoverable costs[60]

---

54 RP-ECJ 74(1); RP-CFI 92(1).

55 Case 14/84 Rev *Hansen (née Meyer) v Economic and Social Committee* [1985] ECR 1381. Such an application cannot be made at all since the award of costs has the authority of res judicata.

56 [1975] ECR 495.

57 [1967] ECR 113.

58 Above (note 32), order of 26 May 1967, unreported.

59 Usually it is the party in whose favour costs were awarded but this is not invariable: in *Acciaierie San Michele SpA v High Authority* (above, note 32) and Case 130/75 *Prais v Council* [1976] ECR 1589 (unreported order of 24 May 1977), the party ordered to pay the costs applied.

60 Case 17/68 *Reinarz v Commission* [1970] ECR 1.

and the Court has frequently stated that it does not tax the costs due from the parties to their own lawyers or advisers.[61] In consequence, the usual order sought in the application is for the Court to fix the sum due by way of recoverable costs at a specified amount. This amount is normally expressed in the currency of one of the member states which is, it would seem, the currency of account used by the party awarded costs in its initial claim. In *Europem-ballage Corpn and Continental Can Co Inc v Commission (No 2)*[62] the Court held that, since 'only lawyers entitled to practise before a court of a Member State may represent parties other than the States and the institutions of the Community before the Court of Justice, the fixing by the Court of the costs recoverable under Article 73 of the Rules of Procedure must be effected on the basis of the national currencies of the Member States'. This appears to mean nothing more than that the order will be expressed in one of those currencies and, in fact, the Court seems invariably to follow the currency mentioned in the applicant's form of order.

Apart from claiming that costs be fixed at a specified amount, the applicant may also claim that the other party be ordered to bear a particular head of costs[63] but, even so, the amount claimed under that head should be specified. When a global amount is claimed, it should be itemised and, in all cases, the claim should be supported by evidence and argument to show that the criteria of recoverability have been fulfilled. In addition, the parties may apply for an authenticated copy of the Court's order for use in enforcing it.[64]

B Procedure

The ECJ's Rules of Procedure say only that, once the application for taxation has been made, the chamber to which the case has been assigned shall make an order 'after hearing the opposite party and the Advocate General'.[65] The CFI's Rules of Procedure provide that the matter shall be decided by the CFI 'after hearing the opposite party'.[66] The normal course of the procedure is for the other party to the dispute over costs to reply in writing to the application for taxation.[67] There are no preparatory enquiries, although the Court no doubt has power to order a measure of enquiry where necessary, and no hearing. In cases before the ECJ the advocate general delivers his opinion in the Deliberation Room and it is not circulated to the parties.[68] The Court then makes the

---

61 See, for example, Case 4/73 *Nold Kohlen-und-Baustoffgrosshandlung v Commission* (above, note 49); *Kali-Chemie AG v Commission* (above, note 22); Case 28/77 *Tepea BV v Commission* [1978] ECR 1391; *Ireks-Arkady GmbH v Council and Commission* (above, note 38); *DGV v EEC* (above, note 35); Case 65/87 *Pfizer International Inc v Commission* (above, note 40).

62 Above (note 56), para 3 of the order.

63 Eg *Maudet v Commission* (above, note 31; fees for acceptance of service); *Badische Anilin- und Sodafabrik AG v Commission* (above, note 29: supplementary costs including those in respect of an expert's report); *Oberthür v Commission* (above, note 37; travel and subsistence expenses incurred by the party).

64 RP-ECJ 74(2); RP-CFI 92(2).

65 RP-ECJ 74(1): for an example of assignment to a chamber, see Case 238/78 *Ireks-Arkady GmbH v Council and Commission* [1981] ECR 1719.

66 RP-CFI 92(1). In cases heard by a chamber of the CFI the application for taxation would be heard and determined by that chamber, the reference in RP-CFI 92(1) to the CFI being also a reference to the relevant chamber: see RP-CFI 11(2).

67 In *Kali-Chemie v Commission* (above, note 22) it seems that the applicant was allowed to lodge a supplement to the application and the other party allowed to reply to it, there being no suggestion that it was inadmissible. In *Maudet v Commission* (above, note 31) it seems that the Court allowed the applicant to reply in writing to the other party's observations.

68 See, for example, the *Dietz* case and *Oberthür v Commission* (above, notes 24 and 37).

order, from which no appeal lies.[69] Since the order taxing the costs takes into account all the circumstances of the case up to and including the taxation itself, no separate order for the costs of the taxation proceedings is made:[70] the costs of those proceedings are included in the taxation order either by addition to the amount to be paid by the party ordered to pay the costs or by deduction from that amount (where, for some reason, the Court considers that the party awarded the costs should bear those of the taxation proceedings). Since the order only specifies the amount recoverable by way of costs and, if the applicant has so requested, orders an authenticated copy to be given to him, there is no need to interpret it.[71]

C   Taxation of costs

In relation to legal fees, the Court does not tax the fees payable by a party to its own lawyers; it is concerned with the amount of the fees that may be recovered from the party ordered to pay the costs.[72] Although the Court fixes the costs recoverable on the basis of the national currencies of the member states[73] because only lawyers entitled to practise before a court of a member state may represent parties other than a member state or Community institution, it is not bound, for the same reason, to fix the costs according to the scale applied in one of the member states[74] or in accordance with that agreed between the applicant and its lawyers[75] or by reference to the level usually received by the party ordered to pay the costs on occasions when it is successful.[76] There is no scale laid down by Community law so the fixing of the amount due is left to the discretion of the Court. It appears to settle on a sum which seems to it to be fair,[77] appropriate[78] or reasonable.[79] In *Ireks-Arkady GmbH v Council and Commission*[80] the criteria to be taken into account were put in this way: 'the Court must undertake a free appreciation of the facts of the dispute having regard to its object and nature, its importance from the point of view of Community law and the difficulties of the proceedings, the amount of work which the litigation may have caused the lawyers and what the dispute may

69 RP-ECJ 74(1); RP-CFI 92(1).
70 Eg Case 318/82 *Leeuwarder Papierwarenfabriek BV v Commission* [1985] ECR 3727 (para 5). In *Tepea BV v Commission* (above, note 61) however, it seems that each party was ordered to bear its own costs in the taxation proceedings.
71 Cf Case 17/68 *Reinarz v Commission* (above, note 60).
72 Eg Case 318/82 *Leeuwarder Papierwarenfabriek* (above, note 70) para 2.
73 The *Europemballage* case (above, note 56).
74 *Ireks-Arkady GmbH v Council and Commission* (above, note 38) para 2 of the order; *DGV v EEC* (above, note 35); *Leeuwarder Papierwarenfabriek v Commission* (above, note 70) para 2; Case 321/85 *Schwiering v Court of Auditors* [1986] ECR 3199 (unreported order of 15 June 1988, para 3). While not obliged to apply a national scale of legal fees, the Court is not prevented from taking into account the general level of fees in a member state.
75 *Nold Kohlen-und-Baustoffgrosshandlung v Commission* (above, note 49) para 1; the *Leeuwarder* case (ibid) para 2; the *Schwiering* case (ibid) para 3.
76 Case 148/87 *Frydendahl Pedersen A/s v Commission* [1988] ECR 4993 (unreported order of 13 March 1989).
77 *Tepea BV SpA v Commission* (above, note 61): 'ex aequo et bono'; *Acciaierie San Michele v Commission* (above, note 32): 'equitable'.
78 Case 130/75 *Prais v Council* (above, note 59); *Papiers Peints v Commission* (above, note 31); *Ireks-Arkady GmbH v Commission and Council* and *DGV v EEC* (above, notes 38 and 35).
79 Case C-225/87-Costs *Belardinelli v Court of Justice* [1989] ECR 2353 (unreported order of 26 March 1990).
80 Ibid, para 3 of the order.

have meant to the parties in financial terms'.[81] The Court may also take into account any legal aid due.[82]

At least since the *Europemballage* case,[83] the sum awarded by the Court has not been itemised and, in some of the early reported cases, it is not even stated in the report. In a few cases, it appears to have excluded expenses, probably because there was agreement on them and the dispute between the parties centred on the lawyers' fees recoverable.[84] For this reason, it is difficult to define with accuracy how, in exercising its discretion, the Court assesses the criteria to be taken into account. Most problems seem to arise in connection with lawyers' fees: in fixing these the Court has had regard to whether the point of law is only of little[85] or average difficulty or not exceptional[86] or did not give rise to a novel point of Community law;[87] whether the party relied to a large extent on arguments put forward by another party;[88] whether the points of law were the same as in other cases in which the same lawyers appeared;[89] whether several cases were joined;[90] the number of pleadings and the time taken to attend the hearing;[91] what is a reasonable remuneration for lawyers or advisers in the member state in question.[92] The legal fees of a party other than

---

81 See the similar phraseology used in *Kali-Chemie AG v Commission* (above, note 22); *Tepea BV v Commission* (above, note 61); *DGV v EEC* (above, note 35); *Nold Kohlen-und-Baustoffgrosshandlung v Commission* (above, note 49); *Europemballage Corpn and Continental Can Co Inc v Commission* (above, note 56); *Ernst Hake & Co v Commission* (above, note 26); Cases 64, 113/76, 167, 239/78, 27, 28, 45/79 *Dumortier Frères SA v Council* [1982] ECR 1748; Case 318/82 *Leeuwarder Papierwarenfabriek v Commission* (above, note 70) para 3; Case 43/83 *De Naeyer v Commission* (above, note 51) para 14; Case 65/87 *Pfizer International Inc v Commission* (above, note 40) para 5 (reference to the economic interests at stake rather than to financial interests). In Case 148/87 *Frydendahl Pedersen* case (above, note 76) reference was made only to the difficulty and circumstances of the case and to a reasonable remuneration of the lawyer or adviser in the member state in question. That seems to be nothing more than a briefer version of the more usual formula (as used in the *Ireks-Arkady* case (ibid)). The reference to 'a reasonable remuneration of the lawyer or adviser in the member state in question' seems to allude not only to what is reasonable having regard to the work involved in the case but also to what is reasonable having regard to the usual level of remuneration in the member state in which the lawyer or adviser in question practises. The same criteria apply whatever the status of the party in whose favour costs were awarded: eg Case C-157/87Dep *GIMELEC v Electroimpex* (above, note 49), where costs were taxed in favour of an intervener.

82 For example, in *Luhleich v Euratom Commission* (above, note 41) the defendant was ordered to pay the costs and, hence, to pay to the Court the sum advanced by it to the applicant by way of legal aid. This sum was paid over and, in the order fixing the costs to be paid by the defendant to the applicant, the Court deducted from the applicant's claim the amount of the legal aid (see also *De Naeyer v Commission* (ibid) paras 14–16).

83 Above (note 56).

84 Eg *Ireks-Arkady GmbH* and *DGV v EEC* (above, notes 38 and 35).

85 Case 321/85 *Schwiering v Court of Auditors* (above, note 74) para 4.

86 *Groupement des Fabricants de Papiers Peints de Belgique v Commission* (above, note 31).

87 Case 65/87 *Pfizer International Inc v Commission* (above, note 40) para 7.

88 *Nold v Commission* (above, note 49).

89 *Ireks-Arkady GmbH v Council and Commission* (above, note 38); Case 260/84 *Minebea Co Ltd v Council* [1987] ECR 1975 (unreported order of 5 July 1988), in relation to the costs of an intervener in several related cases where the points made in the intervener's pleadings were to all intents and purposes the same.

90 *DGV v EEC* and *Dumortier Frères SA v Council* (above, notes 35 and 81).

91 Case 65/87 *Pfizer International Inc v Commission* (above, note 40) para 6, where the case was withdrawn after lodgment of the defence so that the applicant had lodged only the application commencing proceedings and an application for interim relief (both pleadings being in large part similar and the grounds being identical); Cases T-18 and T-24/89 *Tagaras v Court of Justice* [1992] ECR II-153.

92 Case 148/87 *Frydendahl Pedersen A/S v Commission* (above, note 76). Legal fees vary significantly as between the member states. To fix a fair level of reimbursement by reference to the member state with the lowest legal fees or by reference to an average level in the Community would prejudice those persons who, for linguistic or other reasons, feel it necessary or appropriate to

a Community institution are not taxed by reference to the fees paid by a Community institution to an outside lawyer where the latter's role is limited to assisting the institution's agent at the hearing.[93] Where the dispute has been settled, an appropriate reduction in the recoverable costs may be made.[94] It is not excluded that the same criteria may be applied to expenses: in Cases 45 and 49/70 *Bode v Commission*,[95] for example, the party ordered to pay the costs had not in fact contested that the expenses claimed were recoverable but the court awarded them on the ground that they did not appear to it to be excessive.[96] Where costs are awarded to a number of joined parties (eg joint applicants) or where several cases have been joined, the Court may award a global figure to be divided between the parties in whose favour the order is made.[97] The costs, as taxed by the Court, have often been considerably less than the costs claimed.[98]

The right to recover a specific sum by way of recoverable costs accrues only when the order fixing that sum is handed down.[99] For this reason, a claim for interest on the amount awarded, running from the date of judgment in the action, was rejected in the *Europemballage* case.[1] In Case 238/78 *Ireks-Arkady GmbH v Council and Commission* and Cases 241, 242, 246–249/78 *DGV v EEC*,[2] on the other hand, the claim for interest was rejected because, in fixing the costs to be paid, the Court had taken into account all the circumstances relevant at the time of its determination including, one supposes, the delay in paying the costs. At all events, once the order has been made, the party awarded costs may commence proceedings immediately to enforce it and so the risk of losing interest on the sum through further delays is dependent on his diligence.

D   Enforcement

For the purposes of enforcement, as has been remarked, the parties may apply for an authenticated copy of the order. The procedure for enforcement is sketched out in arts 92 of the ECSC Treaty, 192 of the EC Treaty and 164 of the Euratom Treaty and is the same for enforcement of a judgment.[3] Costs necessarily incurred in enforcing the order are paid by the opposite party on the scale in force in the member state in which enforcement takes place.[4] The enforcement procedure comes under the jurisdiction of the competent national

---

retain lawyers or advisers from member states where legal fees are relatively high. In order to work out a fair level of reimbursement, it is therefore appropriate to take into account the general level of legal fees in the member state in which the lawyer or adviser concerned regularly practises.

93 Case 260/84 *Minebea Co Ltd v Council* (above, note 89).
94 Case 43/83 *De Naeyer v Commission* (above, note 51) para 14.
95 [1971] ECR 465 (unreported order of 13 July 1971).
96 In Case 210/81 *Demo-Studio Schmidt v Commission* [1983] ECR 3045 (unreported order of 29 March 1984) the Court accepted various disbursements on the ground that they did not appear excessive or to have been incurred without cause.
97 Cf *DGV v EEC* (above, note 35): costs to be shared among the applicants in several joined cases in proportion to the compensation awarded to each of them; *Dumortier Frères SA v Council* (above, note 81): costs to be shared as above unless the parties agree on some other method of division.
98 For example, in Case 65/87 *Pfizer International Inc v Commission* (above, note 40) the taxed costs were about 9 per cent of the costs claimed.
99 The *Europemballage* case (above, note 56), para 5 of the order.
 1 Ibid.
 2 [1981] ECR 1723 and 1731. See also Case 321 *Schwiering v Court of Auditors* (order of 15 June 1988, para 4).
 3 See chapter 16, pp 534 et seq.
 4 RP-ECJ 71; RP-CFI 89.

authorities and it is for them 'to decide any questions which enforcement may raise without prejudice to the enforceability of the decision in question'.[5] Sums due from the cashier of the Court are paid in Luxembourg francs unless the person entitled to be paid requests payment in the currency of the country where the expenses were incurred or where the steps in respect of which payment is due were taken.[6] Other persons pay in the currency of their country of origin.[7] It is not entirely clear what this is supposed to mean. It is likely that the 'country of origin' will be taken to be that in which lies the party's place of residence, as stated in the pleadings.[8] Since the currency of account (ie that in which the sum fixed by the Court is expressed) is likely to be different, RP-ECJ 75(3) and RP-CFI 93(3) provide that conversions of currency are to be made at the official rates of exchange ruling in Luxembourg on the day of payment.[9]

5 Case 4/73 *Nold Kohlen- und-Baustoffgrosshandlung v Ruhrkohle AG* [1977] ECR 1, para 3 of the order.
6 RP-ECJ 75(1); RP-CFI 93(1).
7 RP-ECJ 75(2); RP-CFI 93(2).
8 Cf Case 28/77 *Tepea BV v Commission* [1978] ECR 1391 where the applicant, who was ordered to pay the costs, stated in its pleadings that its registered office was at The Hague; the Court appears to have held it to its declaration.
9 Cf the order in Case 35/58, above: the currency of account was Belgian francs but the currency of payment Dutch guilders.

CHAPTER 15

Appeals from the CFI

I Scope of the procedure

An appeal may be brought before the ECJ from the following decisions of the CFI:

(1) final decisions;[1]
(2) decisions disposing of the substantive issues in a case in part only;[2]
(3) decisions disposing of a procedural issue concerning a plea of lack of competence or inadmissibility;
(4) decisions dismissing an application to intervene;[3]
(5) decisions granting or refusing interim relief;
(6) decisions granting or refusing a stay of enforcement of a decision of the Council or Commission.[4]

No appeal lies in respect of a decision of the CFI concerning only the amount of the costs to be paid or the identity of the party ordered to pay them[5] or in respect of a decision whether or not to order a measure of enquiry.[5A]

Appeals to the ECJ are limited to points of law irrespective of the nature of the judgment or order appealed against.[6] If the appeal is successful, the judgment or order appealed against is annulled in whole or in part and, to the extent that it is annulled, the matter is then decided by the ECJ or remitted to the CFI for decision in accordance with the judgment of the ECJ on any relevant points of law.[7]

II Time limits

With the exception of the decisions referred to in (4) above, an appeal must be brought within two months of notification of the decision appealed against; in the case of the decisions referred to in (4) above, the period is two weeks.[8] An application to intervene in appeal proceedings must be lodged within three

---

1 Such decisions include: judgments which decide definitively the matters in dispute between the parties; judgments or orders closing the proceedings without any decision on the ground that there is no need to rule on the questions at issue; and orders striking a case from the register.
2 Such as a judgment in an action for damages which determines liability but leaves the issue of quantum to the parties to resolve by agreement.
3 But not, it seems, decisions allowing an intervention.
4 ECSC and EC Statutes, arts 49 and 50; Euratom Statute, arts 50 and 51.
5 ECSC and EC Statutes, art 51 (last sentence); Euratom Statute, art 52 (last sentence).
5A Case C-320/92P *Finsider SpA v Commission* (unreported, per Advocate General Darmon, para 8).
6 ECSC and EC Statutes, art 51; Euratom Statute, art 52.
7 ECSC and EC Statutes, art 54; Euratom Statute, art 55.
8 ECSC and EC Statutes, arts 49 (first subpara) and 50; Euratom Statute, arts 50 (first subpara) and 51. An appeal included in a response to the notice of appeal is not subject to that time-limit: Case C-136/92P *Commission v Lualdi* (unreported, per Advocate General Lenz, paras 113–117).

months of the date on which the appeal was lodged at the Court.[9] As is usual, all time limits are extended by the relevant periods on account of distance.[10] Procedural time limits (such as the periods within which a pleading must be lodged) may be extended by the person setting the time limit.[11]

III   The parties to the appeal

Appeals against the decisions referred to in (1) to (3) above may be brought by (a) any party to the proceedings before the CFI who was unsuccessful, in whole or in part, in its submissions[12] save that interveners (other than member states and Community institutions) may appeal only where the decision appealed against affects them directly; and, save in cases relating to disputes between the Community and its servants, (b) member states and Community institutions who were not parties to the proceedings before the CFI even as interveners.[13] It follows that an appellant who was a party to the proceedings before the CFI (but not an intervener) can appeal only in respect of that part of the relief sought by him in those proceedings in which he was unsuccessful before the CFI. The fact that an argument put forward by him was not accepted by the CFI is not sufficient to found an appeal. Interveners other than member states and Community institutions must, in addition, show that the operative part of the decision appealed against (as opposed to any finding made or argument accepted by the CFI in the reasoning leading up to the operative part) has a direct adverse effect on their position. It is unclear to what extent the requirement that the decision appealed against must affect the appellant intervener directly differs from the usual test for determining whether or not the intervener was entitled to intervene in the proceedings before the CFI in the first place. When an application to intervene is considered in order to determine whether or not it is to be admitted, the intervener's interest in the result of the case is assessed ex ante; when an appeal by an intervener is considered, the intervener's interest can be assessed ex post and it may then become clear whether or not the intervener had in truth a direct and concrete interest in the result of the case. Hence, even if the test for allowing an appeal by an intervener is in principle the same as that for allowing the application to intervene at first instance, it does not necessarily follow that an intervener in the proceedings before the CFI would have capacity to appeal.[14] Member states and Community institutions which were not parties to the proceedings before the CFI (even as interveners) are entitled to appeal without needing to show that the decision of the CFI directly affects them.[15]

Appeals against the decisions referred to in (4) above may be made only by the person whose application to intervene has been dismissed; whereas any

9 RP-ECJ 123.
10 See RP-ECJ 80 and 81(2).
11 RP-ECJ 82.
12 That is, the relief sought or 'form of order'.
13 ECSC and EC Statutes, art 49; Euratom Statute, art 50. Appellant member states and Community institutions who were not parties to the proceedings at first instance are treated as if they had intervened at first instance. The expression 'Community institutions' includes the European Parliament: Case C-70/88 *European Parliament v Council* [1990] ECR I-2041 at 2055 (Advocate General van Gerven).
14 For an example of an appeal brought by an intervener in the proceedings before the CFI, see Case C-98/92P *Union Européenne de Radiodiffusion v La Cinq SA and Commission*, unreported (the case was withdrawn).
15 See ECSC and EC Statutes, art 49 (second subpara); Euratom Statute, art 50 (second subpara).

party to the proceedings before the CFI may appeal against the decisions referred to in (5) and (6) above.[16] It should be observed that, in the case of the decisions referred to in (5) and (6), there is no express requirement that the appellant should have been unsuccessful, in whole or in part, in its claims before the CFI or should be directly affected by the CFI's decision. It makes sense to imply such a requirement: in the ordinary course, a party will not seek to overturn a decision of the CFI which satisfies that party's claims. Even if such a requirement cannot be said to be implied in the Statutes, it may arise by application of the general principle that a party must demonstrate an interest in obtaining the relief sought in proceedings.[17] In relation in particular to the decisions referred to in (5) above, any requirement of an interest in appealing should be applied flexibly: there may be occasions where, for example, a decision to grant interim relief is favourable to the applicant for relief but does not go as far as the applicant would have wished. It should also be noted that member states and Community institutions which were not parties to the proceedings before the CFI cannot appeal against the decisions referred to in (4), (5) and (6) above.

The appeal (occasionally referred to as a 'notice of appeal') is served on all the 'parties to the proceedings' before the CFI and each of them may lodge a response.[18] It follows that all parties to the proceedings before the CFI are automatically parties to the appeal.[19] They appear as respondents to the appeal even where their response supports the appeal. There appears to be no sound reason that the expression 'parties to the proceedings' should exclude interveners in the proceedings before the CFI. At the time of writing, the practice of the ECJ Registry was to accept that such interveners were parties to the appeal and did not need to apply to intervene in the appeal proceedings.[20] The ECJ has rejected the suggestion that that is incorrect and that interveners before the CFI must apply to intervene in the appeal proceedings if they wish to participate in them.[21] In the case of appeals against decisions dismissing an application to intervene or decisions granting or refusing interim relief, it would seem that the 'parties to the proceedings' before the CFI are to be regarded as the parties to, respectively, the intervention and interim relief proceedings. A person who becomes a party to the action before the CFI after the decision in the intervention or interim relief proceedings (that is, an intervener in the action before the CFI) would not, therefore, be a party in the appeal from that decision although interveners in the proceedings before the CFI are ordinarily to be regarded as parties to any appeal made in those proceedings.

A third party to the appeal proceedings may apply to intervene.[22] The application to intervene must be lodged within three months of the date on which the appeal was lodged.[23] Where the appeal is heard by summary

---

16 ECSC and EC Statutes, art 50; Euratom Statute, art 51.

17 See chapter 7, section II.D, p 196.

18 RP-ECJ 114 and 115(1).

19 See also F Hubeau in (1991) C de D Européen 499 at 512.

20 Case C-244/91P *Pincherle v Commission*, 22 December 1993, opinion of Advocate General Darmon (paras 45–46).

21 Ibid para 16; contra Advocate General Darmon (paras 28 and 44–46).

22 RP-ECJ 118, which incorporates RP-ECJ 93.

23 RP-ECJ 123. In a direct action, the time limit for lodging an application to intervene is three months from publication of the notice of the case in the Official Journal: RP-ECJ 93(1). The time limit for lodging an application to intervene in an appeal is therefore much shorter in practice because a third party to the proceedings at first instance is not likely to learn of the initiation of the appeal until the publication of the notice in the Official Journal. Where the

procedure,[24] the application to intervene must be made promptly. The criteria determining the entitlement to intervene and the procedure to be followed in an intervention in appeal proceedings are the same as those in a direct action heard by the ECJ[25] save that an application to intervene in appeal proceedings is dealt with by the ECJ after hearing the advocate general.[26]

IV Initiation of an appeal

An appeal is made by application to the ECJ; the application may be lodged at the Registry of either the ECJ or the CFI.[27] The application (referred to in the Rules of Procedure and hereafter as 'the appeal') must contain:[28]

(1) the name and address of the appellant;
(2) the names of the other parties to the proceedings before the CFI;
(3) the pleas in law and legal arguments relied on;
(4) the form of order sought by the appellant;
(5) the date on which the decision appealed against was notified to the appellant;
(6) the appellant's address for service in Luxembourg and the name of the person who is authorised and has expressed willingness to accept service.

Various documents must be attached to the appeal, including a copy of the decision appealed against, which need not be mentioned here; and the appeal must comply with the general rules governing applications made to the ECJ.[29]

notice is published after the expiry of the three-month period for lodging the application, a third party wishing to intervene may nonetheless be able to rely on that fact as an unforeseeable circumstance entitling him to make an application notwithstanding the expiry of the time limit (and always assuming that the third party had no knowledge beforehand of the initiation of the appeal); see ECSC Statute, art 39 (last subpara); EEC Statute, art 42 (last subpara); Euratom Statute, art 43 (last subpara).

24 As to which, see below pp 476 et seq.
25 See chapter 5 and the approach followed in Case C-242/90P-R *Commission v Albani* [1990] ECR I-4329 (para 5), order of 10 October 1990 (the staff union in question was considered to have an interest to intervene in the appeal proceedings and a consequential interest to intervene in the application for interim relief, made in the context of the appeal proceedings, because the case concerned the immediate consequences of the judgment at first instance; a similar order was made in the main appeal proceedings on 15 November 1990); Case C-107/90P *Hochbaum v Commission* [1992] ECR I-157 (order of 10 October 1990: intervention of a staff union allowed because the grounds relied on by it could raise questions of principle relating to the judicial review of promotion decisions of the appointing authority); *Pincherle v Commission* (above, note 20), opinion of Advocate General Darmon (para 47); Case C-241/91P *Radio Telefis Eireann v Commission* and Case C-242/91P *Independent Television Publications Ltd v Commission*, both unreported (order of 25 March 1992: intervention of Intellectual Property Owners Inc, a non-profit-making association of companies, universities and independent inventors, allowed because its members held extensive portfolios of intellectual property rights which might be affected by the proceedings). As in direct actions, member states and Community institutions may intervene as of right. Intervention in the appeal proceedings is in principle open to persons who were not parties to the proceedings at first instance; the fact that they could have been parties to those proceedings but did not intervene in them is no objection to their intervention in the appeal proceedings.
26 RP-ECJ 123. As a result, the other parties are not heard before the Court decides on the application to intervene and have no means of disputing the Court's decision. In summary proceedings heard by the President of the ECJ, he (not the Court) decides on any application to intervene in those proceedings.
27 RP-ECJ 111(1). Where the application is lodged at the Registry of the CFI, that Registry transmits it immediately to the Registry of the ECJ: RP-ECJ 111(2).
28 RP-ECJ 112(1) and (2).
29 RP-ECJ 112. For a fuller description of the pleading rules relating to appeals see chapter 9, pp 333 et seq.

The scope of the appeal is limited to points of law: (a) lack of competence of the CFI; (b) breach of procedure before the CFI which adversely affects the interests of the appellant; (c) infringement of Community law by the CFI.[30] The appeal may seek to set aside the decision of the CFI, in whole or in part, and the same form of order as that sought at first instance, in whole or in part; a different form of order cannot be claimed and the subject matter of the proceedings before the CFI cannot be changed in the appeal.[31] The language of the appeal is that of the decision appealed against save that the ECJ may authorise use of another language in the same way as it does in direct actions, and member states are entitled to use their own official language.[32] When appeal proceedings are initiated, the Registry of the CFI immediately transmits to the Registry of the ECJ the papers in the case at first instance.[33]

V   Procedural stages

An appeal is dealt with either by summary procedure or by ordinary procedure.

A   Summary procedure

The Statutes provide that appeals from the decisions referred to in (4), (5) and (6) in section I above (that is, decisions dismissing an application to intervene, granting or refusing interim relief or granting or refusing stay of enforcement of a decision of the Council or Commission) are to be heard and determined by summary procedure.[34] The summary procedure referred to is that specified in the Statutes, which provide (in the context of the grant of interim relief in direct actions) that the matter is to be decided by the President of the ECJ, subject to rules laid down in the Rules of Procedure.[35] An appeal may in addition be dealt with summarily when it is wholly or in part clearly inadmissible or clearly unfounded. In that event, it may be dismissed by the Court, in whole or in part, by reasoned order.[36] The Court may so decide at any time and, therefore, before the appeal is served on the parties.

So far as appeals against the decisions referred to in (4), (5) and (6) are concerned, the Rules of Procedure contain no specific provision dealing with the summary procedure to be followed. The Rules applicable to appeals are apt for appeals dealt with under the ordinary procedure. It seems, therefore, that, as the Statutes envisage by summary procedure the procedure followed in respect of applications for interim relief, the provisions of the Rules of Procedure relating to that procedure should be applied mutatis mutandis.[37] Accordingly, after the initiation of the appeal proceedings by lodgment of the appeal, the appeal is served on the other parties to the proceedings before the CFI, as usual, and the President of the ECJ prescribes a short period for the submission by those parties of written or oral observations, depending upon

---

30 ECSC and EC Statutes, art 51; Euratom Statute, art 52.
31 RP-ECJ 113.
32 RP-ECJ 110. See further chapter 2, section II, pp 52 et seq.
33 RP-ECJ 111(2).
34 ECSC and EC Statutes, art 50 (third subpara); Euratom Statute, art 51.
35 ECSC Statute, art 33; EC Statute, art 36; Euratom Statute, art 37.
36 RP-ECJ 119. The order is made on a report from the judge-rapporteur and after hearing the advocate general. See, for example, Case C-126/90P *Viciano v Commission* [1991] ECR I-781; Case C-115/90P *Turner v Commission* [1991] ECR I-1423; Case C-32/92P *Moat v Commission* [1992] ECR I-6379; Case C-318/92P *Moat v Commission* [1993] ECR I-481.
37 See chapter 8, pp 288 et seq., and RP-ECJ 83–86.

the degree of urgency in the case. In the case of appeals against the grant or refusal of interim relief, an interim order may be made in order to preserve the position pending the determination of the appeal.[38] It is to be observed that such an order is itself an interim relief order and the decision whether or not to grant such relief is made in accordance with the usual criteria for the grant of such relief.[39] In contrast, the final decision in the appeal is in principle a decision on the lawfulness of the decision appealed against and is therefore to be made on the basis of different criteria. The President may decide the appeal himself or refer it to the ECJ. The decision on the appeal will take the form of a reasoned order.

In the case of an appeal from a decision dismissing an application to intervene, the President will either confirm the decision or annul it. If the decision is annulled, the President may decide the question himself, in which case the appellant will be allowed to intervene in the proceedings before the CFI by order of the President of the ECJ, or else remit the matter to the CFI. It is unlikely that the second alternative will be appropriate in most cases.

In the case of appeals against decisions granting or refusing interim relief or the suspension of the enforcement of a decision of the Council or Commission, the limitation of the appeal procedure to points of law is likely to be particularly important. The function of the President of the ECJ is limited to reviewing the decision of the CFI (or, more likely, of the President of the CFI) on the grounds of lack of competence, breach of procedure and infringement of Community law.[40] In consequence, the findings of facts made by the CFI (or its President), the assessment of those facts and the assessment of the appropriateness of the relief sought or granted are all matters over which the President of the ECJ has limited powers of review. In effect, apart from lack of competence and breach of procedure, the President of the ECJ's grounds of review seem to be limited to error of law, manifest error of fact and misuse of powers. Further, even where an appeal is successful, it is very likely that the consequence will be that the matter is remitted to the CFI (or its President) for decision unless the ruling of the President of the ECJ on the errors of law in the decision appealed against should reveal that there is only one way in which the application for interim relief or suspension can be decided. Where the President of the ECJ does decide the matter, it is unclear whether any subsequent application (grounded, for example, on a change in circumstances) should be made to the (President of the) CFI or to the (President of the) ECJ. In this respect, a distinction should be drawn between the grant and the refusal of interim relief or suspension. Where the President of the ECJ's decision has the effect that interim relief or suspension is refused, the President of the CFI retains jurisdiction over the question of interim relief or suspension and, where there is a change in circumstances, a subsequent application can be made to the President of the CFI. On the other hand, where the President of the ECJ

---

38 The subject matter of such an order is the decision appealed against and not the matters at issue in the action before the CFI. In consequence, in Cases C-372/90P, C-372/90P-R and C-22/91P *Samenwerkende Electriciteits-Produktiebedrijven NV v Commission* [1991] ECR I-2043 (para 11) the President of the ECJ pointed out that an application for interim relief in respect of an act contested in proceedings before the CFI can be made only in the context of an appeal to the ECJ from a decision made by the CFI (or its President) on that very question. The interim relief that may be granted in the context of an appeal from such a decision is therefore limited in time to the period pending the decision on the appeal and cannot go further (as was claimed in that case), such as for the period pending the judgment of the CFI in the action before it.
39 See chapter 8, pp 238–239 and 241–242.
40 ECSC and EC Statutes, art 51; Euratom Statute, art 52.

makes an order in the appeal proceedings which grants interim relief or suspension, it would appear that, for as long as that decision remains in force, the President of the CFI does not have jurisdiction over the matter unless, in his decision, the President of the ECJ specifies that, in the event of any subsequent change in circumstances, application should be made to the President of the CFI. It would appear that, in order to avoid such a situation (which is, strictly speaking, inconsistent with the essentially appellate function of the President of the ECJ), either the grant of interim relief or suspension should always be remitted to the (President of the) CFI or else, if the President of the ECJ grants such relief, the order should as a matter of course specify that any subsequent application in the matter is to be determined by the (President of the) CFI.

B   Ordinary procedure

The ordinary appeal procedure applies to all appeals with the exception of those dealt with by the summary procedure. The ordinary procedure consists of a written part and an oral part, save that the latter may be dispensed with in accordance with the Rules of Procedure.[41] The ordinary procedure is similar to an action for the annulment of the decision appealed against. The same rules relating to the joinder of cases,[42] service, time limits, assignment of cases to chambers, intervention,[43] stay,[44] the conduct and reopening of the oral procedure, costs, legal aid, discontinuance,[45] interim relief,[46] the form and delivery of judgments, third party proceedings, revision and interpretation of judgments apply as in an ordinary direct action.[47] Preparatory enquiries do not, in principle, form part of the procedure because the appeal is limited to points of law. The different stages of the ordinary procedure are explained below under separate headings. It should be noted that the procedure for obtaining judgment by default in a direct action, when the defendant fails to lodge a defence in time, does not apply in appeal proceedings. In consequence, it would appear that, if the other parties fail to lodge in time any written response opposing the appeal, the appeal must inevitably be upheld and the decision appealed against quashed unless the appeal is manifestly inadmissible or manifestly unfounded.

---

41 ECSC and EC Statutes, art 52; Euratom Statute, art 53.

42 It is doubtful if an appeal can be joined to any proceeding other than another appeal but it cannot be excluded that there may be circumstances in which the similar subject matter and timing of an appeal and a parallel direct action before the ECJ may make joinder of the two cases appropriate.

43 But see above, pp 474–475.

44 See, in particular, RP-ECJ 82a(1)(a) and, for example, Case T-35/89TO1 *Ascasibar Zubizarreta v Albani* [1992] ECR II-1599 (paras 7–8) and Case C-242/90P *Commission v Albani*, 6 July 1993 (appeal proceedings stayed on application pending the outcome of third party proceedings brought before the CFI in respect of the judgment appealed against).

45 See, for example: the *Samenwerkende Electriciteits* case (above, note 38), withdrawal as a result of a compromise; Case C-98/92P *Union Europeéenne de Radiodiffusion v La Cinq SA and Commission*, unreported (order of 21 October 1992: appeal brought by intervener against a decision of the CFI annulling a refusal by the Commission to grant interim relief at the request of La Cinq; the interim relief sought from the Commission would have been directed against the intervener but La Cinq went into liquidation after the commencement of the appeal and withdrew its application to the Commission, thus rendering the continuation of the appeal unnecessary).

46 See below, pp 479–480.

47 RP-ECJ 118.

VI Preliminary issues

The rules relating to appeals exclude the application of RP-ECJ 91 and 92, replacing them with RP-ECJ 119, which enables the Court to dismiss an appeal in whole or in part at any time on the ground that it is in whole or in part clearly inadmissible or clearly unfounded. Although the Court may in principle act under RP-ECJ 119 of its own motion and before the appeal has been served on the other parties to the proceedings before the CFI, at the time of writing the Court had acted almost invariably after the other parties had been given an opportunity to submit written responses to the appeal.[48] The exclusion of RP-ECJ 91 and 92 does not appear to make it impossible to raise any preliminary issue other than a claim that the appeal is clearly inadmissible or clearly unfounded, such as an application for confidential treatment of the pleadings; any such issue must, however, be raised in the body of a party's pleadings in the appeal (the application commencing the appeal, response or, where allowed, the reply, rejoinder or other pleading) and not separately.

VII Interim relief

The making of an appeal does not have suspensory effect.[49] In consequence, unless interim relief is sought from the ECJ, the decision appealed against remains effective and must be complied with even while the appeal is pending. Hence, if subsequent proceedings are commenced before the CFI while the appeal is pending and those subsequent proceedings are affected in some way by the continued effectiveness of the judgment appealed against, the only remedy is to apply to the ECJ for interim relief; an application for interim relief in respect of the judgment appealed against cannot be made to the CFI.[50] Where the decision appealed against declares void a general decision or general recommendation (within the meaning of the ECSC Treaty) or a regulation (within the meaning of the EC and Euratom Treaties), the decision takes effect only as from the date of dismissal of the appeal.[51] Accordingly, interim relief is relevant only where a party to the appeal (presumably a party other than the appellant) seeks to have the effects of the general decision, general recommendation or regulation suspended (or some other form of interim relief) pending the outcome of the appeal.

The circumstances in which an application for interim relief may be made in the context of appeal proceedings can therefore be summarised as follows, using for the purposes of illustration the typical case of an action for annulment decided by the CFI:

(1) if the action is successful and the contested act is annulled by the CFI, the appellant (who is to be supposed to be opposing the annulment of that act) may apply for suspension of the operation of the CFI's judgment, or interim measures as against the judgment;

(2) if the action is successful and involves the making of a declaration that a general decision, general recommendation or regulation is void, the appellant (to the extent that it opposes that declaration, as it is to be

---

48 See the cases referred to in note 36 above.
49 ECSC and EC Statutes, art 53 (first subpara); Euratom Statute, art 54 (first subpara); RP-CFI 83.
50 Case T-77/91R *Hochbaum v Commission* [1991] ECR II-1285 (paras 19–23).
51 ECSC and EC Statutes, art 53 (second subpara); Euratom Statute, art 54 (second subpara).

supposed) need not seek any form of interim relief in respect of that declaration because the judgment appealed against will not take effect unless and until the appeal is dismissed but another party to the appeal proceedings (that is, a party supporting the declaration made by the CFI) may apply for suspension of the effects of the general decision, general recommendation or regulation in order to prevent the statutory postponement of the taking effect of the CFI's judgment from causing serious and irreparable damage pending the determination of the appeal;

(3)   if the action is unsuccessful, the appellant (who is to be supposed to be supporting the annulment of the contested act) may apply for the suspension of the operation of the contested act or interim measures pending the outcome of the appeal.

It will be observed that, in the first situation in which interim relief may be sought, the subject matter of the application will be the judgment appealed against; in the second and third situations, the subject matter of the application will not be the judgment but the acts that were the subject matter of the judgment of the CFI.

In all cases in which interim relief is sought, the same principles apply and the same procedure is followed as in an application for interim relief made to the President of the ECJ in the context of a direct action;[52] the applicant for relief must demonstrate that he or she has a prima facie case (that is, that the case made out in the appeal proceedings for or against the annulment of the decision appealed against is arguable) and that he or she is threatened with serious and irreparable damage if relief is not granted. If relief is granted, it ceases to have effect either on the date specified in the order or on the delivery of final judgment in the appeal[53] unless the order is before then varied or cancelled.[54] Where the final judgment on the appeal remits the case to the CFI, there may still be need for interim relief, in which case application is made to the President of the CFI.

VIII   Written procedure

The written procedure in appeals is set out in outline in chapter 2, section V (p 94), and is dealt with in more detail in chapter 9 (p 333). At this point, it suffices to note that, after the appeal proceedings have been commenced by lodgment of the appeal, notice of the appeal is served on all the parties to the proceedings before the CFI, if necessary after the appeal has been put in order or declared admissible despite the existence of a formal defect.[55] Any party to the proceedings before the CFI may lodge a response to the appeal within two months of service of the notice of appeal.[56] The response must contain: (a) the name and address of the party lodging it; (b) the date on which notice of the appeal was served on him; (c) the pleas in law and legal arguments relied on;

---

52   See chapter 8; RP-ECJ 83–89; Case C-242/90P-R *Commission v Albani* (above, note 25); C-345/90P-R *European Parliament v Hanning* [1991] ECR I-231; C-35/92P-R *European Parliament v Frederiksen* [1992] ECR I-2399.

53   RP-ECJ 86(3).

54   RP-ECJ 84(2) and 87.

55   RP-ECJ 114. In the case of legal and natural persons (that is, parties other than member states and Community institutions), the practice is to serve the appeal on the party at the professional address of the lawyer representing the party at first instance.

56   RP-ECJ 115(1).

(d) the form of order sought; (e) the party's address for service in Luxembourg and the name of the person authorised and willing to accept service.[57] The response must also be accompanied by certain documents which need not be mentioned here.[58] The response may seek to dismiss the appeal, in whole or in part, or to set aside the decision of the CFI, in whole or in part; and the same form of order as that sought by the party before the CFI may be sought, in whole or in part. A different form of order cannot be sought and the subject matter of the proceedings before the CFI cannot be changed in the response.[59] In consequence, a respondent to the appeal cannot claim damages in respect of the making of the appeal.[60] As long as the relief sought by a respondent remains within the scope of the relief sought by him (or her) at first instance, a respondent may rely on any point raised before the CFI in opposition to the appeal, even one on which the CFI did not rule.[61]

The President may allow a further exchange of pleadings (reply and rejoinder or other pleadings) on application made within seven days of service on the party concerned of the other party's latest pleading if he considers it to be necessary.[62] A respondent to the appeal may support or oppose the appeal and may also apply for the decision appealed against to be set aside in whole or in part on the basis of a plea not raised in the appeal.[63] In that event, the appellant and any other party may lodge a reply to that plea.[64] The periods within which any pleading subsequent to the response must be lodged at the Court are fixed by the President.[65] No new plea in law may be raised in any pleading lodged after the response unless it is based on matters of law or of fact which come to light in the course of the appeal proceedings; and, if such a plea is raised, the matter is dealt with in the same way as in a direct action.[66] After the lodgment of the last pleading provided for or, as the case may be, the expiry of the period for lodging that pleading, the written procedure closes and the case is considered by the Court in the light of a preliminary report produced by the judge-rapporteur, as in the case of a direct action.[67]

57 RP-ECJ 115(2). After lodgment of the response, further communications with the party will be made by the Court by registered letter addressed to (or by hand at) the party's address for service in Luxembourg (unless the party fails to provide an address for service in Luxembourg, in which case the second subpara of RP-ECJ 38(2) will be applied).
58 See further, chapter 9, pp 333 et seq.
59 RP-ECJ 116.
60 Case C-35/92P *European Parliament v Frederiksen* [1993] ECR I-991 (paras 34–35).
61 Case C-185/90P *Commission v Gill* [1991] ECR I-4779 at 4803–4804 (Advocate General Jacobs). In Case C-348/90P *European Parliament v Virgili-Schettini* [1991] ECR I-5211 at 5222, Advocate General Lenz considered that the appellant could not raise in the appeal proceedings a point on admissibility known to the CFI but not raised by the appellant at first instance.
62 RP-ECJ 117(1).
63 See, for example, Case C-346/90P *F v Commission* [1992] ECR I-2691 at 2698. If the applicant in the proceedings before the CFI were successful only in part and appealed against that part of the judgment in which it was unsuccessful, the defendant in those proceedings could contest that part of the judgment in which the applicant was successful. An intervener in the proceedings before the CFI may thus seek to set aside the judgment appealed against on grounds not raised by the principal parties if, as appears to be the better view, such an intervener is automatically a party to the appeal proceedings and entitled to lodge a response to the appeal. Interveners in the appeal proceedings merely lodge a statement in intervention (RP-ECJ 93(5), applied by virtue of RP-ECJ 118) and not a response. Having regard to the general principles governing the role of interveners in proceedings before the Court, an intervener in the appeal proceedings cannot challenge the decision appealed against on grounds other than those raised by the principal parties to the appeal.
64 RP-ECJ 117(2).
65 RP-ECJ 117(3). As is usual, those periods may be extended on application: RP-ECJ 82.
66 RP-ECJ 42(2) (applied by virtue of RP-ECJ 118); see chapter 9, pp 327 et seq. Cf Case C-354/92P *Eppe v Commission*, 22 December 1993, per Advocate General Darmon, paras 18–19 and 27.
67 RP-ECJ 121 and 44 (the latter applying by virtue of RP-ECJ 118).

IX   Oral procedure

The Court may dispense with the oral procedure unless one of the parties objects on the ground that the written procedure did not enable him fully to defend his point of view.[68] In principle, the proposal to dispense with the oral procedure is made by the Court and put to the parties but there seems to be no objection to the matter first being raised by one of the parties. If the Court considers that dispensing with the oral procedure may be appropriate, the parties are asked for their views. If any one of the parties objects on the ground that the written procedure did not enable him fully to defend his point of view, the oral procedure must be opened and the proceedings will then continue as in a direct action.[69] If there is no such objection, the Court will proceed to deliberate on its judgment in the case.[70]

X   Judgment

The ECJ may annul a decision of the CFI only on a point of law and, specifically, on the grounds of lack of competence, breach of procedure adversely affecting the interests of the appellant[71] or infringement of Community law.[72] The principle upon which judgment may be given in an appeal can therefore be stated shortly: the ECJ has no competence to put in issue the findings of fact made by the CFI and can only ask whether or not, in the light of those findings, the CFI has correctly applied the law.[73] The application of that principle is not as simple to state. It has been said that a matter decided by the CFI is a matter of law if it restates the existence and extent of a principle of law; and that a challenge directed not to an interpretation of a legal provision but to an assessment of fact is in consequence inadmissible in appeal proceedings.[74] But it has also been said that, although the function of the appeal procedure is limited to removing errors of law in order to avoid divergences in the application and interpretation of the law, breach of Community law (as a ground of appeal) is to be understood as covering all errors of law, including errors of interpretation, erroneous determination of the applicable rule of law and the

---

68 RP-ECJ 120. See, for example, the *Virgili-Schettini* case (above, note 61) at 5221. It should be noted that, although the oral procedure was dispensed with, the advocate general still delivered an opinion.

69 The same limit on the raising of new pleas in law at the hearing applies in appeal proceedings as in a direct action: RP-ECJ 42(2) (applied by virtue of RP-ECJ 118).

70 The judge-rapporteur's report, which takes the place of the report for the hearing, is sent to the parties. As in the case of the dispensing with the oral procedure in direct actions, no practice seems to have emerged regarding the delivery of the advocate general's opinion (see chapter 2, section IV.C, pp 79 et seq). As F Hubeau points out ((1991) C de D Eur 499 at 515, note 31), the explanation for some of the cases where an opinion has been delivered, although the oral procedure has been dispensed with, cannot lie in the fact that the Rules of Procedure in force between 7 June 1989 and 1 September 1991 (when the current rules came into effect) expressly so provided: the opinions in question were delivered after the current rules came into force. The procedure followed in Case C-18/91P *V v European Parliament* [1992] ECR I-3997 suggests either that, as Hubeau suggests (ibid, at note 31*bis*), the ECJ has determined that dispensing with the oral procedure does not involve any dispensing with the advocate general's opinion or that the delivery of an opinion is possible but not obligatory.

71 It would seem, therefore, that an appeal cannot be brought on the ground of a breach of procedure adversely affecting a person other than the appellant. The procedural irregularity must have had an influence on the judgment of the CFI; *Eppe* (above, note 66) per Advocate General Darmon, paras 23–25.

72 ECSC and EC Statutes, art 51; Euratom Statute, art 52.

73 Eg Case C-283/90P *Vidrányi v Commission* [1991] ECR I-4339 (paras 12–13); Case C-132/90P *Schwedler v European Parliament* [1991] ECR I-5745 (paras 9–11); *Hochbaum v Commission* (above, note 25) paras 9 and 16; *F v Commission* (above, note 63) paras 6–7; Case C-115/92P *European Parliament v Volger*, 9 December 1993, para 15.

74 The *Pincherle* case (above, note 20: opinion of Advocate General Darmon, paras 55 and 74).

erroneous characterisation of the facts, resulting in the application of a rule of law to a case that does not fall within it.[75] Another view which has been expressed is that, in an appeal, not only are grounds of fact inadmissible but the ECJ may also take no account of arguments of fact concerning the substance of the case which are raised in support of the parties' pleas in law; the ECJ can examine only the decision appealed against and the procedure before the CFI; and it is bound by the CFI's findings of fact.[76]

To begin with matters of law, not all errors of law result in the quashing or annulment of a decision of the CFI. In general, an error of law made by the CFI is not sufficient to cause its decision to be quashed if the error relates to a conclusion to which the CFI could properly have come in any event[77] or to an alternative ground on which the decision is based.[78] In relation to breach of procedure, a failure to give any or any sufficient reasons is clearly a ground on which a decision of the CFI can be challenged.[79] On the other hand, a failure to give reasons for departing from previous case law is not a defect justifying the annulment of the decision appealed against because the CFI is not bound by case law[80] (although such a departure, if unjustified, may reveal an infringement of Community law). A failure by the CFI to indicate clearly which acts have been annulled is a defect which can be relied on because it prevents the ECJ from verifying whether or not the decision appealed against infringes Community law.[81] A decision of the CFI on whether or not to order a measure of enquiry and, if so, which kind of measure to order is entirely a matter of discretion and therefore appears to provide no basis on which an appeal can be founded even if no reasons are given for the decision[82] unless, presumably, the decision is manifestly unreasonable. The following also do not ground an appeal: a decision of the CFI to deal with an objection to admissibility separately instead of joining it to the substance and a decision requiring the applicant to have his application signed by a lawyer in circumstances where the applicant is himself a lawyer.[83]

Passing now to matters of fact, the furthest that the ECJ can go into matters of fact is to determine whether or not the legal characterisation made by the CFI of the facts found by it is correct.[84] Questions of fact over which the ECJ exercises no appellate jusisdiction include the following: facts which have not been the subject of debate before the CFI;[85] errors of fact relating to the

75 Case C-32/90P *Schwedler v European Parliament* (above, note 73) at 5757 (Advocate General Tesauro). Thus, in his view, an appeal can be based on the allegation that a particular fact is not sufficient in law to produce certain legal consequences (see at 5758 et seq.). See also the *Vidranyi* case (above, note 73) at 4354–4357 (Advocate General Lenz); Case C-145/90P *Costacurta v Commission* [1991] ECR I-5449 at 5459 (Advocate General van Gerven).

76 *European Parliament v Frederiksen* (above, note 60) opinion of Advocate General van Gerven (para 2).

77 Ibid, paras 25–26. In order to avoid an injustice, the ECJ must satisfy itself that the opposing parties would not be successful on some other point put to the CFI before the ECJ decides in favour of the appellant: *Commission v Gill* (above, note 61) at 4803 (Advocate General Jacobs).

78 The *Frederiksen* case (above, note 60), para 31.

79 Eg Case C-68/91P *Moritz v Commission* [1992] ECR I-6849 (paras 21–26 and para 7 of the opinion of Advocate General van Gerven).

80 *Commission v Albani* (above, note 44), opinion of Advocate General van Gerven (para 16).

81 Ibid (paras 24–25).

82 *Moritz v Commission* (above, note 79) at 6870 (Advocate General van Gerven).

83 The *Viciano* case (above, note 36) paras 4–8.

84 Case C-220/91P *Commission v Stahlwerke Peine-Salzgitter AG* [1993] ECR I-2393 (paras 39 and 52); *Commission v Lualdi* (above, note 8) per Advocate General Lenz, para 23; Case C-53/92P *Hilti AG v Commission* (unreported, per Advocate General Jacobs, paras 8–12 and 46–49); Case C-137/92P *Commission v BASF AG* (unreported, per Advocate General van Gerven, paras 9 and 24).

85 The *Pincherle* case (above, note 20: opinion of Advocate General Darmon, para 106). The ECJ cannot consider a ground of appeal based on evidence that was not before the CFI: the *Viciano* case (above, note 36) para 10.

substance of the case, where the issue on the appeal relates to the admissibility of certain claims made at first instance;[86] the question whether or not a delay is reasonable;[87] the finding by the ECJ that the appellant's personal report for a particular period was worse than before;[88] the finding that a hearing in administrative proceedings (in casu, a medical committee) was sufficient;[89] inferences drawn from documents;[90] the finding by the CFI that an assessment made by a medical committee was medical in nature;[91] the finding by the CFI that there is no evidence to support a particular assertion of fact;[92] the finding that the action of a person results from his own choice.[93]

The distinction between matters of facts and matters of law is sometimes difficult to draw. Since a material error of fact may often flow from an error of law (such as an error relating to the admissibility of evidence, the burden or standard of proof and the sufficiency of the evidence in law) and also results in an error of law, a rigid distinction between the points of law on which the ECJ can review a decision of the CFI and the matters of fact in relation to which it cannot do so may not be sustainable in the course of time. In that respect, it should be noted that, in Case C-294/91P *Sebastiani v European Parliament*[94] it was held that errors of fact could not be relied on to contest the decision of the CFI on the substance of the case because, on the basis of the uncontested facts, the CFI could only have dismissed the case. That ruling should not be taken to herald any acceptance by the ECJ that alleged errors of fact can be taken into account in appeal proceedings. The judgment seems instead to have expressed a slightly different principle, namely, that, even if there is a manifest error of fact in the decision appealed against (such that the CFI can be said not to have made a finding of fact at all or not to have observed correctly Community law when making its findings of fact), such an error is not sufficient in itself to cause the decision appealed against to be annulled unless the error is material to the CFI's decision. It is well established that, in an appeal, a ground of appeal which contests a finding of fact or raises an issue of fact is inadmissible.[95]

The appeal may have one of four outcomes:

(1)   the appeal may be dismissed, in which case any limitation on the effect of the decision appealed against, whether imposed under the Statutes or by order of the President of the ECJ, ceases and the decision appealed against may only be reviewed (where appropriate) pursuant to any of the exceptional review procedures applicable to judgments;[96]

(2)   the appeal may be upheld and the decision appealed against annulled[97] without more,[98] in which case the dispute has been decided definitively,

86 Case C-294/91P *Sebastiani v European Parliament* [1992] ECR I-4997 (para 13).

87 The *Pincherle* case (above, note 20) opinion of Advocate General Darmon (para 78).

88 The *Turner* case (above, note 36) para 13.

89 The *Vidranyi* case (above, note 73) paras 14–15.

90 Ibid paras 16–18; *F v Commission* (above, note 63) paras 8–11.

91 *F v Commission* (ibid) paras 17–18.

92 The *Hochbaum* case (above, note 25) para 9.

93 The *Schwedler* case (above, note 73) para 11.

94 Above (note 86), para 14.

95 Case C-378/90P *Pitrone v Commission* [1992] ECR I-2375 (para 12); *V v European Parliament* (above, note 70) paras 15–17 and 42–44.

96 See chapter 16.

97 The Statutes use the word 'quash' (ECSC and EC Statutes, art 54, first subpara; Euratom Statute, art 55, first subpara); the Rules of Procedure use the expression 'set aside' (eg RP-ECJ 113(1)); the case law uses the word 'annul'.

98 An outcome appropriate where, for example, the decision appealed against wrongly annulled the contested act. It may be appropriate for the ECJ to reject formally the respondent's form of order if, in addition to claiming the dismissal of the appeal, it also claims the annulment of the act contested at first instance: eg Case C-345/90P *European Parliament v Hanning* [1992] ECR I-949 (paras 35–38).

subject only to the exceptional review procedures applicable to judgments (which could be invoked only in respect of the judgment of the ECJ);

(3) the appeal may be upheld and the decision appealed against annulled but the ECJ may then make an affirmative ruling on the matters in dispute,[99] in which case, as in (2) above, the dispute has been decided definitively by the ECJ subject only to the exceptional review procedures applicable to the ECJ's judgment;

(4) the appeal may be upheld and the decision appealed against annulled but the matters in dispute may then be remitted by the ECJ to the CFI for it to decide in the light of the ECJ's judgment, in which case proceedings do not come to an end until the CFI has dealt with the matters remitted to it (subject to any further appeal that may be made and to the exceptional review procedures applicable to judgments).[1]

In the case of a successful appeal brought by a member state or Community institution that was not a party to the proceedings at first instance (even as an intervener), the ECJ may, if it considers it to be necessary, state which of the effects of the decision of the CFI which has been quashed shall be considered as definitive in respect of the parties to the litigation.[2] Thus, the ECJ may limit the effect of its judgment, so far as the legal relationship between the parties to the case at first instance is concerned, where it is in the interests of justice to do so.

When the ECJ upholds an appeal, it is not obliged to rule definitively on the case but may in its discretion select any one of the different options open to it.[3] Which option is to be taken depends upon the circumstances. Where the CFI did not rule on all the matters at issue before it, the annulment of its decision cannot lead to a final decision in the case and the matter must be remitted to the CFI for it to rule on the remaining issues unless a ruling on those issues could not affect the outcome. The same applies where the result of annulling the CFI's decision is that it is necessary to reassess the facts in the light of the ECJ's ruling on the relevant legal issues or find further facts.[4] On the other hand, where the result of the appeal leaves no outstanding issues of fact and no issue of law that has not been ventilated at first instance and on appeal, the case can be decided definitively by the ECJ.[5]

---

99 An outcome appropriate where, for example, the ECJ annuls a decision of the CFI wrongly dismissing an action for the annulment of an act: it would not resolve the matters in dispute if the ECJ simply annulled the decision of the CFI.

1 Revision would not apply to the ECJ's judgment: Case C-185/90P-Rev *Gill v Commission* [1992] ECR I-993. It is conceivable that third party proceedings would do so.

2 ECSC and EC Statutes, art 54 (last supbara); Euratom Statute, art 55 (last subpara). The wording of the Statutes reflects that of EC Treaty, art 174 (second subpara) and Euratom Treaty, art 147 (second subpara).

3 Case C-345/90P *European Parliament v Hanning* [1992] ECR I-949 at 977 (Advocate General Darmon).

4 Case C-132/90P *Schwedler v European Parliament* [1991] ECR I-5745 at 5762 (Advocate General Tesauro); Case C-68/91P *Moritz v Commission* [1992] ECR I-6849 (paras 41–42 and at 6879–6880 per Advocate General van Gerven); Case C-36/92P *Samen-werkende Electriciteits produktiebedrijven v Commission* (unreported, per Advocate General Jacobs, para 72).

5 Case C-30/91P *Lestelle v Commission* [1992] ECR I-3755 at 3774 (Advocate General Tesauro) (the ECJ did not in fact agree that the CFI had erred in law); Case C-18/91P *V v European Parliament* [1992] ECR I-3997 (para 52). In the *Hanning* case (above, note 3) at 977, Advocate General Darmon suggested that the matter would have to be remitted to the CFI if a decision on the issues on which it had not ruled would require the ECJ to rule on the facts of the case, thus implying that, if the outstanding issues were matters of law, the case could be decided definitively by the ECJ. There may, however, be circumstances where the outstanding issues of law are highly controversial and, if they have not been considered by the CFI, it may be appropriate to remit the case to the CFI so that any eventual ruling of the ECJ on them is made by it in the exercise of its appellate functions.

XI   Remission to the CFI

When the ECJ sets aside a judgment or order of the CFI and refers the case back to the CFI, the extent of the jurisdiction of the CFI over the case is determined by the judgment referring the matter to the CFI.[6] In particular, the questions of law decided by the ECJ in the appeal proceedings are binding on the CFI;[7] and, where it follows from the ECJ's judgment (but not otherwise) that the facts found in the decision appealed against cannot be relied on, those findings cease to bind the CFI and the parties to the case.[8] Where the decision appealed against was made by a chamber of the CFI, the President of the CFI may assign the case to a different chamber composed of the same number of judges, but is not obliged to do so.[9] Where the decision appealed against was made by the CFI in plenary session, the case must be assigned to the CFI sitting in plenary session.[10] The judgment of the ECJ may reveal that the outstanding issues are easier, or more difficult, to resolve than was apparent at the time of the original judgment at first instance. In that event, it may be more appropriate for the case to be heard and determined by, as the case may be, a smaller, or larger, chamber or by the CFI in plenary session. That decision is not made when the case is assigned to a chamber or to the CFI in plenary session; instead, it may be made by the judges to whom the case has been assigned.[11]

Where the written procedure in the case has already been completed when the judgment of the ECJ remitting the matter to the CFI was delivered, the next step in the procedure before the CFI is that the applicant in the proceedings before the CFI (that is, the party who commenced the action determined at first instance by the CFI) may lodge a statement of written observations within two months of service on him of the judgment of the ECJ.[12] The applicant is not obliged to lodge such a statement. The Rules of Procedure do not indicate what are the consequences if one is not lodged in time. On one view, the onus lies on the applicant to set in motion the procedure to be followed; if, for some reason, he decides not to do so, the effect is the same as if the application had been withdrawn and the proceedings come to an end. On the other view, the remission of the case to the CFI by judgment of the ECJ imposes an obligation on the CFI to determine the dispute in accordance with the ruling of the ECJ and that obligation transcends any private interests of the parties to the litigation. In consequence, the proceedings continue but, in the absence of any statement of written observations from the applicant, the written part of the procedure ends immediately (subject to the right of any intervener to lodge a statement of written observations) and the CFI proceeds

---

6   RP-CFI 117. Where the appeal is decided by the President of the ECJ under the summary procedure, the CFI (in the case of an appeal concerning an application to intervene) or the President of the CFI (in the case of an appeal concerning the grant of interim relief) will be bound by the President of the ECJ's decision on the points of law determined in the appeal.

7   ECSC and EC Statutes, art 54 (second subpara); Euratom Statute, art 55 (second subpara).

8   Case T-43/89RV *Gill v Commission* [1993] ECR II-303 (paras 51–52).

9   RP-CFI 118(1). It would seem that, ordinarily, the case should be heard by a chamber of the same number of judges but it need not be a different chamber from that which delivered the decision appealed against. In elaborating its rules on this point, the CFI wished to establish a flexible system for dealing with the situation: Cruz Vilaça *Yearbook of European law*, vol 10, pp 50–51.

10   RP-CFI 118(2).

11   RP-CFI 118(3), which incorporates RP-CFI 14 and 51. The judge-rapporteur is appointed in the same way as in a direct action: see RP-CFI 13(2), which applies by virtue of RP-CFI 118(3).

12   RP-CFI 119(1)(a).

to the next stage. If the applicant does lodge a statement of written observations in time, the statement is served on the defendant and he is given a period of not less than two months (running from service on him of the ECJ's judgment) within which to lodge his own statement of written observations.[13] If the defendant fails to do so, it does not seem that the applicant can apply for judgment by default. Instead, the written part of the procedure closes (subject to the right of any intervener to lodge a statement of written observations) and the CFI proceeds to the next stage. Where the applicant has lodged a statement of written observations, that statement is served on any intervener in the proceedings at the same time as the intervener is served with any statement of written observations lodged by the defendant. The intervener may lodge a statement of written observations. The time limit for doing so is at most one month from service on him of the statements of the other parties, save where the expiry of that period would require the intervener to lodge the statement within two months of the service on him of the judgment of the ECJ.[14] Thus, the intervener has a minimum of two months from the service of the judgment in which to lodge a statement. The Rules of Procedure envisage only one round of written statements but, if the circumstances justify it, the CFI may allow supplementary statements of written observations to be lodged.[15]

Where the written procedure before the CFI has not been completed by the time of the delivery of the judgment of the ECJ remitting the matter to the CFI, it resumes from the point which it had reached, by means of measures of organisation of procedure adopted by the CFI.[16] The remainder of the written procedure is therefore organised on an ad hoc basis in the light of the circumstances of the case.[17]

The written procedure is conducted in accordance with the rules relating to the form and content of written pleadings applicable in an ordinary direct action, mutatis mutandis.[18] The same rules relating to the joinder of proceedings, legal aid, discontinuance, service, time limits, measures of organisation of procedure, measures of enquiry,[19] stay, the conduct of the oral procedure, the form and content of judgments (including the procedures for rectifying and supplementing a judgment) and costs also apply.[20] Although the Rules of Procedure provide expressly that the procedure shall be conducted in accordance with Title II of the Rules (which covers the aspects of procedure just mentioned),[21] it does not seem to be correct to infer that no provisions other than those contained in that Title can apply. For one thing, the rules relating to the language of the case must still apply, yet those rules are to be found in Title I of the CFI's Rules of Procedure. A more important consideration is that, when the case has been remitted to the CFI, there may still be a need for interim relief pending a final determination of all the issues in the case. Such relief cannot be granted by the ECJ or the President of the ECJ because, after the matter has been remitted to the CFI, the ECJ no longer has jurisdiction over the case. It seems to follow that the application of Title II of the CFI's

---

13 RP-CFI 119(1)(b).
14 RP-CFI 119(1)(c).
15 RP-CFI 119(3). In *Gill v Commission* (above, note 8) para 18, the parties lodged only one set of statements.
16 RP-CFI 119(2).
17 RP-CFI 119(3) also applies.
18 See RP-CFI 43–48, which apply by virtue of RP-CFI 120.
19 *Gill v Commission* (above, note 8) para 64.
20 RP-CFI 120.
21 RP-CFI 120.

Rules of Procedure is without prejudice to the application of the other parts of those Rules, where appropriate.

It does not seem that a third party may be allowed to intervene in the case once it has been remitted to the CFI because the remission of the case does not appear to cause the time for applying to intervene to start running again. On the other hand, if a third party to the proceedings at first instance has intervened in the appeal proceedings, it seems to remain a party to the action after its remission to the CFI as long as the matters remitted to the CFI include matters affecting the position of the intervener (even if those matters relate only to the question of costs).[22]

The steps noted above are apt for dealing with cases where the decision appealed against was a final decision, a decision disposing of the substantive issues in the case in part only or a decision disposing of a procedural issue concerning lack of competence or inadmissibility. Where the decision appealed against dismissed an application to intervene or dealt with an application for some form of interim relief or the stay of enforcement of a decision of the Council or Commission, a less elaborate procedure would be more appropriate. In the somewhat theoretical situation of the remission of the question of an application to intervene, it is likely that the only decision remaining for the CFI to make is to decide definitively on the application. Where necessary, the parties to the proceedings before the CFI could be invited to lodge further written observations on the application to intervene and then the decision would be made. In the case of the grant or refusal of interim relief, it is more likely that there may be a need to hear the parties and obtain further information. In view of the degree of urgency, matters may be expedited by the CFI (more likely, the President of the CFI) fixing the date for a hearing of the matter and asking the parties to state at the hearing their views on particular points that seem to arise from the appeal. Depending upon the complexity of the case and the time available, the lodgment of a single round of written observations before the hearing cannot be excluded.

In its judgment in the case, the CFI disposes of the remaining issues and decides on the costs both of the proceedings before it and of the appeal proceedings before the ECJ[23] save to the extent that the ECJ has already ruled on the latter.[24] The judgment may be the subject of another appeal to the ECJ or to the exceptional review proceedings applicable to all judgments.[25]

---

22 *Gill v Commission* (above, note 8) para 24.
23 RP-CFI 121. The usual rules relating to the award of costs apply: see chapter 14.
24 *Gill v Commission* (above, note 8) paras 66–67; Case T-20/89 *RV Moritz v Commission*, 16 December 1993 (paras 27–28).
25 See further chapter 16.

CHAPTER 16

Judgments and decisions of the Court

I Forms and procedure

Decisions of the Court are generally taken in closed session.[1] Where they concern the Court's own administration, both the advocates general (in the case only of the ECJ) and the Registrar are present, in addition to the judges. The first take part in the discussions and have a vote; the second does not have a vote and may be excluded by the Court.[2] Where the Court sits without the Registrar being present, minutes of the meeting are kept, where necessary, by the most junior judge and are signed by him and the President.[3] Decisions are reached by majority vote and every member of the Court attending is entitled to give his views on the matter under discussion.[4]

Decisions of a judicial nature are made either in an administrative meeting attended by the advocate general (where there is one) or by the judges deliberating alone in camera. As a general rule, the matters decided in the administrative meeting are of a procedural nature while those decided in camera resolve issues of substance in a case. The former are recorded in the minutes of the administrative meeting and, where necessary, are subsequently drawn up in the form of an order; the latter take various forms and may, depending on the nature of the decision and of the proceedings in which it is delivered, be in the form of an order, a judgment or some other decision envisaged in the instruments governing the Court.[5] In any event, the decision can be taken only if:

(1) there is a quorum;[6] if it is found that there is no quorum, the sitting is adjourned by the President until there is one;[7]

---

1 RP-ECJ 27(1); RP-CFI 33(1). The Rules of Procedure use the terms 'deliberate' or 'deliberations' to describe the process of reaching both administrative decisions (RP-ECJ 27(7); RP-CFI 33(7)) and judicial decisions (RP-ECJ 27(2); RP-CFI 33(2)).
2 RP-ECJ 27(7); RP-CFI 33(7).
3 RP-ECJ 27(8); RP-CFI 33(8).
4 Cf RP-ECJ 27(3) and (5); RP-CFI 33(3) and (5).
5 For example: decisions made by the Court in proceedings for interim relief are in the form of an order (eg Case 792/79R *Camera Care Ltd v Commission* [1980] ECR 119); decisions terminating proceedings in an action are usually in the form of a judgment but, where the action is terminated because it is inadmissible, the decision may be in the form of an order under RP-ECJ 92(1) or RP-CFI 111 (eg Cases 114–117/79 *Fournier (née Mazière) v Commission* [1980] ECR 1529) or RP-ECJ 91 or RP-CFI 114 (eg Case 192/80 *Geist v Commission* [1981] ECR 1387) or, more rarely, of a judgment (eg Case 19/72 *Thomik v Commission* [1972] ECR 1155, where there was no hearing); decisions made in proceedings brought under art 95 of the ECSC Treaty or art 228 of the EC Treaty are made in the form of an opinion (eg *Opinion 1/61* [1961] ECR 243 and *Opinion 1/78* [1979] ECR 2871 (Re Draft International Agreements on Natural Rubber) while those made in proceedings brought under arts 103–105 of the Euratom Treaty are made in the form of a ruling (eg *Ruling 1/78* [1978] ECR 2151 (Re Draft Convention on the Physical Protection of Nuclear Material, Facilities and Transport).
6 Seven judges for the full Court, three judges for the chambers: see RP-ECJ 26(2) and (3); RP-CFI 32(2) and (3).
7 RP-ECJ 26(2); RP-CFI 32(2). In the case of the chambers, the President of the Court is informed so that another judge can be designated to complete the chamber: RP-ECJ 26(3); RP-CFI 32(3).

(2)   an uneven number of judges participates in the deliberations and votes;[8] if there is an even number of judges, the most junior judge abstains from taking part in the deliberations (unless he or she is the judge-rapporteur, in which case the duty to abstain falls on the judge immediately senior to him or her);[9] and

(3)   only those judges present at the oral proceedings (if any) take part in the deliberations;[10] if one of the judges dies or is otherwise absent and must be replaced by another judge, who did not attend the hearing or the delivery of the advocate general's opinion, in order to maintain a quorum or restore the uneven number of judges required, the oral procedure must be recommenced.

Since the judges deliberate in secret,[11] there are no interpreters present. Every judge taking part in the deliberations can express his views and the reasons for them[12] and may require that any question be formulated in the language of his choice and communicated in writing to the Court or chamber before being put to the vote.[13] The same seems to apply to administrative meetings. It would appear that, in most cases, the deliberations of the Court or a chamber and the discussions in the administrative meeting are carried out in French, which is the common language of the members of the Court. The deliberations may start in various ways:

(1)   by the presentation, orally or in writing, of the judge-rapporteur's analysis of the case;

(2)   by the presentation of a draft judgment or decision drawn up by the judge-rapporteur;

(3)   by a short discussion between the judges which is intended to determine the overall approach to adopt in the case.

In the first and third cases, the next stage is that the judge-rapporteur produces a draft judgment or decision along the lines indicated in the initial discussions. In

8 ECSC Statute, art 18; EC and Euratom Statutes, art 15.

9 RP-ECJ 26(1); RP-CFI 32(1). See, for example, Case T-26/90 *Società Finanziaria Siderurgica Finsider SpA v Commission* [1992] ECR II-1789 (paras 36–39). The most junior judge may attend both the hearing and the deliberations: the prohibition is on him 'taking part'. This could either mean contributing to the discussion of the case or voting. The French text of RP-ECJ 26(1) (and RP-CFI 32(1)) bars the most junior judge from taking part but allows each of the judges present at the deliberations to express his opinion (RP-ECJ 27(3); RP-CFI 33(3)). This suggests that the extra judge is prevented only from voting, ie participating in the final part of the deliberations, the decision on the Court's view of the matter. Other texts, such as the German, English and Italian versions, are plainly against this interpretation and appear to exclude the most junior judge from giving his views: as the English version expresses it, every judge 'taking part in the deliberations' shall state his opinion (RP-ECJ 27(3); RP-CFI 33(3)) but, where there is an even number of judges, the most junior 'shall abstain from taking part in the deliberations' (RP-ECJ 26(1); RP-CFI 32(1)). For the same reason, it is not possible to construe RP-ECJ 26(1) and RP-CFI 32(1) as referring only to the discussions which immediately precede the vote which determines the decision of the Court or chamber: this may only give formal approval to a conclusion which has already been reached (by an even number of judges) in the earlier discussions. But see Pescatore *Court of Justice of the European Communities* p 11. RP-CFI 32(1) is supplemented by RP-CFI 32(4), which provides that, if the number of judges assigned to a chamber of three or five judges exceeds the appropriate number, the president of the chamber will decide which of the judges will be called on to take part in the judgment.

10 RP-ECJ 27(2); RP-CFI 33(2). This rule does not, of course, apply where the decision is made without the parties being heard.

11 ECSC Statute, art 29; EC Statute, art 32; Euratom Statute, art 33.

12 RP-ECJ 27(3); RP-CFI 33(3).

13 RP-ECJ 27(4); RP-CFI 33(4).

all cases, the draft is discussed in detail at a later meeting and several more may be required before all the points have been thrashed out and the text of the decision has been finalised.[14] The first sentence of RP-ECJ 27(5) and RP-CFI 33(5), respectively, say: 'The conclusions reached by the majority of the Judges after final discussion shall determine the decision of the Court.' The decision need not, therefore, be unanimous. The majority view is determined by a vote, the judges casting their votes in reverse order of precedence.[15] Differences of view on the substance, wording or order of questions or on the interpretation of the voting are resolved by decisions of the Court or chamber,[16] which appears to mean by another vote. The President does not have a casting vote, the number of judges participating being uneven, and dissenting views are not made public.

Under RP-ECJ 64(2) and RP-CFI 82(2), the original of a judgment is signed by the President, the judges who took part in the deliberations and the Registrar. This goes further than the Statutes: the ECSC Statute[17] requires the signature of the President, the judge-rapporteur and the Registrar; the EC and Euratom Statutes[18] require that of the President and of the Registrar only. In Case 5/55 *ASSIDER v High Authority*[19] one judge, who had taken part in the deliberations at which the Court reached its decision and who had signed the operative part of the judgment, was unable to sign the judgment when it was delivered in open court and so the report omits his name. This suggests that a failure to sign the judgment is not a defect sufficient to vitiate it: the decision of the Court or chamber is made when its opinion is formed on the basis of a majority vote in the deliberations; the requirement that the record of the decision, contained in the text of the judgment, be signed is purely formal and has no evidential significance. The same procedure is followed, mutatis mutandis, in respect of all decisions reached in the deliberations whether or not in the form of a judgment, ie the decision is made when the judges vote on, and thereby approve, the decision. At this stage, the decision does not appear to be formally approved by signing the draft or a minute of the decision at the end of the deliberations, as seems to have been the practice at the time of the *ASSIDER* case. In the case of judgments, the original of the judgment is signed just before it is delivered. If, through an oversight, a judge has failed to sign it, the original is subsequently sent to him for signature.

If a judge who participated in the deliberations and the vote were to die after the decision had been made but before it was delivered or, in the alternative, before it was signed by him (as happened in the case of Judge Chloros), this would not, it is thought, affect the validity of the decision or the propriety of delivering it, even if the Court (or chamber) were no longer quorate. Once the decision has been (properly) made, it cannot be unmade by a subsequent event. The delivery of the decision and the signature of the text evidencing it are to this extent mere formalities. They do not affect the reality that a (valid) decision was made.

Signature, in particular, has no legal effect, as can be seen from the case of judgments which, according to RP-ECJ 65 and RP-CFI 83, are (subject to

14 An indication of the way a decision is reached in the deliberations is given by R Lecourt in *Europäische Gerichtsbarkeit und nationale Verfassungsgerichtsbarkeit*, (eds Grewe, Rupp and Schneider) (Nomos, 1981) p 265, and Pescatore, *Court of Justice of the European Communities* pp 22–23.
15 Ie the most junior first: RP-ECJ 27(5), second sentence; RP-CFI 33(5), second sentence.
16 RP-ECJ 27(6); RP-CFI 33(6).
17 Article 31.
18 Articles 34 and 35 respectively.
19 [1954–56] ECR 135 at 145.

certain qualifications affecting judgments of the CFI which are not here relevant) binding from the date of delivery in open court, not from the date of signing. On the other hand, while failure to deliver a judgment properly or at all does not affect the fact that a decision has been reached by the Court (or chamber), it does determine the legal effect of the decision: until delivered, a judgment is not binding and, in consequence, the Court (or chamber) has not yet exhausted its jurisdiction. It is still, therefore, possible for the judges to modify or even alter radically their decision between the time of the vote on the draft judgment, by which it was approved, and the delivery of the judgment in open court. For delivery of a judgment to be effective, there must be substantial compliance with the conditions laid down for delivery, viz reading in open court, the parties having been duly given notice to attend. The rest is practice. Hence there is no requirement that a judgment be delivered in the presence of the judges, the President of the Court (or chamber) reading out the operative part, as is the current practice.

For the purpose of effective delivery, reading out the entire judgment does not appear to be necessary (and is not the practice). It is arguable that, similarly, delivery is not vitiated if the parties are not given due notice to attend because such a defect is in any event perfected by service on them of a certified copy of the judgment. It is this which, for practical purposes, constitutes due notice of the delivery of the judgment because the parties rarely attend the Court at the time the judgment is read out. It is doubtful if this argument can be sustained. The consequence of effective delivery is that the judgment is binding and thereby determines the rights and duties of the parties (albeit, it may be, retrospectively); proceedings can thenceforth be commenced for its enforcement. It is in the interests of the proper administration of justice that the parties are given due notice in advance of the date on which these consequences are settled. If there is no notice, the parties may be led in ignorance to contravene their legal obligations. For the same reasons, the manner in which the judgment is delivered in open court must reveal the essential parts of the judgment which determine the legal position of the parties. The present system, whereby the operative part is read out and complete copies of the judgment are made available to persons attending the Court, satisfies the requirement of due notice. It is not an essential condition of effective delivery that the parties attend the delivery in open court in person or by representation. It is only essential that there be (1) due notice of the date of delivery and (2) due notice, given on the date of delivery, of the essential contents of the judgment. If the parties, being duly forewarned, decline to attend, the consequences are their own. It follows, therefore, that failure to serve the parties with certified copies of the judgment does not affect the legal effects of the judgment, although a party might not, of course, be able to enforce the judgment in a member state.

In contrast to judgments, the position regarding the delivery of other decisions of the Court is unclear. The question is of importance only in the case of orders granting interim relief. Usually the President gives the parties an indication of the date on which the order will be made (if he does not grant or refuse relief immediately) but the order is not read out or delivered in open court. Instead, the text of the order is served on the parties 'forthwith'. The better view seems to be that the order is binding when the parties are given due notice of its terms, but not before. There does not, however, appear to be any clear authority for this and it is arguable that the order is binding immediately it is made.

The form of a judgment[20] is defined in the Statutes and the Rules of

---

20 Set out above: see chapter 2, p 93.

Procedure but no requirements of form and content are laid down with regard to the other types of decisions the Court may make. Of these the most numerous are orders. The form of order made in proceedings for interim relief is not uniform but the tendency is to follow the same basic pattern as judgments: an introductory part setting out the facts, the course taken by the proceedings and the arguments of the parties, followed by the reasoning behind the decision and, lastly, the order made. Other orders, such as those allowing the intervention of a third party, tend to be much shorter and the reasoning behind the decision exiguous or even non-existent. As a general principle, the Court is obliged to give reasons for its decisions, particularly where the decision dismisses a complaint raised before the Court.[21] It appears that the duty to give reasons may be discharged by a reference in the judgment to the reasons given in the advocate general's opinion.[22] Whereas judgments are delivered in open court, orders are simply served on the parties.

II Effect of judgments and orders

The legal consequences of a judgment or order depend in large part on the nature of the proceedings in which it is delivered and in part on the stage in those proceedings at which it is made. For example, an order joining cases is materially different in its effects from an order granting interim relief; and a judgment of a declaratory nature such as is delivered typically in proceedings under art 169 of the EEC Treaty is materially different in its effects from a judgment finding the Community to be liable in damages and requiring a certain sum of money to be paid to the applicant. In more general terms, the characteristic effects of a judgment are that:

(1) the Court is left functus officio;
(2) the parties are bound by the decision (the principle of res judicata);[23] and
(3) the decision can be enforced.[24]

The finality of a judgment in relation to the substance of the litigation, which is exemplified in those characteristics, is the principal distinguishing feature between judgments and orders. The finality of a judgment may be questioned only in exceptional cases and in accordance with procedures listed exhaustively in the procedural rules governing the Court.[25] The circumstances in which the finality of a judgment can be called into question will be described after the application of the characteristic effects of a judgment (in the strict sense) to certain types of judgment and order has been outlined.

---

21 Case C-283/90P *Vidrányi v Commission* [1991] ECR I-4339 (para 29).
22 Case C-59/92 *Hauptzollamt Hamburg-St Annen v Ebbe Sönnischen GmbH* [1993] ECR I-2193. In the early years, the Court occcasionally adopted expressly the reasons given by the advocate general in his opinion on a particular point. The practice died out after a few years and re-emerged in the mid-1980s, possibly as a result of the persuasive efforts of Sir Gordon Slynn. The *Hamburg-St Annen* case was the first in which the Court gave no reasons at all for its ruling other than a general reference to the advocate general's opinion.
23 Eg Case C-56/91 *Greece v Commission* [1993] ECR I-3433, paras 16–17 (rejection of a claim because it contested a finding made in a previous judgment delivered in proceedings between the same parties). Res judicata is discussed in more detail in chapter 7, section II.I p 219.
24 Cf P Pescatore *Introduction à la Science du Droit* para 266. The effect of judgments as a source of Community law is discussed by Lord Mackenzie Stuart and JP Warner in *Europäische Gerichtsbarkeit und nationale Verfassungsgerichtsbarkeit* p 273 and by T Koopmans in *Essays in European Law and Integration* (eds D O'Keeffe and HG Schermers) (Kluwer, 1982) p 11.
25 Case 69/85 *Wünsche Handelgesellschaft GmbH & Co v Germany* [1986] ECR 947 (para 14).

Not all decisions made in the form of a judgment have all the characteristic effects of a judgment in the strict sense. Judgments made in proceedings for a preliminary ruling, for example, do not bind the parties because the nature of the proceedings is non-contentious. It follows that the judgment cannot, strictly speaking, be enforced. This does not mean that it has no legal effect: it is binding on the national court making the reference[26] and, since its effect is declaratory,[27] a judgment interpreting a provision of Community law or finding it to be invalid may also be relied on in other proceedings.[28] Delivery of the judgment does, however, leave the Court functus officio. In consequence, once the Court has pronounced the preliminary ruling, it has exhausted its jurisdiction in the matter and, since the proceedings in which it is delivered are non-contentious, the parties cannot apply to vary the judgment in some way, even though various procedures allowing them to do so in the case of 'judgments' do exist.[29]

In contentious proceedings, judgments are interlocutory,[30] final or mixed. Interlocutory judgments are binding on the parties but do not leave the Court functus officio, final judgment on the matter being reserved for some reason, eg pending production of further evidence,[31] the completion of an administrative procedure,[32] agreement between the parties on the quantum of damages held in the interlocutory judgment to be recoverable,[33] an out-of-court settlement[34] or a re-examination of the dispute by the parties in the light of the legal considerations set out in the interlocutory judgment.[35] In such cases the dispute between the parties may be terminated by agreement between them on the outstanding issues, leaving it unnecessary for the Court to give final judgment on those issues (save in relation to costs)[36] or (in the absence of agreement) the remaining issues may have to be decided by the Court.[37] Sometimes interlocutory judgments decide some issues or heads of claim, leaving others to be decided in the final judgment closing the proceedings,[38] in

26 Eg Case 29/68 *Milch- Fett- und Eierkontor GmbH v Hauptzollamt Saarbrücken (No 2)* [1969] ECR 165 at paras 2–3; Case 52/76 *Benedetti v Munari Fratelli SAS* [1977] ECR 163 at para 26 and at 193 (Advocate General Reischl); Case 112/76 *Manzoni v Fonds National de Retraite des Ouvriers Mineurs* [1977] ECR 1647 at 1662 (Advocate General Warner); *Wünsche Handelgesellschaft GmbH & Co v Germany* (ibid) para 13.
27 Cf Case 61/79 *Amministrazione delle Finanze dello Stato v Denkavit Italiana Srl* [1980] ECR 1205 at 1232 (Advocate General Reischl).
28 Eg Cases 28–30/62 *Da Costa en Schaake NV v Nederlandse Belastingadministratie* [1963] ECR 31 at 38; Case 238/78 *Ireks-Arkady GmbH v Council and Commission* [1979] ECR 2955 at 2990 (Advocate General Capotorti); Case 66/80 *International Chemical Corpn SpA v Amministrazione delle Finanze dello Stato* [1981] ECR 1191 at para 13.
29 Cf Case 13/67 *Firma Kurt A Becher v Hauptzollamt München–Landsbergerstrasse* [1968] ECR 196; Case 40/70 *Sirena Srl v Eda Srl* [1979] ECR 3169; the *Wünsche* case (above, note 25) para 14.
30 Sometimes described in the English version of the Court reports as 'interim': see, for example, Case 149/79 *Commission v Belgium* [1980] ECR 3881.
31 Cases 5, 7, 13-24/66 *Firma E Kampffmeyer v Commission* [1967] ECR 245; Case 30/66 *Firma Kurt A Becher v Commission* [1967] ECR 285; Case 12/68 *X v Audit Board* [1969] ECR 109; Cases 156/79 and 51/80 *Gratreau v Commission* [1980] ECR 3943.
32 Case 31/71 *Gigante v Commission* [1973] ECR 1353.
33 Eg Case 74/74 *Comptoir National Technique Agricole (CNTA) SA v Commission* [1975] ECR 533; *Ireks-Arkady v Council and Commission* (above, note 28).
34 *Gratreau v Commission* (above, note 31).
35 Eg Case 170/78 *Commission v United Kingdom* [1980] ECR 417 (Re Excise Duties on Wine); *Commission v Belgium* (above, note 30).
36 Eg Cases 256, 257, 265, 267/80, 5 and 51/81 and 282/82 *Birra Würrer SpA v Council and Commission* [1987] ECR 789.
37 Eg Case 131/81 *Berti v Commission* [1985] ECR 645.
38 Eg Case 31/71 *Gigante v Commission* [1975] ECR 337; Case 110/75 *Mills v European Investment Bank* [1976] ECR 955 (admissibility); Case 40/82 *Commission v United Kingdom* [1982] ECR 2793 and [1984] ECR 283 (see [1984] ECR at 286).

which case the Court is functus officio so far as the matters on which it has ruled in the interlocutory judgment are concerned, although it remains seised of the dispute as a whole.[39] Final judgments possess all the characteristic effects of a judgment but do not necessarily preclude the reopening of the dispute in subsequent proceedings.[40] Mixed judgments have the effect of an interlocutory judgment in relation to some issues but are final in regard to others.[41] Since, by and large, interlocutory judgments do not exhaust the Court's jurisdiction over the dispute, it is doubtful if the exceptional procedures for modifying the effects of a judgment, which constitute exceptions to the functus officio rule, apply other than to final judgments or to the final parts of mixed judgments. Decisions in the form of a judgment in which the Court holds that there is no need for it to give judgment[42] do not have the effect of a judgment, save in so far as the award of costs is concerned, because the Court does not decide the dispute before it.

Most decisions made in the form of an order do not have the effects of a judgment. Of the ones that do, the most important, if not the only, are orders granting interim relief and those ruling on costs.[43] The effects of such orders may be varied under the procedures applied to 'judgments' on the ground that the Rules of Procedure envisage decisions which have the effects of a judgment and are not just drawn up in that form, but the position is unclear.

The legal effects of a judgment of the Court may in principle be reversed or altered by a change in the law administered by the Court, such as by an amendment of the Treaties.[44] Such a step affects the legal position as defined by the judgment rather than the judgment itself and is therefore to be distinguished from the various procedures which put in question the finality of a judgment. A decision of the ECJ cannot be put in question by any form of appeal (because none exists) or by means of a reference for a preliminary ruling made by a national court.[45] The position is different in relation to decisions of the CFI: the scope for appealing from decisions of the CFI is considered in chapter 15. In addition, in relation to both Courts, there are some cases[46] where there is provision for review of an order made in the event that

---

39 For a classification of interlocutory judgments, see Vandersanden and Barav, Contentieux Communautaire pp 67–68.
40 Eg the judgment in Case 53/72 *Guillot v Commission* [1974] ECR 791 as explained by Advocate General Capotorti in Case 43/74 *Guillot v Commission* [1977] ECR 1309 at 1341.
41 Eg *Kampffmeyer v Commission* (above, note 31); *Becher v Commission* (above, note 31); Case T-48/90 *Giordani v Commission*, 1 July 1993 (in particular, para 92), where the Court estimated the extent of the damages due to the applicant but nonetheless insisted on the parties agreeing the sum to be paid, thus rendering the judgment final on the question of liability but not on the question of quantum.
42 Eg Case 3/54 *ASSIDER v High Authority* [1954–56] ECR 63; Cases 5, 7 and 8/60 *Meroni & Co v High Authority* [1961] ECR 107; Case 103/63 *Rhenania Schiffahrts- und Speditionsgesellschaft mbH v Commission* [1964] ECR 425; Case 75/69 *Firma Ernst Hake & Co v Commission* [1970] ECR 535; Case 74/81 *Rudolf Flender KG v Commission* [1982] ECR 395. There is no need to proceed to judgment if the injury against which the action is directed no longer exists (see Case 14/81 *Alpha Steel Ltd v Commission* [1982] ECR 749 at 775 (Advocate General Reisch); Case 82/85 *Eurasian Corpn Ltd v Commission* [1985] ECR 3603) or never existed in reality. In the latter case the action may, however, be inadmissible. A decision that there is no issue to decide is usually made in the form of an order (eg Case 75/83 *Ferriere San Carlo v Commission* [1983] ECR 3123) unless the oral procedure has been opened, in which case it is made in the form of a judgment.
43 The enforceability of such orders is discussed below.
44 Cf Cases C-106/91, C-110/91, C-152/91 and C-200/91 *Ten Oever v Stichting Bedrijfspensioenfonds*, unreported (opinion of Advocate General van Gerven, para 23).
45 The *Wünsche* case (above, note 25) paras 15–16.
46 Eg legal aid (RP-ECJ 76(4); RP-CFI 96) and interim relief (RP-ECJ 84(2) and 87; RP-CFI 105(2) and 108).

there is a change in circumstances. In the case of judgments, the Rules of Procedure allow:

(1)   rectification, to remove slips and other similar errors;[47]
(2)   the supplementing of a judgment;[48]
(3)   setting aside a judgment given in default of defence;[49]
(4)   review on application by a third party;[50]
(5)   revision on application by a party;[51] and
(6)   interpretation of a judgment.[52]

Of these, only the third, fourth and fifth constitute review proceedings stricto sensu which put in question the finality of a judgment. Although stated to apply to 'judgments', these proceedings, as has been seen, do not all apply to every decision made in the form of a judgment and it is not excluded that they may apply to other decisions which, whatever their form, have the characteristic effects of a judgment.

Judgments are binding, and therefore take effect, from the date of delivery.[53] The precise effect of the judgment depends on the nature of the proceedings in which it was delivered. A judgment delivered in a successful action for damages gives rise to an enforceable obligation on the part of the defendant to compensate. In addition to a declaration of voidness or, as the case may be, a declaration that the defendant has unlawfully failed to act, a judgment annulling an act or finding that the defendant has unlawfully failed to act gives rise to an immediate obligation on the part of the defendant to take the measures necessary to comply with the judgment.[54] Such judgments on occasion provide that the matter is to be remitted to the defendant for it to take appropriate remedial action.[55] Such action may include the award of compensation. The steps taken to comply with the judgment may be the subject of later proceedings.[56] A judgment in a successful action against a member state results in a declaration that the defendant has failed to fulfil its obligations under the Treaty and gives rise to an immediate obligation to take the appropriate steps to remedy the situation (including, where appropriate, the award of compensation) and those steps should be completed as soon as possible.[57]

---

47 RP-ECJ 66; RP-CFI 84.
48 RP-ECJ 67; RP-CFI 85.
49 RP-ECJ 94(4)–(6); RP-CFI 122(4)–(6).
50 RP-ECJ 97; RP-CFI 123–124.
51 RP-ECJ 98–100; RP-CFI 125–127.
52 RP-ECJ 102; RP-CFI 129.
53 RP-ECJ 65; RP-CFI 83.
54 ECSC Treaty, art 34; EC Treaty, art 176; Euratom Treaty, art 149. In principle, the effect of the annulment of an act is to reinstate the status quo ante in legal terms. Where other acts have been adopted on the basis of the annulled act or circumstances have changed in consequence of the annulled act, further action (in addition to the annulment of the contested act) is necessary in order to give effect to the restoration of the legal status quo. The restoration of the legal status quo ante required by the annulment of the contested act does not necessarily mean that in every respect the clock must be turned back to the position as it was when the contested act was adopted: see, for example, Case C-242/90P-R *Commission v Albani* [1990] ECR I-4329 (paras 22–25).
55 Eg Cases 129 and 274/82 *Lux v Court of Auditors* [1984] ECR 4127 (para 23); Case 119/83 *Appelbaum v Commission* [1985] ECR 2423 (para 36); Cases 66–68 and 136–140/83 *Hallet v Commission* [1985] ECR 2459 (para 31).
56 Eg Case 21/86 *Samara v Commission* [1987] ECR 795 (para 4). A judgment requiring the defendant to take action can be performed only in a lawful manner and cannot be regarded as authorising the defendant to take unlawful action: Case 134/84 *Williams v Court of Auditors* [1985] ECR 2225 (para 14).
57 EC Treaty, art 171; Euratom Treaty, art 143. See, for example, Case 131/84 *Commission v Italy* [1985] ECR 3531 (para 7); Case 69/86 *Commission v Italy* [1987] ECR 773 (para 8); Cases 227–230/85 *Commission v Belgium* [1988] ECR 1 (para 11); Case C-75/91 *Commission v Netherlands* [1992] ECR I-549.

As can be seen, although a judgment may be prospective in effect, in the sense that it may impose an obligation as to future conduct (such as a positive obligation to compensate or take remedial action; or a negative obligation to refrain from applying a void act or to refrain from persisting in conduct found to be unlawful), a judgment may also be retrospective in effect to the extent that it determines what the law is and always has been; or finds that an act with all the appearances of lawfulness was in truth unlawful and void since its inception; or declares that past conduct was unlawful. The immediate binding effect of a judgment may thus have significant indirect or secondary effects for the past as well as the future. There are two limitations on the binding effect of judgments. The first applies only to certain judgments of the CFI; the second may be applied by the Court itself in the exercise of its discretion.

A decision of the CFI declaring a general decision or general recommendation, within the meaning of the ECSC Treaty, or a regulation, within the meaning of the EC and Euratom Treaties, to be void does not take effect on the delivery of judgment but only when the period for appealing from the judgment has expired or, if an appeal is brought within that period, as from the date of the dismissal of the appeal by the ECJ.[58] The immediate binding effect of a judgment of the CFI may also be limited in the event of an appeal by an order of the President of the ECJ (or the ECJ itself) granting interim relief pending the outcome of the appeal.[59]

Judgments which are declaratory of the law, typically preliminary rulings and judgments annulling an act, are also retrospective in effect in that they state what the law is and always has been from the date on which the legal provision in question came into effect or from the date when the invalid or annulled act was purportedly adopted.[60] They may thus affect transactions that have already been made and, in the case of judgments finding an act to be invalid or void, may affect future transactions in the period between the delivery of the judgment and the taking of appropriate action by the Community institutions in response to it. The Court therefore has power in certain circumstances to limit the temporal effect of its judgments or define in some other way their future effects.[61] When the

---

58 ECSC Statute, art 53 (as amended by Council Decision 93/350); EC Statute, art 53; Euratom Statute, art 54; RP-CFI 83. The date of dismissal of the appeal is the date of the delivery of the ECJ's judgment on the appeal. The Statutes appear to envisage the dismissal of the appeal in its entirety. If the appeal were upheld as to a part and dismissed as to the rest, so that the contested general decision, recommendation or regulation were found by the ECJ to be void in part only, the judgment of the CFI would arguably take effect as to that part (at least if the CFI had given judgment on different parts of the contested act separately in response to different claims made in the proceedings). In complicated cases it might be necessary for the ECJ to specify which part or parts of the contested act could be regarded as definitive.
59 The Statutes, ibid, first sentence.
60 Eg the *Denkavit Italiana* case (above, note 27) para 16; Case 210/87 *Padovani v Amministrazione delle Finanze* [1988] ECR 6177 (paras 12–13); Case 269/87 *Ventura v Landesversicherungsanstalt Schwaben* [1988] ECR 6411 (para 15); Case C-228/92 *Roquette Frères SA v Hauptzollamt Geldern* (unreported, per Advocate General Darmon). In the case of annulment, see EEC Treaty, art 174 (first sentence); Euratom Treaty, art 146 (first sentence). For the difference between annulment and invalidity, see *Roquette* case per Advocate General Darmon.
61 EC Treaty, art 174, and Euratom Treaty, art 146, second sentence (which expressly apply only where a regulation is held to be void): see, for example, Case 264/82 *Timex Corpn v Council and Commission* [1985] ECR 849 (para 32); Case 45/86 *Commission v Council* [1987] ECR 1493 (para 23); Case 51/87 *Commission v Council* [1988] ECR 5459 (para 22); Case C-65/90 *European Parliament v Council* [1992] ECR I-4593 (paras 22–24). The same approach was followed in relation to a directive in Case C-295/90 *European Parliament v Council* [1992] ECR I-4193 (Re Students' Rights) (paras 22–27). In the case of preliminary rulings, see Case 43/75 *Defrenne v SA Belge de Navigation Aérienne* [1976] ECR 455; Case 61/79 *Denkavit* (ibid); Cases 66, 127 and 128/79 *Amministrazione delle Finanze v Salumi* [1980] ECR 1237; Case 109/79 *Maiseries de Beauce v ONIC* [1980] ECR 2883; Case 145/79 *Roquette Frères v Administration des Douanes* [1980] ECR

Court rules on the consequences of the annulment of an act (and, by parity of reasoning, on the consequences of the invalidity of an act), it is not bound by the proposals of the parties but exercises its discretion in the matter.[62] Thus, in Case 51/87 *Commission v Council*[63] regulations dealing with certain tariff preferences taking the form of the suspension of duties were annulled but, instead of them ceasing to have effect, the Court declared their effects to be definitive: the problem with the regulations was the way in which the preferences had been apportioned, not the principle of the preferences; but, had they ceased to have effect upon the delivery of judgment, the full rate of duty would henceforth have been payable on the goods in question until such time as the Community institutions could remedy the situation. In the same way, in Case 300/86 *van Landschoot v Mera*[64] a provision was declared to be invalid because it was discriminative, the discrimination taking the form of an omission; but the ordinary effect of that declaration would have been that the provision could not be applied at all so, in order to avoid the consequences, the Court held that, pending the introduction of new provisions, the invalid provision should continue to be applied and applied in such a way as to avoid the discrimination that had been found to exist. A limitation on the temporal or other effect of a judgment may be made only in the judgment declaring what the law is; if that judgment imposes no such limitation, a limitation cannot be imposed by any subsequent judgment.[65] Where a measure has been held to be invalid on grounds that are equally applicable to a subsequent measure at issue in a later case, the later measure may be regarded as having been implicitly declared invalid by the earlier judgment; but that will not apply if the scope of the earlier judgment was limited in time, unless the facts in the later case arose before the date of the earlier judgment.[66]

III   Rectification

The Court may, of its own motion or on application by one of the parties, made within two weeks of delivery of the judgment, rectify clerical mistakes, errors in calculation and obvious slips.[67] This is only a slip rule and no correction of a legal error may be made by using this procedure.[68] The parties are informed of a suggested correction to the judgment, whether the initiative comes from the Court itself or one of the parties, and may lodge written observations within a period prescribed by the President.[69] The Court's decision is made in closed

2917; Case 112/83 *Société des Produits de Mais SA v Administration des Douanes* [1985] ECR 719 (paras 17–18); Case 33/84 *Fragd SpA v Amministrazione delle Finanze* [1985] ECR 1605; Case 41/84 *Pinna v Caisse d'Allocations Familiales de la Savoie* [1986] ECR 1; Case 24/86 *Blaizot v University of Liège* [1988] ECR 379 (paras 27–34); Case 300/86 *van Landschoot v Mera NV* [1988] ECR 3443 (paras 22–24); Cases C-38/90 and C-151/90 *R v Lomas* [1992] ECR I-1781 (paras 23–30); Case 262/88 *Barber v Guardian Royal Exchange Assurance Group* [1990] ECR I-1889; *Ten Oever v Stichting Bedrijfspensioenfonds* (above, note 44) opinion of Advocate General van Gerven (paras 13–16).

62 Case C-284/90 *Council v European Parliament* [1992] ECR I-2277 (Re Budgetary Surplus) (para 36).
63 Above (note 61).
64 Above (note 61).
65 Case 309/85 *Blaizot v Belgium* [1988] ECR 355 (paras 12–14).
66 *Fragd v Amministrazione delle Finanze* (above, note 61) paras 12–13 and 16–20.
67 RP-ECJ 66(1); RP-CFI 84(1). The rules applies to corrections made after the delivery of judgment, not before. No formal procedure need be followed in order to correct the text of a judgment or order before it has been delivered.
68 Case 27/76 *United Brands Co v Commission* [1978] ECR 345 at 349.
69 RP-ECJ 66(2); RP-CFI 84(2).

session after hearing the advocate general (where appropriate)[70] and takes the form of a Court order which is annexed to the original of the rectified judgment, a note of the order being entered in the margin of the original.[71]

Where application is made by one of the parties, it should comply with RP-ECJ 37 and 38 or, as the case may be, RP-CFI 43 and 44, mutatis mutandis. In particular the form of order in the application should set out in precise terms the amendment sought and the body of the pleading should explain clearly and succinctly why the judgment should be rectified. The mistakes which can be rectified comprise 'purely material errors in a judgment in cases where no difficulty arises concerning the meaning or scope of the decision'[72] In other words, rectification can be used only to remedy errors which conceal or distort the meaning of the decision but not those which may alter its effect.[73] In consequence, it is not available where the object is to amend a finding of law[74] or, it would seem, a material finding of fact. The procedure does not, therefore, constitute a true exception to the principle of res judicata or to the principle that the Court is functus officio once it has given a final judgment in the matter. An application will be rejected in so far as the applicant seeks to re-argue the case.[75] An order may also be rectified under RP-ECJ 66 and RP-CFI 84.[76]

IV Supplementing a judgment

If the Court omits to give a decision on a particular head of claim or on costs, any party may, within one month of service of the judgment, apply to the Court for it to 'supplement' its judgment. This procedure does not apply to judgments given in proceedings for a preliminary ruling because the scope of such proceedings, which are non-contentious, is determined by the referring court and the parties can take no initiative in them.[77] The application is served on the other parties in the usual manner and the President prescribes a period within which they may lodge written observations.[78] The Rules do not provide for a hearing. It seems, therefore, to be within the discretion of the Court to decide whether or not to hear the parties. The Court decides at the same time on the admissibility of the application and on its merits, after hearing the advocate general (where appropriate).[79]

---

70 RP-ECJ 66(3); RP-CFI 84(3). The CFI's Rules of Procedure are ambiguous in that they make no mention of the advocate general. If the matter came before the Court in plenary session and an advocate general had been designated to assist the Court before judgment, the CFI would have to be assisted by the advocate general in accordance with RP-CFI 17. This does not seem to fall within the category of trivial matters in respect of which no advocate general need be involved because, in proceedings before the ECJ, the advocate general must be heard.
71 RP-ECJ 66(4); RP-CFI 84(4). For an example of a rectification order see Case 1/78 *Kenny v Insurance Officer* [1978] ECR 1510, a reference for a preliminary ruling.
72 Cases 19, 21/60, 2 and 3/61 *Société Fives Lille Cail v High Authority* [1961] ECR 314 at 315.
73 Cf Plouvier (1991) *C de D Eur* 428 at 430.
74 *Fives Lille Cail* (above, note 72) at 315–316; *United Brands Co v Commission* (above, note 68).
75 Eg Cases 52 and 55/65 *Germany v Commission* [1966] ECR 159, order of 13 July 1966, unreported.
76 *United Brands Co v Commission* (above, note 68) at 349: rectification of a rectifying order.
77 *Becker v Hauptzollamt München* (above, note 29); a similar order was also made on 16 May 1968 in Case 25/67 *Milch- Fett- und Eierkontor GmbH v Hauptzollamt Saarbrücken* [1968] ECR 207.
78 RP-ECJ 67; RP-CFI 85. So far as the CFI is concerned, the judgment may be supplemented only if the question of costs remains undecided: cf Case T-50/89 *Sparr v Commission* [1990] ECR II-539.
79 RP-ECJ and RP-CFI, ibid. The CFI's Rules make no mention of the advocate general but, in accordance with RP-CFI 17, the advocate general would have to be heard if the matter were before the Court in plenary session and one had been appointed to assist the Court before the judgment was delivered (see note 70 above).

The application, which may be made by either party, must be made in the usual form.[80] A judgment of the ECJ can be supplemented only where the Court has omitted to give a decision on 'a specific head of claim' or on costs. A 'head of claim', in this context, is not merely an argument put forward by one of the parties and refuted by the other. It must be one of the points in the form of order, ie one of the forms of relief sought by one of the parties, not just a principal argument in favour of the relief sought. Thus, an application cannot be made where the ECJ has merely failed to deal with an argument put to it.[81] The scope of the procedure is not expressly limited to cases where the Court has failed to decide on a point by an oversight. Nonetheless, although it could also be said to apply where, for example, the Court has given judgment on liability in an action for damages and left quantum to be agreed between the parties, it is doubtful if this was the intention: RP-ECJ 67 makes available an exceptional remedy, subject to a comparatively short time limit, which suggests that it applies, in the ordinary way, to the final judgment closing the proceedings. In the case of interlocutory judgments, the action may be continued and the remaining claims disposed of in a final judgment without the need for recourse to any other procedure. Like rectification, the power to supplement a judgment is not a true exception to the res judicata and functus officio principles because, ex hypothesi, the Court has not ruled, and therefore has not discharged its functions, in respect of the claim or claims in question.

It is unclear whether application may be made to supplement an order. Ordinarily the need to do so is likely to arise only in the case of orders made in proceedings for interim relief or those which close an interlocutory procedure and should, therefore, contain a direction as to the award of costs. It is arguable that no specific provision in the Rules of Procedure is necessary because, if the Court or the judge dealing with the matter has omitted to decide it, he remains seised of the issue and, therefore, still has jurisdiction to deal with it; all that is necessary is an (informal) approach designed to jog the Court's or judge's memory. The Rules of Procedure do nothing more than define a procedure for making such an approach in the case of a judgment; nothing prevents either the same procedure being followed by analogy in the case of other decisions or an informal application being made. An alternative argument is that RP-ECJ 67 and RP-CFI 85 apply in the case of all decisions, whatever their form, which share the substantive characteristics of a judgment. In any event, there is no good reason that orders should not be supplemented where need be.

V Judgment by default

A Description of the procedure

The defendant in contentious proceedings before the Court is not obliged to submit a defence. If he has been duly served with the application commencing proceedings and has failed to lodge a defence in the proper form within the time prescribed, the applicant may apply for judgment by default.[82] The

---

80 That is, in accordance with RP-ECJ 37 and 38 or RP-CFI 43 and 44.
81 Cf Case 8/78 *Milac GmbH, Gross- und Aussenhandel v Hauptzollamt Freiburg* [1978] ECR 1721 at 1739 (Advocate General Warner): RP-ECJ 63 'does not mean that a judgment must deal with every argument presented to the Court, whether it is in point or not'.
82 ECSC Statute, art 35; EC Statute, art 38; Euratom Statute, art 39; RP-ECJ 94(1); RP-CFI 122(1).

ECSC Statute limits this procedure to cases in which the Court has unlimited jurisdiction. The procedure is rarely used; the first application was, it seems, in 1984[83] but the first application to be dealt with by the Court was in 1988.[84] This may be due in large part to the willingness of the Court to extend the time for submitting a defence and to the rule in the Statutes[85] that no right may be prejudiced by the expiry of a time limit if there is proof of unforeseeable circumstances or of force majeure. The procedure relating to judgment by default falls into two parts: proceedings for obtaining judgment and proceedings for setting it aside. Where the defendant fails to lodge his rejoinder within the time limit fixed for doing so, the pleadings are nevertheless closed and the procedure carries on as usual.[86] There is no 'judgment in default of rejoinder'.

B Obtaining judgment by default

As soon as the time fixed for lodging the defence has expired[87] without any defence having been lodged, the applicant in the action may submit his application for judgment by default. There is no time limit within which such an application must be lodged. If no defence in any form has been lodged, an application for judgment by default seems to be the only way in which the procedure in the action can be continued because the usual procedural rules in an action presuppose the lodging of a defence. If the failure to lodge a defence within time led to the automatic close of the written procedure (as happens where the reply or rejoinder is not lodged within time),[88] there would be no need to make a second application (one for judgment by default) since the Court could proceed directly to the oral procedure. On the other hand, if a defence has been lodged within time but it is defective (in casu, lacking a form of order), it has been suggested that the applicant may apply for judgment by default and that, in the absence of such an application, the usual procedure in an action is to be followed.[89] It would seem that, if the defect in the defence is essentially formal (as may be the case even with the omission of a form of order, where it is nonetheless clear from the body of the pleading that the defendant does oppose the applicant's claims and has serious arguments of fact and law in support), lodging an application for judgment by default serves no useful purpose and would appear, for that reason, to be inappropriate. If the defence is lodged within time and is not defective but discloses no genuine defence, the situation could in principle be characterised as one where no defence had been lodged. In that event, however, it would be simpler for the applicant to waive the right to lodge a reply and thus cause the written procedure to be closed. The alternative reaction, to apply for judgment by default, apart from being (at this stage) controversial, would be a cumbersome method of dealing with the situation. It would necessitate the making of a separate application (for judgment by default), it would not shorten the proceedings and, as a result of the potential availability of the procedure for setting aside a judgment

---

83 Cases 22 and 24/84 *Commission v Luxembourg*: the action was based on EC Treaty, art 169, and was withdrawn after the opening of the oral procedure because the defendant complied with its obligations under Community law.
84 Case 105/87 *Morabito v European Parliament* [1988] ECR 1707.
85 ECSC Statute, art 39; EC Statute, art 42; Euratom Statute, art 43.
86 RP-ECJ 44(1); RP-CFI 52(2).
87 Ie the period fixed by RP-ECJ 40(1) or RP-CFI 46(1), as extended by the President pursuant to RP-ECJ 40(2) or RP-CFI 46(3).
88 See RP-ECJ 44(1); RP-CFI 52(2).
89 Case C-290/89 *Commission v Belgium* [1991] ECR I-2851 at 2859–2860 (Advocate General Lenz).

obtained by default, would risk giving the defendant an opportunity to recover the situation which the defendant would not otherwise have.

If no defence is lodged within time but the defendant should then request the President to exercise his power under RP-ECJ 40 or, as the case may be, RP-CFI 46 to extend the period for lodging the defence, it is submitted that the request should be rejected. To accede to it would encourage the defendant to procrastinate. Quite apart from the practical objections to prolonging the proceedings, it does not appear that the President has power to extend a time period which has already expired. In any event, it is arguable that the President no longer has power to extend the time for lodging the defence under RP-ECJ 40(2) and RP-CFI 46(3) once proceedings for judgment in default have been commenced: once the application for judgment in default has been lodged, the Court and the President must apply the rules applicable in such proceedings. These do not provide for a subsequent extension of time for lodging the defence. The President could conceivably act under RP-ECJ 40(2) or RP-CFI 46(3) only if it were without prejudice to the application for judgment in default, in which case there would be little point in extending the time limit.

Where the applicant has applied for judgment in default after the expiry of the period but before the President has extended it pursuant to a request made by the defendant before it expired, the position would seem to be the same. It is another matter if the applicant agrees to withdraw the application for judgment in default. The President's powers under RP-ECJ 40(2) or RP-CFI 46(3) would then revive. Understandably, the applicant might only be prepared to do this on condition that the defence were lodged promptly and the costs of the application for judgment in default were borne by the defendant. It would, however, be the sensible course to withdraw the application if the defence really were about to be lodged because the normal procedure in an action is better suited to resolving a contested issue. The procedure for obtaining judgment in default envisages the situation where the defendant really is in default. Because the judgment can later be challenged, it is more efficacious to continue the action when the defendant is capable of lodging a defence. On the other hand, if the defence is lodged, but outside the time limit, it is not a bar to obtaining judgment in default.

The Rules of Procedure lay down no specific requirements relating to the content of the application for judgment by default but, like all pleadings, it must comply with RP-ECJ 37 or, as the case may be, RP-CFI 43 and therefore be signed by the party's agent or lawyer, dated, contain as annexes all documents relied on in it and be lodged together with the required number of copies. It goes without saying that it must be drafted in the language of the case. The application is served on the defendant by the Registry and the President fixes a date for the opening of the oral procedure.[90] If the action has attracted one or more intervening parties, the application should also be served on them. Since it commences an ancillary proceeding in the action, it does not appear to be necessary for the interveners to apply to intervene. Parties intervening in support of the defendant are nevertheless not in a position to supply a defence for him and can only oppose the application.

There is no provision for the submission by the defendant of any written defence or observations concerning the application. It seems, however, that the President would, through the Registrar, inform the defendant of the date and time of the hearing so that he may, if he wishes, attend. The Court may

---

90 RP-ECJ 94(1); RP-CFI 122(1).

then consider whether to order a preparatory enquiry.[91] After the hearing, and having heard the views of the advocate general (where there is one), the Court makes its decision. It is unclear whether the advocate general must give his views in open court or not. In the case of applications for interim relief which are heard and determined by the Court, the decision is also given after hearing the advocate general. The current practice is that he delivers a formal opinion in open court but this has not always been so.[92] On the other hand, judgments in revision proceedings are also delivered after hearing the advocate general[93] but it is not the practice to publish the opinion. The reason may be that the judgment is given in closed session.[94] That is not the case with regard to judgment in default so one is entitled to anticipate that the advocate general would give his opinion in open court, as was done in *Morabito v European Parliament*[95] and Case 68/88 *Commission v Greece*.[96]

The decision to give judgment in default of a defence is taken after considering (i) whether the application commencing the action is admissible; (ii) whether the appropriate formalities have been complied with; and (iii) whether the applicant's claim for relief appears to be well founded.[97] Under the second heading, the Court must consider whether the application commencing proceedings and that for judgment by default were duly served on the defendant and whether, if a defence was lodged, it was not in proper form or was out of time.[98] The Court's consideration of the merits of the application seems to be more profound in scope than in the case of applications for interim relief, where the procedure is summary and it is sufficient that there is a prima facie case for the relief sought. Nevertheless, the Court may give judgment in default if it is satisfied that the applicant's claims 'appear' to be well founded; and the Court's task is in essence to verify whether or not that is so.[99] This does not seem to relieve the Court of the duty to consider the merits of the application with care; it seems to indicate only that the exactitude with which the Court can assess the applicant's case is limited by the fact that it does not benefit from hearing the other side of the story.[1] The fact that the Court has specific power to order a preparatory enquiry[2] suggests that it is entitled not to rely on the applicant's *ipse dixit*: thus, in Case 105/87 *Morabito v European Parliament*[3] the Court made enquiries and looked at documents in order to confirm the applicant's assertions of fact. Since the judgment is delivered without considering a defence (there being none ex hypothesi), the assertions made by the applicant which appear to be well founded are regarded as proved

---

91 RP-ECJ 94(2); RP-CFI 122(2). In *Morabito v European Parliament* (above, note 84) the Court asked the applicant to provide certain information and documents when it opened the oral procedure (see at 1709).
92 See Case 19/59R *Geitling Ruhrkohlen-Verkaufsgesellschaft mbH v High Authority* [1960] ECR 34.
93 RP-ECJ 100(1).
94 Ibid.
95 Above (note 84).
96 [1989] ECR 2965. See also Case C-69/92 *Commission v Luxembourg*, 17 November 1993.
97 RP-ECJ 94(2); RP-CFI 122(2). See, for example, Case T-42/89 *Yorck von Wartenburg v European Parliament* [1990] ECR II-31; *Commission v Luxembourg*, ibid.
98 The requirements of form applicable to the defence are those laid down in RP-ECJ 40 and RP-CFI 46, which also incorporate by reference RP-ECJ 38(2)–(5) and RP-CFI 44(2)–(5), respectively.
99 *Commission v Greece* (above, note 96) para 9.
 1 See, to the same effect, Vandersanden and Barav, op cit, p 66. In *Commission v Greece* (ibid) the only arguments of the defendant that the Court appears to have taken into account were those made in the pre-litigation stage of the proceedings.
 2 RP-ECJ 94(2); RP-CFI 122(2).
 3 [1988] ECR 1707 (para 7).

for the purposes of the proceedings,[4] which does not preclude the possibility of the findings made by the Court when giving judgment by default being reconsidered in the context of proceedings to set that judgment aside.

Judgment by default is enforceable but the Court may grant a stay of execution until it has decided on an application to set the judgment aside and it may make execution conditional on the provision of a security.[5] The Rules make clear that the security may be required before any application to set the judgment aside has been made. It is not clear if a stay of execution may also be ordered. However, since the application to set aside must be made within one month of the service of the judgment on the defendant,[6] it does not seem unfair to the applicant to give judgment and then order its execution to be stayed, without such an application being made, until the time for applying to set it aside has expired.

C Setting judgment aside

The Rules do not say so explicitly but it would seem that only the defendant may apply to set aside a judgment in default. It would appear that an intervener would have to make a fresh application to intervene in the proceedings to set aside because the proceedings in which he had already intervened were closed by the judgment in default. If no application to set aside is made by the defendant, an intervener has no further remedy (save, perhaps revision), not even third party proceedings under RP-ECJ 97 or RP-CFI 123-124, because he had the possibility of opposing the application for judgment in default.

The application to set aside the judgment must be made within one month of the date of service of judgment on the defendant and must be lodged in the form prescribed by RP-ECJ 37–38 or, as the case may be, RP-CFI 43–44.[7] The lodging of such an application does not have the effect of staying the enforcement of the judgment unless the Court decides otherwise.[8] In order to obtain a stay, a separate application must be made.[9] After the application to set aside has been served on the other party, the President prescribes a period within which that party must submit his written observations.[10] Under RP-ECJ 94(5), the proceedings continue in accordance with RP-ECJ 44 et seq. In other words, the procedure for setting aside a judgment made in default of defence takes the form of an action to challenge the judgment which is made within one month of the service of it by an application complying with all the requirements for an application commencing proceedings. Instead of the written proceedings following the normal sequence in a direct action of application, defence, reply, rejoinder, the application to set aside is answered by the other party's observations and the written procedure is then closed.[11] The rest of the

---

4 Ibid.
5 RP-ECJ 94(3); RP-CFI 122(3). The security will be released if no application to set aside is made within time or, if such an application is so made, it fails.
6 RP-ECJ 94(4); RP-CFI 122(4).
7 RP-ECJ 94(4); RP-CFI 122(4).
8 ECSC Statute, art 35; EC Statute, art 38; Euratom Statute, art 39.
9 RP-ECJ 89; RP-CFI 110. The procedure to be followed is the same as that for obtaining any other form of interim measure: see chapter 8.
10 RP-ECJ 94(5); RP-CFI 122(5).
11 Wall *The Court of Justice of the European Communities* p 282 and Vandersanden and Barav, op cit, p 485, consider that pleadings should continue until the rejoinder, seemingly on the basis that RP-ECJ 44, to which RP-ECJ 94(5) refers, mentions the rejoinder. No explanation is given to show why, if RP-ECJ 94(5) did intend to reopen the oral procedure from the beginning, it did not refer to RP-ECJ 41 rather than RP-ECJ 44. The latter actually says 'After the rejoinder . . .', thus indicating that it refers to the course of proceedings after the close of written pleadings.

procedure follows as in a direct action: the Court considers the necessity to order preparatory enquiries, opens the oral procedure, hears the advocate general's opinion and gives judgment.[12] There is no specific provision concerning admissibility. There seems to be a presumption that an application to set aside judgment in default is always admissible. RP-CFI 122(5) provides that the proceedings shall be conducted in accordance with Title II of the CFI's Rules of Procedure, which could be taken to suggest that proceedings follow exactly as in a direct action before the CFI, including the written procedure with its total of four pleadings. However, RP-CFI 122(5) also describes the response to the application to set judgment aside as 'written observations', which suggests that the wholesale incorporation of Title II of the CFI's Rules of Procedure should not be taken too literally. The better view seems to be that, after lodgment of the written observations on the application to set aside, proceedings follow in the same way as before the ECJ.

It would seem that, in theory at least, the Court does not need to decide the issues raised in the original action in order to set aside its judgment. For example, the applicant to set aside (the defendant in the action) may adduce evidence showing that the application commencing proceedings was not in fact served on him or that the originating application was inadmissible. In those circumstances, the Court will not give a decision on the merits of the case when it sets its judgment aside. In the former case the decision to set aside would seem to result in the recommencement of the action, the defendant having to lodge his defence and proceedings continuing as from that point. In the normal course of events, however, one may suppose that the application to set aside will challenge the foundation of the action so that the Court's final decision will settle the original dispute between the parties. It is in this sense that RP-ECJ 94(6) and RP-CFI 122(6) must be understood. Their first sentence provides that the Court's judgment on the application to set aside must not itself be set aside. But this does not preclude continuing the action until final judgment where the application to set aside is based on a matter not material to the admissibility or merits of the action. It is aimed at ensuring finality in the proceedings, not preventing it.

When the Court upholds an application to set aside, its decision takes the form of a judgment and is annexed to the original of the judgment in default, a note of it being made in the margin of the latter.[13]

D Scope of the procedure

It has been suggested[14] that the defendant can only apply to set aside 'judgments' ('*arrêts*') and not orders made by the Court in applications for interim relief, intervention and so forth. Although there is some force in this, the matter remains unclear and can only be considered together with the question, in what proceedings can judgment be given in default?

RP-ECJ 94 and RP-CFI 122 apply where proceedings have been originated by an 'application' which was to have been answered by a 'defence', and the Court's decision is given in the form of a 'judgment'. The right to apply to set aside applies in this context. It is to be noted that RP-ECJ 94 and RP-CFI 122 only show that the application made under them is granted or refused by a

---

12 See Case T-42/89 OPPO *European Parliament v Yorck von Wartenburg* [1990] ECR II-299 which followed the procedure laid down in RP-ECJ 94 because, at that time, the CFI's Rules of Procedure had not yet come into effect.
13 RP-ECJ 94(6); RP-CFI 122(6).
14 Vandersanden and Barav, op cit, p 484.

'judgment'. It does not indicate that the proceedings to which it applies end in a decision in this form, although it is reasonable to suppose that this is the case. The references to an 'application initiating proceedings' and a 'defence' are not reflected in all the language versions of RP-ECJ 94 and RP-CFI 122. Nevertheless they appear to indicate contentious proceedings of an adversarial nature which are terminated in a judgment determining the issues raised in the pleading which starts the action. Thus all non-contentious proceedings, such as references for a preliminary ruling and the like, fall outside the scope of RP-ECJ 94 and RP-CFI 122, although they may end in a judgment.[15] The same applies to proceedings which are not really adversarial, for in them there is no true defendant,[16] such as proceedings for intervention.

Although there are sufficient difficulties arising from the Rules of Procedure to make the point arguable, it seems on balance to be the case that the rules relating to judgment by default apply only to direct actions and not even to interlocutory or ancillary proceedings. The argument that, if this is so, no other proceedings may be terminated by a decision made in default of an answer to the case put by the applicant or the party initiating the procedure, must be rejected. This would plainly be contrary to common sense because it would enable a party to stultify all proceedings simply by remaining silent. Furthermore, it is impliedly contradicted by those provisions empowering the President or the Court to fix a period within which any submissions must be made. But can a party apply to set aside any decision reached in default of submissions from him?

In the case of proceedings for interim relief there is specific provision for this.[17] On the other hand, the Court has power under RP-ECJ 91–92 and RP-CFI 111 and 113–114 to reject an application as inadmissible either at the request of the opposing party[18] or on its own motion.[19] In both cases, but more particularly in the second, the decision may be made without hearing the applicant. There seems to be no provision for reviewing the Court's decision. Decisions made under RP-ECJ 91 or RP-CFI 114 are made after the opposing party has made an application to have the case dismissed. In some respects, therefore, a parallel can be drawn with the procedure envisaged in RP-ECJ 94 and RP-CFI 122: the applicant in the action is the defendant or respondent to the defendant's application and the Court's decision takes the form of a judgment. In contrast the proceedings under RP-ECJ 92 or RP-CFI 111 or 113 may not take this form and are usually terminated by a court order. It does not seem that in either case the Court's decision should be capable of being set aside by applying RP-ECJ 94 or RP-CFI 122 either directly or by analogy.

Most, if not all, interlocutory proceedings cannot be described as being entirely adversarial in character: the fact that the parties only submit observations to the Court indicates that the primary responsibility for ensuring due process lies on the Court itself rather than on them. RP-ECJ 94 and RP-CFI 122, on the other hand, appear to be concerned with the situation where the defendant's concession of the case, deemed in the light of his failure to reply to the applicant's claim, is sufficient justification to decide in favour of the applicant, if his claim is admissible and appears well founded. The Court's

---

15 See, by analogy, Case 40/70 *Sirena Srl v Eda Srl* [1979] ECR 3169, in connection with the interpretation of judgments under RP-ECJ 102.

16 To some extent the hallmark of such proceedings is that the parties only submit observations to the Court.

17 RP-ECJ 84(2); RP-CFI 105(2).

18 RP-ECJ 91; RP-CFI 114.

19 RP-ECJ 92; RP-CFI 111 and 113.

primary duty, after ensuring that the formal conditions for giving judgment have been fulfilled, is to assess the admissibility of the claim. It cannot content itself with the applicant's assurances because admissibility is not a matter which can be properly decided by a concession. On the other hand the court is entitled to accept at face value (or at least without detailed examination) the applicant's assertions as to the merits of the case where the defendant has not seen fit to dispute them.

The position under RP-ECJ 91–92 and RP-CFI 111 and 113–114, as it is in general in interlocutory proceedings, is that the Court cannot content itself with deciding on the basis of an express or implied concession made by one of the parties but must go further and settle the matter as seems right. The defendant's power under RP ECJ 94 or RP-CFI 122 to apply to set aside judgment in default is a residual power to deny the inference from his failure to act that he has consented to judgment being given against him. It counter balances the public interest that justice should not be denied through prevarication by allowing the defendant to remedy the effects of his default by prompt action. Therefore it does not, as a matter of principle, apply where the Court has acted in the context of proceedings which are inquisitorial or quasi-inquisitorial in nature. This does not prevent the defendant from challenging the admissibility of the application in proceedings to set aside a judgment in default: it is the character of the proceedings in which the judgment or decision was given that matters. Proceedings under RP-ECJ 94 and RP-CFI 122 are ex hypothesi adversarial whereas other proceedings in which questions of admissibility may arise are not necessarily so.

VI Third party proceedings

A Description of the procedure

In the procedure of the Court the only person who may be joined compulsorily as a party to proceedings is the defendant. There is no provision for the compulsory joinder of third parties, whether at the application of a party or by the Court on its own motion.[20] Furthermore, the only voluntary form of joinder is intervention. A third party cannot apply to be joined as an applicant or defendant, he can only seek to intervene in support of one side or the other. It is probably for these two reasons that the Statutes allow a third party to apply to have a judgment, which has been given without him being heard, reviewed if it prejudices his rights.[21] This procedure for review is called third party proceedings and may be compared to the procedure for review, revision, which applies in the case of parties, both the original parties to the action and interveners.[22] Revision is possible when a fact relevant to the case is discovered after judgment has been given and it is therefore restricted to the review of issues of fact upon which the Court's decision turned. In third party proceedings, however, all issues, both of fact and of law, may be reviewed. This type of procedure is recognised in a number of member states but its application is not necessarily the same in the context of proceedings before the Court.[23]

---

20 See Cases 9 and 12/60 *Belgium v Société Commerciale Antoine Vloeberghs SA and High Authority* [1962] ECR 171 at 187 (Advocate General Roemer).
21 ECSC Statute, art 36; EC Statute, art 39; Euratom Statute, art 40.
22 See pp 514 et seq.
23 See Cases 42 and 49/59 *Breedband NV v Société des Aciéries du Temple* [1962] ECR 145 and *Belgium v Vloeberghs and High Authority* (above, note 20) at 162 and 188 respectively (Advocate General Roemer).

The Statutes establish the principle that a judgment may be reviewed on application by a third party; RP-ECJ 97 and RP-CFI 123–124 give effect to that principle, the Statutes expressly assigning to the draftsmen of the Rules of Procedure 'the task of defining the conditions governing the admissibility of third party proceedings'.[24] This confers wide powers on the Court, which is responsible for drawing up the Rules of Procedure,[25] but it does not seem that the principle established in the Statutes can be cut down, as opposed to implemented, by the Rules of Procedure.[26] Should the latter be incompatible with the Statutes, they would be inapplicable.[27]

B   Conditions for bringing third party proceedings

The three Statutes set out four conditions for bringing third party proceedings. The EC and Euratom Statutes set out a fifth requirement.

1   The applicant

The application for review is made by a member state, Community institution or any natural or legal person.[28]

2   The subject matter of the application

The application is made 'to contest a judgment'. The meaning of 'judgment' is discussed elsewhere.[29] In brief, it is a final decision in contentious proceedings which is binding on the parties and leaves the Court functus officio regarding the dispute. In consequence, third party proceedings may not be brought in respect of a preliminary ruling.[30]

3   The judgment must have been 'rendered'

The judgment is 'rendered' when the operative part is read out in open court. The date of delivery is recorded on the judgment.[31] Proceedings cannot be commenced before that date, even though the Court has reached agreement on the text of its decision, because, until its delivery, the judgment is not binding[32] and does not therefore constitute a ruling on the dispute.

4   The judgment must have been delivered without the third party having been 'heard'

Not all the texts of the Statutes require the judgment to have been delivered without the third party being 'heard'. For example, the Italian version uses the same phrase used in relation to judgment in default: the third party must not have been 'summoned to appear'.[33] The position with regard to the German

---

24 The *Breedband* case (above, note 23) at 158.
25 ECSC and EC Statutes, art 55; Euratom Statute, art 56.
26 In *Belgium v Vloeberghs and High Authority* (above, note 20) at 188, Advocate General Roemer suggested that the Court could widen or narrow the limits within which applications could be brought with some freedom.
27 The *Breedband* Case (above, note 23) at 157; see also *Belgium v Vloeberghs and High Authority* (ibid) at 181.
28 Article 36 of the ECSC Statute does not mention member states expressly but this omission is purely stylistic: in *Belgium v Vloeberghs and High Authority* (ibid) the application was made by the Belgian government under art 36.
29 See pp 493 et seq.
30 Case 69/85 *Wünsche Handelgesellschaft GmbH & Co v Germany* [1986] ECR 947 (para 14).
31 RP-ECJ 63 and 64(3); RP-CFI 81 and 82(3).
32 RP-ECJ 65; RP-CFI 83.
33 'chiamata in causa'.

version is rather more complicated because the ECSC Statute is, in this respect, worded differently from the other two Statutes, although it would seem that the meaning is the same in all: the third party must not have 'participated' or been 'made a party'.[34] The French text, which is the authentic version in the case of the ECSC Statute,[35] speaks of the third parties not having been 'summoned'.[36] RP-ECJ 97(1)(c) and RP-CFI 123(1)(c) require the third party to explain why he was 'unable to take part' in the action decided by the judgment in question. On one view, that is a slightly different condition from that laid down in the Statutes; on another view, the Rules of Procedure aim to do nothing more than express the condition envisaged in the Statutes.[37]

In the *Breedband* case and *Belgium v Vloeberghs and High Authority*[38] the Court rejected the view that the Statutes overrode the Rules of Procedure (which would open up the possibility of commencing third party proceedings for all persons save defendants who were able to take part in the action) and ruled that third party proceedings can be brought only by (a) someone who was cited as a party but could not participate in the action for some good and sufficient reason and (b) someone who could not intervene.[39] RP-ECJ 97(1)(c) and RP-CFI 123(1)(c) apply to both categories. The Court adopted this approach on the ground that it was in the interests of justice that persons interested in the result of an action pending before the Court should be prevented as far as possible from raising their interest in the case after judgment has been delivered settling the question in dispute.[40]

The first category of persons who may bring third party proceedings appears to cover persons entitled to intervene in the litigation, who may be regarded as being impliedly 'cited' to appear as an intervening party by the notice of the case published in the Official Journal.[41] At least in theory, the first category also covers defendants although it might be thought that, as a matter of principle, they would not be 'third parties'. The position of the defendant in a direct action is unusual in that he is summoned or cited to appear by service on him of the application commencing proceedings. If he takes no part in the action, the applicant may apply for judgment in default and the defendant may in turn apply to set it aside.[42] In consequence, in order to take advantage of third party proceedings, the defendant would have to show why he was unable to apply to set aside. In those proceedings where the judgment in default rules do not apply, there is no right to set the judgment aside other than by way of third party proceedings and so far the problem of the inactive defendant has not arisen.

The second category of persons who may bring third party proceedings appears to envisage those persons without the right to intervene, as opposed to persons with such a right who were for some reason unable to exercise it. The possibility of intervening, even if not exploited, therefore excludes a person

---

34 '*Sie nicht am Streit beteiligt waren*' and '*Rechtsstreit . . . an dem sie nicht teilgenommen haben*'. The German wording of the Statutes is very close to that of RP-ECJ 97(1)(c): '*Sich am Hauptverfahren zu beteiligen*'.

35 *Belgium v Vloeberghs and High Authority* (above, note 20) at 181 (Advocate General Roemer).

36 '*appelées*'.

37 As has been seen, the difference between the wording of the Statutes and the Rules of Procedure is not so obvious in German.

38 Above (notes 23 and 20).

39 See ibid at 158 and 181–187 respectively.

40 Ibid.

41 There is no other sense in which a person other than the defendant can be regarded as being summoned or cited to appear in proceedings before the Court.

42 See RP-ECJ 94; RP-CFI 122.

from the second category.[43] However, in Case C-147/86TO1 *Panhellinia Omospondia Idioktiton Frontistirion Xenon Glosson – POIFXG v Greece and Commission*[44] the Court held that third party proceedings are open only to persons who should or could have taken part in a case. Therefore, if a person has no right to intervene in proceedings, he cannot call into question the judgment in the case by means of third party proceedings.[45]

In the result, the category of persons able to bring third party proceedings is limited to those who are entitled to intervene in the proceedings but who were not able to do so for some good and sufficient reason.

In *Belgium v Vloeberghs and High Authority*[46] Advocate General Roemer put forward the view that the opportunity to intervene might not always prevent the bringing of third party proceedings because intervention is not necessarily an effective way of protecting rights, which is the purpose of third party proceedings.[47] The Court appears to have rejected this argument because intervention proceedings, in substance, enable it to give a ruling on the intervener's case: only if the Court rejects the intervener's arguments and upholds the claims he opposes will the judgment prejudice his rights. In that event, third party proceedings would simply be a repetition of the original action. Intervention is to a large part dependent on the third party knowing that proceedings are pending and that he has an interest in the result of the dispute. Publication of a notice of the case in the Official Journal is intended to bring both factors home to potential interveners and it is to be supposed that a failure to peruse the Official Journal is not sufficient reason to justify not intervening. On the other hand, if the third party's interest in intervening is not reasonably apparent from the notice and any other circumstances known to him, the failure to intervene does not bar third party proceedings.[48]

Under the EC and Euratom Statutes,[49] member states and Community institutions can intervene without showing an interest in the outcome of the case so it would appear, at first sight, that publication of the notice of the case is per se sufficient to put them on notice to intervene.[50] It is arguable that this is

---

43 Cf the approach of Advocate General Mischo in Case 267/80TO *Birra Dreher SpA v Riseria Modenese Srl and Council and Commission* [1986] ECR 3901 at 3908–3910.

44 [1989] ECR 4103 (paras 11–17). See also Case C-147/86TO2 *Panhellinios Syndesmos Idioktiton Frontistirion Xenon Glosson – PALSO v Greece and Commission* [1989] ECR 4111 (paras 11–17); Case C-147/86TO3 *Panhellinos Syndesmos Idioktiton Idiotikon Technikon Epangelmatikon ke Naftikon Scholikon Monadon – PSIITENSM v Greece and Commission* [1989] ECR 4119 (paras 11–17).

45 That case concerned an application commencing third party proceedings brought by various legal and natural persons in respect of a judgment delivered in proceedings under art 169 of the EC Treaty finding that a member state had failed to fulfil its obligations under the EC Treaty. Persons other than member states and Community institutions cannot intervene in such actions. Had it been accepted that, in such cases, persons other than member states and Community institutions could bring third party proceedings, the result would have been to transform proceedings under art 169 of the EC Treaty into an actio popularis by means of third party proceedings. The decision is therefore understandable, although the same result could probably have been achieved by exploiting the fifth condition for bringing third party proceedings. The disadvantage of the approach followed by the Court is that, in actions against member states where the real defendant is a person or body for which the member state is reponsible under Community law but which is largely independent of the member state under national law, the real defendant has no means of being heard by the Court.

46 Above (note 20) at 188–189.

47 He seems to have reneged from this in his subsequent opinion in the *Breedband* case (above, note 23) at 162.

48 Cf *Belgium v Vloeberghs and High Authority* (above, note 20) at 182–183. The requirements as to the contents of the notice have since been changed.

49 Articles 37 and 38 respectively.

50 The *Vloeberghs* case concerned art 34 of the ECSC Statute, which requires every applicant to intervene to show an interest in the outcome.

not in fact so. Due to the fact that intervention is restricted to supporting or opposing the form of order[51] of one of the parties, it would seem that, if the notice does not identify reasonably clearly a basis on which the intervention can be grounded, a failure to intervene is excusable and the possibility of bringing third party proceedings remains open. Some slight support for this view can be drawn from *Belgium v Vloeberghs and High Authority*,[52] where the Court pointed out, in the context of the ECSC Statute, that intervention is in part dependent on the parties' forms of order.[53] The difficulty is that, in the absence of any requirement to show an interest in the outcome of the case, the formulation of the form of order which the intervener must support or reject is no real bar to intervening. However, the very fact that member states and Community institutions can intervene as of right in every case before the Court[54] suggests that, in deciding whether or not a failure to intervene bars the right to commence third party proceedings, the test should be whether the notice of the case (or any other circumstances) revealed some practical justification or interest reasonably sufficient to cause an application to intervene to be made. It should be noted, nonetheless, that third party proceedings apply only where the third party's rights have been prejudiced by the judgment, even where the third party is a member state or Community institution. In consequence it is not possible to commence them in every case in which intervention is possible.

In the *Breedband* case[55] Advocate General Roemer regarded the link between intervention and third party proceedings as reasonable 'having regard to the average importance of the undertaking which may be affected' by actions before the Court. That remark was, of course, uttered in the context of proceedings under the ECSC Treaty and at a time when the impact of Community law was still comparatively minor. It is arguable that, in the light of modern conditions, it is unrealistic to expect every potential litigant to leaf through the Official Journal in order to ensure that no one has commenced proceedings before the Court which may require his intervention. Accordingly, greater latitude should be allowed in so far as the effectiveness or deemed effectiveness of the notice published in the Official Journal is concerned. Even if this could not be accepted as a rule of general application, there is some justification for applying it either in the context of proceedings brought under the EC Treaty, by reason of its wider scope in comparison with the other two Treaties, or by reference to the situation of the litigant, eg if he is a private individual, as opposed to a large company. The current trend in the case law does not, however, support a lenient approach to the efficacy of the notice published in the Official Journal. In Case T-35/89TO1 *Ascasibar Zubizarreta v Albani*[56] it was held that the third party's subjective assessment of the result of the case is not a valid reason for his failure to participate in the proceedings.[57] The test is objective and requires only a construction of the notice published in the Official Journal. As long as the elements of fact and law revealed in the notice would lead a diligent person to think that the judgment might affect his rights, a failure to intervene precludes the bringing of third

---

51 'Submissions' in the English text of the Statutes.
52 Above (note 20) at 182.
53 'Conclusions' in the English text of the judgment.
54 Other than under the ECSC Statute.
55 Above (note 23) at 162.
56 [1992] ECR II-1599 (paras 33–37).
57 See also *Birra Dreher SpA v Riseria Modenese Srl* (above, note 43) at 3910 (Advocate General Mischo).

party proceedings. The facts (if true) that the party supported by the third party failed to persuade the Court or that the Court departed from its previous case law in the contested judgment are not material.

5   The judgment must have prejudiced the third party's rights

This condition is mentioned only in the EC and Euratom Statutes, although it is incorporated in the Rules of Procedure.[58] No question was raised in either the *Breedband* case or *Belgium v Vloeberghs and High Authority* concerning the effect of the omission of this requirement from the ECSC Statute because, no doubt, it also applies to third party proceedings under national law and the parties accepted it for that reason. In any event, the Statutes make it clear that the Rules of Procedure may impose conditions of admissibility, so the precise wording of the ECSC Statute is in this respect of no consequence. The Court accepted in *Belgium v Vloeberghs and High Authority*[59] that this particular condition applied even to third party proceedings under that Statute.

The contested judgment must be prejudicial to a right, not just a legitimate interest.[60] A simple statement of fact in the judgment does not prejudice the third party's rights although it may appear to him to imply some criticism directed to him; there must be a finding, whether of fact or of law, which is either incorporated in the operative part of the judgment or which forms part of the reasoning on which the operative part is based.[61] Where the contested judgment dismisses a claim for damages on the ground that the applicant has assigned the claim to another, the judgment is not prejudicial to the rights of the assignee merely because it is unclear about the true identity of the assignee.[62] A judgment annulling a decision appointing someone to a post for which the applicant in the third party proceedings was not a candidate is not prejudicial to the latter's rights; nor is an interpretation given to a legal provision, so far as third parties to the proceedings are concerned.[63] Since the judgment must be prejudicial to a right, not an interest, it does not seem appropriate to draw too close a parallel with the requirement of an interest in intervention proceedings.[64] Even if a close parallel could be drawn, Advocate General Roemer's acceptance in *Belgium v Vloeberghs and High Authority*[65] of an attack on one's dignity and prestige as a prejudice to one's rights either applies only in the case of member states or must be regarded as having been overruled by Case 40/79 *Mrs P v Commission*.[66]

C   Procedural stages

The application commencing third party proceedings must be lodged within two months of the publication of the judgment in question in the Official Journal.[67] The Rules of Procedure actually say 'where the judgment has been published' etc, thus implying that there is no time limit at all on making the application if it has not been published. The application must comply with the

---

58 RP-ECJ 97(1)(b); RP-CFI 123(1)(b).
59 Above (note 20) at 183.
60 Case 292/84TP *Bolognese v Scharf and Commission* [1987] ECR 3563 (para 7).
61 *Belgium v Vloeberghs and High Authority* (above, note 20) at 183–184 and 190–193 (Advocate General Roemer).
62 *Birra Dreher SpA v Riseria Modenese Srl* (above, note 43) paras 9–10.
63 The *Bolognese* case (above, note 60), paras 8 and 9.
64 See chapter 5, pp 158 et seq.
65 Above (note 20) at 190.
66 [1979] ECR 3299.
67 RP-ECJ 97(1); RP-CFI 123(1).

requirements of RP-ECJ 37–38 or, as the case may be, RP-CFI 43–44 and be made against all the parties to the original case.[68] In addition it must also: (i) specify the judgment contested; (ii) state how it is prejudicial to the applicant's rights; and (iii) give reasons showing why he was unable to take part in the original case.[69] The language of the case is selected, as usual, by applying RP-ECJ 29 or, as the case may be, RP-CFI 35 and may not necessarily be the language of the original proceedings. Once lodged, the application is served on the persons named as defendants in the usual way.[70]

The Rules of Procedure say nothing about the conduct of proceedings after lodgment of the application.[71] It is to be inferred that the form to be followed is that of a normal direct action. Unlike revision proceedings, for example, the defendants do not submit written observations but there is an exchange of pleadings in accordance with RP-ECJ 40–42 or, as the case may be, RP-CFI 46–48. This appears to have happened in both the *Breedband* case and *Belgium v Vloebergh and High Authority* because the judgment records the lodgment of rejoinders.[72] In the same way, the defendants may raise formal objections to the admissibility of the application, pursuant to RP-ECJ 91 or RP-CFI 114.[73] It would also appear to be the case that interested third parties may intervene, despite the fact that they had not done so in the original action. The Court may decide to order a preparatory enquiry and the oral procedure is conducted in the usual way. If, on the other hand, the defendants fail to lodge their defences within the time fixed for doing so, the third party may apply for judgment in default under RP-ECJ 94 or RP-CFI 122. A judgment so obtained may be set aside on application by one of the defendants pursuant to RP-ECJ 94(4)–(6) or RP-CFI 122(4)–(6).

Commencement of third party proceedings does not of itself cause the obligation to comply with the contested judgment to be suspended.[74] RP-ECJ 97(2) and RP-CFI 123(2) provide that the third party may apply for a stay of execution of the judgment contested in the proceedings. Such an application is dealt with in accordance with the rules relating to applications for interim relief.[75] There is nothing in the Rules of Procedure barring an application for other types of interim relief although they are not mentioned specifically in RP-ECJ 97 or RP-CFI 123. Where an appeal pending before the ECJ and an application initiating third party proceedings relate to the same judgment of the CFI, the CFI may (after hearing the parties) stay the third party proceedings until the ECJ has delivered judgment on the appeal[76] or application may be made to the ECJ for it to stay the appeal proceedings pending the outcome of the third party proceedings.[77]

If the Court upholds the third party's arguments, it 'varies' the contested

---

68 Ibid. 'Parties' includes interveners.

69 Ibid.

70 See RP-ECJ 39; RP-CFI 45.

71 Save that RP-CFI 124 provides that the application initiating third party proceedings shall be assigned to the chamber that delivered the judgment which is the subject of the application or to the CFI in plenary session if that judgment was delivered in plenary session. The same procedure is followed as a matter of practice by the ECJ.

72 Above (notes 23 and 20). See also *Birra Dreher SpA v Riseria Modenese Srl* (above, note 43) at 3902.

73 As was done in the *Bolognese* case (above, note 60) para 4; *POIFXG, PALSO* and *PSIITENSM* cases (all above, note 44) para 4.

74 Case C-328/90 *Commission v Greece* [1992] ECR I-425 at 432 (Advocate General Jacobs).

75 See the *Breedband* case (above, note 23) at 167; RP-ECJ 83–89 and RP-CFI 104–110 (dealt with in chapter 8).

76 RP-CFI 123(4).

77 As was done in the *Albani* case (above, note 56) paras 7–8.

judgment accordingly.[78] In consequence the form of order in the application commencing proceedings should set out the precise variation sought. The judgment in the third party proceedings is delivered in the usual way and is binding on all the parties. The original of it is annexed to the original of the contested judgment, a note of the former being made in the margin of the latter.[79] Like all judgments, that given in the third party proceedings may be rectified to remove mistakes in the text,[80] supplemented[81] and interpreted.[82] It cannot be revised pursuant to RP-ECJ 98–100 or RP-CFI 125–127 because its effect is to vary the original judgment. It is that judgment (as varied) which may, however, be made the subject of revision proceedings. By the same token, further third party proceedings, which are likely to be a theoretical rather than a practical proposition, are made against the original judgment as varied.

VII   Revision

A   Description of the procedure

The Statutes provide[83] that the Court may review one of its judgments 'only on discovery of a fact which is of such a nature as to be a decisive factor and which, when the judgment was given, was unknown to the Court and to the party claiming' review. With the exception of proceedings for setting aside a judgment given in default of defence, this is the only procedure whereby a party may seek to have a judgment reviewed by the Court. An alternative method of review is provided in third party proceedings[84] but this applies only if the applicant in them (the 'third party') was not able to take part in the original proceedings, even as an intervener. Revision is not, however, a means of appealing against the judgment in question, even on a point of fact;[85] it is a method of reviewing the judgment in the light of a relevant fact which should have been taken into account by the Court when making its decision but was not because neither the Court itself nor the person applying for revision knew of its existence.[86] Revision is also an inappropriate procedure to invoke where the real purpose is to correct a clerical error in a judgment[87] or dispute the way in which a judgment has been complied with.[88]

B   Conditions for revision of a judgment

There are three conditions for revision of a judgment.[89] They are applied in a restrictive manner because of the nature of revision as an exceptional review procedure which may disapply the principle of res judicata.[90]

---

78 RP-ECJ 97(3); RP-CFI 123(3).
79 Ibid.
80 RP-ECJ 66; RP-CFI 84.
81 RP-ECJ 67; RP-CFI 85.
82 RP-ECJ 102; RP-CFI 129.
83 ECSC Statute, art 38; EC Statute, art 41; Euratom Statute, art 42. See Plouvier (1971) C de D Eur 428 and Del Vecchio in *Studi di Diritto Europeo, in onore di R Monaco* p 227.
84 See pp 507 et seq.
85 Case 116/78 *Bellintani v Commission* [1980] ECR 23; Case T-4/89 Rev *BASF AG v Commission* [1992] ECR II-1591 (para 9).
86 Hence, the application made in Cases C-133 and C-150/87 *Nashua Corpn v Commission and Council* [1990] ECR I-719 (unreported order of 19 May 1988) for the 'revision' of an order refusing the applicant's request for confidential treatment of its pleadings was misconceived because it was in reality an attempt to appeal against the order and did not seek to rely upon any new fact.
87 Case C-295/90 Rev *Council v European Parliament* [1992] ECR I-5299.
88 Case 235/82 Rev *Ferriere San Carlo SpA v Commission* [1986] ECR 1799.
89 Ibid at para 2.
90 Case 267/80 Rev *Riseria Modenese Srl v Council and Commission and Birra Peroni SpA* [1985] ECR 3499 (para 10).

1 Total absence of knowledge on the part of the Court and of the applicant for revision of the existence of a fact prior to the delivery of judgment

Although the Statutes refer to a 'fact' simpliciter and also a 'new fact' it does not seem that this means that revision is justified only where a 'new' decisive issue of fact is revealed. The phrase 'new fact' is there used only in the context of the judgment of the Court finding the application to be admissible, not in relation to the brief description given in the Statutes of the substantive conditions required for a judgment to be revised. 'New fact' really seems to mean 'newly discovered fact': it is 'new' only in the sense that it was hitherto unknown and unconsidered. As the second condition for revision laid down by the Court shows, it is not 'new' in the sense that it came into being after the date of the judgment which is to be revised.

Neither the Court's interpretation of its own case law or of administrative provisions[91] nor the conclusions derived from certain known facts drawn by it in a judgment[92] can be considered to be facts justifying revision. The same applies where the judgment which is the subject of the application for revision was delivered by the ECJ and the judgment relied on to justify revision was delivered by the CFI, or vice versa.[93]

There is no authority that the fact must relate to an issue which the Court had to decide in the earlier proceedings rather than to a new issue. The requirement expressed in the Statutes that it only be 'decisive' suggests that it does not matter that the fact does not relate to an issue decided in the judgment. The cases, none of which has so far been found to be admissible, have tended to involve facts which did relate to such an issue. On the other hand, in the *Polypropylene* cases,[94] which were dismissed as inadmissible on other grounds, the purpose of the revision proceedings was to invoke facts allegedly establishing the non-existence of the act challenged in the proceedings leading up to the contested judgment, an issue that had not been raised previously.

The case law suggests that, in revision proceedings, the fact need not be what could be described as a primary fact but may also constitute evidence of a primary fact. In both Case 56/70 *Fonderie Acciaierie Giovanni Mandelli v Commission*[95] and Case 37/71 Rev *Jamet v Commission*,[96] the facts relied on were in reality further evidence to support an issue of fact in the earlier proceedings. In *Mandelli* it was an Italian government audit report for the years 1958 to 1959 which came to the applicant's notice in 1970. Extracts from the report were produced concerning the applicant's consumption of ferrous scrap in those years. In *Jamet* the applicant, an official, relied on his periodical report, which came to his attention after the date of judgment, in order to reverse a finding of fact concerning the nature of the duties he had performed. In both cases the application was held to be inadmissible, because the existence of the evidence was known to the applicant (*Mandelli*)[97] or the evidence was not a decisive

---

91 The *Bellintani* case (above, note 85) at paras 6 and 7.
92 Case C-403/85 Rev *Ferrandi v Commission* [1991] ECR I-1215 (para 13); the *BASF* case (above, note 85), para 12.
93 *Ferrandi* (ibid) para 13.
94 *BASF v Commission* (above, note 85); Case T-8/89 Rev *DSM NV v Commission* [1992] ECR II-2399; Case T-14/89 Rev *Montecatini SpA (formerly Montedipe SpA) v Commission* [1992] ECR II-2409.
95 [1971] ECR 1.
96 [1973] ECR 295. See also Cases 285/81 R I and II *Geist v Commission* [1984] ECR 1789.
97 The original proceedings, Case 3/67 *Fonderie Acciaierie Giovanni Mandelli v Commission* [1968] ECR 25, concerned two decisions, one assessing the amount of scrap bought and consumed by Mandelli, the other demanding payment of the sum due on this amount by way of contribution to the Scrap Equalisation Fund. Mandelli's declarations of its consumption of scrap were not

factor in the dispute decided by the judgment (*Jamet*). In the *BASF* case[98] the only 'facts' that the Court regarded as capable of being invoked in support of the application for revision were statements made by the Commission at the hearing in another case. Strictly speaking, those 'facts' were (oral) evidence of the real facts capable (it was argued) of establishing the non-existence of the act challenged in the proceedings because, in those statements, the Commission purported to recount events that had already taken place and whose occurrence had not previously been known. It is striking that, nonetheless, the Court did not consider that subsequent press statements made by the Commission confirming the statements made at the hearing were capable of supporting an application for revision: one would have thought that, if a statement that a fact exists can constitute a 'fact' for the purposes of revision proceedings, a subsequent repetition or confirmation of the statement must also be such a 'fact'.[99]

Some support for the view that revision is not a procedure allowing the Court to review its own findings of fact can be drawn from Case 115/73R *Serio v Commission*[1] and the *Bellintani* case[2] but these concerned situations where no new proof was presented in order to overturn a finding of fact in the judgment. They were simply applications for the Court to reconsider the case on the basis of the elements of fact and law at its disposal at the time of the judgment.[3] The discovery of proof of a fact, such as documentary evidence, is, however, just as much a relevant fact as that which it tends to prove. The only objection to allowing evidence to be relied on as a fact justifying revision is that it enables issues of fact resolved in the judgment to be reconsidered. If this is not the object of revision, the procedure is in practice restricted in its scope to cases where the newly discovered fact provides a new basis for deciding the dispute. Yet there is no indication in any of the cases so far decided that revision is so limited. In their present state the authorities suggest that a 'fact' for the purpose of revision is not just a fact stricto senso but the evidence of it; and not just a new issue on which to decide the dispute but (decisive) support for an old one.

The fact relied on must have been unknown both to the Court and to the applicant but it is irrelevant if it was known to another party to the proceedings. In the *Mandelli* case[4] it was the applicant who knew of the facts in

accepted by the High Authority. But the company's records were incomplete. The High Authority therefore had recourse to various indirect methods of finding out the amount of scrap used. The case turned to a large extent on the accuracy of the estimation made by it, given the information available. The primary fact, the amount of scrap consumed, was thus in the knowledge of the parties in the sense that they were aware of its existence. The difficulty lay in proving it. In the revision proceedings the Court rejected Mandelli's application because it knew of the existence of further evidence to support its contentions, not because it knew of the existence of the primary fact before the date of judgment.

98 Above (note 85), in particular paras 10–13.
99 If a statement of fact, or evidence of a fact, is a 'fact' for the purposes of revision proceedings, the time for commencing revision proceedings would start to run as from the first occasion on which the 'fact' came to the knowledge of the applicant. The repetition of the statement or the confirmation or corroboration of the evidence could not cause time to start running again or otherwise extend the time limit for commencing revision proceedings. In consequence, it is unclear what reason of principle or convenience exists for excluding confirmatory or corroborative evidence of a primary fact from the class of matters capable of supporting an application for revision.
1 [1974] ECR 671.
2 Case 116/78 Rev *Bellintani v Commission* [1980] ECR 23.
3 See also Case 13/69 *van Eick v Commission* [1970] ECR 3.
4 Case 56/70 *Fonderie Acciaierie Giovanni Mandelli v Commission* [1971] ECR 1.

question at the time of the judgment. In Case 1/60 *FERAM v High Authority*,[5] on the other hand, it was the Court that knew of the facts while the applicant allegedly did not. It was said that certain documents which had been presented to the Court had not been translated into the language of the case (Italian) so that the applicant could be apprised of their contents.[6] The Court held that the documents were known to it before it gave judgment since they had been lodged before the oral procedure was over; their contents were also known to the Court because (a) they were drawn up in an official Community language and (b) there is what the English text of the judgment describes as an 'irrebuttable presumption of law'[7] that the Court, like all the Community institutions, is cognisant of all the official Community languages.

The absence of knowledge must be total. A failure on the part of the Court or the applicant to appreciate correctly or at all the significance of the fact is nihil ad rem, it is bare knowledge that counts: 'this requirement [ie the first condition] is not . . . satisfied if the fact in question has been referred to in any manner, or simply known, even if not expressly referred to, in the course of the proceedings; prior knowledge of the fact, whether or not fortuitous and, a fortiori, the assessment of its importance by the Court, do not therefore constitute a factor making possible an application for revision'.[8] An application for revision which is based simply on the ground that there are errors of fact in the judgment is not just inadmissible but vexatious.[9] If the applicant has knowledge of the facts relied on, he remains bound by res judicata and is not entitled to ask the Court to reconsider the merits of the case, even where the same issue arises in the context of other proceedings.[10] Thus, in the *Polypropylene* cases[11] the essential facts were known at the date of the contested judgment because the applicants had all been present at the hearing in other proceedings at which the statements constituting the facts relied on were uttered. The applicants could have brought the facts to the attention of the Court before judgment (as other persons in other actions had done) and applied for the oral procedure to be reopened so as to allow them to make, before the delivery of judgment, the points that they were seeking to make in the revision proceedings.

It is unclear whether there must be an absence of actual or constructive knowledge. In the *Mandelli* case[12] the Court rejected the application because (a) the applicant knew of the audit and its scope at the material time, (b) it was given a report of the facts found in 1959 and knew of the existence of an audit report at the time of judgment, although it did not learn of the contents until 1970, and (c) nothing had prevented it from getting hold of the audit report itself during the earlier proceedings or asking the Court to exercise its powers to call for its production.[13] The Court's reasoning thus suggests that, if the applicant is put on notice of the existence of a relevant fact, he cannot

---

5 [1960] ECR 165.
6 As pleaded, the application did not in fact show that any of the conditions for its admissibility had been fulfilled: it did not even identify the facts which the applicant had been prevented from discovering before judgment was given.
7 Or a presumption 'juris et de jure'.
8 The *Bellintani* case (above, note 2) at para 2.
9 Ibid and the *Serio* case (above, note 1).
10 *van Eick v Commission* (above, note 3) and the *Serio* case (ibid).
11 Case T-4/89 Rev *BASF v Commission* [1992] ECR II-1591; Case T-8/89 Rev *DSM NV v Commission* [1992] ECR II-2399; Case T-14/89 Rev *Montecatini SpA (formerly Montedipe SpA) v Commission* [1992] ECR II-2409.
12 Above (note 4).
13 See ECSC Statute, art 24.

subsequently rely on it for the purposes of revision unless he was unable to prove its existence at the material time. In the *FERAM* case[14] the Court drew a distinction between knowledge of the existence of the documents in question and knowledge of their contents. The case is certainly authority for the proposition that it does not lie in the mouth of a Community institution to say that it was not aware of the existence of a document or of its contents as long as it is written in an official Community language. The decision leaves it unclear whether a Community institution (or any other person for that matter) can say that it was not aware of the contents of a document in its possession, which it had not read, and whether possession of a document in a foreign language (sc the language of a third country in the case of a Community institution) may equally be relied on to justify ignorance of its contents or its very existence.

If, as is suggested, evidence constitutes a fact justifying revision, the *Mandelli* case is not to be regarded as authority for the existence of a doctrine of constructive knowledge: the applicant had actual knowledge of the existence of the fact (the proof which the audit report comprised) as well as knowledge of the primary facts which it tended to prove. On this basis it is questionable whether there is any material distinction between the contents of a document and the document itself: both are facts for the purpose of revision. Indeed, it is arguable that the only true fact is the document, whether it constitutes the primary fact or evidence of the primary fact. Knowledge of its contents goes to appreciation of its relevance to the case, not to appreciation of its existence and, as the Court seemed to suggest in the *Bellintani* case, it is only the latter that matters. By the same process of reasoning, knowledge of the existence of a document whose relevance cannot be determined because it is drawn up in a language incomprehensible to its possessor, is a bar to applying for revision in reliance on the fact constituted by or proved in the document. Lest it be thought that this is an unduly restrictive approach, it should be borne in mind that careful preparation of a case would avoid the situation in which a relevant fact is not put before the Court because, while its existence is known, its significance is not appreciated. Even in the case of documents in a foreign tongue, it is an elementary precaution to find out what they mean. At all events, the cases do not appear to support the existence of a doctrine of constructive knowledge.

2   At the time of the delivery of judgment the Court must have been unaware of a fact already in existence

Although the Statutes[15] actually refer to a 'new fact', it is now well established that the fact must have been in existence at the time of judgment.[16] In Case 28/64 Rev *Müller v Council and Euratom Council*[17] the application was based on a decision of the defendant made almost two years after the Court had given judgment. The Court held that it did not relate to the period before judgment and so the application was inadmissible. On the other hand, in Case 56/75 Rev *Elz v Commission*[18] the original action had been one for damages arising from the alleged wrongful delay on the part of the defendant in transmitting a summons issued by a Belgian court to the applicant. The action was dismissed on the ground that there was no evidence of any damage arising from the

---

14   Above (note 5).
15   ECSC Statute, art 38; EC Statute, art 41; Euratom Statute, art 42.
16   Eg Case 267/80 Rev *Riseria Modenese Srl v Council, Commission and Birra Peroni SpA* [1985] ECR 3499 (para 10).
17   [1967] ECR 141.
18   [1977] ECR 1617.

wrongful act. Just over a year later a Belgian court gave judgment confirming a decision of a lower court delivered prior to the commencement of the action. The applicant relied on the former as the basis of the claim for revision. The Court appeared to reject the defendant's argument that a 'new fact' had to be something that was in existence before the judgment sought to be revised was handed down: it held that 'the mere fact that the judgment of the [Belgian court] was subsequent to the judgment of the Court cannot of itself prevent the first-mentioned judgment from being considered as the discovery of a new fact'.[19] The reason for this appears to have been that the Belgian judgment only confirmed the decision of the lower court and drew the inevitable consequences of doing so. It was therefore a repetition or reaffirmation of a fact that was in existence prior to the delivery of the judgment sought to be revised. That fact was known to the Court and the parties at the time of judgment and the application for revision was dismissed as being inadmissible. Where the fact is evidence of a primary fact, it does not seem that it can be used as the basis of an application for revision only if it came into existence before the date of judgment. In Case C-403/85 Rev *Ferrandi v Commission*,[20] for example, the Court considered that the only facts capable of being relied on were medical reports made after the date of the contested judgment (the application was dismissed as inadmissible on other grounds). The reports related to the applicant's medical condition in the period at issue in the proceedings leading up to the contested judgment. They therefore constituted proof of facts already in existence before the delivery of that judgment.

3   The unknown fact must be of such a nature as to be a decisive factor as regards the outcome of the case

The fact must, in other words, 'be capable of altering the decision of the court of which revision is sought'.[21] In consequence, if the unknown fact relates to an issue of fact or law which was only an additional but not decisive factor in the judgment,[22] does not contradict a finding made by the Court,[23] reaffirms a fact known at the time of the judgment[24] or simply fails to establish the point which the applicant seeks to make,[25] the application for revision will be rejected. The test of decisiveness is, in short, its bearing on the operative part of the judgment, not its relevance to other points canvassed in the judgment.

C   Procedural stages

An application for revision must be made within ten years of the date of the judgment in question[26] and within three months of the date on which the applicant received knowledge of the facts on which the application is based.[27] This time limit cannot be extended by reason of the behaviour of the defendant to the application; the time limits in proceedings for revision are particularly important and must be observed strictly because revision creates an exception

---

19 Ibid para 7 of the judgment.
20 [1991] ECR I-1215 (para 12).
21 The *Bellintani* case (above, note 2) at para 2. See also Case 107/79 Rev *Schuerer v Commission* [1983] ECR 3805; *Riseria Modenese Srl v Birra Peroni SpA* (above, note 16) para 12.
22 Case 40/71 *Richez-Parise v Commission* [1972] ECR 73.
23 Case 37/71 Rev *Jamet v Commission* [1973] ECR 295.
24 The *Elz* case (above, note 18) and Cases 285/81 RI and II *Geist v Commission* [1984] ECR 1789.
25 The *BASF* case (above, note 11).
26 ECSC Statute, art 38; EC Statute, art 41; Euratom Statute, art 42.
27 RP-ECJ 98; RP-CFI 125. See, for example, Case C-403/85 Rev *Ferrandi v Commission* [1991] ECR I-1215 (para 12).

to the principles of res judicata and legal certainty.[28] The application must be made in the form specified by RP-ECJ 37–38 or, as the case may be, RP-CFI 43–44. It must also:[29]

(1)   identify the judgment contested;
(2)   indicate the points on which it is contested;
(3)   set out the facts on which the application is based; and
(4)   indicate the nature of the evidence showing:
   (a)   that the facts justify revision; and
   (b)   that the application was lodged within three months of those facts coming to light.

The application is made by a 'party'.[30] This seems to cover all persons bound by the judgment in question, ie the original parties to the action and interveners. There seems to be no logic in restricting capacity to make the application to the original parties to the action: all those who are bound by the judgment have just as great an interest in seeing its revision. The application is made against all the parties to the original judgment.[31] The interveners (if any) would therefore be defendants in the proceedings for revision.

The application is made to the Court which delivered the judgment whose revision is sought. That is so even where the judgment was delivered by the ECJ but jurisdiction at first instance over the cause of action in question has since then been entrusted to the CFI.[32] In the case of judgments of the CFI, the application for revision is assigned to the chamber which delivered the judgment contested in the application for revision or to the CFI sitting in plenary session if it was a judgment of the plenary session.[33] If a judgment of the CFI is the subject both of an appeal to the ECJ and an application for revision (made to the CFI), the CFI may, after hearing the parties, stay the revision proceedings until the ECJ has delivered judgment on the appeal.[34] In principle, a judgment delivered by the ECJ on appeal is not subject to revision because the ECJ has no jurisdiction over issues of fact. Where the judgment on appeal has upheld the CFI's judgment or annulled it in part only, an application for revision relating to the matters in respect of which the CFI's judgment is final is properly to be dealt with by the CFI. Where the judgment on appeal has remitted the case to the CFI, any new facts may, and should, be raised in the proceedings before the latter and not in revision proceedings before the ECJ.[35] It seems only to be where the ECJ annuls the CFI's judgment and decides the case itself that revision proceedings can be brought before the ECJ: in that event, there would not be any judgment of the CFI which could be revised.

That aspect apart, the procedure for dealing with an application for revision is not clearly set out in the Rules of Procedure. It would seem that the application should be made by separate document. In the *Richez-Parise* case[36]

---

28   The *Richez-Parise* case (above, note 22) at 86 (Advocate General Roemer).
29   RP-ECJ 99(1); RP-CFI 126(1). For an example of a failure to comply with those requirements, see Case 235/82 Rev *Ferriere San Carlo SpA v Commission* [1986] ECR 1799.
30   ECSC Statute, art 38; EC Statute, art 41; Euratom Statute, art 42.
31   RP-ECJ 99(2); RP-CFI 126(2).
32   *Ferrandi v Commission* (above, note 27).
33   RP-CFI 127(1). The same procedure is followed by the ECJ as a matter of practice.
34   RP-CFI 128. See the parallel situation in third party proceedings: p 513. Where the matter has been remitted to the CFI by the ECJ and a party seeks the revision of the judgment of the ECJ on the appeal, the CFI may stay the proceedings before it pending the outcome of the revision proceedings before the ECJ: Case T-43/89RV *Gill v Commission* [1993] ECR II-303 (para 17).
35   Case C-185/90P-Rev *Gill v Commission* [1992] ECR I-993; Case T-43/89RV *Gill v Commission*, ibid (para 16).
36   Above (note 22).

the pleading commencing proceedings was drawn up in the form of an application claiming damages with an alternative claim that, if the defendant should rely on res judicata to bar the claim for damages, the application should be regarded as one for revision. The Court held that 'The application therefore comprises two distinct actions governed by different rules as regards both procedure and judgment'.[37] It nevertheless decided to settle both claims in the same judgment, largely because the claim for revision was made in the alternative and sought in substance the same result as the claim for damages. In addition, it should be observed that the revision claim was plainly out of time so there was no need to consider the other grounds of admissibility. The conclusion to be drawn appears to be that an application for revision may not be inadmissible merely because it has been made in the same document as another application[38] but that it ought to be made separately and should in any event be regarded in procedural terms as severed from the other application.

It will be noted that in *Richez-Parise* the defendant lodged its objection to the admissibility of the damages claim and its written observations in the revision proceedings in separate documents. Furthermore the Court opened the oral procedure in the former without prejudice to its decision on the admissibility of the latter.

Once the application has been lodged at the Court it will be served on all the parties named in it, in the usual way, as a matter of course. The next step is for the Court to decide on the admissibility of the application. The Statutes[39] expressly provide that the procedure commences with a judgment of the Court recording the existence of a new fact, recognising that its character is such as to justify laying the case open to revision and declaring that the application is admissible on this ground. It does not seem to be possible for the decision on admissibility to be made at the same time as the decision on the merits of the application. In the *Bellintani* case[40] the Court explained the compulsory division of the procedure into two stages as being due to the strictness of the conditions to be fulfilled for revision, which defeats the force of res judicata.

The decision on admissibility is made 'having regard to the written observations of the parties'.[41] This indicates that the defendants to the application must be given an opportunity to submit written observations and this has been done in all the cases so far decided. This stage of the proceedings has in practice been limited to allowing the defendants to reply to the application; the exchange of pleadings found in a direct action does not, therefore, take place at this stage.[42] It is doubtful if the Rules of Procedure should be interpreted as excluding the possibility of further written observations should the Court feel it to be necessary. Equally, there is no provision in the rules for a hearing. So far as can be seen from the reports, the practice is to dispense with hearing oral argument from the parties.[43] Nonetheless, it does not seem that the Court lacks the power to hear them if it thinks it right to do so. In principle measures of

---

37 Ibid at para 2.
38 There is no provision in the Rules of Procedure similar to RP-ECJ 83(3) and RP-CFI 104(3), which apply to applications for interim relief.
39 ECSC Statute, art 38; EC Statute, art 41; Euratom Statute, art 42.
40 Above (note 2) at para 3.
41 RP-ECJ 100(1); RP-CFI 127(2).
42 In *Richez-Parise* (above, note 22) the applicant was allowed to reply but the report does not say whether this was allowed in relation to the written observations on the application for revision as well as to the objection to the admissibility of the damages claims. The inference is that the reply was only to the latter.
43 In *Richez-Parise* (ibid) the oral procedure was opened expressly without prejudice to the Court's decision in the revision proceedings.

enquiry, which are also not provided for at this stage, are not necessary because admissibility is determined by reference only to the contents of the application. The applicant must in that document discharge the burden that lies on him of showing that the conditions for admissibility have been met. On the other hand, since the judgment on admissibility must establish the existence of the 'new' fact, and the evidence set out in the application might conceivably be testimony, it may be assumed that the Court may, in certain circumstances, order a preparatory enquiry. If this does happen, it would seem right that the parties be allowed to present (oral) observations in order to allow them to comment on the results of the preparatory enquiry.

In proceedings before the ECJ, the Court's decision on admissibility is given in closed session, in the form of a judgment, after hearing the advocate general.[44] The significance of this is that, in derogation from RP-ECJ 64(1), the judgment is not delivered in open court and the parties are not given notice to attend to hear it, although it is served on them. It is not the practice to publish the advocate general's views. The only case in which this was done was *Richez-Parise*[45] but there the situation was unusual because the revision claim was pleaded in the alternative to the damages action and so both had to be canvassed in the opinion. For the same reason the judgment was given in open court. In proceedings before the CFI, the decision on admissibility is not required to be made in closed session. There is provision for hearing the advocate general before the decision is made. That applies only where an advocate general has been assigned to the case; it does not imply that there must always be an advocate general in revision proceedings. Lastly, the CFI's decision on admissibility is not required to take the form of a judgment.[46]

If the Court decides that the application is admissible, the next stage is for it to give judgment on the merits.[47] The decision on admissibility is not to prejudice the decision on the merits.[48] This suggests that the scope of the enquiry into admissibility is limited, as the Statutes indicate, to finding out if the fact in question exists and whether its character is such as to justify revision, not whether it does in substance do so. The test at the stage of admissibility seems to be whether or not the fact could determine an issue of fact or law upon which the decision in the case turned. If, on that basis, the application is admissible, the Court is not prevented by its decision on admissibility from later finding that the fact lacked decisive character.

The Rules of Procedure say little about the procedure to be followed if the Court finds the application for revision to be admissible. There is so far no case in which this has happened and, in consequence, no example to refer to. RP-ECJ 100(2) and RP-CFI 127(3) simply say that the Court shall give its decision on the merits of the application 'in accordance with these Rules'. It may be that the vagueness of RP-ECJ 100(2) and RP-CFI 127(3) is intentional and designed to allow the Court a discretion in determining the future course of proceedings which is not constrained by reference to a specific procedural sequence.

Since the application for revision must, pursuant to RP-ECJ 38 and RP-CFI 44, have set out the grounds on which revision is sought (ie the merits of the application) and any necessary preparatory enquiries should have been

44 RP-ECJ 100(1).
45 Above (note 22).
46 RP-CFI 127(2). In *BASF AG v Commission* (above, note 11) (see para 17) the decision was made in the form of a reasoned order under RP-CFI 111.
47 RP-ECJ 100(2); RP-CFI 127(3).
48 RP-ECJ 100(1); RP-CFI 127(2).

undertaken in connection with the admissibility of the application (in order to establish the existence of the fact), it would seem possible for the Court to consider the merits immediately after giving judgment upholding admissibility. Such a possibility is all the more apparent in the case of proceedings before the CFI, where the decision on admissibility need not take the form of a judgment: it is therefore possible for the CFI to come to a decision on admissibility which is expressed in the form of an order or, alternatively, not even written down at that stage but recorded in the eventual judgment on the substance. On the other hand, to proceed immediately to consider the merits might preclude the submission of argument from the parties. There therefore seem to be two basic interpretations of what is the correct procedure to follow.

If the parties have presented their arguments on the merits of the application during the first stage of proceedings, the Court should, after deciding that the application is admissible, open the oral procedure in order to hear oral argument from the parties and (where there is one) the advocate general's opinion on the merits of the application. The opinion should be delivered in the usual way and the judgment given in open court. In the alternative, if the defendant's written observations at the first stage are restricted to the question of admissibility, the Court should reopen the written procedure after giving judgment on admissibility, in order to allow all the parties to submit written observations on the merits. It is unclear if there should simply be submission of observations or a fully fledged exchange of pleadings as in a direct action. The former seems the preferable solution because the proceedings will be between the applicant, on the one hand, and all the other parties including interveners, on the other. In this situation, it is simpler if written observations alone are submitted. The Court then decides whether to hold a preparatory enquiry.[49] The oral procedure is opened in the usual way and, after the advocate general (if there is one) has delivered his opinion, the Court gives judgment.[50]

Once again, in the absence of authority, it is impossible to be dogmatic about the correct procedure to follow. The determining factor seems to be whether or not there has been full written argument concerning the merits of the application at the first stage of the proceedings. As has been indicated, the application itself must canvass both admissibility and the merits. The question whether the defendant's written observations should also do so depends in part on the covering letter sent by the Registrar with the copy of the application when it is served on the defendants. The Court may, through him, invite the defendants to submit observations only on admissibility. When this happens the parties should be given the opportunity to submit written observations on the merits if the Court decides that the application is admissible. On the other hand, if no such direction is given in the Registrar's letter, the defendants should argue the merits unless the application is blatantly inadmissible. In this way the second stage of proceedings may be abbreviated.

It may be said that the Court should either accept written observations or hear oral argument on the merits in the second stage, but not both. The general pattern of procedure before the Court is marked by reliance on written pleadings with oral argument being used to supplement them and, in particular, to allow the parties to answer their opponent's pleadings directly before the Court. In cases where written observations are lodged, the hearing is often the only opportunity to answer another party's pleadings. For example, in the

---

49 As has been seen, since the judgment (or, in the case of the CFI, order or other decision) finding the application to be admissible must establish the existence of the fact relied on, measures of enquiry should not strictly be necessary at this stage.

50 Vandersanden and Barav, op cit, at p 515.

first stage of revision proceedings, the applicant is not given an opportunity to answer the defendant's observations. In consequence, it seems right to restrict the situations where parties are not given an opportunity to reply to those cases in which the Rules of Procedure are reasonably clear. Therefore, in the second stage of revision proceedings, there ought to be a hearing, particularly where the written procedure is restricted to the lodgment of observations.

Whatever is the correct procedure, when the Court does give judgment, it is annexed to the original of the judgment sought to be revised, if the application is upheld, and a note of the revising judgment is made in the margin of the original.[51] The same happens where a judgment is rectified[52] or where judgment in default is set aside.[53] It would seem that revision has retrospective effect and relates back to the date at which the revised judgment was delivered. The reason for this is that the object of reviewing a judgment in revision proceedings is its replacement. Since the time limit for applying for revision is ten years after the date of judgment,[54] the effects of revision may be drastic but, if the procedure does not result in the review of the original judgment from the date of its delivery, it can only be of theoretical value in a large number of cases.

D   Scope of the procedure

The specific reference in both the Statutes and Rules of Procedure to revision of a *judgment* implies that the procedure is available only in proceedings which terminate in a decision which may properly be described as such and which therefore complies with the requirements of Chapter 4 of Title II of the ECJ's Rules of Procedure or Chapter 5 of Title 2 of the CFI's Rules of Procedure. This would exclude revision of, for example, decisions granting interim relief, which are made in the form of an order[55] and opinions delivered by the ECJ pursuant to art 228 of the EC Treaty. However, in Case 150/87 *Nashua Corpn v Council*[56] an application was made for the revision of a Court order refusing a request for confidential treatment of the applicant's pleadings. The application was dismissed as inadmissible because the conditions required by the Statutes had not been satisfied but not on the ground that such an application could not be made in respect of such an order. Further, it seems to be the case that some judgments may not be susceptible to revision. In Case 40/70 *Sirena Srl v Eda Srl*[57] the Court rejected an application made under RP-ECJ 102 for the interpretation of a judgment given in proceedings under art 177 of the EC Treaty[58] because such proceedings are non-contentious and initiated by the national court making the reference. It is for the national court to decide on the principle and purpose of the reference and also to determine whether sufficient guidance has been received from the Court. The proper procedure to adopt, where there is uncertainty concerning the interpretation of a judgment given in response to a reference for a preliminary ruling is, therefore, a second reference for a preliminary ruling, made by the national court, and not an application for interpretation made by a party under RP-ECJ 102. In Case

---

51 RP-ECJ 100(3); RP-CFI 127(4).
52 See RP-ECJ 66(4); RP-CFI 84(4).
53 See RP-ECJ 94(6); RP-CFI 122(6).
54 ECSC Statute, art 38; EC Statute, art 41; Euratom Statute, art 42.
55 See RP-ECJ 86(1); RP-CFI 107(1).
56 Reported sub nom Cases 133/87 and 150/87 *Nashua Corpn v Commission and Council* [1990] ECR I-719 (unreported order of 19 May 1988).
57 [1979] ECR 3169.
58 [1971] ECR 69.

69/85 *Wünsche Handelgesellschaft GmbH & Co v Germany*[59] the Court gave an even firmer indication that the exceptional review procedures set out in the Statutes (including revision) do not apply to preliminary rulings because there are no parties to such proceedings. Thus, where a hitherto unknown fact comes to the notice of the national court, it should make a second order for reference, if it thinks it appropriate to do so.[60] It does not seem to be possible for the parties to the proceedings before it to apply directly to the Court for the judgment given in response to the first order for reference to be revised. The reason why this is so lies in the nature of proceedings under art 177, which have often been described as a dialogue between the national court and the Court.

The approach of the Court in the *Sirena* and *Wünsche* cases suggests that the true test for determining the scope of revision proceedings is not whether the decision in question is headed by the word 'judgment' but whether it is in substance a judgment, within the meaning of the Statutes and the Rules of Procedure, for the purpose of revision.

On the basis of those cases it is possible to say that one of the features of a 'judgment' in the context of revision is that it is delivered in contentious proceedings. This excludes all preliminary rulings and similar references for interpretation from the scope of revision proceedings. One can go further and identify, as a second feature, that the judgment must have the force of res judicata. Although it is often said in the cases that revision is an exception to the doctrine of res judicata, that is not a particularly helpful criterion. A decision granting or refusing interim relief, for example, has such force, although it is made in the form of an order. On the other hand, it may be varied or cancelled where circumstances change,[61] so there is no real need for revision. The situation may arise, however, where an application in a direct action is rejected as inadmissible under RP-ECJ 92 or RP-CFI 111 or 113 by a decision in the form of an order and it is not possible to lodge another application before the expiry of a relevant time limit. Again, the order has the force of res judicata. Theoretically, if a newly discovered fact is relevant to the issue of admissibility, a second application can be lodged but this time it would be rejected as inadmissible on the ground that it was made out of time. It is therefore in the interests of the applicant to seek to have the previous decision overturned by bringing revision proceedings.

In the absence of authority, whether he can do so or not is uncertain. In principle, however, it would seem that he cannot because, as in the case of a decision granting or refusing interim relief, the newly discovered fact may ground a subsequent application. In the example given, that application would be inadmissible by reason of the additional fact that it is out of time. But, as a matter of law, the earlier order does not preclude a subsequent application grounded on a newly discovered fact. It may be inferred that, for the purposes of revision, a 'judgment' has not only the force of res judicata but is also final in the sense that the Court is functus officio and cannot consider an *originating* application concerning the same matter, even in the presence of different facts. On this basis, revision is really an exception to the rule that the Court is functus officio once it has given a final decision in an action. It would seem from the *Nashua* case[62] that procedural decisions may also have the degree of finality required to render them subject to revision. However, it is more likely that such decisions can always be revisited where there are new

---

59 [1986] ECR 947 (para 14).
60 Ibid para 15.
61 See RP-ECJ 84(2), 87 and 88; RP-CFI 105(2), 108 and 109.
62 Above (note 56).

facts (that is to say, a new element for the Court to take into consideration, whether or not it is one that existed at the time when the decision was made) and do not require a formal procedure for that purpose.

It has been suggested[63] that in the case of a judgment given in case of default of defence, the defendant can apply for its revision only after the time for applying to set aside the judgment has passed. This is clearly so if it be accepted that revision only applies to decisions which are final in the sense given above because the Court is not functus officio in the matter until the time limit for setting its judgment aside has expired. In practice the likelihood that a defendant would rely on revision rather than apply to set aside is rather far-fetched because, in the latter case, the Court re-hears the dispute and any new facts are in consequence admissible.[64] If an application for revision were made when it was still possible to apply to set aside, it might be argued that this would be a misuse of procedure and that, by analogy to the relationship between intervention and third party proceedings,[65] the defendant is restricted to an application to set aside while the time for doing so is still running. The Court's decision on the application to set aside cannot itself be set aside[66] but it would seem that it may be the subject of revision proceedings. Conversely, the Rules of Procedure do not state that a judgment on an application for revision cannot itself be revised and there is nothing in them which suggests unambiguously that judgment cannot be given in default and, if so given, subsequently set aside.

The objection to the revision of a revising judgment, apart from its extreme unlikelihood in practice and the theoretical possibility of an endless series of revising judgments, is that in theory the purpose of revision is the amendment of the original judgment and so its juridical identity merges with that of the judgment it revises.[67] At most there can be an application for the revision of the original judgment *as revised* but not for a revision of the revising judgment. The objection to applying the rules relating to judgment in default is slightly different. It is unclear whether the written procedure in revision proceedings can be said to include a 'defence' within the meaning of RP-ECJ 94 or RP-CFI 122. It appears to be more likely that it would comprise the lodging of written observations only. This factor cannot be said to indicate that the Court is unable to give judgment at all, whether on admissibility or the merits, if the defendants to the application refrain from submitting written observations. Instead it suggests that the adversarial nature of the procedure is not so strong as to justify a decision being made on the basis of the default of one party.[68]

VIII　Interpretation of judgments

A　Description of the procedure

The Statutes provide[69] that, if the meaning or scope of a judgment is in doubt, the Court shall construe it on application by a party or a Community institution showing an interest therein. The English version is taken from the

---

63 Vandersanden and Barav, op cit, pp 505–506.
64 See RP-ECJ 94; RP-CFI 122.
65 See pp 510–511.
66 RP-ECJ 94(6); RP-CFI 122(6).
67 It will be observed that RP-ECJ 100(3) and RP-CFI 127(4) are in the same terms as, respectively, RP-ECJ 66(4) and RP-CFI 84(4).
68 See under 'Judgment by default', above pp 505–507.
69 ECSC Statute, art 37; EC Statute, art 40; Euratom Statute, art 41.

German text of the Statutes; other versions such as the French and Italian refer to a 'difficulty', rather than doubt, in the correct interpretation of the judgment. The French version must naturally be preferred as far as the ECSC Statute is concerned.[70] There does not seem to be any difference in substance between the two terms 'difficulty' and 'doubt'. The procedure for obtaining the interpretation of a judgment need not be initiated where a dispute concerning the interpretation of the judgment arises in the context of, or as an incidental question in, a different dispute between the parties which can be brought before the Court by a different procedure.[71] The possibility of applying to the Court for it to interpret its judgment has been described as an exception to the functus officio rule rather than the principle of res judicata.[72] Thus, it is not an exception to the finality of judgments in the same sense as is the procedure for revising a judgment[73] because the Court does not review its decision or settle new matters of dispute.[74] It simply clarifies the meaning and scope of its judgment.

Conditions for applying for interpretation

Three conditions can be identified for the making of an application for interpretation: the application must relate to the 'meaning or scope' of a judgment; the meaning or scope must be in 'doubt'; and the applicant must have an interest in the matter.

1 The subject matter of the application

The purpose of the procedure has been said to be to obtain a clear elaboration of the will of the Court expressed in the judgment, or 'how the Court as a whole conceived its exact line of thought in the case'[75] and a parallel has been drawn with the interpretation of legislation.[76] For this reason the 'scope' of the judgment, in the context of these proceedings, has been narrowly construed. In *High Authority v Collotti and European Court of Justice*[77] the application was made primarily in order to find out whether the judgment in question was binding on persons who were not parties to the case. As Advocate General Roemer pointed out, this did relate to the scope of the judgment, taken literally, but the answer depended on an interpretation of the Treaty, which gave the Court its powers, not on the will of the Court as expressed in its judgment. A similar situation arose in *Gesellschaft für Getreidehandel mbH v Commission*,[78] where the problem was whether the judgment bound national courts, and in Case 9/81-Interpretation *Court of Auditors v Williams*,[79] where

---

70 See Case 70/63A *High Authority v Collotti and European Court of Justice* [1965] ECR 275 at 281 (Advocate General Roemer).
71 Case 135/87 *Vlachou v Court of Auditors* [1988] ECR 2901, paras 10–15 and at 2907 (Advocate General Lenz), where the applicant sought the annulment of a decision, inter alia, on the ground that it failed to comply with an earlier judgment of the Court, thus giving rise in the context of that annulment action to the issue of the true meaning of the earlier judgment.
72 See Case 5/55 *ASSIDER v High Authority* [1954–56] ECR 135 at 147 (Advocate General Lagrange) and Case 110/63A *Willame v Euratom Commission* [1966] ECR 287 at 295 (Advocate General Gand).
73 See pp 525–526.
74 The *ASSIDER* case (above, note 72) at 143–144 and 147 (Advocate General Lagrange).
75 *High Authority v Collotti and ECJ* (above, note 70) at 282 (Advocate General Roemer).
76 Case 24/66A *Gesellschaft für Getreidehandel mbH v Commission* [1973] ECR 1599 at 1606 (Advocate General Reischl).
77 Above (note 70).
78 Above (note 76).
79 [1983] ECR 2859 (paras 9–13).

the application concerned the interpretation of the judgment in relation to another case. In all three cases the application was held to be inadmissible, the Court stating that the basis for the application for an interpretation is 'the obscurity or ambiguity affecting the meaning or scope of the judgment itself in settling the particular case before the Court'[80] and that 'scope' meant the scope 'as regards the relationship between the parties' to the case, not the general effect of the judgment on others[81] or its effect on legal questions raised in another case.[82] The Court may therefore be called upon to clarify the extent of any obligation its judgment lays on the party[83] but not its application to a given set of facts,[84] nor its execution, application or other consequences.[85]

The only parts of the judgment that may be interpreted are those that express the Court's decision: the operative part and those grounds set out in the judgment which are essential for reaching the conclusion in the operative part. These constitute the actual decision and the Court cannot be called upon to interpret other parts of the judgment which supplement or explain them[86] or, a fortiori, points not decided by the judgment.[87] Advocate General Lagrange appears to have adopted a narrower approach in his opinion in the *ASSIDER* case,[88] where he said that interpretation was restricted to the part of the judgment which is res judicata, in principle the operative part only. As a general rule, the operative part of judgments is to be interpreted in the light of the reasoning preceding it.[89] If the judgment does not decide a particular issue (for example, because it has already been decided in a previous case) but is concerned only with the consequences to be drawn from it, the application for interpretation is inadmissible in so far as it relates to that issue.[90]

2   Doubt

For the application to be admissible the proper interpretation of the Court's judgment must be 'in doubt' or give rise to a 'difficulty'. In the *ASSIDER* case[91] the Court held that it was sufficient that the parties give different meanings to the wording of the judgment; it was not necessary for there to be a dispute between them. Advocate General Lagrange said that the difficulty must be 'concrete' or specific and such as to interfere with the enforcement of the judgment; a Community institution could apply even though the parties were themselves agreed as to its correct meaning.[92] To some extent this was followed by Advocate General Roemer in *High Authority v Collotti and European Court of Justice*.[93] He took the view that the fact that the doubt arose between different departments or officials of the High Authority, the applicant, as opposed to a difference of opinion between the parties or between one party and a Community institution which was not a party, was not in itself a ground for holding

---

80 *High Authority v Collotti and ECJ* (above, note 70) at 279.
81 The *Getreidehandel* case (above, note 76) at para 4.
82 *Court of Auditors v Williams* (above, note 79).
83 Cases 41, 43 and 44/73 *Société Anonyme Générale Sucrière v Commission* [1977] ECR 445.
84 *Willame v Euratom Commission* (above, note 72) at 291.
85 Ibid; *Court of Auditors v Williams* (above, note 79); Case 206/81A *Alvarez v European Parliament* [1983] ECR 2865; Cases 146 and 431/85-Interpretation *Maindiaux v Economic and Social Committee and Diezler* [1988] ECR 2003 (paras 6–8).
86 The *ASSIDER* case (above, note 72) at 142; the *Maindiaux* case (ibid) para 6.
87 The *Maindiaux* case (ibid) paras 6–8.
88 Above (note 72) at 147–148.
89 Case 135/77 *Bosch v Hauptzollamt Hildesheim* [1978] ECR 855.
90 The *Getreidehandel* case (above, note 76); the *Maindiaux* case (above, note 85), paras 7–8.
91 Above (note 72) at 142.
92 Ibid at 147.
93 Above (note 70) at 281.

the application to be inadmissible: it was sufficient if the applicant put forward serious reasons showing that a judgment could be interpreted in different ways. Nonetheless, the difficulty must still relate to the meaning or scope of the judgment in settling the dispute before the Court.[94] The existence of agreement between parties as to the correct interpretation of the judgment is a bar to an application made by one of the parties.[95]

For the purposes of admissibility it is sufficient to allege the existence of an ambiguity or uncertainty in the judgment[96] although, as Advocate General Roemer pointed out in *High Authority v Collotti and European Court of Justice*, there must be some basis for the allegation and, as Advocate General Lagrange pointed out in *ASSIDER*,[97] the ambiguity or uncertainty must relate to the part of the judgment which can be interpreted. The question whether the allegation is founded relates to the substance of the application, not to its admissibility.[98] Whether the operative part of the judgment is ambiguous or uncertain is to be determined by examining it in the context of the form of order in the original action and the reasoning set out in the judgment supporting the operative part.[99] If the judgment is found to be clear, there is nothing to interpret and the case should be dismissed.[1]

3 Interest

Only one of the parties to the case or a Community institution can apply for a judgment to be interpreted and, in both cases, the applicant must show that he has an interest in having the judgment interpreted. The Court has construed 'party' broadly so as to include any person bound by the judgment in question. Further, in the *ASSIDER* case[2] the applicant sought an interpretation of the judgment in Case 2/54 *Italy v High Authority*,[3] to which it was not a party. Nevertheless, ASSIDER was held to be entitled to apply for interpretation because:[4]

'where several actions are brought against the same decision of the High Authority and where, as the result of one of those actions, the decision is annulled, the applicants in the other actions may be regarded as "parties" to the action within the meaning of Article 37 [of the ECSC Statute], subject expressly to the condition that the applicant has cited in his previous application the same ground on which the judgment to be interpreted has annulled the decision or as in the present case has declared the application well-founded.'

What had happened was that, in Case 3/54 *ASSIDER v High Authority*,[5] ASSIDER had claimed that part of a High Authority decision should be

---

94 Ibid at 279.
95 *Willame v Euratom Commission* (above, note 72) at 291.
96 Ibid at 292.
97 Above (note 72) at 147.
98 *Willame v Euratom Commission* (above, note 72) at 291. But, as Advocate General VerLoren van Themaat pointed out in *Alvarez v European Parliament* (above, note 85) at 2877 and 2878, the borderline between inadmissibility and lack of substance is not clear. In Cases 100, 146 and 153/87 *Basch v Commission* [1989] ECR 447 at 456, Advocate General Jacobs regarded the absence of doubt about the meaning of the judgment as going to admissibility.
99 *Willame* ibid at 292.
1 Case 5/55 *ASSIDER v High Authority* [1954–56] ECR 135 at 148 (Advocate General Lagrange).
2 Ibid.
3 [1954–56] ECR 37.
4 *ASSIDER* (above, note 1) at 141–142.
5 [1954–56] ECR 63.

annulled because it infringed art 30 of the ECSC Convention on the Transitional Provisions. The same argument was put forward by the Italian government in Case 2/54 *Italy v High Authority*[6] and held by the Court to be well founded. But the Court did not formally annul the decision because it had already done so, for different reasons, in Case 1/54 *France v High Authority*.[7] For the same reason it did not give judgment at all in Case 3/54. Subsequently, in correspondence with ASSIDER, the High Authority cited the decision in Case 2/54 as an authoritative interpretation of the Convention on the Transitional Provisions, but ASSIDER disagreed with the conclusions the High Authority drew from the judgment and applied to the Court for an interpretation of it in order to clear the matter up. Had the Court given judgment in Case 3/54, either repeating the reasoning adopted in Case 2/54 or incorporating it by reference, the application would not have given rise to any difficulty. It was the fact that the Court had not, in formal terms, annulled the decision in either case that created the problem, albeit that, in substance, the Court's acceptance of the arguments in favour of annulment used in Case 2/54 covered precisely the point raised by ASSIDER in its own action. Advocate General Lagrange found the solution to the problem in the principle of res judicata, the effect of the annulment in Case 1/54 being erga omnes.[8] The Court agreed with him in principle, looking at the substance of the legal position rather than the form. Nevertheless, it seems that, if ASSIDER's claim had been inadmissible, it would not have been considered a party to Case 2/54. The principle in the *ASSIDER* case applies only where the Court does not give judgment solely because the point has already been decided in a previous case. Thus the application in the *Getreidehandel* case[9] was inadmissible, inter alia, because the subsequent case raised no issue that was decided in the first case but further issues flowing from the effects of that decision. Where cases have been joined for the purpose of giving judgment, of course, all the parties in all the joined cases are parties to the judgment.[10]

In the *ASSIDER* case[11] the Court found that the applicant had an interest in obtaining an interpretation of the judgment because (i) the question 'which of the two contending interpretations is correct?' was of direct concern to it and (ii) the only way of settling the question was by applying for interpretation. In subsequent cases the problem of interest is lost sight of, but it would seem that the applicant must show that there is something more than an academic interest in finding out what the Court really meant that lies behind the application. Clearly a dispute over the enforcement of the judgment gives sufficient interest to ground an application even though the Court cannot rule on such a dispute in those proceedings.[12] In the case of interveners, the interest that they have in intervening in the case seems to be sufficient for the purpose of making an application for interpretation.[13] On the other hand, it is difficult to see what interest a Community institution, which was not a party to the original action, may have. The only case in which a Community institution did

---

6 [1954–56] ECR 37.
7 [1954–56] ECR 1.
8 *ASSIDER* (above, note 1) at 146.
9 Case 24/66A *Getreidehandel v High Authority* [1973] ECR 1599.
10 See Cases 41, 43 and 44/73 *Société Anonyme Général Sucrière v Commission* [1977] ECR 445.
11 Above (note 1) at 141.
12 Case 206/81A *Alvarez v European Parliament* [1983] ECR 2865 at 2875–2876 (Advocate General VerLoren van Themaat).
13 Cases 146 and 431/85-Interpretation *Maindiaux v Economic and Social Committee and Diezler* [1988] ECR 2003 (para 4).

apply for interpretation although it was not a party, seems to have been Case 70/63A *High Authority v Collotti and European Court of Justice*.[14] The application was rejected as inadmissible on the ground that it was not concerned with the proper construction of the Court's judgment but with its legal effects so the case gives little guidance. What it does seem to show, however, is that, since interpretation is restricted to clarifying the decision settling the dispute before the Court, an applicant institution, not being a party, has to show some interest in the question raised in the dispute and settled in the judgment.

C Procedural stages

There is no time limit for applying for the interpretation of a judgment.[15] The application can be made only by one of the parties to the case closed by the judgment (including interveners)[16] or by a Community institution.[17] The application must be made against all the parties to the case in which the judgment in question was given.[18] Where the application is made in respect of a judgment given in one of a number of cases which were joined for the purpose of giving judgment, every party in every one of the joined cases must be cited in the application.[19] The reason is that the object is to cite as parties to the interpretation proceedings all those bound by the judgment in question so that they will be equally bound by the interpreting judgment. The applicant cannot limit the scope of the application by pleading that the interpretation should affect only him.[20] Due to the fact that the application must be made against all the parties to the original case, it would seem that it must ordinarily be made by separate document (although the Rules of Procedure do not expressly so provide); otherwise, the other parties to the original case might have to be made parties to another action solely by reason of the inclusion in the application commencing proceedings in that action of a claim for the interpretation of the judgment in question.[21]

The application must comply with RP-ECJ 37–38 or, as the case may be, RP-ECJ 43–44. In addition, it must specify the judgment to be interpreted and the passages of which interpretation is sought.[22] In the *Getreidehandel* case[23] Advocate General Reischl took the view that it is sufficient if, from the overall content of the application, it is clear what part of the judgment the applicant has in mind. It does not seem necessary, therefore, to quote the relevant extract from the Court's judgment. On the other hand, the general rules of pleadings before the Court apply and the applicant is restricted to the request for interpretation as it is formulated in the application. He cannot extend the scope of the request after it has been served on the other parties, at least in the

---

14 [1965] ECR 275.
15 The *ASSIDER* case (above, note 1) at 140.
16 The *Maindiaux* case (above, note 13) para 4.
17 ECSC Statute, art 37; EC Statute, art 40; Euratom Statute, art 41.
18 RP-ECJ 102(1), last sentence; RP-CFI 129(1), last sentence.
19 See the *Générale Sucrière* case (above, note 10).
20 Ibid para 29.
21 An application for interpretation was included in an application for annulment in Cases 100, 146 and 153/87 *Basch v Commission* [1989] ECR 447 but regarded by Advocate General Jacobs as being inadmissible for other reasons (see at 456). However, as pointed out in Case 135/87 *Vlachou v Court of Auditors* [1988] ECR 2901, the mere fact that an action gives rise to an issue as to the interpretation of an earlier judgment does not mean that that issue can be decided only by proceedings for interpretation.
22 RP-ECJ 102(1); RP-CFI 129(1); *Alvarez v European Parliament* (above, note 12) at 2877–2878 (Advocate General VerLoren van Themaat).
23 Above (note 9) at 1605.

absence of a valid reason for omitting the additional claim from the application.[24] The form of order in the application should therefore make clear the respects in which the judgment requires interpretation. In some cases it also appears to have set out the applicant's own formulation of what the correct interpretation should be. This does not appear to be essential as long as the various contending interpretations of the judgment are set out in the body of the application.

The application is served on the persons named in it in the usual way and they are invited to submit their written observations on it.[25] The fact that the defendants must be heard is said to mark the contentious nature of the proceedings, despite the fact that there is no exchange of pleadings as in a direct action or any need for a lis between the parties.[26] The Rules of Procedure do not expressly exclude a further exchange since they specify only that the parties must be given an opportunity to submit their observations. It is not even stated whether the observations are written or oral or both. Until recently, the Court's practice has been to close the pleadings after the lodgment of the defendant's observations and then to open the oral procedure. There are no preparatory enquiries because the proceedings are limited to finding out what the Court's judgment means and that is a question of law. The oral procedure consists of the hearing and the advocate general's opinion (where there is one), which is delivered, as is usual, in open Court. In *Alvarez v European Parliament*,[27] Advocate General VerLoren van Themaat pointed out that the Rules of Procedure do not specify the form in which the parties are to submit their observations and the advocate general is to deliver his opinion. Where, therefore, there is no oral procedure stricto sensu and the parties do not present their observations at a public hearing, the advocate general does not present his opinion formally in open court but may do so either in writing or orally. In that case there does not seem to have been a hearing in the usual sense, although the parties were heard, and the advocate general did not deliver an opinion but presented his views in the form of written 'observations'.

In principle, the Court's decision is given in the form of a judgment[28] and delivered in open Court, the parties being given notice to attend and being served with certified copies.[29] The requirement that the decision be given in the form of a judgment could be construed as applicable only when the application is admissible and the earlier judgment interpreted. In practice, the decision has taken the form of a judgment in other circumstances, such as where the application has been rejected as inadmissible[30] or has been found to be admissible but dismissed on the merits.[31] It would seem that the decision will take the form of an order if the oral procedure has not been opened and, presumably, the application has been dismissed. Otherwise, it is required to take the form of a judgment only if the application is admissible and well founded. Where the case is admissible but is dismissed on the merits, the Court

---

24 Case 110/63A *Willame v Euratom Commission* [1966] ECR 287 at 291 and 297 (Advocate General Gand).
25 RP-ECJ 102(2); RP-CFI 129(3).
26 *Willame v Euratom Commission* (above, note 24) at 295 (Advocate General Gand); see also the *ASSIDER* case (above, note 1) at 149 (Advocate General Lagrange).
27 Above (note 12) at 2874.
28 RP-ECJ 102(2); RP-CFI 129(3).
29 RP-ECJ 64; RP-CFI 82.
30 Eg the *Getreidehandel* case (above, note 9).
31 Eg *Willame v Euratom Commission* (above, note 24).

states in the operative part of the judgment closing the interpretation proceedings that the application does not give rise to an interpretation of the judgment in question, not that it is unambiguous and certain.[32] Where the application is successful, the original of the interpreting judgment is annexed to the original of the judgment interpreted and a note of the former is made in the margin of the latter.[33] An interpreting judgment is binding on all the parties to the original action in so far as they are affected either by the passage of the judgment which the Court has interpreted or by another passage which is exactly the same.[34]

Although the procedure has been described as one designed to obtain an interpretation of an obscure provision in a judgment from the very court which gave the judgment,[35] this does not mean that the same judges must be involved. In *High Authority v Collotti and European Court of Justice*[36] the initial judgment had been delivered by the First Chamber but it was the full Court that heard and determined the application for interpretation. The point about the composition of the Court was raised by one of the parties but does not figure in the judgment. Advocate General Roemer, however, seems to have taken the view that a decision of a chamber is a decision of the Court.[37] If judgments are regarded as decisions, not of the judges individually or collectively, but of the Court as a judicial body, the problem of the composition of the tribunal deciding the case does not arise. Where the application for interpretation is made to the CFI, it is assigned to the chamber which delivered the judgment to be interpreted or to the full Court, if the judgment was delivered by the CFI sitting in plenary session.[38] Where the same judgment of the CFI is the subject at the same time of an appeal to the ECJ and an application for interpretation brought before the CFI, the CFI may, after hearing the parties, stay the interpretation proceedings until the ECJ has decided the appeal.[39]

Interpretation proceedings are contentious in form rather than in nature.[40] Nonetheless, intervention is possible, albeit unusual because, in principle, the dispute about the interpretation of the judgment should be of interest only to the parties to the judgment.[41] On the other hand, it does not seem that the rules relating to judgment by default and, in particular, setting aside such a judgment apply where the defendant fails to submit his observations in time.[42] Revision cannot apply because there is no issue of fact in proceedings for the interpretation of a judgment. On the other hand, there seems no objection to applying for interim measures (but not the suspension of the operation of a measure adopted by an institution, with the exception of a decision of the Court) pending the interpreting judgment, nor do third party proceedings appear to be excluded although they are not likely to occur in practice.

32 Ibid at 293; see XII Rec at 420.
33 RP-ECJ 102(2); RP-CFI 129(3).
34 The *Générale Sucrière* case (above, note 10), para 29; see also the *ASSIDER* case (above, note 1) at 149 (Advocate General Lagrange).
35 The *ASSIDER* case (ibid) at 147 (Advocate General Lagrange).
36 Above (note 14).
37 Ibid at 282.
38 RP-CFI 129(2).
39 RP-CFI 129(4). See the parallel situation in third party proceedings: p 513.
40 RP-ECJ 102(2); RP-CFI 129(3); see the *ASSIDER* case (above, note 1) at 145.
41 In Case 9/81-Interpretation *Court of Auditors v Williams* [1983] ECR 2859 (para 7) a third party to the original judgment was allowed to intervene because the interpretation was requested specifically in relation to another case between the applicant for interpretation and the intervener.
42 See pp 500 et seq.

D   Scope of the procedure

The meaning of the word 'judgment' is discussed elsewhere.[43] In Case 40/70 *Sirena Srl v Eda Srl*[44] the Court dismissed as inadmissible an application for the interpretation of a judgment delivered in proceedings under art 177 of the EC Treaty on the ground that such proceedings are non-contentious in character and it is for the national court making the reference to decide whether the Court's ruling gives it adequate guidance in the matter. If it has not, the remedy is for the national court to make a second order for reference.[45] In essence, it seems, a judgment is a final decision in contentious proceedings which is binding on the parties and leaves the Court functus officio in the matter, ie it has exhausted its jurisdiction once it has given judgment.[46]

IX   Execution and enforcement of judgments

Judgments are binding from the date of their delivery,[47] ie from the time the operative part is read out in open court.[48] The conditions for their enforcement are laid down in the Treaties,[49] which provide[50] that enforcement is governed by the rules of civil procedure[51] in force in the member state in whose territory the judgment is executed. It seems that enforcement is conditional on there being appended to the judgment the order for its enforcement. This is done by the national authority designated for this purpose. This operation should be performed automatically, the only formality being verification of the authenticity of the judgment.[52] Once the order for enforcement has been appended to the judgment, the party concerned may proceed to enforce it, in accordance with national law, by bringing the matter directly before the competent authority.[53] The courts of the country in which execution takes place have jurisdiction over complaints that enforcement is being carried out in an irregular manner but only the Court can order the suspension of the enforcement of one of its own decisions.[54] All those to whom a judgment is addressed are directly concerned by the way in which it is executed.[55] Application for the

---

43 See pp 493 et seq.
44 [1979] ECR 3169.
45 See also Case 13/67 *Firma Kurt A Becher v Hauptzollamt München Landsbergerstrasse* [1968] ECR 187 at 196–197; Case 135/77 *Robert Bosch GmbH v Hauptzollamt Hildesheim* [1978] ECR 855.
46 In Case 17/68 *Reinarz v Commission* [1970] ECR 1, an application was made for the interpretation of an order fixing the amount of costs recoverable in earlier proceedings. The Court did not reject it as inadmissible on the ground that the order was not a 'judgment' so that, as in the *Sirena* case, a substantive test was adopted. The order fixing costs was final and fulfilled the other conditions of a judgment.
47 RP-ECJ 65; RP-CFI 83.
48 RP-ECJ 64(1); RP-CFI 82(1).
49 ECSC Treaty, art 44; EC Treaty, art 187; Euratom Treaty, art 159.
50 ECSC Treaty, art 92; EC Treaty, art 192; Euratom Treaty, art 164.
51 The EC and Euratom Treaties, ibid; the ECSC Treaty simply refers to 'the legal procedure in force'.
52 This is done by producing an authenticated copy of the judgment which is obtainable, on request, from the Court subject to the payment of Registry charges: see IR 20.
53 In the United Kingdom the procedure for enforcing decisions of the Court is set out in the European Communities (Enforcement of Community Judgments) Order 1972 (SI 1972/1590), which provides that the High Court (as defined) is to register forthwith, upon application, any judgment to which the Secretary of State has appended an order for enforcement. Once registered, the judgment has the same force and effect, for all purposes of execution, as if it had been made by the High Court.
54 See Case 4/73 *J Nold Kohlen- und Baustoffgrosshandlung v Ruhrkohle AG* [1977] ECR 1.
55 Case T-38/89 *Hochbaum v Commission* [1990] ECR II-43 (para 9).

suspension of the enforcement of a decision of the Court is made to whichever of the ECJ and the CFI delivered the judgment under RP-ECJ 89 or, as the case may be, RP-CFI 110.[56] Costs necessarily incurred by a party in enforcing a judgment or order of the Court are borne by the opposing party and are calculated by reference to the scale in force in the member state in which the judgment or order is executed.[57]

It has been suggested[58] that only judgments which impose a pecuniary obligation on persons other than States can be enforced. The basis for this appears to be that, under the EC Treaty, judgments are enforceable 'under the conditions' laid down in the article of the Treaty covering the enforcement of 'decisions of the Council or of the Commission which impose a pecuniary obligation on persons other than States' (art 192). In fact, the parallel provision in the ECSC Treaty, art 92 refers to 'decisions of the [Commission] which impose a pecuniary obligation' simpliciter and contains no limitation to 'persons other than States'. On this ground alone it is arguable that judgments delivered in actions brought under the ECSC Treaty can be enforced against a member state, at least if they impose a pecuniary obligation. In addition, art 164 of the Euratom Treaty refers generally to enforcement without specifying decisions imposing a pecuniary obligation or those made against persons other than member states. Hence neither limitation can be said to apply to judgments made in actions brought under the Euratom Treaty.

However, it is doubtful if the enforcement of judgments of the Court under the EC Treaty is restricted as suggested. Article 192 of the EC Treaty sets out in the opening sentence the decisions of the Council or Commission to which it applies. There then follows a description of the conditions upon which enforcement of the decisions so defined may be effected. The opening sentence defines the scope of these provisions and, because it makes no mention of judgments of the Court, they do not apply to judgments, which are covered by art 187. Had the intention been to limit enforcement to judgments imposing a pecuniary obligation on a person other than a member state, one would expect to see such a limitation in this article but its scope is not cut down by any restrictive definition of the type of judgments to which it refers. Since it is this article which governs the scope of the enforceability of judgments of the Court, there is no reason to apply the additional restrictions which may be found in the Treaty provision determining the scope of the enforceability of the acts of other institutions. A more powerful objection lies in the fact that, in any event, enforcement of a judgment is governed by the rules of *civil* procedure in the member state in question. If these rules do not provide for enforcement against the state, cadit quaestio.

In the nature of things, however, judgments made against member states are almost invariably delivered in actions brought under art 169 of the EC Treaty in respect of a failure by a member state to fulfil an obligation under the Treaty. This procedure, if successful, results in a declaration and an obligation, arising under art 171 of the Treaty, to take the necessary measures to comply with the judgment. The result is that the competent national authorities are directly bound not to apply any measures incompatible with the Treaty and, if necessary, to take positive steps to apply Community law,[59] without it being necessary to enforce the judgment. Furthermore, since the

---

56 See chapter 8, pp 246–247.
57 RP-ECJ 71; RP-CFI 89.
58 Vandersanden and Barav, op cit, p 65.
59 See, for example, Case 48/71 *Commission v Italy* [1972] ECR 527 (Re Export Tax on Art Treasures (No 2)) (paras 7–8).

object of the judgment is to obtain a finding that a member state has not fulfilled its obligations, the operative part does not contain an order (save as to costs) which is susceptible of enforcement. Judgments given in proceedings for a preliminary ruling are also not enforceable because no order is made which binds the parties; the judgment does, however, bind the referring court.[60]

All the Treaties say that 'judgments' of the Court are enforceable. This suggests that Court orders cannot be enforced. Court orders are not generally susceptible of enforcement but this is not so, in particular, in the case of orders granting interim relief or awarding costs. So far as the latter are concerned, the Statutes expressly envisage that the Court shall 'adjudicate' on costs;[61] RP-ECJ 74(2) and RP-CFI 92(2) provide that the parties may, for the purpose of enforcing it, apply for an authenticated copy of the order made determining the costs recoverable. In *J Nold Kohlen- und Baustoffgrosshandlung v Ruhrkohle AG*,[62] the Court deduced from this that its decisions on costs are enforceable. The order concerned the enforcement of an earlier order fixing the costs recoverable in an action under the ECSC Treaty. The same reasoning seems to apply to actions under the other Treaties. There is no similar decision concerning the enforcement of orders granting interim relief although there are several provisions in the Rules of Procedure which envisage that orders (other than those concerning costs) may be enforced.[63] Clearly, if an order granting interim relief cannot be enforced, there is a serious gap in the web of legal protection woven in the Treaties. It is doubtful, however, if the gap really exists.

The Treaties appear to envisage that decisions granting interim relief are enforceable because they expressly empower the Court to make such decisions, which would be pointless if they had no effect. The problem arises because, under the Statutes and Rules of Procedure, the exercise of the Court's power to order interim relief is delegated to the President or the Judge replacing him (who may refer the matter back to the Court) and the decision is made in the form of what the Rules of Procedure[64] describe as a 'reasoned order' rather than a 'judgment'. The question is, therefore, whether a 'reasoned order' granting interim relief is a 'judgment' within the meaning of the Treaties. Hitherto, in interpreting the word 'judgment', the Court has adopted a substantive rather than a terminological test.[65] The hallmarks of a judgment can be said to be that it binds the parties, leaves the Court functus officio in the matter[66] and can be enforced. Orders granting interim relief certainly bind the parties and the judge deciding the matter is left functus officio, rebus sic stantibus;[67] the intention of the Treaties seems to be that such decisions are enforceable and this is expressly envisaged in the Rules of Procedure.[68] There appears to be no reason of substance, therefore, that a terminological disparity between the Treaties and the Rules of Procedure should result in the unenforceability of orders granting interim relief.

---

60 Eg Case 52/76 *Benedetti v Munari Fratelli SAS* [1977] ECR 163 at para 26 and at 193 (Advocate General Reischl); Case 112/76 *Manzoni v FNROM* [1977] ECR 1647 at 1662 (Advocate General Warner); Case 69/85 *Wünsche Handelsgesellschaft GmbH & Co v Germany* [1986] ECR 947 (para 13); Case C-364/92 *SAT Fluggesellschaft mbH v Eurocontrol*, 19 January 1994, para 14.
61 ECSC Statute, art 32; EC Statute, art 35; Euratom Statute, art 36.
62 Above (note 54) at para 3.
63 Eg RP-ECJ 16(5), 48(2) and (4), and 86(2); RP-CFI 24(5), 69(2) and (4), and 107(2).
64 RP-ECJ 86(1); RP-CFI 107(1).
65 Cf *Reinarz v Commission* (above, note 46); *Sirena Srl v Eda Srl* (above, note 44).
66 Cf the *ASSIDER* case (above, note 1) at 147 (Advocate General Lagrange).
67 RP-ECJ 87; RP-CFI 108.
68 RP-ECJ 86(2); RP-CFI 107(2).

Under IR 22(2), where a party is directed by a judgment or order to pay costs to the Court's cashier and fails to comply within the period prescribed, the Registrar shall 'apply for payment of the costs to be enforced'. This appears to mean that the Registrar proceeds to enforce the judgment or order in the appropriate state by asking the competent national authority to append to it the order for its enforcement. On the other hand, where the Court orders the repayment to it of legal aid, the reimbursement of avoidable costs or the return of advance payments made to witnesses or experts by way of legal aid, payment of the sum due is to be demanded by registered letter signed by the Registrar.[69] If the sum due is not paid within the period prescribed, the Court's order cannot be enforced directly: the Registrar must, according to IR 22(2), first request the Court to make an 'enforceable decision' and then seek its enforcement under the Treaties.[70] This necessarily implies that the Court order requiring the sums in question to be paid is not itself enforceable. Why this should be so is obscure.

---

69 IR 22(1).
70 The English version of IR 22(2) actually says: 'the Registrar . . . shall request the Court to make an enforceable decision and to order its enforcement'. This is the same as the German text but the French and Italian versions make more sense because they clearly provide that it is the Registrar who applies for enforcement of the 'enforceable decision' delivered by the Court at his request.

CHAPTER 17

Forms of action

I Introduction

The Court exercises its powers under the conditions and for the purposes provided for in the Treaties and any other treaties and Acts modifying and supplementing them.[1] Its jurisdiction is defined not only in the Treaties but also in a number of other instruments (conventions and agreements etc, but primarily secondary legislation). Specific limits are placed on its jurisdiction by art 31 of the Single European Act and art L of the EU Treaty; and those limits must be borne in mind when considering whether or not an action lies before the Court.[2] The most important forms of action[3] are discussed at length in the leading textbooks[4] and need no more than a brief sketch here. Other proceedings have not been the subject of detailed commentary and are therefore described at greater length. Not all procedures are covered, partly because it is difficult to be comprehensive given the fragmented nature of the corpus of relevant texts, partly because some procedures are of no practical importance or interest.

II Common procedures

A Actions for annulment

1 Nature of the action

Under the EC and Euratom Treaties,[5] an action for annulment can be brought by:

(1) a member state;

---

1 ECSC Treaty, art 3; EC Treaty, art 4(1); Euratom Treaty, art 3(1); EU Treaty, art E.
2 In brief, art 31 of the Single European Act provides that, in relation to that Act, the Court's jurisdiction extends only to Title II and art 32 of the Act. It is likely that, in reality, the Court's power to interpret Community law also covers art 31 itself and art 3(1), both of which are referred to in art 32. The broad effect of art 31 is to exclude political co-operation and the activities of the European Council (comprising heads of state or of government and the President of the Commission) from judicial review. Art L of the EU Treaty provides that the Court's jurisdiction extends to the provisions of the EU Treaty amending the ECSC, EC and Euratom Treaties and to arts K.3(2)(c) and L to S of the EU Treaty only, thus excluding jurisdiction over the remaining provisions of the EU Treaty.
3 Ie actions for annulment, failure to act, damages, default by a member state and preliminary rulings.
4 See, for example, Bebr *Development of Judicial Control of the European Communities*; Hartley *The Foundations of European Community Law*; Joliet *Le Droit Institutionnel des Communautés Européennes: Le Contentieux*; Schermers and Waelbroeck *Judicial Protection in the European Communities*; Vandersanden and Barav *Contentieux Communautaires*; Vaughan (ed) *Law of the European Communities*, part 2.
5 Articles 173 and 146 respectively.

(2)   the Council;
(3)   the Commission;
(4)   the European Parliament (but only for the purpose of protecting its prerogatives);[6]
(5)   the European Central Bank (but only for the purpose of protecting its prerogatives);[7] or
(6)   any natural or legal person.

The defendant in the proceedings is the author of the act challenged in the action. The following may be challenged:

(1)   acts of the Council, the Commission or the European Central Bank other than recommendations or opinions;[8]
(2)   acts adopted jointly by the European Parliament and the Council, other than recommendations and opinions;
(3)   acts of the European Parliament intended to produce legal effects vis-à-vis third parties;[9] and
(4)   acts of the Court of Auditors.[10]

Acts adopted by a national authority cannot be challenged even if they are adopted in the context of the decision-making process in the Community.[11] A claim arising out of a contract with a Community institution is not properly the subject of an action for annulment.[12] A legal or natural person can only challenge (i) 'a decision addressed to that person' or (ii) 'a decision which, although in the form of a regulation or a decision addressed to another person, is of direct and individual concern to the former'.

Under art 33 of the ECSC Treaty, an action for annulment can be brought by a member state, the Council, 'undertakings or the associations referred to in Article 48'[13] or the European Parliament (but only for the purpose of protecting its prerogatives).[14] The defendant in the action is always the Commission because proceedings can be brought only against an act adopted by it. Member states, the Council and the European Parliament may challenge a decision or recommendation of the Commission but undertakings and associations may challenge only 'decisions or recommendations concerning them which are individual in character' or 'general decisions or recommendations which they consider to involve a misuse of powers affecting them'.

---

6 EU Treaty, arts G(E)(53) and I(13), implementing Case C-70/88 *European Parliament v Council* [1990] ECR I-2041 (para 27); Case C-65/90 *European Parliament v Council* [1992] ECR I-4593 (paras 10–15).
7 See the amendment of art 173 introduced by the EU Treaty, art G(E)(53).
8 Articles 189 and 161 of the EC and Euratom Treaties, respectively, define the acts which may be adopted by the Council and the Commission. The classification adopted is not the same as that used in the ECSC Treaty.
9 Articles 173 and 146, as amended by the EU Treaty, art G(E)53, implementing in relation to the European Parliament Case 294/83 *Parti Ecologiste 'Les Verts' v European Parliament* [1986] ECR 1339 (paras 23–25); Case 78/85 *Group of the European Right v European Parliament* [1986] ECR 1753 (paras 10–11); Case 34/86 *Council v European Parliament* [1986] ECR 2155.
10 Cases 193 and 194/87 *Maurissen v Court of Auditors* [1989] ECR 1045 (para 42 and at 1063–1065, Advocate General Darmon).
11 Case C-97/91 *Oleificio Borelli SpA v Commission* [1992] ECR I-6313 (paras 9–13); Cases C-181 and C-248/91 *European Parliament v Council and Commission* [1993] ECR I-3685 (para 12).
12 Case 43/84 *Maag v Commission* [1985] ECR 2581 (para 26).
13 Undertakings are defined in art 80 of the Treaty
14 The Parliament was included by an amendment introduced by the EU Treaty, art H(13), which thereby acted on the Court's ruling in Case C-70/88 *European Parliament v Council* (above, note 6) para 27.

The ECSC Treaty contains two other provisions which open a right to claim the annulment of an act of a Community institution. The first is art 38, which provides that such an action may be brought by either a member state or the Commission against an 'act' of the Parliament or the Council. Natural or legal persons have no right of action.[15] The second provision is art 63(2), which provides that a purchaser of coal and steel may institute proceedings for the annulment of an act of the Commission restricting or prohibiting temporarily dealings between the purchaser and Community undertakings.[16] This right of action is said to be 'without prejudice to Article 33', which indicates that the conditions imposed by art 33 relating to the grounds which may be relied on and the time limit for commencing proceedings both apply. It does not seem, however, that the limitation on the type of act which may be challenged under art 33 applies in the context of art 63(2).

2 Time limits

The time limit for bringing proceedings under art 173 of the EC Treaty or art 146 of the Euratom Treaty is two months, running from (i) publication of the measure, (ii) notification to the applicant or, in the absence of notification, (iii) the day on which the measure challenged 'came to the knowledge' of the applicant. The time limit for bringing proceedings under arts 33 or 63(2) of the ECSC Treaty is one month from the notification or publication of the contested act. Proceedings under art 38 of the ECSC Treaty must be brought within one month of the publication of the act, where it is adopted by the Parliament, or, in the case of an act of the Council, one month of its notification to the member states or the Commission.[17]

3 Grounds

The grounds which may be relied on in support of a claim for annulment under art 173 of the EC Treaty, art 146 of the Euratom Treaty or art 33 of the ECSC Treaty are:

(1) lack of competence;
(2) infringement of an essential procedural requirement;
(3) infringement of the relevant Treaty or of any rule of law relating to its application; or
(4) misuse of powers.

Under art 33 of the ECSC Treaty, where the action is brought by an undertaking or association against a general decision or recommendation, the only ground which may be relied on is misuse of powers (which includes misuse of procedure) and any other ground relied on is inadmissible.[18] The grounds which may be relied on in an action under art 63(2) of the ECSC Treaty are the same as those which may be invoked in an action under art 33. The only grounds which may be relied on under art 38 of the ECSC Treaty are lack of competence and infringement of an essential procedural requirement.

---

15 The *Group of the European Right* case (above, note 9) para 10.
16 Decisions taken under art 63(2) must be notified to the purchaser and the undertakings concerned individually unless they concern 'all or a large number of undertakings', in which case publication may be substituted for notification: ECSC Statute, art 43.
17 For an example of such an action see Case 230/81 *Luxembourg v European Parliament* [1983] ECR 255.
18 Case 8/55 *Fédération Charbonnière de Belgique v High Authority* [1954–56] ECR 245 at 258; Case 250/83 *Finsider v Commission* [1985] ECR 131 (para 4); Cases 32, 52 and 57/87 *Industrie Siderurgiche Associate (ISA) v Commission* [1988] ECR 3305 (paras 7–8).

In an action for annulment based on only one Treaty, claims concerning the infringement of another Treaty are admissible because of the need for a complete and consistent review of the lawfulness of the contested act.[19]

4 The Court's powers of review

In reviewing the lawfulness of the decision or recommendation challenged before it in proceedings under art 33 of the ECSC Treaty (and also art 63(2)), the Court cannot examine 'the evaluation of the situation, resulting from the economic facts or circumstances, in the light of which the Commission took its decisions or made its recommendations'. However, the Court's powers of review are not so restricted where the ground relied on by the applicant is either misuse of powers or a manifest failure to observe the provisions of the Treaty or any rule of law relating to its application. In the context of actions under art 173 of the EC Treaty, it is for similar reasons occasionally said that, in the course of judicial review, the Court is not empowered to substitute its own appreciation of the facts for that of the body which adopted the contested act, particularly in relation to economic matters.[20] In that context, an appreciation of the facts is not the same as a finding of fact; the expression usually refers to the inferences (very often inferences as to future consequences) drawn from primary facts. Where the act challenged in the proceedings is one whose adoption involved complex economic assessments, the Court's powers of review are limited to (a) infringement of any procedural rules applicable in the course of the adoption of the act, including the obligation to give reasons, (b) material error of fact, (c) manifest error of assessment or (d) misuse of powers.[21]

5 Result of the action

Under all three Treaties a successful action for annulment results in a declaration made by the Court to the effect that the measure challenged is void.[22] Such a declaration has the immediate effect of restoring the status quo, in legal terms, by destroying the existence in law of the annulled act ab initio. The immediate consequence of the declaration may therefore be to cause a sale to be completed where the contested act had interrupted its completion.[23] Under the ECSC Treaty,[24] the Court is enjoined to 'refer the matter back' to the Commission which is then bound to 'take the necessary steps to comply with the judgment'. If it fails to do so within a reasonable time, an action for damages may be brought before the Court.[25] The EC and Euratom Treaties[26] provide that the defendant institution's obligation to take the necessary measures to comply with the judgment does not affect possible liability for non-contractual damage and that, where the measure annulled is a regulation, the Court 'shall, if it considers this necessary, state which of the effects of the regulation which it has declared void shall be considered as definitive'.

---

19 Case C-62/88 *Greece v Council* [1990] ECR I-1527 (para 8, contra Advocate General Darmon at 1537).
20 Eg Case C-225/91 *Matra SA v Commission* [1993] ECR I-3203 (para 23).
21 Case T-7/92 *SA Asia Motor France v Commission*, 29 June 1993 (para 33). The precise formulation of the limitation placed on the Court's powers varies from case to case: in the *Matra* case (ibid) paras 24–25, the grounds of review were limited to manifest error of fact, misuse of powers and infringement of procedure.
22 ECSC Treaty, art 34; EC Treaty, art 174; Euratom Treaty, art 147.
23 Case 264/81 *Savma SpA v Commission* [1984] ECR 3915 (para 23).
24 Article 34.
25 Ibid.
26 Articles 174 and 176, and 147 and 149, respectively.

In brief, the position under all three Treaties is that a declaration that a measure is void gives rise to an immediate obligation under the Treaties which binds the defendant institution, but not the Court, to take the steps necessary to give effect to the judgment;[27] for example, to revoke or cease to apply a decision confirming the measure annulled[28] or compensate the loss suffered by the applicant[29] or review the applicant's situation in the light of the judgment.[30] The Court may not make any specific order regarding the implementation of the judgment[31] but it may make such declarations in the judgment as are necessary in conjunction with the annulment of the measure.[32] The Court has no jurisdiction to pronounce upon any eventual obligations of the national authorities arising from the annulment of the contested act.[33] The judgment affects both the parties to the case and persons directly affected by the measure annulled[34] who have an interest in the way the defendant institution complies with the judgment.[35] The effect of annulment is ex tunc[36] and erga omnes[37] but the Court has express power under the EC and the Euratom Treaties to restrict the retrospective effect of the judgment, or define in some other way its future effects, so as to ensure that allowance is made for, in particular, acquired rights.[38] This reflects a general principle of legal certainty inherent in the Community legal order[39] and seems, therefore, to apply also to actions under the ECSC Treaty.

B   Failure to act

1   Nature of the action

Under the EC and Euratom Treaties[40] the member states, Community institutions[41] and (in relation to areas falling within its field of competence) the

---

27 EC Treaty, art 176; Euratom Treaty, art 149. Eg Case 75/77 *Mollet v Commission* [1978] ECR 897 (para 23). Although the obligation accrues immediately, execution is not necessarily immediate: see Case 266/82 *Turner (née Krecké) v Commission* [1984] ECR 1 (para 5).
28 Cases 45 and 49/70 *Bode v Commission* [1971] ECR 465 (para 12).
29 Case 76/79 *Karl Könecke Fleischwarenfabrik GmbH & Co KG v Commission* [1980] ECR 665 (para 15).
30 Case 65/83 *Eridini v Council* [1984] ECR 211 (para 22).
31 Case 141/84 *De Compte v European Parliament* [1985] ECR 1951 (para 22); Case 53/85 *AKZO Chemie BV and AKZO Chemie UK Ltd v Commission* [1986] ECR 1965 (para 23).
32 Case 17/78 *Deshormes (née La Valle) v Commission* [1979] ECR 189 at 211.
33 Cases C-121 and C-122/91 *CT Control (Rotterdam) BV v Commission*, 6 July 1993 (para 57).
34 Eg Case 34/65 *Mosthaf v Euratom Commission* [1966] ECR 521; but see Cases 15–33, 52, 53, 57–109, 116, 117, 123, 132, 135–137/73 *Schots (née Kortner) v Council, Commission and European Parliament* [1974] ECR 177 (para 36).
35 Cf Case 30/76 *Küster v European Parliament* [1976] ECR 1719.
36 Case 155/78 *Miss M v Commission* [1980] ECR 1797 at 1814 (Advocate General Capotorti).
37 *Küster v European Parliament* (above, note 35) at 1731–1732 (Advocate General Reischl); Case 4/79 *Société Coopérative Providence Agricole de la Champagne v ONIC* [1980] ECR 2823 at 2868 (Advocate General Mayras).
38 Case 91/75 *HZA Göttingen v Miritz* [1976] ECR 217 at 238 (Advocate General Trabucchi).
39 Case 61/79 *Amministrazione delle Finanze delle Stato v Denkavit Italiana Srl* [1980] ECR 1205 (para 17); Cases 66, 127 and 128/79 *Amministrazione delle Finanze delle Stato v Salumi Srl* [1980] ECR 1237; Case 811/79 *Amministrazione delle Finanze delle Stato v Ariete* [1980] ECR 2545; Case 826/79 *Amministrazione delle Finanze delle Stato v MIRECO* [1980] ECR 2559. For examples of cases where the Court has limited the effects of its judgment, and the reasons relied on to justify doing so, see Case 43/75 *Defrenne v SABENA* [1976] ECR 455 (paras 69–75), a reference for a preliminary ruling, and Case 264/82 *Timex Corpn v Council and Commission* [1985] ECR 849 (para 32), an action for annulment, and more generally chapter 16, section II, pp 497–498.
40 Articles 175 and 148 respectively. A request to act made under Euratom Treaty, art 148 (which is to the same effect as EC Treaty, art 175), may be combined with a request under Euratom Treaty, art 53: Case C-107/91 *Empresa Nacional de Urânio SA v Commission* [1993] ECR I-599 (paras 10 and 21).
41 For the position of the European Parliament, see Case 13/83 *European Parliament v Council* [1985] ECR 1513 (paras 17–18); Case 302/87 *European Parliament v Council* [1988] ECR 5615.

European Central Bank[42] may bring proceedings before the Court, should either the European Parliament, the Council, the Commission or the European Central Bank, in breach of the Treaty, fail to act, in order to have the infringement established; any natural or legal person may 'complain to the Court of Justice that an institution of the Community has failed to address to that person any act other than a recommendation or an opinion'. In both cases proceedings may be brought before the Court only if (i) the defendant has first been called on to act, (ii) it has failed to define its position within two months of being called on to act and (iii) the action is brought within two months of the failure to define its position.

Under art 35 of the ECSC Treaty, member states, the Council, undertakings or associations may commence proceedings before the Court against the failure of the Commission to adopt a decision or recommendation in two situations: where the Commission is required by the Treaty or rules laid down for its implementation to adopt a decision or recommendation; and where it has power (but is not required) so to act. In the latter event, because the Commission has failed to exercise a power but has not failed to discharge a duty, the failure to act is actionable only if it constitutes a misuse of powers.[43] In both cases the person or body concerned must first take the matter up with the Commission. Proceedings must be brought within one month 'against the implied decision of refusal which is to be inferred from the silence of the [Commission] on the matter'. This implied decision is deemed to have been taken at the end of two months from the time the matter was first put to the Commission. If, within that time, the Commission has adopted an express decision or recommendation, an action for annulment may be brought under art 33 of the ECSC Treaty, if need be. In substance, art 35 sets out a procedure for obtaining an implied decision which can then be annulled in proceedings before the Court.

In all cases the defendant must first be called upon to act before proceedings can be commenced. That is done by giving the defendant formal notice calling on it to act in a specified way.[44]

2   *Result of the proceedings*

The object of the action is to obtain a judgment of the Court establishing that the failure to act is unlawful and thereby forcing the defendant institution to act. As in the case of a successful action for annulment, judgment in favour of the applicant gives rise to an obligation under the Treaties whereby the defendant institution is required to take the steps necessary to comply with the Court's judgment[45] but not to any immediate consequential order by the Court, such as an order to make a payment.[46] In consequence, if the defendant defines its position after the commencement of proceedings but before the delivery of judgment (even in a way that does not satisfy the applicant), the action no longer has any purpose;[47] if the defendant defines its position before

---

42 EC Treaty, art 175, as amended by EU Treaty, art G(E)(54).
43 Case 95/86 *Ferriere San Carlo SpA v Commission* [1987] ECR 1413 (paras 5–7).
44 Eg Case 25/85 *Nuovo Campsider v Commission* [1986] ECR 1531 (para 8).
45 EC Treaty, art 176; Euratom Treaty, art 149; Case 377/87 *European Parliament v Council* [1988] ECR 4017 (para 9); Case 383/87 *Commission v Council* [1988] ECR 4051.
46 *De Compte v European Parliament* (above, note 31) para 22; Case C-25/91 *Pesqueras Echebastar SA v Commission* [1993] ECR I-1719 (para 14).
47 Cases C-15 and C-108/91 *Buckl & Söhne OHG v Commission* [1992] ECR I-6061 (paras 13–18).

the commencement of proceedings (albeit after the expiry of the period within which it is to define its position), the action is inadmissible.[48]

C   Default by a member state

1   Nature of the action

Under the EC and Euratom Treaties only the Commission or a member state can bring proceedings against a member state in respect of a failure to fulfil a Treaty obligation. The Commission must first give the member state concerned an opportunity to submit its observations on the matter and then deliver a reasoned opinion. It is only if the member state fails to comply with the reasoned opinion that proceedings may be brought before the Court.[49] The commencement of proceedings is a matter of discretion for the Commission and the Commission's motives in commencing proceedings are not relevant.[50] Before a member state can bring proceedings, it must first bring the matter before the Commission. The action before the Court can be started once the Commission has delivered a reasoned opinion or, in the absence thereof, at the expiry of three months from the date when the matter was brought before it.[51] Proceedings may be brought directly before the Court by the Commission or a member state, without going through the pre-litigation procedure, in the circumstances envisaged in arts 93(2) and 225 of the EC Treaty and 38 and 82 of the Euratom Treaty.

Actions brought in respect of a failure by a member state to fulfil a Treaty obligation follow a procedure under the ECSC Treaty which is different from that prescribed in the EC and Euratom Treaties. Under art 88 of the ECSC Treaty, it is for the Commission to establish in a reasoned decision that a member state has failed to fulfil an obligation under the Treaty. The member state concerned then has two months from notification within which to commence proceedings against that decision. The action is one in which the Court has unlimited jurisdiction so it has full powers of review and may amend the decision if it finds that it cannot be upheld in its entirety. If the member state fails to comply with the Commission's decision or brings an unsuccessful action against it, the Commission may then, with the assent of the Council, either suspend payment of sums due to the member state under the Treaty or take measures to authorise other member states to take measures, to correct the effects of the infringement of the Treaty obligation. The member state concerned may challenge decisions which adopt either expedient and, in the ensuing action, the Court again has unlimited jurisdiction.

2   Subject matter of the proceedings

In proceedings under the EC and Euratom Treaties, the subject matter of the action is defined in the reasoned opinion sent to the member state by the Commission before the commencement of proceedings, which must set out in a coherent and detailed fashion the matters of complaint;[52] but, even if the

---

48 Case 48/65 *Lütticke v Commission* [1966] ECR 19 at 27–28; *Pesqueras Echebastar SA v Commission* (above, note 46) paras 11–13 (but in Case C-41/92 *Liberal Democrats v European Parliament*, unreported (case withdrawn by order of 10 June 1993), Advocate General Darmon considered that the existence of a definition of position goes to the substance of the case, see para 44 of his opinion).
49 EC Treaty, art 169; Euratom Treaty, art 141.
50 Case 415/85 *Commission v Ireland* [1988] ECR 3097 (Re Zero-Rating) (para 9).
51 EC Treaty, art 170; Euratom Treaty, art 142.
52 Case 274/83 *Commission v Italy* [1985] ECR 1077 (paras 19–21).

matters of complaint specified in the reasoned opinion are remedied before the commencement of proceedings, the Commission still has an interest in pursuing the action, not least with the object of establishing the potential liability of the member state in damages to persons injured by its default.[53] If the member state concedes the matter, including the right to claim damages against it, it is still for the Court to establish the existence of the member state's default because, otherwise, member states could bring the proceedings to an end and forestall any adverse finding by the Court simply by making a concession.[54] It is not a defence for the member state to allege that the legislative or other measure with which it is said to have failed to comply was unlawful unless the measure in question is vitiated by particularly serious and evident defects such that it can be said to be non-existent[55] or the measure has been challenged in pending proceedings.

The subject matter of proceedings under the ECSC Treaty is the decision of the Commission finding that the member state concerned has failed to fulfil an obligation under that Treaty or defining the steps to be taken in order to correct the effects of the infringement.

2 Result of the action

The object of an action against a member state in respect of a failure to fulfil a Treaty obligation under the EC and Euratom Treaties is to obtain a judgment declaring that there was such a failure. This, in turn, gives rise to a further Treaty obligation binding the defendant member state to take the measures necessary to comply with the judgment.[56] Under the EU Treaty, if the Commission considers that the member state concerned has not taken the measures necessary to comply with the judgment, it must first give the member state an opportunity to submit its observations on the point and then issue a reasoned opinion specifying the points on which the member state has failed to comply with the judgment and setting a time limit for compliance. If the member state fails to comply within that time limit, the Commission may commence proceedings before the Court with the specific object of obtaining an order from the Court requiring the member state to pay a lump sum or penalty payment.[57] Quite apart from that, it appears that a member state is liable in damages without need for proof of fault in respect of any loss arising after the date of the Court's judgment from the failure to fulfil the Treaty obligation found by the Court in that judgment or at least from any failure to comply with that judgment; the member state concerned would also appear to be liable in respect of loss arising before the date of the judgment but it is at the time of writing unclear whether or not fault need be shown in order to attach liability.[58]

The object of proceedings under the ECSC Treaty is to obtain the annulment or modification of the contested decision. A successful action against a Commission decision finding that the member state concerned has failed to fulfil an obligation under the Treaty expunges that finding. A successful action against a Commission decision defining the measures to be taken to correct the

---

53 Case 103/84 *Commission v Italy* [1986] ECR 1759 (paras 8–9).
54 Case C-243/89 *Commission v Denmark* [1993] ECR I-3353 (para 30).
55 Case C-74/91 *Commission v Germany* [1992] ECR I-5437 (paras 10–11).
56 EC Treaty, art 171; Euratom Treaty, art 143.
57 EC Treaty, art 171, and Euratom Treaty, art 143, as amended by EU Treaty, arts G(E)(51) and I(12). The Commission must specify the amount of the lump sum or penalty payment claimed.
58 Cases C-6 and C-9/90 *Francovich v Italy* [1991] ECR I-5357.

effects of such an infringement results in the annulment or (where the Court exercises its unlimited jurisdiction) the amendment of those measures. It does not result in the expunging of the finding that the member state concerned did fail to fulfil its obligations.

D   Actions for damages

1   Nature of the action

The EEC and Euratom Treaties provide[59] that the Court has jurisdiction over actions for compensation for damage caused by the Community otherwise than in the context of a contractual relationship with the injured party and that, in the case of such non-contractual liability, 'the Community shall, in accordance with the general principles common to the laws of the Member States, make good any damage caused by its institutions or by its servants in the performance of their duties'; the Community's contractual liability is governed by the law applicable to the contract.[60] The same applies in respect of damage caused by the European Investment Bank[61] or by the European Central Bank or its servants in the performance of their duties.[62] The Community is not liable in respect of the acts or defaults of the authorities of the member states.[63] The admissibility of an action for damages may in certain instances be subject to the exhaustion of national remedies but, for that to be so, the national remedies must be effective.[64] Where the applicant has different causes of action against a national authority and a Community institution arising out of the same facts, the fact that proceedings could have been brought against the former is not a bar to a claim for damages made against the latter.[65]

Under the ECSC Treaty an action for damages may be brought against the Commission in respect of (i) failure to comply within a reasonable time with a judgment declaring a decision or recommendation of the Commission to be void[66] and (ii) breach of professional secrecy.[67] An action may be brought against the Community in respect of (i) a wrongful act or omission on the part of the Community in the performance of its functions and (ii) a personal wrong committed by a servant of the Community in the performance of his duties.[68]

---

59 EC Treaty, arts 178 and 215; Euratom Treaty, arts 151 and 188.

60 Where an action for damages arises out of a contractual relationship which national law deems to exist even in the absence of a contract, the matter does not fall within the Court's exclusive jurisdiction over disputes concerning non-contractual liability: Case 232/84 *Commission v Tordeur* [1985] ECR 3223 (paras 19–21).

61 Case C-370/89 *Société Générale d'Entreprises Electromécaniques v European Investment Bank* [1992] ECR I-6211.

62 EC Treaty, art 215, as amended by EU Treaty, art G(E)(78).

63 Case C-97/91 *Oleificio Borelli SpA v Commission* [1992] ECR I-6313 (para 20). But an action may be brought in respect of damage comprising sums overcharged by a national administrative body in purported exercise of Community law where there is no way of recovering such sums under national law: Case 20/88 *Roquette Frères v Commission* [1989] ECR 1553 (paras 14–16).

64 Case 175/84 *Krohn & Co Import-Export GmbH & Co v Commission* [1986] ECR 753 (paras 27–29).

65 Case 281/84 *Zuckerfabrik Bedburg AG v Council and Commission* [1987] ECR 49 (para 12).

66 Article 34. Any undertaking or group of undertakings which considers itself injured directly by the failure to comply with the judgment may apply to the Court for a declaration that the decision or recommendation involved a fault rendering the Community liable; proceedings may also be brought under ECSC Treaty, art 40: Cases C-363/88 and C-364/88 *Finanziaria Siderurgiche Finsider SpA v Commission* [1992] ECR I-359 (paras 14–15 and 24).

67 Article 47.

68 Article 40. The previous annulment of the act causing the loss is not a condition of liability under art 40: Case C-220/91P *Commission v Peine-Salzgitter AG* [1993] ECR I-2393 (paras 21–25). The question of liability in damages under the ECSC Treaty was the subject of prolonged and detailed consideration in that case and at first instance (reported sub nom. Case T-120/89 *Stahlwerke Peine-Salzgitter AG v Commission* [1991] ECR II-279).

2 Conditions establishing liability

In general terms, liability in an action for damages is established where there is proof of unlawful conduct on the part of the defendant, damage and a causal connection between the damage claimed and the alleged unlawful conduct.[69] Where legislative action involving measures of economic policy causes damage, the Community does not incur non-contractual liability unless there has been a sufficiently flagrant violation of a superior rule of law for the protection of the individual.[70] A basic distinction must therefore be drawn between loss arising from administrative action and loss arising from legislative action.

In relation to the former, liability may arise from: an act causing physical damage otherwise than by way of legal right; improper or unjustified exercise (or failure to exercise) of an administrative power;[71] failure to perform a duty imposed by law which confers correlative rights or legitimate expectations on the injured party;[72] failure to supervise or control adequately or at all, or failure to establish any or any adequate system of supervision or control of, the conduct of subordinate persons or bodies as required by a normal standard of care;[73] failure to comply with the rules relating to health and safety at work or, more generally, failure to exercise due diligence concerning the safety measures necessary in order to prevent accidental injury to persons present on the premises of the Community institutions;[74] failure to take reasonable steps to warn the injured party of circumstances which are such as to put him or her at risk;[75] unjustified failure to correct inaccurate information supplied to the injured party;[76] failure to exercise the diligence required of an employer;[77] infringement of a superior rule of law for the protection of the individual.[78]

In relation to loss arising from legislative action or inaction, the illegality of the conduct of the institution concerned and even the annulment of the legislative act in question may not be sufficient to ground liability. For liability to arise, the act in question must infringe a superior legal norm, such as a general principle of Community law,[79] a Treaty provision[80] or a legislative measure whose observance was mandatory when the act in question was adopted. That superior rule of law must be intended for the protection of the injured party or of the interests of a class of persons encompassing the injured party[81] (liability does not arise if the superior rule of law is merely intended to

---

69 See, for example, Cases 9 and 12/60 *Société Commercial Antoine Vloeberghs SA v High Authority* [1961] ECR 197 at 216–217; Case 4/69 *Alfons Lütticke GmbH v Commission* [1971] ECR 325 (para 10).

70 Case 5/71 *Aktien Zuckerfabrik Schöppenstedt v Council* [1971] ECR 975 (para 11); Case C-63/89 *Les Assurances du Crédit et Compagnie Belge d'Assurances Crédit SA v Council and Commission* [1991] ECR I-1799 (para 12); Cases C-104/89 and C-37/90 *Mulder v Council and Commission* [1992] ECR I-3061 (para 12).

71 Cases 5, 7 and 13–24/66 *Kampffmeyer v Commission* [1967] ECR 245 at 262.

72 *Vloeberghs v High Authority* (above, note 69) at 216–217.

73 Cases 326/86 and 66/88 *Francesconi v Commission* [1989] ECR 2087.

74 Case C-308/87 *Grifoni v Euratom* [1990] ECR I-1203 (paras 8 and 14).

75 Case 145/83 *Adams v Commission* [1985] ECR 3539 (paras 41–44).

76 Cases 19, 20, 25 and 30/69 *Richez-Parise v Commission* [1970] ECR 325 (paras 38–39). But compare Case C-353/88 *Briantex v EEC and Commission* [1989] ECR 3623 (paras 8–12).

77 Cases 169/83 and 136/84 *Leussinck-Brummelhuis v Commission* [1986] ECR 2801 (para 15); Case 180/87 *Hamill v Commission* [1988] ECR 6141.

78 *Kampffmeyer v Commission* (above, note 71) at 260–263.

79 Eg Case 74/74 *CNTA v Commission* [1975] ECR 533 (paras 42–47: the protection of legitimate expectations).

80 Eg Case 238/78 *Ireks-Arkady v Council and Commission* [1979] ECR 2955 (para 11).

81 Eg Case C-152/88 *Sofrimport v Commission* [1990] ECR I-2477 (para 26).

protect other interests than those of the injured party[82] or the common interest, in circumstances where the common interest does not require specific individuals to be compensated).[83] Finally, the infringement of that superior rule of law must be sufficiently flagrant or serious, such as where there is a grave and manifest disregard of the limits placed on the exercise of the powers of the institution concerned[84] or conduct verging on the arbitrary.[85] Individuals may be required within reasonable limits to bear the losses arising from even void legislative acts[86] but damage arising from behaviour that can be characterised as fault does not fall within what a person can normally expect and is recoverable.[87]

3 Damage

Damages are recoverable in respect of direct physical or economic loss (such as loss of profit)[88] as well as for non-material loss (such as shock, disturbance, uneasiness and damage to reputation).[89] The amount of the former must be proved by evidence;[90] the amount of the latter is fixed by the Court ex aequo et bono[91] save that, if the Court feels that a declaration made in the judgment is sufficient to compensate for any non-material loss, no award of damages will be made.[92] Where the loss arises from the conduct of the applicant as well as the defendant, or the applicant has also received some benefit from the acts complained of, the applicant's share of responsibility or the benefit received by him or her may be taken into account in diminution of the liability of the defendant.[93]

4 Award of damages

In some cases the Court has decided the question of liability and left the question of quantum to be agreed between the parties (subject to the possibility of bringing the matter back to the Court in the event of a failure to reach

---

82 *Vloeberghs v High Authority* (above, note 69) at 216–217.
83 Cases 9 and 11/71 *Compagnie d'Approvisionnement v Commission (No 2)* [1972] ECR 391 (paras 32–34). Thus, a failure to respect the distribution of powers between the institutions is not sufficient for liability to attach: Case C-282/90 *Industrie- en Handelsonderneming Vreugdenhil v Commission* [1992] ECR I-1937 (paras 20–22).
84 Eg the *Sofrimport* case (above, note 81), para 27; the *Mulder* cases (above, note 70) paras 16–21.
85 Eg Cases 116 and 124/77 *Amylum v Council and Commission* [1979] ECR 3497 (para 19). Arbitrary conduct is not a necessary condition of liability: Case C-220/91P *Commission v Peine-Salzgitter AG* (above, note 68) para 51.
86 Eg Case T-120/89 *Peine-Salzgitter AG v Commission* (above, note 68) at paras 131–136.
87 Case C-220/91P *Commission v Peine-Salzgitter AG* (above, note 68) para 58.
88 Eg the *Kampffmeyer* case (above, note 71) at 263–266; the *Mulder* cases (above, note 70) paras 23–34. For the quantum of damages in personal injury cases, see Case C-308/87 *Grifoni v EAEC*, 3 February 1994.
89 Eg the *Hamill* case (above, note 77) paras 11–13. Non-material loss may be occasioned where a person is placed in a position of uncertainty and worry concerning his or her personal reputation (in casu, where the Commission had done nothing to contradict harmful press reports tending to lower the applicant in the esteem of the public): Case T-59/92 *Caronna v Commission*, 26 October 1993 (para 106).
90 Eg Case T-27/90 *Latham v Commission* [1991] ECR II-35 (para 43).
91 Eg Case C-343/87 *Culin v Commission* [1990] ECR I-225 (paras 27–29); Case T-63/89 *Latham v Commission* [1991] ECR II-19 (para 39); Case T-27/90 *Latham v Commission* (ibid) para 51.
92 Eg Case T-37/89 *Hanning v European Parliament* [1990] ECR II-463 (para 83); the *Culin* case (ibid) para 26; the *Caronna* case (above, note 89) para 107; Case T-58/92 *Moat v Commission*, 16 December 1993, para 71.
93 Eg *Adams v Commission* (above, note 75) para 53; Case 229/84 *Sommerlatte v Commission* [1986] ECR 1805 (paras 26–28). For the situation where loss arises in part from the action of a third party, see Case C-201/86 *Spie-Batignolles v Commission* [1990] ECR I-197 at 201–204 (Advocate-General van Gerven).

agreement).[94] The obligation to pay damages arises on the date the Court gives judgment finding the defendant liable and it is therefore from this date that interest on the judgment debt starts to run and by reference to this date that the damages recoverable are converted into the currency of payment.[95] At present the Court awards interest at 6%.[96]

Interest on the judgment debt is to be distinguished from default interest, which is damages for wrongful delay in the performance of an obligation. A claim for default interest is one in respect of damage arising before the action commences, as opposed to relief in the event that the defendant delays in paying the judgment debt. Claims for default interest have arisen mostly in staff cases.[97] The obligation to pay default interest arises only where the amount of the principal sum owed is certain or can at least be ascertained on the basis of established objective criteria or, possibly, where there has been an unjustified delay in determining the amount due.[98] The rate awarded by the Court tends to be 6%.[99] No reason has been given why this should be so. Since the claim is, in substance, one for damages for delay in performance, a more logical rate would be that applied by the courts in the country where the obligation should have been performed.[1] The cases are in some disarray so far as concerns the date on which default interest starts to run. It is likely that the Court's approach is to fix a date which seems to it to be equitable in all the circumstances. On the other hand, there is adequate authority for arguing that the correct date is that when the performance falls due or when the creditor makes an express or implied demand that the debtor perform the obligation.[2]

E Interim relief

All the Treaties provide that, in proceedings before the Court, application may be made to it for the adoption of a measure of interim relief. This is discussed in detail in chapter 8.

94 Eg Cases 256, 257, 265, 267/80, 5 and 51/81 and 282/82 *Birra Wührer v Council and Commission* [1984] ECR 3693 (para 35); Case C-152/88 *Sofrimport v Commission* [1992] ECR I-153.
95 Cf Cases 64 and 113/76, 167 and 239/78, 27, 28 and 45/79 *Dumortier v Council* [1979] ECR 3091 and [1982] ECR 1733; *Birra Wührer v Council and Commission* (ibid) para 34.
96 Eg the *Ireks-Arkady GmbH* case (above, note 80); Cases 241, 242 and 245–250/78 *DGV v Council and Commission*, Cases 261 and 262/78 *Interquell Starke-Chemie GmbH & Co KG and Diamalt AG v Council and Commission*, Cases 64, 113/76, 167, 239/78 and 27, 28, 45/79 *Frères Dumortier SA v Council* [1979] ECR 3017, 3045 and 3091; *Birra Wührer* (ibid) para 37. The reason 6% was fixed upon is obscure. In *Leussinck-Brummelhuis v Commission* (above, note 77) at 2820, Advocate General Slynn said that it was appropriate for the Court to adopt rates of interest reflecting contemporary financial realities. On interest generally, see Case C-136/92P *Commission v Lualdi* (unreported, per Advocate General Lenz).
97 Eg Cases 27 and 39/59 *Campolongo v High Authority* [1960] ECR 391; Case 115/76 *Leonardini v Commission* [1978] ECR 735; Case 114/77 *Jacquemart v Commission* [1978] ECR 1697; Case 152/77 *B v Commission* [1979] ECR 2819; Cases 63 and 64/79 *Boizard v Commission* [1980] ECR 2975; Case 40/79 *P v Commission* [1981] ECR 361; Case 785/79 *Pizziolo v Commission* [1981] ECR 969; Case 185/80 *Garganese v Commission* [1981] ECR 1785; Case 9/81 *Williams v Court of Auditors* [1982] ECR 3301.
98 Case 174/83 *Ammann v Council* [1986] ECR 2647 (para 19); Case 175/83 *Culmsee v Economic and Social Committee* [1986] ECR 2667 (para 19); Case 176/83 *Allo v Commission* [1986] ECR 2687 (para 19); Case 233/83 *Agostini v Commission* [1986] ECR 2729 (para 19); Case 264/83 *Delhez v Commission* [1986] ECR 2749 (para 20); Cases 176 and 177/86 *Houyoux v Commission* [1987] ECR 4333 at 4346 (Advocate General Cruz Vilaça); Cases 314 and 315/86 *de Szy-Tarisse v Commission* [1988] ECR 6013 (paras 33 and 36).
99 However, in the *Mulder* cases (above, note 70), para 36, interest was awarded at 7% and 8%; and in Case T-48/90 *Giordani v Commission*, 1 July 1993 (para 92), interest was awarded at 8%.
1 Cf Case 131/8 *Berti v Commission* [1985] ECR 645 (paras 19–21): interest awarded at the rate prescribed by the relevant Belgian legislation.
2 Eg Case 158/79 *Roumengous (née Carpentier) v Commission* [1985] ECR 39 (para 11); Cases 532, 534, 567, 600, 618, 660/79 and 543/79 *Amesz v Commission* [1985] ECR 55 (para 14); Case 737/79 *Battaglia v Commission* [1985] ECR 71 (para 10); Cases 176 and 177/86 *Houyoux v Commission* [1987] ECR 4333 (para 18).

F   Staff cases

1   Nature of the action

The Court's jurisdiction over disputes between the Community and its officials or servants was originally based on art 42 of the ECSC Treaty and the contract of employment made with the official or servant concerned.[3] Under the EC and Euratom Treaties,[4] jurisdiction is defined by reference to the limits and conditions laid down in the Staff Regulations and Conditions of Employment, which apply to all persons employed directly by the Communities[5] and those claiming under them,[6] and former employees, where the claim arises from the past employment relationship with the Community (as in the case of a dispute over pension payments).[7] Persons claiming rights under the Staff Regulations or Conditions of Employment may also bring proceedings before the Court.[8] In addition, the staff of certain bodies, set up by act of the Council, which are separate from the institutions, are governed by their own Conditions of Employment.[9] These rules follow the same basic pattern as the rules relating to persons employed by the institutions. Apart from the Court's general jurisdiction over disputes, the President is given power to appoint a doctor to an Invalidity Committee should the official concerned fail to do so.[10] No procedure is laid down for applying and it seems that application may be made informally in writing by any interested party.[11]

The Court's jurisdiction is exclusive and the basis of the service relationship between the Community and its officials or servants (other than local staff) is not dependent upon decisions of national courts.[12] The jurisdiction of the Court is exercised at first instance by the CFI. The principal limitation on the Court's jurisdiction is that an official or servant can bring an action before the Court only in respect of an act adversely affecting him which is adopted by or on behalf of the employing institution or body; disputes arising between an

---

3 See Case 1/55 *Kergall v Common Assembly* [1954–56] ECR 151.

4 Articles 179 and 152 respectively.

5 Regulation No 259/68 of 29 February 1968 (OJ No L56 of 4 March 1968, p 1), as amended. The Staff Regulations and Conditions of Employment apply to employees of the Community to differing degrees. Local agents, for example, are dealt with in arts 79 to 81 of the Conditions of Employment which basically provide that conditions of employment shall be determined in accordance with current rules and practice in the place of employment; disputes are submitted to the 'competent court in accordance with the laws in force in the place' of employment. Not all persons employed by the institutions may, therefore, bring proceedings directly before the Court.

6 Eg Cases 75 and 117/82 *Razzouk and Beydoun v Commission* [1984] ECR 1509.

7 Case 9/75 *Meyer-Burckhardt v Commission* [1975] ECR 1171; Case 48/76 *Reinarz v Commission and Council* [1977] ECR 291 (paras 9–10).

8 Eg Case 123/84 *Klein v Commission* [1985] ECR 1907. Whether or not a person actually is an official or other servant of the Communities or otherwise has rights under the Staff Regulations or Conditions of Employment goes to the substance of the case and not to the entitlement to bring proceedings before the Court.

9 Eg Council Regulations No 1859 and 1860/76 of 29 June (OJ No L214 of 6 August 1976, p 1 and 24), as amended, which lay down the conditions of employment of staff of the European Centre for the Development of Vocational Training and of the European Foundation for the Improvement of Living and Working Conditions, respectively.

10 Article 7 of Annex II of the Staff Regulations.

11 The European Investment Bank Staff Regulations similarly provide that the President shall appoint the Chairman of the Conciliation Board in the event that the two other members of the Board are unable to agree on the appointment themselves (art 41). Under Annex I of the Convention of 19 April 1972 establishing the European University Institute (OJ No C29 of 9 February 1976, p 1) the Court may be requested to rule on disputes between the Institute and its staff.

12 Case 65/74 *Porrini v EAEC and Comont* [1975] ECR 319 (para 15).

official or servant and an institution or body other than that employing him appear to be dealt with under the other articles of the Treaty, where appropriate.[13]

2 Commencement of proceedings

Proceedings cannot be commenced before the Court unless a preliminary procedure, set out in the Staff Regulations and Conditions of Employment (which refer to the Staff Regulations), has been completed. The purpose of that procedure is to enable and encourage an amicable settlement of the difference which has arisen between the official or servant concerned and the administration.[14] The preliminary procedure serves no purpose in cases where the administration has no power to alter the decision of which the official or servant complains.[15] In such cases, the action before the Court can, and should, be begun within three months[16] of notification of the decision complained of; if the official or servant concerned nonetheless goes through the preliminary procedure, his eventual action before the Court is, in principle, inadmissible (because it is out of time) but the Court has accepted the admissibility of such actions on the ground that the Staff Regulations are in this respect obscure and misleading so that it would be inequitable to deprive the official or servant of his rights.[17] Subject to the above, an action can be brought before the Court only if the administration has first rejected (by express or implied decision) a complaint submitted to it by the official or servant concerned;[18] and the action must be commenced within three months of that decision.[19] The official or servant can commence proceedings before the Court immediately after having submitted the complaint to the administration on condition that the application to the Court is accompanied by an application for interim relief; in such circumstances, the Court may decide on the latter but stays the main action until the complaint has been rejected by express or implied decision.[20] The object of that procedure is to get over the problem which arises where urgent action is required in order to preserve the official or servant from serious and irreparable damage flowing from the matters complained of. The Court alone is in a position to grant the necessary interim relief but the opportunity to do so might be lost if the official or servant were required to go through the preliminary procedure before being able to apply to the Court for interim relief.

3 Subject matter and result of the proceedings

The scope of the action before the Court is not limited by the terms of the complaint submitted to the administration but the legal basis and subject matter of the action must be the same.[21] That apart, the arguments set out in

---

13 Cf Case 48/79 *Ooms v Commission* [1979] ECR 3121. For general consideration of 'act adversely affecting' the applicant, see Cases T-6 and T-52/92 *Reinarz v Commission*, 26 October 1993, paras 35–44.
14 Eg Case 58/75 *Sergy v Commission* [1976] ECR 1139 (para 32); *Reinarz v Commission*, ibid (para 96).
15 Typically cases where the decision complained of is made by a selection board.
16 As extended by any relevant periods of grace.
17 Eg Case 34/80 *Authié v Commission* [1981] ECR 665 (paras 6–8).
18 The procedure for submitting a complaint and dealing with it is set out in art 90(2) and (3) of the Staff Regulations.
19 Staff Regulations, art 91(2) and (3). The limitation period applies also in the case of claims for compensation: eg Case 257/85 *Dufay v European Parliament* [1987] ECR 1561 (paras 21–23); Case 317/85 *Pomar v Commission* [1987] ECR 2467.
20 Staff Regulations, art 91(4).
21 Eg the *Sergy* case (above, note 14) para 33; see further chapter 7, section II.G. It is not necessary for there to be express concordance between the complaint and the action; but, at the least, it must be possible to discern in sufficient detail in the complaint a plea made in the action: the *Reinarz* case (above, note 13) para 96.

the complaint may be expanded by the addition of further arguments in the course of the proceedings before the Court.[22] The action concerns the lawfulness of the act of the administration of which the official or servant complains; and damages may be claimed for loss arising from the employment relationship.[23] Strictly speaking, the action is not brought against the administration's rejection of the complaint made by the official or servant in the course of the preliminary procedure; it is brought against the initial decision of the administration which provoked the making of the complaint. A decision rejecting a complaint merely confirms the act complained of; but, where the reasons for the act complained of appear only in the decision rejecting the complaint, it is common to see the latter annulled (if the applicant wins the case), thus bringing in its train the invalidity of the act complained of. In disputes of a financial character, the Court has unlimited jurisdiction.[24] When the Court annuls the act complained of, it cannot define the steps that the defendant must take in order to comply with the judgment, whether it has unlimited jurisdiction in the case[25] (unless the order still leaves the defendant a margin of discretion)[26] or not;[27] but it may make appropriate declarations in the course of the judgment.[28]

G   References for a preliminary ruling

1   Nature of the proceedings

Under the Treaties[29] and several conventions[30] the Court has jurisdiction to give preliminary rulings, ie authoritative pronouncements on a question of Community law which arises in proceedings before a national court and is referred to the Court for decision before the national court gives judgment.

22 Eg Case 133/88 *Martinez v European Parliament* [1989] ECR 689 (para 10).
23 Eg Case 401/85 *Schina v Commission* [1987] ECR 3911 (para 9). For an example of a case concerning which damages claims arise from the employment relationship and which do not, see Case 180/87 *Hamill v Commission* [1988] ECR 6141.
24 Staff Regulations, art 91(1). Eg Case 24/79 *Oberthür v Commission* [1980] ECR 1743 (para 14); *Houyoux v Commission* (above, note 2) para 16.
25 Case T-156/89 *Mordt v Court of Justice* [1991] ECR II-407 (para 150).
26 Case T-73/89 *Barbi v Commission* [1990] ECR II-619 (para 38).
27 Case 162/84 *Vlachou v Court of Auditors* [1986] ECR 481 at 487 (Advocate General Lenz).
28 Eg the *Mordt* case (above, note 25) para 141; Case T-59/92 *Caronna v Commission*, 26 October 1993, paras 40–41.
29 ECSC Treaty, art 41; EC Treaty, art 177; Euratom Treaty, art 150. See also chapter 2, section VI.
30 The most important is the Convention on Jurisdiction and the Enforcement of Judgments in Civil and Commercial Matters, signed at Brussels on 27 September 1968, as amended: see the Protocol on its interpretation by the Court, signed at Luxembourg on 3 June 1971 (OJ No L304 of 30 October 1978, p 1), as amended (referred to as the 'Brussels Convention Protocol'). A consolidated version of the Brussels Convention Protocol is published in OJ No C189 of 28 July 1990, p 25. The procedure is also to be found in the Protocol on the Interpretation by the Court of Justice of the Convention of 29 February 1968 on the mutual recognition of companies, firms and legal persons (see Bulletin of the European Communities, 1969, No 2); the European Patent Convention (OJ No L17 of 1976, p 1) which, in art 73, provided that the Court has jurisdiction to rule on the interpretation of the Convention and on the validity and interpretation of measures implementing it other than national measures; the Agreement relating to Community Patents of 15 December 1989, arts 2(2) and 3 (OJ No L401 of 30 December 1989, p 1), which replaced pro tanto the European Patent Convention; and the First Protocol annexed to the Convention on the Law applicable to Contractual Obligations (OJ No L 48 of 20 February 1989 p 1, referred to as 'the Rome Convention Protocol'). The Agreement on the European Economic Area provides in art 107 and Protocol 34 for member states of the European Free Trade Area to allow their courts or tribunals to ask the Court to decide on the interpretation of a provision of the Agreement. Such rulings of the Court will be binding: *Opinion* 1/92 [1992] ECR I-2821 (para 37).

The notion of a preliminary ruling is a decision of the Court on one or more of the matters set out in the provisions referred to above which is in issue before a national court or tribunal; the decision is made before the national court gives judgment, not after, so that it has the benefit of an authoritative statement of Community law when resolving the dispute before it. The preliminary ruling procedure falls naturally into two parts: the procedure before the referring court before, during and after the making of the reference to the Court; and the procedure before the Court. The same procedure before the Court is followed in relation to all references for a preliminary ruling irrespective of the legal provision making the procedure available.[31] That procedure is described in more detail elsewhere.[32]

The right, and in some cases the duty, to make an order referring a matter for a preliminary ruling is granted to, or imposed on, the courts or tribunals envisaged in (as the case may be) the Treaties, the Convention Protocols or the Agreement relating to Community Patents. It is not a right of the parties before the national court or tribunal (although the latter may validly refer a matter to the Court for a preliminary ruling, at the request of the parties, if it believes it appropriate to do so). The object of the preliminary ruling procedure is not to determine the rights of the parties to the proceedings[33] but to lead to an authoritative ruling on a question of Community law. The procedure is 'dominated by the concept of the public interest',[34] which explains why the power to refer lies in the hands of the national courts or tribunals and also why the procedure itself is non-contentious, the parties appearing in order to submit their observations, not as parties stricto sensu, but more as amici curiae. The procedure cannot be fettered by any restraints imposed by another national body, whether or not its character is judicial. Hence instructions laid down by a national authority, whether they relate to the exercise of the right or duty to refer or simply lay down guidelines as to the practice to be adopted in referring, have no effect and do not bind the referring court or tribunal;[35] and the national court cannot be constrained from making a reference by any rule of national constitutional law reserving to another court the task of finding provisions of national law to be unconstitutional.[36]

2 Subject matter of the reference

Articles 177 and 150 of the EC and Euratom Treaties, respectively, provide that the Court has 'jurisdiction to give preliminary rulings concerning: (a) the interpretation of this Treaty;[37] (b) the validity and interpretation of acts of the institutions of the Community and of the ECB;[38] (c) the interpretation of the

---

31 RP-ECJ 103(2).   **32** See chapter 2, section VI.

33 Case 13/61 *Kledingverkoopbedrijf De Geus en Uitdenbogerd v Robert Bosch GmbH* [1962] ECR 45 at 61 (Advocate General Lagrange).

34 Case 127/73 *BRT v SABAM* [1974] ECR 51 at 69 (Advocate General Mayras); Case C-364/92 *SAT Fluggesellschaft mbH v Eurocontrol*, 19 January 1994, para 9.

35 See Case 166/73 *Firma Rheinmuhlen-Düsseldorf v Einfuhr- und Vorratsstelle für Getreide und Futtermittel* [1974] ECR 33.

36 Case C-348/89 *Mecanarte-Metalurgica de Lagoa Lda v Chefe do Serviço da Conferencia Final da Alfandego do Porto* [1991] ECR I-3277 (paras 44–49).

37 Ie the EC and Euratom Treaties, the annexes and protocols thereto, and any amending provisions, including the Acts by which new member states accede to the Community (see also the Merger Treaty, art 30). A Treaty may also exclude the possibility of interpretation by the Court: see Single European Act, art 31; EU Treaty, art L.

38 International agreements entered into by the Community are acts of the institutions for these purposes: see, for example, *Opinion 1/91* [1991] ECR I-6079, para 38. Acts of the European Central Bank are included in art 177 as a result of an amendment effected by the EU Treaty, art G(E)(56).

statutes of bodies established by an act of the Council'.[39] The only difference between the EC and Euratom Treaties relates to the last: under art 177 the Court has jurisdiction to interpret the statutes of the bodies in question 'where those statutes so provide';[40] under art 150 it has jurisdiction 'save where those statutes provide otherwise'.

Article 41 of the ECSC Treaty provides that the Court has 'sole jurisdiction to give preliminary rulings on the validity of acts of the High Authority and of the Council where such validity is in issue in proceedings brought before a national court or tribunal'. It would seem that only acts having legal effect can be the subject matter of a reference.[41] Although the scope of the procedure under art 41 is in principle limited to the validity of an act, the Court has construed it as applying also to the interpretation of acts.[42]

The Brussels Convention Protocol and Rome Convention Protocol (which are alone of practical importance) provide only for references concerning the interpretation of the Conventions in question and certain protocols to those Conventions. In the case of the Rome Convention Protocol, the Court's interpretative jurisdiction is described as 'concerning interpretation of the provisions contained in the instruments referred to in' art 1 of the Protocol[43] with the object of enabling a reference for a preliminary ruling to be made where the question of interpretation before the referring court relates directly to a provision of national law which transposes into national law, or merely corresponds to, a provision of the Rome Convention.[44] The Agreement relating to Community Patents provides for references of two kinds: references made by the Common Appeal Court established by the Protocol on Litigation 'whenever there is a risk of an interpretation of this Agreement being inconsistent with that Treaty' (that is, the EC Treaty);[45] and (b) references made by certain named national courts concerning the interpretation of the provisions on jurisdiction applicable to actions relating to Community patents brought before national courts, contained in Part VI, Chapter I, of the Community Patent Convention and in the Protocol on Litigation.[46] References made by the Common Appeal Court appear to be concerned not so much with the interpretation of either the Agreement relating to Community Patents or the EC Treaty as with establishing the existence or otherwise of an inconsistency between a particular interpretation of that Agreement and the EC Treaty.

'Acts' of the Community institutions, as envisaged in this context by the Treaties, cover all measures adopted under or purportedly pursuant to the Treaties, including conventions to which the Community is a party[47] and the

---

39 The instruments governing organisations which have been set up on the basis of international agreements concluded by the member states and not on the basis of the Treaties or measures adopted by the Community institutions cannot be the subject of a reference to the Court for their interpretation: Case 44/84 *Hurd v Jones* [1986] ECR 29 (para 20).
40 Eg art 14 of the Rules of the Administrative Commission on Social Security for Migrant Workers (OJ No C 68 of 21 August 1973, p 25).
41 Case 168/82 *ECSC v Fallimento Ferriere St Anna SpA* [1983] ECR 1681 (para 2).
42 Case 36/83 *Mabanaft GmbH v Hauptzollamt Emmerich* [1984] ECR 2497 at 2530 (Advocate General Slynn); Case 172/84 *Celestri & Co SpA v Ministry of Finance* [1985] ECR 963 (para 12); Case C-221/88 *ECSC v Acciaierie e Ferriere Busseni SpA* [1990] ECR I-495 (paras 8–17).
43 See art 2 of the Protocol.
44 See the Tizzano Report on the Protocol on the Interpretation by the Court of the Rome Convention, para 33 (OJ No C219 of 3 September 1990, p 1 at pp 12–13).
45 Article 2(2).
46 Article 3.
47 Cf Case 87/75 *Conceria Daniele Bresciani v Amministrazione Italiana delle Finanze* [1976] ECR 129; Case 12/86 *Demirel v Stadt Schwabisch Gmund* [1987] ECR 3719, paras 6–12 and at 3739–3742 (Advocate General Darmon), a 'mixed' agreement where it was for the member states to give effect to the commitments of the Community. For more detailed consideration of this question, see Chevallier and Maidani, Guide Pratique Article 177 CEE (1982), pp 27 et seq.

acts of international bodies set up by international agreement in which the Community institutions have participated.[48] The Court has jurisdiction to entertain references made in respect of the validity or interpretation of all acts of the institutions without exception,[49] subject to express provision otherwise in the Treaties.[50] Where the reference concerns the validity of such an act, it is irrelevant that the act could have been, but was not, challenged in an action for annulment.[51] The mere fact that an act of an institution has been incorporated by reference into national legislation or a contract does not deprive the Court of jurisdiction.[52] On the other hand, the Court does not have jurisdiction to entertain references concerning an agreement negotiated and concluded by bodies governed by private law acting within the framework of functions attributed to them under national law (even where the agreement is a condition for the entry into force of Community legislation)[53] or an agreement concluded by a Community institution with an employment agency.[54]

3 The referring court

The chief distinction between the different provisions conferring on the Court jurisdiction to deliver preliminary rulings is that the Treaties open the preliminary ruling procedure to all national courts whereas the Brussels and Rome Convention Protocols and the Agreement relating to Community Patents restrict it to certain named national courts.[55] In consequence, an order for reference purportedly made under the Convention Protocols or that Agreement by a court not envisaged by them is inadmissible and the case will be removed from the Register.[56] On the other hand, the fact that the Treaties refer simply to 'a national court or tribunal', leaves it unclear precisely which courts are envisaged. This is a matter of Community law, not national law, to be determined on the basis of the true construction of the Treaties.

48 Case C-192/89 *Sevince v Staatsecretaris van Justitie* [1990] ECR I-3461 (paras 7–12), decisions of the Council of Association set up under an Association Agreement; Case C-188/91 *Deutsche Shell AG v Hauptzollamt Hamburg-Harburg* [1993] ECR I-363 (paras 13–19), recommendations and arrangements made by a mixed commission set up between the Community and EFTA.

49 Case C-322/88 *Grimaldi v Fonds des Maladies Professionnelles* [1989] ECR 4407 (paras 8–9).

50 See in that connection Single European Act, art 31; EU Treaty, art L.

51 Case C-197/91 *Frutticoltori Associati Cuneesi v Associazione tra Produttori Ortofrutticoli Piemontesi* [1993] ECR I-2639 (para 10); contra, Case C-188/92 *TWD Textilwerke Deggendorf GmbH v Germany* (unreported) per Advocate General Jacobs.

52 Cases C-297/88 and C-197/89 *Dzodzi v Belgium* [1990] ECR I-3763 (paras 31–37); Case C-231/89 *Gmurzynska-Bscher v Oberfinanzdirektion Köln* [1990] ECR I-4003 (paras 24–25); Case C-384/89 *Ministère Public v Tomatis and Fulchirion* [1991] ECR I-127; Case C-88/91 *Federazione Italiana dei Consorzi Agrari v Azienda di Stato er gli Interventi nel Mercato Agricolo* [1992] ECR I-4035 (paras 6–10).

53 Case 152/83 *Demouche v Fonds de Garantie Automobile and Bureau Central Français* [1987] ECR 3833 (paras 18–20).

54 Case 232/84 *Commission v Tordeur* [1985] ECR 3223 at 3226 (Advocate General VerLoren van Themaat).

55 Brussels Convention, art 37; Brussels Convention Protocol, arts 2 and 3; Rome Convention Protocol, art 2; Agreement relating to Community Patents, arts 2(2) and 3(2). In the case of the Rome Convention Protocol, subject to a declaration to the contrary by the United Kingdom, the United Kingdom courts empowered to make references exclude courts ruling on decisions handed down by courts operating in European territories situated outside the United Kingdom for the international relations of which the United Kingdom is responsible: see Rome Convention, art 27(2)(b) and 27(4); Tizzano Report (above, note 44) para 34(b).

56 Eg Case 43/76, order of 30 June 1976 (unreported); Case 80/83 *Habourdin v Italocremona* [1983] ECR 3639.

The definition of a court or tribunal is not tied to the nature of its jurisdiction, whether civil, criminal or administrative,[57] but to whether the body making the reference 'is called upon to give judgment in proceedings intended to lead to a decision of a judicial nature' and which it is 'under a legal duty to try'.[58] However, even an advisory body may be a 'court or tribunal' within the meaning of the Treaties, if the proceedings leading up to and including the decision given in response to its advice can be considered as constituting a single procedure which is judicial in character.[59]

Certain difficulties have arisen over bodies of a private or quasi-public nature such as an arbitral tribunal with jurisdiction over disputes concerning a private pension fund,[60] an appeal committee set up by a private association representing the medical profession[61] and an arbitrator appointed pursuant to a contractual arbitration clause.[62] These cases indicate that a number of factors must be taken into account when deciding whether or not a particular body is a 'court or tribunal'. In particular, it seems clear that it is the nature of the functions performed by the body in the proceedings in which the reference is made that is the determining factor, not the functions performed in general or at other times.[63] The other factors referred to by the Court are these:

(1)   the composition of the body must be determined by an exercise of or entail a 'significant degree of involvement' on the part of public authority;
(2)   the body must be entrusted by law with the exercise of certain powers or responsibilities of a public law nature, in particular those relating to the implementation of Community law;
(3)   its jurisdiction over the dispute in question must be compulsory and not consensual;
(4)   its procedure must be similar to that of ordinary courts;
(5)   it must apply rules of law; and
(6)   its decision must bind the parties and therefore be enforceable.

On the basis of those criteria, references have been accepted from an industrial arbitration board,[64] a compensation board for criminal injuries,[65] a permanent committee with jurisdiction over cases concerning local taxes[66] and a body which exercised judicial functions but was in an administrative sense part of a government department;[67] references have not been accepted from a consultative committee on exchange control which was an organ of the national

---

57 Cf Case 82/71 *Pubblico Ministero v SAIL* [1972] ECR 119 (para 5); Case 199/82 *Amministrazione delle Finanze v San Giorgio* [1983] ECR 3595 (paras 7–9). See generally Alexander and Grabandt (1982) 19 CMLRev 413.
58 Case 138/80 *Borker* [1980] ECR 1975 (para 4).
59 Case 36/73 *Nederlandse Spoorwegen NV v Minister van Verkeer en Waterstaat* [1973] ECR 1299, particularly per Advocate-General Mayras at 1317–1320.
60 Case 61/65 *Vaassen (née Gobbels) v Beambtenfonds voor het Mijnbedrijf* [1966] ECR 261.
61 Case 246/80 *Broekmeulen v Huisarts Registratie Commissie* [1981] ECR 2311.
62 Case 102/81 *Nordsee Deutsche Hochseefischerei GmbH v Reederei Mond Hochseefischerei Nordstem A G & Co KG* [1982] ECR 1095.
63 See also Case 14/86 *Pretore di Salò v X* [1987] ECR 2545 (para 7 and at 2556, Advocate General Mancini).
64 Case 109/88 *Handels- og Kontorfunktionaerernes Forbund i Danmark v Dansk Arbejdsgiverforening* [1989] ECR 3199 (paras 7–9).
65 Case 186/87 *Cowan v Trésor Public* [1989] ECR 195, in particular at 204 (Advocate General Lenz).
66 Case C-109/90 *NV Giant v Gemeente Overijse* [1991] ECR I-1385, in particular at 1391 (Advocate General Jacobs).
67 Case C-67/91 *Direccion General de Defensa de la Competencia v Asociación Española de Banca Privada* [1992] ECR I-4785 at 4809 (Advocate General Jacobs).

Treasury[68] and from the head of the national fiscal administration.[69] If proceedings start before a body which is not a 'court or tribunal' as so defined, but they subsequently come before another body which does have capacity to refer a matter to the Court, a reference can be made.[70]

In the case of references made under the Treaties, the referring court or tribunal must be a court or tribunal 'of a member state'. Where the court or tribunal is located in a region of a member state which is part of the Community or subject to Community law only in certain respects, a reference may be made only in relation to matters of Community law which are applicable within the jurisdiction of that court or tribunal.[71]

An allied question concerns the constitution and jurisdiction of the referring court. As far as national law is concerned, the referring court should, of course, be correctly constituted and have jurisdiction over the matters in dispute; and the same seems to be required by Community law. In Case 65/81 *Reina v Landeskreditbank Baden-Württemberg*,[72] it was argued that the order for reference was inadmissible because the referring court was incorrectly composed when it made the order. The Court accepted that it was for it to consider whether it was duly seised of a matter brought before it by a national court or tribunal but went on to hold that it was not for it to determine whether the order seising it was taken in accordance with national law: 'the Court is therefore bound by a decision of a court or tribunal of a Member State referring a matter to it, in so far as that decision has not been rescinded on the basis of a means of redress provided for by national law'. Similarly, in Cases C-13/91 and C-113/91 *Debus*,[73] the Court held that, in principle and in the absence of exceptional circumstances, it is not for the Court to verify the jurisdiction of national courts under national rules of procedure. In effect, the Court trusts to the national procedures to sort out any dispute relating to the constitution or jurisdiction of the referring court.

4 The power to request a preliminary ruling

Under the terms of the EC and Euratom Treaties,[74] a national court or tribunal 'may' request a preliminary ruling on a question of Community law 'if it considers that a decision on the question is necessary to enable it to give judgment' and must do so if it is a court or tribunal 'against whose decisions there is no judicial remedy under national law'. In the same way, the Brussels Convention Protocol and the Agreement relating to Community Patents distinguish between courts and tribunals which 'shall' or 'must' refer if they consider that a decision on the question is necessary and those which 'may' do so.[75] The Rome Convention Protocol provides only that a court 'may' make a reference.[76] The ECSC Treaty is worded rather differently: the Court has 'sole jurisdiction to give preliminary rulings on the validity of acts of the [Commission] and of the Council where such validity is in issue in proceedings brought

68 Case 318/85 *Unterweger* [1986] ECR 955.
69 Case C-24/92 *Corbiau v Administration des Contributions* [1993] ECR I-1277.
70 Case 65/77 *Razanatsimba* [1977] ECR 2229; the *Nordsee* case (above, note 62) paras 14–15.
71 Cases C-100/89 and C-101/89 *Kaefer and Procacci v France* [1990] ECR I-4647, paras 8–10 and at 4658 (Advocate General Mischo); Case C-355/89 *Department of Health and Social Security v Barr and Montrose Holdings Ltd* [1991] ECR I-3479 (paras 6–10).
72 [1982] ECR 33 (paras 6–8).
73 [1992] ECR I-3617 (para 8). See also Case C-10/92 *Balocchi v Ministero delle Finanze dello Stato*, 20 October 1993 (paras 15–17).
74 Articles 177 and 150, respectively.
75 Brussels Convention Protocol, art 3; Agreement relating to Community Patents, art 3(2)–(4).
76 Article 2.

before a national court or tribunal'. As a general principle, when the validity of an act adopted by a Community institution is at issue before a national court or tribunal, that court or tribunal is bound to refer the matter to the Court, unless it considers that the arguments in favour of concluding that the act in question is invalid are unfounded, because only the Court has jurisdiction to declare such an act to be invalid.[77] In consequence, in cases where the issue of invalidity is raised, any discretion of the national court is largely removed, whichever is the Treaty under which the reference is to be made.

In the Treaties and the other instruments conferring on national courts jurisdiction to request a preliminary ruling, the expressions 'where such a question [that is, a referable question] is raised' (or the equivalent) and 'if it considers that a decision on the question is necessary to enable it to give judgment' set out the two preconditions for the exercise of, as the case may be, the discretion or duty of the national court to make a reference.

A referable question is raised in proceedings before a national court where it arises as an issue in the proceedings. It may be raised by the parties or, subject to any national rule of procedure preventing the national court from raising a point which has not been raised by one of the parties to the proceedings,[78] by the national court of its own motion. Where the question is raised by a party, the national court is not obliged to accept that the first condition has been satisfied: it is entitled to verify for itself that a referable question does in truth arise in the proceedings.[79] To a large extent, whether or not the first condition has been satisfied is an objective test: either the proceedings give rise to a referable question, or they do not. On one view, a referable question never arises in situations where the point of Community law in question has already been decided by the Court: if the issue has been resolved, it cannot give rise to a question in any real sense. However, the Court has accepted that national courts are always free to make a reference to the Court, if they think it appropriate, even in circumstances where the 'question' has already been dealt with by the Court in an identical case or is the subject of a settled line of decisions of the Court, albeit not necessarily in identical cases.[80] Accordingly, the fact that the referable 'question' relates to a matter that has already been decided by the Court goes in principle to the second condition and not to the first.

Whereas the fulfilment of the first condition is essentially verifiable objectively, the fulfilment of the second condition is a matter that is entirely for the subjective appreciation of the national court before whom are pending the proceedings in the context of which the referable question has arisen.[81] In the

---

77 Case 314/85 *Foto-Frost v Hauptzollamt Lübeck-Ost* [1987] ECR 4199 (paras 14–20 and at 4214–4221, Advocate General Mancini).
78 On one view, a national court cannot be precluded from raising a point of Community law of its own motion because it is the general duty of national courts to ensure that the rule of law is observed and it is their particular duty to ensure that Community law is observed by virtue of art 5 of the EC Treaty. Even points of Community law that are of particular importance to private parties, such as matters of European Community competition law, are not intended simply to protect private interests or confer private law rights; the rights conferred by Community law on individuals are conferred on them in large part in the public interest. At the very least, any national procedural rule precluding a national court from taking a point not raised by the parties would be sustainable only if it applied to any such point and not just to points of Community law.
79 Case 283/81 *CILFIT Srl v Minister of Health* [1982] ECR 3415, para 9.
80 Ibid paras 13–15.
81 Eg Case 59/85 *Netherlands v Reed* [1986] ECR 1283 at 1286–1287 (Advocate General Lenz); Case 298/87 *Smanor SA* [1988] ECR 4489 (para 9); Case C-127/92 *Enderby v Frenchay Health Authority and Secretary of State for Health*, 27 October 1993 (para 10).

same way, the different question that must be considered by the Common Appeal Court when deciding whether or not to make a reference under art 2(2) of the Agreement relating to Community Patents (whether or not there is a risk of an interpretation of the Agreement being inconsistent with the EEC Treaty) is a matter for that Court. In making its appraisal, the national court or tribunal cannot be bound by the views expressed by other national authorities because it is exercising a power given it by the Treaties (or the Convention Protocols) which is governed exclusively by Community law and for the consequences of which it alone is responsible.[82] Hence, one court or tribunal cannot make a reference in order to obtain a ruling that may be of benefit to another court or tribunal, even if to do so would expedite the resolution of the dispute before the latter.[83]

In relation to the second condition, the Court has construed the necessity for a decision on the referable question as indicating the necessity for a decision by the Court itself (not the national court or tribunal); and the case law therefore refers to the 'necessity for a preliminary ruling'.[84] The necessity for a preliminary ruling logically raises two different questions: the necessity for a decision on the question of Community law raised in the proceedings to enable the national court to give judgment in those proceedings; and the necessity for the question of Community law to be decided by the Court rather than by the national court itself. In neither respect is the test of 'necessity' given a strict construction.

So far as the necessity for a decision on the question of Community law is concerned, it is sufficient if that question is 'relevant' to the issue before the national court;[85] there is no requirement that a decision on the question of Community law be a sine qua non of the delivery of judgment in the proceedings before the national court. The classic illustration of that point is Case 33/74 *van Binsbergen v Bestuur van de Bedrijfsvereniging voor de Metallnijverheid*,[86] where the question of Community law raised in the proceedings had nothing whatever to do with the substance of the dispute before the referring court; it related only to the right of audience before the referring court of the person representing one of the parties. That case shows that the second condition for making a reference may be satisfied in respect of a point arising incidentally in the proceedings before the referring court, one that it is not, strictly speaking, 'necessary' for the referring court to decide in order to give judgment. In relation to the necessity for a preliminary ruling to decide the question of Community law (as opposed to a decision of the national court itself), the matter is entirely one of discretion for the national court seised with the case, as can be seen from the Court's acceptance that, even where the question of Community law is one that has already been the subject of a ruling of the Court

---

82 Case 244/80 *Foglia v Novello (No 2)* [1981] ECR 3045 (paras 15–16); Case 232/82 *Baccini v ONEM* [1983] ECR 583 (para 11); Case 170/82 *ONCV v Ramel Sàrl* [1983] ECR 1319 (para 8).

83 Case 338/85 *Fratelli Pardini SpA v Ministero del Commercio con l'Estero* [1988] ECR 2041, paras 10–14 and at 2056–2060 (Advocate General Darmon), where the problem arose in connection with the grant of interim relief.

84 Cf Case C-83/91 *Meilicke v ADV/ORGA AG* [1992] ECR I-4871 (para 23). In some cases, such as Case 180/83 *Moser v Land Baden-Württemberg* [1984] ECR 2539 (para 6), the English version of the judgment refers to the 'need' for a preliminary ruling, but the French version (which sets out the form of words which the judges would have agreed) uses the term 'necessary'.

85 In the case law of the Court, the term 'relevant' is invariably used to describe this part of the test: see, for example, the *Pardini* case (above, note 83) para 8; Case C-368/89 *Crispoltoni v Fattoria Autonoma Tabacchi di Città di Castello* [1991] ECR I-3695 (para 10); the *Enderby* case (above, note 81) para 10.

86 [1974] ECR 1299.

in another case, the national court remains free to request a preliminary ruling, if it thinks it appropriate.[87]

Where a referable question has been raised in the proceedings before the national court or tribunal and where that court or tribunal considers both that the question raised is 'relevant' and that a preliminary ruling is 'necessary' to decide it, the decision to make a reference is then a matter of discretion or of duty, depending upon whether the provision conferring the power to make a reference admits of a discretion or imposes a duty. That seems to follow from the fact that, by way of example, the discretion conferred by art 177 of the EC Treaty indicated by the word 'may' operates once the preconditions have been satisfied and is therefore separate from those conditions. That degree of discretion is therefore additional to the discretion accorded to the national court or tribunal when deciding whether or not the second condition has been satisfied. In consequence, the discretion accorded to certain national courts or tribunals implies the existence of an entitlement on their part to refrain from making a reference and, instead, to decide a question of Community law raised before them even in circumstances where the conditions for making a reference have been satisfied. However, it is more usual to assimilate the discretion implied by the word 'may' to the discretion of the national court or tribunal regarding the fulfilment of the second condition for making a reference, no doubt because it seems illogical for a national court to determine that a preliminary ruling is 'necessary' but then to exercise its discretion and decide the referable question itself.

5   The discretion to make a reference

The courts and tribunals which retain a discretion whether or not to make a reference are identified by name or description in the Brussels and Rome Convention Protocols and in the Agreement relating to Community Patents. In the EC and Euratom Treaties, the principle is that all courts and tribunals having the power to make a reference possess a discretion, and not a duty, to do so unless (i) they are a court or tribunal 'against whose decisions there is no judicial remedy under national law';[88] or (ii) the matter at issue is the validity of an act of a Community institution, in which case a reference must be made unless the national court or tribunal is confident that the act in question is valid.[89] The very wide discretion accorded to national courts when deciding whether or not to make a reference in cases where they are not bound to do so means that it is for the national court alone to decide whether or not a question of Community law raised before it is material, whether or not a reference is

---

87 The *CILFIT* case (above, note 79) para 15. The underlying assumption is that the earlier ruling of the Court, while dealing with an identical point of Community law, was made in the context of a different case and that there may therefore be room for doubt whether or not the ruling is entirely applicable to the case before the national court. If the ruling of the Court relates to the same case (such as where a reference was made by an appellate court at an earlier stage in the proceedings and, subsequently, the matter was remitted to a lower court for final decision), the binding effect of the ruling of the Court or of the decision of a higher court made in the light of that ruling may relieve the lower court of the power to make a further reference on the same point: Case 166/73 *Rheinmühlen-Düsseldorf v Einfuhr- und Vorratsstelle für Getreide und Futtermittel* [1974] ECR 33 (para 4). A further reference may, however, be made by the referring court (or, it must be supposed, by an appellate court or a lower court – the latter when the matter is remitted to it by a higher court – in the same proceedings) in order to elucidate the meaning of the Court's ruling: Case 69/85 *Wünsche v Germany* [1986] ECR 947 (para 15).

88 Such courts and tribunals are considered in the next section.

89 See the text to note 77 above.

necessary in order to decide it and at what stage in the proceedings it is appropriate to make the reference; and that discretion is not limited otherwise than by considerations of procedural organisation and efficiency to be assessed by that court.[90]

The earliest point at which a reference can be made is, of course, when the national court or tribunal is first seised of the case (or when the referable question first arises in the proceedings). It has been doubted whether a reference may be made in ex parte proceedings. The consensus of opinion is that it is preferable for references to be made after all the parties have been heard but that is not a condition for making a reference (it is a matter lying within the discretion of the referring court); and a reference made without the parties, or all of them, being heard is nonetheless admissible.[91] Further, the Court has indicated that, as a matter of practice, it is preferable if the reference is made after the referring court has found the facts and decided any relevant questions of national law.[92] It is nonetheless within the discretion of the national court or tribunal to make a reference before finding the facts or deciding any relevant questions of national law, or on the basis of a hypothesis, if it thinks it appropriate.[93] The latest point at which a reference may be made is immediately before the national court or tribunal gives judgment in the case before it or on the issue of Community law in question. The object of the preliminary ruling procedure is to obtain a ruling on a point of Community law which is before the national court: if the national court is not, or is no longer, seised with such an issue (because, for example, the proceedings before it have come to an end), it cannot make that issue the subject of a reference for a preliminary ruling:[94] the right to make a reference is that of the court with the issue in question pending before it.

Although the exercise of the power to make a reference is governed exclusively by Community law,[95] the Court has not laid down any particular guidelines as to the exercise of the discretion to make a reference other than that it is preferable for references to be made after the relevant facts have been found and any points of national law decided and after the parties have been heard.[96] Nonetheless, those considerations do not restrict in any way the

---

90 Cases 36, 71/80 *Irish Creamery Milk Suppliers Association v Ireland* [1981] ECR 735 (paras 5–9); Case 278/82 *Rewe-Handelsgesellschaft Nord v Hauptzollamt Flensburg* [1984] ECR 721 (para 8); the *Moser* case (above, note 84) para 6; Cases 209–213/84 *Ministére Public v Asjés* [1986] ECR 1425 (para 10); Cases 98, 162, 258/85 *Bertini v Regione Lazio* [1986] ECR 1885 (para 8); the *Gmurzynska-Bscher* case (above, note 52), para 19.

91 *Pretore di Salò v X* (above, note 63), in particular at para 13 and 2559 (Advocate General Mancini); Case 228/87 *Pretura Unificata di Torino v X* [1988] ECR 5099 at 5108–5110 (Advocate General Lenz); Cases C-277, C-318 and C-319/91 *Ligur Carni Srl v Unità Sanitarie Locali nos. XV e XIX*, unreported (opinion of Advocate General Darmon, paras 12–14); the *Balocchi* case (above, note 73), paras 13–14 and the opinion of Advocate General Jacobs (paras 16–18).

92 The *Irish Creamery* case (above, note 90); the *Meilicke* case (above, note 84) para 26.

93 In relation to references made without finding the facts or deciding matters of domestic law, see, for example: Case 72/83 *Campus Oil Ltd v Minister for Industry and Energy* [1984] ECR 2727 (paras 9–11); the *Pretore di Salò* case (above, note 63), paras 10–11. In relation to references made on the basis of a hypothesis, see, for example: the *Enderby* case (above, note 81) para 12 (the Court is obliged to answer without questioning the basis for the hypothesis unless there is manifestly no connection between the question referred and the reality or subject matter of the dispute before the referring court). As can be seen from cases such as *Meilicke* (above, note 84) and Cases C-320 to C-322/90 *Telemarsicabruzzo SpA v Circostel* [1993] ECR I-393 (paras 6–9), a failure to define properly the factual and legal matrix of the questions referred may lead the Court to decline to give an answer.

94 The *Pardini* case (above, note 83) para 11). See, for example, the situation that arose in Case C-339/89 *Alsthom Atlantique v Sulzer* [1991] ECR I-107 at 116 (Advocate General van Gerven).

95 Case 244/80 *Foglia v Novello (No 2)* (above, note 82) para 16.

96 See above text to notes 91 to 93.

discretion of the national court. That reflects the fact that the referring court is accorded by Community law 'the widest power' to make a reference, reflecting the fact (constantly reiterated in the case law) that the court before whom the dispute is pending alone bears the responsibility for the case before it.[97]

6   The obligation to make a reference

Whereas the Brussels Convention Protocol and the Agreement relating to Community Patents distinguish reasonably clearly between the courts or tribunals which must refer and those which may, the position with regard to the EC and Euratom Treaties is not so obvious. Cases where the issue is one of the validity of an act of a Community institution aside, the criterion determining the existence of the obligation to refer is that there is no judicial remedy under national law against the decision of the court or tribunal concerned. It would seem that, in this context, that criterion is satisfied where the parties to the proceedings before the national court or tribunal in question have no means of obtaining as of right a reconsideration of any decision made by that court or tribunal on the question of Community law raised in the proceedings (or on the wider issue to which that question relates) by another national court or tribunal. In particular, exceptional proceedings which may be invoked by, for example, a party on the discovery of a new fact or by a third party with an interest in the case do not constitute judicial remedies which may relieve the national court or tribunal of the obligation to make a reference. However, even where there is no judicial remedy under national law against a decision of the national court or tribunal, the Court has accepted that there may be circumstances in which the obligation to refer does not apply.

Case 107/76 *Hoffmann-La Roche AG v Centrafarm Vertriebsgesellschaft Pharmazeutischer Erzeugnisse mbH*[98] concerned an interlocutory application for an injunctive form of relief. Under German law such applications may be made before the commencement of the action and are heard and determined ex parte in cases where there is urgency. If the order is granted, the defendant can appeal to the same court for the matter to be considered again in the light of full argument. There is then an appeal to a higher court which is the court of last instance so far as the interlocutory application is concerned, but the plaintiff can and, under German law, must, if so required by the defendant, bring an action for a permanent form of relief. In the *Hoffmann-La Roche* case, the plaintiff had applied for an interlocutory injunction restraining the defendant from infringing its trademark rights. The defendant raised a defence under Community law and the question arose whether the court of last instance in the proceedings was bound to make a reference concerning that point, even though it would have to be decided again in the main proceedings. The Court held that a court of last instance is not bound to refer a question of Community law raised in interlocutory proceedings before it, provided that each of the parties is entitled to institute proceedings or require proceedings to be instituted on the substance of the case and that, during such proceedings, the question of Community law may be re-examined and be the subject of a reference under art 177.

A similar problem arose in Cases 35 and 36/82 *Morson and Jhanjan v Netherlands*.[99] There two nationals of Surinam residing in the Netherlands had their applications for a resident's permit turned down by the Secretary of State, thus

97 Eg the *Pardini* case (above, note 83) paras 8–9.
98 [1977] ECR 957; see in particular para 6.
99 [1982] ECR 3723 (paras 8–10).

making them liable to deportation. They applied to the president of the local civil court for an injunction restraining the Secretary of State from deporting them pending the review of his decision by the competent administrative court. The injunction proceedings were appealed to the highest civil court, which referred two questions to the Court. The first was whether it was obliged to make the reference and the second concerned the point of Community law before it. It seems that one of the criteria for granting an injunction was the applicant's chances of success in the proceedings for reviewing the Secretary of State's decision. In contrast to the situation in the *Hoffmann-La Roche* case, those proceedings were before an administrative court with a jurisdiction separate and independent from the court hearing the interlocutory proceedings. The Court repeated, in substance, what it had said in *Hoffmann-La Roche*.

The burden of the Court's decision in both cases is that the test to be applied is neither formal nor technical. The crucial factor is whether the question of Community law can effectively be re-examined in proceedings on the substance of the case. If the interlocutory proceedings terminate in a provisional decision and the question of Community law arises for consideration in the action itself, the provisional decision does not in substance amount to a decision against which there is no judicial remedy under national law for the purposes of the Treaties. But if the applicant is disqualified from instituting proceedings, or the question of Community law does not arise, on the substance of the case, or if events have or will have made a decision on the question wholly academic or pointless, the question must be referred because, to all intents and purposes, the interlocutory decision is one against which there is no judicial remedy. This does not mean that such a decision can become final if a party refrains from continuing the proceedings. It often happens that the parties accept the decision on a point of law delivered in interlocutory proceedings as settling the dispute between them. Nevertheless, as long as it lies within the power of one of the parties to have that decision re-examined, it cannot be said that there is no judicial remedy under national law against it. Nonetheless, while the national court may not be obliged to make a reference in interim relief proceedings, there is nothing to prevent it from doing so, should it consider it appropriate, as long as the outcome of the reference would be relevant to the proceedings before it.[1]

It is unclear whether the same reasoning applies to cases where there is no right of appeal but an appeal may be allowed by the exercise of a discretionary power. This situation does not seem to arise in most of the member states. Where it does, it would appear that the obligation to refer exists unless a right to appeal has already been opened by the exercise of a discretion or the existence of some rule or practice which effectively prevents the discretion from being exercised so as to exclude the possibility of an appeal.[2]

Given that there is no effective remedy against its decisions under national law, a court of last instance is still not bound to refer any and every question of Community law that comes before it. In Cases 28–30/62 *Da Costa en Schaake NV v Nederlandse Belastingadministratie*[3] the Court held: 'although the third paragraph of Article 177 unreservedly requires courts or tribunals of a Member State against whose decisions there is no judicial remedy under national law . . . to refer to the Court every question of interpretation raised before them,

1 Case 30/87 *Bodson v Pompes Funèbres des Régions Liberées* [1988] ECR 2479 at 2490–2491 (Advocate General Cruz Vilaça); Case C-159/90 *Society for the Protection of Unborn Children Ireland Ltd v Grogan* [1991] ECR I-4685 (para 13 and at 4706, Advocate General van Gerven).
2 See Bebr *Development of Judicial Control* pp 375–376.
3 [1963] ECR 31 at 38.

the authority of an interpretation under Article 177 already given by the Court may deprive the obligation of its purpose and thus empty it of its substance. Such is the case especially when the question raised is materially identical with a question which has already been the subject of a preliminary ruling in a similar case.' In Case 283/81 *CILFIT Srl v Minister of Health*[4] the Court took this a stage further. It held that courts of last instance enjoy the same power as other national courts or tribunals to assess the question whether a decision on a point of Community law is necessary to give judgment in a case. They are not, therefore, bound to refer a question raised before them whose answer, whatever it is, can have no effect on the result of the case. But once a court of last instance finds that a decision on a point of Community law is necessary to decide the case before it, it is obliged to make a reference unless: (i) the point is materially identical to a question which has already been decided in proceedings for a preliminary ruling arising out of a similar case or there is an established body of case law concerning the point, whatever the nature of the proceedings (whether direct actions or references for a preliminary ruling) in which it was laid down and even if the questions at issue were not strictly identical; (ii) the correct application of Community law is so evident that it leaves no reasonable doubt.

In concluding that the latter situation exists, a national court must be convinced that the matter is equally evident to courts in other member states and to the Court itself, taking into account the nature of Community law and the special difficulties that its interpretation presents, in particular:

(1)   the fact that Community law is drafted in several languages, each of which is authentic, so an interpretation of a text of Community law requires a comparison of the different language versions;

(2)   even where the different language versions are in agreement, Community law has its own terminology and the expressions it uses may not have the same meaning as in national law; and

(3)   each provision of Community law must be placed in context and interpreted in the light of Community law, taken as a whole and with regard to its objectives and the state of its development at the time the provision is to be applied.

7   Procedural steps before national courts pending the preliminary ruling

The Statutes provide that the referring court 'suspends its proceedings and refers a case to the Court',[5] suggesting that the making of a reference is necessarily accompanied by the suspension of the proceedings in which the question referred arose for consideration and that, while the reference is pending before the Court, the proceedings before the national courts are at an end. The nature and extent of the suspension of the national proceedings that is consequential upon the making of a reference must be seen in the light of the purpose of the preliminary ruling procedure: it is intended to assist the referring court in coming to a decision; a preliminary ruling requested or delivered after the delivery of judgment by the national court is pointless. The suspension of the national proceedings therefore goes no further than is necessary in order to preserve the effectiveness of the preliminary ruling eventually given by the Court. In consequence, it applies essentially so as to prevent the question referred, or the wider issue in the case to which it relates,

---

4   [1982] ECR 3415.
5   EC Statute, art 20; Euratom Statute, art 21.

from being decided by the referring court (or any other national court or tribunal in the same proceedings between the same parties) until the preliminary ruling has been delivered. To that extent, the making of the reference can be regarded as operating so as to disseise the national courts of jurisdiction over the dispute until the matter is remitted to them upon delivery of the preliminary ruling. That does not mean that no steps at all can be taken in the national proceedings while the preliminary ruling is pending. On the contrary, there seems to be no impediment to the taking of further procedural steps as long as the limited purpose of the suspension envisaged in the Statutes is respected. There are two procedural steps likely to be contemplated or taken while a preliminary ruling is pending which merit particular comment: the grant of interim relief; and steps to withdraw the reference or appeal against the decision to make a reference.

The suspension of proceedings envisaged in the Statutes does not preclude the national court from granting interim relief, where it is appropriate to do so, pending the outcome of the reference.[6] Ordinarily, the usual criteria for the grant of interim relief employed by the national court in question apply as long as they do not discriminate against the protection of rights under Community law or make the protection of such rights impossible in practice or excessively difficult.[7] Slightly different considerations come into play where an act of a national body is challenged before a national court on the ground that it implements an unlawful act of a Community institution. In those circumstances, the national court has power to suspend the operation of the former by way of interim relief if the issue of the validity of the latter is referred to the Court. The grant of interim relief is therefore conditional upon the making of a reference. National law governs the making of the application for relief and the procedure for dealing with it but interim relief can be granted only if the national court entertains serious doubts about the validity of the act of the Community institution and suspension must be temporary (and only until the preliminary ruling has been delivered). In other respects, the criteria applied by the Court itself in interim relief cases must be applied by the national court: there must be urgency, in the sense of a threat of serious and irreparable damage (other than purely financial loss, save in exceptional cases) to the party seeking relief which is likely to materialise before the delivery of the preliminary ruling; the national court must take into account the interests of the Community in having its measures applied and not set aside without proper guarantees; and, where suspension would involve a financial risk for the Community, the national court must be able to require adequate guarantees from the party seeking relief, such as a desposit of money, bank guarantee or other security.[8]

The Court remains seised of the order for reference, even if the parties to the proceedings before the national court settle the case, unless and until the referring court withdraws it. Apart from situations where the proceedings before the national court are discontinued or withdrawn by the parties while the preliminary ruling is pending, it is not clear whether or not the referring court entertains any residual jurisdiction to withdraw the reference once the decision to make it has been made. In principle, it would appear that a reference may be withdrawn by the referring court or tribunal only if there has

---

6 Eg Case C-213/89 *R v Secretary of State for Transport, ex p Factortame Ltd* [1990] ECR I-2433.
7 Ibid at 2462–2464 (Advocate General Tesauro).
8 Cases C-143/88 and C-92/89 *Zuckerfabrik Süderdithmarschen AG v Hauptzollamt Itzehoe* [1991] ECR I-415 (paras 18–32).

been a material change in circumstances since the decision to make a reference: namely, the discontinuance or withdrawal of the proceedings before the referring court, the discovery of a new fact or matter indicating that the referring court had no jurisdiction to make the reference (such as where it is subsequently discovered that there is no genuine dispute between the parties) or the quashing of the order for reference on appeal.

In Case 13/61 *Kledingverkoopbedrijf De Geus v Robert Bosch GmbH*[9] it was questioned whether the Court could entertain an order for reference once the national court's decision making it had been appealed to a higher national court. The Court pointed out in its judgment that, just as the making of the order for reference does not affect the possibility of appealing the referring court's decision, so the making of an appeal does not affect the Court's jurisdiction over the order for reference: national law is, in this respect, separate and distinct from Community law. In Case 127/73 *BRT v SABAM*[10] the Court held that, in the event of an appeal being made, the preliminary ruling procedure continues nevertheless 'as long as the request of the national court has neither been withdrawn nor become devoid of object'.[11] In consequence, while the mere making of an appeal has no effect on the preliminary ruling procedure, unless the referring court itself asks for proceedings to be stayed pending the result of the appeal or, under national law, the making of the appeal has the effect of suspending the referring court's order[12] (in which case the Court's practice is to stay the proceedings before it), it is only if the referring court's decision is reversed on appeal that the preliminary ruling procedure ends. In any event, the staying of proceedings, withdrawal of the order for reference, or removal of the case from the Register can only be made at the formal request of a competent person, either the referring court or the appeal court whose decision reverses that of the referring court.[13]

Just as the making of a reference to the Court does not preclude the possibility of appealing that decision to a higher national court, so a decision refusing to make a reference may in principle be the subject of an appeal. In either case, the appeal may be based on the usual grounds of appeal accepted by the national legal order but subject to the particular features of the preliminary ruling procedure. In other words, the appeal may in principle be based on lack of jurisdiction to make a reference or error of law in general (including an erroneous finding that the court or tribunal lacks jurisdiction to make a reference) and procedural irregularities (such as the irregular constitution of the referring court or tribunal). Instances where an appeal may lie may also be inferred from the situations where the Court itself will refuse to entertain a reference or decline to answer a question that has been referred.[14] In principle, however, the scope for appealing from a decision of a national court or tribunal making or refusing to make a reference is limited to those matters falling outside the area of discretion accorded to the national court or tribunal. Further, it does not seem that a national court hearing such an appeal can itself make a reference (save in regard to questions of Community law arising in the appeal itself) or amend the terms of the order for reference

---

9 [1962] ECR 45 at 49–50; see also Case 146/73 *Firma Rheinmuhlen Düsseldorf v Einfur- und Vorratsstelle für Getreide and Futtermittel* [1974] ECR 139 (para 3).

10 [1974] ECR 51 (paras 8–9).

11 'Devoid of object' is misleading. The French text of the judgment says '*mise à néant*': see Case 106/77 *Amministrazione delle Finanze dello Stato v Simmenthal SpA* [1978] ECR 629 (para 10).

12 This was the situation in, for example, Case 822/79, later withdrawn, and Case 152/83 *Demouche v Fonds de Garantie Automobile* [1987] ECR 3833.

13 Case 31/68 *Chanel SA v Cepeha Handelsmaatschappij NV* [1970] ECR 403; Cases 2–4/82 *Delhaize v Belgium* [1983] ECR 2973 (paras 8–9).

14 See below, pp 567 et seq.

made by the referring court unless and until it is itself seised with the dispute out of which the question of Community law arises.[15]

8   The handling of the reference[16]

The Court will not investigate whether or not there are any additional questions for which a preliminary ruling may be 'necessary'[17] but it may review the referring court's appraisal for the purpose of determining whether or not it has jurisdiction to rule on the questions that have been referred. The Court does so only on the basis of the terms of the order for reference, referring where necessary to the file of the case; only if it is manifest on the face of the former (as explained by the latter) that a ruling on the question of Community law is not necessary to give judgment in the case will the Court reject the reference as inadmissible.[18] In particular the Court has emphasised that it does not have jurisdiction to entertain a reference which does not correspond to an objective requirement inherent in the resolution of a dispute[19] or which bears no relation to the actual nature of the case or the subject matter of the action before the referring court.[20]

The Court is obliged to rule on the questions referred to it as long as they fall within its jurisdiction,[21] even though the reference appears to be irrelevant.[22] In particular, the Court has no power to apply a rule of Community law to a particular case or decide on the compatibility of national law with Community law; the most that it can do is provide the national court with information concerning the interpretation or validity of provisions of Community law which may assist the national court in deciding the dispute before it.[23] The ruling delivered by the Court states the law as it is and always has been and as it must be applied by the referring to court even to legal relationships arising before the date of the preliminary ruling unless the Court exercises its power to limit the scope of its judgment.[24]

---

15 Cf Case 338/85 *Fratelli Pardini SpA v Ministero del Commercio con l'Estero* [1988] ECR 2041 (para 10).

16 See chapter 2, section VI.

17 Eg Case 126/86 *Gimenez Zaera v Instituto Nacional de la Seguridad Social y Tesoreria General de la Seguridad Social* [1987] ECR 3697 (para 7).

18 Case 244/80 *Foglia v Novello (No 2)* [1981] ECR 3045 (paras 17–21). The case is discussed at greater length in the following articles: Bebr (1980) 17 CMLRev 525 and (1982) 19 CMLRev 421; Barav (1980) 5 ELRev 443 and (1982) Rev Trim Dr Eur 431; Wyatt (1981) 6 ELRev 447 and (1982) 7 ELRev 186. See also Case 13/68 *Salgoil SpA v Italian Ministry of Foreign Trade* [1968] ECR 453 at 459, Case 126/80 *Salonia v Poidomani* [1981] ECR 1563 (para 6); Case 149/82 *Robards v Insurance Officer* [1983] ECR 171 (para 19); Cases 286/82 and 26/83 *Lüisi and Carbone v Ministero del Tesoro* [1984] ECR 377 at 412–413 (Advocate General Mancini); Case 180/83 *Moser v Land Baden Württemberg* [1984] ECR 2539; Case C-343/90 *Dias v Director da Alfandega do Porto* [1992] ECR I-4673 (paras 18–20); Case C-292/92 *Hünermund*, 15.12.93, paras 8–10; Case C-364/92 *Eurocontrol*, 19.1.94, para 13; Case C-331/92 *Gestion Hotelera* (per Advocate General Lenz, paras 13–14).

19 *Foglia v Novello (No 2)* (ibid) para 18; Case C-83/91 *Meilicke v ADV/ORGA AG* [1992] ECR I-4871.

20 *Salonia v Poidomani* (above, note 18); Case C-67/91 *Direccion General de Defensa de la Competencia v Asociación Española de Banca Privada et al* [1992] ECR I-4785 (para 26); Case C-127/92 *Enderby v Frenchay Health Authority and Secretary of State for Health*, 27 October 1993 (para 12).

21 Eg Case C-231/89 *Gmurzynska-Bscher v Oberfinanzdirektion Köln* [1990] ECR I-4003 (paras 20–22); the *Dias* case (above, note 18) paras 16–18, which sets out the circumstances in which the Court may decline to answer a question referred to it. See also chapter 7, section II.A.

22 Case 239/84 *Gerlach & Co BV, Internationale Expeditie v Minister for Economic Affairs* [1985] ECR 3507 (paras 6–8).

23 Eg Case 107/83 *Ordre des Avocats au Bureau de Paris v Klopp* [1984] ECR 2971 (para 14); Case 137/84 *Ministère Public v Mutsch* [1985] ECR 2681 (para 6); Case 296/84 *Sinatra v FNROM* [1986] ECR 1047 (para 11).

24 Eg Case 309/85 *Barra v Belgium and City of Liège* [1988] ECR 355 (paras 11–14); Case 24/86 *Blaizot v University of Liège* [1988] ECR 379 (paras 27–34); Case C-163/90 *Administration des Douanes et Droits Indirects v Legros* [1992] ECR I-4625 (paras 28–36). See further chapter 16, section II, pp 497–498.

H   Fines and penalties

Under the ECSC Treaty[25] the Court has 'unlimited jurisdiction in appeals against pecuniary sanctions and periodic penalty payments imposed under this Treaty'. The EC Treaty[26] provides that the Court may, by regulation adopted jointly by the European Parliament and the Council or by the Council alone, be given unlimited jurisdiction in regard to the penalties provided for in such regulation. Provision is made in regulations providing for the abolition of discrimination in transport rates and conditions;[27] the imposition of penalties in competition cases;[28] and, in relation to disputes which are financial in character, under the Communities' Staff Regulations.[29] It should be noted that the Court's unlimited jurisdiction under the Staff Regulations is wider than that under other regulations or the ECSC Treaty because it is not restricted to cases where a fine or penalty is imposed; disputes which are financial in character include any dispute in which a sum is claimed.

Strictly speaking, the effect of granting the Court unlimited jurisdiction is not to confer on it a form of action but to enlarge the jurisdiction of the Court in disputes before it. In general terms, where the Court has unlimited jurisdiction, it has power not only to annul but also to increase or reduce the penalty imposed.[30] It may also make a general order addressed to the defendant (in casu, an order requiring the defendant to review the applicant's administrative situation) even though, in an ordinary action for annulment, it could not order the defendant to take specific measures to implement the judgment;[31] and the Court may exercise its unlimited jurisdiction of its own motion and in the absence of any formal claim for the particular relief granted by the Court.[32] The Court's unlimited jurisdiction does not, however, appear to entitle it to substitute its own view of what is an appropriate penalty for that of the administration in the absence of a manifest error or misuse of powers or a procedural defect, such as a failure to provide adequate reasons for the choice actually made[33] (it should be emphasised that that appears to apply in relation to the choice between different *types* of penalty; the Court retains unlimited jurisdiction in relation to the *gravity* of the penalty imposed). Generalities apart, in cases where, unlike the Staff Regulations, the Court's unlimited jurisdiction applies only to

25   Article 36; see also art 66(6) and art 43 of the ECSC Statute.
26   Article 172, as amended by art G(E)(51) of the EU Treaty.
27   Council Regulation No 11 of 27 June 1960, art 25(2) (OJ 1121/1960, English Special Edition 1959–1962, p 60), implemented pursuant to EC Treaty, art 79(3).
28   Council Regulation No 17 of 6 February 1962, art 17 (OJ 204/1962, English Special Edition 1959–1962, p 87), which implements EC Treaty, arts 85 and 86; Council Regulation No 1017/68 of 19 July 1968, art 24 (OJ No L175/1 of 23 July 1968, English Special Edition 1968(I), p 302), on the application of the EC competition rules to transport by rail, road and inland waterway; Council Regulation No 4056/86 of 22 December 1986, art 21 (OJ 1986 No L378/4), applying the competition rules to maritime transport; Council Regulation No 3975/87 of 14 December 1987, art 14 (OJ 1987 No L374/1), applying the competition rules to air transport; Council Regulation No 4064/89 of 21 December 1989, art 16 (OJ 1989 No L395/1), on merger control (see the corrected version published in OJ 1990 No L257/14).
29   Article 91(1).
30   Cf Case 8/56 *ALMA v High Authority* [1957–58] ECR 95 at 99 and at 102 (Advocate General Lagrange).
31   Case T-73/89 *Barbi v Commission* [1990] ECR II-619 (para 38).
32   Cases 176 and 177/86 *Houyoux v Commission* [1987] ECR 4333 (para 16): grant of compensation for maladministration. The case law is, however, inconsistent: compare Case 24/79 *Oberthür v Commission* [1980] ECR 1743 (para 14); Case 150/84 *Bernardi v European Parliament* [1986] ECR 1375 at 1382 (Advocate General Darmon); Case 267/85 *Luttgens v Commission* [1986] ECR 3417, para 6 and at 3429 (Advocate General Cruz Vilaça).
33   Case 228/83 *F v Commission* [1985] ECR 275 (paras 34 and 40).

the imposition of a fine or penalty, it applies only to the gravity of the fine or penalty imposed.

The existence of the Court's unlimited jurisdiction in respect of the imposition of a fine or penalty means that, in principle, an action can be brought under the provisions referred to above simply in order to seek a reduction of the fine or penalty and without alleging that the decision imposing it is void.[34] Such an action is one for the annulment or quashing of the fine or penalty alone. It is more usual, however, to seek the annulment of both the fine or penalty and the findings underpinning it. In such a case, the application is one for the annulment of the decision imposing the fine or penalty, pursuant to the appropriate Treaty provision concerning actions for annulment, coupled with a claim that the fine or penalty be reduced, under the Court's unlimited jurisdiction.[35] If the claim for the annulment of the decision is successful, the Court's unlimited jurisdiction in relation to the fine or penalty need not be invoked because the latter falls with the annulment of the decision. On the other hand, if the decision is upheld, the Court's unlimited jurisdiction is of particular importance because it enables the Court to alter the fine or penalty on the basis of factual or legal grounds that are ex hypothesi insufficient to bring about the annulment of the decision imposing the fine or penalty. The Court's unlimited jurisdiction is an extension of its powers of review in an action for annulment. Hence, in Case 9/56 *Meroni & Co Industrie Metallurgiche SpA v High Authority*,[36] an action brought under art 36 of the ECSC Treaty, the Court annulled the Decision imposing the penalty in application of art 33. Strictly speaking, therefore, reliance on its unlimited jurisdiction is relevant only to the alteration of the fine or penalty, not the annulment of the legal basis for imposing it. When challenging the legality of the decision imposing the penalty, reliance may be placed on the unlawfulness of a measure of general effect upon which the decision in question was based.[37]

I Arbitration

All three Treaties provide, in the same terms, that the Court has jurisdiction 'to give judgment pursuant to any arbitration clause contained in a contract concluded by or on behalf of the Community, whether that contract be governed by public or private law'.[38] The existence and extent of the Court's jurisdiction is derived from the arbitration clause itself and cannot be excluded by any rule of the proper law of the contract.[39] Under the EC and Euratom Treaties, the effect of the arbitration clause is to confer exclusive jurisdiction on the Court, so far as the courts of member states are concerned.[40] The arbitration clause must be contained in a contract concluded by the

---

34 Cf Cases 2–10/63 *Società Industriale Acciaierie San Michele v High Authority* [1963] ECR 327 at 341.
35 For an example of the reduction of a fine under the Court's unlimited jurisdiction, see Case 41/85 *Sideradria SpA – Industria Metallurgica v Commission* [1986] ECR 3917 (para 12).
36 [1957–58] ECR 133.
37 This is the so-called plea or exception of illegality. It is referred to in art 36 of the ECSC Treaty, which expresses a principle of general application: see *Meroni & Co v High Authority* (ibid) at 140.
38 ECSC Treaty, art 42; EC Treaty, art 181; Euratom Treaty, art 153. Those provisions necessarily imply the existence of power on the part of each Community, exercised by its institutions, to conclude contracts governed either by public or by private law: Case C-249/87 *Mulfinger v Commission* [1989] ECR 4127 (para 10).
39 Case C-209/90 *Commission v Feilhauer* [1992] ECR I-2613 (paras 12–14).
40 EC Treaty, art 183; Euratom Treaty, art 155. See Case 65/74 *Porrini v EAEC and Comont* [1975] ECR 319 at 333 (Advocate General Reischl).

Community.[41] The Court appears to have jurisdiction in the case of an agreement to arbitrate a dispute before (or, more properly, to submit any dispute to) the Court where the dispute arises from a contract even though the arbitration or jurisdiction clause was made after the contract had been made.[42] It is not clear whether a mere agreement to arbitrate a dispute before the Court is sufficient (such as an agreement made by the Community and another person to submit to arbitration by the Court a dispute as to the non-contractual liability of a party to the arbitration agreement) or whether there must be a contract concluded by or on behalf of the Community to which the agreement to arbitrate and the dispute that is the subject of the arbitration relate. The proper law of the contract determines the rights, obligations and liabilities of the parties, including the Community.[43] That law is the national law governing the contract[44] but Community law may also be relevant.[45] Actions under an arbitration clause take the form of an ordinary direct action and the procedural law applicable is contained in the Rules of Procedure and the other instruments governing the Court. Only parties to the arbitration clause can be parties to the action.[46] Where the Court has jurisdiction under the arbitration clause, mistaken reliance by the applicant on another provision of Community law does not make the action inadmissible.[47] The Court may adjudicate upon claims arising from the contract containing the arbitration clause or claims that are directly connected with the obligations arising from that contract.[48] The Court does not have jurisdiction over other claims and cannot take them into account by way of set-off or counterclaim even if a national court could do so.[49] In other respects, the relief that the Court may order is that which is available under the law governing the substance of the dispute.[50]

J   Disputes between member states

1   Nature of the proceedings

All three Treaties provide that the Court has jurisdiction over disputes between member states which relate to the subject matter of the Treaty and

---

41 Cf Case C-142/91 *Cebag BV v Commission* [1993] ECR I-553 (paras 10–14), where the arbitration agreement was set out in a regulation and incorporated in the contract.
42 In Case 109/81 *Pace (née Porta) v Commission* [1982] ECR 2469 (in particular, para 10), the situation was different in that the contracts made prior to the making of the arbitration clause simply formed part of the factual matrix of the dispute.
43 EC Treaty, art 215 (first subpara); Euratom Treaty, art 188 (first subpara). See Case 318/81R *Commission v CODEMI* [1985] ECR 3693.
44 Eg Case 426/85 *Commission v Zoubek* [1986] ECR 4057. The proper law of the contract may be indicated in the contract itself but, in the absence of express provision to that effect, is identified in accordance with the principles of private international law common to the member states. Contractual provisions expressing the common intention of the parties regarding the proper law of the contract take precedence over any other criterion that might be used to identify the proper law (such other criteria may be used only where the contract is silent): the *CODEMI* case (ibid) para 21.
45 Eg Case 123/84 *Klein v Commission* [1985] ECR 1907; Case 251/84 *Centrale Marketinggesellschaft der Deutschen Agrarwirtschaft mbH v EEC* [1986] ECR 217.
46 Case 23/76 *Luigi Pellegrini & Co SAS v Commission* [1976] ECR 1807 (para 31).
47 *Pace (née Porta) v Commission* (above, note 42) at 2486 (Advocate General Capotorti).
48 The *Zoubek* case (above, note 44) para 11.
49 Ibid; Case C-330/88 *Grifoni v EAEC* [1991] ECR I-1045 (para 20).
50 The *Zoubek* case (above, note 44) para 13.

are referred to it under a special agreement between the parties.[51] The ECSC Treaty, art 89, also provides that 'any dispute between member states concerning the application of this Treaty which cannot be settled by another procedure provided for in this Treaty may be submitted to the Court on application by one of the States which are parties to the dispute'. This provision gives the Court compulsory jurisdiction over disputes between member states and enables one member state to bring a default action directly before the Court even in the absence of an agreement between the parties to the dispute to submit it to the Court. The EC and Euratom Treaties similarly provide that the member states may not submit a dispute concerning the interpretation or application of the Treaty to any method of settlement other than those provided for in the relevant Treaty.[52] In consequence, although the Treaty provisions conferring jurisdiction on the Court in relation to disputes submitted by special agreement are in principle permissive (that is, they enable but do not oblige the member states to submit a matter to the Court by special agreement), there may be situations in which a dispute cannot be settled otherwise than by submission to the Court pursuant to a special agreement.

In the case of disputes submitted to the Court by special agreement, the extent of the Court's jurisdiction over such disputes is defined by the special agreement but the procedural law applicable is contained in the Rules of Procedure and the other instruments governing the Court. Proceedings would normally take the form of a direct action. The relief which may be ordered should be apparent from the terms of the agreement.[53] The form of an action under the Court's compulsory jurisdiction under the ECSC Treaty is that of an ordinary direct action. The ECSC Treaty does not, however, specify what relief the Court may grant. In the absence of authority, it is arguable that, under the Court's compulsory jurisdiction, it can only grant a declaration concerning the correct interpretation to be given to the Treaty.[54] The better view, however, seems to be that the Court's power to grant relief depends on the nature of the dispute and the relief sought by the parties; in the nature of things the most appropriate form of relief might often prove to be a declaration but another form of relief is not excluded.

2 *Procedural aspects*

Article 41 of the ECSC Statute provides that, in disputes brought before the Court under art 89, that is to say both those under its compulsory jurisdiction and those under a special agreement, the other member states shall be notified by the Registrar of the subject matter of the dispute forthwith. They may then

51 ECSC Treaty, art 89; EC Treaty, art 182; Euratom Treaty, art 154. One such agreement is the Agreement of 21 March 1955 on the establishment of through international railway tariffs: see art 16 (OJ 1955/701, English Special Edition 1952–1958, p 25). Another example is the Agreement relating to Community Patents, signed at Luxembourg on 15 December 1989: see art 14(2)–(3) (OJ No L401 of 30 December 1989, p 1). The creation of the CFI was effected without prejudice to any such agreement between the member states: see Single European Act, Declaration on the Court of Justice.

52 EC Treaty, art 219; Euratom Treaty, art 193.

53 Thus, under art 14(3) of the Agreement relating to Community Patents, it is apparent that the Court may only dismiss the action or make a declaration that a contracting state has failed to fulfil an obligation under the Agreement. In the latter event, the contracting state concerned is subject to a duty to take the necessary measures to comply with the Court's judgment. As in the case of an action against a member state under art 169 of the EC Treaty (see section II.C above pp 544 et seq), it is not for the Court to determine what those measures are.

54 ECSC Statute, art 42.

intervene as of right. There is no indication of a time limit on the right of intervention and none is expressly laid down in the Rules of Procedure for such actions. It is, nevertheless, strongly arguable that the normal rules for intervening, contained in RP-ECJ 93, apply and these include a three-month time limit running as from the date of publication of the notice of the case in the Official Journal. If a state does intervene, the interpretation given by the Court in its judgment is binding on that State.[55] It is not clear whether other persons, such as the Community institutions, undertakings or associations, may also intervene. The most likely interpretation of the Statute is that, while the member states are given a right to intervene, other persons can intervene only if they can show an interest in the result of the case.[56] It is equally possible that the Court may construe the Statute strictly and decide that only member states can intervene on the basis that the object of art 89 is to provide a procedure for the resolution of disputes involving the contracting Parties to the Treaty alone. Disputes submitted under art 89 are heard by the Court in plenary session only.[57]

The EC and Euratom Statutes do not contain any special provision concerning intervention in disputes submitted by special agreement. There are two possible explanations of this: either the normal rules in a direct action apply or the intention was to exclude intervention altogether on the ground that disputes under the relevant provisions of these Treaties can come before the Court only by special agreement. It is arguable that, as a matter of principle, the parties to such an action can only be the parties to the special agreement unless there is specific provision otherwise, as in the case of the ECSC Statute. Against this, it may be said that an intervener is not in the same procedural position as an applicant or a defendant and there is, therefore, no real reason to exclude intervention, at least by other member states and Community institutions, which normally have a right to intervene,[58] particularly in such cases as these, where the Community public interest is involved.

K   Disputes concerning members of the Commission and of the Court of Auditors and the Ombudsman

The Court has jurisdiction over applications made by the Council or the Commission for a ruling that a member of the Commission should be compulsorily retired or deprived of his right to a pension or other benefit; the grounds for so ruling are breach by the member concerned of any of the obligations arising from his (or her) office.[59] Application may be made in respect of acts or defaults committed after the member has ceased to hold office which constitute a breach of any continuing obligation. In that event, the only penalty would be deprivation of the right to a pension or other benefit. The Court may also compulsorily retire a member of the Commission, again on application by the Council or the Commission if he no longer fulfils the conditions required for the performance of his duties or if he has been guilty of serious misconduct.[60] In

55 Ibid.
56 Cf ECSC Statute, art 34: 'natural or legal persons establishing an interest in the result of *any* case submitted to the Court may intervene in that case' (emphasis added).
57 ECSC Statute, art 41.
58 EC Statute, art 37; Euratom Statute, art 38.
59 ECSC Treaty, art 9(2) (as amended by the EU Treaty); EC Treaty, art 157(2) (as amended); Euratom Treaty, art 126(2) (as amended); see also Treaty Establishing a Single Council and a Single Commission of the European Communities ('the Merger Treaty'), art 10.
60 ECSC Treaty, art 12a (as amended by the EU Treaty); EC Treaty, art 160 (as amended); Euratom Treaty, art 129 (as amended); see also Merger Treaty, art 13. See, for example, Decision No 76/619 of 19 July 1976 (OJ No L201/31 of 27 July 1976).

the same way, the Court of Auditors may apply to the Court for a ruling that one of its members no longer fulfils the conditions required for office or no longer meets the obligations arising from office, thus causing the member concerned to be deprived of office or of the right to a pension or other benefit.[61] The ECSC, EC and Euratom Treaties, as amended by the EU Treaty, provide for the appointment by the European Parliament of an Ombudsman who is empowered to investigate complaints of maladministration in the conduct of the Community institutions and other bodies (with the exception of the ECJ and the CFI in respect of their judicial role). The Ombudsman is appointed after each election of the European Parliament for the duration of that Parliament's term of office and is eligible for reappointment. However, although the Parliament has power to appoint the Ombudsman and may decline to renew the appointment, the Parliament does not have power to dismiss him (or her). The Ombudsman may be dismissed before the expiry of his (or her) term of appointment only by the Court, on application made by the European Parliament, and only on the grounds that the Ombudsman no longer fulfils the conditions required for the performance of his (or her) duties or that he (or she) is guilty of serious misconduct.[62] No specific procedure is laid down for such applications and the Court's decisions do not appear to be published. On basic principles, the procedure is adversarial in the sense that the person in respect of whom the application is made must be given an opportunity to be heard before any decision adversely affecting him (or her) is made by the Court.[63]

L   Plea of illegality

The last paragraph of art 36 of the ECSC Treaty provides that, in an action brought against a Commission decision imposing a pecuniary sanction or ordering a periodic penalty payment, 'a party may, under the same conditions as in the first paragraph of Article 33 of this Treaty, contest the legality of the decision or recommendation which that party is alleged not to have observed'. The EC and Euratom Treaties contain a similar provision[64] which is not expressly restricted in its application to actions against decisions imposing a penalty. Both Treaties provide that, notwithstanding the expiry of the period laid down for commencing an action for annulment, any party may, in proceedings in which a regulation is in issue, plead the grounds specified in the Treaty for seeking the annulment of an act of an institution in order to invoke before the Court of Justice the inapplicability of that regulation.[65] Those

---

61 ECSC Treaty, art 45b(7) (formerly art 78(e)(8)); EC Treaty, art 188b(7) (formerly art 206(8)); Euratom Treaty, art 160b(7) (formerly art 180(8)). Those provisions were introduced by the Treaty Amending Certain Financial Provisions of the Treaties Establishing the European Communities and of the Treaty Establishing a Single Council and a Single Commission of the European Communities (OJ No L359/1 of 31 December 1977) and were transposed to their current position in the Treaties by the EU Treaty (arts H(14), G(E)(59) and I(14), respectively).

62 ECSC Treaty, art 20d(1) and (2); EC Treaty, art 137d(1) and (2); Euratom Treaty, art 107d(1) and (2).

63 Different considerations arise where, for example, the reason why the application is made is because the person concerned has through accident or illness become incapable of functioning. In any event, the Court lies under a duty to ascertain the facts before making any decision.

64 Articles 184 and 156 respectively, the former as amended by the EU Treaty, art G(E)(58).

65 Under the EC Treaty, art 184 (as amended), the regulation in question may be one adopted jointly by the European Parliament and the Council or one adopted by any one of the Council, the Commission or the European Central Bank. Under the Euratom Treaty, art 156, the regulation in question is one adopted by the Council or the Commission.

provisions, although dissimilar in wording, express the same general principle[66] which applies even in the absence of an express Treaty provision[67] and which the Court has defined as 'conferring upon any party to proceedings the right to challenge, for the purpose of obtaining the annulment of a decision of direct and individual concern to that party, the validity of previous acts of the institutions which form the legal basis of the decision which is being attacked, if that party was not entitled . . . to bring a direct action challenging those acts by which it was thus affected without having been in a position to ask that they be declared void'.[68] Since member states and Community institutions do have locus standi to challenge acts of general effect, it is unclear to what extent they may plead the illegality of such a measure after the expiry of the time limit for bringing an action for annulment, although the Court appears to have accepted that they can.[69] A party cannot rely on the way in which the act of general effect is interpreted and applied, as opposed to its unlawfulness.[70]

This principle, the plea of illegality, does not create an independent right of action but is simply a plea which may be raised in proceedings brought directly before the Court under some other provision of the Treaty; it does not apply where the matter is raised before a national court[71] and is of no purpose if the applicant's main claims are inadmissible.[72] The plea can be raised only in respect of acts of a Community institution which are of general effect (even if they are not in the form of a regulation), not individual decisions;[73] and it may be raised only if and to the extent that the measure of general effect provides the legal basis of the measure whose annulment is sought in the action.[74] The theory behind the plea is that the act of general effect which is in question cannot itself be challenged directly in an action for annulment; it is only when

66 *Meroni & Co v High Authority* (above, note 36) at 140–141; Case 10/56 *Meroni & Co v High Authority* [1957–58] ECR 157 at 162–163; Case 15/57 *Compagnie des Hauts Fourneaux de Chasse v High Authority* [1957–58] ECR 211 at 224–225 (see also at 235–237, Advocate General Lagrange).

67 See Case 20/71 *Sabbatini née Bertoni v European Parliament* [1972] ECR 345 and at 354 (Advocate General Roemer).

68 Case 92/78 *Simmenthal SpA v Commission* [1979] ECR 777 (para 39); Case 262/80 *Andersen v European Parliament* [1984] ECR 195 (para 6).

69 Case 32/65 *Italy v Council and Commission* [1966] ECR 389, see also at 414 (Advocate General Roemer); Case 181/85 *France v Commission* [1987] ECR 689 at 703 (Re Countervailing Charge on French Ethyl Alcohol) (Advocate General Slynn); Case 204/86 *Greece v Council* [1988] ECR 5323 at 5343–5345 (Advocate General Mancini).

70 Case 18/62 *Barge v High Authority* [1963] ECR 259 at 280.

71 Cases 31 and 33/62 *Milchwerke Heinz Wöhrmann & Sohn KG and Alfons Lütticke GmbH v Commission* [1962] ECR 501 at 507.

72 Case 33/80 *Albini v Council and Commission* [1981] ECR 2141 (para 17); Cases 89 and 91/86 *L'Etoile Commerciale and Comptoir National Technique Agricole v Commission* [1987] ECR 3005 (para 22).

73 Case 3/59 *Germany v High Authority* [1960] ECR 53 at 61; Case 21/64 *Macchiorlati Dalmas and Figli v High Authority* [1965] ECR 175 at 187; Case 156/77 *Commission v Belgium* [1978] ECR 1881 at para 22; the *Simmenthal* case (above, note 68), para 41; Case 76/83 *Usines Gustave Boel and Fabrique de Fer de Maubeuge v Commission* [1984] ECR 859 (para 4); Case 270/82 *Estel NV v Commission* [1984] ECR 1195 (para 11); Case 151/83 *Société Aciéries et Laminoires de Paris v Commission* [1984] ECR 3519 (para 9); Case 67/84 *Sideradria SpA v Commission* [1985] ECR 3983 (para 15); Cases T-6 and T-52/92 *Reinarz v Commission*, 26 October 1993 (para 56). A general measure is one which applies to categories of situations defined by reference to objective criteria (and not by reference to particular facts which are peculiar to a particular case) and which affects the legal position of categories of persons defined in a general and abstract manner: see, for example, the *Reinarz* case.

74 The *Gustave Boel* case (ibid) para 5; Cases 140, 146, 221 and 226/82 *Walzstahl-Vereinigung & Thyssen AG v Commission* [1984] ECR 951 (para 20); *Aciéries et Laminoires de Paris v Commission* (ibid); Cases 87 and 130/77, 22/83, 9 and 10/84 *Salerno v Commission and Council* [1985] ECR 2523 (para 36); the *Reinarz* case (ibid) para 57.

the effect of the act takes the concrete form of a decision of direct and individual concern to the party that he acquires an interest in challenging the lawfulness of the act of general effect, in order to obtain the annulment of the decision.[75] The plea enables the party to take advantage of the illegality of the act of general effect, despite the expiry of the time limit for seeking its annulment, but does not result in the annulment of that act.[76] It follows that there must be a direct link between the lawfulness of the subject matter of the plea and the lawfulness of the decision whose annulment is sought.[77] The unlawfulness of the act of general effect may be based on any of the grounds which could have been relied on had an action for its annulment been brought.[78]

M   Judicial review of co-operation with the national authorities

1   *Nature of the proceedings*

The Court has jurisdiction to review the discharge by each Community institution of its duty of sincere co-operation with national courts and tribunals which are seised with proceedings concerning the alleged infringement of Community law.[79] The jurisdiction is relatively novel. The recognition of its existence arose from the failure by the Commission to respond to requests made by a national court in a case before it for the production of evidence relating to the dispute before the national court. The Commission's refusal to produce the information and evidence sought seems to have been based on the Protocol on the Privileges and Immunities of the European Communities, attached to the Treaty Establishing a Single Council and Single Commission of the European Communities of 8 April 1965. In consequence, the basis for the jurisdiction and the procedure to be followed are analogous to cases where the Court waives the immunity of the Community under that Protocol.[80]

2   *Procedure*

The prerequisite for the commencement of proceedings before the Court is that (i) a national judicial authority seised with proceedings concerning the alleged infringement of Community law has made a request to a competent Community institution for the production of evidence (whether in the form of documents, testimony or other) which is relevant to the proceedings and considered by the national authority to be necessary for its decision, and (ii) the Community institution concerned has refused to comply with that request.

---

75 The fact that the act of general effect is implemented by another act which is of general effect in form (such as a regulation), rather than an act having the form of an individual decision, does not preclude reliance on the principle as long as the implementing act is challengeable: *France v Commission* (above, note 69) at 702 (Advocate General Slynn). The applicant may not in every case have a reasonable interest in relying on the plea: see Cases 39, 43, 85 and 88/81 *Halyvourgiki Inc v Commission* [1982] ECR 593 at 628 (Advocate General VerLoren van Themaat).

76 Cf Case 9/56 *Meroni & Co v High Authority* (above, note 36); Case 10/56 *Meroni & Co v High Authority* (above, note 66) see also at 183 (Advocate General Roemer); *Compagnie des Hauts Fourneaux de Chasse v High Authority, Germany v High Authority* (above, note 66) at 67 (Advocate General Lagrange); *Milchwerke Heinz Wöhrmann & Sohn KG v Commission* (above, note 71).

77 *Macchiorlatti Dalmas and Figli v High Authority* (above, note 73) at 187–188; *Italy v Council and Commission* (above, note 69) and see also at 414 (Advocate General Roemer); Cases 25 and 26/65 *SIMET and FERAM v High Authority* [1967] ECR 33 at 44; Cases 154, 205, 206, 226–228, 263, 264/78, 31, 39, 83 and 85/79 *Valsabbia SpA v Commission* [1980] ECR 907 (para 9).

78 The Treaties, ECSC Treaty, art 36; EC Treaty, art 184; Euratom Treaty, art 156; see also *Valsabbia SpA v Commission* (ibid) para 10.

79 Case C-2/88 Imm *Zwartveld* [1990] ECR I-3365 (para 23).

80 See section VI.A below.

The author of the request must, it seems, be a judicial and not an administrative body; but it cannot be excluded that, where an investigation into an alleged infringement of Community law is being carried out by an administrative body, a failure on the part of a Community institution to co-operate may be dealt with by application to a national judicial authority for it to request the institution to co-operate. Similarly, the matter in dispute before the national authority must concern the existence or otherwise of an infringement of Community law but it cannot be excluded that the procedure may be extended to other matters.[81] The competent Community institution is the one which is in possession of the evidence in question or the one to whom the person whose testimony is sought is attached as an official or temporary or other agent. A refusal to comply with the request which is based on incompetence or impossibility to respond to the request (such as where the national authority has approached the wrong institution or where the evidence no longer exists) would seem to preclude taking matters further unless the national authority considers that the institution concerned has rejected the request erroneously or improperly. Otherwise, such a request may be refused on the basis of some legitimate ground connected with the protection of the rights of third parties or where the disclosure of the information or evidence sought would be capable of interfering with the functioning and independence of the Community, in particular, by jeopardising the accomplishment of the tasks entrusted to it.[82] In that event, the national authority may apply to the Court for it to review the lawfulness of the refusal.

If there has been such a request and it has been refused, the national judicial authority concerned may apply to the Court in writing for it to make an appropriate order addressed to the institution concerned. The application to the Court should be made in one of the Court's official languages and should set out the reasons on which it is based.[83] The relief sought may, it seems, be expressed in general terms: it does not seem that the Court's jurisdiction is limited to granting or refusing a specific form of relief, such as an application for an order that a certain person be heard as a witness by the national judicial authority. On the other hand, the more general the relief sought the more necessary it is that the national authority set out clearly in its application the circumstances giving rise to it and the purpose to be served by it. The application is then served on the institution concerned and, if the Court thinks fit, on the member states or any other Community institution for them to lodge written observations on the application.[84] In cases of urgency, the matter may be dealt with solely on the basis of written observations or, if necessary, solely on the basis of an oral hearing at which the member states and Community institutions may have an opportunity to address the Court. The Court may

81 Cf the situation in Case 180/87 *Hamill v Commission* [1988] ECR 6141, where the Court held that a Community institution was bound to provide certain information to the police of a member state in connection with an investigation into certain alleged criminal offences which appear to have had nothing to do with Community law. Once a duty on the part of a Community institution to co-operate with a national authority has been established, the procedure described here seems necessarily to apply in order to ensure that the performance of the duty can be secured.

82 The *Zwartveld* case [1990] ECR I-4405 (para 11).

83 As in the case of references for a preliminary ruling, it does not seem to be necessary for the national authority to send to the Court the usual number of copies of the application, as would ordinarily be necessary under RP-ECJ 37(1) or RP-CFI 43(1).

84 In the *Zwartveld* case (above, note 79), the Court requested the Community institutions and the member states to submit observations but, at that stage, the very existence of the procedure was in doubt. It would seem to be appropriate for the Court to continue that practice in future cases, at least until there is a sufficient body of case law dealing with the essential points of principle.

also invite the parties to the proceedings before the national authority to submit observations but it does not seem that those parties have any right to submit observations: in principle, the procedure is like references for a preliminary ruling in that it constitutes a form of judicial co-operation between the national authority and the Court. There may, however, be circumstances in which it would be appropriate to hear the parties to the proceedings before the national authority. The national authority itself may be invited by the Court to comment on the position taken up by the Community institution concerned[85] but does not otherwise take part in the proceedings. It is not necessary for there to be an oral hearing.

3 Result of the proceedings

The function of the Court is to review the decision of the Community institution concerned to refuse to comply with the national authority's request. Where the Court concludes that the refusal is unjustified, its decision does not necessarily result in the immediate disclosure to the national authority of the information and evidence requested: it may be necessary for the Court itself to go through the disputed material in order to decide which parts must be disclosed to the national authority and which are protected from disclosure.[86] If the institution concerned fails to make out a case for its refusal to comply with the national authority's request, the Court has power to order the institution to disclose documents and permit its officials or servants to give evidence before the national authority.[87] If the parties submitting observations to the Court have made no claim for costs, no order for costs will be made.[88] It is unclear what order would be made if the parties have claimed costs. By analogy with references for a preliminary ruling, the Community institutions and member states participating in the proceedings should bear their own costs.

III Special procedures under the ECSC Treaty

A Decisions concerning fundamental and persistent disturbances in the economy of a member state

1 Nature of the proceedings

Article 37 of the ECSC Treaty provides that a member state may complain to the Commission when an act or failure to act of the latter is considered by the member state to be 'of such a nature as to provoke fundamental and persistent disturbances in its economy'. Proceedings may then be brought before the Court in respect of any decision taken by the Commission to end the situation or any express or implied decision refusing to recognise the existence of the situation. The Court has jurisdiction to determine whether the decision challenged is 'well founded'. If it declares the decision void, the Commission must take the necessary steps to comply with its obligations under art 37. The form of the action is the same as that for an action for annulment; the operative part of the Court's judgment can only dismiss the claim entirely or annul the

---

85 As happened in the *Zwartveld* case [1990] ECR I-3365 (para 12).
86 See the *Zwartveld* case (above, note 82).
87 The *Zwartveld* case ibid.
88 Ibid para 14.

Commission's decision,[89] so the form of order in the application commencing proceedings can, in consequence, only claim annulment and costs. But the Court has very broad powers of review;[90] proceedings under art 37 'necessarily entail an assessment both of the existence of the disturbed situation recognised by the [Commission] and the necessity and appropriateness of the decision adopted by the [Commission]'.[91] The decision adopted by the Commission must satisfy the following conditions: it must be 'necessary' and 'appropriate' and must, therefore, (i) 'constitute a *proper remedy* to the disturbed situation caused by (the Commission's) action or failure to act' and (ii) 'safeguard the *essential* interests of the Community'. The object of art 37 is to enable national interests to be reconciled with the general interests of the Community and the Court's role is to review the Commission's 'power to arbitrate' between these interests.[92]

2   Procedure

Neither the ECSC Statute nor the Rules of Procedure contain any special provisions relating to this procedure, although art 39 of the former lays down that proceedings must be commenced within one month of the notification or publication of the decision in question.[93] Proceedings therefore follow the course of an ordinary direct action. In view of their special nature, proceedings brought under art 37 cannot be combined with another procedure, such as an action for annulment.[94] Only the member state in which the economic disturbance has occurred or threatens to occur is entitled to raise the matter with the Commission because it alone is 'capable of appreciating whether the economic situation requires application of Article 37'.[95] It alone has sufficient interest to challenge before the Court an express or implied decision of the Commission refusing to recognise the existence of the disturbance[96] or one which is regarded as being insufficient to cope with the situation.[97] On the other hand, all the member states have sufficient interest to challenge a Commission decision which accedes to a request made by a member state. Undertakings and associations of undertakings cannot, however, invoke art 37 because, in the proceedings before the Court, the political responsibilities of the member states and the Commission are under examination.[98]

A necessary condition of the admissibility of an application made by the member state experiencing or threatened with the economic disturbance in question is that the member state has raised the matter with the Commission 'in such a manner that the latter cannot fail to understand the purpose of the

---

89 Cases 2 and 3/60 *Niederrheinische Bergwerks AG v High Authority* [1961] ECR 133 at 152 (Advocate General Lagrange).
90 Unlimited jurisdiction, per Advocate General Lagrange (ibid) and Case 13/63 *Italy v Commission* [1963] ECR 165 at 183.
91 The *Niederrheinische Bergwerks* case (above, note 89) at 147.
92 Ibid at 145–146.
93 In fact time will start to run either from the day after notification or the fifteenth day after publication: see RP-ECJ 80(1) and 81(1). There are difficulties in the case of an implied decision. Applying art 35 of the ECSC Treaty by analogy, such a decision is to be implied from the Commission's silence over a period of two months.
94 Case 19/58 *Germany v High Authority* [1960] ECR 225, see at 201 (Advocate General Lagrange), and the *Niederrheinische Bergwerks* case (above, note 89) at 147.
95 The *Niederrheinische Bergwerks* case (above, note 89) at 144.
96 Cases 27-29/58 *Compagnie des Hauts Fourneaux et Fonderies de Givors v High Authority* [1960] ECR 241 at 258, and (above, note 89) at 145.
97 The *Niederrheinische Bergwerks* case (ibid).
98 Ibid at 146–147.

request'.[99] In the absence of such a request, a member state cannot bring proceedings under art 37 against a decision which is alleged to have provoked a disturbance in the economy; it can only challenge a subsequent refusal to recognise the existence of the disturbance or a failure to take adequate measures to end it.[1] Although an application made by an undertaking or association of undertakings is inadmissible, the possibility that a natural or legal person may intervene in proceedings commenced by a member state has not been excluded by the Court. Intervention is, however, conditional on the applicant to intervene establishing an interest in the result of the case.

B Supplementary jurisdiction

Article 43 of the ECSC Treaty provides that the Court (i) 'shall have jurisdiction in any other case provided for by a provision supplementing this Treaty' and (ii) 'may also rule in all cases which relate to the subject matter of this Treaty where jurisdiction is conferred on it by the law of a Member State'. The second possibility does not appear to have been made use of by any member state. The first depends for its effectiveness on the existence of a provision entrusting the Court with jurisdiction over a particular matter.[2]

C Proceedings against decisions concerning concentrations

1 Nature of the proceedings

The Commission is given extensive powers to control concentrations between undertakings of which one at least is covered by art 80 of the Treaty. If it finds that a concentration is unlawful, it has power under art 66(5) to order the separation of the undertakings involved or of their assets, the cessation of joint control or any other measures it considers appropriate to return the undertakings or assets in question to independent operation and restore normal conditions of competition. Article 66(5) provides: 'any person directly concerned may institute proceedings against such decisions, as provided in Article 33'. By 'such decisions', art 66(5) means both the decision finding the concentration to be unlawful and the decision ordering the return of the undertakings or assets to independent operation and restoring normal conditions of competition.[3]

An action brought under art 66(5) is a simple direct action for annulment. Article 33 defines the grounds of annulment which may be relied on and the time limit for commencing proceedings. There are, however, three significant differences between an action for annulment brought under art 33 and one brought under art 66(5).

The first is that an applicant under the latter provision must fulfil two conditions: he must be (i) a person and (ii) directly concerned by the decision challenged in the action. The significance of this is that the ECSC Treaty normally reserves rights of action to undertakings or associations of undertakings. The former are defined in art 80 of the Treaty as undertakings 'engaged in production in the coal or the steel industry within the territories' covered by the Community and, so far as arts 65 and 66 are concerned,

---

99 *Germany v High Authority* (above, note 94) at 201 (Advocate General Lagrange).
1 Ibid at 233.
2 Eg Case 6/60 *Humblet v Belgium* [1960] ECR 559, where the Court had jurisdiction by virtue of the combined effect of art 43 and art 16 of the Protocol on the Privileges and Immunities of the European Coal and Steel Community.
3 Case 12/63 *Schlieker v High Authority* [1963] ECR 85 at 89.

undertakings or agencies 'regularly engaged in distribution other than sale to domestic consumers or small craft industries'. In referring simply to a 'person', art 66(5) creates a more broadly based right of action which can be relied on by any natural person or body having the characteristics of legal personality. The specific intention behind the form of words in art 66(5) seems to have been to allow undertakings not covered by the Treaty (and hence not falling within the definitions set out in art 80) to challenge Commission decisions which affect concentrations involving such undertakings.[4] Nonetheless, it does not seem that the word 'person' in art 66(5) is to be interpreted as meaning them only: it is equally apt to cover natural or legal persons in general. The practical limitation on this right of action is to be found in the second condition for bringing proceedings: the applicant must be 'directly concerned' by the decision challenged. That requirement is similar to the locus standi requirements in proceedings brought by an undertaking or association under art 33 of the ECSC Treaty (the contested act must 'concern' an applicant) and proceedings brought by a legal or natural person (not a member state or Community institution) under art 173 of the EC Treaty (the contested act must be of 'direct and individual concern' to the applicant).

The second distinctive feature of proceedings under art 66(5) is that the Court is expressly given unlimited jurisdiction 'to assess whether the transaction effected is a concentration'. This means that the Court is not, to this extent, bound by the limitation of its powers of review under art 33, where it may not examine 'the evaluation of the situation, resulting from economic facts or circumstances, in the light of which the [Commission] took its decisions'. Nonetheless, unlimited jurisdiction extends only to review of the finding that the transaction is a concentration, not to the finding that it is unlawful. The extent of the Court's power to review the latter finding depends on the extent of the Commission's discretion in applying art 66.

The last distinctive feature is that the commencement of proceedings under art 66(5) has suspensory effect. Normally actions do not[5] but the Court may grant interim relief in order to preserve the position pending judgment. The possibility of prescribing interim measures is not excluded by art 66(5) but the need to do so would arise only in exceptional cases: usually, where a Commission decision is challenged before the Court, the only form of interim relief which is sought is suspension of the operation of the decision but this follows automatically from the commencement of proceedings under art 66(5).

2   *Procedural aspects*

The Treaty provides that proceedings may not be commenced 'until the measures provided for above' (ie the consequential measures prescribed in order to unscramble the unlawful concentration) 'have been ordered, unless the [Commission] agrees to the institution of separate proceedings against the decision declaring the transaction unlawful'. This is a little obscure. Article 66(5) makes it quite clear that there is a right of action against both the decision finding the concentration to be unlawful and the decision ordering consequential measures. The former may be challenged because a declaration that a concentration is unlawful has its own intrinsic effects which may affect the rights and interests of the undertakings involved. The Treaty appears to envisage, however, that the right of action is exercised jointly against both decisions unless the Commission consents to a separate application. Under art

4 Cf ibid at 93 (Advocate General Roemer).
5 See art 39.

33, which is to this extent incorporated by reference, proceedings must be brought within one month of the notification or publication of the decision challenged. Combining this with a literal interpretation of art 66(5), it is arguable that, if the Commission fails to order consequential measures within one month of notifying or publishing the decision finding the concentration to be unlawful and withholds its consent to the commencement of proceedings against that decision within time, it may effectively prevent an applicant from challenging the decision. In the event that consequential measures are ordered, the applicant is then barred by the effluxion of time from disputing the unlawfulness of the concentration and can only challenge the consequential measures adopted to reverse its effects. If no consequential measures are adopted, all possibility of relief is excluded and the undertakings involved may find themselves subject to measures taken under national law pursuant to the declaration of unlawfulness.[6]

It is difficult to believe that this situation was intended by the draftsman of the Treaty. To begin with, it does not seem that the adoption of consequential measures after the expiry of the time limit for challenging the declaration of unlawfulness does affect the right to challenge the latter. Since proceedings may not be instituted until the consequential measures have been adopted, it necessarily follows that time for challenging the declaration of unlawfulness does not begin to run until the notification or publication of the decision prescribing such measures. Time may start to run before this decision is adopted, if the Commission agrees to the commencement of separate proceedings against the declaration of unlawfulness. This agreement makes the right of action exercisable and so time starts from the date that assent is communicated to the applicant. Where the Commission does not intend to prescribe any consequential measures, it seems to follow that, without its consent to the commencement of separate proceedings, the right of action under art 66(5) is not exercisable and, therefore, time does not start to run.

This may leave the undertakings concerned in a difficult position if they are of the opinion that the transaction is not a concentration at all or is not unlawful. The solution seems to be to request the Commission to agree to the commencement of proceedings against the declaration of unlawfulness. If the Commission refuses to give its consent or fails to respond to the request, proceedings may be brought under arts 33 or 35, as the case may be. Such proceedings may be commenced only by an undertaking or association of undertakings envisaged in the Treaty. It would appear that the basis of any such action would be the claim that the Commission had failed lawfully to exercise its discretion to consent to the commencement of separate proceedings: the Commission is bound to exercise its powers in a manner which respects the objectives of the Treaty and the principles of law upon which it is founded; where no consequential measures are to be adopted, the only reason for withholding consent to separate proceedings would be to prevent the undertakings concerned from challenging the declaration of unlawfulness; this is an unlawful exercise of the Commission's powers because its sole objective is to deprive a person of the legal protection afforded by the Treaty.

---

6 It is doubtful if an undertaking, within the meaning of art 80, or an association of undertakings could avoid this result by bringing proceedings under art 33 instead; although it is arguable that the right of action under art 33 is preserved for such undertakings or associations, the right under art 66(5) being intended primarily to protect persons unable to bring proceedings under art 33, the specific features of the action under art 66(5) (ie unlimited jurisdiction and suspensory effect) indicate that it has exclusive application so far as unlawful concentrations are concerned.

D   Opinions

1   *Nature of the proceedings*

Article 95 of the ECSC Treaty provides, inter alia, that the Treaty may be amended where unforeseen difficulties in its application or fundamental economic or technical changes directly affecting the common market in coal and steel make it necessary to 'adapt the rules for the High Authority's exercise of its powers'. Amendments are proposed jointly by the Commission[7] and the Council, the latter acting by what is now a ten-twelfths majority,[8] and then submitted to the Court for its opinion. If the Court finds them to be compatible with the fourth paragraph of art 95, they are then submitted to the Parliament and come into effect if they are approved by a majority of three-quarters of the votes cast and two-thirds of its members. This method of amending the Treaty is to be contrasted with that set out in art 96, which provides that any member state or the High Authority may propose amendments. The proposal is considered by the Council which must then decide whether to call a conference of representatives of the governments of the member states to consider it. This decision must be made by a two-thirds majority. The amendments to be made to the Treaty must be agreed by all participants in the conference and enter into force after being ratified by all the member states. As can be seen, the Court's role in the procedure under art 95 is particularly important: the proposed amendment can be submitted to the Parliament for its approval only if the Court finds that it complies with the fourth paragraph of art 95. If not, the proposal is lost. Article 95 provides that, in making this assessment, the Court has 'full power to assess all points of fact and of law'.

2   *Summary of the procedure*

The Rules of Procedure are particularly brief in their exposition of the procedure to be followed in cases brought under art 95. The request for an opinion must be submitted jointly by the Commission and the Special Council of Ministers.[9] As soon as the request has been lodged, the President designates one of the judges to act as rapporteur.[10] After hearing the advocates general,[11] the Court delivers a reasoned opinion in closed session, not in open court.[12] The opinion is signed by the President, the judges who took part in the deliberations and the Registrar.[13] It is then served on the Commission, the Council and the Parliament but not, it seems, on the member states.[14]

The Rules of Procedure say no more than this. Nevertheless, it does not seem correct to conclude that the Court is confined only to what is expressed in them. For example, art 95 of the ECSC Treaty makes clear that the Court is empowered to make an assessment of the facts. The Rules of Procedure, on the other hand, say nothing about its powers in this context to order measures of enquiry. The inference is that the Court may rely, if need be, on the powers set out in the Statute, applying the detailed provisions concerning measures of

7 The Commission replaced the High Authority. For this procedure, see Bebr *Development of Judicial Control in the European Communities* (1981) pp 346 et seq.
8 Article 95, as last amended by art 13 of the Spanish and Portuguese Acts of Accession.
9 RP-ECJ 109.
10 RP-ECJ 108(1). RP-ECJ 108 is incorporated in its entirety, see the second paragraph of RP-ECJ 109.
11 RP-ECJ 108(2).
12 Ibid.
13 RP-ECJ 108(3).
14 RP-ECJ 109.

enquiry to be found in the Rules of Procedure by analogy. The very absence of a precise description of the formal steps in the procedural sequence suggests that the Court is free to adopt the course which seems to it to be the best in the circumstances.

In order to see what is the Court's practice, one turns to the decided cases. So far three opinions have been given under art 95.[15] All were delivered in the years 1959 to 1961. Since then the Court has also delivered several opinions in the context of the analogous procedure under art 228 of the EC Treaty.[16] There appears in principle to be little difference in substance between these two proceedings, at least from the procedural point of view, and one may anticipate that the Court, in any future proceedings under art 95, is likely to follow the pattern set by the cases under art 228, in terms of both procedure and the layout of the opinion.

3 Commencement of proceedings

The reports of the cases under art 95 set out in extenso the text of the request for an opinion. It is signed by the Presidents of the Council of Ministers and of the High Authority (now the Commission), being submitted jointly by both institutions. There are no rules concerning the form and content of the request. It is not, therefore, obligatory that it should be signed by both Presidents, as long as it is signed by a person representing the institutions who has authority to do so.[17] In the body of the request there is set out (i) the text of the proposed amendment, (ii) the reasons for it and an explanation of its scope and (iii) the reasons the Commission and the Council consider the proposal to comply with the requirements of art 95. In *Opinion 1/60* and *Opinion 1/61*[18] there were annexed certain legal considerations relating to the request which had been put to the Council and an extract from the minutes of the Council meeting at which the proposal was adopted, respectively. The latter is of particular importance because the request should set out some proof that the proposal was adopted by the majority required by art 95.

On the first occasion that a request was submitted to the Court, no particular title was assigned to the case but, on the two subsequent occasions, the proceedings were entitled *Opinion 1/60* and *Opinion 1/61*. This usage has also been adopted in proceedings under art 228 of the EC Treaty. The Rules of Procedure do not set out the number of copies of the request which must be lodged. It may be presumed that the usual rules in RP-ECJ 37(1) apply, ie that the original must be accompanied by five certified copies for the use of the Court. Since there are no other parties to the proceedings, no other copies need be lodged. It would also seem that translations of the request and its annexes into all the Community languages must be produced, pursuant to RP-ECJ 37(2). All the requirements set out in RP-ECJ 37 should, in any event, be met by pleadings submitted to the Court in all proceedings. There is no indication of what the language of the proceedings is or should be. Clearly any of the languages used in proceedings before the Court may be used. In *Ruling 1/78*,[19]

---

15 *Procedure for amendment pursuant to the third and fourth paragraphs of Article 95 of the ECSC Treaty* [1959] ECR 259, hereafter referred to as *Opinion 1/59*; *Opinion 1/60* [1960] ECR 39; *Opinion 1/61* [1961] ECR 243.

16 See, pp 588 et seq.

17 In the first request for an opinion which, for the sake of brevity, will be called *Opinion 1/59*, the Vice-President of the High Authority signed. Under the current Rules of Procedure, it would seem that the request should be signed by an agent: see RP-ECJ 37(1).

18 Above, note 15.

19 [1978] ECR 2151 (Re the Draft Convention on the Physical Protection of Nuclear Materials, Facilities and Transport).

which was a case under art 103 of the Euratom Treaty, a footnote in the report indicates that the language of the proceedings was French. On the other hand, in *Opinion 1/78*,[20] a case under art 228 of the EC Treaty, the report gives as the languages of the proceedings all the then official Community languages.[21] In practice the language of the case is of little importance in proceedings under art 95 of the ECSC Treaty because the Community institutions are deemed to be cognisant of all the official Community languages.[22] It is arguable that French should invariably be the language of proceedings under art 95 simply because the authentic text of the ECSC Treaty is the French version[23] and the proposed amendment will therefore have to be drawn up in that language. From a practical point of view there is much to be said for this but it cannot be described as a legal requirement. Unlike the procedure under art 228 of the EC Treaty and art 103 of the Euratom Treaty, a member state cannot be directly involved in the proceedings. However, even if a particular official Community language is selected as the language of the proceedings, it seems to be within the power of the Court to accept submissions from a member state, where this occurs, in that country's own official language.[24]

4   The hearing of the parties

There is no provision for the submission of written or oral observations or pleadings or indeed for the service of the request for an opinion on anyone. Article 95 envisages a procedure which involves only three Community institutions, the joint makers of the request and the Court itself, and which appears to exclude participation by the member states. This does not necessarily mean that the Court will refuse to hear the views of a member state. In *Opinion 1/61*[25] the government of the Netherlands informed the Court why it was opposed to the amendment, after having obtained the agreement of the Council to do so. It is arguable that the member states can make representations to the Court, even if asked to do so by the latter, only with the consent of the Council on the ground that, properly speaking, proceedings are internal to the Community institutions involved and that the interests of the member states are represented by the Council. It is uncertain if this is correct. What seems beyond doubt is that it is only the Council and the Commission that have a right, which can only be exercised jointly, to submit a request to the Court. No other person or body is given the capacity or right to make representations to the Court. On the other hand, the Court has power to request information,[26] which it has used in the context of proceedings under art 95. In *Opinion 1/59*[27] the Court requested the production of the Council minutes relating to the proposal. It also relied on a letter from the Secretary General of the Council but it is unclear from the report if this was sent by him of his own accord or pursuant to a request from the Court. In *Opinion 1/61*[28] the Court put a series of questions to the Commission and the Council concerning both the texts of the

20 [1979] ECR 2871.
21 But not Irish, which can be used only in proceedings before the Court.
22 See Case 1/60 *FERAM v High Authority* [1960] ECR 165. This presumption does not appear to extend to Irish.
23 See art 100.
24 See RP-ECJ 29(2)(c): RP-ECJ 29(3)(fourth subpara) may also be applicable if the making of submissions by a member state is to be regarded as an 'intervention' in the proceedings, which is unclear.
25 Above, note 15, see at 257.
26 See, for example, ECSC Statute, art 24.
27 Above, note 15 at 269.
28 Above, note 15 see at 257 and 264–269.

proposed amendment and the necessity for it. The first question relating to the latter, for example, asks what were the legal, economic or political reasons for the failure to reduce or prevent coal imports from third countries.

The inference seems to be that, while there is no right to make written submissions to the Court save in the request for an opinion itself, the Court may call for both information and argument on specific matters that it feels require clarification before it delivers its opinion. In the first instance those enquiries should be directed to the Commission and Council but there is nothing which suggests that the Court cannot also approach a member state, at least for the purpose of requiring information from it. In the same way, there is no right to be heard by the Court but it may, if it thinks it right to do so, invite the Commission and the Council to make oral submissions, as it has done in the context of proceedings under art 228 of the EC Treaty.[29] Whereas a power to request information from a member state may be derived from art 24 of the ECSC Statute, it is unclear whether there is also a power to invite a member state to make oral submissions. In *Opinion 1/92*,[30] a case under art 228 of the EC Treaty, the Court gave leave for the European Parliament to submit observations at the Parliament's request; but that was in the context of RP-ECJ 107(1), which provides for the submission of written observations.

5   Measures of enquiry

The power of the Court under art 95 to assess all points of fact necessarily implies that it may order measures of enquiry. Hitherto, as has been seen, these have been restricted to requests to the High Authority and the Council to produce documents or make submissions on certain aspects specified by the Court. Although it would appear that the Court's powers go further, it does not seem that it is likely to exercise them. In *Opinion 1/59*[31] the Court declined to examine in detail one issue of fact on the ground that 'such an investigation could end in legally conclusive results only if it followed from a full hearing of all sides ('*un débat contradictoire*'), a procedure which would go well beyond the limits laid down by Article 95'. Two conclusions can be drawn from this. Firstly, the Court is not likely to take upon itself the burden of examining witnesses and of making its own investigations into the facts; instead it will rely to a great extent on the assessments made by the Commission and the Council, checking them in the light of any documentary evidence and against the replies given to specific questions which may be put to the Commission and the Council by the Court itself. Secondly, since proceedings under art 95 do not involve 'a full hearing of all sides', all the various ancillary proceedings set out in the Statute and the Rules of Procedure, such as intervention, judgment by default and so forth, have no application.

6   Result of the proceedings

The views of the advocates general are heard by the Court in camera and are not published. The Court's opinions in cases under art 95 reflect the contemporary style of drafting and would no doubt today take a form more akin to the opinions which have been delivered under art 228 of the EEC Treaty. Once the Court has delivered its opinion, it is functus officio and the proceedings are at an end. It is a reasonable inference that the Court may act to correct slips in the

---

29   See *Opinion 1/78* (above, note 20) at 2879 and 2902, para 17.
30   [1992] ECR I-2821.
31   Above, note 15 see at 271.

text of the opinion[32] but it does not seem that it is possible to reopen proceedings by way of revision or even to apply for a formal interpretation by the Court of its opinion. No order for costs is made because the proceedings are non-contentious.

IV   Special procedures under the EC Treaty

A   Disputes concerning the European Investment Bank

Article 180 of the Treaty gives the Court jurisdiction over three categories of dispute concerning the activities of the European Investment Bank ('the EIB').[33]

1   Disputes concerning the obligations of member states

The first category concerns the fulfilment by member states of obligations under the EIB's Statute. The model of the proceedings is the default action against a member state brought under arts 169 and 170 of the Treaty. Article 180 provides that the EIB's Board of Directors enjoys the Commission's powers under the former but says nothing about the possibility of proceedings being commenced by a member state or some other person (for example, a Community institution). In these circumstances, the most that can be said is that the course of proceedings is the same as under art 169, the Board of Directors being substituted for the Commission. However, it does not seem that proceedings may also be commenced by any other natural or legal person.[33A] When proceedings are commenced by a person other than the EIB's Board of Directors, it is unclear whether they derogate from art 170, as in the case of art 93, or not. Since there is no express reference to art 170 in art 180, it is to be presumed that proceedings can be begun without first referring the matter to the Board of Directors. In other respects, proceedings are the same as those under arts 169 and 170.

2   Disputes concerning the Board of Governors

Any member state, the Commission or the EIB's Board of Directors may commence proceedings for the annulment of a 'measure' adopted by the Board of Governors of the EIB. The proceedings are the same, mutatis mutandis, as those under art 173. Normally it would be supposed that, although not defined, the word 'measure' must be taken as indicating an act having legal consequences: it is difficult to see how it could otherwise be annulled. The matter is not entirely free from doubt because other texts of art 180 refer to 'resolutions' and 'deliberations'.[34] It seems likely that the Treaty means the former. In Case 85/86R *Commission v Board of Governors of the EIB*,[35] Advocate General Mancini suggested that the contested measure does not have to cause or be capable of causing adverse effects for it to be open to challenge; but the Court did not rely on that ground, holding instead that the measure in

---

32 By analogy to RP-ECJ 66(1).

33 Article 180 does not list exhaustively the situations in which the Court has jurisdiction over the activities of the EIB: see Case 110/75 *Mills v EIB* [1976] ECR 955 (paras 16–17); Case C-370/89 *Société Générale d'Entreprises Electro-mécaniques et al v EIB* [1992] ECR I-6211 (para 17).

33A Case T-460/93 *Tête v European Investment Bank*, 26 November 1993.

34 *Beschlüsse, délibérations, deliberazioni.*

35 [1988] ECR 1281 (para 13 and at 1299).

question might affect the applicant's rights. It would seem that any resolution of the Board of Governors is open to be annulled on one of the grounds mentioned in art 173, at least if the applicant can demonstrate sufficient interest. The action is brought against the Board of Governors of the EIB, as an organ of the EIB, and not against the EIB itself, in much the same way as an action for annulment under art 173 of the EC Treaty is brought against the institution which adopted the contested act and not against the Community.[36] If the applicant is successful, the contested measure is declared void.[37]

3 Disputes concerning the Board of Directors

Any member state or the Commission may commence proceedings for the annulment of a 'measure' adopted by the EIB's Board of Directors. The word 'measure' again seems to mean 'resolution'. Although the action is said to be brought 'under the conditions laid down in Article 173', this seems to refer to the model to be used and not the grounds for annulment: these are specified 'solely' to be 'non-compliance with the procedure provided for in Article 21(2), (5), (6) and (7) of the Statute of the Bank'. This refers to decisions of the Board of Directors concerning the grant of a loan or guarantee. It follows that the 'measures' or 'resolutions' which can be attacked are those to which art 21(2) and (5) to (7) inclusive of the EIB's Statute applies and no other.

B Disputes concerning national central banks

The EU Treaty amended arts 173, 175, 176, 177 and 215 so as to extend the Court's jurisdiction to acts and defaults of the European Central Bank ('the ECB').[38] In addition, it amended art 180 of the EC Treaty so as to add a new subparagraph (d) conferring on the Court jurisdiction in respect of disputes concerning the fulfilment by national central banks of obligations under the EC Treaty and the Statute of the European System of Central Banks.[39] As in the case of the first form of action envisaged in art 180,[40] the model of the proceedings is the default action against a member state under arts 169 and 170 of the Treaty. Article 180(d) provides that the powers of the Council of the ECB in respect of national central banks are the same as those of the Commission in respect of member states under art 169. Thus, the proceedings are the same as in an action under art 169 with the Council of the ECB substituted for the Commission and the national central bank in question substituted for the defendant member state. As in the case of the first form of action envisaged in art 180, the Treaty does not state that proceedings can be begun only by the Council of the ECB. The possibility therefore remains that another person with sufficient interest (the Commission or a member state) may bring proceedings. Article 180(d) says that, if the Court finds that a national central bank has failed to fulfil an obligation under the Treaty, that bank 'shall be required to take the necessary measures to comply with the judgment of the Court of Justice'. Thus, the effect of the judgment is essentially the same as that in an action under art 169. Although art 180(d) does not make similar provision in respect of a finding that a national central bank has failed to fulfil its obligation under the Statute of the European System of Central Banks, it is implicit that the result of such a finding would be the same.

---

36 Case 85/86 *Commission v Board of Governors of the EIB* [1986] ECR 2215.
37 Case 85/86R *Commission v Board of Governors of the EIB* [1988] ECR 1281.
38 See section II.A, B, D and G above.
39 The Statute is set out in a Protocol to the EU Treaty.
40 See section IV.A(1) above.

C   Opinions

1   *Nature of the proceedings*

Article 228(6) of the EC Treaty (as amended by the EU Treaty)[41] allows, but does not require, the Council, the Commission or a member state to apply to the Court for an opinion as to whether a proposed agreement between the Community and one or more states or an international organisation is compatible with the provisions of the Treaty. In this context 'agreement' means any undertaking entered into by entities subject to international law which has binding force, irrespective of its formal designation.[42] Where the Court's view is that it is incompatible with the Treaty, the agreement can enter into force only in accordance with art N of the EU Treaty, ie pursuant to an amendment of the Treaty.[43] The purpose of this procedure was explained by the Court in the first opinion it delivered under art 228 as being 'to forestall complications which would result from legal disputes concerning the compatibility with the Treaty of international agreements binding upon the Community. In fact, a possible decision of the Court to the effect that such an agreement is, either by reason of its content or of the procedure adopted for its conclusion, incompatible with the provisions of the Treaty could not fail to provoke, not only in a Community context but also in that of international relations, serious difficulties and might give rise to adverse consequences for all interested parties, including third countries.'[44]

Although no time limit is laid down for the submission of a request for an opinion, it would seem that it must be made before the agreement in question is 'concluded'.[45] If made after that event, it is inadmissible. Conclusion does not mean that the discussions concerning the substance of the agreement are at an end and that the text has been finalised.[46] For example, in *Opinion 1/76*[47] the negotiations had been completed and the draft text had been initialled before the request was lodged. The critical point is that at which the Community becomes bound in international law by the agreement. The request may be lodged at any time before that point, even if the text of the agreement has not been settled and negotiations have only just begun.[48] In *Opinion 1/78*[49] it was argued that, in the absence of a draft text, the agreement cannot be considered to be an 'agreement envisaged', which is the phrase used in art 228; the least that is necessary to provide the basis for a request is a preliminary draft text. It is no doubt arguable that the term 'agreement envisaged' in fact refers to the Treaty itself, ie the only condition for making the request, in this sense, is that the agreement be one whose conclusion is provided for in the Treaty.[50] In consequence, the request may be lodged at any time. The Court rejected the claim that the request in *Opinion 1/78* was inadmissible on the ground that it had enough information at its disposal to form 'a sufficiently certain judgment'

---

41 Before the amendments introduced by the EU Treaty, the relevant provision was EC Treaty, art 228(1).
42 *Opinion 1/75* [1975] ECR 1355 at 1359–1360. For this procedure, see Bebr *Development of Judicial Control in the European Communities* (1981) pp 351 et seq.
43 Before the EU Treaty came into force, the agreement could enter into force only in accordance with art 236 of the EC Treaty, which was in effect replaced by art N of the EU Treaty.
44 *Opinion 1/75* (above, note 42) at 1360–1361.
45 See art 228(1)–(5) and ibid at 1361.
46 *Opinion 1/75* (above, note 42).
47 [1977] ECR 741 at 744.
48 *Opinion 1/78* (above, note 20).
49 Ibid.
50 See the first para of art 228(1).

on the question raised in the request.[51] This suggests that admissibility is a function of the question raised in the request so that the earliest date on which a request may be admissible is that on which the preparation of the agreement is sufficiently advanced to enable the Court to decide the question put by the maker of the request. Even if there is no text to refer to, it may be enough that the subject matter of the agreement is known or that there is sufficient background material.

Opinion 1/78 arose out of a dispute between the Commission and the Council concerning how the negotiations on the agreement in question were to be conducted by the Community. It was argued that this made the request inadmissible and even a misuse of procedure because the real purpose was to air the difference of opinion between the Commission, on one hand, and the Council and all the member states on the other. The Court rejected this, saying that 'a judgment on the compatibility of an agreement with the Treaty may depend not only on provisions of substantive law but also on those concerning the powers, procedure or organisation of the institutions of the Community'.[52] It went on to hold that the Commission had an interest in lodging its request immediately after its disagreement with the Council, regarding the question of the power to negotiate and conclude the agreement, had become apparent: 'Indeed, when a question of powers is to be determined it is clearly in the interests of all the States concerned including non-member countries, for such a question to be clarified as soon as any particular negotiations are commenced.'[53] Apart from the problem of negotiating the agreement, RP-ECJ 107(2) expressly provides that the opinion 'may deal not only with the question whether the envisaged agreement is compatible with the provisions of the EEC Treaty but also with the question whether the Community or any Community institution has the power to enter into that agreement'. In *Opinion 1/75*[54] the Court in consequence found that the mere fact that the request was made in order to obtain the Court's opinion on the extent of the Community's powers to conclude the agreement 'cannot be sufficient of itself to render the request inadmissible': 'The compatibility of an agreement with the provisions of the Treaty must be assessed in the light of all the rules of the Treaty, that is to say, both those rules which determine the extent of the powers of the institutions of the Community and the substantive rules.'[55] Thus, the Court has jurisdiction under art 228 to consider the respective competences of the Community and the member states even in relation to an international agreement which can be ratified only by the member states.[56]

The questions which may be raised in the request are 'all questions capable of submission for judicial consideration, either by the Court of Justice or possibly by national courts, in so far as such questions give rise to doubt either as to the substantive or formal validity of the agreement with regard to the Treaty'.[57] The reason for this is that the purpose of the procedure under art 228 is to preclude the compatibility of the agreement with the Treaty from being challenged in subsequent proceedings. It would seem, therefore, that the Court's opinion is binding in relation to the questions canvassed by it in any subsequent proceedings unless there is a new factor which would require a

51 Above (note 20) para 34.
52 Ibid para 30.
53 Ibid para 35.
54 Above (note 42) at 1360.
55 Ibid; see also *Opinion 1/78* (above, note 20) para 30.
56 *Opinion 2/91*, 19 March 1993 (OJ No C109 of 19 April 1993, p 1).
57 *Opinion 1/75* (above, note 42) at 1361.

reassessment of the position. On the other hand, it is not the Court's function to give a definitive interpretation of the text of the disputed agreement in proceedings under art 228.[58] Hence, any interpretation it may have adopted is not binding in subsequent proceedings and the fact that a different interpretation is used in practice is sufficient to re-open any question of compatibility decided by the Court in an opinion. The possibility of making a series of requests concerning the same agreement, as different problems concerning its compatibility with the Treaty are seen to arise, was impliedly accepted by the Court in *Opinion 1/78*.[59]

2   *Procedure*

Proceedings are commenced by the lodgment at the Court of the request for an opinion. Only the Council, the Commission or one of the member states can lodge a request.[60] No requirements as to its form or contents are laid down in the Rules of Procedure or elsewhere. In contrast to the cases decided under art 95 of the ECSC Treaty, the reports of those brought under art 228 of the EC Treaty do not appear to set out the text of the request. Like requests made under art 95, however, it seems that those made under art 228 comprise: (i) the text of the agreement in question or sufficient background documents and information to enable the Court to form a view, if there is no agreed text or draft; (ii) an explanation of the context of the agreement and its scope; (iii) the reasons why the maker of the request considers that the agreement may or may not be compatible with the Treaty. The request must be signed by someone authorised to do so on behalf of the maker of the request, such as its agent, and comply in general with the requirements of RP-ECJ 37. It is unclear how many copies of the request should be lodged and what should be the language of the proceedings. RP-ECJ 105(1), which deals with applications made under art 103 of the Euratom Treaty, states that four copies should be lodged. There is no reason that this rule should apply in the present context. It seems reasonable to apply RP-ECJ 37(1), with the effect that the original of the request should be lodged together with five copies for the use of the Court and one for every other party to the proceedings. Here a 'party' to the proceedings is a party on whom the request is to be served in accordance with the Rules of Procedure. Where the request is lodged by the Council or the Commission the usual rules relating to lodgment of a pleading by a Community institution apply.[61] The report of *Opinion 1/78*[62] sets out as the languages of the proceedings all the official Community languages. In *Ruling 1/78*,[63] however, which was a case under art 103 of the Euratom Treaty, the language of the proceedings was apparently French. It would seem that any language which may be used in proceedings before the Court can be chosen but, in the case of observations from a member state, the Court may authorise use by it of a different language from that of the proceedings.[64]

After the request is lodged at the Court it is served in the usual way. The parties on whom it may be served are specified by the Rules of Procedure: the Commission only, when the request is made by the Council; the Council and the member states, when it is made by the Commission; the Council, the

---

58 *Opinion 1/76* (above, note 47) para 20.
59 Above (note 20).
60 EC Treaty, art 228(6), as amended.
61 See, inter alia, RP-ECJ 37(2).
62 Above, note 20.
63 Above, note 19.
64 See RP-ECJ 29(2)(c).

Commission and all the other member states, when it is made by one of the member states.[65] As soon as the request has been lodged the President designates a judge to act as rapporteur.[66] The case is not assigned to an advocate general because all the advocates general are heard by the Court. The President also prescribes a period for the lodgment of written observations on the request by the parties served with it.[67] It seems a little odd that the member states should be barred from submitting observations when the Council makes the request but not when it is made by the Commission. Nevertheless, that is what the Rules of Procedure say and, as with proceedings under art 95 of the ECSC Treaty, those under art 228 would appear to exclude in principle the possibility of intervention, together with all the other ancillary proceedings in a direct action. Nonetheless, in *Opinion 1/92*[68] the Court allowed the European Parliament to submit written observations in response to a request made by the Parliament. It would therefore seem that the Court may entertain written observations from a Community institution or a member state on whom the request for an opinion has not been served. The Court may either invite such an institution or member state to submit observations or, as in *Opinion 1/92*, allow the submission of observations in response to a request made by the institution or state concerned.

By way of written procedure the Rules provide only for the request and the written observations submitted in response to it. No rules are laid down concerning the form and content of the written observations but it seems that they should comply with RP-ECJ 37. It does not seem to be necessary for them to end with a 'form of order', or suggested response to be given by the Court to the request. So far all the proceedings under art 228 have been initiated by the Commission but, apart from the Council, only a few member states submitted written observations.[69] There is no provision for preparatory enquiries or a hearing. Silence does not in this case indicate that the Court has no further powers. The better view seems to be that the precise route taken by the proceedings is left to the discretion of the Court. In any event, its practice indicates that it is not restricted to a literal interpretation of the Rules of Procedure. There seems to be no bar to the submission, by the maker of the request, of additional observations[70] or annexes to it[71] and the Court has also on occasion asked one or all of the parties which have submitted written observations to provide it with information[72] or reply to questions.[73] It would appear that the Court may also require member states which have not submitted written observations to supply any information which it considers necessary for the proceedings.[74]

Although the Court is not given express power to assess questions of fact, as it has in proceedings under art 95 of the ECSC Treaty,[75] it may be inferred that, should the need arise, it may order measures of enquiry but that it is

65 RP-ECJ 107(1).
66 RP-ECJ 108(1).
67 RP-ECJ 107(1).
68 Above (note 30).
69 For example, four of the member states in *Opinion 1/75* (above, note 42), two in *Opinions 1/76* (above, note 47) and *1/78* (above, note 20), three in *Opinion 1/91* [1991] ECR I-6079, eight in *Opinion 2/91* (above, note 56).
70 See *Opinion 1/76* (ibid) at 744.
71 See *Opinion 1/78* (above, note 20) at 2879.
72 See *Opinion 1/76* (above, note 47) at 754.
73 See *Opinion 1/78* (above, note 20); *Opinion 1/91* (above, note 69).
74 EC Statute, art 21.
75 See p 582.

unlikely to exercise such powers, beyond requests for documents and further information, on the ground that the nature of proceedings under art 228 does not lend itself to the resolution of disputed questions of fact.[76] In *Opinion 1/78*[77] the Court invited the Council, the Commission and the two member states which had submitted written observations to present oral argument. Only the Council and the Commission responded to this invitation and the hearing was held in camera. It does not seem that there is any right to make oral submissions to the Court. It is for the Court to decide whom to invite to address it. The opinions of the advocates general are heard by the Court in closed session[78] and are not published. The Court's opinion, which must be reasoned, is also delivered in closed session[79] and the parties are not therefore given notice to attend to hear it. It is signed by the President, the judges who took part in the deliberations and by the Registrar; it is then served on the Council, the Commission and all the member states.[80] After having delivered the opinion the Court is functus officio although it is reasonable to assume that it retains power to correct slips in the text of the opinion.[81] It does not seem that proceedings can be reopened by way of revision or even for the purpose of obtaining a formal interpretation by the Court of its opinion. No order for costs is made because the proceedings are non-contentious.

V   Special procedures under the Euratom Treaty

The Euratom Treaty contains a number of provisions setting out special procedures in specific areas covered by the Treaty: the grant of patent licences; the enforcement of basic health and safety standards; inspections and sanctions under the safeguard rules; the verification of agreements or contracts made with a third country, an international organisation or a national of a third country, in order to ensure their compatibility with the Treaty. As far as the enforcement of basic health and safety standards is concerned, art 38 of the Treaty simply provides for an abbreviated procedure for applying under arts 141 or 142 for a declaration that the defendant member state has failed to fulfil its obligations under the Treaty. Under this procedure the formal preliminaries of such actions are omitted and, in order to commence proceedings, the applicant merely lodges its application at the Court. The abbreviated procedure under art 38 is reserved for cases of urgency, where there are exceptional circumstances.[82] The same applies when a member state does not comply with a Commission directive requiring it to take steps to bring to an end an infringement of art 79, which requires that records be kept of ores, source materials and special fissile materials in order to document their use, production and transport.[83] In consequence, none of these areas will be considered separately.

---

76 See *Opinion 1/59* (above, note 15) at 271.
77 Above (note 20) see at 2879 and 2902, para 17.
78 RP-ECJ 108(2); see also *Opinion 1/76* (above, note 47) at 744 and *Opinion 1/78* (ibid) at 2880.
79 RP-ECJ 108(2).
80 RP-ECJ 108(3).
81 By analogy to RP-ECJ 66(1).
82 Case 187/87 *Saarland v Minister for Industry, Post and Telecommunications and Tourism* [1988] ECR 5013 (para 15).
83 Article 82.

A Applications to fix the terms of a licence

Article 12 of the Treaty provides that member states, persons or undertakings[84] have a right to obtain (i) 'non-exclusive licences under patents, provisionally protected patent rights, utility models or patent applications owned by the Community' and (ii) 'sub-licences under patents, provisionally protected patent rights, utility models or patent applications, where the Community holds contractual licences conferring power' to grant them. In both cases entitlement to the licence or sub-licence is dependent on the applicant being 'able to make effective use of the inventions covered thereby'. The application is made to the Commission which lies under a duty to grant such licences or sub-licences on terms to be agreed with the licensees. If no agreement on the terms is reached, the applicant, whom the English version of art 12 describes as a 'licensee', may apply to the Court 'so that appropriate terms may be fixed'.

Although art 12 provides for a direct application to the Court, no special procedure for such an action appears to have been laid down in the Treaty, the Euratom Statute or the Rules of Procedure. Article 144 of the Treaty says that the Court has unlimited jurisdiction in 'proceedings instituted under Article 12 to have the appropriate terms fixed for the granting by the Commission of licences or sub-licences'. This means only that the Court is not limited to reviewing the legality of any action taken by the Commission but may itself exercise a discretion of its own regarding the fixing of appropriate terms; and that the Court is not constrained to give its decision only in terms of the prayers set out in the pleadings of one or the other party. There seems to be no time limit on the making of the application.

In the absence of any precise authority on the point, it seems right to use the model of an ordinary direct action, the application being one for the Court to 'fix the appropriate terms' of the licence or sub-licence in question, the defendant being the Commission. The form of order in the application should nevertheless specify the precise terms sought by the applicant. Whether the form of order in the defence should content itself with a prayer that the application be dismissed with costs or should also specify the defendant's preferred terms is unclear. Since the applicant has a right to be granted the licence or sub-licence and the dispute relates to its terms, it does not seem that, if the action is admissible, the Court can simply dismiss it if it takes the view that the applicant is wrong in relation to the terms he has suggested: it must decide what are the appropriate terms of the licence or sub-licence. For the Commission to plead that those suggested by the applicant are wrong or inappropriate would be of little assistance to the Court. It therefore seems incumbent on the Commission to put forward its own suggestions so that the Court can balance both sides of the case and come to a conclusion with the full benefit of the views of the opposing parties.

B Appeals against decisions of the Euratom Arbitration Committee

1 Nature of the proceedings

The Treaty provides for the communication to the Commission of information which is of use to the Community by 'amicable agreement'[85] or

---

84 This phrase appears with great frequency throughout the Treaty. 'Persons' and 'undertakings' are defined in art 196 as being 'any natural person' and 'any undertaking or institution . . . whatever its public or private legal status', respectively, which 'pursues all or any of its activities in the territories of Member States within the field specified in the relevant chapter of this Treaty'. Various provisions, such as arts 10 and 104, indicate that both are distinct from 'international organisations' and 'nationals of third countries'.

85 Articles 14–15.

compulsorily.[86] In the same way, the Commission is empowered to make use of inventions either with the consent of the applicant for the patent or utility model to which they relate or, without his consent, by arbitration or compulsorily.[87] Where no amicable agreement can be reached, non-exclusive licences may be granted either to the Community or Joint Undertakings accorded this right by art 48 or to persons or undertakings who have applied for them to the Commission.[88] The conditions attaching to the grant of the licences vary as between these two categories. Provision is made for the submission to the Euratom Arbitration Committee of disputes concerning the grant or the terms of a licence. There may then be an appeal to the Court from any decision of the Arbitration Committee which, if successful, would result in the setting aside of the latter's decision.

2   *Proceedings before the Arbitration Committee*

The procedure for obtaining grant of a licence compulsorily or by arbitration starts when the Commission gives notice of its intention to secure the grant of a licence to a person or body falling within one of these categories in accordance with art 17. The notice is served on the proprietor of the patent, provisionally protected patent right, utility model or patent application ('the proprietor') and must specify the name of the applicant and the scope of the licence.[89] A condition precedent to the service of the notice is that an attempt has been made to obtain grant of the licence by amicable agreement and that this attempt has failed. Within one month of receipt of the notice the proprietor may propose to the Commission and, where appropriate, the applicant, that a special agreement be concluded to refer the matter to the Arbitration Committee created by art 18.[90] If either the Commission or the applicant should refuse to enter into this arbitration agreement, the matter ends there because the Commission cannot then require the member state concerned or its appropriate authority to grant the licence or cause it to be granted[91] and there is no other relevant provision for securing grant of the licence under the Treaty.

On the other hand, if the Commission and, where appropriate, the applicant, agree to enter the arbitration agreement, the matter comes up before the Arbitration Committee. The agreement must set out the matters in dispute, the questions on which the arbitrators will have to rule and the basis for deciding the composition of the arbitration board dealing with the case.[92] Proceedings are conducted in one of the Community official languages chosen by the proprietor. The arbitration board may authorise partial or total use of another official language at the request of one of the parties, other than the Commission, after hearing the views of the other party.[93] The Arbitration Committee's Rules of Procedure are contained in Council Regulation No 7/63 of 3 December 1963[94] and provide that it sits in arbitration boards of three arbitrators. One of them is the Chairman or one of the two Vice-Chairmen of the Committee; each of the parties chooses one of the other two arbitrators

---

86 Article 16.
87 Articles 16(4) and 17(1).
88 Article 17(1).
89 Article 19.
90 Article 20, para 1.
91 Article 20, para 2.
92 Article 11(2) of Regulation No 7/63 (below, note 94).
93 Ibid, art 12.
94 OJ English Special Edition 1963–1964, p 56; JO No 180 of 10 December 1963, p 2849.

from among the 12 members of the Committee. When a dispute is referred to the Committee, the Chairman acts as chairman of the arbitration board for that case or appoints one of the Vice-Chairmen to fulfil that function. The chairman of the arbitration board then sets a time limit, which may be extended on application, for the appointment (in writing) by each party to the dispute of the members of the Committee chosen to act as arbitrator.[95] Alternatively, the parties may specify in the arbitration agreement that they wish the case to be decided by only one arbitrator or by an arbitration board consisting of five arbitrators, the parties nominating two each in addition to its chairman.[96] As can be seen, the rules envisage only two parties to the proceedings. It is unclear what role in them the applicant for the licence plays. The Treaty seems to make it clear that proceedings are commenced by the Commission and the right to seek grant of the licence rests with it. The applicant appears to have no direct right against the proprietor but, at most, the power to cause the Commission to exercise its powers. It would seem that the applicant, where one exists, must be a party to the arbitration agreement so that he is bound by and may rely on it and, in particular, the Arbitration Committee's decision. On the other hand, he has no right to be heard by the Committee.

The arbitration board decides whether there is an exchange of written pleadings before the hearing, its chairman fixing the number and the time limits. Pleadings are addressed to the Registrar of the Arbitration Committee and he ensures their service on the other party. After all the pleadings have been submitted (or after the time limit fixed has expired without their submission),[97] the chairman fixes the date and time of the hearing.[98] The way proceedings are conducted is decided by the arbitration board: it has a broad discretion in assessing facts and may carry out an inspection if it considers it advisable.[99] The hearing is held in private unless the arbitration board decides otherwise with the consent of the parties.[1] The hearing ends when the parties have finished explaining their cases but the arbitration board retains power until an award has been made to reopen the hearing (i) where fresh evidence has come to light which may have a decisive influence on the outcome or (ii) where, after a more thorough examination, it wishes to have certain points clarified.[2] Article 23 of Regulation No 7/63 provides that, in accordance with the Treaty and the general principles common to the laws of the member states, 'the arbitration board shall decide *ex aequo et bono*'. The award is drawn up in writing and must be reasoned unless the arbitration agreement provides otherwise.[3]

Article 20 of the Treaty provides that, when the dispute is referred to the Arbitration Committee, it makes its decision[4] if it 'finds that the request from the Commission complies with the provisions of Article 17'. It is unclear whether this 'request' is to be regarded as the notice provided for in art 19 or the Commission's initial proposal to the proprietor suggesting the grant of a licence by amicable agreement. Either possibility is arguable, although the former may be the more likely. A third possibility is that 'request' refers to the

---

95 Ibid, art 10.
96 Ibid, art 11(1).
97 Ibid, art 15.
98 Ibid, art 14.
99 Ibid, arts 17 and 18.
 1 Ibid, art 19.
 2 Ibid, art 20.
 3 Ibid, art 22.
 4 In fact, as has been seen, the decision is made by an arbitration board composed of members of the Committee.

Commission's written or oral submission to the Arbitration Committee. The Committee's decision must do three things: grant the licence to the applicant; specify its terms; and lay down the remuneration to which the proprietor is entitled. The Committee's power to decide these matters is, however, subject to any agreement on them reached between the parties.[5] After a year, the decision may be revised by the Committee but only in so far as it relates to the terms of the licence, if there are new facts justifying it doing so.[6]

3　Scope of the appeal

An appeal may be brought against the decision of the Arbitration Committee within one month of the service of the decision on the appellant. The making of the appeal suspends the effect of the decision. The Court's jurisdiction is limited to examining the formal validity of the decision and reviewing the Arbitration Committee's interpretation of the Treaty.[7] Final decisions of the Arbitration Committee have the force of res judicata and are enforceable[8] in accordance with the relevant rules of civil procedure in force in the member state in which enforcement is carried out. The only formality is verification of the authenticity of the decision by the competent national authority.[9] The Treaty does not indicate what is the precise distinction between a 'decision' and a 'final decision'. The dichotomy does not seem to lie between final decisions in the sense of 'judgments', to use the terminology applied to decisions of the Court, and decisions of a procedural nature ('orders') because art 18 of the Treaty clearly states that the appeal to the Court lies against 'decisions' of the Arbitration Committee. Taken in this way, any decision of the arbitration board dealing with the procedure to be followed in the case could be appealed. There therefore seem to be two alternative interpretations of the Treaty: either 'decisions' and 'final decisions' mean the same or the former become final only once the time limit for appeal to the Court has expired without an appeal having been lodged, alternatively, once the decision has been confirmed by the Court. The latter interpretation seems preferable and is supported by art 20 of the Euratom Statute, which provides that decisions of the Arbitration Committee become final if the Court rejects the appeal.

4　Procedure

Article 20 of the Euratom Statute provides that appeals from decisions of the Arbitration Committee are to be 'addressed' to the Registrar. This only means that they are sent to him. The use of the word 'appeal' is not reflected in all the language versions of the Euratom Treaty and Statute. A more accurate term might be 'review'. Nevertheless, the usage of the official English texts will be followed here. The application originating the appeal must contain:[10]

5　Euratom Treaty, art 20.
6　Ibid, art 23.
7　Article 18.
8　Ibid.
9　As far as the United Kingdom is concerned, see paras 3 and 4 of the European Communities (Enforcement of Community Judgments) Order 1972 (SI 1972/1590): on application by the party entitled to enforce it, the High Court registers any such decision to which the Secretary of State has appended an order for enforcement. Once registered, the decision has the same force and effect, for the purposes of execution, as a High Court judgment.
10　There are variations between the Statute and the Rules of Procedure but not all are reflected in the different language versions of the texts. This is one occasion on which the precise words used to describe the contents of the application should be regarded with care. It is better to interpret them broadly, as giving an indication of what is required. Apart from art 20 of the Statute and RP-ECJ 101 the contents of the application are also to be determined by reference to RP-ECJ 37(3) and (4) and 38(2), (3) and (5), which are incorporated by reference, by RP-ECJ 101(2).

(1)   the date;
(2)   the name and permanent address of the applicant;
(3)   the 'description' of the signatory (ie his capacity);
(4)   a reference to the decision against which the appeal is brought;
(5)   the names and description of the respondents;[11]
(6)   the subject matter of the dispute;[12]
(7)   the pleas in law relied on;[13]
(8)   the form of order sought; and
(9)   an address for service in Luxembourg and the name of a person authorised and willing to accept service.

It must be accompanied by:

(1)   a certified copy of the Arbitration Committee's opinion;
(2)   all documents relied on in support of the application, together with a schedule listing them;
(3)   a practising certificate showing that the lawyer acting for the applicant is entitled to practise before the Court of a member state;[14] and
(4)   where the application is made by a legal person governed by private law, the instrument or instruments constituting and regulating it (or a recent extract from the register of companies, firms or associations or any other proof of the applicant's existence in law) and proof that the authority to act granted to the applicant's lawyer has been properly conferred on him by someone authorised for this purpose.

Rules of Procedure do not refer expressly in this context to RP-ECJ 37(1), which provides that the original of every pleading must be signed by the party's agent or lawyer and that it must be accompanied by all annexes and the required number of copies. There is also no reference to RP-ECJ 38(7), which deals with defective applications. In the case of applications under art 18 of the Euratom Treaty, this provision would cover only defects relating to items (3) and (4), in the two lists given above, respectively. Despite the absence of any express reference, it is to be inferred that these provisions apply. The usual rules relating to the language of the case also apply[15] although it is to be expected that the same language will be used as in the proceedings before the Arbitration Committee. As soon as the application has been lodged, the Registrar requests the Arbitration Committee Registry to transmit to the Court the papers in the case.[16] The request is made by registered letter, enclosing a form for acknowledgment of its receipt.[17] If the request were to be refused, it does not seem as though the Court has power to require the production of the Arbitration Committee's file. It may be supposed that the rules relating to requests of documents would apply by analogy and that the Court would simply take formal note of the refusal and continue with the proceedings.[18] The application is served on the other parties

---

11 The Statute specifies the respondents but RP-ECJ 101(1)(d) refers to the 'parties'. Since the applicant has already been catered for, it is to be supposed that 'respondents' is meant. The English text of the Statute also mentions only the 'names' of the respondents. Both it and the Rules of Procedure do, in fact, seem to require the respondents to be identified in the application (see, for example, the French text of both).
12 RP-ECJ 101(1)(e) says 'a summary of the facts'.
13 Article 20 of the Statute requires 'a brief statement of the grounds'.
14 See chapter 9, p 318.
15 See RP-ECJ 29–30.
16 RP-ECJ 101(3).
17 IR 5(2).
18 Euratom Statute, art 22.

to the proceedings before the Arbitration Committee in the usual way.[19] On the assumption that RP-ECJ 38(7) does apply to these proceedings, service is effected as soon as the application has been put in order or the Court has declared it to be admissible, notwithstanding failure to comply with RP-ECJ 38(3)–(6). It has been suggested that the Court has an implied power to declare an application admissible despite any defect of a purely formal nature; a defect of substance, which would prevent the application being declared admissible and served on the other parties before it is put in order, is one which would prevent or hinder the respondent(s) in answering the case made out in the application.[20] RP-ECJ 101(4) incorporates by reference RP-ECJ 40. Hence the usual rules as to the service and contents of the defence apply. It will be observed that the requirements relating to the contents of the application do not include reference to the evidence relied on by the applicant. The same applies to the contents of the defence because the Court has no jurisdiction to review the arbitrators' findings of fact.

There is no provision for service of written pleadings after the defence. RP-ECJ 101 does not mention any other provisions in the Rules between RP-ECJ 40 and RP-ECJ 55. It thus excludes the possibility of a preparatory enquiry, no doubt because this falls outside the Court's jurisdiction in these proceedings. Therefore, after service of the defence, the pleadings are closed. It would seem that, instead of serving a defence, stricto sensu, the respondent may raise a preliminary objection under RP-ECJ 91. There appears to be no advantage in adopting this course because the preliminary objection would have to be followed by the other party's answer before the oral procedure could commence. In consequence, the written procedure would be longer than normal because it would involve three pleadings rather than two. The oral procedure and judgment stage of proceedings follow as in a direct action and there is no need to go into them here.[21] The Court's decision is given in the form of a judgment[22] and the usual rules relating to judgments apply: it may be rectified,[23] supplemented,[24] interpreted,[25] reviewed on the application of a third party[26] or revised.[27] After judgment has been given (or after the case has been removed from the Court's Register, as the case may be) the Arbitration Committee's papers are returned to it by the Registrar.[28]

5   *Result of the proceedings*

If the Court rejects the application for review, the decision of the Arbitration Committee becomes final,[29] binds the parties and may be executed.[30] If, on the other hand, the Court sets the decision aside, it may remit the case to the Committee.[31] The wording of, for example, the French text of the Rules of Procedure suggests that the Court must remit 'if need be'. In any event, as long as the Court has annulled the decision, even if it has not remitted the matter to

19 RP-ECJ 39; see RP-ECJ 101(4).
20 See chapter 7, p 222.
21 RP-ECJ 101(4).
22 RP-ECJ 101(5).
23 RP-ECJ 66.
24 RP-ECJ 67.
25 RP-ECJ 102.
26 RP-ECJ 97.
27 RP-ECJ 98–100.
28 IR 5(2).
29 Euratom Statute, art 20.
30 Euratom Treaty, art 18.
31 RP-ECJ 101(5).

the Committee, any of the parties may apply to the Committee to reopen the case. This means that the Committee must go through the process of reaching a decision a second time, conforming to the Court's judgment on points of law.[32]

C Actions for the grant of a licence

Where the proprietor of a patent, provisionally protected patent right, utility model or patent application does not propose that the matter be referred to the Arbitration Committee, the Commission may apply to the member state concerned or to its appropriate authority for grant of the licence.[33] The member state (or the appropriate authority) must only consider whether the conditions laid down by art 17 of the Treaty for the grant of a licence have been complied with. Its assessment is made after hearing the proprietor's view, although otherwise the procedure to be followed is left to national law. If art 17 has not been complied with, the member state or appropriate authority concerned must refuse to grant the licence or cause it to be granted and notify the Commission of its decision. The Commission then has two months in which to bring the matter before the Court. The same applies if no information regarding the grant of the licence is 'forthcoming' within four months of the date of the Commission's request.[34] It is unclear whether time starts to run from the date on which the request was drawn up or the date on which it was made, in the sense of served on the member state or the appropriate national authority. The better view seems to be the latter.

No special procedure is laid down for this action. It is to be presumed that it will take the form of an ordinary direct action. The defendant will be the member state or national authority concerned. Article 21 provides that the proprietor 'must be heard in the proceedings before the Court'. This suggests that he is a party and should also be cited as a defendant to the application. The applicant for the licence may also take part in the proceedings but only as an intervener. Article 21 says that it is the Commission which may bring the action so it would not be correct to name the applicant for the licence as an applicant in the proceedings before the Court. The judgment of the Court is restricted to determining whether or not the conditions set out in art 17 have been fulfilled and the form of order should be framed accordingly. If art 17 has been complied with, the defendant is enjoined to 'take such measures as enforcement of that judgment require',[35] ie grant the licence or cause it to be granted.

It is unclear whether the decision of the member state or appropriate authority under art 21 is restricted to the simple grant of a licence or whether it may also specify its terms and the remuneration due to the proprietor. At first sight it might be thought that all three elements were comprised in the phrase 'grant the licence' but art 20 does distinguish between them when specifying the contents of the Arbitration Committee's decision. To complicate matters even more, art 22(1) envisages an agreement between the proprietor and the licensee on the amount of 'compensation' due to the former. It can therefore be argued that, under art 21, only the grant of the licence and its terms can be decided, the question of remuneration being left to the parties to decide in accordance with the procedure set out in art 22. Alternatively, all three

---

32 Euratom Statute, art 20.
33 Euratom Treaty, art 21.
34 Ibid. The silence is presumed to be a refusal to grant the licence.
35 Ibid.

elements can be settled by the member state or the appropriate authority but the question of remuneration is not binding on the parties. The former appears to be the more likely, but both approaches presuppose that the 'compensation' mentioned in art 22 is the same as the 'remuneration' mentioned in art 20. This interpretation is not sanctified by any authority. It could equally well be said that art 22 deals, for example, with a lump sum compensation due to the proprietor, not income from exploitation of the licence, and that it applies not only in the context of art 21 but also where the proprietor does agree to submit the grant of the licence to arbitration. The writer favours the first view but one cannot at this point be dogmatic. On this basis, the question of remuneration is decided by amicable agreement between the proprietor and the licensee.

In the absence of agreement, the parties may conclude a special agreement to refer the matter to the Arbitration Committee. This time the Commission does not appear to be a party unless it is or represents the licensee. By agreeing to arbitration, the parties are taken to have waived the right to institute any proceedings other than those under art 18, ie an appeal to the Court from the Arbitration Committee's decision. Since the waiver is derived from the Treaty,[36] it is enforceable even if, under national law, an exclusive jurisdiction clause in an arbitration agreement cannot ordinarily oust the jurisdiction of the Courts.[37] As has been said, the appeal to the Court is restricted to a review of the formal validity of the decision and of the interpretation of the Treaty provisions by the Arbitration Committee.[38] The consequences of a failure to conclude an arbitration agreement vary depending on the party responsible for the failure. If the licensee, the licence is deemed void; there is no provision, however, preventing the licensee from re-applying for a licence. If the proprietor, compensation is determined by the appropriate national authority.[39] Decisions of that authority may be revised by it any time after the lapse of a year, if there are new facts to justify it, the revision relating to the terms of the licence.[40]

D Inspections

The Commission has power to send inspectors into the territories of the member states for the purpose of ensuring the application of the safeguards provided for in arts 77 et seq of the Treaty and compliance with art 77 itself.[41] The inspectors have right of access at all times 'to all places and data and to all persons who, by reason of their occupation, deal with materials, equipment or installations subject to the safeguards provided for'. If the inspection is opposed, however, whether it be by the member state itself or the person or undertaking in question, the inspector cannot simply force his way in. Instead, the Commission may either: (i) apply to the President of the Court for an order that the inspection be carried out compulsorily (the President must make a decision within three days of receiving the application); or (ii) if there is danger in delay, issue a written order to proceed with the inspection. In this event the order, which is made in the form of a decision, must be submitted to the President of the Court without delay for his ex post facto approval.[42] Article 81 provides that 'after the order or decision has been issued, the authorities of the

---

36 Article 22(1).
37 Cf, as far as England is concerned, *Scott v Avery* (1856) 5 HL Cas 811, 25 LJ Ex 308.
38 Euratom Treaty, art 18.
39 Ibid, art 22(2).
40 Ibid, art 23.
41 Ibid, art 81.
42 Ibid.

State concerned shall ensure that the inspectors have access to the places specified in the order or decision'.

The Rules of Procedure say little. Applications to the President, whether they seek an order requiring inspection or approval of a Commission decision, must set out the name and address of the persons or undertakings to be inspected, an indication of what is to be inspected and of the purpose of the inspection.[43] That is all. To this may be added the requirements of RP-ECJ 37. It would seem that the basic form of the application should follow that set out in RP-ECJ 38, mutatis mutandis. The form of order will seek an order requiring inspection or approving the Commission decision, as the case may be. In the latter event, the decision should be annexed to the application. The language of the proceedings will be the official language of the member state of which the defendant to the application is a national.[44]

The application is heard by the President of the Court or, if he is absent or prevented from sitting, by the president of one of the chambers or a judge, in accordance with the rules laid down in RP-ECJ 11.[45] The Rules of Procedure make no provision for the submission of written or oral argument to the President. In the case of applications for an order requiring inspection this is in practical terms excluded by the necessity to give the order within three days of the lodgment of the application. It is possible, however, to conceive of a situation in which there has already been considerable contact between the Commission and the person or undertaking subject to the inspection so that the latter is in a position to argue the case at short notice. Strictly speaking, in the absence even of any provision for service of the application, the President has the power to grant or reject it without hearing the other side, but, as a matter of practice, he should allow representations to be made to him as long as this would not jeopardise the effectiveness of any order to be made.

The relative simplicity of proceedings also suggests that the President's function is to ensure that the formal requirements for the exercise of the Commission's powers of inspection have been met and that is all. In the case of applications for approval of a decision requiring inspection, the President must also consider whether there really was danger in delay but it is likely that the Commission would be allowed a broad measure of discretion in assessing the situation, given its technical nature. The decision is made in the form of a reasoned order from which no appeal lies and it is served on the parties.[46] It would appear that the President may make an order for inspection conditional on the lodging of a security.[47] The making of the order does not, however, prejudice proceedings which may be brought before the Court to challenge the inspection;[48] the purpose of the President's order is only to cause the authorities of the member state to ensure the access required for the inspection or to give formal approval to the Commission's own decision to the same effect, it does not validate an unlawful decision to make an inspection.

---

43 RP-ECJ 90(1).
44 RP-ECJ 29(2). Should it not be a national of any member state, it would appear to be sufficient to frame the application in the official language of the member state in which the inspection is to take place.
45 RP-ECJ 90(2).
46 RP-ECJ 90(2) and 86(1).
47 RP-ECJ 86(2).
48 RP-ECJ 86(4).

E   Sanctions

1   Sanctions under art 83

Where a person or undertaking breaches obligations relating to the safeguards envisaged in the Treaty, the Commission may impose sanctions.[49] Its decision to do so may be challenged by bringing a direct action against the Commission before the Court. The Court has unlimited jurisdiction in such proceedings.[50] Lodgment of the application automatically suspends enforcement of the decision but the Court may order the decision to be enforced forthwith on application by the Commission or any member state concerned.[51] No specific procedure is laid down for such an application. It is to be supposed, although there is no authority for saying so, that the rules applying to applications for interim relief would apply, mutatis mutandis. Several points should be noted:

(1)   the application seeks the immediate enforcement of the decision in question and so it is to be considered as a request for the adoption of interim measures within the meaning of art 158 of the Euratom Treaty;

(2)   the defendant in the action is the Commission but the application for relief may be made either by it or by a member state, ie a person who is not a party to the proceedings; the right to apply is granted directly by art 83(2) of the Treaty and so there appears to be no necessity for the member state to intervene or be cited as a party;

(3)   power to grant relief is given to the Court but, as in the case of arts 157 and 158, this does not appear to prevent the President from making the order; and

(4)   the order cannot prejudice the outcome of the action.

Article 83(2) also provides that there shall be 'an appropriate legal procedure to ensure the protection of interests that have been prejudiced'. The significance of this is not particularly clear. It may have been intended as a pious exhortation. So far as is known, however, there is no special procedure for protecting interests that have been prejudiced, at least in Community law; but the interests of all persons concerned can and should be taken into account by the Court when making its decision. At the time of writing, an application had been made under art 83(2) in only one case: Case C-308/90 *Advanced Nuclear Fuels GmbH v Commission*.[52] The application was made by the defendant in the proceedings in the defence and by separate document. As in the case of any application for interim relief, it does not seem appropriate for the application to be made in the defence. The application was heard by the Court in plenary session. It was unopposed but an order was made nonetheless. In cases where the application is unopposed, it is still necessary to make an order for two reasons: first, since the sanctions in dispute are suspended automatically by virtue of art 83(2) upon commencement of proceedings before the Court, the suspensory effect of the commencement of proceedings may be lifted only by Court order and not by the consent of the person concerned; secondly, the requirement that there be 'an appropriate legal procedure to ensure the protection of interests that have been prejudiced' implies that the Court must scrutinise all applications for the removal of the mandatory suspension of the sanctions in question in order to ensure that its removal is objectively justified.

---

49   Article 83(1). Eg Decisions 90/413 and 90/465 (OJ No L209, p 27, and L241, p 14),which were at issue in Case C-308/90 *Advanced Nuclear Fuels GmbH v Commission* [1993] ECR I-309.
50   Article 144(b).
51   Article 83(2).
52   [1990] ECR I-4499 and above, note 49.

2 Other sanctions

In the case of infringements of the Treaty by a person or undertaking which do not fall within the scope of art 83, the procedure for imposing sanctions is somewhat different. The Commission must first call upon the member state 'having jurisdiction' over the person or undertaking in question to impose sanctions in accordance with national law.[53] If the member state fails to comply within a period fixed by the Commission for doing so, the Commission may start proceedings before the Court 'to have the infringement of which the person or undertaking is accused established'.[54] It is unclear if the Commission can do so where the member state has purported to take action but it has had no effect. It seems that, as long as sanctions have in fact been imposed, art 145 of the Treaty has been complied with and the Commission can do nothing more. The Treaty does not, however, appear to prevent the Commission from specifying a particular form of sanction to be taken by the member state, as long as it is compatible with national law. The injunction in art 145 relates to the means to be used: national law rather than Community law.

The proceedings brought by the Commission before the Court take the form of a normal direct action, the defendant being the author of the alleged infringement of the Treaty. It seems implicit in art 145 that the object of the action is to establish (i) that the defendant has committed the breach of the Treaty specified in the application and (ii) that this breach falls outside the scope of art 83. There is no express authority for saying that the Court can order the defendant to cease its violation of the Treaty if it finds in favour of the Commission. In consequence, it is difficult to see what practical advantage, aside from an award of costs, the Commission can gain. The implication seems to be that the Commission can seek to enforce the Court's judgment under art 164, but this presupposes that there is an order which can be enforced. A finding cannot be executed, therefore the Court must require, and the Commission must claim in its form of order, that the defendant take specific steps in order to comply with the Treaty; alternatively, the Court must itself impose, and the Commission claim, specific sanctions against the defendant. Neither possibility is expressly envisaged in the Treaty and both the Statute and the Rules of Procedure are silent on the matter.

F Special procedures under arts 103–105

Articles 103 to 105 of the Euratom Treaty lay down rules designed to ensure that the objectives of the Treaty are not frustrated by agreements or contracts entered into by the member states, a person or an undertaking with a third country, an international organisation or a national of a third country (hereafter, for the sake of brevity, referred to as 'agreements'). Although the Treaty is not precise in this respect, it is to be inferred that the makers of such agreements, other than the member states, are persons and undertakings who are subject to the jurisdiction of a member state.[55] It is to be noted that the agreements covered by these articles are those made with persons or bodies outside the Community, not within it. Each article relates to a different situation. Article 103 applies in the case of agreements about to be made by a

---

53 Article 145.
54 Ibid.
55 See, for example, RP-ECJ 106(2), which applies to proceedings under the last paragraph of arts 104 and 105 of the Euratom Treaty and which provides that the application commencing proceedings is to be served on 'the State to which the respondent person or undertaking belongs'. In that context, the word 'State' means 'member state'.

member state and sets out a 'Community supervisory procedure'[56] for the prior examination of their compatibility with the Treaty, the member state concerned refraining from concluding it until the procedure has terminated. Article 104 applies to agreements made or renewed by a person or undertaking after the entry into force of the Treaty and provides for the communication to the Commission of information relating to them so that the Commission may verify that they 'do not contain clauses impeding the implementation of this Treaty'. The Commission has power to apply to the Court for a ruling on compatibility with the Treaty. Under art 105, the Treaty cannot be invoked to prevent the implementation of agreements concluded before its entry into force by a member state, person or undertaking but agreements concluded by a person or undertaking between the signature and the entry into force of the Treaty cannot be invoked as grounds for failure to implement the Treaty 'if, in the opinion of the Court of Justice, ruling on an application from the Commission, one of the decisive reasons on the part of either of the parties in concluding the agreement or contract was an intention to evade the provisions' of the Treaty.

1   Proceedings under art 103

i   Nature of the proceedings   The member states must give the Commission a copy of the draft agreement[57] or contract which is to be concluded with the third country, international organisation or national of a third country 'to the extent that such agreements or contracts concern matters within the purview of this Treaty'.[58] It is unclear whether the phrase 'to the extent that' relates to the member states' draft agreements taken as a whole, in which case it is only those agreements 'which concern matters within the purview' of the Treaty which must be communicated to the Commission, or whether it refers to each draft agreement, in which case it is only that part of it which concerns 'matters within the purview' of the Treaty which must be communicated to the Commission. The better view seems to be the former.[59] Both interpretations leave it largely within the hands of the member state in question to decide whether or not to commence proceedings under art 103 in the sense that it must determine what the 'purview' of the Treaty is and whether the proposed agreement concerns matters that fall within it. It does not seem, however, that any particularly profound study of the question is necessary: 'purview' is not a technical term requiring a specific, restricted interpretation, it simply indicates the scope of the Treaty. If a member state were to fail to communicate a draft that, viewed objectively, did concern matters within the purview of the Treaty, this would constitute a breach of its obligations under the Treaty. If part only of the agreement concerns such matters, the entire text should nevertheless be communicated to the Commission.

If the Commission finds that the agreement 'contains clauses which impede the application of this Treaty', it must 'make its comments known' to the member state within one month of receipt of the draft. Once those comments have been received within the time limit, the member state has a choice between satisfying the objections raised by the Commission (if any) or applying to the Court for it to rule on 'the compatibility of the proposed clauses

56 See *Ruling 1/78* [1978] ECR 2151, para 3.
57 'Agreement' is probably to be construed in the same way as the Court indicated in *Opinion 1/75* [1975] ECR 1355 at 1359–1360.
58 Article 103.
59 Under RP-ECJ 105(2) the complete text of the agreement must accompany the member state's application to the Court.

with the provisions of this Treaty'. The member state cannot conclude the agreement until it has complied either with the Commission's objections or with the Court's ruling. Should it neither satisfy the Commission's objections nor apply to the Court for a ruling, but conclude the agreement, the Commission may commence proceedings under art 141 of the Euratom Treaty, or another member state under art 142, for a declaration that it has failed to fulfil its obligations under the Treaty. It is arguable that, unless the agreement does impede the application of the Treaty, the Commission is not empowered to make its comments known and the member state is not obliged to comply with any criticisms of the agreement made in them. If the Commission does not therefore specify in what way the application of the Treaty is impeded, the member state may ignore its comments altogether and conclude the agreement without waiting for a ruling from the Court. The alternative view is that the Commission may submit comments if it believes the clauses to be incompatible with the Treaty and the member state must either comply with its objections or apply to the Court; in the particular case where the Commission finds that the agreement impedes the application of the Treaty, art 103 merely imposes a time limit for the submission of the Commission's comments.

It is doubtful if this alternative interpretation of art 103 is correct because, if so, there would be no time limit at all for submission of the Commission's comments in the event that it found the agreement to be incompatible with the Treaty but not a hindrance to its application. The member state might therefore have to wait indefinitely before being in a position to conclude the agreement. It seems more likely that the two phrases 'impedes the application of the Treaty' and 'compatibility with the provisions of the Treaty' form the positive and negative of the same concept. In consequence, incompatibility with the Treaty is the same as impeding its application. If the Commission does not make its comments on the agreement known to the member state within one month of receiving a copy of it, the member state is entitled to assume that it is regarded by the Commission as being compatible with the Treaty and that it may be concluded. If the Commission submits comments between the expiry of the time limit and conclusion of the agreement, it would seem that the member state is still bound to comply with the Commission's objections or apply to the Court. Expiry of the one-month period simply gives the member state the green light to conclude the agreement but it does not appear to prevent the agreement from subsequently being regarded as contrary to the Treaty. As soon as the member state is on notice that the Commission regards the agreement as being incompatible with the Treaty, the green light has turned, if not to red, then to amber, even if the Commission's comments are late in time. It no longer lies in the mouth of the member state to say that it is unaware of the likelihood of a breach of its obligations under the Treaty if it goes ahead and concludes the agreement. Hence, a refusal to make use of the opportunity provided by the procedure in art 103 can be regarded as being contrary to its spirit and objectives. To rely on the formal point that the Commission had not made its comments known in time would subvert the purpose of art 103, which is to provide a procedure for ensuring that an agreement does not impede the application of the Treaty, because it is incompatible with it, by means of a preliminary examination of the agreement before it is concluded. Compliance with the Commission's objections and, a fortiori, with the Court's ruling, provides a good defence to a later charge that the member state failed to fulfil its obligations under the Treaty when it concluded the agreement. It is therefore in the interest of the member state to comply with the Commission's objections (or apply to the Court) even if they are made out of time.

Should the member state decline to satisfy the Commission's objections or apply to the Court but evince an intention to conclude the agreement, the Commission may commence proceedings under art 141 (or another member state under art 142) and apply for an order restraining the member state from concluding the agreement pending trial of the action by way of interim relief.[60] It is no defence in these proceedings that the member state, rightly, believed the agreement to be compatible with the Treaty. The object of art 103 is to make the Commission, in the first instance, and the Court, in the final instance, the sole judges of the question, not the member state, although there is no formal appeal from the Commission to the Court. Even if the member state were found to be right, it would still be in breach of the Treaty by taking the law into its own hands. If the member state complies with the Commission's objections, matters proceed no further, save that the agreement can be concluded. In the alternative, the member state may apply to the Court for a ruling at any time after receiving the Commission's comments. There is no time limit on making the application although there may be practical encouragements for it to act with due dispatch so that it can conclude the agreement. The Court itself must adjudicate 'urgently' on the application.[61] In the only case so far decided under art 103, the Court delivered its ruling in just over four months from the commencement of proceedings.[62]

This case arose over a dispute between the Council and the Commission relating to the necessity for the Community to be a party to a Convention on the Physical Protection of Nuclear Materials, Facilities and Transports. The Belgian government became concerned and formally communicated the draft text of the Convention to the Commission. The Commission informed the Belgian government of its comments over a month after the draft text had been sent to it, but the report does not make it clear whether it was within a month of receiving the draft text. In the Commission's view the member states could not subscribe to one of the articles in the draft without impeding the application of the Treaty and the only satisfactory solution was for the Community to be a party to the Convention. The Belgian government then referred the matter to the Court. This type of dispute is not the kind that appears to be envisaged by art 103 because, to some extent, the disagreement seems to have lain between the Council and the other member states, on the one hand, and the Commission and the Belgian government, on the other. The Court nevertheless held that the application was admissible because, under art 103, 'the Court's examination must take account of all the relevant rules of the Treaty whether they concern questions of substance, of jurisdiction or of procedure'.[63] The effect of this is to broaden the scope of the procedure so that it applies to the type of situation covered by art 228 of the EC Treaty,[64] for which there is no precise equivalent in the Euratom Treaty. The difference is that, under art 103, only a member state can seise the Court.

ii Procedure   No special procedural rules governing the procedure before the Court are laid down in the Euratom Statute. The Rules of Procedure provide that four certified copies of the application must be lodged[65] and that it must be accompanied by the draft of the agreement or contract in question, the

---

60 See chapter 8.
61 Article 103.
62 *Ruling 1/78* (above, note 56).
63 Ibid para 5.
64 See pp 588 et seq.
65 RP-ECJ 105(1).

observations concerning the draft, served by the Commission on the applicant, and all other supporting documents.[66] No further requirements concerning the application are laid down in the Rules of Procedure. Like all pleadings, however, it must comply with RP-ECJ 37, except with regard to the number of copies to be lodged. The language of the proceedings may be any of those which can be used before the Court. It is to be expected that it will be the applicant's official language.[67] By analogy with the position in cases under art 95 of the ECSC Treaty and art 228 of the EC Treaty,[68] it appears that the application should set out (i) the background and scope of the agreement in question and (ii) the applicant's reasons supporting or contesting the Commission's comments. These should make clear the points on which the Court's ruling is sought.

RP-ECJ 105(1) provides that the application is to be served (in the usual way) on the Commission and RP-ECJ 105(2) states that the Commission shall lodge its observations within a period of ten days.[69] There is no express provision for service on any other Community institution or member state or for the submission of observations by them. It is to be inferred that at this stage the proceedings concern only the applicant and the Commission. The period of ten days may be extended by the President, no doubt on application by the Commission, after the views of the applicant have been heard.[70] A certified copy of the Commission's observations is served on the applicant but the Rules say no more about their form and content. As is usual, however, they must comply with RP-ECJ 37. The Commission's observations in *Ruling 1/78* appear to have included a form of order, or suggested response to the questions raised by the applicant,[71] but this does not seem to be essential.

As soon as the application has been lodged, the President designates a judge to act as rapporteur and, when this has been done, the First Advocate General assigns the case to an advocate general.[72] It is also provided that the agents and advisers of the applicant and the Commission 'shall be heard if they so request'.[73] This appears to give the applicant and the Commission a right to be heard at their request. It does not, however, seem to exclude any power of the Court to invite them to make oral submissions should they not exercise this right. Similarly, the written part of the proceedings is in principle restricted to the applicant's application and the Commission's observations on it. No other Community institution or member state[74] has a right to submit written or oral observations to the Court. It would seem nevertheless that the Court may invite further written observations from the two parties to the proceedings and oral (if not also written) submissions from persons who are not parties. In addition, the Court may order a measure of enquiry should it consider this to be necessary. As an illustration, reference may be made to *Ruling 1/78*.[75] There the Court exercised its power under art 22 of the Euratom Statute, requiring the Belgian government and the Council to submit documents. The latter was not, of course, a party to the proceedings. It also invited the Council to attend

66 RP-ECJ 105(2).
67 In *Ruling 1/78* (above, note 56) it was French.
68 See pp 582 et seq and 588 et seq.
69 Time running from the service of the application on it.
70 RP-ECJ 105(2).
71 Above (note 56) at 2162.
72 RP-ECJ 105(3).
73 RP-ECJ 105(4). In *Ruling 1/78* (above, note 56) the parties were heard in the Deliberation Room, ie in camera (see at 2157.)
74 Or any other person or body.
75 Above (note 56) at 2156–2157.

the hearing, which it did, submitting its own oral observations on the case and replying to questions put by the Court.

It is unclear if the character of proceedings under art 103 is the same as that of proceedings under art 95 of the ECSC Treaty, ie they do not involve a 'full hearing of all sides', which would appear to entrain both a thorough investigation of disputed facts and the application of the various ancillary proceedings, such as intervention and judgment by default, to be found in a normal direct action.[76] On balance it would seem that this is not so because, unlike art 95, art 103 does envisage a situation where there is a dispute between two parties: the applicant and the Commission. For the same reason the proceedings under art 103 are not directly comparable to those under art 228 of the EC Treaty, which do not arise from a formal difference of opinion envisaged in the Treaty. It is therefore arguable that proceedings under art 103 attract the various ancillary procedures applicable in contentious proceedings, mutatis mutandis. On this basis there may well exist the possibility of intervention. The difficulty here lies in the time limit for intervening: three months from publication of the notice of the case in the Official Journal.[77] The Treaty and the Rules of Procedure envisage a swift, abbreviated procedure. A person wishing to intervene must therefore move fast but, if prevented from intervening by, for example, tardy publication of the notice, the possibility of third party proceedings may remain open.[78]

There are three difficulties in the way of the application of third party proceedings in the present context, two of principle and one purely practical. The practical difficulty is that, whether or not the Court's ruling finds the agreement to be compatible with the Treaty, it is impossible to see what interest, other than a theoretical one, there can be in having the ruling reversed after the member state has, in reliance on it, concluded the agreement.[79] The two objections of principle are that third party proceedings, according to art 40 of the Euratom Statute, apply where the Court's decision is 'prejudicial to the rights' of the third party and only in the case of 'judgments'. It would certainly seem to be prejudicial to the rights of a member state or Community institution if another member state were to be allowed to conclude an agreement that was (mistakenly) believed by the Court to be compatible with the Treaty. The Court's ruling is not, of course, in formal terms a judgment but the true test appears to be whether it is one in substance.[80] The substantive conditions for defining a decision of the Court as a judgment are discussed elsewhere.[81] In the present context it would seem that a ruling of the Court under art 103 can be considered a judgment because it gives a final, binding decision on a dispute between the parties.

The Court's ruling is delivered in closed session after the advocate general has been heard.[82] His opinion is not published and is delivered in camera.[83] Since the ruling is not given in open court, the parties are not given notice to attend when it is handed down. It is signed by the President and all the judges who took part in the deliberations but not, apparently, by the Registrar,[84] and served on the parties. In *Ruling 1/78* the Court made no order for costs. The

---

76 See *Opinion 1/59* [1959] ECR 259 at 271.
77 RP-ECJ 93(1).
78 RP-ECJ 97.
79 The same objection applies to revision of the ruling.
80 See Case 40/70 *Sirena Srl v Eda Srl* [1979] ECR 3169.
81 See chapter 16, pp 493 et seq.
82 RP-ECJ 105(4).
83 See *Ruling 1/78* (above, note 56) at 2157.
84 Ibid at 2181.

reason may have been that neither party asked for them. As a matter of principle, however, there is nothing to suggest that costs cannot be ordered. The fact that this is not done in opinions delivered under art 95 of the ECSC Treaty and art 228 of the EC Treaty appears to be irrelevant, given the difference in nature of the proceedings. Although the proceedings are contentious it does not seem that they are truly adversarial, with the result that the rules relating to judgment by default and, more particularly, setting aside such a judgment, do not apply. Naturally, if the Commission fails to submit any written observations and does not ask to be heard, the Court can still give its ruling. But if this happens, the Commission cannot seek to have the ruling set aside in reliance, whether directly or by analogy, on RP-ECJ 94(4)–(6). The reason is that the proceedings involve the public interest in ensuring that the application of the Treaty is not impeded, rather than purely private interests. Hence the Commission does not, strictly speaking, reply to the applicant but submits observations to the Court to aid the discharge of its task. A concession by the Commission is nihil ad rem in so far as the disposal of the case is concerned and so the basis for the application of the judgment by default provisions, together with the corresponding right to apply to set aside, is lacking. On the other hand, it would appear that the Court may correct slips in the text of the ruling and may give a decision on its interpretation.[85]

2 Proceedings under art 104

i Nature of the proceedings Article 104 falls into two parts. The first sentence declares that 'no person or undertaking concluding or renewing' an agreement after the entry into force of the Treaty 'may invoke that agreement or contract in order to evade the obligations imposed by this Treaty'. The rest of the article contains the procedure for vetting such agreements. The Commission is empowered to request the communication to it, by the member states, of all information relating to agreements falling within the purview of the Treaty which were concluded by a person or undertaking with a third country, international organisation or national of a third country after its entry into force. The Commission can exercise this power only 'for the purpose of verifying that such agreements or contracts do not contain clauses impeding the implementation of this Treaty'. The Commission may apply to the Court for a ruling on the compatibility of the agreement with the Treaty. There appears to be no duty binding the Commission to make the application or any time limit within which it must do so. The purpose of the procedure appears to be to resolve disputes arising over alleged conflicts between the agreement in question and the obligations imposed by the Treaty.

ii Procedure RP-ECJ 106(1) provides that RP-ECJ 37 et seq apply 'in a corresponding manner'. The proceedings therefore take the form of a direct action initiated by the Commission. Since there is a wholesale incorporation of the rules relating to direct actions, there would appear to be no special features applying to proceedings under art 104, save one. RP-ECJ 106(2) states that the Commission's application 'shall be served on the State to which the respondent person or undertaking belongs'. The precise significance of this is obscure in a number of respects. It is clear that the application is made against the 'person or undertaking' who has concluded (or renewed) the agreement in question. He, she or it is therefore the defendant. What is unclear is whether service of the application on the member state makes it a party to the proceedings and, if so, whether it is also a defendant. As is always the case in the absence of any authority, there is no certain answer, but there seem to be two alternative interpretations of the rule:

(1)   RP-ECJ 106(2) provides for what could be described as the automatic intervention of a member state in the proceedings: service does make the member state a party so there is no need for it to apply to intervene in the proceedings; on the other hand, it is not a defendant but has the option of supporting the case made out by either the Commission or the defendant. As far as the conduct of the written procedure is concerned, the member state simply lodges written observations.[86]

(2)   Service of the application does not make a member state a party to the proceedings but puts it on notice of their commencement so that it may apply to intervene.

There are arguments for and against both these interpretations. The objection to the first is that it requires much to be implied into the Rules of Procedure; the objection to the second is that all the member states would have adequate notice of the existence of the proceedings through the information in the Official Journal so that a special procedure for giving notice to a member state would seem to be pointless. The relative oddity of RP-ECJ 106(2) could be explicable if there were no general right of intervention at all but this seems to be contradicted by RP-ECJ 106(1).

The next problem is to consider which member state is to be served with the application. The English text of RP-ECJ 106(2) seems to have been inspired by the German version. The French text, on the other hand, refers to the member state '*dont ressortit*', and the Italian to the member state '*di cui sono soggetti*', the person or undertaking against whom proceedings are brought. All appear to indicate the member state to whose jurisdiction the respondent is subject. An undertaking incorporated in one member state with a branch in another can be said to 'belong' to, or be subject to, the jurisdiction of both, albeit to different degrees. Very much the same applies to the person who is a citizen of one member state but lives in another and, perhaps, works in a third. As far as proceedings under art 104 of the Euratom Treaty are concerned, one possible method of identifying the appropriate member state is by reference to the obligation to provide information to the Commission. The member state so bound is likely to be the one with whom the respondent has the closest connection. This may not necessarily be so and it may be more appropriate to work the other way round and look for the member state with the closest relevant connection to the respondent. In the case of a natural person, the connection might be permanent or habitual residence, in that of an undertaking the principal place of business (in so far as the agreement in question is concerned); but it is also arguable that the connection need only be incidental, eg by reference to the place of performance of the terms of the agreement or any part of them, which may make the respondent subject to the health and safety at work legislation of a particular member state. Naturally one cannot be dogmatic about the correct meaning of RP-ECJ 106(2), given the present lack of authority. It should be noted that, while the singular is used in the Rules, there seems to be no reason that a number of member states may not have equal claims to jurisdiction over the respondent, particularly in the case of an undertaking whose activities span more than one.

---

86 See, by analogy, RP-ECJ 93(5).

Service is, of course, the responsibility of the Court. While it may adopt the safest course of serving every member state to which the respondent may reasonably be regarded as 'belonging', failure to serve a particular member state may be construed as indicating the Court's view as to the proper construction of RP-ECJ 106(2).[87] In any event, failure to serve a member state which should have been served is not such a factor as to prejudice the conduct of proceedings as between the Commission and the respondent, nor is it such a defect of procedure as to vitiate them. Each party is responsible for conducting his own side of the case and failure to serve a member state does not in itself deprive the Commission or the respondent of the ability to do so. From the point of view of the member state, the mistaken failure to serve it can be remedied by an application to intervene. If there is no general right of intervention, failure to serve may provide the basis for an application originating third party proceedings.

The Rules of Procedure do not specify the form taken by the Court's decision. Article 104 of the Euratom Treaty refers to a 'ruling' but the incorporation by reference of the rules relating to direct actions indicates that it is, in substance at least, if not in name, a judgment.

3 Proceedings under art 105

Like art 104, art 105 falls into two parts. The first provides that the provisions of the Treaty do not prevent the implementation of agreements concluded before its entry into force by member states, persons or undertakings, where they have been communicated to the Commission not later than 30 days after the Treaty came into effect. The second part relates only to agreements concluded between the signature of the Treaty and its entry into force by a person or undertaking, but not a member state. Such agreements cannot be 'invoked as grounds for failure to implement this Treaty' if the Court rules that 'one of the decisive reasons on the part of either of the parties in concluding the agreement or contract was an intention to evade the provisions of this Treaty'. This is a question of fact rather than one of law. As in the case of art 104, proceedings for obtaining a ruling from the Court can be commenced only by the Commission and the same procedure applies.

VI   Special procedures under other instruments

A   Privileges and immunities

The Protocol on the Privileges and Immunities of the European Communities, which is annexed to the Treaty Establishing a Single Council and a Single Commission of the European Communities, gives effect to the provision in art 28 of that Treaty, that the European Communities 'shall enjoy in the territories of the Member States such privileges and immunities as are necessary for the performance of their tasks'.[88] That provision replaced the parallel provisions in the ECSC, EEC and Euratom Treaties and the similar Protocols attached thereto. Article 1 of the Protocol provides that: 'The premises and buildings of the Communities shall be inviolable. They shall be exempt from search, requisition, confiscation or expropriation. The property and assets of the Communities shall not be the subject of any administrative or legal

---

87 There would be consultation between the Registrar and the Court over whom to serve.
88 The Protocol was amended by a Protocol of the EU Treaty so as to cover the European Central Bank, the members of its organs and its staff.

measure of constraint without the authorisation of the Court of Justice.' Until the immunity of the Community (and the other persons or bodies covered by the Protocol) is lifted by the Court or, expressly, by the institution concerned, the operation of such measures of constraint remains suspended.[89] The Court may also waive the immunity accorded to the officials or other servants employed by it whenever waiver appears to it not to be contrary to the interests of the Community[90] but this is an administrative rather than a judicial function.

The expression 'administrative or legal measure of constraint' appears to cover all public authority acts, other than those of a Community institution, which constitute an intervention in the sphere of interest of a Community institution, such as a request to inspect the premises of an institution for an official purpose,[91] or enforce against the Community a decision which alters its legal position, such as an attachment or garnishee order intended to ensure payment to a person (the creditor) of a debt owed by another (the debtor) who is a creditor of the Community.[92] In the case of attachment or garnishee orders, the Court's jurisdiction under the Protocol is limited to considering whether or not the measure of constraint is likely to interfere with the proper functioning and independence of the Community; the remaining aspects of the proceedings are governed by the applicable national law.[93] In considering that question, the fact that the money or assets which are the subject of the measure of constraint belong, as a matter of national law, to the debtor, for whom they are held by the Community, is of no account.[94] On the other hand, the measure of constraint is not likely to interfere with the proper functioning and independence of the Community where it relates to assets or money which are due by the Community to the debtor and have already been allocated by the Community to payment to the debtor, whether the debtor be an official or servant of the Community to whom sums are owed by the Community by way of salary or a member state to whom sums are owed by the Community by way of rent.[95]

There is no specific procedure for applying for authorisation. Any person or national authority which is competent under national law to carry out the measure of constraint in question may apply for authorisation to do so.[96] An application for authorisation must be made in any case where the privileges or immunities of the Communities preclude the enforcement of a measure of constraint because, otherwise, a refusal by the institution concerned to comply with the measure of constraint is lawful, cannot be attacked in an action for annulment and does not give rise to a claim for damages.[97] Application should be made only after the institution concerned has been asked and has declined to comply voluntarily with the measure of constraint.[98] If the institution

89 Case C-182/91 *Forafrique Burkinabe SA v Commission* [1993] ECR I-2161 (paras 14 and 17). A failure by the institution concerned to take up a position on the enforcement of a measure of constraint does not constitute the lifting of the Community's immunity (para 18).

90 Protocol, art 18.

91 Cf Case 2/68 *Ufficio Imposte di Consumo di Ispra v Commission* [1968] ECR 435.

92 Case 4/62 *Re a Garnishee Order against the High Authority* [1962] ECR 41; Case 64/63 *Potvin v Van de Velde* [1963] ECR 47.

93 Case 1/87SA *Universe Tankship Co Inc v Commission* [1987] ECR 2807 (para 3).

94 Case 1/88SA *Générale de Banque SA v Commission* [1989] ECR 857 (para 9).

95 Ibid para 13. Where the financial interests of third parties might be affected by payment by the Community, the third parties concerned should have recourse to the remedies available to them under the applicable national law in the attachment or garnishee proceedings (para 15).

96 *Ufficio Imposte di Consumo* (above, note 91) at 438.

97 The *Forafrique Burkinabe* case (above, note 89) paras 14–17 and 22.

98 Case SA 1/71 *Application for authorisation to serve an attachment order on the EC Commission* [1971] ECR 363; the *Universe Tankship* case (above, note 93) para 5.

concerned does not in fact object to complying with the measure of constraint, the application is pointless and will be dismissed as such.[99] The application should be framed like one commencing proceedings in a direct action and proceedings take the same form.[1]

B Interpretative rulings

Various instruments confer on the Court jurisdiction to give interpretative rulings at the request of a person or persons other than a national court.

1 The Protocol on the Interpretation of the Convention on Jurisdiction and the Enforcement of Judgments in Civil and Commercial Matters

i Nature of the proceedings Article 4 of the Brussels Convention Protocol, as amended[2] empowers the Court to give rulings on the interpretation of the Convention itself, the two Protocols annexed thereto and the conventions by which Denmark, Greece, Ireland, Portugal, Spain and the United Kingdom acceded to the Convention.[3] The power to deliver such rulings is additional to the power to deliver preliminary rulings on interpretation at the request of a court in one of the contracting states.[4] The essential difference between these two proceedings for obtaining an authoritative ruling from the Court on the interpretation of the Convention or one of the other instruments mentioned, lies in the fact that the preliminary ruling is delivered as a step in proceedings before a national court concerning the application of the instrument in question to a concrete case, whereas the ruling delivered under art 4 of the Protocol on Interpretation is made outside the context of pending litigation in a contracting state.

ii The power to request a ruling Article 4(1) states that 'the competent authority of a Contracting State' may request a ruling. Article 4(3) defines the competent authority as 'the Procurators-General of the Courts of Cassation of the Contracting States, or any other authority designated by a Contracting State'. In consequence, in countries possessing a court of cassation, the procurator-general, if any, is empowered directly by the Protocol to request a ruling. In other contracting states, no person has this power unless designated by that state. No procedure is laid down for making such a designation. The matter appears to be covered by national law. In the report on the Protocol produced by Mr P Jenard,[5] it is said that the contracting states are empowered to designate more than one authority competent to request a ruling. Article 4(1) and (3) is not clear on this point but there seems to be no compelling reason for construing the reference to 'competent authority' (in the singular) so as to exclude the plural. By the same token, it would appear that contracting states in which there is a procurator-general in the court of cassation are not

---

99 The *Universe Tankship* case (above, note 93), paras 6–7; Case C-40/90SA *Herbosch*, unreported order of 7 November 1990 (the Commission had not raised any objection to the enforcement by a creditor of a garnishee order obtained from a national court on the ground that the enforcement of the order would not interfere with its functioning).

1 Case 2/68 *Ufficio Imposte de Consumo di Ispra v Commission* [1968] ECR 435 (see also per Advocate General Roemer).

2 See the amended version published in OJ No C189 of 28 July 1990, p 25 and Appendix, below, p 717.

3 Articles 1 and 4(1) of the Protocol.

4 Article 2 of the Protocol; see section II.G, above pp 552 et seq.

5 OJ C59 of 5 March 1979, p 66; see p 69.

prevented from appointing another person competent to request a ruling, in addition to the procurator-general. On the other hand, the latter's power to request a ruling, cannot, it seems, be excluded or amended without a revision of the Protocol.

The power to request a ruling applies 'if judgments given by the courts of that State' (ie the state of the authority competent to request a ruling) 'conflict with the interpretation given either by the Court of Justice or in a judgment of one of the courts of another Contracting State referred to in point 1 or 2 of Article 2'.[6] The power is discretionary[7] and no guidelines for its exercise are laid down in the Protocol. In the Jenard report,[8] it is said that it is for the competent authority to decide whether it is advisable to refer a matter to the Court and that 'it will presumably not do so unless the national judgment includes reasons which might lead to an interpretation different from that previously given by the Court of Justice or by a foreign court. If there are no factors involved which make it likely that the principles established in the decided cases would be changed, the national authority could always seek to clarify the point of law by appealing in its own country in accordance with the procedure there in force.'

The French version of the report is not to the same effect. It suggests that the usual method of dealing with a judgment which is in conflict with the case law of the Court or the courts of another contracting state, and which is not appealed by one of the parties, will be an appeal under national law at the motion of the competent authority. This presupposes that such an appeal is possible under national procedural law, which was indeed the case for all of the six original contracting states, save the Federal Republic of Germany. On this basis, the problem of interpretation would come before the Court by way of a reference for a preliminary ruling and the procedure envisaged in art 4 of the Protocol would be used only in exceptional cases where it was not possible under national law to bring the matter before a national court with power to make a reference under art 2 of the Protocol. At all events, the Protocol itself is silent on how the discretion to refer under art 4 should be exercised. The matter is for the competent authority alone to decide. A request for a ruling would not, it would seem, be inadmissible simply because the matter might have been brought before the Court by another route. As long as the basic conditions determining the existence of the power are fulfilled, the exercise of that power cannot be questioned, at least by the Court. It is, however, arguable that the existence of a power to request a ruling carries with it a responsibility to ensure that the power is exercised in order to prevent the emergence of a divergent body of case law: the competent authority cannot stand by and do nothing because this would defeat the purpose of the Convention as a whole and the existence of the power to request a ruling in particular.

Apart from the designation of the competent authority, whether by the Protocol itself, in the case of procurators-general of national courts of cassation, or by the contracting state, the basic conditions for requesting a ruling are the following:

(1)   there must be at least one judgment of a court in the contracting state of the competent authority;
(2)   it must conflict with the interpretation of the Convention or the other instruments referred to in art 1 of the Protocol given by either:

6   Article 4(1).
7   Ibid. The French and Italian versions are more emphatic than the English text: '*L'autorité compétent . . . a la faculté*'; '*L'autorità competente . . . ha facoltà*'.
8   Above, note 5 at 69–70.

(a)   the Court, or
(b)   one of the courts of another contracting state referred to in points 1 or 2 of art 2; and

(3)   both the judgment of the court in the competent authority's contracting state and the judgments with which it is in conflict must have the force of res judicata.

It is to be observed that, so far as the first condition is concerned, the judgment may be delivered by *any* court in the competent authority's own contracting state. It does not matter if the court is one which could or could not have referred the matter to the Court for a preliminary ruling. The fact that the Protocol refers to a 'judgment' does not mean that decisions delivered in a form other than that of a 'judgment' as defined under national procedural law cannot give rise to a request for a ruling. Other language versions of art 4(1) of the Protocol refer simply to 'decisions' and, like the Convention itself, the Protocol must in any event be given an interpretation independent of the concepts prevailing in any one contracting state.[9] In order for the second condition to be fulfilled, the judgment of the court in the competent authority's contracting state must interpret or apply the Convention or other instrument in a manner which is at variance with the interpretation given by the Court, whether in response to a request for a preliminary ruling or a request under art 4 of the Protocol, or by a court in any one of the other contracting states. So far as the latter is concerned, a conflict with the interpretation given by *any* court in another contracting state is insufficient: the conflict must arise in relation to an interpretation given by one of the courts specified in points 1 and 2 of art 2 of the Protocol. The courts mentioned in point 3 of art 2 appear to be excluded only when they exercise the powers envisaged in art 37 of the Convention. It would also appear that a variation between judgments delivered by courts in different parts of a contracting state (such as, in the case of the United Kingdom, England and Scotland) could not ground a request for a ruling under art 4: they are all courts in the same contracting state, although they may not be in the same jurisdiction for the purpose of applying the Convention. The third basic condition is linked to art 4(2) of the Protocol, which provides that the ruling given in response to the request for interpretation 'shall not affect the judgments which gave rise to the request for interpretation'. This seems to apply to all of the judgments in question. The Jenard report explains[10] that the object of the ruling is simply to ensure the uniform interpretation of the Convention and the other instruments in question wherever *existing* judgments are in conflict but it is not intended to affect the position of the parties to those judgments and so 'cannot give rise to any fresh proceedings, even where otherwise an extraordinary avenue of appeal might be appropriate'.

iii   Procedure   No rules are laid down governing the form and content of the request made by the competent authority. It would appear that it should be made in writing and should indicate that the basic conditions for making the request have been fulfilled. The object of the request is to obtain a ruling which will settle the variation in interpretation which has arisen. In consequence, the nature of the variation should be identified. This may require the

---

9   Article 25 of the Convention defines 'judgment' as 'any judgment given by a court or tribunal of a Contracting State, whatever the judgment may be called, including a decree, order, decision or writ of execution, as well as the determination of costs or expenses by an officer of the court'.
10   Above (note 5) at 69–70.

competent authority to annex to the request the text of the judgment of the national court in question and, if necessary, any background material which will explain the context in which the judgment was delivered: even though the Court's ruling cannot affect the parties to the judgment, it can only appreciate the question of interpretation raised if the factual elements of the case are established. After the request has been lodged at the Court, the Court's Registrar notifies it to the contracting states, the Commission and the Council, which then have two months running from the date of notification in which to submit statements of case or written observations to the Court.[11] No rules are laid down concerning the form and content of the statement of case or written observations. It would appear that the same rules apply, mutatis mutandis, as in the case of written observations in references for a preliminary ruling. From this point on, the remainder of the proceedings follows as in the case of a preliminary ruling.[12] It does not seem that a failure to submit written observations is a bar to the submission of oral observations at the hearing. It should be observed that only the contracting states, the Commission and the Council may submit observations. No one else is entitled to do so, not even, so it would seem, the competent authority making the request. The Court gives judgment in the usual way. No order for costs is made and no fees may be levied in the proceedings.[13]

The Jenard report[14] has this to say of the effects of the Court's judgment: 'it may be wondered what are the implications of a ruling on interpretation given on the basis of art 4. The ruling certainly is not binding on the parties. It must be acknowledged that such a ruling has no force in law, and that accordingly nobody is bound by it. But clearly it will have the greatest persuasive authority and will for the future constitute the guideline for all Community courts. In this respect it may be compared with the decision on a "pourvoi dans l'intérêt de la loi". Such a decision is binding on nobody, but constitutes a decision of principle of the greatest importance for the future, and one which judges will generally follow.'

2   *The First Protocol on the Interpretation of the Convention on the Law applicable to Contractual Obligations*

In wording to all intents and purposes the same as that of art 4 of the Brussels Convention Protocol, art 3 of the Rome Convention Protocol empowers the Court to give rulings on the interpretation of the provisions of the Rome Convention itself, the Convention on accession to the Rome Convention by states which become members of the Community after the date on which the Rome Convention was open for signature, and the Rome Convention Protocol.[15] Such rulings may be requested by the competent authority of a contracting state, defined in the Protocol as the Procurators-General of the Supreme Courts of Appeal of the contracting states or any other authority designated by a contracting state.[16] The preconditions for requesting such a ruling,[17] the

---

11 Article 4(4) of the Protocol.
12 Article 5(1) of the Protocol and RP-ECJ 103(2).
13 Article 4(5) of the Protocol.
14 Above (note 5) at 70.
15 For the text of the relevant provisions of the Rome Convention Protocol, see OJ No L48 of 20 February 1989, p 1, and the Appendix, p 714 below. The Court's jurisdiction under the Rome Convention Protocol was conferred on it pursuant to the Second Protocol to the Rome Convention. The reasons for the existence of two Protocols concerning the Court's interpretative jurisdiction are set out in the Tizzano report on the protocols on the interpretation by the Court of the Rome Convention (OJ No C219 of 3 September 1990, p 1).
16 Article 3(1) and (3).
17 Article 3(1).

procedure to be followed[18] and the effects of such a ruling[19] are the same as in the case of interpretative rulings requested under the Brussels Convention Protocol.

3 The Agreement relating to Community Patents

i Nature of the proceedings Article 2(3) of the Agreement[20] empowers the Court to give a ruling in response to a request made by a member state or the Commission. Such a request may be made only if the applicant for a ruling 'considers that a decision of the Common Appeal Court (established by the Protocol on Litigation) which closes the procedure before it does not comply with the principle stated in' art 2(1) and (2) of the Agreement. That principle is in fact set out in art 2(1) and is to the effect that no provision of the Agreement may be invoked against the application of the EC Treaty. Article 2(2) of the Agreement gives effect to that principle by imposing on the Common Appeal Court the obligation to request the Court for a preliminary ruling 'whenever there is a risk of an interpretation of this Agreement being inconsistent with' the EC Treaty. The preconditions for the making of such a request are, in consequence, that: the Common Appeal Court has made a decision which closes the procedure before it; and the applicant for the ruling considers that that decision produces, or risks producing, an inconsistency between the Agreement and the EC Treaty. The first condition is satisfied only if the decision in question is final and leaves the Common Appeal Court functus officio. The second condition is satisfied where, in the subjective opinion of the applicant for the ruling, there is an inconsistency or a risk of one. It should be noted that the making by the Common Appeal Court of a reference to the Court for a preliminary ruling does not preclude expressly the subsequent request for a ruling under art 2(3). That might be regarded as implicit in the reference in art 2(3) to art 2(2): if the Common Appeal Court has already considered that there was a risk of an inconsistency and had taken the precaution of obtaining a preliminary ruling from the Court before making a final decision, why should a member state or the Commission need to request a ruling under art 2(3)? However, there is a sound reason that the obtaining of a preliminary ruling cannot, as a matter of principle, preclude a subsequent request under art 2(3): the member state concerned or the Commission might consider that, in interpreting or applying the Court's preliminary ruling, the Common Appeal Court had perpetuated the inconsistency or produced another one.

ii Procedure There is no express time limit for the making of a request. It cannot be excluded that the Court may rule that a request must be made within a reasonable period after the delivery by the Common Appeal Court of the decision in question. On the other hand, the principle that the Agreement should not give rise to inconsistencies with the EC Treaty is mandatory and, arguably, should not be subject to any time limit for establishing whether or not such an inconsistency has arisen. In practice, it does not seem that the absence of express provision for a time limit will cause any difficulties: if a decision of the Common Appeal Court should lead to an inconsistency or risk of an inconsistency between the Agreement and the EC Treaty, that

---

18 Articles 3(4) and (5) and 4.
19 Article 3(2).
20 See OJ No L401 of 30 December 1989, p 1, and the Appendix at p 718 below.

situation will sooner or later give rise to litigation which may result in a request for a preliminary ruling made to the Court under arts 2(2) or 3 of the Agreement; or else to an opportunity for a request to be made by a member state or the Commission under art 2(3) concerning some later decision of the Common Appeal Court.

The proceedings are subject to the EC Statute and the Court's Rules of Procedure.[21] No rules are expressly laid down concerning the form and content of the request but, as a matter of principle, it should comply with RP-ECJ 37. The request should set out the reasons the applicant for a ruling considers that the conditions for making the request have been satisfied and the ruling sought. From the nature of the proceedings, it is implicit that the only ruling that can be sought in such a request is a ruling that the interpretation of the Agreement adopted by the Common Appeal Court is inconsistent with the EC Treaty. When the request is made by the Commission, the notice of the request is given by the Registrar of the Court to the Council and to the member states; when the request is made by a member state, notice of it is given to the other member states, the Council and the Commission.[22] It is implicit that a copy of the request will be served on those given notice. The correct number of copies of the request to be provided to the Court can be inferred from the number of persons to whom notice is to be given.[23] Those given notice of the request have two months within which to submit statements of case or written observations to the Court.[24] Time starts to run from notification to them of the making of the request, which should therefore be accompanied by service of the request itself. Time is extended by the usual periods of grace on account of distance[25] but there is no provision for obtaining an extension of time from the President of the Court. By analogy with the time limits for submitting written observations in references for a preliminary ruling, the period cannot be extended by the President or anyone else. The reference to 'statements of case or written observations' reflects the terms used in art 20 of the EC Statute to describe the written observations lodged by member states and Community institutions in references for a preliminary ruling. Such pleadings must be lodged in writing and may for the sake of convenience be entitled, and take the form of, written observations as in references for a preliminary ruling. The written observations should include as a form of order the ruling that the person lodging the observations wishes the Court to make, which may support or oppose the ruling sought by the applicant. There is no provision for preparatory enquiries or a hearing. The former appear to be unnecessary because the issue before the Court is essentially one of law. There is, however, scope for the Court to exercise its discretion and ask the member states or Community institutions to provide information or answer questions. In the same way, it seems to be within the discretion of the Court to invite the member states and Community institutions concerned to address the Court orally, should the Court think it appropriate. In the ordinary course, it may be anticipated that there would be a hearing or at least a further exchange of written observations after the lodgment of the observations submitted in

---

21 Article 4(1) of the Agreement. Article 4(2) provides for the adaptation and supplementing of the Rules of Procedure, where necessary. At the time of writing, no changes in the Rules of Procedure had been made to deal expressly with proceedings under art 2(3) of the Agreement.
22 Article 2(3) of the Agreement.
23 See RP-ECJ 37(1).
24 Article 2(3) of the Agreement.
25 See p 207.

response to the request; otherwise, the Court would not have the benefit of comment by the parties on the points made by the other parties in response to the request.[26] There is no provision for the delivery of an opinion by the advocate general. On the assumption that the proceedings are properly to be considered to be a reference for interpretation, the usual rules applicable to references for a preliminary ruling would apply.[27] No fees are levied or any costs or expenses awarded in respect of the proceedings.[28] Like references for a preliminary ruling, the proceedings do not have the character of litigation inter partes but are dominated by the public interest in avoiding inconsistencies between the Agreement and the EC Treaty. The exceptional procedures for reviewing judgments of the Court do not, in consequence, apply. On the other hand, unlike references for a preliminary ruling, there seems to be no good reason why an application cannot be made to the Court for an interpretation of the ruling given by it in response to a request under art 2(3) of the Agreement.

The Court's ruling will establish whether or not the decision of the Common Appeal Court in question gives rise to an inconsistency between the Agreement and the EC Treaty. In either event, the ruling does not affect the decision of the Common Appeal Court which gave rise to the request so far as the parties to that decision are concerned.[29] The effect of the ruling is, nonetheless, to determine the future interpretation and application of the Agreement by indicating the existence or otherwise of an inconsistency between the two instruments.

4 The Agreement on the European Economic Area

Article 111(3) provides that contracting parties to the EEA Agreement may agree to request the Court to give a ruling on the interpretation of provisions of the Treaty which are identical in substance to corresponding rules of the EC or ECSC Treaties or to acts adopted in application of the EC or ECSC Treaties. For such a request to be made, there must not only be agreement between the contracting parties concerned to submit the matter to the Court but also a dispute between those contracting parties concerning the case law regarding the relevant provisions of the EEA Agreement. The Court is not entrusted with the function of settling that dispute; it merely provides an interpretation of the relevant provisions but that interpretation is binding on the contracting parties and the Joint Committee set up under the EEA Agreement.[30] Thus, the ruling given by the Court does not affect in any way the outcome of the cases which have given rise to the dispute.[31] No special procedure governing such proceedings exists. It seems likely that the procedure to be followed is the same as that where a dispute is submitted to the Court by special agreement between the member states.[32]

---

26 See the practice followed in regard (for example) to the delivery of opinions under art 228 of the EEC Treaty: section IV.C above.

27 See RP-ECJ 103(2), second subpara.

28 Article 2(3) of the Agreement.

29 Ibid.

30 *Opinion 1/92* [1992] ECR I-2821 (paras 34–35). For the text of the EEA Agreement see OJ No L1 of 3 January 1994 pp 3 et seq.

31 No doubt, if one of them were still under appeal when the Court gave its ruling, the appellate court would be obliged to take that ruling into account when deciding the appeal.

32 See section II.J above pp 570 et seq.

C   Miscellaneous

Under a number of conventions and agreements[33] the Court or its President are empowered to make certain appointments, generally the chairman or members of an arbitration board. It would appear that application is made by letter to the person given the power of appointment.

D   The Community trade mark

Regulation No 40/94,[34] provides for the registration of a Community trade mark. Among the consequential arrangements is a system of legal remedies which involves the Court. The jurisdiction conferred on the Court by the Regulation is exercised at first instance by the CFI in accordance with Council Decision 88/591, as amended.[35]

In the first place, the Court has jurisdiction to hear appeals from appeal decisions of the Boards of Appeals created by the Regulation.[36] The Court's jurisdiction is wider than that in an ordinary action for annulment because it can either annul or alter the contested decision.[37] An action for the annulment or alteration of such a decision must be brought within two months of the date of notification of the contested decision to the parties to the proceedings before the Board of Appeal.[38] The action can be brought only by a party to the proceedings before the Board of Appeal who has been adversely affected by the contested decision.[39] The grounds on which the action can be based are: lack of competence; infringement of an essential procedural requirement; infringement of the EC Treaty; infringement of Regulation No 40/94; infringement of any rule of law relating to the application of the Treaty or that Regulation; misuse of power.[40] Commencement of such an action within time has the effect of preventing the contested decision from taking effect until judgment in the action.[41] The Regulation makes no express provision for the grant of interim relief. In many cases, no such relief may be appropriate as a result of the automatic suspension of the operation of the contested decision caused by the commencement of the action. However, it would seem that proceedings before the Court take the form of an ordinary direct action and therefore, in principle, interim relief is available where appropriate. The action must be commenced by a written application in the usual form and the written procedure and all successive stages in the proceedings follow as in a direct action. As in any such action, an appeal lies to the ECJ from a decision of the CFI. The Regulation

---

33 Eg art 29 of the Convention of 19 April 1972 setting up the European University Institute (OJ C29 of 9 February 1976, p 1), which provides that the President may appoint the arbitration body to be called on to settle disputes arising between the contracting states or between one or more contracting states and the Institute. Annex 1 of the Convention provides that the Court may itself be designated as the arbitration body. Similar powers were given to the Court under art 8(4) of the EC Treaty, which has ceased to have effect, and art 1(3) of the Protocol on certain provisions relating to France, attached to the EC Treaty.

34 20 December 1993, OJ No L11 of 14 January 1994, p 1. The Regulation entered into force on the 60th day after publication in the Official Journal (see art 143(1)), that is, on 14 March 1994.

35 See the 17th recital to the preamble to the Regulation.

36 Regulation No 40/94, art 63(1).

37 Ibid art 63(3).

38 Art 63(5). That period would be extended by the usual periods of grace on account of distance.

39 Art 63(4).

40 Art 63(2).

41 Art 62(3). If the action is successful, the contested decision never comes into effect unless it is merely altered by the Court, in which case it comes into effect in its altered form; if the action is unsuccessful, the contested decision comes into effect on the day of delivery of judgment in the action.

provides that 'The Office (that is, the Office for Harmonisation in the Internal Market (trade marks and designs) created by the Regulation) shall be required to take the necessary measures to comply with the judgment of the Court of Justice'.[42] Thus, the outcome of the action is not only to annul or alter or uphold a decision of the Board of Appeal but also to impose a specific obligation on the Office to comply with the judgment. That obligation applies as between the parties to the proceedings; it does not appear to apply to third parties or to other actual or potential proceedings. Nonetheless, it may be surmised that a judgment of the Court may well guide the future actions of the Office in other cases.

Final decisions of the Office fixing the amount of costs are enforceable subject to compliance with certain formalities.[43] Enforcement may be suspended only by a decision of the Court.[44] The procedure to be followed appears to be the same as that appropriate when seeking suspension of the enforcement of a decision of the Court or of any measure adopted by another Community institution.[45]

The Court has jurisdiction to give judgment pursuant to any arbitration clause contained in a contract concluded by the Office.[46] That jurisdiction appears to be exercised in the same way as the parallel jurisdiction of the Court under the Treaties.[47]

The Court also has jurisdiction in disputes relating to the non-contractual liability of the Office.[48] That jurisdiction is exercised in the same way as the jurisdiction of the Court over the non-contractual liability of the Communities.[49]

Lastly, the Court has jurisdiction to entertain applications for the removal from office of members of the Boards of Appeal.[50] Such an application is made by the body appointing the member concerned (that is, the Council) and must set out the serious grounds justifying the member's removal from office. That jurisdiction is exercised in the same way as the parallel jurisdiction over members of the Commission.[51]

---

42 Art 63(6).
43 Art 82(1) to (3).
44 Art 82(4).
45 RP-ECJ 89; RP-CFI 110. See chapter 8, pp 246 et seq.
46 Regulation No 40/94, art 114(2).
47 See pp 569 et seq.
48 Regulation No 40/94, art 114(3) to (4).
49 See pp 546 et seq.
50 Regulation No 40/94, art 131(1).
51 See pp 572 et seq.

Appendix

Protocol on the Statute of the Court of Justice of the European Coal and Steel Community

Article 1

The Court of Justice established by Article 7 of the Treaty shall be constituted and shall function in accordance with the provisions of this Treaty and of this Statute.

TITLE I

JUDGES

Oath of Office

Article 2

Before taking up his duties each Judge shall, in open court, take an oath to perform his duties impartially and conscientiously and to preserve the secrecy of the deliberations of the Court.

Privileges and Immunities

Article 3[1]

The Judges shall be immune from legal proceedings. After they have ceased to hold office, they shall continue to enjoy immunity in respect of acts performed by them in their official capacity, including words spoken or written.

The Court, sitting in plenary session, may waive the immunity.

Where immunity has been waived and criminal proceedings are instituted against a Judge, he shall be tried, in any of the Member States, only by the court competent to judge the members of the highest national judiciary.

Disqualifications

Article 4

The Judges may not hold any political or administrative office.

They may not engage in any occupation, whether gainful or not, unless exemption is exceptionally granted by the Council, acting by a two-thirds majority.

They may not acquire or retain, directly or indirectly, any interest in any business related to coal and steel during their term of office and for three years after ceasing to hold office.

---

1 Article 3 contained a fourth paragraph which was repealed by the second paragraph of art 28 of the Treaty Establishing a Single Council and a Single Commission of the European Communities (the 'Merger Treaty') and effectively replaced by art 21 of the Protocol on the Privileges and Immunities of the European Communities, which provides:

> Articles 12 to 15 and Article 18 shall apply to the Judges, the Advocates-General, the Registrar and the Assistant Rapporteurs of the Court of Justice, without prejudice to the provisions of Article 3 of the Protocols on the Statute of the Court of Justice concerning immunity from legal proceedings of Judges and Advocates-General.

Remuneration

Article 5[2]

Termination of Appointment

Article 6

Apart from normal replacement, the duties of a Judge shall end on his death or resignation.

Where a Judge resigns, his letter of resignation shall be addressed to the President of the Court for transmission to the President of the Council. Upon this notification a vacancy shall arise on the bench.

Save where Article 7 applies, a Judge shall continue to hold office until his successor takes up his duties.

Article 7

A Judge may be deprived of his office only if, in the unanimous opinion of the other Judges, he no longer fulfils the requisite conditions.

The President of the Council, the President of the High Authority and the President of the Assembly shall be notified thereof by the Registrar.

A vacancy shall arise on the bench upon this notification.

Article 8

A Judge who is to replace a member of the Court whose term of office has not expired shall be appointed for the remainder of his predecessor's term.

TITLE II

ORGANISATION

Article 9

The Judges, the Advocates-General and the Registrar shall be required to reside at the place where the Court has its seat.

Article 10[3]

The Court shall be assisted by [six] Advocates-General and a Registrar.

Advocates-General

Article 11

It shall be the duty of the Advocate-General, acting with complete impartiality and independence, to make, in open court, oral and reasoned submissions on cases brought before the Court, in order to assist the Court in the performance of the task assigned to it in Article 31 of this Treaty.

Article 12[4]

The Advocates-General shall be appointed for a term of six years in the same manner as the Judges. Every three years there shall be a partial replacement. [Three

---

2 Article 5 was repealed by art 8(3)(a) of the Merger Treaty and effectively replaced by Article 6 thereof, which provides:

> The Council shall, acting by a qualified majority, determine the salaries, allowances and pensions of the President and members of the Commission, and of the President, Judges, Advocates-General and Registrar of the Court of Justice. It shall also, again by a qualified majority, determine any payment to be made instead of remuneration.

3 See art 4(2)(b) of the Convention on Certain Institutions Common to the European Communities and art 32a of the ECSC Treaty, as last amended pursuant to the Act of Accession of Spain and Portugal, art 18.

4 See art 4(2) of the Convention on Certain Institutions Common to the European Communities and art 32b of the ECSC Treaty, as amended.

Advocates-General shall be replaced on each occasion.] The provisions of [the third paragraph of Article 32a and the fourth paragraph of Article 32b of this Treaty] and the provisions of Article 6 of this Statute shall apply to the Advocates-General.

Article 13

The provisions of Articles 2 to 5 and of Article 8 shall apply to the Advocates-General.

An Advocate-General may be deprived of his office only if he no longer fulfils the requisite conditions. The decision shall be taken by the Council, acting unanimously, after the Court has delivered its opinion.

Registrar

Article 14[5]

The Court shall appoint its Registrar and lay down the rules governing his service, account being taken of the provisions of Article 15. The Registrar shall take an oath before the Court to perform his duties impartially and conscientiously and preserve the secrecy of the deliberations of the Court.

Article 15[6]

Staff of the Court

Article 16[7]

1   Officials and other servants shall be attached to the Court to enable it to function. They shall be responsible to the Registrar under the authority of the President.

2   On a proposal from the Court, the Council may, acting unanimously, provide for the appointment of Assistant Rapporteurs and lay down the rules governing their service. The Assistant Rapporteurs may be required, under conditions laid down in the rules of procedure, to participate in preparatory inquiries in cases pending before the Court and to cooperate with the Judge who acts as Rapporteur.

The Assistant Rapporteurs shall be chosen from persons whose independence is beyond doubt and who possess the necessary legal qualifications; they shall be appointed by the Council. They shall take an oath before the Court to perform their duties impartially and conscientiously and to preserve the secrecy of the deliberations of the Court.

Functioning of the Court

Article 17

The Court shall remain permanently in session. The duration of the judicial vacations shall be determined by the Court with due regard to the needs of its business.

Composition of the Court

Article 18[8]

The Court shall sit in plenary session. It may, however, form [. . .] Chambers, each consisting of three [or five] Judges, either to undertake certain preparatory enquiries or to adjudicate on particular categories of cases in accordance with rules laid down for these purposes.

---

5 The second paragraph was repealed by the second paragraph of art 28 of the Merger Treaty and effectively replaced by art 21 of the Protocol on the Privileges and Immunities of the European Communities: see footnote 1, above.

6 Article 15 was repealed by art 8(3)(a) of the Merger Treaty and effectively replaced by art 6 thereof: see footnote 2, above.

7 As amended by art 8(3)(b) of the Merger Treaty.

8 See art 4(2) of the Convention on Certain Institutions Common to the European Communities, art 32 of the ECSC Treaty, as amended.

Decisions of the Court shall be valid only when an uneven number of its members is sitting in the deliberations. Decisions of the full Court shall be valid if seven members are sitting. Decisions of the Chambers shall be valid only if three Judges are sitting: in the event of one of the Judges of a Chamber being prevented from attending, a Judge of another Chamber may be called upon to sit in accordance with conditions laid down in the rules of procedure.

Actions brought by States or by the Council shall in all cases be tried in plenary session.

Special Rules

Article 19

No Judge or Advocate-General may take part in the disposal of any case in which he has previously taken part as agent or adviser or has acted for one of the parties, or on which he has been called upon to pronounce as a member of a court or tribunal, of a commission of inquiry or in any other capacity.

If, for some special reason, any Judge or Advocate-General considers that he should not take part in the judgment or examination of a particular case, he shall so inform the President. If, for some special reason, the President considers that any Judge or Advocate-General should not sit or make submissions in a particular case, he shall notify him accordingly.

Any difficulty arising as to the application of this Article shall be settled by decision of the Court.

A party may not apply for a change in the composition of the Court or of one of its Chambers on the grounds of either the nationality of a Judge or the absence from the Court or from the Chamber of a Judge of the nationality of that party.

TITLE III

PROCEDURE

Representation of and Assistance to the Parties

Article 20[9]

The States and the institutions of the Community shall be represented before the Court by an agent appointed for each case; the agent may be assisted by a lawyer entitled to practise before a court of a Member State.

Undertakings and all other natural or legal persons must be assisted by a lawyer entitled to practise before a court of a Member State.

Such agents and lawyers shall, when they appear before the Court, enjoy the rights and immunities necessary to the independent exercise of their duties, under conditions laid down in rules drawn up by the Court and submitted for the approval of the Council, acting unanimously.

As regards such lawyers who appear before it, the Court shall have the powers normally accorded to courts of law, under conditions laid down in those rules.

University teachers being nationals of a Member State whose law accords them a right of audience shall have the same rights before the Court as are accorded by this Article to lawyers entitled to practise before a court of a Member State.

Stages of Procedure

Article 21

The procedure before the Court shall consist of two parts: written and oral.

The written procedure shall consist of the communication to the parties and to the institutions of the Community whose decisions are in dispute of applications, statements of case, defences and observations, and of replies, if any, as well as of all papers and documents in support or of certified copies of them.

Communications shall be made by the Registrar in the order and within the time laid down in the rules of procedure.

---

9 The third paragraph was amended by art 8(3)(c) of the Merger Treaty.

The oral procedure shall consist of the reading of the report presented by a Judge acting as Rapporteur, the hearing by the Court of witnesses, experts, agents, and lawyers entitled to practise before a court of a Member State and of the submissions of the Advocate-General.

Applications
Article 22

A case shall be brought before the Court by a written application addressed to the Registrar. The application shall contain the name and address of the party and the description of the signatory, the subject matter of the dispute, the submissions and a brief statement of the grounds on which the application is based.

The application shall be accompanied, where appropriate, by the decision the annulment of which is sought or, in the case of proceedings against an implied decision, by documentary evidence of the date on which the request was lodged. If the documents are not submitted with the application, the Registrar shall ask the party concerned to produce them within a reasonable period, but in that event the rights of the party shall not lapse even if such documents are produced after the time limit for bringing proceedings.

Transmission of Documents
Article 23

Where proceedings are instituted against a decision of one of the institutions of the Community, that institution shall transmit to the Court all the documents relating to the case before the Court.

Preparatory Enquiries
Article 24

The Court may require the parties, their representatives or agents or the Governments of the Member States to produce all documents and to supply all information which the Court considers desirable. Formal note shall be taken of any refusal.

Article 25

The Court may at any time entrust any individual, body, authority, committee or other organisation it chooses with the task of holding an inquiry or giving an expert opinion; to this end it may compile a list of individuals or bodies approved as experts.

Hearing to be Public
Article 26

The hearing in court shall be public, unless the Court decides otherwise for serious reasons.

Minutes
Article 27

Minutes shall be made of each hearing and signed by the President and the Registrar.

Hearings
Article 28[10]

The cause list shall be established by the President.

Witnesses may be heard under conditions laid down in the rules of procedure. They may be heard on oath.

During the hearings the Court may also examine experts, persons entrusted with holding an inquiry, and the parties themselves. The latter, however, may address the Court only through their representatives or their lawyers.

---

10 The fifth paragraph was amended by art 8(3)(c) of the Merger Treaty.

Where it is established that a witness or expert has concealed facts or falsified evidence on any matter on which he has testified or been examined by the Court, the Court is empowered to report the misconduct to the Minister of Justice of the State of which the witness or expert is a national, in order that he may be subjected to the relevant penal provisions of the national law.

With respect to defaulting witnesses the Court shall have the powers generally granted to courts and tribunals, under conditions laid down in rules drawn up by the Court and submitted for the approval of the Council, acting unanimously.

Secrecy of the Deliberations of the Court

Article 29

The deliberations of the Court shall be and shall remain secret.

Judgments

Article 30

Judgments shall state the reasons on which they are based. They shall contain the names of the Judges who took part in the deliberations.

Article 31

Judgments shall be signed by the President, the Judge acting as Rapporteur and the Registrar. They shall be read in open court.

Costs

Article 32

The Court shall adjudicate upon costs.

Summary Procedure

Article 33

The President of the Court may, by way of summary procedure, which may, in so far as necessary, differ from some of the rules contained in this Statute and which shall be laid down in the rules of procedure, adjudicate upon applications to suspend execution, as provided for in the second paragraph of Article 39 of this Treaty, or to prescribe interim measures in pursuance of the last paragraph of Article 39, or to suspend enforcement in accordance with the third paragraph of Article 92.

Should the President be prevented from attending, his place shall be taken by another Judge under conditions laid down in the rules provided for in Article 18 of this Statute.

The ruling of the President or of the Judge replacing him shall be provisional and shall in no way prejudice the decision of the Court on the substance of the case.

Intervention

Article 34

Natural or legal persons establishing an interest in the result of any case submitted to the Court may intervene in that case.

Submissions made in an application to intervene shall be limited to supporting or requesting the rejection of the submissions of one of the parties.

Judgment by Default

Article 35

Where the defending party in proceedings in which the Court has unlimited jurisdiction, after having been duly summoned, fails to file written submissions in defence, judgment shall be given against that party by default. An objection may be lodged against the judgment within one month of it being notified. The objection shall not have the effect of staying enforcement of the judgment by default unless the Court decides otherwise.

Third Party Proceedings

Article 36

Natural or legal persons and the institutions of the Community may, in cases and under conditions to be determined by the rules of procedure, institute third-party proceedings to contest a judgment recorded without their being heard.

Interpretation

Article 37

If the meaning or scope of a judgment is in doubt, the Court shall construe it on application by any party or any institution of the Community establishing an interest therein.

Revision of a Judgment

Article 38

An application for revision of a judgment may be made to the Court only on discovery of a fact which is of such a nature as to be a decisive factor, and which, when the judgment was given, was unknown to the Court and to the party claiming the revision.

The revision shall be opened by a judgment of the Court expressly recording the existence of a new fact, recognising that it is of such a character as to lay the case open to revision and declaring the application admissible on this ground.

No application for revision may be made after the lapse of ten years from the date of the judgment.

Time Limits

Article 39

The proceedings provided for in Articles 36 and 37 of this Treaty must be instituted within the time limit of one month provided for in the last paragraph of Article 33.

Periods of grace based on considerations of distance shall be laid down in the rules of procedure.

No right shall be prejudiced in consequence of the expiry of a time limit if the party concerned proves the existence of unforeseeable circumstances or of force majeure.

Periods of Limitation

Article 40

Proceedings provided for in the first two paragraphs of Article 40 of this Treaty shall be barred after a period of five years from the occurrence of the event giving rise thereto. The period of limitation shall be interrupted if proceedings are instituted before the Court or if prior to such proceedings an application is made by the aggrieved party to the relevant institution of the Community. In the latter event the proceedings must be instituted within the time limit of one month provided for in the last paragraph of Article 33; the provisions of the last paragraph of Article 35 shall apply where appropriate.

Special Rules relating to Disputes between Member States

Article 41

Where a dispute between Member States is brought before the Court under Article 89 of this Treaty, the other Member States shall be notified forthwith by the Registrar of the subject matter of the dispute.

Each Member State shall have the right to intervene in the proceedings.

The disputes referred to in this Article must be dealt with in plenary session.

Article 42

If a State intervenes in a case before the Court as provided for in the preceding Article, the interpretation contained in the judgment shall be binding upon that State.

Proceedings by Third Parties

Article 43

Decisions taken by the High Authority under Article 63(2) of this Treaty must be notified to the purchaser and to the undertakings concerned; if the decision concerns all or a large number of undertakings, publication may be substituted for individual notification.

Appeals may be brought, under Article 36 of this Treaty, by any person on whom a periodic penalty payment has been imposed under the fourth subparagraph of Article 66(5).

TITLE IV[11]

THE COURT OF FIRST INSTANCE OF THE EUROPEAN COMMUNITIES

Rules concerning the members of the Court of First Instance and its organization

Article 44

Articles 2, 3, 4, 6 to 9, the first paragraph of Article 13, Article 17, the second paragraph of Article 18 and Article 19 of this Statute shall apply to the Court of First Instance and its members. The oath referred to in Article 2 shall be taken before the Court of Justice and the decisions referred to in Articles 3, 4 and 7 shall be adopted by that Court after hearing the Court of First Instance.

Registrar and staff

Article 45

The Court of First Instance shall appoint its Registrar and lay down the rules governing his service. Articles 9 and 14 of this Statute shall apply to the Registrar of the Court of First Instance *mutatis mutandis*.

The President of the Court of Justice and the President of the Court of First Instance shall determine, by common accord, the conditions upon which officials and other servants attached to the Court of Justice shall render their services to the Court of First Instance to enable it to function. Certain officials or other servants shall be responsible to the Registrar of the Court of First Instance under the authority of the President of the Court of First Instance.

Procedure before the Court of First Instance

Article 46

The procedure before the Court of First Instance shall be governed by Title III of this Statute, with the exception of Articles 41 and 42.

Such further and more detailed provisions as may be necessary shall be laid down in the Rules of Procedure established in accordance with Article 32d(4) of this Treaty.

Notwithstanding the fourth paragraph of Article 21 of this Statute, the Advocate-General may make his reasoned submissions in writing.

Article 47

Where an application or other procedural document addressed to the Court of First Instance is lodged by mistake with the Registrar of the Court of Justice it shall be transmitted immediately by that Registrar to the Registrar of the Court of First Instance; likewise, where an application or other procedural document addressed to the Court of Justice is lodged by mistake with the Registrar of the Court of First Instance, it shall be transmitted immediately by that Registrar to the Registrar of the Court of Justice.

11 Title IV was inserted by Decision 88/591, art 5.

Where the Court of First Instance finds that it does not have jurisdiction to hear and determine an action in respect of which the Court of Justice has jurisdiction, it shall refer that action to the Court of Justice; likewise, where the Court of Justice finds that an action falls within the jurisdiction of the Court of First Instance, it shall refer that action to the Court of First Instance, whereupon that Court may not decline jurisdiction.

Where the Court of Justice and the Court of First Instance are seised of cases in which the same relief is sought, the same issue of interpretation is raised or the validity of the same act is called in question, the Court of First Instance may, after hearing the parties, stay the proceedings before it until such time as the Court of Justice shall have delivered judgment. Where applications are made for the same act to be declared void, the Court of First Instance may also decline jurisdiction in order that the Court of Justice may rule on such applications. In the cases referred to in this subparagraph, the Court of Justice may also decide to stay the proceedings before it; in that event, the proceedings before the Court of First Instance shall continue.

Article 48
Final decisions of the Court of First Instance, decisions disposing of the substantive issues in part only, or disposing of a procedural issue concerning a plea of lack of competence or inadmissibility, shall be notified by the Registrar of the Court of First Instance to all parties as well as all Member States and the Community institutions even if they did not intervene in the case before the Court of First Instance.

Appeals to the Court of Justice
Article 49
An appeal may be brought before the Court of Justice, within two months of the notification of the decision appealed against, against final decisions of the Court of First Instance and decisions of that Court disposing of the substantive issues in part only, or disposing of a procedural issue concerning a plea of lack of competence or inadmissibility.

Such an appeal may be brought by any party which has been unsuccessful, in whole or in part, in its submissions. However, interveners other than the Member States and the Community institutions may bring such an appeal only where the decision of the Court of First Instance directly affects them.

With the exception of cases relating to disputes between the Community and its servants, an appeal may also be brought by Member States and Community institutions which did not intervene in the proceedings before the Court of First Instance. Such Member States and institutions shall be in the same position as Member States or institutions which intervened at first instance.

Article 50
Any person whose application to intervene has been dismissed by the Court of First Instance may appeal to the Court of Justice within two weeks of the notification of the decision dismissing the application.

The parties to the proceedings may appeal to the Court of Justice against any decision of the Court of First Instance made pursuant to the second or third paragraphs of Article 39 or the third paragraph of Article 92 of the Treaty within two months from their notification.

The appeal referred to in the first two paragraphs of this Article shall be heard and determined under the procedure referred to in Article 33 of this Statute.

Article 51
An appeal to the Court of Justice shall be limited to points of law. It shall lie on the grounds of lack of competence of the Court of First Instance, a breach of procedure before it which adversely affects the interests of the appellant as well as the infringement of Community law by the Court of First Instance.

No appeal shall lie regarding only the amount of the costs or the party ordered to pay them.

Procedure before the Court

Article 52

Where an appeal is brought against a decision of the Court of First Instance, the procedure before the Court of Justice shall consist of a written part and an oral part. In accordance with conditions laid down in the Rules of Procedure the Court of Justice, having heard the Advocate-General and the parties, may dispense with the oral procedure.

Suspensory effect

Article 53[12]

Without prejudice to the second and third paragraphs of Article 39 of this Treaty, an appeal shall not have suspensory effect.

By way of derogation from Article 44 of the Treaty, decisions of the Court of First Instance declaring a general decision or general recommendation to be void shall take effect only as from the date of expiry of the period referred to in the first paragraph of Article 49 of this Statute, or if an appeal shall have been brought within that period, as from the date of dismissal of the appeal, without prejudice, however, to the right of a party to apply to the Court of Justice pursuant to the second and third paragraphs of Article 39 of the Treaty, for the suspension of the effects of the act which has been declared void or for the prescription of any other interim measure.

The decision of the Court of Justice on the appeal

Article 54

If the appeal is well founded, the Court of Justice shall quash the decision of the Court of First Instance. It may itself give final judgment in the matter, where the state of the proceedings so permits, or refer the case back to the Court of First Instance for judgment.

Where a case is referred back to the Court of First Instance, that Court shall be bound by the decision of the Court of Justice on points of law.

When an appeal brought by a Member State or a Community institution, which did not intervene in the proceedings before the Court of First Instance, is well founded the Court of Justice may, if it considers this necessary, state which of the effects of the decision of the Court of First Instance which has been quashed shall be considered as definitive in respect of the parties to the litigation.

Rules of Procedure

Article 55[13]

The Court of Justice shall adopt its rules of procedure. These shall require the unanimous approval of the Council. The rules of procedure shall contain all the provisions necessary for applying and, where required, supplementing this Statute.

Transitional Provision

Article 56[14]

Immediately after the oath has been taken, the President of the Council shall proceed to choose by lot the Judges and the Advocates-General whose terms of office are to expire at the end of the first three years in accordance with Article 32 of this Treaty.

---

12 As amended by Decision 93/350, art 2.
13 As amended by art 8(3)(d) of the Merger Treaty and renumbered by art 6 of Decision 88/591 (formerly art 44).
14 Formerly art 45. Renumbered by Decision 88/591, art 6.

Protocols on the Statute of the Court of Justice of the European Community and the European Atomic Energy Community: Consolidated Text[15]

Article 1
The Court established by [Article 4 of the EC Treaty, Article 3 of the Euratom Treaty] shall be constituted and shall function in accordance with the provisions of this Treaty and of this Statute.

TITLE I
JUDGES AND ADVOCATES-GENERAL

Article 2
Before taking up his duties each Judge shall, in open court, take an oath to perform his duties impartially and conscientiously and to preserve the secrecy of the deliberations of the Court.

Article 3
The Judges shall be immune from legal proceedings. After they have ceased to hold office, they shall continue to enjoy immunity in respect of acts performed by them in their official capacity, including words spoken or written.

The Court, sitting in plenary session, may waive the immunity.

Where immunity has been waived and criminal proceedings are instituted against a Judge, he shall be tried, in any of the Member States, only by the Court competent to judge the members of the highest national judiciary.

Article 4
The Judges may not hold any political or administrative office.

They may not engage in any occupation, whether gainful or not, unless exemption is exceptionally granted by the Council.

When taking up their duties, they shall give a solemn undertaking that, both during and after their term of office, they will respect the obligations arising therefrom, in particular the duty to behave with integrity and discretion as regards the acceptance, after they have ceased to hold office, of certain appointments or benefits.

Any doubt on this point shall be settled by decision of the Court.

Article 5
Apart from normal replacement, or death, the duties of a Judge shall end when he resigns.

Where a Judge resigns, his letter of resignation shall be addressed to the President of the Court for transmission to the President of the Council. Upon this notification a vacancy shall arise on the bench.

Save where Article 6 applies, a Judge shall continue to hold office until his successor takes up his duties.

Article 6
A Judge may be deprived of his office or of his right to a pension or other benefits in its stead only if, in the unanimous opinion of the Judges and Advocates-General of the

---

15 Apart from references to Treaty provisions, the only difference between the two Protocols is that the Euratom Statute comprises an additional provision, contained in art 20, with the result that the subsequent articles are numbered differently from the EC Statute.

Court, he no longer fulfils the requisite conditions or meets the obligations arising from his office. The Judge concerned shall not take part in any such deliberations.

The Registrar of the Court shall communicate the decision of the Court to the President of the Assembly and to the President of the Commission and shall notify it to the President of the Council.

In the case of a decision depriving a Judge of his office, a vacancy shall arise on the bench upon this latter notification.

Article 7

A Judge who is to replace a member of the Court whose term of office has not expired shall be appointed for the remainder of his predecessor's term.

Article 8

The provisions of Articles 2 to 7 shall apply to the Advocates-General.

TITLE II

ORGANISATION

Article 9

The Registrar shall take an oath before the Court to perform his duties impartially and conscientiously and to preserve the secrecy of the deliberations of the Court.

Article 10

The Court shall arrange for replacement of the Registrar on occasions when he is prevented from attending the Court.

Article 11

Officials and other servants shall be attached to the Court to enable it to function. They shall be responsible to the Registrar under the authority of the President.

Article 12

On a proposal from the Court, the Council may, acting unanimously, provide for the appointment of Assistant Rapporteurs and lay down the rules governing their service. The Assistant Rapporteurs may be required, under conditions laid down in the rules of procedure, to participate in preparatory inquiries in cases pending before the Court and to cooperate with the Judge who acts as Rapporteur.

The Assistant Rapporteurs shall be chosen from persons whose independence is beyond doubt and who possess the necessary legal qualifications; they shall be appointed by the Council. They shall take an oath before the Court to perform their duties impartially and conscientiously and to preserve the secrecy of the deliberations of the Court.

Article 13

The Judges, the Advocates-General and the Registrar shall be required to reside at the place where the Court has its seat.

Article 14

The Court shall remain permanently in session. The duration of the judicial vacations shall be determined by the Court with due regard to the needs of its business.

Article 15[16]

Decisions of the Court shall be valid only when an uneven number of its members is sitting in the deliberations. Decisions of the full Court shall be valid if seven members are sitting. Decisions of the Chambers shall be valid only if three Judges are sitting; in the event of one of the Judges of a Chamber being prevented from attending, a Judge of another Chamber may be called upon to sit in accordance with conditions laid down in the rules of procedure.

16 As amended by art 20 of the Act of Accession of Denmark, Ireland and the United Kingdom.

Article 16
No Judge or Advocate-General may take part in the disposal of any case in which he has previously taken part as agent or adviser or has acted for one of the parties, or on which he has been called upon to pronounce as a member of a court or tribunal, of a commission of inquiry or in any other capacity.

If, for some special reason, any Judge or Advocate-General considers that he should not take part in the judgment or examination of a particular case, he shall so inform the President. If, for some special reason, the President considers that any Judge or Advocate-General should not sit or make submissions in a particular case, he shall notify him accordingly.

Any difficulty arising as to the application of this Article shall be settled by decision of the Court.

A party may not apply for a change in the composition of the Court or of one of its Chambers on the grounds of either the nationality of a Judge or the absence from the Court or from the Chamber of a Judge of the nationality of that party.

TITLE III
PROCEDURE

Article 17
The States and the institutions of the Community shall be represented before the Court by an agent appointed for each case; the agent may be assisted by an adviser or a lawyer entitled to practise before a court of a Member State.

Other parties must be represented by a lawyer entitled to practise before a court of a Member State.

Such agents, advisers and lawyers shall, when they appear before the Court, enjoy the rights and immunities necessary to the independent exercise of their duties, under conditions laid down in the rules of procedure.

As regards such advisers and lawyers who appear before it, the Court shall have the powers normally accorded to courts of law, under conditions laid down in the rules of procedure.

University teachers being nationals of a Member State whose law accords them a right of audience shall have the same rights before the Court as are accorded by this Article to lawyers entitled to practise before a court of a Member State.

Article 18
The procedure before the Court shall consist of two parts: written and oral.

The written procedure shall consist of the communication to the parties and to the institutions of the Community whose decisions are in dispute of applications, statements of case, defences and observations, and of replies, if any, as well as of all papers and documents in support or of certified copies of them.

Communications shall be made by the Registrar in the order and within the time laid down in the rules of procedure.

The oral procedure shall consist of the reading of the report presented by a Judge acting as Rapporteur, the hearing by the Court of agents, advisers and lawyers entitled to practise before a court of a Member State and of the submissions of the Advocate-General, as well as the hearing, if any, of witnesses and experts.

Article 19
A case shall be brought before the Court by a written application addressed to the Registrar. The application shall contain the applicant's name and permanent address and the description of the signatory, the name of the party against whom the application is made, the subject matter of the dispute, the submissions and a brief statement of the grounds on which the application is based.

The application shall be accompanied, where appropriate, by the measure the annulment of which is sought or, in the circumstances referred to in [Article 175 of the EC Treaty, Article 148 of the Euratom Treaty], by documentary evidence of the date on which an institution was, in accordance with that Article, requested to act. If the documents are not submitted with the application, the Registrar shall ask the party concerned to produce them within a reasonable period, but in that event the rights of the party shall not lapse even if such documents are produced after the time limit for bringing proceedings.

Article 20 (Euratom)

A case governed by Article 18 of this Treaty shall be brought before the Court by an appeal addressed to the Registar. The appeal shall contain the name and permanent address of the applicant and the description of the signatory, a reference to the decision against which the appeal is brought, the names of the respondents, the subject matter of the dispute, the submissions and a brief statement of the grounds on which the appeal is based.

The appeal shall be accompanied by a certified copy of the decision of the Arbitration Committee which is contested.

If the Court rejects the appeal, the decision of the Arbitration Committee shall become final.

If the Court annuls the decision of the Arbitration Committee, the matter may be reopened, where appropriate, on the initiative of one of the parties in the case, before the Arbitration Committee. The latter shall conform to any decisions on points of law given by the Court.

Article 20 (EC), 21 (Euratom)

In the cases governed by [Article 177 of the EC Treaty, Article 150 of the Euratom Treaty], the decision of the court or tribunal of a Member State which suspends its proceedings and refers a case to the Court shall be notified to the Court by the court or tribunal concerned. The decision shall then be notified by the Registrar of the Court to the parties, to the Member States and to the Commission, and also to the Council if the act the validity or interpretation of which is in dispute originates from the Council.

Within two months of this notification, the parties, the Member States, the Commission and, where appropriate, the Council, shall be entitled to submit statements of case or written observations to the Court.

Article 21 (EC), 22 (Euratom)

The Court may require the parties to produce all documents and to supply all information which the Court considers desirable. Formal note shall be taken of any refusal.

The Court may also require the Member States and institutions not being parties to the case to supply all information which the Court considers necessary for the proceedings.

Article 22 (EC), 23 (Euratom)

The Court may at any time entrust any individual, body, authority, committee or other organisation it chooses with the task of giving an expert opinion.

Article 23 (EC), 24 (Euratom)

Witnesses may be heard under conditions laid down in the rules of procedure.

Article 24 (EC), 25 (Euratom)

With respect to defaulting witnesses the Court shall have the powers generally granted to courts and tribunals and may impose pecuniary penalties under conditions laid down in the rules of procedure.

Article 25 (EC), 26 (Euratom)

Witnesses and experts may be heard on oath taken in the form laid down in the rules of procedure or in the manner laid down by the law of the country of the witness or expert.

Article 26 (EC), 27 (Euratom)

The Court may order that a witness or expert be heard by the judicial authority of his place of permanent residence.

The order shall be sent for implementation to the competent judicial authority under conditions laid down in the rules of procedure. The documents drawn up in compliance with the letters rogatory shall be returned to the Court under the same conditions.

The Court shall defray the expenses, without prejudice to the right to charge them, where appropriate, to the parties.

Article 27 (EC), 28 (Euratom)

A Member State shall treat any violation of an oath by a witness or expert in the same manner as if the offence had been committed before one of its courts with jurisdiction in civil proceedings. At the instance of the Court, the Member State concerned shall prosecute the offender before its competent court.

Article 28 (EC), 29 (Euratom)

The hearing in court shall be public, unless the Court, of its own motion or on application by the parties, decides otherwise for serious reasons.

Article 29 (EC), 30 (Euratom)

During the hearings the Court may examine the experts, the witnesses and the parties themselves. The latter, however, may address the Court only through their representatives.

Article 30 (EC), 31 (Euratom)

Minutes shall be made of each hearing and signed by the President and the Registrar.

Article 31 (EC), 32 (Euratom)

The cause list shall be established by the President.

Article 32 (EC), 33 (Euratom)

The deliberations of the Court shall be and shall remain secret.

Article 33 (EC), 34 (Euratom)

Judgments shall state the reasons on which they are based. They shall contain the names of the Judges who took part in the deliberations.

Article 34 (EC), 35 (Euratom)

Judgments shall be signed by the President and the Registrar. They shall be read in open court.

Article 35 (EC), 36 (Euratom)

The Court shall adjudicate upon costs.

Article 36 (EC), 37 (Euratom)

The President of the Court may, by way of summary procedure, which may, in so far as necessary, differ from some of the rules contained in this Statute and which shall be laid down in the rules of procedure, adjudicate upon applications to suspend execution, as provided for in [Article 185 of the EC Treaty, Article 157 of the Euratom Treaty], or to prescribe interim measures in pursuance of [Article 186, Article 158], or to suspend enforcement in accordance with the last paragraph of [Article 192, Article 164].

Should the President be prevented from attending, his place shall be taken by another Judge under conditions laid down in the rules of procedure.

The ruling of the President or of the Judge replacing him shall be provisional and shall in no way prejudice the decision of the Court on the substance of the case.

Article 37 (EC), 38 (Euratom)

Member States and institutions of the Community may intervene in cases before the Court.

The same right shall be open to any other person establishing an interest in the result of any case submitted to the Court, save in cases between Member States, between institutions of the Community or between Member States and institutions of the Community.

Submissions made in an application to intervene shall be limited to supporting the submissions of one of the parties.

Article 38 (EC), 39 (Euratom)

Where the defending party, after having been duly summoned, fails to file written submissions in defence, judgment shall be given against that party by default. An objection may be lodged against the judgment within one month of it being notified. The objection shall not have the effect of staying enforcement of the judgment by default unless the Court decides otherwise.

Article 39 (EC), 40 (Euratom)

Member States, institutions of the Community and any other natural or legal persons may, in cases and under conditions to be determined by the rules of procedure, institute third-party proceedings to contest a judgment rendered without their being heard, where the judgment is prejudicial to their rights.

Article 40 (EC), 41 (Euratom)

If the meaning or scope of a judgment is in doubt, the Court shall construe it on application by any party or any institution of the Community establishing an interest therein.

Article 41 (EC), 42 (Euratom)

An application for revision of a judgment may be made to the Court only on discovery of a fact which is of such a nature as to be a decisive factor, and which, when the judgment was given, was unknown to the Court and to the party claiming the revision.

The revision shall be opened by a judgment of the Court expressly recording the existence of a new fact, recognising that it is of such a character as to lay the case open to revision and declaring the application admissible on this ground.

No application for revision may be made after the lapse of ten years from the date of the judgment.

Article 42 (EC), 43 (Euratom)

Periods of grace based on considerations of distance shall be determined by the rules of procedure.

No right shall be prejudiced in consequence of the expiry of a time limit if the party concerned proves the existence of unforeseeable circumstances or of force majeure.

Article 43 (EC), 44 (Euratom)

Proceedings against the Community in matters arising from non-contractual liability shall be barred after a period of five years from the occurrence of the event giving rise thereto. The period of limitation shall be interrupted if proceedings are instituted before the Court or if prior to such proceedings an application is made by the aggrieved party to the relevant institution of the Community. In the latter event the proceedings must be instituted within the period of two months provided for in [Article 173 of the EC Treaty, Article 146 of the Euratom Treaty]; the provisions of the second paragraph of [Article 175 of the EC Treaty, Article 148 of the Euratom Treaty] shall apply where appropriate.

TITLE IV[17]

THE COURT OF FIRST INSTANCE OF THE EUROPEAN COMMUNITIES

Article 44 (EC), 45 (Euratom)

Articles 2 to 8, and 13 to 16 of this Statute shall apply to the Court of First Instance and its members. The oath referred to in Article 2 shall be taken before the Court of Justice and the decisions referred to in Articles 3, 4 and 6 shall be adopted by that Court after hearing the Court of First Instance.

17 Title IV was inserted by Decision 88/591, arts 7 and 9.

Article 45 (EC), 46 (Euratom)

The Court of First Instance shall appoint its Registrar and lay down the rules governing his service. Articles 9, 10 and 13 of this Statute shall apply to the Registrar of the Court of First Instance *mutatis mutandis*.

The President of the Court of Justice and the President of the Court of First Instance shall determine, by common accord, the conditions under which officials and other servants attached to the Court of Justice shall render their services to the Court of First Instance to enable it to function. Certain officials or other servants shall be responsible to the Registrar of the Court of First Instance under the authority of the President of the Court of First Instance.

Article 46 (EC), 47 (Euratom)

The procedure before the Court of First Instance shall be governed by Title III of this Statute, with the exception of Article 20 [and 21 of the Euratom Statute].

Such further and more detailed provisions as may be necessary shall be laid down in the Rules of Procedure established in accordance with [Article 168a(4) of the EC Treaty, Article 140a(4) of the Euratom Treaty].

Notwithstanding the fourth paragraph of Article 18 of this Statute, the Advocate-General may make his reasoned submissions in writing.

Article 47 (EC), 48 (Euratom)

Where an application or other procedural document addressed to the Court of First Instance is lodged by mistake with the Registrar of the Court of Justice it shall be transmitted immediately by that Registrar to the Registrar of the Court of First Instance; likewise, where an application or other procedural document addressed to the Court of Justice is lodged by mistake with the Registrar of the Court of First Instance, it shall be transmitted immediately by that Registrar to the Registrar of the Court of Justice.

Where the Court of First Instance finds that it does not have jurisdiction to hear and determine an action in respect of which the Court of Justice has jurisdiction, it shall refer that action to the Court of Justice; likewise, where the Court of Justice finds that an action falls within the jurisdiction of the Court of First Instance, it shall refer that action to the Court of First Instance, whereupon that Court may not decline jurisdiction.

Where the Court of Justice and the Court of First Instance are seised of cases in which the same relief is sought, the same issue of interpretation is raised or the validity of the same act is called in question, the Court of First Instance may, after hearing the parties, stay the proceedings before it until such time as the Court of Justice shall have delivered judgment. Where applications are made for the same act to be declared void, the Court of First Instance may also decline jurisdiction in order that the Court of Justice may rule on such applications. In the cases referred to in this subparagraph, the Court of Justice may also decide to stay the proceedings before it; in that event, the proceedings before the Court of First Instance shall continue.

Article 48 (EC), 49 (Euratom)

Final decisions of the Court of First Instance, decisions disposing of the substantive issues in part only or disposing of a procedural issue concerning a plea of lack of competence or inadmissibility, shall be notified by the Registrar of the Court of First Instance to all parties as well as all Member States and the Community institutions even if they did not intervene in the case before the Court of First Instance.

Article 49 (EC), 50 (Euratom)

An appeal may be brought before the Court of Justice, within two months of the notification of the decision appealed against, against final decisions of the Court of First Instance and decisions of that Court disposing of the substantive issues in part only or disposing of a procedural issue concerning a plea of lack of competence or inadmissibility.

Such an appeal may be brought by any party which has been unsuccessful, in whole or in part, in its submissions. However, interveners other than the Member States and the Community institutions may bring such an appeal only where the decision of the Court of First Instance directly affects them.

With the exception of cases relating to disputes between the Community and its servants, an appeal may also be brought by Member States and Community institutions which did not intervene in the proceedings before the Court of First Instance. Such Member States and institutions shall be in the same position as Member States or institutions which intervened at first instance.

Article 50 (EC), 51 (Euratom)

Any person whose application to intervene has been dismissed by the Court of First Instance may appeal to the Court of Justice within two weeks of the notification of the decision dismissing the application.

The parties to the proceedings may appeal to the Court of Justice against any decision of the Court of First Instance made pursuant to [Article 185 or 186 or the fourth paragraph of Article 192 of the EC Treaty, Article 157 or 158 of the third paragraph of Article 164 of the Euratom Treaty] within two months from their notification.

The appeal referred to in the first two paragraphs of this Article shall be heard and determined under the procedure referred to in [Article 36, Article 37] of this Statute.

Article 51 (EC), 52 (Euratom)

An appeal to the Court of Justice shall be limited to points of law. It shall lie on the grounds of lack of competence of the Court of First Instance, a breach of procedure before it which adversely affects the interests of the appellant as well as the infringement of Community law by the Court of First Instance.

No appeal shall lie regarding only the amount of the costs or the party ordered to pay them.

Article 52 (EC), 53 (Euratom)

Where an appeal is brought against a decision of the Court of First Instance, the procedure before the Court of Justice shall consist of a written part and an oral part. In accordance with conditions laid down in the Rules of Procedure the Court of Justice, having heard the Advocate-General and the parties, may dispense with the oral procedure.

Article 53 (EC), 54 (Euratom)

Without prejudice to [Articles 185 and 186 of the EC Treaty, Articles 157 and 158 of the Euratom Treaty], an appeal shall not have suspensory effect.

By way of derogation from [Article 187 of the EC Treaty, Article 159 of the Euratom Treaty], decisions of the Court of First Instance declaring a regulation to be void shall take effect only as from the date of expiry of the period referred to in the first paragraph of [Article 49, Article 50] of this Statute or, if an appeal shall have been brought within that period, as from the date of dismissal of the appeal, without prejudice, however, to the right of a party to apply to the Court of Justice, pursuant to [Articles 185 and 186 of the EC Treaty, Articles 157 and 158 of the Euratom Treaty], for the suspension of the effects of the regulation which has been declared void or for the prescription of any other interim measure.

Article 54 (EC), 55 (Euratom)

If the appeal is well founded, the Court of Justice shall quash the decision of the Court of First Instance. It may itself give final judgment in the matter, where the state of the proceedings so permits, or refer the case back to the Court of First Instance for judgment.

Where a case is referred back to the Court of First Instance, that Court shall be bound by the decision of the Court of Justice on points of law.

Where an appeal brought by a Member State or a Community institution, which did not intervene in the proceedings before the Court of First Instance, is well founded the Court of Justice may, if it considers this necessary, state which of the effects of the decision of the Court of First Instance which has been quashed shall be considered as definitive in respect of the parties to the litigation.

Article 55 (EC), 56 (Euratom)[18]

The rules of procedure of the Court provided for in [Article 188 of the EC Treaty, Article 160 of the Euratom Treaty] shall contain, apart from the provisions contemplated by this Statute, any other provisions necessary for applying and, where required, supplementing it.

Article 56 (EC), 57 (Euratom)

The Council may, acting unanimously, make such further adjustments to the provisions of this Statute as may be required by reason of measures taken by the Council in accordance with the last paragraph of [Article 165 of the EC Treaty, Article 137 of the Euratom Treaty].

Article 57 (EC), 58 (Euratom)

Immediately after the oath has been taken, the President of the Council shall proceed to choose by lot the Judges and the Advocates-General whose terms of office are to expire at the end of the first three years in accordance with the second and third paragraphs of [Article 167 of the EC Treaty, Article 139 of the Euratom Treaty].

18 The following arts (originally EEC Statute, arts 44 to 46; Euratom Statute, arts 45 to 47) were renumbered by Decision 88/591, arts 8 and 10.

Council Decision 88/591 establishing a Court of First Instance of the European Communities[19]

Preamble

. . . Whereas Article 32d of the ECSC Treaty, Article 168a of the EEC Treaty and Article 140a of the EAEC Treaty empower the Council to attach to the Court of Justice a Court of First Instance called upon to exercise important judicial functions and whose members are independent beyond doubt and possess the ability required for performing such functions;

Whereas the aforesaid provisions empower the Council to give the Court of First Instance jurisdiction to hear and determine at first instance, subject to a right of appeal to the Court of Justice on points of law only and in accordance with the conditions laid down by the Statutes, certain classes of action or proceeding brought by natural or legal persons;

Whereas, pursuant to the aforesaid provisions, the Council is to determine the composition of that Court and adopt the necessary adjustments and additional provisions to the Statutes of the Court of Justice;

Whereas, in respect of actions requiring close examination of complex facts, the establishment of a second court will improve the judicial protection of individual interests;

Whereas it is necessary, in order to maintain the quality and effectiveness of judicial review in the Community legal order, to enable the Court to concentrate its activities on its fundamental task of ensuring uniform interpretation of Community law;

Whereas it is therefore necessary to make use of the powers granted by Article 32d of the ECSC Treaty, Article 168a of the EEC Treaty and Article 140a of the EAEC Treaty and to transfer to the Court of First Instance jurisdiction to hear and determine at first instance certain classes of action or proceeding which frequently require an examination of complex facts, that is to say actions or proceedings brought by servants of the Communities and also, in so far as the ECSC Treaty is concerned, by undertakings and associations in matters concerning levies, production, prices, restrictive agreements, decisions or practices and concentrations, and so far as the EEC Treaty is concerned, by natural or legal persons in competition matters . . .

Article 1

A Court, to be called the Court of First Instance of the European Communities, shall be attached to the Court of Justice of the European Communities. Its seat shall be at the Court of Justice.

Article 2

1   The Court of First Instance shall consist of 12 members.

2   The members shall elect the President of the Court of First Instance from among their number for a term of three years. He may be re-elected.

3   The members of the Court of First Instance may be called upon to perform the task of an Advocate-General. It shall be the duty of the Advocate-General, acting with complete impartiality and independence, to make, in open court, reasoned submissions on certain cases brought before the Court of First Instance in order to assist the Court of First Instance in the performance of its task. The criteria for selecting such cases, as well as the procedures for designating the Advocates-General, shall be laid down in the Rules of Procedure of the Court of First Instance. A member called upon to perform the task of Advocate-General in a case may not take part in the judgment of the case.

4   The Court of First Instance shall sit in chambers of three or five judges. The composition of the chambers and the assignment of cases to them shall be

---

19   24 October 1988, OJ No L 319 of 25 November 1988 p 4, amended by corrigendum published in OJ No L 241 of 17 August 1989 p 4 and by Council Decision 93/350 of 8 June 1993, OJ No L 144 of 16 June 1993 p 21. A corrected version of Decision 88/591 was published in OJ No C 215 of 21 August 1989 p 1 but it does not include the amendments later made by Decision 93/350. Those parts of Decision 88/591 which made amendments to the Statutes of the Court have been incorporated in the Statutes and are not set out here.

5 governed by the Rules of Procedure. In certain cases governed by the Rules of Procedure the Court of First Instance may sit in plenary session.
Article 21 of the Protocol on Privileges and Immunities of the European Communities and Article 6 of the Treaty establishing a Single Council and a Single Commission of the European Communities shall apply to the members of the Court of First Instance and to its Registrar.

Article 3[20]

The Court of First Instance shall exercise at first instance the jurisdiction conferred on the Court of Justice by the Treaties establishing the Communities and by the acts adopted in implementation thereof, save as otherwise provided in an act setting up a body governed by Community law:

(a) in disputes as referred to in Article 179 of the EEC Treaty and Article 152 of the EAEC Treaty;
(b) in actions brought by natural or legal persons pursuant to the second paragraph of Article 33, Article 35, the first and second paragraphs of Article 40 and Article 42 of the ECSC Treaty;
(c) in actions brought by natural or legal persons pursuant to the second paragraph of Article 173, the third paragraph of Article 175 and Articles 178 and 181 of the EEC Treaty.
(d) in actions brought by natural or legal persons pursuant to the second paragraph of Article 146, the third paragraph of Article 148 and Articles 151 and 153 of the EAEC Treaty.

Article 4[21]

Save as hereinafter provided, Articles 34, 36, 39, 44 and 92 of the ECSC Treaty, Articles 172, 174, 176, 184 to 187 and 192 of the EEC Treaty and Articles 49, 83, 144b, 147, 149, 156 to 159 and 164 of the Euratom Treaty shall apply to the Court of First Instance.

Article 11

The first President of the Court of First Instance shall be appointed for three years in the same manner as its members. However, the Governments of the Member States may, by common accord, decide that the procedure laid down in Article 2(2) shall be applied.

The Court of First Instance shall adopt its Rules of Procedure immediately upon its constitution.

Until the entry into force of the Rules of Procedure of the Court of First Instance, the Rules of Procedure of the Court of Justice shall apply *mutatis mutandis*.

Article 12

Immediately after all members of the Court of First Instance have taken oath, the President of the Council shall proceed to choose by lot the members of the Court of First Instance whose terms of office are to expire at the end of the first three years in accordance with Article 32d(3) of the ECSC Treaty, Article 168a(3) of the EEC Treaty, and Article 140a(3) of the EAEC Treaty.

Article 13

This Decision shall enter into force on the day following its publication in the *Official Journal of the European Communities*, with the exception of Article 3, which shall enter into force on the date of the publication in the *Official Journal of the European Communities* of the ruling by the President of the Court of Justice that the Court of First Instance has been constituted in accordance with law.

Article 14

Cases referred to in Article 3 of which the Court of Justice is seised on the date on which that Article enters into force but in which the preliminary report provided for in Article 44(1) of the Rules of Procedure of the Court of Justice has not yet been presented shall be referred to the Court of First Instance.

20 As amended by Decision 93/350, art 1(1) and (2).
21 As amended by Decision 93/350, art 1(3).

Council Decision 93/350 amending
Council Decision 88/591[22]

Preamble

. . . Whereas the attachment to the Court of Justice of a Court of First Instance by Decision 88/591/ECSC, EEC, Euratom is intended, by the establishment of a second court, in particular in respect of actions requiring close examination of complex facts, to improve the judicial protection of individual interests and to maintain the quality and effectiveness of judicial review in the Community legal order by enabling the Court of Justice to concentrate its activities on its fundamental task, of ensuring uniform interpretation of Community law;

Whereas, with the same end in view, it is appropriate, taking into account past experience to enlarge the jurisdiction transferred to the Court of First Instance to hear and determine at first instance certain classes of action or proceeding brought by natural or legal persons;

Whereas Decision 88/591/ECSC, EEC, Euratom should therefore be amended in consequence . . .

Article 3

This Decision shall enter into force on the first day of the second month following that of its publication in the *Official Journal of the European Communities*; however, in respect of actions brought by natural or legal persons pursuant to the second paragraph of Article 33, Article 35 and the first and second paragraphs of Article 40 of the ECSC Treaty and which concern acts relating to the application of Article 74 of the said Treaty in respect of actions brought by natural or legal persons pursuant to the second paragraph of Article 173, the third paragraph of Article 175 and Article 178 of the EEC Treaty and relating to measures to protect trade within the meaning of Article 113 of that Treaty in the case of dumping and subsidies, its entry into force shall be deferred to a date that the Council shall fix by unanimous decision.

The provisions relating to actions brought under Article 42 of the ECSC Treaty, Article 181 of the EEC Treaty or Articles 153 of the EAEC Treaty shall apply only to contracts concluded after the entry into force of this Decision.

Article 4

Cases falling within the scope of Article 3 of Decision 88/591/ECSC, EEC, Euratom, as amended by this Decision, of which the Court of Justice is seised on the date on which this Decision enters into force but in which the preliminary report provided for in Article 44(1) of the Rules of Procedure of the Court of Justice has not yet been presented, shall be referred to the Court of First Instance.

---

22 8 June 1993, OJ No L 144 of 16 June 1993 p 21. Those parts of the Decision which made amendments to Decision 88/591 and the ECSC Statute have been incorporated in the text of those instruments and are not set out here.

Rules of Procedure of the Court of Justice of the European Communities[23]

Interpretation

Article 1

In these Rules:

'ECSC Treaty' means the Treaty establishing the European Coal and Steel Community;

'ECSC Statute' means the Protocol on the Statute of the Court of Justice of the European Coal and Steel Community;

'EEC Treaty' means the Treaty establishing the European Economic Community;

'EEC Statute' means the Protocol on the Statute of the Court of Justice of the European Economic Community;

'Euratom Treaty' means the Treaty establishing the European Atomic Energy Community (Euratom);

'Euratom Statute' means the Protocol on the Statute of the Court of Justice of the European Atomic Energy Community.

For the purposes of these Rules, 'institutions' means the institutions of the European Communities and the European Investment Bank.

TITLE I

ORGANISATION OF THE COURT

Chapter 1

Judges and Advocates-General

Article 2

The term of office of a Judge shall begin on the date laid down in his instrument of appointment. In the absence of any provisions regarding the date, the term shall begin on the date of the instrument.

Article 3

1   Before taking up his duties, a Judge shall at the first public sitting of the Court which he attends after his appointment take the following oath:

'I swear that I will perform my duties impartially and conscientiously; I swear that I will preserve the secrecy of the deliberations of the Court.'

2   Immediately after taking the oath, a Judge shall sign a declaration by which he solemnly undertakes that, both during and after his term of office, he will respect the obligations arising therefrom, and in particular the duty to behave with integrity and discretion as regards the acceptance, after he has ceased to hold office, of certain appointments and benefits.

Article 4

When the Court is called upon to decide whether a Judge no longer fulfils the requisite conditions or no longer meets the obligations arising from his office, the President shall invite the Judge concerned to make representations to the Court, in closed session and in the absence of the Registrar.

---

23 Original rules contained in OJ L350 28.12.74 p1 (as amended by OJ L238 21.9.79 p1; OJ L199 20.7.81 p1; OJ L165 24.6.87 p1; OJ L241 17.8.89 p1). Rules replaced in OJ L176 4.7.91; corrected in OJ L383 29.12.92 p 117. The preamble to the Rules has been omitted.

Article 5

Articles 2, 3 and 4 of these Rules shall apply to Advocates-General.

Article 6

Judges and Advocates-General shall rank equally in precedence according to their seniority in office.

Where there is equal seniority in office, precedence shall be determined by age.

Retiring Judges and Advocates-General who are reappointed shall retain their former precedence.

Chapter 2

Presidency of the Court and constitution of the Chambers

Article 7

1   The Judges shall, immediately after the partial replacement provided for in Article 32b of the ECSC Treaty, Article 167 of the EEC Treaty and Article 139 of the Euratom Treaty, elect one of their number as President of the Court for a term of three years.
2   If the office of the President of the Court falls vacant before the normal date of expiry thereof, the Court shall elect a successor for the remainder of the term.
3   The elections provided for in this Article shall be by secret ballot. If a Judge obtains an absolute majority he shall be elected. If no Judge obtains an absolute majority, a second ballot shall be held and the Judge obtaining the most votes shall be elected. Where two or more Judges obtain an equal number of votes the oldest of them shall be deemed elected.

Article 8

The President shall direct the judicial business and the administration of the Court; he shall preside at hearings and deliberations.

Article 9

1   The Court shall set up Chambers in accordance with the provisions of the second paragraph of Article 32 of the ECSC Treaty, the second paragraph of Article 165 of the EEC Treaty and the second paragraph of Article 137 of the Euratom Treaty and shall decide which Judges shall be attached to them.
     The composition of the Chambers shall be published in the Official Journal of the European Communities.
2   As soon as an application initiating proceedings has been lodged, the President of the Court shall assign the case to one of the Chambers for any preparatory inquiries and shall designate a Judge from that Chamber to act as Rapporteur.
3   The Court shall lay down criteria by which, as a rule, cases are to be assigned to Chambers.
4   These Rules shall apply to proceedings before the Chambers.
     In cases assigned to a Chamber the powers of the President of the Court shall be exercised by the President of the Chamber.

Article 10

1   The Court shall appoint for a period of one year the Presidents of the Chambers and the First Advocate-General.
     The provisions of Article 7(2) and (3) shall apply.
     Appointments made in pursuance of this paragraph shall be published in the Official Journal of the European Communities.
2   The First Advocate-General shall assign each case to an Advocate-General as soon as the Judge-Rapporteur has been designated by the President. He shall take the necessary steps if an Advocate-General is absent or prevented from acting.

Article 11

When the President of the Court is absent or prevented from attending or when the office of President is vacant, the functions of President shall be exercised by a President of a Chamber according to the order of precedence laid down in Article 6 of these Rules.

If the President of the Court and the Presidents of the Chambers are all prevented from attending at the same time, or their posts are vacant at the same time, the functions of President shall be exercised by one of the other Judges according to the order of precedence laid down in Article 6 of these Rules.

Chapter 3

Registry

Section 1—The Registrar and Assistant Registrars

Article 12

1 The Court shall appoint the Registrar. Two weeks before the date fixed for making the appointment, the President shall inform the Members of the Court of the applications which have been made for the post.
2 An application shall be accompanied by full details of the candidate's age, nationality, university degrees, knowledge of any languages, present and past occupations and experience, if any, in judicial and international fields.
3 The appointment shall be made following the procedure laid down in Article 7(3) of these Rules.
4 The Registrar shall be appointed for a term of six years. He may be reappointed.
5 The Registrar shall take the oath in accordance with Article 3 of these Rules.
6 The Registrar may be deprived of his office only if he no longer fulfils the requisite conditions or no longer meets the obligations arising from his office; the Court shall take its decision after giving the Registrar an opportunity to make representations.
7 If the office of Registrar falls vacant before the normal date of expiry of the term thereof, the Court shall appoint a new Registrar for a term of six years.

Article 13

The Court may, following the procedure laid down in respect of the Registrar, appoint one or more Assistant Registrars to assist the Registrar and to take his place in so far as the Instructions to the Registrar referred in Article 15 of these Rules allow.

Article 14

Where the Registrar and the Assistant Registrars are absent or prevented from attending or their posts are vacant, the President shall designate an official or other servant to carry out the duties of Registrar.

Article 15

Instructions to the Registrar shall be adopted by the Court acting on a proposal from the President.

Article 16

1 There shall be kept in the Registry, under the control of the Registrar, a register initialled by the President, in which all pleadings and supporting documents shall be entered in the order in which they are lodged.
2 When a document has been registered, the Registrar shall make a note to that effect on the original and, if a party so requests, on any copy submitted for the purpose.
3 Entries in the register and the notes provided for in the preceding paragraph shall be authentic.
4 Rules for keeping the register shall be prescribed by the Instructions to the Registrar referred to in Article 15 of these Rules.

5   Persons having an interest may consult the register at the Registry and may obtain copies or extracts on payment of a charge on a scale fixed by the Court on a proposal from the Registrar.

The parties to a case may on payment of the appropriate charge also obtain copies of pleadings and authenticated copies of judgments and orders.

6   Notice shall be given in the Official Journal of the European Communities of the date of registration of an application initiating proceedings, the names and addresses of the parties, the subject matter of the proceedings, the form of order sought by the applicant and a summary of the pleas in law and of the main supporting arguments.

7   Where the Council or the Commission is not a party to a case, the Court shall send to it copies of the application and of the defence, without the annexes thereto, to enable it to assess whether the inapplicability of one of its acts is being invoked under the third paragraph of Article 36 of the ECSC Treaty, Article 184 of the EEC Treaty or Article 156 of the Euratom Treaty.

Article 17

1   The Registrar shall be responsible, under the authority of the President, for the acceptance, transmission and custody of documents and for effecting service as provided for by these Rules.

2   The Registrar shall assist the Court, the Chambers, the President and the Judges in all their official functions.

Article 18

The Registrar shall have custody of the seals. He shall be responsible for the records and be in charge of the publications of the Court.

Article 19

Subject to Articles 4 and 27 of these Rules, the Registrar shall attend the sittings of the Court and of the Chambers.

Section 2—Other departments

Article 20

1   The officials and other servants of the Court shall be appointed in accordance with the provisions of the Staff Regulations.

2   Before taking up his duties, an official shall take the following oath before the President, in the presence of the Registrar:

'I swear that I will perform loyally, discreetly and conscientiously the duties assigned to me by the Court of Justice of the European Communities'.

Article 21

The organisation of the departments of the Court shall be laid down, and may be modified, by the Court on a proposal from the Registrar.

Article 22

The Court shall set up a translating service staffed by experts with adequate legal training and a thorough knowledge of several official languages of the Court.

Article 23

The Registrar shall be responsible, under the authority of the President, for the administration of the Court, its financial management and its accounts; he shall be assisted in this by an administrator.

Chapter 4

Assistant Rapporteurs

Article 24

1 Where the Court is of the opinion that the consideration of, and preparatory inquiries in, cases before it so require, it shall, pursuant to Article 16 of the ECSC Statute and Article 12 of the EEC and Euratom Statutes, propose the appointment of Assistant Rapporteurs.
2 Assistant Rapporteurs shall in particular assist the President in connection with applications for the adoption of interim measures and assist the Judge-Rapporteurs in their work.
3 In the performance of their duties the Assistant Rapporteurs shall be responsible to the President of the Court, the President of a Chamber or a Judge-Rapporteur, as the case may be.
4 Before taking up his duties, an Assistant Rapporteur shall take before the Court the oath set out in Article 3 of these Rules.

Chapter 5

The working of the Court

Article 25

1 The dates and times of the sittings of the Court shall be fixed by the President.
2 The dates and times of the sittings of the Chambers shall be fixed by their respective Presidents.
3 The Court and the Chambers may choose to hold one or more sittings in a place other than that in which the Court has its seat.

Article 26

1 Where, by reason of a Judge being absent or prevented from attending, there is an even number of Judges, the most junior Judge within the meaning of Article 6 of these Rules shall abstain from taking part in the deliberations unless he is the Judge-Rapporteur. In that case the Judge immediately senior to him shall abstain from taking part in the deliberations.
2 If after the Court has been convened it is found that the quorum of seven Judges has not been attained, the President shall adjourn the sitting until there is a quorum.
3 If in any Chamber the quorum of three Judges has not been attained, the President of that Chamber shall so inform the President of the Court who shall designate another Judge to complete the Chamber.

Article 27

1 The Court and Chambers shall deliberate in closed session.
2 Only those Judges who were present at the oral proceedings and the Assistant Rapporteur, if any, entrusted with the consideration of the case may take part in the deliberations.
3 Every Judge taking part in the deliberations shall state his opinion and the reasons for it.
4 Any Judge may require that any questions be formulated in the language of his choice and communicated in writing to the Court or Chamber before being put to the vote.
5 The conclusions reached by the majority of the Judges after final discussion shall determine the decision of the Court. Votes shall be cast in reverse order to the order of precedence laid down in Article 6 of these Rules.
6 Differences of view on the substance, wording or order of questions, or on the interpretation of the voting shall be settled by decision of the Court or Chamber.

7   Where the deliberations of the Court concern questions of its own administration, the Advocates-General shall take part and have a vote. The Registrar shall be present, unless the Court decides to the contrary.
8   Where the Court sits without the Registrar being present it shall, if necessary, instruct the most junior Judge within the meaning of Article 6 of these Rules to draw up minutes. The minutes shall be signed by that Judge and by the President.

Article 28

1   Subject to any special decision of the Court, its vacations shall be as follows:
—from 18 December to 10 January,
—from the Sunday before Easter to the second Sunday after Easter,
—from 15 July to 15 September.
During the vacations, the functions of President shall be exercised at the place where the Court has its seat either by the President himself, keeping in touch with the Registrar, or by a President of Chamber or other Judge invited by the President to take his place.
2   In a case of urgency, the President may convene the Judges and the Advocates-General during the vacations.
3   The Court shall observe the official holidays of the place where it has its seat.
4   The Court may, in proper circumstances, grant leave of absence to any Judge or Advocate-General.

Chapter 6

Languages

Article 29

1   The language of a case shall be Danish, Dutch, English, French, German, Greek, Irish, Italian, Portuguese or Spanish.
2   The language of a case shall be chosen by the applicant, except that:

(a) where the defendant is a Member State or a natural or legal person having the nationality of a Member State, the language of the case shall be the official language of that State; where that State has more than one official language, the applicant may choose between them;
(b) at the joint request of the parties the Court may authorise another of the languages mentioned in paragraph (1) of this Article to be used as the language of the case for all or part of the proceedings;
(c) at the request of one of the parties, and after the opposite party and the Advocate-General have been heard, the Court, may, by way of derogation from sub-paragraphs (a) and (b), authorise another of the languages mentioned in paragraph (1) of this Article to be used as the language of the case for all or part of the proceedings; such a request may not be submitted by an institution of the European Communities.

In cases to which Article 103 of these Rules applies, the language of the case shall be the language of the national court or tribunal which refers the matter to the Court.
3   The language of the case shall in particular be used in the written and oral pleadings of the parties and in supporting documents, and also in the minutes and decisions of the Court.
Any supporting documents expressed in another language must be accompanied by a translation into the language of the case.
In the case of lengthy documents, translations may be confined to extracts. However, the Court or Chamber may, of its own motion or at the request of a party, at any time call for a complete or fuller translation.
Notwithstanding the foregoing provisions, a Member State shall be entitled to use its official language when intervening in a case before the Court or when taking part in any reference of a kind mentioned in Article 103. This provision shall apply both to written statements and to oral addresses. The Registrar shall cause any such statement or address to be translated into the language of the case.

4　Where a witness or expert states that he is unable adequately to express himself in one of the languages referred to in paragraph (1) of this Article, the Court or Chamber may authorise him to give his evidence in another language. The Registrar shall arrange for translation into the language of the case.

5　The President of the Court and the Presidents of Chambers in conducting oral proceedings, the Judge-Rapporteur both in his preliminary report and in his report for the hearing, Judges and Advocates-General in putting questions and Advocates-General in delivering their opinions may use one of the languages referred to in paragraph (1) of this Article other than the language of the case. The Registrar shall arrange for translation into the language of the case.

Article 30

1　The Registrar shall, at the request of any Judge, of the Advocate-General or of a party, arrange for anything said or written in the course of the proceedings before the Court or a Chamber to be translated into the languages he chooses from those referred to in Article 29(1).

2　Publications of the Court shall be issued in the languages referred to in Article 1 of Council Regulation No 1.

Article 31

The texts of documents drawn up in the language of the case or in any other language authorised by the Court pursuant to Article 29 of these rules shall be authentic.

Chapter 7

Rights and obligations of agents, advisers and lawyers

Article 32

1　Agents representing a State or an institution, as well as advisers and lawyers, appearing before the Court or before any judicial authority to which the Court has addressed letters rogatory, shall enjoy immunity in respect of words spoken or written by them concerning the case or the parties.

2　Agents, advisers and lawyers shall enjoy the following further privileges and facilities:

　(a)　papers and documents relating to the proceedings shall be exempt from both search and seizure; in the event of a dispute the customs officials or police may seal those papers and documents; they shall then be immediately forwarded to the Court for inspection in the presence of the Registrar and of the person concerned;

　(b)　agents, advisers and lawyers shall be entitled to such allocation of foreign currency as may be necessary for the performance of their duties;

　(c)　agents, advisers and lawyers shall be entitled to travel in the course of duty without hindrance.

Article 33

In order to qualify for the privileges, immunities and facilities specified in Article 32, persons entitled to them shall furnish proof of their status as follows:

(a)　agents shall produce an official document issued by the State or institution which they represent; a copy of this document shall be forwarded without delay to the Registrar by the State or institution concerned;

(b)　advisers and lawyers shall produce a certificate signed by the Registrar. The validity of this certificate shall be limited to a specified period, which may be extended or curtailed according to the length of the proceedings.

Article 34

The privileges, immunities and facilities specified in Article 32 of these Rules are granted exclusively in the interests of the proper conduct of proceedings.

　The Court may waive the immunity where it considers that the proper conduct of proceedings will not be hindered thereby.

Article 35

1   Any adviser or lawyer whose conduct towards the Court, a Chamber, a Judge, an Advocate-General or the Registrar is incompatible with the dignity of the Court, or who uses his rights for purposes other than those for which they were granted, may at any time be excluded from the proceedings by an order of the Court or Chamber, after the Advocate-General has been heard; the person concerned shall be given an opportunity to defend himself.

     The order shall have immediate effect.

2   Where an adviser or lawyer is excluded from the proceedings, the proceedings shall be suspended for a period fixed by the President in order to allow the party concerned to appoint another adviser or lawyer.

3   Decisions taken under this Article may be rescinded.

Article 36

The provisions of this Chapter shall apply to university teachers who have a right of audience before the Court in accordance with Article 20 of the ECSC Statute and Article 17 of the EEC and Euratom Statutes.

TITLE II

PROCEDURE

Chapter 1

Written procedure

Article 37

1   The original of every pleading must be signed by the party's agent or lawyer.

     The original, accompanied by all annexes referred to therein, shall be lodged together with five copies for the Court and a copy for every other party to the proceedings. Copies shall be certified by the party lodging them.

2   Institutions shall in addition produce, within time-limits laid down by the Court, translations of all pleadings into the other languages provided for by Article 1 of Council Regulation No 1. The second sub-paragraph of paragraph (1) of this Article shall apply.

3   All pleadings shall bear a date. In the reckoning of time-limits for taking steps in proceedings, only the date of lodgment at the Registry shall be taken into account.

4   To every pleading there shall be annexed a file containing the documents relied on in support of it, together with a schedule listing them.

5   Where in view of the length of a document only extracts from it are annexed to the pleading, the whole document or a full copy of it shall be lodged at the Registry.

Article 38

1   An application of the kind referred to in Article 22 of the ECSC Statute and Article 19 of the EEC and Euratom Statutes shall state:

(a) the name and address of the applicant;
(b) the designation of the party against whom the application is made;
(c) the subject matter of the proceedings and a summary of the pleas in law on which the application is based;
(d) the form of order sought by the applicant;
(e) where appropriate, the nature of any evidence offered in support.

2   For the purpose of the proceedings, the application shall state an address for service in the place where the Court has its seat and the name of the person who is authorised and has expressed willingness to accept service.

     If the application does not comply with these requirements, all service on the party concerned for the purpose of the proceedings shall be effected, for so long as the defect has not been cured, by registered letter addressed to the agent or lawyer of that party. By way of derogation from Article 79, service shall then be deemed to be duly effected by the lodging of the registered letter at the post office of the place where the Court has its seat.

3   The lawyer acting for a party must lodge at the Registry a certificate that he is entitled to practise before a court of a Member State.
4   The application shall be accompanied, where appropriate, by the documents specified in the second paragraph of Article 22 of the ECSC Statute and in the second paragraph of Article 19 of the EEC and Euratom Statutes.
5   An application made by a legal person governed by private law shall be accompanied by:

   (a) the instrument or instruments constituting or regulating that legal person or a recent extract from the register of companies, firms or associations or any other proof of its existence in law;
   (b) proof that the authority granted to the applicant's lawyer has been properly conferred on him by someone authorised for the purpose.

6   An application submitted under Articles 42 and 89 of the ECSC Treaty, Articles 181 and 182 of the EEC Treaty and Articles 153 and 154 of the Euratom Treaty shall be accompanied by a copy of the arbitration clause contained in the contract governed by private or public law entered into by the Communities or on their behalf, or, as the case may be, by a copy of the special agreement concluded between the Member States concerned.
7   If an application does not comply with the requirements set out in paragraphs (3) to (6) of this Article, the Registrar shall prescribe a reasonable period within which the applicant is to comply with them whether by putting the application itself in order or by producing any of the abovementioned documents. If the applicant fails to put the application in order or to produce the required documents within the time prescribed, the Court shall, after hearing the Advocate-General, decide whether the non-compliance with these conditions renders the application formally inadmissible.

Article 39

The application shall be served on the defendant. In a case where Article 38(7) applies, service shall be effected as soon as the application has been put in order or the Court has declared it admissible notwithstanding the failure to observe the formal requirements set out in that Article.

Article 40

1   Within one month after service on him of the application, the defendant shall lodge a defence, stating:

   (a) the name and address of the defendant;
   (b) the arguments of fact and law relied on;
   (c) the form of order sought by the defendant;
   (d) the nature of any evidence offered by him.

   The provisions of Article 38(2) to (5) of these Rules shall apply to the defence.
2   The time-limit laid down in paragraph (1) of this Article may be extended by the President on a reasoned application by the defendant.

Article 41

1   The application initiating the proceedings and the defence may be supplemented by a reply from the applicant and by a rejoinder from the defendant.
2   The President shall fix the time-limits within which these pleadings are to be lodged.

Article 42

1   In reply or rejoinder a party may offer further evidence. The party must, however, give reasons for the delay in offering it.
2   No new plea in law may be introduced in the course of proceedings unless it is based on matters of law or of fact which come to light in the course of the procedure.

If in the course of the procedure one of the parties puts forward a new plea in law which is so based, the President may, even after the expiry of the normal procedural time-limits, acting on a report of the Judge-Rapporteur and after hearing the Advocate-General, allow the other party time to answer on that plea.

The decision on the admissibility of the plea shall be reserved for the final judgment.

Article 43

The President may, at any time, after hearing the parties and the Advocate-General, if the assignment referred to in Article 10(2) has taken place, order that two or more cases concerning the same subject matter shall, on account of the connection between them, be joined for the purposes of the written or oral procedure or of the final judgment. The cases may subsequently be disjoined.

Article 44

1   After the rejoinder provided for in Article 41(1) of these Rules has been lodged, the President shall fix a date on which the Judge-Rapporteur is to present his preliminary report to the Court. The report shall contain recommendations as to whether a preparatory inquiry or any other preparatory step should be undertaken and whether the case should be referred to the Chamber to which it has been assigned under Article 9(2).

The Court shall decide, after hearing the Advocate-General, what action to take upon the recommendations of the Judge-Rapporteur.

The same procedure shall apply:

(a) where no reply or no rejoinder has been lodged within the time-limit fixed in accordance with Article 41(2) of these Rules;
(b) where the party concerned waives his right to lodge a reply or rejoinder.

2   Where the Court orders a preparatory inquiry and does not undertake it itself, it shall assign the inquiry to the Chamber.

Where the Court decides to open the oral procedure without an inquiry, the President shall fix the opening date.

Article 44a

Without prejudice to any special provisions laid down in these Rules, and except in the specific cases in which, after the pleadings referred to in Article 40(1) and, as the case may be, in Article 41(1) have been lodged, the Court, acting on a report from the Judge-Rapporteur, after hearing the Advocate-General and with the express consent of the parties, decides otherwise, the procedure before the Court shall also include an oral part.

Chapter 2

Preparatory inquiries

Section 1—Measures of inquiry

Article 45

1   The Court, after hearing the Advocate-General, shall prescribe the measures of inquiry that it considers appropriate by means of an order setting out the facts to be proved. Before the Court decides on the measures of inquiry referred to in paragraph (2)(c), (d) and (e) the parties shall be heard.

The order shall be served on the parties.

2   Without prejudice to Articles 24 and 25 of the ECSC Statute, Articles 21 and 22 of the EEC Statute or Articles 22 and 23 of the Euratom Statute, the following measures of inquiry may be adopted:

(a) the personal appearance of the parties;
(b) a request for information and production of documents;
(c) oral testimony;
(d) the commissioning of an expert's report;
(e) an inspection of the place or thing in question.

3   The measures of inquiry which the Court has ordered may be conducted by the
     Court itself, or be assigned to the Judge-Rapporteur.
        The Advocate-General shall take part in the measures of inquiry.
4   Evidence may be submitted in rebuttal and previous evidence may be amplified.

Article 46

1   A Chamber to which a preparatory inquiry has been assigned may exercise the
     powers vested in the Court by Articles 45 and 47 to 53 of these Rules; the powers
     vested in the President of the Court may be exercised by the President of the
     Chamber.
2   Articles 56 and 57 of these Rules shall apply to proceedings before the Chamber.
3   The parties shall be entitled to attend the measures of inquiry.

Section 2—The summoning and examination of witnesses and experts

Article 47

1   The Court may, either of its own motion or an application by a party, and after
     hearing the Advocate-General, order that certain facts be proved by witnesses.
     The order of the Court shall set out the facts to be established.
        The Court may summon a witness of its own motion or on application by a party
     or at the instance of the Advocate-General.
        An application by a party for the examination of a witness shall state precisely
     about what facts and for what reasons the witness should be examined.
2   The witness shall be summoned by an order of the Court containing the following
     information:

   (a) the surname, forenames, description and address of the witness;
   (b) an indication of the facts about which the witness is to be examined;
   (c) where appropriate, particulars of the arrangements made by the Court for
       reimbursement of expenses incurred by the witness, and of the penalties
       which may be imposed on defaulting witnesses.

        The order shall be served on the parties and the witnesses.
3   The Court may make the summoning of a witness for whose examination a party
     has applied conditional upon the deposit with the cashier of the Court of a sum
     sufficient to cover the taxed costs thereof; the Court shall fix the amount of the
     payment.
        The cashier shall advance the funds necessary in connection with the examin-
     ation of any witness summoned by the Court of its own motion.
4   After the identity of the witness has been established, the President shall inform
     him that he will be required to vouch the truth of his evidence in the manner laid
     down in these Rules.
        The witness shall give his evidence to the Court, the parties having been given
     notice to attend. After the witness has given his main evidence the President may,
     at the request of a party or of his own motion, put questions to him.
        The other Judges and the Advocate-General may do likewise.
        Subject to the control of the President, questions may be put to witnesses by the
     representatives of the parties.
5   After giving his evidence, the witness shall take the following oath:

     'I swear that I have spoken the truth, the whole truth and nothing but the
     truth.'

        The Court may, after hearing the parties, exempt a witness from taking the oath.
6   The Registrar shall draw up minutes in which the evidence of each witness is
     reproduced.
        The minutes shall be signed by the President or by the Judge-Rapporteur
     responsible for conducting the examination of the witness, and by the Registrar.
     Before the minutes are thus signed, witnesses must be given an opportunity to
     check the content of the minutes and to sign them.
        The minutes shall constitute an official record.

Article 48

1   Witnesses who have been duly summoned shall obey the summons and attend for examination.

2   If a witness who has been duly summoned fails to appear before the Court, the Court may impose upon him a pecuniary penalty not exceeding ECU 5,000 and may order that a further summons be served on the witness at his own expense.

    The same penalty may be imposed upon a witness who, without good reason, refuses to give evidence or to take the oath or where appropriate to make a solemn affirmation equivalent thereto.

3   If the witness proffers a valid excuse to the Court, the pecuniary penalty imposed on him may be cancelled. The pecuniary penalty imposed may be reduced at the request of the witness where he establishes that it is disproportionate to his income.

4   Penalties imposed and other measures ordered under this Article shall be enforced in accordance with Articles 44 and 92 of the ECSC Treaty, Articles 187 and 192 of the EEC Treaty and Articles 159 and 164 of the Euratom Treaty.

Article 49

1   The Court may order that an expert's report be obtained. The order appointing the expert shall define his task and set a time-limit within which he is to make his report.

2   The expert shall receive a copy of the order, together with all the documents necessary for carrying out his task. He shall be under the supervision of the Judge-Rapporteur, who may be present during his investigation and who shall be kept informed of his progress in carrying out his task.

    The Court may request the parties or one of them to lodge security for the costs of the expert's report.

3   At the request of the expert, the Court may order the examination of witnesses. Their examination shall be carried out in accordance with Article 47 of these Rules.

4   The expert may give his opinion only on points which have been expressly referred to him.

5   After the expert has made his report, the Court may order that he be examined, the parties having been given notice to attend.

    Subject to the control of the President, questions may be put to the expert by the representatives of the parties.

6   After making his report, the expert shall take the following oath before the Court :

    'I swear that I have conscientiously and impartially carried out my task.'

    The Court may, after hearing the parties, exempt the expert from taking the oath.

Article 50

1   If one of the parties objects to a witness or to an expert on the ground that he is not a competent or proper person to act as witness or expert or for any other reason, or if a witness or expert refuses to give evidence, to take the oath or to make a solemn affirmation equivalent thereto, the matter shall be resolved by the Court.

2   An objection to a witness or to an expert shall be raised within two weeks after service of the order summoning the witness or appointing the expert; the statement of objection must set out the grounds of objection and indicate the nature of any evidence offered.

Article 51

1   Witnesses and experts shall be entitled to reimbursement of their travel and subsistence expenses. The cashier of the Court may make a payment to them towards these expenses in advance.

2   Witnesses shall be entitled to compensation for loss of earnings, and experts to fees for their services. The cashier of the Court shall pay witnesses and experts their compensation or fees after they have carried out their respective duties or tasks.

Article 52

The Court may, on application by a party or of its own motion, issue letters rogatory for the examination of witnesses or experts, as provided for in the supplementary rules mentioned in Article 125 of these Rules.

Article 53

1 The Registrar shall draw up minutes of every hearing. The minutes shall be signed by the President and by the Registrar and shall constitute an official record.
2 The parties may inspect the minutes and any expert's report at the Registry and obtain copies at their own expense.

Section 3—Closure of the preparatory inquiry

Article 54

Unless the Court prescribes a period within which the parties may lodge written observations, the President shall fix the date for the opening of the oral procedure after the preparatory inquiry has been completed.

Where a period had been prescribed for the lodging of written observations, the President shall fix the date for the opening of the oral procedure after that period has expired.

Chapter 3

Oral procedure

Article 55

1 Subject to the priority of decisions provided for in Article 85 of these Rules, the Court shall deal with the cases before it in the order in which the preparatory inquiries in them have been completed. Where the preparatory inquiries in several cases are completed simultaneously, the order in which they are to be dealt with shall be determined by the dates of entry in the register of the applications initiating them respectively.
2 The President may in special circumstances order that a case be given priority over others.

The President may in special circumstances, after hearing the parties and the Advocate-General, either on his own initiative or at the request of one of the parties, defer a case to be dealt with at a later date. On a joint application by the parties the President may order that a case be deferred.

Article 56

1 The proceedings shall be opened and directed by the President, who shall be responsible for the proper conduct of the hearing.
2 The oral proceedings in cases heard in camera shall not be published.

Article 57

The President may in the course of the hearing put questions to the agents, advisers or lawyers of the parties.

The other Judges and the Advocate-General may do likewise.

Article 58

A party may address the Court only through his agent, adviser or lawyer.

Article 59

1 The Advocate-General shall deliver his opinion orally at the end of the oral procedure.
2 After the Advocate-General has delivered his opinion, the President shall declare the oral procedure closed.

Article 60

The Court may at any time, in accordance with Article 45(1), after hearing the Advocate-General, order any measure of inquiry to be taken or that a previous inquiry be repeated or expanded. The Court may direct the Chamber or the Judge-Rapporteur to carry out the measures so ordered.

Article 61

The Court may after hearing the Advocate-General order the reopening of the oral procedure.

Article 62

1   The Registrar shall draw up minutes of every hearing. The minutes shall be signed by the President and by the Registrar and shall constitute an official record.
2   The parties may inspect the minutes at the Registry and obtain copies at their own expense.

Chapter 4

Judgments

Article 63

The judgment shall contain:
—a statement that it is the judgment of the Court,
—the date of its delivery,
—the names of the President and of the Judges taking part in it,
—the name of the Advocate-General,
—the name of the Registrar,
—the description of the parties,
—the names of the agents, advisers and lawyers of the parties,
—a statement of the forms of order sought by the parties,
—a statement that the Advocate-General has been heard,
—a summary of the facts,
—the grounds for the decision,
—the operative part of the judgment, including the decision as to costs.

Article 64

1   The judgment shall be delivered in open court; the parties shall be given notice to attend to hear it.
2   The original of the judgment, signed by the President, by the Judges who took part in the deliberations and by the Registrar, shall be sealed and deposited at the Registry; the parties shall be served with certified copies of the judgment.
3   The Registrar shall record on the original of the judgment the date on which it was delivered.

Article 65

The judgment shall be binding from the date of its delivery.

Article 66

1   Without prejudice to the provisions relating to the interpretation of judgments the Court may, of its own motion or on application by a party made within two weeks after the delivery of a judgment, rectify clerical mistakes, errors in calculation and obvious slips in it.
2   The parties, whom the Registrar shall duly notify, may lodge written observations within a period prescribed by the President.
3   The Court shall take its decision in closed session after hearing the Advocate-General.
4   The original of the rectification order shall be annexed to the original of the rectified judgment. A note of this order shall be made in the margin of the original of the rectified judgment.

Article 67

If the Court should omit to give a decision on a specific head of claim or on costs, any party may within a month after service of the judgment apply to the Court to supplement its judgment.

The application shall be served on the opposite party and the President shall prescribe a period within which that party may lodge written observations.

After these observations have been lodged, the Court shall, after hearing the Advocate-General, decide both on the admissibility and on the substance of the application.

Article 68

The Registrar shall arrange for the publication of reports of cases before the Court.

Chapter 5

Costs

Article 69

1   A decision as to costs shall be given in the final judgment or in the order which closes the proceedings.

2   The unsuccessful party shall be ordered to pay the costs if they have been applied for in the successful party's pleadings.

    Where there are several unsuccessful parties the Court shall decide how the costs are to be shared.

3   Where each party succeeds on some and fails on other heads, or where the circumstances are exceptional, the Court may order that the costs be shared or that the parties bear their own costs.

    The Court may order a party, even if successful, to pay costs which the Court considers that party to have unreasonably or vexatiously caused the opposite party to incur.

4   The Member States and institutions which intervene in the proceedings shall bear their own costs.

    The Court may order an intervener other than those mentioned in the preceding sub-paragraph to bear his own costs.

5   A party who discontinues or withdraws from proceedings shall be ordered to pay the costs if they have been applied for in the other party's pleadings. However, upon application by the party who discontinues or withdraws from proceedings, the costs shall be borne by the other party if this appears justified by the conduct of that party.

    Where the parties have come to an agreement on costs, the decision as to costs shall be in accordance with that agreement.

    If costs are not claimed, the parties shall bear their own costs.

6   Where a case does not proceed to judgment the costs shall be in the discretion of the Court.

Article 70

Without prejudice to the second sub-paragraph of Article 69(3) of these Rules, in proceedings between the Communities and their servants the institutions shall bear their own costs.

Article 71

Costs necessarily incurred by a party in enforcing a judgment or order of the Court shall be refunded by the opposite party on the scale in force in the State where the enforcement takes place.

Article 72

Proceedings before the Court shall be free of charge, except that:

    (a) where a party has caused the Court to incur avoidable costs the Court may, after hearing the Advocate-General, order that party to refund them;

(b) where copying or translation work is carried out at the request of a party, the cost shall, in so far as the Registrar considers it excessive, be paid for by that party on the scale of charges referred to in Article 16(5) of these Rules.

Article 73

Without prejudice to the preceding Article, the following shall be regarded as recoverable costs:

(a) sums payable to witnesses and experts under Article 51 of these Rules;
(b) expenses necessarily incurred by the parties for the purpose of the proceedings, in particular the travel and subsistence expenses and the remuneration of agents, advisers or lawyers.

Article 74

1　If there is a dispute concerning the costs to be recovered, the Chamber to which the case has been assigned shall, on application by the party concerned and after hearing the opposite party and the Advocate-General, make an order, from which no appeal shall lie.

2　The parties may, for the purposes of enforcement, apply for an authenticated copy of the order.

Article 75

1　Sums due from the cashier of the Court shall be paid in the currency of the country where the Court has its seat.

　　At the request of the person entitled to any sum, it shall be paid in the currency of the country where the expenses to be refunded were incurred or where the steps in respect of which payment is due were taken.

2　Other debtors shall make payment in the currency of their country of origin.

3　Conversions of currency shall be made at the official rates of exchange ruling on the day of payment in the country where the Court has its seat.

Chapter 6

Legal aid

Article 76

1　A party who is wholly or in part unable to meet the costs of the proceedings may at any time apply for legal aid.

　　The application shall be accompanied by evidence of the applicant's need of assistance, and in particular by a document from the competent authority certifying his lack of means.

2　If the application is made prior to proceedings which the applicant wishes to commence, it shall briefly state the subject of such proceedings.

　　The application need not be made through a lawyer.

3　The President shall designate a Judge to act as Rapporteur. The Chamber to which the latter belongs shall, after considering the written observations of the opposite party and after hearing the Advocate-General, decide whether legal aid should be granted in full or in part, or whether it should be refused. The Chamber shall consider whether there is manifestly no cause of action.

　　The Chamber shall make an order without giving reasons, and no appeal shall lie therefrom.

4　The Chamber may at any time, either of its own motion or on application, withdraw legal aid if the circumstances which led to its being granted alter during the proceedings.

5　Where legal aid is granted, the cashier of the Court shall advance the funds necessary to meet the expenses.

　　In its decision as to costs the Court may order the payment to the cashier of the Court of the whole or any part of amounts advanced as legal aid.

　　The Registrar shall take steps to obtain the recovery of these sums from the party ordered to pay them.

Chapter 7

Discontinuance

Article 77

If, before the Court has given its decision, the parties reach a settlement of their dispute and intimate to the Court the abandonment of their claims, the President shall order the case to be removed from the register and shall give a decision as to costs in accordance with Article 69(5), having regard to any proposals made by the parties on the matter.

This provision shall not apply to proceedings under Articles 33 and 35 of the ECSC Treaty, Articles 173 and 175 of the EEC Treaty or Articles 146 and 148 of the Euratom Treaty.

Article 78

If the applicant informs the Court in writing that he wishes to discontinue the proceedings, the President shall order the case to be removed from the register and shall give a decision as to costs in accordance with Article 69(5).

Chapter 8

Service

Article 79

Where these Rules require that a document be served on a person, the Registrar shall ensure that service is effected at that person's address for service either by the dispatch of a copy of the document by registered post with a form for acknowledgment of receipt or by personal delivery of the copy against a receipt.

The Registrar shall prepare and certify the copies of documents to be served, save where the parties themselves supply the copies in accordance with Article 37(1) of these Rules.

Chapter 9

Time-limits

Article 80

1   Any period of time prescribed by the ECSC, EEC or Euratom Treaties, the Statutes of the Court or these Rules for the taking of any procedural step shall be reckoned as follows:

   (a) where a period expressed in days, weeks, months or years is to be calculated from the moment at which an event occurs or an action takes place, the day during which that event occurs or that action takes place shall not be counted as falling within the period in question;
   (b) a period expressed in weeks, months or in years shall end with the expiry of whichever day in the last week, month or year is the same day of the week, or falls on the same date, as the day during which the event or action from which the period is to be calculated occurred or took place. If, in a period expressed in months or in years, the day on which it should expire does not occur in the last month, the period shall end with the expiry of the last day of that month;
   (c) where a period is expressed in months and days, it shall first be reckoned in whole months, then in days;
   (d) periods shall include official holidays, Sundays and Saturdays;
   (e) periods shall not be suspended during the judicial vacations.

2   If the period would otherwise end on a Saturday, Sunday or an official holiday, it shall be extended until the end of the first following working day.

   A list of official holidays drawn up by the Court shall be published in the Official Journal of the European Communities.

Article 81

1   The period of time allowed for commencing proceedings against a measure adopted by an institution shall run from the day following the receipt by the person concerned of notification of the measure or, where the measure is published, from the 15th day after publication thereof in the Official Journal of the European Communities.

2   The extensions, on account of distance, of prescribed time-limits shall be provided for in a decision of the Court which shall be published in the Official Journal of the European Communities.

Article 82

Any time-limit prescribed pursuant to these Rules may be extended by whoever prescribed it.

The President and the Presidents of Chambers may delegate to the Registrar power of signature for the purpose of fixing time-limits which, pursuant to these Rules, it falls to them to prescribe or of extending such time-limits.

Chapter 10

Stay of proceedings

Article 82a

1   The proceedings may be stayed:

(a) in the circumstances specified in the third paragraph of Article 47 of the ECSC Statute, the third paragraph of Article 47 of the EEC Statute and the third paragraph of Article 48 of the Euratom Statute, by order of the Court or of the Chamber to which the case has been assigned, made after hearing the Advocate-General;

(b) in all other cases, by decision of the President adopted after hearing the Advocate-General and, save in the case of references for a preliminary ruling as referred to in Article 103, the parties.

The proceedings may be resumed by order or decision, following the same procedure.

The orders or decisions referred to in this paragraph shall be served on the parties.

2   The stay of proceedings shall take effect on the date indicated in the order or decision of stay or, in the absence of such indication, on the date of that order or decision.

While proceedings are stayed time shall cease to run for the purposes of prescribed time-limits for all parties.

3   Where the order or decision of stay does not fix the length of stay, it shall end on the date indicated in the order or decision of resumption or, in the absence of such indication, on the date of the order or decision of resumption.

From the date of resumption time shall begin to run afresh for the purposes of the time-limits.

TITLE III

SPECIAL FORMS OF PROCEDURE

Chapter 1

Suspension of operation or enforcement and other interim measures

Article 83

1   An application to suspend the operation of any measure adopted by an institution, made pursuant to the second paragraph of Article 39 of the ECSC Treaty, Article 185 of the EEC Treaty or Article 157 of the Euratom Treaty, shall be admissible only if the applicant is challenging that measure in proceedings before the Court.

An application for the adoption of any other interim measure referred to in the third paragraph of Article 39 of the ECSC Treaty, Article 186 of the EEC Treaty or Article 158 of the Euratom Treaty shall be admissible only if it is made by a party to a case before the Court and relates to that case.

2 An application of a kind referred to in paragraph (1) of this Article shall state the subject matter of the proceedings, the circumstances giving rise to urgency and the pleas of fact and law establishing a prima facie case for the interim measures applied for.

3 The application shall be made by a separate document and in accordance with the provisions of Articles 37 and 38 of these Rules.

Article 84

1 The application shall be served on the opposite party, and the President shall prescribe a short period within which that party may submit written or oral observations.

2 The President may order a preparatory inquiry.

The President may grant the application even before the observations of the opposite party have been submitted. This decision may be varied or cancelled even without any application being made by any party.

Article 85

The President shall either decide on the application himself or refer it to the Court.

If the President is absent or prevented from attending, Article 11 of these Rules shall apply.

Where the application is referred to it, the Court shall postpone all other cases, and shall give a decision after hearing the Advocate-General. Article 84 shall apply.

Article 86

1 The decision on the application shall take the form of a reasoned order, from which no appeal shall lie. The order shall be served on the parties forthwith.

2 The enforcement of the order may be made conditional on the lodging by the applicant of security, of an amount and nature to be fixed in the light of the circumstances.

3 Unless the order fixes the date on which the interim measure is to lapse, the measure shall lapse when final judgment is delivered.

4 The order shall have only an interim effect, and shall be without prejudice to the decision of the Court on the substance of the case.

Article 87

On application by a party, the order may at any time be varied or cancelled on account of a change in circumstances.

Article 88

Rejection of an application for an interim measure shall not bar the party who made it from making a further application on the basis of new facts.

Article 89

The provisions of this Chapter shall apply to applications to suspend the enforcement of a decision of the Court or of any measure adopted by another institution, submitted pursuant to Articles 44 and 92 of the ECSC Treaty, Articles 187 and 192 of the EEC Treaty or Articles 159 and 164 of the Euratom Treaty.

The order granting the application shall fix, where appropriate, a date on which the interim measure is to lapse.

Article 90

1 An application of a kind referred to in the third and fourth paragraphs of Article 81 of the Euratom Treaty shall contain:

(a) the names and addresses of the persons or undertakings to be inspected;
(b) an indication of what is to be inspected and of the purpose of the inspection.

2   The President shall give his decision in the form of an order. Article 86 of these Rules shall apply.

    If the President is absent or prevented from attending, Article 11 of these Rules shall apply.

Chapter 2

Preliminary issues

Article 91

1   A party applying to the Court for a decision on a preliminary objection or other preliminary plea not going to the substance of the case shall make the application by a separate document.

    The application must state the pleas of fact and law relied on and the form of order sought by the applicant; any supporting documents must be annexed to it.

2   As soon as the application has been lodged, the President shall prescribe a period within which the opposite party may lodge a document containing a statement of the form of order sought by that party and its pleas in law.

3   Unless the Court decides otherwise, the remainder of the proceedings shall be oral.

4   The Court shall, after hearing the Advocate-General, decide on the application or reserve its decision for the final judgment.

    If the Court refuses the application or reserves its decision, the President shall prescribe new time-limits for the further steps in the proceedings.

Article 92

1   Where it is clear that the Court has no jurisdiction to take cognisance of an action or where the action is manifestly inadmissible, the Court may, by reasoned order, after hearing the Advocate-General and without taking further steps in the proceedings, give a decision on the action.

2   The Court may at any time of its own motion consider whether there exists any absolute bar to proceeding with a case, and shall give its decision in accordance with Article 91(3) and (4) of these Rules.

Chapter 3

Intervention

Article 93

1   An application to intervene must be made within three months of the publication of the notice referred to in Article 16(6) of these Rules.

    The application shall contain:

(a) the description of the case;
(b) the description of the parties;
(c) the name and address of the intervener;
(d) the intervener's address for service at the place where the Court has its seat;
(e) the form of order sought, by one or more of the parties, in support of which the intervener is applying for leave to intervene;
(f) except in the case of applications to intervene made by Member States or institutions, a statement of the reasons establishing the intervener's interest in the result of the case.

The intervener shall be represented in accordance with the first and second paragraphs of Article 20 of the ECSC Statute and with Article 17 of the EEC and Euratom Statutes.

    Articles 37 and 38 of these Rules shall apply.

2   The application shall be served on the parties.

    The President shall give the parties an opportunity to submit their written or oral observations before deciding on the application.

    The President shall decide on the application by order or shall refer the application to the Court.

3   If the President allows the intervention, the intervener shall receive a copy of every document served on the parties. The President may, however, on application by one of the parties, omit secret or confidential documents.

4   The intervener must accept the case as he finds it at the time of his intervention.

5   The President shall prescribe a period within which the intervener may submit a statement in intervention.

The statement in intervention shall contain:

(a) a statement of the form of order sought by the intervener in support of or opposing, in whole or in part, the form of order sought by one of the parties;

(b) the pleas in law and arguments relied on by the intervener;

(c) where appropriate, the nature of any evidence offered.

6   After the statement in intervention has been lodged, the President shall, where necessary, prescribe a time-limit within which the parties may reply to that statement.

Chapter 4

Judgments by default and applications to set them aside

Article 94

1   If a defendant on whom an application initiating proceedings has been duly served fails to lodge a defence to the application in the proper form within the time prescribed, the applicant may apply for judgment by default.

The application shall be served on the defendant. The President shall fix a date for the opening of the oral procedure.

2   Before giving judgment by default the Court shall, after hearing the Advocate-General, consider whether the application initiating proceedings is admissible, whether the appropriate formalities have been complied with, and whether the application appears well founded. The Court may order a preparatory inquiry.

3   A judgment by default shall be enforceable. The Court may, however, grant a stay of execution until the Court has given its decision on any application under paragraph (4) to set aside the judgment, or it may make execution subject to the provision of security of an amount and nature to be fixed in the light of the circumstances; this security shall be released if no such application is made or if the application fails.

4   Application may be made to set aside a judgment by default.

The application to set aside the judgment must be made within one month from the date of service of the judgment and must be lodged in the form prescribed by Articles 37 and 38 of these Rules.

5   After the application has been served, the President shall prescribe a period within which the other party may submit his written observations.

The proceedings shall be conducted in accordance with Articles 44 et seq of these Rules.

6   The Court shall decide by way of a judgment which may not be set aside. The original of this judgment shall be annexed to the original of the judgment by default. A note of the judgment on the application to set aside shall be made in the margin of the original of the judgment by default.

Chapter 5

Cases assigned to Chambers

Article 95

1   The Court may assign to a Chamber any appeal brought against a decision of the Court of First Instance pursuant to Article 49 of the ECSC Statute, Article 49 of the EEC Statute and Article 50 of the Euratom Statute; any reference for a preliminary ruling of a kind mentioned in Article 103 of these Rules and any other case, with the exception of those brought by a Member State or an institution, in so far as the difficulty or the importance of the case or particular circumstances are not such as to require that the Court decide it in plenary session.

2   The decision so to assign a case shall be taken by the Court at the end of the
        written procedure upon consideration of the preliminary report presented by the
        Judge-Rapporteur and after the Advocate-General has been heard.
            However, a case may not be so assigned if a Member State or an institution,
        being a party to the proceedings, has requested that the case be decided in
        plenary session. In this sub-paragraph the expression 'party to the proceedings'
        means any Member State or any institution which is a party to or an intervener in
        the proceedings or which has submitted written observations in any reference of a
        kind mentioned in Article 103 of these Rules.
            The request referred to in the preceding sub-paragraph may not be made in
        proceedings between the Communities and their servants.
3   A Chamber may at any stage refer a case back to the Court.

Article 96

(*repealed*)

Chapter 6

Exceptional review procedures

Section 1—Third-party proceedings

Article 97

1   Articles 37 and 38 of these Rules shall apply to an application initiating third-
        party proceedings. In addition such an application shall:

(a) specify the judgment contested;
(b) state how that judgment is prejudicial to the rights of the third party;
(c) indicate the reasons for which the third party was unable to take part in the
     original case.

The application must be made against all the parties to the original case.
    Where the judgment has been published in the Official Journal of the
European Communities, the application must be lodged within two months of
the publication.

2   The Court may, on application by the third party, order a stay of execution of the
        judgment. The provisions of Title III, Chapter 1, of these Rules shall apply.
3   The contested judgment shall be varied on the points on which the submissions of
        the third party are upheld.
            The original of the judgment in the third-party proceedings shall be annexed to
        the original of the contested judgment. A note of the judgment in the third-party
        proceedings shall be made in the margin of the original of the contested
        judgment.

Section 2—Revision

Article 98

An application for revision of a judgment shall be made within three months of the date
on which the facts on which the application is based came to the applicant's knowledge.

Article 99

1   Articles 37 and 38 of these Rules shall apply to an application for revision. In
        addition such an application shall:

(a) specify the judgment contested;
(b) indicate the points on which the judgment is contested;
(c) set out the facts on which the application is based;
(d) indicate the nature of the evidence to show that there are facts justifying
     revision of the judgment, and that the time-limit laid down in Article 98 has
     been observed.

2   The application must be made against all parties to the case in which the contested judgment was given.

Article 100

1   Without prejudice to its decision on the substance, the Court, in closed session, shall, after hearing the Advocate-General and having regard to the written observations of the parties, give in the form of a judgment its decision on the admissibility of the application.

2   If the Court finds the application admissible, it shall proceed to consider the substance of the application and shall give its decision in the form of a judgment in accordance with these Rules.

3   The original of the revising judgment shall be annexed to the original of the judgment revised. A note of the revising judgment shall be made in the margin of the original of the judgment revised.

Chapter 7

Appeals against decisions of the Arbitration Committee

Article 101

1   An application initiating an appeal under the second paragraph of Article 18 of the Euratom Treaty shall state:

(a) the name and address of the applicant;
(b) the description of the signatory;
(c) a reference to the arbitration committee's decision against which the appeal is made;
(d) the description of the parties;
(e) a summary of the facts;
(f) the pleas in law of and the form of order sought by the applicant.

2   Articles 37(3) and (4) and 38(2), (3) and (5) of these Rules shall apply.
     A certified copy of the contested decision shall be annexed to the application.

3   As soon as the application has been lodged, the Registrar of the Court shall request the arbitration committee registry to transmit to the Court the papers in the case.

4   Articles 39, 40, 55 et seq of these Rules shall apply to these proceedings.

5   The Court shall give its decision in the form of a judgment. Where the Court sets aside the decision of the arbitration committee it may refer the case back to the committee.

Chapter 8

Interpretation of judgments

Article 102

1   An application for interpretation of a judgment shall be made in accordance with Articles 37 and 38 of these Rules. In addition it shall specify:

(a) the judgment in question;
(b) the passages of which interpretation is sought.

The application must be made against all the parties to the case in which the judgment was given.

2   The Court shall give its decision in the form of a judgment after having given the parties an opportunity to submit their observations and after hearing the Advocate-General.

The original of the interpreting judgment shall be annexed to the original of the judgment interpreted. A note of the interpreting judgment shall be made in the margin of the original of the judgment interpreted.

Chapter 9

Preliminary rulings and other references for interpretation

Article 103

1   In cases governed by Article 20 of the EEC Statute and Article 21 of the Euratom Statute, the procedure shall be governed by the provisions of these Rules, subject to adaptations necessitated by the nature of the reference for a preliminary ruling.

2   The provisions of paragraph (1) shall apply to the references for a preliminary ruling provided for in the Protocol concerning the interpretation by the Court of Justice of the Convention of 29 February 1968 on the mutual recognition of companies and legal persons and the Protocol concerning the interpretation by the Court of Justice of the Convention of 27 September 1968 on jurisdiction and the enforcement of judgments in civil and commercial matters, signed at Luxembourg on 3 June 1971, and to the references provided for by Article 4 of the latter Protocol.

The provisions of paragraph (1) shall apply also to references for interpretation provided for by other existing or future agreements.

3   In cases provided for in Article 41 of the ECSC Treaty, the text of the decision to refer the matter shall be served on the parties in the case, the Member States, the Commission and the Council.

These parties, States and institutions may, within two months from the date of such service, lodge written statements of case or written observations.

The provisions of paragraph (1) shall apply.

Article 104

1   The decisions of national courts or tribunals referred to in Article 103 shall be communicated to the Member States in the original version, accompanied by a translation into the official language of the State to which they are addressed.

2   As regards the representation and attendance of the parties to the main proceedings in the preliminary ruling procedure the Court shall take account of the rules of procedure of the national court or tribunal which made the reference.

3   Where a question referred to the Court for a preliminary ruling is manifestly identical to a question on which the Court has already ruled, the Court may, after informing the court or tribunal which referred the question to it, hearing any observations submitted by the persons referred to in Article 20 of the EEC Statute, Article 21 of the Euratom Statute and Article 103(3) of these Rules and hearing the Advocate-General, give its decision by reasoned order in which reference is made to its previous judgment.

4   Without prejudice to paragraph (3) of this Article, the procedure before the Court in the case of a reference for a preliminary ruling shall also include an oral part. However, after the statements of case or written observations referred to in Article 20 of the EEC Statute, Article 21 of the Euratom Statute and Article 103(3) of these Rules have been submitted, the Court, acting on a report from the Judge-Rapporteur, after informing the persons who under the aforementioned provisions are entitled to submit such statements or observations, may, after hearing the Advocate-General, decide otherwise, provided that none of those persons has asked to present oral argument.

5   It shall be for the national court or tribunal to decide as to the costs of the reference.

In special circumstances the Court may grant, by way of legal aid, assistance for the purpose of facilitating the representation or attendance of a party.

Chapter 10

Special procedures under Articles 103 to 105 of the Euratom Treaty

Article 105

1   Four certified copies shall be lodged of an application under the third paragraph of Article 103 of the Euratom Treaty. The Commission shall be served with a copy.

2   The application shall be accompanied by the draft of the agreement or contract in question, by the observations of the Commission addressed to the State concerned and by all other supporting documents.

The Commission shall submit its observations to the Court within a period of 10 days, which may be extended by the President after the State concerned has been heard.

A certified copy of the observations shall be served on that State.

3   As soon as the application has been lodged the President shall designate a Judge to act as Rapporteur. The First Advocate-General shall assign the case to an Advocate-General as soon as the Judge-Rapporteur has been designated.

4   The decision shall be taken in closed session after the Advocate General has been heard.

The agents and advisers of the State concerned and of the Commission shall be heard if they so request.

Article 106

1   In cases provided for in the last paragraph of Article 104 and the last paragraph of Article 105 of the Euratom Treaty, the provisions of Articles 37 et seq of these Rules shall apply.

2   The application shall be served on the State to which the respondent person or undertaking belongs.

Chapter 11

Opinions

Article 107

1   A request by the Council for an Opinion under Article 228 of the EEC Treaty shall be served on the Commission. Such a request by the Commission shall be served on the Council and on the Member States. Such a request by a Member State shall be served on the Council, the Commission and the other Member States.

The President shall prescribe a period within which the institutions and Member States which have been served with a request may submit their written observations.

2   The Opinion may deal not only with the question whether the envisaged agreement is compatible which the provisions of the EEC Treaty but also with the question whether the Community or any Community institution has the power to enter into that agreement.

Article 108

1   As soon as the request for an Opinion has been lodged, the President shall designate a Judge to act as Rapporteur.

2   The Court sitting in closed session shall, after hearing the Advocates-General, deliver a reasoned Opinion.

3   The Opinion, signed by the President, by the Judges who took part in the deliberations and by the Registrar, shall be served on the Council, the Commission and the Member States.

Article 109

Requests for the Opinion of the Court under the fourth paragraph of Article 95 of the ECSC Treaty shall be submitted jointly by the Commission and the Council.

The Opinion shall be delivered in accordance with the provisions of the preceding Article. It shall be communicated to the Commission, the Council and the European Parliament.

TITLE IV

Appeals against decisions of the Court of First Instance

Article 110

Without prejudice to the arrangements laid down in Article 29(2)(b) and (c) and the fourth sub-paragraph of Article 29(3) of these Rules, in appeals against decisions of the

Court of First Instance as referred to in Articles 49 and 50 of the ECSC Statute, Articles 49 and 50 of the EEC Statute and Articles 50 and 51 of the Euratom Statute, the language of the case shall be the language of the decision of the Court of First Instance against which the appeal is brought.

Article 111

1   An appeal shall be brought by lodging an application at the Registry of the Court of Justice or of the Court of First Instance.
2   The Registry of the Court of First Instance shall immediately transmit to the Registry of the Court of Justice the papers in the case at first instance and, where necessary, the appeal.

Article 112

1   An appeal shall contain:

(a) the name and address of the appellant;
(b) the names of the other parties to the proceedings before the Court of First Instance;
(c) the pleas in law and legal arguments relied on;
(d) the form of order sought by the appellant.

Article 37 and Article 38(2) and (3) of these Rules shall apply to appeals.
2   The decision of the Court of First Instance appealed against shall be attached to the appeal. The appeal shall state the date on which the decision appealed against was notified to the appellant.
3   If an appeal does not comply with Article 38(3) or with paragraph (2) of this Article, Article 38(7) of these Rules shall apply.

Article 113

1   An appeal may seek:
—to set aside, in whole or in part, the decision of the Court of First Instance;
—the same form of order, in whole or in part, as that sought at first instance and shall not seek a different form of order.
2   The subject matter of the proceedings before the Court of First Instance may not be changed in the appeal.

Article 114

Notice of the appeal shall be served on all the parties to the proceedings before the Court of First Instance. Article 39 of these Rules shall apply.

Article 115

1   Any party to the proceedings before the Court of First Instance may lodge a response within two months after service on him of notice of the appeal. The time-limit for lodging a response shall not be extended.
2   A response shall contain :

(a) the name and address of the party lodging it;
(b) the date on which notice of the appeal was served on him;
(c) the pleas in law and legal arguments relied on;
(d) the form of order sought by the respondent.

Article 38(2) and (3) of these Rules shall apply.

Article 116

1   A response may seek:
—to dismiss, in whole or in part, the appeal or to set aside, in whole or in part, the decision of the Court of First Instance;
—the same form of order, in whole or in part, as that sought at first instance and shall not seek a different form of order.
2   The subject matter of the proceedings before the Court of First Instance may not be changed in the response.

Article 117

1   The appeal and the response may be supplemented by a reply and a rejoinder or any other pleading, where the President, on application made within seven days of service of the response or of the reply, considers such further pleading necessary and expressly allows it in order to enable the party concerned to put forward its point of view or in order to provide a basis for the decision on the appeal.

2   Where the response seeks to set aside, in whole or in part, the decision of the Court of First Instance on a plea in law which was not raised in the appeal, the appellant or any other party may submit a reply on that plea alone within two months of the service of the response in question. Paragraph (1) shall apply to any further pleading following such a reply.

3   Where the President allows the lodging of a reply and a rejoinder, or any other pleading, he shall prescribe the period within which they are to be submitted.

Article 118

Subject to the following provisions, Articles 42(2), 43, 44, 55 to 90, 93, 95 to 100 and 102 of these Rules shall apply to the procedure before the Court of Justice on appeal from a decision of the Court of First Instance.

Article 119

Where the appeal is, in whole or in part, clearly inadmissible or clearly unfounded, the Court may at any time, acting on a report from the Judge-Rapporteur and after hearing the Advocate-General, by reasoned order dismiss the appeal in whole or in part.

Article 120

After the submission of pleadings as provided for in Articles 115(1) and, if any, Article 117(1) and (2) of these Rules, the Court may, acting on a report from the Judge-Rapporteur and after hearing the Advocate-General and the parties, decide to dispense with the oral part of the procedure unless one of the parties objects on the ground that the written procedure did not enable him fully to defend his point of view.

Article 121

The report referred to in Article 44(1) shall be presented to the Court after the pleadings provided for in Article 115(1) and where appropriate Article 117(1) and (2) of these Rules have been lodged. The report shall contain, in addition to the recommendations provided for in Article 44(1), a recommendation as to whether Article 120 of these Rules should be applied. Where no such pleadings are lodged, the same procedure shall apply after the expiry of the period prescribed for lodging them.

Article 122

Where the appeal is unfounded or where the appeal is well founded and the Court itself gives final judgment in the case, the Court shall make a decision as to costs.

In proceedings between the Communities and their servants:

—Article 70 of these Rules shall apply only to appeals brought by institutions;

—by way of derogation from Article 69(2) of these Rules, the Court may, in appeals brought by officials or other servants of an institution, order the parties to share the costs where equity so requires.

If the appeal is withdrawn Article 69(5) shall apply.

When an appeal brought by a Member State or an institution which did not intervene in the proceedings before the Court of First Instance is well founded, the Court of Justice may order that the parties share the costs or that the successful appellant pay the costs which the appeal has caused an unsuccessful party to incur.

Article 123

An application to intervene made to the Court in appeal proceedings shall be lodged before the expiry of a period of three months running from the date on which the appeal was lodged. The Court shall, after hearing the Advocate-General, give its decision in the form of an order on whether or not the intervention is allowed.

Miscellaneous provisions
Article 124
1   The President shall instruct any person who is required to take an oath before the Court, as witness or expert, to tell the truth or to carry out his task conscientiously and impartially, as the case may be, and shall warn him of the criminal liability provided for in his national law in the event of any breach of this duty.

2   The witness shall take the oath either in accordance with the first sub-paragraph of Article 47(5) of these Rules or in the manner laid down by his national law.

Where his national law provides the opportunity to make, in judicial proceedings, a solemn affirmation equivalent to an oath as well as or instead of taking an oath, the witness may make such an affirmation under the conditions and in the form prescribed in his national law.

Where his national law provides neither for taking an oath nor for making a solemn affirmation, the procedure described in paragraph (1) shall be followed.

3   Paragraph (2) shall apply mutatis mutandis to experts, a reference to the first sub-paragraph of Article 49(6) replacing in this case the reference to the first sub-paragraph of Article 47(5) of these Rules.

Article 125
Subject to the provisions of Article 188 of the EEC Treaty and Article 160 of the Euratom Treaty and after consultation with the Governments concerned, the Court shall adopt supplementary rules concerning its practice in relation to:

    (a) letters rogatory;
    (b) applications for legal aid;
    (c) reports of perjury by witnesses or experts, delivered pursuant to Article 28 of the ECSC and Euratom Statutes and Article 27 of the EEC Statute.

Article 126
These Rules replace the Rules of Procedure of the Court of Justice of the European Communities adopted on 4 December 1974 (Official Journal of the European Communities No L350, of 28 December 1974, p 1), as last amended on 15 May 1991.[24]

Article 127
These Rules, which are authentic in the languages mentioned in Article 29(1) of these Rules, shall be published in the Official Journal of the European Communities and shall enter into force on the first day of the second month following their publication.
    Done at Luxembourg, 19 June 1991.

ANNEX I

Decision on official holidays[25]
Article 1
For the purposes of Article 80(2) of the Rules of Procedure the following shall be official holidays:

New Year's Day;
Easter Monday;
1 May;
Ascension Day;
Whit Monday;
23 June;
24 June, where 23 June is a Sunday;
15 August;
1 November;
25 December;
26 December.

---

24 OJ L176 4.7.91 p 27.
25 The preamble to the Decisions has been omitted.

The official holidays referred to in the first paragraph hereof shall be those observed at the place where the Court of Justice has its seat.

Article 2
Article 80(2) of the Rules of Procedure shall apply only to the official holidays mentioned in Article 1 of this Decision.

Article 3
This Decision, which shall constitute Annex I to the Rules of Procedure, shall enter into force on the same day as those Rules.

It shall be published in the Official Journal of the European Communities.

Done at Luxembourg, 19 June 1991.

ANNEX II

Decision on extension of time-limits on account of distance[25]

Article 1
In order to take account of distance, procedural time-limits for all parties save those habitually resident in the Grand Duchy of Luxembourg shall be extended as follows:
—for the Kingdom of Belgium: two days;
—for the Federal Republic of Germany, the European territory of the French Republic and the European territory of the Kingdom of the Netherlands: six days;
—for the European territory of the Kingdom of Denmark, for the Hellenic Republic, for Ireland, for the Italian Republic, for the Kingdom of Spain, for the Portuguese Republic (with the exception of the Azores and Madeira) and for the United Kingdom: 10 days;
—for other European countries and territories: two weeks;
—for the autonomous regions of the Azores and Madeira of the Portuguese Republic: three weeks;
—for other countries, departments and territories: one month.

Article 2
This Decision, which shall constitute Annex II to the Rules of Procedure, shall enter into force on the same day as those Rules.

It shall be published in the Official Journal of the European Communities.

Done at Luxembourg, 19 June 1991.

Supplementary Rules[26]

CHAPTER I

LETTERS ROGATORY

Article 1

Letters rogatory shall be issued in the form of an order which shall contain the names, forenames, description and address of the witness or expert, set out the facts on which the witness or expert is to be examined, name the parties, their agents, lawyers or advisers, indicate their address for service and briefly describe the subject matter of the dispute.

Notice of the order shall be served on the parties by the Registrar.

Article 2

The Registrar shall send the order to the competent authority named in Annex I of the Member State in whose territory the witness or expert is to be examined. Where necessary, the order shall be accompanied by a translation into the official languages of the Member State to which it is addressed.

The authority named pursuant to the first paragraph shall pass on the order to the judicial authority which is competent according to its national law.

The competent judicial authority shall give effect to the letters rogatory in accordance with its national law. After implementation the competent judicial authority shall transmit to the authority named pursuant to the first paragraph the order embodying the letters rogatory, any documents arising from the implementation and a detailed statement of costs. These documents shall be sent to the Registrar of the Court.

The Registrar shall be responsible for the translation of the documents into the language of the case.

Article 3

The Court shall defray the expenses occasioned by the letters rogatory without prejudice to the right to charge them, where appropriate to the parties.

CHAPTER II

LEGAL AID

Article 4

The Court, by any order by which it decides that a person is entitled to receive legal aid, shall order that a lawyer be appointed to act for him.

If the person does not indicate his choice of lawyer, or if the Court considers that his choice is unacceptable, the Registrar shall send a copy of the order and of the application for legal aid to the authority named in Annex II, being the competent authority of the State concerned.

The Court, in the light of the suggestion made by that authority, shall of its own motion appoint a lawyer to act for the person concerned.

Article 5

The Court shall advance the funds necessary to meet expenses. It shall adjudicate on the lawyer's disbursements and fees; the President may, on application by the lawyer, order that he receive an advance.

---

26 OJ 1974 No L 350/29, as amended in 1981 (OJ No L 282/1 of 5 October 1981); and 1987 (OJ No L 165 of 24 June 1987 p 4).

CHAPTER III

REPORTS OF PERJURY BY A WITNESS OR EXPERT

Article 6
The Court, after hearing the Advocate-General, may decide to report to the competent authority referred to in Annex III of the Member State, whose courts have penal jurisdiction in any case of perjury on the part of a witness or expert before the Court, account being taken of the provisions of Article [124] of the Rules of Procedure.

Article 7
The Registrar shall be responsible for communicating the Decision of the Court.
The Decision shall set out the facts and circumstances on which the report is based.

FINAL PROVISIONS

Article 8
These Supplementary Rules replace the Supplementary Rules of 9 March 1962 (OJ, 1962, p 1113).

Article 9
These Rules, which shall be authentic in the languages referred to in Article 29(1) of the Rules of Procedure, shall be published in the *Official Journal of the European Communities*.
These Rules shall enter into force on the date of their publication.

ANNEX I

List referred to in the first paragraph of Article 2

Belgium
The Minister of Justice
Denmark
The Minister of Justice
Germany
The Federal Minister of Justice
Greece
The Minister of Justice
Spain
The Minister of Justice
France
The Minister of Justice

Ireland
The Minister of Justice
Italy
The Minister of Justice
Luxembourg
The Minister of Justice
Netherlands
The Minister of Justice
Portugal
The Minister of Justice
United Kingdom
The Secretary of State

ANNEX II

List referred to in the second paragraph of Article 4

Belgium
The Minister of Justice
Denmark
The Minister of Justice
Germany
Bundesrechtsanwaltskammer
Greece
The Minister of Justice
Spain
The Minister of Justice
France
The Minister of Justice
Ireland
The Minister of Justice
Italy
The Minister of Justice

Luxembourg
The Minister of Justice
Netherlands
Algemene Raad van de Nederlandse
Orde van Advocaten
Portugal
The Minister of Justice
United Kingdom
The Law Society, London
(for applicants resident in England or Wales)
The Law Society of Scotland, Edinburgh
(for applicants resident in Scotland)
The Incorporated Law Society of
Northern Ireland, Belfast
(for applicants resident in Northern Ireland)

ANNEX III

List referred to in Article 6

Belgium
The Minister of Justice
Denmark
The Minister of Justice
Germany
The Federal Minister of Justice
Greece
The Minister of Justice
Spain
The Minister of Justice
France
The Minister of Justice
Ireland
The Attorney General
Italy
The Minister of Justice

Luxembourg
The Minister of Justice
Netherlands
The Minister of Justice
Portugal
The Minister of Justice
United Kingdom
Her Majesty's Attorney General, for witnesses or experts
resident in England and Wales
Her Majesty's Advocate, for witnesses or experts resident in Scotland
Her Majesty's Attorney General, for witnesses or experts
resident in Northern Ireland

Instructions to the Registrar[27]

SECTION ONE

RESPONSIBILITIES OF THE REGISTRY

Article 1

1   The Registry shall be open to the public from Monday to Friday from 10 am to 12 noon and from 3 pm to 6 pm, except on the official holidays listed in Annex I to the Rules of Procedure.

Outside the opening hours of the Registry procedural documents may be validly lodged with the janitor, who shall record the date and time of such lodging.

2   In any event the Registry shall at every public hearing held by the Court or a Chamber be open to the public half an hour before the hearing begins.

Article 2

The Registrar shall be responsible for maintaining the files of pending cases and for keeping them fully up to date.

Article 3

1   The Registrar shall be responsible for drawing up minutes of judgments, orders and other decisions. He shall submit them to the responsible Judges for their signatures.

2   The Registrar shall ensure that where the ECSC, EEC or Euratom Treaty, the ECSC, EEC or Euratom Statute, the Rules of Procedure or any other act giving powers to the Court of Justice provide for a document to be served, a notice to be given or a communication to be made the steps are carried out in accordance with the Rules of Procedure; the documents, notices and communications shall be sent by registered post, accompanied by a note signed by the Registrar giving the number of the case and the registration number of the document, together with a brief indication as to its nature. A copy of the note shall be appended to the original document.

3   The parties shall be served with the pleadings and other documents relating to the proceedings.

Where a document is very bulky and only one specimen of it is lodged at the Registry, the Registrar shall, after consulting the Judge-Rapporteur, inform the parties by registered letter that the document may be inspected by them at the Registry.

4   Where in the submission in the application originating proceedings it is contended that an act of a Community institution not being a party to the action is illegal, the Registrar shall transmit a copy of the application to the institution in accordance with the second paragraph of Article 18 of the Statutes of the Court of Justice of the EEC and the Euratom and the second paragraph of Article 21 of the Statute of the Court of Justice of the ECSC.

The Registrar shall not transmit other written pleadings to the institution, unless the institution has been allowed to intervene in accordance with Article 93(4) of the Rules of Procedure.

Article 4

1   A party who has lodged a procedural document at the Registry shall, if he so requests, be given a receipt.

2   Unless otherwise expressly authorized by the President or the Court, the Registrar shall decline to accept or, as the case may be, shall without delay return by

---

27 OJ 1974 No L 350/33; see also OJ 1982 No C 39/35.

registered post any pleading or other document not provided for in the Rules of
Procedure or not worded in the language of the case.

3   On a procedural document which has been lodged on a date other than the date of
its registration, a note shall be made stating that it has been so lodged.

Article 5

1   The Registrar shall, after consulting the President and the Judge-Rapporteur,
take all measures necessary for implementing Article 38(7) of the Rules of
Procedure. He shall prescribe the period mentioned in that Article and shall
communicate it to the person concerned by registered letter with a form for
acknowledgment of receipt.

If the person concerned does not comply with the directions of the Registrar,
the latter shall refer the matter to the President of the Court.

2   Requests to the Registrar of the Arbitration Committee pursuant to Article
101(3) of the Rules of Procedure shall be sent by registered letter with a form for
acknowledgment of receipt.

The papers shall be returned to the Registry of the Arbitration Committee after
the Decision of the Court is pronounced or after the case is removed from the
Court Register.

Article 6

1   Where a Decision or order is delivered in open court a note to that effect shall be
made at the foot of the text; the note shall be in the language of the case and shall
read as follows:

'Delivered in open court on . . . (date)
(Signature)   (Signature)
Registrar   President'

2   The notes in the margins to judgments, as required by Articles 66(4), 94(6), 97(3)
and 102(2) of the Rules of Procedure, shall be made in the language of the case;
the President and the Registrar shall initial them.

Article 7

1   Before every public hearing of the Court or a Chamber the Registrar shall draw
up a cause list in the respective language of each case.
This list shall contain:
—the date, hour and place of the hearing;
—the references to the cases which will be called;
—the names of the parties;
—the names and descriptions of the parties' agents, advisers and lawyers.
The cause list shall be displayed at the entry to the courtroom.

2   The Registrar shall draw up in the respective language of each case the minutes of
every public hearing.
The minutes shall contain:
—the date and place of the hearing;
—the names of the Judges, Advocates-General and Registrar present;
—the reference to the case;
—the names of the parties;
—the names and descriptions of the parties' agents, advisers and lawyers;
—the names, forenames, descriptions and permanent addresses of the witnesses
or experts examined;
—an indication of the evidence produced at the hearing;
—an indication of the documents lodged by the parties in the course of the
hearing;
—the decision of the Court, the Chamber or the President of the Court or
Chamber, given at the hearing.
If the oral procedure in the case extends over several successive hearings, it
may be reported in a single set of minutes.

Article 8
The Registrar shall ensure that a person or body responsible for making an investigation or giving an expert opinion in accordance with Article 49 of the Rules of Procedure is in possession of the material necessary for carrying out his task.

Article 9
Certificates as provided for in Article 33(b) of the Rules of Procedure shall be delivered to the adviser or lawyer concerned if he so requests, where this step is required for the proper conduct of proceedings.

The certificates shall be drawn up by the Registrar.

Article 10
For the purposes of Article 32 of the Rules of Procedure, an extract from the cause list shall be transmitted in advance to the Minister of Foreign Affairs of the place where the Court is sitting.

SECTION TWO

KEEPING OF THE REGISTER

Article 11
The Registrar shall be responsible for keeping up to date the Register of cases brought before the Court.

Article 12
Where an application originating proceedings is registered, the case shall be given a serial number followed by a mention of the year and a statement of either the name of the applicant or the subject matter of the application. Cases shall be referred to by their serial numbers.

An application for the adoption of interim measures shall be given the same serial number as the principal action, followed by the letter 'R'.

Article 13
The pages of the Register shall be numbered in advance.

At regular intervals the President and the Registrar shall check the Register and initial it in the margin against the last entry.

Article 14
The procedural documents in cases brought before the Court, including documents lodged by the parties and documents served by the Registrar, shall be entered in the Register.

An annex which has not been lodged at the same time as the procedural document to which it relates shall be separately registered.

Article 15
1   Entries in the Register shall be made chronologically in the order in which the documents to be registered are lodged; they shall be numbered consecutively.
2   Procedural documents shall be registered as soon as they are lodged at the Registry.
     Documents drawn up by the Court shall be registered on the day of issue.
3   The entry in the Register shall contain the information necessary for identifying the document and in particular:
     —the date of registration;
     —the reference to the case;
     —the nature of the document;
     —the date of the document.
     The entry shall be made in the language of the case; numbers shall be written in figures and usual abbreviations shall be permitted.
4   Where a correction is made in the Register a note to that effect, initialled by the Registrar, shall be made in the margin.

Article 16

The registration number of every document drawn up by the Court shall be noted on its first page.

A note of the registration, worded as follows, shall be stamped on the original of every document lodged by the parties:

'Registered at the Court of Justice under No . . .
Luxembourg, . . . day of . . . 19 . . .'

This note shall be signed by the Registrar.

SECTION THREE

SCALE OF CHARGES OF THE REGISTRY OF THE COURT

Article 17

No registry charges may be imposed save those referred to in this section.

Article 18

Registry charges may be paid either in cash to the cashier of the Court or by bank transfer to the Court account at the bank named in the demand for payment.

Article 19

Where the party owing Registry charges has been granted legal aid, Article 76(5) of the Rules of Procedure shall apply.

Article 20

Registry charges shall be as follows:

(a) for an authenticated copy of a judgment or order, a certified copy of a procedural document or set of minutes, an extract from the Court Register, a certified copy of the Court Register or a certified copy made pursuant to Article 72(b) of the Rules of Procedure: Lfrs 60 a page;

(b) for a translation made pursuant to Article 72(b) of the Rules of Procedure: Lfrs 500 a page.

No page shall contain more than 40 lines.

This scale applies to the first copy; the charge for further copies shall be Lfrs 50 for each page or part of a page.

The charges referred to in this Article shall as from 1 January 1975 be increased by 10% each time the cost-of-living index published by the Government of the Grand Duchy of Luxembourg is increased by 10%.

Article 21

1   Where pursuant to Articles 47(3), 51(1) and 76(5) of the Rules of Procedure an application is made to the cashier of the Court for an advance payment, the Registrar shall direct that particulars of the costs for which the advance payment is required be delivered.

   Witnesses must supply evidence of their loss of earnings and experts must supply a note of fees for their services.

2   The Registrar shall order payment by the cashier of the Court of sums payable pursuant to the preceding paragraph, against a receipt or other proof of payment. Where he is of the opinion that the amount applied for is excessive, he may of his own motion reduce it or order payment by instalments.

3   The Registrar shall order the cashier of the Court to refund the costs of letters rogatory payable in accordance with Article 3 of the Supplementary Rules to the authority designated by the competent authority referred to in Article 2 of those rules, in the currency of the State concerned against proof of payment.

4   The Registrar shall order the cashier of the Court to make the advance payment referred to in the second paragraph of Article 5 of the Supplementary Rules of Procedure, subject to the second sub-paragraph of paragraph 2 of this Article.

Article 22

1   Where sums paid out by way of legal aid pursuant to Article 76(5) of the Rules of Procedure are recoverable, payment of the sums shall be demanded by registered letter, signed by the Registrar. The letter shall state not only the amount payable but also the method of payment and the period prescribed.

The same provision shall apply to the implementation of Article 72(a) of the Rules of Procedure and Article 21(1), (3) and (4) of these instructions.

2   If the sums demanded are not paid within the period prescribed by the Registrar, he shall request the Court to make an enforceable Decision and to order its enforcement in accordance with Articles 44 and 92 of the ECSC Treaty, 187 and 192 of the EEC Treaty or 159 and 164 of the Euratom Treaty.

Where a party is by a judgment or order directed to pay costs to the cashier of the Court, the Registrar shall, if the costs are not paid within the period prescribed, apply for payment of the costs to be enforced.

SECTION FOUR

PUBLICATIONS OF THE COURT

Article 23

The Registrar shall be responsible for the publications of the Court.

Article 24

There shall be published in the languages referred to in Article 1 of Council Regulation No 1 'Reports of Cases before the Court' which shall, subject to a decision to the contrary, contain the judgments of the Court together with the submissions of the Advocates-General and the opinions given and the interim orders made in the course of the calendar year.

Article 25

The Registrar shall cause the following to be published in the *Official Journal of the European Communities:*

(a) notices of applications originating proceedings, as referred to in Article 16(6) of the Rules of Procedure;
(b) notices of the removal of cases from the Register;
(c) subject to a decision by the Court to the contrary, the operative part of every judgment and interim order;
(d) the composition of the Chambers;
(e) the appointment of the President of the Court;
(f) the appointment of the Registrar;
(g) the appointment of the Assistant Registrar and the Administrator.

FINAL PROVISIONS

Article 26

These instructions replace the instructions issued by the Court of Justice of the European Communities on 23 June 1960 (OJ, 1960, p 1417) as amended by the Decisions of the Court of 6 April 1962 (OJ, 1962, p 1115) and 13 July 1965 (OJ, 1965, p 2413).

Article 27

These instructions, which are authentic in the languages referred to in Article 29(1) of the Rules of Procedure, shall be published in the *Official Journal of the European Communities.*

Rules of Procedure of the Court of First Instance of the European Communities[28]

Interpretation

Article 1

In these Rules:

'ECSC Treaty' means the Treaty establishing the European Coal and Steel Community;

'ECSC Statute' means the Protocol on the Statute of the Court of Justice of the European Coal and Steel Community;

'EEC Treaty' means the Treaty establishing the European Community;

'EEC Statute' means the Protocol on the Statute of the Court of Justice of the European Economic Community;

'Euratom Treaty' means the Treaty establishing the European Atomic Energy Community (Euratom);

'Euratom Statute' means the Protocol on the Statute of the Court of Justice of the European Atomic Energy Community.

For the purposes of these Rules, 'institutions' means the institutions of the European Communities and the European Investment Bank.

TITLE I

ORGANISATION OF THE COURT OF FIRST INSTANCE

Chapter 1

President and Members of the Court of First Instance

Article 2

1   Every Member of the Court of First Instance shall, as a rule, perform the function of Judge.

Members of the Court of First Instance are hereinafter referred to as 'Judges'.

2   Every Judge, with the exception of the President, may, in the circumstances specified in Articles 17 to 19, perform the function of Advocate-General in a particular case.

References to the Advocate-General in these Rules shall apply only where a Judge has been designated as Advocate-General.

Article 3

The term of office of a Judge shall begin on the date laid down in his instrument of appointment. In the absence of any provision regarding the date, the term shall begin on the date of the instrument.

Article 4

1   Before taking up his duties, a Judge shall take the following oath before the Court of Justice of the European Communities:

'I swear that I will perform my duties impartially and conscientiously; I swear that I will preserve the secrecy of the deliberations of the Court.'

---

28 OJ L 136 30.5.91 p 1; corrected in OJ L 317 of 19 November 1991 p 34. These Rules replaced the Rules published in OJ C 136 of 5 June 1990 p 1. The preamble to the Rules has been omitted.

2   Immediately after taking the oath, a Judge shall sign a declaration by which he solemnly undertakes that, both during and after his term of office, he will respect the obligations arising therefrom, and in particular the duty to behave with integrity and discretion as regards the acceptance, after he has ceased to hold office, of certain appointments and benefits.

Article 5

When the Court of Justice is called upon to decide, after consulting the Court of First Instance, whether a Judge of the Court of First Instance no longer fulfils the requisite conditions or no longer meets the obligations arising from his office, the President of the Court of First Instance shall invite the Judge concerned to make representations to the Court of First Instance, in closed session and in the absence of the Registrar.

The Court of First Instance shall state the reasons for its opinion.

An opinion to the effect that a Judge of the Court of First Instance no longer fulfils the requisite conditions or no longer meets the obligations arising from his office must receive the votes of at least seven Judges of the Court of First Instance. In that event, particulars of the voting shall be communicated to the Court of Justice.

Voting shall be by secret ballot; the Judge concerned shall not take part in the deliberations.

Article 6

With the exception of the President of the Court of First Instance and of the Presidents of the Chambers, the Judges shall rank equally in precedence according to their seniority in office.

Where there is equal seniority in office, precedence shall be determined by age.

Retiring Judges who are re-appointed shall retain their former precedence.

Article 7

1   The Judges shall, immediately after the partial replacement provided for in Article 32d of the ECSC Treaty, Article 168a of the EEC Treaty and Article 140a of the Euratom Treaty, elect one of their number as President of the Court of First Instance for a term of three years.

2   If the office of President of the Court of First Instance falls vacant before the normal date of expiry thereof, the Court of First Instance shall elect a successor for the remainder of the term.

3   The elections provided for in this Article shall be by secret ballot. If a Judge obtains an absolute majority he shall be elected. If no Judge obtains an absolute majority, a second ballot shall be held and the Judge obtaining the most votes shall be elected. Where two or more Judges obtain an equal number of votes the oldest of them shall be deemed elected.

Article 8

The President of the Court of First Instance shall direct the judicial business and the administration of the Court of First Instance. He shall preside at plenary sittings and deliberations.

Article 9

When the President of the Court of First Instance is absent or prevented from attending or when the office of President is vacant, the functions of President shall be exercised by a President of a Chamber according to the order of precedence laid down in Article 6.

If the President of the Court of First Instance and the Presidents of the Chambers are all prevented from attending at the same time, or their posts are vacant at the same time, the functions of President shall be exercised by one of the other Judges according to the order of precedence laid down in Article 6.

Chapter 2

Constitution of the Chambers and designation of Judge-Rapporteurs and Advocates-General

Article 10

1   The Court of First Instance shall set up the Chambers composed of three or five judges and shall decide which Judges shall be attached to them.
2   The composition of the Chambers shall be published in the Official Journal of the European Communities.

Article 11

1   Cases before the Court of First Instance shall be heard by Chambers composed in accordance with Article 10.
     Cases may be heard by the Court of First Instance sitting in plenary session under the conditions laid down in Articles 14, 51, 106, 118, 124, 127 and 129.
2   In cases coming before a Chamber, the term 'Court of First Instance' in these Rules shall designate that Chamber.

Article 12

1   Subject to the provisions of Article 14, disputes between the Communities and their servants shall be assigned to Chambers of three Judges.
     Other cases shall, subject to the provisions of Article 14, be assigned to Chambers of five Judges.
2   The Court of First Instance shall lay down criteria by which, as a rule, cases are to be assigned to Chambers composed of the same number of Judges.

Article 13

1   As soon as the application initiating proceedings has been lodged, the President of the Court of First Instance shall assign the case to one of the Chambers.
2   The President of the Chamber shall propose to the President of the Court of First Instance, in respect of each case assigned to the Chamber, the designation of a Judge to act as Rapporteur; the President of the Court of First Instance shall decide on the proposal.

Article 14

Whenever the legal difficulty or the importance of the case or special circumstances so justify, a case may be referred to the Court of First Instance sitting in plenary session or to a Chamber composed of a different number of Judges.
     Any decision to refer a case shall be taken under the conditions laid down in Article 51.

Article 15

The Court of First Instance shall appoint for a period of one year the Presidents of the Chambers.
     The provisions of Article 7(2) and (3) shall apply.
     The appointments made in pursuance of this Article shall be published in the Official Journal of the European Communities.

Article 16

In cases coming before a Chamber the powers of the President shall be exercised by the President of the Chamber.

Article 17

When the Court of First Instance sits in plenary session, it shall be assisted by an Advocate-General designated by the President of the Court of First Instance.

Article 18

A Chamber of the Court of First Instance may be assisted by an Advocate-General if it is considered that the legal difficulty or the factual complexity of the case so requires.

Article 19

The decision to designate an Advocate-General in a particular case shall be taken by the Court of First Instance sitting in plenary session at the request of the Chamber before which the case comes.

The President of the Court of First Instance shall designate the Judge called upon to perform the function of Advocate-General in that case.

Chapter 3

Registry

Section 1 – The Registrar

Article 20

1   The Court of First Instance shall appoint the Registrar.
     Two weeks before the date fixed for making the appointment, the President of the Court of First Instance shall inform the Judges of the applications which have been submitted for the post.
2   An application shall be accompanied by full details of the candidate's age, nationality, university degrees, knowledge of any languages, present and past occupations and experience, if any, in judicial and international fields.
3   The appointment shall be made following the procedure laid down in Article 7(3).
4   The Registrar shall be appointed for a term of six years. He may be reappointed.
5   Before he takes up his duties the Registrar shall take the oath before the Court of First Instance in accordance with Article 4.
6   The Registrar may be deprived of his office only if he no longer fulfils the requisite conditions or no longer meets the obligations arising from his office; the Court of First Instance shall take its decision after giving the Registrar an opportunity to make representations.
7   If the office of Registrar falls vacant before the usual date of expiry of the term thereof, the Court of First Instance shall appoint a new Registrar for a term of six years.

Article 21

The Court of First Instance may, following the procedure laid down in respect of the Registrar, appoint one or more Assistant Registrars to assist the Registrar and to take his place in so far as the Instructions to the Registrar referred to in Article 23 allow.

Article 22

Where the Registrar is absent or prevented from attending and, if necessary, where the Assistant Registrar is absent or so prevented, or where their posts are vacant, the President of the Court of First Instance shall designate an official or servant to carry out the duties of Registrar.

Article 23

Instructions to the Registrar shall be adopted by the Court of First Instance acting on a proposal from the President of the Court of First Instance.

Article 24

1   There shall be kept in the Registry, under the control of the Registrar, a register initialled by the President of the Court of First Instance, in which all pleadings and supporting documents shall be entered in the order in which they are lodged.
2   When a document has been registered, the Registrar shall make a note to that effect on the original and, if a party so requests, on any copy submitted for the purpose.
3   Entries in the register and the notes provided for in the preceding paragraph shall be authentic.
4   Rules for keeping the register shall be prescribed by the Instructions to the Registrar referred to in Article 23.

5   Persons having an interest may consult the register at the Registry and may obtain copies or extracts on payment of a charge on a scale fixed by the Court of First Instance on a proposal from the Registrar.

       The parties to a case may on payment of the appropriate charge also obtain copies of pleadings and authenticated copies of orders and judgments.

6   Notice shall be given in the Official Journal of the European Communities of the date of registration of an application initiating proceedings, the names and addresses of the parties, the subject matter of the proceedings, the form of order sought by the applicant and a summary of the pleas in law and of the main supporting arguments.

7   Where the Council or the Commission is not a party to a case, the Court of First Instance shall send to it copies of the application and of the defence, without the annexes thereto, to enable it to assess whether the inapplicability of one of its acts is being invoked under the third paragraph of Article 36 of the ECSC Treaty, Article 184 of the EEC Treaty or Article 156 of the Euratom Treaty.

Article 25

1   The Registrar shall be responsible, under the authority of the President, for the acceptance, transmission and custody of documents and for effecting service as provided for by these Rules.

2   The Registrar shall assist the Court of First Instance, the President and the Judges in all their official functions.

Article 26

The Registrar shall have custody of the seals. He shall be responsible for the records and be in charge of the publications of the Court of First Instance.

Article 27

Subject to Articles 5 and 33, the Registrar shall attend the sittings of the Court of First Instance.

Section 2—Other departments

Article 28

The officials and other servants whose task is to assist directly the President, the Judges and the Registrar shall be appointed in accordance with the Staff Regulations. They shall be responsible to the Registrar, under the authority of the President of the Court of First Instance.

Article 29

The officials and other servants referred to in Article 28 shall take the oath provided for in Article 20(2) of the Rules of Procedure of the Court of Justice before the President of the Court of Justice in the presence of the Registrar.

Article 30

The Registrar shall be responsible, under the authority of the President of the Court of First Instance, for the administration of the Court of First Instance, its financial management and its accounts; he shall be assisted in this by the departments of the Court of Justice.

Chapter 4

The working of the Court of First Instance

Article 31

1   The dates and times of the sittings of the Court of First Instance shall be fixed by the President.

2   The Court of First Instance may choose to hold one or more sittings in a place other than that in which the Court of First Instance has its seat.

Article 32

1 Where, by reason of a Judge being absent or prevented from attending, there is an even number of Judges, the most junior Judge within the meaning of Article 6 shall abstain from taking part in the deliberations unless he is the Judge-Rapporteur. In this case, the Judge immediately senior to him shall abstain from taking part in the deliberations.

2 If, after the Court of First Instance has been convened in plenary session, it is found that the quorum of seven Judges has not been attained, the President of the Court of First Instance shall adjourn the sitting until there is a quorum.

3 If in any Chamber the quorum of three Judges has not been attained, the President of that Chamber shall so inform the President of the Court of First Instance who shall designate another Judge to complete the Chamber.

4 If in any Chamber of three or five Judges the number of Judges assigned to that Chamber is higher than three or five respectively, the President of the Chamber shall decide which of the Judges will be called upon to take part in the judgment of the case.

Article 33

1 The Court of First Instance shall deliberate in closed session.

2 Only those Judges who were present at the oral proceedings may take part in the deliberations.

3 Every Judge taking part in the deliberations shall state his opinion and the reasons for it.

4 Any Judge may require that any question be formulated in the language of his choice and be communicated in writing to the other Judges before being put to the vote.

5 The conclusions reached by the majority of the Judges after final discussion shall determine the decision of the Court of First Instance. Votes shall be cast in reverse order to the order of precedence laid down in Article 6.

6 Differences of view on the substance, wording or order of questions, or on the interpretation of a vote shall be settled by decision of the Court of First Instance.

7 Where the deliberations of the Court of First Instance concern questions of its own administration, the Registrar shall be present, unless the Court of First Instance decides to the contrary.

8 Where the Court of First Instance sits without the Registrar being present it shall, if necessary, instruct the most junior Judge within the meaning of Article 6 to draw up minutes. The minutes shall be signed by this Judge and by the President.

Article 34

1 Subject to any special decision of the Court of First Instance, its vacations shall be as follows:
—from 18 December to 10 January;
—from the Sunday before Easter to the second Sunday after Easter;
—from 15 July to 15 September.
During the vacations, the functions of President shall be exercised at the place where the Court of First Instance has its seat either by the President himself, keeping in touch with the Registrar, or by a President of Chamber or other Judge invited by the President to take his place.

2 In a case of urgency, the President may convene the Judges during the vacations.

3 The Court of First Instance shall observe the official holidays of the place where it has its seat.

4 The Court of First Instance may, in proper circumstances, grant leave of absence to any Judge.

Chapter 5

Languages

Article 35

1 The language of a case shall be Danish, Dutch, English, French, German, Greek, Irish, Italian, Portuguese or Spanish.

2   The language of the case shall be chosen by the applicant, except that:

(a) at the joint request of the parties the Court of First Instance may authorise another of the languages mentioned in paragraph (1) of this Article to be used as the language of the case for all or part of the proceedings;

(b) at the request of one of the parties, and after the opposite party and the Advocate-General have been heard, the Court of First Instance may, by way of derogation from sub-paragraph (a), authorise another of the languages mentioned in paragraph (1) of this Article to be used as the language of the case for all or part of the proceedings; such a request may not be submitted by an institution.

3   The language of the case shall be used in the written and oral pleadings of the parties and in supporting documents, and also in the minutes and decisions of the Court of First Instance.

Any supporting documents expressed in another language must be accompanied by a translation into the language of the case.

In the case of lengthy documents, translations may be confined to extracts. However, the Court of First Instance may, of its own motion or at the request of a party, at any time call for a complete or fuller translation.

Notwithstanding the foregoing provisions, a Member State shall be entitled to use its official language when intervening in a case before the Court of First Instance. This provision shall apply both to written statements and to oral addresses. The Registrar shall cause any such statement or address to be translated into the language of the case.

4   Where a witness or expert states that he is unable adequately to express himself in one of the languages referred to in paragraph (1) of this Article, the Court of First Instance may authorise him to give his evidence in another language. The Registrar shall arrange for translation into the language of the case.

5   The President in conducting oral proceedings, the Judge-Rapporteur both in his preliminary report and in his report for the hearing, Judges and the Advocate-General in putting questions and the Advocate-General in delivering his opinion may use one of the languages referred to in paragraph (1) of this Article other than the language of the case. The Registrar shall arrange for translation into the language of the case.

Article 36

1   The Registrar shall, at the request of any Judge, of the Advocate-General or of a party, arrange for anything said or written in the course of the proceedings before the Court of First Instance to be translated into the languages he chooses from those referred to in Article 35(1).

2   Publications of the Court of First Instance shall be issued in the languages referred to in Article 1 of Council Regulation No 1.

Article 37

The texts of documents drawn up in the language of the case or in any other language authorised by the Court of First Instance pursuant to Article 35 shall be authentic.

Chapter 6

Rights and obligations of agents, advisers and lawyers

Article 38

1   Agents representing a State or an institution, as well as advisers and lawyers, appearing before the Court of First Instance or before any judicial authority to which it has addressed letters rogatory, shall enjoy immunity in respect of words spoken or written by them concerning the case or the parties.

2   Agents, advisers and lawyers shall enjoy the following further privileges and facilities:

   (a) papers and documents relating to the proceedings shall be exempt from both search and seizure; in the event of a dispute the customs officials or police may seal those papers and documents; they shall then be immediately forwarded to the Court of First Instance for inspection in the presence of the Registrar and of the person concerned;

   (b) agents, advisers and lawyers shall be entitled to such allocation of foreign currency as may be necessary for the performance of their duties;

   (c) agents, advisers and lawyers shall be entitled to travel in the course of duty without hindrance.

Article 39

In order to qualify for the privileges, immunities and facilities specified in Article 38, persons entitled to them shall furnish proof of their status as follows:

(a) agents shall produce an official document issued by the State or institution which they represent; a copy of this document shall be forwarded without delay to the Registrar by the State or institution concerned;

(b) advisers and lawyers shall produce a certificate signed by the Registrar. The validity of this certificate shall be limited to a specified period, which may be extended or curtailed according to the length of the proceedings.

Article 40

The privileges, immunities and facilities specified in Article 38 are granted exclusively in the interests of the proper conduct of proceedings.

The Court of First Instance may waive the immunity where it considers that the proper conduct of proceedings will not be hindered thereby.

Article 41

1   Any adviser or lawyer whose conduct towards the Court of First Instance, the President, a Judge, or the Registrar is incompatible with the dignity of the Court of First Instance, or who uses his rights for purposes other than those for which they were granted, may at any time be excluded from the proceedings by an order of the Court of First Instance; the person concerned shall be given an opportunity to defend himself.

   The order shall have immediate effect.

2   Where an adviser or lawyer is excluded from the proceedings, the proceedings shall be suspended for a period fixed by the President in order to allow the party concerned to appoint another adviser or lawyer.

3   Decisions taken under this Article may be rescinded.

Article 42

The provisions of this Chapter shall apply to university teachers who have a right of audience before the Court of First Instance in accordance with Article 20 of the ECSC Statute and Article 17 of the EEC and Euratom Statutes.

TITLE II

Procedure

Chapter 1—Written Procedure

Article 43

1   The original of every pleading must be signed by the party's agent or lawyer.

   The original, accompanied by all annexes referred to therein, shall be lodged together with five copies for the Court of First Instance and a copy for every other party to the proceedings. Copies shall be certified by the party lodging them.

2   Institutions shall in addition produce, within time-limits laid down by the Court of First Instance, translations of all pleadings into the other languages provided for by Article 1 of Council Regulation No 1. The second sub-paragraph of paragraph (1) of this Article shall apply.

3   All pleadings shall bear a date. In the reckoning of time-limits for taking steps in proceedings only the date of lodgment at the Registry shall be taken into account.

4   To every pleading there shall be annexed a file containing the documents relied on in support of it, together with a schedule listing them.

5   Where in view of the length of a document only extracts from it are annexed to the pleading, the whole document or a full copy of it shall be lodged at the Registry.

Article 44

1   An application of the kind referred to in Article 22 of the ECSC Statute and Article 19 of the EEC and Euratom Statutes shall state:

(a)   the name and address of the applicant;
(b)   the designation of the party against whom the application is made;
(c)   the subject matter of the proceedings and a summary of the pleas in law on which the application is based;
(d)   the form of order sought by the applicant;
(e)   where appropriate, the nature of any evidence offered in support.

2   For the purposes of the proceedings, the application shall state an address for service in the place where the Court of First Instance has its seat and the name of the person who is authorised and has expressed willingness to accept service.

    If the application does not comply with these requirements, all service on the party concerned for the purposes of the proceedings shall be effected, for so long as the defect has not been cured, by registered letter addressed to the agent or lawyer of that party. By way of derogation from Article 100, service shall then be deemed to have been duly effected by the lodging of the registered letter at the post office of the place where the Court of First Instance has its seat.

3   The lawyer acting for a party must lodge at the Registry a certificate that he is entitled to practise before a court of a Member State.

4   The application shall be accompanied, where appropriate, by the documents specified in the second paragraph of Article 22 of the ECSC Statute and in the second paragraph of Article 19 of the EEC and Euratom Statutes.

5   An application made by a legal person governed by private law shall be accompanied by:

(a)   the instrument or instruments constituting and regulating that legal person or a recent extract from the register of companies, firms or associations or any other proof of its existence in law;
(b)   proof that the authority granted to the applicant's lawyer has been properly conferred on him by someone authorised for the purpose.

6   If an application does not comply with the requirements set out in paragraphs (3) to (5) of this Article, the Registrar shall prescribe a reasonable period within which the applicant is to comply with them whether by putting the application itself in order or by producing any of the above-mentioned documents. If the applicant fails to put the application in order or to produce the required documents within the time prescribed, the Court of First Instance shall decide whether the non-compliance with these conditions renders the application formally inadmissible.

Article 45

The application shall be served on the defendant. In a case where Article 44(6) applies, service shall be effected as soon as the application has been put in order or the Court of First Instance has declared it admissible notwithstanding the failure to observe the formal requirements set out in that Article.

Article 46

1 Within one month after service on him of the application, the defendant shall lodge a defence, stating:

    (a) the name and address of the defendant;
    (b) the arguments of fact and law relied on;
    (c) the form of order sought by the defendant;
    (d) the nature of any evidence offered by him.

    The provisions of Article 44(2) to (5) shall apply to the defence.

2 In proceedings between the Communities and their servants the defence shall be accompanied by the complaint within the meaning of Article 90(2) of the Staff Regulations of Officials and by the decision rejecting the complaint together with the dates on which the complaint was submitted and the decision notified.

3 The time-limit laid down in paragraph (1) of this Article may be extended by the President on a reasoned application by the defendant.

Article 47

1 The application initiating the proceedings and the defence may be supplemented by a reply from the applicant and by a rejoinder from the defendant.

2 The President shall fix the time-limits within which these pleadings are to be lodged.

Article 48

1 In reply or rejoinder a party may offer further evidence. The party must, however, give reasons for the delay in offering it.

2 No new plea may be introduced in the course of proceedings unless it is based on matters of law or of fact which come to light in the course of the procedure.

    If in the course of the procedure one of the parties puts forward a new plea in law which is so based, the President may, even after the expiry of the normal procedural time-limits, acting on a report of the Judge-Rapporteur and after hearing the Advocate-General, allow the other party time to answer on that plea.

    Consideration of the admissibility of the plea shall be reserved for the final judgment.

Article 49

At any stage of the proceedings the Court of First Instance may, after hearing the Advocate-General, prescribe any measure of organisation of procedure or any measure of inquiry referred to in Articles 64 and 65 or order that a previous inquiry be repeated or expanded.

Article 50

The President may, at any time, after hearing the parties and the Advocate-General, order that two or more cases concerning the same subject-matter shall, on account of the connection between them, be joined for the purposes of the written or oral procedure or of the final judgment. The cases may subsequently be disjoined.

Article 51

In the cases specified in Article 14, and at any stage in the proceedings, the Chamber hearing the case may, either on its own initiative or at the request of one of the parties, propose to the Court of First Instance sitting in plenary session that the case be referred to the Court of First Instance sitting in plenary session or to a Chamber composed of a different number of Judges. The Court of First Instance sitting in plenary session shall, after hearing the parties and the Advocate-General, decide whether or not to refer a case.

Article 52

1 Without prejudice to the application of Article 49, the President shall, after the rejoinder has been lodged, fix a date on which the Judge-Rapporteur is to present his preliminary report to the Court of First Instance. The report shall contain

recommendations as to whether measures of organisation of procedure or measures of inquiry should be undertaken and whether the case should be referred to the Court of First Instance sitting in plenary session or to a Chamber composed of a different number of Judges.

2   The Court of First Instance shall decide, after hearing the Advocate-General, what action to take upon the recommendations of the Judge-Rapporteur.

The same procedure shall apply:

(a) where no reply or no rejoinder has been lodged within the time- limit fixed in accordance with Article 47(2);

(b) where the party concerned waives his right to lodge a reply or rejoinder.

Article 53

Where the Court of First Instance decides to open the oral procedure without undertaking measures of organisation of procedure or ordering a preparatory inquiry, the President of the Court of First Instance shall fix the opening date.

Article 54

Without prejudice to any measures of organisation of procedure or measures of inquiry which may be arranged at the stage of the oral procedure, where, during the written procedure, measures of organisation of procedure or measures of inquiry have been instituted and completed, the President shall fix the date for the opening of the oral procedure.

Chapter 2

Oral Procedure

Article 55

1   Subject to the priority of decisions provided for in Article 106, the Court of First Instance shall deal with the cases before it in the order in which the preparatory inquiries in them have been completed. Where the preparatory inquiries in several cases are completed simultaneously, the order in which they are to be dealt with shall be determined by the dates of entry in the register of the applications initiating them respectively.

2   The President may in special circumstances order that a case be given priority over others.

The President may in special circumstances, after hearing the parties and the Advocate-General, either on his own initiative or at the request of one of the parties, defer a case to be dealt with at a later date. On a joint application by the parties the President may order that a case be deferred.

Article 56

The proceedings shall be opened and directed by the President, who shall be responsible for the proper conduct of the hearing.

Article 57

The oral proceedings in cases heard in camera shall not be published.

Article 58

The President may in the course of the hearing put questions to the agents, advisers or lawyers of the parties.

The other Judges and the Advocate-General may do likewise.

Article 59

A party may address the Court of First Instance only through his agent, adviser or lawyer.

Article 60

Where an Advocate-General has not been designated in a case, the President shall declare the oral procedure closed at the end of the hearing.

Article 61

1 Where the Advocate-General delivers his opinion in writing, he shall lodge it at the Registry, which shall communicate it to the parties.
2 After the delivery, orally or in writing, of the opinion of the Advocate-General the President shall declare the oral procedure closed.

Article 62

The Court of First Instance may, after hearing the Advocate-General, order the reopening of the oral procedure.

Article 63

1 The Registrar shall draw up minutes of every hearing. The minutes shall be signed by the President and by the Registrar and shall constitute an official record.
2 The parties may inspect the minutes at the Registry and obtain copies at their own expense.

Chapter 3

Measures of organisation of procedure and measures of inquiry

Section 1—Measures of organisation of procedure

Article 64

1 The purpose of measures of organisation of procedure shall be to ensure that cases are prepared for hearing, procedures carried out and disputes resolved under the best possible conditions. They shall be prescribed by the Court of First Instance, after hearing the Advocate-General.
2 Measures of organisation of procedure shall, in particular, have as their purpose:

   (a) to ensure efficient conduct of the written and oral procedure and to facilitate the taking of evidence;
   (b) to determine the points on which the parties must present further argument or which call for measures of inquiry;
   (c) to clarify the forms of order sought by the parties, their pleas in law and arguments and the points at issue between them;
   (d) to facilitate the amicable settlement of proceedings.

3 Measures of organisation of procedure may, in particular, consist of:

   (a) putting questions to the parties;
   (b) inviting the parties to make written or oral submissions on certain aspects of the proceedings;
   (c) asking the parties or third parties for information or particulars;
   (d) asking for documents or any papers relating to the case to be produced;
   (e) summoning the parties' agents or the parties in person to meetings.

4 Each party may, at any stage of the procedure, propose the adoption or modification of measures of organisation of procedure. In that case, the other parties shall be heard before those measures are prescribed.

   Where the procedural circumstances so require, the Registrar shall inform the parties of the measures envisaged by the Court of First Instance and shall give them an opportunity to submit comments orally or in writing.

5 If the Court of First Instance sitting in plenary session decides to prescribe measures of organisation of procedure and does not undertake such measures itself, it shall entrust the task of so doing to the Chamber to which the case was originally assigned or to the Judge-Rapporteur.

   If a Chamber prescribes measures of organisation of procedure and does not undertake such measures itself, it shall entrust the task to the Judge-Rapporteur.

   The Advocate-General shall take part in measures of organisation of procedure.

Section 2—Measures of inquiry

Article 65

Without prejudice to Articles 24 and 25 of the ECSC Statute, Articles 21 and 22 of the EEC Statute or Articles 22 and 23 of the Euratom Statute, the following measures of inquiry may be adopted:

(a) the personal appearance of the parties;
(b) a request for information and production of documents;
(c) oral testimony;
(d) the commissioning of an expert's report;
(e) an inspection of the place or thing in question.

Article 66

1   The Court of First Instance, after hearing the Advocate-General, shall prescribe the measures of inquiry that it considers to be appropriate by means of an order setting out the facts to be proved. Before the Court of First Instance decides on the measures of inquiry referred to in Article 65(c), (d) and (e) the parties shall be heard.

The order shall be served on the parties.

2   Evidence may be submitted in rebuttal and previous evidence may be amplified.

Article 67

1   Where the Court of First Instance sitting in plenary session orders a preparatory inquiry and does not undertake such an inquiry itself, it shall entrust the task of so doing to the Chamber to which the case was originally assigned or to the Judge-Rapporteur.

Where a Chamber orders a preparatory inquiry and does not undertake such an inquiry itself, it shall entrust the task of so doing to the Judge-Rapporteur.

The Advocate-General shall take part in the measures of inquiry.

2   The parties may be present at the measures of inquiry.

Section 3—The summoning and examination of witnesses and experts

Article 68

1   The Court of First Instance may, either of its own motion or on application by a party, and after hearing the Advocate-General and the parties, order that certain facts be proved by witnesses. The order shall set out the facts to be established.

The Court of First Instance may summon a witness of its own motion or on application by a party or at the instance of the Advocate-General.

An application by a party for the examination of a witness shall state precisely about what facts and for what reasons the witness should be examined.

2   The witness shall be summoned by an order containing the following information:

(a) the surname, forenames, description and address of the witness;
(b) an indication of the facts about which the witness is to be examined;
(c) where appropriate, particulars of the arrangements made by the Court of First Instance for reimbursement of expenses incurred by the witness, and of the penalties which may be imposed on defaulting witnesses.

The order shall be served on the parties and the witnesses.

3   The Court of First Instance may make the summoning of a witness for whose examination a party has applied conditional upon the deposit with the cashier of the Court of First Instance of a sum sufficient to cover the taxed costs thereof; the Court of First Instance shall fix the amount of the payment.

The cashier of the Court of First Instance shall advance the funds necessary in connection with the examination of any witness summoned by the Court of First Instance of its own motion.

4   After the identity of each witness has been established, the President shall inform him that he will be required to vouch the truth of his evidence in the manner laid down in paragraph (5) of this Article and in Article 71.

The witness shall give his evidence to the Court of First Instance, the parties having been given notice to attend. After the witness has given his main evidence the President may, at the request of a party or of his own motion, put questions to him.

The other Judges and the Advocate-General may do likewise.

Subject to the control of the President, questions may be put to witnesses by the representatives of the parties.

5 Subject to the provisions of Article 71, the witness shall, after giving his evidence, take the following oath:

'I swear that I have spoken the truth, the whole truth and nothing but the truth.'

The Court of First Instance may, after hearing the parties, exempt a witness from taking the oath.

6 The Registrar shall draw up minutes in which the evidence of each witness is reproduced.

The minutes shall be signed by the President or by the Judge-Rapporteur responsible for conducting the examination of the witness, and by the Registrar. Before the minutes are thus signed, witnesses must be given an opportunity to check the content of the minutes and to sign them.

The minutes shall constitute an official record.

Article 69

1 Witnesses who have been duly summoned shall obey the summons and attend for examination.

2 If a witness who has been duly summoned fails to appear before the Court of First Instance, the latter may impose upon him a pecuniary penalty not exceeding 5,000 ECU and may order that a further summons be served on the witness at his own expense.

The same penalty may be imposed upon a witness who, without good reason, refuses to give evidence or to take the oath or where appropriate to make a solemn affirmation equivalent thereto.

3 If the witness proffers a valid excuse to the Court of First Instance, the pecuniary penalty imposed on him may be cancelled. The pecuniary penalty imposed may be reduced at the request of the witness where he establishes that it is disproportionate to his income.

4 Penalties imposed and other measures ordered under this Article shall be enforced in accordance with Articles 44 and 92 of the ECSC Treaty, Articles 187 and 192 of the EEC Treaty and Articles 159 and 164 of the Euratom Treaty.

Article 70

1 The Court of First Instance may order that an expert's report be obtained. The order appointing the expert shall define his task and set a time-limit within which he is to make his report.

2 The expert shall receive a copy of the order, together with all the documents necessary for carrying out his task. He shall be under the supervision of the Judge-Rapporteur, who may be present during his investigation and who shall be kept informed of his progress in carrying out his task.

The Court of First Instance may request the parties or one of them to lodge security for the costs of the expert's report.

3 At the request of the expert, the Court of First Instance may order the examination of witnesses. Their examination shall be carried out in accordance with Article 68.

4 The expert may give his opinion only on points which have been expressly referred to him.

5 After the expert has made his report, the Court of First Instance may order that he be examined, the parties having been given notice to attend.

Subject to the control of the President, questions may be put to the expert by the representatives of the parties.

6   Subject to the provisions of Article 71, the expert shall, after making his report, take the following oath before the Court of First Instance:

'I swear that I have conscientiously and impartially carried out my task.'

The Court of First Instance may, after hearing the parties, exempt the expert from taking the oath.

Article 71

1   The President shall instruct any person who is required to take an oath before the Court of First Instance, as witness or expert, to tell the truth or to carry out his task conscientiously and impartially, as the case may be, and shall warn him of the criminal liability provided for in his national law in the event of any breach of this duty.

2   Witnesses and experts shall take the oath either in accordance with the first sub-paragraph of Article 68(5) and the first sub-paragraph of Article 70(6) or in the manner laid down by their national law.

3   Where the national law provides the opportunity to make, in judicial proceedings, a solemn affirmation equivalent to an oath as well as or instead of taking an oath, the witnesses and experts may make such an affirmation under the conditions and in the form prescribed in their national law.

Where their national law provides neither for taking an oath nor for making a solemn affirmation, the procedure described in the first paragraph of this Article shall be followed.

Article 72

1   The Court of First Instance may, after hearing the Advocate-General, decide to report to the competent authority referred to in Annex III to the Rules supplementing the Rules of Procedure of the Court of Justice of the Member State whose courts have penal jurisdiction in any case of perjury on the part of a witness or expert before the Court of First Instance, account being taken of the provisions of Article 71.

2   The Registrar shall be responsible for communicating the decision of the Court of First Instance. The decision shall set out the facts and circumstances on which the report is based.

Article 73

1   If one of the parties objects to a witness or to an expert on the ground that he is not a competent or proper person to act as witness or expert or for any other reason, or if a witness or expert refuses to give evidence, to take the oath or to make a solemn affirmation equivalent thereto, the matter shall be resolved by the Court of First Instance.

2   An objection to a witness or to an expert shall be raised within two weeks after service of the order summoning the witness or appointing the expert; the statement of objection must set out the grounds of objection and indicate the nature of any evidence offered.

Article 74

1   Witnesses and experts shall be entitled to reimbursement of their travel and subsistence expenses. The cashier of the Court of First Instance may make a payment to them towards these expenses in advance.

2   Witnesses shall be entitled to compensation for loss of earnings, and experts to fees for their services. The cashier of the Court of First Instance shall pay witnesses and experts their compensation or fees after they have carried out their respective duties or tasks.

Article 75

1   The Court of First Instance may, on application by a party or of its own motion, issue letters rogatory for the examination of witnesses or experts.

2 Letters rogatory shall be issued in the form of an order which shall contain the name, forenames, description and address of the witness or expert, set out the facts on which the witness or expert is to be examined, name the parties, their agents, lawyers or advisers, indicate their addresses for service and briefly describe the subject matter of the dispute.

Notice of the order shall be served on the parties by the Registrar.

3 The Registrar shall send the order to the competent authority named in Annex I to the Rules supplementing the Rules of Procedure of the Court of Justice of the Member State in whose territory the witness or expert is to be examined. Where necessary, the order shall be accompanied by a translation into the official language or languages of the Member State to which it is addressed.

The authority named pursuant to the first sub-paragraph shall pass on the order to the judicial authority which is competent according to its national law.

The competent judicial authority shall give effect to the letters rogatory in accordance with its national law. After implementation the competent judicial authority shall transmit to the authority named pursuant to the first sub-paragraph the order embodying the letters rogatory, any documents arising from the implementation and a detailed statement of costs. These documents shall be sent to the Registrar.

The Registrar shall be responsible for the translation of the documents into the language of the case.

4 The Court of First Instance shall defray the expenses occasioned by the letters rogatory without prejudice to the right to charge them, where appropriate, to the parties.

Article 76

1 The Registrar shall draw up minutes of every hearing. The minutes shall be signed by the President and by the Registrar and shall constitute an official record.

2 The parties may inspect the minutes and any expert's report at the Registry and obtain copies at their own expense.

Chapter 4

Stay of proceedings and declining of jurisdiction by the Court of First Instance

Article 77

Without prejudice to Article 123(4), Article 128 and Article 129(4), proceedings may be stayed:

(a) in the circumstances specified in the third paragraph of Article 47 of the ECSC Statute, the third paragraph of Article 47 of the EEC Statute and the third paragraph of Article 48 of the Euratom Statute;

(b) where an appeal is brought before the Court of Justice against a decision of the Court of First Instance disposing of the substantive issues in part only, disposing of a procedural issue concerning a plea of lack of competence or inadmissibility or dismissing an application to intervene;

(c) at the joint request of the parties.

Article 78

The decision to stay proceedings shall be made by order of the Court of First Instance, after hearing the parties and the Advocate-General. The Court of First Instance may, following the same procedure, order that the proceedings be resumed. The orders referred to in this Article shall be served on the parties.

Article 79

1 The stay of proceedings shall take effect on the date indicated in the order of stay or, in the absence of such an indication, on the date of that order.

While proceedings are stayed time shall, except for the purposes of the time-limit prescribed in Article 115(1) for an application to intervene, cease to run for the purposes of prescribed time-limits for all parties.

2   Where the order of stay does not fix the length of the stay, it shall end on the date indicated in the order of resumption or, in the absence of such indication, on the date of the order of resumption.

From the date of resumption time shall begin to run afresh for the purposes of the time-limits.

Article 80

Decisions declining jurisdiction in the circumstances specified in the third paragraph of Article 47 of the ECSC Statute, the third paragraph of Article 47 of the EEC Statute and the third paragraph of Article 48 of the Euratom Statute shall be made by the Court of First Instance by way of an order which shall be served on the parties.

Chapter 5

Judgments

Article 81

The judgment shall contain:
—a statement that it is the judgment of the Court of First Instance;
—the date of its delivery;
—the names of the President and of the Judges taking part in it;
—the name of the Advocate-General, if designated;
—the name of the Registrar;
—the description of the parties;
—the names of the agents, advisers and lawyers of the parties;
—a statement of the forms of order sought by the parties;
—a statement, where appropriate, that the Advocate-General delivered his opinion;
—a summary of the facts;
—the grounds for the decision;
—the operative part of the judgment, including the decision as to costs.

Article 82

1   The judgment shall be delivered in open court; the parties shall be given notice to attend to hear it.
2   The original of the judgment, signed by the President, by the Judges who took part in the deliberations and by the Registrar, shall be sealed and deposited at the Registry; the parties shall be served with certified copies of the judgment.
3   The Registrar shall record on the original of the judgment the date on which it was delivered.

Article 83

Subject to the provisions of the second paragraph of Article 53 of the ECSC Statute, the second paragraph of Article 53 of the EEC Statute and the second paragraph of Article 54 of the Euratom Statute, the judgment shall be binding from the date of its delivery.

Article 84

1   Without prejudice to the provisions relating to the interpretation of judgments, the Court of First Instance may, of its own motion or on application by a party made within two weeks after the delivery of a judgment, rectify clerical mistakes, errors in calculation and obvious slips in it.
2   The parties, whom the Registrar shall duly notify, may lodge written observations within a period prescribed by the President.
3   The Court of First Instance shall make its decision in closed session.
4   The original of the rectification order shall be annexed to the original of the rectified judgment. A note of this order shall be made in the margin of the original of the rectified judgment.

Article 85

If the Court of First Instance should omit to give a decision on costs, any party may within a month after service of the judgment apply to the Court of First Instance to supplement its judgment.

The application shall be served on the opposite party and the President shall prescribe a period within which that party may lodge written observations.

After these observations have been lodged, the Court of First Instance shall decide both on the admissibility and on the substance of the application.

Article 86

The Registrar shall arrange for the publication of cases before the Court of First Instance.

Chapter 6

Costs

Article 87

1   A decision as to costs shall be given in the final judgment or in the order which closes the proceedings.

2   The unsuccessful party shall be ordered to pay the costs if they have been applied for in the successful party's pleadings.

     Where there are several unsuccessful parties the Court of First Instance shall decide how the costs are to be shared.

3   Where each party succeeds on some and fails on other heads, or where the circumstances are exceptional, the Court of First Instance may order that the costs be shared or that each party bear its own costs.

     The Court of First Instance may order a party, even if successful, to pay costs which it considers that party to have unreasonably or vexatiously caused the opposite party to incur.

4   The Member States and institutions which intervened in the proceedings shall bear their own costs.

     The Court of First Instance may order an intervener other than those mentioned in the preceding sub-paragraph to bear his own costs.

5   A party who discontinues or withdraws from proceedings shall be ordered to pay the costs if they have been applied for in the other party's pleadings. However, upon application by the party who discontinues or withdraws from proceedings, the costs shall be borne by the other party if this appears justified by the conduct of that party.

     Where the parties have come to an agreement on costs, the decision as to costs shall be in accordance with that agreement.

     If costs are not claimed in the written pleadings, the parties shall bear their own costs.

6   Where a case does not proceed to judgment, the costs shall be in the discretion of the Court of First Instance.

Article 88

Without prejudice to the second sub-paragraph of Article 87(3), in proceedings between the Communities and their servants the institutions shall bear their own costs.

Article 89

Costs necessarily incurred by a party in enforcing a judgment or order of the Court of First Instance shall be refunded by the opposite party on the scale in force in the State where the enforcement takes place.

Article 90

Proceedings before the Court of First Instance shall be free of charge, except that:

    (a)   where a party has caused the Court of First Instance to incur avoidable costs, the Court of First Instance may order that party to refund them;

   (b) where copying or translation work is carried out at the request of a party, the cost shall, in so far as the Registrar considers it excessive, be paid for by that party on the scale of charges referred to in Article 24(5).

Article 91

Without prejudice to the preceding Article, the following shall be regarded as recoverable costs:

   (a) sums payable to witnesses and experts under Article 74;
   (b) expenses necessarily incurred by the parties for the purpose of the proceedings, in particular the travel and subsistence expenses and the remuneration of agents, advisers or lawyers.

Article 92

1   If there is a dispute concerning the costs to be recovered, the Court of First Instance hearing the cases shall, on application by the party concerned and after hearing the opposite party, make an order, from which no appeal shall lie.

2   The parties may, for the purposes of enforcement, apply for an authenticated copy of the order.

Article 93

1   Sums due from the cashier of the Court of First Instance shall be paid in the currency of the country where the Court of First Instance has its seat.

     At the request of the person entitled to any sum, it shall be paid in the currency of the country where the expenses to be refunded were incurred or where the steps in respect of which payment is due were taken.

2   Other debtors shall make payment in the currency of their country of origin.

3   Conversions of currency shall be made at the official rates of exchange ruling on the day of payment in the country where the Court of First Instance has its seat.

Chapter 7

Legal Aid

Article 94

1   A party who is wholly or in part unable to meet the costs of the proceedings may at any time apply for legal aid.

     The application shall be accompanied by evidence of the applicant's need of assistance, and in particular by a document from the competent authority certifying his lack of means.

2   If the application is made prior to proceedings which the applicant wishes to commence, it shall briefly state the subject of such proceedings.

     The application need not be made through a lawyer.

     The President of the Court of First Instance shall designate a Judge to act as Rapporteur. The Chamber to which the latter belongs shall, after considering the written observations of the opposite party, decide whether legal aid should be granted in full or in part, or whether it should be refused. The Chamber shall consider whether there is manifestly no cause of action.

     The Chamber shall make an order without giving reasons, and no appeal shall lie therefrom.

Article 95

1   The Court of First Instance, by any order by which it decides that a person is entitled to receive legal aid, shall order that a lawyer be appointed to act for him.

2   If the person does not indicate his choice of lawyer, or if the Court of First Instance considers that his choice is unacceptable, the Registrar shall send a copy of the order and of the application for legal aid to the authority named in Annex II to the Rules supplementing the Rules of Procedure of the Court of Justice, being the competent authority of the State concerned.

3   The Court of First Instance, in the light of the suggestions made by that authority, shall of its own motion appoint a lawyer to act for the person concerned.

Article 96
The Court of First Instance may at any time, either of its own motion or on application, withdraw legal aid if the circumstances which led to its being granted alter during the proceedings.

Article 97
1   Where legal aid is granted, the cashier of the Court of First Instance shall advance the funds necessary to meet the expenses.
2   The Court of First Instance shall adjudicate on the lawyer's disbursements and fees; the President may, on application by the lawyer, order that he receive an advance.
3   In its decision as to costs the Court of First Instance may order the payment to the cashier of the Court of First Instance of the whole or any part of amounts advanced as legal aid.
     The Registrar shall take steps to obtain the recovery of these sums from the party ordered to pay them.

Chapter 8

Discontinuance

Article 98
If, before the Court of First Instance has given its decision, the parties reach a settlement of their dispute and intimate to the Court of First Instance the abandonment of their claims, the President shall order the case to be removed from the register and shall give a decision as to costs in accordance with Article 87(5) having regard to any proposals made by the parties on the matter.

This provision shall not apply to proceedings under Articles 33 and 35 of the ECSC Treaty, Articles 173 and 175 of the EEC Treaty or Articles 146 and 148 of the Euratom Treaty.

Article 99
If the applicant informs the Court of First Instance in writing that he wishes to discontinue the proceedings, the President shall order the case to be removed from the register and shall give a decision as to costs in accordance with Article 87(5).

Chapter 9

Service

Article 100
Where these Rules require that a document be served on a person, the Registrar shall ensure that service is effected at that person's address for service either by the dispatch of a copy of the document by registered post with a form for acknowledgment of receipt or by personal delivery of the copy against a receipt.

The Registrar shall prepare and certify the copies of documents to be served, save where the parties themselves supply the copies in accordance with Article 43(1) .

Chapter 10

Time-limits

Article 101
1   Any period of time prescribed by the ECSC, EEC or Euratom Treaties, the Statutes of the Court of Justice or these Rules for the taking of any procedural step shall be reckoned as follows:

(a) Where a period expressed in days, weeks, months or years is to be calculated from the moment at which an event occurs or an action takes place, the day during which that event occurs or that action takes place shall not be counted as falling within the period in question;

(b) A period expressed in weeks, months or in years shall end with the expiry of whichever day in the last week, month or year is the same day of the week, or falls on the same date, as the day during which the event or action from which the period is to be calculated occured or took place. If, in a period expressed in months or in years, the day on which it should expire does not occur in the last month, the period shall end with the expiry of the last day of that month;

(c) Where a period is expressed in months and days, it shall first be reckoned in whole months, then in days;

(d) Periods shall include official holidays, Sundays and Saturdays;

(e) Periods shall not be suspended during the judicial vacations.

2   If the period would otherwise end on a Saturday, Sunday or official holiday, it shall be extended until the end of the first following working day.

The list of official holidays drawn up by the Court of Justice and published in the Official Journal of the European Communities shall apply to the Court of First Instance.

Article 102

1   The period of time allowed for commencing proceedings against a measure adopted by an institution shall run from the day following the receipt by the person concerned of notification of the measure or, where the measure is published, from the 15th day after publication thereof in the Official Journal of the European Communities.

2   The extensions, on account of distance, of prescribed time-limits provided for in a decision of the Court of Justice and published in the Official Journal of the European Communities shall apply to the Court of First Instance.

Article 103

1   Any time-limit prescribed pursuant to these Rules may be extended by whoever prescribed it.

2   The President may delegate power of signature to the Registrar for the purpose of fixing time-limits which, pursuant to these Rules, it falls to them to the President prescribe, or of extending such time-limits.

TITLE III

Special forms of procedure

Chapter 1

Suspension of operation or enforcement and other interim measures

Article 104

1   An application to suspend the operation of any measure adopted by an institution, made pursuant to the second paragraph of Article 39 of the ECSC Treaty, Article 185 of the EEC Treaty or Article 157 of the Euratom Treaty, shall be admissible only if the applicant is challenging that measure in proceedings before the Court of First Instance.

An application for the adoption of any other interim measure referred to in the third paragraph of Article 39 of the ECSC Treaty, Article 186 of the EEC Treaty or Article 158 of the Euratom Treaty shall be admissible only if it is made by a party to a case before the Court of First Instance and relates to that case.

2   An application of a kind referred to in paragraph (1) of this Article shall state the subject matter of the proceedings, the circumstances giving rise to urgency and the pleas of fact and law establishing a prima facie case for the interim measures applied for.

3   The application shall be made by a separate document and in accordance with the provisions of Articles 43 and 44.

Article 105

1   The application shall be served on the opposite party, and the President of the Court of First Instance shall prescribe a short period within which that party may submit written or oral observations.

2   The President of the Court of First Instance may order a preparatory inquiry.
       The President of the Court of First Instance may grant the application even before the observations of the opposite party have been submitted. This decision may be varied or cancelled even without any application being made by any party.

Article 106

The President of the Court of First Instance shall either decide on the application himself or refer it to the Chamber to which the case has been assigned in the main proceedings or to the Court of First Instance sitting in plenary session if the case has been assigned to it.

If the President of the Court of First Instance is absent or prevented from attending, he shall be replaced by the President or the most senior Judge, within the meaning of Article 6, of the bench of the Court of First Instance to which the case has been assigned.

Where the application is referred to a bench of the Court of First Instance, that bench shall postpone all other cases and shall give a decision. Article 105 shall apply.

Article 107

1   The decision on the application shall take the form of a reasoned order. The order shall be served on the parties forthwith.

2   The enforcement of the order may be made conditional on the lodging by the applicant of security, of an amount and nature to be fixed in the light of the circumstances.

3   Unless the order fixes the date on which the interim measure is to lapse, the measure shall lapse when final judgment is delivered.

4   The order shall have only an interim effect, and shall be without prejudice to the decision on the substance of the case by the Court of First Instance.

Article 108

On application by a party, the order may at any time be varied or cancelled on account of a change in circumstances.

Article 109

Rejection of an application for an interim measure shall not bar the party who made it from making a further application on the basis of new facts.

Article 110

The provisions of this Chapter shall apply to applications to suspend the enforcement of a decision of the Court of First Instance or of any measure adopted by another institution, submitted pursuant to Articles 44 and 92 of the ECSC Treaty, Articles 187 and 192 of the EEC Treaty or Articles 159 and 164 of the Euratom Treaty.

The order granting the application shall fix, where appropriate, a date on which the interim measure is to lapse.

Chapter 2

Preliminary issues

Article 111

Where it is clear that the Court of First Instance has no jurisdiction to take cognisance of an action or where the action is manifestly inadmissible, the Court of First Instance may, by reasoned order, after hearing the Advocate-General and without taking further steps in the proceedings, give a decision on the action.

Article 112

The decision to refer an action to the Court of Justice, pursuant to the second paragraph of Article 47 of the ECSC Statute, the second paragraph of Article 47 of the EEC Statute and the second paragraph of Article 48 of the Euratom Statute, shall, in the case of manifest lack of competence, be made by reasoned order and without taking any further steps in the proceedings.

Article 113

The Court of First Instance may at any time of its own motion consider whether there exists any absolute bar to proceeding with it, and shall give its decision in accordance with Article 114(3) and (4).

Article 114

1   A party applying to the Court of First Instance for a decision on admissibility, on lack of competence or other preliminary plea not going to the substance of the case shall make the application by a separate document.

The application must contain the pleas of fact and law relied on and the form of order sought by the applicant; any supporting documents must be annexed to it.

2   As soon as the application has been lodged, the President shall prescribe a period within which the opposite party may lodge a document containing a statement of the form of order sought by that party and its pleas in law.

3   Unless the Court of First Instance otherwise decides, the remainder of the proceedings shall be oral.

4   The Court of First Instance shall, after hearing the Advocate-General, decide on the application or reserve its decision for the final judgment. It shall refer the case to the Court of Justice if the case falls within the jurisdiction of that Court.

If the Court of First Instance refuses the application or reserves its decision, the President shall prescribe new time-limits for further steps in the proceedings.

Chapter 3

Intervention

Article 115

1   An application to intervene must be made within three months of the publication of the notice referred to in Article 24(6).

2   The application shall contain:

(a) the description of the case;

(b) the description of the parties;

(c) the name and address of the intervener;

(d) the intervener's address for service at the place where the Court of First Instance has its seat;

(e) the form of order sought, by one or more of the parties, in support of which the intervener is applying for leave to intervene;

(f) except in the case of applications to intervene made by Member States or institutions, a statement of the reasons establishing the intervener's interest in the result of the case.

Articles 43 and 44 shall apply.

3   The intervener shall be represented in accordance with the first and second paragraphs of Article 20 of the ECSC Statute and with Article 17 of the EEC and Euratom Statutes.

Article 116

1   The application shall be served on the parties.

The President shall give the parties an opportunity to submit their written or oral observations before deciding on the application.

The President shall decide on the application by order or shall refer the decision to the Court of First Instance. The order must be reasoned if the application is dismissed.

2   If the President allows the intervention, the intervener shall receive a copy of every document served on the parties. The President may, however, on application by one of the parties, omit secret or confidential documents.

3   The intervener must accept the case as he finds it at the time of his intervention.

4   The President shall prescribe a period within which the intervener may submit a statement in intervention.
The statement in intervention shall contain:

   (a) a statement of the form of order sought by the intervener in support of or opposing, in whole or in part, the form of order sought by one of the parties;
   (b) the pleas in law and arguments relied on by the intervener;
   (c) where appropriate, the nature of any evidence offered.

5   After the statement in intervention has been lodged, the President shall, where necessary, prescribe a time-limit within which the parties may reply to that statement.

Chapter 4

Judgments of the Court of First Instance delivered after its decision has been set aside and the case referred back to it

Article 117

Where the Court of Justice sets aside a judgment or an order of the Court of First Instance and refers the case back to that Court, the latter shall be seised of the case by the judgment so referring it.

Article 118

1   Where the Court of Justice sets aside a judgment or an order of a Chamber, the President of the Court of First Instance may assign the case to another Chamber composed of the same number of Judges.

2   Where the Court of Justice sets aside a judgment delivered or an order made by the Court of First Instance sitting in plenary session, the case shall be assigned to that Court as so constituted.

3   In the cases provided for in paragraphs (1) and (2) of this Article, Articles 13(2), 14 and 51 shall apply.

Article 119

1   Where the written procedure before the Court of First Instance has been completed when the judgment referring the case back to it is delivered, the course of the procedure shall be as follows:

   (a) Within two months from the service upon him of the judgment of the Court of Justice the applicant may lodge a statement of written observations;
   (b) In the month following the communication to him of that statement, the defendant may lodge a statement of written observations. The time allowed to the defendant for lodging it may in no case be less than two months from the service upon him of the judgment of the Court of Justice;
   (c) In the month following the simultaneous communication to the intervener of the observations of the applicant and the defendant, the intervener may lodge a statement of written observations. The time allowed to the intervener for lodging it may in no case be less than two months from the service upon him of the judgment of the Court of Justice.

2   Where the written procedure before the Court of First Instance had not been completed when the judgment referring the case back to the Court of First Instance was delivered, it shall be resumed, at the stage which it had reached, by means of measures of organisation of procedure adopted by the Court of First Instance.

3   The Court of First Instance may, if the circumstances so justify, allow supplementary statements of written observations to be lodged.

Article 120

The procedure shall be conducted in accordance with the provisions of Title II of these Rules.

Article 121

The Court of First Instance shall decide on the costs relating to the proceedings instituted before it and to the proceedings on the appeal before the Court of Justice.

Chapter 5

Judgments by default and applications to set them aside

Article 122

1   If a defendant on whom an application initiating proceedings has been duly served fails to lodge a defence to the application in the proper form within the time prescribed, the applicant may apply to the Court of First Instance for judgment by default.

   The application shall be served on the defendant. The President shall fix a date for the opening of the oral procedure.

2   Before giving judgment by default the Court of First Instance shall consider whether the application initiating proceedings is admissible, whether the appropriate formalities have been complied with, and whether the application appears well founded. It may order a preparatory inquiry.

3   A judgment by default shall be enforceable. The Court of First Instance may, however, grant a stay of execution until it has given its decision on any application under paragraph (4) of this Article to set aside the judgment, or it may make execution subject to the provision of security of an amount and nature to be fixed in the light of the circumstances; this security shall be released if no such application is made or if the application fails.

4   Application may be made to set aside a judgment by default.

   The application to set aside the judgment must be made within one month from the date of service of the judgment and must be lodged in the form prescribed by Articles 43 and 44.

5   After the application has been served, the President shall prescribe a period within which the other party may submit his written observations.

   The proceedings shall be conducted in accordance with the provisions of Title II of these Rules.

6   The Court of First Instance shall decide by way of a judgment which may not be set aside. The original of this judgment shall be annexed to the original of the judgment by default. A note of the judgment on the application to set aside shall be made in the margin of the original of the judgment by default.

Chapter 6

Exceptional Review Procedures

Section 1—Third-party proceedings

Article 123

1   Articles 43 and 44 shall apply to an application initiating third-party proceedings. In addition such an application shall:

   (a) specify the judgment contested;
   (b) state how that judgment is prejudicial to the rights of the third party;
   (c) indicate the reasons for which the third party was unable to take part in the original case before the Court of First Instance.

   The application must be made against all the parties to the original case.

   Where the judgment has been published in the Official Journal of the European Communities, the application must be lodged within two months of the publication.

2   The Court of First Instance may, on application by the third party, order a stay of execution of the judgment. The provisions of Title III, Chapter 1, shall apply.

3   The contested judgment shall be varied on the points on which the submissions of the third-party are upheld.

The original of the judgment in the third-party proceedings shall be annexed to the original of the contested judgment. A note of the judgment in the third- party proceedings shall be made in the margin of the original of the contested judgment.

4   Where an appeal before the Court of Justice and an application initiating third-party proceedings before the Court of First Instance contest the same judgment of the Court of First Instance, the Court of First Instance may, after hearing the parties, stay the proceedings until the Court of Justice has delivered its judgment.

Article 124

The application initiating third-party proceedings shall be assigned to the Chamber which delivered the judgment which is the subject of the application; if the Court of First Instance sitting in plenary session delivered the judgment, the application shall be assigned to it.

Section 2—Revision

Article 125

Without prejudice to the period of ten years prescribed in the third paragraph of Article 38 of the ECSC Statute, the third paragraph of Article 41 of the EEC Statute and the third paragraph of Article 42 of the Euratom Statute, an application for revision of a judgment shall be made within three months of the date on which the facts on which the application is based came to the applicant's knowledge.

Article 126

1   Articles 43 and 44 shall apply to an application for revision. In addition such an application shall:

(a) specify the judgment contested;
(b) indicate the points on which the application is based;
(c) set out the facts on which the application is based;
(d) indicate the nature of the evidence to show that there are facts justifying revision of the judgment, and that the time-limits laid down in Article 125 have been observed.

2   The application must be made against all parties to the case in which the contested judgment was given.

Article 127

1   The application for revision shall be assigned to the Chamber which delivered the judgment which is the subject of the application; if the Court of First Instance sitting in plenary session delivered the judgment, the application shall be assigned to it.

2   Without prejudice to its decision on the substance, the Court of First Instance shall, after hearing the Advocate-General, having regard to the written observations of the parties, give its decision on the admissibility of the application.

3   If the Court of First Instance finds the application admissible, it shall proceed to consider the substance of the application and shall give its decision in the form of a judgment in accordance with these Rules.

4   The original of the revising judgment shall be annexed to the original of the judgment revised. A note of the revising judgment shall be made in the margin of the original of the judgment revised.

Article 128

Where an appeal before the Court of Justice and an application for revision before the Court of First Instance concern the same judgment of the Court of First Instance, the Court of First Instance may, after hearing the parties, stay the proceedings until the Court of Justice has delivered its judgment.

Section 3—Interpretation of judgments

Article 129

1   An application for interpretation of a judgment shall be made in accordance with Articles 43 and 44. In addition it shall specify:

(a) the judgment in question;
(b) the passages of which interpretation is sought.

The application must be made against all the parties to the case in which the judgment was given.

2   The application for interpretation shall be assigned to the Chamber which delivered the judgment which is the subject of the application; if the Court of First Instance sitting in plenary session delivered the judgment, the application shall be assigned to it.

3   The Court of First Instance shall give its decision in the form of a judgment after having given the parties an opportunity to submit their observations and after hearing the Advocate-General.

The original of the interpreting judgment shall be annexed to the original of the judgment interpreted. A note of the interpreting judgment shall be made in the margin of the original of the judgment interpreted.

4   Where an appeal before the Court of Justice and an application for interpretation before the Court of First Instance concern the same judgment of the Court of First Instance, the Court of First Instance may, after hearing the parties, stay the proceedings until the Court of Justice has delivered its judgment.

Miscellaneous Provisions

Article 130

These Rules, which are authentic in the languages mentioned in Article 35(1), shall be published in the Official Journal of the European Communities. They shall enter into force on the first day of the second month from the date of their publication.

Done at Luxembourg on 2 May 1991.

Articles 1 to 5 of the Protocol on the Interpretation of the Convention on Jurisdiction and the Enforcement of Judgments in Civil and Commercial Matters[29]

Article 1[30]

The Court of Justice of the European Communities shall have jurisdiction to give rulings on the interpretation of the Convention on Jurisdiction and the Enforcement of Judgments in Civil and Commercial Matters and of the Protocol annexed to that Convention, signed at Brussels on 27 September 1968, and also on the interpretation of the present Protocol.

The Court of Justice of the European Communities shall also have jurisdiction to give rulings on the interpretation of the Convention on the accession of the Kingdom of Denmark, Ireland and the United Kingdom of Great Britain and Northern Ireland to the Convention of 27 September 1968 and to this Protocol.

The Court of Justice of the European Communities shall also have jurisdiction to give rulings on the interpretation of the Convention on the accession of the Hellenic Republic to the Convention of 27 September 1968 and to this Protocol, as adjusted by the 1978 Convention.

The Court of Justice of the European Communities shall also have jurisdiction to give rulings on the interpretation of the Convention on the Accession of the Kingdom of Spain and the Portuguese Republic to the Convention of 27 September 1968 and to this Protocol, as adjusted by the 1978 Convention and the 1982 Convention.

Article 2[31]

1   The following courts may request the Court of Justice to give preliminary rulings on questions of interpretation:

—In Belgium: la Cour de Cassation—het Hof van Cassatie and le Conseil d'Etat—de Raad van State;
—in Denmark: højesteret;
—in the Federal Republic of Germany: die obersten Gerichtshöfe des Bundes;
—in Greece: the ανώτατα δικαστήρια;
—in Spain: el Tribunal Supremo;
—in France: la Cour de Cassation and le Conseil d'État;
—in Ireland: the Supreme Court;

---

29 The Convention on Jurisdiction and the Enforcement of Judgments in Civil and Commercial Matters was signed by the six original Member States on 27 September 1968 (for the original text, see OJ No L 299/32 of 31 December 1972). The Protocol on the Interpretation of the Convention by the Court was signed on 3 June 1971 (see OJ No L 204/28 of 2 August 1975). A Convention on the accession of Denmark, Ireland and the United Kingdom to the 1968 Convention was signed on 9 October 1978 ('the 1978 Accession Convention') and consequential amendments were made to the text of the 1968 Convention and the Protocol on its interpretation (see OJ No L 304 of 30 October 1978). A Convention on the accession of Greece to the 1968 Convention ('the 1982 Accession Convention'), which made corresponding changes to both it and the Protocol, was signed on 25 October 1982 (see OJ No L 388 of 31 December 1982). Further changes were made by the Convention of 26 May 1989 on the accession of Spain and Portugal to the 1968 Convention (see OJ No L 285 of 3 October 1989 p 1—'the 1989 Accession Convention'). A consolidated version of the 1968 Convention and the Protocol was published in OJ No C 189 of 28 July 1990. It is from this version that the following extracts have been taken.
30 The second paragraph was added by Article 30 of the 1978 Accession Convention, the third paragraph by Article 10 of the 1982 Accession Convention and the fourth paragraph by Article 24 of the 1989 Accession Convention.
31 Point 1 was amended by Article 31 of the 1978 Accession Convention, Article 11 of the 1982 Accession Convention and Article 25 of the 1989 Accession Convention.

—in Italy: la Corte Suprema di Cassazione;

—in Luxembourg: la Cour supérieure de Justice when sitting as Cour de Cassation;

—in the Netherlands: de Hoge Raad;

—in Portugal: o Supremo Tribunal de Justiça and o Supremo Tribunal Administratiro;

—in the United Kingdom: the House of Lords and courts to which application has been made under the second paragraph of Article 37 or under Article 41 of the Convention.[32]

2   The courts of the Contracting States when they are sitting in an appellate capacity.

3   In the cases provided for in Article 37 of the Convention, the courts referred to in that Article.

Article 3

1   Where a question of interpretation of the Convention or of one of the other instruments referred to in Article 1 is raised in a case pending before one of the courts listed in point 1 of Article 2, that court shall, if it considers that a decision on the question is necessary to enable it to give judgment, request the Court of Justice to give a ruling thereon.

2   Where such a question is raised before any court referred to in point 2 or 3 of Article 2, that court may, under the conditions laid down in paragraph 1, request the Court of Justice to give a ruling thereon.

Article 4

1   The competent authority of a Contracting State may request the Court of Justice to give a ruling on a question of interpretation of the Convention or of one of the other instruments referred to in Article 1 if judgments given by courts of that State conflict with the interpretation given either by the Court of Justice or in a judgment of one of the courts of another Contracting State referred to in point 1 or 2 of Article 2. The provisions of this paragraph shall apply only to judgments which have become *res judicata*.

2   The interpretation given by the Court of Justice in response to such a request shall not affect the judgments which give rise to the request for interpretation.

3   The Procurators-General of the Courts of Cassation of the Contracting States, or any other authority designated by a Contracting State, shall be entitled to request the Court of Justice for a ruling on interpretation in accordance with paragraph 1.

4   The Registrar of the Court of Justice shall give notice of the request to the Contracting States, to the Commission and to the Council of the European Communities; they shall then be entitled within two months of the notification to submit statements of case or written observations to the Court.

5   No fees shall be levied or any costs or expenses awarded in respect of the proceedings provided for in this Article.

Article 5

1   Except where this Protocol otherwise provides, the provisions of the Treaty establishing the European Economic Community and those of the Protocol on the Statute of the Court of Justice annexed thereto, which are applicable when the Court is requested to give a preliminary ruling, shall also apply to any proceedings for the interpretation of the Convention and the other instruments referred to in Article 1.

2   The Rules of Procedure of the Court of Justice shall, if necessary, be adjusted and supplemented in accordance with Article 188 of the Treaty establishing the European Economic Community.

---

32 Article 37 of the Convention is set out below. Article 41 refers to courts hearing appeals on a point of law from a judgment given on appeal by the applicant against a refusal to enforce a judgment given in a Contracting State. In the case of the United Kingdom, the appeal against refusal is heard by one of the courts referred to in Article 37. The appeals envisaged in Article 41 are therefore heard by the next highest court competent to hear appeals on a point of law.

Article 37 of the Convention on Jurisdiction and the Enforcement of Judgments in Civil and Commercial Matters

Article 37[33]

An appeal against the decision authorizing enforcement shall be lodged in accordance with the rules governing procedure in contentious matters:

—in Belgium, with the tribunal de première instance or rechtbank van eerste aanleg;
—in Denmark, with the landsret;
—in the Federal Republic of Germany, with the Oberlandesgericht;
—in Greece, with the Σφετείο;
—in Spain, with the Audencia Provincial;
—in France, with the cour d'appel;
—in Ireland, with the High Court;
—in Italy, with the corte d'appello;
—in Luxembourg, with the Cour supérieure de justice sitting as a court of civil appeal;
—in the Netherlands, with the arrondissementsrechtbank;
—in Portugal, with the Tribunal da Relação;
—in the United Kingdom:

1   in England and Wales, with the High Court of Justice, or in the case of a maintenance judgment with the Magistrates' Court;
2   in Scotland, with the Court of Session, or in the case of a maintenance judgment with the Sheriff Court;
3   in Northern Ireland, with the High Court of Justice, or in the case of a maintenance judgment with the Magistrates' Court.

The judgment given on the appeal may be contested only:
—in Belgium, Greece, Spain, France, Italy, Luxembourg and in the Netherlands, by an appeal in cassation;
—in Denmark, by an appeal to the højesteret, with the leave of the Minister of Justice;
—in the Federal Republic of Germany, by a Rechtsbeschwerde;
—in Ireland, by an appeal on a point of law to the Supreme Court;
—in Portugal, by an appeal on a point of law;
—in the United Kingdom, by a single further appeal on a point of law.

33 As amended by Article 17 of the 1978 Accession Convention, Article 5 of the 1982 Accession Convention and Article 11 of the 1989 Accession Convention.

First Protocol on the Interpretation by the Court of Justice of the European Communities of the Convention on the Law Applicable to Contractual Obligations[34]

Article 1

The Court of Justice of the European Communities shall have jurisdiction to give rulings on the interpretation of:

(a) the Convention on the law applicable to contractual obligations, opened for signature in Rome on 19 June 1980, hereinafter referred to as 'the Rome Convention';

(b) the Convention on accession to the Rome Convention by the States which have become Members of the European Communities since the date on which it was opened for signature;

(c) this Protocol.

Article 2

Any of the courts referred to below may request the Court of Justice to give a preliminary ruling on a question raised in a case pending before it and concerning interpretation of the provisions contained in the instruments referred to in Article 1 if that court considers that a decision on the question is necessary to enable it to give judgment:

(a) —in Belgium: la Cour de cassation (her Hof van Cassatie) and le Conseil d'Etat (de Raad van State);

—in Denmark: Højesteret;

—in the Federal Republic of Germany: die obersten Gerichtshöfe des Bundes;

—in Greece: Τα ανώτατα Δικαστήρια;

—in Spain: el Tribunal Supremo;

—in France: la Cour de cassation and le Conseil d'Etat;

—in Ireland: the Supreme Court;

—in Italy: la Corte suprema di cassazione and il Consiglio di Stato;

—in Luxembourg: la Cour Supérieure de Justice, when sitting as Cour de cassation;

—in the Netherlands: de Hoge Raad;

—in Portugal: o Supremo Tribunal de Justiça and o Supremo Tribunal Administrativo;

—in the United Kingdom: the House of Lords and other courts from which no further appeal is possible;

(b) the courts of the Contracting States when acting as appeal courts.

Article 3

1   The competent authority of a Contracting State may request the Court of Justice to give a ruling on a question of interpretation of the provisions contained in the instruments referred to in Article 1 if judgments given by courts of that State conflict with the interpretation given either by the Court of Justice or in a judgment of one of the courts of another Contracting State referred to in Article 2. The provisions of this paragraph shall apply only to judgments which have become *res judicata*.

2   The interpretation given by the Court of Justice in response to such a request shall not affect the judgments which gave rise to the request for interpretation.

---

34 OJ No L 48 of 20 February 1989 p 1.

3   The Procurators-General of the Supreme Courts of Appeal of the Contracting States, or any other authority designated by a Contracting State, shall be entitled to request the Court of Justice for a ruling on interpretation in accordance with paragraph 1.

4   The Registrar of the Court of Justice shall give notice of the request to the Contracting States, to the Commission and to the Council of the European Communities; they shall then be entitled within two months of the notification to submit statements of case or written observations to the Court.

5   No fees shall be levied or any costs or expenses awarded in respect of the proceedings provided for in this Article.

Article 4

1   Except where this Protocol otherwise provides, the provisions of the Treaty establishing the European Economic Community and those of the Protocol on the Statute of the Court of Justice annexed thereto, which are applicable when the Court is requested to give a preliminary ruling, shall also apply to any proceedings for the interpretation of the instruments referred to in Article 1.

2   The Rules of Procedure of the Court of Justice shall, if necessary, be adjusted and supplemented in accordance with Article 188 of the Treaty establishing the European Economic Community.

Article 5

This Protocol shall be subject to ratification by the Signatory States. The instruments of ratification shall be deposited with the Secretary-General of the Council of the European Communities.

Article 6

1   To enter into force, this Protocol must be ratified by seven States in respect of which the Rome Convention is in force. This Protocol shall enter into force on the first day of the third month following the deposit of the instrument of ratification by the last such State to take this step. If, however, the Second Protocol conferring on the Court of Justice of the European Communities certain powers to interpret the Convention on the law applicable to contractual obligations, opened for signature in Rome on 19 June 1980, concluded in Brussels on 19 December 1988, enters into force on a later date, this Protocol shall enter into force on the date of entry into force of the Second Protocol.

2   Any ratification subsequent to the entry into force of this Protocol shall take effect on the first day of the third month following the deposit of the instrument of ratification, provided that the ratification, acceptance or approval of the Rome Convention by the State in question has become effective.

Article 7

The Secretary-General of the Council of the European Communities shall notify the Signatory States of:

(a) the deposit of each instrument of ratification;
(b) the date of entry into force of this Protocol;
(c) any designation communicated pursuant to Article 3(3);
(d) any communication made pursuant to Article 8.

Article 8

The Contracting States shall communicate to the Secretary-General of the Council of the European Communities the texts of any provisions of their laws which necessitate an amendment to the list of courts in Article 2(a).

Article 9

This Protocol shall have effect for as long as the Rome Convention remains in force under the conditions laid down in Article 30 of that Convention.

Article 10

Any Contracting State may request the revision of this Protocol. In this event, a revision conference shall be convened by the President of the Council of the European Communities.

Article 11

This Protocol, drawn up in a single original in the Danish, English, French, German, Greek, Irish, Italian, Portuguese and Spanish languages, all ten texts being equally authentic, shall be deposited in the archives of the General Secretariat of the Council of the European Communities. The Secretary-General shall transmit a certified copy to the Government of each Signatory State.

Second Protocol Conferring on the Court of Justice of the European Communities Certain Powers to Interpret the Convention on the Law Applicable to Contractual Obligations[35]

Article 1

1 The Court of Justice of the European Communities shall, with respect to the Rome Convention, have the jurisdiction conferred upon it by the First Protocol on the interpretation by the Court of Justice of the European Communities of the Convention on the law applicable to contractual obligations, opened for signature in Rome on 19 June 1980, concluded in Brussels on 19 December 1988. The Protocol on the Statute of the Court of Justice of the European Communities and the Rules of Procedure of the Court of Justice shall apply.

2 The Rules of Procedure of the Court of Justice shall be adapted and supplemented as necessary in accordance with Article 188 of the Treaty establishing the European Economic Community.

Article 2

This Protocol shall be subject to ratification by the Signatory States. The instruments of ratification shall be deposited with the Secretary-General of the Council of the European Communities.

Article 3

This Protocol shall enter into force on the first day of the third month following the deposit of the instrument of ratification of the last Signatory State to complete the formality.

Article 4

This Protocol, drawn up in a single original in the Danish, Dutch, English, French, German, Greek, Irish, Italian, Portuguese and Spanish languages, all ten texts being equally authentic, shall be deposited in the archives of the General Secretariat of the Council of the European Communities. The Secretary-General shall transmit a certified copy to the Government of each signatory.

35 OJ No L 48 of 20 February 1989 p 17.

Agreement Relating to Community Patents[36]

Article 2

Relationship with the Community legal order

1 No provision of this Agreement may be invoked against the application of the Treaty establishing the European Economic Community.

2 In order to ensure the uniformity of the Community legal order, the Common Appeal Court established by the Protocol on Litigation shall request the Court of Justice of the European Communities to give a preliminary ruling in accordance with Article 177 of the Treaty establishing the European Economic Community whenever there is a risk of an interpretation of this Agreement being inconsistent with that Treaty.

3 Where a Member State or the Commission of the European Communities considers that a decision of the Common Appeal Court which closes the procedure before it does not comply with the principal stated in the foregoing paragraphs, it may request the Court of Justice of the European Communities to give a ruling. The ruling given by the Court of Justice in response to such request shall not affect the decision by the Common Appeal Court which gave rise to the request. The Registrar of the Court of Justice shall give notice of the request to the Member States, to the Council and, if the request is made by a Member State, the Commission of the European Communities; they shall then be entitled within two months of the notification to submit statements of case or written observations to the Court. No fees shall be levied or any costs or expenses awarded in respect of the proceedings provided for in this paragraph.

Article 3

Interpretation of provisions on jurisdiction

1 The Court of Justice of the European Communities shall have jurisdiction to give preliminary rulings concerning the interpretation of the provisions on jurisdiction applicable to actions relating to Community patents before national courts, contained in Part VI, Chapter I, of the Community Patent Convention and in the Protocol on Litigation.

2 The following courts shall have the power to request the Court of Justice to give a preliminary ruling on any question of interpretation as defined in paragraph 1:

(a) —in Belgium: la Cour de cassation (het Hof van Cassatie) and le Conseil d'État (de Raad van State);
—in Denmark: Højesteret;
—in the Federal Republic of Germany: die obersten Gerichtshöfe des Bundes;
—in Greece: τα ανώτατα Δικαστήρια;
—in Spain: el Tribunal supremo;
—in France: la Cour de cassation and le Conseil d'État;
—in Ireland: an Chúirt Uachtarach (the Supreme Court);
—in Italy: la Corte suprema di cassazione;
—in Luxembourg: la Cour supérieure de justice when sitting as Cour de cassation;
—in the Netherlands: de Hoge Raad;

---

36 Done at Luxembourg on 15 December 1989 (89/695/EEC), OJ No L 401 of 30 December 1989 p 1.

    —in Portugal: o Supremo Tribunal de Justiça;
    —in the United Kingdom: the House of Lords;
(b) the courts of the Contracting States when ruling on appeals.

3   Where such a question is raised in a case before one of the courts listed in paragraph 2(a), that court must, if it considers that a decision on the question is necessary to enable it to give a judgment, request the Court of Justice to give a ruling thereon.

4   Where such a question is raised before one of the courts referred to in paragraph 2(b), that court may, under the conditions laid down in paragraph 1, request the Court of Justice to give a ruling thereon.

Article 4

Rules of Procedure of the Court of Justice

1   The Protocol on the Statute of the Court of Justice of the European Economic Community and the Rules of Procedure of the Court of Justice shall apply to any proceedings referred to in Articles 2 and 3.

2   The Rules of Procedure shall be adapted and supplemented, as necessary, in conformity with Article 188 of the Treaty establishing the European Economic Community.

Article 14

Disputes between Contracting States

1   Any dispute between Contracting States concerning the interpretation of application of this Agreement which is not settled by negotiation shall be submitted, at the request of one of the States concerned, to the Select Committee or to the Administrative Committee as the case may be. The body to which the dispute is submitted shall endeavour to bring about agreement between the States concerned.

2   If agreement is not reached within six months from the date when the Select Committee or the Administrative Committee was seised of the dispute, any one of the States concerned may submit the dispute to the Court of Justice of the European Communities.

3   If the Court of Justice finds that a Contracting State has failed to fulfil an obligation under this Agreement, that State shall be required to take the necessary measures to comply with the judgment of the Court of Justice.

Council Regulation (EC) No 40/94 on the Community Trade Mark[37]

Preamble:

. . . Whereas it is necessary to ensure that parties who are affected by decisions made by the Office are protected by the law in a manner which is suited to the special character of trade mark law; whereas to that end provision is made for an appeal to lie from decisions of the examiners and of the various divisions of the Office;

Whereas if the department whose decision is contested does not rectify its decision it is to remit the appeal to a Board of Appeal of the Office, which is to decide on it; whereas decisions of the Boards of Appeal are, in turn, amenable to actions before the Court of Justice of the European Communities, which has jurisdiction to annul or to alter the contested decision;

Whereas under Council Decision 88/591/ECSC, EEC, Euratom of 24 October 1988 establishing a Court of First Instance of the European Communities, as amended by Decision 93/350/Euratom, ECSC, EEC of 8 June 1993, that Court shall exercise at the first instance the jurisdiction conferred on the Court of Justice by the Treaties establishing the Communities – with particular regard to appeals lodged under the second sub-paragraph of Article 173 of the EC Treaty – and by the acts adopted in implementation thereof, save as otherwise provided in an act setting up a body governed by Community law; whereas the jurisdiction which this Regulation confers on the Court of Justice to cancel and reform decisions of the appeal courts shall accordingly be exercised at the first instance by the Court in accordance with the above Decision.

Article 62

Decisions in respect of appeals

. . .

3   The decisions of the Boards of Appeal shall take effect only as from the date of expiration of the period referred to in Article 63(5) or, if an action has been brought before the Court of Justice within that period, as from the date of rejection of such action.

Article 63

Actions before the Court of Justice

1   Actions may be brought before the Court of Justice against decisions of the Boards of Appeal on appeals.
2   The action may be brought on grounds of lack of competence, infringement of an essential procedural requirement, infringement of the Treaty, of this Regulation or of any rule of law relating to their application or misuse of power.
3   The Court of Justice has jurisdiction to annul or to alter the contested decision.
4   The action shall be open to any party to proceedings before the Board of Appeal adversely affected by its decision.
5   The action shall be brought before the Court of Justice within two months of the date of notification of the decision of the Board of Appeal.

---

37 20 December 1993, OJ No 11 of 14 January 1994 p 1. The Regulation entered into force on the 60th day following publication in the Official Journal (see art 143(1)), that is, on 14 March 1994.

6   The Office shall be required to take the necessary measures to comply with the judgment of the Court of Justice.

Article 82

Enforcement of decisions fixing the amount of costs

1   Any final decisions of the Office fixing the amount of costs shall be enforceable.
2   Enforcement shall be governed by the rules of civil procedure in force in the State in the territory of which it is carried out. The order for its enforcement shall be appended to the decision, without other formality than verification of the authenticity of the decision, by the national authority which the Government of each Member State shall designate for this purpose and shall make known to the Office and to the Court of Justice.
3   When these formalities have been completed on application by the party concerned, the latter may proceed to enforcement in accordance with the national law, by bringing the matter directly before the competent authority.
4   Enforcement may be suspended only by a decision of the Court of Justice. However, the courts of the country concerned shall have jurisdiction over complaints that enforcement is being carried out in an irregular manner.

Article 114

Liability

1   The contractual liability of the Office shall be governed by the law applicable to the contract in question.
2   The Court of Justice shall be competent to give judgment pursuant to any arbitration clause contained in a contract concluded by the Office.
3   In the case of non-contractual liability, the Office shall, in accordance with the general principles common to the laws of the Member States, make good any damage caused by its departments or by its servants in the performance of their duties.
4   The Court of Justice shall have jurisdiction in disputes relating to compensation for the damage referred to in paragraph 3.
5   The personal liability of its servants towards the Office shall be governed by the provisions laid down in their Staff Regulations or in the Conditions of Employment applicable to them.

Article 131

Independent of the members of the Boards of Appeal

1   The members, including the chairmen, of the Boards of Appeal shall be appointed, in accordance with the procedure laid down in Article 120, for the appointment of the President of the Office, for a term of five years. They may not be removed from office during this term, unless there are serious grounds for such removal and the Court of Justice, on application by the body which appointed them, takes a decision to this effect. Their term of office shall be renewable.

Agreement on the European Economic Area, Articles 107, 110, 111(3) and Protocol 34[38]

Article 107

Provisions on the possibility for an EFTA State to allow a court or tribunal to ask the Court of Justice of the European Communities to decide on the interpretation of an EEA rule are laid down in Protocol 34.

Article 110

Decisions under this Agreement by the EFTA Surveillance Authority and the EC Commission which impose a pecuniary obligation on persons other than States, shall be enforceable. The same shall apply to such judgments under this Agreement by the Court of Justice of the European Communities, the Court of First Instance of the European Communities and the EFTA Court.

Enforcement shall be governed by the rules of civil procedure in force in the State in the territory of which it is carried out. The order for its enforcement shall be appended to the decision, without other formality than verification of the authenticity of the decision, by the authority which each Contracting Party shall designate for this purpose and shall make known to the other Contracting Parties, the EFTA Surveillance Authority, the EC Commission, the Court of Justice of the European Communities, the Court of First Instance of the European Communities and the EFTA Court.

When these formalities have been completed on application by the party concerned, the latter may proceed to enforcement, in accordance with the law of the State in the territory of which enforcement is to be carried out, by bringing the matter directly before the competent authority.

Enforcement may be suspended only by a decision of the Court of Justice of the European Communities, as far as decisions by the EC Commission, the Court of First Instance of the European Communities or the Court of Justice of the European Communities are concerned, or by a decision of the EFTA Court as far as decisions by the EFTA Surveillance Authority or the EFTA Court are concerned. However, the courts of the States concerned shall have jurisdiction over complaints that enforcement is being carried out in an irregular manner.

Article 111

3   If a dispute concerns the interpretation of provisions of this Agreement, which are identical in substance to corresponding rules of the Treaty establishing the European Economic Community and the Treaty establishing the European Coal and Steel Community and to acts adopted in application of these two Treaties and if the dispute has not been settled within three months after it has been brought before the EEA Joint Committee, the Contracting Parties to the dispute may agree to request the Court of Justice of the European Communities to give a ruling on the interpretation of the relevant rules.

If the EEA Joint Committee in such a dispute has not reached an agreement on a solution within six months from the date on which this procedure was initiated or if, by then, the Contracting Parties to the dispute have not decided to ask for a ruling by the Court of Justice of the European Communities, a Contracting Party may, in order to remedy possible imbalances,

—either take a safeguard measure in accordance with Article 112(2) and following the procedure of Article 113;
—or apply Article 102 *mutatis mutandis*.

---

38 The text of the Agreement, the Decision of the Council and the Commission on its conclusion and the Final Act are published in OJ No L 1 of 3 January 1994. The Agreement entered into force on 1 January 1994: see ibid p 606.

Protocol 34

On the possibility for courts and tribunals of EFTA States to request the Court of Justice of the European Communities to decide on the interpretation of EEA rules corresponding to EC rules

Article 1

When a question of interpretation of provisions of the Agreement, which are identical in substance to the provisions of the Treaties establishing the European Communities, as amended or supplemented, or of acts adopted in pursuance thereof, arises in a case pending before a court or tribunal of an EFTA State, the court or tribunal may, if it considers this necessary, ask the Court of Justice of the European Communities to decide on such a question.

Article 2

An EFTA State which intends to make use of this Protocol shall notify the Depositary and the Court of Justice of the European Communities to what extent and according to what modalities the Protocol will apply to its courts and tribunals.

Article 3

The Depositary shall notify the Contracting Parties of any notification under Article 2.

Index